T0234442

Lecture Notes in Artificial Intelligence   8864

Subseries of Lecture Notes in Computer Science

LNAI Series Editors

Randy Goebel
  University of Alberta, Edmonton, Canada
Yuzuru Tanaka
  Hokkaido University, Sapporo, Japan
Wolfgang Wahlster
  DFKI and Saarland University, Saarbrücken, Germany

LNAI Founding Series Editor

Joerg Siekmann
  DFKI and Saarland University, Saarbrücken, Germany

More information about this series at http://www.springer.com/series/1244

Ana L.C. Bazzan · Karim Pichara (Eds.)

Advances in Artificial Intelligence – IBERAMIA 2014

14th Ibero-American Conference on AI
Santiago de Chile, Chile, November 24–27, 2014
Proceedings

 Springer

Editors
Ana L.C. Bazzan
Universidade Federal do Rio Grande do Sul
Porto Alegre
Brazil

Karim Pichara
Pontifica Universidad Católica (PUC)
Santiago de Chile
Chile

ISSN 0302-9743
ISBN 978-3-319-12026-3
DOI 10.1007/978-3-319-12027-0

ISSN 1611-3349 (electronic)
ISBN 978-3-319-12027-0 (eBook)

Library of Congress Control Number: 2014952189

LNCS Sublibrary: SL7 – Artificial Intelligence

Springer Cham Heidelberg New York Dordrecht London

Printed on acid-free paper

Springer is part of Springer Science+Business Media (www.springer.com)

Computer Vision

Luis Enrique Sucar	Instituto Nacional de Astrofísica, Óptica y Electrónica, Mexico
José Manuel Menéndez	Universidad Politécnica de Madrid, Spain

Bio-inspired Computing

Camelia Chira	Technical University of Cluj-Napoca, Romania
Luis Correia	Universidade de Lisboa, Portugal
Marcilio Souto	University of Orléans, France

Information and Knowledge Processing Knowledge Discovery and Data Mining

Ana Gabriela Maguitman	Universidad Nacional del Sur, Argentina
Gisele Pappa	Universidade Federal de Minas Gerais, Brazil

Applications of AI

Ana Cristina Bicharra García	Universidade Federal Fluminense, Brazil
Fernando Koch	Samsung Research Institute, Brazil

Knowledge Engineering, Knowledge Representation, and Probabilistic Reasoning

Fabio Cozman	Universidade de São Paulo, Brazil
Guillermo Simari	Universidad Nacional del Sur, Argentina
Renata Wassermann	Universidade de São Paulo, Brazil

Machine Learning

Paulo Cortez	Universidade do Minho, Portugal
Joao Gama	University of Porto, Portugal
Estevam Rafael Hruschka Junior	Federal University of São Carlos, Brazil

Agent-Based Modeling and Simulation

Jaime Sichman	Universidade de São Paulo, Brazil
Giuseppe Vizzari	University of Milano-Bicocca, Italy

Multi-Agent Systems

Juan Carlos Burguillo	University of Vigo, Spain
Valérie Camps	University of Toulouse – IRIT, France
Jomi Fred Hubner	Universidade Federal de Santa Catarina, Brazil
Carles Sierra	IIIA-CSIC, Spain

Organization

IBERAMIA 204 was organized by the Pontifica Universidad Católica, Chile. The conference was sponsored by the main Ibero-American artificial intelligence and computer science societies:

Associação Portuguesa para Inteligência Artificial	APPIA
Asociación Española de Inteligencia Artificial	AEPIA
Sociedad Argentina de Informática	SADIO
Sociedad Colombiana de Computacion	SCC
Sociedad Cubana de Matemática y Computación	SCMC
Sociedad Iberoamericana de Inteligencia Artificial	IBERAMIA
Sociedad Mexicana de Inteligencia Artificial	SMIA
Sociedade Brasileira de Computação	SBC
Sociedad Peruana de Inteligencia Artificial	SPIA

Organizing Committee

Program Chair

Ana L.C. Bazzan — Instituto de Informática, Universidade Federal do Rio Grande do Sul, Brazil

Organization Chair

Karim Pichara — Pontifica Universidad Católica, Chile

Area Chairs

Ambient Intelligence

Juan Botía — Universidad de Murcia, Spain
Paulo Novais — Universidade do Minho, Portugal

AI in Education, Affective Computing and Human-Computer Interaction

Silvana Aciar — Instituto de Informática, Universidad Nacional de San Juan, Argentina
Silvia Schiaffino — Universidad Nacional del Centro de la Provincia de Buenos Aires, Argentina
Rosa Vicari — Universidade Federal do Rio Grande do Sul, Brazil

Table 2. Papers by area

Area	Submissions	Accepted	Acceptance Rate
Agent-based modeling and simulation	6	2	0.33
AI in education, affective computing, and human-computer interaction	7	4	0.57
Ambient intelligence	3	3	1.00
Applications of AI	14	6	0.43
Bio-inspired computing	12	7	0.58
Computer vision	2	-	0.00
Fuzzy systems	3	2	0.67
Information and knowledge processing/ knowledge discovery and data mining	11	5	0.45
Knowledge engineering, knowledge representation and probabilistic reasoning	8	3	0.38
Machine learning	11	6	0.55
Multi-agent systems	12	4	0.33
Natural language processing	19	5	0.26
Papers from area chairs	16	11	0.69
Planning and scheduling	3	1	0.33
Robotics	9	5	0.56

The editors would like to thank: the authors for submitting their work to IBERAMIA; the Area Chairs, Program Committee members, and additional reviewers for their hard work and valuable time; the sponsors; and Springer Verlag for agreeing to print this volume.

We also thank our keynote speakers: Professor Guillermo Simari (Universidad Nacional del Sur in Bahia Blanca, Argentina), Professor Blai Bonet (Universidad Simón Bolívar, Venezuela), and Pavlos Protopapas (University of Pennsylvania, USA).

Thanks also to the IBERAMIA executive committee and to the secretariat for its guidance and support, the team responsible for maintaining the website, and the local organizers as well as the Pontifica Universidad Católica, Chile.

Ana L.C. Bazzan
Karim Pichara

Preface

IBERAMIA is the biennial Ibero-American Conference on Artificial Intelligence (AI). In 2014, IBERAMIA was held in Santiago (Chile), from November 24 to 27. This conference is supported by the main Ibero-American societies of artificial intelligence, and provides researchers from Portugal, Spain, and countries in Latin America the opportunity to meet AI researchers from all over the world. Since its first edition (Barcelona, 1988), IBERAMIA has expanded its scope to become a well-recognized international conference in the AI field, with papers published in English by Springer in the LNCS/LNAI series since the sixth edition (Lisbon, 1998).

The technical structure of the conference is composed of the main technical sessions, keynote talks, and workshops.

The organizational structure of the scientific program of IBERAMIA is as follows: the conference is organized along several areas of AI and computational intelligence, each coordinated by two or three Area Chairs (ACs) who are experts in a particular area. ACs are responsible to select the Program Committee (PC) members. In total, IBERAMIA has involved 34 ACs, almost 300 PC members (from 30 countries, including 19 that are outside the Ibero-American geographical area), and an extra number of additional reviewers. Their names appear on pages VII, IX, and XVII respectively.

This year we have introduced one innovation, which is to try to provide as much feedback as possible to authors by doing our best to have each paper reviewed by more than four reviewers. We have succeeded in this task in more than 50% of the papers, as shown in Table 1.

Table 1. Number of reviews per paper

Number of reviews per paper	Number of papers
2	1
3	56
4	41
5	35
6	3

IBERAMIA 2014 received 136 submissions from 27 countries (among these, 16 are not within the Ibero-American area). From the total, 64 were accepted for presentation and publication in this volume. Statistics per area are shown in Table 2. We believe that this volume represents a fine contribution to the current research on several areas of AI.

Natural Language Processing

Manuel Montes-y-Gómez | Instituto Nacional de Astrofísica, Óptica y Electrónica, Mexico
Aline Villavicencio | Universidade Federal do Rio Grande do Sul, Brazil

Planning and Scheduling

Felipe Meneguzzi | Pontifícia Universidade Católica do Rio Grande do Sul, Brazil
Eva Onaindia | Universitat Politècnica de València, Spain

Fuzzy Systems

Andrea Tettamanzi | University of Nice Sophia Antipolis, France
Andrés Soto | Bityvip Technology, Spain

Robotics

Luiz Chaimowicz | Universidade Federal de Minas Gerais, Brazil
Luis Paulo Reis | Universidade do Minho, Portugal

Program Committee

Silvana Aciar | Instituto de Informática, Universidad Nacional de San Juan, Argentina
Emmanuel Adam | Université de Valenciennes, France
Nuria Agell | ESADE, URL, Spain
Eneko Agirre | University of the Basque Country, Spain
Tayseer Al-Shanableh | Near East University, Cyprus
Igor Alexander | Imperial College London, UK
Vania Almeida | INESC Porto, Portugal
Laura Alonso Alemany | Universidad Nacional de Córdoba, Argentina
Sandra Aluisio | Universidade de São Paulo, Brazil
Fred Amblard | CNRS IRIT – Université des Sciences Sociales Toulouse 1, France
Anca Andreica | UBB, Romania
Luis Antunes | GUESS/Universidade de Lisboa, Portugal
Manuel Armada | Spanish Council for Scientific Research, Spain
Marcelo Gabriel Armentano | ISISTAN, Facultad de Ciencias Exactas, UNICEN/CONICET, Argentina
Priscilla Avegliano | IBM Research, Brazil
Asier Aztiria | University of Mondragón, Spain
Javier Bajo | Universidad Politécnica de Madrid, Spain
Javier Bajo Pérez | Universidad Politécnica de Madrid, Spain
Silvia Baldiris | Universitat de Girona, Spain
Tiago Baptista | Universidade de Coimbra, Portugal

Guilherme Barreto	Universidade Federal do Ceará, Brazil
Leliane Barros	Universidade de São Paulo, Brazil
Ana L.C. Bazzan	Universidade Federal do Rio Grande do Sul, Brazil
Carlos Bento	Universidade de Coimbra, Portugal
Magda Bercht	Universidade Federal do Rio Grande do Sul, Brazil
Flavia Bernardini	Universidade Federal Fluminense – Polo Rio das Ostras, Brazil
Albert Bifet	University of Waikato, New Zealand
Fernando Bobillo	University of Zaragoza, Spain
Olivier Boissier	ENS Mines Saint-Etienne, France
Blai Bonet	Universidad Simón Bolívar, Venezuela
Sergio Borger	IBM Research, Brazil
Juan Botía	Universidad de Murcia, Spain
Rodrigo Braga	Universidade Federal de Santa Catarina, Brazil
Agnès Braud	University of Strasbourg, France
Ramón Brena	Tecnológico de Monterrey, Mexico
Sofia Brenes	Google, USA
Facundo Bromberg	Universidad Tecnológica Nacional, Argentina
Alberto Bugarín	University of Santiago de Compostela, Spain
Juan Carlos Burguillo	University of Vigo, Spain
Davide Buscaldi	Université Paris 13, France
Dídac Busquets	Imperial College London, UK
Aleksander Byrski	AGH University of Science and Technology, Poland
Daniel Cabrera-Paniagua	Universidad de Valparaíso, Chile
Heloisa Camargo	
Valérie Camps	University of Toulouse – IRIT, France
Carlos Cardonha	IBM Research, Brazil
Jaime Cardoso	INESC Porto, Portugal
Luis Carriço	Universidade de Lisboa, Portugal
Alexandre Carvalho	LIAAD INESC Porto, Portugal
Andre Carvalho	Universidade de São Paulo, Brazil
Ana Casali	Universidad Nacional de Rosario – CIFASIS, Argentina
Jose Cascalho	Universidade dos Açores, Portugal
Luis Fernando Castillo	Universidad de Caldas, Colombia
Rita María Castillo Ortega	Universidad de Granada, Spain
Rocío Luján Cecchini	Universidad Nacional del Sur, Argentina
Loic Cerf	Universidade Federal de Minas Gerais, Brazil
Mario Chacon	New York University Abu Dhabi, UAE
Luiz Chaimowicz	Universidade Federal de Minas Gerais, Brazil
Chee Seng Chan	University of Malaya, Malaysia
Carlos Chesñevar	Universidad Nacional del Sur, Argentina

Fernando Koch — Samsung Research Institute, Brazil
Andrew Koster — Samsung Research Institute, Brazil
Jaroslaw Kozlak — AGH University of Science and Technology, Poland
Salvador Landeros — Universidad Nacional Autónoma de México, Mexico
Nuno Lau — University of Aveiro, Portugal
João Leite — Universidade Nova de Lisboa, Portugal
Jim Little — UBC, Canada
Fernando Lobo — University of the Algarve, Portugal
Magalí Teresinha Longhi — Universidade Federal do Rio Grande do Sul, Brazil
Ana Carolina Lorena — Federal University of São Paulo, Brazil
Carlos Martín Lorenzetti — Universidad Nacional del Sur, Argentina
Michael Luck — King's College London, UK
Teresa Ludermir — Universidade Federal de Pernambuco, Brazil
Beatriz López — Universitat de Girona, Spain
Itzamá López Yáñez — Instituto Politécnico Nacional, Mexico
Ana Gabriela Maguitman — Universidad Nacional del Sur, Argentina
Benedita Malheiro — Instituto Superior de Engenharia do Porto, Portugal
Nuno Mamede — Spoken Language Systems Laboratory, Portugal
Nuno Marques — Universidade Nova de Lisboa, Portugal
Sarajane Marques Peres — Universidade de São Paulo, Brazil
Goreti Marreiros — Instituto Superior de Engenharia do Porto, Portugal
Luis Marti — PUC-Rio, Brazil
María Vanina Martínez — University of Oxford, UK
Vicente Matellan — Universidad de León, Spain
Luis Matias — University of Porto, Portugal
Jorge Maturana — UACH, Chile
Wagner Meira Jr. — Universidade Federal de Minas Gerais, Brazil
Felipe Meneguzzi — Pontifícia Universidade Católica do Rio Grande do Sul, Brazil
José Manuel Menéndez — Universidad Politécnica de Madrid, Spain
Juan Julián Merelo — Universidad de Granada, Spain
Luiz Merschmann — UFOP, Brazil
Domingo Mery — Pontificia Universidad Católica, Chile
Pedro Meseguer — IIIA-CSIC, Spain
Fabien Michel — LIRMM – Université Montpellier II, France
Diego Milone — Universidad Nacional del Litoral, Argentina
Maria-Carolina Monard — Universidade de São Paulo, Brazil

Manuel Montes-Y-Gómez	Instituto Nacional de Astrofísica, Óptica y Electrónica, Mexico
Eduardo Morales	Instituto Nacional de Astrofísica, Óptica y Electrónica, Mexico
António Paulo Moreira	University of Porto, Portugal
Carlos Morell	Universidad Central de Las Villas, Cuba
Julian Moreno	Universidad Nacional de Colombia, Colombia
Plinio Moreno	Instituto de Sistemas e Robótica, Instituto Superior Técnico, Portugal
Rafael Murrieta	UIUC, USA
Andres Muñoz	UCAM, Spain
Susana Nascimento	Universidade Nova de Lisboa, Portugal
Roberto Navigli	Sapienza University of Rome, Italy
José Neira	University of Zaragoza, Spain
Adolfo Neto	Universidade Tecnológica Federal do Paraná, Brazil
M.C. Nicoletti	Federal University of Sao Cãrlos, Brazil
Pablo Noriega	IIIA-CSIC, Spain
Paulo Novais	Universidade do Minho, Portugal
Luís Nunes	Instituto Universitário de Lisboa (ISCTE-IUL), Instituto de Telecomunicações, Portugal
Pedro Nuñez	Universidad de Extremadura, Spain
Colm O'Riordan	GALWAY
José Ángel Olivas Varela	Universidad de Castilla-La Mancha, Spain
Elaine H.T. Oliveira	Universidade Federal do Amazonas, Brazil
José Luis Oliveira	University of Aveiro, Portugal
Márcia Oliveira	LIAAD INESC Porto, Portugal
Eva Onaindia	Universitat Politécnica de València, Spain
Manuel Ortega Cantero	Universidad de Castilla-La Mancha, Spain
Fernando Osório	Universidade de São Paulo, Brazil
Patricia Paderewski	Universidade de Granada, Spain
Muntsa Padró	Universidade Federal do Rio Grande do Sul, Brazil
Aline Paes Carvalho	Universidade Federal Fluminense, Brazil
Luis Paes Leme	Universidade Federal Fluminense, Brazil
Gisele Pappa	Universidade Federal de Minas Gerais, Brazil
Thiago Pardo	Universidade de São Paulo, Brazil
Gabriella Pasi	University of Milano-Bicocca, Italy
Juan Pavón	Universidad Complutense de Madrid, Spain
Max Pereira	University of Porto, Portugal
Ted Petersen	University of Minnesota in Duluth, USA
Marcelo Pimenta	Universidade Federal do Rio Grande do Sul, Brazil
David Pinto	Universidad Autónoma de Puebla, Mexico

Fabio Piva	Samsung Research Institute, Brazil
Alexandre Plastino	Universidade Federal Fluminense, Brazil
Aurora Pozo	UFPR, Brazil
Ronaldo Prati	UFABC, Brazil
Edson Prestes	Universidade Federal do Rio Grande do Sul, Brazil
Carlos Ramisch	Aix Marseille Université, France
Carlos Ramos	Instituto Superior de Engenharia do Porto, Portugal
Thomas Reichherzer	University of West Florida, USA
Luis Paulo Reis	Universidade do Minho, Portugal
Solange Rezende	Universidade de São Paulo, Brazil
Fernando Ribeiro	Universidade do Minho, Portugal
Márcio Ribeiro	Universidade de São Paulo, Brazil
Rita Ribeiro	University of Porto, Portugal
Jan Richter	IBM Research, Australia
Mariano Rivera	CIMAT, Mexico
Luís Rocha	Indiana University, USA
Rui Rocha	Universidade de Coimbra, Portugal
Josemar Rodrigues de Souza	Universidade do Estado da Bahia, Brazil
Ricardo O. Rodriguez	Universidad de Buenos Aires, Argentina
Oswaldo Rojas	Universidad Nacional de Colombia, Colombia
Roseli Romero	Universidade de São Paulo, Brazil
Agostinho Rosa	IST, Portugal
Alejandro Rosete Suárez	CUJAE, Cuba
Rosaldo Rossetti	University of Porto, Portugal
Paolo Rosso	Universitat Politècnica de València, Spain
Cristian Rusu	Pontificia Universidad Católica de Valparaíso, Chile
Luis Salgado	Universidad Autónoma de Madrid, Spain
Nayat Sanchez-Pi	ADDLabs, Universidade Federal Fluminense, Brazil
João Sarraipa	UNINOVA, Portugal
Silvia Schiaffino	Universidad Nacional del Centro de la Provincia de Buenos Aires, Argentina
Klamer Schutte	Netherlands Organisation for Applied Scientific Research TNO, Netherlands
Ivan Serina	University of Brescia, Italy
Emilio Serrano	Universidad Politécnica de Madrid, Spain
Jaime Sichman	Universidade de São Paulo, Brazil
Carles Sierra	IIIA-CSIC, Spain
Sara Silva	Universidade Nova de Lisboa, Portugal
Moser Silva Fagundes	Pontifícia Universidade Católica do Rio Grande do Sul, Brazil

Denis Wolf   Universidade de São Paulo, Brazil
Dina Wonsever   Universidad de la República, Uruguay
Cornelio Yannez Marquez   Instituto Politécnico Nacional, Mexico
Neil Yorke-Smith   American University of Beirut, Lebanon
Bianca Zadrozny   IBM Research, Brazil
Daniela Zaharie   UVT, Romania
Victor Zamudio   Instituto Tecnológico de León, Mexico
Cleber Zanchettin   Universidade Federal de Pernambuco, Brazil
Gerson Zaverucha   UFRJ, Brazil

Additional Reviewers

Alvares Cherman, Everton   Hoedlmoser, Michael
Alvares, Luis Otavio   Hoey, Jesse
Armentano, Marcelo Gabriel   Iruskieta, Mikel
Baldiris Navarro, Silvia Margarita Jubertie, Sylvain
Beloglazov, Anton   Koshiyama, Adriano Soares
Bifet, Albert   Landeros, Salvador
Borges, Henrique   Lopez De Lacalle, Oier
Bugarín, Alberto   Lopez-Monroy, Adrián Pastor
Carvalho, Veronica   Lorenzetti, Carlos Martín
Casali, Ana   Loula, Angelo
Castro, Pablo   Maciel, Cristiano
Cecchini, Rocío Luján   Marchi, Jerusa
Cobe, Raphael   Mery, Domingo
Coelho, Frederico   Moncecchi, Guillermo
Correa Da Silva, Flavio S.   Mucientes, Manuel
Croitoru, Madalina   Neto, Adolfo
De Bona, Glauber   Nicoletti, M.C.
Delgado, Myriam   Oliveira, Allysson
Dias De Assuncao, Marcos   Oliveira, Eugénio
Dias, Douglas Mota   Olivetti De França, Fabrício
Eyharabide, Victoria   Osborne, John
Ferraz, Inhauma   P. Rocha, Honovan
Ferreira, Liliana   Patrão, Diogo
Fillottrani, Pablo   Pilehvar, Mohammad Taher
Finger, Marcelo   Pintea, Camelia
Flores, Enrique   Pinto, Fábio
Godo, Lluis   Pitangui, Cristiano
Goldbarg, Elizabeth   Poria, Soujanya
Goldbarg, Marco   Prado, Adriana
Gomez, Sergio Alejandro   Primo, Tiago
Gonzalez, Carina   Ralha, Célia Ghedini
Gonçalves, Eder Mateus   Rangel, Francisco
Grinblat, Guillermo Luis   Rodrigues, Mário

Rodriguez, Alejandro
Rodríguez-Fdez, Ismael
Rosá, Aiala
Salgado, Luis
Santos, António-Paulo
Santos, Elder
Sapkota, Upendra
Silva, Alexandre
Silva, Filipe
Soto, Axel
Sousa, Armando
Spolaôr, Newton
Stegmayer, Georgina

Sánchez, Fernando
Tohmé, Fernando
Tomassi, Diego
Torres-Méndez, Luz Abril
Trigueiros, Paulo
Uriarte, Abril
Valverde-Rebaza, Jorge Carlos
Vianna, Luis G.R.
Villatoro-Tello, Esau
Vinyals, Meritxell
Viterbo, Jose
Wanderley, Maria Fernanda

Contents

Fuzzy Systems

Knowledge Discovery and Data Mining

Bio-inspired Computing

Agent-Based Modelling and Simulation

AI in Education, Affective Computing, and Human-Computer Interaction

Knowledge Engineering, Knowledge Representation and Probabilistic Reasoning

A Parsing Approach to SAT

José M. Castaño[✉]

Depto. de Computación, FCEyN, UBA, Buenos Aires, Argentina
jcastano@dc.uba.ar

Abstract. We present a parsing approach to address the problem of propositional satisfiability (SAT). We use a very simple translation from formulae in conjunctive normal form (CNF) to strings to be parsed by an Earley type algorithm. The parsing approach enables both a SAT and an ALL-SAT solver. The parsing algorithm is based in a model of automata that uses multiple stacks, presented here with a grammar characterization. The time complexity of the algorithm is polynomial, where the degree of the polynomial is dependent on the number of stacks used. It is not dependent on the length of the input nor properties of the grammar. However the number of stacks used might be a function on the number of variables and this is an open question. The number of stacks effectively used in practice is dependent on ordering of variables and clauses. A prototype of the parser was implemented and tested.

Keywords: SAT · ALL-SAT · Multi-stack automata · Earley parsing

Introduction

Propositional satisfiability (SAT) solving has many practical applications ranging from artificial intelligence to software verification. Search-based techniques in SAT solving have been enormously successful. State-of-the-art SAT solvers are based on the DPLL (Davis-Putnam-Logemann-Loveland) algorithm. Current research in this area involves refinements and extensions of the DPLL technique. Little effort has gone into investigating alternative techniques.

The relationship between logic formulae and automata was formally considered as early as in [3,8] and also in [21,22]. However the relationship of SAT to formal languages and related automata was mainly related to NP-hard or NP-complete results. Most attempts to extend the descriptive power of CFGs at least turned out in an NP-hard/complete result [1,11,13–15,20].

There is an accepted view that many problems require machinery above the context-free realm. A number of formalisms have been proposed generalizing properties of context-free machinery. Such models used *control* devices, where the control device is a context-free grammar (see [6,23,24] regarding control languages). Also equivalent models of automata with additional pushdown stacks were proposed: [5,10,16,24]. They form hierarchies of levels of languages, where a language of level k properly includes a language of level k-1. The complexity of the recognition problem is dependent on the language level, for a level k language: $\mathcal{O}(n^{3 \cdot 2^{k-1}})$ [24].

© Springer International Publishing Switzerland 2014
A.L.C. Bazzan and K. Pichara (Eds.): IBERAMIA 2014, LNAI 8864, pp. 3–14, 2014.
DOI: 10.1007/978-3-319-12027-0_1

In this paper we use a grammar formalism where the control of the derivation is performed by a sequence of stacks. The use of multiple stacks with different writing/reading constraints has been analyzed [23]. A number of constraints are imposed here on the operations available on the sequence of stacks. These constraints aim to restrict the descriptive power of the generative devices used. This grammar formalism is capable to model the language of satisfiable propositional formulae (SAT). The work presented here focuses on the use of multiple-stack for SAT solving. The use of a parsing algorithm to address SAT is as far as we know a totally ignored approach. Approaching SAT as a parsing approach offers some advantages, like the use of memoization, with regards to a search backtracking method like DPLL.

The model of automata presented here is intended to be able to model problems which are beyond context-free and are essentially in NP. Probably the most studied problem in NP is propositional satisfiability (SAT) [2]. In terms of formal languages it is related to unrestricted crossing dependencies as represented by the language of satisfiable propositional formulae (SAT) as shown by Satta in [14].

The rest of the article is organized as follows: we present in Section 1 the grammatical formalism Multiple Global Indexed Grammars. In Section 2 we show the descriptive power of this formalism considering the language of satisfiable propositional formula L_{sat}. In section 3 we introduce a recognition algorithm specifically designed for L_{sat} and show that the particular recognition problem is in P, where the degree of the polynomial is determined by the number of stacks used but it is not dependent on properties of the grammar or the length of the input. However, the universal recognition problem is NP-complete, where the universal recognition problem is the one to decide for a given grammar G and string w, whether G generates w.

1   Multiple Global Indexed Languages (MGILs)

We present here Multiple Global Index Languages. We define Multiple Global Index grammars (MGIGs) which are conceived as a modification (not an extension because they do not include GILs) to Global Index Grammars [4]. A proper extension to GIGs can be defined easily. We keep GIG's requirement that writing in a stack is restricted to reading of the input, and similarly the derives relation requires leftmost derivation.

Definition 1. *A MGIG is a 6-tuple $G = (N, T, S, \#, P, O)$ where $N, T, S, \#$ are as defined in GIGs, P is a finite set of productions, having the following form, where A denotes a non-terminal α a possibly empty sequence of non-terminals and terminals, t and u are terminals.*

        a. $A \underset{\epsilon}{\rightarrow} \alpha$ (epsilon or CF)   c. $A \underset{\bar{t}}{\rightarrow} uB|B|\epsilon$ (pop terminal word t)

        b. $A \underset{t}{\rightarrow} uB|u$ (push word t)   d. $A \underset{\bar{t}\&t_s}{\rightarrow} uB|B|\epsilon$ (pop t and push suffix t_s)

O is an order relation over T that is used in the derivation relation.

There are several characteristics to notice. Productions type (a.) are essentially context-free. Push productions (b) require the first element in the right-hand side to be a terminal (or token, a sequence of terminals). Also what is pushed onto the list of stacks is a terminal or sequence of terminals. This restriction on *push* rules is a crucial property of GIGs and MGIGs. MGIGs (unlike GIGs) allow productions for pushing and popping operations with at most one non terminal in the right side. This is a departure from GIGs and this is the reason why MGIGs are not a proper extension of GIGs. This restriction is used to constrain the operations on the list of stacks. Pop productions (c,d) remove the corresponding word from the top of the least ordered stack. Pop-push productions (d), pop a word and push a suffix of this word. Derivations in MGIGs are similar to those in GIGs except that instead of modifying a string of indices, several sequences of stored stacks can be modified, but only one at a time, in both cases they require leftmost derivation.

Sentential forms are strings in $(T^*\#)^+(N \cup T)^*$. The relation *derives* $\Rightarrow$ on sentential forms is defined as follows: let t, u be in T, w, y be in T^* let α and γ be in $(N \cup T)^*$, let η be in $(T^*\#)^+$ i.e. possible empty multi-stacks. Given a sequence of stacks $\eta_k\#_k, \ldots, \eta_1\#_1$, ts denotes the set of non empty top of stacks: $ts(\eta_k\#_k, \ldots, \eta_1\#_1) = \{t_k, \ldots, t_1\}$. The derives relation uses an order O relation over T:

1. If $A \rightarrow \alpha$ is a production (context-free) then, there are no changes in the multi-stack: $\eta_k\#_k, \ldots, \eta_1\#_1wA\gamma \Rightarrow \eta_k\#_k, \ldots, \eta_1\#_1w\alpha\gamma$

2. If $A \underset{t}{\rightarrow} \alpha$ is a *push* production then t is inserted in the corresponding stack i where the u_i is the least element in ts greater than or equal to t, $1 \leq i \leq k$:
   - $if \exists u_i \in ts : t \leq_O u_i \wedge (\forall t_j \in ts : t \leq_O t_j \implies u_i \leq_O t_j)$ then
   - $-$ $\eta_k, \ldots, \mathbf{u_iy_i}\#_i, \ldots, \eta_1\#_1wA\gamma \Rightarrow \eta_k, \ldots, \mathbf{t_iu_iy_i}\#_i, \ldots, \eta_1\#_1w\alpha\gamma$
   - else $\eta_k\#_k, \ldots, \eta_1\#_1wA\gamma \Rightarrow t_{k+1}\#_{k+1}\eta_k\#_k, \ldots, \eta_1\#_1w\alpha\gamma$
   (t is now the greatest top element in the multi-stack, and a new stack will be added at $k + 1$).

3. If $A \underset{\bar{t}}{\rightarrow} \alpha$ is a production (a *pop* production) and t is the least element of the top of stacks ts then remove t from the top of its stack. Say t is at the stack i formally $t_i \in ts \wedge (\forall t_j \in ts : t_i \leq_O t_j)$, where $1 \leq i \leq k$:
   - then $\eta_k, \ldots, \mathbf{t_iy_i}\#_i, \ldots, \eta_1\#_1wA\gamma \Rightarrow \eta_k, \ldots, \mathbf{y_i}\#_i, \ldots, \eta_1\#_1w\alpha\gamma$

4. If $A \underset{\bar{t}\&t_s}{\rightarrow} \alpha$ is a production (*pop&push*) then t is removed from its stack i, ts' is obtained after a first step derivation and then the non empty suffix t_s is pushed to the corresponding order stack j, where $1 \leq i \leq k$ and $1 \leq j \leq k$:
   - then:
   $$\eta_k, \ldots, \mathbf{t_iy_i}\#_i, \ldots, \eta_1\#_1wA\gamma \Rightarrow \eta_k, \ldots, \mathbf{y_i}\#_i, \ldots, \mathbf{t_sy_j}\#_j, \ldots, \eta_1\#_1w\alpha\gamma$$

   this derivation might be easier interpreted as two steps combined, given t_s might be pushed into the same stack from which t is removed:

   $$\eta_k, \ldots, \mathbf{t_iy_i}\#_i, \ldots, \eta_1\#_1wA\gamma \Rightarrow \eta_k, \ldots, \mathbf{y_i}\#_i, \ldots, \eta_1\#_1w\alpha\gamma \Rightarrow$$
   $$\eta_k, \ldots, \mathbf{t_sy_j}\#_j, \ldots, \eta_1\#_1w\alpha\gamma$$

The reflexive and transitive closure of $\Rightarrow$ is denoted, as usual by $\overset{*}{\Rightarrow}$. We define the language L of a MGIG, G, $L(G)$ to be: $\{w \,|\, \#S \overset{*}{\Rightarrow} \#w,$ where w is in $T^*\}$ and we call L a MGIL.

It is clear that the acceptance condition relies on the sequence of stacks to be empty. In other words, all the dependencies have to be matched. It should be noted that MGIGs (unlike GIGs) require a regular backbone for push and pop productions. These restrictions aim to mitigate the added power of the sequence of stacks and simplify the parsing algorithm. In many other formalisms [5,20,23] there are different restrictions on writing and reading from the additional stacks. Decoupling the selection of the stacks from the transition function and using an ordering relation to select the reading and writing stacks is as far as we know a novelty regarding restrictions on reading and writing to multiple stacks and provides a different hierarchy of languages. Unlike relying on a fixed order of stacks the order relation O over T is used to determine the stack to be selected for reading and/or writing. The use of O shows a possible way to accommodate expected valuations to be matched with clauses using ordering of variables and clauses.

2   SAT as an Abstract Language

We present in this section a grammar and an example of derivation. This construction is inspired on a reduction of SAT to LCFRS in [14].

In order to represent formulae to be parsed, we perform the following translation. Given an arbitrary instance of SAT, a formula in CNF with a set of variables $\{x_1, ..., x_n\}$ and a set of clauses $\{c_1, ..., c_k\}$, map each variable to $i \in [1, ..., n]$. For each clause c, replace each literal $l_j, ..., l_m$ by ia if it is a positive literal and by ib if it is a negated literal. Disjunction is not represented by a string and conjunction is represented by white space. We assume that strings have to be ordered by the initial integer in each clause. Therefore, a string like $1a2b\ 1b2a\ 1b3a\ 2a3b\ 2b3a$ is a mapping from a formula: $(x \vee \neg y) \wedge (\neg x \vee y) \wedge (\neg x \vee z) \wedge (y \vee \neg z) \wedge (\neg y \vee z)$, where x corresponds to 1, y to 2 and z to 3.

We define a set of Multiple Global Indexed Grammars for any given n that generates the corresponding language as follows:

Definition 2. *(GSAT$_n$)*
$G_{SATn} = (N, T, S_1, \#, P, O)$, *where for a given* $n \in \mathbb{N}$
$T = \{ia, ib, ia\omega, ib\omega \mid 1 \leq i \leq n\}$
$N = \{S_i, A_i, B_i \mid 1 \leq i \leq n\}$
$P = P_{cf} \cup P_{cfn} \cup P_{lex1} \cup P_{lex2} \cup P_{lex3}$
$P_{cf} = \{S_i \rightarrow A_i S_{i+1}, S_i \rightarrow B_i S_{i+1}\}$ *for* $S_i, A_i, B_i \in N, i < n$
$P_{cfn} = \{S_n \rightarrow A_n, S_n \rightarrow B_n\}$
$P_{lex1} = \{A_i \rightarrow ia A_i | ia\omega A_i | \epsilon, B_i \rightarrow ib B_i | ib\omega B_i | \epsilon\}$,
$P_{lex2} = \{A_i \xrightarrow{\omega} ib\omega A_i, B_i \rightarrow ia\omega B_i\}$,
$P_{lex3} = \{A_i \xrightarrow[ia\omega]{} A_i, A_i \xrightarrow[ia]{} A_i, B_i \xrightarrow[ib\omega]{} B_i, B_i \xrightarrow[ib]{} B_i, A_i \xrightarrow[ib\omega\&\omega]{} A_i, B_i \xrightarrow[ia\omega\&\omega]{} B_i\}$
O *is lexicographic order of* i *prefixes in* $\mathbb{N}$.

The set of terminals and productions is defined using the variable i and a regular expression notation, where ω stands for an ordered sequence of pairs of integers and the characters a, b. Therefore $ia\omega$ defines as tokens or terminals in the language those tokens with prefix ia, e.g. $1a2b$ or $1a3a4b$. This is the same use of a terminal V (or *verb*), that defines verbs in a grammar for natural language. Another similar example is the use of **int** which defines integers in a context-free grammar for arithmetic expressions. Regular expressions were also used in extended context-free grammars (e.g. [12]). Each sequence of numbers and letters (a clause) is a *token* (in a parsing sense) or a *terminal* in a grammar sense. The same use is made for those terminals pushed into the additional stack. Therefore production $A_1 \rightarrow 1b\omega A_1$ is equivalent to a set including productions like $A_1 \underset{2a}{\rightarrow} 1b2aA_1, A_1 \underset{2b3a}{\rightarrow} 1\overset{\omega}{b2}b3aA_1$. Such productions require that words generated have a non empty suffix to be pushed in the auxiliary multi-stack. Those suffixes pushed in the multi-stack have to be matched later to continue the derivation. A *unit* terminal like $1b$ cannot be generated using productions with non-terminal A_1, but only with a production with non-terminal B_1: $B_1 \rightarrow 1bB_1$. The lexicographic order O is restricted to those prefixes in words that are in $\mathbb{N}$. Therefore $3a7b <_O 5b7b$, but $3a7b \leq_O 3b$ and $3b \leq_O 3a7b$.

Grammar G_{sat_n} allows two non deterministic choices for each variable i, either the non terminal A_i or the non terminal B_i, each of them representing respectively a *True* or *False* assignment to the corresponding variable. Therefore if non terminal A_1 is chosen in the derivation, clause $1a2b$ has a valid assignment, but clause $1b2a$, requires non terminal A_2 to be chosen at the next step and this is forced by pushing $2a$ to the multi-stack. The multi-stack is the data structure used to book those parts of the clause that need to be satisfied later on when the right order to assign the corresponding truth value is reached. On the other hand if non terminal B_1 is chosen in the derivation clause $1a2b$ has not a valid assignment yet, therefore $2b$ is pushed onto the multi-stack and forces a derivation with non-terminal B_2.

Example 1. (Unsuccessful derivation).
$\#S_1 \Rightarrow \#B_1S_2 \Rightarrow$ **2b** $\#1a2b\ B_1S_2 \Rightarrow$ **2a3a 2b** $\#1a2b\ 1a2a3a\ B_1S_2 \Rightarrow$
$2a3a\ 2b\ \#1a2b\ 1a2a3a\ 1b2a\ B_1S_2 \Rightarrow 2a3a\ 2b\ \#1a2b\ 1a2a3a\ 1b2a\ 1b3a\ B_1S_2 \Rightarrow$
$2a3a\ 2b\ \#1a2b\ 1a2a3a\ 1b2a\ 1b3a\ S_2 \Rightarrow 2a3a\ 2b\ \#1a2b\ 1a2a3a\ 1b2a\ 1b3a\ B_2S_3 \Rightarrow$
3a $\#$**2b** $\#1a2b\ 1a2a3a\ 1b2a\ 1b3a\ B_2S_3 \Rightarrow 3a\ \#1a2b\ 1a2a3a\ 1b2a\ 1b3a\ B_2S_3 \Rightarrow$
3b 3a $\#1a2b\ 1a2a3a\ 1b2a\ 1b3a\ 2a3b\ B_2S_3 \Rightarrow$
$3b\ 3a\ \#1a2b\ 1a2a3a\ 1b2a\ 1b3a\ 2a3b\ 2b3a\ B_2S_3 \Rightarrow$
$3b\ 3a\ \#1a2b\ 1a2a3a\ 1b2a\ 1b3a\ 2a3b\ 2b3a\ S_3 \Rightarrow$
$3b\ 3a\ \#1a2b\ 1a2a3a\ 1b2a\ 1b3a\ 2a3b\ 2b3a\ B_3 \Rightarrow$
$3a\ \#1a2b\ 1a2a3a\ 1b2a\ 1b3a\ 2a3b\ 2b3a\ B_3$

In example 1 we consider the string $1a2b\ 1a2a3a\ 1b2a\ 1b3a\ 2a3b\ 2b3a$ which cannot be generated by a sequence of B_i, because the multi-stack cannot be emptied. It can be observed the use of productions type *pop-push* with non terminal B_2. This string is successfully derived using a sequence of A_i's.

We have shown in Example 1 how a conflict driven by previous variable assignment prevents the derivation to continue. It also should be noted how conflicts can be encoded in the Multiple Stack in the derivation. It can be easily seen that the grammar enforces and controls through the multiple stack the truth value assignments for each clause and formula that the grammar generates. In other words if a *translated formula* is generated by the grammar then it is a satisfiable formula. On the other direction, it can be seen that if a *translated formula* is satisfiable then there is a derivation for the encoding of the formula that represents the truth assignments for the formula. Following this sketch it can be shown that $L(G_{sat_n})$ is the language of satisfiable propositional formula with n variables L_{sat_n}. The construction is done in polynomial time as can be easily verified, therefore, MGIL universal recognition is NP-hard. Alternatively, it can be seen that a particular grammar can be encoded for each instance of a formula, following the general specifications provided in G_{sat_n}, as it is done in may reductions to SAT.

This brings back the issue of time complexity both for LCFRS and equivalent formalisms: they are acknowledged to define *polynomially* recognizable languages, however the degree of the polynomial is dependent of the rank/fan-out of the system. The rank or the fan-out of LCFRS allow to encode k variable values for a propositional formula as was shown in [14]. Therefore the universal recognition problem was shown to be NP-complete, and it is equivalent to explore the complete space of truth value assignments. However as it can be observed from Example 1, the number of stacks in MGILs are not determined by the grammar as in LCFRS, but are determined by each particular derivation. Different derivations for the same string might use different number of stacks. The upper boundary for the number of stacks in a language like L_{sat_n}, is bound by the number of variables from the formula. However this would imply that at every variable choice (A_i, B_i), a new stack is added. This seems an unlikely situation. The interesting question is then whether the number of stacks used when parsing L_{sat} is a function of $|V|$, the cardinality of the set of variables in a propositional formula, and if so which is the function.

3   An Earley Parsing Algorithm for SAT

3.1   Graph-Structured Stacks and Multiple Stack Operations

Graph-structured stacks [19] were used to compute the operations corresponding to each individual stack configurations. A graph structured stack is a directed acyclic graph. It is a device for efficiently handling of non-determinism in stack operations.

If all the possible stack configurations in a GIG (and therefore MGIG) derivation were to be represented, the number of possible configurations would grow exponentially with the length of the input. MGIGs graph structured stack is simpler than GIGs because cannot combine non-terminal dependencies with additional stacks dependencies. MGIGs graph structured stack is more complex than GIGs' in that the top of the stack is represented by an ordered set of pointers to the graph structured stack instead of a single pointer. The least ordered node is accessible for pop operations. All other nodes in the set are accessible for push operations but only one can be chosen and this node is determined by the given order in the grammar. Figure 1 (left) represents this idea of multi-stack graph.

In order to represent properly alternative derivations allowed by a MGIG the pushed word (w_i) and its positional index (p_i) are used to represent nodes in the stack. Therefore the same *word*, pushed at different positions in the input, will be represented as two different nodes in the graph. It is also necessary to distinguish, a word pushed into different stacks in different multi-stack configurations. A unique identifier id is used for each created stack. Therefore, a node n_j will be represented by a triple: (w_i, p_i, id).

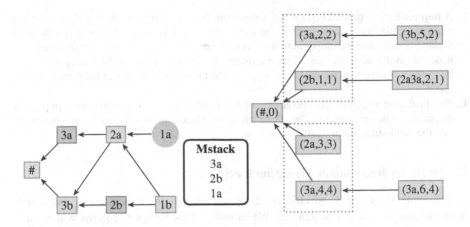

Fig. 1. Simple representation (left).The multi-stack graph for derivation 1 (right).

The pair w_i, p_i represents the word pushed into the stack identified by id. For instance, the graph in Figure 1 (right) is constructed while processing the following words from Example 1, presented here with their positional indices as subscripts:

$1a2b_1$ $1a2a3a_2$ $1b2a_3$ $1b3a_4$ $2a3b_5$ $2b3a_6$

The upper part of the graph corresponds to the derivation that uses non terminals B_1 and B_2, and the lower part of the graph corresponds to the derivation that uses non terminals A_1 and A_2. Dotted rectangles represent multi-stacks with more than a node in the multi-stack. The upper part multi-stack corresponds to the multi-stack configuration after the first B_2 derivation. The lower part multi-stack is produced after processing the word $1b3a$ at position 4, using $A's$ non terminals.

We detail here the algorithm to update the graph structured stack (line numbers refer to Algorithm 1 in the Appendix). It uses four parameters: 1) the input multi-stack ms represented by an ordered list $[n_0, \ldots, n_k]$ of nodes in the graph (line 7), 2) the ordering O defined in the grammar, 3) μ the operation on the multi-stack defined by current production 4) p current input position (line 1). The graph is represented as an adjacency list (line 4). The unique id that identifies each individual stack is represented by the global variable cid (line 5) The output returned by Update is the set of possible configurations of the multi-stack (i.e. a set of ordered lists of nodes), corresponding to the possible configurations of top elements of the multiple stack after a derivation step.

There are 4 possible modifications to the multiple stack according to the value of μ in the production used in the derivation. Modifications of the multiple stack reflect the conditions on the derivation that were specified in Section 1.

1. μ is ϵ. Do nothing, the set returned contains only the input multi-stack with no modification (lines 8 to 10).
2. A **push** production (lines 11-22): μ is a word or token t. Traverse the multi-stack list ms, until a node n_i is found such that $t \leq_O n_i$. A new node n_t is created and the adjacency list and the multi-stack ms are updated. If the list is exhausted (there was no n_i such that $t \leq_O n_i$, then the new node n_t is added to the multi-stack being the last element in the list. The output is returned with a single element (line 15 or 19-21).

3. A **pop** production (lines 23-31) μ is $\bar{t}$. Check whether t matches n_0 the first element in the multi-stack list, the least element in the input multi-stack (line 23). If this is not the case nothing is done and the empty output set is returned (line 31). If there is a match then the nodes n_j in the adjacency list of n_0 are returned. For each n_j in the adjacency list a new multi-stack is obtained, replacing n_o by n_j, in the multi-stack list ms in the corresponding order.

4. The final case specifies the operations on the multi-stack corresponding to a **pop-push** derivation. μ has to match n_0, but there has to be a non-empty suffix of n_0 that is pushed into the multi-stack (lines 32-49).

3.2 An Earley Recognition Algorithm for SAT

The following algorithm is specifically designed for the grammar G_{SATn} and it will not be correct for MGILs in general. We modify CFLs Earley [7] items which have the following shape: $[A \rightarrow \alpha \bullet \beta, i, j]$ adding a parameter Δ that corresponds to an ordered list pointers to accessible nodes in the graph-structured stack. Also the operator μ, corresponding to MGILs productions is added to the item. Therefore Earley items for MGILs are as follows: $[\Delta, A \underset{\mu}{\rightarrow} \alpha \bullet \beta, i, j]$. Δ is $\langle n_0, ..., n_k \rangle$, where n_i is a node in the graph structured stack and $n_0 \leq n_j \leq n_k$ for any n_0, n_j, n_k in Δ. In other words Δ is an ordered lists of nodes.

Main properties of Earley's algorithm for CFLs remains unchanged. We use here *Parsing Schemata*, a framework that allows high-level specification and analysis of parsing algorithms [17,18]. This framework enables the analysis of relations between different parsing algorithms by means of the relations between their respective parsing schemata.

Due to space constraints, we present parsing schemata rather informally here. Parsing Schemata are a generalization (or uninstantiation) of a parsing system. A parsing system specifies the set of items that represent partial specifications of parse results and a set of deduction steps that allow to derive new items from already known items. Deduction (inference) steps are of the form $\dfrac{\eta_1, ..., \eta_k}{\xi}$ which means that if all the required antecedents η_i are present, then the consequent ξ is generated by the parser. The acceptance conditions are represented by the goal item that encodes the recognition of a sentence. Therefore a sentence is recognized if we can reach a goal item starting from an initial (Axiom) item.

Initial item (Axiom), and stop conditions (Goal item) for the MGIG parser require the *empty multi-stack* node represented as: $\langle (\#, 0) \rangle$.

Inference rules correspond to Earley operations **predictor, scanner, completer**. Predictor[1] and Completer do not introduce any change on the multi-stack. These operations just pass the corresponding multiple-stack information. However each Completer operation may pass a different multiple stack Δ_k upwards. The important change is made on the scanner operation, where the multi-stack Δ_j is updated. In this case if the production makes any change on the multiple stack the operation is performed. At the

---

[1] We are ignoring scanning of ϵ in pop-operations. This can be introduced either modifying the predictor operation or performing scanning with a dummy symbol in these cases.

prediction operation, constraints on the value of the lowest node in the multi-stack are checked against current values of A. In this case if $A = S_i$, then $n_0 \geq_O i$.

Item form: $[\Delta, A \underset{\mu}{\to} \alpha \bullet \beta, i, j]$

Axioms: $[\langle (\#, 0) \rangle, S' \to \bullet S, 0, 0]$

Goals: $[\langle (\#, 0) \rangle, S' \to S \bullet, 0, n]$

Inference rules:

Scanning $$\frac{[\langle n_0, ..., n_m \rangle_j, A \underset{\mu}{\to} \alpha \bullet w_{j+1} \beta, i, j]}{[\Delta_{j+1}, A \underset{\mu}{\to} \alpha w_{j+1} \bullet \beta, i, j+1]} \quad Update(\mu, \langle n_0, ..., n_m \rangle_j) = \Delta_{j+1}$$

Prediction $$\frac{[\langle n_0, ..., n_m \rangle_j, A \underset{\mu_i}{\to} \alpha \bullet B\beta, i, j]}{[\langle n_0, ..., n_m \rangle_j, B \underset{\mu_j}{\to} \bullet \gamma, i, j]} \quad B \to \gamma, test(n_0, A)$$

Completion $$\frac{[\_, A \underset{\mu_i}{\to} \alpha \bullet B\beta, i, j] \quad [\Delta_k, B \underset{\mu_j}{\to} \gamma \bullet, j, k]}{[\Delta_k, A \underset{\mu_i}{\to} \alpha B \bullet \beta, i, k]}$$

Fig. 2. An Earley MGIL deductive parsing system to recognize SAT

The set of valid items $\mathcal{V}$ defines the invariant of Earley algorithm for CFLs.
$$\mathcal{V}_{CFL} = \{[A \to \alpha \bullet \beta, i, j] | S \overset{*}{\Rightarrow} a_1...a_i A\gamma \wedge \alpha \overset{*}{\Rightarrow} a_{i+1}...a_j\}$$
In the case of MGILs the set of valid items is defined by the following invariant:
$$\mathcal{V}_{MGIL} = \{[\langle n_0, ..., n_m \rangle_j, A \underset{\mu_i}{\to} \alpha \bullet \beta, i, j] | \#S \overset{*}{\Rightarrow} \Delta_1 \# a_1...a_i A\gamma \wedge \Delta_1 \# \alpha \overset{*}{\Rightarrow}$$
$\Delta_2 \# a_{i+1}...a_j\} \wedge \Delta_2$ where the ordered top of stacks in Δ_2 is $\langle n_0, ..., n_m \rangle$.
The proof of this invariant has as corollary the correctness of the algorithm.

The recognition algorithm we have presented here has time complexity bounded by the number of multi-stacks required, the asymptotic time complexity is $\mathcal{O}(n^{3 \cdot k})$, where n is the size of the input and k is the maximum number of multi-stacks used, in particular in the completion step of the algorithm. This can be easily observed considering that all the possible combinations on multi-stacks is bound by the combination of a single multi-stack parameter Δ_k which is transmitted to the completed item. Note that the item target of the completion operation (non terminal A at the left hand side) has the multi-stack parameter underspecified. This is the case because the values of these parameters can be ignored at completion. There are three positional indexes, which determine the classic cubic time of Earley for CFLs.

This complexity is similar to LCFRS complexity where the degree of the polynomial is dependent on the rank and fan-out (e.g. $\mathcal{O}(n^{f \cdot (r+1)})$ [9]) in the sense that the determining factor is the number of multiple stacks used. It is also similar to $\mathcal{O}(n^{3 \cdot 2^{k-1}})$ time complexity of multiple context-free grammars[24] (or the equivalent multiple pushdown automata). But in the case of LCFRS, this is a tight bound, because all possible dependencies have to be set by the grammar and transmitted in the derivation through the spine. In the case of MGIGs, dependencies are introduced by the input, and the number of stacks to be used will be dependent on the given order, its correlation with the ordering of the input and the number of dependencies per word.

4   Conclusions and Discussion

We have presented a grammar formalism that uses multiple stacks that can be used to recognize the language of satisfiable propositional formulae L_{sat_n}. An Earley recognition algorithm for this class of languages was given. We have shown that MGILs membership recognition is bound by the number of stacks used in the multi-stack. Unlike LCFRLs the number of multi-stacks is not equal to the number of variables in the formula (see [14]). The number of stacks in the multi-stack is dependent on the particular sentence instance and the particular derivation even for a language like L_{sat_n}. A prototype of the parser was implemented in python and tested with a limited number of manually coded examples. In order to test it on proper benchmarks to compare running time with efficient algorithms, an optimized version of the algorithm needs to be implemented. From running time in hand coded examples and minimal benchmark examples (20 variable formulae in SATLIB), it was observed that the implementation of Earley items set was not adequate and consumed important processing time even with small items sets. The number of items generated, which dominates the time complexity analysis, had important variations regarding the ordering of variables used in the translation of the formula. However its size remained relatively small. We are re-implementing the algorithm in order to solve the detected efficiency issues and be able to compare running time with state-of-the-art solvers using a reasonable benchmarks. Problems with efficiency were related to items representation, and its related access time in the set representation. In the future, agenda-driven chart-based parsers can be used to implement different sat-solving strategies.

Acknowledgments. The algorithm was implemented by Agustín S. Gutiérrez as part of his M.Sc. Thesis.

Appendix

4.1   The Algorithm to Update the Multi-Stack

Algorithm 1. Operations on the Multi-Stack

1: Update(O,μ,p,MStack)
2: Let O be the order defined in the grammar, μ the production operator and $1 \leq p \leq n$
3: Let MStack be $[(w_0, p_0, id_0), ..., (w_k, p_k, id_k)]$, where $w_0 \leq_O w_j \leq_O w_k$
4: Let $AdjL$ be the adjacency list used to represent the graph
5: Let cid be the identifier of each individual stack, for any w_0, w_j, w_k in MStack.
6:   $least = (w_0, p_0, id_0)$
7:   Out = $\{\}$
8:   **if** $\mu = epsilon$ **then**
9:       Add MStack to Out
10:      **return** Out
11: **if** $\mu \in T^+$ **then**
12:      **for** (w_i, p_i, id_i) in MStack **do**
13:          **if** $\mu \leq_O w_i$ **then**
14:              Add (w_i, p_i, id_i) to AdjL[(μ, p, id_i)]
15:              Remove (w_i, p_i, id_i) from MStack
16:              Add (μ, p, id_i) to MStack
17:              Add MStack to Out
18:              **return** Out
19:      Add $(\#, 0)$ to AdjL[(μ, p, cid)] ($\forall w_i, \mu > w_i$)
20:      Add (μ, p, cid) to MStack and MStack to Out
21:      $cid = cid + 1$
22:      **return** Out
23: **if** $\mu \in \bar{y}, y \in T^+$ **then**
24:      **if** match(y, w_0) **then**
25:          Remove $least$ from MStack
26:          **for** prevnode in AdjL[$least$] **do**
27:              Copy MStack to NMStack
28:              **if** prevnode is not $(\#, 0)$ **then**
29:                  Add prevnode to NMStack
30:              Add NMStack to Out
31:          Return Out
32: **if** $\mu \in \bar{y}|x$ **then**
33:      **if** $match(y, w_0)$, x matches a non-empty suffix sw_0 from w_0 excluding matching part
    then
34:          Remove $least$ from MStack
35:          **for** prevnode in AdjL[$least$] **do**
36:              Copy MStack to NMStack
37:              **if** prevnode is not $(\#, 0)$ **then**
38:                  Add prevnode to NMStack
39:              **for** (w_j, p_j, id_j) in NMStack **do**
40:                  **if** $sw_0 \leq_O w_j$ **then**
41:                      Add (w_j, p_j, id_j) to AdjL[(sw_0, p_0, id_j)]
42:                      Remove (w_j, p_j, id_j) from NMStack
43:                      Add (sw_0, p_0, id_j) to NMStack
44:                      Add NMStack to Out
45:                      **break**
46:                  Add $(\#, 0)$ to AdjL[(sw_0, p_0, cid)] (there was no (w_j, p_j) in MStack s.t.
    $sw_0 \leq_O w_j$)
47:                  Add (sw_0, p_i, cid) to NMStack and NMStack to Out
48:                  $cid = cid + 1$
49:          **return** Out

References

1. Barton, G.E.: Computational complexity in two-level morphology. In: Proc. of the 24th ACL, pp. 53–59, New York (1986)
2. Biere, A., Heule, M., van Maaren H., Walsh, T. (eds): Handbook of Satisfiability. IOS Press (2009)
3. Büchi, J.R.: Weak second-order arithmetic and finite automata. Zeit. Math. Logik. Grund. Math., 66–92 (1960)
4. Castaño, J.: Global index grammars and descriptive power. Journal of Logic, Language and Information 13, 403–419 (2004)
5. Cherubini, A., Breveglieri, L., Citrini, C., Reghizzi, S.: Multipushdown languages and grammars. International Journal of Foundations of Computer Science 7(3), 253–292 (1996)
6. Dassow, J., Păun, G., Salomaa, A.: Grammars with controlled derivations. In: Rozenberg, G., Salomaa, A. (eds.) Handbook of Formal Languages, vol. 2. Springer, Berlin (1997)
7. Earley, J.: An Efficient Context-free Parsing Algorithm. Communications of the ACM 13, 94–102 (1970)
8. Elgot, C.C.: Decision problems of automata design and related arithmetics. Transactions of the American Mathematical Society (1961)
9. Gómez-Rodríguez, C., Kuhlmann, M., Satta, G.: Efficient parsing of well-nested linear context-free rewriting systems. In: Human Language Technologies: The 2010 Annual Conference of the North American Chapter of the Association for Computational Linguistics, HLT 2010, pp. 276–284. Association for Computational Linguistics, Stroudsburg (2010)
10. Khabbaz, N.A.: A geometric hierarchy of languages. Journal of Computer and System Sciences 8(2), 142–157 (1974)
11. Neuhaus, P., Broker, N.: The complexity of recognition of linguistically adequate dependency grammars. In: Proceedings of the 35th Annual Meeting of the Association for Computational Linguistics, pp. 337–343. Association for Computational Linguistics, Madrid (1997)
12. Purdom Jr, P.W., Brown, C.A.: Parsing extended LR(k) grammars. Acta Informatica 15(2), 115–127 (1981)
13. Ristad, E.S.: Computational complexity of current GPSG theory. In: Proc. of the 24th ACL, pp. 30–39, New York (1986)
14. Satta, G.: Recognition of Linear Context-Free Rewriting Systems. In: ACL, pp. 89–95 (1992)
15. Satta, G.: Some computational complexity results for synchronous context-free grammars. In: Proceedings of HLT/EMNLP 2005, pp. 803–810 (2005)
16. Seki, H., Matsumura, T., Fujii, M., Kasami, T.: On multiple context-free grammars. Theoretical Computer. Science, 191–229 (1991)
17. Shieber, S., Schabes, Y., Pereira, F.: Principles and implementation of deductive parsing. Journal of Logic Programming 24, 3–36 (1995)
18. Sikkel, K.: Parsing schemata. Springer (1997)
19. Tomita, M.: An efficiente augmented-context-free parsing algorithm. Computational Linguistics 13, 31–46 (1987)
20. La Torre, S., Madhusudan, P., Parlato, G.: A robust class of context-sensitive languages. In: LICS, pp. 161–170. IEEE Computer Society (2007)
21. Vardi, M.Y.: Logic and Automata: A Match Made in Heaven. In: Baeten, J.C.M., Lenstra, J.K., Parrow, J., Woeginger, G.J. (eds.) ICALP 2003. LNCS, vol. 2719, pp. 64–65. Springer, Heidelberg (2003)
22. Vardi, M.Y., Wolper, P.: Automata-theoretic techniques for modal logics of programs. J. Comput. Syst. Sci. 32, 183–221 (1986)
23. Wartena, C.: Storage products and linear control of derivations. Theory of Computing Systems 42(2), 157–186 (2008)
24. Weir, D.: A geometric hierarchy beyond context-free languages. Theoretical Computer Science 104(2), 235–261 (1992)

Inconsistency-Tolerant Reasoning in Datalog$^\pm$ Ontologies via an Argumentative Semantics

Maria Vanina Martinez[1], Cristhian Ariel David Deagustini[2,3]([✉]),
Marcelo A. Falappa[2,3], and Guillermo Ricardo Simari[2]

[1] Department of Computer Science, University of Oxford, Oxford, UK
[2] Artificial Intelligence Research and Development Laboratory Department
of Computer Science and Engineering, Universidad Nacional del Sur,
Alem 1253, 8000 Bahía Blanca, Buenos Aires, Argentina
caddeagustini@gmail.com
[3] Consejo Nacional de Investigaciones Científicas y Técnicas, Buenos Aires, Argentina

Abstract. The Semantic Web provides an effective infrastructure that allows data to be easily shared and reused across applications. At its core is the description of ontological knowledge using ontological languages which are powerful knowledge representation tools with good decidability and tractability properties; Datalog$^\pm$ is one of these tools. The problem of inconsistency has been acknowledged in both the Semantic Web and Database Theory communities. Here we introduce elements of defeasible argumentative reasoning in Datalog$^\pm$, consequences to represent statements whose truth can be challenged leading to a better handling of inconsistency in ontological languages.

Keywords: Defeasible Argumentation · Inconsistency-tolerant reasoning · Datalog$^\pm$

1 Introduction and Motivation

The Semantic Web provides an effective infrastructure that allows data to be shared and reused across applications. At its core is the description of ontological knowledge using ontological languages which are powerful knowledge representation tools, since their decidability and tractability properties makes them attractive for handling practical applications. In particular, Datalog$^\pm$ [9] is a family of ontology languages which enables a modular rule-based style of knowledge representation. Datalog$^\pm$ provides the capability of representing fragments of first-order logic so that answering a Boolean Conjunctive query Q under a set Σ of Datalog$^\pm$ rules for an input database I is equivalent to checking whether Q is classically entailed from $I \cup \Sigma$. Furthermore, its properties of decidability of query answering and good query answering complexity in the data complexity allow to realistically assume that the database I is the only really large object in the input. These properties and its expressive power make Datalog$^\pm$ very useful in scenarios such as Ontology Querying, Web Data Extraction, and Ontology-based Data Access.

The problem of inconsistency in ontologies has been acknowledged in both the Semantic Web and Database Theory communities, and several methods have been developed to deal with it. The most widely accepted semantics for querying inconsistent

A.L.C. Bazzan and K. Pichara (Eds.): IBERAMIA 2014, LNAI 8864, pp. 15–27, 2014.
DOI: 10.1007/978-3-319-12027-0_2

databases is that of *consistent answers* [1] (or *AR* semantics in [19]), which yields the set of atoms that can be derived despite all possible ways of repairing the inconsistency. This semantics is based on the *"when in doubt, throw it out"* principle. We argue that the process of conflict resolution could be carried out through logical reasoning, using as much information as possible to weigh out conflicting pieces of information.

We introduce in Datalog$^\pm$ elements of defeasible reasoning that have already shown practical results [12,17], allowing consequences to represent statements whose acceptance can be challenged. Section 3 presents *defeasible* Datalog$^\pm$ ontologies extending classical Datalog$^\pm$ ontologies with defeasible atoms and defeasible *tuple-generating dependencies* (or TGDs) which are used as inference rules in Datalog$^\pm$. Defeasible atoms represent statements that can be challenged, while defeasible TGDs represent a weaker connection between pieces of information. Conflicts among derived atoms are resolved through an argumentative dialectical process. The argumentation-based reasoning mechanism described in Section 4 consider reasons for and against potential conclusions and decides which are the ones that can be obtained (warranted) from the knowledge base. In Section 5, we show that this extension allows to entail atoms that are not yielded by several inconsistency-tolerant semantics from the literature, including *AR* and several others designed to be sound approximations of *AR*; yet, we are guaranteed that a very important property holds: no conflicting atoms can be entailed – we call this the *NCE property*. We then go on to show how to obtain sound approximations (that also enjoy the NCE property) to a family of semantics called *k*-defeaters [7].

2   Preliminaries on Datalog$^\pm$ Ontologies

First, we briefly recall some basics on Datalog$^\pm$ [9], namely, on relational databases, (Boolean) conjunctive queries ((B)CQs), tuple-generating dependencies (TGDs), negative constraints, the chase, and ontologies in Datalog$^\pm$.

We assume (i) an infinite universe of *(data) constants* Δ (which constitute the "normal" domain of a database), (ii) an infinite set of *(labeled) nulls* Δ_N (used as "fresh" Skolem terms, which are placeholders for unknown values, and can thus be seen as variables), and (iii) an infinite set of variables $\mathcal{V}$ (used in queries, dependencies, and constraints). Different constants represent different values (*unique name assumption*), while different nulls may represent the same value. We assume a lexicographic order on $\Delta \cup \Delta_N$, with every symbol in Δ_N following all symbols in Δ. We denote by $\mathbf{X}$ sequences of variables $X_1, \ldots, X_k$ with $k \geq 0$. We assume a *relational schema* $\mathscr{R}$, which is a finite set of *predicate symbols* (or simply *predicates*). A *term t* is a constant, null, or variable. An *atomic formula* (or *atom*) $\mathbf{a}$ has the form $P(t_1, \ldots, t_n)$, where P is an n-ary predicate, and $t_1, \ldots, t_n$ are terms. A *database (instance) I* for a relational schema $\mathscr{R}$ is a (possibly infinite) set of atoms with predicates from $\mathscr{R}$ and arguments from Δ.

Given a relational schema $\mathscr{R}$, a *tuple-generating dependency (TGD)* σ is a first-order formula $\forall \mathbf{X} \forall \mathbf{Y} \, \Phi(\mathbf{X}, \mathbf{Y}) \rightarrow \exists \mathbf{Z} \, \Psi(\mathbf{X}, \mathbf{Z})$, where $\Phi(\mathbf{X}, \mathbf{Y})$ and $\Psi(\mathbf{X}, \mathbf{Z})$ are conjunctions of atoms over $\mathscr{R}$ (without nulls), called the *body* and the *head* of σ, respectively. Satisfaction of TGDs are defined via *homomorphisms*, which are mappings $\mu : \Delta \cup \Delta_N \cup \mathcal{V} \rightarrow \Delta \cup \Delta_N \cup \mathcal{V}$ such that (i) $c \in \Delta$ implies $\mu(c) = c$, (ii) $c \in \Delta_N$ implies $\mu(c) \in \Delta \cup \Delta_N$, and (iii) μ is naturally extended to atoms, sets of atoms, and conjunctions of atoms. A TGD σ is satisfied in a database I for $\mathscr{R}$ iff, whenever there exists a homomorphism h that maps the atoms of $\Phi(\mathbf{X}, \mathbf{Y})$ to atoms of I, there exists an extension h' of h that maps the atoms of $\Psi(\mathbf{X}, \mathbf{Z})$ to atoms of I. A TGD σ is *guarded* iff an atom in its body contains all universally quantified variables of σ. Since TGDs can be reduced to TGDs with only single atoms in their heads, in the sequel, every TGD has without loss of generalization a single atom in its head.

A *conjunctive query (CQ)* over $\mathscr{R}$ has the form $Q(\mathbf{X}) = \exists \mathbf{Y}\, \Phi(\mathbf{X}, \mathbf{Y})$, where $\Phi(\mathbf{X}, \mathbf{Y})$ is a conjunction of atoms (possibly equalities, but not inequalities) with the variables $\mathbf{X}$ and $\mathbf{Y}$, and possibly constants, but without nulls. A *Boolean CQ (BCQ)* over $\mathscr{R}$ is a CQ of the form $Q()$, often written as the set of all its atoms, without quantifiers. The set of *answers* for a CQ Q to I and Σ, denoted $ans(Q, I, \Sigma)$, is the set of all tuples $\mathbf{a}$ such that $\mathbf{a} \in Q(B)$ for all $B \in mods(I, \Sigma)$. The *answer* for a BCQ Q to I and Σ is *Yes*, denoted $I \cup \Sigma \models Q$, iff $ans(Q, I, \Sigma) \neq \emptyset$. Note that query answering under general TGDs is undecidable [3], even when the schema and TGDs are fixed [8]. Decidability of query answering for the guarded case follows from a bounded tree-width property. The data complexity of query answering in this case is P-complete (see [9] for details).

The chase algorithm for a database I and a set of TGDs Σ consists of an exhaustive application of the TGDs [9] in a breadth-first (level-saturating) fashion, which outputs a (possibly infinite) chase for I and Σ. The (possibly infinite) chase relative to TGDs is a *universal model*, i.e., there exists a homomorphism from $chase(I, \Sigma)$ onto every $B \in mods(I, \Sigma)$ [9]. This implies that BCQs Q over I and Σ can be evaluated on the chase for I and Σ, i.e., $I \cup \Sigma \models Q$ is equivalent to $chase(I, \Sigma) \models Q$.

A *negative constraint* (or simply *constraint*) γ is a first-order formula of the form $\forall \mathbf{X} \Phi(\mathbf{X}) \rightarrow \bot$, where $\Phi(\mathbf{X})$ (called the *body* of γ) is a conjunction of atoms over $\mathscr{R}$ (without nulls). Under the standard semantics of query answering of BCQs in Datalog$^\pm$ with TGDs, adding negative constraints is computationally easy, as for each constraint $\forall \mathbf{X} \Phi(\mathbf{X}) \rightarrow \bot$, we only have to check that the BCQ $\exists \mathbf{X} \Phi(\mathbf{X})$ evaluates to false in I under Σ; if one of these checks fails, then the answer to the original BCQ Q is true, otherwise the constraints can simply be ignored when answering the BCQ Q. In this work we restrict our attention to binary denial constraints. As we will show later, this class of constraints suffices for the formalization of the concept of conflicting atoms.

As another component, the Datalog$^\pm$ language has special types of *equality-generating dependencies (EGDs)*. Without loss of generality we do not consider EGDs in this work, since for our purposes they can also be modeled via negative constraints (see [9] for details). We usually omit the universal quantifiers in TGDs, negative constraints, and we implicitly assume that all sets of dependencies and/or constraints are finite.

Datalog$^\pm$ Ontologies. A *Datalog$^\pm$ ontology* $KB = (I, \Sigma)$, where $\Sigma = \Sigma_T \cup \Sigma_{NC}$, consists of a database I, a set of TGDs Σ_T, and a set of negative constraints Σ_{NC}. We say KB is *guarded* (resp., *linear*) iff Σ_T is guarded (resp., linear). Example 1 (used in the sequel as a running example) illustrates a simple Datalog$^\pm$ ontology.

Example 1. Consider the following simple Datalog$^\pm$ ontology $KB = (I, \Sigma_T \cup \Sigma_{NC})$:
$I = \{collaborates(will, fbi), security\_agency(fbi), psychiatrist(hannibal, will),$
$\quad victim(abigail)\}$
$\Sigma_{NC} = \{risky\_job(P) \wedge unstable(P) \rightarrow \bot\}$

$$\Sigma_T = \{collaborates(P,A) \rightarrow works\_in(A,P), in\_therapy(P) \rightarrow unstable(P),$$
$$lives\_depend\_on(A) \wedge works\_in(A,P) \rightarrow risky\_job(P),$$
$$psychiatrist(S,P) \rightarrow in\_therapy(P), security\_agency(A) \rightarrow lives\_depend\_on(A)\}.$$

3   Defeasible Datalog$^\pm$ Ontologies

Here we extend Datalog$^\pm$ ontologies to allow defeasible reasoning. First, to represent statements whose acceptance can be challenged, we consider the existence of a set of *defeasible atoms*; thus, the database instance of a defeasible Datalog$^\pm$ ontology consists of two parts, a set of facts (*i.e.,* strict knowledge) and a set of defeasible atoms.

Second, we also want to add defeasibility to express weaker connections between pieces of information than in TGDs; thus, we extend the language accordingly. *Defeasible TGDs* are rules of the form $\Upsilon(\mathbf{X},\mathbf{Y}) \vdash \exists \mathbf{Z}\, \Psi(\mathbf{X},\mathbf{Z})$, where $\Upsilon(\mathbf{X},\mathbf{Y})$ and $\Psi(\mathbf{X},\mathbf{Z})$ are conjunctions of atoms. As in DeLP's defeasible rules [15], defeasible TGDs are used to represent weaker connections between the body and the head of a rule. Unlike strict (traditional) TGDs, acceptance of the body of a defeasible rule does not always lead to the acceptance of the head, which means that consequences of such rule can be challenged. For our running Example 1, we can represent the information that if A is a security agency then it is the case that the lives of people depend on A as a defeasible TGD instead of a strict one, reflecting that the connection between the two atoms holds in general but is weak in nature. Defeasible TGDs are written using the symbol " $\vdash$ ", while the classical (right) arrow " $\rightarrow$ " is reserved to *strict* TGDs and NCs.

Then, a *defeasible* Datalog$^\pm$ *ontology KB* consists of a (finite) set F of *ground atoms*, called *facts*, a set D of *defeasible atoms*, a finite set of TGDs Σ_T, a finite set of defeasible TGDs Σ_D, and a finite set of binary negative constraints Σ_{NC}. The following example shows a defeasible Datalog$^\pm$ ontology that encodes the knowledge from Example 1 changing some of the facts and TGDs to defeasible ones.

Example 2. The information from the ontology presented in Example 1 can be better represented by the following defeasible Datalog$^\pm$ ontology $KB = (F, D, \Sigma'_T, \Sigma_D, \Sigma_{NC})$, where $F = \{collaborates(will, fbi), security\_agency(fbi), psychiatrist(hannibal, will)\}$ and $D = \{victim(abigail)\}$. Note that we have changed the fact stating that *abigail* is a victim to a defeasible atom since some suspicious actions from her indicate that she may be an accomplice instead. The sets of TGDs, and defeasible TGDs are now given by the following sets; note that we have changed some of the TGDs into defeasible TGDs to make clear that the connection between the head and body is weaker.

$$\Sigma_{T'} = \{collaborates(P,A) \rightarrow works\_in(A,P), psychiatrist(S,P) \rightarrow in\_therapy(P)\}$$
$$\Sigma_D = \{in\_therapy(P) \vdash unstable(P), lives\_depend\_on(A) \wedge works\_in(A,P) \vdash risky\_job(P),$$
$$security\_agency(A) \vdash lives\_depend\_on(A)\}$$

As in classical Datalog$^\pm$, derivations from a defeasible Datalog$^\pm$ ontology rely in the application of (strict or defeasible) TGDs. Given a defeasible Datalog$^\pm$ ontology *KB* the classical application of a TGD applies almost directly to defeasible TGDs and ontologies. The difference is that for a (strict or defeasible) TGD σ to be applicable there must exist a homomorphism mapping the atoms in the body of σ into $F \cup D$. The *application of* σ on *KB* generates a new atom from the head of σ if it is not already in $F \cup D$, in the same way as explained in Section 2. The following definitions follow similar ones first introduced in [22]. Here we adapt the notions to defeasible Datalog$^\pm$ ontologies.

Definition 1. Let $KB = (F, D, \Sigma_T, \Sigma_D, \Sigma_{NC})$ be a defeasible Datalog$^\pm$ ontology and L an atom. An *annotated derivation* ∂ of L from *KB* consists of a finite sequence $[R_1, R_2, \ldots, R_n]$ such that R_n is L, and each atom R_i is either: (*i*) R_i is a fact or defeasible atom, *i.e.*, $R_i \in F \cup D$, or (*ii*) there exists a TGD $\sigma \in \Sigma_T \cup \Sigma_D$ and a homomorphism h such that $h(head(\sigma)) = R_i$ and σ is applicable to the set of all atoms and defeasible atoms that appear before R_i in the sequence. When no defeasible atoms and no defeasible TGDs are used in a derivation, we say the derivation is a *strict derivation*, otherwise it is a *defeasible derivation*.

Note that there is non-determinism in the order in which the elements in a derivation appear. Syntactically distinct derivations are, however, equivalent for our purposes. When no confusion is possible, we assume that a unique selection has been made.

We say an atom a is strictly derived from *KB* iff there exists a strict derivation for a from *KB*, denoted with $KB \vdash a$, and a is defeasibly derived from *KB* iff there exists a defeasible derivation for a from *KB* and no strict derivation exists, denoted with $KB \vdash\!\!\!\sim a$.

A derivation ∂ for L is *minimal* if no proper sub-derivation ∂' of ∂ (every member of ∂' is a member of ∂) is also an annotated derivation of L. Considering minimal derivations in a defeasible derivation avoids the insertion of unnecessary elements that will weaken its ability to support the conclusion by possibly introducing unnecessary points of conflict. Given a derivation ∂ for L, there exists at least one minimal sub-derivation $\partial' \subseteq \partial$ for an atom L. Thus, we only consider minimal derivations.

Example 3. From the defeasible Datalog$^\pm$ ontology in Example 2, we can get the following (minimal) annotated derivation for atom *unstable(will)*:
$\partial = [psychiatrist(hannibal, will), psychiatrist(S, P) \rightarrow in\_therapy(P),$
$\quad in\_therapy(will), in\_therapy(P) \vdash\!\!\!\sim unstable(P), unstable(will)]$
Then, we have $KB \vdash in\_therapy(will)$ (following from the fact that Will has a psychiatrist) and $KB \vdash\!\!\!\sim unstable(will)$ (by means of the defeasible rule that says that a person in therapy generally is unstable).

We now show that classical query answering in defeasible Datalog$^\pm$ ontologies is equivalent to query answering in Datalog$^\pm$ ontologies.

Proposition 1. Let L be a ground atom, $KB = (F, D, \Sigma_T, \Sigma_D, \Sigma_{NC})$ be a defeasible Datalog$^\pm$ ontology, $KB' = (F \cup D, \Sigma'_T \cup \Sigma_{NC})$ is a classical Datalog$^\pm$ ontology where $\Sigma'_T = \Sigma_T \cup \{\Upsilon(\mathbf{X}, \mathbf{Y}) \rightarrow \exists \mathbf{Z}\, \Psi(\mathbf{X}, \mathbf{Z}) \mid \Upsilon(\mathbf{X}, \mathbf{Y}) \vdash\!\!\!\sim \exists \mathbf{Z}\, \Psi(\mathbf{X}, \mathbf{Z})\}$. Then, $KB' \models L$ iff $KB \vdash L$ or $KB \vdash\!\!\!\sim L$.

Proposition 1 states the equivalence between derivations from defeasible Datalog$^\pm$ ontologies and entailment in traditional Datalog$^\pm$ ontologies whose database instance corresponds to the union of facts and defeasible atoms, and the set of TGDs corresponds to the union of the TGDs and the strict version of the defeasible TGDs. As a direct consequence, all the existing work done for Datalog$^\pm$ directly applies to defeasible Datalog$^\pm$. In particular, it is easy to specify a defeasible Chase procedure over defeasible Datalog$^\pm$ ontologies, based on the revised notion of application of (defeasible) TGDs, whose result is a *universal model*. Therefore, a (B)CQ Q over a defeasible Datalog$^\pm$ ontology can be evaluated by verifying that Q is a classical consequence of the chase obtained from the defeasible Datalog$^\pm$ ontology. Despite this equivalence, the main reason, for defining a defeasible extension of Datalog$^\pm$ ontologies, is that defeasible knowledge and reasoning allows the possibility of managing conflicts in a more sensible way; *i.e.*, aspects of the nature of the different pieces of knowledge in conflict and/or the way they are derived from previous knowledge can be considered in the process of conflict resolution. For this reason, in the following section we propose an argumentation-based procedure to answer queries in defeasible Datalog$^\pm$ ontologies.

4   Argumentation-Based Reasoning in Defeasible Datalog$^\pm$

Conflicts in defeasible Datalog$^\pm$ ontologies come, as in classical Datalog$^\pm$, from the violation of negative constraints. Intuitively, two atoms are in conflict relative to a defeasible Datalog$^\pm$ ontology whenever they are both derived from the ontology (either strictly o defeasible) and together map to the body of a negative constraint.

Definition 2. Given a set of negative constraints Σ_{NC}, two ground atoms (possibly with nulls) a and b are said to be *in conflict* relative to Σ_{NC} iff there exists an homomorphism h such that $h(body(\upsilon)) = a \wedge b$ for some $\upsilon \in \Sigma_{NC}$.

In what follows, we say that a set of atoms is a *conflicting* set of atoms relative to Σ_{NC} if and only if there exist at least two atoms in the set that are in conflict relative to Σ_{NC}, otherwise will be called *non-conflicting*. Whenever is clear from the context we omit the set of negative constraints.

Example 4. Consider the set $\Sigma_{NC} = \{risky\_job(P) \wedge unstable(P) \rightarrow \bot\}$ of negative constraints from Example 3. In this case, the set of atoms $\{unstable(will), risky\_job(will)\}$ is a conflicting set relative to Σ_{NC}. However, this is not the case for the set $S = \{collaborates(will, fbi), psychiatrist(hannibal, will), security\_agency(fbi)\}$.

Given a defeasible Datalog$^\pm$ ontology $KB = (F, D, \Sigma_T, \Sigma_D, \Sigma_{NC})$, sets F and Σ_T are used to represent non-defeasible information, as it is the case with facts and strict rules in DeLP [15, 16]. Therefore, we require F to be *representationally coherent*, that is F must be non-conflicting with respect to Σ_{NC} and furthermore given KB there cannot be strict derivations for conflicting atoms.

Whenever defeasible derivations of conflicting atoms exist, we use, as in DeLP, a dialectical process to decide which information prevails, *i.e.*, which piece of information is such that no acceptable reason can be put forward against it. Reasons are supported by arguments. An argument is an structure that supports a claim from evidence through the use of a reasoning mechanism. Maintaining the intuition that led to the classic definition of arguments in [27], given a defeasible Datalog$^\pm$ ontology, an argument $\mathscr{A}$ for a claim L is a minimal (under $\subseteq$) set of facts, defeasible atoms, TGDs, and defeasible TGDs contained in *KB*, such that *L* is derived from it and no conflicting atoms can be derived from it, and $\mathbb{A}_{KB}$ denotes the set of all arguments that can be built from *KB*.

Answers to atomic queries are supported by arguments built from the ontology. However, it is possible to build arguments for conflicting atoms, and so arguments can *attack* each other. We now adopt the definitions of counter-argument and attacks for defeasible Datalog$^\pm$ ontologies from [15]. First, an argument $\langle \mathscr{B}, L' \rangle$ is a sub-argument of $\langle \mathscr{A}, L \rangle$ if $\mathscr{B} \subseteq \mathscr{A}$. Argument $\langle \mathscr{A}_1, L_1 \rangle$ counter-argues, rebuts, or attacks $\langle \mathscr{A}_2, L_2 \rangle$ at literal *L*, iff there exists a sub-argument $\langle \mathscr{A}, L \rangle$ of $\langle \mathscr{A}_2, L_2 \rangle$ such that *L* and L_1 conflict.

Example 5. Consider derivation ∂ from Example 3 and let $\mathscr{A}$ be the set of (defeasible) atoms and (defeasible) TGDs used in ∂. $\mathscr{A}$ is an argument for *unstable(will)*. Also, we can obtain a minimal derivation ∂' for *risky_job(will)* where $\mathscr{B}$, the set of (defeasible) atoms and (defeasible) TGDs used in ∂', is such that no conflicting atoms can be defeasibly derived from $\mathscr{B} \cup \Sigma_T$. As $\{unstable(will), risky\_job(will)\}$ is conflicting relative to Σ_{NC}, we have that $\langle \mathscr{A}, unstable(will) \rangle$ and $\langle \mathscr{B}, risky\_job(will) \rangle$ attack each other.

Once the attack relation is established between arguments, it is necessary to analyze whether the attack is strong enough so one of the arguments can *defeat* the other. Given an argument $\mathscr{A}$ and a counter-argument $\mathscr{B}$, a comparison criterion is used to determine if $\mathscr{B}$ is preferred to $\mathscr{A}$ and, therefore, *defeats* $\mathscr{A}$. Different preference criteria can be applied for this purpose; *specificity* [28] is often used in the defeasible reasoning and argumentation literature. In the presence of defeasible atoms, specificity might not always return the intended results — other preference criteria have been developed for such cases [15,22]. For our defeasible Datalog$^\pm$ framework, unless otherwise stated, we assume an arbitrary preference criterion $\succ$ among arguments.

Let $\langle \mathscr{A}_1, L_1 \rangle$ and $\langle \mathscr{A}_2, L_2 \rangle$ be two arguments. We say that argument $\langle \mathscr{A}_1, L_1 \rangle$ is a defeater of $\langle \mathscr{A}_2, L_2 \rangle$ iff there exists a sub-argument $\langle \mathscr{A}, L \rangle$ of $\langle \mathscr{A}_2, L_2 \rangle$ such that $\langle \mathscr{A}_1, L_1 \rangle$ counter-argues $\langle \mathscr{A}, L \rangle$ at *L*, and either $\langle \mathscr{A}_1, L_1 \rangle \succ \langle \mathscr{A}, L \rangle$ (it is a proper defeater) or $\langle \mathscr{A}_1, L_1 \rangle \not\succ \langle \mathscr{A}, L \rangle$, and $\langle \mathscr{A}, L \rangle \not\succ \langle \mathscr{A}_1, L_1 \rangle$ (it is a blocking defeater).

Definition 3. Given a defeasible Datalog$^\pm$ ontology *KB* defined over a relational schema $\mathscr{R}$, a *Datalog$^\pm$ argumentation framework* $\mathfrak{F}$ is a tuple $\langle \mathscr{L}_{\mathscr{R}}, \mathbb{A}_{KB}, \succ \rangle$, where $\succ$ specifies a preference relation defined over $\mathbb{A}_{KB}$.

To decide whether an argument $\langle \mathscr{A}_0, L_0 \rangle$ is undefeated within a Datalog$^\pm$ argumentation framework, all its defeaters must be considered, and there may exist defeaters for their counter-arguments as well. An *argument line* for $\langle \mathscr{A}_0, L_0 \rangle$ is defined as a sequence of arguments that starts at $\langle \mathscr{A}_0, L_0 \rangle$, and every element in the sequence is a defeater of its predecessor in the line [15]. Note that for defeasible Datalog$^\pm$ ontologies arguments in an argumentation line can contain both facts and defeasible atoms.

Different argumentation systems can be defined by setting a particular criterion for proper attack or defining the admissibility of argumentation lines. Here, we adopt the one from [15], which states that an argumentation line has to be finite, and no argument is a sub-argument of an argument used earlier in the line; furthermore, when an argument $\langle \mathscr{A}_i, L_i \rangle$ is used as a blocking defeater for $\langle \mathscr{A}_{i-1}, L_{i-1} \rangle$ during the construction of an argumentation line, only a proper defeater can be used for defeating $\langle \mathscr{A}_i, L_i \rangle$.

The dialectical process considers all possible admissible argumentation lines for an argument, which together form a dialectical tree. Dialectical trees for defeasible

Datalog$^\pm$ ontologies are defined following [15], and we adopt the notion of coherent dialectical tree from [22], which ensures that the use of defeasible atoms is *coherent* in the sense that conflicting defeasible atoms are not used together in supporting (or attacking) a claim. We denote with $Args(\mathscr{T})$ the set of arguments in $\mathscr{T}$.

Argument evaluation, *i.e.*, determining whether the root node of the tree is defeated or undefeated, is done by means of a *marking* or *labelling* criterion, similar to the grounded semantics in abstract argumentation frameworks [2,13]. Each node in an argument tree is labelled as either defeated (D) or undefeated (U). We denote the root of $\mathscr{T}(\langle \mathscr{A},L \rangle)$ with $root(\mathscr{T}(\langle \mathscr{A},L \rangle))$, and $marking(N)$, where N is a node in a dialectical tree, denotes the value of the marking for node N (either U or D). Deciding whether a node is defeated or undefeated depends on whether or not all its children are defeated: (1) if node N is a leaf then $marking(N) = U$, (2) node N is such that $marking(N) = D$ iff at least one of its children that is marked with U, and (3) node N is such that $marking(N) = U$ iff all its children are marked with D.

Definition 4. Let KB be a defeasible Datalog$^\pm$ ontology and $\mathfrak{F}$ the corresponding Datalog$^\pm$ argumentation framework. An atom L is *warranted* in $\mathfrak{F}$ (through $\mathscr{T}$) iff there exists an argument $\langle \mathscr{A},L \rangle$ such that $marking(root(\mathscr{T}(\langle \mathscr{A},L \rangle))) = U$. We say that L is entailed from KB (through $\mathfrak{F}$), denoted with $KB \models_{\mathfrak{F}} L$, iff it is *warranted* in $\mathfrak{F}$.

Example 6. Continuing with KB from Example 2, consider its corresponding Datalog$^\pm$ argumentation framework $\mathfrak{F}$, the atom *unstable*(*will*) is warranted through $\mathfrak{F}$ under the assumption that arguments $\mathscr{A}$ and $\mathscr{B}$ from Example 5 are such that $\mathscr{A} \succ \mathscr{B}$.

The following proposition establishes that no conflicting sets of atoms can be entailed/warranted from a Datalog$^\pm$ argumentation framework.

Proposition 2. *Let* $KB = (F,D,\Sigma_T,\Sigma_D,\Sigma_{NC})$ *be a defeasible Datalog$^\pm$ ontology. No two atoms L_1 and L_2 that are warranted in $\mathfrak{F}$ are conflicting relative to Σ_{NC}.*

We regard this property as desirable for inconsistency-tolerant reasoning mechanisms which is related to a similar one introduced in [10]. We formalize it as follows.

Non-Conflicting Entailment (NCE). Given a knowledge base $\mathscr{K}$ and a set of binary negative constraints Σ_{NC}, any entailment operator $\models$ satisfies the NCE property iff for any two atoms L_1 and L_2 $\mathscr{K} \models L_1$ and $\mathscr{K} \models L_2$ are non-conflicting relative to Σ_{NC}.

5   A Comparison with Inconsistency-Tolerant Semantics

Although query answering in Datalog$^\pm$ does not contemplate the possibility of returning meaningful answers in the presence of conflicts, a variety of inconsistency-tolerant semantics have been developed in the last decade for ontological languages, including lightweight Description Logics (DLs), such as $\mathscr{EL}$ and *DL-Lite* [7,19], and several fragments of Datalog$^\pm$ [20]. In this section we analyze entailment in defeasible Datalog$^\pm$ ontologies in relation to several inconsistency-tolerant semantics for ontological languages: *AR* semantics [19], *CAR* semantics [19], *IAR*, *k*-support [7], and *ICAR* semantics that are sound approximations of *AR* and of *CAR*, respectively, and finally, the k-defeater semantics [6] that comprises a family of complete approximation of *AR*.

We present the basic concepts needed to understand the different semantics on Datalog$^\pm$ ontologies and then show how entailment under such semantics compare to entailment on defeasible Datalog$^\pm$. We first recall the notion of *repair*; in relational databases a repair is a model of the set of integrity constraints that is maximally close, *i.e.*, *"as close as possible"* to the original database. Different notions of repairs have been developed depending on the meaning of "closeness" used and on the type of constraints. For a Datalog$^\pm$ ontology $KB = (I, \Sigma_T \cup \Sigma_{NC})$, repairs are maximal subsets of I such that their consequences with respect to Σ_T are non-conflicting relative Σ_{NC}.

AR Semantics. The *AR* semantics corresponds to the notion of *consistent answers* in relational databases [1]. Intuitively, an atom L is said to be *AR*-consistently entailed from a Datalog$^\pm$ ontology KB, denoted $KB \models_{AR} L$ iff L is classically entailed from every ontology that can be built from every possible repair.

CAR Semantics. Another definition of repairs was also proposed in [19] that includes knowledge that comes from the closure of the database instance with respect to the set of TGDs. Since the closure of an inconsistent ontology yields the whole language, they define the *consistent closure* of an ontology $KB = (I, \Sigma_T \cup \Sigma_{NC})$ as the set $CCL(KB) = \{\alpha \mid \alpha \in \mathcal{H}(\mathscr{L}_{\mathscr{R}}) \, s.t. \, \exists S \subseteq I$ and $mods(S, \Sigma_T \cup \Sigma_{NC}) \neq \emptyset$ and $(S, \Sigma_T) \models \alpha\}$. A *Closed ABox repair* of a Datalog$^\pm$ ontology KB is a consistent subset I' of $CCL(KB)$ such that it maximally preserves the database instance [19]. It is said that an atom L is *CAR*-consistently entailed from a Datalog$^\pm$ ontology KB, denoted by $KB \models_{CAR} L$ iff L is classically entailed from every ontology built from each possible closed ABox repair.

The following result shows that every atom that is *AR*-consistently (resp., *CAR*-consistently) entailed from a Datalog$^\pm$ ontology $KB = (I, \Sigma_T \cup \Sigma_{NC})$ is also entailed from the defeasible Datalog$^\pm$ ontology $KB' = (\emptyset, I, \Sigma_T, \emptyset, \Sigma_{NC})$ constructed from KB. This transformation from Datalog$^\pm$ to defeasible Datalog$^\pm$ is without loss of generality; the inconsistency-tolerant semantics that we study here assume that the knowledge contained in I is somehow *challengeable* as it can be in conflict once considered together with the set of constraints. Defeasible Datalog$^\pm$ ontologies allow to express both strict and defeasible knowledge, however the strict part is assumed to be consistent in itself (in particular, it could be empty), therefore, to make a fair comparison between approaches we need to translate the data contained in I to defeasible atoms.

Theorem 1. *Let $KB = (I, \Sigma_T \cup \Sigma_{NC})$ be a Datalog$^\pm$ ontology, $KB' = (\emptyset, I, \Sigma_T, \emptyset, \Sigma_{NC})$ be a defeasible Datalog$^\pm$ ontology and $\mathfrak{F} = \langle \mathscr{L}_{\mathscr{R}}, \mathbb{A}_{KB'}, \succ \rangle$. Then, (i) if $KB \models_{AR} L$ then $KB' \models_{\mathfrak{F}} L$, and (ii) if $KB \models_{CAR} L$ then $KB' \models_{\mathfrak{F}} L$.*

The converse does not hold. In our running example, *unstable*(*will*) is not entailed by *AR* neither by *CAR* since every (closed) ABox repair either entails *unstable*(*will*) or *risky_job*(*will*), but not both. However, as shown in Example 6, it is entailed from KB as $\mathscr{A} \succ \mathscr{B}$. Depending on the preference criterion, it could be the case that *unstable*(*will*) would not be entailed, in which case *risky_job*(*will*) could be, or neither would be. The results from Theorem 1 directly extends to the sound approximations for *AR* and *ICAR* defined in [19] and the family of k-support semantics from [7].

Finally, we analyze the k-defeater semantics from [7]. Given a Datalog$^\pm$ ontology $KB = (I, \Sigma_T \cup \Sigma_{NC})$, an atom L is entailed from KB under the k-defeater semantics, $KB \models_{k\text{-}def} L$, for some $k \geq 0$, iff no set of facts with size smaller than k is such that it *contradicts* every minimal set from I that yields L. From an argumentation point of view, this semantics looks for counter-arguments for L up to a certain size – the size of an argument being the number of (defeasible) atoms used. If no such argument can be found, L is entailed from KB. Conflicting atoms could be entailed from KB for any k (except for that in which converges to AR), therefore it does not enjoy the NCE property.

In the following, consider $\succ_{k\text{-}def}$, a preference criterion such that $\mathscr{A} \succ_{k\text{-}def} B$ iff the number of facts and defeasible atoms used in $\mathscr{A}$ is less than or equal to k, for any $k \geq 0$.

Theorem 2. *Let $KB = (I, \Sigma_T \cup \Sigma_{NC})$ be a Datalog$^\pm$ ontology, $KB' = (\emptyset, I, \Sigma_T, \emptyset, \Sigma_{NC})$ be a defeasible Datalog$^\pm$ ontology, $\mathfrak{F} = \langle \mathscr{L}_{\mathscr{R}}, \mathbb{A}_{KB'}, \succ \rangle$, and $\mathfrak{F}' = \langle \mathscr{L}_{\mathscr{R}}, \mathbb{A}_{KB'}, \succ_{k\text{-}def} \rangle$. Then, (i) if $KB' \models_{\mathfrak{F}} L$ then $KB \models_{0\text{-}def} L$, and (ii) for any $0 \leq k < k'$ if $KB' \models_{\mathfrak{F}'} L$ then $KB \models_{k\text{-}def} L$, where k' is the point where AR and k-defeater semantics coincide.*

Statement (i) from Theorem 2 shows, unsurprisingly, that independently of the preference criterion defined over $\mathbb{A}_{KB'}$, $\models_{\mathfrak{F}}$ is a sound approximation to 0-defeaters, which corresponds to the *brave* semantics in which anything that can be classically entailed from some repair is *consistently* entailed from the ontology. Furthermore, given Proposition 2, this approximation is not only sound but it also satisfies the NCE property.

More interesting is statement (ii) showing that, using $\succ_{k\text{-}def}$, argumentation-based entailment on defeasible Datalog$^\pm$ is a sound approximation of the k-defeater semantics for every k (up to the point where k-defeater coincides with AR). Furthermore, since Proposition 2 ensures the NCE property independently of the preference criterion, we have obtained a family of semantics that soundly approximate the k-defeater semantics and ensure that no conflicting atoms can be entailed from a defeasible ontology.

6   Related Work

Within Artificial Intelligence, many efforts to deal with inconsistent information have been developed in the last four decades. Frameworks such as default logic [26] can be used to represent a database DB with integrity constraints IC as a default logic theory where the background theory consists of the IC and the facts in D constitutes the defaults rules, *i.e.*, a fact in D is assumed to be true if it can be assumed to be true. Argumentation [13, 15, 23, 27] has been used for handling uncertainty and inconsistency by means of reasoning about how contradictory arguments defeat each other.

The most widely accepted semantics for querying a possibly inconsistent database is that of *consistent answers*, which yields the set of tuples (atoms) that appear in the answer to the query over *every* possible repair, which we have discussed in more detail in Section 5. More recently, Ontology-based Data Access approach to data integration, has led to a resurgence of interest in this area, specially focusing on the development of efficient inconsistency-tolerant reasoning and query answering in DLs and other ontology languages. Lately, several works have focused on inconsistency handling for different classes of DLs, adapting and specializing general techniques previously considered for traditional logics [18, 21, 24]. In [19], the adaptation of CQA for *DL-Lite* ontologies and several sound and complete approximation are studied. Computing consistent answers is an inherently hard problem, [19] shows co-NP completeness for ground atomic queries in *DL-Lite*, though some works identify cases for very simple ontologies and restricted queries (within the *DL-Lite* family) for which tractable results can be obtained [6]. In [20], an alternative semantics called k-lazy is proposed, which relaxes the notion of repairs by adopting a compromise between quality of answers and tractability for fragments of Datalog$^\pm$. Section 5 presents some preliminary comparison between these semantics and our approach, a more detailed analysis is leave for future work.

Finally, more recently, there have been several developments in combining argumentation methods with description logics in order to overcome inconsistency and incoherence in such ontological languages, such as the work of [29] and [11]. In [29] an argumentation framework for reasoning and management in (inconsistent or incoherent) description logic ontologies, based Besnard and Hunter's framework [5], is proposed. In [11], on the other hand, Dung's abstract frameworks are used instead, and consistent answers under de *ICR* semantics [6] are obtained by means of obtaining the sets of accepted answers under some of the classical argumentation semantics. The main difference with our approach is that these frameworks are based on classical logic consequences and therefore, in the end answers and repairs are equivalent to those obtained for particular semantics of CQA, whose relationship we have discussed in Section 5.

7 Conclusions

We have introduced the idea of defeasible reasoning over Datalog$^\pm$ ontologies by introducing the construction of arguments, the definition of conflict using the negative constrains available in the system, and completing the argumentative infrastructure by characterizing defeat employing a preference criterion that has remained as an abstract element to be instantiated. The dialectical process to decide what arguments are warranted is done applying the classic techniques of argumentation theory. Furthermore, we show how such approach ensures the reasonableness of the answers given by it, as no conflicting atoms can be entailed/warranted in it [4, 25].

We have also shown that atoms entailed from a Datalog$^\pm$ ontology, under well-known inconsistency-tolerant semantics, namely *AR* and *CAR* semantics, and sound approximations of these, are also entailed from the corresponding defeasible Datalog$^\pm$ ontology that includes the database instance of the ontology as defeasible atoms. Moreover, we have shown that the converse property does not hold in general, and therefore argumentation-based query answering for defeasible Datalog$^\pm$ ontologies allows to produce answers that though are involved in conflicts, and therefore are not consistent answers, the ontology contains enough information in order to warrant them. Furthermore, we show how to construct a Datalog$^\pm$ argumentation framework that yields a semantics that is a sound approximation to the k-defeaters semantics from [6], that enjoys the property of never entailing conflicting atoms.

Future work will involve a full complexity study of argumentation-based entailment for defeasible Datalog$^\pm$ ontologies to complete the comparison with the different inconsistent-tolerant semantics and better understand possible implementation problems for the framework [14].

Acknowledgments. This work was partially supported by CONICET Argentina, SeGCyT Universidad Nacional del Sur in Bahia Blanca, UK Engineering and Physical Sciences Research Council (EPSRC) grant EP/J008346/1 (PrOQAW).

References

1. Arenas, M., Bertossi, L.E., Chomicki, J.: Consistent query answers in inconsistent databases. In: Proc. of PODS, pp. 68–79 (1999)
2. Baroni, P., Caminada, M., Giacomin, M.: An introduction to argumentation semantics. Knowledge Eng. Review **26**(4), 365–410 (2011)
3. Beeri, C., Vardi, M.Y.: The implication problem for data dependencies. In: Even, S., Kariv, O. (eds.) Automata, Languages and Programming. LNCS, vol. 115, pp. 73–85. Springer, Heidelberg (1981)
4. Besnard, P., Hunter, A.: Elements of Argumentation. MIT Press (2008)
5. Besnard, P., Hunter, A.: A logic-based theory of deductive arguments. Artif. Intell. **128**(1–2), 203–235 (2001)
6. Bienvenu, M.: On the complexity of consistent query answering in the presence of simple ontologies. In: Proc. of AAAI (2012)
7. Bienvenu, M., Rosati, R.: Tractable approximations of consistent query answering for robust ontology-based data access. In: Proc. of IJCAI (2013)
8. Calì, A., Gottlob, G., Kifer, M.: Taming the infinite chase: Query answering under expressive relational constraints. In: Proc. of KR, pp. 70–80 (2008)
9. Calì, A., Gottlob, G., Lukasiewicz, T.: A general Datalog-based framework for tractable query answering over ontologies. J. Web Sem. **14**, 57–83 (2012)
10. Caminada, M., Amgoud, L.: On the evaluation of argumentation formalisms. Artif. Intell. **171**(5–6), 286–310 (2007)
11. Croitoru, M., Vesic, S.: What Can Argumentation Do for Inconsistent Ontology Query Answering? In: Liu, W., Subrahmanian, V.S., Wijsen, J. (eds.) SUM 2013. LNCS, vol. 8078, pp. 15–29. Springer, Heidelberg (2013)
12. Deagustini, C.A.D., Dalibón, S.E.F., Gottifredi, S., Falappa, M.A., Chesñevar, C.I., Simari, G.R.: Relational databases as a massive information source for defeasible argumentation. Knowl. Based Syst. **51**, 93–109 (2013)
13. Dung, P.M.: On the acceptability of arguments and its fundamental role in nonmonotonic reasoning, logic programming and n-person games. Artif. Intell. **77**, 321–357 (1995)
14. Dunne, P., Wooldridge, M.: Complexity of Abstract Argumentation. In: Argumentation in Artificial Intelligence, pp. 85–104. Springer (2009)
15. García, A.J., Simari, G.R.: Defeasible logic programming: An argumentative approach. TPLP **4**(1–2), 95–138 (2004)
16. García, A.J., Simari, G.R.: Defeasible logic programming: Delp-servers, contextual queries, and explanations for answers. Argument & Computation **5**(1), 63–88 (2014)
17. Gómez, S.A., Chesñevar, C.I., Simari, G.R.: Ontoarg: A decision support framework for ontology integration based on argumentation. Expert Syst. Appl. **40**(5), 1858–1870 (2013)
18. Huang, Z., van Harmelen, F., ten Teije, A.: Reasoning with inconsistent ontologies. In: Proc. of IJCAI, pp. 354–359 (2005)
19. Lembo, D., Lenzerini, M., Rosati, R., Ruzzi, M., Savo, D.F.: Inconsistency-tolerant semantics for description logics. In: Hitzler, P., Lukasiewicz, T. (eds.) RR 2010. LNCS, vol. 6333, pp. 103–117. Springer, Heidelberg (2010)
20. Lukasiewicz, T., Martinez, M.V., Simari, G.I.: Inconsistency handling in Datalog+/- ontologies. In: Proc. of ECAI, pp. 558–563 (2012)

21. Ma, Y., Hitzler, P.: Paraconsistent Reasoning for OWL 2. In: Polleres, A., Swift, T. (eds.) RR 2009. LNCS, vol. 5837, pp. 197–211. Springer, Heidelberg (2009)
22. Martinez, M.V., García, A.J., Simari, G.R.: On the use of presumptions in structured defeasible reasoning. In: Proc. of COMMA, pp. 185–196 (2012)
23. Prakken, H., Sartor, G.: Argument-based extended logic programming with defeasible priorities. J. Appl. Non-Classical Logics 7(1) (1997)
24. Qi, G., Du, J.: Model-based revision operators for terminologies in description logics. In: Proc. of IJCAI, pp. 891–897 (2009)
25. Rahwan, I., Simari, G.R.: Argumentation in Artificial Intelligence. Springer (2009)
26. Reiter, R.: A logic for default reasoning. Artif. Intel. 13(1–2), 81–132 (1980)
27. Simari, G.R., Loui, R.P.: A mathematical treatment of defeasible reasoning and its implementation. Artif. Intell. 53(2–3), 125–157 (1992)
28. Stolzenburg, F., García, A.J., Chesñevar, C.I., Simari, G.R.: Computing generalized specificity. J. of Applied Non-Classical Logics 13(1), 87–113 (2003)
29. Zhang, X., Lin, Z.: An argumentation framework for description logic ontology reasoning and management. J. Intell. Inf. Syst. 40(3), 375–403 (2013)

A Labeled Abstract Bipolar Argumentation Framework

Maximiliano Celmo David Budán[1,2]([⊠]), Ignacio Viglizzo[2],
and Guillermo Ricardo Simari[1]

[1] Artificial Intelligence Research and Development Laboratory,
Department of Computer Science and Engineering, Universidad Nacional del Sur, Alem 1253,
8000 Bahía Blanca, Buenos Aires, Argentina
[2] Consejo Nacional de Investigaciones Científicas y Técnicas, Av. Rivadavia 1917,
Ciudad Autónoma de Buenos Aires, Argentina
{mcdb,grs}@cs.uns.edu.ar, viglizzo@gmail.com

Abstract. Argumentation is a form of reasoning where a claim is accepted or
rejected according to the analysis of the arguments for and against it; furthermore,
it provides a reasoning mechanism able to handle contradictory, incomplete and
uncertain information in real-world situations. We combine *Bipolar Argumentation Frameworks* (an extension of Dung's work) with an *Algebra of Argumentation
Labels* modeling two independent types of interaction between arguments, representing meta-information associated with arguments, and introducing an acceptability notion that will give more information for arguments acceptability.

1 Introduction

The evolution of applications based on argumentation mechanisms is requiring the
development of more sophisticated tools to implement them. In recent years, the
research in argumentation theory has produced significant results on abstract and structured systems. Argumentation theories are applied in many areas such as legal reasoning [3], Semantic Web [17], recommender systems [14], autonomous agents and
multi-agent systems [20], and many others [5, 19].

Several argument-based formalisms have emerged to study the different relations
among arguments. In [12], Dung proposes *Abstract Argumentation Frameworks* to
model real-world situations by representing the attack relations between abstract entities called arguments, providing different acceptability semantics to determine which
sets of arguments are acceptable. Subsequently, Cayrol and Lagasquie-Schiex in [10]
extended Dung's framework taking into account two independent types of interaction between arguments: attack and support. Considering this, *Bipolar Argumentation
Frameworks* (*BAF*s) allow to model situations in which an argument reinforces another
giving more reasons to believe in it; moreover, they adapt Dung's acceptability semantics adding the consideration of the support relationship between arguments.

Although these formalizations model certain aspects of real-world situations, they
do not provide tools to represent the particular features of arguments, such as its
strength, reliability, temporal availability, among others. In certain applications, it is

© Springer International Publishing Switzerland 2014
A.L.C. Bazzan and K. Pichara (Eds.): IBERAMIA 2014, LNAI 8864, pp. 28–40, 2014.
DOI: 10.1007/978-3-319-12027-0_3

necessary to consider further details to obtain more refined results. In [8], a formalization was presented that allows to attach descriptive information to arguments through a structure called *argumentation labels*. These labels are affected by the existing relations among arguments; to reflect that, an algebraic structure called *algebra of argumentation labels* was proposed, combining and propagating the information associated to arguments. Acceptability is then defined taking into account the qualities associated with the arguments. We present a new version of *BAF* taking into account the properties associated with the arguments, increasing the representational capabilities of this formalization; in addition, we will introduce an acceptability notion in which we will get more information about arguments acceptability.

This paper is structured as follows. In Section 2, we present an example to motivate and illustrate the objectives of our work; in Section 3, we have included an introduction to bipolar argumentation frameworks; then, a particular abstract algebra for handling the labels associated with the arguments is presented in Section 4; next, in Section 5, an new version of BAF is presented to represent argument attributes; finally, in Section 6 we discuss related work, and in Section 7 we conclude and propose future work.

2 Running Example

The aim of this work is to increase the representational capability of *BAF*s, using labels to represent features associated with arguments, such as relevance degree, reliability degree, measure of strength, or temporal availability, among many others, using the information to refine the acceptability process, providing additional details. To motivate the usefulness of our formalization, in the context of agent and multi-agents systems, we introduce an example where the formalism could help achieve a better behavior.

Consider the following scenario where an agent is looking for an apartment to rent, and in considering candidates she analyzes different arguments in favor and against renting it. To reach a decision she evaluates these arguments according to her preferences, assigning each of them an assessment of its relevance.

A *She should rent it, the apartment has a good location since it is near of her work.* [0.5]

B *The apartment is located in an well illuminated and safe area.* [0.8]

C *The property is in a quiet area, because most of the neighbors are retirees and peaceful people.* [0.6]

D *The apartment is small; therefore, she should not rent it.* [0.7]

E *Despite the apartment size, the spaces are well distributed.* [0.4]

F *She should not rent it, since the apartment seems to have humidity problems.* [0.9]

G *There are rumors that a nightclub will open in the area, so the area will not be quiet anymore.* [0.5]

H *The humidity problems are difficult and costly to resolve.* [0.7]

I *Laws forbid the opening of a nightclub in this urban area.* [0.9]

J *The person responsible for maintenance is committed to fixing the humidity problem at a low cost.* [0.8]

K *A renowned architect designed the building, so that the distribution of the spaces is optimal.* [0.3]

This example illustrates how the knowledge used to decide can be naturally structured as arguments, and to reach a decision it is necessary to consider the relationships among these arguments. The interactions between arguments can be given as support (*e.g.*, A and B) or conflict (*e.g.*, A and F). Each *pro* and *con* has associated descriptive features that weight over the final decision. Clearly, the agent analyzes the arguments in favor and against renting the apartment according to her preferences; therefore, the arguments endorsing certain characteristics have different relevance according to these preferences showing the need of representing additional information. Arguments in conflict are evaluated and the position of best argument becomes supported, but the one who loses remains the same. In this proposal, we consider how the features of both arguments are affected; for instance, the relevance of an argument providing support to a decision should not be the same when it is free of counterarguments as when it is controversial.

Next we will present our formalism that includes the possibility of using labels to represent additional information associated with arguments, and of combining and propagating these labels according to the interactions of support and conflict between arguments; the extra information associated with the arguments is used to inform the acceptability process. Subsequently, we will instantiate the proposed formalization to model the example presented in this section.

3   Bipolar Argumentation Frameworks

It is natural to consider bipolarity In the analysis of the argumentation process. Abstracting away from the inner structure of the arguments, this framework as proposed by Amgoud *et al.* in [2] (that we slightly modify below), redefines Dung's notion of acceptability [12] distinguishing two independent forms of interaction: support and attack (see [11] for a survey). Note that in [2] all attacking arguments defeat the attacked argument, while in the extension we propose in the next section, attacks can be successful or not; we adapted some of the definitions below to reflect this.

Definition 1 (Bipolar Argumentation Framework). *A   Bipolar   Argumentation Framework (BAF) is a 3-tuple* $\Phi = \langle AR, \rightarrow, \dashrightarrow \rangle$*, where AR is a set of arguments,* $\rightarrow$ *and* $\dashrightarrow$ *are disjoint binary relations on AR called attack and support relation respectively.*

Notation: Consider $A \in AR$. The set $\{A_i \in AR \mid A_i \rightarrow A\}$ is denoted by $S^{\rightarrow}(A)$ and the set $\{A_i \in AR \mid A_i \dashrightarrow A\}$ is denoted by $S^{\dashrightarrow}(A)$.

Definition 2 (Bipolar argumentation graph). *Given a BAF* $\Phi = \langle AR, \rightarrow, \dashrightarrow \rangle$*, we define a directed graph* G_Φ *by taking as nodes the elements in AR, and two types of arcs: one for the attack relation (represented by plain arrows), and one for the support relation (represented by dashed arrows). We define:*

- *A path from A to B is a sequence of arguments* $P = A_1, \ldots, A_n$ *such that* $A = A_1 \, R_1 \, A_2 \, R_2 \, A_3 \ldots A_{n-1} \, R_{n-1} \, A_n = B$*, with* $R_i \in \{\rightarrow, \dashrightarrow\}$*,* $1 \leq i \leq n-1$*. The length of the path P is* $n-1$ *(the number of edges that are used in the path), denoted by* ℓ^P*;* $P(A, B)$ *denotes the set of all possible paths from an argument A to an argument B.*

- *The* defeat number of the path *(resp. support number of the path)* $P = A_1 \ldots A_n$, *with* $A_1 \, R_1 \, A_2 \, R_2 \, A_3 \ldots A_{n-1} \, R_{n-1} \, A_n$, *is the number of* $R_i =\longrightarrow$ *(resp.* $R_i =$--$\rightarrow$ *), denoted* $n^{\rightarrow}(P)$ *(resp.* $n^{\text{--}\rightarrow}(P)$*).*

We considered *well-founded* BAFs, *i.e.*, there is no infinite path in them (and therefore no cycles, no self-attacking, and no self-supporting arguments exist). This implies there are arguments A such that $S^{\rightarrow}(A) = S^{\text{--}\rightarrow}(A) = \emptyset$; these arguments are called *leaves*.

Example 1. *Now, we model the scenario described in the motivation example through a BAF* $\Phi = \langle AR, \rightarrow, \text{--}\rightarrow \rangle$, *where:*

$AR = \{A, B, C, D, E, F, G, H, I, J, K\}$
$\rightarrow = \{(D, A), (F, A), (E, D), (G, C), (I, G), (J, H)\}$
$\text{--}\rightarrow = \{(B, A), (C, A), (H, F), (K, E)\}$

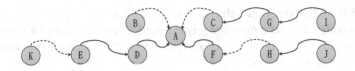

Fig. 1. Bipolar argumentation graph for our running example

The interaction between the two relations allowed Amgoud *et al.* [2] to introduce direct and indirect attackers and defenders, together with direct and indirect supporters.

Definition 3 (Direct and Indirect Attackers, Defenders and Supporters) *Let* $A \in AR$:
- *The* direct attackers *of* A *are the elements of* $S^{\rightarrow}(A)$.
- *The* direct defenders *of* A *are the direct attackers of the elements of* $S^{\rightarrow}(A)$.
- *The* indirect attackers *of* A *are the arguments* A_i *such that* $\exists P \in P(A_i, A)$ *with* $n^{\rightarrow}(P) = 2k + 1$ *for some* $k \geq 0$ *and* A_i *is not a direct attacker of* A.
- *The* indirect defenders *of* A *are the elements* A_i *such that* $\exists P \in P(A_i, A)$ *with* $n^{\rightarrow}(P) = 2k$ *for some* $k \geq 1$ *and* A_i *is not a direct defender of* A.
- *The* direct supporters *of* A *are the elements of* $S^{\text{--}\rightarrow}(A)$.
- *The* indirect supporters *of* A *are the* A_i *such that* $\exists P \in P(A_i, A)$ *with* $n^{\text{--}\rightarrow}(P) = \ell^P \geq 2$.

We call attackers (defenders, supporters) of an argument to both the direct and indirect attackers (respectivelly, defenders, supporters) of that argument.

Definition 4 (Set–defense). *Let* $S \subseteq AR$ *be a set of arguments, and* $A \in AR$. *The set* S *defends* A *if there exists in* S *a direct or indirect attacker of each attacker of* A. *Note that an argument that doesn't have attackers is trivially defended by the empty set.*

Example 2. *(Continued Example 1) On the BAF of Figure 1, we have:*

The path K --$\rightarrow$ $E \rightarrow D \rightarrow A$ *has* $n^{\rightarrow}(P) = 2$ *and* $n^{\text{--}\rightarrow}(P) = 1$.
The path $J \rightarrow H$ --$\rightarrow$ $F \rightarrow A$ *has* $n^{\rightarrow}(P) = 2$ *and* $n^{\text{--}\rightarrow}(P) = 1$.
The path $I \rightarrow G \rightarrow C$ --$\rightarrow$ A *has* $n^{\rightarrow}(P) = 2$ *and* $n^{\text{--}\rightarrow}(P) = 1$.

The path B $\dashrightarrow$ A *has* $n^{\rightarrow}(P) = 0$ *and* $n^{\dashrightarrow}(P) = 1$.
The direct and indirect attackers of A *are* $\{D,F\}$ *and* $\{G,H\}$ *respectively.*
The direct and indirect supporters of A *are* $\{C,B\}$ *and* $\emptyset$ *respectively.*
The direct and indirect defenders of A *are* $\{E\}$ *and* $\{J,I,K\}$ *respectively.*
Examples of defense sets for A *are* $\{E,J,I\}$ *and* $\{K,J,I\}$. *The maximal defense set for* A *with respect to inclusion is* $\{K,E,J,I\}$.

Cayrol and Lagasquie-Schiex in [10] argued that a set of arguments must be in some sense coherent to model one side of an intelligent dispute. The coherence of a set of arguments is analyzed *internally* (a set of arguments in which an argument attacks another in the set is not acceptable), and *externally* (a set of arguments which contains both a supporter and an attacker for the same argument is not acceptable). The internal coherence is captured extending the definition of *conflict free set* proposed in [12], and external coherence is captured with the notion of *safe* set.

Definition 5 (Conflict-free and Safe). *Let* $S \subseteq AR$ *be a non empty set of arguments. Then,* S *is a* conflict-free set *if there are no arguments* A, B $\in S$ *such that* A *is an attacker of* B; *and* S *is* safe *if there is no* B $\in AR$ *such that* S *contains both an attacker of* B *and either* S *contains a supporter of* B, *or* B $\in S$.

Property 1. *Let* $S \subseteq AR$ *be a set of arguments. Then, (i) if* S *is safe, then* S *is conflict-free; (ii)* S *is conflict-free and closed for* $\dashrightarrow$, *then* S *is safe. A set* S *of arguments is closed for* $\dashrightarrow$ *if* A $\dashrightarrow$ B *and* A $\in S$, *then* B $\in S$.

From the notions of coherence, and extending the propositions introduced in [12], Cayrol and Lagasquie-Schiex in [10] proposed different new semantics for the acceptability.

Definition 6 (Stable extension). *Let* $\Phi = \langle AR, \rightarrow, \dashrightarrow \rangle$ *be a BAF. Let* $S \subseteq AR$ *be a set of arguments.* S *is a* stable extension *of* Φ *if* S *is conflict-free and for all* A $\notin S$, *there is an attacker of* A *in* S.

Property 2. *Let* $\Phi = \langle AR, \rightarrow, \dashrightarrow \rangle$ *be a BAF. Let* S *be a stable extension of* Φ. *If* S *is safe, then it is closed for* $\dashrightarrow$.

Example 3. *(Continued Example 2) The set* $S_1 = \{B,F\}$ *is conflict free but not safe. Also,* S_1 *is not a stable extension, since* G $\notin S_1$ *and there is no attacker of* G *in it. The set* $S_2 = \{A,B,C,E,I,J,K\}$ *is conflict free and closed by* $\dashrightarrow$, *then it is safe. In addition,* S_2 *is a stable extension since it is conflict-free and there is an attacker for all arguments that not belong to* S_2 *(the argument D is defeated by E, the argument F and H is defeated by J, and the argument G es defeated by J).*

Cayrol *et al.* in [10] proposed three different definitions for admissibility. The most general is based on Dung's admissiblity definition; then, they extended the notion of d-admissibility notion taking into account external coherence. Finally, external coherence is strengthened by requiring that admissible sets be closed for $\dashrightarrow$.

Definition 7 (Admissibility in BAF). *Let* $\Phi = \langle AR, \rightarrow, \dashrightarrow \rangle$ *be a BAF. Let* $S \subseteq AR$ *be a set of arguments. The admissibility of a set* S *is defined as follows:*

- *S is d-admissible if S is conflict-free and defends all its elements.*
- *S is s-admissible if S is safe and defends all its elements.*
- *S is c-admissible if S conflict-free, closed for $\dashrightarrow$ and defends all its elements.*

Definition 8 (Preferred extension). *Let $\Phi = \langle AR, \rightarrow, \dashrightarrow \rangle$ be a BAF. Let $S \subseteq AR$ be a set of arguments. S is a d-preferred (resp. s-preferred, c-preferred) extension if S is maximal (for set-inclusion) among the d-admissible (resp. s-admissible, c-admissible) subsets of AR.*

Example 4. *(Continued Example 3) From definitions 7 and 8, we determine that:*

$S_2 = \{A, B, C, E, I, J, K\}$ is a maximal d-admissible set, so S_2 is a d-preferred extension. $S_3 = \{B, K, E, J\}$ is another d-admissible set, but not a maximal one. S_2 is also a maximal s-admissible set, so it is an s-preferred extension. $S_4 = \{B, C, J\}$ is an s-admissible set, but not an s-preferred extension, since it is not maximal. S_2 is a maximal c-admissible set, therefore S_2 is a c-preferred extension. $S_5 = \{E, K\}$ is a c-admissible set, but not a c-preferred extension, since it is not maximal.

Based on the arguments acceptability under the stable and preferred semantics, since she has sufficient reasons to believe it is a good decision she decides to rent.

4 Algebra of Argumentation Labels

The use of labels gives us the possibility of representing distinctive features of arguments; moreover, these labels will be changing according to the existing relations between arguments. Our example shows that there exists a support relation between B and A, so A is strengthened by B. Since there exists an attack relation between F and A, A is weakened by F.

To represent argument features like the relative strength, reliability, or preference, it is common to use a numerical scale, normalizing this scale to the real interval $[0, 1]$. Generalizing this approach, we can abstract the definitions below to a partially ordered set with a least element $\perp$ representing the lowest possible strength and $\top$ for the maximum degree attainable by an attribute; thusly, our definition will be able to accommodate different specific cases required by different applications. To operate with these elements, we borrow operations from *fuzzy logic* [21, 22], a well researched set of tools for making inferences when the available information is approximate rather than exact.

Definition 9 (Algebra of Argumentation Labels). *An algebra of argumentation labels is a 6-tuple which has the form $A = \langle A, \leq, \oplus, \ominus, \top, \perp \rangle$, where:*

- *A is a set of argumentation labels called the* domain *of labels.*
- *$\leq$ is a partial order relation on A (that is, a reflexive, antisymmetric, and transitive).*
- *$\oplus : A \times A \rightarrow A$ is called a* support operation *which satisfies:*
  $\alpha \oplus \beta = \beta \oplus \alpha$, for all $\alpha, \beta \in A$ (commutativity).
  if $\alpha \leq \beta$, then $\alpha \oplus \gamma \leq \beta \oplus \gamma$, for all $\alpha, \beta \in A$ (monotonicity).
  $\alpha \oplus (\beta \oplus \gamma) = (\alpha \oplus \beta) \oplus \gamma$, for all $\alpha, \beta \in A$ (associativity).

- $\ominus : A \times A \to A$ *is called a* conflict operation *which satisfies:*

    $\alpha \ominus \beta \leq \alpha$, *for all* $\alpha \in A$.

    $\alpha \ominus \alpha = \bot$, *for all* $\alpha \in A$.

    $\alpha \ominus \bot = \alpha$, *for all* $\alpha \in A$ *(right neutral element).*

    if $\alpha \ominus \beta = \bot$ *and* $\beta \ominus \alpha = \bot$, *then* $\alpha = \beta$, *for all* $\alpha, \beta \in A$.

    if $(\alpha \oplus \beta) < \top$, *then* $((\alpha \oplus \beta) \ominus \beta) = \alpha$.

    $\bot \ominus \alpha = \bot$, *for all* $\alpha \in A$.

- $\top$ *is the greatest element of A, while* $\bot$ *is the least one. Furthermore,* $\bot$ *is the neutral element for* $\oplus$: $\alpha \oplus \bot = \alpha$, *for all* $\alpha \in A$.

The support operation is a T-conorm. Notice that from the definition it follows that if an argument has a label with value $\alpha \oplus \beta$ because it has supported the values of other arguments, and then it is attacked by an argument with value β, its value becomes reduced to α. Thus, the conflict operation is in some sense an inverse of the support operation. Since the operations are limited to values between $\top$ and $\bot$, some information will be lost, and we cannot have a proper inverse operation.

5 Labeled Bipolar Argumentation Frameworks

As we noted before, BAFs allow us to model the relationships of support and attack between arguments; however, it is not possible to represent any additional characteristics of arguments. To expand the representation capabilities of the argumentative structures, we will incorporate labels; these labels hold specific information regarding each argument, and the results obtained using the algebra of argumentative labels produced by the interactions that combine and propagate them. Through these labels it is possible to refine the acceptability process and offer more information in a compact way.

Definition 10 (**Labeled Bipolar Argumentation Framework**). *A Labeled Bipolar Argume-ntation Framework (L-BAF) is a tuple* $\Psi = \langle AR, \to, \dashrightarrow, A, \mathscr{F} \rangle$, *where* $\langle AR, \to, \dashrightarrow \rangle$ *is a Bipolar Argumentation Framework, A is a Algebra of Argumentation Labels, and* $\mathscr{F}$ *is a function that assigns an attribute to each element of AR; i.e.,* $\mathscr{F} : AR \longrightarrow A$.

Definition 11 (**Labeling of a BAF**). *Given a Labeled Bipolar Argumentation Framework* Ψ, *and the bipolar argumentation graph associated with it, we proceed to determine a label for each argument. Each label for an argument* A *is composed of three elements in the algebra* A: $\langle \alpha_A, \mu_A, \delta_A \rangle$, *where* α_A *is the original value of the attribute assigned to the argument by the function* $\mathscr{F}$ *of definition 10,* μ_A *accounts for the aggregation of the attributes of the arguments supporting* A, *and* δ_A *is obtained after taking the attacks into account. Let* A *be an argument, then the values are obtained as follows:*

- $\alpha_A = \mathscr{F}(A)$ *for all* $A \in AR$.
- *If* $S^{\dashrightarrow}(A) = \emptyset$, *then* $\mu_A = \alpha_A$.
- *If* $S^{\to}(A) = \emptyset$, *then* $\delta_A = \mu_A$.

- *If $S^{\dashrightarrow}(A) \neq \emptyset$, then $\mu_A = \alpha_A \oplus (\oplus_{i=1}^{n} \delta_{Ai})$, with $A_i \in S^{\dashrightarrow}(A)$.*
- *If $S^{\rightarrow}(A) \neq \emptyset$, then $\delta_A = \mu_A \ominus (\oplus_{i=1}^{m} \delta_{Bi})$, with $B_i \in S^{\rightarrow}(A)$.*

In definition 11, we start labeling the arguments using the given attribute α and then going from the leaves (where μ and δ coincide with α) to the rest of the nodes. For a given node, we first determine μ (that is α reinforced by the values of its supporting arguments) and then δ, where μ is weakened by the values of the attacking arguments. For each $A \in AR$, the triple $\langle \alpha_A, \mu_A, \delta_A \rangle$ is called the *label* of A.

Proposition 1. *Let Ψ be a labeled bipolar argumentation framework. Then for all $A \in AR$, the labels $\langle \alpha_A, \mu_A, \delta_A \rangle$ satisfy: i) $\mu_A \geq \delta_A$; ii) $\mu_A \geq \alpha_A$; and iii) If $\mu_A = \bot$, then $\delta_A = \alpha_A = \bot$ as well.*

Proof:
i) $\mu_A \geq \delta_A$: δ_A *is defined as μ_A in the case in which $S^{\rightarrow}(A) = \emptyset$. If $S^{\rightarrow}(A) \neq \emptyset$ then by Def 11, $\delta_A = \mu_A \ominus (\oplus_{B_i \in S^{\rightarrow}(A)} \delta_{B_i})$, which is less or equal than μ_A by Def 9.*
ii) *Since $\bot \leq \beta$ for all $\beta \in A$, it follows that for any $\alpha, \alpha = \alpha \oplus \bot \leq \alpha \oplus \beta$, so since by definition μ_A is either α_A or $\alpha_A \oplus (\oplus_{B_i \in S^{\dashrightarrow}(A)} \delta_{Ai})$ then $\mu_A \geq \alpha_A$.*
iii) *If $\mu_A = \bot$, then by i), δ_A must be $\bot$ as well. By definition μ_A is either α_A (in which case $\alpha_A = \bot$) or $\alpha_A \oplus (\oplus_{B_i \in S^{\dashrightarrow}(A)} \delta_{Ai})$. We saw in the proof of ii) that $\alpha \oplus \beta \geq \alpha$ for all $\alpha, \beta \in A$ so we get in the second case that $\bot = \mu_A \geq \alpha_A$ therefore $\alpha_A = \bot$.*

Unlike what happens in the original BAF, in our proposal the attack does not mean always a defeat. It is a weakening of the value of the attribute which can result in a defeat, a weakening, or a strengthening.

Definition 12 (Arguments Status). *Let $\Psi = \langle AR, \rightarrow, \dashrightarrow, A, \mathscr{F} \rangle$ be a L-BAF. Let A be an argument in AR. The argument A is assigned one of three possible status accordingly to their associated labels:*

- *Defeated iff $\delta_A = \bot$.*
- *Weakened iff $\bot < \delta_A < \alpha_A$.*
- *Strengthened iff $\alpha_A \leq \delta_A$.*

From the definitions immediately follows:

Proposition 2. *Argument status is unique in a L-BAF.*

Having extra information associated with arguments introduces the possibility of analyzing the argumentation model. If the algebra of labels is a subset of the real numbers, then we can calculate the coefficients of conflict and support of the model, which give an indication of the efficiency of attacks and supports; these notions are defined below.

Definition 13 (Conflict and Support coefficients). *Let $\Psi = \langle AR, \rightarrow, \dashrightarrow, A, \mathscr{F} \rangle$ be a L-BAF. Let $| \rightarrow |$ and $| \dashrightarrow |$ be the cardinalities of the attack and support relation respectively. Then:*

- *The conflict coefficient is* $\omega^{\rightarrow} = \begin{cases} \frac{\sum_{\{A \in AR \mid S^{\rightarrow}(A) \neq \emptyset\}} \mu_A - \delta_A}{|\rightarrow|} & \text{iff } |\rightarrow| \neq 0, \\ 0 & \text{otherwise.} \end{cases}$

– *The* support coefficient *is* $\omega^{-\rightarrow} = \begin{cases} \frac{\sum_{\{A \in AR \mid S^{-\rightarrow}(A) \neq 0\}} \mu_A - \alpha_A}{|-\rightarrow|} & \text{iff } |-\rightarrow| \neq 0, \\ 0 & \text{otherwise.} \end{cases}$

Example 5. *Now we add labels to our running example. The domain of labels A is the real interval $[0,1]$ and represents a normalized relevance value, where $\top = 1$ is the maximum relevance, while $\bot = 0$. For $\beta, \gamma \in A$ the operators of support and conflict over labels associated with arguments, are specified in the Relevance Attribute Table.*

Relevance Attribute Table	
$\beta \oplus \gamma = \min(\beta + \gamma, 1)$	The support operator states that if we have more than one argument for a conclusion, its relevance value is the sum of the relevance of the arguments that support it. This is a T-conorm.
$\beta \ominus \gamma = \max(\beta - \gamma, 0)$	This conflict operator reflects that the relevance value of a conclusion is weakened by the relevance of its contradiction satisfying the conditions in definition 1.

AR	A	B	C	D	E	F	G	H	I	J	K
α	0.5	0.8	0.6	0.7	0.4	0.9	0.5	0.7	0.9	0.8	0.3

The attribute α is given by the table below. The set $S_6 = \{D, G, H\}$ is the set of defeated arguments, the set $S_7 = \{A\}$ is the set of weakened arguments, and the set $S_8 = \{B, C, E, F, I, J, K\}$ is the set of strengthened arguments. Then, the main argument that supports the conclusion of renting the apartment is weakened to a relevance degree of $0.1/1$, so the agent decides not rent the apartment.

The conflict coefficient is $\omega^{\rightarrow} = 0.46$, while $\omega^{-\rightarrow} = 0.2$, so we can conclude that, in this model, the level of weakening effected over the arguments is greater than the level of strengthening on them.

In a L-BAF we distinguish two types of attacks producing different results: defeat and weakening. Based on this difference it is possible derive from a L-BAF two kinds of BAFs, defined as follows:

Definition 14 (Defeating Bipolar Argumentation Framework in L-BAF.) *Let Ψ be a labeled bipolar argumentation framework. The defeating Bipolar Argumentation Framework based on Ψ is the 3-tuple $\langle AR, \rightarrow, --\rightarrow \rangle$, where $\rightarrow$ is the defeat relation defined by $\{(A, B) \in \rightarrow \mid \delta_B = \bot \text{ and } \delta_A \neq \bot\}$.*

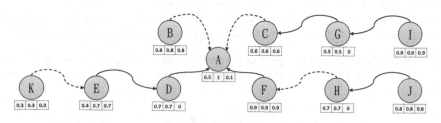

Fig. 2. Example for labeled bipolar argumentation graph

Definition 15 (Weakening Bipolar Argumentation Framework in L-BAF). *Let* Ψ *be a labeled bipolar argumentation framework. The* Weakening Bipolar Argumentation Framework *based on* Ψ *is the 3-tuple* $\langle AR', \twoheadrightarrow, \dashrightarrow' \rangle$*, where AR' is the set of undefeated arguments:* $\{A \in AR | \delta_A \neq \bot\}$*,* $\twoheadrightarrow = \twoheadrightarrow \cap (AR' \times AR')$ *and* $\dashrightarrow' = \dashrightarrow \cap (AR' \times AR')$*.*

Example 6. (*Continued Example 6*) *In this example we show the resulting BAFs derived from our L-BAF, discriminating the two kinds of attacks (defeat and weakening). First, we instantiate the BAF with the defeat relation* $\twoheadrightarrow = \{(E,D), (J,H), (I,G)\}$*.*

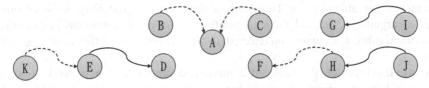

The set $S_2 = \{A,B,C,E,I,J,K\}$ *is a stable extension and safe, so it is closed for* $\dashrightarrow$*. In addition, S_2 is a d-preferred, c-preferred and s-preferred extension. Based on the arguments acceptability under the stable and preferred extensions, the agent will decide to rent the apartment, since there are sufficient reasons to believe that it is a good decision.*

Finally, we calculate the BAF with the weakening relation $\twoheadrightarrow = \{(F,A)\}$*, the set of arguments* $AR' = \{A,B,C,E,F,I,J,K\}$*, and support relation* $\dashrightarrow' = \{(K,E), (B,A), (C,A)\}$*.*

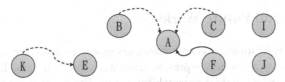

The set $S_9 = \{B,C,E,F,I,J,K\}$ *is a stable extension but not safe. In addition, S_9 is d-preferred extension, but there are not c-preferred nor s-preferred extensions. Based on the arguments acceptability under the stable and d-preferred extension, the agent will decide to not rent the apartment, since now F appears in the extension, while A does not. We can notice F is in the set of strengthened arguments, with a value of (0.9). In this model, no attack diminishes sensibly this argument, so the agent should not rent the apartment.*

Whenever two opposing arguments A and B appear in stable or preferred extensions, and a decision must be taken choosing between them, we may now appeal to the new information provided by the labels. We can compare δ_A with δ_B, and choose the argument with the highest value. If this does not solve the conflict, we can still use the values of μ and α to break the tie.

6 Related Work

In [18], Pollock points out the fact that, in defeasible reasoning, most semantics ignore the issue of the inner force of arguments, *i.e.*, that some arguments support their conclusions more strongly. But once we acknowledge that arguments can differ in strength and conclusions can differ in their degree of justification, things become more complicated. In particular, he introduces the notion of diminishers, which are defeaters that cannot completely defeat their target, but instead lower the degree of justification of that argument. Both of these ideas motivate and resonate in our work here.

Dunne *et al.* in [13] explore a natural extension of Dung's well-known model of argument systems in which attacks are associated with a weight, indicating the relative strength of the attack. Cayrol and Lagasquie-Schiex in [9] argue that argumentation is based on the exchange and valuation of interacting arguments, followed by the selection of the most acceptable of them. They propose the notion of graduality in the selection of the best arguments, *i.e.*, to be able to partition the set of the arguments in more than the two usual subsets, accepted and rejected, in order to represent different acceptability levels.

In [4], Barringer et al. presented a numerical argumentation network to study the relationships of support and attack between arguments; they considered both the strength of the arguments, and the strength that carries the attack and support between themselves as well. This work pays close attention to the definitions of support and attacks between arguments, and to the treatment of cycles in such an argumentative network.

It is important to observe that the features or properties associated with an argument can vary over time and in because of that become affected by a variety of characteristics that influence in the real world, as the reliability of a given source does [7, 16].

7   Conclusion and Future Works

In argumentation applications, it is sometimes necessary to associate additional information to arguments to accurately represent features of the arguments in consideration with the goal of determining their acceptability status. For instance, in an agent implementation, it would be beneficial to establish a relevance degree associated with the arguments representing the agent's preferences; or, in a recommender systems, it is interesting to provide recommendations together with a measure of the uncertainty or the reliability degree associated with it.

We focused on the development of the framework called *Labeled Bipolar Argumentation Framework*, combining the representation capabilities provided by the *Bipolar Argumentation Framework* and the manipulation of additional labels using an algebra developed with this purpose. Interactions between arguments have associated operations defined on the algebra, allowing to propagate information in the labeled bipolar argumentation framework. In this enhanced framework it is possible to determine the acceptability of sets arguments, and additional data justifying their acceptability status.

We are currently working to determine how useful our framework is to represent preference between arguments, and how the setting of a threshold of acceptability based on context constraints affects the semantic results. In addition, we will study the internal structure of arguments and how to obtain a measure of an argument's strength based on it. Following the ideas introduced in [6], we will extend our proposal of using meta-argumentation to instantiate a bipolar argumentation framework and represent defeasible support, allowing that this relation be attacked.

Finally, we are developing an implementation of L-BAF instantiating it in the existing DeLP system [1] as a basis; the resulting implementation will be exercised in different domains requiring to model extra information associated with the arguments, taking as motivation studies of P-DeLP [1, 15].

References

1. Alsinet, T., Chesñevar, C.I., Godo, L., Sandri, S., Simari, G.R.: Formalizing argumentative reasoning in a possibilistic logic programming setting with fuzzy unification. International Journal of Approximate Reasoning **48**(3), 711–729 (2008)
2. Amgoud, L., Cayrol, C., Lagasquie-Schiex, M.C., Livet, P.: On bipolarity in argumentation frameworks. International Journal of Intelligent Systems **23**(10), 1062–1093 (2008)
3. Amgoud, L., Prade, H.: Using arguments for making and explaining decisions. Artificial Intelligence **173**(3), 413–436 (2009)
4. Barringer, H., Gabbay, D., Woods, J.: Temporal, numerical and meta-level dynamics in argumentation networks. Argument & Computation **3**(2–3), 143–202 (2012)
5. Bench-Capon, T., Dunne, P.E.: Argumentation in artificial intelligence. Artificial Intelligence **171**(10), 619–641 (2007)
6. Boella, G., Gabbay, D.M., van der Torre, L.W., Villata, S.: Support in abstract argumentation. In: Computational Models of Argument (LNCS), pp. 111–122 (2010)
7. Budán, M.C.D., Lucero Gómez, M.J., Chesñevar, C.I., Simari, G.R.: Modelling time and reliability in structured argumentation frameworks. In: Proceedings of the 13th International Conference on Principles of Knowledge Representation and Reasoning, pp. 578–582 (2012)
8. Budán, M.C.D., Lucero, M.J.G., Simari, G.R.: An aif-based labeled argumentation framework. In: Beierle, C., Meghini, C. (eds.) FoIKS 2014. LNCS, vol. 8367, pp. 117–135. Springer, Heidelberg (2014)
9. Cayrol, C., Lagasquie-Schiex, M.C.: Graduality in argumentation. Journal of Articial Intelligence Research (JAIR) **23**, 245–297 (2005)
10. Cayrol, C., Lagasquie-Schiex, M.C.: On the acceptability of arguments in bipolar argumentation frameworks. In: Godo, L. (ed.) ECSQARU 2005. LNCS (LNAI), vol. 3571, pp. 378–389. Springer, Heidelberg (2005)
11. Cohen, A., Gottifredi, S., García, A.J., Simari, G.R.: A survey of different approaches to support in argumentation systems. The Knowledge Engineering Review (FirstView 2013)
12. Dung, P.M.: On the acceptability of arguments and its fundamental role in nonmonotonic reasoning, logic programming and n-person games. Artif. Intell. **77**(2), 321–357 (1995)
13. Dunne, P.E., Hunter, A., McBurney, P., Parsons, S., Wooldridge, M.: Weighted argument systems: Basic definitions, algorithms, and complexity results. Artif. Intell. **175**(2), 457–486 (2011)
14. García, A.J., Chesñevar, C.I., Rotstein, N.D., Simari, G.R.: Formalizing dialectical explanation support for argument-based reasoning in knowledge-based systems. Expert Syst. with Apps **40**(8), 3233–3247 (2013)
15. García, A.J., Simari, G.R.: Defeasible logic programming: An argumentative approach. TPLP **4**(1–2), 95–138 (2004)
16. Godo, L., Marchioni, E., Pardo, P.: Extending a temporal defeasible argumentation framework with possibilistic weights. In: del Cerro, L.F., Herzig, A., Mengin, J. (eds.) JELIA 2012. LNCS, vol. 7519, pp. 242–254. Springer, Heidelberg (2012)

---

[1] See http://lidia.cs.uns.edu.ar/delp

17. Gómez, S.A., Chesñevar, C.I., Simari, G.R.: Ontoarg: A decision support framework for ontology integration based on argumentation. Expert Syst. with Apps **40**(5), 1858–1870 (2013)
18. Pollock, J.L.: Defeasible reasoning and degrees of justification. Argument and Computation **1**(1), 7–22 (2010)
19. Rahwan, I., Simari, G.R.: Argumentation in Artificial Intelligence. Springer (2009)
20. van der Weide, T.L., Dignum, F., Meyer, J-JCh., Prakken, H., Vreeswijk, G.A.W.: Multi-criteria argument selection in persuasion dialogues. In: McBurney, Peter, Parsons, Simon, Rahwan, Iyad (eds.) ArgMAS 2011. LNCS, vol. 7543, pp. 136–153. Springer, Heidelberg (2012)
21. Zadeh, L.A.: Fuzzy sets. Information and Control **8**(3), 338–353 (1965)
22. Zimmermann, H.: Fuzzy set theory and its applications, 2nd revised edn. Springer (1992)

On Supporting Strong and Default Negation
in Answer-Set Program Updates

Martin Slota[1], Martin Baláž[2], and João Leite[1]([✉])

[1] CENTRIA and Departamento de Informática, Universidade Nova de Lisboa, Lisbon, Portugal
[2] Faculty of Mathematics, Physics and Informatics, Comenius University, Bratislava, Slovakia
jleite@fct.unl.pt

Abstract. Existing semantics for answer-set program updates fall into two categories: either they consider only *strong negation* in heads of rules, or they primarily rely on *default negation* in heads of rules and optionally provide support for strong negation by means of a syntactic transformation.

In this paper we pinpoint the limitations of both these approaches and argue that both types of negation should be first-class citizens in the context of updates. We identify principles that plausibly constrain their interaction but are not simultaneously satisfied by any existing rule update semantics. Then we extend one of the most advanced semantics with direct support for strong negation and show that it satisfies the outlined principles as well as a variety of other desirable properties.

1 Introduction

The increasingly common use of rule-based knowledge representation languages in highly dynamic and information-rich contexts, such as the Semantic Web [2], requires standardised support for updates of knowledge represented by rules. Answer-set programming [3,4] forms the natural basis for investigation of rule updates, and various approaches to answer-set program updates have been explored throughout the last 15 years [5–18].

The most straightforward kind of conflict arising between an original rule and its update occurs when the original conclusion logically contradicts the newer one. Though the technical realisation and final result may differ significantly, depending on the particular rule update semantics, this kind of conflict is resolved by letting the newer rule prevail over the older one. Actually, under most semantics, this is also the *only* type of conflict that is subject to automatic resolution [5,7,8,11,12,15,16].

From this perspective, allowing for both *strong* and *default negation* to appear in heads of rules is essential for an expressive and universal rule update framework

J. Leite and M. Slota were partially supported by FCT under project PTDC/EIA-CCO/121823/2010. The collaboration between the co-authors resulted from the Slovak–Portuguese bilateral project supported by APVV agency under SK-PT-0028-10 and by FCT under FCT/2487/3/6/2011/S.
A preliminary version of this paper appeared as [1]. An extended version of this paper with all the proofs is available at http://arxiv.org/abs/1404.6784

A.L.C. Bazzan and K. Pichara (Eds.): IBERAMIA 2014, LNAI 8864, pp. 41–53, 2014.
DOI: 10.1007/978-3-319-12027-0_4

[9]. While strong negation is the natural candidate here, used to express that an atom *becomes explicitly false*, default negation allows for more fine-grained control: the atom only *ceases to be true*, but its truth value may not be known after the update. The latter also makes it possible to move between any pair of epistemic states by means of updates, as illustrated in the following example:

Example 1 (Railway crossing [9]). Take the following logic program used to choose an action at a railway crossing (where ¬ (reps. ∼) denotes strong (resp. default) negation):

$$\text{cross} \leftarrow \neg\text{train}. \qquad \text{wait} \leftarrow \text{train}. \qquad \text{listen} \leftarrow \sim\text{train}, \sim\neg\text{train}.$$

The intuitive meaning of these rules is as follows: one should cross if there is evidence that no train is approaching; wait if there is evidence that a train is approaching; listen if there is no such evidence. Consider a situation where a train is approaching, represented by the fact (train.). After this train has passed by, we want to update our knowledge to an epistemic state where we lack evidence with regard to the approach of a train. If this was accomplished by updating with the fact (¬train.), we would cross the tracks at the subsequent state, risking being killed by another train that was approaching. Therefore, we need to express an update stating that all past evidence for an atom is to be removed, which can be accomplished by allowing default negation in heads of rules. In this scenario, the intended update can be expressed by the fact (∼train.).

Concerning the support of negation in rule heads, existing rule update semantics fall into two categories: those that only allow for strong negation, and those that primarily consider default negation. As illustrated above, the former are unsatisfactory as they render many belief states unreachable by updates. As for the latter, they optionally provide support for strong negation by means of a syntactic transformation. Two such transformations are known, both based on the principle of coherence: if an atom p is true, its strong negation $\neg p$ cannot be true simultaneously, so $\sim\neg p$ must be true, and also vice versa, if $\neg p$ is true, then so is $\sim p$. The first transformation, introduced in [19], encodes this principle directly by adding, to both the original program and its update, the following two rules for every atom p: $\sim\neg p \leftarrow p$. and $\sim p \leftarrow \neg p$. This way, every conflict between an atom p and its strong negation $\neg p$ directly translates into two conflicts between the objective literals p, $\neg p$ and their default negations. However, the added rules lead to undesired side effects that stand in direct opposition with basic principles underlying updates. Specifically, despite the fact that the empty program does not encode any change in the modelled world, the stable models assigned to a program may change after an update by the empty program. This undesired behaviour is addressed in an alternative transformation from [9] that encodes the coherence principle more carefully. Nevertheless, this transformation also leads to undesired consequences, as demonstrated in the following example:

Example 2 (Faulty sensor). Suppose that we collect data from sensors and multiple sensors are used to supply information about the critical fluent p. In case of a malfunction of one of the sensors, we may end up with an inconsistent logic program consisting of the following two facts: p. and $\neg p$. At this point, no stable model of the program exists. If a problem is found in the sensor that supplied the first fact $(p.)$, after the sensor is repaired, this information needs to be reset by updating the program with the fact $(\sim p.)$. Following the common pattern in rule updates, where recovery from conflicting states is always possible, this update should be sufficient to assign a stable model to the updated program. However, the transformational semantics for strong negation of [9] still does not provide any stable model – we remain without a valid epistemic state when one should exist.

In this paper we address the combination of strong and default negation in the context of rule updates. We formulate a generic desirable principle that is violated by the existing approaches. Then we show how two distinct definitions of one of the most well-behaved rule update semantics [11, 12] can be equivalently extended with support for strong negation while satisfying the formulated principle and retaining the formal and computational properties of the original semantics. Our main contributions are as follows: *a*) based on Example 2, we introduce the *early recovery principle* that captures circumstances under which a stable model after a rule update should exist; *b*) we extend the *well-supported semantics for rule updates* [12] with direct support for strong negation; *c*) we define a fixpoint characterisation of the new semantics, based on the *refined dynamic stable model* semantics for rule updates [11]; *d*) we show that the defined semantics enjoy the early recovery principle as well as a range of desirable properties for rule updates known from the literature.

This paper is organised as follows: In Sect. 2 we present logic programs, generalise the well-supported semantics from the class of normal programs to extended ones and define the rule update semantics from [11, 12]. In Sect. 3, we establish the early recovery principle, define the new rule update semantics for strong negation and show that it satisfies the principle. In Sect. 4 we introduce other established rule update principles and show that the proposed semantics satisfies them. We discuss our findings and conclude in Sect. 5.

2 Background

Logic Programs. We assume that a countable set of propositional atoms $\mathcal{A}$ is given and fixed. An *objective literal* is an atom $p \in \mathcal{A}$ or its strong negation $\neg p$. We denote the set of all objective literals by $\mathcal{L}$. A *default literal* is an objective literal preceded by $\sim$ denoting default negation. A *literal* is either an objective or a default literal. We denote the set of all literals by $\mathcal{L}^*$. As a convention, double negation is absorbed, so that $\neg\neg p$ denotes the atom p and $\sim\sim l$ denotes the objective literal l. Given a set of literals S, we introduce the following notation: $S^+ = \{ l \in \mathcal{L} \mid l \in S \}$, $S^- = \{ l \in \mathcal{L} \mid \sim l \in S \}$, $\sim S = \{ \sim L \mid L \in S \}$. An *extended rule* is a pair $\pi = (\mathsf{H}_\pi, \mathsf{B}_\pi)$ where H_π is a literal, referred to as the *head of* π, and B_π is a finite set of literals, referred to as the *body of* π. Usually we write π as $(\mathsf{H}_\pi \leftarrow \mathsf{B}_\pi^+, \sim\mathsf{B}_\pi^-.)$. A *generalised rule* is an extended rule that contains no occurrence of $\neg$, i.e., its head and body consist only of atoms and their default negations. A *normal rule* is a generalised rule that has an atom in the head. A *fact* is an extended rule whose body is empty and a *tautology* is any extended rule π such that $\mathsf{H}_\pi \in \mathsf{B}_\pi$. An *extended (generalised, normal) program* is a set of extended (generalised, normal) rules. An *interpretation* is a consistent subset of the set of objective literals, i.e., a subset of $\mathcal{L}$ not containing both p and $\neg p$ for any atom p. The satisfaction of an objective literal l, default literal $\sim l$, set of literals S, extended rule π and extended program P in an interpretation J is defined as usual: $J \models l$ iff $l \in J$; $J \models {\sim}l$ iff $l \notin J$; $J \models S$ iff $J \models L$ for all $L \in S$; $J \models \pi$ iff $J \models B_\pi$ implies $J \models H_\pi$; $J \models P$ iff $J \models \pi$ for all $\pi \in P$. Also, J is a *model of P* if $J \models P$, and P is *consistent* if it has a model.

Definition 1 (Stable model). *Let P be an extended program. The set $[\![P]\!]_{\mathsf{SM}}$ of stable models of P consists of all interpretations J such that $J^* = \mathsf{least}(P \cup \mathsf{def}(J))$ where $\mathsf{def}(J) = \{ {\sim}l. \mid l \in \mathcal{L} \setminus J \}$, $J^* = J \cup {\sim}(\mathcal{L} \setminus J)$ and $\mathsf{least}(\cdot)$ denotes the least model of the argument program with all literals treated as propositional atoms.*

A *level mapping* ℓ is a function that maps every atom to a natural number. Also, for any default literal ${\sim}p$, where $p \in \mathcal{A}$, and finite set of atoms and their default negations S, $\ell({\sim}p) = \ell(p)$, $\ell^\downarrow(S) = \min \{ \ell(L) \mid L \in S \}$ and $\ell^\uparrow(S) = \max \{ \ell(L) \mid L \in S \}$.

Definition 2 (Well-supported model of a normal program). *Let P be a normal program and ℓ a level mapping. An interpretation $J \subseteq \mathcal{A}$ is a well-supported model of P w.r.t. ℓ if the following conditions are satisfied: 1. J is a model of P and 2. For every atom $p \in J$ there exists a rule $\pi \in P$ such that $H_\pi = p \wedge J \models B_\pi \wedge \ell(H_\pi) > \ell^\uparrow(B_\pi)$. The set $[\![P]\!]_{\mathsf{WS}}$ of well-supported models of P consists of all interpretations $J \subseteq \mathcal{A}$ such that J is a well-supported model of P w.r.t. some level mapping.*

Proposition 1 ([20]). *Let P be a normal program. Then, $[\![P]\!]_{\mathsf{WS}} = [\![P]\!]_{\mathsf{SM}}$.*

Well-Supported Models for Extended Programs. The well-supported models for normal logic programs can be generalised in a straightforward manner to deal with strong negation while maintaining their tight relationship with stable models (c.f. Proposition 1). This will come useful when we discuss adding support for strong negation to semantics for rule updates. We extend level mappings from atoms and their default negations to all literals: An *(extended) level mapping* ℓ maps every objective literal to a natural number. Also, for any default literal ${\sim}l$ and finite set of literals S, $\ell({\sim}l) = \ell(p)$, $\ell^\downarrow(S) = \min \{ \ell(L) \mid L \in S \}$ and $\ell^\uparrow(S) = \max \{ \ell(L) \mid L \in S \}$.

Definition 3 (Well-supported model of an extended program). *Let P be an extended program and ℓ a level mapping. An interpretation J is a well-supported model of P w.r.t. ℓ if the following conditions are satisfied: 1. J is a model of P and 2. For every objective literal $l \in J$ there exists a rule $\pi \in P$ such that $H_\pi = l \wedge J \models B_\pi \wedge \ell(H_\pi) > \ell^\uparrow(B_\pi)$. The set $[\![P]\!]_{\mathsf{WS}}$ of well-supported models of P consists of all interpretations J such that J is a well-supported model of P w.r.t. some level mapping.*

Proposition 2. *Let P be an extended program. Then, $[\![P]\!]_{\mathsf{WS}} = [\![P]\!]_{\mathsf{SM}}$.*

Rule Updates. Rule update semantics assign stable models to a pair or sequence of programs where each component represents an update of the preceding ones. Formally, a *dynamic logic program* (DLP) is a finite sequence of extended programs and by $\mathsf{all}(\boldsymbol{P})$ we denote the multiset of all rules in the components of $\boldsymbol{P}$. A rule update semantics S assigns a *set of S-models*, denoted by $[\![\boldsymbol{P}]\!]_{\mathsf{S}}$, to $\boldsymbol{P}$.

We focus on semantics based on the causal rejection principle [5,7–9,11,12,16] which states that a rule is *rejected* if it is in a direct conflict with a more recent rule. The basic conflict between rules π and σ occurs when their heads are complementary, i.e. when $H_\pi = {\sim}H_\sigma$. Based on such conflicts and on a stable model candidate, a *set of rejected rules* can be determined and it can be verified that the candidate is indeed stable w.r.t. the remaining rules.

We define the most mature of these semantics, providing two equivalent definitions: the *refined dynamic stable models* [11], or *RD-semantics*, defined using a fixpoint equation, and the *well-supported models* [12], or *WS-semantics*, based on level mappings.

Definition 4 (RD-semantics [11]). *Let $P = \langle P_i \rangle_{i<n}$ be a DLP without strong negation. Given an interpretation J, the multisets of rejected rules $\mathrm{rej}_{\geq}(P,J)$ and of default assumptions $\mathrm{def}(P,J)$ are defined as follows:*

$$\mathrm{rej}_{\geq}(P,J) = \left\{ \pi \in P_i \mid i < n \wedge \exists j \geq i \, \exists \sigma \in P_j : H_\pi = {\sim}H_\sigma \wedge J \models B_\sigma \right\} \ ,$$
$$\mathrm{def}(P,J) = \left\{ ({\sim}l.) \mid l \in \mathcal{L} \wedge \neg(\exists \pi \in \mathrm{all}(P) : H_\pi = l \wedge J \models B_\pi) \right\} \ .$$

Let J^* and $\mathrm{least}(\cdot)$ be defined as before. The set $[\![P]\!]_{\mathrm{RD}}$ of RD-models of P consists of all interpretations J such that $J^* = \mathrm{least}\left([\mathrm{all}(P) \setminus \mathrm{rej}_{\geq}(P,J)] \cup \mathrm{def}(P,J)\right)$.

Definition 5 (WS-semantics [12]). *Let $P = \langle P_i \rangle_{i<n}$ be a DLP without strong negation. Given an interpretation J and a level mapping ℓ, the multiset of rejected rules $\mathrm{rej}_\ell(P,J)$ is defined as follows:*

$$\mathrm{rej}_\ell(P,J) = \left\{ \pi \in P_i \mid i < n \wedge \exists j > i \, \exists \sigma \in P_j : H_\pi = {\sim}H_\sigma \wedge J \models B_\sigma \wedge \ell(H_\sigma) > \ell^\uparrow(B_\sigma) \right\} \ .$$

The set $[\![P]\!]_{\mathrm{WS}}$ of WS-models of P consists of all interpretations J such that for some level mapping ℓ, the following conditions are satisfied: 1. J is a model of $\mathrm{all}(P) \setminus \mathrm{rej}_\ell(P,J)$ and 2. For every $l \in J$ there exists some rule $\pi \in \mathrm{all}(P) \setminus \mathrm{rej}_\ell(P,J)$ such that $H_\pi = l \wedge J \models B_\pi \wedge \ell(H_\pi) > \ell^\uparrow(B_\pi)$.

Unlike most other rule update semantics, these semantics can properly deal with tautological and other irrelevant updates, as illustrated in the following example:

Example 3 (Irrelevant updates). Consider the DLP $P = \langle P, U \rangle$ where programs P, U are as follows: $P = \{\, \mathrm{day} \leftarrow {\sim}\mathrm{night.}, \mathrm{night} \leftarrow {\sim}\mathrm{day.}, \mathrm{stars} \leftarrow \mathrm{night}, {\sim}\mathrm{cloudy.}, {\sim}\mathrm{stars.} \,\}$ and $U = \{\, \mathrm{stars} \leftarrow \mathrm{stars.} \,\}$. Program P has the single stable model $J_1 = \{\, \mathrm{day} \,\}$ and U contains a single tautological rule, i.e. it does not encode any change in the modelled domain. Thus, we expect that P also has the single stable model J_1. However, many rule update semantics, such as those introduced in [5,7–10,13,15,16,18], are sensitive to this or other tautological updates, introducing or eliminating models of the original program. In this case, the unwanted model candidate is $J_2 = \{\, \mathrm{night}, \mathrm{stars} \,\}$ and it is neither an RD- nor a WS-model of P, though the reasons for this are technically different under these two semantics. It is not difficult to verify that, given an arbitrary level mapping ℓ, the set of default assumptions and the respective sets of rejected rules are as follows: $\mathrm{def}(P,J_2) = \{\, ({\sim}\mathrm{cloudy.}), ({\sim}\mathrm{day.}) \,\}$, $\mathrm{rej}_{\geq}(P,J_2) = \{\, (\mathrm{stars} \leftarrow \mathrm{night}, {\sim}\mathrm{cloudy.}),$ $({\sim}\mathrm{stars.}) \,\}$, and $\mathrm{rej}_\ell(P,J_2) = \emptyset$. Note that $\mathrm{rej}_\ell(P,J_2)$ is empty because, independently of ℓ, no rule π in U satisfies the condition $\ell(H_\pi) > \ell^\uparrow(B_\pi)$, so there is no rule that could reject another rule. Thus, the atom stars belongs to J_2^* but does not belong to $\mathrm{least}([\mathrm{all}(P) \setminus \mathrm{rej}_{\geq}(P,J_2)] \cup \mathrm{def}(P,J_2))$, so J_2 is not an RD-model of P. Furthermore, no model of $\text{all}(P) \setminus \text{rej}_\ell(P, J_2)$ contains stars, so J_2 cannot be a WS-model of P. Furthermore, the resilience of RD- and WS-semantics is not limited to empty and tautological updates, but extends to other irrelevant updates as well [11, 12]. For example, consider the DLP $P' = \langle P, U' \rangle$ where $U' = \{\,(\text{stars} \leftarrow \text{venus.}), (\text{venus} \leftarrow \text{stars.})\,\}$. Though the updating program contains non-tautological rules, it does not provide a bottom-up justification of any model other than J_1 and, indeed, J_1 is the only RD- and WS-model of P'.

We also note that the two presented semantics for DLPs without strong negation provide the same result regardless of the particular DLP to which they are applied.

Proposition 3 ([12]). *Let P be a DLP without strong negation. Then,* $[\![P]\!]_{\text{WS}} = [\![P]\!]_{\text{RD}}$.

When dealing with a single program, strong negation can be reduced away by treating all objective literals as atoms and adding, for each atom p, the integrity constraint $(\leftarrow p, \neg p.)$ to the program [4]. However, this transformation does not serve its purpose when adding support for strong negation to causal rejection semantics for DLPs because integrity constraints have empty heads, so according to these rule update semantics, they cannot be used to reject any other rule. For example, a DLP such as $\langle \{\, p., \neg p.\,\}, \{\, p.\,\} \rangle$ would remain without a stable model even though the DLP $\langle \{\, p., {\sim} p.\,\}, \{\, p.\,\} \rangle$ does have a stable model. To capture the conflict between opposite objective literals l and $\neg l$ in a way that is compatible with causal rejection semantics, a slightly modified syntactic transformation can be performed, translating such conflicts into conflicts between objective literals and their default negations. Two such transformations have been suggested in the literature [9, 19], both based on the principle of coherence. For any extended program P and DLP $\boldsymbol{P} = \langle P_i \rangle_{i<n}$ they are defined as follows:

$$P^\dagger = P \cup \{\, {\sim}\neg l \leftarrow l. \mid l \in \mathcal{L} \,\}, \quad \boldsymbol{P}^\dagger = \langle P_i^\dagger \rangle_{i<n},$$

$$P^\ddagger = P \cup \{\, {\sim}\neg \mathsf{H}_\pi \leftarrow \mathsf{B}_\pi. \mid \pi \in P \wedge \mathsf{H}_\pi \in \mathcal{L} \,\}, \quad \boldsymbol{P}^\ddagger = \langle P_i^\ddagger \rangle_{i<n}.$$

These transformations lead to four possibilities for defining the semantics of a DLP $\boldsymbol{P}$: $[\![\boldsymbol{P}^\dagger]\!]_{\text{RD}}$, $[\![\boldsymbol{P}^\ddagger]\!]_{\text{RD}}$, $[\![\boldsymbol{P}^\dagger]\!]_{\text{WS}}$ and $[\![\boldsymbol{P}^\ddagger]\!]_{\text{WS}}$. We discuss these in the subsequent section.

3 Direct Support for Strong Negation in Rule Updates

The problem with existing semantics for strong negation in rule updates is that those based on the first transformation ($\boldsymbol{P}^\dagger$) sometimes assign too many models, while those based on the second ($\boldsymbol{P}^\ddagger$) sometimes do not assign any model when one should exist.

Example 4 (Undesired side effects of the first transformation). Consider the DLP $\boldsymbol{P}_1 = \langle P, U \rangle$ where $P = \{\, p., \neg p.\,\}$ and $U = \emptyset$. Since P has no stable model and U does not encode any change in the represented domain, it should follow that $\boldsymbol{P}_1$ has no stable model either. However, $[\![\boldsymbol{P}_1^\dagger]\!]_{\text{RD}} = [\![\boldsymbol{P}_1^\dagger]\!]_{\text{WS}} = \{\{p\}, \{\neg p\}\}$, i.e. two models are assigned to $\boldsymbol{P}_1$ when using the first transformation to add support for strong negation. To verify this, observe that $\boldsymbol{P}_1^\dagger = \langle P^\dagger, U^\dagger \rangle$ where $P^\dagger = \{\, p., \neg p., {\sim} p \leftarrow \neg p., {\sim}\neg p \leftarrow p.\,\}$ and $U^\dagger = \{\, {\sim} p \leftarrow \neg p., {\sim}\neg p \leftarrow p.\,\}$. Consider $J_1 = \{\, p\,\}$. Then, we have $\text{rej}_{\geq}(\boldsymbol{P}_1^\dagger, J_1) = \{\,\neg p., {\sim}\neg p \leftarrow p.\,\}$ and $\text{def}(\boldsymbol{P}_1^\dagger, J_1) = \emptyset$, so it follows that $least([\text{all}(\boldsymbol{P}_1^\dagger) \setminus \text{rej}_{\geq}(\boldsymbol{P}_1^\dagger, J_1)] \cup$

$\text{def}(\boldsymbol{P}_1^\dagger, J_1)) = \{p, \sim\neg p\} = J_1^*$. In other words, J_1 belongs to $[\![\boldsymbol{P}_1^\dagger]\!]_{\text{RD}}$ and in an analogous fashion it can be verified that $J_2 = \{\neg p\}$ also belongs there. A similar situation occurs with $[\![\boldsymbol{P}_1^\dagger]\!]_{\text{WS}}$ since the rules that were added to the more recent program can be used to reject facts in the older one.

Thus, the problem with the first transformation is that an update by an empty program, which does not express any change in the represented domain, may affect the original semantics. This behaviour goes against basic and intuitive principles underlying updates, grounded already in the classical belief update postulates [21, 22] and satisfied by virtually all belief update operations [23] as well as by the vast majority of existing rule update semantics, including the original RD- and WS-semantics.

This undesired behaviour can be corrected by using the second transformation. The more technical reason is that it does not add any rules to a program in the sequence unless that program already contains some original rules. However, its use leads to another problem: sometimes *no model* is assigned when in fact a model should exist.

Example 5 (Undesired side effects of the second transformation). Consider Example 2, formalised as DLP $\boldsymbol{P}_2 = \langle P, V \rangle$ where $P = \{p., \neg p.\}$ and $V = \{\sim p.\}$. One expects that since V resolves the conflict present in P, a stable model should be assigned to $\boldsymbol{P}_2$. However, $[\![\boldsymbol{P}_2^\ddagger]\!]_{\text{RD}} = [\![\boldsymbol{P}_2^\ddagger]\!]_{\text{WS}} = \emptyset$. To verify this, observe that $\boldsymbol{P}_2^\ddagger = \langle P^\ddagger, V^\ddagger \rangle$ where $P^\ddagger = \{p., \neg p., \sim p., \sim\neg p.\}$ and $V^\ddagger = \{\sim p.\}$. Given an interpretation J and level mapping ℓ, we conclude that $\text{rej}_\ell(\boldsymbol{P}_2^\ddagger, J) = \{p.\}$, so the facts $(\neg p.)$ and $(\sim\neg p.)$ both belong to the program $\text{all}(\boldsymbol{P}_2^\ddagger) \setminus \text{rej}_\ell(\boldsymbol{P}_2^\ddagger, J)$. Consequently, this program has no model and it follows that J cannot belong to $[\![\boldsymbol{P}_2^\ddagger]\!]_{\text{WS}}$. Similarly it can be shown that $[\![\boldsymbol{P}_2^\ddagger]\!]_{\text{RD}} = \emptyset$.

Based on this example, in the following we formulate a generic *early recovery principle* that formally identifies conditions under which *some* stable model should be assigned to a DLP. For the sake of simplicity, we concentrate on DLPs of length 2 which are composed of facts. We discuss a generalisation of the principle to DLPs of arbitrary length and containing other rules than just facts in Sect. 5. After introducing the principle, we define a semantics for rule updates which directly supports both strong and default negation and satisfies the principle.

We begin by defining, for every objective literal l, the sets of literals $\bar{l} = \{\sim l, \neg l\}$ and $\overline{\sim l} = \{l\}$. Intuitively, for every literal L, $\overline{L}$ denotes the set of literals that are in conflict with L. Furthermore, given two sets of facts P and U, we say that U *solves all conflicts in* P if for each pair of rules $\pi, \sigma \in P$ such that $\text{H}_\sigma \in \overline{\text{H}_\pi}$ there is a fact $\rho \in U$ such that either $\text{H}_\rho \in \overline{\text{H}_\pi}$ or $\text{H}_\rho \in \overline{\text{H}_\sigma}$.

Considering a rule update semantics S, the new principle simply requires that when U solves all conflicts in P, S will assign *some model* to $\langle P, U \rangle$. Formally:

Early recovery principle: If P is a set of facts and U is a consistent set of facts that solves all conflicts in P, then $[\![\langle P, U \rangle]\!]_{\text{S}} \neq \emptyset$.

We conjecture that rule update semantics should generally satisfy the above principle. In contrast with the usual behaviour of belief update operators, the nature of existing rule update semantics ensures that recovery from conflict is always possible, and this principle simply formalises and sharpens the sufficient conditions for such recovery.

Our next goal is to define a semantics for rule updates that not only satisfies the outlined principle, but also enjoys other established properties of rule updates identified over the years. As for the original semantics for rule updates, we provide two equivalent definitions, one based on a fixed point equation and the other one on level mappings.

To directly accommodate strong negation in the RD-semantics, we first need to look more closely at the set of rejected rules $\text{rej}_\geq(P, J)$, particularly at the fact that it allows conflicting rules within the same component of P to reject one another. This behaviour, along with the constrained set of defaults $\text{def}(P, J)$, is used to prevent tautological and other irrelevant cyclic updates from affecting the semantics. However, in the presence of strong negation, rejecting conflicting rules within the same program has undesired side effects. For example, the early recovery principle requires that some model be assigned to the DLP $\langle \{p., \neg p.\}, \{\sim p\} \rangle$ from Example 5, but if the rules in the initial program reject each other, then the only possible stable model to assign is $\emptyset$. However, such a stable model would violate the causal rejection principle since it does not satisfy the initial rule $(\neg p.)$ and there is no rule in the updating program that overrides it.

To overcome the limitations of this approach to the prevention of tautological updates, we disentangle rule rejection per se from ensuring that rejection is done without cyclic justifications. We introduce the set of rejected rules $\text{rej}^-_>(P, S)$ which directly supports strong negation and does not allow for rejection within the same program. Prevention of cyclic rejections is done separately by using a customised immediate consequence operator $T_{P,J}$. Given a stable model candidate J, instead of verifying that J^* is the least fixed point of the usual consequence operator, as done in the RD-semantics using $\text{least}(\cdot)$, we verify that J^* is the least fixed point of $T_{P,J}$.

Definition 6 (Extended RD-semantics). *Let* $P = \langle P_i \rangle_{i<n}$ *be a DLP. For an interpretation* J *and set of literals* S, *the multiset of rejected rules* $\text{rej}^-_>(P, S)$, *the remainder* $\text{rem}(P, S)$ *and the consequence operator* $T_{P,J}$ *are defined as follows:*

$$\text{rej}^-_>(P, S) = \left\{ \pi \in P_i \mid i < n \wedge \exists j > i \, \exists \sigma \in P_j : \mathsf{H}_\sigma \in \overline{\mathsf{H}_\pi} \wedge \mathsf{B}_\sigma \subseteq S \right\},$$

$$\text{rem}(P, S) = \text{all}(P) \setminus \text{rej}^-_>(P, S),$$

$$T_{P,J}(S) = \left\{ \mathsf{H}_\pi \mid \pi \in (\text{rem}(P, J^*) \cup \text{def}(J)) \right.$$
$$\left. \wedge \mathsf{B}_\pi \subseteq S \wedge \neg \left(\exists \sigma \in \text{rem}(P, S) : \mathsf{H}_\sigma \in \overline{\mathsf{H}_\pi} \wedge \mathsf{B}_\sigma \subseteq J^* \right) \right\}.$$

Furthermore, $T^0_{P,J}(S) = S$ *and for every* $k \geq 0$, $T^{k+1}_{P,J}(S) = T_{P,J}(T^k_{P,J}(S))$. *The set* $[\![P]\!]^-_{\text{RD}}$ *of extended RD-models of* P *consists of all interpretations* J *such that* $J^* = \bigcup_{k \geq 0} T^k_{P,J}(\emptyset)$.

Adding support for strong negation to the WS-semantics is done by modifying the set of rejected rules $\text{rej}_\ell(P, J)$ to account for the new type of conflict. Additionally, to ensure that rejection of a literal L cannot be based on the assumption that some conflicting literal $L' \in \overline{L}$ is true, a rejecting rule σ must satisfy the stronger condition $\ell^\downarrow(\overline{L}) > \ell^\uparrow(\mathsf{B}_\sigma)$. Finally, to prevent defeated rules from affecting the resulting models, we require that all supporting rules belong to $\text{rem}(P, J^*)$.

Definition 7 (Extended WS-semantics). *Let* $P = \langle P_i \rangle_{i<n}$ *be a DLP. For interpretation* J *and a level mapping* ℓ, *the multiset of rejected rules* $\text{rej}^-_\ell(P, J)$ *is defined by:*
$$\text{rej}^-_\ell(P, J) = \{ \pi \in P_i \mid i < n \wedge \exists j > i \, \exists \sigma \in P_j : \mathsf{H}_\sigma \in \overline{\mathsf{H}_\pi} \wedge J \models \mathsf{B}_\sigma \wedge \ell^\downarrow(\overline{\mathsf{H}_\pi}) > \ell^\uparrow(\mathsf{B}_\sigma) \}.$$

Table 1. Desirable properties of rule update semantics

Generalisation of stable models	$[\![\langle P\rangle]\!]_{\mathsf{S}} = [\![P]\!]_{\mathsf{SM}}.$
Primacy of new information	If $J \in [\![\langle P_i\rangle_{i<n}]\!]_{\mathsf{S}}$, then $J \models P_{n-1}.$
Fact update	A sequence of consistent sets of facts $\langle P_i\rangle_{i<n}$ has the single model $\{\, l \in \mathcal{L} \mid \exists i < n : (l.) \in P_i \wedge (\forall j > i : \{\neg l., \sim l.\} \cap P_j = \emptyset)\,\}.$
Support	If $J \in [\![P]\!]_{\mathsf{S}}$ and $l \in J$, then there is some rule $\pi \in \mathrm{all}(P)$ such that $\mathsf{H}_\pi = l$ and $J \models \mathsf{B}_\pi.$
Idempotence	$[\![\langle P, P\rangle]\!]_{\mathsf{S}} = [\![\langle P\rangle]\!]_{\mathsf{S}}.$
Absorption	$[\![\langle P, U, U\rangle]\!]_{\mathsf{S}} = [\![\langle P, U\rangle]\!]_{\mathsf{S}}.$
Augmentation	If $U \subseteq V$, then $[\![\langle P, U, V\rangle]\!]_{\mathsf{S}} = [\![\langle P, V\rangle]\!]_{\mathsf{S}}.$
Non-interference	If U and V are over disjoint alphabets, then $[\![\langle P, U, V\rangle]\!]_{\mathsf{S}} = [\![\langle P, V, U\rangle]\!]_{\mathsf{S}}.$
Immunity to empty updates	If $P_j = \emptyset$, then $[\![\langle P_i\rangle_{i<n}]\!]_{\mathsf{S}} = \left[\!\!\left[\langle P_i\rangle_{i<n \wedge i \neq j}\right]\!\!\right]_{\mathsf{S}}.$
Immunity to tautologies	If $\langle Q_i\rangle_{i<n}$ is a sequence of sets of tautologies, then $[\![\langle P_i \cup Q_i\rangle_{i<n}]\!]_{\mathsf{S}} = [\![\langle P_i\rangle_{i<n}]\!]_{\mathsf{S}}.$
Causal rejection principle	For every $i < n$, $\pi \in P_i$ and $J \in [\![\langle P_i\rangle_{i<n}]\!]_{\mathsf{S}}$, if $J \not\models \pi$, then there exists some $\sigma \in P_j$ with $j > i$ such that $\mathsf{H}_\sigma \in \overline{\mathsf{H}_\pi}$ and $J \models \mathsf{B}_\sigma.$

The set $[\![P]\!]_{\mathsf{WS}}^{\neg}$ of extended WS-models of P consists of all interpretations J such that for some level mapping ℓ, the following conditions are satisfied: 1. J is a model of $\mathrm{all}(P) \setminus \mathrm{rej}_\ell^{\neg}(P, J)$ and 2. For every $l \in J$ there exists some rule $\pi \in \mathrm{rem}(P, J^*)$ such that $\mathsf{H}_\pi = l \wedge J \models \mathsf{B}_\pi \wedge \ell(\mathsf{H}_\pi) > \ell^{\uparrow}(\mathsf{B}_\pi).$

The following theorems establish that the two defined semantics are equivalent, that they coincide with the original on DLPs without strong negation, and, unlike the transformational semantics for strong negation, the new semantics satisfy the early recovery principle.

Theorem 1. *Let P_1 be a DLP and P_2 be a DLP without strong negation. Then, $[\![P_1]\!]_{\mathsf{WS}}^{\neg} = [\![P_1]\!]_{\mathsf{RD}}^{\neg}$ and $[\![P_2]\!]_{\mathsf{WS}}^{\neg} = [\![P_2]\!]_{\mathsf{RD}}^{\neg} = [\![P_2]\!]_{\mathsf{WS}} = [\![P_2]\!]_{\mathsf{RD}}.$*

Theorem 2. *The extended RD-semantics and extended WS-semantics satisfy the early recovery principle.*

4 Properties

The various approaches to rule updates [5,7–18] share a number of basic characteristics, significantly differing in their technical realisation and classes of supported inputs, and desirable properties such as immunity to tautologies are violated by many of them.

Table 1 lists several generic properties proposed for rule updates that have been identified and formalised throughout the years [5,8,9,11]. The rule update semantics we defined in the previous section enjoys all of them, while retaining the same computational complexity as the stable models.

Theorem 3. *The extended RD-semantics and extended WS-semantics satisfy all properties listed in Table 1.*

Theorem 4. *Let P be a DLP. The problem of deciding whether some $J \in [\![P]\!]_{WS}^{\neg}$ exists is NP-complete. Given a literal L, the problem of deciding whether for all $J \in [\![P]\!]_{WS}^{\neg}$ it holds that $J \models L$ is coNP-complete.*

5   Concluding Remarks

In this paper we have identified shortcomings in the existing semantics for rule updates that fully support both strong and default negation, and proposed a generic *early recovery principle* that captures them formally. Subsequently, we provided two equivalent definitions of a new semantics for rule updates. We have shown that the newly introduced rule update semantics constitutes a strict improvement upon the state of the art in rule updates as it enjoys the following combination of characteristics, unmatched by any previously existing semantics:

– It allows for both strong and default negation in heads of rules, making it possible to move between any pair of epistemic states by means of updates;
– It satisfies the *early recovery principle* which guarantees the existence of a model whenever all conflicts in the original program are satisfied;
– It enjoys all rule update principles and desirable properties reported in Table 1;
– It does not increase the computational complexity of the stable model semantics upon which it is based.

However, the early recovery principle, as it is formulated in Sect. 3, only covers a single update of a set of facts by another set of facts. Can it be generalised further without rendering it too strong? Certain caution is appropriate here, since in general the absence of a stable model can be caused by odd cycles or simply by the fundamental differences between different approaches to rule update, and the purpose of this principle is not to choose which approach to take.

Nevertheless, one generalisation that should cause no harm is the generalisation to iterated updates, i.e. to sequences of sets of facts. Another generalisation that appears very reasonable is the generalisation to *acyclic DLPs*, i.e. DLPs such that all(P) is an acyclic program. An acyclic program has at most one stable model, and if we guarantee that all potential conflicts within it certainly get resolved, we can safely conclude that the rule update semantics should assign some model to it. We formalise these ideas in what follows.

A program P is *acyclic* [24] if for some level mapping ℓ, such that for every $l \in \mathcal{L}$, $\ell(l) = \ell(\neg l)$, and every rule $\pi \in P$ it holds that $\ell(H_\pi) > \ell^\uparrow(B_\pi)$. Given a DLP $P = \langle P_i \rangle_{i<n}$, we say that *all conflicts in P are solved* if for every $i < n$ and each pair of rules $\pi, \sigma \in P_i$ such that $H_\sigma \in \overline{H_\pi}$ there is some $j > i$ and a fact $\rho \in P_j$ such that either $H_\rho \in \overline{H_\pi}$ or $H_\rho \in \overline{H_\sigma}$.

Generalised early recovery principle: If $\mathsf{all}(P)$ is acyclic and all conflicts in P are solved, then $[\![P]\!]_\mathsf{S} \neq \emptyset$.

Note that this generalisation of the early recovery principle applies to a much broader class of DLPs than the original one. We illustrate this in the following example:

Example 6 (Recovery in a stratified program). Consider the following programs programs P, U and V: $P = \{ p \leftarrow q, {\sim}r., {\sim}p \leftarrow s., q., s \leftarrow q. \}$, $U = \{ \neg p., r \leftarrow q., \neg r \leftarrow q, s. \}$, and $V = \{ {\sim}r. \}$. Looking more closely at program P, we see that atoms q and s are derived by the latter two rules inside it while atom r is false by default since there is no rule that could be used to derive its truth. Consequently, the bodies of the first two rules are both satisfied and as their heads are conflicting, P has no stable model. The single conflict in P is solved after it is updated by U, but then another conflict is introduced due to the latter two rules in the updating program. This second conflict can be solved after another update by V. Consequently, we expect that some stable model be assigned to the DLP $\langle P, U, V \rangle$.

The original early recovery principle does not impose this because the DLP in question has more than two components and the rules within it are not only facts. However, the DLP is acyclic, as shown by any level mapping ℓ with $\ell(p) = 3$, $\ell(q) = 0$, $\ell(r) = 2$ and $\ell(s) = 1$, so the generalised early recovery principle does apply. Furthermore, we also find the single extended RD-model of $\langle P, U, V \rangle$ is $\{ \neg p, q, \neg r, s \}$, i.e. the semantics respects the stronger principle in this case.

It is no coincidence that the extended RD-semantics respects the stronger principle in the above example – the principle is generally satisfied by the semantics introduced in this paper.

Theorem 5. *The extended RD-semantics and extended WS-semantics satisfy the generalised early recovery principle.*

Both the original and the generalised early recovery principle can guide the future addition of full support for both kinds of negations in other approaches to rule updates, such as those proposed in [10,13,15,18], making it possible to reach any belief state by updating the current program. Furthermore, adding support for strong negation is also interesting in the context of recent results on program revision and updates that are performed on the *semantic level*, ensuring syntax-independence of the respective methods [25–28], in the context of finding suitable condensing operators [29], and unifying with updates in classical logic [30].

References

1. Slota, M., Baláž, M., Leite, J.: On strong and default negation in logic program updates. In: Procs. of NMR 2014. INFSYS Research Report Series, vol. 1843–14-01, pp. 73–81. TU Wien (2014)

2. Berners-Lee, T., Hendler, J., Lassila, O.: The semantic web. Sci. Am. **284**(5), 28–37 (2001)
3. Gelfond, M., Lifschitz, V.: The stable model semantics for logic programming. In: Procs. of ICLP 1988, pp. 1070–1080. MIT Press (1988)
4. Gelfond, M., Lifschitz, V.: Classical negation in logic programs and disjunctive databases. New Generation Computing **9**(3–4), 365–385 (1991)
5. Leite, J.A., Pereira, L.M.: Generalizing Updates: From Models to Programs. In: Dix, J., Moniz Pereira, L., Przymusinski, T.C. (eds.) LPKR 1997. LNCS (LNAI), vol. 1471, pp. 224–246. Springer, Heidelberg (1998)
6. Alferes, J.J., Leite, J.A., Pereira, L.M., Przymusinska, H., Przymusinski, T.C.: Dynamic logic programming. In: Procs. of KR 1998, pp. 98–111. Morgan Kaufmann (1998)
7. Alferes, J.J., Leite, J.A., Pereira, L.M., Przymusinska, H., Przymusinski, T.C.: Dynamic updates of non-monotonic knowledge bases. The Journal of Logic Programming **45**(1–3), 43–70 (2000)
8. Eiter, T., Fink, M., Sabbatini, G., Tompits, H.: On properties of update sequences based on causal rejection. Theory and Practice of Logic Programming (TPLP) **2**(6), 721–777 (2002)
9. Leite, J.A.: Evolving Knowledge Bases, vol. 81. Frontiers of Artificial Intelligence and Applications. IOS Press (2003)
10. Sakama, C., Inoue, K.: An abductive framework for computing knowledge base updates. Theory and Practice of Logic Programming (TPLP) **3**(6), 671–713 (2003)
11. Alferes, J.J., Banti, F., Brogi, A., Leite, J.A.: The refined extension principle for semantics of dynamic logic programming. Stud. Logica. **79**(1), 7–32 (2005)
12. Banti, F., Alferes, J.J., Brogi, A., Hitzler, P.: The Well Supported Semantics for Multidimensional Dynamic Logic Programs. In: Baral, C., Greco, G., Leone, N., Terracina, G. (eds.) LPNMR 2005. LNCS (LNAI), vol. 3662, pp. 356–368. Springer, Heidelberg (2005)
13. Zhang, Y.: Logic program-based updates. ACM Transactions on Computational Logic **7**(3), 421–472 (2006)
14. Šefránek, J.: Irrelevant Updates and Nonmonotonic Assumptions. In: Fisher, M., van der Hoek, W., Konev, B., Lisitsa, A. (eds.) JELIA 2006. LNCS (LNAI), vol. 4160, pp. 426–438. Springer, Heidelberg (2006)
15. Delgrande, J.P., Schaub, T., Tompits, H.: A Preference-Based Framework for Updating Logic Programs. In: Baral, C., Brewka, G., Schlipf, J. (eds.) LPNMR 2007. LNCS (LNAI), vol. 4483, pp. 71–83. Springer, Heidelberg (2007)
16. Osorio, M., Cuevas, V.: Updates in answer set programming: An approach based on basic structural properties. Theory and Practice of Logic Programming **7**(4), 451–479 (2007)
17. Šefránek, J.: Static and dynamic semantics: Preliminary report. In: Procs. of MICAI 2011, pp. 36–42 (2011)
18. Krümpelmann, P.: Dependency semantics for sequences of extended logic programs. Logic Journal of the IGPL **20**(5), 943–966 (2012)
19. Alferes, J.J., Pereira, L.M.: Update-programs can update programs. In: Dix, J., Pereira, L.M., Przymusinski, T. C. (eds.) Procs. of NMELP 1996. LNCS, vol. 1216, 110–131. Springer, Heidelberg (1996)
20. Fages, F.: A new fixpoint semantics for general logic programs compared with the well-founded and the stable model semantics. New Generation Computing **9**(3/4), 425–444 (1991)
21. Keller, A.M., Winslett, M.: On the use of an extended relational model to handle changing incomplete information. IEEE Trans. Software Eng. **11**(7), 620–633 (1985)
22. Katsuno, H., Mendelzon, A.O.: On the difference between updating a knowledge base and revising it. In: Procs. of KR 1991, pp. 387–394. Morgan Kaufmann Publishers (1991)
23. Herzig, A., Rifi, O.: Propositional belief base update and minimal change. Artif. Intell. **115**(1), 107–138 (1999)
24. Apt, K.R., Bezem, M.: Acyclic programs. New Generation Computing **9**(3/4), 335–364 (1991)

25. Delgrande, J., Schaub, T., Tompits, H., Woltran, S.: A model-theoretic approach to belief change in answer set programming. ACM Transactions on Computational Logic (TOCL) 14(2), 14:1–14:46 (2013)
26. Slota, M., Leite, J.: The rise and fall of semantic rule updates based on se-models. Theory and Practice of Logic Programming FirstView, 1–39 (January 2014)
27. Slota, M., Leite, J.: Robust equivalence models for semantic updates of answer-set programs. In: Procs. of KR 2012, pp, 158–168. AAAI Press (2012)
28. Slota, M., Leite, J.: On semantic update operators for answer-set programs. In: Procs. of ECAI 2010. Frontiers in Artificial Intelligence and Applications, vol. 215, 957–962. IOS Press (2010)
29. Slota, M., Leite, J.: On condensing a sequence of updates in answer-set programming. In: Procs. of IJCAI 2013. IJCAI/AAAI (2013)
30. Slota, M., Leite, J.: A Unifying Perspective on Knowledge Updates. In: del Cerro, L.F., Herzig, A., Mengin, J. (eds.) JELIA 2012. LNCS, vol. 7519, pp. 372–384. Springer, Heidelberg (2012)

On the Use of Agreement Technologies
for Multi-criteria Decision Making
within a BDI Agent

Cecilia Sosa Toranzo, Marcelo Errecalde, and Edgardo Ferretti[✉]

Laboratorio de Investigación y Desarrollo en Inteligencia Computacional
Departamento de Informática, Universidad Nacional de San Luis,
Ejército de los Andes 950, D5700HHW San Luis, Argentina
{csosatoranzo,merreca,ferretti}@unsl.edu.ar

Abstract. The BDI model, as a practical reasoning architecture aims at making decisions about what to do based on cognitives notions as beliefs, desires and intentions. However, during the decision making process, BDI agents also have to make background decisions like choosing what intention to achieve next from a set of possibly conflicting desires; which plan to execute from the plans that satisfy a given intention; and whether it is necessary or not to reconsider current intentions. Likewise, agreement technologies have proven to be effective mechanisms to reach agreements between agents with different preferences, as well as to conciliate different criteria within a single agent. Therefore, in this work, we present an abstract framework which incorporates agreement technologies in decision processes within BDI agents. Besides, from the mechanisms belonging to the research field of agreement technologies, a voting-based approach is also proposed.

Keywords: Agreement technologies · Multi-criteria decision making · BDI architecture · Voting

1 Introduction

Nowadays, many social mechanisms that help human beings to interact, like *argumentation* or *voting*, have become building-blocks of complex computational systems composed by several components working together. Despite the fact that this kind of mechanisms have been widely studied separately, in the last years, the idea of studying them as a whole from a holistic perspective, has arisen the new paradigm of the so-called, *Agreement Technologies* (AT).

Artificial Intelligent Agents and *Multi-Agent Systems* are for certain the research fields where AT has been extensively investigated and used to solve real-world problems. It is worth noting, that the primary goal of agents acting in the real world is deciding what action to accomplish in a given situation. This kind of reasoning that is oriented towards action is called *Practical Reasoning* (PR). In this respect, the Belief-Desires-Intentions (BDI) architecture is very

© Springer International Publishing Switzerland 2014
A.L.C. Bazzan and K. Pichara (Eds.): IBERAMIA 2014, LNAI 8864, pp. 54–65, 2014.
DOI: 10.1007/978-3-319-12027-0_5

relevant because it has been successfully applied to deal with real-world problems [1], its functioning is easily understandable given its similarity to human reasoning, and it provides a well-defined theoretical underpinning [2].

As a practical reasoning architecture, BDI aims at making decisions about what to do based on cognitives notions as beliefs, desires and intentions. However, during the decision making process, BDI agents also have to make background decisions like choosing what intention to achieve next from a set of possibly conflicting desires; which plan to execute from the plans that satisfy a given intention; and whether it is necessary or not to reconsider current intentions. Making these decisions typically involves multiple criteria.

With respect to the aforementioned research lines, viz. AT and PR architectures, we think that these research areas have been widely studied in the last years in a separate manner, but few efforts have been made to integrate AT mechanisms within PR architectures. That is why, we present an abstract framework (Sect. 3) which integrates in a systematic manner AT mechanisms to support multi-criteria decision making within the inner decision processes of BDI agents (Sect. 2). Likewise, a voting-based instantiation of this framework is proposed (Sect. 4) and exemplified in the TILEWORLD domain (Sect. 5). Finally, Sect. 6 draws the conclusions and briefly describes possible future work.

2   BDI Model

Belief-Desires-Intentions models have been inspired from the philosophical tradition on understanding *practical reasoning* [2]. This kind of reasoning can be conceived as the process of deciding what action perform next to accomplish a certain goal. Practical reasoning involves two important processes: deciding *what* states of the world to achieve and *how* to do it. The first process is known as *deliberation* and it results in a set of intentions. The second process, so-called *means-ends reasoning*, involves generating actions sequences to achieve intentions.

The mental attitudes of a BDI agent on its beliefs, desires and intentions, represent its informational state, motivational state and decision state, respectively. The BDI architecture defines its cognitive notions as follows:

- **Beliefs:** Partial knowledge the agent has about the world.
- **Desires:** The states of the world that the agent would ideally like to achieve.
- **Intentions:** Desires (states of the world) that the agent has been *committed* (dedicated resources) to achieve.

These cognitive notions are implemented as data structures in the BDI architecture. The interpreter of this architecture performs deliberation and means-ends reasoning by manipulating these data structures and its simpler version is shown in Algorithm 1, as proposed in [3].

A usual problem in designing PR agents lies in getting a good balance among deliberation, means-ends reasoning and actions execution. It is clear that, in some point in time, an agent should drop some of its intentions, because they were already achieved, they are impossible to be achieved or it makes no sense to do it, etc.

Likewise, when opportunities arise to achieve new desires, the agent should generate intentions to accomplish them. Thus, as mentioned above, it is important for an agent to *reconsider its intentions*. However, intentions reconsideration is costly in terms of time and computational resources. It can happen that some of the actions from the executing plan might fail in achieving the intended results, hence *replanning* capabilities should be provided.

Algorithm 1. Agent control loop

1: **while** true **do**
2:     observe the world;
3:     update internal world model;
4:     deliberate about what
        intention to achieve next;
5:     use means-ends reasoning to
        get a plan for the intention;
6:     execute the plan;
7: **end while**

---

3   Integration Framework

As mentioned above, a BDI agent comprises two fundamental processes, namely, deliberation and means-ends reasoning, which are followed by a plan execution stage. Within these processes the following inner decisions can be made:

- CHOICE AMONG CONFLICTING DESIRES: *deliberation* requires to commit to an intention from among conflicting desires.
- CHOICE BETWEEN PLANS: during *means-ends reasoning* it might be necessary to choose from among plans which achieve the same intention, that is, deciding which action perform to achieve a particular intention.
- INTENTIONS RECONSIDERATION: during the *execution* process, decisions should be made with respect to whether reconsider or not current intentions based on the dynamics of the environment, and if so, if new intentions should be adopted or current intentions should be dropped.

All in all, our BDI architecture will incorporate an *Inner Decision Making Component (IDMC)* which will make inner decisions with respect to the different alternatives and the multiple criteria provided to the agent. In our proposal, to select the best alternative from a given set of alternatives, the agent will have the $select(\cdot, \cdot, \cdot)$ function that will return the choice made by the IDMC. This function will be used (within this framework) in all the inner decision processes a BDI agent has. It will receive as input parameters: (1) a set A of candidate alternatives, (2) the set C containing the criteria that will be used to compare alternatives among each other, and (3) the preferences $\mathcal{P}$, composed by a preference order among criteria and a preference order among the possible values an alternative can take for each particular criterion.

In the following subsections, there will be described in more detail those functions called in the BDI interpreter, which use $select(\cdot, \cdot, \cdot)$ function, to make the inner decisions mentioned at the beginning of this section.

3.1   Deliberation

Deliberation process can be considered as composed by two functions:

– *options*(·,·): which returns a set of *acceptable options* (desires) considering the agent's belief.

– *filter*(·,·,·): which returns the set of alternatives the agent has committed to. Once desires have been obtained by using *options*(·,·) function, the agent may find conflicting options since the desires set might not be consistent. Hence, the agent must *choose* one alternative among the competing ones to commit to. Then, *filter*(·,·,·) function will accept those non-conflicting options and from among the conflicting ones, only one will be selected. Next, the agent will commit to the surviving options (intentions) of the filtering process. To select one of the conflicting desires, the agent will call *select*(·,·,·) within *filter*(·,·,·) function, whose generic algorithm is shown in Algorithm 2. It is worth noting that in simplest cases, where all the alternatives are conflicting among each other (see example in Sect. 5), *filter*(·,·,·) function is directly conceived as the *select*(·,·,·) function.

Algorithm 2. Filtering of alternatives

function:
filter(beliefs B, desires D, intentions I)
return I
1: C ← selection criteria
2: $\mathcal{P}$ ← user's preferences
3: $D' ← D$
4: **while** $D' \neq \emptyset$ **do**
5:    d ← remove-any(D')
6:    **if** feasible(d,B) **then**
7:      **for all** $d' \in D$ **do**
8:        **if** competing(d,d') **then**
9:          add(d',A)
10:          remove(d', D')
11:        **end if**
12:      **end for**
13:      **if** A = $\emptyset$ **then**
14:        add(d,I)
15:      **else**
16:        add(d,A)
17:        a_I ← select(A,C,$\mathcal{P}$)
18:        add(a_I,I)
19:      **end if**
20:    **end if**
21: **end while**
22: **return** I

3.2 Means-ends Reasoning

Means-ends reasoning is the process aiming to decide how to achieve an *end* (*i.e.*, an intention) by means of the actions available to the agent. In Artificial Intelligence community, means-ends reasoning is best known as *planning*. A planning algorithm outputs a "plan", that is, the sequence of actions to be performed.

In the BDI interpreter, means-ends reasoning is achieved by calling *plan*(·,·) function. In Algorithm 1, *plan*(·,·) function would be called in line 5. This function, based on beliefs and current intentions together with the actions available to the agent, determines a plan to achieve the intentions. On the grounds that several plans may exist to achieve a certain intention, a choice among them should be made considering issues like: cost execution (physical resources needed), time execution, sensitivity to changes in the environment, etc. The implementation of *plan*(·,·) function based on *select*(·,·,·) function is presented in Algorithm 3.

3.3 Execution

One design issue in BDI agents concerns defining the intention reconsideration policy [3]. This policy will define under which circumstances the BDI agent will use computational resources to deliberate about its intentions. At present there is no consensus on when or how an agent should reconsider its intentions. Current proposals consider the agents' *commitment levels*, which range from *cautious* agents (which reconsider their intentions after each action execution) to *bold* agents (that perform no reconsideration until the current plan has been completely executed).

In [4], the efficiency of these policies in different kind of environments are investigated, but the intention reconsideration policy is defined in the agent's design stage, which makes impossible to modify this policy in execution time. It is clear that this is not a practical solution for agents operating in dynamic and changing environments. In this respect, in [5], it is proposed a framework that allows the agent to choose by itself what policy to follow based on the current state of the world. The main idea underlying this work is that an intention reconsideration policy can be conceived as a meta-level control process which selects whether to deliberate or to act. This proposal is based on the *discrete deliberation scheduling* framework, where deliberations are treated as if they were actions.

In [5], the proposed model incorporates decision making in the intention reconsideration process of a BDI agent. To determine the best possible action, the maximum expected utility is considered which means considering only one criterion to solve the decision problem. In this way, our work extends [5] to apply multi-criteria decision making when choosing between acting or deliberating.

Integrating the BDI model with the discrete deliberation scheduling framework, from a multi-criteria point of view, involves implementing $reconsider(\cdot, \cdot)$ function. In this way, a distinction should be made between external actions and inner actions. External actions, Ac_{ext}, change the agent's environment, whereas inner actions, Ac_{int}, affect the agent's internal state. It holds that the set of actions $Ac = Ac_{ext} \cup Ac_{int}$ and it is assumed that $Ac_{ext} \cap Ac_{int} = \emptyset$. As it can be observed in Algorithm 4, in this model, the agent must choose between a default

---

Algorithm 3. Planning

function:
$plan(beliefs\ B, intentions\ I)$
return π

```
 1: C ← selection criteria
 2: P ← user's preferences
 3: for i ∈ I do
 4:     P ← finding-plans(B,i)
 5:     if singleton(P) then
 6:         add(p ∈ P,Ps)
 7:     else
 8:         p ← select(P,C,P)
 9:         add(p,Ps)
10:     end if
11: end for
12: π ← sort(Ps)
13: return π
```

Algorithm 4. Intention Reconsideration

function:
$reconsider(beliefs\ B, intentions\ I)$
return $bool$

```
 1: C ← selection criteria
 2: P ← user's preferences
 3: get current plan π from I
 4: if π = ∅ then
 5:     return true
 6: end if
 7: a_def ← π[0]
 8: A ← {a_def, a_del}
 9: a_selec ← select(A, C, P)
10: if a_selec = a_del then
11:     return true
12: end if
13: return false
```

action $a_{def} \in Ac_{ext}$ (acting) or an inner action $a_{del} \in Ac_{int}$ (deliberating). Let $Plan$ be the set of plans available to the agent, and let $\pi \in Plan$ be a plan composed by actions $\pi[0], \ldots, \pi[n-1]$, where $\pi[i] \in A_{ext}$ and n denotes the plan length. In any execution time it holds that a_{def} is $\pi[0]$.

The use of the BDI model makes the treatment of deliberation at a very abstract level, since deliberation is considered as a way of changing the intentions set and is referred as a simple inner action. When $reconsider(\cdot, \cdot)$ function returns true, this means that deliberating was decided, while if it returns false, this means that acting was chosen. In order to decide between both meta-actions, the agent should be provided well-established comparison criteria, then it has to compute the actions values considering their consequences and it also has to estimate the benefit of deliberating for a_{del}.

In the following section, a concrete voting-based approach is proposed to instantiate the abstract framework presented in this section. The voting-based mechanism will be implemented by the IDMC, which will return to the BDI interpreter the choice made, as result of the inner decision making process.

4   Voting-Based Instantiation

Several voting methods have been proposed, from which Duncan Black's rule [6] is a remarkable proposal given the properties it satisfies. This rule states that if a Condorcet winner exists it should be chosen; if not, Borda count should be used instead.

In order to instantiate the abstract framework proposed in Sect. 3 with Duncan Black's rule as a concrete mechanism for the IDMC, it should be adapted for a unique agent so as to be applied to the components that interact to make a decision in the agent's modular mind. Given that distributed decision making methods can also be applied in cases where a consensus among different points of view is needed, if we consider a group of agents (each one with its own preferences) as a unique decision maker with several decision criteria, we fall under multi-criteria decision making. In this way, the agent will be provided with:

1. A *criteria* set $C = \{C_1, C_2, ..., C_n\}$.
   For each criterion C_i there exists a 3-tuple $\langle O_{C_i}, P_{C_i}, \Theta_{C_i} \rangle$ where:
   - O_{C_i} is the set of *possible values* (consequences) an alternative can take with respect to criterion C_i.
   - P_{C_i} are the *preferences* on the possible values from criterion C_i.
   - Θ_{C_i} is the threshold representing the minimum value an alternative should take with respect to C_i to be acceptable. Therefore, all the alternatives with lower values than Θ_{C_i} are rejected with respect to C_i.
2. A *criteria weighting* function $w : C \to [0,1]$, such that $w(C_i)$ represents how important is C_i for the decision maker.
3. A set, $A = \widetilde{A} \cup \{a_R\}$, of candidate *alternatives* to be chosen.
   - $\widetilde{A}$ is the set of acceptable alternatives generated from information received from the environment.
   - Rejection alternative, a_R, is a *particular* alternative that, if chosen, represents the case where all the alternatives are rejected.

- Each numeric or symbolic value $C_j(a_i)$ represents the value of alternative a_i with respect to C_j, where $C_j(a_i) \in O_{C_j}$.
- The *valuation* of each alternative a_i, $v(a_i) = (v_{C_1}(a_i), ..., v_{C_n}(a_i))$, is computed from preferences among its values with respect to each criterion, where $v_{C_j}(a_i) = P_{C_j}(C_j(a_i))$.

4. A *choice method*, Duncan Black's rule in our case.

Pairwise Voting. Given two alternatives $a_j, a_k \in A$, a pairwise voting among each other consists of calculating de number of votes that each alternative gets for each criterion in C and to select the one with more votes. The number of votes associated to each criterion C_i are calculated as indicated in (1), where k is an arbitrary constant used to scale the number of votes per criterion. To determine if the votes associated to C_i are given to one alternative or the other, their f_{C_i} values are compared, which represent their importance with respect to criterion C_i. These values are usually referred as the alternatives' strength. Function $f_{C_i} : A \to \mathbb{R}$ is formally defined as shown in (2).

$$V_C(C_i) = \frac{w(C_i)}{\sum_{C_j \in C} w(C_j)} \times k \qquad (1)$$

Based on f_{C_i} it can be determined if an alternative a_j *is preferred* to an alternative a_k according to criterion C_i, which will be denoted as $a_j \succ_{C_i} a_k$, if and only if $f_{C_i}(a_j) > f_{C_i}(a_k)$. The number of votes that alternative a_j gets in a pairwise voting against alternative a_k can be calculated as the sum of votes of all those criteria where alternative a_j is preferred to alternative a_k. If $V_{par}(a_j, a_k)$ represents this value and it is considered that $C_{a_k}^{a_j} = \{C_i \in C | a_j \succ_{C_i} a_k\}$ is the criteria set where alternative a_j is preferred to alternative a_k, V_{par} can be defined as a function $V_{par} : A \times A \to \mathbb{R}$, as shown in (3).

$$f_{C_i}(a_j) = \begin{cases} P_{C_i}(C_i(a_j)) & \text{if } a_j \in \tilde{A}, \\ \theta_{C_i} & \text{if } a_j = a_R \end{cases} \qquad (2) \qquad V_{par}(a_j, a_k) = \sum_{C_i \in C_{a_k}^{a_j}} V_C(C_i) \qquad (3)$$

Criteria may exist where both alternatives (a_j, a_k) have the same strength, and hence, their corresponding votes are not given to neither of them. The total amount of votes corresponding to those criteria where both alternatives have the same strength will be denoted as $\tilde{V}_{par}(a_j, a_k)$. This value can be computed as follows: $\tilde{V}_{par}(a_j, a_k) = K - (V_{par}(a_j, a_k) + V_{par}(a_k, a_j))$ based on function V_{par}, where K is the sum of the votes corresponding to all the criteria in C.

In this way, based on V_{par}, it can be stated that an alternative a_j will be *preferred* to another alternative a_k in a pairwise voting, if and only if $V_{par}(a_j, a_k) > V_{par}(a_k, a_j)$ and it will be denoted as $a_j \succ a_k$. When this concept is extended to pairwise voting among all possible pairs of alternatives, in some cases it will be possible to determine a *Condorcet winner*. An alternative $a_j \in A$ is a Condorcet winner in A, if and only if $a_j \succ a_k$ for all $a_k \in A$, and $k \neq j$. It can thus be seen, that determining a Condorcet winner implies in this case to find an alternative $a_j \in A$ whose value $V_{par}(a_j, a_k)$ is greater than $V_{par}(a_k, a_j)$ for each of the remaining alternatives $a_k \in A - \{a_j\}$.

Borda Count. In order to compute this count, the ordering of the alternatives should be considered with respect to their strength, for each criterion $C_i \in C$. Based on this ordering, $C_B(a_j, C_i)$ is defined as the amount of points (ranking position) that Borda assigns to alternative a_j in respect to criterion C_i. Given that two alternatives may be equally strong with respect to a particular criterion C_i, the indifference relation among alternatives will be admitted. It is denoted, $a_j \sim a_k$, and both alternatives will receive the average value of the points corresponding to their positions in the preference ranking. The whole amount of votes $V_B(a_j)$ received by an alternative a_j, is computed considering that the votes each criterion gets correspond to the amount of voters having this preference. Formally:

$$V_B(a_j) = \sum_{C_i \in C} C_B(a_j, C_i) V_C(C_i) \tag{4}$$

Algorithm 5 chooses an alternative following Black's rule described above.

Algorithm 5. Computation for alternatives selection (Voting)

---

function:
$select$(alternatives A, criteria C, preferences Γ (three-tuple $\langle O_{C_i}, P_{C_i}, \Theta_{C_i} \rangle$ and weights $w(C_i)$ per C_i.))
return alt-$select$
1: Calculating $V_C(C_i)$ for all criterion C_i
2: Getting $f_{C_i}(a_j)$ for all $a_j \in A$ for each criterion C_i
3: For every pair of distinct alternatives $a_j, a_k \in A$, to compute $V_{par}(a_j, a_k)$
4: **if** $\exists\, a* \in A / V_{par}(a*, a_k) > V_{par}(a_k, a*) \forall a_k \in A - \{a*\}$ **then**
5:     alt-$select \leftarrow a*$
6: **else**
7:     Ordering all alternatives by each criterion C_i
8:     For each alternative a_j get $C_B(a_j, C_i)$, relative to its position in the ordering of C_i
9:     For all $a_j \in A$ computing $V_B(a_j)$
10:     alt-$select \leftarrow \arg\max V_B(a_j)$
11: **end if**
12: **return** alt-$select$

---

5 Example: The Tileworld

The TILEWORLD experimental domain [7] is a grid environment containing agents, tiles, holes and obstacles. The agent's objective consists of scoring as many points as possible by pushing the tiles into the holes to fill them in. This environment is dynamic, so that holes and tiles may randomly appear and disappear.

A BDI agent for the TILEWORLD can be implemented as follows: the agent's beliefs consist of its perceptions about the objects locations, as well as the score and time-out time for all the holes. Desires represent the holes to be filled in, and the current intention (IH) is filling a particular hole right now. The means-end reasoner basically is a special-purpose route planner, which guides the agent to a particular tile that must be pushed into the hole to be filled in. The agent gets its perception and then update its beliefs. If $reconsider(\cdot, \cdot)$ function returns true, the agent should deliberate about what intention to achieve next. During deliberation it gets its reachable holes (options), *i.e.*, those which are not surrounded by obstacles and their time-out times are higher or equal to the distances from the agent to the holes. Then, filtering stage takes place where one of the reachable holes is selected and becomes the IH. Figure 1 shows a hypothetical scene in which the framework proposed in Sect. 3 will be used.

5.1   Filtering

In this case, all options are conflicting among each other, since it is not possible to fill in more than one hole at a time. Hence, all reachable holes will serve as input to $selec(\cdot, \cdot, \cdot)$ function. Since the agent has to commit to one of the options, rejection alternative is not considered. In this way, $A = \{h_1, h_2, h_3, h_4, h_5\}$ and $C = \{C_1 = \text{score}, C_2 = \text{timeout}, C_3 = \text{distAgent}, C_4 = \text{tileAvail (distance to the}$ nearest tile)$\}$. Table 1 presents preference $w(C_i)$ and the number of votes V_C (Equation 1, with $k=1000$) for each criterion. For criteria C_1 and C_2, preferences $P_{C_i}(C_i(a)) = C_i(a)$ and for criteria C_3 and C_4, $P_{C_i}(C_i(a)) = \frac{1}{C_i(a)}$. Table 2 shows the alternatives and their respective values for each criterion.

Based on the preferences (P_{C_i}) of each criterion, by using Equation 2 the strength of each alternative (f_{C_i}) can be calculated as shown in Table 3. These strengths are used in the pairwise voting among alternatives by means of $V_{par}(\cdot, \cdot)$ function, tabulated in Table 4. Since there is no Condorcet winner, an ordering of the alternatives according to each criterion should be performed (Table 5), in order to compute Borda count. Taking into account these orderings, points $C_B(\cdot, \cdot)$ are assigned to each alternative, as shown in Table 6. Then, for each alternative the total number of votes $V_B(\cdot)$ is computed. Finally, hole h_5 is chosen by Borda count as it can be observed in Figure 2.

5.2   Planning

Once a hole has been selected to fill in, plans to achieve this intention are selected. As it can be observed from Fig. 3 and Table 7, the means-ends reasoner provides four plans to fill in hole h_5. The criteria set provided for plan selection would be $C = \{C_1 = \text{length}, C_2 = \text{cost}, C_3 = \text{timeoutTile}\}$. Criterion C_1 is the number of actions within the plan. C_2 represents the plan cost which is calculated as the sum of its actions costs: if the agent maintains the same orientation, the action cost is 1 but if agent's orientation is changed, action cost is 2. Finally, C_3 is the time-out time of the tile selected in the plan to fill in the hole. In this stage, Black's rule is applied similarly than in the filtering stage. Table 8 shows the weighting function and the number of votes for each criterion. Likewise, Table 9 reports the values and strengths for each alternative with respect to each criterion. From the pairwise voting from among all the alternatives (Table 10), "plan p_4" becomes the Condorcet winner and is thus chosen to fill in hole h_5.

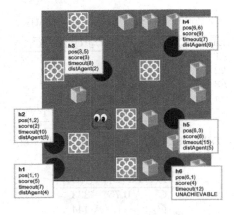

Fig. 1. Tileworld scene

$$V_\mathcal{B}(h1) = 2 \times 400 + 0.5 \times 200 + 2 \times 300 + 2 \times 100 = 1700$$

$$V_\mathcal{B}(h2) = 0 \times 400 + 3 \times 200 + 3 \times 300 + 4 \times 100 = 1900$$

$$V_\mathcal{B}(h3) = 1 \times 400 + 2 \times 200 + 4 \times 300 + 2 \times 100 = 2200$$

$$V_\mathcal{B}(h4) = 4 \times 400 + 0.5 \times 200 + 0 \times 300 + 2 \times 100 = 1900$$

$$V_\mathcal{B}(h5) = 3 \times 400 + 4 \times 200 + 1 \times 300 + 0 \times 100 = 2300$$

Fig. 2. Borda count

Table 1. Preferences and number of votes per criterion

Criteria	$w(C_i)$	$V_C(C_i)$
C_1	1	400
C_2	0.5	200
C_3	0.75	300
C_4	0.25	100

Table 2. Alternatives values for each criterion

Alternatives	C_1	C_2	C_3	C_4
$h1$	5	7	4	2
$h2$	2	10	3	1
$h3$	3	8	2	2
$h4$	9	7	6	2
$h5$	6	15	5	2

Table 3. Alternatives strength with respect to each criterion

Alternatives	f_{C_1}	f_{C_2}	f_{C_3}	f_{C_4}
$h1$	5	7	0.25	0.5
$h2$	2	10	0.33	1
$h3$	3	8	0.5	0.5
$h4$	9	7	0.17	0.5
$h5$	6	15	0.2	0.33

Table 4. Pairwise voting

V_{par}	h_1	h_2	h_3	h_4	h_5
h_1		400	400	300	400
h_2	600		300	600	400
h_3	500	700		500	400
h_4	400	400	400		500
h_5	600	600	600	500	

5.3 Intention Reconsideration

The fact that holes appear and disappear causes the agent to change its intentions. For example, when the set of holes dot not change while the agent is executing a plan, then there is no need to deliberate; but if the set of holes do change, this might mean that IH has disappeared or that a closer hole has appeared; thus, intentions reconsideration is necessary. To achieve this behavior, it is important to consider appropriate criteria to determine whether these changes have occurred or not. Once the criteria and preferences have been chosen, to decide whether to reconsider or not will be determined by Black's rule as shown in previous sections for filtering and planning stages.

Table 5. Ordering of the alternatives according to each criterion

Criteria	Ordering of the alternatives
C_1	$h_4 \succ h_5 \succ h_1 \succ h_3 \succ h_2$
C_2	$h_5 \succ h_2 \succ h_3 \succ h_1 \sim h_4$
C_3	$h_3 \succ h_2 \succ h_1 \succ h_5 \succ h_4$
C_4	$h_2 \succ h_1 \sim h_3 \sim h_4 \succ h_5$

Table 6. Points assigned to each alternative

Alternatives	$C_B(C_1)$	$C_B(C_2)$	$C_B(C_3)$	$C_B(C_4)$
$h1$	2	0.5	2	2
$h2$	0	3	3	4
$h3$	1	2	4	2
$h4$	4	0.5	0	2
$h5$	3	4	1	0

Table 7. Plans to fill in hole h_5

$p_1 = \langle \uparrow, \rightarrow, \uparrow, \rightarrow, \uparrow, \rightarrow, \downarrow, \downarrow \rangle$
$p_2 = \langle \downarrow, \rightarrow, \uparrow, \leftarrow, \uparrow, \rightarrow, \rightarrow, \uparrow, \rightarrow, \downarrow \rangle$
$p_3 = \langle \uparrow, \uparrow, \uparrow, \rightarrow, \rightarrow, \downarrow, \leftarrow, \downarrow, \rightarrow, \uparrow, \rightarrow, \downarrow \rangle$
$p_4 = \langle \uparrow, \uparrow, \rightarrow, \rightarrow, \uparrow, \rightarrow, \downarrow, \downarrow \rangle$

Table 8. Preferences and number of votes per criterion

Criteria	$w(C_i)$	$V_C(C_i)$
C_1	0.75	333
C_2	1	444
C_3	0.5	222

Table 9. Alternatives' strength and values per criterion

Alternatives	C_1	C_2	C_3	f_{C_1}	f_{C_2}	f_{C_3}
h_1	8	13	12	0.12	0.076	0.08
h_2	10	17	17	0.1	0.058	0.058
h_3	12	19	12	0.08	0.052	0.8
h_4	8	11	12	0.12	0.09	0.8

Table 10. Pairwise voting among alternatives

V_{par}	p_1	p_2	p_3	p_4
p_1		999	777	0
p_2	0		777	0
p_3	0	222		0
p_4	444	999	777	

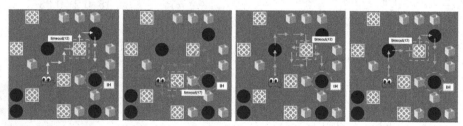

Fig. 3. Plans p_1, p_2, p_3, p_4

6 Conclusion

In this work, we have presented an abstract framework that integrates AT from a multi-criteria approach, within the inner decision making processes (IDMPs) of a BDI agent. Besides, a concrete voting-based instantiation was implemented. In this way, in addition to giving concrete implementation details of the IDMPs within a BDI agent, different criteria and preferences were aggregated to get a solution to a multi-criteria decision problem.

Some of the issues mentioned above have been tackled in previous works. Casali *et al.* [8] present a general framework to define graded BDI agent architectures, where degrees in BDI models are used to set different levels of preferences or rejections on desires and preferences at intentions level to model the cost/benefit trade-off of reaching a goal. In [9], argumentation is used with desire and planning rules, to give a formal account on how consistent sets of intentions can be obtained from a conflicting set of desires. In opposition to [8,9], our framework identifies three processes involving inner decision making, including intention reconsideration function, and it can be instantiated with different agreement mechanisms like voting, argumentation, negotiation, auctions, etc.

In this context, the paper at hand can be considered an extension of the argumentation-based framework presented in [10]. The abstraction process of the components involved is completely defined and its adequacy as abstract framework is effectively proven, viz. a new voting-based instantiation is implemented including more stages of the inner processes than the ones considered in [10]. This is not a secondary aspect; our abstract framework offers a unified framework where different ATs can be easily and coherently integrated. In this way, the advantages that these mechanisms exhibit separately can be integrated and their potential weaknesses simultaneously diminished. Thus, for instance, voting mechanisms can guarantee the achievement of certain theoretical desirable properties in the obtained outcomes for a particular stage of the IDMP, at a relatively low computational cost. Otherwise, argumentation mechanisms can provide an ideal support in those stages of the inner agent process, where the particularities of the domain require a rationally justifiable position of the steps/arguments involved in reaching a conclusion/decision. That "inter mechanism" comparisons will be the focus of our future work, where the abstract framework will be used to integrate and compare different AT technologies at the different stages of the inner agent process in difficult real problems requiring that kind of integration.

References

1. Benfield, S.S., Hendrickson, J., Galanti, D.: Making a strong business case for multiagent technology. In: 5th AAMAS (2006)
2. Bratman, M., Israel, D., Pollack, M.: Plans and resource bounded reasoning. Computational Intelligence **4**(4), 349–355 (1988)
3. Wooldridge, M.: Reasoning about Rational Agents. The MIT Press (2000)
4. Kinny, D.N.: Commitment and effectiveness of situated agents. In: 12th International Joint Conference on Artificial Intelligence (IJCAI), pp. 82–88 (1991)
5. Schut, M., Wooldridge, M., Parsons, S.: The theory and practice of intention reconsideration. JETAI **16**(4), 261–293 (2004)
6. Black, D.: The Theory of Committees and Elections. CUP, Campridge (1958)
7. Pollack, M.E., Ringuette, M.: Introducing the tileworld: Experimentally evaluating agent architectures. In: 8th AAAI, pp. 183–189 (1990)
8. Casali, A., Godo, L., Sierra, C.: A graded BDI agent model to represent and reason about preferences. Artifical Intelligence **175**(7-8), 1468–1478 (2011)
9. Amgoud, L.: A Formal Framework for Handling Conflicting Desires. In: Nielsen, T.D., Zhang, N.L. (eds.) ECSQARU 2003. LNCS (LNAI), vol. 2711, pp. 552–563. Springer, Heidelberg (2003)
10. Sosa-Toranzo, C., Errecalde, M., Ferretti, E.: A framework for multi-criteria argumentation-based decision making within a BDI agent. JCS&T 14(1) (2014)

Planning and Scheduling

Real-Time Pathfinding in Unknown Terrain
via Reconnection with an Ideal Tree

Nicolás Rivera[1]([⊠]), León Illanes[2], and Jorge A. Baier[2]

[1] Department of Informatics, King's College London, London, UK
nicolas.rivera@kcl.ac.uk
[2] Departmento de Ciencia de la Computación, Pontificia Universidad Católica de Chile,
Santiago, Chile

Abstract. In real-time pathfinding in unknown terrain an agent is required to solve a pathfinding problem by alternating a time-bounded deliberation phase with an action execution phase. Real-time heuristic search algorithms are designed for general search applications with time constraints but unfortunately in pathfinding they are known to produce poor-quality solutions. In this paper we propose p-FRIT$_{RT}$, a real-time version of FRIT, a recently proposed algorithm able to produce very good-quality solutions in pathfinding under strict, but not fully real-time constraints. The idea underlying p-FRIT$_{RT}$ draws inspiration from bug algorithms, a family of pathfinding algorithms. Yet, as we show, p-FRIT$_{RT}$ is able to outperform a well-known bug algorithm and is able to solve graph search problems that are more general than pathfinding. p-FRIT$_{RT}$ also outperforms significantly—generating solutions six times shorter when time constraints are tight—a previously proposed real-time version of FRIT and the real-time heuristic search algorithm that is considered to have state-of-the-art performance in real-time pathfinding.

1 Introduction

Pathfinding in an a priori unknown terrain is an important problem, with applications ranging from videogames to robotics. In many of those applications, time is a very limited resource. One example is videogames, where characters are required to move fluently but game developers are not willing to design pathfinding algorithms which would spend more than one millisecond per game cycle, for all simultaneously moving characters [1]. Under such time constraints it is often not possible to compute complete solutions offline before all agents have to be moved.

Real-Time heuristic search algorithms, as conceived by Korf [2], solve general search problems—including pathfinding—and are designed to produce movements given a constant time bound for planning. However, it is known that in pathfinding applications they generate poor-quality solutions, because they rely on a heuristic function that needs to be updated for several states in the search space [3]. When time constraints are tight, the agent is required to re-visit many states before completing search, generating *scrubbing*-like behavior [1].

Recently, Rivera *et al.* [4] proposed FRIT (Follow and Reconnect with the Ideal Tree), a general search algorithm that performs very well at pathfinding in unknown terrain, requiring very little time resources. Unfortunately FRIT cannot produce an action

© Springer International Publishing Switzerland 2014
A.L.C. Bazzan and K. Pichara (Eds.): IBERAMIA 2014, LNAI 8864, pp. 69–80, 2014.
DOI: 10.1007/978-3-319-12027-0_6

given a constant time bound. In a follow-up paper [5], however, they proposed FRIT_{RT}, a fully real-time version of FRIT. In their evaluation they showed that in pathfinding, the resulting algorithm outperformed a state-of-the-art real-time heuristic search algorithm. However, the quality of the solutions produced could be up to one order of magnitude *worse* than those obtained by its predecessor, unless significant time was given per move.

In this paper we propose a real-time version of FRIT_{RT}, p-FRIT_{RT}, that unlike FRIT_{RT}, is able to produce solutions comparable to those of FRIT in pathfinding. The key idea underlying this algorithm draws inspiration from a family of algorithms known as *bug algorithms* [6], which are pathfinding-specific algorithms that imitate the behavior of bugs by "going around" obstacles as they move. Our version of FRIT_{RT} is designed to restrict to borders too; specifically, it restricts reconnection search—a key phase of FRIT—to only expand nodes that are in the border of obstacles.

We prove that our algorithm always finds a solution in a general class of problems which subsumes pathfinding in 8-connected grids. In an experimental evaluation on game map benchmarks, we show that p-FRIT_{RT} improves upon FRIT_{RT} significantly and that it is able to outperform a bug algorithm.

The outline of the paper is as follows. In the next section we present background knowledge, including FRIT and FRIT_{RT}. Then we present our algorithm, p-FRIT_{RT}, and prove it always terminates. Next, we present our experimental evaluation. The paper finishes with an analysis of related work and conclusions.

2   Preliminaries

A search problem is a tuple $P = (G, c, s_{start}, g)$, where $G = (S, A)$ is a directed graph that represents the search space. The set S represents the *states* and the arcs in A represent all available actions. We define the successors of s as $Succ(s) = \{s' \mid (s, s') \in A\}$. State $s_{start} \in S$ is the *initial state* and state $g \in S$ is the *goal state*. A standard assumption in real-time search is that S is finite, that A does not contain elements of the form (s, s), that G is such that g is reachable from all states reachable from s_{start}. In addition, we have a non-negative cost function $c : A \to \mathbb{R}$ which associates a cost with each of the available actions.

Given a subset T of S we define the frontier of T as $\partial T = \{s \in S \setminus T : \exists t \in T \text{ such that } (t, s) \in A\}$. Intuitively, ∂T corresponds to the states that surround the region of states T, i.e., it contains the neighbors of states in T that are not in T. A subset T of S is said connected if for every pair of vertices s, t in T there exists a path that only uses states in T that connects s and t and vice versa.

The objective in *offline* search is to compute a path from s_{start} to g. Heuristic search algorithms solve search problems using a heuristic function to guide search. A heuristic for a search graph G is a non-negative function $h : S \to \mathbb{R}$ such that $h(s)$ estimates the distance between state s and state g, $d_G(s, g)$. We say that h is *admissible* iff $h(s) \leq d_G(s, g)$, for every $s \in S$. Furthermore, h is *consistent* if for every $(s, t) \in A$ it holds that $h(s) \leq c(s, t) + h(t)$, and furthermore that $h(g) = 0$. It is simple to prove that consistency implies admissibility.

Below we assume familiarity with the heuristic-search algorithm A* [7], which ranks states in its search frontier with a function $f(s) = g(s) + h(s)$, where $g(s)$ is the cost of a path from s_{start} to s, and h is the heuristic. We may refer to $h(s)$ and $g(s)$ as, respectively the h-value and g-value of s.

A pathfinding problem in an $n \times m$ grid can represented as a search problem by representing each cell as a state. Specifically, the set of states is defined by $\{0, 1, \ldots, n, n+1\} \times \{0, 1, \ldots, m, m+1\}$, where cells of the form $(0, x)$, $(n+1, x)$, $(x, 0)$, or $(x, m+1)$, for some x, are *border cells* and are regarded as *obstacles*. In this paper we focus on 8-connected grids, which are such that each of the cells have eight possible neighbors (two horizontal, two vertical, and four diagonal neighbors). Formally, we denote by $dist(s, t)$ the euclidean distance between s and t, and we say that $(s, t) \in A$ if and only if $dist(s, t) \leq \sqrt{2}$. For any pair such that $(s, t) \in A$, we define $c(s, t) = dist(s, t)$ if neither s nor t are obstacles. If s is an obstacle, then $c(s, t) = \infty$ and $c(t, s) = \infty$, for every suitable t. Finally, we assume $Obs \subseteq S$ contains all obstacle cells.

Our pathfinding algorithm will restrict search to states that are adjacent to an obstacle. To that end, we define an order for successor states. Specifically, $Succ(s, i)$ denotes the i-th successor of s, such that two successive successors are adjacent to each other. Formally, $Succ(s, i) = s + \delta_i$, for $i \in \{1, \ldots, 8\}$, where δ_i is the i-th element of the following vector,

$$\delta = \big((1, 0)\ (1, 1)\ (0, 1)\ (-1, 1)\ (-1, 0)\ (-1, -1)\ (0, -1)\ (1, -1) \big),$$

defines the 8 successors of a cell in clockwise order.[1] In addition, for simplicity, we define $Succ(s, 0) \overset{\text{def}}{=} Succ(s, 8)$ and $Succ(s, 9) \overset{\text{def}}{=} Succ(s, 1)$. Finally, if $Succ(s, i) \notin S$, we say $Succ(s, i)$ is undefined, which may only happen for an s that lies in the border of the grid, which we defined above as obstacles.

An admissible and consistent heuristic often used in 8-connected grid navigation is the octile distance, which is an analogue of the Manhattan distance in 4-connected grids.

2.1 Real-Time Heuristic Search

Real-time search algorithms move an agent from the initial state to the goal. They are given a bounded amount of time for deliberating, independent of the size of the problem, after which the agent is expected to move. After such a move, more time is given for deliberation and the loop repeats.

Real-time *heuristic* search algorithms are akin to heuristic search algorithms and thus guide search with a heuristic. An example is Real-Time Adaptive A* (RTAA*) [8], which in pathfinding problems in unknown terrain can be described using the following algorithm. (1) Set s to s_{start}. (2) Observe the environment, updating Obs and c. (3) Carry out a bounded A* search that will not extract the goal from $Open$ or expand more than k states. (4) Set $next$ to arg $\min_{t \in Open} g(t) + h(t)$. (5) Set $h(s) \leftarrow f(next) - g(s)$, for every s in $Closed$. (6) Follow the path identified by A* towards $next$; update Obs while moving; stop if an obstacle is blocking the path or if $next$ is reached. Step 5 is called the *learning step*, in which it makes h more informed. It can be shown that Step 5 preserves heuristic consistency [8], which implies RTAA* always terminates.

---

[1] We chose this particular δ for convenience but any vector that allows defining the successors in a clockwise order will work, as well as any vector that reflects a counter-clockwise order.

RTAA* and many other generalizations of LRTA* (e.g., [9–11]) perform poorly in the presence of *heuristic depressions* [3,12]. A heuristic depression is an area of the search space in which the heuristic function returns values that are much lower than the actual cost required to reach a goal state.

2.2   FRIT and FRIT$_{RT}$

Follow and Reconnect with the Ideal Tree (FRIT) [4], is a family of algorithms for solving search problems in unknown search graphs. FRIT is a framework for general search problems but since the focus of this paper is pathfinding we describe it using pathfinding notions, differing slightly from [4].

In an unknown terrain the search graph G is not known to the agent at the outset; instead, the agent knows the dimensions of the grid and the start and goal cells, and furthermore believes that the search graph is given by G_M, which intuitively defines an idealistic pathfinding problem in which the set of obstacles is a subset of the obstacles in G. Specifically, G_M is a search graph that materializes the free-space assumption [13], in which unobserved cells whose blockage status is unknown are assumed obstacle-free.

In its initialization, FRIT defines a so-called *ideal tree*, $\mathcal{T}$, which contains each non-border cell and is defined via *parent pointers*, which point from children nodes to parent nodes. Specifically, each cell s in $\mathcal{T}$, except for the goal cell, has a parent pointer $p(s)$ such that $p(s)$ is a state not in Obs. In addition, given any cell s in $\mathcal{T}$, there exists a natural n such that $p^n(s) = g$. In other words, by "following" the parent pointers from any cell s in $\mathcal{T}$, one eventually reaches the goal in the idealistic world defined by G_M.

For pathfinding in unknown terrain we can generate an initial ideal tree using a consistent heuristic h, setting $p(s) = \arg\min_{t \in Succ(t)} c(s,t) + h(t)$, for every non-border cell which is not the goal cell. Moreover, the parent pointers do not need to be set explicitly for every cell but rather computed when needed. Fig. 1(a) illustrates the ideal tree defined for an 8-connected grid.

To solve a pathfinding problem, FRIT follows the parent pointers of the ideal tree, observing the environment as it moves, until it discovers that this is not possible because a newly discovered obstacle is blocking the path the pointers define. When this happens it invokes a search procedure whose objective is to find a path connecting the current state to a state that is connected to the ideal tree. We call this search *reconnection search*.

Reconnection search can be carried out with any graph search algorithm. The goal condition is the only aspect that is rather different: instead of looking for a specific goal state, reconnection search needs to verify whether or not a state is connected to the search graph, which can be done verifying that there exists a path to the goal state via p pointers. After reconnection, the p pointers define a forest, and the current state is in the ideal tree $\mathcal{T}$.

FRIT(BFS) [4] is the simplest instance of FRIT. It uses breadth-first search (BFS) for reconnection and was shown to have very good performance in pathfinding, with very little time requirements. Fig. 1(b)-(d) shows a few iterations of FRIT(BFS) on a pathfinding problem.

Unfortunately, FRIT(BFS), unlike standard real-time search algorithms, is not able to produce an action given a time bound. This is because BFS takes time bounded by the *size of the search graph* to return a solution. To address this pitfall, Rivera *et al.* [5] proposed to use a real-time search algorithm for reconnection search. In particular, when RTAA* is used for reconnection, one produces $FRIT_{RT}$ (RTAA*).

Algorithm 1. $FRIT_{RT}$ (RTAA*): FRIT with RTAA* reconnection.

Input: A search graph G_M, an initial state s_{start}, and a goal state g
1 **Initialization:** Let $\mathcal{T}$ be an ideal tree for G_M.
2 Set s to s_{start}.
3 Set c to 0 and the color of each state in G_M to 0.
4 **while** $s \neq g$ **do**
5   Observe the environment around s.
6   **for each** *newly discovered inaccesible state o* **do**
7   ⌊ Prune from $\mathcal{T}$ any arcs that lead to o, and add o to *Obs*.
8   **if** $p(s) = null$ **then**
9          $c \leftarrow c + 1$
10   ⌊ Call RTAA*, using $INTREE[c]$ as termination condition.
11   **Movement:** Move the agent from s to $p(s)$ and set s to the new position of the agent.

Algorithm 1 shows the pseudo-code for $FRIT_{RT}$ (RTAA*). Line 10 invokes a slightly modified version of RTAA* (Algorithm 3), which differs from its original in (1) that it sets the parent pointers following the path traversed by the agent, and (2) that it uses function $INTREE[c]$ to determine whether or not a state is connected to the ideal tree. A simplified version of the pseudo-code of $INTREE[c]$ is shown in Algorithm 2. It is simplified because it still may need a number of iterations bounded by the size of the graph. We can modify $INTREE[c]$ to make it real-time, making it return *false* if there is no more time for a new iteration in the main loop. If time constraints are extremely tight $INTREE[c]$ will return *false* almost always. This is no problem since RTAA* is still guaranteed to lead the agent to the goal state. For more details on this discussion we refer the reader to [5]. In the next section we will show that this implementation of $INTREE[c]$ will not guarantee termination; this will motivate a new version of $INTREE[c]$.

Algorithm 2. $INTREE[c]$ function

Input: a vertex s
1 **while** $s \neq g$ **do**
2   Paint s with color c.
3   **if** $p(s) = null$ *or* $p(s)$ *has color c* **then**
4   ⌊ **return false**
5   ⌊ $s \leftarrow p(s)$
6 **return true**

An important aspect of using a real-time search algorithm for reconnection is what heuristic to use. In contrast to the traditional use of real-time search algorithms, which is to guide the agent to the goal, here RTAA* is used to find a reconnecting path. Rivera *et al.* [5] defined the concept of *admissible reconnecting heuristic*. By using them termination is guaranteed. In addition, they showed that both the null heuristic ($h(s) = 0$, for every $s \in S$), and the octile distance are admissible reconnecting heuristics and hence can be used along with $FRIT_{RT}$. Experimentally, they showed that best results in pathfinding are obtained with the null heuristic. The intuition for this is that, upon reconnection, search must be guided away from heuristic depressions rather than towards the goal. The null heuristic seems to better serve that purpose.

Algorithm 3. Real-Time Adaptive A* for FRIT

Input: A search problem P, and a heuristic function h.
Effect: The agent is moved from the initial state to a goal state if a trajectory exists

1 $h_0 \leftarrow h$
2 $s_{current} \leftarrow s_0$
3 **while** $s_{current} \notin G$ **do**
4   A$\star$ (k)
5   **if** $Open = \emptyset$ **then return** no-solution
6      $s_{next} \leftarrow \arg\min_{s \in Open} f(s)$
7   **for each** $s \in Closed$ **do**
8          $h(s) \leftarrow f(s_{next}) - g(s)$
9   Follow the path connecting $s_{current}$ and s_{next} that was identified by A$\star$ and that can be extracted by following the back pointers from s_{next}. Update Obs while moving. Stop if an obstacle is detected in the path or if s_{next} is reached.
10   Assuming $\sigma = s_0 s_1, \ldots s_n$ is the path traversed in this iteration, make $\mathrm{p}(s_i) = s_{i+1}$ for every $i \in \{0, \ldots, n-1\}$.
11   Set $s_{current}$ to the current position of the agent.

2.3 Bug Algorithms

Bug algorithms [6] are pathfinding algorithms for continuous 2D terrain. Unlike real-time heuristic search algorithms, they do not work in general search problems and do not exploit heuristics.

An algorithm relevant to our evaluation is Bug2 [14], which behaves as follows. First it defines a straight line connecting the initial position with the final position, which henceforth we call *m-line*. During execution Bug2 follows the m-line until encountering an obstacle or reaching the goal. If an obstacle is encountered, it saves the position at which the obstacle was hit in a variable called *hit point* and then starts following the boundary of the obstacle (either clockwise or counterclockwise) until the m-line is encountered again. Then, if the current position is closer to the goal than the hit point, the agent starts following the m-line again and the process repeats.

The trajectories generated by Bug2 "go around" obstacles. In the pathfinding problem defined by Fig. 1, there are two trajectories that can be returned by Bug2, depending on the side that is chosen when the obstacle in F6 is observed.

3 A Pathfinding-Specific Version of FRIT$_{RT}$

FRIT$_{RT}$ was shown in [5] to have to have good performance in pathfinding relative to other real-time heuristic search algorithms. Indeed, its performance was shown to be comparable to that of daRTAA* [12], which is considered state-of-the-art in real-time pathfinding. Nevertheless, there are situations in which paths returned by FRIT$_{RT}$ have a large number of steps; much larger than those returned by pathfinding-specific

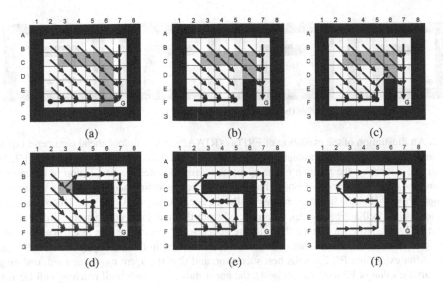

Fig. 1. An execution of FRIT (BFS) when solving the pathfinding problem of moving an agent from cell F2 to cell F7. The gray areas represent obstacles that have not been detected yet by the agent. The position of the agent is shown by the dot. The arrows are a representation of the ideal tree as maintained by FRIT. The first few moves, (a)-(b), trivially follow the ideal tree moving the agent from F2 to F5. In (b), the ideal tree has been updated by removing edges that go through the observed obstacles. (c) shows the agent in the same location after the reconnection through BFS has been completed connecting F5 to D6 through F6. (d)-(e) show the next few stages of the search after reconnection is performed. After (e), the rest of the search is straightforward and the search effort is minimal. The path followed by the agent throughout the whole execution is shown in (f).

algorithms like Bug2 or even FRIT(BFS). There are two reasons for this. First, reconnection is carried out using a standard real-time search algorithm (in this case, RTAA*), the agent may be required to revisit some states many times while reconnecting.

The second reason explaining poor behavior of $FRIT_{RT}$ is that the search space considered by $FRIT_{RT}$ during reconnection is large. An illustration is given in Fig. 2. In that situation the path followed $FRIT_{RT}$ (RTAA*) covers a complete *area* underneath the obstacle, while a bug algorithm would only move on the *perimeter* of that obstacle. As a general conclusion, $FRIT_{RT}$ (RTAA*) may return solution paths whose size is quadratic on the size of paths returned by pathfinding-specific bug algorithms.

Our approach to reducing the search space is strongly inspired by the design principle of bug algorithms. We propose to restrict the reconnection search space only to states that are in the border of an obstacle. This can be ensured by replacing the A* search in RTAA* by Algorithm 4, which in Line 10 guarantees that a state is added to *Open* only if it has a neighbor which is an obstacle too. We call the resulting algorithm p-$FRIT_{RT}$. It is not hard to verify that p-$FRIT_{RT}$ (RTAA*) solves the problem of Fig. 2 in 19 steps.

A rather important detail to notice is that since Algorithm 4 only considers states next to obstacles, RTAA*'s learning rule applies only to those states. Although Algorithm 4 imposes a clockwise order to look for new open states, any order can be

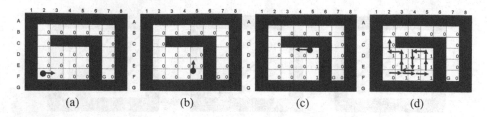

Fig. 2. An illustration of the execution of FRIT$_{RT}$ (RTAA*), run with lookahead parameter equal to 1, at solving a pathfinding problem whose start state is cell F2, and whose goal cell is F7. In (a)-(d), the dot shows the position of the agent, the arrow denotes the next action to be carried out, and the number in the cell denotes the value of the reconnecting heuristic that we use in this example ($h = 0$). For the first three moves (a)-(b) the agent follows the ideal tree. Once it reaches F5, the obstacle cell at F6 becomes disconnected from the tree and reconnection is initiated via running RTAA*. Now we assume the cells are added to A* priority queue in clockwise order, starting from the top cell, and that, moreover ties are broken in the priority queue in the same order. After expanding F5, E5 is the best successor, and thus the agent moves upward, updating the heuristic value of F5 to 1. Analogously, the agent moves upwards until reaching cell D5 (c). D5's best successor is D4, and due to tie-breaking rules the agent moves downward, then left, and then upwards again, following the path shown in (d).

implemented. On the other hand, in order to ensure that FRIT$_{RT}$ always reaches the goal, the INTREE[c] function needs modification. As mentioned above, if time constraints are tight INTREE[c] will return **false** most of the times putting reconnection at risk. Since Algorithm 4 only inserts into $Open$ states that are next to an obstacle, RTAA* moves the agent only through those states. If the goal state is not adjacent to a wall and the agent does not have enough time to check whether states are connected to the ideal tree then it may end up looping forever around an obstacle. To address this, we propose a modification of the INTREE[c] function, shown in Algorithm 5.

Algorithm 4. Bounded A* lookahead restricted to follow walls

---

1 **procedure** A* (k)
2   **for each** $s \in S$ **do** $g(s) \leftarrow \infty$
3      $g(s_{current}) \leftarrow 0$; $Open \leftarrow \emptyset$
4   Insert $s_{current}$ into $Open$
5      $expansions \leftarrow 0$
6   **while** *each $s' \in Open$ with minimum f-value is such that* INTREE[c](s') *is not true and expansions $< k$* **do**
7   Remove state s with smallest f-value from $Open$
8   Insert s into $Closed$
9   **for** i *in* $1, \ldots, 8$ **do**
10   **if** $Succ(s, i-1) \in Obs$ or $Succ(s, i+1) \in Obs$ **then**
11   **if** $g(s') > g(s) + c(s, s')$ **then**
12                     $g(s') \leftarrow g(s) + c(s, s')$
13                     $s'.\text{back} = s$
14   **if** $s' \in Open$ **then** remove s' from $Open$
15   Insert s' in $Open$
16         $expansions \leftarrow expansions + 1$

Algorithm 5. Modified INTREE[c] function

Input: a vertex s
1 $s' \leftarrow s$
2 **if** sp(s') = *null* **then**
3 | **return false**
4 **else**
5 | $s' \leftarrow$ sp(s')
6 **while** $s' \neq g$ **do**
7 | Paint s' with color c.
8 | **if** p(s') = *null* or p(s') *has color c* **then**
9 | | **return false**
10 | $s' \leftarrow$ p(s')
11 | sp(s) $\leftarrow$ p(s')
12 **return true**

Algorithm 5 introduces a new attribute for states called the *super parent* sp. At the outset of each reconnection (i.e., each call of RTAA* in Algorithm 1) we set sp(s) = s for every s. The idea of Algorithm 5 is now that if the agent does not have enough time to complete the INTREE[c] process from a state s and it had to move, if we perform the INTREE[c] function again from s, we can recover the work done starting the search from sp(s) instead of s. It is easy yet important to observe that if we repeat Algorithm 5 from the same state a sufficient number of times the algorithm will eventually return true if the state is connected to the goal state.

3.1 Theoretical Analysis

In this section we prove that p-FRIT$_{RT}$ is *correct*; i.e., that it guides an agent to the goal when a solution exists. Though p-FRIT$_{RT}$ was designed for pathfinding, we extend it now to a more general class of graphs. Below, $G = (S, A)$ is an undirected graph, i.e., one in which $(s, s') \in A$ if and only if $(s', s) \in A$.

We say that $B \subset S$ is a *fence* with respect to state s and goal state g if $g \notin B$, B is a connected graph and whenever there is a path from s to g then $\partial B \cap L(s, B)$ is connected, where $L(s, B)$ is the set of all vertices reachable by a path from s without using states of B. The idea of the fence is that the agent cannot cross it but can "skirt around it". Note that, for technical reasons, B is a fence in the trivial cases when $s \in B$ or B cuts all paths from s to g.

We say G is *nice* with respect to state s and goal state g, if every $B \subset V$ is a fence with respect to s and g. A graph is nice (with respect to g) if it is nice with respect to s and g for all $s \in S$. As a way of example an $n \times m$ grid that has a solution is nice.

Remark 1. This simple observation about the definition of fence is the key to prove that the algorithm always finds a solution. Let G be a connected, nice undirected graph with g the goal state. Let s be a state such that $\pi = s s_1 \ldots s_n g$ is a path from s to g. Let B be a fence w.r.t. s and g, and $s \notin B$ but $s_i \in B$ for some i (the reader should think B as a set of obstacles that cut the path π). We can always reconstruct a new path P' with the following idea, let N be the greater N such that $s_N \in B$, then $s_{N+1} \in \partial B$ (note that s_{N+1} might be g), then we can construct a path starting from s, then move along the path until we hit B, then move through states in ∂B until we reach s_{N+1} and continue using π again.

Theorem 1. *Consider a search problem P, and assume that at every moment, the current search graph G_M is nice. Then the algorithm finds a solution.*

To prove Theorem 1 we use the following intermediate result.

Lemma 1. *Suppose that from the current state p-FRIT$_{RT}$ follows the path defined by the p pointers and that when the agent reaches state s the path becomes blocked by an obstacle. Then reconnection search can find a reconnecting path to the ideal tree.*

Proof. Recall that when the ideal tree is disconnected then the agent runs RTAA* using the modified version of A* in Algorithm 4 which restricts to states next to an obstacle. Let G_M be the current graph, let x be the obstacle in the path that was being followed and let B be the set of all obstacles connected with x. Since G_M is nice, and B is a fence the agent can move on the wall of B. By Remark 1, there exists a set of states on the wall of B, say U, such that the vertices of U are connected with g and thus if the agent can identify them, it can reconnect to the ideal tree. Finally, even though it may take several runs of Algorithm 5 from the same vertex, a connected vertex is eventually recognized since the graph is finite and connected. RTAA* will make the agent move on the wall of B until it recognizes a state of U connected to the ideal tree.

Proof (Of theorem 1). Let T be the ideal tree defined by the p pointers after a reconnection or at the beginning of the algorithm. Moreover, let s be the position of the agent after such reconnection. Let π be the path in T that goes from s to g. Recall the agent will follow π until it reaches g or finds an obstacle. Now assume an obstacle is found, and let G_M be the known graph at the point the agent found the obstacle. The above lemma says that we can reconnect the tree on G_M, recovering a new tree that connects the position of the agent with the goal state. Since the initial tree T connects the initial position with g (in the initial known graph) and the set of connected components of obstacles is finite, we repeat the argument inductively, finishing the proof.

4   Experimental Evaluation

We implemented our algorithm over the same codebase of FRIT. The objective of our experimental evaluation was to compare p-FRIT$_{RT}$ (RTAA*) with the state of the art in real-time pathfinding, which is represented by daRTAA* and FRIT (RTAA*). The objective of our evaluation was not to establish a relationship between p-FRIT$_{RT}$ and the state of the art in bug algorithms. However, for reference we also include a comparison with Bug2, which we is easy to implement.

We evaluated over 12 game maps from N. Sturtevant's pathfinding repository [15]. The maps we considered come from the games *Dragon Age*, and *StarCraft*.[2] We generated 500 problems for each of them. We ran the real-time algorithms in 9 lookahead configurations $(1, 2, 4, 8, 16, 32, 64, 128, 512)$. We assume the agent can observe the blockage status of its neighbor cells. All experiments were run on a Linux 2.00GHz QuadCore Intel Xeon machine with 128MB of RAM.

---

[2] **Map details.** Dragon Age: brc202d, orz702d, orz900d, ost000a, ost000t and ost100d; sizes: 481×530, 939×718, 656×1491, 969×487, 971×487, and 1025×1024 resp. StarCraft: ArcticStation, Enigma, Inferno, JungleSiege, Ramparts and WheelofWar; sizes: 768×768, 768×768, 768×768, 768×768, 512×512 and 768×768 resp.

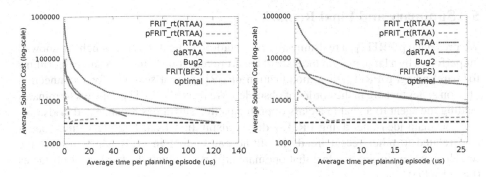

Fig. 3. A comparison of p-FRIT$_{RT}$, FRIT$_{RT}$ (RTAA), and the state-of-the-art daRTAA* over 12 standard game maps. The plot on the right-hand side is a zoomed version of the one on the left.

Figure 3 compares solution quality obtained by the various algorithms. FRIT(BFS) is not a real-time algorithm and its average solution cost is included in the plots for reference only. On the other hand, Bug2 returns a single solution in very little time; it is shown in the figure as a horizontal line, rather than a simple dot, for clarity. As well, "optimal" is the average optimal solution (obtained using RTAA* using an infinite lookahead parameter) and it is included for reference as a horizontal line.

p-FRIT$_{RT}$ significantly outperforms the real-time search algorithms daRTAA* and FRIT$_{RT}$ (RTAA*) with respect to average time spent per search episode. In fact, for lookahead equal to 1 p-FRIT$_{RT}$ (RTAA*) generates a solution that is 6.9 times cheaper than that produced by daRTAA* and 8.3 times better than the one returned by FRIT$_{RT}$ (RTAA*). For other values of the lookahead parameter we observe a similar behavior. For example, for lookahead 16, the solution returned by p-FRIT$_{RT}$ (RTAA*) is 2.7 times cheaper than that produced by daRTAA* and 4.5 times better than the one returned by FRIT$_{RT}$ (RTAA*). For lack of space we omit total runtime plots. However, p-FRIT$_{RT}$ (RTAA*) clearly outperforms the other real-time search algorithms on that metric. For example, it is 5.52, 23.62, and 2.81 times faster than daRTAA* for lookaheads 1, 16, and 512, respectively, and on average 9.81 times faster than daRTAA*, 22.8 times faster than RTAA*, and 7.55 times faster than FRIT$_{RT}$ (RTAA*).

The average cost of the solutions returned by Bug2 is 6,546, with an average runtime of 2,317 μs. p-FRIT$_{RT}$ (RTAA*), on the other hand, obtains solutions of cost 7,629 on average for lookahead parameter 16, with an average runtime of 4,777 μs. For lookahead parameter 32, p-FRIT$_{RT}$ (RTAA*) obtains an average solution of cost 4,210 with an average total runtime of 4,008 μs. The best average solution cost obtained by p-FRIT$_{RT}$ (RTAA*) is for a lookahead equal to 64, which yields an average solution of cost 3,225—about half of the cost obtained by Bug2—, with a runtime of 4,838 μs.

We conclude that p-FRIT$_{RT}$ significantly outperforms the state of the art in real-time heuristic search for pathfinding tasks. Given sufficient time, p-FRIT$_{RT}$ may also return solutions substantially better than those obtained by Bug2 and thus should be preferred in situations in which time constraints allow for at least 64 node expansions.

5 Summary and Final Remarks

We presented p-FRIT$_{RT}$, a real-time algorithm tailored to pathfinding which we showed outperforms by a large margin the state of the art in real-time heuristic search algorithms for pathfinding. p-FRIT$_{RT}$ is a modification of FRIT$_{RT}$ that searches for reconnection only on states that are in the border of obstacles. We proved p-FRIT$_{RT}$ always terminates leading the agent to a goal in a class of problems that subsumes 8-connected grids.

The main idea underlying FRIT$_{RT}$ draws inspiration from bug algorithms, but is also related to other recent trends in offline pathfinding in grids which restrict the search space exploiting the fact that optimal paths must touch the borders of obstacles (i.e., [16, 17]).

References

1. Bulitko, V., Björnsson, Y., Sturtevant, N., Lawrence, R.: Applied Research in Artificial Intelligence for Computer Games. In: Real-time Heuristic Search for Game Pathfinding, pp. 1–30. Springer (2011)
2. Korf, R.E.: Real-time heuristic search. Artificial Intelligence **42**(2–3), 189–211 (1990)
3. Ishida, T.: Moving target search with intelligence. In: Proc. of the 10th National Conf. on Artificial Intelligence (AAAI), pp. 525–532 (1992)
4. Rivera, N., Illanes, L., Baier, J.A., Hernández, C.: Reconnecting with the ideal tree: An alternative to heuristic learning in real-time search. In: Proc. of the 6th Symposium on Combinatorial Search (SoCS) (2013)
5. Rivera, N., Illanes, L., Baier, J.A., Hernández, C.: Reconnection with the ideal tree: A new approach to real-time search. Journal of Artificial Intelligence Research **50**, 235–264 (2014)
6. LaValle, S.M.: Planning algorithms. Cambridge University Press (2006)
7. Hart, P.E., Nilsson, N., Raphael, B.: A formal basis for the heuristic determination of minimal cost paths. IEEE Transactions on Systems Science and Cybernetics **4**(2), 100–107 (1968)
8. Koenig, S., Likhachev, M.: Real-time Adaptive A*. In: Proc. of the 5th Int'l Joint Conf. on Autonomous Agents and Multi Agent Systems (AAMAS), pp. 281–288 (2006)
9. Hernández, C., Meseguer, P.: LRTA*(k). In: Proc. of the 19th int'l Joint Conf. on Artificial Intelligence (IJCAI), pp. 1238–1243 (2005)
10. Hernández, C., Meseguer, P.: Improving LRTA*(k). In: Proc. of the 20th Int'l Joint Conf. on Artificial Intelligence (IJCAI), pp. 2312–2317 (2007)
11. Koenig, S., Sun, X.: Comparing real-time and incremental heuristic search for real-time situated agents. Autonomous Agents and Muti-Agent Systems **18**(3), 313–341 (2009)
12. Hernández, C., Baier, J.A.: Avoiding and escaping depressions in real-time heuristic search. Journal of Artificial Intelligence Research **43**, 523–570 (2012)
13. Zelinsky, A.: A mobile robot exploration algorithm. IEEE Transactions on Robotics and Automation **8**(6), 707–717 (1992)
14. Lumelsky, V.J., Stepanov, A.A.: Path-planning strategies for a point mobile automaton moving amidst unknown obstacles of arbitrary shape. Algorithmica **2**, 403–430 (1987)
15. Sturtevant, N.R.: Benchmarks for grid-based pathfinding. IEEE Transactions Computational Intelligence and AI in Games **4**(2), 144–148 (2012)
16. Harabor, D.D., Grastien, A.: Online graph pruning for pathfinding on grid maps. In: Proc. of the 26th AAAI Conf. onArtificial Intelligence (AAAI) (2011)
17. Uras, T., Koenig, S., Hernández, C.: Subgoal graphs for optimal pathfinding in eight-neighbor grids. In: Proc. of the 23rd Int'l Conf. on Automated Planning and Scheduling (ICAPS) (2013)

Natural Language Processing

The Influence of Syntactic Information
on Hedge Scope Detection

Guillermo Moncecchi[1](✉), Jean-Luc Minel[2], and Dina Wonsever[1]

[1] Instituto de Computación, Facultad de Ingeniería, Universidad de la República,
Montevideo, Uruguay
gmonce@fing.edu.uy
[2] Laboratoire MoDyCo, UMR 7114 CNRS, Université Paris Ouest Nanterre La
Défense, Nanterre, France

Abstract. In this paper we elaborate over the use of sequential supervised learning methods on the task of hedge cue scope detection. We address the task using a learning methodology that proposes the use of an iterative, error-based approach to improve classification performance. We analyze how the incorporation of syntactic constituent information to the learning and post-processing steps produces a performance improvement of almost twelve points in terms of F-score over previously unseen data.

1 Introduction

The use of speculative language poses an interesting problem for Natural Language Processing (NLP), since it potentially reflects the subjective position of the writer towards the truth value of certain facts; when the fact is extracted or used for inference, this certainty information should not be lost. *Hedging*, a term first introduced by Lakoff (1973) to describe the use of 'words whose job is to make things fuzzier or less fuzzy' is 'the expression of tentativeness and possibility in language use' (Hyland, 1995), and is extensively used in scientific writing. Several authors have studied the phenomenon of speculation from philosophical, logical and linguistic points of view, generating a rich and heterogeneous theory about speculative language. All this body of work should aid in the construction of an NLP system for speculative sentence detection.

The most common approach in the NLP literature (see, for example, Farkas et al. (2010)) to speculative language detection within scientific writing is through hedge detection: the presence of lexical tentativeness or possibility marks ('hedge cues') within a sentence is considered an indicator of speculation. The linguistic devices used to express hedging are diverse: besides modal verbs, epistemic lexical verbs (such as 'suggest' or 'indicate that'), adjectives ('likely'), adverbs ('probably'), and even nouns ('possibility') are frequently used to express uncertainty. For example, in the following sentence, the modal verb 'may' is epistemically used to avoid bald assertion:

Example 1. Since clinical remission has been observed in a significant fraction of DLCL cases, these markers <u>may</u> serve as critical tools for sensitive monitoring of minimal residual disease and early diagnosis of relapse.

© Springer International Publishing Switzerland 2014
A.L.C. Bazzan and K. Pichara (Eds.): IBERAMIA 2014, LNAI 8864, pp. 83–94, 2014.
DOI: 10.1007/978-3-319-12027-0_7

The sentence expresses speculation, and the hedge 'may' serves to show the possibility of a certain procedure. But there is another fact within the sentence (that clinical remission have been observed in many cases) which is not hedged, so marking the whole sentence as speculative could lead to the wrong assumption that this fact is merely a possibility. The notion of *hedge scope* (Morante et al., 2009; Vincze et al., 2008) captures the idea that it is possible that only a fragment of a sentence is hedged. In the previous example, we could consider that the scope of the 'may' hedge cue could be the verb phrase that starts with the very word[1]:

Example 2. Since clinical remission has been observed in a significant fraction of DLCL cases, these markers {may serve as critical tools for sensitive monitoring of minimal residual disease and early diagnosis of relapse}.

Hedges, when lexically marked, can be considered linguistic operators, therefore inducing a scope. However, the very notion of hedge scope is introduced for the Bioscope corpus annotation (Vincze, 2008), and is never formally defined, presenting instead a series of criteria to identify them, based mainly on syntax. We have previously suggested (Moncecchi et al., 2013) defining hedge scope as *the part of meaning in the sentences that is hedged*, i.e. where the tentativeness or possibility holds. From this perspective, scope is a *semantic* notion, that can be, however, strongly related with syntax.

In this paper we show how we applied supervised sequential learning methods to the task of scope detection. In particular, we want to analyze how the incorporation of different linguistic information (including lexical and syntactic information) to the learning and post-processing steps allowed to improve prediction performance[2]. To achieve this improvement we propose an iterative methodology, where errors committed on a held out corpus are inspected and general rules (mostly based on expert knowledge on syntax) are proposed to solve them. These rules are incorporated as features for the learning process.

In the next section we review previous work on hedge cue identification and scope detection, with special emphasis on this second task. Section 3 presents the learning methodology. In section 4 we analyze performance improvement after incorporating diverse learning attributes, mainly from syntactic scope information, and discuss when these improvements hold on previously unseen data. Finally, we analyze the presented approach, suggesting future lines of research.

2   Related Work

The first approaches to speculation detection aimed to classify each sentence as speculative or not speculative. Medlock and Briscoe (2007), for example,

---

[1] In this work, hedge cues will be underlined and their scope marked with brackets, annotated with the name of the hedge cue in case there are multiply nested scopes.

[2] Obviously, for scope to be detected we have first to identify sentence hedge cues; in this paper (for space reasons), we assume that this step is completed, and use gold-standard hedge cues, concentrating on the problem of scope detection.

proposed to use a semi-supervised learning approach to solve this binary classification task. Morante et al. (2009), adapting previous work on negation detection, reduced speculation detection to hedge cue identification: a sentence would be considered speculative if it included one or more hedge cues.

For the scope detection task, Morante et al. (2009) proposed to address it as a case of *sequential classification*: given a sentence and a hedge cue within it, classify each sentence token, indicating if it is part of the hedge scope, using a so-called FOL marking: assign class F to the first token of the predicted scope, and L the last one, marking every other token with class O. The classifier input included both the sentence and the hedge cue since a sentence could include two or more cues. For this task, only those sentences where a hedge cue had been found were used as learning instances.

Several works have been presented using this same approach, specially during the CoNLL-2010 Shared Task (Farkas et al., 2010), ranging from pure rule-based studies, based on sentence syntactic structure (Ozgur et al., 2009; Ovrelid et al., 2010; Velldal et al., 2010), to machine learning and hybrid systems (Morante et al., 2010), incorporating lexical and syntactical information. However, the task of scope resolution is still far from resolved: the best reported result for the CoNLL evaluation corpus is a F-measure of 0.696 (Velldal et al., 2012), using gold-standard hedge cues.

3   Methodology

To address the sequential learning task of scope detection, we followed a learning methodology that starts with an initial guess of attributes for supervised learning and a learning method, and builds a classifier; this classifier is in turn evaluated on a held out corpus, and errors are handled to an expert, who proposed rules for solving, based on present or proposed lexical, positional or syntactic attributes. In this section we briefly explain the process. For a detailed explanation see Moncecchi et al. (2013; 2010; 2012).

We used the abstracts section of the Bioscope corpus (Vincze et al., 2008) as a learning source and for evaluation purposes. We first divided the corpus into a 80% training corpus and a 20% evaluation corpus; since we were using an iterative methodology, we further separated a 10% held out corpus from the training set, and used it for tuning.

Following previous studies, we addressed scope detection as a sequential learning task, using FOL classes for each token. Table 1 shows a scope learning instance for the following sentence:

Example 3. This finding {suggests that the BZLF1 promoter may be regulated by the degree of squamous differentiation}.

The input format is the standard learning format used in the CoNLL Shared Tasks (Buchholz, 2006). For each hedge cue in a sentence, a learning instance is generated. In the previous example, the hedge cue is the word 'suggests' (you can see it marked with a B value for the 'Hedge cue' attribute in Tables 1-2), while its scope is the text span between tokens 3 and 16. There is another, different, learning instance coming from the same sentence, originated by the hedge cue 'may' spanning from tokens 5 to 16 (according to the Bioscope corpus annotation guidelines). Each learning instance could include an arbitrary number of additional attributes, resulting, for example, from lexical or syntactical analysis.

To evaluate classifier performance, we took a perfect-match approach: we considered an evaluation instance as correctly identified only if every token in the sentence were correctly classified. This means that, for the case of scope detection, the scope was considered correctly detected if both the first and last token of the scope were correctly marked. Classification performance was measured in terms of the traditional figures of precision, recall, and F-score. For the scope detection task, these three numbers coincided, since every False Positive (instances with incorrectly classified scope), implied a False Negative (instances where the correct scope was not identified).

The sequential learning process acts as expected: from the learning instances, a model is constructed using a learning method. We used linear-chain Conditional Random Fields, a statistical method, since it had produced state-of-the-art result in many sequential learning tasks (Lafferty, 2001). Besides the usual lexical or syntactical attributes related to each word (e.g. POS tags, lemmas, syntax tree parent), we introduced a special type of attributes, which we called *knowledge rules*. Their name comes from the fact that they try to model a prediction on the target classes, given an instance, product of an expert rule. For example, a rule that states 'the scope of the keyword 'may' is the same as the scope of the parent node of the hedge cue in the syntax tree', would be represented by an attribute (with exactly the same possible values as the target class), whose F and L tokens will be, respectively, the first and last token of the syntax scope of the parent node of 'may'. Note that these knowledge rules are *not* post-processing rules, but just learning attributes. The learning method will decide if they are relevant for learning, just as any other attribute. We will see some examples later in this article.

In the next section we show how we defined a base classifier and incrementally improved it. Since our procedure is based on analyzing errors, we used a held out corpus to evaluate improvements; classifier measurement on the evaluation corpus was only done after finishing the iterative process. At the end of the section, we will show how each classifier performed on the evaluation corpus, so as to measure if the improvements on the held out corpus hold.

4 Classification Improvement

4.1 Baseline Classifier

What we considered as learning attributes for our baseline classifier were the same lexical attributes (word, lemma, and part-of-speech class[3]) we used for

---

[3] We applied the GENIA tagger (Tsuruoka et al., 2005) to the original corpus to get the lexical information for each word, and the Stanford Parser (Klein et al., 2003) to get each sentence syntax tree.

hedge cue identification, adding the hedge cue attribute learned in the previous step; all four attributes were considered in a window of size 5, centered in the current token. Figure 1 shows the learning instance for this classifier, for our previous example. This classifier also includes a set of post-processing rules that are fired when one (or both) scope limits could not be identified: when we transform the task of scope detection into a sequential classification one and use a FOL format, it is possible that not exactly one F and one L class are predicted for an instance. In this case, we know for sure that the correct scope could not be identified, and should try to back off to a simpler guess. The set of rules we used to modify the classifier results on evaluation data to correct those cases were a slightly modified form of the rules presented by Morante et al. (2009).

This baseline classifier, including the post-processing rules, obtained an F-score of 0.66 on the held out corpus.

Table 1. Base classifier attributes

Token	Word	Lemma	POS	Hedge cue	Scope
1	This	This	DT	O	O
2	finding	finding	NN	O	O
3	suggests	suggest	VBZ	B	F
4	that	that	IN	O	O
5	the	the	DT	O	O
6	BZLF1	BZLF1	NN	O	O
7	promoter	promoter	NN	O	O
8	may	may	MD	O	O
9	be	be	VB	O	O
10	regulated	regulate	VBN	O	O
11	by	by	IN	O	O
12	the	the	DT	O	O
13	degree	degree	NN	O	O
14	of	of	IN	O	O
15	squamous	squamous	JJ	O	O
16	differentiation	differentiation	NN	O	L
17	.	.	.	O	O

4.2 Iteration 1: Adding Syntax Information

We observed that most scopes were associated with the sentence syntactic constituents, particularly those that included the hedge cue (this was reasonable, since the corpus annotation guidelines were mostly based on syntax). For example, the scope of a lexical verb such as 'suggest' matched the parent component of the hedge cue in the parse tree, as the parse tree in Figure 1 shows:

To improve classification, we included as a learning attribute a knowledge rule stating that the scope of the hedge cue was the syntactic scope of the parent of the hedge cue (i.e. the parent in the parse tree of its first word), modulo final periods. Or, in terms of attribute values:

in_hc_parent_scope = F if the token is the first word of the parent of the HC
                     = L if the token is the last word of the parent of the HC
                     = O otherwise

```
(ROOT
  (S
    (NP (DT This) (NN finding))
    (VP (VBZ suggests)
      (SBAR (IN that)
        (S
          (NP (DT the) (NN BZLF1) (NN promoter))
          (VP (MD may)
            (VP (VB be)
              (VP (VBN regulated)
                (PP (IN by)
                  (NP
                    (NP (DT the) (NN degree))
                    (PP (IN of)
                      (NP (JJ squamous) (NN differentiation)))))))))))
    (. .)))
```

Fig. 1. Parsing tree for sentence 3. The scope of the hedge cue is shown in bold.

Since this criterion does not hold for every part-of-speech (and not even for every use of the verb, as, for example, passive voice construction or raising verbs cases show), we also included as a learning attribute the part-of-speech of the hedge cue parent. Table 2 shows the classifier attributes for the 'suggest' hedge cue in sentence 3. We can see that the in_hc_parent_scope rule matches the cue scope; that does not happen in the case of the hedge cue 'may', where the syntactic scope starts with the hedge cue, while the hedge scope starts with token 5, according to annotation guidelines. We expected that the classifier could confirm or discard a correlation between the knowledge rule and the scope, based on training data, as it does with every other attribute.

Table 2. Learning Instance after Iteration 1 for sentence 3, hedge cue 'suggests'

Token	Word	Lemma	POS	HC	PPOS	in-PScope	Scope
1	This	This	DT	O	VP	O	O
2	finding	finding	NN	O	VP	O	O
3	suggests	suggest	VBZ	B	VP	F	F
4	that	that	IN	O	VP	O	O
5	the	the	DT	O	VP	O	O
6	BZLF1	BZLF1	NN	O	VP	O	O
7	promoter	promoter	NN	O	VP	O	O
8	may	may	MD	O	VP	O	O
9	be	be	VB	O	VP	O	O
10	regulated	regulate	VBN	O	VP	O	O
11	by	by	IN	O	VP	O	O
12	the	the	DT	O	VP	O	O
13	degree	degree	NN	O	VP	O	O
14	of	of	IN	O	VP	O	O
15	squamous	squamous	JJ	O	VP	O	O
16	differentiation	differentiation	NN	O	VP	L	L
17	.	.	.	O	VP	O	O

After a grid search for the best attributes and fine-tuning learning parameters (w.r.t performance on the held-out corpus), we obtained a classifier with an F-measure of 0.705 on the held out corpus, improving by four points with respect to the base classifier.

4.3 Iteration 2: Adding Ancestors in the Syntax Tree

After the previous iteration, we elaborated a list of the 116 errors the classifier had committed in the held-out corpus and tried to understand why it had been wrong. As we have already said, this method could be applied because attributes for learning corresponded quite directly with a few observable properties related to the linguistic phenomenon we aimed to study.

Analyzing these errors, we found that assuming that only parent scopes were related with hedge scopes was not enough. In some cases, such as those of passive voice use, hedge scopes matched the syntactic scope of ancestors in the tree other than the parent. To cope with this, we added the same syntactic information for hedge cue grandparents and great-grandparents in the syntax tree, and their part-of-speech tags, exactly the same way we did in the previous section. We fed the classifier with all of them in the form of knowledge rules, and let it select which scope to use, depending on the remaining attributes. Performance, again, improve clearly, yielding a 0.740 F-score, eight points above the baseline, and four points above the previous iteration.

4.4 Iteration 3: Adjusting Ancestor Scopes

Until this iteration we had assumed that syntactic scopes matched hedge scopes, i.e. that we could find an ancestor of the hedge cue in the syntax tree whose scope matched the scope of the hedge cue. Studying classification errors, we found that this assumption was not always true. In this iteration we aimed to see whether this was a general problem, and whether we could adjust constituent scopes to achieve concordance.

We first studied, for every hedge cue in the training corpus, if its hedge scope matched the syntactic scope of one of its ancestors, resulting from the sentence parsing. We found that for about 80% of the hedge cues this was actually true. To improve this matching, we studied the cases of misalignment where they accounted for a greater proportion and greater number of instances. We found two main causes for misalignments: the scope of the hedge cue included several non-nested scopes, not allowing a characterization of the hedge scope in terms of syntactic scopes, or the hedge scope matched just a portion of an ancestor scope, excluding some subconstituents. In both cases, scopes should be modified (adding or eliminating subcomponents) to match hedge scopes. Consider, for example, the following sentence:

Example 4. Our results lend further support to the {hypothesis that inflammatory and immune responses of monocytes/macrophages may be modulated at the molecular level by signals originating from tissue structural cells such as fibroblasts}.

Its syntactic analysis tree (partially depicted in Figure 2), shows that the hedge cue scope (shown underlined) includes the parent noun phrase of the hedge cue (excluding the initial determiner) and the clause to the right of the grand-parent constituent. We can observe that this mismatch was probably originated by an incorrect parsing decision. The clause starting with 'that inflammatory...' could be considered within the syntactic scope of the NP clause headed by the noun hedge cue 'hypothesis'. Several other, similar errors appeared in the held out corpus.

Recall that to obtain sentence constituents we used an external parser: therefore, it was not possible (in our working scenario) to correct parsing errors such as the one shown. However, analyzing the relation between hedge scopes and syntactic constituents in the training corpus it was possible for us to derive a series of rules to 'correct' the extracted features and adjust the syntactic scopes based mainly on lexical information. This procedure did not aim to derive a correct parse, but only to produce better features for the task, in certain clearly identified cases. Similar comments could be made to those cases where the syntax constituent was correctly derived, but, due to annotation idiosyncrasies, certain parts should not be included in the hedge scope.

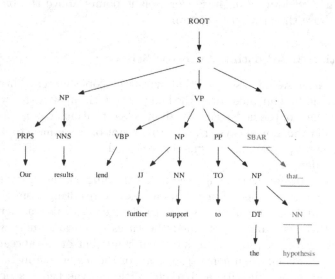

Fig. 2. Hedge scope for sentence 4

After looking at several of these mismatches, we modified our definition of 'constituent scope', incorporating several rules to cope with specific, 'pathological' cases. Once again, performance improved on the held out corpus, but this time only by 1.5 points, giving an F-measure of 0.756.

4.5   Iteration 4: Handling Misclassified Examples

Another source of errors beside wrong scope selection and mismatches between hedge and syntactic scopes, were the cases where the classifier failed to classify one sentence token as the first element of the scope and one token as the last one. In these cases, we could be sure that this evaluation instances would be misclassified, because they were 'badly-formed', since they did not meet the very definition of scope. After the last iteration, more than half of classification errors corresponded to these cases.

As we have previously mentioned, these cases were handled using post-processing rules, based mainly in positional and lexical information. Since we had available the sentence syntax structure, we decided to modify these rules and base them on syntax, probably reflecting better the corpus annotation guidelines. We ended using only three post-processing rules:

- If the hedge cue is a conjugated verb (except when in passive voice or in the case of raising verbs such as 'seem'), use the next verb phrase up in the syntax tree that includes it.
- If the hedge cue is 'or', 'neither' or 'either', use the first noun phrase that includes it.
- In every other case, use the first clause that includes the hedge cue.

After modifying post-processing rules, performance dramatically improved by more than ten percentage points, obtaining a 0.860 F-measure value.

4.6   Iteration 5: Post-processing Rules

After we had studied the three types of errors identified in section 4.3 and modified the classifier attributes and post-processing rules, improving classification, we had only 49 errors left. We studied these errors, and identified several patterns where the classifier did not manage to predict the correct scopes. We found that in most cases these errors probably corresponded to situations where, despite having enough attributes, the absence of enough training data prevented the classifier to infer them. To try to solve this problem, we took a rule-based approach: we ignored the classifier predictions and deterministically assigned the scope limits. We had to be careful about being very precise in the determination of the situations these rules fired, the avoid introducing false positives. After applying these rules, and fine tuning parameters, performance improved to its best value on the held out corpus with 0.885 in terms of F-measure.

4.7   Results on the Evaluation Corpus

To estimate the performance of our classifier, we rebuilt the classifiers in each one of the methods iteration, this time training on the whole training corpus (also including sentences in the held out corpus). We do not only wish to estimate the prediction ability of our best classifier on future data, but also to evaluate if the application of the methodology actually produced a performance improvement after each iteration, when faced with unseen data. This is of particular importance for our method: since improvement was based on errors on a held out corpus, we risked overfitting our built classifiers to this corpus. Table 3 summarizes the results[4].

---

[4] Note that these results are not comparable with state-of-the art numbers, since most of them are calculated on the evaluation corpus of the CoNLL 2010 Shared Task,

Table 3. Scope detection: results on evaluation data. Number in parenthesis show results on the held out corpus.

Classifier	F-score
Baseline	0.737 (0.664)
It. #1 (Adding syntax info)	0.749 (0.705)
It. #2 (Adding ancestors)	0.802 (0.740)
It. #3 (Adjusting ancestors scopes)	0.800 (0.756)
It. #4 (Handling misclassified examples)	**0.852** (0.860)
It. #5 (Post-processing rules)	0.831 (**0.885**)

It can be observed that improvements in the held out corpus hold for the evaluation corpus, except for iteration #3 and #5. In both cases, overfitting occurred. It seems that specific rules used to adjust scopes or even final results were too tailored to solve errors in the held out corpus, and actually harmful for the overall performance on unseen data. On the other hand, general decisions, such as the addition of new syntax attributes or a general modification of post-processing rules clearly improved performance. At the end of the day, the best classifier improved performance by more than twelve points in term of F-measure, compared to the baseline classifier.

5   Final Remarks

In this article we presented a series of experiment on the detection of hedge scopes, and showed how we improved classifier performance incorporating attributes resulting from syntactic analysis. All the results presented suggest that the methodology proposed successfully identified syntax information as an important predictor of hedge scopes, clearly improving baseline results for scope detection.

However, there were still several instances that could not be correctly classified, especially those that did not correspond with the scope of any ancestor of the hedge cue. We found that the classification method used was highly successful in finding the correlation between syntactic scopes and hedge scopes, when that was possible. In almost every case the correct ancestor in the tree was selected by the classifier to be used as the hedge scope, independently of the hedge cue part-of-speech tag. Adjusting the original syntactic scope of the hedge cue ancestor to exclude or add certain spans (such as certain prepositional phrases or clauses at the end or at the beginning of the scope) seemed useful to improve classification, but produced no improvement on the evaluation data. We think that the absence of clear annotation rules for the selected corpus, indicating when they should be included or excluded acted as a source of ambiguity, and we found several corpus instances where the reasons for pruning or not pruning

which, for example, includes full articles. Actually, we evaluated our methods against the CoNLL corpus, obtaining competitive results. See Moncecchi et al. (2013) for details.

the hedge scope were not clear. The rules for scope pruning that we developed were based purely on data observation, causing an overfit to the training corpus.

Another source of hedge scope detection errors was syntax parsing. Several of the remaining errors on the held out corpus corresponded to cases such as the one presented in section 4.4, where syntax constituents were incorrectly identified by the parser, yielding wrong syntactic scopes and consequently wrong hedge scopes. Improving parsing results would almost surely imply improving hedge scope identification.

In future research, we plan to apply this methodology to similar phenomena involving cues and scope, such as negation, event recognition, factuality or modality identification. Previous work on those topics suggests that they present several similarities and relation with syntax, with respect to the here addressed phenomenon of hedging.

References

Buchholz, S., Marsi, E.: Conll-x shared task on multilingual dependency parsing. In: Proceedings of the Tenth Conference on Computational Natural Language Learning, pp. 149–164. Association for Computational Linguistics (2006)

Farkas, R., Vincze, V., Móra, G., Csirik, J., Szarvas, G.: The CoNLL-2010 shared task: Learning to detect hedges and their scope in natural language text. In: Proceedings of the Fourteenth Conference on Computational Natural Language Learning, pp. 1–12. Association for Computational Linguistics, Uppsala (2010)

Hyland, K.: The author in the text: Hedging scientific writing. Hongkong Papers in Linguistics and Language Teaching 18, 33–42 (1995)

Klein, D., Manning, C.D.: Accurate unlexicalized parsing. In: ACL 2003: Proceedings of the 41st Annual Meeting on Association for Computational Linguistics, pp. 423–430. Association for Computational Linguistics, Morristown (2003)

Lafferty, J., McCallum, A., Pereira, F.: Conditional random fields: Probabilistic models for segmenting and labeling sequence data. In: Proceedings of ICML 2001, pp. 282–289 (2001)

Lakoff, G.: Hedges: A study in meaning criteria and the logic of fuzzy concepts. Journal of Philosophical Logic 2(4), 458–508 (1973)

Medlock, B., Briscoe, T.: Weakly supervised learning for hedge classification in scientific literature. In: Proceedings of the 45th Annual Meeting of the Association of Computational Linguistics (2007)

Moncecchi, G.: Recognizing Speculative Language in Research Texts., Phd. Thesis, Universidad de la República, Montevideo, Uruguay - Université Paris Ouest Nanterre La Défense (2013)

Moncecchi, G., Minel, J.L., Wonsever, D.: Enriching the bioscope corpus with lexical and syntactic information. In: Workshop in Natural Language Processing and Web-based Tecnhologies 2010, pp. 137–146 (November 2010)

Moncecchi, G., Minel, J.L., Wonsever, D.: Improving speculative language detection using linguistic knowledge. In: Proceedings of the Workshop on Extra-Propositional Aspects of Meaning in Computational Linguistics. p. 37–46. Association for Computational Linguistics, Jeju (2012)

Morante, R., Daelemans, W.: Learning the scope of hedge cues in biomedical texts. In: Proceedings of the BioNLP 2009 Workshop, pp. 28–36. Association for Computational Linguistics, Boulder (June 2009)

Morante, R., Van Asch, V., Daelemans, W.: Memory-based resolution of in-sentence scopes of hedge cues. In: Proceedings of the Fourteenth Conference on Computational Natural Language Learning, pp. 40–47. Association for Computational Linguistics, Uppsala (July 2010)

Øvrelid, L., Velldal, E., Oepen, S.: Syntactic scope resolution in uncertainty analysis. In: Proceedings of the 23rd International Conference on Computational Linguistics, COLING 2010, pp. 1379–1387. Association for Computational Linguistics, Strouds-burg (2010)

Özgür, A., Radev, D.R.: Detecting speculations and their scopes in scientific text. In: EMNLP, Singapore (2009)

Tsuruoka, Y., Tateishi, Y., Kim, J.-D., Ohta, T., McNaught, J., Ananiadou, S., Tsujii, J.: Developing a Robust Part-of-Speech Tagger for Biomedical Text. In: Bozanis, P., Houstis, E.N. (eds.) PCI 2005. LNCS, vol. 3746, pp. 382–392. Springer, Heidelberg (2005)

Velldal, E., Øvrelid, L., Oepen, S.: Resolving speculation: Maxent cue classification and dependency-based scope rules. In: Proceedings of the Fourteenth Conference on Computational Natural Language Learning. pp. 48–55. Association for Computational Linguistics, Uppsala (July 2010)

Velldal, E., Øvrelid, L., Read, J., Oepen, S.: Speculation and negation: Rules, rankers, and the role of syntax. In: Computational Linguistics, pp. 1–64 (February 2012)

Vincze, V., Szarvas, G., Farkas, R., Mora, G., Csirik, J.: The bioscope corpus: biomed-ical texts annotated for uncertainty, negation and their scopes. BMC Bioinformatics 9(suppl. 11), S9+ (2008)

A Straightforward Author Profiling
Approach in MapReduce

Suraj Maharjan[✉], Prasha Shrestha, Thamar Solorio, and Ragib Hasan

University of Alabama at Birmingham, Birmingham, Alabama
{suraj,prasha,solorio,ragib}@cis.uab.edu

Abstract. Most natural language processing tasks deal with large amounts of data, which takes a lot of time to process. For better results, a larger dataset and a good set of features are very helpful. But larger volumes of text and high dimensionality of features will mean slower performance. Thus, natural language processing and distributed computing are a good match. In the PAN 2013 competition, the test runtimes for author profiling range from several minutes to several days. Most author profiling systems available now are either inaccurate or slow or both. Our system, written entirely in MapReduce, employs nearly 3 million features and still manages to finish the task in a fraction of time than state-of-the-art systems and with better accuracy. Our system demonstrates that when we deal with a huge amount of data and/or a large number of features, using distributed systems makes perfect sense.

1   Introduction

In natural language processing (NLP) as with any task, producing good results takes higher precedence over getting the results faster. But most of the time the runtime performance is so overlooked that it is almost never mentioned in publications. A good approach is of course of utmost importance to get good results. But if testing out the approach takes a large amount of time, we will be spending our time waiting for results rather than improving our approach or trying out newer ones. Also, a good runtime performance is important to have practical solutions.

By nature, most NLP tasks such as parsing, POS tagging, and named entity recognition are computationally expensive. When we perform these tasks on large datasets, we have to wait hours, even days, to see preliminary results. However, since most of the work in NLP entails performing the same tasks over and over again on different texts, the tasks can be easily parallelized and distributed. Theoretically, each document or independent piece of text could be computed on a single machine, which would allow the whole work to be completed within the time taken for a single document.

The PAN workshop series is one of the few shared tasks where the test runtimes for the systems submitted to the competition are published. There are different tracks in the competition, namely, plagiarism detection, authorship attribution and author profiling. We chose the author profiling task because along with the runtimes being very high for some systems, the accuracy for this task was very

© Springer International Publishing Switzerland 2014
A.L.C. Bazzan and K. Pichara (Eds.): IBERAMIA 2014, LNAI 8864, pp. 95–107, 2014.
DOI: 10.1007/978-3-319-12027-0_8

low and we wanted to see if we could improve along these two fronts. Moreover, author profiling is in itself an important problem. Analyzing of an author's profile is useful in fields such as security, forensics, literary research, and marketing. In forensics, finding out the profile of the author of an email containing threats, spam or malware can help to narrow down the number of suspects. Another scenario where author profiling can be useful is when there are a lot of old texts for which the author is unknown. If we are to directly perform authorship attribution, the list of authors will be too long. If we profile the author of the text first, we can cut down the list of prospective authors on which authorship attribution can then be performed. In the field of marketing, companies can target their ad campaigns at certain groups of people who match the demographics and profile of current customers. Author profiling can also be applied to the feedback on online shopping websites and on reviews of their products [1].

Although author profiling has many practical applications, it is also time intensive. Having a large amount of training data helps in generating a good model for the profile of an author. In the PAN 2013 competition [1], the size of training data was 2.2GB. Other previous works do not generally mention their data sizes. However, they do mention the number of files in their dataset. Estival et al. [2] have used 9,836 email messages of at least 200 words each. Schwartz et al. [3] have performed what they claim to be the largest study on Facebook data. They have trained their system on 700 million words. These statistics show that the task of author profiling usually deals with a large quantity of data. For this reason, author profiling tasks are generally very slow.

Most authors do not mention how long their system takes to run, so we are unable to compare directly against them. In the PAN 2013 competition, however, even to get results from an already trained model, it took up to 17 days for some systems. The time required for training these models was not reported. There were 312,500 training documents, while there were only 33,600 test documents. The number of training documents is nearly 10 times more than the number of test documents. Also, all of the methods used in the competition are supervised learning methods; so all of the systems must have performed model training. Thus training is bound to have required more time by an order of magnitude. Here, we have taken on the same task as of the PAN 2013 competition i.e. given a document, finding out the age and gender of the author. Although in the competition, the focus was more on accuracy than on speed, we have given both equal emphasis. We have used nearly 3 million n-gram features, which produce a well-rounded representation of the text. Finding and using this large number of features for a large data set consumes a huge amount of time and memory. So, we have used Hadoop MapReduce so that even with large number of features, we can run our experiments with on all of the data in an acceptable amount of time. We also developed a web interface for users, so that they can submit a sample text to our system and get a response in real time.[1]

The contributions of this paper are threefold. First of all, we show that by using MapReduce we can dramatically increase the runtime performance of an

---

[1] http://coral-projects.cis.uab.edu:8080/authorprofile/

author profiling system. Since most NLP systems deal with large amounts of data and most of these systems are parallelizable at least on the document level, we believe that this increase in performance will translate to any such system if parallelization is used. Secondly, we were also able to improve on the best accuracy of the competition, even though we used simple features as compared to other systems. Finally, our system is useful for someone who wants to use distributed computing for NLP but does not want to get into MapReduce. The Naive Bayes implementation and other jobs that we wrote can be useful in that scenario. The tokenizer, filter, IDF counter, and Naive Bayes implementation can all be used fairly easily by someone who does not have any knowledge of MapReduce. Our code is freely available for use and extension.

2   Related Work

The PAN Overview paper for author profiling [1] outlines all of the methods used by the participants in the competition. All of the approaches use a combination of several linguistic features such as lexical, stylistic, syntactic and readability features. Since the dataset contains a lot of spam, some of the approaches also use a spam filter. Some have used URLs and emoticons as features as well, while others simply removed them. Although the training runtimes are not reported, the PAN competition organizers have listed the testing runtimes for them, which range from 10.26 mins to 11.78 days. Since all of the approaches use supervised learning, we believe it is safe to assume that the training runtimes are a lot higher than the test ones. The winning approach for the English language data was by Meina et al. [4] also used Naive Bayes for classification. Their testing runtime was 4.44 days. The winning approach in Spanish was by Santosh et al. [5] and they used decision trees for classification. Their tests took 4.86 hours. The overall winner was the system by Lopez-Monroy et al. [6] and they used second level meta-features. Their testing runtime was comparatively low at 38.31 mins.

Schwartz et al. [3] explored gender, age and five personality traits on data obtained from Facebook users. They used n-grams and LDA topics as features and obtained an accuracy of 91.9% for gender. They modeled age as a continuous variable and obtained linear regression coefficient R of 0.84. Estival et al. [2] collected English email texts and along with gender, age and personality traits, they also tried to predict the first language and the country of the authors. They tried experimenting with a variety of classifiers including SVMs using SMO, Random Forest and rule based learners among others. While no one classifier was best for all traits, SMO performed the best for both age and gender. They obtained accuracy of 56.46% and 69.26% for age and gender respectively.

The accuracy obtained by the above two systems is a lot higher than any of the systems in the PAN 2013 competition. This might be due to the difference in the dataset. The PAN data is mostly blogs, which while mostly informal, retains a little more formality than say, Facebook statuses. In blogs, people have to write on a certain topic and are restricted in the kind of language that they can use. In Facebook statuses and messages, people are completely free to express themselves and use any kind of language. So, they are more likely to use words that are predictive of their profiles. We have further explored this overall low accuracy in later sections.

We also wanted to compare the runtime performance of our system with other author profiling systems implemented in MapReduce. But we could not find any such research. However, there were papers that dealt with using MapReduce for natural language processing tasks. Eidelman et al. [7] have investigated the use of MapReduce for large-margin structured learning. They used MapReduce for statistical machine translation and showed that their approach scaled linearly with the size of the data.

3   Dataset

We have used the dataset provided in the PAN 2013 competition. The data has been collected from different blog posts where the authors also mention their age and gender [1]. There are a total of 236,600 files in the English dataset and 75,900 files in the Spanish dataset of the PAN 2013 training corpus. There are 3 classes across age: 10s, 20s and 30s and 2 classes for gender: male and female. We considered this as a 6 class problem rather than considering the 2 sets of classes independently. The distribution for these 6 classes for both English and Spanish is shown in Table 1. The dataset is balanced across gender and imbalanced across age. The size of training, early bird and test datasets are shown in Table 2. PAN has a provision in which during the course of the task, participants' software can be pre-evaluated against a separate test dataset, called the early bird dataset. The datasets are large and will take a large amount of time to process by using standard off-the shelf machine learning toolkits.

Table 1. Training, Early bird, Test documents distribution

Age	Gender	English			Spanish		
		Training	Early Bird	Test	Training	Early Bird	Test
10s	male	8600	740	888	1250	120	144
10s	female	8600	740	888	1250	120	144
20s	male	42900	3840	4608	21300	1920	2304
20s	female	42900	3840	4608	21300	1920	2304
30s	male	66800	6020	7224	15400	1360	1632
30s	female	66800	6020	7224	15400	1360	1632
Total		236600	21200	25440	75900	6800	8160

Table 2. Sizes of the Dataset

Language	Training	Early Bird	Test
English	1.8 GB	135 MB	168 MB
Spanish	384 MB	34 MB	40 MB
Total	2.2 GB	169 MB	209 MB

4   MapReduce for Author Profiling

We have built our system by using MapReduce on Hadoop. We chose MapReduce because it provides a high level abstraction for writing distributed applications. Programmers do not have to manage the communication as with MPI or p-threads. Hadoop handles race conditions, fault tolerance, deadlock, and failures automatically so that programmers can focus on the application rather than the on the cluster details. Similarly, Hadoop Distributed File System (HDFS) provides a distributed file system, which takes care of the data distribution and replication. This provides a benefit over some other cluster management software such as SGE, because for SGE, we have to manage the data ourselves. All parts of our system have been written as MapReduce jobs, from preprocessing to training and testing, which are described below.

4.1   Preprocessing

Since the PAN 2013 dataset is in XML format, we removed all the XML tags. Most of the training and test files were very small in size: only a few kilobytes. Hadoop is optimized to work with large files rather than with lots of small files. So, we merged them into larger sequence files with the filename as key and the file content as value. The tokenizer job (Algorithm 1) takes this sequence file, removes all HTML tags from it, changes all the tokens to lowercase and finally generates unigrams, bigrams and trigrams. This is a map only process and not having a reducer eliminates shuffle and sort that could have hindered the speed.

4.2   IDF Counts and Filtering

Algorithm 2 works on the n-gram tokens generated in the tokenization phase. IdfMapper emits the partial count of each unique token in the document and IdfReducer sums these counts grouped by keys. We also used combiner in between mapper and reducer which performs local aggregation and hence reduces data transfer across the network, thus making the process faster. The output of this phase are the tokens with their IDF scores, which are passed on to the filtering job (algorithm 3). The filtering job first creates a dictionary file as a mapping between tokens and their unique integer id. It also has an entry for *UNSEEN_TOKEN*, which accounts for any unseen tokens that we may encounter in the test documents. It then reads the idf files and based on the threshold supplied, filters out infrequent tokens. After obtaining the final tokens, TFIDFVectorizeMapper (algorithm 4) creates term frequency-inverse document frequency (TF-IDF) vectors for each document by making use of the dictionary file and idf scores.

4.3   Training

For training, we used Naive Bayes as our classifier. We explored Mahout's Naive Bayes implementation, but it did not meet our requirements. First of all, to use it we

Algorithm 1. Document Tokenizer	**Algorithm 2.** IDF Count
1: **class** TOKENIZERMAPPER	1: **class** IDFMAPPER
2: **method** MAP(docname a, doc d)	2: **method** MAP(docname a, tokens T)
3: tokens $T \leftarrow$ new TUPLE	3: uniqueWords $U \leftarrow$ new LIST
4: **for all** term $t \in$ TOKENIZE(d) **do**	4: **for all** term $t \in$ tokens T **do**
5: T.ADD(t)	5: **if** term $t \notin U$ **then**
6: **end for**	6: EMIT(term t, count 1)
7: EMIT(docname a, tokens T)	7: U.ADD(t)
8: **end method**	8: **end if**
9: **end class**	9: **end for**
	10: **end method**
	11: **end class**
	1: **class** IDFREDUCER
	2: **method**
	REDUCE(term t, counts[$c_1, c_2...$])
	3: idf $i \leftarrow 0$
	4: **for all** count $c \in$ counts [$c_1, c_2...$] **do**
	5: $i \leftarrow i + c$
	6: **end for**
	7: EMIT(term t, idf i)
	8: **end method**
	9: **end class**

have to have the training and test data together so that it can create the dictionary file and vectors. So, the vector creation process needs to be done by combining the training and test sets. The resulting vector is subdivided into training and test sets by Mahout and the ratio of training and test can be given to it as parameters. But in a lot of cases, we have separate training and test data like in the PAN competition. Also, as of Mahout version 0.7, the Naive Bayes implementation does not consider prior probability and unseen words. Although Mahout can be frustrating due to lack of proper documentation, it has implementations for a lot of machine learning algorithms and is worth exploring.

We wrote our own Naive Bayes classifier in MapReduce. We did use Mahout's *Vector* class in order to take advantage of *mahout-math*, Mahout's well-designed math library. Also, Mahout's Naive Bayes is well-structured, so we based our class structure upon it. The TrainNBMapper reads in the vectors per document created by TFIDFVectorizeMapper, groups the vectors by their class labels, and then computes frequencies of tokens per class label, total tokens in a class and vocabulary size. During the mapping phase, it extracts class labels from document names and maps them to unique integer values. It then emits the class label id as key and the TF-IDF vector as value.

At the clean up stage, we emit a special key -1 to indicate that this key holds the partial counts for documents with the same class label. Finally the reducer needs to sum up the vectors grouped by the label id for which we used Mahout's

---

Algorithm 3. Filter out Least Frequent Tokens

```
1: class FilterLeastFrequenMapper
2:   method Setup
3:     H ← new HashSet
4:     Read dictionary file
5:     H.Add(tokens ∈ dictionary file)
6:   end method
7:   method Map(docname a, tokens T)
8:     finalTokens F ← new Tuple
9:     for all term t ∈ tokens T do
10:      if term t ∈ H then
11:        F.Add(t)
12:      end if
13:    end for
14:    Emit(docname a, finalTokens F)
15:  end method
16: end class
```

Algorithm 4. TF-IDF Vectorizer

```
1: class TFIDFVectorizeMapper
2:   method Setup
3:     H ← new HashMap
4:     IDF ← new HashMap
5:     Read dictionary file
6:     H.Add(tokens, id ∈ dictionary file)
7:     Read idf file
8:     IDF.Add(tokens, idf ∈ idf file)
9:   end method
10:  method Map(docname a, tokens T)
11:    vector V                          ←
         new RandomSparseVector
12:    Compute token count
13:    for all unique term t ∈ tokens T do
14:      V.Set(H.get(t), tfIdfScore(t))
15:    end for
16:    Emit(docname a, vector V)
17:  end method
18: end class
```

VectorSumReducer. These final vectors hold all the information we need for Naive Bayes. After completion of this phase, we read in all of the final vectors and create a Naive Bayes Model and then save it to a model file. This model file also contains other details like vocabulary count, total number of classes and Laplace smoothing coefficient.

4.4 Testing

We tested our system on both the early bird dataset and the test dataset released by PAN 2013. Similar to what we did with the training files, we first removed the XML tags from the test files and then converted them to sequence files. Algorithm 6 takes the sequence file as input. The TestNBMapper loads the model created during the training phase, the dictionary file and the idf scores files. Then TestNBMapper tokenizes the test document and creates TF-IDF vectors using dictionary and idf files. It then computes the scores for each class label using the model and emits the actual label and the score vector. After the completion of this process, we read in all the score vectors and used Mahout's ResultAnalyzer to compute accuracy and create the confusion matrix.

5 Experimental Settings

After we had our MapReduce jobs in place, we performed our experiments on our local cluster. It consists of a master node and 7 slave nodes, each node having 16 cores and 12GB memory. We are running Hadoop version 1.0.4 and Mahout version 0.7.

Algorithm 5. Naive Bayes Training	**Algorithm 6.** Naive Bayes Testing
1: **class** TRAINNBMAPPER	1: **class** TESTNBMAPPER
2: **method** SETUP	2: **method** SETUP
3: priorPbVector $P \leftarrow$ new VECTOR	3: dictionary $D \leftarrow$ new HASHMAP
4: **end method**	4: $IDF \leftarrow$ new HASHMAP
5: **method** MAP(docname a, vector v)	5: READ dictionary file
6: $l \leftarrow$ EXTRACTLABEL(a)	6: D.ADD($tokens, id \in$ dictionary file)
7: $P\{l\} \leftarrow P\{l\} + 1$	7: READ idf file
8: EMIT(label index l, vector v)	8: IDF.ADD($tokens, idf \in$ idf file)
9: **end method**	9: model $M \leftarrow$ load Model
10: **method** CLEANUP	10: vectorClassifier C $\leftarrow$
11: EMIT(-1, priorpb vector P)	new NBCLASSIFIER(M)
12: **end method**	11: **end method**
13: **end class**	12: **method** MAP(docname a, doc d)
	13: COMPUTE TOKEN COUNT
	14: CREATE TEST VECTORS T
	15: $l \leftarrow$ EXTRACTLABEL(a)
	16: vector $V \leftarrow C$.CLASSIFY(T)
	17: EMIT(actual label l, vector V)
	18: **end method**
	19: **end class**

5.1 Features

Our method is based upon an n-gram model and we worked with unigrams, bigrams and trigrams. We filtered out the least frequent n-grams and used the rest as features. In the English training dataset, there were 71,710,553 unique n-gram tokens for 236,600 authors. In the Spanish dataset, there were 11,920,013 unique n-gram tokens for 75,900 authors. We removed all of the tokens that were not used by at least 10 of the authors for English and 2 of the authors for Spanish. We then created bigrams and trigrams from those tokens. After this, we were left with 2,908,894 n-gram tokens for English and 2,806,922 n-gram tokens for Spanish, each of which acts as a feature. This is a very large number of features and it can be computationally intensive to calculate values for all of them. It is almost impossible to imagine using this many features with a single machine and to expect results in a reasonable amount of time.

5.2 Classification Algorithm

To choose our classification method, we first divided the training dataset from the PAN 2013 Competition in 60:40 ratio. We created a unigram model of the text and trained a Logistic Regression classifier and a Naive Bayes classifier provided by Mahout [8]. We obtained 29.01% and 38.61% accuracy by using Logistic Regression and Naive Bayes respectively. From these preliminary results, since the difference of accuracy between these methods was so high, we chose Naive Bayes as our classification method.

6   Results

Figures 1(a) to 1(b) show the runtimes for the whole process, including testing and training. The CPU time denotes the total time taken by the process to run on all the CPUs available in the cluster. This value should be comparable to the time taken to run the MapReduce tasks on a single CPU. The task of creating IDF was the most time consuming and as expected it was also the task in which the speedup is truly remarkable. For a task that would have taken at least 1085 minutes as evidenced by CPU time, our system finished it within 55.79 minutes. The total amount of time taken for the whole process was just 72.12 minutes, which is a lot less than the time most of the participant's approach took just for testing. Although both our system and the system used by Meina et al. [4] use Naive Bayes, their testing required 4.44 days, while ours required just 2.86 minutes. However, even our individual machines had high computational power and all the participants in the contest might not have access to such powerful machines.

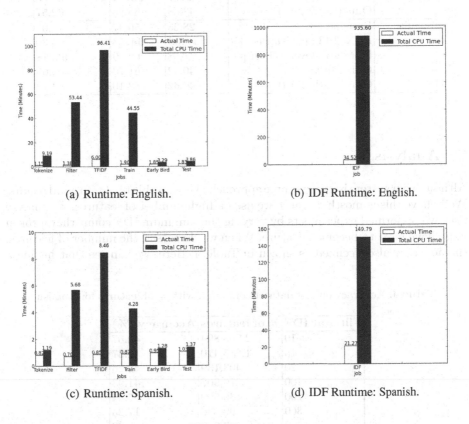

(a) Runtime: English.   (b) IDF Runtime: English.

(c) Runtime: Spanish.   (d) IDF Runtime: Spanish.

Fig. 1. Runtime

The accuracy of our system, the majority class baseline and the accuracy of best systems for English [4], Spanish [5] and overall [4] in the PAN 2013 Competition are shown in Table 3. In both the early bird and actual test datasets, our accuracy is a lot higher than the baseline for both languages. For age and gender individually, we have the highest accuracy for English in the age category only. But, our overall accuracy and the accuracy for English is the highest, while it is in the top 3 for Spanish. However, the participants in the PAN'13 competition did not have the early bird or test datasets available to them and could not have made any changes based upon them.

Table 3. Accuracy on Test data

Language	System	Total (%)	Age (%)	Gender (%)
English	Baseline	28.40	56.80	50.00
	PAN 2013 English Best [4]	38.94	59.21	64.91
	PAN 2013 Overall Best [6]	38.13	56.90	**65.72**
	Ours (Test)	**42.57**	**65.62**	61.66
	Ours (Early Bird)	43.88	65.80	62.57
Spanish	Baseline	28.23	56.47	50.00
	PAN 2013 Spanish Best [5]	**42.08**	**64.73**	64.30
	PAN 2013 Overall Best [6]	41.58	62.99	**65.58**
	Ours (Test)	40.32	61.73	64.63
	Ours (Early Bird)	40.62	62.10	64.79

7   Analysis

Although our system is a very simple approach, we were able to obtain good results. We believe this is mostly because we used a high number of features. To analyze this, we performed experiments by varying the minimum IDF count that a token must have for it to become a feature. When we decreased the number of features, the accuracy also declined as shown in Table 4. Here, we can see that having a

Table 4. Accuracy on test dataset compared with # of features for English

Filter at IDF	# of features	Accuracy (%)
10	2,908,894	42.57
15	1,885,410	42.37
20	1,403,139	42.26
100	276,902	41.93
200	136,999	37.34
300	90,836	17.23
400	67,938	7.80
500	54,330	5.93
1000	27,151	4.66

large number of features is surely helpful, although the increase in accuracy is not necessarily linear.

We also performed experiments with different types of features and weighing schemes. Our original system runs with the following parameters and settings: n-grams of words with n from 1 to 3, tf-idf weighing scheme, filter at 10 and no pre-processing applied. As shown in Table 3, the accuracy with this setting is 42.57%. We performed different experiments with one of these parameters changed. The changed parameter, its setting and the accuracy obtained are shown in Table 5. When we used character n-grams instead, the accuracy dropped by more than 11%. Although character n-grams represent the writing style of an author and are helpful, people of certain age or gender group are more likely to use certain words than to collectively use a certain style of writing. When unigrams, bigrams and trigrams were used separately, the accuracy was again lower than when they were used together. We obtained the highest accuracy when using bigrams, although we had similar accuracy with all three. When we stemmed the words and also filtered out stopwords, the accuracy again decreased. Stemming and stopword filtering causes a loss of information about the syntactic structure of a text, which is important. We also experimented by using only stopwords as features and again obtained very low accuracy. Although just the syntactic information is not powerful enough in determining the age and gender of an author, it is certainly helpful. When we used term frequency as a weighing scheme rather than using TF-IDF, the accuracy was much lower than that of our original system. Using TF-IDF assigns weight based not only upon how frequently a word is used by an author but also upon how common the word is among other authors. So, it makes sense for TF-IDF to be the better weighing scheme.

Table 5. Accuracy comparison for different parameter settings for English dataset

Parameter	Setting	Accuracy (%)
N-gram	Character Bigrams and Trigrams	31.20
N-gram	Word Unigrams	39.99
N-gram	Word Bigrams	41.17
N-gram	Word Trigrams	39.70
N-gram	Stopword Unigrams	29.14
Weighing Scheme	TF	36.12
Preprocessing	Stopwords filtered and Porter Stemming	35.82

Although we performed well and obtained overall best accuracy in the PAN 2013 competition, the accuracy on this data is generally very low when compared to author profiling done on Facebook [3] and email data [2]. When we analysed the PAN data for possible reasons, we found out that the data contains a lot of spam and some mixed language documents as well, containing both English, Spanish and even some other languages. Along with this, some of the files are very short and do not even contain 5 words. Also, since the data has been collected from blogs, there is no guarantee that authors of the text will provide their correct age and gender. We even found cases where an author mentions his age in the text but it is different from what the file has been labeled as. All these shortcomings of the dataset can introduce errors in the model.

8 Discussion and Future Work

We were able to run everything, which would have taken at least a day at best, within 1.5 hours for the whole process from preprocessing to testing. We were able to outperform all of the systems in the PAN 2013 competition in terms of both speed and combined overall accuracy in the whole corpus. Along with that, even by using a simple approach, we were able to obtain good results. We believe this is in part, because we used a high number of features. Using distributed computing allowed us to use lots of features, which we could not have done with single machine computation.

One aspect we can improve on is cleaning the training data. Although we filtered out a lot of words, we need to filter out some of the documents as well. Removing spam-like documents from our dataset is likely to improve our results. Another aspect is that although we have used a large number of features, they are simple features. In the future, we will look at adding more sophisticated features and making them work in MapReduce. That way, we will be able to test to see if our system obtains even higher accuracy with sophisticated features, while retaining the speed.

As with this task, most NLP tasks deal with a lot of data. People resort to random sampling in order to decrease the amount of data, as done by participants of the PAN 2013 competition. Although filtering the dataset might be useful, random sampling is rarely so. Generally, having a good amount of properly labeled data is helpful in creating good models. So, having to resort to using only a small sample of the data due to computational constraints will keep a system from performing at its best. Our results are a good indication that for most NLP tasks, distributed computing is the way to go.

Acknowledgments. This research was partially funded by The Office of Naval Research under grant N00014-12-1-0217 and by The National Science Foundation under grant 1350360.

References

1. Rangel, F., Rosso, P., Koppel, M., Stamatatos, E., Inches, G.: Overview of the author profiling task at PAN: In: Notebook Papers of CLEF 2013 LABs and Workshops, CLEF-2013, Valencia, Spain, pp. 23–26 (September 2013)
2. Estival, D., Gaustad, T., Pham, S.B., Radford, W., Hutchinson, B.: Author profiling for english emails. In: Proceedings of the 10th Conference of the Pacific Association for Computational Linguistics, pp. 263–272 (2007)

3. Schwartz, H.A., Eichstaedt, J.C., Kern, M.L., Dziurzynski, L., Ramones, S.M., Agrawal, M., Shah, A., Kosinski, M., Stillwell, D., Seligman, M.E.P., Ungar, L.H.: Personality, gender, and age in the language of social media: The open-vocabulary approach. PLoS ONE 8, e73791 (2013)
4. Meina, M., Brodzinska, K., Celmer, B., Czoków, M., Patera, M., Pezacki, J., Wilk, M.: Ensemble-based classification for author profiling using various features. In: Notebook Papers of CLEF 2013 LABs and Workshops, CLEF-2013, Valencia, Spain (September 2013)
5. Santosh, K., Bansal, R., Shekhar, M., Varma, V.: Author profiling: Predicting age and gender from blogs. In: Notebook Papers of CLEF 2013 LABs and Workshops, CLEF-2013, Valencia, Spain (September 2013)
6. López-Monroy, A.P., Montes-y Gómez, M., Escalante, H.J., Villaseñor-Pineda, L., Villatoro-Tello, E.: INAOE's participation at PAN'13 : Author profiling task. In: Notebook Papers of CLEF 2013 LABs and Workshops, CLEF-2013, Valencia, Spain (September 2013)
7. Eidelman, V., Wu, K., Ture, F., Resnik, P., Lin, J.: Mr. MIRA: Open-source large-margin structured learning on MapReduce. ACL System Demonstrations (2013)
8. Owen, S., Anil, R., Dunning, T., Friedman, E.: Mahout in action. Manning (2011)

Extraction of Relation Descriptors for Portuguese Using Conditional Random Fields

Sandra Collovini[(✉)], Lucas Pugens, Aline A. Vanin, and Renata Vieira

Pontifícia Universidade Católica do Rio Grande do Sul - PUCRS,
Faculdade de Informática, Av. Ipiranga, Porto Alegre, RS 6681, Brazil
{sandra.abreu,lucas.pugens}@acad.pucrs.br,
aline.vanin@ymail.com, renata.vieira@pucrs.br

Abstract. An important task in Information Extraction is Relation Extraction. Relation Extraction (RE) is the task of detecting and characterizing the semantic relations between entities in the text. This work proposes a new process for the extraction of any relation descriptors between Named Entities (NEs) in the Organization domain, for the Portuguese language, using the Conditional Random Fields (CRF) model. For example, from the following sentence fragment *"Microsoft headquartered in Redmond, [...]"*, we can extract the relation descriptor *"headquartered-in"*, that relates the NEs *"Microsoft"* and *"Redmond"*. We evaluated different features configurations for CRF; the best results were obtained with the inclusion of the *semantic feature* based on the NE category, since this feature could express, in a better way, the kind of relationship between the pair of NEs we want to identify. The proposed process achieved F-measure rates of 45% and 53%, considering the extraction of complete and partial matching, respectively.

Keywords: Information Extraction · Relation Extraction · Named Entity · Named Entity Recognition · Natural Language Processing · Conditional Random Fields

1 Introduction

In many extraction tasks, there is a need to relate known entities, such as Person, Organization and Location. Rather than finding just occurrences of Organization and Person in a news article, Relation Extraction (RE) aims also at identifying if there is, for example, an "acquisition" relation between them [1]. However, the whole RE process is not a trivial task. RE system aims at identifying and classifying semantic relations that occur between (pairs of) entities recognized in a given text [2].

The task of RE from text is one of the main challenges in Information Extraction (IE), given the required language knowledge and the sophistication of the employed language processing techniques. This task contributes with several areas, such as Question Answering, Information Retrieval, summarization, semantic Web annotation, construction and extension of lexical resources and ontologies.

Given the importance of exploring relations for a more accurate understanding of language, the need of further advances in techniques for identifying and extracting

© Springer International Publishing Switzerland 2014
A.L.C. Bazzan and K. Pichara (Eds.): IBERAMIA 2014, LNAI 8864, pp. 108–119, 2014.
DOI: 10.1007/978-3-319-12027-0_9

them emerged; thus, the establishment of the RE task was necessary. There is an increasing interest in RE, mostly motivated by the exponential growth of information available through the Web, which makes the tasks of researching and using such massive amount of data impossible through manual means. That context makes RE an even more complex and relevant research area [3].

For some languages, such as English, there is extensive research and literature regarding RE [4, 5, 6, 7, 8, 9, 10, 11, 12, 13, 14, 15, 16, 17, 18], while for Portuguese there are fewer references to existing work dealing with RE [19, 20, 21, 22, 23, 24, 25, 26]. Moreover, for works in Portuguese, it is not possible to reuse the same tasks for resources and databases developed for English, what limits considerably the advances in the research for Portuguese.

Among the available RE techniques, the Conditional Random Fields (CRFs) models stand out in the statistical machine learning. CRFs are undirected graphical models used to calculate the conditional probability of values on designated output nodes, given values assigned to other designated input nodes [27]. The literature has presented the CRF model as a good alternative, since it has been efficiently applied in several tasks of sequential text processing, including the RE task [5, 6, 7].

In this work, we propose a new process for the extraction of any relation descriptors between Named Entities (NEs) in the Organization domain for Portuguese language, using the CRF model. The relation descriptor to which we refer is the portion of the text that describes the explicit relation between the two NEs, for example, in the sentence *"Facebook co-founder Mark Zuckerberg"*, we can extract the relation descriptor *"co-founder"* that occurs between the NEs *"Facebook"* and *"Mark Zuckerberg"*. We do not have knowledge of any previous work of RE using CRF for Portuguese.

Unlike Open Information Extraction approach [28], in this work the extracted relations that depend on the domain of Organization and the arguments of these relations are the named entities, which also describe the field of study. The Organization domain was chosen because of its potential applicability to different areas such as Natural Language Processing (NLP), Competitive Intelligence, Risk Management, Sales and Marketing, among others.

This work is organized as follows. In Section 2, we discuss the related works. The corpus utilized is described in Section 3. The RE process is detailed in Section 4. In Section 5, the experimental evaluation of the proposed process, the results and the error analysis are presented. Finally, Section 6 presents concluding remarks.

2   Related Work

There is great interest in applying CRFs for a wide range of areas, such as NLP, bioinformatics, computational vision, and others. Among NLP applications, the FIGER system of Entity Recognition [29] stands out, which used CRF in the segmentation stage. In [4], CRF is applied to extract relations between knowledge elements, involving the relation types: "preorder", "illustration" and "analogy". Banko and Etzioni [5] present the O-CRF system based in a CRF model. The authors show that many relations can be categorized using a compact set of lexicon-syntactic patterns. Li et al. [6]

apply the CRF model for extraction of specific relations descriptors between two entities based on general relations.

RE for Portuguese systems is usually rule-based [19, 20, 21]. These systems generally do not make use of machine learning techniques, contrary to the situation for English; they applied simple heuristics that explore evidences of relations between NEs in the texts, comprising lexical, syntactic and semantic analysis, entity types and information from external sources. From the external sources, it is worth highlighting Wikipedia in Portuguese, that provides a great number of structured information, as well as ontologies which provide names. A study on the state of the art of RE was published in [30], situating the Portuguese language within the NLP research field.

In the literature for the Portuguese language, there are three systems of RE between NEs [19, 20, 21] that took part in the Recognition of Relation between Named Entities (ReRelEM) [31] track of HAREM[1]. The REMBRANDT system (Recognition of Named Entities Based on Relations and Detailed Text Analysis) [19] was developed to recognize all types of NEs and relationship between them. This system makes use of Portuguese Wikipedia as an external resource, as well as some grammar rules. The SeRELeP (Recognition of Relations for the Portuguese language) system [20] aimed at recognizing three relation types: "identity", "inclusion" and "location". The steps for identification/classification of NEs were carried out by PALAVRAS parser [32]. SEI-Geo [21] is an extraction system that deals with Named Entity Recognition (NER) concerning only the Location category and its relations. Besides these systems, Batista et al.'s [22] work stands out among the papers dealing with RE for Portuguese. These authors propose an approach of distantly supervised RE between two entities in articles written in Portuguese from Wikipedia.

We defined the extraction of relation descriptors that occur between pairs of NEs of the Organization domain from texts in Portuguese according to Li et al. [6]. In our work, the parameters of the relation have been previously defined (Organization, Person and Location). Moreover, the main challenge of this research is to extract relation descriptors that express any type of relation between the NEs in Portuguese, differently from Li et al.'s [6] work, in which the relation descriptors in English are extracted considering pre-defined classes of relations ("employment" and "personal/social").

Based on the previous works for the English language that apply the CRF model [4, 5, 6, 29], we adapted some of the features used to induce the model for Portuguese. Also, new features were developed based on syntactic rules. In order to clarify the relation descriptor, a fragment of a sentence is shown in (1), in which the NEs *"Ronaldo Lemos"* and *"Creative Commons"* represent the parameters of the relation. In (2), we present the correspondent relation descriptor.

1. *"No próximo Sábado, Ronaldo Lemos, diretor do Creative Commons, irá participar de um debate [...]"*
   (*"Next Saturday, Ronaldo Lemos, director of Creative Commons, will participate in a debate [...]"*)

2. Descriptor Relation: *diretor de o (director of the)*

---

[1] http://www.linguateca.pt/

3   Reference Corpus

In this work, we used a subset of the Golden Collections (GCs) from the two HAREM conferences; in these texts, the NEs were manually annotated. We only analyzed texts that deal with the Organization domain, such as opinion, journalistic, and politic texts, among others. A sum of 516 relation instances was selected to compound the reference corpus (see Table 1). The small amount of instances is due to the difficulty in the manual annotation of the data.

We added to these texts the annotation of the relation descriptors that occur between pairs of NEs that have already been annotated in each sentence of the texts. The manual annotation of the relation descriptors was performed by two linguists, and resulted in four sets of data (ORG-ORG, ORG-PERS, ORG-LOCAL, and ORG-PERS-LOCAL[2]), which were defined according to the categories of the pairs of NEs.

The total number of relation instances and the number of positive and negative instances in each data set are summarized in Table 1. Positive instances are those that explicit relation descriptor between the two NEs. Such instances have been classified as verbal (the main descriptive element is a verb) and non-verbal (the main descriptive element is not a verb), and they are accounted in Table 2. Examples of non-verbal (i.e., expressing an institutional bond relation) and verbal (i.e., expressing the act of founding an Organization) instances are illustrated in Table 3.

Table 1. Number of instances in each data set

Data set	Total	positive	Negative
ORG-ORG	175	90	85
ORG-PERS	171	105	66
ORG-LOCAL	170	109	61
ORG-PERS-LOCAL	516	304	212

Table 2. Classification of relations for each data set

Data Set	Total	Verbal	Non-Verbal
ORG-ORG	90	66	24
ORG-PERS	105	45	60
ORG-LOCAL	109	37	72
ORG-PERS-LOCAL	304	148	156

Table 3. Relation Instance of the ORG-PERS data set

Relation Type	Relation Instance	Relation Descriptor
Non-Verbal	3. *"Mário Vaz, **diretor da** Central Globo [...]"*	***diretor de a***
	(*"Mário Vaz, **director of the** Central Globo [...]"*)	(***director of the***)
Verbal	4. *"Amílcar Cabral **criou o** Partido Africano [...]"*	***criou o***
	(*"Amílcar Cabral **created the** Partido Africano[...]"*)	(***created the***)

---

[2] ORG-PERS-LOCAL data set is the union of the other three data sets.

4   Proposed Process

In this section, we present the process for the extraction of relation descriptors between NEs in Portuguese texts. The steps of pre-processing, the extraction of features and the generation of the CRF model are presented in the next subsections.

4.1   Pre-processing

The first step of the proposed process is tagging the data, when the reference corpus is annotated on Part-Of-Speech (POS), syntactic and semantic information. In this work, the texts have been annotated with the parser PALAVRAS [32], which provides such information. For example, the parser PALAVRAS assigns semantic tags for most nouns, proper names, verbs and some adjectives, such as the semantic tag job/title.

Pre-processing step also involves the NER task for identifying the NEs' categories Person, Organization and Location; they were found to be the most relevant to the Organization domain [33]. As described in Section 3, the reference corpus that we used already had the annotations of the NEs; thus, there was no need for applying an automatic NER system.

At last, in the step for representing the relation instances, the words that compound the relation descriptors were tagged according to the BIO notation [34]. Then, we defined the set of labels {B-REL, I-REL, O}, in which B-REL indicates the beginning of the relation descriptor; I-REL indicates that it is part of the relation descriptor; and O indicates that it is not a part of it. This set of labels was applied to every word of the annotated relation instances (positive and negative) of the four data sets, resulting in a vector with the BIO labels of each word. As an example, we present in (5) the BIO vector corresponding to the sentence fragment shown in (1).

1.   ... Ronaldo_Lemos ,   diretor   de   o   Creative_Commons ...

5. BIO vector: [... O   O   B-REL I-REL I-REL   O ...]

4.2   Features Definition

Distinct sets of features were defined based on the literature [4, 5, 6, 8, 29] and some of them were adapted to Portuguese, as there are not many resources developed for this language. New features based in syntactic information (appositive and direct object), have also been developed, as shown in Table 4.

In the case of CRF for RE, feature vectors were generated for the NEs and also for the words between them. To clarify, we illustrated in (7) the vector corresponding to the *phrasal sequence features* of the fragment of a sentence with the POS tag that is presented in (6):

6. "Ronaldo_Lemos<PROP>, director<N> de<PREP> o<DET> Creative_Commons<PROP>"

7. Vector: ["PROP , N   PREP DET   PROP" ; "N   PREP DET   PROP"]

Table 4. Features sets

Features sets	Description
POS features	- POS tag of the current word in an observation window of 5 words. - 2 consecutive POS tags of the words in an observation window of words.
Lexical Item *features*	- canonic form of the current word in an observation window of 5 words. - 2 consecutive canonic forms of the words in an observation window of 5 words. - number of words in the segment[3].
Syntactic features	- syntactic tag of the current word in an observation window of 5 words. - 2 consecutive syntactic tags of the words in an observation window of 5 words. - if the current word is the head[4] of the segment. - if the current word is in the appositive[5] in an observation window of 5 words. - if the current word is the head of the appositive. - if the current word functions as the direct object[6].
Patterns features	- if the current word is a verb in an observation window of 5 words. - if the current word is a verb followed whether by a preposition, by an article or by a preposition plus an article. - if the current word is a noun and the next one is a preposition. - if the current word is an adverb, or if it is followed whether by a preposition or by a preposition plus an article.
Phrasal sequence features	- POS labels of the sequence of words between the two NEs. - POS labels of the two NEs and also of the words between them.
Semantic features	- if the current word has the semantic tag job/title provided by parser PALAVRAS in an observation window of 5 words. - if the current word is an NE, return to the NE category.
Dictionary features	- list of typical Person titles and jobs, and list of Location words.

4.3   Generation of the Conditional Random Fields Model

This step uses the BIO vector as input, along with features vectors that describe each instance of the input data relation. The CRF model is generated from the features vectors; for every feature it is attributed certain weight, resulting in a weight matrix. Starting from the generated matrix, the CRF is capable of classifying correctly the words that indicate an explicit relation in new texts, which were not tagged yet.

5   Experimental Evaluation

In this section we present the experimental evaluation, which aims at applying the CRF model in the learning step based on the defined features. For the implementation

---

[3] A segment contains the pair of NEs and the sequence of words between them.
[4] 'Head' is the term of the sentence whose properties or relations are designed by the predicate.
[5] Appositive is one or more terms that refer to a noun or pronoun, therefore explaining it.
[6] Direct object is the direct complement of a transitive verb.

of the CRF algorithm, we used the NLTK[7] and Mallet[8] libraries. We performed the cross validation method considering 5-folds in all of the data sets, due to their reduced size, which implies in a very small number of test instances when considering only 10% for testing.

The evaluation followed two criteria: partial matching, when the relation descriptor must be, at least, the same word labeled as *B-REL* in the true relation descriptor; and complete matching, when the relation descriptor extracted is exactly the same as the one manually annotated. In order to have a better understanding of these criteria, Table 5 is presented for the evaluation of the descriptor *"concordar com o"* (*"agree with the"*) from the ORG-ORG set. Note that this descriptor is considered complete matching when the sequence of words that forms it is annotated with *B-REL* label followed by *I-REL* labels, and it is considered partial matching when at least the verb *"concordar"* (*"agree"*) receives the *B-REL* label, followed or not by *I-REL* labels.

Table 5. Example of the evaluation criteria for descriptors from the ORG-ORG data set

Relation Instance	Complete matching	Partial matching
8. *"[...] o PSD passa entre as sombras, ou, em muitos casos, **concordando com o** Governo [...]"* (*"[...] PSD is in the shadows or, in many cases, it **agrees with the** Government [...]"*)	concordar <B-REL> com <I-REL> o <I-REL>	concordar <B-REL> com <O> o <O>

5.1   Experimental Setup

One of the main objectives of this work is to study different features associated with positive and negative instances of the reference corpus. In order to do that, different configurations of input features for the CRF model have been evaluated as follows:

- F1=POS: *POS features* set;
- F2=F1+LEX: addition of *lexical features* set;
- F3=F2+SINT: addition of *syntactic features* set;
- F4=F3+PAD: addition of *patterns features* set;
- F5=F4+FR: addition of *phrasal sequence features* set;
- F6=F5+SEM: addition of *semantic features* set.

The *dictionary features* were used in all experiments, therefore only in few of the bases. For the ORG-PERS data set, a list of jobs was utilized, and for the ORG-LOCAL data set, a list of localization cues was used.

5.2   Results

In this section, we present the results of the RE process applying the CRF model, considering the configurations described in Section 5.1. The performance measures

---

[7] http://nltk.org/
[8] http://mallet.cs.umass.edu/

were: number of correct (#C), Recall (R), Precision (P) and F-measure (F). We also measured the significance level reached for every feature configuration in relation to the previous configuration through a T-test [35].

Overall, the best results in the classification of correct relation descriptors were obtained with the F6 configuration for all data sets. Especially in the *semantic feature* based on the NE category, since this feature could express, in a better way, the kind of relationship between the pair of NEs we want to identify.

Table 6 presents the results of all different configurations for the ORG-ORG data set. The F5 configuration showed significant gains in Precision compared to the previous configuration (level of confidence of 0.950) for both complete and partial matching relation descriptors.

Table 6. Comparison of different configurations for ORG-ORG data set. * indicates that the current value is statistically better than the value expressed in the previous row.

ORG-ORG	Complete matching				Partial matching			
(5-folds)	#C	R	P	F	#C	R	P	F
F1=POS	23	0.25	0.41	0.31	36	0.40	0.65	0.49
F2=F1+LEX	19	0.21	0.44	0.28	28	0.31	0.65	0.42
F3=F2+SINT	24	0.26	0.46	0.33	36	0.40	0.69	0.50
F4=F3+PAD	24	0.26	0.40	0.32	**41**	**0.45**	0.69	0.54
F5=F4 +FR	24	0.26	0.53*	0.35	36	0.40	**0.80***	0.53
F6=F5 +SEM	**27**	**0.30**	**0.56**	**0.39**	38	0.42	0.79	**0.55**

In the results for the ORG-PERS data set, we increased significantly the Precision in the F2 configuration for complete matching descriptors in relation to the previous configuration (level of confidence of 0.990), as illustrated in Table 7. The F3 configuration presented gains in Recall for partial matching descriptors compared to the previous configuration (level of confidence of 0.950).

Table 7. Comparison of different configurations for ORG-PERS data set

ORG-PERS	Complete matching				Partial matching			
(5-folds)	#C	R	P	F	#C	R	P	F
F1=POS	33	0.31	0.41	0.35	51	0.48	0.63	0.55
F2=F1+LEX	37	0.35	0.58*	0.44	44	0.41	0.69	0.52
F3=F2+SINT	47	0.44	0.65	0.53	**56**	**0.53***	0.77	**0.63**
F4=F3+PAD	45	0.42	0.61	0.50	56	0.53	0.76	0.62
F5=F4+FR	45	0.42	0.64	0.51	55	0.52	0.78	0.62
F6=F5+SEM	**50**	**0.47**	**0.71**	**0.57**	**56**	**0.53**	**0.80**	**0.63**

The results for the ORG-LOCAL data set, shown in Table 8, presented gains for the complete matching descriptors: F2 configuration increased both the Precision and the F-measure (level of confidence of 0.950 and 0.975, respectively). The F6 configuration also stood out in Precision compared to the previous configuration (level of confidence of 0.950).

Table 8. Comparison of different configurations for ORG-LOCAL data set

ORG-LOCAL	Complete matching				Partial matching			
(5-folds)	#C	R	P	F	#C	R	P	F
F1=POS	30	0.27	0.50	0.35	40	0.36	0.66	0.47
F2=F1+LEX	41	0.37	0.64*	0.47*	**47**	**0.43**	0.73	**0.54**
F3=F2+SINT	39	0.35	0.60	0.45	46	0.42	0.71	0.53
F4=F3+PAD	37	0.33	0.57	0.42	44	0.40	0.68	0.50
F5=F4+FR	39	0.35	0.66	0.46	43	0.39	0.72	0.51
F6=F5+SEM	**43**	**0.39**	**0.76***	**0.52**	45	0.41	**0.80**	**0.54**

Finally, Table 9 presents gains of the F2 configuration compared to the previous one for the ORG-PERS-LOCAL set (level of confidence of 0.995): for the complete matching descriptors, the rates of Recall, Precision and F-measure increased.

Table 9. Comparison of different configurations for ORG-PERS-LOCAL data set

ORG-PERS-LOCAL	Complete matching				Partial matching			
(5-folds)	#C	R	P	F	#C	R	P	F
F1=POS	71	0.23	0.38	0.28	120	0.39	0.64	0.48
F2=F1+LEX	101	0.33*	0.57*	0.42*	129	0.41	0.69	0.52
F3=F2+SINT	105	**0.34**	0.56	0.42	**132**	**0.43**	0.71	0.53
F4=F3+PAD	104	**0.34**	0.57	0.42	**132**	**0.43**	0.72	**0.54**
F5=F4+FR	101	0.33	0.62	0.43	117	0.38	0.72	0.49
F6=F5+SEM	**106**	**0.34**	**0.64**	**0.45**	125	0.41	**0.75**	0.53

5.3   Error Analysis

In the evaluation of results, we noticed the identification of false-positive examples, which are relation descriptors formed by words that do not express a relation between the NEs. In general, the data sets present only few cases of false-positives; it occurs due to the fact that the CRF model is very precise in the process of tagging the relation descriptors.

One of the main errors in the classification of examples as false-positives was the identification of verbal relation descriptors that do not express an explicit relation between pairs of NEs. This kind of error occurred most frequently in the ORG-ORG data set. Most of the descriptors from this set are verbal; thus, such result is coherent. Table 10 illustrates a false-positive example (9) from the ORG-ORG data set, in which the NE *"Associação Industrial do Viseu"* was interpreted as referent to the verb *"ser"* (*"to be"*), when, in fact, its referent is the previous NE *"Almeida Henriques"*.

We also performed an analysis of the false-negative examples, relation descriptors that express a relation between the NEs and that have not been tagged in the data sets. In Table 10, we show a false-negative example of verbal relation descriptor (10) of the ORG-LOCAL data set. In this example, there were elements interposed between the NE *"Legião da Boa Vontade"* and the relation descriptor *"foi fundada no"* (*"was founded in"*), a fact that made its identification more difficult.

Table 10. Examples of extracted relation descriptor

Relation instance	Output Classification	Reference Classification
9. *"Almeida Henriques, presidente da Associação Industrial do Viseu, é o novo rosto do Conselho."* (*"Almeida Henriques, president of the Associação Industrial do Viseu, is the new face of the Conselho."*)	ser <B-REL>	ser <O>
10. *"A Legião da Boa Vontade, instituição educacional, cultural e beneficiente, **foi fundada no** Brasil [...]"* (*"The Legião da Boa Vontade, educational, cultural and beneficent institution, **was founded in** Brazil [...]"*)	ser <O> fundar <O> em <O> o <O>	ser <B-REL> fundar <I-REL> em <I-REL> o <I-REL>

6   Concluding Remarks

We proposed a process for the extraction of relation descriptors between NEs, from the Portuguese language, applying the CRF model. Unlike other works for Portuguese [19, 20, 21, 22], the relations classified by the CRF model are not known; only the NEs' categories were previously defined. To the best of our knowledge, this work is the first one to use Linear-chain CRFs for RE to Portuguese. Due to the lack of common data, it is difficult to make a comparison with other works. However, we can get an idea of the levels achieved in other studies for Portuguese (Table 11).

Table 11. Results of the RE works for Portuguese

Works	Corpora	Results (%)
SeRELeP	HAREM/ReRelEM GC	All relations F=36%
REMBRANDT	HAREM/ReRelEM GC	All relations F=45%
SEI-Geo	HAREM/ReRelEM GC	All relations F=27%
Batista et al.	DBpedia: 97.988 sentences	Relation average F=55.6%
Proposed Process	subset from HAREM GCs	ORG-PERS-LOCAL: Complete matching F=45% Partial matching F=53%

We can see in Table 11 that our results are not distant from other works dealing with Portuguese; SeRELeP, REMBRANT and SEI-Geo considered three specific relations from ReRelEM; Batista et al. [22] defined ten relation types from DBPédia; and our process treats any explicit relations between NEs.

In this work, different feature configurations for CRF were defined and evaluated. We are now able to conclude that the *semantic feature* based on the NE category provides us with relevant information for the extraction of relation descriptors.

In future works, we intend to apply other machine learning techniques for RE, such as K-Nearest-Neighbors [22] and Support Vector Machine [18], as well as to analyze the potential of each feature, and to broaden the scope of the text for the observation of features not only between NEs, but also before and after the descriptor. We also look forward to performing an extension of the proposed process for other language.

Acknowledgments. We thank the FAPERGS and CAPES for their financial support.

References

1. Sarawagi, S.: Information Extraction. Foundations and Trends in Databases **1**(3), 261–377 (2008)
2. Jurafsky, D., Martin, J.H.: Speed and Language Processing: An Introduction to Natural Language Processing, Computational Linguistics and Speech Recognition. Prentice Hall series in Artificial Inteligence, 2nd edn. Pearson Education Ltd., London (2009)
3. Etzioni, O., Fader, A., Christensen, J., Soderland, S.: Mausam: Open Information Extraction: the second generation. In: Twenty-second International Joint Conference on Artificial Intelligence, IJCAI, pp. 3–10 (2011)
4. Chen, Y., Zheng, Q., Wang, W., Chen, Y.: Knowledge element relation extraction using conditional random fields. In: CSCWD, pp 245–250 (2010)
5. Banko, M., Etzioni, O.: The tradeoffs between open and traditional relation extraction. In: McKeown, K., Moore, J.D., Teufel, S., Allan, J., Furui, S. (eds) ACL, The Association for Computer, Linguistics, Bulgaria, pp. 28–36 (2010)
6. Li, Y., Jiang, J., Chieu, H.L., Chai, K.M.A.: Extracting relation descriptors with conditional random fields. In: Proceedings of 5th International Joint Conference on NLP. Asian Federation of NLP, Chiang Mai, pp. 392–400 (2011)
7. Culotta, A., McCallum, A., Betz, J.: Integrating probabilistic extraction models and data mining to discover relations and patterns in text. In: Proceedings of the Main Conference on Human Language Technology Conference of the North American chapter of the Association of Computational Linguistics, HLT-NAACL 2006, pp. 296–303. Association for Computational Linguistics, Stroudsburg (2006)
8. Mintz, M., Bills, S., Snow, R., Jurafsky, D.: Distant supervision for relation extraction without labeled data. In: Proceedings of the joint conference of the 47th Annual Meeting of the ACL and the 4th International Joint Conference on NLP of the AFNLP, ACL 2009, vol. 2, pp. 1003–1011. Association for Computational Linguistics, Stroudsburg (2009)
9. Agichtein, E., Gravano, L.: SNOWBALL: Extracting relations from large plain-text collections. In: 5th ACM International Conference on Digital Libraries, pp 85–94 (2000)
10. Brin, S.: Extracting patterns and relations from the World Wide Web. In: Atzeni, P., Mendelzon, A.O., Mecca, G. (eds.) WebDB 1998. LNCS, vol. 1590, pp. 172–183. Springer, Heidelberg (1999)
11. Etzioni, O., Cafarella, M.J., Downey, D., Kok, S., Popescu, A.M., Shaked, T., Soderland, S., Weld, D.S., Yates, A.: Web-scale information extraction in knowitall: preliminary results. In: WWW, pp. 100–110 (2004)
12. Fader, A., Soderland, S., Etzioni, O.: Identifying relations for open information extraction. In: EMNLP, pp. 1535–1545 (2011)
13. Hasegawa, T., Sekine, S., Grishman, R.: Discovering relations among named entities from large corpora. In: ACL 2004: Proceedings of the 42nd Annual Meeting on Association for Computational Linguistics, pp. 415. Association for Computational Linguistics (2004)
14. Hobbs, J.R., Appelt, D., Bear, J., Israel, D., Kameyama, M., Stickel, M., Tyson, M.: Fastus: a cascaded finite-state transducer for extracting information from natural-language text. In: Roche, E., Schabes, Y. (eds.) Finite-state Language Processing, pp. 383–406. MIT Press, Cambridge (1997)
15. Hoffmann, R., Zhang, C., Ling, X., Zettlemoyer, L.S., Weld, D.S.: Knowledge-based Weak Supervision for Information Extraction of Overlapping Relations, pp. 541–550. ACL, Stroudsburg (2011)
16. Sun, A.: A two-stage bootstrapping algorithm for relation extraction. In: Proceedings of RANLP 2009—recent advances in NLP, Borovets, Bulgaria (2009)

17. Wu, F., Weld, D.S.: Open information extraction using Wikipedia. In: ACL, Stroudsburg, pp. 118–127 (2010)
18. Culotta, A., Sorensen, J.: Dependency tree kernels for relation extraction. In: Proceedings of the 42nd Meeting of the Association for Computational Linguistics (ACL 2004), main volume, Barcelona, pp. 423–429 (2004)
19. Cardoso, N.: REMBRANDT — Reconhecimento de Entidades Mencionadas Baseado em Relações e ANálise Detalhada do Texto. In: Mota, C., Santos, D. (eds) Segundo HAREM, Chap. 11. Linguateca, pp. 195–211 (2008)
20. Brucksen, M., Souza, J.G.C., Vieira, R., Rigo, S.: Sistema SeRELeP para o Reconhecimento de Relações entre Entidades Mencionadas. In: Mota, C., Santos, D. (eds) Segundo HAREM, Chap. 14. Linguateca, pp. 247–260 (2008)
21. Chaves, M.S.: Geo-ontologias e padrões para reconhecimento de locais e de suas relações em textos: o SEI-Geo no Segundo HAREM. In: Mota, C., Santos, D. (eds) Segundo HAREM, Chap. 13. Linguateca, pp. 231–245 (2008)
22. Batista, D.S., Forte, D., Silva, R., Martins, B., Silva, M.: Extracção de relações semânticas de textos em português explorando a DBpédia e a Wikipédia. Linguamatica 5(1), 41–57 (2013)
23. Santos, D., Mamede, N., Baptista, J.: Extraction of family relations between entities. In: Barbosa, L. S., Correia, M. P. (ed) Proceedings of the INForum 2010—II Simpósio de Informática, Braga, Portugal, pp. 549–560 (2010)
24. Taba, L.S., de Mcdeiros Caseli, H.: Automatic Hyponymy Identification from Brazilian Portuguese Texts. In: Caseli, H., Villavicencio, A., Teixeira, A., Perdig\{a}o, F. (eds.) PROPOR 2012. LNCS, vol. 7243, pp. 186–192. Springer, Heidelberg (2012)
25. Ferreira, L., Oliveira, C., Teixeira, A., Cunha, J.: Extração de informação de relatórios médicos. Linguamatica 1(1), 89–101 (2009)
26. Oliveira, H. G., Costa, H., Gomes, P.: Extracção de conhecimento léxico-semântico a partir de resumos da Wikipédia. In: Barbosa, L. S., Correia, M. P. (ed) Proceedings of the INForum 2010—II Simpósio de Informática, Braga, Portugal, pp. 537–548 (2010)
27. Lafferty, J.D., McCallum, A., Pereira, F.C.N.: Conditional Random Fields: probabilistic models for segmenting and labeling sequence data. In: Proceedings of the Eighteenth International Conference on Machine Learning, ICML 2001, pp. 282–289. Morgan Kaufmann Publishers Inc., San Francisco (2001)
28. Banko, M., Cafarella, M.J., Soderl, S., Broadhead, M., Etzioni, O.: Open information extraction from the Web. In: IJCAI, pp. 2670–2676 (2007)
29. Ling, X., Weld, D.S.: Fine-grained entity recognition. In: Proceeding of the Twenty-Sixty AAAI Conference on Artificial Intelligence, AAAI, Toronto, Ontario, Canada (2012)
30. Abreu, S.C., Bonamigo, T.L., Vieira, R.: A review on relation extraction with an eye on portuguese. Journal of the Brazilian Computer Society 19, 553–571 (2013)
31. Freitas, C., Santos, D., Oliveira, H.G., Carvalho, P., Mota, C.: Relações semânticas do ReRelEM: além das entidades no Segundo HAREM, Chap. 4. Linguateca, pp. 75–94 (2008)
32. Bick, E.: The parsing system PALAVRAS. In: Automatic Grammatical Analysis of Portuguese in a Constraint Grammar Frame-work. University of Arhus, Arhus (2000)
33. Collovini, S., Grando, F., Souza, M., Freitas, L., Vieira, R.: Semantic relations extraction in the organization domain. In: Proceedings of IADIS International Conference on Applied Computing, Rio de Janeiro, pp. 99–106 (2011)
34. Ramshaw, L.A., Marcus, M.P.: Text chunking using transformation-based learning. In: Proceedings of the Third ACL Workshop on Very Large Corpora, Cambridge, MA, USA, pp. 82–94 (1995)
35. Hogg, R.V., Craig, A.T.: Introduction to Mathematical Statistics. Macmillan, New York (1978)

Content and Style Features for Automatic Detection of Users' Intentions in Tweets

Helena Gómez-Adorno[1]([⊠]), David Pinto[2], Manuel Montes[3],
Grigori Sidorov[1], and Rodrigo Alfaro[4]

[1] Centro de Investigación en Computación, Instituto Politécnico
Nacional, Mexico, Mexico
helena.adorno@gmail.com, sidorov@cic.ipn.mx
[2] Facultad de Ciencias de la Computación,Benemérita Universidad
Autonóma de Puebla, Puebla, Mexico
dpinto@cs.buap.mx
[3] Coordinación de Ciencias Computacionales, Instituto de Astrofísica,
Óptica y Electrónica, Puebla, Mexico
mmontesg@ccc.inaoep.mx
[4] Escuela de Ingeniería Informática,Pontificia Universidad Católica
de Valparaíso, Valparaíso, Chile
rodrigo.alfaro@ucv.cl

Abstract. The aim of this paper is to evaluate the use of content and
style features in automatic classification of intentions of Tweets. For this
we propose different style features and evaluate them using a machine
learning approach. We found that although the style features by themselves are useful for the identification of the intentions of tweets, it is
better to combine such features with the content ones. We present a set
of experiments, where we achieved a 9.46 % of improvement on the overall performance of the classification with the combination of content and
style features as compared with the content features.

Keywords: Short texts · Text classification · Twitter · Detection of
intention

1 Introduction

Nowadays, social networks have become an important interaction media among
worldwide users. Among the most used social networks is Twitter, a microblogging social network, with over 200 million users and about 400 million posts
per day [1]. Twitter is used for various purposes by a large number of users,
which may found themselves overwhelmed with the constantly growing amount

This work was done under partial support of the Mexican Government (CONACYT-
134186, CONACYT grant #308719, SNI, COFAA-IPN, SIP-IPN 20144274) and
FP7-PEOPLE-2010-IRSES: "Web Information Quality Evaluation Initiative (WIQ-
EI)" European Commission project 269180.

© Springer International Publishing Switzerland 2014
A.L.C. Bazzan and K. Pichara (Eds.): IBERAMIA 2014, LNAI 8864, pp. 120–128, 2014.
DOI: 10.1007/978-3-319-12027-0_10

of received messages. In our personal experience, this is a major problem when the messages are accessed via mobile devices.

Some studies of Twitter identify that people use microblogging to talk about their daily activities and to seek or share information [2], making it a rich source for text analysis in several areas. Therefore, classification of tweets is an active research field. There are numerous research works on this social network in the area of sentiment analysis [3–5], predicting box office revenues [6] or the outcome of political elections [7], among others.

The classification of Twitter users intentions [8] is becoming a new opportunity area of research. Our aim is to identify intention or purpose of users typing a tweet. "Intention" is defined as an "agent's specific purpose in performing an action or series of actions, the end or goal that is aimed at" [9]. The automatic classification of tweets into intention categories may improve navigation and search for twitter users, especially when using a mobile device. In order to classify the user intention we use a taxonomy of 8 categories of the main user intentions in Twitter proposed in [10]. This taxonomy allows to classify messages in categories such as News Report (NR), News Opinion (NO), Publicity (PU), General Opinion (GO), Share Location/Event (SL), Chat (CH), Question (QU) and Personal Message (PM).

Most of the systems and approaches implemented to automatically detect the intention of the twitter message use a content based representation (raw word representation, user meta-information) as features to build a model for intention detection [10,11]. The contribution of this paper consists in analyzing the relevance of content and style attributes for this task. Based on tasks such as Authorship Attribution [12], Profiling [13] and Sentiment Analysis [5,14] we consider that the style plays an important role and complements the content information. The style information depends on the presence of pronouns, adjectives, verbal time, url and hashtags. We build a tweet representation extracting a set of content (words, words n-grams) and style (presence of hashtags, presence of emoticons, POS tags) features, which are subsequently used in a machine learning algorithm in order to built a classifier based on several labeled examples.

The obtained results show that the models created with the content and style features together overcome the results of the models using only words as features. Besides, the models created with the style features are domain independent, since they are no longer based on specific words but only on the language structure.

The rest of this paper is organized as follows. First we present an overview of related works on twitter text classification in Section 2. In Section 3 we explain our strategy for feature selection. In Section 4 the experimental setup is described and the obtained results are discussed. Finally, conclusions and future work directions are given in Section 5.

2   Related Work

There are a lot of research work in topic text classification (e.g. health, education, politics), hashtag recommendation, sentiment analysis; but there are a lack of studies where user intentions in Twitter are identified. In [2] the authors analyze the aggregate behavior across communities of users to describe a community intention. They also propose a user intention taxonomy based on the link structure of a community network. Even though, it does not propose an automatic methodology, this work laid the foundations of the task of detection of user intentions in Twitter.

In [15] the authors classify the tweets based on their content in 9 different twitter content type categories. They study in which way the tweets' content varies according to the users activity, personal networks and usage patterns. In the same way, in [8] the authors present a taxonomy of tweets purposes. Their aim was to identify user purposes in writing single tweets. Although, both works present an interesting taxonomy for detection of user intention in writing single tweets, none of them present an automatic method for classification.

With the purpose of improving of information filtering, in [11] the authors classify tweets in 5 general types of content (related to intention). They propose an automatic method using a set of domain-specific features extracted from the author's profile and text. In addition, they claim that corporate and personal Twitter users have different intentions. Such features, in comparison to the style features proposed here require external resources and user profile information.

In [10] the authors define a user intention taxonomy and an automatic classification model. They transform the tweets into a Vector Space Model, where the words are the features represented by the ("exists" or "does not exists") boolean values. Their results show that the tweets emitting an opinion were easily confused and consequently achieve low classification performance. There is a high overlap between two categories, thus leading to confusion of the classifier, given that the *News Opinion* tweets contain much of the content that the *News Report* expresses. By analyzing this phenomenon we propose the use of the style features which will be useful in this problem, since it has been proven to be helpful features in some related problems [11,16].

Another related problem is addressed in [16], where the authors use features related to certain content keywords in order to identify real-time intentions tweets. For this binary problem (tweet express or does not express an intention) the authors use a classification algorithm with the content keywords features, certain verbs, temporal expressions and POS tags with their position with respect to the content keywords. The POS features used in this task were useful, when they are employed in conjunction with other features.

3   Feature Selection

The aim of this work is to evaluate content and style features to identify user intentions when writing a single tweet. The features were selected taking into account the way in which each of them may represent certain classes. For example, Twitter users express themselves differently when sharing a *Personal Message* (PM) or *Chats* (CH) than when posting *News Reports* (NR) or *Publicity* (PU). In general, PM tweets tend to have mentions to other users and emoticons, while NR tweets are written in a clear form and usually using URLs to complement the news. In this sense a feature for discriminating PM tweets may be the use of mentions and emoticons, and viceversa the absence of such features will possibly discriminate NR tweets.

Let us consider the use of POS tags in tweets. For example, for the intention *Share Location/Event* (SL), we observe that the use of the verb in the gerund form is used frequently. Hence, we decided to label the tweets with their POS tags. The POS tags provide grammatical information of the words in the messages; in this way the classifier may be able to identify, say, SL messages by the presence of verbs in gerund forms among others. Interrogative pronouns are also identified by the POS tagger. Such words are useful for the identification of *Question Messages* (QU).

For the case of the opinion tweets (*News Opinion* and *General Opinion*), our hypothesis is that the presence of adjectives to express an opinion is very important. Therefore, these classes can be identified by the presence of such grammatical category. In the same way, function words (pronouns, prepositions, conjunctions, determiners, auxiliary verbs) have been effectively used for capturing author style in the task of authorship attribution [17]. We believe that function words tags may also be helpful features for the identification of user intentions in tweets.

Formally, tweets are represented as a vector $V = \{f_1, f_2, f_3, ..., f_n\}$, where n is the total number of features f_i. The set of features is divided into two subsets V_1, $V_2 \subset V$ where V_1 represents the content features and V_2 represents the style features. An explanation of the details for each subset follows.

3.1 Subset of Content Features

The content features are represented by the words in the message, so we use bag-of-words and n-grams representations for these features. In order to assign weights to each feature, we have evaluated three different weight schemata: the term frequency (TF), the term frequency/inverse document frequency (TF/IDF), and the term presence (TP). Nevertheless, the performance of the classifier is practically the same for all types of values, probably due to the length of the tweet, which is 140 characters maximum. Hence, we decided to use the TP for the values of each feature; the presence of a word is identified with the value 1 and it's absence with the value 0.

3.2 Subset of Style Features

In this section we present the style features used in this work. For this purpose we extracted 4 style features, which were previously used in the related task of sentiment analysis [4]. For each tweet we identify: (a) initial mentions (presence of @*user* at the beginning of the tweet), (b) mention inside the message (presence of @*user* inside the tweet), (c) URL, and (d) Emoticons. The four previous features have binary values (BF, binary features), in the sequel 4BF, so the presence or absence of each one is identified with the values 1 or 0 respectively in the feature vector. Words and punctuation marks are also included in the features vector in the same way as the 4 previously explained features, indicating their presence and their absence with 1 and 0, respectively.

In addition, tweets are grammatically tagged using Freeling[1] for Spanish, obtaining the Part-Of-Speech (POS) tags of each word in the tweet. Freeling uses the EAGLES[2] Standard in order to represent the grammatical information of words. Each label is composed of at most 8 digits, where the first digit represents the grammatical category and the rest of the digits represent the attributes of each grammatical category. The total number of POS tags used was 240. The POS tags become additional features in the feature set, and the presence or absence of each one is indicated with the values 1 or 0 in the feature vectors, respectively.

4   Experimental Results

In this section we describe the experimental setup and the results obtained when evaluating the different features considered in our approach.

4.1   Experimental Setup

The dataset used in this study is the one described in [10]. The dataset consists of 5,209 messages manually classified by the authors of [10] into the following classes: News Report (NR), News Opinion (NO), Publicity (PU), General Opinion (GO), Share Location/Event (SL), Chat (CH), Question (QU) and Personal Message (PM). The class distribution given in Figure 1. The tweets are written in Spanish and contain mentions referring to: *Banco Santander* (a bank), *Pontificia Universidad Católica de Valparaíso* (a university), *El Mercurio* (a newspaper), *La Tercera* (a newspaper), *Movistar* (a telecommunication company) and a set of random tweets.

We used seven different configurations for our test dataset. First, we evaluated the classification performance when using only the content features (only words unigrams or words + word bigrams + word trigrams). Second, the classification performance was evaluated with the style features (only 4BF or POS + 4BF or POS + POS bigrams + POS trigrams + 4BF). Finally, we have mixed the content and style features, obtaining two different feature sets: words + POS + 4BF or Word_POS + Word_POS bigrams + Word_POS trigrams + 4BF. So, each feature type was evaluated independently in order to determine which one is most suitable for this task. Thereafter, the combination of the types of features was evaluated in order to assess whether they complement each other to improve the classification accuracy.

For the classification process we used a machine learning approach. The experiments were conducted using the SVM algorithm provided in the WEKA[3] data mining tool. The training phase was performed on the entire data set using

---

[1] http://nlp.lsi.upc.edu/freeling/
[2] http://nlp.lsi.upc.edu/freeling/doc/tagsets/tagset-es.html
[3] http://www.cs.waikato.ac.nz/ml/weka/

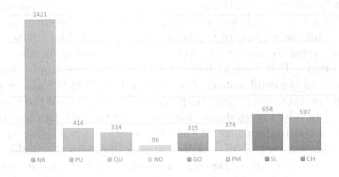

Fig. 1. Class distribution in the dataset.

tenfold cross-validation. The evaluation metrics used were the $F1$ and $F1_\mu$ measures :

$$F1 = 2 \cdot \frac{precision \cdot recall}{precision + recall} \tag{1}$$

$$F1_\mu = 2 \cdot \frac{precision_\mu \cdot recall_\mu}{precision_\mu + recall_\mu} \tag{2}$$

where:
tp =number of true positives (correct class prediction),
tn =number of true negatives (correct negative prediction),
fp =number of false positives (incorrect class prediction),
fn =number of false negatives (incorrect negative prediction),
$i =$ number of classes,

$$precision = \frac{tp}{tp + fp}, \tag{3}$$

$$recall = \frac{tp}{tp + fn}, \tag{4}$$

$$precision_\mu = \frac{\sum_{i=1}^{|c|} tp_i}{\sum_{i=1}^{|c|} tp_i + fp_i}, \tag{5}$$

$$recall_\mu = \frac{\sum_{i=1}^{|c|} tp_i}{\sum_{i=1}^{|c|} tp_i + fn_i}. \tag{6}$$

4.2   Evaluation

In this section we present the evaluation of the classification using the above-mentioned seven feature sets. With this experiment we aimed to assess the benefits of using style features such as POS and POS n-grams over content features such as words and word n-grams.

As mentioned in section 3, in Figure 2 the label 4BF refers to the four features previously presented: initial mention, mention inside the message, URL, emoticons. The labels "words and words n-gram" refer to the entire set of words of the corpus and the n-gram of words, with $n = 1, 2, 3$. The labels "POS and POS n-grams" refer to the set of POS tags corresponding to the words and the n-grams of such POS tags with $n = 1, 2, 3$. Finally, the label "(Word_POS) n-grams" refers to the combination of a word and its POS tag as one feature.

The results presented in Figure 2 depict the $F1_\mu$ measure of the classification over the data sets. The Figure shows that the use of the 4BF by themselves does not outperform the performance of the classification when using the content features. On the contrary, POS + 4BF features improves the performance by 6.49% over the words' features. Besides, the combination of a word with its POS tag plus the 4BF achieves a 9.46% of improvement over the Words features.

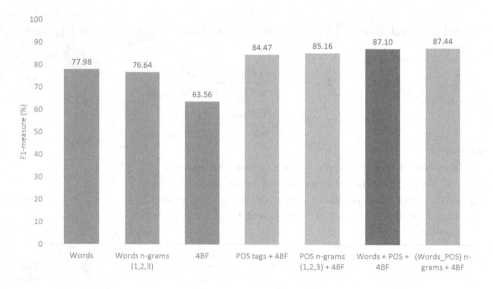

Fig. 2. Classification performance obtained with different feature sets

Table 1 presents the detailed results, in $F1$ measure terms, for each type of feature sets per class. We can observe that the 4BF by themselves do not identify the tweets in the classes *Publicity, Question, News Opinion* and *General Opinion*. On the other hand, such features are able to identify the classes *News Report* and *Chat* with 81.4% and 68.1% of $F1$ measures, respectively. In addition, the style features (POS n-grams + 4BF) outperform the content features (words and word n-grams) in almost all classes, with the exception of the *General Opinion* and *Publicity* classes. The class that benefits the most from the style features is *Question*, achieving an $F1$ measure of 87.5% with such features and only 53.6% with the content features. Other classes such as *News Report, Personal Messages, Share Location* and *Chat* also benefit from the style features. On the contrary, such classes as *Publicity*, *News Opinion*, and *General Opinion* need both the content features and the style features in order to improve the classification performance.

In Table 1, is observed that the use of POS features for the classes *Publicity*, *News Opinion*, and *General Opinion* did not result in an improvement of the classification. It is possible that the tagger does not identify well the grammatical tags due to the use of an informal language in tweets. These phenomena may bring as a result a decrease of the classification accuracy.

Table 1. $F1$ measures obtained with the different configuration of the feature set

Features	NR	PU	QU	NO	GO	PM	SL	CH
Words	88.6	80.0	53.6	49.7	39.4	48.6	94.8	62.9
Word n-grams	87.8	79.5	41.5	40.9	22.6	48.5	93.7	62.0
4BF	81.4	0.00	0.00	0.00	0.00	58.1	24.2	68.1
POS tags + 4BF	93.4	71.7	87.6	48.7	34.3	62.4	95.7	80.3
POS tag n-grams + 4BF	94.4	74.9	87.6	40.0	44.0	63.5	96.7	80.3
Words + POS tags + 4BF	95.4	80.4	**88.0**	53.6	**48.7**	68.4	96.9	81.4
(Word_POS) n-grams + 4BF	**95.6**	**80.7**	**88.0**	**55.6**	46.3	**68.4**	**97.1**	**82.9**

5   Conclusion and Future Work

We have presented an approach for automatic classification of tweets taking into account user intention categories. We used style and content features of tweets. This kind of classification can be used for filtering out tweets by user interests and facilitate queries and navigation.

Experimental results show that the POS features improve the performance of the classification as compared with only the words features. Besides, the combination of the word with its POS tag performs significantly better with this set of classes.

We are currently working on the selection of new features that could improve the classification of certain classes such as *News Opinion*, *General Opinion* and *Personal Message*. For example, we consider other style features, such as syntactic *n*-grams, that were successfully used in the task of authorship attribution and author profiling [18].

References

1. Wickre, K.: Celebrating #Twitter7. Twitter Blog (2013), https://blog.twitter.com/2013/celebrating-twitter7
2. Java, A., Song, X., Finin, T., Tseng, B.: Why we twitter: Understanding microblogging usage and communities. In: Proceedings of the 9th WebKDD and 1st SNA-KDD 2007 Workshop on Web Mining and Social Network Analysis. ACM (2007)

3. Agarwal, A., Xie, B., Vovsha, I., Rambow, O., Passonneau, R.: Sentiment analysis of Twitter data. In: Proceedings of the Workshop on Languages in Social Media. ACL, Stroudsburg (2011)
4. Pandey, V., Iyer, C.: Sentiment analysis of microblogs. Technical report (2009)
5. Jain, H., Mogadala, A., Varma, V.: Sielers : Feature analysis and polarity classification of expressions from Twitter and SMS data. In: Proceedings of the Seventh International Workshop on Semantic Evaluation (SemEval 2013). Second Joint Conference on Lexical and Computational Semantics (*SEM), vol. 2. ACL (2013)
6. Asur, S., Huberman, B.A.: Predicting the future with social media. In: Proceedings of the 2010 IEEE/WIC/ACM International Conference on Web Intelligence and Intelligent Agent Technology, vol. 1. IEEE Computer Society (2010)
7. Diakopoulos, N.A., Shamma, D.A.: Characterizing debate performance via aggregated Twitter sentiment. In: Proceedings of the SIGCHI Conference on Human Factors in Computing Systems. ACM (2010)
8. Alhadi, A.C., Staab, S., Gottron, T.: Exploring user purpose writing single tweets. In: WebSci 2011: Proceedings of the 3rd International Conference on Web Science. ACM (2011)
9. Website: Wikipedia, the free encyclopedia (2014), http://en.wikipedia.org/wiki/Intention
10. Martis, M., Alfaro, R.: Clasificación automática de la intención del usuario en mensajes de Twitter. In: I Workshop en Procesamiento Automatizado de Textos y Corpora, Sausalito, Viña del (March 2012)
11. Sriram, B., Fuhry, D., Demir, E., Ferhatosmanoglu, H., Demirbas, M.: Short text classification in Twitter to improve information filtering. In: Proceedings of the 33rd International ACM SIGIR Conference on Research and Development in Information Retrieval. ACM (2010)
12. Stamatatos, E.: A survey of modern authorship attribution methods. J. Am. Soc. Inf. Sci. Technol. 60(3) (2009)
13. Rangel, F., Rosso, P.: Use of language and author profiling: Identification of gender and age. Natural Language Processing and Cognitive Science (2013)
14. Barbosa, L., Feng, J.: Robust sentiment detection on Twitter from biased and noisy data. In: Proceedings of the 23rd International Conference on Computational Linguistics: Posters. ACL, pp. 36–44 (2010)
15. Naaman, M., Boase, J., Lai, C.H.: Is it really about me?: Message content in social awareness streams. In: Proceedings of the 2010 ACM Conference on Computer Supported Cooperative Work. ACM (2010)
16. Banerjee, N., Chakraborty, D., Joshi, A., Mittal, S., Rai, A., Ravindran, B.: Towards analyzing micro-blogs for detection and classification of real-time intentions. In: Breslin, J.G., Ellison, N.B., Shanahan, J.G., Tufekci, Z., (eds.) Proceedings of International AAAI Conference on Weblogs and Social Media. The AAAI Press (2012)
17. Zhao, Y., Zobel, J.: Effective and Scalable Authorship Attribution Using Function Words. In: Lee, G.G., Yamada, A., Meng, H., Myaeng, S.-H. (eds.) AIRS 2005. LNCS, vol. 3689, pp. 174–189. Springer, Heidelberg (2005)
18. Sidorov, G., Velasquez, F., Stamatatos, E., Gelbukh, A., Chanona-Hernández, L.: Syntactic n-grams as machine learning features for natural language processing. Expert Syst. Appl. 41(3) (2014)

Size Does Not Matter. Frequency Does. A Study of Features for Measuring Lexical Complexity

Rodrigo Wilkens[✉], Alessandro Dalla Vecchia[✉], Marcely Zanon Boito,
Muntsa Padró, and Aline Villavicencio

Institute of Informatics, Federal University of Rio Grande do Sul,
Porto Alegre, Brazil
{rodrigo.wilkens,advecchia,mzboito,muntsa.padro,
avillavicencio}@inf.ufrgs.br

Abstract. Lexical simplification aims at substituting complex words by simpler synonyms or semantically close words. A first step to perform such task is to decide which words are complex and need to be replaced. Though this is a very subjective task, and not trivial at all, there is agreement among linguists of what makes a word more difficult to read and understand. Cues like the length of the word or its frequency in the language are accepted as informative to determine the complexity of a word. In this work, we carry out a study of the effectiveness of those cues by using them in a classification task for separating words as simple or complex. Interestingly, our results show that word length is not important, while corpus frequency is enough to correctly classify a large proportion of the test cases (F-measure over 80 %).

Keywords: Lexical simplification · Lexical complexity · Feature selection

1 Introduction

Text Simplification (TS) is an area which has attracted much attention in recent years [1–4]. An important application is to make texts more accessible to people with comprehension disabilities as on the Practical Simplification of English Text project which focuses on aphasic patients.

Text Simplification typically addresses lexical and/or syntactic simplification, and in this paper we focus on the former. A common pipeline for a Lexical Simplification system, according to [5], includes at least three major components: (i) complexity analysis: a selection of words or phrases in a text that are considered complex for the reader and/or task at hand; (ii) substitute lookup: a search for adequate replacement for words or phrases deemed complex in context, e.g., taking synonyms (with the same sense) from a thesaurus or finding similar words in a corpus using distributional similarity metrics; and (iii) context-based ranking: the ranking of candidate substitutes according to their simplicity to the reader.

In this paper we focus in the very first step of this pipeline: determining whether a word is complex and should be replaced for a simpler synonym or

© Springer International Publishing Switzerland 2014
A.L.C. Bazzan and K. Pichara (Eds.): IBERAMIA 2014, LNAI 8864, pp. 129–140, 2014.
DOI: 10.1007/978-3-319-12027-0_11

similar word. For this task, heuristics such as the frequency of the word in pre-defined lists or the word length to detect complex words have been usually adopted. Either explicitly or as part of measures such as Flesch readability tests [6]. Nevertheless, it is important to determine the characteristics that reflect the complexity of a word. There are several studies about such a classification, but not so many data-driven experiments supporting them. Thus, we propose to use machine learning techniques to learn a supervised classifier for distinguishing complex and simple words according to lexical features. The final goal is to see how these features affect the performance of classifiers, determining which are the most relevant for the task. The results show that the length of the word, classically considered as an important cue for complexity, is not a good feature for the classifiers. On the other hand, frequency of the word in reference corpora is an informative feature, especially when combining frequency from simple and general corpora.

This paper starts with a review of related work in §2. The methodology, features and data are presented in §3 and 4, followed by the results in §5. §6 wraps up with the conclusions and future work.

2   Text Simplification

There are numerous studies on TS, most of them focusing on English (e.g. [3, 7, 8]) using as basis frequency, context and syntactic information. Frequency-based methods, as [9], usually simplify a text on a word by word basis, by first generating a list of synonyms using a dictionary (e.g. WordNet), and then selecting the one with the highest frequency in a reference list. Word sense disambiguation is not performed, due to the assumption that less frequent words only have one specific meaning, in this way they are complex. This method also relies on the availability of resources like WordNet and a psycholinguistic database frequency list, which are not available for every language.

The approaches based on context automatically learn simpler counterparts for complex words using parallel or comparable corpus. For instance [10] work with two collections: English Wikipedia (EW) and Simple English Wikipedia (SEW)[1]. The method does not assume any specific alignment or correspondence between individual EW and SEW articles and is suitable for other cases where there is a simplified corpus in the same domain. Their sentence simplification system consists of two main stages: rule extraction and simplification. In the first stage, simplification rules are extracted from corpora consisting of an ordered word pair along with a score indicating the similarity between the words. In the second stage, the system decides whether to apply a rule (i.e., transform the original word into the simplified one), based on contextual information. The complexity of a word is based on two measures: corpus complexity and lexical complexity. The evaluation dataset contained 65 sentences. Each was simplified by their system and the baseline, resulting in 130 simplification examples (consisting of an original and a simplified sentence).

---

[1] Only about 2% of the EW articles have been simplified.

Syntactic approaches, as [11], usually are composed by two layers. The first indicates the complexity level of a constituent based on features like average size of prepositional phrases, number of words, number of verb phrases and average size of words. The second implements simplification operations (e.g. split the sentence, change a discourse marker by a simpler and more frequent one, change passive to active voice, invert the order of the clauses) and executes them when recommended by the first layer.

Many of these works focus on English and similar initiatives are often missing for other languages like Portuguese and Spanish. In this context, the Simplext [12] and PorSimples [13] projects present pioneer work. The Simplext project [12] aims at producing an ubiquitous text simplification system for Spanish. It explores the frequency of words as a reading measure, so the procedure for text simplification consists of replacing low frequency words by others whose linguistic use is widespread. The PorSimples project [13] aimed at producing Brazilian Portuguese text simplification tools for promoting digital inclusion and accessibility for people with low levels of literacy. To help readers process documents available on the web, two high-level tools were designed: (1) a browser plugin to automatically simplify texts on the web for the end-user and (2) an authoring tool to support authors in the process of producing simple texts.

2.1 Lexical Simplification

The Lexical Simplification (LS) problem can be defined as replacing words with easier alternatives [14], so that the text becomes easier to comprehend. An important point is that the meaning of the original text cannot be altered, and should remain fluent. Many LS approaches are based on machine translation [15–19] from a source complex text monolingually to a target simpler text. One strategy to perform this approach consists of training a translation system with a text and its manually simplified version. An alternative strategy is to identify replacement patterns using big monolingual corpora (e.g. "X found a solution to Y" means "X solved Y") [15,17,20]. Other approaches in LS use features to identify the complexity level, for instance, the number of syllables and frequency (from a reference corpus)[21]. [8] defines LS in three phases: identify difficulty words (using web frequency as an estimate of how familiar words are to readers); generate candidate substitutions (based on dictionaries), and choose the best substitution (replacing only if a new word has a Google n-gram frequency higher than the original word and the two words have the same part-of-speech).

[22] approximate simplicity with word frequency, so that a cognitively simpler lexical form is the one that is more frequent in the language. In the case of one-word substitutes or common collocations, they uses the frequency in WordNet [23] and the lexical form as a metric to rank the substitutes. In the case of multi-words or syntactically complex substitutes, they apply relevance rules[2].

---

[2] Based on (de)compositional semantic criteria and attempting to identify a unique content word in the substitute that better approximates the whole lexical form.

Lexical Simplification needs standard datasets, for allowing direct comparison among different proposals. In this sense, [14] discuss how to create ground truth models used in the evaluation of the LS task. This dataset consists of 201 words, which were chosen at random. For each of the words, 10 sentences were retrieved that contained the word or a conjugated form of the word. The sentences were selected from the Internet Corpus of English produced by Sharoff [24], obtained by sampling data from the Web. To transform this to a Lexical Simplification dataset, they first removes those of the 201 words that are on a list of "easy words". After removal there were 43 words, or 430 sentences, remaining.

In this work we adopt features that are widely used in the TS literature as representative of word complexity [9,13,14,22]. However the contribution of this work is in determining quantitavely how indicative these features really are of word complexity.

3   Methodology

In this work, we focus on the study of features for assessing lexical complexity. To do so, we propose to use a set of simple word-level features and perform a classification task using supervised machine learning methods. We study the performance of different algorithms in this classification task and determine which of the defined features are more important to determine lexical complexity.

The basic idea is to produce vectors of features of simple and complex words to build classifiers and analyze the impact of each feature in the success of the classification of a word as complex. Figure 1 shows the the pipeline adopted in these experiments.

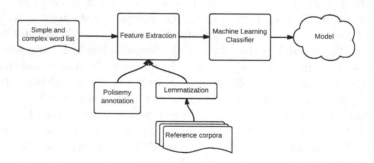

Fig. 1. Word Complexity Pipeline

As most previous work on lexical complexity focuses on English, for the sake of comparability, we first apply the methodology to English to assess which features perform best. Secondly, to investigate to what extend these results hold crosslinguistically, we perform parallel experiments with Portuguese. For the latter, as there are less resources available, some of them had to be induced such as the gold standard (see §4).

3.1 Features

For the classification task we encode information relative to each word as a feature vector. Since our focus is lexical complexity, we propose a set of simple features with information just about the word, not the context, to classify a word as simple or complex, and consider the lemmatized words to take into account purely lexical issues. The features we experiment with are based on traditional intuitions about what makes a word simple:

Word length (W_{length}) as the number of characters of each word in the training corpora, based on the assumption that the longer the word, the more complex it is. For instance, [22] approximate word frequency with word size and [10] used it to smooth frequency information.

Frequency of word in a general corpus ($Freq_{WaC}$) using the frequency of each word in Web (described in §4.2). It is the most widely used feature in lexical simplification, and often a common baseline [7].

Frequency of word in Childes ($Freq_{Childes}$) as the frequency of each word in the CHILDES [25] corpora (described in §4.2, assuming that words appearing in child-directed or child-produced speech are simple.[3]

Frequency of word in complex and simple corpora as discussed in §4.2. We follow [10] who used the frequency in a simple corpus ($Freq_{simple}$) and the frequency in a complex corpus ($Freq_{complex}$).

Number of synsets in WordNet ($Num_{Synsets}$) represents the number of synonyms for each word in the training corpora, to assess the impact of word polysemy, introducing a feature that is based on the semantics of the word. WordNet 3.0 [23] is used for English and openWordNet-PT[4] [26] for Portuguese.

3.2 Classifiers

Our approach applied five widely used supervised learning algorithms from different classes from the Weka toolkit[5] [27]. The performances of the models are estimated with 10-fold cross-validation, using their default configurations: a decision tree, *C4.5 (J48)*, *Naive Bayes (NB)* *Naive Bayes Network (NBN)*, *Support Vector Machines (SVM)*, and *Adaptive Boosting (AB)*, which is considered less susceptible to overfitting.

---

[3] [13] used newspaper articles targeted to children.
[4] https://github.com/arademaker/openWordnet-PT/
[5] http://www.cs.waikato.ac.nz/ml/weka/

4 Data

4.1 Gold Standard

To have equivalent gold standards for English and Portuguese for classifying simple and complex words we infer both of them from other existing resources.

English

Semeval 2012 [5] was devoted to evaluate Lexical Simplification in context for English. In the frame of this shared task, a manually developed gold standard was created[6]. The gold standard consists of a list of synonyms sorted from simpler to complex. From that list, we infer a gold standard of simple/complex words. By taking the ranked list organized as a gradient of synonyms from more complex to simpler and assuming the top ranked word is the simplest and the word at the bottom of the rank is the more complex. In our case we are not interested in synonymy between words but rather in a binary decision of whether they are simple or complex. In order to ensure a reasonable separation between simple and complex words we discard too short lists[7]. Since words can be repeated in different lists the number of final words in complex and simple classes can be different. To balance the classes we discard some examples, keeping only 489 words (for each class) that were observed in longer lists.

Portuguese

For Portuguese, we infer our gold standard from a parallel corpus formed by texts from the series *Coleção é Só o Começo*. The books in this collection were simplified by linguists targeting people with low reading skills. The original and the simplified version of each book were used to create a parallel corpus.[8]

To create a gold standard from this corpus, we assume that words that appear much more frequently in the simplified texts than in the original texts are considered simple, while those that are more frequent in the original versions are more complex. This simple assumption can introduce errors, but we see it as a starting point to create gold standards from corpora, which could be easily applied to other languages.

We lemmatized and PoS tagged all corpora using FreeLing [28]. Then the *keyness* [29] for each lemma belonging to open classes (nouns, verbs, adjectives and adverbs) was computed as its membership to either the original or the simplified text. *Keyness* gives us two sorted excluding lists: one of words that

---

[6] http://www.cs.york.ac.uk/semeval-2012/task1

[7] With this threshold (less than 4 items per list) we intend to avoid words with similar complexity levels.

[8] This initiative is a collaboration between different publishers and the Ministry of Education and Culture of Brazil, and the texts we used in this work were kindly made available by L&PM Publishing Company.

are representative of the original texts and one of the simplified texts. These two lists can be seen as list of complex and simple words. Since the size of the lists may be different, we choose the first 900 words of each list.

4.2 Corpora

The reference corpora used to extract frequency features for our classification task are listed below and a summary is in Table 1:

General corpora as a reference of the frequency of the word in the language. In this work we use subsets of the web-crawled corpora ukWaC [30] for English and brWaC [31] for Portuguese containing from 200 to 300 million words.

Simple corpora as Simple English Wikipedia (SEW) for English and for Portuguese we combine texts from different sources, Diário Gaúcho [32], Zero Hora *natural* [33] and books for children[9].

Complex corpora as English Wikipedia for English and for Portuguese a combination of the newspaper Folha de São Paulo[10], Europarl [34], Machado de Assis corpus[11] and Zero Hora *original*[12] [33].

Childes corpus [25] contains transcriptions of child-directed and child-produced talks. We used frequency of words produced by children in both English and Portuguese.

Table 1. Number of tokens, types and type-token ratio (TTR) in each reference corpus

Corpus	English			Portuguese		
	Tokens	Types	TTR	Tokens	Types	TTR
General corpora	2,000M	3.8M	0.002	3,000M	2,7M	0.008
Simple corpora	2.7M	173K	0.064	317K	26K	0.083
Complex corpora	3.0M	197K	0.065	86M	634K	0.007
Childes	2.1M	35.7K	0.016	177K	5.9K	0.033

5 Results

Table 2 shows the average F-measure results for the task for both languages to measure the impact of each feature. As baselines we adopted the average

---

[9] A Domínio Público initiative, all of them designed using a popular subset of language. Note that the corpus described in §4.1 is not used as reference since it is used to create the gold standard lists).

[10] http://www.linguateca.pt/cetenfolha/

[11] We choose Machado de Assis corpus because it is contains several works of an author acknowledged to have used a very rich vocabulary. It is available as a Domínio Público initiative from the Brazilian government.

[12] This corpus is composed of two sets, the original articles from and their manually targeted versions for low literacy subjects. We use the latter as *simple* corpus and the former as *complex*.

word length and frequency in general corpus, measured in terms of average F1: for English $W_{length}=0.67$ and $Freq_{WaC}=0.52$, and for Portuguese $W_{length}=0.51$ and $Freq_{WaC}=0.50$.

We train the classifiers using each feature alone, the combination $Freq_{simple}$ and $Freq_{complex}$ which are often used together in the literature, and the combination of all features (last line).

The use of all features improves the best results for each language, obtained with J48 for English and NBN and J48 for Portuguese. For the best classifiers for each language, frequency consistently outperformed word length, and the estimated prediction agreement between the J48 for word length and frequency in Childes, for instance, was 74.84% for English and 81.67% for Portuguese.

In terms of the two languages, for English we obtain better results (F1=0.82 in the best case) than for Portuguese (F1=0.64) perhaps due to the difference in size and quality of data available for the experiment.

Table 2. Average F-measure for English and Portuguese respectively

Features	English					Portuguese				
	SVM	J48	NB	NBN	AB	SVM	J48	NB	NBN	AB
W_{length}	0.67	0.67	0.66	0.67	0.67	0.51	0.49	0.53	0.33	0.52
$Freq_{simple}$	0.70	0.71	0.48	0.71	0.71	0.62	0.62	0.41	0.62	0.62
$Freq_{complex}$	0.66	0.68	0.49	0.68	0.69	0.53	0.57	0.38	0.58	0.58
$Freq_{simple}$ & $Freq_{complex}$	0.70	0.73	0.50	0.70	0.71	0.53	0.62	0.40	0.63	0.61
$Freq_{Childes}$ (simple)	0.76	0.78	0.59	0.77	0.78	0.61	0.62	0.41	0.62	0.62
$Freq_{WaC}$ (general)	0.39	0.79	0.60	0.79	0.78	0.49	0.60	0.40	0.60	0.60
$Num_{Synsets}$	0.65	0.65	0.58	0.63	0.63	0.55	0.54	0.50	0.53	0.54
all	0.42	0.82	0.62	0.79	0.79	0.43	0.63	0.43	0.64	0.62

Studying in detail the features that perform better for English, we see that the best results obtained when using only one feature ($Freq_{Childes}$ or $Freq_{WaC}$) are almost as high as their combination (0.77-0.79). In order to better study the influence of these features we removed one feature at a time and evaluated the classifiers. The worst results are achieved with J48 using all features and leaving out $Num_{Synsets}$ for both languages. For English the average F1=0.83 and for Portuguese F1=0.64. In this case, the only features that showed to be important were again $Freq_{Childes}$ and $Freq_{WaC}$[13]. Only when removing one of these features the results significantly decreased while the other features did not lead to a variation in F1 when removed. This supports the conclusion that $Freq_{Childes}$ and $Freq_{WaC}$ are the most important features for this task.

Regarding Portuguese, the main conclusions are very similar: for classifiers trained only on one feature the best results are obtained using $Freq_{simple}$, $Freq_{Childes}$ and $Freq_{WaC}$ and these differences are not statistically significant.

---

[13] To confirm the significance of $Freq_{Childes}$ and $Freq_{WaC}$ in the task an Information Gain evaluation was also performed. It confirms the frequencies as the best features (in English the best one is $Freq_{WaC}$ followed by $Freq_{Childes}$ and $Freq_{simple}$, and in Portuguese the best one is $Freq_{simple}$ followed by $Freq_{Childes}$ and $Freq_{WaC}$).

5.1 Discussion

The results showed that, contrary to what is generally assumed, word length is not a good cue to separate simple and complex words. On the other hand, frequency is a much more informative cue. In that line, it is also interesting that Childes and general corpus frequencies are the best predictors. Indeed, when using just these two features with J48 we obtain F1=0.83 for English, which is better than using just one of these features but equivalent to using all features. Thus, it is clear that the best option for our task is to use word frequency from a general large corpus combined with frequency from a simple corpus, in this case approximated as Childes corpora.

Interestingly, for Portuguese the use of a simple corpus as reference led to good results while for English it did not. This may be partly explained by the specific corpora used as simple and complex in each language: for English, we used Simple Wikipedia which contains paraphrases where a complex term from Wikipedia is simplified in a SEW sentence still containing that same term but along with an explanation or definition for it. As a consequence Simple Wikipedia still contains many of the same complex words found in the original Wikipedia. On the other hand, the corpora that we used as simple for Portuguese are texts more focused on using simple vocabulary.

Furthermore, note that using Childes as a reference corpus is informative for this task. The hypothesis behind that is that a word that appears often in child-produced or child-directed sentences is more likely to be universally understood.

The influence of Polysemy ($Num_{Synsets}$) on the other hand was not as informative. This may be partly due to polysemy and frequency often co-occuring in the lexicon of a language, where some of the most frequent words are often also very polysemic (e.g. *make, do, go*). The role of polysemy needs to be further investigated as the frequency features adopted in this work may already convey some of its contribution. Additionally, the use of WordNet as basis for determining polysemy is affected by limitations in coverage in relation to the target words.

Finally, regarding the fact that classifier performance is much better for English than for Portuguese, a manual error revision showed that, in many cases, the error source is the gold standard. Since it was induced automatically from corpus, some words are not correctly classified, while other words can be considered neutral. As future work we plan to improve the Portuguese gold standard for further evaluation of classifier performance.

6 Conclusions and Future Work

In this work we examined the ability of a set of lexical, distributional and semantic features to classify words as simple or complex. One of our contributions is to quantify the predicting power of these features, which have been widely assumed in the literature to be related to word complexity. Moreover we performed this investigation in two languages, adopting similar evaluation setups to compare whether the impact of these features holds crosslinguistically.

An interesting result of this research is that word length, contrary to what is normally assumed in the literature, does not seem to be a good predictor of complexity. On the other hand, using just two frequency features (one from a general corpus and the other from Childes or a simple corpus) we obtained very good results, specially for English, getting the best results when combining both of them in a classifier. Therefore, when deciding the complexity of a word, frequency plays a very important role, and classification improves if the frequency in general language (in our case obtained from web corpora, $ukWaC$ and $brWaC$) is combined with the frequency in a simple language corpus.

To further investigate the difference in results found between the two languages, as future work we plan to refine the Portuguese gold standard with manual annotation. We also intend to extend the feature set using other frequency sources to classify simple and complex words, such as Oxford 3000. Finally, we plan to examine classifier performance with ensemble approaches and to apply the classifiers learned with these features in a real simplification application, in an extrinsic evaluation of the method.

Acknowledgments. We would like to thank to Instituto de Informática for the support in this research. Part of the results presented by this paper were obtained through the project named *Simplificação Textual de Expressões Complexas* sponsored by Samsung Eletronica da Amazonia Ltda., under the terms of Law number 8.248/91. This work was also partly supported by CNPq (482520/2012-4, 312184/2012-3, 551964/2011-1), PNPD (2484/2009), CAPES (707/11) and FAPERGS.

References

1. Max, A.: Writing for language-impaired readers. In: Gelbukh, A. (ed.) CICLing 2006. LNCS, vol. 3878, pp. 567–570. Springer, Heidelberg (2006)
2. Siddharthan, A., Nenkova, A., McKeown, K.: Syntactic simplification for improving content selection in multi-document summarization. In: Proc. of the 20th International Conference on Computational Linguistics, p. 896. ACL (2004)
3. Carroll, J., Minnen, G., Canning, Y., Devlin, S., Tait, J.: Practical simplification of english newspaper text to assist aphasic readers. In: Proc. of the AAAI-98 Workshop on Integrating Artificial Intelligence and Assistive Technology, pp. 7–10 (1998)
4. Chandrasekar, R., Doran, C., Srinivas, B.: Motivations and methods for text simplification. In: Proc. of the 16th Conference on Computational linguistics, pp. 1041–1044. ACL (1996)
5. Specia, L., Jauhar, S.K., Mihalcea, R.: Semeval-2012 task 1: English lexical simplification. In: Proc. of the First Joint Conference on Lexical and Computational Semantics, pp. 347–355 (2012)
6. Flesch, R.: A new readability yardstick. Journal of Applied Psychology **32**(3), 221–233 (1948)
7. Devlin, S., Unthank, G.: Helping aphasic people process online information. In: Proceedings of the 8th International ACM SIGACCESS Conference on Computers and Accessibility, pp. 225–226. ACM (2006)

8. Leroy, G., Kauchak, D., Mouradi, O.: A user-study measuring the effects of lexical simplification and coherence enhancement on perceived and actual text difficulty. International Journal of Medical Informatics **82**(8), 717–730 (2013)

9. De Belder, J., Deschacht, K., Moens, M.F.: Lexical simplification. In: Proceedings of ITEC2010: 1st International Conference on Interdisciplinary Research on Technology, Education and Communication (2010)

10. Biran, O., Brody, S., Elhadad, N.: Putting it simply: a context-aware approach to lexical simplification. In: Proceedings of the 49th Annual Meeting of the ACL: Human Language Technologies, pp. 496–501 (2011)

11. Gasperin, C., Maziero, E., Specia, L., Pardo, T., Aluisio, S.M.: Natural language processing for social inclusion: a text simplification architecture for different literacy levels. In: Proceedings of SEMISH-XXXVI Seminário Integrado de Software e Hardware, pp. 387–401 (2009)

12. Saggion, H., Martínez, E.G., Etayo, E., Anula, A., Bourg, L.: Text simplification in simplext. making text more accessible. Procesamiento del lenguaje natural 47, 341–342 (2011)

13. Aluísio, S.M., Specia, L., Pardo, T.A., Maziero, E.G., Fortes, R.P.: Towards brazilian portuguese automatic text simplification systems. In: Proceedings of the 8th ACM symposium on Document engineering, pp. 240–248. ACM (2008)

14. De Belder, J., Moens, M.-F.: A dataset for the evaluation of lexical simplification. In: Gelbukh, A. (ed.) CICLing 2012, Part II. LNCS, vol. 7182, pp. 426–437. Springer, Heidelberg (2012)

15. Lin, D., Pantel, P.: DIRT - Discovery of Inference Rules from Text. In: Proc. of ACM Conference on Knowledge Discovery and Data Mining (KDD-01). San Francisco, USA pp. 323–328 (2001)

16. Barzilay, R., McKeown, K.R.: Extracting paraphrases from a parallel corpus. In: Proceedings of the 39th Annual Meeting on Association for Computational Linguistics, pp. 50–57. ACL (2001)

17. Shinyama, Y., Sekine, S., Sudo, K.: Automatic paraphrase acquisition from news articles. In: Proceedings of the second International Conference on Human Language Technology Research, pp. 313–318. Morgan Kaufmann Publishers Inc. (2002)

18. Barzilay, R., Lee, L.: Learning to paraphrase: an unsupervised approach using multiple-sequence alignment. In: Proc. of the 2003 Conference of the North American Chapter of the Association for Computational Linguistics on Human Language Technology, pp. 16–23 (2003)

19. Pang, B., Knight, K., Marcu, D.: Syntax-based alignment of multiple translations: Extracting paraphrases and generating new sentences. In: Proc. of the 2003 Conference of the North American Chapter of the Association for Computational Linguistics on Human Language Technology, pp. 102–109 (2003)

20. Ibrahim, A., Katz, B., Lin, J.: Extracting structural paraphrases from aligned monolingual corpora. In: Proceedings of the Second International Workshop on Paraphrasing, pp. 57–64. ACL (2003)

21. Lal, P., Ruger, S.: Extract-based summarization with simplification. In: Proceedings of the ACL Workshop on Text Summarisation: DUC, Philadelphia, USA (2002)

22. Amoia, M., Romanelli, M.: Sb: mmsystem-using decompositional semantics for lexical simplification. In: Proceedings of the First Joint Conference on Lexical and Computational Semantics, pp. 482–486 (2012)

23. Fellbaum, C.: WordNet: An Electronic Lexical Database (Language, Speech, and Communication). MIT Press, Cambridge (1998)

24. Sharoff, S.: Open-source corpora: Using the net to fish for linguistic data. International Journal of Corpus Linguistics **11**(4), 435–462 (2006)
25. MacWhinney, B.: The CHILDES Project: The database. vol. 2. Psychology Press (2000)
26. de Paiva, V., Rademaker, A., de Melo, G.: Openwordnet-pt: An open brazilian wordnet for reasoning. In: Proceedings of the 24th International Conference on Computational Linguistics (2012)
27. Hall, M., Frank, E., Holmes, G., Pfahringer, B., Reutemann, P., Witten, I.H.: The weka data mining software: An update. SIGKDD Explor. Newsl. **11**(1), 10–18 (2009)
28. Padró, L., Stanilovsky, E.: Freeling 3.0: Towards wider multilinguality. In: Proceedings of the Language Resources and Evaluation Conference (LREC). ELRA, Istanbul (2012)
29. Scott, M., Tribble, C.: Textual patterns: key words and corpus analysis in language education. John Benjamins publishing company, Amsterdam (2006)
30. Baroni, M., Bernardini, S., Ferraresi, A., Zanchetta, E.: The wacky wide web: a collection of very large linguistically processed web-crawled corpora. Language Resources and Evaluation **43**(3), 209–226 (2009)
31. Boos, R., Prestes, K., Villavicencio, A., Padró, M.: brWaC: a WaCky corpus for Brazilian Portuguese. In: Proceedings of PROPOR 2014, São Carlos, Brazil (2014)
32. Finatto, M.J.B., Scarton, C.E., Rocha, A., Aluísio, S.: Características do jornalismo popular: avaliação da inteligibilidade e auxílio à descrição do gênero. In: Proceedings of the 8th Brazilian Symposium in Information and Human Language Technology (2011)
33. Caseli, H.M., Pereira, T.F., Specia, L., Pardo, T.A., Gasperin, C., Aluísio, S.: Building a brazilian portuguese parallel corpus of original and simplified texts. In: Proceedings of CICLing (2009)
34. Koehn, P.: Europarl: A parallel corpus for statistical machine translation. In: Proceedings of the 10th Machine Translation Summit, pp. 79–86 (2005)

A Dempster-Shafer Theoretic Approach
to Understanding Indirect Speech Acts

Tom Williams[1]([⊠]), Rafael C. Núñez[2], Gordon Briggs[1], Matthias Scheutz[1],
Kamal Premaratne[2], and Manohar N. Murthi[2]

[1] Human-Robot Interaction Laboratory, Tufts University, 200 Boston Avenue,
Medford, MA02155, USA
{williams,gbriggs,mscheutz}@cs.tufts.edu
[2] Department of Electrical and Computer Engineering, University of Miami,
1251 Memorial Drive, Coral Gables, FL33146, USA
nunez@umiami.edu,{kamal,mmurthi}@miami.edu

Abstract. Understanding *Indirect Speech Acts (ISAs)* is an integral
function of human understanding of natural language. Recent attempts
at understanding ISAs have used rule-based approaches to map utterances to deep semantics. While these approaches have been successful in
handling a wide range of ISAs, they do not take into account the uncertainty associated with the utterance's context, or the utterance itself.
We present a new approach for understanding ISAs using the Dempster-
Shafer theory of evidence and show how this approach increases the
robustness of ISA inference by (1) accounting for uncertain implication
rules and context, (2) fluidly adapting rules given new information, and
(3) enabling better modeling of the beliefs of other agents.

Keywords: Speech act theory · Intention understanding · Dempster-
Shafer theory

1 Introduction

People do not often directly express their intentions. For various social reasons (e.g. politeness [2]) they instead use linguistic strategies such as *Indirect
Speech Acts (ISAs)*, i.e., utterances whose intended meanings differ from their
literal meanings. Two approaches have been proposed for handling ISAs in computational systems. The *inferential* approach reasons about possible intended
meanings by considering observed speech acts in the current context as part of
a broader plan that captures the agent's goals and intentions [9]. In contrast,
the *idiomatic* approach leverages the fact that certain ISA forms are *conventionalized*, i.e., that they are directly associated with an inferred meaning, largely
independent of context [15]. Both approaches have advantages and disadvantages: the inferential approach requires the ability to infer interlocutors' possible
plans, which can be quite computationally expensive, while the idiomatic approach is limited to ISAs for which conventionalized meanings exist. We contend

© Springer International Publishing Switzerland 2014
A.L.C. Bazzan and K. Pichara (Eds.): IBERAMIA 2014, LNAI 8864, pp. 141–153, 2014.
DOI: 10.1007/978-3-319-12027-0_12

that there are three capabilities necessary for robust understanding of conventionalized ISAs through the idiomatic approach:

C1: Uncertainty. An agent must not assume perfect knowledge of the contexts in which an indirect interpretation applies. The conventionalized meaning of an ISA is not always the intended meaning; sometimes "I'd love some cake" is simply a statement expressing a desire, and not an indirect request for someone to give you cake. Since an agent might not always be able to determine the true intended meaning of an utterance, it should ascribe a level of confidence to each of its interpretations, based on the contextual factors that provide evidence for each interpretation. Furthermore, it is important that an agent be able to represent and reason about its own uncertainty and ignorance, and be able to act appropriately when uncertainty is identified.

C2: Adaptation. Since an agent should be able to learn new ISAs, and since it may not know the precise scenarios in which new ISAs should be used, an agent should be able to learn and adapt new rules, using feedback from interlocutors to adjust its beliefs as to when the rules it knows apply. For example, consider the following dialogue:

DATA: Are you certain you do not wish to talk about your mother?

GEORDI: Why do you ask that?

DATA: You are no doubt feeling emotional distress as a result of her disappearance. Though you claimed to be "just passing by," that is most likely an excuse to start a conversation about this uncomfortable subject. Am I correct?

GEORDI: Well, no. Sometimes "just passing by" means "just passing by."

DATA: Then I apologize for my premature assumption...

GEORDI: Data, maybe you gave up too fast.

DATA: I do not understand.

GEORDI: When I said "just passing by" means "just passing by," I didn't really mean it.

DATA: My initial assumption was correct. You do wish to speak of your mother.

Short dialogue from Star Trek: The Next Generation. "Interface"

In the space of this short dialogue, an agent (i.e., the android "Data") must make several adaptations. First, he must alter his beliefs about the ISA "just passing by" based on feedback from Geordi that the ISA's literal meaning had been the correct interpretation. Then, he must at least partially revert to his previous beliefs, as well as alter his belief as to when $said(X, Y) \rightarrow means(X, Y)$.

C3: Belief modeling. An agent should be able to model interlocutors' beliefs: the interpretation of an ISA *uttered by an interlocutor* should be based not on the *robot's* beliefs about, for example, its capabilities and obligations, but rather on its *interlocutor's* beliefs.

In this paper, we present a novel approach that addresses the three aforementioned capabilities to robustly handle idiomatic ISAs. We first give a brief overview of Dempster-Shafer (DS) theory and DS rule-based inference before presenting the DS theoretic approach to ISA understanding. We then compare this approach to previous work, and conclude with an outlook for future work.

2 Indirect Speech Act (ISA) Modeling

Suppose a robot were told "I would love a coffee." This utterance was likely generated due to some intention to communicate something to the robot. This intention was likely formed due to some contextual factors, whether environmental (e.g., the interlocutor was tired) or dialogic (e.g., the robot had just asked the interlocutor "Would you like a coffee?").

We see two distinct ways to model these contextual effects. **(A)** They could be modeled as part of the user's intentions; the relationship between the robot and its interlocutor may, e.g., cause the interlocutor to form the intention to avoid production of utterances that could be insulting to the robot. **(B)** Alternatively, context could directly affect utterance production, and the information the interlocutor intends to communicate as well as the context that dictates whether and how the information is conveyed could be treated as separate factors leading to the production of the utterance. We have chosen approach **(B)**, using a graphical model with random variables C, U and I such that I depends on C and U depends on C and I. Here, C, I and U represent distributions over possible contexts, intentions and utterances, respectively. From this model, we are interested in inferring the interlocutor's intentions given the current context and the produced utterance. The Bayesian approach to this inference problem would be to calculate $P(U, I, C) = P(U|I, C) \cdot P(I|C) \cdot P(C)$. To calculate $P(I|U, C)$ given an utterance u and context c, one would then formulate:

$$P(I|U = u, C = c) = \frac{P(U = u|I, C = c) \cdot P(I|C = c) \cdot P(C = c)}{\sum_{i \in I} P(U = u, I = i, C = c)}.$$

However, $P(U|I, C)$ is at least as hard to calculate as $P(I|U, C)$, for two reasons. First, we do not have access to the distribution over an interlocutor's intentions as we cannot look inside his or her head. Second, one would need a table containing priors on all combinations of intentions and contexts; a table that could not be realistically represented unless sparse representations were used. Even if such a table could be constructed, it is unclear where its values would come from. An example of a Bayesian approach to utterance interpretation can be found in [3]. However, this work appears to only engage in speech act classification and not semantic analysis of utterances.

3 DS-Based Inference for ISAs

Because the direct Bayesian approach of inferring $P(I|U, C)$ by way of $P(U|I, C)$, $P(I|C)$, and $P(C)$ (i.e., the conditional probability of utterances occurring given intentions and context, the conditional probability of intentions given context, and the prior distribution of contexts) does not make the inference problem any easier, we instead tackle $P(I|U, C)$ directly. To do so, we create rules of the form $u \wedge c \Rightarrow_{[\alpha, \beta]} i$. Here, u is an utterance, c is a context, i is an intention, and $[\alpha, \beta]$, where $0 \leq \alpha \leq \beta \leq 1$, is the uncertainty interval associated with the rule.

3.1 Dempster-Shafer (DS) Theory

DS theory is an uncertainty processing framework often interpreted as an extension of the Bayesian framework [8,13]. Its notions of belief and plausibility bear a close relationship to the inner and outer measures in probability theory [4].

Basic Notions in DS Theory Frame of Discernment. In DS theory, the discrete set of elementary events of interest related to a given problem is called the *Frame of Discernment (FoD)*. We take the FoD to be the finite set of mutually exclusive events $\Theta = \{\theta_1, \theta_2, \ldots, \theta_N\}$. The power set of Θ is denoted by $2^\Theta = \{A : A \subseteq \Theta\}$.

Basic Belief Assignment. A *Basic Belief Assignment (BBA)* is a mapping $m_\Theta(\cdot) : 2^\Theta \to [0,1]$ such that $\sum_{A \subseteq \Theta} m_\Theta(A) = 1$ and $m_\Theta(\emptyset) = 0$. The BBA measures the support assigned to propositions $A \subseteq \Theta$ *only*. The subsets of A with nonzero mass are referred to as *focal elements*, and comprise the *core* $\mathcal{F}_\Theta$. The triple $\mathcal{E} = \{\Theta, \mathcal{F}_\Theta, m_\Theta(\cdot)\}$ is called the *Body of Evidence (BoE)*.

Belief, Plausibility, and Uncertainty. Given a BoE $\{\Theta, \mathcal{F}, m\}$, the *belief* $\mathrm{Bl} : 2^\Theta \to [0,1]$ is $\mathrm{Bl}(A) = \sum_{B \subseteq A} m_\Theta(B)$. So, $\mathrm{Bl}(A)$ captures the total support that can be committed to A without also committing it to the complement A^c of A. The *plausibility* $\mathrm{Pl} : 2^\Theta \to [0,1]$ is $\mathrm{Pl}(A) = 1 - \mathrm{Bl}(A^c)$. So, $\mathrm{Pl}(A)$ corresponds to the total belief that does not contradict A. The *uncertainty* of A is $[\mathrm{Bl}(A), \mathrm{Pl}(A)]$.

Conditional Fusion Equation (CFE). The evidence from two sources having the BBAs $m_j(\cdot)$ and $m_k(\cdot)$ can be fused using various fusion strategies. A robust fusion strategy is the *Conditional Fusion Equation (CFE)* [11].

Uncertain Logic. Uncertain logic, a DS-based extension of classical logic which deals with propositions whose truth is uncertain, handles expressions of the following form [6,7]:

$$\varphi(x), \text{ with uncertainty } [\alpha, \beta],\ 0 \leq \alpha \leq \beta \leq 1, \tag{1}$$

where $\varphi(x)$ is a proposition which contains a reference to individual x, $x \in \mathcal{D} = \{x_1, x_2, \ldots, x_n\}$, a finite set of individuals. A DS model for expression (1) can be defined over the logical FoD $\Theta_{\varphi,x} = \{\varphi(x) \times \mathbf{1}, \varphi(x) \times \mathbf{0}\}$, which contains two mutually exclusive elements: our confidence that the proposition φ applies and does not apply to x, respectively. When no confusion can arise, we represent these two elements as $\{x, \overline{x}\}$. Then the information in (1) can be captured by the following DS model over $\Theta_{\varphi,x}$: $m(x) = \alpha$; $m(\overline{x}) = 1 - \beta$; $m(\Theta_{\varphi,x}) = \beta - \alpha$. In general, we could also model the uncertainty of propositions $\varphi_i \in \{\varphi_1, \ldots, \varphi_M\}$ applying to particular elements $x_j \in \Theta_x$, i.e.,

$$\varphi_i(x_j), \text{ with uncertainty } [\alpha_{i,j}, \beta_{i,j}],\ 0 \leq \alpha_{i,j} \leq \beta_{i,j} \leq 1, \tag{2}$$

via a model defined over the FoD $\Theta_{\varphi_i, x_j} = \{\varphi_i(x_j) \times \mathbf{1}, \varphi_i(x_j) \times \mathbf{0}\} = \{x_{i,j}, \overline{x}_{i,j}\}$.

CFE-Based Logical Operators. We can now define logic operations such as NOT ($\neg$), AND ($\wedge$), and OR ($\vee$) [6,7]. Whenever possible we define operations in a simple unquantified first-order logic model (e.g., based on (1)) instead of (2)), but extension to more complex cases and simplification into propositional logic are straightforward.

Logical Negation. Logical negation of uncertain proposition $\varphi(x)$ in (1) and its corresponding DS model are $\neg\varphi(x)$, with uncertainty $[1 - \beta, 1 - \alpha]$, and

$$m(x) = 1 - \beta; \quad m(\overline{x}) = \alpha; \quad m(\Theta_{\varphi,x}) = \beta - \alpha. \tag{3}$$

Logical AND/OR. Consider M logic predicates, each providing a statement regarding the truth of x with respect to the proposition $\varphi_i(\cdot)$ in (2). Then, the corresponding DS models for $\varphi_i(x)$ are, for $i = 1, 2, \ldots, M$:

$$m_i(x) = \alpha_i; \quad m_i(\overline{x}) = 1 - \beta_i; \quad m_i(\Theta_{\varphi_i,x}) = \beta_i - \alpha_i. \tag{4}$$

The DS model for the logical AND and OR of the statements in (4) can be defined as:

$$m_\wedge(\cdot) = \bigcap_{i=1}^{M} m_i(\cdot); \quad m_\vee(\cdot) = \left(\bigcap_{i=1}^{M} m_i^c(\cdot) \right)^c, \tag{5}$$

respectively, where $\bigcap$ denotes an appropriate fusion operator. When the CFE (with appropriate parameters) is used as the fusion operator, consistency with classical logic can be achieved [7]. In the case of CFE-Based Logical Operators, logical AND when $M = 2$ is defined as:

$$m(x) = \underline{\alpha}; \quad m(\overline{x}) = 1 - \underline{\beta}; \quad m(\Theta_{\varphi_1,x} \times \Theta_{\varphi_2,x}) = \underline{\beta} - \underline{\alpha}, \tag{6}$$

where $\underline{\alpha} = \min(\alpha_1, \alpha_2)$ and $\underline{\beta} = \min(\beta_1, \beta_2)$, and logical OR is defined as:

$$m(x) = \overline{\alpha}; \quad m(\overline{x}) = 1 - \overline{\beta}; \quad m(\Theta_{\varphi_1,x} \times \Theta_{\varphi_2,x}) = \overline{\beta} - \overline{\alpha}, \tag{7}$$

where $\overline{\alpha} = \max(\alpha_1, \alpha_2)$ and $\overline{\beta} = \max(\beta_1, \beta_2)$. Hereafter, $m_1 \otimes m_2$ denotes the DS model corresponding to the uncertain logic operation $\varphi_1(\cdot) \wedge \varphi_2(\cdot)$.

Logical Implication. Given two logic statements $\varphi_1(\cdot)$ and $\varphi_2(\cdot)$, an implication rule in classical logic takes the form $\varphi_1(x) \Rightarrow \varphi_2(y) \equiv \neg\varphi_1(x) \vee \varphi_2(y) \equiv \neg (\varphi_1(x) \wedge \neg\varphi_2(y))$, where $x_i \in \Theta_x$ and $y_j \in \Theta_y$.

As shown in [6], the DS model for the uncertain implication $\varphi_1(\cdot) \Rightarrow \varphi_2(\cdot)$ over the true-false FoD $\{1, 0\}$ may be defined using (7) and (3):

$$m_{\varphi_1 \to \varphi_2}(1) = \alpha_R; \quad m_{\varphi_1 \to \varphi_2}(0) = 1 - \beta_R;$$
$$m_{\varphi_1 \to \varphi_2}(\{1, 0\}) = \beta_R - \alpha_R, \tag{8}$$

where $\alpha_R = \max(1 - \beta_1, \alpha_2)$ and $\beta_R = \max(1 - \alpha_1, \beta_2)$. Thus, the implication rule's uncertainty interval is $[\alpha_R, \beta_R]$. This DS model provides us with an important inference tool. Suppose DS models for the implication rule and antecedent are known. We then obtain the following DS model for the consequent [6]:

$$\alpha_2 = \begin{cases} \alpha_R, & \text{if } \alpha_R > 1 - \beta_1; \\ 0, & \text{if } \alpha_R = 1 - \beta_1; \\ \text{no solution}, & \text{otherwise}; \end{cases} \text{ and } \beta_2 = \begin{cases} \beta_R, & \text{if } \beta_R > 1 - \alpha_1; \\ \text{no solution}, & \text{otherwise}. \end{cases} \tag{9}$$

Inference. Inference in uncertain logic shares the fundamental principles of classical logic, and adds the possibility of attaching, tracking, and propagating uncertainties that may arise on premises and/or rules. The model in (9) can be used as an uncertain Modus Ponens (MP) rule [7]. We use $m_2 = m_1 \odot m_{12}$ to express that the BBA m_2 is obtained after applying MP when the BBAs of the antecedent m_1 and the implication $m_{12} = m_{\varphi_1 \to \varphi_2}$ are known.

Symbolic Dempster-Shafer Operators. In [14], Tang et al. produce another candidate set of operators for Logical AND, OR, Implication, and Modus Ponens (their operator for logical negation is equivalent to that defined by Núñez et al).

Logical AND/OR. Tang et al. define the DS model for logical AND as:

$$m(x) = \alpha_1 * \alpha_2; \quad m(\overline{x}) = 1 - (\beta_1 * \beta_2);$$
$$m(\Theta_{\varphi_1,x} \times \Theta_{\varphi_2,x}) = (1 - m(\overline{x})) - m(x), \tag{10}$$

and OR as:

$$m(x) = \frac{\alpha_1 + \alpha_2}{2}; \quad m(\overline{x}) = \frac{(1-\beta_1) + (1-\beta_2)}{2};$$
$$m(\Theta_{\varphi_1,x} \times \Theta_{\varphi_2,x}) = (1 - m(\overline{x})) - m(x), \tag{11}$$

Logical Implication. Tang et al. define logical implication as

$$m(x) = \frac{(1-\alpha_1) + \alpha_2}{2}; \quad m(\overline{x}) = \frac{\beta_1 + (1-\beta_2)}{2};$$
$$m(\Theta_{\varphi_1,x} \times \Theta_{\varphi_2,x}) = (1 - m(\overline{x})) - m(x), \tag{12}$$

allowing the consequent to be calculated as

$$\alpha_2 = \alpha_1 * \alpha_R; \quad \beta_2 = \beta_R. \tag{13}$$

This as well can also be used as an uncertain Modus Ponens rule [14].

3.2   Inferring Intentions

Let $\Theta_U = \{u_1, u_2, \ldots, u_{Nu}\}$ be the set of all utterances an agent may interpret, and $\Theta_C = \{c_1, c_2, \ldots, c_{Nc}\}$ be the set of all contextual items. Also, let $\Theta_I = \{i_1, i_2, \ldots, i_{Ni}\}$ be the set of atomic intentions an interlocutor may be trying to communicate. Using the uncertain logic framework described above, we can define the BBAs $m_u(\cdot), m_c(\cdot), m_i(\cdot)$ over the FoDs $\Theta_U, \Theta_C, \Theta_I \times \{1, 0\}$ respectively. The information required to calculate $m_i(\cdot)$ is available to the agent: its natural language understanding system can provide a distribution over possible utterances heard (yielding m_u), its knowledge base can provide a distribution over different contextual items being believed (yielding m_c), and information regarding the uncertainty of $(u \wedge c) \Rightarrow i$ can be encoded in a table M indexed by utterance u and contextual item c, defining a BBA $m_{uc \to i}$. Using these three BBAs, we can obtain a model for the uncertainty of intention i through MP by computing $m_i(\cdot) = ((m_u \otimes m_c) \odot m_{uc \to i})(\cdot)$ defined over the FoD $\Theta_I \times \{1, 0\}$.

While recent approaches to ISA understanding (e.g., [1]) use only the first applicable rule found, we instead combine multiple applicable rules, as multiple rules may produce different beliefs regarding the same hypothesis. For example, one rule may produce an inference that an interlocutor does not want coffee as he rarely drinks it, while another may produce an inference that he does because he just stated how tired he was. Fusing these results yields a single inference that paints a better picture of the agent's confidence. We can obtain a DS model produced by n applicable rules of the type $(u \wedge c) \Rightarrow i$ by combining n BBAs:

$$m_\psi(\cdot) = \bigcap_{u \in \Theta_u, c \in \Theta_c} ((m_u \otimes m_c) \odot m_{uc \to i})(\cdot), \tag{14}$$

where $\cap$ refers to some generic fusion operator (e.g., the CFE). Since each BBA resulting from the application of MP in the equation above is defined over the FoD $\Theta_I \times \{1, 0\}$, so is the resulting fused DS model m_ψ.

3.3   Algorithm

Given the BoEs $\{\Theta_U, m_u\}$ and $\{\Theta_C, m_c\}$, which encode the uncertainty as to the truthfulness of utterance u and context c respectively, and a list of applicable rules R, Algorithm 1 infers the intended meaning of u. The algorithm first collects the consequents resulting from the application of u and c to rule r into the set S, and then groups these consequents using $group(S)$ such that the consequents in each group are all on the same FoD (for example, a consequent $wants(jim, coffee)[0.1, 0.3]$ would be in the same group as $wants(jim, coffee)[0.7, 0.9]$ but in a different group than $wants(jim, tea)[0.4, 0.6]$). This allows the constituents of each group to be fused using the CFE, or to be processed using MP. Finally, the fused consequents resulting from this step are collected into ψ, which is returned.

Algorithm 1. getIntendedMeaning($\{\Theta_U, m_u\}, \{\Theta_C, m_c\}, R$)

1: $\{\Theta_U, m_u\}$: BoE of candidate utterances
2: $\{\Theta_C, m_c\}$: BoE of relevant contextual items
3: R: Currently applicable rules
4: $S = \emptyset$
5: **for all** $r \in R$ **do**
6:     $S = S \cup \{(m_u \otimes m_c) \odot m_{r=uc \to i}\}$
7: **end for**
8: $G = group(S)$
9: $\psi = \emptyset$
10: **for all** group $g_i \in G$ **do**
11:     $\psi = \psi \cup \{\bigcap_{j=0}^{|g_i|} g_{i_j}\}$
12: **end for**
13: **return** ψ

Our approach is similar to that of [1], who express each rule as a tuple $(\tilde{C}, \tilde{U}, [[U]]_C)$ where $\tilde{C}$ is a set of contextual constraints, $\tilde{U}$ is an utterance form, and $[[U]]_C$ is a set of belief updates to be made if $\tilde{U}$ and $\tilde{C}$ match the current utterance and context. Rules are sequentially compared against utterances and contexts. If a matching rule is found, its consequent is immediately returned. As only one rule is ever applied, specific rules are written for particular combinations of contextual items, and are arranged in descending order of specificity. This differs from the DS-theoretic approach, in which the consequents from all applicable rules are combined; instead of a single rule encoding all pieces of context that evidence a given intention, multiple rules are used.

4   Evaluation

We will now present an evaluation of our algorithm and demonstrate the capabilities facilitated by our approach. The evaluation of a system at this stage of the natural language pipeline is difficult, as the performance of the algorithm is tightly coupled with the performance of components that precede it in the natural language pipeline (e.g., speech recognition, parsing, semantic analysis). We thus take the same approach to evaluation as previous work, i.e., through a case study that demonstrates the behavior of our algorithm. We will now show how our algorithm works towards the capabilities necessary for robust understanding of conventionalized ISAs, and then compare our algorithm to previous work.

4.1   Handling Uncertainty

Consider a robot speaking with interlocutor Jim. Suppose Jim says to the robot: "I need coffee". From the robot's perspective, this utterance is represented as $Stmt(jim, self, needs(jim, coffee))$. In this representation, the three arguments represent the speaker of the utterance (in this case, Jim), the receiver (in this case, the robot ("self")), and the conveyed message (in this case, *Jim needs coffee*). Suppose the robot knows two pragmatic rules. In both rules, $[\alpha_{R_i}, \beta_{R_i}]$ represents the belief and plausibility of rule i.

First, if B believes A is a barista, then telling A that B needs coffee indicates that B wants A to believe that B wants A to get them coffee.

$$r^0_{[\alpha_{R_0}, \beta_{R_0}]} = \frac{(Context : believe(B, barista(A)))}{(Utterance : Stmt(B, A, need(A, coffee)))} {(Intention : want(B, believe(A, want(B, get\_for(A, B, coffee)))))}$$

Second, if B believes C is thirst quenching, telling A that B needs C indicates that B wants A to believe that B is thirsty.

$$r^1_{[\alpha_{R_1}, \beta_{R_1}]} = \frac{(Context : believe(B, quenches(C, thirst)))}{(Utterance : Stmt(B, A, need(A, C)))} {(Intention : want(B, believe(A, thirsty(B))))}$$

Our approach affords the first capability of an ideal system, i.e., the ability to handle uncertain contextual and dialogical information, and to recognize and reason about one's own ignorance. To demonstrate this, suppose the robot strongly believes the following:

(a) Jim believes coffee is thirst quenching: $bel(jim, quenches(coffee, thirst))$ [1.0, 1.0],   (b) Jim just said he needs a coffee: $Stmt(jim, self, need(jim, coffee))$ [0.9, 0.9], and (c) Jim may or may not think the robot is a barista: $bel(jim, barista(self)$ $[\alpha_b, \beta_b]$.

Applying rules r^0 and r^1 will produce a BBA that encompasses information from two consequents, namely:

$$c_0 = want(jim, bel(self, want(jim, get\_for(self, jim, coffee))))$$
$$c_1 = want(jim, bel(self, thirsty(jim))).$$

The degree to which c_0 and c_1 are believed depends on the logic models and operators that are being used. In our example, we use Núñez and Tang's operators (see Section 3.1 above). Although Núñez' logic models can be parameterized to enforce certain logic properties, for ease of explanation we only consider the CFE-based classically consistent uncertain logic operators defined in [7]. Table 1 contains some cases that illustrate how the uncertainty in the two consequents changes depending on the set of logic models and fusion operators, the degree to which the robot believes the interlocutor believes the robot is a Barista (b), and the degree to which the robot believes the two rules r^0 and r^1 hold.

Table 1. Comparison of operators under Tang and Núñez

	$b[\alpha, \beta]$	$r^0[\alpha, \beta]$	$r^1[\alpha, \beta]$	Fusion	$c_0[\alpha, \beta]$	$c_1[\alpha, \beta]$	λ_0	λ_1
1	[0.9,0.9]	[0.85,0.9]	[0.7,0.85]	Núñez	[0.85,0.90]	[0.70,0.85]	0.41	0.17
2	[0.9,0.9]	[0.85,0.9]	[0.7,0.85]	Tang	[0.69,0.90]	[0.63,0.85]	0.18	0.11
3	[0.1,0.1]	[0.1,0.1]	[0.5,0.5]	Núñez	N/A	[0.50,0.50]	N/A	0.00
4	[0.1,0.1]	[0.1,0.1]	[0.5,0.5]	Tang	[0.01,0.10]	[0.05,0.50]	0.56	0.07
5	[0.5,0.5]	[0.1,0.5]	[0.5,0.5]	Núñez	N/A	N/A	N/A	N/A
6	[0.5,0.5]	[0.1,0.5]	[0.5,0.5]	Tang	[0.05,0.5]	[0.45,0.5]	0.07	0.002
7	[0.002,0.002]	[0.99,0.99]	[0.99,0.99]	Núñez	[0.99,0.99]	[0.99,0.99]	0.92	0.92
8	[0.002,0.002]	[0.99,0.99]	[0.99,0.99]	Tang	[0.002,0.99]	[0.80,0.99]	0.00001	0.35

Note that our approach can modulate its interpretation of utterances based on the certainty of the relevant utterance, contextual factors, and pragmatic rules. However, an ideal system should also explicitly reason about its own ignorance. Since we are using a DS-theoretic approach, we can use the consequents' uncertainty intervals to determine whether or not the agent needs to ask for clarification. Specifically, we use the ambiguity measure defined in [6]:

$$\lambda = 1 + \frac{\beta}{1 + \beta - \alpha} log_2 \frac{\beta}{1 + \beta - \alpha} + \frac{1 - \alpha}{1 + \beta - \alpha} log_2 \frac{1 - \alpha}{1 + \beta - \alpha}.$$

For example, for the interval $[0.6, 0.9]$, $\lambda = 1 + \frac{0.9}{1.3} log_2 \frac{0.9}{1.3} + \frac{0.4}{1.3} log_2 \frac{0.4}{1.3} = 0.11$. $\lambda \to 0$ as uncertainty grows and as α and $1 - \beta$ grow closer together. Using this equation, we generate a clarification request if $\lambda \leq 0.1$. This makes use of information that is unavailable to the Bayesian approach.

We will now briefly compare Tang and Núñez' fusion operators before discussing the other capabilities afforded by our approach. Referring to Table 1, one of the most visible results, is that there are several cases in which Núñez' operators do not return a solution (see rows 3 and 6). This is expected since, based on the CFE-based classically consistent logic models, a Modus Ponens does not return a result if there is not enough evidence in the antecedent that supports making a conclusion. In most cases, this lack of supporting evidence is shown as very low values for λ_0 and λ_1 when using Tang's operators, with the only exception being the case of λ_0 in row 4, where the very low uncertainty in the antecedent translates into a very low uncertainty in the consequent.

A second difference between Tang and Núñez' operators is that Tang's operators seem to be slightly more conservative in the allocation of evidence. This can be seen in rows 1 and 2, where the uncertainty intervals associated with c_0 and c_1 are wider when Tang's operators are used.

A more important difference between these operators is evidenced in rows 7 and 8. In the scenarios depicted in these rows, the application of Modus Ponens based on Núñez' operators leads to a potentially problematic high confidence in the consequents c_0 and c_1. Note that, in row 7, the very small uncertainty associated with the antecedent (which suggests that it is false) is not reflected in the resulting uncertainty for the consequent c_0. Furthermore, λ_0 renders a high value, preventing the automatic request of additional evidence by the robot. Due to the more conservative allocation of evidence of Tang's operators, this problem is not visible in row 8. In light of this, we prefer the use of Tang's logical operators in the domain of ISA understanding and pragmatic inference. Using Núñez' operators in this domain could be enabled by a different parameterization of the uncertain logic (e.g., with CFE coefficients that relax some classical logic properties), or by incorporating additional components in the reasoning system (e.g., additional logic rules) aimed at solving the above mentioned issue.

4.2 Adaptation

The second capability of an ideal system is the ability to adapt old rules and learn new ones. We currently assume that the initial beliefs and plausibilities of our rules and contextual items are given, but we do allow rules to be adapted based on user feedback. Upon receiving a corrected rule from a user, it is compared against all current rules. Those whose antecedents and consequents are on the same frames as the antecedents and consequents of the new rule may be updated using the Conditional Update Equation (CUE) as defined in [11]. For example, if rule r^i is on interval $[0.8, 0.8]$, and a correction states that in the current context, $[\alpha_{R_i}, \beta_{R_i}]^i$ should be $[0.5, 0.9]$, the CUE will update the rule's uncertainty to $r^i_{[0.53, 1.0]}$ (a substantial increase in uncertainty). Although the proposed approach only allows for adaptation of rules, it could easily be extended to allow for the addition of new rules, which would initially have very high levels of uncertainty and would become less uncertain with exposure to applications of the rule.

4.3   Belief Modeling

The third capability of an ideal system is the ability to reason about other agents beliefs. Rules such as r^0 and r^1 are formulated in terms of the *interlocutor's* beliefs; to determine what interlocutor J is trying to communicate, J's utterances must be evaluated in the context of J's beliefs. For example, if J says he needs coffee, the likelihood that he is trying to order a coffee should be modulated not by the *robot's* belief that it is a barista, but instead by J's beliefs; if J has no reason to think the robot is a barista, his statement should not be viewed as a coffee order even if the robot has barista training. Belief modeling also allows natural representation of interlocutors' beliefs about the robot's abilities and social roles. For example, the robot may need general rules (e.g., Equation 15) that suggest that a statement such as "I need a coffee" is only an indirect request if its interlocutor believes the robot to be able and obligated to get them coffee.

$$\frac{(Context : bel(B, obligated(A, give(A, B, C))))}{(Intention : want(B, bel(A, want(B, give(A, B, C)))))} \tag{15}$$

4.4   Comparison to Previous Work

While ISAs have been studied for nearly forty years in philosophy and linguistics [10, 12], few computational approaches have been presented for modeling idiomatic ISAs in situated contexts (e.g., [1, 15]). We believe that the DS theoretic approach represents a significant advance over existing approaches.

Wilske and Kruijff's proposal maps indirect requests to action requests [15], and models ambiguity and adaptation: certain utterance types and dialogue contexts will prompt a clarification request whose result determines whether the agent will change its belief. However, such changes are all-or-nothing, which can lead to shifts in belief of unwarranted magnitude. Wilske and Kruijff attempt to rectify this problem by always allowing a chance for the agent to ask for clarification, so unwarranted belief shifts can be reversed. However, this can lead to superfluous questions (when the agent is fairly certain) and incorrect interpretations (when the agent has a belief that is certain and incorrect).

DeVault and Stone presented *COREF*, a dialog system that uses observed dialog features to learn the appropriate interpretations of utterances. While COREF learns to identify the appropriate meaning of an utterance, this consists of resolving lexical, referential, and dialog-move ambiguities in a simple shape-identification game; COREF does not show evidence of handling ISAs.

Some systems that handle conventionalized ISAs also handle unconventionalized ISAs using plan reasoning [1, 5]. These approaches first attempt to handle conventionalized ISAs via rule-based systems that map incoming utterances to deep semantics according to context, and then handle unconventionalized ISAs using plan-reasoning. These approaches do not handle uncertainty or adaptation.

Table 2. Comparison of new and existing work

	Wilske	Hinkelman	Briggs	DeVault	Proposed
Conventional ISAs	•	•	•		•
Unconventional ISAs		•	•		
Handles uncertain context					•
Handles uncertain utterances				•	•
Handles uncertain rules					•
Robust rule combination			•		•
Models agent's ignorance	•				•
Adaptation of existing rules	•			•	•
Learning of new rules				•	
Uses belief modeling			•		•

5 Conclusion

We have presented a novel approach for robustly handling ISAs using DS-theoretic uncertain logical inference, and have shown (1) how the proposed algorithm robustly deals with uncertainty in implication rules and dialogic and environmental context, (2) how belief modeling allows the algorithm to better resolve ISAs, and (3) how rules can be adapted. Table 2 demonstrates that this approach comes closer than previous approaches to satisfying these capabilities.

Currently, our algorithm only handles conventionalized ISAs. A logical next step is to use a hierarchical approach like that described by [1]. While Briggs et al. attempt to understand an ISA inferentially only if a conventionalized form does not exist, we would also need to attempt to understand ISAs inferentially if idiomatic analysis only produced consequents with very low belief and/or high uncertainty. It would also be advantageous to extend the adaptation algorithm to learn *new* ISAs when a correction is provided for which an existing rule does not exist. Future work includes determining which set of fusion operators is preferable, and then performing a large scale evaluation of performance under that set of fusion operators when integrated into a cognitive robotic architecture.

Acknowledgments. This work was funded in part by ONR grants #N00014-11-1-0493 and #N00014-10-1-0140, and in part by NSF grants #1111323 and #1038257.

References

1. Briggs, G., Scheutz, M.: A hybrid architectural approach to understanding and appropriately generating indirect speech acts. In: Proceedings of the 27th AAAI Conference on Artificial Intelligence (July 2013)
2. Brown, P.: Politeness: Some Universals in Language Usage, vol. 4. Cambridge University Press (1987)
3. Chien, A.Y.-H., Soo, V.-W.: Inferring pragmatics from dialogue contexts in simulated virtual agent games. In: Beer, M., Brom, C., Dignum, F., Soo, V.-W. (eds.) AEGS 2011. LNCS, vol. 7471, pp. 123–138. Springer, Heidelberg (2012)

4. Fagin, R., Halpern, J.Y.: A new approach to updating beliefs. In: Uncertainty in Artificial Intelligence. pp. 347–374. Elsevier Science Publishers (1991)
5. Hinkelman, E.A., Allen, J.F.: Two constraints on speech act ambiguity. In: Proceedings of the 27th annual meeting on Association for Computational Linguistics. pp. 212–219. Association for Computational Linguistics (1989)
6. Núñez, R.C., Dabarera, R., Scheutz, M., Briggs, G., Bueno, O., Premaratne, K., Murthi, M.N.: DS-Based Uncertain Implication Rules for Inference and Fusion Applications. In: 16th International Conference on Information Fusion (July 2013)
7. Núñez, R.C., Scheutz, M., Premaratne, K., Murthi, M.N.: Modeling Uncertainty in First-Order Logic: A Dempster-Shafer Theoretic Approach. In: Proceedings of the 8th Int. Symposium on Imprecise Probability: Theories and Applications (July 2013)
8. Pearl, J.: Probabilistic reasoning in intelligent systems: networks of plausible inference. Morgan Kaufmann Publishers Inc., San Francisco (1988)
9. Perrault, C.R., Allen, J.F.: A plan-based analysis of indirect speech acts. Computational Linguistics 6(3–4), 167–182 (1980)
10. Pinker, S., Nowak, M.A., Lee, J.J.: The logic of indirect speech. Proceedings of the National Academy of Sciences 105(3), 833–838 (2008)
11. Premaratne, K., Murthi, M.N., Zhang, J., Scheutz, M., Bauer, P.H.: A Dempster-Shafer theoretic conditional approach to evidence updating for fusion of hard and soft data. In: 12th Int. Conf. on Information Fusion, pp. 2122–2129 (July 2009)
12. Searle, J.R.: Indirect speech acts. Syntax and semantics 3, 59–82 (1975)
13. Shafer, G.: A Mathematical Theory of Evidence. Princeton University Press (1976)
14. Tang, Y., Hang, C.W., Parsons, S., Singh, M.P.: Towards argumentation with symbolic Dempster-Shafer evidence. In: COMMA, pp. 462–469 (2012)
15. Wilske, S., Kruijff, G.J.: Service robots dealing with indirect speech acts. In: IEEE/RSJ International Conference on Intelligent Robots and Systems, pp. 4698–4703. IEEE (2006)

Identification of Bilingual Suffix Classes for Classification and Translation Generation

Karimbi Mahesh Kavitha[1,3]([⊠]), Luís Gomes[1,2],
and José Gabriel Pereira Lopes[1,2]

[1] CITI (NOVA LINCS), Faculdade de Ciências e Tecnologia,
Universidade Nova de Lisboa, Quinta da Torre, 2829-516 Caparica, Portugal
{k.mahesh,gpl}@fct.unl.pt, luismsgomes@gmail.com
[2] ISTRION BOX-Translation and Revision, Lda., Parkurbis,
6200-865 Covilhã, Portugal
[3] Department of Computer Applications, St. Joseph Engineering College,
Vamanjoor, Mangalore, 575 028 , India
kavitham@sjec.ac.in

Abstract. We examine the possibility of learning bilingual morphology using the translation forms taken from an existing, manually validated, bilingual translation lexicon. The objective is to evaluate the use of bilingual stem and suffix based features on the performance of the existing Support Vector Machine based classifier trained to classify the automatically extracted word-to-word translations. We initially induce the bilingual stem and suffix correspondences by considering the longest sequence common to orthogonally similar translations. Clusters of stem-pairs characterised by identical suffix-pairs are formed, which are then used to generate out-of-vocabulary translations that are identical to, but different from, the previously existing translations, thereby completing the existing lexicon. Using the bilingual stem and suffix correspondences induced from the augmented lexicon we come up with 5 new features that reflects the (non)existence of morphological coverage (agreement) between a term and its translation. Specifically, we examine and evaluate the use of suffix classes, bilingual stem and suffix correspondences as features in selecting correct word-to-word translations from among the automatically extracted ones. With a training data of approximately 35.8K word translations for the language pair English-Portuguese, we identified around 6.4K unique stem pairs and 0.25K unique suffix pairs. Further, experimental results show that the newly added features improved the word-to-word classification accuracy by 9.11% leading to an overall improvement in the classifier accuracy by 2.15% when all translations (single- and multi-word translations) were considered.

Keywords: Bilingual suffix classes · Translation classification · Support vector machine · Lexicon augmentation · OOV terms

1 Introduction

Translation Lexicons are known to improve the quality of parallel corpora alignment at sub-sentence granularity, the quality of newly extracted translations, and

A.L.C. Bazzan and K. Pichara (Eds.): IBERAMIA 2014, LNAI 8864, pp. 154–166, 2014.
DOI: 10.1007/978-3-319-12027-0_13

as a consequence, machine translation and cross language information retrieval. High coverage lexicons with correct translations contribute positively to the improvement of application's quality. In the current study, we focus on bilingual morphology learning (stem and suffix correspondences) using the English (EN) - Portuguese (PT) bilingual translation lexicon acquired by adopting the extraction techniques [1], [2], [3], [4] applied on an aligned parallel corpora [5]. Further, we evaluate its usage in improving the accuracy of an existing SVM-based classifier trained to classify automatically extracted EN-PT translations as correct or incorrect based on the existing manually validated entries that are marked as 'accepted' or 'rejected'.

In our previous work on translation classification [6], we proposed an automatic SVM based classifier, trained upon a set of manually classified entries that classifies the extracted term pairs as correct or incorrect. This classification phase, prior to validation was introduced with an intention to improve the validation productivity, enabling 5,000 validated entries per day per validator, thereby contributing to significant decrease in the time consumed on manual validation. In this paper, we discuss and evaluate the use of suffix classes and bilingual stem and suffix mappings (added as 5 new features) on the performance of the existing classifier trained to classify automatically extracted translations as correct and incorrect ones.

1.1   The Existing Bilingual Translation Lexicon

We observe that not all of the extracted translations are good enough to be used for subsequent learning, a few inadequate extractions (multi-word translations) are discussed in [6]. In the context of word-to-word translations, inadequacy is attributed to syntactic (inflectional) or/and semantic (stem context) disagreements, a few of which are as follows. The extracted translation candidate *transported* ⟺ *transportar*, labelled manually as 'rejected', is an example indicating disagreements in morphological inflection, while on the other hand, *transported* ⟺ *transformação* is an example indicating inappropriate stem contexts. The correct translations being *transported* ⟺ (*transportou, transportaram, transportados, transportado, transportada, transportadas*), or *transport* ⟺ (*transportar* (from the translation perspective of the word in PT), the first example points out to the underlying disagreement between the suffix, *ed* in first language (EN) and the suffix, *ar* in second language (PT) and can be used as a feature characterising 'rejected' entries. The latter example indicates a disagreement in stem translations (or semantics), as, *transported* should translate into one of the above mentioned forms (or the translation *transformação* is acceptable provided its EN counterpart is *transformation*). Further, the candidate translation extracted, *observation* ⟺ *observações*, manually labelled as 'rejected', instantiates translation candidates, where, inflections do not match in number (singular noun vs plural noun). These observations stress on the need to bilingual morphological learning and the associated feature extraction (using both the accepted and rejected translations) that will enable the classification of the extracted translations with the accuracy nearing that achieved with human validation.

In our previous work, we have classified the extracted translations (both word-to-word and multi-word translations) using the SVM-based classifier trained with the features, such as, occurrence frequencies of terms in the aligned segments, orthographic similarity measured using Levenshtein Distance, longest common sequence and using the normalised length ratio. Further, the features indicating translation coverage was used to uncover the existence of translation gaps (missing translations in one language with respect to the other language and vice-versa)[6]. However, certain translation candidates (such as those discussed above), manually labelled as 'rejected', were misclassified by the classifier as 'accepted'. This is because, the morphological based features (reflecting the underlying (dis)agreements between bilingual stems and suffixes) were not considered in training the classifier, leading to false positives. To avoid such classifier errors, we adapt the translation coverage based features to represent the morphological coverage in candidate translations considering bilingual stem correspondence and the suffix correspondence induced from the bilingual morphology learning (Subsection 3.1). We include four additional features (hereafter, morphological coverage feature), that looks for the stem and its translation (likewise, considering suffix and its translation) to reflect whether the morphological gap exists in the bilingual pair to be validated. Further, whether the bilingual stems and suffixes belong to the same cluster is indicated using a binary valued feature. The performance of the classifier trained with these additional features when tested on word-to-word translations is evaluated. Table 1 provides a

Table 1. Translation Patterns in the extracted lexicon

Term (EN)	Term (PT)			
ensure	assegurar	zelar	garantir, garantem	permitir
	asseguram			permitam
	assegurem			permitem
ensures	assegura		garanta	permite
	assegure		garante	permita
ensured	asseguradas,		garantidas, garantido	
	assegurados,			
	assegurado,			
	assegurou			
	asseguraram		garantidos	
ensuring	assegurando		garantindo	permitindo

sample listing of the 'accepted' translations existing in the lexicon for each of the *word forms* corresponding to *ensure*. Although the translations seem exhaustive, it is observable that some similar patterns are missing such as, *'garantam'* for *'ensure'*, *'garantiu, garantiram, garantidos'*, *'permitidas, permitido, permitidos, permitidas, permitidas permitiu, permitiram'* for *'ensured'*, which are possible translations as well. Also, we may see that almost all of the translation forms identical to *ensure* ⇔ *zelar* are absent. Generally we may see that, a word (*noun or verb*) in English (en) can have several different forms and it is unlikely that all the different forms of that word or the corresponding translations are seen during the translation extraction process. Thus, the bilingual lexicon acquired is incomplete with respect to all possible translation forms. This is because extractions cannot handle what is not in a parallel corpora. Moreover, they are not able to extract everything. In this regard, we first complete the translation lexicon with respect to the available translations by generating identical translation forms different from the currently existing ones.

A closer look at the lexicon entries for one-to-one word translations reveal near orthographic similarities among each group of terms in the source language vocabulary and such similarities extend to their translations as well. For example, considering the EN part of the bilingual pairs in the columns (1,2), (1, 4) and (1,5) of the Table 1, we observe that each of the words in EN share the same set of suffixes *-e, -es, - ed* and *-ing* with the stem *ensur*. Extending this observation to include their corresponding translations, we see that, a word ending with *-ed* in EN translates as a word ending with *-adas, -ados, -ado, -ou, -aram* (columns (1,2) in 4th row, with the stems *ensur* ⇔ *assegur*) or as a word ending with *-idas, -ido, -idos* (columns (1,4) with the stems *ensur* ⇔ *garant* in 4th row). Similarly, word ending with *-e* in EN translates as a word ending with *-ar* (columns (1,2) with the stems *ensur* ⇔ *assegur* and columns (1,3) with the stems *ensur* ⇔ zel, in 2nd row), or as a word ending with *-ir* (columns (1,4) with the stems *ensur* ⇔ *garant* and columns (1,5) with the stems *ensur* ⇔ *permit*, in 2nd row). This enables us to suggest *permitidas, permitido* and *permitidos* as translations for the word *ensured*, based on the observation that *-ir* attaches to the stem *permit* and that *-ir, -idas, -ido, -idos* co-occur with the same stem (*garant*, for example), just as, *-ar, -adas, -ados, -ado, -ou, -aram* co-occur with same stem *assegur*. By similar observations, we initially induce the bilingual stem and suffix correspondences by considering the longest sequence common to orthographically similar translations. Further, we choose productive bilingual segments and form clusters of stem-pairs characterised by identical suffix-pairs. The stem-pairs and the suffix-pairs are then directly concatenated to generate out-of-vocabulary translations that are identical to, but different from, the previously existing translations, thereby completing the existing lexicon. Now, using the augmented lexicon, bilingual stem and suffix correspondences are identified and induced, bilingual suffix classes are formed, based on which we come up with 5 new features that looks for morphological coverage between a term and its translation.

In the Section 2, we present the related works relevant to bilingual morphology learning and translation classification. In the Section 3, we discuss classification of word-to-word translations by introducing the approach used in learning bilingual suffix classes (Subsection 3.1), followed by discussion on the extraction of features used in classification (Subsection 3.2). The data set and the tools used in classification are described in Section 4. Results of clustering and classification, and their analysis are presented in Sections 5 and 6. Conclusions drawn based on the results and a bit on future work are discussed in Section 7.

2   Related Work

2.1   Bilingual Morphology Learning

Analysing the raw texts for identifying similarities in the structure of words in a language enable acquisition of morphology. Further, learning suffixes and suffixation operations from corpus or a lexicon of a language improves word coverage by allowing new words to be generated. While a few of such studies use supervised approaches [7], others, that exploit the Minimum Description Length principle [8], [9], or target resource-poor languages [10], and agglutinative languages[11], mostly focus on morphological learning considering monolingual data. We take up the learning task considering bilingual data, by using specifically the translation examples taken from validated bilingual translation lexicon. We believe that bilingual data can facilitate appropriate segmentations by reducing ambiguities and complexities as decompositions will be guided by not just the frequent forms occurring in one language but also by their translated forms as well.

One of the earliest works utilising bilingual translations [12] compares to some extent with our work in the way the bilingual segment correspondences are identified. Common and different parts of strings between known words and their translations represent the example strings, referred as Piece of Word (PW) and Pair of Piece of Word (PPW). The bilingual pairs of these extracted example strings maintained as PPW dictionary form the basis of the prediction process. The predicted translation(s) are ranked based on the correct or erroneous prediction frequency of PPW [1]. In our work, we consider the bilingual segments to be valid only if they occur as bilingual stems (suffixes) for at least 2 unique translations in the lexicon. Further, we group the induced suffix pairs attached to the same stem pair. Using those grouped suffix pairs as features, we further cluster the stem pairs. The resulting clusters with bags of stem-pairs and bags of suffix-pairs enable us to generate new translations by directly concatenating the stem-pairs and the suffix-pairs.

Gispert et al., [13] show that translations for unseen verb forms can be generated by generalising them using verb forms seen in training data. Verbs are identified using rules incorporating word forms, POS-tags and word lemmas and are classified to the lemma of their head verb, such that they belong to only one class with such a classification done for each language separately. To translate an unseen verb form, the verb is classified into the lemma of its head word and all the tuples representing translation of that class of verbs (in training data) are identified. New target verb form is generated by replacing the personal pronoun in the seen form with the personal pronoun in the expression to be translated. The suggested translation is weighed based on the frequency of its occurrence in the training data. In case of any ambiguity in generalisation of verb forms, the

---

[1] Number of times PPW has been used in correct or erroneous prediction.

approach over generates all possible forms, leaving the target language model to decide on the best translation alternative. Further, dealing language-specific problems while translating from EN to a morphologically rich languages by identifying morphological relationships that are left uncaptured by current Statistical Machine Translation models, the possibilities of morphology derivation by separating the task from the translation model are discussed. Proper derivations into the text are introduced by simplifying morphological information (or parts of it), followed by a morphology generation by means of a classification model which makes use of a set of relevant features for each simplified morphology word and its context. The study reveals that the main source of potential improvement lies in verb form morphology as this morphological category is seen to exhibit more derivation in Romance languages. We generate unseen forms using the induced morphological correspondences by relying merely on the lexical similarities and the existing translation forms. From the generation perspective, we generate all possible translations as long as the induced morphological correspondences belong to the same cluster, validate them, and use them in subsequent learning. Also, learning and generation is not restricted to verbs and also does not depend on POS-tagging. Similar to their work, we isolate the task of morphology learning and generation from the translation model.

2.2 SVM-Based Classification Approaches in Selecting Translations

SVM, introduced by [14] is a learning machine based on the Structural Risk Minimization principle and mapping of input vectors into high-dimensional feature space. Good learning is possible by adequate feature identification that appropriately represent the knowledge implicit in data. SVM had been successfully used for translation related tasks such as learning translation model for extracting word sequence correspondences (phrase translations) [15] and automatic annotation of cognate pairs [16].

The use of Support Vector Machines in selecting correct translations is not restricted to our work. For selecting appropriate entries[2] into a dictionary from aligned expressions, Kutsumi et. al. [17], use morphemes, part of speech, semantic markers obtained by consulting EDR concept dictionary, and upper-level semantic markers as the means for representing linguistic information. In our experiments, only the lexical similarities between translation pairs are used in extracting the features. For a bilingual pair to be classified as correct, we require that there exists morphological translation coverage, i.e., stem pairs and the suffix pairs should be translations. Further, they should belong to the same cluster.

3 Classification as a Vaiidation Task

We consider the classification of word-to-word translation candidates that were extracted from aligned parallel corpora[3] for language pairs EN-PT. For this

---

[2] Complex proper noun phrases of the English-Japanese pair
[3] DGT-TM - https://open-data.europa.eu/en/data/dataset/dgt-translation-memory

purpose, we first extract the features that characterise each such translation [6]. Additionally, we extract 4 features that indicates if the bilingual pair to be validated has morphological coverage, by considering the stem of the bilingual pair under consideration and its translation (similarly, considering the suffix and its translation). Further, the fact that the bilingual stems and suffixes belong to the same class or not is indicated using a binary-valued feature.

3.1 Extracting the Bilingual Correspondences

Decompositon. Decomposition slightly resembles the notion of suffix pairs and the associated approach underlying their acquisition as proposed by Gaussier [18]. The initial decomposition is based on the longest common sequence applied to the similar translations[4]. For example, considering translation forms such as *ensuring ⇔ assegurando* and *ensured ⇔ assegurou*, we assume a segmentation as given below:

[*ensur ⇔ assegur*] + [*ing ⇔ ando*] and [*ensur ⇔ assegur*] + [*ed ⇔ ou*], yielding the stem pair *ensur ⇔ assegur* with a pair of bilingual suffixes, (*ing ⇔ ando, ed ⇔ ou*).

For each of the decompositions identified, we retain candidate segments satisfying the following criteria:

- Stem pair made of stems with a minimum of 4 characters. The minimum base length criteria proposed in [18] is relaxed to 4 characters to avoid the removal of stem pairs, such as, *rais ⇔ aument, fast ⇔ rápid*.
- Each candidate stem pair should at least attach to one pair of bilingual suffixes. For example, *ensur ⇔ assegur* is retained as the bilingual suffixes, *ing ⇔ ando* and *ed ⇔ ou* attaches to it. But as there are no translation forms similar to *ensure ⇔ zelar* (see Table 1), we discard it.
- Each pair of bilingual suffixes should attach to at least two unique stem pairs. For example, the pair of bilingual suffixes, (*ing ⇔ ando, ed ⇔ ou*), is considered valid if, there exists at least another stem pair, *declar ⇔ declar*, induced from the translations, for instance, *declaring ⇔ declarando* and *declared ⇔ declarou* such that there exists a decomposition as below: [*declar ⇔ declar*] + [*ing ⇔ ando*] and [*declar ⇔ declar*] + [*ed ⇔ ou*].

Grouping. For each of the stem pairs obtained in the previous step, we identify all candidate suffix translation pairs associated with the corresponding stem pair using the pair of bilingual suffixes identified in the previous step.

For example, the candidate suffix translation pairs that associate with the candidate stem translation pair ('ensur', 'assegur') obtained from the segmentation of the bilingual pairs *ensure ⇔ assegurem, ensured ⇔ assegurou* and *ensuring ⇔ assegurando* would be as follows:

('ensur', 'assegur') : ('e', 'em'), ('ing', 'ando'), ('ed', 'ou').

Europarl - http://www.statmt.org/europarl/
OPUS (EUconst, EMEA) - http://opus.lingfil.uu.se/
[4] Similar in the 1st and the 2nd language

Each such grouping indicates suffix pair replacement operations applicable to the associated stem pairs enabling the transformation of one translation form by another.

Clustering. A cluster is a group of suffix pairs that are attached to a common set of stem pairs. The induced stem pairs characterised by suffix pairs (features) are clustered using the clustering tool namely CLUTO[5]. CLUTO is a toolkit that allows clustering low and high dimensional data sets by providing three different classes of clustering algorithms such as, partition, agglomerative and graph-partitioning. The partition and agglomerative clustering, is driven by a total of seven different criterion functions that are described and analysed in [19]. In the experiments presented here, partition approach was adopted for clustering. The *doc2mat*[6] tool provides the necessary conversion of data to be clustered into matrix form. We applied the clustering and analysis algorithms implemented in CLUTO to do a 10, 15, 20, 50, 100 way clustering analysis and the best results were obtained with 50 clusters.

The clustering results are further analysed manually to further identify the sub-clusters from among the clustered results. New translations are generated by directly concatenating the stem pairs and suffix pairs belonging to the same cluster. These newly generated pairs are validated manually and used as training data in the subsequent iteration. Finally around 63 suffix classes were identified consisting of 254 different suffix pairs.

3.2 Morphological Coverage Feature

The bilingual suffix classes identified using the method discussed in Subsection 3.1 are used to extract features for training the SVM based classifier in addition to the orthographic similarity based features (here used as baseline) discussed in [6].

To represent the morphological coverage, first we construct two separate key-word trees for the words in EN and in PT taken from the bilingual pairs labelled as accepted in the training data. Each keyword tree is constructed using the stem part of the word. Similarly, we represent the training and the test set using their stems. Now, the procedure for identifying coverage (with respect to stems) follows the Aho-corasick set-matching algorithm [20] that checks if a stem in the key-word tree (constructed from the bilingual training data separately for EN and PT terms) occurs in the bilingual pair to be validated. If they occur, we check whether they are accepted stem translation pairs.

To represent the coverage based on suffixes, two more key-word trees are constructed separately for suffixes in EN and PT, that are learnt from the accepted training data using the procedure described in Subsection 3.1. Using the Aho-corasick set-matching algorithm we check if the the bilingual pair to be validated ends with the suffix in the keyword tree (constructed from the learnt bilingual

---

[5] http://glaros.dtc.umn.edu/gkhome/views/cluto
[6] http://glaros.dtc.umn.edu/gkhome/files/fs/sw/cluto/doc2mat.html

suffixes separately for EN and PT terms). If they end with the suffixes in the keyword tree, we check whether the matched suffixes are the translations belonging to the same class.

4 Experimental Setup

To extract the features, we used data consisting of a set of bilingual pairs in EN-PT solely representing word-to-word translations, collected from an existing bilingual lexicon whose entries are tagged as being accepted. SVM based tool namely LIBSVM[7] was used to learn the classifier. In the experiments discussed, the radial basis function kernel, with parameters g=32, C=0.5 was used. The values presented for g and C reflect the best cross-validation rate.

For the SVM based classification experiments, we used training set consisting of 209,739 accepted single word translations and 72,136 rejected pairs (i.e, 95% each of the total word-pairs labelled as accepted and rejected). The test set consisted of 14,093 samples (remaining 5%).

5 Results and Discussion

The overview of the data used in learning bilingual suffix classes and the clustering statistics are depicted in Table 2.

Table 2. Overview of the data and Clustering statistics

Description	Statistics
Unique Bilingual examples (training data)	35,891
Partitions for clustering	50
Unique stem pairs identified	6,644
Unique suffix pairs identified	254
New bilingual pairs generated	4,279
Correct bilingual pairs generated	3,862
Incorrect bilingual pairs generated	306

Table 3 depicts sample suffix pairs automatically identified from the clustered results returned by CLUTO, which are further used in extracting the features for training the classifier. Of the 4,279 new bilingual pairs generated (Table 2), 3,862 pairs were correct ones, 306 were spurious translations (due to irregular forms) and the remaining 111 pairs indicate over-generations. Incorrect generations correspond to irregular forms in EN, PT or in both languages. An example is the spuriously generated translation 'selled' ⇔ 'vendidos'. Additionally, other

---

[7] A library for support vector machines - Software available at http://www.csie.ntu.edu.tw/~cjlin/libsvm

Table 3. Translation patterns representing various bilingual suffix classes

Class	Suffix pairs	Stem pairs
4	(al, ivo), (al, iva), (al, ivos), (al, ivas), (ally, ivamente)	remedi ⟺ correct
12	(ence, ência), (ences, ências)	prefer ⟺ prefer
17	(", er), (", erem), (", am), (", em), (s, e), (s, a), (ed, ida), (ed, idas), (ed, ido), (ed, idos), (ed, eram), (ed, eu), (ing, endo), (ing, er)	answer ⟺ respond
32	(e, ar), (e, arem), (e, am), (e, em), (es, e), (es, a), (ed, ada), (ed, adas), (ed, ado), (ed, ados), (ed, aram), (ed, ou), (ing, ando), (ing, ar)	encourag ⟺ estimul

faulty entries are attributed to over-generations as in 'awesomes' ⟺ 'assombrosas', 'attainables' ⟺ 'obtidas' indicating translations generated for adjectives that have no plural forms in English. Some of the errors occurred as no sufficient forms were seen in training data causing stem pairs to be classified under inappropriate classes. An example for this is the incorrectly generated bilingual pair 'pushs' ⟺ 'empurra' as stem pair ('push', 'empurr') was misclassified under class 33.

6   Evaluation

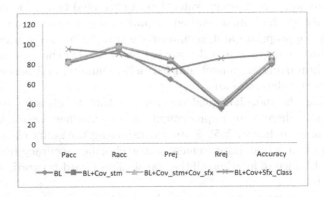

Fig. 1. Precision and Recall with different features

Figure 1 shows the precision (P_{acc}, P_{rej}), recall (R_{acc}, R_{rej}) and the accuracy of the estimated classifier in predicting each of the classes (accepted, *acc* and rejected, *rej*) while using different features. By adapting the features indicating morphological coverage with respect to bilingual stems and suffixes, the accuracy attained is 82.74% which shows an improvement of 4.53% over the baseline (BL) when no such features were used [6].

Micro-average Recall (μ_R), Micro-average Precision (μ_P), and Micro-average f-measure (μ_F)[8] are used to assess the global performance over both classes.

---

[8] Computed as discussed in [6]

Table 4. Performance of classifier on EN-PT word-word-translations for different features

Features	μ_P	μ_R	μ_F	Accuracy
BaseLine	73.91	65.38	69.38	79.15
BaseLine, $Coverage_{stm}$	82.05	67.03	73.79	81.80
BaseLine, $Coverage_{stm}$, $Coverage_{sfx}$	83.61	68.64	75.39	82.74
BaseLine, $Coverage$, $SuffixClass$	83.97	87.1	85.51	88.26

Table 4 shows the μ_P, μ_R and μ_F obtained in classifying word-to-word translations with various features. The morphological coverage added with the class information enabled a micro-average f-measure of 85.51%, almost 15% above BL.

The underlying morphological knowledge about highly reliable translation pairs was exploited in deciding if newly extracted bilingual pairs are correct.

7   Conclusion

In this paper, we have discussed the use of bilingual stem and suffix correspondences in classifying EN-PT word-to-word translations. The fact that, automatically extracted translation equivalents after human validation, are used for iteratively aligning, extracting and validating new translation pairs is the motivation behind our work. Moreover, evaluation of extracted translation equivalents depends heavily on the human evaluator, and hence incorporation of an automated filter for appropriate and inappropriate translation pairs prior to human evaluation tremendously reduces this work, thereby saving the time involved and progressively improving alignment and extraction quality, and hence contributing to improve translation quality.

By adapting the morphological coverage feature to classify word-to-word translations, we achieved an improvement in the classifier accuracy by 3.59% over the BL, and further by 5.52% upon considering the suffix class based feature. This led to an overall improvement in the classifier accuracy by 2.15% over the accuracy obtained in [6] when all the translations (word-to-word, multi-word) are considered.

In future, we intend to experiment with other language pairs such as EN-FR. Further, the possibility of pivoting the transformations learnt from EN-PT and EN-FR to FR-PT shall be studied.

Acknowledgements K.M. Kavitha and Luís Gomes gratefully acknowledge the Research Fellowship by FCT/MCTES with Ref. nos., SFRH/BD/64371/2009 and SFRH/BD/65059/2009, respectively. The authors would like to acknowledge ISTRION project (Ref. PTDC/EIA-EIA/114521/2009) funded by FCT/MCTES that provided other means for the research carried out, thank CITI, FCT/UNL for providing partial financial assistance to participate in IBERAMIA 2014, and ISTRION BOX - Translation & Revision, Lda., for the data and valuable consultation received while preparing this manuscript.

References

1. Aires, J., Lopes, G.P., Gomes, L.: Phrase translation extraction from aligned parallel corpora using suffix arrays and related structures. In: Lopes, L.S., Lau, N., Mariano, P., Rocha, L.M. (eds.) EPIA 2009. LNCS, vol. 5816, pp. 587–597. Springer, Heidelberg (2009)
2. Brown, P.F., Pietra, V.J.D., Pietra, S.A.D., Mercer, R.L.: The mathematics of statistical machine translation: Parameter estimation. Computational Linguistics 19(2), 263–311 (1993)
3. Lardilleux, A., Lepage, Y.: Sampling-based multilingual alignment. In: Proceedings of Recent Advances in Natural Language Processing, pp. 214–218 (2009)
4. Gomes, L., Pereira Lopes, J.G.: Measuring spelling similarity for cognate identification. In: Antunes, L., Pinto, H.S. (eds.) EPIA 2011. LNCS, vol. 7026, pp. 624–633. Springer, Heidelberg (2011)
5. Gomes, L., Lopes, G.P.: Parallel texts alignment. In: New Trends in Artificial Intelligence, 14th Portuguese Conference in Artificial Intelligence, EPIA 2009, Aveiro, pp. 513–524 (October 2009)
6. Kavitha, K.M., Gomes, L., Lopes, G.P.: Using svms for filtering translation tables for parallel corpora alignment. In: 15th Portuguese Conference in Arificial Intelligence, EPIA 2011, pp. 690–702 (October 2011)
7. Déjean, H.: Morphemes as necessary concept for structures discovery from untagged corpora. In: Proceedings of the Joint Conferences on New Methods in Language Processing and Computational Natural Language Learning, pp. 295–298. Association for Computational Linguistics (1998)
8. Goldsmith, J.: Unsupervised learning of the morphology of a natural language. Computational Linguistics 27(2), 153–198 (2001)
9. Creutz, M., Lagus, K.: Unsupervised discovery of morphemes. In: Proceedings of the ACL 2002 Workshop on Morphological and Phonological Learning, vol. 6, pp. 21–30. Association for Computational Linguistics (2002)
10. Hammarström, H., Borin, L.: Unsupervised learning of morphology. Computational Linguistics 37(2), 309–350 (2011)
11. Monson, C., Carbonell, J., Lavie, A., Levin, L.: Paramor and morpho challenge 2008. In: Peters, C., Deselaers, T., Ferro, N., Gonzalo, J., Jones, G.J.F., Kurimo, M., Mandl, T., Peñas, A., Petras, V. (eds.) CLEF 2008. LNCS, vol. 5706, pp. 967–974. Springer, Heidelberg (2009)
12. Momouchi, H.S.K.A.Y. Tochinai, K.: Prediction method of word for translation of unknown word. In: Proceedings of the IASTED International Conference, Artificial Intelligence and Soft Computing, Banff, Canada, July 27-August 1 1997, p. 228. Acta Pr. (1997)
13. de Gispert, A., Marino, J.B.: On the impact of morphology in English to Spanish statistical MT. Speech Communication 50(11–12), 1034–1046 (2008)
14. Vapnik, V.: The Nature of Statistical Learning Theory. Data Mining and Knowledge Discovery, 1–47 (2000)
15. Sato, K., Saito, H.: Extracting word sequence correspondences based on support vector machines. Journal of Natural Language Processing 10(4), 109–124 (2003)
16. Bergsma, S., Kondrak, G.: Alignment-based discriminative string similarity. In: Annual Meeting-ACL, vol. 45, p. 656 (2007)
17. Kutsumi, T., Yoshimi, T., Kotani, K., Sata, I., Isahara, H.: Selection of entries for a bilingual dictionary from aligned translation equivalents using support vector machines. In: Proceedings of Pacific Association for Computational Linguistics

18. Gaussier, É.: Unsupervised learning of derivational morphology from inflectional lexicons. In: Proceedings of ACL 1999 Workshop: Unsupervised Learning in Natural Language Processing (1999)
19. Zhao, Y., Karypis, G.: Evaluation of hierarchical clustering algorithms for document datasets. In: Proceedings of the Eleventh International Conference on Information and Knowledge Management, pp. 515–524. ACM (2002)
20. Gusfield, D.: Algorithms on strings, trees, and sequences: computer science and computational biology, pp. 52–61. Cambridge Univ. Pr. (1997)

Machine Learning

Association Rules to Help Populating a Never-Ending Growing Knowledge Base

Rafael Garcia Leonel Miani[1(✉)], Saulo D. de S. Pedro[2], and Estevam R. Hruschla Jr.[2]

[1] Federal Institute of São Paulo, Votuporanga, Brazil
`rafagami@gmail.com`
[2] Federal University of São Carlos, São Carlos, Brazil

Abstract. Large and continuous growing knowledge bases (KBs) have been widely studied in recent years. A major challenge in this field is how to develop techniques to help populating such KBs and improve their coverage. In this context, this work proposes an "association rules"-base approach. We applied an association rule mining algorithm to discover new relations between the instances and categories, to populate a KB. Considering that automatically constructed KBs are often incomplete, we modified traditional support criteria, creating the MSC measure, to deal with missing values. Experiments showed that an association rule mining algorithm, with and without the modified support calculation, brings relevant rules and can play an interesting role in the process of increasing a large growing knowledge base.

Keywords: Association rules · Missing values · Large knowledge base · Knowledge base extension · Never-ending learning

1 Introduction

From the past few years, we are facing the rise of large knowledge bases (KBs) [1]. In this field, many systems, such as YAGO [2], Cyc [3], DBpedia [4] and NELL [5], were developed aiming to automatically (or semi-automatically) build these KBs.

NELL (Never-Ending Language Learning) is a computer system that runs 24 hours per day, 7 days per week, extracting information from web text to populate and extend its own KB. The main goal of the system is to learn to read the web better each day and to store the gathered knowledge in a never-ending growing KB. The system takes advantage of many different components like CPL [6], CSEAL [7], Prophet [8], OntExt [9], and Conversing Learning [10], in order to be self-supervised and avoid semantic drifting [11]. NELL's knowledge base is represented by an ontology-based structure characterized by categories, relations and their instances.

Since NELL's KB continuously grows each day, it does not contain all instances of every category, neither all instances of every relation described in the ontology. Also, some relations may never occur for some specific instances. So, NELL's KB contains many missing values. To extract rules from a knowledge base having such missing values properties, we have two main options: i) exploring new approaches when using frequent-item-set-based algorithms; ii) trying relational rule extraction approaches (as the one presented in [12], for instance). In this work, we focus on the first possibility.

© Springer International Publishing Switzerland 2014
A.L.C. Bazzan and K. Pichara (Eds.): IBERAMIA 2014, LNAI 8864, pp. 169–181, 2014.
DOI: 10.1007/978-3-319-12027-0_14

The main idea behind the work described in this paper is to show how we can help NELL populating its own knowledge base using association rule mining algorithms [13]. We aim at using facts (knowledge) already stored in NELL's KB as input to a frequent-item-set-based algorithm, thus, discovering new relations and instances that NELL's algorithms were not able to get from web text before. The proposed approach can make use of any association rules mining algorithm, but in the experiments described in this paper we've used NARFO algorithm [14].

There are two main reasons that explain the presence of missing values in a large and continuous growing knowledge base like NELL. First, some instances were not extracted yet from the web by NELL's algorithms, i.e., they are not available at the moment (but should be in the future). Second, a specific relation between two categories might be defined in the ontology, but may never occur in web text, thus, no instances will be extracted by NELL's algorithms. This will be explained later.

In this context, in our approach we modified traditional support measure, creating an adapted measure called MSC. We also have to analyze extracted rules to verify which one is a valid rule that can be used to help to populate the KB. Our approach differs from traditional association rule algorithms on how to interpret and weight the extracted rules. Usually, a rule is considered strong if both support and confidence measures are greater than a threshold, and the higher support and confidence of a rule, the stronger the rule. As NELL's ontology grows each day, daily learning just a small portion of what can be learned, a rule with high confidence must be carefully analyzed, as it could bring wrong knowledge, as NELL does not have all instances to every category yet. Therefore, those rules (with high confidence) need to be carefully inspected before being considered useful.

In our proposed approach, in addition to use the new proposed measure, we automate the assessment of extracted rules by using a Conversing Learning [10] approach. After analyzing the association rules, the relevant ones are used to populate the KB, replacing missing values. The main contributions of this work are:

1. A method, based on association rules, to populate a continuously growing KB;
2. A new approach to deal with missing values in a large and continuously growing knowledge base;
3. New method to rules' support assessment, called MSC measure.
4. Results on the use of Conversing Learning [10] to automatically assess the validity and usability of learned association rules.

2   Related Work

Large and continuously growing knowledge bases have been widely explored in recent years. YAGO [2], YAGO2 [15] (which extend YAGO to deal with spatio-temporal dimension), Cyc [3], DBpedia [4], ReVerb [16], BabelNet [17] and NELL [5] are some examples of systems that deal with a large growing knowledge bases. How to develop methodologies to help populating such KBs and improving their coverage is still a challenge.

In [18], a large scale knowledge base is built from a Chinese Wiki Encyclopedia. [19] developed *Elementary*, a knowledge base construction system that combines diverse resources and techniques via machine learning and statistical inference. A knowledge base construction that extracts information from text and learns a probabilistic model of that information using Tractable Markov Logic (TML) was developed in [20]. The work proposed in [21] described *Sherlock*, which learns First-Order Horn Clauses from web texts. Other studies can be found in [7, 8, 9, 22, 23].

We propose the use of association rule mining to help NELL populate its own KB. Our approach is based on the use of NARFO algorithm [14], which is a generalized association rule algorithm that uses an ontology as background knowledge. Its implementation is based on *Apriori* [13], but also deals with the problem of generalized association rules [24], which is very helpful to navigate through instances and domains of NELL's ontology.

Some similar works that use association rule mining to extend ontologies or knowledge bases were developed in [25] and [1]. The first one uses association rules under an existing ontology, the Finnish General Upper Ontology YSO [26], in order to improve it by populating more relationships between its concepts. [1] produced AMIE, an association rule mining algorithm under incomplete evidence. AMIE focuses on discovering relations like if *motherOf (m; c)* ∧ *marriedTo(m; f)* → *fatherOf (f; c)*. The work described in our paper also aims to discover relations like these.

Association rule is a widely used approach in the field of data mining. Many association rules algorithms were developed due to different purposes. Nevertheless, as stated in [29], many of them are used based on databases that do not contain missing values, differently from what happens in NELL's KB and other large and continuously growing KBs.

Missing values have been widely studied for many years. According to [27], there are some reasons that explain why they occur in datasets:

- Values recorded are missing because they were too small or too large to be measured;
- Values recorded are missing because they have been forgotten, they have been lost or they were not available.

In both ways, the presence of missing values results in loss of information, difficulties in inducing association rules, and also, difficulties to get useful rules. Thus, minimum support and confidence values are usually reduced in most approaches [27].

There are some strategies to deal with the problem of missing values for association rule mining. In [27], the authors apply a technique in which an itemset with missing values is not considered, i. e., it is disabled. For that, they created a new measure definition to support calculation. In [28], all items corresponding to attributes with missing values are set to zero. An algorithm (called ~AR) was proposed in [29], in which missing values are replaced by a probability distribution over possible values represented by existing data. XMiner [28] is an association rule algorithm based on [25] that also brings the concept of extensible itemsets to deal with missing values.

The works presented in [31, 32] both focused on the problem of missing values for association rule mining. In [31], a Markov-chain based Missing Value Estimation (MC-MVE) method was proposed. The work proposed in [32] developed an iterative way to extract association rules for inferring missing values based on the algorithm created by [27].

Fig. 1. Example of Ontology subset

In the context of NELL's ontology, missing values occur either because they are not available at the moment, or because the relation may never happen. NELL's algorithms extract relations between categories, like *athleteplaysport (X,Y)* and *athleteplaytournament (X, Z)*. So, by transitivity, we can induce that if an athlete X plays a sport Y and if the same athlete X plays a tournament Z, then this tournament (Z) is related to that sport (Y). However, NELL could extract relations like *athleteplaysport (Lebron_James, basketball)*, *athleteplaytournament* (kevin_garnett, nba) and *athleteplaytournament (Lebron_James,nba)*. Notice that, in this given example, NELL did not extract the relation between *kevin_garnett* and the sport he plays and, thus, this value will be missing in the KB (*kevin_garnett* is also a basketball player). Another kind of missing value that NELL's KB has is when the relation between two categories did not occur and will never happen. Following along these lines, this paper focuses on dealing with two kind of missing values:

1. Missing values that are missing because they are not available yet;
2. Missing values caused by relations between two specific categories that may never happen.

3   Methodology

To perform our empirical investigation, we extracted a subset of NELL's KB (as the one shown in Fig. 1, for instance). Then, instances were inserted for each category and relation. However, the dataset consists of many empty cells as the relation between two categories was not discovered yet or because the relation might never happen. And it resulted in a missing-values-rich dataset.

To cope with missing values, we substituted them by a 'mv' value. An ontology, based on the domains and instances of the dataset, was created. After that, the data was ready to be used by the association rule algorithm.

3.1   Execution

The use of the association rule algorithm (NARFO) has the following goals in our work: 1) Extract association rules that can be used to update the knowledge base; and 2) Extract and assess association rules by using a new method for support calculation (MSC measure) and comparing to the traditional method. We modified NARFO algorithm support calculation, not considering missing values to a specific itemset domain, in order to deal with missing values. This method is called MSC measure.

Table 1. Example to support calculation

Table 1a			Table 1b	
SportsLeague	Sport	Trophy	Itemset	MSC-based Support value
Nba	Basketball		Nba	4/6 = 0.667
Nba		nba_championship	Nhl	2/6 = 0.333
		nba_championship	Basketball	2/3 = 0.667
Nba		nba_championship	Hockey	1/3 = 0.333
Nba	Basketball	nba_championship	nba_championship	4/4 = 1
Nhl			Nba, basketball	2/6 = 0.333
Nhl	Hockey		Nhl, hockey	1/6 = 0.167
			Nba, nba_championship	3/7 = 0.428
			Nba, basketball , nba_championship	1/7 = 0.142

Consider the toy dataset shown in Table 1a, which contains instances of three different categories (*SportsLeague, Sport and Trophy*). Empty cells in Table 1a represent missing values. So, when calculating MSC, the algorithm does not count missing values to calculate an itemset support value. In Table 1a, *Sportsleague* category has a single empty cell, and this is not considered during support calculation. *Sport* and *trophy* categories have, respectively, four and three empty cells. Table 1b presents itemsets support values (calculated based on Algorithm 1) using MSC measure.

```
For each itemset{
   missingCount := 0;
   weight := getWeigth(itemset);
   For each row in the itemset Domain{
     If (all items == missing)
       Then
          missingCount := missingCount + 1;
   }
   support := weight/(numberRows - missingCount);
   addItemSet(itemset,support);
   support := 0;
}
```

[**Algorithm 1.** Pseudo-code of MSC measure calculation algorithm]

MSC measure computation (described in Algorithm 1) is as follows, for an *n-itemset*, the algorithm discards a missing value if *n items* in the *itemset* are not present. For example, in *1-itemset*, if one missing value is found, the instance containing the missing value is not considered to support calculation. For a *2-itemset*, both items in the domain have to be missing to discard them. The algorithm continues performing this task until no more *itemset* can be found.

For each *itemset* found, the algorithm gets the number of rows in which all items in the current *itemset* appear. Then, it checks the number of rows containing all missing values in the domains of the present *itemset*. Finally, it calculates the support of the *itemset* by the equation shown in Algorithm 1.

3.2   Analyzing Rules

After extracting association rules, we analyze extracted rules to check if a rule can help extending NELL's knowledge base. So, unlikely in traditional association rules algorithms, which consider strong rules the ones with higher support and confidence, we noticed that some rules that have high confidence, specially, could not be good examples of rules to populate and grow the KB, since NELL's KB did not contain all instances and relations yet. And this is one important contribution in this work.

Consider Table 2 as another example. Imagine that NELL's algorithms extracted some instances and relations about *Players*, *Sports* and *Sportsleagues* as shown in Table 2. Based on those instances, it is possible to conclude that a traditional association rule mining algorithm would probably extract the following rule: if *playerPlaysSport (X, Soccer)* then *playerPlaysChampionship (X, italian_championship)*. Notice that, based on Table 2, this rule may have high support and confidence, but it carries wrong information. Why does it occur? It does, mainly because NELL's KB does not have all instances and relations yet. So, an important task is to analyze the discovered association rules and use only the useful ones.

Table 2. Example of instances from players, sports and championships

Player	Sport	SportsLeague
Kaka	Soccer	Italian_championship
Pirlo	Soccer	Italian_championship
Messi	Soccer	
Hernanes	Soccer	Italian_championship
Cavani	Soccer	
Gilardino		Italian_championship
Cristiano_Ronaldo	Soccer	

To evaluate the extracted rules, and automatically (with no need of any feedback from the user) identify the useful ones, we made use of Conversing Learning 9, which is a NELL component capable of autonomously evaluate instances and relations on the KB by having "conversations" with human beings (social network users) and understanding whether those humans would assess a rule as a valid or an invalid rule. NELL's Conversing Learning component may use Twitter and Yahoo Answers to validate rules. In this work, however, only Twitter was used to evaluate extracted rules. Therefore, association rules extracted that are considered relevant rules by Twitter's users are selected to update NELL's KB.

3.3   Populating (Updating) the KB Using Extracted Rules

Having the association rules approved by the Conversing Learning component, the positive examples (correct and useful rules) are used to populate the KB. To this purpose, we get each useful association rule that Conversing Learning brought, verify where an instance with the antecedent(s) values appear and update the dataset with the value(s) of the consequent(s) of the rule. As an example, consider the first rule shown in Table 3 (*playerPlaysLeague (X, nba)* → *playerPlaysSport (X, basketball)*). Using this rule, all *NBA players* (already present in the KB) having a missing value in relation *playerPlaysSport* would have the missing value substituted by *basketball*.

Table 3 shows some of the extracted association rules and the approved rules (useful rules given by Twitter users) that will help populating the KB. Note that three extracted rules are not considered useful, due to the incomplete KB that does not contain all possible relations between two or more domains.

Table 3. Extracted Association rules

Association Rules	Useful rule
playerPlaysLeague (X, nba) → playerPlaysSport (X, basketball)	Yes
playerPlaysSport (X, basketball) → playerPlaysLeague (X, nba)	No
playerPlaysLeague (X, nba) → playerWinTrophy(X, nba_championship)	No
playerWinTrophy (X, nba_championship) → playerPlaysLeague (X, nba)	Yes
playerPlaysSport(X, Soccer) → playerPlaysLeague (X, italian_championship)	No
playerPlaysLeague (X, italian_championship) → playerPlaysSport(X, Soccer)	Yes

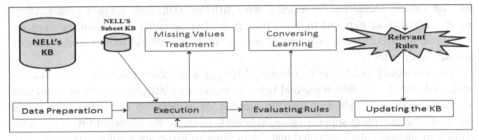

Fig. 2. Methodology representation

With the populated knowledge base, we ran the algorithm again so we can check if new rules could be discovered to help again to iteratively populate the knowledge base. This is done because we are proposing this approach to be used to help a never-ending growing knowledge base system. The experiments and results are shown in next section. Figure 2 describes the sequence of steps taken to achieve results described in the next section.

4   Experiments

The experiments performed in this work show how effective and efficient the use of association rules mining can be to help populating a large and continuously growing knowledge base.

To perform experiments, we used a subset of NELL's KB. This subset is represented in the ontology illustrated in Fig. 1. Notice that this is only a small piece of NELL's ontology that we choose to perform our experiments. The selected subset of the ontology has eight categories (ellipses in Figure 1) and has relations between *Athlete* and the other categories as shown in the graphical representation (arrows in Fig. 1).

The dataset, with instances for the ontology depicted in Fig. 1, contains many missing values. As aforementioned, there are two causes for the missing values: instances are not available yet or instances might not exist. So these experiments were performed having the following main purposes:

- **Experiment 1:** Verify how association rules can help growing the KB containing missing values and replace them using the discovered relations as base for inference;
- **Experiment 2:** Check if MSC measure brings new helpful knowledge to help populating the KB.

Experiment 1 did not consider missing values while finding frequent *itemsets*. So rules are extracted by the algorithm and could be used to populate the KB, by replacing missing values with the instances brought by the extracted rules.

Experiment 2 was performed to check if the MSC measure (described in section 3) has influence on extracting association rules in a large knowledge base with so many missing values. Therefore, we tested it with different minimum support values, varying from 0.04 (four percent) to 0.015 (one point five percent). These values were selected due the KB characteristic and to investigate how it would impact in the number of discovered rules.

We also would like to verify whether different association rules would be discovered, and also, to see which method behaves better with different levels of minimum support. Experiments showed that the number of association rules discovered gets higher as the minimum support value decreases. Running the algorithm with different minimum support values revealed that the number of association rules extracted using MSC measure is bigger than compared with traditional method. Such behavior occurred for all minimum support values tested.

An interesting fact could be observed. Although Experiment 2 extracted more association rules than Experiment 1, Experiment 2 didn't induce some rules that were induced in Experiment 1. There is a particular reason for that behavior: as the new support calculation method makes *itemsets* support higher, the confidence of each rule decreases. Thus, the second method brings new rules that were not present in the first one. This is result of discarding *itemsets* having missing values in all domains, as explained in section 3.

Fig. 3 brings a comparison between these two approaches with different support values, describing the number of association rules extracted by each one. Fig. 4 illustrates the amount of different rules discovered in both experiments. It can be observed that the number of rules in the approach with MSC measure increases very much as the minimum support value decreases. The discard of missing values during support calculation makes the support higher, and this is the explanation for this fact.

In Fig. 4, a similar behavior has occurred (as in the experiments described in Fig. 3). As the minimum support values decreases, the number of different rules extracted by Experiment 2 increases. Different rules mean rules extracted in one experiment that were not extracted in the other one. Some rules extracted by the algorithm are in Table 4.

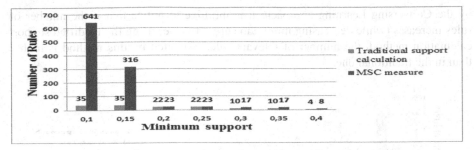

Fig. 3. Number of rules by each approach

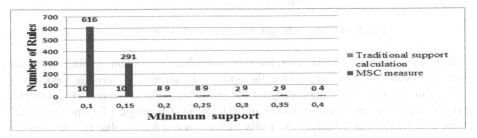

Fig. 4. Number of different rules extracted by each method

Table 4. Rules discovered in experiments

	Association Rules	Measure values	Method
1	*playerPlaysSport(X,basketball)* → *playerPlaysLeague(X,nba)*	sup=0.06666667 conf=1.0	Traditional
2	*playerPlaysLeague(X,nfl)* → *playerPlaysSport(X ,football)*	sup=0.08888889 conf=0.57777774	MSC Measure
3	*playerPlaysforTeam(X,spurs)* → *playerPlaysLeague(X,nba)*	sup=0.021276595 conf=0.8085106	MSC Measure
4	*playerPlaysforTeam(X,yankees)* → *playerPlaysLeague(X,mlb)*	sup=0.01904762 conf=1.0	Traditional

Table 4, shows some rules extracted by the approaches used in these experiments. Note that, although the first rule has higher support and confidence values than the minimum values expected, this rule bring wrong information as there are other players who play basketball in other leagues. This is result of the KB's characteristic at the moment experiments were performed and reveals that rules must be analyzed not only based on support and confidence values. Rules 2 and 4 were extracted by both methods. But the third rule was only extracted by the approach using MSC measure. Using traditional methods, the support of that *itemset* is low and the rule was not generated. However, discarding missing values, as we propose, the *itemset* support gets higher and the rule is generated.

After performing these experiments, each discovered association rule is evaluated, using Conversing Learning, which is another NELL's component. Fig. 5 shows the amount of relevant rules extracted by those two methods used to populate the KB. Considering Table 4, rules 2, 3 and 4 were validated and rule only rule 1 was rejected by the Conversing Learning approach. It is intuitive to notice that if the number of rules increases (while decreasing minimum support value) using the modified support calculation method, the number of relevant rules extracted by this method is higher than in the traditional one.

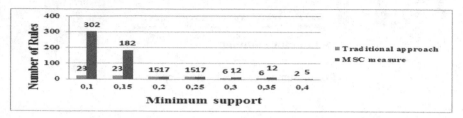

Fig. 5. Number of relevant rules discovered by each method

As a next step in the experiments, the knowledge base was updated using the *useful* association rules to populate it. After the update, the number of missing values was reduced in different levels depending on the minimum support degree. For example, using minimum support values 0.025 and 0.015 the percentage of empty cells decreased in 4.23% and 7.37%, respectively. This is not a fixed value for those minimum support values, as it can vary depending on the used dataset and on the amount of missing values on it. Although this number is not expressive, the relevant discovered rules can be used to populate the KB as new instances and relations are inserted on it each day.

An important result found when performing these tests is that, in this kind of KB, as the association rule mining algorithm was executed with smaller minimum support values each time, the amount of rules increased as expected. But, differently from traditional association rule mining algorithms, which might not consider these rules strong (as they are not very present in the dataset), many rules found with small support value are significant and could be used to help to populate the KB.

The experiments described in this section empirically demonstrated the validity of the use of association rule to help to populate a continuously growing large knowledge base, as well as how missing values are present in this kind of KB and why is it crucial to deal with them. In additions, revealed how a new support measure calculation (MSC measure) impacts the number and the quality of extracted rules.

5   Conclusion and Future Works

Many large and continuously growing knowledge bases face the problem of getting new category instances and relation instances to populate them, thus improving their coverage. In this context, we propose the use of an association rule mining algorithm to help NELL to populate its own KB. To perform that, we tackled the missing value problem, which is common in this kind of KB and has special properties in this context. Thus, our approach takes into consideration that missing values should not be considered in the process of finding frequent *itemsets*, when using traditional support and confidence calculation approach. In addition, we proposed modifying the support calculation method discarding the missing values. The proposed approach also incorporates the idea of conversing learning to automatically filter useful and not useful induced rules and uses the useful ones to automatically populate the KB, contributing to the never-ending learning process.

The experiments demonstrated that the analysis of the extracted rules is a very significant step as it was capable of preventing the propagation of wrong information as described in sections 3 and 4. After analyzing the rules, the KB was updated replacing empty cells by the new discovered instances induced by the association rules.

As future work, we intend to focus on some issues that were not explored in this paper, as well as further investigate the proposed approach. Some interesting topics not yet covered in this paper are:

- Consider generalization in the process of mining association rules in a large and continuously growing knowledge base;
- Improve the preprocessing of association rules extraction to discover irrelevant rules and not consider them during the execution;
- Deal with homonyms and check how they affect the process of extract association rules;
- Considering temporal data in the process of extraction association rules.

References

1. Galágarra, L., Teflioudi, C., Hose, K., Suchanek, F.M.: AMIE: Association Rule Mining under Incomplete Evidence in Ontological Knowledge Bases. In: Proc. of the 22nd Int. Conf. of World Wide Web, pp. 413–422. ACM, New York (2013)
2. Suchanek, F.M., Kasneci, G., Weikum, G.: Yago: a core of semantic web. In: 16th Proc. of the Int. Conf. of World Wide Web, pp. 697–706. ACM, New York (2007)
3. Matuszek, C., Cabral, J., Witbrock, M., DeOliveira, J.: An Introduction to the Syntax and Content of Cyc. In: Proc. of 2006 AAAI Spring Symp. on Formalizing and Compiling Background Knowledge and Its Applications to Knowledge Representation and Question Answering, pp. 44–49 (2006)
4. Bizer, C., Lehmann, J., Kobilarov, G., Auer, S., Becker, C., Cyganiak, R., Hellmann, S.: DBpedia – a crystallization point for the web of data. J. of Web Seman. 7, 154–165 (2009)
5. Carlson, A., Betteridge, J., Kisiel, B., Settles, B., Hruschka Jr., E.R., Mitchell, T.M.: Toward an Architecture for Never-Ending Language Learning. In: 24th Proc. of the Conf. on Artificial Intelligence, pp. 1306–1313. AAAI Press, Atlanta (2010)
6. Carlson, A., Betteridge, J., Hruschka Jr., E.R., Mitchell, T.M.: Coupling Semi-Supervised Learning of Categories and Relations. In: Proc. of the NAACL HLT 2009 Work. on Semi-supervised Learning for Natural Language Processing, pp. 1–9. ACL, New Jersey (2009)
7. Carlson, A., Betteridge, J., Wang, R.C., Hruschka Jr., E.R., Mitchell, T.M.: Coupled Semi-Supervised Learning for Information Extraction. In: 3rd Int. Conf. on Web Search and Data Mining (WSDM), pp. 101–110. ACM, New York (2010)
8. Appel, A.P., Hruschka Jr., E.R.: Prophet – a link-predictor to learn new rules on NELL. In: 11th Proc. of the Int. Conf. on Data Mining Work., pp. 917–924. IEEE (2011)

9. Mohamed, T.P., Hruschka Jr., E.R., Mitchell, T.M.: Discovering Relations between Noun Categories. In: Proc. of the 8th Conf. on Emp. Methods in Natural Language Processing, pp. 1447–1455. Association for Computational Linguistics, Stroudsburg (2011)

10. Pedro, S.D., Hruschka Jr., E.R.: Conversing Learning: Active Learning and Active Social Interaction for Human Supervision in Never-Ending Learning Systems. In: Pavón, J., Duque-Méndez, N.D., Fuentes-Fernández, R. (eds.) IBERAMIA 2012. LNCS, vol. 7637, pp. 231–240. Springer, Heidelberg (2012)

11. Curran, J.R., Murphy, T., Scholz, B.: Minimising semantic drift with mutual exclusion bootstrapping. In: Proc. of the 10th Conf. of the Pacific Association for Computational Linguistics, pp. 172–180 (2007)

12. Gardner, M., Talukdar, P.P., Kisiel, B., Mitchell, T.: Improving Learning and Inference in a Large Knowledge-base using Latent Syntactic Cues. In: Proc. of the Conference on Empirical Methods in Natural Language Processing, pp. 833–838 (2013)

13. Agrawal, R., Imielinski, T., Swami, A.M.: Mining Association Rules between Sets of Items in Large Databases. In: 19th ACM SIGMOD Annual Conference on Management of Data, pp. 207–216 ACM, New York (1993)

14. Miani, R.G., Yaguinuma, C.A., Santos, M.T., Biajiz, M.: NARFO Algorithm: Mining Non-redundant and Generalized Association Rules Based on Fuzzy Ontologies. In: Filipe, J., Cordeiro, J. (eds.) Enterprise Information Systems. LNBIP, vol. 24, pp. 415–426. Springer, Heidelberg (2009)

15. Hoffart, J., Suchanek, F.M., Berberich, K., Weikum, G.: YAGO2: A spatially and temporally enhanced knowledge base from Wikipedia. J. Art. Intelligence. 196, 28–61 (2012)

16. Etzioni, O., Fader, A., Christensen, J., Soderland, S., Mausam, M.: Open Information Extraction: the Second Generation. In: 22nd Proc. of the IJCAI, pp. 3–10 (2011)

17. Navigli, R., Ponzetto, S.P.: BabelNet: building a very large multilingual semantic network. In: 48th Proc. of the Annual Meeting of the Assoc. for Comp. Ling., pp. 216–225 (2010)

18. Wang, Z., Wang, Z., Li, J., Pan, J.Z.: Building a Large Scale Knowledge Base from Chinese Wiki Encyclopedia. In: Pan, J.Z., Chen, H., Kim, H.-G., Li, J., Wu, Z., Horrocks, I., Mizoguchi, R., Wu, Z. (eds.) JIST 2011. LNCS, vol. 7185, pp. 80–95. Springer, Heidelberg (2012)

19. Niu, F., Zhang, C., Ré, C., Shavlik, J.: Elementary: Large-scale Knowledge-base Construction via Machine Learning and Statistical Inference. J. on Sem. Web and Inf. Sys. 8, 42–73 (2012)

20. Kiddon, C., Domingos, P.: Knowledge Extraction and Joint Inference Using Tractable Markov Logic. In: Proc. of the 2nd Joint Work. on Automatic Knowledge Base Construction and Web-scale Knowledge Extraction, pp. 79–83. ACL (2012)

21. Schoenmackers, S., Etzioni, O., Weld, D.S.: Learning First-Order Horn Clauses from Web Text. In: Proc. of the Conf. on Empirical Methods in Natural Language Processing, pp. 1088–1098 (2010)

22. Ji, H., Grishman, R.: Knowledge Base Population: Successful Approaches and Challenges. In: Proc. of the 49th Annual Meet. of the Assoc. for Comp. Ling., pp. 1148–1158 (2011)

23. Lao, N., Mitchell, T., Cohen, W.W.: Random Walk Inference and Learning in a Large Scale Knowledge Base. In: 8th Proc. of the Conf. on Empirical Methods in Natural Language Processing, pp. 529–539. Assoc. for Computational Linguistics, Stroudsburg (2011)

24. Srikant, R., Agrawal, R.: Mining Generalized Association Rules. In: Proceedings of the International Conference of Very Large Knowledge Bases, pp. 407–419 (1995)

25. Kauppinen, T., Kuittinen, H., Seppälä, K., Tuominen, J., Hyvönen, E.: Extending an Ontology by Analyzing Annotation Co-occurrences in a Semantic Cultural Heritage Portal. In: Proc. of the 3rd Work. on Collective Int. at the Asian Sem. Web Conf., Bangkok (2008)

26. Hyvönen, E., Viljanen, K., Tuominen, J., Seppälä, K.: Building a national semantic web ontology and ontology service infrastructure –the FinnONTO approach. In: Bechhofer, S., Hauswirth, M., Hoffmann, J., Koubarakis, M. (eds.) ESWC 2008. LNCS, vol. 5021, pp. 95–109. Springer, Heidelberg (2008)
27. Ragel, A., Cremilleux, B.: Treatment of Missing Values for Association Rules. In: 2nd Pacific-Asia Conf. on Knowledge Disc. and Data Mining, Melbourne, pp. 258–270 (1998)
28. Hahsler, M., Grün, B., Hornik, K.: arules – A Computational Environment for Mining Association Rules and Frequent Item Sets. J. of Statistics Software 14, 1–25 (2005)
29. Nayak, J.R., Cook, D.J.: Approximate Association Rule Mining. In: Proceedings of 14th FLAIRS Conference, pp. 259–263. AAAI, Key West (2001)
30. Calders, T., Goethals, B., Mampaey, M.: Mining Itemsets in the Presence of Missing Values. In: Proc. of the 22nd Annual ACM Symposium on Applied Computing, pp. 404–408 (2007)
31. Chen, R.H., Fan, C.M.: Treatment of Missing Values for Association Rule-Based Tool Commonality Analysis in Semiconductor Manufacturing. In: Proc. of the 8th IEEE Int. Conf. on Automation Science and Engineering, pp. 886–891. IEEE, Seoul (2012)
32. Hong, T.P., Wu, C.W.: Mining rules from incomplete dataset with high missing rate. J. of Expert Systems with Applications: An International Journal 38, 3931–3936 (2011)

Likelihood Function for Multi-target Color Tracking Using Discrete Finite Mixtures

Sergio Hernandez$^{(\boxtimes)}$ and Matias Hernandez

Universidad Católica del Maule, Talca, Chile
shernandez@ucm.cl, matiasfh@gmail.com
http://www.eici.ucm.cl/Academicos/shernandez/

Abstract. Color-based object trackers have been proved robust and versatile in visual tracking applications. There are different techniques used in the literature to compare the color similarity between the current object being tracked and a reference model and the most common being a Gaussian approximation of the color histogram distribution and a distance measure based on the Bhattacharyya coefficient to accomplish for the target correspondence task. This approach requires constant updating in order to preserve the invariability of the color model and therefore requires ad-hoc techniques for estimating the parameters of the Gaussian likelihood and the histogram update model. In this paper, we present a more general approach to color-based object tracking using a finite mixture of discrete multivariate distributions. More particularly, the Dirichlet Compound Multinomial (DCM) or Polya density is used to directly model random color histograms from a single target. Conversely, a mixture of Polya distributions is proposed as a multi-target color likelihood. The approach presented in this work only requires to estimate the parameters of the DCM mixture, with a single component of the mixture representing the color distribution of a single object. We demonstrate the improvement obtained with this method compared to the more traditional Gaussian assumption in real scenes, solving complex problems like changes in illumination and perspective.

1   Introduction

Detecting and tracking color objects in video frames are two important tasks in automatic video surveillance as well as other applications such as gesture-based interfaces, augmented reality and grape seeds phenolics tracing among others. Also, in the past few years there has been an increased interest in other application domains such as medical applications, robotics, interactive games and business intelligence among others [1]. The main goal of this type of implementation is to efficiently extract useful information such as the position and velocity of one ore more objects in sequences of images or video streams.

There are several challenges that have to be addressed in order to accomplish the task of tracking moving objects. In constrained scenarios, the target and the background objects can be designed to be easily distinguishable. However, it still remains a complex challenge to detect and track targets in uncontrolled

© Springer International Publishing Switzerland 2014
A.L.C. Bazzan and K. Pichara (Eds.): IBERAMIA 2014, LNAI 8864, pp. 182–193, 2014.
DOI: 10.1007/978-3-319-12027-0_15

environments. Moreover, there might be several targets that can interact each other, creating a complex dynamic estimation problem.

In either case, the task of video tracking basically consists of establishing the relationship between an object of interest with a reference model that describes the appearance of the target. The reference model can make use of high-level, mid-level or low-level descriptors. Color histograms are low-level descriptors which are widely used in this context because of their invariance to translation and rotation and at the same time are and robust to partial occlusions.

One popular method to perform color object tracking is the Mean-Shift algorithm [2]. The method consists of computing the color histogram of a target using a kernel density estimate and then iteratively finding the mode of the distribution in a new video frame. The Mean-Shift algorithm can be efficiently implemented by only using the first moments of the distribution, however the search process is conducted deterministically so the method is prone to fail when the background exhibits a similar color distribution or the tracked object is completely occluded.

In the other hand, probabilistic techniques such as the Kalman filter or the particle filter algorithm can recursively estimate the state of a target using the history of previous measurements. The dynamic behaviour of the target can be modelled as being linear or non-linear but one common assumption is to model the observations as Gaussian with additive noise [3]. In this regard, assuming conditional independence between different sub-regions of the image and approximating the Bhattacharyya distance of the regions and the reference histogram by a Gaussian distribution has succeeded in many complex tracking scenarios [4,5].

One of the problems of this approach arises from the Gaussian assumption of the likelihood. Under this assumption, the observation noise is a design parameter and cannot be estimated from data. We present a novel approach to model the color histogram using the Dirichlet Compound Multinomial (Polya) distribution. In this approach, a set of histograms can be collected from manual or automated detections and the parameters of the observation model can be effectively estimated from data.

2   Particle Filter Color Tracking

The state space model is a probabilistic representation of a partially observed dynamical system. In the context of target tracking, at time k the state (i.e. position and velocity) of the target x_k follows a dynamic model $f(\cdot)$. The observed variables y_k are related to the hidden state through another function $g(\cdot)$. The model can be summarized as follows:

$$x_k = f(x_{k-1}, v_k) \qquad \text{dynamic model}$$
$$y_k = g(x_k, w_k) \qquad \text{observation model}$$

where v_k and w_k are the dynamic and observation noise respectively.

Particle filters are Monte Carlo techniques specifically designed for sequential Bayesian estimation of state space models with non-linear dynamics and non-Gaussian observations. Using this technique we can recursively estimate the posterior distribution of the hidden path $x_{1:k}$ given observations $y_{1:k}$, and more specifically the marginal or *filtering distribution* $p(x_k|y_{1:k})$. This process is also known in the literature as recursive Bayesian estimation or *Bayesian filtering* [6] and consists of a prediction step (Equation 1) and another update step (Equation 2).

$$p(x_k|y_{1:k-1}) = \int p(x_k|x_{k-1})p(x_{k-1}|y_{1:k-1})\, dx_{k-1} \tag{1}$$

$$p(x_k|y_{1:k}) = \frac{p(y_k|x_k, y_{1:k-1})p(x_k|y_{1:k-1})}{p(y_k|y_{1:k-1})} \tag{2}$$

Because of the intractability of the model, the particle filter algorithm uses a weighted estimate of the posterior pdf.

$$p(x_k|y_{1:k}) \approx \sum_j^{N_s} w_k^j \delta(x_k - x_k^j)$$

where $\delta(x_k - x_k^j)$ is the Dirac delta function and w_k^j are importance weights. Futhermore, it is common to use the transition prior as importance or sampling density, so at any time step k we can recursively generate new samples with weights:

$$w_k^j \propto w_{k-1}^j p(y_k|x_k) \tag{3}$$

3   Color Observation Model

The Bhattacharyya coefficient is a widely used similarity measure for color distributions. However, it has been recently noticed that the choice of the distance measure and the parameters of the base distribution may affect the quality in the performance of tracking systems [7]. Subsection 3.1 describes the Gaussian/Bhattacharyya observation model and Subsection 3.2 describes the Polya color model.

3.1   Gaussian/Bhattacharyya Likelihood

The distance D_k (see Equation 4) is based on the Bhattacharyya coefficient and measures the dissimilarity between two probability distributions. The distance D_k obeys the triangle inequality and therefore can be used to determine the relative closeness between two color histograms being considered. If we now consider two histograms $\mathbf{y}_k = (y_1, \ldots, y_{N_b})_k$ and $\mathbf{y}^* = (y_1, \ldots, y_{N_b})^*$ each having N_b bins, then the Bhattacharyya distance is defined as:

$$D_k = \sqrt{1 - \sum_{i=1}^{N_b} \sqrt{y_i^* y_i}} \tag{4}$$

In [4] the authors proposed a probabilistic framework based on the particle filter algorithm, where a second-order autoregressive model is used to model the dynamic behaviour of the target and the color histogram of the candidate regions in the HSV color space is used to model the likelihood of the observations.

The Gaussian density for the likelihood function of the measured color histograms is given by:

$$p(\mathbf{y}_k|x_k) \approx \mathcal{N}(D_k; 0, \sigma^2) \tag{5}$$

$$p(\mathbf{y}_k|x_k) = \frac{1}{\sqrt{2\pi}\sigma} \exp\left\{-\frac{D_k^2}{2\sigma^2}\right\} \tag{6}$$

where D_k is the distance between the reference histogram $\mathbf{y}^*$ of the tracked object and the histogram $\mathbf{y}_k$ computed from the current region that will be tested against. As noted before, the squared standard deviation σ^2 of the Gaussian density Equation 5 is a design parameter and cannot be estimated from data. Several values for σ have been reported in the literature, but none of them estimate this value from data.

3.2   Dirichlet Compound Multinomial Likelihood (Polya)

The multinomial distribution can be used to specify the probability of a vector with discrete elements $\mathbf{y} = (y_1, \ldots, y_{N_b})$, containing counts on each one of the N_b bins of the color histogram. We can now write down the probability of a color histogram given certain parameter vector $\boldsymbol{\theta} = (\theta_1, \ldots, \theta_{N_b})$ as:

$$p(\boldsymbol{y}|\boldsymbol{\theta}) = \frac{n!}{\prod_i y_i!} \prod_i \theta_i^{y_i} \tag{7}$$

where $n = \sum_i y_i$ correspond to the total number of pixels in the ROI.

The maximum likelihood estimate can be calculated from a set of D histograms $\boldsymbol{Y} = \{\boldsymbol{y}_1, \ldots, \boldsymbol{y}_D\}$ using:

$$\hat{\theta}_i = \frac{\sum_d y_{di}}{\sum_j \sum_d y_{dj}} \tag{8}$$

Whenever the number of bins is fixed and each one of the bins are independent, a multinomial likelihood can be used to correctly model color histograms. This is not a difficult assumption for color histograms with a large number of bins, where each pixel can be regarded as a random sample from a frequency distribution. However, under the multinomial model the probabilities for each bin must remain constant over the D histograms.

Another problem related to the multinomial model is related to the independence assumption within each one of the bins. In the text modelling community the term word "burstiness" is used to represent the co-occurrence of the same word within a single document. In order to cope with the extra variation across the collected histograms and the probability of having repeated occurrences of the same color in a single histogram, the $\boldsymbol{\theta}$ parameter can be also treated as a random vector with distribution on the simplex. The Dirichlet distribution is a probability density function over distributions and can therefore be used as prior for the multinomial data. The generative model now use a N_b-dimensional hyper-parameter vector $\boldsymbol{\alpha}$ such that:

$$p(\boldsymbol{\theta}|\boldsymbol{\alpha}) = \frac{\Gamma(\sum_i \alpha_i)}{\prod_i \Gamma(\alpha_i)} \prod_i \theta_i^{\alpha_i - 1} \tag{9}$$

Following [8], the marginal likelihood of a single color histogram can be written as:

$$p(\boldsymbol{y}|\boldsymbol{\alpha}) = \int p(\boldsymbol{y}|\boldsymbol{\theta})p(\boldsymbol{\theta}|\boldsymbol{\alpha})d\boldsymbol{\theta} \tag{10}$$

There is no closed form for the maximum likelihood value of $\boldsymbol{\alpha}$. A lower of bound for the gradient of the log-likelihood was proposed in [8], leaving the following update rule:

$$\alpha_i = \alpha_i' \frac{\sum_d \{\Psi(y_{di} + \alpha_i) - \Psi(\alpha_i)\}}{\sum_d \{\Psi(\sum_i y_{di} + \alpha_i) - \Psi(\sum_i \alpha_i)\}} \tag{11}$$

Integrating out the $\boldsymbol{\theta}$ parameter in Equation 10, the likelihood function does not depend on the multinomial parameter anymore. Therefore, we can now write the likelihood of a new histogram $\mathbf{y}_k$ as follows:

$$p(\mathbf{y}_k|x_k) = \frac{n!}{\prod_i y_i!} \frac{\Gamma(n+1)\Gamma(\sum_i \alpha_i)}{\Gamma(\sum_i y_i + \alpha_i)} \prod_i \frac{\Gamma(y_i + \alpha_i)}{\Gamma(y_i + 1)\Gamma(\alpha_i)} \tag{12}$$

with α being a N_b dimensional parameter vector representing the color distribution of the target x_k.

4   Multi-target Color Tracking

In the probabilistic tracking framework, we would like to take samples from a sampling density that creates uniformly weighted samples. However, computing an optimal importance distribution is also intractable so the likelihood function is used to give more importance to samples that are closer to the true state (see Equation 3). Therefore a better likelihood function should increase the effective sampling size.

Nevertheless, extending the particle filter framework for multi-target tracking is far from being straightforward and complicated Markov Chain Monte Carlo strategies are required to cope with the changing dimensionality of the state vector. Apart from the difficulties of coping with target birth and death as well as handling occlusions and overlapping, the probabilistic model has to successfully maintain a multi-modal distribution for the color measurements from multiple targets [9], in which case the filtering distribution can be written as:

$$p(x_k|y_{1:k}) = \sum_m^M \pi_{km} p_m(x_k|y_{1:k}) \tag{13}$$

4.1 Mixture Color Likelihood

In the case of color likelihoods, the data from the multiple targets is also not continuous but discrete so we can now consider a mixture of M Polya distributions with parameter $A = \{\alpha_1, \ldots, \alpha_M\}$, where each component of the mixture is a Dirichlet Compound Multinomial distribution with parameter α_m that represents the color distribution of a single target.

The prior distribution for the multinomial parameter θ using the mixture model can be written as:

$$p(\theta|A, \pi) = \sum_m \pi_m \frac{\Gamma(\sum_i \alpha_{mi})}{\prod_i \Gamma(\alpha_{mi})} \prod_i \theta_i^{\alpha_{mi}-1} \tag{14}$$

where $\pi = (\pi_1, \ldots, \pi_M)$ is a vector containing the mixture weights according to the following normalization constraint $\sum_m \pi_m = 1$.

The marginal likelihood of the observed data given the mixture prior is now:

$$p(y|A, \pi) = \sum_m \pi_m p(y|\alpha_m) \tag{15}$$

The multi-modal observation likelihood can now be written as:

$$p(y_k|x_k) = \frac{n!}{\prod_i y_i!} \sum_m \pi_m \frac{\Gamma(n+1)\Gamma(\sum_i \alpha_{mi})}{\Gamma(\sum_i y_i + \alpha_{mi})} \prod_i \frac{\Gamma(y_i + \alpha_{mi})}{\Gamma(y_i + 1)\Gamma(\alpha_{mi})} \tag{16}$$

Off-line estimation of the mixture model can be performed with the *Expecation-Maximization* (E-M) algorithm [10, 11]. The log-likelihood $\log p(Y|A, \pi)$ of the observed histograms $Y = \{y_1, \ldots, y_K\}$ now contains the logarithm of the summation over the mixture components, which leaves parameter estimation intractable. However, this problem is alleviated by considering the expectation $\gamma(z) = E[z|Y, A, \pi]$ of an auxiliary variable denoted $z_k = (z_1, \ldots, z_M)$. A full derivation of the E-M procedure is out of the scope of this paper and can be found in [12], however an outline of the EM algorithm is presented as follows:

In order to determine the number of mixture components M, a criteria such as the Bayesian Information Criteria (BIC) can be used to assess the trade-off between the goodness of fit and the model complexity, defined as:

$$BIC = -2\log p(Y|A, \pi) + M\log(K) \tag{17}$$

where M is the number of mixture components and K is the number of histograms or data points.

Algorithm 1. EM algorithm for parameter estimation of the Polya mixture model

---
Require: π, A, TOL
  while $\log p(Y|A, \pi) - \log p(Y|A', \pi') < TOL$ **do**
    $\pi' \leftarrow \pi, A' \leftarrow A$
    E-Step : Evaluate the expectation $\gamma(z)$.
    M-Step : Calculate A and π.
  end while

---

5 Experiments

This section compares the performance of the proposed Polya likelihood with the standard Gaussian/Bhattacharyya approach. The first experiment makes use of color histograms from a Region of Interest (ROI) taken from a face detector and compares the performance of the two likelihood approaches for comparing a new ROI with an arbitrary region in the same image. The second experiment also uses color histograms from a face detector but comparison is made under changing light conditions. A third experiment takes color histograms from a person detector in a surveillance video and the collected data is used to estimate the parameters of a Polya mixture model.

5.1 Experiment 1

The first step is to obtain the ROI in a set of frames and create the color histograms used for parameter estimation. The ROI was captured by means of the well known Viola-Jones detector [13] and a Gaussian likelihood was created with a single histogram y^* (reference frame) and the design parameter $\sigma = 0.22$. 2-D color histograms in the HSV color space were considered and histogram equalization was performed for image enhancement. Figure 1 shows one ROI captured in this experiment and the corresponding 8×8 bins histogram.

Instead of considering a single histogram, we collected 200 histograms and estimated the Polya parameter α iterating Equation 11 with a maximum number of 1000 iterations and tolerance $1e-6$. After the learning step, detections in new images having the same lighting conditions than the reference frame were

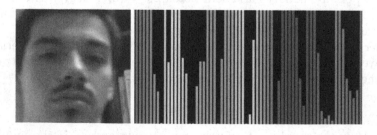

Fig. 1. Captured ROI and 2 channels color histogram

used to compare the performance of the Polya and the Gaussian/Bhattacharyya likelihood. Channels H-S were used to create 2-D histograms with 8 bins per channel. Figure 2 shows the ROC curve for the two likelihood approaches. The AUC (Area Under the Curve) values for each ROC curve in Figure2 are 0.991600 for the Gaussian/Bhattacharyya likelihood and 1.0000 for the proposed Polya likelihood.

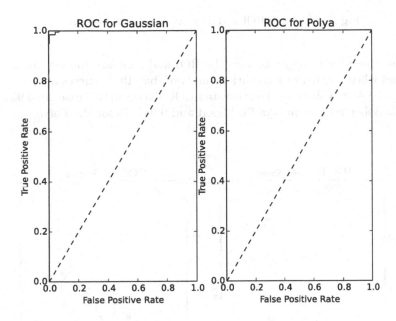

Fig. 2. ROC curves for data generated from color histograms with constant illumination

The results in Figure 2 show little difference between the two approaches. The performance of the Gaussian/Bhattacharyya is good enough since there are no changes in the lighting conditions. However, there is a slightly improved performance for the Polya likelihood, confirming previous results using a Dirichlet likelihood for human skin detection [14].

5.2 Experiment 2

In this experiment we use the same setup as the previous example but we now consider an environment with changing lighting conditions.

Figure 3 shows one ROI captured with its corresponding 8×8 bins histogram.

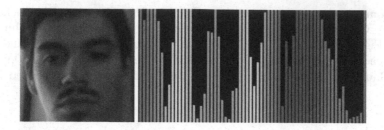

Fig. 3. Captured ROI and 2 channels color histogram

We use the color histograms from the ROI and compare the two likelihood approaches when the lighting conditions are variable. ROC curves are shown in Figure 4. The AUC values for the generated ROC curves in this case are 0.954550 for the Gaussian/Bhattacharyya likelihood and 0.984175 for the Polya.

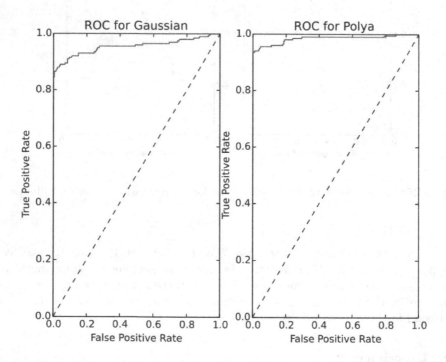

Fig. 4. ROC curves for data generated from color histograms with non-constant illumination

This experiment shows that our method outperforms the classical approach using a Gaussian distribution as the color likelihood. This Gaussian likelihood uses a single histogram $\mathbf{y}*$ to represent an object of interest, so it cannot cope with the multiple modalities arising from the changing lighting conditions. Instead, a single Polya distribution with parameter α estimated from a set of color histograms can hold the varying information of the environment and target.

5.3 Experiment 3

As mentioned before, for this experiment we create a set of color histograms gathered from multiple targets. In this case, we used the Histogram of Oriented Gradients (HOG) descriptor and a linear SVM to detect the ROI [15]. The data is taken from the PETS 2013 Benchmark Database [1] and more specifically the *S2.L1 Walking* track.

Using this dataset we gather a collection of color histograms from the ROIs marked by the detector, as shown in Figure 5. The HOG detector used a 8×8 sliding window and a scale factor of 1.05. For each frame, the detector get a varying number of detections and for each detection we get a set of histograms. When the detection process finishe, we have a set of histograms represeting all the detection in each frame. This set is then used to estimate the A and π parameters of the Polya mixture model using the E-M algorithm.

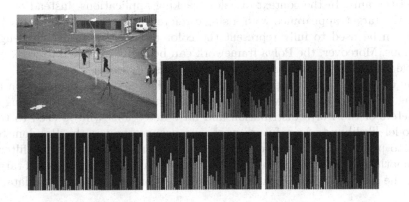

Fig. 5. Captured ROIs and color histogram for each ROI in a frame of the PETS database

As seen in Figure 6(a), in the case of a Polya mixture with $M = 7$ components, the E-M algorithm successfully identified the parameters of the model. Figure 6(a) shows the log-likelihood after 100 iterations and Figure 6(b) shows the BIC for the different numbers of mixture components M. The BIC score indicates that $M = 10$ can be regarded as a model with a good trade-off between complexity and goodness of fit.

---

[1] http://www.cvg.rdg.ac.uk/PETS2013/a.html

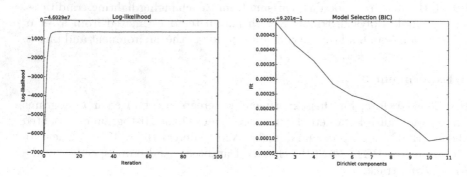

Fig. 6. Log-likelihood and model selection for the mixture of Polya distributions generated from the multi-target color histograms

6 Conclusions

Compared to the standard Gaussian likelihood, the Dirichlet Compound Multinomial (Polya) distribution has noticeable advantages as a generative model for color histograms. In the context of color tracking applications, instead of comparing the target appearance with a single reference histogram, the Polya likelihood can be used to fully represent the color distribution under challenging conditions. Moreover, the Polya framework can be easily extended to work with multiple targets when using mixtures of Polya distributions.

One drawback of this approach arises from the separation of detection and learning. Missed detections will not be taken into account when estimating the parameters of the Polya distribution and false detections will be used to train the model likelihood. As a future work, we propose to use the Random Sets theory to perform joint detection, tracking and learning. In that case, filtering and smoothing recursions can be used to estimate an unknown number of targets and at the same time to learn the model observation parameters from data.

Acknowledgments. This paper is funded entirely by FONDEF IDeA CA12i10236 Estimación de la Madurez Fenólica de la Uva en base a Imágenes de la Semilla (Estimation of Phenolic Maturity based on Grape Seed Images). Marco Mora, Claudio Fredes, Sergio Hernandez. National Commission for Science and Technological Research (CONICYT), Government of Chile.

References

1. Maggio, E., Cavallaro, A.: Video Tracking. Theory and Practice. John Wiley & Sons (2011)
2. Comaniciu, D., Meer, P.: Mean shift: A robust approach toward feature space analysis. IEEE Trans. Pattern Anal. Mach. Intell. **24**, 603–619 (2002)
3. Isard, M., Blake, A.: Condensation : Conditional density propagation for visual tracking. Int. J. Comput. Vision **29**, 5–28 (1998)

4. Pérez, P., Hue, C., Vermaak, J., Gangnet, M.: Color-based probabilistic tracking. In: Heyden, A., Sparr, G., Nielsen, M., Johansen, P. (eds.) ECCV 2002, Part I. LNCS, vol. 2350, pp. 661–675. Springer, Heidelberg (2002)
5. Czyz, J., Ristic, B., Macq, B.: A particle filter for joint detection and tracking of color objects. Image Vision Comput. **25**, 1271–1281 (2007)
6. Särkkä, S.: Bayesian filtering and smoothing, vol. 3. Cambridge University Press (2013)
7. Dunne, P., Matuszewski, B.: Choice of similarity measure, likelihood function and parameters for histogram based particle filter tracking in cctv grey scale video. Image Vision Comput. **29**, 178–189 (2011)
8. Minka, T.P.: Estimating a dirichlet distribution. Technical report (2003)
9. Vermaak, J., Doucet, A., Perez, P.: Maintaining multimodality through mixture tracking. In: Proceedings of the Ninth IEEE International Conference on Computer Vision 2003, vol. 2, pp. 1110–1116 (2003)
10. Sjölander, K., Karplus, K., Brown, M., Hughey, R., Krogh, A., Mian, I., Haussler, D.: Dirichlet mixtures: a method for improved detection of weak but significant protein sequence homology. Computer Applications in the Biosciences: CABIOS **12**, 327–345 (1996)
11. Holmes, I., Harris, K., Quince, C.: Dirichlet multinomial mixtures: Generative models for microbial metagenomics. PLoS ONE **7** (2012)
12. Rigouste, L., Cappé, O., Yvon, F.: Inference and evaluation of the multinomial mixture model for text clustering. Information Processing & Management **43**, 1260–1280 (2007)
13. Viola, P.A., Jones, M.J.: Robust real-time face detection. Intl. Journal of Computer Vision **57**, 137–154 (2004)
14. Bouguila, N., Ziou, D.: Dirichlet-based probability model applied to human skin detection. In: Proceedings of the IEEE International Conference on Acoustics, Speech, and Signal Processing, (ICASSP 2004), vol. 5, p. V-521-4 (2004)
15. Dalal, N., Triggs, B.: Histograms of oriented gradients for human detection. In: IEEE Computer Society Conference on Computer Vision and Pattern Recognition, CVPR 2005, vol. 1, pp. 886–893 (2005)

Evaluating ReliefF-Based Multi-Label Feature Selection Algorithm

Newton Spolaôr and Maria Carolina Monard[✉]

Laboratory of Computational Intelligence, Institute of Mathematics and Computer Science, University of São Paulo, São Carlos, Brazil
newtonspolaor@gmail.com, mcmonard@icmc.usp.br

Abstract. In multi-label learning, each instance is associated with multiple labels, which are often correlated. As other machine learning tasks, multi-label learning also suffers from the curse of dimensionality, which can be mitigated by feature selection. This work experimentally evaluates four multi-label feature selection algorithms that use the filter approach. Three of them are based on the ReliefF algorithm, which takes into account interacting features. The quality of the selected features is assessed by three different learning algorithms. Evaluating multi-label learning algorithms is a complicated task, as multiple evaluation measures, which might optimize different loss functions, should be considered. To this end, $General_B$, a baseline algorithm which learns by only looking at the multi-labels of the dataset, is used as a reference. Results show that feature selection contributed to improve the performance of classifiers initially worse than $General_B$ and highlight ReliefF-based algorithms in some experimental settings.

Keywords: Multi-label learning · Feature selection · Feature ranking · Filter approach · Information Gain · Systematic review

1 Introduction

Multi-label learning refers to problems where an instance (example) can be assigned to a set of labels (the multi-label of the instance). This differs from single-label learning where every instance can be assigned to only one label. Single-label learning is called binary whenever there are only two possible such labels, and it is called multi-class whenever there are more than two labels. An important difference between multi-class and multi-label learning is that labels in multi-class learning are mutually exclusive, while labels in multi-label learning are often correlated. Thus, multi-label learning is more challenging and difficult to solve and evaluate than single-label learning.

Multi-label learning algorithms suffer from the curse of dimensionality, which can be mitigated by dimensionality reduction tasks, such as Feature Selection (FS). FS aims to find a small number of features that describes the dataset as

© Springer International Publishing Switzerland 2014
A.L.C. Bazzan and K. Pichara (Eds.): IBERAMIA 2014, LNAI 8864, pp. 194–205, 2014.
DOI: 10.1007/978-3-319-12027-0_16

well as, or even better than the original set of features does [7]. These benefits have recently supported multi-label learning in many papers [6,10,12,14,15].

This work experimentally evaluates three ReliefF (RF) and one Information Gain (IG)-based multi-label FS methods. The quality of the selected features is assessed in terms of the performance of the classifiers built by three multi-label learning algorithms. As evaluating multi-label classifiers is a difficult task [18], this work pioneers the use of $General_B$ [9], a multi-label baseline algorithm which learns by only looking at the multi-labels of the dataset, as an evaluation reference. Results show that feature selection contributed to improve the performance of classifiers initially worse than $General_B$ and highlight ReliefF-based algorithms in some experimental settings.

The rest of this work is organized as follows: Section 2 describes multi-label learning and FS. Section 3 summarizes related work on multi-label feature selection. The four FS methods used in this work are presented and evaluated in Sections 4 and 5, respectively. Section 6 concludes and highlights future work.

2 Background

This section presents basic concepts of multi-label learning and feature selection.

2.1 Multi-Label Learning

Let D be a dataset composed of N examples $E_i = (\mathbf{x}_i, Y_i)$, $i = 1 \ldots N$. Each example E_i is associated with a feature vector $\mathbf{x}_i = (x_{i1}, x_{i2}, \ldots, x_{iM})$ described by M features (attributes) X_j, $j = 1 \ldots M$, and its multi-label Y_i, which consists of a subset of labels $Y_i \subseteq L$, where $L = \{y_1, y_2, \ldots, y_q\}$ is the set of q labels. Table 1 shows this representation. In this scenario, the multi-label classification task consists in generating a classifier H which, given an unseen instance $E = (\mathbf{x}, ?)$, is capable of accurately predicting its multi-label Y, i.e., $H(E) \rightarrow Y$.

Table 1. Multi-label data

	X_1	X_2	$\ldots$	X_M	Y
E_1	x_{11}	x_{12}	$\ldots$	x_{1M}	Y_1
E_2	x_{21}	x_{22}	$\ldots$	x_{2M}	Y_2
$\vdots$	$\vdots$	$\vdots$	$\ddots$	$\vdots$	$\vdots$
E_N	x_{N1}	x_{N2}	$\ldots$	x_{NM}	Y_N

Multi-label learning methods can be organized into two main categories [17]: (i) problem transformation methods, in which the multi-label learning problem is decomposed into a set of single-label (binary or multi-class) learning tasks; and (ii) algorithm adaptation methods, such as $BRkNN$-b [16], which adapt specific learning algorithms to handle multi-label datasets directly. The key philosophy of the problem transformation methods is to fit data to algorithms, while the one of the algorithm adaptation methods is to fit algorithms to data [18].

Methods that transform the multi-label classification problem into either several binary classification problems, such as the Binary Relevance (BR) approach, or one multi-class classification problem, such as the Label Powerset (LP) approach, fall within the first category.

The BR approach decomposes the multi-label learning problem into multiple binary classification problems, one per label. In each single-label learning problem, examples associated with the label are regarded as positive and the others as negative. Any single-label algorithm can be used as the base algorithm. Afterwards, a labeling criteria to predict the set of labels (the multi-label) of a new instance, based on the output of the binary classifiers, is used. Although BR suffers by ignoring label correlation, some attempts have been made to consider label dependence, such as the learning algorithm $BR+$ [1] used in this work. Another deficiency is the fact that a large number of binary classifiers have to be built whenever the number of labels q is large, which may cause the imbalance problem in the binary data. LP, in turn, transforms a multi-label dataset into a multi-class one by mapping each distinct multi-label Y into a unique class value. Although label dependence is partially considered by LP, the multi-class data is frequently imbalanced. Furthermore, LP only handles multi-labels which are already present in the training data.

Evaluation Measures. In multi-label learning, performance evaluation of the classifiers built by the learning algorithms is much more complicated than in single-label learning, as each instance can have multiple labels simultaneously. Moreover, unlike single-label classification where the prediction of a new instance has only two possible outcomes, correct or incorrect, multi-label classification should also take into account *partially* correct prediction. To this end, several evaluation measures, which optimize different loss functions, have been proposed.

A complete discussion on multi-label performance measures is out of the scope of this work, and can be found in [17]. In what follows, we briefly describe the four multi-label evaluation measures used in this work.

F-measure (FM), *Hamming Loss* (HL) and *Accuracy* (AC), defined by Equations 1 to 3, are example-based evaluation measures, where Δ represents the symmetric difference of two sets, Y_i and Z_i are the true and the predicted multi-labels respectively. On the other hand, *Micro-averaged F-measure* (F_b), defined by Equation 4, is a label-based measure, where $T_{P_{y_i}}$, $F_{P_{y_i}}$, $T_{N_{y_i}}$ and $F_{N_{y_i}}$ represent, respectively, the number of true/false positives/negatives for a label $y_j \in L$. In this equation, $F_{*y_j} = \sum_{j=1}^{q} F_{P_{y_j}} + \sum_{j=1}^{q} F_{N_{y_j}}$.

$$FM(H, D) = \frac{1}{|D|} \sum_{i=1}^{|D|} \frac{2|Y_i \cap Z_i|}{|Z_i| + |Y_i|}.(1) \qquad AC(H, D) = \frac{1}{|D|} \sum_{i=1}^{|D|} \frac{|Y_i \cap Z_i|}{|Y_i \cup Z_i|}.(3)$$

$$HL(H, D) = \frac{1}{|D|} \sum_{i=1}^{|D|} \frac{|Y_i \Delta Z_i|}{|L|}.(2) \qquad F_b(H, D) = \frac{2 \sum_{j=1}^{q} T_{P_{y_j}}}{2 \sum_{j=1}^{q} T_{P_{y_j}} + F_{*y_j}}.(4)$$

All these evaluation measures range in the interval $[0,1]$. For *Hamming Loss*, the smaller the value, the better the multi-label classifier performance is, while for the other measures, greater values indicate better performance.

2.2 Feature Selection

Regardless of the multi-label learning approach, any FS method addresses a few relevant issues, such as the interaction with the learning algorithm and the feature importance measure. Three approaches determine different interactions between a FS method and the learning algorithm: wrapper, embedded and filter [7]. The first two approaches strongly interact with the learning algorithm. On the other hand, filters use general properties of the dataset to remove unimportant features from it, regardless of the learning algorithm. Thus, the features chosen using the filter approach may not be the best ones for a specific learning algorithm, as is the case for the wrapper and embedded approaches. This work evaluates filter FS methods based on the single-label Information Gain and ReliefF measures.

IG evaluates each feature X_j, $j = 1 \ldots M$, according to the dependence between the feature X_j and a single label, as defined by Equation 5. To do so, IG calculates the difference between the entropy of the dataset D and the weighted sum of the entropy of each subset $D_v \subseteq D$, where D_v consists in the set of examples where X_j has the value v. Discretization is applied to numerical features before using IG. In this work, the Minimum Description Length discretization [4] is used.

$$IG\left(D, X_j\right) = entropy\left(D\right) - \sum\nolimits_v \frac{|D_v| \, entropy\left(D_v\right)}{|D|}. \tag{5}$$

RF rewards a feature for having different values on a pair of similar instances (neighbors) from different classes, as well as penalizes it for having different values on similar instances from the same class [3,11]. The main advantage of ReliefF over the strictly univariate measure IG is that it considers the effect of interacting features, as all features are used to search for similar instances. Moreover, as RF deals with numerical data directly, no discretization is needed.

3 Related Work on Multi-Label Feature Selection

Feature selection has been an active research topic in supervised learning, with many related publications and comprehensive surveys [7]. Although most publications are related to single-label learning, a number of papers have recently reported FS results that support multi-label learning.

Aiming at capturing a wide, replicable and rigorous overview of the topic, the systematic literature review process [5] for multi-label FS, instantiated in [13], was updated to take into account the interaction with the learning algorithm approaches — Section 2.2. Table 2 summarizes the 72 publications found. As can be observed, the filter approach has been the most usual choice in multi-label FS. The Supplementary Material (SM) available at http://www.labic.icmc. usp.br/pub/mcmonard/ExperimentalResults/IBERAMIA2014.pdf lists the bibliographical references, as well as the approach related to each paper.

Table 2. Number of related publications per feature selection approach (*total* = 72)

approach	#publications (%)
filter	50 (69,44%)
embedded	10 (13,89%)
wrapper	7 (9,72%)
unrecognized	5 (6,94%)

4   Feature Selection Methods Evaluated

In this work, the following four multi-label FS methods, which fall within the filter approach, are evaluated:

1. ReliefF combined with Binary Relevance (*RF-BR*);
2. ReliefF combined with Label Powerset (*RF-LP*);
3. Multi-label ReliefF (*RF-ML*);
4. Information Gain combined with Binary Relevance (*IG-BR*).

RF-BR and *IG-BR* use *BR* to transform the multi-label dataset into q binary datasets, one per label, before using a feature importance measure: *RF* or *IG*. Then, each algorithm applies its measure in each binary dataset and averages the measure value (score) of each feature X_j, $j = 1 \ldots M$, across all labels. The resulting feature ranking sorts the M averaged values in descending order of importance. As both methods follow the standard *BR* approach [6,14], which works with one label at a time, no label relation is considered.

RF-LP directly applies ReliefF in the multi-class dataset obtained by the *LP* problem transformation approach [6,14]. As each distinct class value from this single-label dataset maps a specific multi-label Y from the original dataset, one can note that a kind of label relation is taken into account by *RF-LP*.

ReliefF has been extended to take into account label relations in multi-label feature selection [10,12,15]. In this work, we use the *RF-ML* algorithm proposed in [15], which focus on filter FS to support non-hierarchical ("flat") multi-label learning. *RF-ML* extends ReliefF for regression problems (RReliefF) by using a dissimilarity function specific for multi-labels, as well as dealing with multi-label instances directly. Both extensions enable *RF-ML* to perform multi-label feature selection based on *RF* without any problem transformation.

In particular, the *RF-ML* dissimilarity function models the probability that the predictions of two instances are different [3,11]. Thus, different from the original ReliefF, only one search for similar instances (neighbors) is needed for each instance. In this work, we set the normalized *Hamming Distance* (*HD*) between the multi-labels Y_i and Y_j – Equation 6 – as the dissimilarity function.

$$HD(Y_i, Y_j) = \frac{|Y_i \cup Y_j| - |Y_i \cap Y_j|}{q}. \tag{6}$$

The complexity of the ReliefF-based algorithms (as $RF\text{-}ML$) is bound to the search for the k nearest instances [11], i.e., $O(N^2.M)$, where N is the number of instances and M is the number of features. $RF\text{-}BR$ clearly has a higher complexity than $RF\text{-}LP$ and $RF\text{-}ML$, i.e., $O(N^2.M.q)$, as it has to conduct the search q times, one per label. $RF\text{-}LP$ is slightly more expensive than $RF\text{-}ML$ due to its inherent problem transformation approach.

$IG\text{-}BR$ complexity is $O(N.M.q)$, as the algorithm estimates q times the single-label measure IG for each feature X_j, $j = 1 \ldots M$. As can be observed, $RF\text{-}BR$ has the highest complexity of the four evaluated algorithms. Although $IG\text{-}BR$ does not have quadratic complexity, it is the unique evaluated algorithm that has additional cost due to its discretization procedure.

In this work, each FS method yields a feature ranking from which the subsets of the best features $X' \subset X$, $|X'| = 10\%M, 20\%M, \ldots, 90\%M$, are chosen. These subsets are used to describe reduced versions of the original multi-label datasets, which are then submitted to three multi-label learning algorithms to evaluate the quality of the selected features in terms of classification performance.

5   Experimental Evaluation

In this work, the following three multi-label learning algorithms are used:

- Binary Relevance k Nearest Neighbor, extension b ($BRkNN\text{-}b$)
- Binary Relevance (BR)
- Binary Relevance Plus ($BR+$)

briefly described in Section 5.2, evaluate the quality of the features selected by the four FS algorithms in 10 benchmark multi-label datasets. In addition, the multi-label baseline classifier $General_B$, briefly presented in Section 5.3, is considered as a reference of the four evaluation measures used in this work – Section 2.1. All algorithms have been implemented in the Mulan framework[1], a multi-label learning package based on Weka[2].

5.1   Multi-Label Datasets

Table 3 summarizes the characteristics of the 10 datasets used in this work. For each dataset it shows: dataset name (Dataset); dataset domain (Domain); number of instances (N); number of features (M); feature type ($Type$); number of labels ($|L|$); label cardinality (LC), which is the average number of labels associated with each instance; label density (LD), which is the cardinality normalized by $|L|$; and the number of different multi-labels (#Diff).

---

[1] http://mulan.sourceforge.net
[2] http://www.cs.waikato.ac.nz/ml/weka/

Table 3. Dataset description

Dataset	Domain	N	M	$Type$	$|L|$	LC	LD	#Diff
1-*Cal500*	music	502	68	numeric	174	26.044	0.150	502
2-*Corel5k*	image	5000	499	discrete	374	3.522	0.009	3175
3-*Corel16k001*	image	13766	500	discrete	153	2.859	0.019	4803
4-*Emotions*	music	593	72	numeric	6	1.869	0.311	27
5-*Fapesp*	text	332	8669	discrete	66	1.774	0.027	206
6-*Genbase**	biology	662	1185	discrete	27	1.252	0.046	32
7-*Llog-f**	text	1253	1004	discrete	75	1.375	0.018	303
8-*Magtag5k*	music	5260	68	numeric	136	4.839	0.036	4163
9-*Scene*	image	2407	294	numeric	6	1.074	0.179	15
10-*Yeast*	biology	2417	103	numeric	14	4.237	0.303	198

Except for datasets *5-Fapesp* and *8-Magtag5k*, the other datasets are available in the Mulan[3] and Meka[4] repositories. In particular, *5-Fapesp* was built by members of our research laboratory[5] by extracting features from stories (instances) from a scientific magazine, which in turn were annotated by the staff magazine according to the scientific branch(es) reported (labels). Dataset *8-Magtag5k*[6] is further described in [8]. Furthermore, *6-Genbase** and *7-Llog-f** are pre-processed versions of the publicly available datasets in which an identification feature and unlabeled instances, respectively, were removed.

5.2   Multi-Label Learning Algorithms and Settings

An empirical study carried out in [16] highlights the lazy algorithm *BRkNN-b* as an improved single-label k-Nearest Neighbor (*kNN*) adaptation to classify multi-label instances [16]. The main *BRkNN-b* parameter consists in the number of nearest neighbors k. For each dataset in Table 3, k was set as the one that maximizes the *Example-based F-measure* of the *BRkNN-b* classifiers built using All Features (AF), *i.e.*, without FS. These values were found in a preliminary study, in which k was varied in the interval [1..27] with step 2 and in the interval [29..99] with step 10. The k value used for each dataset, denoted as (dataset ID, k), were: $[(1, 59), (2, 21), (3, 49), (4, 15), (5, 29), (6, 1), (7, 13), (8, 17), (9, 27), (10, 21)]$. The k parameter of the ReliefF-based algorithms was set in the same way. Note, however, that this experimental setup clearly favors the classifiers built using AF – the original datasets.

BR+ extends *BR* to take into account label relations during learning [1]. The main idea is to put the learning algorithm in charge of identifying some label relations in the dataset. To do so, *BR+* also builds q binary classification problems for training, one per single label y_i, $i = 1 \ldots q$, but augments the dataset by including the remaining single labels y_j, $y_j \neq y_i$, as additional features. Afterwards, the q predictions performed by a base single-label classification algorithm are combined to obtain the multi-label of an unseen instance.

---

[3] http://mulan.sourceforge.net/datasets.html

[4] http://meka.sourceforge.net/#datasets

[5] The dataset can be obtained from the authors.

[6] http://tl.di.fc.ul.pt/t/magtag5k.zip

BR and $BR+$ are applied using Naive Bayes (NB) as the base single-label classification algorithm, resulting respectively in the learning algorithms BR-NB and $BR+(NB)$. NB scales better to high dimensionality than kNN, motivating us to include it as an alternative algorithm to evaluate the FS results. In this work, $BR+(NB)$ uses the dynamic update strategy [1] during its prediction phase. Therefore, by following a dynamic order based on the earliest binary classifiers confidences, the values of the additional features are updated with the new binary predictions as they are obtained.

All remaining parameters related to the learning and FS algorithms were executed with default values.

5.3 Multi-Label Baseline Classifier $General_B$

As a reference, we use $General_B$ [9], a simple baseline learning algorithm which learns by only looking at the multi-labels of the dataset. As $General_B$ does not necessarily concentrates on optimizing specific loss functions, it can be used as a global baseline for the difficult task of evaluating multi-label predictions.

The rationale behind $General_B$ is very simple. It consists in ranking the q single labels in L according to their individual relative frequencies in the multi-labels in order to include the σ most frequent labels in the predicted multi-label Z. To obtain a representative Z, $General_B$ defines σ as the closest integer value of the label cardinality LC – Section 5.1. In case of ties (single labels with the same frequency), the label co-occurrence measure chooses the label which maximizes its co-occurrence with better ranked labels.

5.4 Results and Discussion

All experimental results were obtained according to the 10-fold cross-validation strategy. For each evaluation measure described in Section 2.1, results for the classifiers constructed by the learning algorithms $BRkNN$-b, $BR+(NB)$ and BR-NB in the original datasets (4 measures $\times$ 3 classifiers = 12 cases), as well as the results of the classifiers built using the 10% up to 90% most important features ranked by each FS method (4 FS methods $\times$ 9 percentage of features $\times$ 3 classifiers = 108 cases) were tabulated with the correspondent standard deviation. Due to lack of space, in what follows the main results are discussed. Tables with all tabulated results can be found in the SM at http://www.labic. icmc.usp.br/pub/mcmonard/ExperimentalResults/IBERAMIA2014.pdf.

Table 4 shows an overview of the results obtained by the three classifiers using the original datasets (*i.e.*, all features) compared with the ones obtained by $General_B$. An empty cell in this table means that the corresponding evaluation measure value is better than the one from $General_B$, although it is not the best overall classifiers.

Although the $BRkNN$-b classifiers reached the best values overall more often, for two datasets (2-$Corel5k$ and 3-$Corel16k001$) the four evaluation measures are worse than the ones from $General_B$. The same happens with the $BR+(NB)$ and BR-NB classifiers in dataset 1-$Cal500$, as well as with the BR-NB classifiers in

Table 4. Summarized results from the classifiers built using all features: ⇓ indicates evaluation measure values worse than or equal to the corresponding values from $General_B$, whereas ★ indicates best values overall

	BRkNN-b				BR+(NB)				BR-NB			
	FM	HL	AC	F_b	FM	HL	AC	F_b	FM	HL	AC	F_b
1-Cal500	★	★	★	★	⇓	⇓	⇓	⇓	⇓	⇓	⇓	⇓
2-Corel5k	⇓	⇓	⇓	⇓	★	★	★	★				
3-Corel16k001	⇓	⇓	⇓	⇓	★	⇓	★			⇓		★
4-Emotions		★			★		★	★				
5-Fapesp	★	⇓					★	★	⇓	★	⇓	⇓
6-Genbase*	★	★	★	★								
7-Llog-f*		★	★	★	★	⇓				⇓		
8-Magtag5k	★	★	★	★		⇓		⇓	⇓	⇓	⇓	⇓
9-Scene	★	★	★	★								
10-Yeast	★	★	★	★					⇓	⇓		⇓

dataset 8-*Magtag5k*. Even though it is not expected that all evaluation measures of a specific classifier should be better than the ones obtained by $General_B$, as different evaluation measures might optimize different loss functions, failing to improve all measures should call our attention to the quality of the classifier built using the dataset.

FS can be an alternative to remove features that harm the performance of these classifiers. To this end, a comparison similar to the one in Table 4 is carried out by replacing the classifiers built using AF with the classifiers built using the features selected by the FS methods *RF-ML*, *RF-LP*, *RF-BR* and *IG-BR*. As shown in the supplementary material, all methods contribute to improve the performance of most of the classifiers initially worse than $General_B$ for all evaluation measures. In what follows, some of these improvements are described.

In dataset 1-*Cal500*, the *BR-NB* classifiers outperformed $General_B$ in terms of the evaluation measure *Hamming Loss*, by using the subsets composed of $|X'| = 10\%M$ of the best features ranked by the three ReliefF-based FS methods. Another improvement regarding the *BR-NB* classifiers is obtained in dataset 8-*Magtag5k*, as the feature subsets $X' \subset X$, $|X'| = 20\%M$ obtained by these FS methods led to classifiers better than $General_B$ in terms of all evaluation measures. It was observed that *IG-BR* also supported building a few *BR-NB* classifiers better than $General_B$ in these datasets.

Furthermore, FS supported the improvement of the *BRkNN-b* classifiers in datasets 2-*Corel5k* and 3-*Corel16k001*. In the former dataset, the *BRkNN-b* classifiers built using the feature subsets X', $|X'| = 10\%M, 20\%M$, yielded by all FS methods outperformed $General_B$ in terms of *F-measure*, *Accuracy* and *Micro-averaged F-measure*. A similar achievement is obtained in the latter dataset with the subsets X', $|X'| = 10\%M, \ldots, 40\%M$.

It should be emphasized that feature selection is often related to the trade-off between classification performance and number of features. To this end, we compared the results obtained by 10% up to 90% of the most important features selected by the 4 FS methods. We used the Friedman's statistical test [2] with significance level $\alpha = 0.05$. The null hypothesis states that the performances of the classifiers built using a number of selected features are equivalent in terms of an evaluation measure. Whenever the null hypothesis was rejected, we proceeded with the Nemenyi post-hoc test, which states that the performance of two classifiers is significantly different if the corresponding average ranks differ by at least a Critical Difference (CD). When multiple classifiers are compared, these results can be visually represented with a simple diagram. Due to lack of space, Figure 1 shows the diagram for the *BR+(NB)* classifiers evaluated by *F-measure* and built using the feature subsets X', $|X'| = 10\%M$. The remaining ones can be found in the supplementary material.

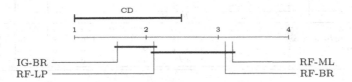

Fig. 1. Comparison of the *F-measure* values of the *BR+(NB)* classifiers built using the best $|X'| = 10\%M$ features according to the Nemenyi test. Groups of classifiers that are not significantly different (at $\alpha = 0.05$) are connected.

Table 5 summarizes the cases where significant differences were found for each evaluation measure and number of features. Although *IG-BR* stands up more often, it can be observed that in most cases the null hypothesis is not rejected. In other words, considering the 4 evaluation measures × 9 percentage of features = 36 cases for each learning algorithm, few significant differences were found: 10 for *BRkNN-b*; 2 for *BR+(NB)* and 2 for *BR-NB*.

Table 5. Differences with significance level $\alpha = 0.05$ (sbt: significantly better than)

$|X'|$	*F-measure*	*Hamming loss*	*Accuracy*	F_b
		BRkNN-b		
30%				IG-BR sbt RF-ML
60%				IG-BR sbt RF-ML
70%	IG-BR sbt RF-ML		IG-BR sbt RF-ML	IG-BR sbt RF-ML
80%	IG-BR sbt RF-BR	RF-ML sbt RF-BR	IG-BR sbt RF-BR	IG-BR sbt RF-BR
90%	IG-BR sbt RF-ML			
		BR+(NB)		
10%	IG-BR sbt RF-ML and RF-BR			
90%		RF-BR sbt IG-BR		
		BR-NB		
10%	IG-BR sbt RF-ML	RF-ML sbt IG-BR		

The Friedman's test also gives us information about the best classifiers built after FS by the rankings averaged across all datasets. Table 6 summarizes the results, which can be found in the SM. Each symbol identifies a FS method: + (*IG-BR*), * (*RF-ML*), o (*RF-LP*), × (*RF-BR*). Classifiers with at least one significant difference — Table 5 — are shaded, whereas "/" separates ties.

As can be observed, the FS method *IG-BR* (+) is more often ranked first by *BRkNN-b* (28 times out of 36). On the other hand, *RF-LP* (o) is more often ranked first by *BR-NB* (22 times out of 36), while *BR+(NB)* ranks first both FS methods, *IG-BR* and *RF-LP* (18 and 15 times respectively out of 36). Moreover,

Table 6. Best FS methods according to the average rankings of the evaluation measures from each classification algorithm (last columns: frequency of the best average rankings)

$|X'|$	10%	20%	30%	40%	50%	60%	70%	80%	90%	+	*	o	×
					BRkNN-b								
F-measure	o	+/o	+	+	+	+	+	+	+	8		2	
Hamming loss	*	*	+	*	o	+	+	*	+	4	4	1	
Accuracy	o	+/o	+	+/o	+	+	+	+	+	8		3	
F_b	+	o/×	+	+	+	+	+	+	+	8		1	1
					BR+(NB)								
F-measure	+	o	+	+	+	o	+	*/o	+	6	1	3	
Hamming loss	o	o	o	×	o	×	o	*	×	1	5		2
Accuracy	+	o	+	+	+/o	o	+	*/o	+/*	6	2	4	1
F_b	+	o	+	+	+	+/o	+	o	×	6		3	1
					BR-NB								
F-measure	+	o	o	o	o	o	+/o	o	o	2		8	
Hamming loss	*	o	*	*/×	×	*	*/×	*/o	*		6	2	3
Accuracy	+	o	o	o	+	o	+	o	o	3		6	
F_b	+	o	o	o	+/×	o	+/×	o	o	3		6	2

for $|X'| = 10\%M, \ldots, 40\%M$, the FS method *RF-ML* (*) supported building some of the best *BRkNN-b* and *BR-NB* classifiers in terms of the *Hamming loss* measure. This could be related to the use of the *Hamming dissimilarity function* by *RF-ML*.

6   Conclusion

This work experimentally evaluated four ReliefF and Information Gain-based multi-label feature selection algorithms in 10 benchmark datasets. Classifiers built using the features selected by each algorithm were compared with each other, as well as with the ones obtained by the multi-label baseline *General$_B$*.

All FS methods contribute to improve the performance of some classifiers which are worse than *General$_B$* when all features are used. It should be emphasized that this achievement was obtained using the filter FS approach, which is not directly biased to any classification algorithm.

By comparing the FS methods, although for some evaluation measures *IG-BR* led to significantly better classifiers in a few cases, a significant difference was not found in most of the comparisons. Furthermore, ReliefF-based algorithms, such as *RF-LP* and *RF-ML*, supported building some of the classifiers ranked first in specific settings.

As future work, we plan to graphically explore multi-label data properties, such as label relations, to complement the evaluation of FS algorithms.

Acknowledgments. This research was supported by the So Paulo Research Foundation (FAPESP), grant 2011/02393-4.

References

1. Cherman, E.A., Metz, J., Monard, M.C.: Incorporating label dependency into the binary relevance framework for multi-label classification. Expert Systems with Applications **39**(2), 1647–1655 (2012)

2. Demšar, J.: Statistical comparison of classifiers over multiple data sets. Journal of Machine Learning Research **7**(1), 1–30 (2006)
3. Demšar, J.: Algorithms for subsetting attribute values with Relief. Machine Learning **78**, 421–428 (2010)
4. Fayyad, U.M., Irani, K.B.: Multi-interval discretization of continuous-valued attributes for classification learning. In: International Joint Conference on Artificial Intelligence, pp. 1022–1029 (1993)
5. Kitchenham, B.A., Charters, S.: Guidelines for performing systematic literature reviews in software engineering. EBSE-2007-01 Technical Report. 65 pg. Evidence-based Software Engineering (2007)
6. Kong, D., Ding, C., Huang, H., Zhao, H.: Multi-label ReliefF and F-statistic feature selections for image annotation. In: IEEE Conference on Computer Vision and Pattern Recognition, pp. 2352–2359 (2012)
7. Liu, H., Motoda, H.: Computational Methods of Feature Selection. Chapman & Hall/CRC (2008)
8. Marques, G., Domingues, M.A., Langlois, T., Gouyon, F.: Three current issues in music autotagging. In: Conference of the International Society for Music Information Retrieval, pp. 795–800 (2011)
9. Metz, J., de Abreu, L.F.D., Cherman, E.A., Monard, M.C.: On the estimation of predictive evaluation measure baselines for multi-label learning. In: Pavón, J., Duque-Méndez, N.D., Fuentes-Fernández, R. (eds.) IBERAMIA 2012. LNCS, vol. 7637, pp. 189–198. Springer, Heidelberg (2012)
10. Pupo, O.G.R., Morell, C., Soto, S.V.: ReliefF-ML: An extension of reliefF algorithm to multi-label learning. In: Ruiz-Shulcloper, J., Sanniti di Baja, G. (eds.) CIARP 2013, Part II. LNCS, vol. 8259, pp. 528–535. Springer, Heidelberg (2013)
11. Robnik-Šikonja, M., Kononenko, I.: Theoretical and empirical analysis of ReliefF and RReliefF. Machine Learning **53**(1–2), 23–69 (2003)
12. Slavkov, I., Karcheska, J., Kocev, D., Kalajdziski, S., Džeroski, S.: Extending reliefF for hierarchical multi-label classification. In: Workshop on New Frontiers in Mining Complex Patterns - European Conference on Machine Learning/Principles and Practice of Knowledge Discovery in Databases, pp. 156–167 (2013)
13. Spolaôr, N., Monard, M.C., Lee, H.D.: A systematic review to identify feature selection publications in multi-labeled data. ICMC Technical Report No 374. 31 pg., University of São Paulo (2012)
14. Spolaôr, N., Cherman, E.A., Monard, M.C., Lee, H.D.: A comparison of multi-label feature selection methods using the problem transformation approach. Electronic Notes in Theoretical Computer Science **292**, 135–151 (2013)
15. Spolaôr, N., Cherman, E.A., Monard, M.C., Lee, H.D.: ReliefF for multi-label feature selection. In: Brazilian Conference on Intelligent Systems, pp. 6–11 (2013)
16. Spyromitros, E., Tsoumakas, G., Vlahavas, I.P.: An empirical study of lazy multilabel classification algorithms. In: Darzentas, J., Vouros, G.A., Vosinakis, S., Arnellos, A. (eds.) SETN 2008. LNCS (LNAI), vol. 5138, pp. 401–406. Springer, Heidelberg (2008)
17. Tsoumakas, G., Katakis, I., Vlahavas, I.P.: Mining multi-label data. In: Maimon, O., Rokach, L. (eds.) Data Mining and Knowledge Discovery Handbook, pp. 667–685. Springer (2010)
18. Zhang, M.L., Zhou, Z.H.: A review on multi-label learning algorithms. IEEE Transactions on Knowledge and Data Engineering **99**, 1–59 (2013)

Recursive Dependent Binary Relevance Model for Multi-label Classification

Thomas W. Rauber[✉], Lucas H. Mello, Victor F. Rocha,
Diego Luchi, and Flávio Miguel Varejão

Departamento de Informática, Centro Tecnológico,
Universidade Federal do Espírito Santo, Vitória 29060-970, Brazil
{thomas,fvarejao}@inf.ufes.br, victor.rocha@aluno.ufes.br,
{lmello,dluchi}@ninfa.inf.ufes.br

Abstract. A recursive dependent binary relevance model for multi-label classification is proposed where the predicted label of a pattern is obtained in an iterative process. The motivation behind this strategy is the simultaneous intrinsic dependency of the labels and the fact that predicted labels in the final decision by themselves are estimates which can be re-estimated to improve their robustness.

1 Introduction

The classical single-label multi-class classification problem associates a pattern vector x from domain $\mathcal{X}$ with exactly one out of m possible labels $\ell_j, j = 1, \ldots, m$. A training set[1] $S = \left\{ (x^1, y^1), \ldots, (x^n, y^n) \right\}$ consists of pattern-label pairs (x^k, y^k) where the desired output y^k is one of the possible m labels. A common practice is to code the class membership of the pattern as a vector y^k from domain $\mathcal{Y}$ of length m where the components are binary values. This is called one-out-of-m coding. Only one of the binary values has value one, i.e. $y_j^k = 1$, the remaining $(m - 1)$ values are zero, hence the associated class information of pattern x^k becomes $y^k = (y_1^k, \ldots, y_{j-1}^k, y_j^k, y_{j+1}^k, \ldots y_m^k)$. This strategy has an important advantage, namely that the labels become patterns in a newly created vector space. Besides, for instance, when an Euclidean metric is used to measure a distance between two labels, the mutual distance among all single-labels becomes $\sqrt{2}$, thus not introducing any biased proximity relationships among the labels.

A straightforward extension to the multi-label case is to allow that more than one component of y^k can have the value one which indicates that is belongs simultaneously to these classes.

The presented work is an extension of the dependent binary relevance model for multi-label classification proposed in [6]. The predicted labels produced by this model are considered as an intermediate estimation that can be used to re-estimate the labels again. The experimental results suggest that this strategy generally improves the performance criterion of the multi-label classifier.

---

[1] Superscripts of individual patterns and labels mean indices.

© Springer International Publishing Switzerland 2014
A.L.C. Bazzan and K. Pichara (Eds.): IBERAMIA 2014, LNAI 8864, pp. 206–217, 2014.
DOI: 10.1007/978-3-319-12027-0_17

The rest of this paper is organized as follows: in Section 2 the necessary nomenclature of multi-label classification is introduced, in Section 3 the method of dependent binary relevance is reviewed. Section 4 presents the proposed iterative re-estimation of the class labels, in Section 5 experimental results are given and finally in Section 6 conclusions are drawn and future work is pointed out.

2 Multi-label Classification

In multi-label classification [9] the classification task becomes a map $h : \mathcal{X} \rightarrow \mathcal{Y}$, $x \mapsto y$. The multidimensional feature space $\mathcal{X}$ can be any composition of symbolic, numerical discrete and numerical continuous features,[2] whereas the class domain becomes $\mathcal{Y} = \{0, 1\}^m$. The training set is redefined as n pairs of pattern vectors and m-dimensional binary label vectors as $S = \{(x^1, y^1), \ldots, (x^n, y^n)\}$, with $y_j^k \in \{0, 1\}$.

2.1 Binary Relevance Classifier

If the interdependency of the labels is ignored, for each of the m labels an individual classifier $h_j^{\mathrm{BR}} : \mathcal{X} \rightarrow \{0, 1\}$, $x \mapsto y_j$, $j = 1, \ldots, m$ can be constructed. This approach is commonly called *binary relevance* classifier (BR) [6]. There is an analogy between the Naive Bayes classifier in single-label classification which ignores dependencies among the components of the feature vector x and BR which does the same on the class label side. The BR classifier can be any classical pattern recognition dichotomizer architecture, e.g. K-Nearest Neighbor, Multi-layer Perceptron, Support Vector Machine or Logistic regression [10].

2.2 Classifier Chains

Introducing dependencies among the labels, the classifier chain (CC) approach [7] successively increments the number of used labels to predict the next label in the chain. The process is initiated by a classifier $h_1^{\mathrm{CC}} : \mathcal{X} \rightarrow \{0, 1\}$, $x \mapsto y_1$ that is basically a BR classifier. The second classifier in the chain uses the feature vector x together with the first label. $h_2^{\mathrm{CC}} : \mathcal{X} \times \{0, 1\} \rightarrow \{0, 1\}$, $(x, y_1) \mapsto y_2$. In the training phase the true label y_1 is used, whereas in the prediction phase the estimated label $\hat{y}_1$ from h_1^{CC} is used for the mapping, such that $(x, \hat{y}_1) \mapsto y_2$. Hence there are m classifiers that use from zero to $(m-1)$ labels as additional features, such that in training phase $h_j^{\mathrm{CC}} : \mathcal{X} \times \{0, 1\}^{j-1} \rightarrow \{0, 1\}$, $(x, y_1, \ldots, y_{j-1}) \mapsto y_j$, $j = 1, \ldots, m$ and in the prediction phase $h_j^{\mathrm{CC}} : \mathcal{X} \times \{0, 1\}^{j-1} \rightarrow \{0, 1\}$, $(x, \hat{y}_1, \ldots, \hat{y}_{j-1}) \mapsto y_j$, $j = 1, \ldots, m$.

---

[2] "Attribute" is a synonym of "feature", preferentially used in the machine learning community.

2.3 Classifier Stacking

Consider again the output $\hat{\boldsymbol{y}} = \boldsymbol{h}^{\mathrm{BR}}(\boldsymbol{x})$ of the BR classifier of Section 2.1, which is the independent estimate of all m labels. Classifier stacking (STA) [3] considers all these m labels as additional features that are merged with the original feature vector $\boldsymbol{x}$. The second level of the classifier stack is composed of m classifiers $h_j^{\mathrm{STA}} : \mathcal{X} \times \{0,1\}^m \rightarrow \{0,1\}$, $(\boldsymbol{x}, \hat{\boldsymbol{y}}) \mapsto y_j, j = 1, \ldots, m$ that learn a single label. In the training phase the true label y_j of the pattern is known. Even if the estimated label $\hat{y}_j = h_j^{\mathrm{BR}}(\boldsymbol{x})$ from the first level of the stack could be different, it is used as a feature. For prediction purposes, the first classifier level delivers the estimate $\hat{\boldsymbol{y}}^{(0)}$ which is then fed together with the unknown pattern $\boldsymbol{x}$ into the second level to provide the final estimate $\hat{\boldsymbol{y}}^{(1)}$.

2.4 Nested Stacking

The only difference of nested stacking (NS) [8] to classifier chains of Section 2.2 is that in the training phase the estimated labels are used instead of the true labels, such that the jth classifier in the chain is realizing the mapping $h_j^{\mathrm{NS}} :$ $\mathcal{X} \times \{0,1\}^{j-1} \rightarrow \{0,1\}$, $(\boldsymbol{x}, \hat{y}_1, \ldots, \hat{y}_{j-1}) \mapsto y_j, j = 1, \ldots, (m-1)$ during the training. The prediction is identical to that of CC.

2.5 Evaluation Metrics of Predicted Labels

The crisp zero-one error outcome of a single-label multi-class classifier must be substituted by an evaluation metric that measures the discrepancy between the m-dimensional expected vector $\boldsymbol{y}$ and the result $\boldsymbol{h}(\boldsymbol{x})$ of the classification. The Hamming loss is defined as

$$\mathrm{HammingLoss}(\boldsymbol{y}, \boldsymbol{h}(\boldsymbol{x})) = \frac{1}{m} \sum_{j=1}^{m} [y_j \neq h_j(\boldsymbol{x})], \tag{1}$$

where the symbol $[.]$ is the Iverson bracket, such that the Hamming loss counts the true occurrences of the argument predicate.

The Subset$_{0/1}$ accuracy [1] detects a strict coincidence of the true and estimated labels as

$$\mathrm{Subset}_{0/1}(\boldsymbol{y}, \boldsymbol{h}(\boldsymbol{x})) = [\boldsymbol{y} = \boldsymbol{h}(\boldsymbol{x})]. \tag{2}$$

The subset *loss* is the complement of the subset accuracy.

The F_1 index is defined as the harmonic mean of the precision and recall which can be obtained from the estimated performance of a dichotomizer and has the following definition

$$F_1(\boldsymbol{y}, \boldsymbol{h}(\boldsymbol{x})) = \frac{2 \sum_{j=1}^{m} [y_j = 1 \text{ and } h_j(\boldsymbol{x}) = 1]}{\sum_{j=1}^{m} ([y_j = 1] + [h_j(\boldsymbol{x}) = 1])}. \tag{3}$$

Finally the Jaccard index is defined as

$$\mathrm{Jaccard}(\boldsymbol{y}, \boldsymbol{h}(\boldsymbol{x})) = \frac{\sum_{j=1}^{m} [y_j = 1 \text{ and } h_j(\boldsymbol{x}) = 1]}{\sum_{j=1}^{m} [y_j = 1 \text{ or } h_j(\boldsymbol{x}) = 1]}. \tag{4}$$

3 Dependent Binary Relevance

The model presented in [6] is the *dependent binary relevance* classifier (DBR). Its superiority over BR comes from the fact that the class labels are not considered independent. The difference with respect to the chaining and stacking approaches is that all but one label y_j is used to estimate this same label. Two groups of classifiers are defined that compose the DBR.

3.1 Dependent Label Classifier

A single label predictor is defined as follows: The original feature space $\mathcal{X}$ is expanded by $(m - 1)$ dimensions by merging all but a single[3] label y_j as new features $\boldsymbol{y}_{\bar{j}} := (y_1, \ldots, y_{j-1}, y_{j+1}, \ldots, y_m)$. Hence the new feature space is $\mathcal{X}^{\text{new}} = \mathcal{X} \times \{0,1\}^{(m-1)}$ The mapped domain is the feature space $\mathcal{Y}^{\text{new}} = \{0,1\}$ of the predicted label y_j.

The label predictors are defined for each label, hence there are m classifiers $h_j^{\text{DBR}} : \mathcal{X} \times \{0,1\}^{(m-1)} \to \{0,1\}, (\boldsymbol{x}, \boldsymbol{y}_{\bar{j}}) \mapsto y_j, j = 1, \ldots, m$. If the training phase is considered, theoretically all m desired labels y_j are available to train all m classifiers h_j^{DBR}. In the prediction phase however, only an unknown pattern $\boldsymbol{x}$ is given. As a consequence all $(m - 1)$ labels $\boldsymbol{y}_{\bar{j}}$ of classifier h_j^{DBR} must be estimated in order to provide the label features for the DBR classifier as $\hat{\boldsymbol{y}}_{\bar{j}} := (\hat{y}_1, \ldots, \hat{y}_{j-1}, \hat{y}_{j+1}, \ldots, \hat{y}_m)$. This job is performed by m independent BR classifiers, described next.

3.2 Binary Relevance Label Estimator

In order to compose the label vector $\boldsymbol{y}_{\bar{j}}$ that is needed besides the pattern $\boldsymbol{x}$ as the DBR input for classifier h_j^{DBR} described in the previous section, each individual component $y_i, i \in \bar{j}$ is provided by a BR classifier h_i^{BR}. Since all m DBR h_j^{DBR} need all but a single label, it is only necessary to estimate all m labels $y_j, j = 1, \ldots, m$ once, and then use them as desired by the DBR. Hence m BR classifiers are defined $h_j^{\text{BR}} : \mathcal{X} \to \{0,1\}, \boldsymbol{x} \mapsto y_j, j = 1, \ldots, m$. The complete DBR multi-label classifier architecture is illustrated in fig. 1

4 Recursive Dependent Binary Relevance

In the DBR architecture described above, a first estimate $\hat{\boldsymbol{y}}^{(0)}$ of the complete label vector $\boldsymbol{y}$ is obtained by the m BR classifiers. The estimator $\hat{\theta}$ is a function of the pattern vector $\boldsymbol{x}$, hence one can define

$$\hat{\boldsymbol{y}}^{(0)} = \hat{\theta}^{\text{BR}}(\boldsymbol{x}). \tag{5}$$

---

[3] The connotation $\bar{j}$ is used to express all $(m - 1)$ complementary labels indices $\{1, 2, \ldots, j - 1, j + 1, \ldots, m\}$ of label y_j.

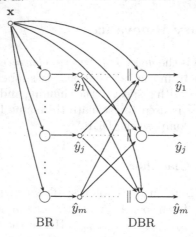

Fig. 1. Architecture of the dependent binary relevance classifier (DBR). In the first layer the binary relevance classifiers (BR) provide the class labels individually. The next layer provides all final estimated labels $\hat{y}_j$. The dotted line is the label *not* used by the DBR.

The estimator $\hat{\theta}^{\mathrm{BR}}$ simply composes the result of the m BR classifiers h_j^{BR}. The final estimate $\hat{\boldsymbol{y}}^{(1)}$ of the label vector needed in multi-label classification in the DBR architecture is a function of the pattern vector $\boldsymbol{x}$, jointly with the estimate $\hat{\boldsymbol{y}}^{(0)}$ obtained from the BR estimator. This defines the DBR estimator as

$$\hat{\boldsymbol{y}}^{(1)} = \hat{\theta}^{\mathrm{DBR}}(\boldsymbol{x}, \hat{\boldsymbol{y}}^{(0)}). \tag{6}$$

The estimator $\hat{\theta}^{\mathrm{DBR}}$ composes the result of the m DBR classifiers h_i^{DBR}. The key idea of this work is to consider the estimate $\hat{\boldsymbol{y}}^{(1)}$ not as the final guess of the label vector, but as an initial estimate which can recursively be fed into the DBR estimator in an iterative manner. Note that the recursive estimation will not achieve an independent self-agreement among the labels of the labels $\boldsymbol{y}$ since the estimation is always jointly based on the distribution of the feature vector $\boldsymbol{x}$. Two versions of the update strategy of the estimated labels are proposed. The first re-estimates the labels only when a complete current label vector is available. This is called batch re-estimation. The second uses re-estimated labels as soon as they become available. This is called stochastic re-estimation.

4.1   Batch Recursive Dependent Binary Relevance

The batch version re-estimates the current labels $\hat{\boldsymbol{y}}^{(\tau+1)}$ based on the feature vector $\boldsymbol{x}$ and the previous label estimate $\hat{\boldsymbol{y}}^{(\tau)}$ as

$$\hat{\boldsymbol{y}}^{(\tau+1)} = \hat{\theta}^{\mathrm{DBR}}(\boldsymbol{x}, \hat{\boldsymbol{y}}^{(\tau)}), \tau \geq 1. \tag{7}$$

The batch version of the recursive dependent binary relevance classifier is illustrated in fig. 2.

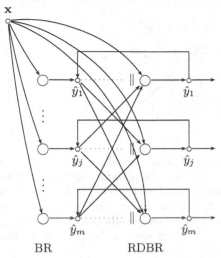

x

BR   RDBR

Fig. 2. Architecture of the recursive dependent binary relevance classifier (RDBR), batch version. The second layer provides the mutually dependent estimates obtained by the DBR estimator which are recursively fed into the DBR. The feedback to obtain $\hat{\boldsymbol{y}}^{(\tau+1)}$ is only performed when the complete estimated label vector from the current iteration $\hat{\boldsymbol{y}}^{(\tau+1)}$ has been calculated.

4.2 Stochastic Recursive Dependent Binary Relevance

As soon as a single new label estimate $\hat{y}_j^{(\tau+1)}$ at the current iteration $\tau + 1$ has been estimated by RDBR, it could immediately be used to estimate the other labels $\hat{y}_{\bar{j}}^{(\tau+1)}$. This method constitutes the stochastic version of the recursive dependent binary relevance as $\hat{\boldsymbol{y}}^{(\tau)}$ as

$$\hat{\boldsymbol{y}}^{(\tau+1)} = \hat{\theta}^{\mathrm{DBR}}(\boldsymbol{x}, \hat{\boldsymbol{y}}^{(\tau)}, \hat{\boldsymbol{y}}^{(\tau+1)}), \tau \geq 1. \tag{8}$$

The sequence of the updated labels is arbitrary at each recursion, so as to avoid a possible bias related to the class labels. The difference between the batch RDBR and stochastic RDBR is explained in fig. 3.

The strategy of RDBR is to try to repeat the re-estimation until a convergence $\hat{\boldsymbol{y}}^{(\tau+1)} = \hat{\boldsymbol{y}}^{(\tau)}$ has been reached. The rationale behind this method is that this stable value of the estimated label vector should plausibly be more robust, since it explores the mutual dependencies among the labels many times, until reaching an agreement.

A natural upper bound of the number of iterations is $\tau_{\max} = 2^m$ which is the cardinality of the power set of all m labels, since a repeated label estimation $\hat{\boldsymbol{y}}^{(\tau_p)} = \hat{\boldsymbol{y}}^{(\tau_q)}, \tau_p < \tau_q$ at the latest occurs after $\tau_{\max}$ iterations. For a large number of labels this exponential bound must be completed by a simpler stopping criterion, for instance a fixed maximum number of iterations or a heuristic performance criterion based on a validation set.

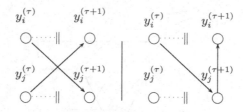

Fig. 3. Basic idea of the recursive dependent binary relevance classifier (RDBR), stochastic version. In the left side the update strategy of the batch version is shown. A label $\hat{y}_i^{(\tau+1)}$ is estimated, based exclusively on the label estimates of the previous estimates $\hat{y}_j^{(\tau)}$. In the right side the update strategy of the stochastic version is shown. A label $\hat{y}_i^{(\tau+1)}$ is estimated, based on the label estimates of the previous estimates and on the current estimates $\hat{y}_j^{(\tau+1)}$, as soon as they become available.

5 Experimental Results

The main work to which the experiments are compared is [6]. Therefore, the same databases are used, in a first experiment the same base classifiers, the same strategy to obtain the hyperparameters of the base classifiers and the same performance criteria in order to allow a fair evaluation of the method proposed in this work. In related relevant work, e.g. [11], [5], [4], the idea of recursive label re-estimation could not be identified. In table 1 the databases used in the experiments are listed, together with their relevant statistical information. The experiments are first performed with the logistic regression classifier proposed in [6]. An additional test is done with a 1-Nearest-Neighbor classifier as base learner.

Table 1. Benchmark databases used in the multi-label classification experiments. The database names Emotions, Genbase and Mediamill were abbreviated to Emot, Genb and Media respectively.

Dataset	Bibtex	Emot	Enron	Genb	Image	Media	Medical	Reuters	Scene	Slashdot	Yeast
Attributes	1836	72	1001	1185	135	120	1449	243	294	1079	103
Examples	7395	593	1702	662	2000	5000	978	7119	2407	3782	2417
Labels	159	6	53	27	5	101	45	7	6	22	14
Cardinality	2.40	1.87	3.38	1.25	1.24	4.27	1.25	1.24	1.07	1.18	4.24

The experiments compare the classifiers binary relevance of Section 2.1, classifier chain of Section 2.2, dependent binary relevance of Section 3, the batch and the stochastic version of the recursive dependent binary relevance of Section 4.1 and Section 4.2. The stacking approach of Section 2.3 and the nested stacking Section 2.4 were not considered here, since they showed inferior performance in [6] and since the technique proposed here is a direct extension of the

DBR. The evaluation metrics are those presented in Section 2.5, Hamming loss Eq. (1), subset accuracy Eq. (2), F_1 index Eq. (3) and Jaccard index Eq. (4). The maximum allowed iterations of the RDBR technique was set to $\tau_{\max} = 5$.

5.1 Logistic Regression

Logistic regression (LR) is the base learner employed firstly. A public implementation in form of the `liblinear` [2] library is used. Using regularization, the learning of the coefficients w of the regressor is formulated as the unconstrained optimization

$$\min_{w}(w \cdot w) + C \sum_{k=1}^{n} \log(1 + \exp(-y^k w \cdot x^k)), \qquad (9)$$

where again n training pairs (x^k, y^k) are used and C is the regularization parameter. As proposed in [6], this parameter is associated to each base learner and is found by sequentially testing candidate values for C within the set $\{10^p | p = -3, \ldots, 3\}$. The performance criterion was the estimated accuracy with a balanced two-fold cross validation, and taking the mean over five runs. The results for the logistic regression base learner are presented in table 2, table 3, table 4 and table 5. The tables show the performance criteria for each database and for

Table 2. Hamming Loss, Logistic regression base learner

Dataset	Bibtex	Emot	Enron	Genb	Image	Media	Medical	Reuters	Scene	Slashdot	Yeast	Avg. Rank
BR	.012	.2348	.0444	.0094	.2514	.0276	.0091	.0459	.099	.0363	.1975	2.50
DBR	.0119	.2423	.0462	.0093	.2425	.0294	.0088	.0552	.2012	.0611	.216	3.46
RDBR-S	.012	.2379	.0446	.0102	.2288	.0294	.0087	.047	.1159	.0415	.2059	2.77
RDBR-B	.0134	.2401	.046	.0094	.2451	.0316	.0088	.0553	.2012	.0611	.2351	4.18
CC	.012	.2365	.0442	.0081	.2471	.0274	.009	.0454	.1027	.0362	.211	2.09

Table 3. Subset accuracy, Logistic regression base learner

Dataset	Bibtex	Emot	Enron	Genb	Image	Media	Medical	Reuters	Scene	Slashdot	Yeast	Avg. Rank
BR	.1763	.1788	.1275	.7783	.2315	.0976	.6953	.7438	.5293	.3913	.1551	3.15
DBR	.1808	.2309	.1568	.7931	.248	.124	.7218	.7561	.5351	.4096	.1572	3.63
RDBR-S	.1842	.2832	.1463	.7764	.295	.1094	.7362	.7744	.6261	.4373	.1874	2.54
RDBR-B	.0848	.2545	.1598	.7931	.2650	.1010	.7218	.7561	.5355	.4098	.1572	3.50
CC	.18	.2544	.1416	.8083	.26	.1484	.7147	.766	.663	.436	.192	2.18

Table 4. F-Measure, Logistic regression base learner

Dataset	Bibtex	Emot	Enron	Genb	Image	Media	Medical	Reuters	Scene	Slashdot	Yeast	Avg. Rank
BR	.3697	.4618	.55	.8722	.4547	.5964	.7999	.8412	.5957	.4532	.615	3.55
DBR	.3602	.6022	.5882	.8777	.4203	.5901	.8245	.8695	.6747	.5616	.6062	2.59
RDBR-S	.3625	.5689	.5787	.8677	.4371	.581	.8299	.8679	.6678	.5101	.6076	3.09
RDBR-B	.1780	.6097	.588	.8767	.4315	.5521	.8245	.8692	.6748	.5617	.6012	2.86
CC	.3612	.5549	.5794	.8862	.446	.5997	.8111	.8619	.7087	.5047	.5994	2.91

Table 5. Jaccard index aka Example-Based Accuracy, Logistic regression base learner

Dataset	Bibtex	Emot	Enron	Genb	Image	Media	Medical	Reuters	Scene	Slashdot	Yeast	Avg. Rank
BR	.3159	.392	.4415	.8512	.3955	.4721	.7732	.8168	.579	.4374	.5053	3.82
DBR	.3108	.5059	.4791	.8583	.3748	.4723	.7983	.84	.6271	.518	.4926	2.82
RDBR-S	.3134	.4925	.4688	.8463	.4002	.4648	.806	.8444	.6574	.4915	.5013	2.54
RDBR-B	.1488	.5177	.4795	.8575	.3880	.4358	.7982	.8397	.6273	.5182	.4840	3.09
CC	.3111	.4778	.4699	.869	.3972	.4861	.7868	.8378	.6973	.4872	.4972	2.73

the sake of simplicity, the batch version of RDBR was named RDBR-B and the stochastic version of RDBR was named RDBR-S. The average rank is shown in the last row. The results suggest a potential improvement of the RDBR method, especially considering the subset accuracy which is a crisp measure of matching between target label vectors and estimated label vectors.

5.2 1-Nearest-Neighbor

The estimation of the hyperparameter C of the logistic regression Eq. (9) might have an unpredictable influence on the results presented so far. It is difficult to judge the performance of each multi-label classifier, if each of the methods had the opportunity to be tuned to the data in this preliminary estimation of C. With the objective to exclude possible misjudgments, a very simple, although very justifiable base classifier in the form of the 1-NN rule is employed. As well known the error is bound by twice the Bayes error if sufficient data is available. It might not be the best possible architecture, but it allows a comparison of the different techniques without having to consider additional parameters. The results for the 1-Nearest-Neighbor base learner are presented in table 6, table 7, table 8 and table 9. The performance scores differ considerably between the logistic regression and 1-NN. For instance for 'bibtex', LR scored for the subset accuracy around 0.18 against 0.1 for 1-NN, whereas for 'genbase', LR scored 0.78 against 0.97 for 1-NN. RDBR and CC suggest their superiority over DBR and BR, considering a better average rank in 7 or more out of 8 cases. Moreover, the stochastic version of RDBR seems to be clearly better than the batch version.

Table 6. Hamming Loss, 1-Nearest-Neighbor base learner

Dataset	Bibtex	Emot	Enron	Genb	Media	Medical	Image	Reuters	Scene	Slashdot	Yeast	Avg. Rank
BR	.0239	.235	.0677	.0011	.0303	.019	.2359	.0398	.1112	.0745	.2432	3.00
DBR	.0249	.235	.0689	.0015	.0303	.0192	.2359	.0398	.1112	.0735	.2432	3.69
RDBR-S	.0236	.235	.0671	.0012	.0303	.019	.2359	.0398	.1112	.0729	.2432	2.36
RDBR-B	.0245	.235	.0688	.0015	.0303	.0192	.2359	.0398	.1112	.0735	.2432	3.50
CC	.0238	.235	.0673	.001	.0303	.019	.2359	.0398	.1112	.0732	.2432	2.45

Table 7. Subset accuracy, 1-Nearest-Neighbor base learner.

Dataset	Bibtex	Emot	Enron	Genb	Media	Medical	Image	Reuters	Scene	Slashdot	Yeast	Avg. Rank
BR	.0914	.2679	.1017	.9728	.2408	.4908	.376	.859	.629	.2319	.2131	3.13
DBR	.0913	.2679	.1005	.9683	.2408	.4928	.376	.859	.629	.2303	.2131	3.64
RDBR-S	.0945	.2679	.1228	.9698	.2408	.501	.376	.859	.629	.2467	.2131	2.55
RDBR-B	.0914	.2679	.1005	.9683	.2408	.4928	.376	.859	.629	.2303	.2131	3.50
CC	.0952	.2679	.1251	.9743	.2408	.504	.376	.859	.629	.243	.2131	2.18

Table 8. F-Measure, 1-Nearest-Neighbor base learner

Dataset	Bibtex	Emot	Enron	Genb	Media	Medical	Image	Reuters	Scene	Slashdot	Yeast	Avg. Rank
BR	.2447	.598	.4142	.9913	.6422	.6558	.5197	.8874	.6896	.2864	.5751	3.04
DBR	.2464	.598	.4293	.9902	.6422	.6348	.5197	.8874	.6896	.2745	.5751	3.32
RDBR-S	.2463	.598	.4359	.9913	.6422	.6465	.5197	.8874	.6896	.2877	.5751	2.59
RDBR-B	.2464	.598	.429	.9902	.6422	.6352	.5197	.8874	.6896	.2745	.5751	3.32
CC	.2460	.598	.4324	.9928	.6422	.6469	.5197	.8874	.6896	.2836	.5751	2.73

Table 9. Jaccard index aka Example-Based Accuracy, 1-Nearest-Neighbor base learner.

Dataset	Bibtex	Emot	Enron	Genb	Media	Medical	Image	Reuters	Scene	Slashdot	Yeast	Avg. Rank
BR	.1973	.5136	.3252	.9875	.5473	.6134	.4824	.8802	.6744	.2721	.4817	3.09
DBR	.1984	.5136	.3349	.9855	.5473	.5983	.4824	.8802	.6744	.2625	.4817	3.59
RDBR-S	.1997	.5136	.3472	.9868	.5473	.6098	.4824	.8802	.6744	.2771	.4817	2.55
RDBR-B	.1986	.5136	.3348	.9855	.5473	.5986	.4824	.8802	.6744	.2626	.4817	3.41
CC	.1998	.5136	.3451	.989	.5473	.611	.4824	.8802	.6744	.2731	.4817	2.36

5.3   Recursion Depth of Label Estimation

An interesting analysis is the evolution of the classifier performance when considering the recursive re-estimation of the class labels. The subset accuracy performance criterion is used to juxtapose the DBR and RDBR methods and observe its evolution when incrementing the number of iterations. Since DBR calculates the labels only once, after the first iteration its value stays invariant. It can be observed that the stochastic RDBR converges very quickly to a stable value of the performance score. For this selection of databases one could also observe a complete stabilization of the estimated class labels much earlier than the natural upper bound 2^m, although this cannot be generalized.

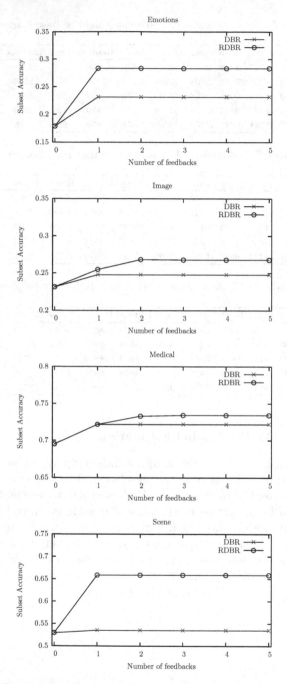

Fig. 4. RDBR Convergence Analysis. Comparison between the DBR and stochastic RDBR classifiers, considering the subset accuracy. Iteration zero is the score of the BR base classifiers. A difference already in the first iteration can be explained by the stochastic update method. If the batch methods had been used, in the first iteration the score of DBR and RDBR would be identical.

6   Conclusions

This work presented an extension to the dependent binary relevance classifier for multi-label classification. Instead of considering the outcome of the DBR as the final estimate, the estimated class labels are fed again into the DBR classifier in order to try to reach a stable value. Experimental results suggest the potential to improve partially the performance scores obtained by previous methods. Future work will try to refine the method and obtain a more theoretical formulation and will investigate the convergence of the proposed method.

References

1. Cheng, W., Hüllermeier, E., Dembczynski, K.J.: Bayes optimal multilabel classification via probabilistic classifier chains. In: Proceedings of the 27th International Conference on Machine Learning (ICML 2010), pp. 279–286 (2010)
2. Fan, R.E., Chang, K.W., Hsieh, C.J., Wang, X.R., Lin, C.J.: LIBLINEAR: A library for large linear classification. Journal of Machine Learning Research 9, 1871–1874 (2008)
3. Godbole, S., Sarawagi, S.: Discriminative methods for multi-labeled classification. In: Dai, H., Srikant, R., Zhang, C. (eds.) PAKDD 2004. LNCS (LNAI), vol. 3056, pp. 22–30. Springer, Heidelberg (2004)
4. Madjarov, G., Gjorgjevikj, D., Deroski, S.: Two stage architecture for multi-label learning. Pattern Recognition 45(3), 1019–1034 (2012). http://www.sciencedirect.com/science/article/pii/S0031320311003487
5. Madjarov, G., Kocev, D., Gjorgjevikj, D., Deroski, S.: An extensive experimental comparison of methods for multi-label learning. Pattern Recognition 45(9), 3084–3104 (2012). http://www.sciencedirect.com/science/article/pii/S0031320312001203, best Papers of Iberian Conference on Pattern Recognition and Image Analysis (IbPRIA 2011)
6. Montañes, E., Senge, R., Barranquero, J., Ramón Quevedo, J., del Coz, J.J., Hüllermeier, E.: Dependent binary relevance models for multi-label classification. Pattern Recognition 47(3), 1494–1508 (2014)
7. Read, J., Pfahringer, B., Holmes, G., Frank, E.: Classifier chains for multi-label classification. Machine Learning 85(3), 333–359 (2011)
8. Senge, R., del Coz, J.J., Hüllermeier, E.: Rectifying classifier chains for multi-label classification. In: Henrich, A., Sperker, H.C. (eds.) LWA 2013 Workshop Lernen, Wissen & Adaptivität, pp. 162–169 (2013)
9. Tsoumakas, G., Katakis, I.: Multi-label classification: An overview. International Journal of Data Warehousing and Mining (IJDWM) 3(3), 1–13 (2007)
10. Wu, X., Kumar, V., Quinlan, J.R., Ghosh, J., Yang, Q., Motoda, H., McLachlan, G.J., Ng, A., Liu, B., Philip, S.Y., et al.: Top 10 algorithms in data mining. Knowledge and Information Systems 14(1), 1–37 (2008)
11. Zhang, M.L., Zhang, K.: Multi-label learning by exploiting label dependency. In: Proceedings of the 16th ACM SIGKDD International Conference on Knowledge Discovery and Data Mining, pp. 999–1008. ACM (2010)

An Experimental Evaluation of Sentiment Analysis on Financial News Using Prior Polarity Words

Eduardo Campos and Edson Matsubara[✉]

Laboratório de Inteligência Artificial (LIA), Federal University of Mato Grosso do Sul, Computer College, Campo Grande, Brazil
efc@brturbo.com.br, edsontm@facom.ufms.br

Abstract. Throughout the past decade, extensive research on text classification has produced fast and accurate algorithms. Most of these algorithms are based on bag-of-words representations, which generate high dimensional data. However, just a few supervised learning methods, such as SVMs, can efficiently handle high dimensional data. To overcome this limitation we propose the use of prior polarity words (PPW) in order to create a compact and representative feature set for financial news classification. Using this approach it is possible to reduce feature sets from thousands to less than tens of features without compromising the accuracy of the text classifier. We measured accuracy, precision, recall, F-measure and ROC AUC of text classifiers using PPW. Classifier using PPW was able to topping all results when compared with a wide range of feature selection methods. By adopting PPW, Support Vector Machines and Naive Bayes performed consistently better than using the full feature set. PPW also turned Naive Bayes comparable to SVMs, as indicated by the improved performance scores in all measures tested.

Keywords: Text categorization · Knowledge engineering · Feature selection

1 Introduction

Financial analysts and stockbrokers (or financial advisers) are continuously connected to financial news. A single breaking news stories can dramatically affect the market and ignoring it can incur huge cost in money and/or opportunity. Rapid response to such news can provide a strong earning opportunity. Fast and accurate text classifiers would not only benefit financial analysts and advisers, but would assist the development of automatic or semi-automatic stockbrokers.

However, texts must be converted into a structured format. This conversion usually requires pre-processing steps such as stemming, removal of stop words, and Luhn's cut offs. The pre-processing texts are then converted into a bag-of-words (BOW) representation. When the resulting high-dimensional data is a problem, it can be handled by feature selection methods. The fully processed

© Springer International Publishing Switzerland 2014
A.L.C. Bazzan and K. Pichara (Eds.): IBERAMIA 2014, LNAI 8864, pp. 218–228, 2014.
DOI: 10.1007/978-3-319-12027-0_18

data can then be input to a preferred machine learning method, which usually requires some parameter adjustment. The final result can be an accurate text classifier.

Many real world problems, require accurate, fast classification and learning by easily implemented algorithms. Just being accurate is not enough. Such algorithms may not be realized in practice, but the requirements can be realized by improving the feature representation. Therefore, rather than developing new learning methods, the present study focuses on improving the quality of feature sets.

This study borrows elements from an established task in computational linguistics named sentiment analysis. According to [18], sentiment analysis is the task of identifying positive and negative opinions, emotions, and evaluations. Most work on sentiment analysis has been done on text expressions. Sentiment analysis work with lexicons of positive and negative words and phrases. In these lexicons, entries are tagged with their a priori *prior polarity*: out of context, does the word seem to evoke something positive or something negative. For example, *optimism* has a positive prior polarity, and *pessimism* has a negative prior polarity. The goal of this study is construct a set of prior polarity words to represent texts in a bag-of-words representation.

We propose an annotation scheme to extract prior-polarity words from positive and negative financial news and represent them in a bag-of-words vector. According to the experimental results, the proposed approach can improve the accuracy of machine learning algorithms and can reduce the size of feature sets from thousands to tens of features. The representation enhances the classification performance of SVMs and Naive Bayes (NB), and shown to be highly effective.

The rest of the paper is organized as follows: Section 2 provides the essential background and reviews related work. Section 3, presents the annotation scheme. In Section 4, we apply the annotation scheme to a Brazilian financial news source and show the prior polarity words extracted. Section 5 experimentally compares our proposal to a range of feature selection methods. Section 6, discusses the advantages of our proposal over the competing techniques. The paper concludes with Section 7.

2 Textual Representation

Data can be represented in many ways, but are usually input to machine learning algorithms in structured tabular format. Texts, on the other hand, are represented in richer but unstructured format. When converting texts to a structured format information is generally lost. Therefore, a crucial problem in text classifiers is representing textual data in a suitable format for machine learning algorithms, which can then deliver highly accurate classifiers. A very simple and successful strategy is the Bag-of-Words (BOW) approach [5, 10, 16].

In BOW text representation, the bag (containing the words) is represented as a vector E. Each word of the text corpora is an attribute A_i and the number of attributes n is the number of different words in the text corpora. The values can be simple as the word presence or absense (binary representation, one or zero) or more informative as weighted frequency as *tfidf* [13]. In this study we considered the term frequency in the document. Grammar and word order are ignored. Although the BOW representation loses huge quantities of information it has proven very effective in many applications.

The simplicity of BOW comes at a price. In this representation, a single text can extend into a very sparse vector containing tens or hundreds of thousands of attributes [8]. In the financial text classification problem treated in this study, 16 thousand attributes were obtained from text collected during on month (April 2013). The OHSUMED dataset[1] of peer-reviewed medical literature, yields 11 thousand attributes when converted to a two class problem.

Since many unnecessary attributes are inserted into feature sets, a data cleaning step is required prior to processing. Meaningless attributes are commonly excluded by tag removal, stop word removal, stemming, and Luhn's cut offs.

To improve generalization and avoid 'over fitting', the high dimensionality of this feature space must be reduced by extracting relevant features. Dimensionality is commonly reduced by feature selection, as explained in the next section.

2.1 Feature Selection

In the BOW approach, the number of words often exceeds the number of training documents. Feature selection is necessary when seeking a computationally efficient classifier. Besides ensuring computational efficiency, well-chosen features improve the classification accuracy in most text domains [5]. Other potential benefits of feature selection are facilitating data understanding and data visualization, reducing the measurement and storage requirements and defying the curse of dimensionality [8].

According to [16], feature selection reduces the extent of over-fitting. Experiments have shown that when the number of training examples and attributes are similar, the over-fitting problem is alleviated. However, when removing attributes, care is required to prevent the removal of potentially useful information from the text document.

Feature selection methods are divided into two broad categories: wrapper and filter methods. Some researchers have proposed an additional category, embedded methods. Wrappers use a machine learning algorithm to select subsets of attributes based on their predictive power. Filters select subsets of attributes independently of the chosen predictor. In embedded methods, features are selected during the classifier training process. Guyon and Elisseeff [8] tested well-known feature selection methods on 15 benchmarks datasets, including 20 Newsgroups and Reuters-21578. They concluded that wrapper methods yield stronger predictor than filter methods, but the improvements are not always significant. Other researchers have criticized wrappers as computationally expensive 'brute force' methods.

Gabrilovich and Markovitch [6] consider redundant features in the text categorization problem. They proposed an aggressive feature selection, and

---

[1] http://davis.wpi.edu/~xmdv/datasets/ohsumed.html

experimentally demonstrated an improvement in SVM. They also proposed a measure that predicts the usefulness of feature selection. Interestingly, this paper shows that C4.5 (decision tree) significantly outperforms SVM and KNN. Decision tree has a built-in feature selection method based on Information Gain (IG), which may (at least partly) explain these results.

Forman[5] conducted an extensive empirical study of feature selection in text classification. He evaluated 12 filtering feature selection methods on a benchmark of 229 2-class text classification problems collected from Reuters, TREC, OHSUMED, WebACE, and Whizbang. Several important findings were presented in Forman's paper: as the class skew increases, the outputs of SVMs vary more widely; Bi-Normal Separation (BNS) revealed surprising performance of a new feature selection metric, and selecting the two best performing metrics can be sub-optimal, since their weaknesses are probably correlated.

2.2   Text Classification and Sentiment Analysis in Financial News

Schumaker and Chen [14] employed a SVM to predict the stock price 20 min after the financial news and stock quotes had been publicizes by news wire. They tested three textual representations: BOW, noun phrases, and named entities. Named entities and noun phrases proved more effective than BOW. The highest return yielded by a simulated trading engine was 2.06%.

In the systems proposed above predictions are not accompanied by explanatory hypotheses. If the system is to be used for recommendations, hypothesis generation is an important feature. Chan and Franklin [2] proposed a text-based decision support system (DSS) whose prediction are supported by explanatory hypotheses using Hidden Markov Models. The system relies on two feature sets, adjacent events and a set of information-theoretic functions. The accuracy of this approach (up to 92.5%) proved significantly higher than that of similar approaches.

Another important topic is the management of losses due to movements in the financial market prices, known as financial market risk. Groth and Muntermann [7] predicted the future volatility of the market using corporate disclosures. They trialled an intra day risk management using k-NN, Neural Networks, SVMs and NB classifiers, and reported that SVMs delivered superior results.

The use of sentiment analysis in financial news has been studied before by [15]. They paired the financial news article prediction system (AZFinText) with a sentiment analyis tool and increased the trading return in more than 3%. The entire corpus of financial news articles is represented by their proper nouns in binary as suggested on [14], and each news article is evaluated by Opinion-Finder [17] to identify its polarity. Complementary, the study on [20] presents the correlation blog/news variables and stock markets.

Another interesting work is presented on [1]. The authors used Twitter moods to predict stock market. The accuracy of their proposal is 86% in prediction the daily up and down changes in the closing prices.

In [12], the authors construct manualy a small polarity dictionary from stock market news which is incremented by using semi-supervised learning methods. The results were validated with financial experts analysis.

3   Annotation Scheme: Obtaining Prior Polarity Words (PPW)

Marking the polarity of expressions involves the human annotators under some annotation scheme. Usually the labels are *positive, negative, both,* or *neutral.* From our experience, deciding whether a text is *positive* or *negative* is faster than *neutral* or *both.* Also, according to [19], in a contextual polarity task, "the presence of neutral instances greatly degrades the performance ..." and they propose a two-step approach to recognize contextual polarity. Based on this finding, our annotation scheme use just positive and negative labels.

In our annotation scheme, we used financial domain experts to select important financial news characterizing good (positive) and bad (negative) from our text corpora. However, good news is subjective and depends on the company. For example, recent news from Reuters follows:

> *NEW YORK (Reuters) - A data breach at Target Corp that exposed the credit card information of tens of millions of holiday shoppers was a major black eye for the retailer. In its wake, investors and analysts are circling companies that could benefit from a major upgrade in credit card technology.*

Is this news positive or negative? What constitutes good and bad news is not always obvious. The distinction is further blurred by neutral news with no positive or negative connotation. Thus, deciding whether news is positive or negative may be excessively labouring and time demanding for the domain expert. For this reason, we based the important features purely on certain positive and negative news. After many attempts, we proceeded through the following annotation scheme:

1. Instruct the domain experts about prior polarity words.
2. Scrutinize the titles of articles and select those that are strongly related to the positive and negative class value. We just take the articles with high confidence whether the article is positive or negative. If the domain expert doubts whether the article belongs to positive or negative, the article is excluded from the procedure.
3. Split the articles into two folds, a positive and a negative fold. Create a single list of words for each fold. Create a lexicographically ordered list of unique words, one word per line. By implementing this step, the domain expert is not required to pen mark important words on each text. Since a single word can appear hundreds of times in the text collection, the same word will be repeatedly marked by the domain expert, which is time intensive and wasteful.

4. Hand a printout of the listed words to the domain expert. The domain expert marks the important words characterize the class.
5. Perform stemming and convert the stem into the infinitive form of the word (or a more readable form of the word). This step removes inflections and derivations of the same word. For readability and time saving purposes, the stem should be preceded by the infinitive form of the word.
6. Aided by the domain expert, refine the list if necessary, using simple tools such as Linux/Unix grep to search for texts containing the selected words.

Once the list of words is defined, the PPW is ready to be represented as a bag of words. The next section, demonstrates the result of this annotation scheme.

4   PPW on a Real World Problem

Since our domain expert is Brazilian our proposal was evaluated on Brazilian Portuguese Finance News. Our domain expert identified the Portal EXAME Abril http://exame.abril.com.br/topicos/bolsas as an important source of Brazilian financial news. Using a PHP script, we collected 1009 texts from 2nd of January to 31st March 2013, removing all HTML tags and stopwords[2].

Our work proceeded through the steps detailed in the previous section. After step 4, our list of informative words numbered 373. Stemming reduced this number to 74 words (37 positive words and 37 negative words). The 37 positive words are listed below (Portuguese words translated to English words):

Acceleration Above High Reach Advance Benefit Good Buy Grow Defensive Demand Performance Jump Dividend Raise Stable Stimulus Expansion Favourable Strong Gain Boost Invest Lead Profit Maximum Best Opportunity Optimism Positive Potential Protection Record Recovery Profitable Rise Appreciation

The 37 negative words were:

Below Attention Low Fall Sink Bankruptcy Correction Crisis Decline Deduction Melt Slowdown Down Discount Debt Shrink Speculation Collapse Weak Less Minimum Negative Burden Losses Pessimism Worse Damage Worry Drop Readjustment Realize Retreat Reduce Risk Suffer Sell Volatile

As a preliminary work, the proposed approach just considered single words (monograms) and the approach does not treat compound words. The words in both lists represent a domain expert generalization of positive and negative financial news.

---

[2] http://snowball.tartarus.org/algorithms/portuguese/stop.txt

5   Experimental Evaluation on Real Data Sets

We collected of 331 financial news from 1st April to 30th April 2013. Among these texts, 228 were labelled by our domain expert (117 negative, 111 positive, and 103 ignored). The texts were obtained from Portal EXAME Abril http://exame.abril.com.br/topicos/bolsas. Taking care of overlapping avoidance of training and test set, the data used to evaluate the method were collected over a different period from those used to construct PPW. The texts were preprocessed by HTML tag removal, stopword removal, and stemming. The machine learning algorithms, were multinomial naive Bayes (NB) from WEKA [9] and support vector machines (SVM) from LIBSVM [3]. We selected SVM on account of its superior performance in previously reported text classification problems. Alternatively, the NB classifier is a popular choice because it is fast and easily implemented.

The results reported in this section use NB with default parameters. For SVM we used a gaussian kernel adjusting the parameter as recommended on [11] and implemented on additional scripts on the implementation of LIBSVM. When using SVM on full dataset the parameters were $c = 32$ and $g = 3.0517578125e - 05$, on PPW dataset the parameters were $c = 128$ and $g = 3.0517578125e - 05$.

The feature selection methods (Information Gain, Gain Ratio, Symmetrical Uncertainty, and Correlation) are available from WEKA. We have newly implemented the Bi-Normal Separation (BNS) based on Forman's recommendation [5].

The results were analysed in terms of accuracy, precision, recall, F-measure, and ROC AUC since each serves different purposes. All results were obtained using 10-fold cross validation. Each of the following sections answers a question that guided the experimental evaluation and the significance test.

5.1   Does PPW Outperform a Full Feature Set?

Figure 5 shows of the accuracy, precision, recall, F-measure (F1) and ROC AUC obtained by the multinomial NB (Fig. 1) classifier and SVM (Fig. 2) using the full dataset and the dataset with PPW. Clearly PPW improves the performance of NB in all measures. We applied a paired t-test ($p = 0.05$) on this result and there is a significant difference.

SVM is already accurate classifier using the complete dataset, even though PPW shows better results on accuracy, precision and AUC. Performing a paired t-test there are significant differences ($p = 0.05$) on precision and recall, which indicates that PPW is better than complete dataset on precision and it is worst on recall. When calibrating classifier, changing its classification threshold, precision and recall are considered trade offs, therefore these significant differences are not conclusive.

Our experimental results support the claim that SVMs are very robust in high dimensional problems [10]. The performance of SVM and NB on the unfiltered dataset is plotted in Figure 3. Clearly SVM outperformed NB. Therefore we conclude that, in the absence of feature selection, SVM is more suitable for our

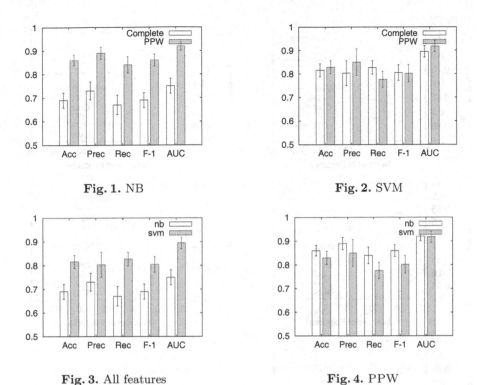

Fig. 1. NB

Fig. 2. SVM

Fig. 3. All features

Fig. 4. PPW

Fig. 5. Complete dataset (16501 features) and PPW dataset (74 features). Vertical lines on the top of each bar indicates standard error.

problem than NB. However, under PPW, interestingly NB achieved competitive results to SVM. When performing paired t-test the differences are not significant ($p = 0.05$) confirming our hypothesis that NB and SVM are competitive in this set up (Figure 4).

5.2 How Sensitive is PPW to the Number of Available Features, Relative to Other Feature Selection Methods?

The performance of feature selection algorithms generally depends on the number of features. Performance may improve or decline as the number of features increases. To verify whether any of the evaluated feature selection methods was compromised by the fixed number of features, we varied the number of features from 10 to 70 and again recorded the AUC, F1, accuracy, precision and recall of all methods. The results are plotted in Figure 6.

It wouldn't be fair to compare methods with different number of features. The proposed feature set, PPW, has a fixed set of 74 features. In order to vary this number and allow a fair comparison between methods PPW and other feature selection methods, we applied Information Gain feature selection to PPW

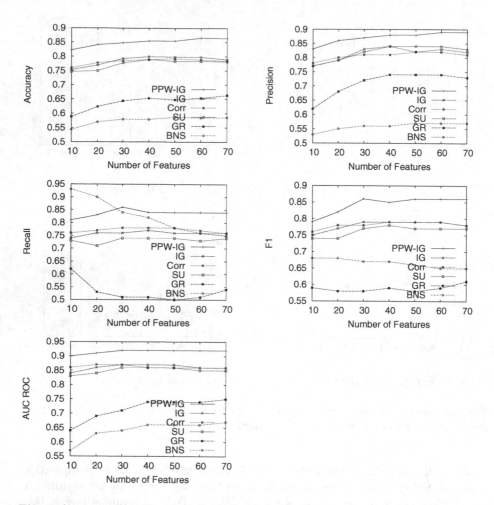

Fig. 6. Accuracy, Precision, Recall, F1 and ROC AUC shown in an increasing order of features from 10 to 70 features

(PPW-IG) in this comparison. Among the feature selection methods, PPW scored highest in all measures except for recall, which was topped by BNS with 10 and 20 features.

The accuracy, precision and recall scores of classifiers can depend on the classifier score threshold [4]. For this reason, the ROC AUC is useful measure. In the ROC AUC plot Figure 6, the highest AUC score was achived by PPW-IG at 30 features. This score was unchanged at higher feature number, indicating that the performances of PPW-IG is maximized at 30 PPW features. Therefore if desired, we could reduce the number of features from 74 to 30. This result suggests that the method could be further investigated and improved.

6 Conclusions

In this paper, we present an experimental evaluation using PPW on finance text classification problem. We also propose an annotation scheme to obtain PPW to represet texts in a more compact and representative way. We applied the annotation scheme in Brazilian financial texts and compared to results of PPW on a range of feature selection methods. The PPW is consistently superior than all feature selection methods tested. Surprisingly, combined with PPW, the NB classifier is comparable to SVM. According to our results using just 30 features (Fig. 6 AUC ROC and F1), it is possible to achieve accurate classifiers, which can be the starting point for developing fast and accurate text classifiers for big data or any data intensive problem.

As future work, we plan to extend the experimental evaluation to other datasets on financial news and include more domain expert annotators. According to the results in our experimental section, the difference between human annotation and automated annotation is significant. Our future goal is to reduce this difference by studying PPW extracted by the proposal of this work and automatic feature selection methods using semi-supervised learning methods and active learning.

References

1. Bollen, J., Mao, H., Zeng, X.: Twitter mood predicts the stock market. Journal of Computational Science 2(1), 1–8 (2011), http://www.sciencedirect.com/science/article/pii/S187775031100007X
2. Chan, S.W., Franklin, J.: A text-based decision support system for financial sequence prediction. Decision Support Systems 52(1), 189–198 (2011), http://www.sciencedirect.com/science/article/pii/S0167923611001230
3. Chang, C.C., Lin, C.J.: Libsvm: A library for support vector machines. ACM Trans. Intell. Syst. Technol. 2(3), 27:1–27:27 (2011), http://doi.acm.org/10.1145/1961189.1961199
4. Fawcett, T.: An introduction to roc analysis. Pattern Recogn. Lett. 27(8), 861–874 (2006), http://dx.doi.org/10.1016/j.patrec.2005.10.010
5. Forman, G.: An extensive empirical study of feature selection metrics for text classification. J. Mach. Learn. Res. 3, 1289–1305 (2003), http://dl.acm.org/citation.cfm?id=944919.944974
6. Gabrilovich, E., Markovitch, S.: Text categorization with many redundant features: Using aggressive feature selection to make svms competitive with c4.5. In: Proceedings of the Twenty-first International Conference on Machine Learning, ICML 2004, p. 41. ACM, New York (2004), http://doi.acm.org/10.1145/1015330.1015388
7. Groth, S.S., Muntermann, J.: An intraday market risk management approach based on textual analysis. Decision Support Systems 50(4), 680–691 (2011), http://www.sciencedirect.com/science/article/pii/S0167923610001430, (enterprise Risk and Security Management: Data, Text and Web Mining)
8. Guyon, I., Elisseeff, A.: An introduction to variable and feature selection. J. Mach. Learn. Res. 3, 1157–1182 (2003), http://dl.acm.org/citation.cfm?id=944919.944968

9. Hall, M., Frank, E., Holmes, G., Pfahringer, B., Reutemann, P., Witten, I.H.: The weka data mining software: An update. SIGKDD Explor. Newsl. 11(1), 10–18 (2009), http://doi.acm.org/10.1145/1656274.1656278

10. Joachims, T.: Text categorization with suport vector machines: Learning with many relevant features. In: Proceedings of the 10th European Conference on Machine Learning, ECML 1998, Chemnitz, Germany, April 21-23, pp. 137–142 (1998)

11. Keerthi, S.S., Lin, C.J.: Asymptotic behaviors of support vector machines with gaussian kernel. Neural Comput. 15(7), 1667–1689 (2003), http://dx.doi.org/10.1162/089976603321891855

12. Mizumoto, K., Yanagimoto, H., Yoshioka, M.: Sentiment analysis of stock market news with semi-supervised learning. In: 2012 IEEE/ACIS 11th International Conference on Computer and Information Science (ICIS), pp. 325–328. IEEE (2012)

13. Robertson, S.: Understanding inverse document frequency: on theoretical arguments for idf. Journal of Documentation 60(5), 503–520 (2004)

14. Schumaker, R.P., Chen, H.: Textual analysis of stock market prediction using breaking financial news: The azfin text system. ACM Trans. Inf. Syst. 27(2), 12:1–12:19 (2009), http://doi.acm.org/10.1145/1462198.1462204

15. Schumaker, R.P., Zhang, Y., Huang, C.N., Chen, H.: Evaluating sentiment in financial news articles. Decis. Support Syst. 53(3), 458–464 (2012), http://dx.doi.org/10.1016/j.dss.2012.03.001

16. Sebastiani, F.: Machine learning in automated text categorization. ACM Comput. Surv. 34(1), 1–47 (2002), http://doi.acm.org/10.1145/505282.505283

17. Wilson, T., Hoffmann, P., Somasundaran, S., Kessler, J., Wiebe, J., Choi, Y., Cardie, C., Riloff, E., Patwardhan, S.: Opinionfinder: A system for subjectivity analysis. In: Proceedings of HLT/EMNLP on Interactive Demonstrations, HLT-Demo 2005, pp. 34–35. Association for Computational Linguistics, Stroudsburg (2005), http://dx.doi.org/10.3115/1225733.1225751

18. Wilson, T., Wiebe, J., Hoffmann, P.: Recognizing contextual polarity in phrase-level sentiment analysis. In: Proceedings of the Conference on Human Language Technology and Empirical Methods in Natural Language Processing, HLT 2005, pp. 347–354. Association for Computational Linguistics, Stroudsburg (2005), http://dx.doi.org/10.3115/1220575.1220619

19. Wilson, T., Wiebe, J., Hoffmann, P.: Recognizing contextual polarity: An exploration of features for phrase-level sentiment analysis. Comput. Linguist. 35(3), 399–433 (2009), http://dx.doi.org/10.1162/coli.08-012-R1-06-90

20. Zhang, W., Skiena, S.: Trading strategies to exploit blog and news sentiment. In: ICWSM (2010)

A Language Model for Improving the Graph-Based Transcription Approach for Historical Documents

Graciela Lecireth Meza-Lovón[✉]

Universidad La Salle, Arequipa, Perú
gracielamezalovon@ulasalle.edu.pe

Abstract. Language Models (LMs) capture the contextual dependencies of a language and assign higher probabilities to well-formed sequences of words. For that reason, LMs have been commonly used in generic handwriting recognition, improving recognition results. In this paper, we present the integration of a Language Model along with a dictionary into a graph-based recognizer, which aims at transcribing handwritten historical documents. The results of such integration show a significant improvement on word accuracy when applied to our corpora.

Keywords: Language model · Bigram · Dictionary · Text transcription · Handwriting recognition · Support vector machines

1 Introduction

Over the last decade, worldwide libraries have shown an increased interest in digitalizing and storing handwritten historical documents resulting in the creation of large image databases. Most of the stored document images are not transcribed, which causes queries to be mostly restricted to author, title or subject, and prevents people from performing more specialized queries, such as those based on the content of the documents.

In spite of the great deal of research conducted on generic handwriting recognition in the last decade [1][5][6][7][13], the transcription of handwritten historical documents has remained mostly unexplored. In fact, initial research on historical documents did not aim at querying arbitrary words, but querying previously defined specific words. In this context, Rath et al. [15][16][17] proposed a word spotting method based on Dynamic Time Warping and clustering techniques. Leydier et al. [10][11][12] used gradient features in a segmentation-free approach that tolerates spatial variations of a queried word image and a candidate word image. Zhang et al. [25] used semi-Markov conditional random fields on Chinese handwritten documents. However, the aforementioned research did not pursue full transcriptions.

Pioneer work on transcribing ancient documents, including a post-editing module, was made by Toselli et al. [23] and Romero et al. [19][20], who proposed

© Springer International Publishing Switzerland 2014
A.L.C. Bazzan and K. Pichara (Eds.): IBERAMIA 2014, LNAI 8864, pp. 229–241, 2014.
DOI: 10.1007/978-3-319-12027-0_19

a transcription system based on Hidden Markov Models, whose performance was improved by the feedback given by experts. That feedback updated the system's parameters and yielded more accurate outputs.

Meza-Lovon [14] proposed a graph-based transcription approach, which instead of learning isolated word models, learned character models. This functionality allowed the system to recognize words, even if they did not appear in the training data. Despite this advantage, the graph-based approach includes neither a language model nor a dictionary.

Language models capture the word dependencies of a language and assign higher probabilities to meaningful and grammatically correct sequences of words. Therefore, language models are an important component in tasks such as machine translation, speech recognition, text recognition and word spotting. In the context of generic handwritten recognition, language models have been extensively used in improving recognition rates as shown in [2][4][21][24].

In this paper, we integrate a language model into the graph-based approach. Furthermore, we include a dictionary which is employed to propose alternative words to the one offered by the graph-based recognizer. The language model, along with the dictionary, is used to create a wordnet, from which the most likely transcription is obtained. Our experiments show that the results from the graph-based approach are remarkably improved when using the language model and the dictionary.

This paper is organized as follows: Sec. 2 provides an overview of the whole process. Sec. 3, Sec. 4 and Sec. 5 describe the pre-processing methods, the extraction of gradient features and the classifier we used in this approach. In Sec. 6 we describe the graph-based approach applied to word recognition. Later, in Sec. 7 we describe the integration of our language model and our dictionary into the graph-based approach. Finally, we present experiments and results in Sec. 8, as well as conclusions and future work in Sec. 9.

2   Overview

Like most recognition systems, our proposal has three stages, namely, data preparation or pre-processing, feature extraction and learning/recognition. We briefly describe such stages and illustrate them in Fig. 1.

The pre-processing stage aims at not only improving the quality of images, but also dividing page images into word images. To this end, several pre-processing tasks are performed; namely, correcting the skew of text-lines, splitting page images into text-line images, correcting the slant of handwriting, normalizing text-line images, and finally, cutting text-line images into word images.

In the feature extraction stage, feature vectors containing information about the gradients of the pixels of images are created. More precisely, images are divided vertically and horizontally into equal-sized zones, and for them, the magnitudes of the gradients of their pixels are accumulated according the directions of their gradients.

Furthermore, a Support Vector Machine (SVM) is used to learn from character images. It is important to clarify that during training, the SVM learns from a collection of feature vectors which are computed from character images; however, in the recognition stage, the SVM receives feature vectors which are obtained from subimages of word images.

The recognition is a two-step stage. In the first step, for each word image of a text-line image, a graph is constructed. Roughly speaking, a word image is divided into frames whose starting points are used to label the nodes of the graph. Edges are associated to a certain number of consecutive frames, which altogether constitute a subimage. This subimage is feature extracted and passed to a SVM, which provides a probability class which, in turn is used to compute the cost of the edges. Then using the Dijisktra algorithm, the most likely sequence of characters is obtained, which ideally is a valid word.

In the second recognition step, a language model and a dictionary that was previously created with the training data is used. The language model employed in this work is a bigram and is useful to capture contextual properties of the Spanish language. On the other hand, a dictionary provides alternative words to the word produced by the graph-based recognizer. The bigram, along with the dictionary, cooperates to create a wordnet from which the most likely sequence of words is finally obtained.

3   Data Pre-processing

In this work, data pre-processing aims at improving the quality of the images of our corpora as well as splitting the page images into word images. For doing so, we increased the contrast of the images, such that their text areas stand out from their background areas. Also, we fixed the skew of the pages by applying a two-step heuristic: in the first step we simulated text-line rotations using angles ranging from $-18°$ to $18°$. In the second step, we chose the angle α that produced the horizontal projection profile with both the greatest variance and the highest peak, and then we rotated the page image using the angle α.

We also split the page images into text-line images. First, we computed the horizontal projection profiles of the page images; then we identified the profiles' valleys, which mostly correspond to the spaces between lines. Finally we used such valleys as cut points for obtaining text-lines.

Furthermore, the slant of text-line images was corrected, first by detecting the angle α between the handwriting and the y-coordinate, and then by smearing the image in question using the detected angle. More precisely, the angle α was estimated using central moments μ as follows, $\alpha = \arctan(\mu_{11}/\mu_{02})$; $\mu_{gh} = \sum_{x=1}^{N} \sum_{y=1}^{N} (x-x_c)^g (y-y_c)^h p(x,y)$, where x_c and y_c are the centroid coordinates of the image and $p(x,y)$ is the pixel intensity at position (x,y). The smearing step was performed applying the shear transform to every pixel (x,y), obtaining for each of them a new position (x',y') in which, $x' = x - (y - y_c)\tan(\alpha)$ and $y' = y$.

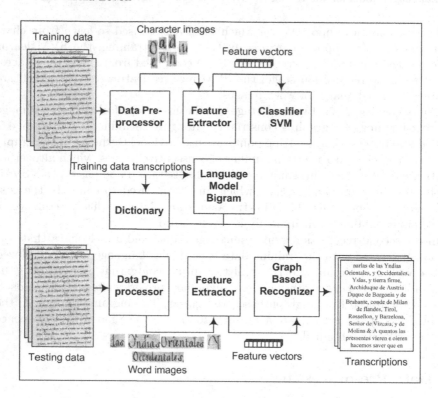

Fig. 1. Overview of the transcription system improved by a language model and a dictionary

In order to make the recognition process image size-invariant, all text-line images must keep the same height proportions. This means that the height of the ascender areas of all text-line images must be the same, as well as that of the descender and central areas. The ratios for computing the new height of areas of interest are given by a user. This procedure was explored in greater detail in [14].

Finally, the text-line images were divided into word images. To do so, we took advantage of the fact that the inter-word spaces of our data sets are greater than the intra-word spaces. Based on this observation, we performed a procedure based on projection profiles, which is very similar to that of splitting page images, but instead of computing the horizontal projection profile, we computed the vertical one.

4   Feature Extraction: Gradient Features

Gradient features were reported to provide high recognition rates when applied to handwritten images [9][22]. According to Fujisawa et al. [8], both the gradient magnitude s and direction θ of a pixel (x, y) are estimated via

$$s(x,y) = \sqrt{\triangle u^2 + \triangle v^2}$$

and

$$\theta(x,y) = \arctan\left(\frac{\triangle v}{\triangle u}\right),$$

respectively, where

$$\triangle u = \frac{\partial p}{\partial x} = p(x+1, y+1) - p(x,y),$$

and

$$\triangle v = \frac{\partial p}{\partial y} = p(x+1, y) - p(x, y+1).$$

The direction space (angle space) was quantized into 32 angle intervals of $\pi/16$ each. For computing the feature vector $\mathbf{F}$ of an image, we divided the image vertically and horizontally into non-overlapping zones of the same size, and for each zone $z_i, i = 1, 2, \ldots, B$, we accumulated the magnitudes of the gradients of its pixels in their corresponding direction intervals. Thus, for each zone z_i, we obtained a 32-feature vector $\mathbf{f}_{z_i}$ and consequently $\mathbf{F} = (\mathbf{f}_{z_1} \ldots, \mathbf{f}_{z_B})$, where B represents the number of zones in which the image was divided.

5 Learning: Support Vector Machines

One of the learning models that performs well on most classification tasks is Support Vector Machines (SVMs) [3]. The SVM learning scheme finds a hyperplane which provides the maximal distance between the hyperplane and the closest input samples of two classes. The problem of finding such hyperplane can be formulated as an optimization problem subject to some restrictions. Also, SVMs are based on the kernel trick which uses a kernel function for mapping the input data into a higher dimensional space where a linear separation is feasible.

Although SVMs were initially proposed for binary classification, there are some extensions for solving the multi-class problem. Those extensions are mostly based on both the one-versus-all approach consisting in training different binary classifiers which distinguish one class from the rest; and the one-versus-one approach which builds binary classifiers for distinguishing between every pair of classes.

In this work, a SVM is used for learning isolated characters that correspond to letters of the Spanish alphabet.

6 Word Recognition: Graph-Based Approach

In our work, a word image is considered as a sequence of frames, $f_1, f_2, \ldots, f_N$, where each frame f_i has a starting point p_i, that corresponds to the x-coordinate where the frame starts. The frames are the same height of the text-line image and are of fixed width given by a user. This is illustrated in Fig. 2.

Fig. 2. A word image split into frames

The word recognition approach consists of two procedures, namely, the representation of a word image as a graph and the search of the best sequence of characters in the created graph. The first procedure is described in the following section.

6.1 Graph-Based Representation of Word Images

Before building the graph, we determined the width of the frames and estimated the minimum m and maximum M number of frames that any character spreads out.

In the graph, each node is associated to the starting point p_i of a frame f_i and has at most $(M-m+1)$ leaving edges. Furthermore, each edge is associated to: a) a number n of consecutive frames that must be taken from the starting point p_i, where $n = [m, \ldots, M], n \in N$; b) a subimage that starts at position p_i of the word image and whose width is determined by its corresponding number of consecutive frames (note that p_i is the start node of the edge in question) c) the most likely class for the subimage; and d) an estimated cost, which is based on the class probability given by the SVM.

The procedure to build the graph for a word image is described below:

1. We create node p_i. Note that, the first node we add is p_1 and corresponds to zero x-coordinate of the text-line image.
2. For each node p_i without leaving edges, we add $(M - m + 1)$ edges.
3. For each edge e whose cost was not estimated, we obtain the feature vector of its corresponding subimage as described in Sec. 4. Then, the SVM provides both the most likely class and the class probability denoted by p (without substript) for the feature vector. Subsequently, we compute the cost c as follows $c = f \times \left(\frac{1}{\ln p}\right)$, where f is the number of frames tied up to the edge. Finally, for edge e, we add its end node $p_n, n = i + k + 1$.
4. We repeat step 2 and 3 until we reach $p_N + 1$.

Figs. 3(a), 3(b) and 3(c) shows this procedure.

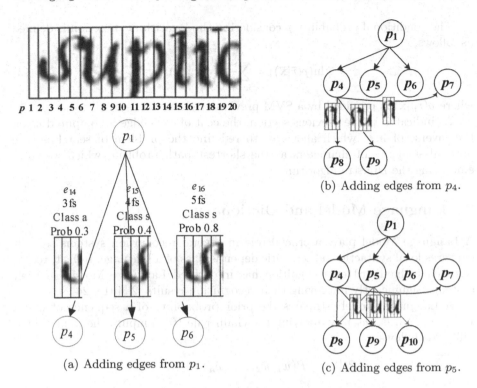

(a) Adding edges from p_1.

(b) Adding edges from p_4.

(c) Adding edges from p_5.

Fig. 3. Graph-based Approach

6.2 Search of the Optimal Sequence of Characters

A word image is considered as a sequence of feature vectors $\overline{\mathbf{x}} = (\mathbf{x_1}, \ldots, \mathbf{x_T})$, where $\mathbf{x_t} \in \mathbb{R}^d$. Furthermore, a word transcription $\overline{l}$ is a sequence of characters, $\overline{l} = (l_1, \ldots, l_N)$ where $l_n \in \Sigma$ (spanish alphabet) for all n, $1 \leq n \leq N$. Thus $\overline{l} \in \Sigma^*$ (set of all finite-length sequences over Σ). In our approach, word recognition aims at searching for a sequence of characters $\overline{l}' \in \Sigma^*$, with the highest conditional probability,

$$\overline{l}' = \arg\max_{\overline{l} \in \Sigma^*} p(\overline{l}|\overline{\mathbf{x}}) \qquad (1)$$

Since the number of possible sequences is exponential in the number of events, it is not feasible to perform an exhaustive search. Thus in this work we solve Eq. 1 by assuming that $\overline{l}'$ is the path of the graph with the highest conditional probability. We denote the graph of interest by G and its optimal path by $\overline{r}'$. Furthermore, we use the logarithmic function in order to avoid the product probabilities from vanishing. Hence Eq. 1 is reformulated as shown below,

$$\overline{r}' = \arg\max_{\overline{r} \in G} \ln(p(\overline{r}|\overline{\mathbf{x}})) \qquad (2)$$

where $\overline{r} = (r_1, \ldots, r_N)$ is one of the paths of graph G.

The conditional probability p considering the logarithmic function is defined as follows,

$$\ln(p(\overline{r}|\overline{\mathbf{x}})) = \sum_{n=1}^{N} \ln(p(r_n|\mathbf{x})). \tag{3}$$

where $p(r_n|\mathbf{x})$ is provided by a SVM previously trained.

As indicated in the previous section, the cost of each edge is computed using the inverse of $\ln p$, which allows us to redefine the problem of searching the optimal sequence of characters as the shortest path problem, which we solve employing the Dijkstra algorithm.

7   Language Model and Dictionary

A Language Model plays a crucial role in several recognition systems since it captures local syntactic and semantic dependencies of a language. In fact, recent research in handwritten recognition has integrated Language Models in their systems, significantly improving their recognition results [2][4][18][24].

A Language Model estimates the prior probability of a sequence of words $W = (w_1, w_2, \ldots, w_n)$ by applying the chain rule (to compute the joint probability) as follows

$$P(W) = P(w_1, w_2, \ldots, w_n)$$
$$= P(w_1) \cdot \prod_{i=2}^{n} P(w_i|w_1, \ldots, w_{i-1}) \tag{4}$$

However, in order to compute the joint probability $P(W)$ of the entire word sequence, the conditional probability $P(w_i|w_1, \ldots, w_{i-1})$ needs all the previous history, i.e., the sequence of previous words $w_1, \ldots, w_{i-1}$. Accordingly, such computation would require enough training data for every single sentence a person could create, which is not viable. Therefore, most approaches for language models restrict the word-history used in the computation of $P(W)$. For example n-grams restrict their history to the n previous words.

In our transcription system, we employed a specific n-gram called bigram which estimates the probability based only on the preceding word. Formally, bigrams approximate $P(W)$ as follows,

$$P(W) = P(w_1) \cdot \prod_{i=2}^{n} P(w_i|w_{i-1}), \tag{5}$$

where $P(w_i|w_{i-1})$ is estimated via,

$$P(w_i|w_{i-1}) = \frac{C(w_{i-1}w_i)}{C(w_{i-1})}, \tag{6}$$

where $C(w_{i-1}w_i)$ and $C(w_{i-1})$ are the number of occurrences of the sequence $w_{i-1}w_i$ and the word w_{i-1}, respectively.

In the same vein, the words produced by the graph-based recognizer may be non valid words, i.e., sequences of characters that do not represent words of the Spanish language. The use of a dictionary allows us to provide valid word choices to the sequence of characters given by the recognizer.

Furthermore, the Language Model and the dictionary were constructed using the training data, so that the dictionary is open, i.e., it could not contain all the words of the testing set. Accordingly, during the construction of the wordnet out-of-the-dictionary words produced by the graph-based recognizer were included as well. The probability of word transitions are obtained from the bigram. Fig. 4 illustrates this procedure.

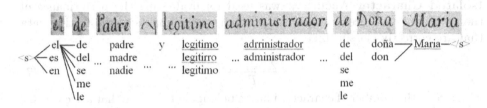

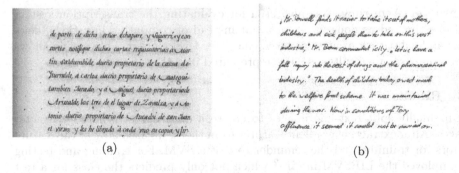

Fig. 4. A wordnet for a text-line image of ECA corpus

8 Experiments and Results

8.1 Corpora

We employed both the ECA corpus [14] and the IAMDB corpus[1]. ECA contains 500 page images of handwritten Spanish text written by a single author; while IAMDB consists of 1539 pages of scanned English text, 5685 sentences, written by 657 writers. Samples of both corpora are shown in Fig. 5.

(a)   (b)

Fig. 5. Fragments of a page from a) ECA and b) IAMDB

---

[1] http://www.iam.unibe.ch/fki/databases/iam-handwriting-corpus

Table 1 summarizes the statistics of our corpora and shows the number of samples used in the experiments.

Table 1. Statistics of ECA and IAMDB

	Number of			Number of Characters SVM		Number of
	pages	lines	characters	training	testing	Characters GBM
ECA	50	9982	39498	7150	795	31553
IAMDB	50	531	15636	2814	313	12509

8.2 Evaluation Metrics

Isolated Character Accuracy was used for evaluating the performance of the SVM and computes the percentage of character images in the testing data that are correctly classified, i.e.,

$$\frac{\sum_{c=1}^{K} S_c}{T} \tag{7}$$

where S_c is the number of character images belonging to class c that are correctly classified, and T is the number of testing samples.

Word Accuracy, denoted by W_{ACC}, was used for assessing the performance of the transcription system and is defined as,

$$W_{ACC} = 100 * (1 - WER). \tag{8}$$

The word error rate WER is computed as follows,

$$WER = \frac{i + s + d}{T}, \tag{9}$$

where i, s and d are the number of inserted, substituted and deleted words required to convert the transcription given a system into the true transcription of the testing data.

Character Accuracy, was also used for evaluating the transcription system and is estimated as done for W_{ACC}, but instead of computing insertions, deletions and substitutions at word level, character level is used. This metric allows us to compare our results with those presented in [14].

8.3 Results

We manually split text-line images to create a database of isolated character images. After extracting gradient features from them, we used 90% of the feature vectors for training, and the reminder to test a SVM. For training and testing we employed the LIBSVM library[2] which not only predicts the class for a test pattern, but also provides the probabilities associated with each class.

The best isolated character accuracies for ECA and IAMDB were obtained using a radial basis kernel. The results are presented in Table 2.

---

[2] http://www.csie.ntu.edu.tw/~cjlin/libsvm/

Table 2. Results for ECA and IAMDB using SVM

Isolated Character Accuracy (%)	
ECA	IAMDB
96.58±2.65%	90.36±3.24%

It is worth mentioning that for some non frequent letters such as 'z' and 'x', we obtained an isolated character accuracy of 92% and 89%. We assume that those low percentages respond to insufficient training data for those characters.

On the other hand, the word accuracy achieved by incorporating the language model into the Graph-Based Model(GBM) is shown in Table 3.

Table 3. Main Results for our method using ECA and IAMDB

	Character Accuracy(%)		Word Accuracy(%)	
	ECA	IAMDB	ECA	IAMDB
GBM without LM	79.30	72.57	70.64	60.23
GBM with LM	83.67	76.01	75.14	66.08

The graph-based approach integrated with a language model and a dictionary increased the word accuracy by approximately 4% in both corpora.

9   Conclusions and Future Work

In this work, we integrated a Language Model and a dictionary into the graph-based transcription proposed by [14]. Experiments were conducted on IAMBD, a laboratory-made corpus, as well as on ECA, a real-world data set. Results show that recognition results can be significantly improved by including a Language Model and a dictionary into the system. Furthermore, we observed that some uncommon characters in Spanish language, such as 'z' and 'x' have an insufficient number of instances for training, which results in classes that are undertrained by the SVM. We think this effect can be reduced by including classifiers capable of learning incrementally.

Acknowledgments. The authors would like to thank Cátedra CONCYTEC, Perú for their financial support (Grant No.158-2013-CONCYTEC-OAJ).

References

1. Burger, T., Kessentini, Y., Paquet, T.: Dempster-shafer based rejection strategy for handwritten word recognition. In: Proc. 2011 Int. Conf. on Document Analysis and Recognition (ICDAR 2011), pp. 528–532 (2011)
2. Chowdhury, S., Garain, U., Chattopadhyay, T.: A weighted finite-state transducer (wfst)-based language model for online indic script handwriting recognition. In: 2011 International Conference on Document Analysis and Recognition (ICDAR), pp. 599–602 (September 2011)
3. Cortes, C., Vapnik, V.: Support-vector networks. Maching Learning 20(3), 273–297 (1995)
4. Fischer, A., Frinken, V., Bunke, H., Suen, C.Y.: Improving hmm-based keyword spotting with character language models. In: ICDAR, pp. 506–510 (2013)
5. Frinken, V., Bunke, H.: Self-training for handwritten text line recognition. In: Bloch, I., Cesar Jr., R.M. (eds.) CIARP 2010. LNCS, vol. 6419, pp. 104–112. Springer, Heidelberg (2010)
6. Frinken, V., Fischer, A., Bunke, H.: Combining neural networks to improve performance of handwritten keyword spotting. In: El Gayar, N., Kittler, J., Roli, F. (eds.) MCS 2010. LNCS, vol. 5997, pp. 215–224. Springer, Heidelberg (2010)
7. Frinken, V., Fischer, A., Bunke, H., Fornés, A.: Co-training for handwritten word recognition. In: Proc. 2011 Int. Conf. on Document Analysis and Recognition (ICDAR 2011), pp. 314–318 (2011)
8. Fujisawa, Y., Shi, M., Wakabayashi, T., Kimura, F.: Handwritten numeral recognition using gradient and curvature of gray scale image. In: Proc. 5th Int. Conf. on Document Analysis and Recognition (ICDAR 1999), pp. 277–300 (1999)
9. He, C.L.: Error Analysis of a Hybrid Multiple Classifier System for Recognizing Unconstrained Handwritten Numerals. PhD thesis, Computer Science Department, Concordia University, Montreal, Canada (September 2010)
10. Leydier, Y., Lebourgeois, F., Emptoz, H.: Omnilingual Segmentation-freeWord Spotting for Ancient Manuscripts Indexation. In: Proc. 8th Int. Conf. on Document Analysis and Recognition (ICDAR 2005), pp. 533–537 (2005)
11. Leydier, Y., Lebourgeois, F., Emptoz, H.: Text search for medieval manuscript images. Pattern Recogntion 40(12), 3552–3567 (2007)
12. Leydier, Y., Ouji, A., LeBourgeois, F., Emptoz, H.: Towards an omnilingual word retrieval system for ancient manuscripts. Pattern Recognition 42(9), 2089–2105 (2009)
13. Liwicki, M., Bunke, H.: Feature selection for HMM and BLSTM based handwriting recognition of whiteboard notes. Int. Journal on Pattern Recognition and Artificial Intelligence 23(5), 907–923 (2009)
14. Meza-Lovón, G.L.: A graph-based approach for transcribing ancient documents. In: Pavón, J., Duque-Méndez, N.D., Fuentes-Fernández, R. (eds.) IBERAMIA 2012. LNCS, vol. 7637, pp. 210–220. Springer, Heidelberg (2012)
15. Rath, T.M., Manmatha, R.: Features for word spotting in historical manuscripts. In: Proc. 7th Int. Conf. on Document Analysis and Recognition (ICDAR 2003), pp. 218–222. IEEE Computer Society (2003)
16. Rath, T.M., Manmatha, R.: Word image matching using dynamic time warping. In: IEEE Computer Society Conf. on Computer Vision and Pattern Recognition, vol. 2, pp. 521–527 (2003)
17. Rath, T.M., Manmatha, R.: Word spotting for historical documents. Int. Journal on Document Analysis and Recognition, 139–152 (2007)

18. Romero, V., Andreu Sanchez, J.: Category-based language models for handwriting recognition of marriage license books. In: 2013 12th International Conference on Document Analysis and Recognition (ICDAR), pp. 788–792 (August 2013)
19. Romero, V., Pastor, M.: Computer Assisted Transcription of Text Images. In: Multimodal Interactive Pattern Recognition and Applications. Springer (2011)
20. Romero, V., Rodríguez-Ruiz, L.: Computer Assisted Transcription: General Framework. In: Multimodal Interactive Pattern Recognition and Applications. Springer (2011)
21. Roy, U., Sankaran, N., Sankar, K., Jawahar, C.: Character n-gram spotting on handwritten documents using weakly-supervised segmentation. In: 2013 12th International Conference on Document Analysis and Recognition (ICDAR), pp. 577–581 (August 2013)
22. Sagheer, M.W., He, C.L., Nobile, N., Suen, C.Y.: Holistic Urdu handwritten word recognition using support vector machine. In: Proc. of the 9th International Conference on Pattern Recognition (ICPR 2010), pp. 1900–1903 (2010)
23. Toselli, A.H., Romero, V., Pastor, M., Vidal, E.: Multimodal interactive transcription of text images. Pattern Recognition 43(5), 1814–1825 (2010)
24. Wang, Q.-F., Yin, F., Liu, C.-L.: Integrating language model in handwritten chinese text recognition. In: 10th International Conference on Document Analysis and Recognition, ICDAR 2009, pp. 1036–1040 (July 2009)
25. Zhang, H., Zhou, X.-D., Liu, C.-L.: Keyword spotting in online chinese handwritten documents with candidate scoring based on semi-crf model. In: 2013 12th International Conference on Document Analysis and Recognition (ICDAR), pp. 567–571 (August 2013)

Dynamically Adaptive Genetic Algorithm
to Select Training Data for SVMs

Michal Kawulok and Jakub Nalepa[(✉)]

Institute of Informatics, Silesian University of Technology, Gliwice, Poland
{michal.kawulok,jakub.nalepa}@polsl.pl

Abstract. This paper addresses an important problem of training set selection for support vector machines (SVMs). It is a critical step in case of large and noisy data sets due to high time and memory complexity of the SVM training. There have been several methods proposed so far, in majority underpinned with the analysis of data geometry either in the input or kernel space. Here, we propose a new dynamically adaptive genetic algorithm (DAGA) to select valuable training sets. We demonstrate that not only can DAGA quickly select the training data, but in addition it dynamically determines the desired training set size without any prior information. We analyze the impact of the support vectors ratio, defined as the percentage of support vectors in the training set, on the DAGA performance. Also, we investigate and discuss the possibility of incorporating reduced SVMs into the proposed algorithm. Extensive experimental study shows that DAGA offers fast and effective training set optimization that is independent on the entire training set size.

1 Introduction

Support vector machines (SVM) [1] have been attracting attention of researchers over the years due to their applicability to a variety of pattern recognition problems. Their main limitation lies in high training complexity, which makes them virtually inapplicable in case of huge amounts of training samples. SVM training is a constrained quadratic programming (QP) problem of $O(n^3)$ time and $O(n^2)$ memory complexity, where n is the number of samples in the training set. Based on a labeled training set, SVMs determine a hyperplane that linearly separates two classes in a higher-dimensional kernel space. It is defined by a small subset of the vectors from the entire training set, termed *support vectors* (SVs). This hyperplane is used to classify the unseen vectors of the same dimensionality as the training data. The classification time depends on the number of selected SVs. Thus, it should be kept low to speed up the classification.

Since the classification is based on a subset of the training set, some attempts have been made to refine the training sets and use only those samples, from which the SVs are most likely to be selected. State-of-the-art techniques are focused either on random selection or analysis of data geometry in the input space or in the kernel spaces. In our earlier work, we proposed to use a genetic algorithm (GA) for selecting valuable data from the training set [2]. This is an effective

© Springer International Publishing Switzerland 2014
A.L.C. Bazzan and K. Pichara (Eds.): IBERAMIA 2014, LNAI 8864, pp. 242–254, 2014.
DOI: 10.1007/978-3-319-12027-0_20

approach, but it requires that the size of the refined training set is given before-hand. This problem was recently addressed in our adaptive genetic algorithm (AGA), which adaptively sets its various parameters during the search [3].

In this paper, we propose a new dynamically adaptive genetic algorithm to select training data for SVMs. We investigate the impact of the SVs ratio (i.e., the percentage of SVs in the training set) on the DAGA performance. Depending on it, and on the fitness growth, the enlargement factor of the reduced training set is dynamically adapted during the search. In this way, the desired size of the reduced set is determined quickly in a single DAGA run, which makes the algorithm extremely efficient in terms of convergence and classification capabilities.

The paper is organized as follows. State of the art regarding training set reduction techniques is outlined in Section 2. The details of the adaptive method are outlined in Section 3, and the results obtained in our experimental study are presented and discussed in Section 4. Section 5 concludes the paper.

2   Related Literature

Reducing the SVM training set has been given a considerable research attention over the years. Numerous approaches emerged to tackle the problem of handling large and noisy sets. Joachims proposed to split the QP optimization problem into sub-problems to decrease the overall training time [4]. However, the increasing size of real-world sets in various domains, including bioinformatics, genomics, document categorization and more [5], makes this technique virtually inapplicable in practice. There are methods that approximate the answer of a non-linear kernel machine in a low-dimensional randomized feature space [6].

Balcázar et al. [7] proposed to sample a subset of a large set randomly to create a smaller SVM training set. This approach was the basis of other randomized sampling methods [8], including reduced support vector machines (RSVMs) [9], later applied and enhanced in many works [10]. RSVMs select a small subset randomly to build a thin rectangular kernel matrix rather than the full kernel matrix, which significantly reduces the computational complexity of the training. Thus, the SVs are determined out of a small randomly selected subset, but the hyperplane is optimized using the entire training set.

There exist a number of algorithms analyzing the data geometry to determine an appropriate training set [11]. In [12], crisp clusters along with safety regions are found, and samples positioned inside the single-class clusters are rejected, since they do not contribute to determining the decision hyperplane. Intuitively, the clustering should be performed near the decision boundary to boost its performance and decrease the execution time. Clearly, this hyperplane is unknown before the SVM training. However, it may be estimated based on the samples heterogeneity measured with entropy [13]. Another approach to estimate the decision boundary is to classify the training data based on their mutual Mahalanobis distances, and use only the misclassified vectors for training [14].

In data structure analysis, the hierarchical clustering is performed for each class independently [15]. Then, the interior samples from each cluster are removed based on the Mahalanobis distance, calculated in either input or kernel space. Finally, the exterior samples that are distant from the opposite class clusters are discarded. It is based on the observation that these samples have neglectable influence on the position of the final decision boundary. The desired number of clusters in each class is not known *a priori*, and can be estimated based on finding the point of the maximum curvature of the merge distance plot [16].

Embedding the training data using convex hulls and selecting refined sets based on the Hausdorff distance between opposite class clusters was discussed in [17]. The method based on the convex-concave hull analysis was recently discussed in [18]. In [19], samples are interpreted as a graph and subject to β-skeleton algorithm. The techniques based on the analysis of the minimum enclosing ball and the smallest enclosing ball with a ring region were presented in [20,21]. Active learning algorithms operate on large unlabeled sets, and dynamically determine labels for the samples [22]. It was shown that these approaches select the labels near the separating hyperplane, as the clustering methods [23]. The mentioned geometry-based approaches are dependent on the training set size which is a significant drawback in case of very large data sets.

Evolutionary algorithms to select a valuable SVM training set have not been explored extensively so far. A novel genetic algorithm (GA), which was not dependent on the training set size, was proposed in [2]. In the GA, a population of N solutions (individuals) evolves with time. Each solution, i.e., a *chromosome*, represents a subset of $2K$ training samples from the entire training set. The population is successively improved in the biologically-inspired algorithm during consecutive generations, in which chromosomes are selected, crossed-over and mutated. The *fitness* of each individual corresponds to the objective function of the optimization problem. The most important shortcoming of the GA is an unclear selection of the chromosome size $2K$ to ensure the proper convergence speed, exploration and exploitation capabilities, and to cope with noisy data sets. This issue was addressed in our recent works [3,24].

3   Dynamically Adaptive Genetic Algorithm

The general goal of DAGA is to determine a desired size and content of the SVM training set. Hence, from the entire set T, which contains t samples belonging to two classes C_A and C_B, t' ones are selected to form a refined training set T'. In DAGA, every sample in T' is defined by a single element of the chromosome. To avoid biasing the set, K samples are selected from C_A and C_B, thus $t' = 2K$. The DAGA symbols used in this paper are summarized in Tab. 1.

The initial population of N individuals is created based on random sampling (Alg. 1, line 1). From each class, K distinct vectors are selected randomly to create a new individual p_i. This selection is independent from t, which means that DAGA does not depend on the training set size.

Table 1. The DAGA symbols used in this paper

N	Population size
p_i	The i-th individual
$\eta(p_i)$	Fitness of the i-th individual
η_B	Best fitness in the population
η_P	Best fitness in the previous generation
η_I	Best fitness before the last increase of K
K	Number of samples of class C_A and C_B in a given individual
δ_K	Increase factor of K (i.e., $K_{i+1} = \delta_K \cdot K_i$)
c_s	Stable chromosome size counter
s	Number of SVs found during SVM training
ϱ_{SV}	SVs ratio (s/t')
$\mathcal{T}_{SV}$	Threshold for the SVs ratio (ϱ_{SV})
Δ_T	Total improvement of η_B achieved after increasing K
Δ_R	Recent (i.e., compared with the previous generation) improvement of η_B
G_i	The i-th generation
$\mathcal{T}_s$	Minimum number of generations between consecutive increases of K
T	Entire training set
t	Number of samples in the entire training set
T'	Refined training set
t'	Number of samples in the refined training set

Algorithm 1. Dynamically Adaptive Genetic Algorithm (DAGA).

1: Initialize population of size N;
2: $c_s \leftarrow 0$; $p_{best} \leftarrow$ **null**; $\eta_I \leftarrow 0$; $\eta_P \leftarrow 0$; $\eta_B \leftarrow 0$;
3: **repeat**
4:      Determine N pairs (p_a, p_b);   ▷ Pre-selection
5:      **for all** (p_a, p_b) **do**
6:          $p_c \leftarrow$ Crossover(p_a, p_b, K);
7:          $p_c \leftarrow$ Compensate(p_c, T, K);
8:          $p_c \leftarrow$ Mutate(p_c);
9:          $\eta(p_c) \leftarrow$ FindFitness(p_c, T);
10:          $\eta_B \leftarrow$ UpdateBestFitness(p_c);
11:      **end for**
12:      Form the next generation G;   ▷ Post-selection
13:      Adapt the DAGA parameters;   ▷ See Fig. 2
14: **until** StopCondition();
15: **return** solution with the highest fitness η_B;

3.1   Genetic Operators

The population is subject to iterative transformation using genetic operators. From each generation G_i, N pairs are selected for recombination (Alg. 1, line 4) to create the children pool. There have been numerous efficient selection schemes proposed for balancing the exploration and exploitation of the solution space [25]. In this paper, we utilized the high-low fit scheme [26], which was shown to be asymptotically best in terms of the classification score [2].

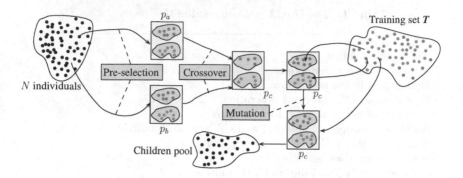

Fig. 1. Creation of a child p_c in DAGA

For each (p_a, p_b), a new individual p_c is generated using crossover, compensation (if necessary), and mutation (Alg. 1, lines 6–8; see also Fig. 1). During the crossover, p_a and p_b create a temporary chromosome consisting of $t_a + t_b \leq 4K$ samples, from which $t_c \in [\max(t_a, t_b), 2K]$ distinct ones are selected randomly (the value of t_c is also selected randomly from the given range). As K may be increased between subsequent generations, p_a and p_b may contain less than t_c distinct samples. In such a case, the compensation procedure is run, which consists in drawing the missing samples from the entire set T. This creates p_c which is subsequently subject to mutation with the probability $\mathcal{P}_m$, consisting in substituting its vectors from both C_A and C_B with the random T samples.

SVM is trained using the refined set defined by p_c and its fitness $\eta(p_c)$ is determined based on the area under curve (AUC) obtained for T. The individuals from the children pool and the generation G_i are selected to form G_{i+1} (Alg. 1, line 12). Here, the N best individuals are chosen from the set of size $2N$ containing the individuals from the previous generation and their child solutions.

3.2   Dynamic Adaptation

The dynamic adaptation of the DAGA parameters is outlined in Fig. 2. It is worth noting that it is dynamic, i.e., the adaptation parameters are dynamically changed during the search. First, it is verified whether K should be increased. It may be done only once in $\mathcal{T}_s$ generations to prevent too rapid growth that would jeopardize the convergence. The training set is not enlarged, if the fitness has not grown since the last increase ($\Delta_T = 0$). Also, if the recent fitness improvement (Δ_R) is significant (greater than $0.5 \cdot \Delta_T$), then the increase is delayed.

The most important condition for the increase, which makes it possible to adapt to the data, is the analysis of the SVs ratio ($\varrho_{SV} = s/t'$) in the refined training set computed for the best individual p_B, where s is the number of SVs found during SVM training. If there are a small number of SVs in a training set (ratio below $\mathcal{T}_{SV}$), then there is no point in enlarging this set. Based on ϱ_{SV}, δ_K is determined and K is updated. DAGA is stopped when the fitness does not grow in a given number of generations, and the chromosome size is not increased.

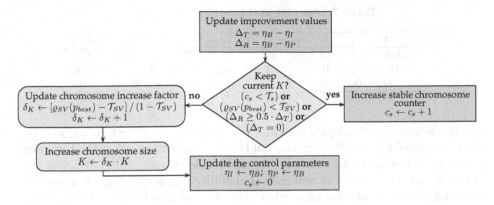

Fig. 2. Adapting the DAGA parameters

4 Experimental Validation

DAGA was compared with several state-of-the-art methods: (1) random sampling (RS-SVM) [7], (2) RSVM [27] with smooth SVM, (3) data structure analysis (SR-DSA) [15], (4) GA (GASVM) [2], and (5) the adaptive GA (AGA) [3]. We optimize the training set using GA and DAGA for SVMs (GASVM and DAGASVM) and RSVMs (GARSVM and DAGARSVM). For SVM and RSVM, we used the LIBSVM implementations, while the remaining methods were written in C++ and run on an Intel Xeon 3.2 GHz computer with 16 GB RAM.

4.1 Experimental Setup

The experiments were conducted based on three data sets: (1) *2D* – an artificial set of 6371 points positioned on a 500×500 surface (used for training and validation), (2) *Skin* – real-world data derived from the ECU skin image database [2,28], and (3) *Adult* benchmark set from the UCI repository[1]. The *Skin* data set consists of the training set T (93455 pixels) in the RGB color space and the validation set V (560732 pixels). For the *Adult* set, we skipped the samples with missing data, and the set was split into training (15082 vectors) and validation (15080 vectors) sets. The presented scores were obtained for V's.

We used SVMs with the RBF kernel: $K(u, v) = \exp\left(-\gamma \|u - v\|^2\right)$, whose parameters (i.e., C and γ) were determined using a grid search [29]. These values are given in Tab. 2, along with maximum DAGASVM execution times (τ). C and γ were found independently for SVMs and RSVMs as in [30]. Also, we present the SR-DSA settings (c is the final number of clusters in the clustering step, and λ denotes the percentage of internal samples removed from each cluster).

The population size was set to a small $N = 10$ value to reduce the time required for a single generation, which increases the adaptation speed. Similarly,

---

[1] http://archive.ics.uci.edu/ml/datasets.html

Table 2. Settings used for different data sets

Data set	γ	C	γ_{RSVM}	C_{RSVM}	c	λ (%)	τ (sec.)
Adult	0.1	0.1	10	1	505	92	600
Skin	1	10	1	0.01	125	99.95	1500
2D	100	10	10	1	255	80	30

the initial number of samples per class was small ($K = 10$), which reduced the time consumed for a single test (i.e., validation of an individual) at the beginning of the DAGA process. All tests were repeated at least $n = 5$ times ($5 \leq n \leq 30$), if not stated otherwise. The mutation probability was set to $\mathcal{P}_m = 0.3$, and the minimal number of generations without the chromosome increase was $\mathcal{T}_s = 3$.

4.2 Support Vectors Ratio

Here, we investigated the impact of the SVs ratio determined for each training set. We selected the SVs ratio threshold $\mathcal{T}_{SV}$ based on the 2D set (see Fig. 3). For each presented value we ran 10 tests, and the averaged results along with the deviations are shown in the graph. We examined the overall DAGA execution time and AUC obtained for the best individual. It is clear that too large value of $\mathcal{T}_{SV}$ reduces the optimization time at the cost of the classification score, while small values make DAGA harder to converge. Hence, in all our experiments we used $\mathcal{T}_{SV} = 0.25$, which we found satisfactory also for other data sets.

4.3 Classification Accuracy Analysis

In Tab. 3, we compare the AUC values obtained for the investigated methods, and show the results obtained for SVM trained using the entire set. It is worth noting that the SVM classification speed is linearly dependent on s, thus a large s affects the performance. We ran GASVM with a number of samples per class in a training set corresponding to the average value delivered by DAGASVM.

The results show that DAGASVM is competitive compared with other methods in terms of the classification score. For Adult, it is AGA which delivered the highest AUC, however its deviation is larger than in the case of DAGASVM, which indicates that it is more dependent on the selection of the initial population. It is easy to see that the refined set size is increased faster in DAGASVM to explore new regions of the solution space. This approach aims at obtaining a valuable set (possibly larger) in a shorter time (see Skin and 2D). It is easy to note that GASVM gave satisfactory results for each data set. However, the refined training set size here is not known beforehand (it does not change during the GA run). Thus, this method needs to be run multiple times (for various K's) to determine a desired number of samples in the refined training set. Similarly, SR-DSA resulted in high AUC values obtained in a short time. Nevertheless, if its parameters are not tuned very carefully, then its performance drastically drops. It is easy to see that SVMs trained using the entire sets resulted in very

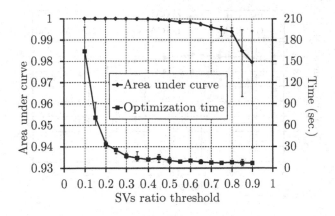

Fig. 3. Optimization time and final AUC for the *2D* data set for different T_{SV}'s

Table 3. Results obtained using various methods

		SVM	SR-DSA [15]	GASVM [2]	AGA [3]	DAGASVM
Adult	AUC (in %)	88.7607	82.7171	88.531 $\pm 4.2 \cdot 10^{-4}$	89.2020 $\pm 19 \cdot 10^{-4}$	89.2011 $\pm 6.8 \cdot 10^{-4}$
	t'	15082	751	2074	64 ± 20	2073.3 ± 453.3
	s	7536	369	2074 ± 0	64 ± 19	1704 ± 471.3
	τ (in sec.)	71	16.2	10346 ± 1443	600	600
Skin	AUC (in %)	71.4187	93.0851	94.3248 $\pm 2.2 \cdot 10^{-4}$	93.9299 $\pm 8.5 \cdot 10^{-4}$	94.3166 $\pm 5.0 \cdot 10^{-4}$
	t'	560732	144	754	64 ± 20	753.2 ± 308.2
	s	61480	11	542.7 ± 30.2	29 ± 8	393.9 ± 186.2
	τ (in sec.)	22195	5.6	12313 ± 2950	1500	1500
2D	AUC (in %)	99.9980	99.5733	99.9987 $\pm 3.6 \cdot 10^{-4}$	97.8285 $\pm 51.71 \cdot 10^{-4}$	99.9976 $\pm 3.6 \cdot 10^{-4}$
	t'	6371	573	435	38 ± 6	435 ± 5.39
	s	279	142	217.6 ± 7.13	36 ± 6	209 ± 9.04
	τ (in sec.)	0.6	1.07	1268.4 ± 977.1	30	30

high numbers of SVs (which increases the classification time). Also, *Skin* data set appeared to be quite noisy, since the AUC obtained for the entire set is low. Clearly, utilizing the entire (noisy) set T for training may result in poor classification of unseen data. This is addressed by our algorithm, since it continuously removes "bad" samples from refined sets during the optimization process.

The results for various K's are presented in Figs. 4–6. DAGASVM proved to be robust and resulted in high AUC scores with small deviations. For the *Skin* set, RSVM performance drops for larger K's, and then grows again. The first tendency is caused by the decrease in the number of tests, while the second trend is attributed to the fact that for larger K's, the RSVM is generally better. Furthermore, for the *Skin* set, the effectiveness of GASVM and RS-SVM drops for $K > 320$. This is

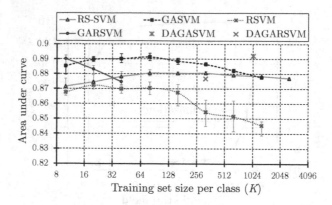

Fig. 4. AUC obtained using different optimization strategies for *Adult* set

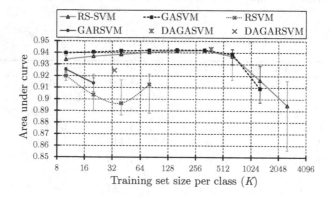

Fig. 5. AUC obtained using different optimization strategies for *Skin* set

certainly caused by the time limit, as the tests consume much more time for larger K's, but also by noisy data that make it harder to select valuable sets of a larger size. This problem was also discussed in [2].

Examples of the visualized results for *2D* set are shown in Fig. 7. White and black dots indicate samples from T, whereas the crosses (colors are swapped for clarity) – samples selected to T'. It can be observed that the vectors genetically selected to the training set do not follow any uniform geometric pattern. This indicated that the analysis of data geometry for selecting a refined training set may be insufficient in case of difficult (e.g., noisy) data sets.

4.4   Incorporating RSVM into DAGA

The results show that incorporating RSVM into the GA-based approaches results in low classification scores. Poor scores of RSVM-based methods (RSVM, GARSVM and DAGARSVM) are attributed to their longer training times,

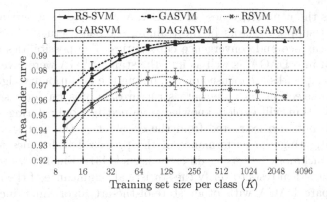

Fig. 6. AUC obtained using different methods for *2D* data set

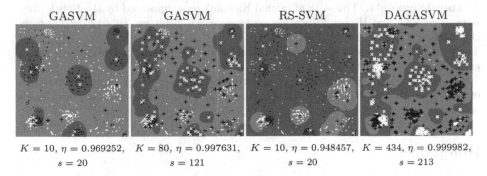

GASVM	GASVM	RS-SVM	DAGASVM
$K = 10$, $\eta = 0.969252$, $s = 20$	$K = 80$, $\eta = 0.997631$, $s = 121$	$K = 10$, $\eta = 0.948457$, $s = 20$	$K = 434$, $\eta = 0.999982$, $s = 213$

Fig. 7. Training sets selected using RS-SVM, GASVM, and DAGASVM

which result in less tests executed within the time limit. Results for GARSVM are presented only for three smallest K's (Figs. 4–6). In the remaining cases the first generation was not finished within the assumed time. It is clear that GASVM is competitive compared with other methods, however it is DAGASVM which finds the desired size of the training set in a single run. As mentioned earlier, GASVM would have to be run multiple times to determine the minimum feasible (allowing to obtain a high classification score) size of the refined training set.

5   Conclusions and Future Work

In this paper we introduce a new dynamically adaptive genetic algorithm for SVM training set selection, which adapts its parameters to the presented data set in a dynamic manner. In this way, not only does it select the most valuable subset from the entire set and reduce the overall training time, but it also determines the desired size of this subset. An extensive experimental study clearly demonstrates the competitiveness of DAGA. We showed that setting a proper percentage of support vectors in the training set has a crucial impact on the DAGA performance and convergence capabilities. The possibilities of incorporating RSVM into DAGA as well as into the standard GA were investigated.

Our ongoing works are focused on combining the evolutionary algorithms for training data selection with the data structure analysis for local search. This memetic algorithm will exploit knowledge gained not only during the genetic optimization, but also extracted from the data set in the first step. Also, we aim at investigating the performance of the proposed techniques for a larger number of benchmark sets using different kernels [31]. Finally, we plan to perform some statistical tests to verify the statistical significance of the results [32], and to compare DAGA with other state-of-the-art algorithms, including our MA [24].

Acknowledgments. The work of Michal Kawulok was supported by the Polish Ministry of Science and Higher Education under research grant no. IP2012 026372 from the Science Budget 2013–2015.

The work of Jakub Nalepa was supported by the National Science Centre under research grant no. DEC-2013/09/N/ST6/03461.

This work was performed using the infrastructure supported by POIG.02.03.01-24-099/13 grant: "GeCONiI–Upper Silesian Center for Computational Science and Engineering".

References

1. Cortes, C., Vapnik, V.: Support-Vector Networks. Mach. Learn. **20**(3), 273–297 (1995)
2. Kawulok, M., Nalepa, J.: Support vector machines training data selection using a genetic algorithm. In: Gimel'farb, G., Hancock, E., Imiya, A., Kuijper, A., Kudo, M., Omachi, S., Windeatt, T., Yamada, K. (eds.) SSPR & SPR 2012. LNCS, vol. 7626, pp. 557–565. Springer, Heidelberg (2012)
3. Nalepa, J., Kawulok, M.: Adaptive genetic algorithm to select training set for support vector machines. In: EvoIASP, EvoApp. LNCS. Springer (in press, 2014)
4. Joachims, T.: Making large-scale SVM learning practical. In: Schölkopf, B., Burges, C.J.C., Smola, A.J. (eds.) Advances in Kernel Methods, pp. 169–184. MIT Press (1999)
5. Rodriguez-Lujan, I., Cruz, C.S., Huerta, R.: Hierarchical linear support vector machine. Patt. Recogn. **45**(12), 4414–4427 (2012)
6. Le, Q., Sarlos, T., Smola, A.: Fastfood - approximating kernel expansions in log-linear time. In: Proc. ICML (2013)
7. Balcázar, J., Dai, Y., Watanabe, O.: A Random Sampling Technique for Training Support Vector Machines. In: Abe, N., Khardon, R., Zeugmann, T. (eds.) ALT 2001. LNCS (LNAI), vol. 2225, pp. 119–134. Springer, Heidelberg (2001)
8. Ferragut, E., Laska, J.: Randomized sampling for large data applications of SVM. In: Int. Conf. on Mach. Learning and App., vol. 1, pp. 350–355 (2012)

9. Lee, Y.J., Huang, S.Y.: Reduced support vector machines: A statistical theory. IEEE Trans. on Neural Networks **18**(1), 1–13 (2007)
10. Chang, C.C., Pao, H.K., Lee, Y.J.: An RSVM based two-teachers-one-student semi-supervised learning algorithm. Neural Networks **25**, 57–69 (2012)
11. Chien, L.J., Chang, C.C., Lee, Y.J.: Variant methods of reduced set selection for reduced support vector machines. J. Inf. Sci. Eng. **26**(1), 183–196 (2010)
12. Koggalage, R., Halgamuge, S.: Reducing the number of training samples for fast support vector machine classification. Neural Information Process. Lett. and Reviews **2**(3), 57–65 (2004)
13. Shin, H., Cho, S.: Neighborhood property-based pattern selection for SVMs. Neural Comput. **19**(3), 816–855 (2007)
14. Abe, S., Inoue, T.: Fast Training of Support Vector Machines by Extracting Boundary Data. In: Dorffner, G., Bischof, H., Hornik, K. (eds.) ICANN 2001. LNCS, vol. 2130, pp. 308–313. Springer, Heidelberg (2001)
15. Wang, D., Shi, L.: Selecting valuable training samples for SVMs via data structure analysis. Neurocomputing **71**, 2772–2781 (2008)
16. Salvador, S., Chan, P.: Determining the number of clusters/segments in hierarchical clustering/segmentation algorithms. In: Proc. IEEE ICTAI, pp. 576–584 (2004)
17. Wang, J., Neskovic, P., Cooper, L.N.: Training data selection for SVMs. In: Adv. in Natural Comp., pp. 554–564. Springer (2005)
18. Lopez-Chau, A., Li, X., Yu, W.: Convex-concave hull for classification with SVM. In: Proc. IEEE ICDMW, pp. 431–438 (2012)
19. Zhang, W., King, I.: Locating support vectors via β-skeleton technique. In: Int. Conf. on Neural Inf. Process., pp. 1423–1427 (2002)
20. Tsang, I.W., Kwok, J.T., Cheung, P.M.: Core vector machines: Fast SVM training on very large data sets. J. of Machine Learning Research **6**, 363–392 (2005)
21. Zeng, Z.Q., Xu, H.R., Xie, Y.Q., Gao, J.: A geometric approach to train SVM on very large data sets. Intell. Sys. and Knowl. Eng. **1**, 991–996 (2008)
22. Musicant, D.R., Feinberg, A.: Active set support vector regression. IEEE Trans. on Neural Networks **15**(2), 268–275 (2004)
23. Schohn, G., Cohn, D.: Less is more: Active learning with support vector machines. In: Int. Conf. on Mach. Learning, pp. 839–846 (2000)
24. Nalepa, J., Kawulok, M.: A memetic algorithm to select training data for support vector machines. In: Proc. of the 2014 Conf. on Genetic and Evolutionary Computation, GECCO 2014, pp. 573–580. ACM (2014)
25. Nalepa, J., Czech, Z.J.: New Selection Schemes in a Memetic Algorithm for the Vehicle Routing Problem with Time Windows. In: Tomassini, M., Antononi, A., Daolio, F., Buesser, P. (eds.) ICANNGA 2013. LNCS, vol. 7824, pp. 396–405. Springer, Heidelberg (2013)
26. Elamin, E.E.A.: A proposed genetic algorithm selection method. In: 1st National Symposium (NITS) (2006)
27. Lee, J.S., Kuo, Y.M., Chung, P.C., Chen, E.L.: Naked image detection based on adaptive and extensible skin color model. Pattern Recognit. **40**, 2261–2270 (2007)
28. Phung, S.L., Chai, D., Bouzerdoum, A.: Adaptive skin segmentation in color images. In: Proc. IEEE ICASSP, pp. 353–356 (2003)
29. Hsu, C.W., Chang, C.C., Lin, C.J., et al.: A practical guide to support vector classification (2003)

30. Lin, K.M., Lin, C.J.: A study on reduced support vector machines. IEEE Trans. on Neural Networks **14**(6), 1449–1459 (2003)
31. Simiński, K.: Transformation of Input Domain for SVM in Regression Task. In: Gruca, A., Czachórski, T., Kozielski, S. (eds.) Man-Machine Interactions 3. AISC, vol. 242, pp. 423–430. Springer, Heidelberg (2014)
32. Demšar, J.: Statistical comparisons of classifiers over multiple data sets. J. Mach. Learn. Res. **7**, 1–30 (2006)

Fuzzy Systems

Forecasting in Fuzzy Time Series by an Extension of Simple Exponential Smoothing

Fábio José Justo dos Santos[1,2(✉)] and Heloisa de Arruda Camargo[1]

[1] Federal University of São Carlos, São Carlos, Brazil
[2] Federal Institute of Education,
Science and Technology of São Paulo, São Paulo, Brazil
{fabio_santos,heloisa}@dc.ufscar.br

Abstract. Fuzzy Time Series was introduced to improve the forecasting made by statistical methods in vague or imprecise data and in time series with few samples available. However, the integration of these concepts is a little explored area. In this paper we introduced a new forecast model composed by a pre-processing method and a predicting method. The pre-processing method is responsible for analyzing the data and defining a suitable structure of representation. The predicting method is based on the combination of fuzzy time series concepts with the simple exponential smoothing, a traditional statistical method for prediction. The experiments performed with the TAIEX index show that, besides obtaining better accuracy rates when compared with other methods available in the literature, the predictions made over the whole time series had the same behavior and trends than the real data.

Keywords: Fuzzy time series · Simple exponential smoothing · Forecasting

1 Introduction

In the last years, Fuzzy Time Series (FTS) has been used in many forecasting problems, especially when the data in the Time Series (TS) are represented by linguistic terms, are vague, imprecise or when there are few samples available. Since it was introduced by Song and Chinson [1,2,3], several proposals have been presented to extend the main concepts with applications in different areas. Basically, the FTS follow three steps: (1) fuzzification of crisp values; (2) derivation of Fuzzy Logical Relationships (FLR); and (3) calculation of the forecasted value. In Uslu et al. [4], the authors use genetic algorithm to fuzzify and to derivate the FLR. The calculation of forecasted values considers the frequency of each FLR, but do not consider when the FLR occurred. A hybrid system with concepts of support vector machines, neural network and linguistic fuzzy rules is presented by Stepnicka et al. [5] to deal forecasting problems. Chatterjee et al. [6] presented a second order forecast model to multi-attribute time series. In [7] a forecasting method for FTS based on k-means is introduced.

In the literature, several researches in FTS focus on forecasting without the preprocessing of the data [8,9,10]. However, the preprocessing has an important role to improve the forecasting accuracy rate. Without the preprocessing, the forecast in FTS

© Springer International Publishing Switzerland 2014
A.L.C. Bazzan and K. Pichara (Eds.): IBERAMIA 2014, LNAI 8864, pp. 257–268, 2014.
DOI: 10.1007/978-3-319-12027-0_21

can be prejudiced by outliers and by fuzzy sets that represent inadequately the distribution of the data over the entire time series.

Some works have reported better accuracy in forecasted values by FTS than by traditional statistics methods [5], particularly in TS with few samples or irregular behavior. However, the integration of FTS concepts with the traditional statistical methods is a little explored area. An important feature frequently neglected in FTS research is the updating of obtained knowledge with the arrival of new samples. In a FTS with variation in its behavior, the update of FLR identified during the training can be essential for a good accuracy on the new forecasts. Therefore, this research arises to overcome this lack in FTS. Besides keeping the FLR base updated with the arrival of new samples, allowing the forecasting model to follow the new tendencies of the time series, the proposed model is composed of a preprocessing method and a forecasting method. The pre-processing method aims at removing the outliers and creating a suitable representation by means of linguistic terms that reflects the real structure of the data. The forecasting method is defined using a combination of FLR concepts with the extension of simple exponential smoothing, a traditional statistical method. The obtained results confirm the effectiveness of the proposal.

The remaining of this paper is organized as follows. Section 2 presents the basic concepts of fuzzy time series and simple exponential smoothing. The proposed forecasting model is introduced in Section 3. In Section 4 the results and comparisons among the proposed method and other techniques found in the literature are presented. Section 5 summarizes the main conclusions and gives indications for future work.

2   Basic Concepts

2.1   Fuzzy Time Series

Based on Zadeh's works [11,12], a fuzzy set A in the universe of discourse $U = \{u_1, u_2, ..., u_n\}$, can be defined by $A = f_A(u_1)/u_1 + f_A(u_2)/u_2 + \cdots + f_A(u_n)/u_n$ where f_A is the membership function of the fuzzy set A, $f_A: U \to [0,1]$, and $f_A(u_i)$ denotes the value of membership of u_i in the fuzzy set A, where $1 \leq i \leq n$. In the sequence, the basic definitions about fuzzy time series are presented [1,2,3]:

Definition 1: Let $Y(t)$ $(t = ..., 0, 1, 2, ...)$, a subset of $\mathbb{R}$, be the universe in which fuzzy sets $f_i(t)$ $(i = 1, 2, ...)$ are defined. If $F(t)$ is a collection of $f_i(t)(i = 1, 2, ...)$, then, $F(t)$ is called a fuzzy time series on $Y(t)$.

Definition 2: If $F(t)$ is caused by $F(t-1), F(t-2), ..., F(t-n)$, then the fuzzy logical relationship between them can be represented by a high order fuzzy logical relationship as $F(t-1), F(t-2), ..., F(t-n) \to F(t)$ and it is called the nth-order fuzzy time series model.

According to Song and Chinson [3], the forecasting process in FTS follows five steps: (1) specify the universe of discourse U on which the fuzzy sets will be defined; (2) partition U into several equal length intervals for defining the fuzzy sets; (3) if the historical data are linguistic values, go to Step 4; otherwise fuzzify the data; (4) forecast the linguistic value; (5) defuzzify the linguistic value attained in Step 4.

2.2   Simple Exponential Smoothing

Proposed by Brown and Meyer [13], the Simple Exponential Smoothing ponders past observations by means of exponentially decreasing weights. The forecasting value is defined by Equation 1:

$$\bar{d}_{t+1} = \sum_{i=0}^{t-1} \alpha(1-\alpha)^i d_{t-i} + (1-\alpha)^t d_0 \tag{1}$$

Where t is the index of most recent sample, $\bar{d}_{t+1}$ is the forecasted value for the time $t+1$, d_{t-i} is the crisp value at time $t-i$, and α is the smoothing factor and should attend the constraint $0 \le \alpha \le 1$. If α is equal to 1, the forecasted value is equal to the most recent sample, that is, the sample at time t. If α is near 0, than the forecasted value have more influence of the oldest sample, that is, the first sample of time series.

3   Proposed Forecasting Model

In this section we present a forecasting model developed from the integration of fuzzy time series concepts with simple exponential smoothing of statistical area. The model is composed by two main processes: (1) pre-processing and; (2) forecasting method.

3.1   Pre-processing Method

The pre-processing is based on [14] and its purpose is to analyze the data to allow a better linguistic representation of TS and, in this way, improve the accuracy of forecasting values. This method consists of four main steps shown in Figure 1.

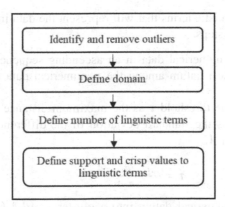

Fig. 1. Steps of the pre-processing method

The existence of one or more outliers in the sample data can exert a negative influence in all remaining steps in the process. Thus, consider the existence of n historical data in $Y(t)$, where $t = 0,1,2,\dots,n$. The first step to detect an outlier is define the square matrix H as in Equation 2.

$$H = x(x^T x)^{-1} x^T \tag{2}$$

where

$$x = \begin{bmatrix} 1 & d_0 \\ 1 & d_1 \\ 1 & d_2 \\ \vdots & \vdots \\ 1 & d_n \end{bmatrix} \tag{3}$$

and d_i for $i = 0, 1, \ldots, n$ are the observed values in the time series. In the sequence, the *Residual Student* index is computed by Equation 4 for each sample in the time series [15].

$$RStudent_i = \frac{e_i}{\hat{\sigma}^{(i)}\sqrt{1-h_i}} \tag{4}$$

In Equation 4, $\hat{\sigma}^{(i)}$ is the standard deviation without the ith sample of time series, h_i is the ith diagonal element in the matrix H, and e_i is defined by Equation 5, where d_i is the ith sample of the time series. In this work, the ith observed sample is an outlier, when the $RStudent_i$ is equal or greater than 2.5. This value was defined after the execution of some preliminary experiments.

$$e_i = d_i - \frac{\sum_{t=0}^{n} d_t}{n} \tag{5}$$

Once the outliers have been identified and removed, the universe of discourse D is defined according to Equation 6, where D_{min} is the minimum value in the observed values, D_{max} is the maximum and σ is the standard deviation of the historical data.

$$D = [D_{min} - \sigma, D_{max} + \sigma] \tag{6}$$

The number of linguistic terms that will represent the data in the time series is defined by the following steps.

Step 1. Sort the n numerical data in an ascending sequence as $d_0, d_1, d_2, \ldots, d_n$, where d_0 is the smallest datum among the n numerical data and d_n is the highest datum.

Step 2. Calculate the threshold τ as the maximum distance to fuse clusters using Equation 7, where δ is the standard deviation of the difference between the sorted samples defined in Step 1.

$$\tau = \frac{\sum_{i=1}^{n-1}(d_{i+1} - d_i)}{n-1} + \delta \tag{7}$$

Step 3. Put each numerical datum into a cluster as $\{d_1\}, \{d_2\}, \ldots, \{d_i\}, \ldots, \{d_n\}$, where the symbol "{ }" denotes a cluster.

Step 4. Assume that there are p clusters. Calculate the center of cluster k by the arithmetic mean of all data that belong to it, for $1 \leq k \leq p$.

Step 5. Calculate the distance between clusters k and $k + 1$ by Equation 8, where $k = 1, 2, 3, \ldots, p - 1$.

$$distance_{k,k+1} = |cluster\_center_k - cluster\_center_{k+1}| \tag{8}$$

Step 6. If the shortest distance between two clusters is less than τ, then join the clusters into only one cluster and go back to Step 4. Otherwise, stop the algorithm.

In order to reflect the real structure of data, the parameter p resulting from the previous algorithm will be used as input to indicate the number of clusters in the fuzzy c-means [16]. After its execution, the centroids found will be used to represent the linguist terms of FTS. Thus, the parameters of the membership functions that represents the linguistic terms are defined as follows:

- The linguistic terms L_j, for $1 < j < p$, are represented by triangular fuzzy sets, whose center is the center of cluster j;
- The left-limit and the right-limit of the support of linguistic terms L_j, where $1 < j < p$, are defined by the cluster center $j - 1$ and $j + 1$, respectively;
- The linguistic term L_1 is represented by a trapezoidal membership function with values equal to 1 in the interval $[D_{min} - \sigma, center\_cluster_1]$, where σ is the standard deviation of the series and D_{min} is the minimum value in the observed data;
- The left-limit and the right-limit of the support of L_1 are defined, respectively, by $D_{min} - \sigma$ and $center\_cluster_2$;
- The linguistic term L_p is also represented by a trapezoidal membership function, with values equal to 1 in the interval $[center\_cluster_p, D_{max} + \sigma]$, where σ is the standard deviation of the series and D_{max} is the maximum value in the observed data;
- The left-limit and the right-limit of the support of L_p are defined by $center\_cluster_{p-1}$ and $D_{max} + \sigma$, respectively;

After the pre-processing of the time series, the fuzzification of data is performed and the FLR are derived to make predictions as presented in the next subsection.

3.2   Forecasting Method

In general, the forecasting methods by means of time series consider that, from the observations and analysis of available samples, it is possible to predict the values and, therefore, the future behavior of the series. However, several time series have different behavior along the entire observation period. The proposed model consider that the most recent samples should have more influence in the process of forecasting than the earliest samples and, for this, uses the statistical technique called simple exponential smoothing. Besides, other important feature of the proposed model is the update of the FLR base with the arrival of new samples, i.e., after the acquisition of knowledge from training data, the model is updated by derivation of new FLR with the arrival of new samples. This feature allows the method to enhance the accuracy rate in scenarios where the series present a different behavior when compared with the training data. The proposed forecasting method is composed by four steps: (1) fuzzification of the original data; (2) extraction of a FLR base formed by second order FLR with three consequents; (3) forecasting value using the integration of FLR with the simple exponential smoothing concepts; (4) update the FLR base.

After the definition of fuzzy sets in the pre-processing phase, the fuzzification of the time series consists of finding the linguistic term that better represents each crisp value of the series. The derivation of fuzzy logical relationships from the fuzzified FTS, as proposed in this work, uses an extension of the traditional definition of FLR presented in the Section 2.1. In this proposal, we use second order FLR with three linguist terms in the consequent where the reverse simple exponential smoothing will be applied. Thus, the knowledge is represented by a FLR base composed by $n-4$ fuzzy logical relationships of the form presented in Equation 9.

$$L_t, L_{t+1} \rightarrow L_{t+2}, L_{t+3}, L_{t+4} \tag{9}$$

where L_t is the linguistic term in time t, $t = 1, 2, ..., n-4$, and n is the number of observed data in the FTS. With three linguistic terms in the consequent of FLR, it is possible to better identify the future trends over forecasted values. However, previous experiments have suggested that by considering more than three terms in the consequent of FLR, the accuracy rate starts to decrease.

Once the FLR base has been defined, the predictions are performed from the last two linguistic terms in the FTS, L_n and L_{n-1}. The FLR in the base with the antecedents L_n and L_{n-1} will be used in the calculation of the forecasted value. Differently than the original method [13], in which the exponential smoothing is applied over the past values of the entire time series, in the proposed method a modified version of exponential smoothing is introduced. In this work, the smoothing is performed both on the three crisp values that represent the linguistic terms in the consequents of each FLR being used in the forecasting and on the FLR themselves, so that the most recent ones have higher influence than the oldest ones. Suppose that a FLR of the form presented in Equation 9 will be used in the forecasting. This FLR then, generates a smoothing value S, defined by Equation 10.

$$S = (1-\alpha)^2 l_{t+2} + \alpha(1-\alpha) l_{t+3} + \alpha l_{t+4} \tag{10}$$

where α is the smoothing factor, l_{t+2}, l_{t+3} and l_{t+4} represents the crisp values of the corresponding linguistic terms L_{t+2}, L_{t+3} and L_{t+4}, respectively and ,as in Equation 1, the constraint $0 \leq \alpha \leq 1$ should be observed.

Consider that there are m FLR in the base with the terms L_{n-1} and L_n in the antecedents, and q is the index of the most recent value S_j, $j = 0, 1, ..., q$, defined by Equation 10. The forecasted value d_{n+1} is calculated as presented in Equation 11.

$$d_{n+1} = \alpha \sum_{i=0}^{q-1} (1-\alpha)^i S_{q-i} + (1-\alpha)^q S_0 \tag{11}$$

where S_0 refers to the value defined by the oldest FLR with antecedents L_{n-1} and L_n in the base. Similarly to Equation 1, the α value should attend the constraint $0 \leq \alpha \leq 1$.

The continuous update of FLR base is also an important feature to attain the good accuracy in the proposed method. The arrival of new samples can mean a change in the behavior of time series. Thus, after the arrival of each new sample, a new FLR with two antecedents and three consequents is added to the FLR base. In the next section the experiments performed are described. The results show that the accuracy rate of the proposed method was better than other methods available in the literature.

4   Experiments

To validate the proposed method, four experiments with the Taiwan Stock Exchange (TAIEX) index between 2001 and 2004 were performed and compared with other methods in the literature. The training was performed with the data from January to October of each year, and the data between November and December were used in the tests. Table 1 shows the amount of samples, the domain and number of linguistic terms of each time series obtained from the pre-processing.

Table 1. Pre-processing in TAIEX index between 2001 and 2004

Time Series	Samples	Domain	Linguistic Terms	Samples Trainning	Test
TAIEX 2001	244	[2732.30; 6818.20]	52	201	43
TAIEX 2002	248	[3190.59; 7121.75]	49	205	43
TAIEX 2003	249	[3580.74; 6666.89]	49	206	43
TAIEX 2004	250	[4861.44; 7489.53]	48	205	45

The next step after the pre-processing is the fuzzification of the crisp values values in the original observed data. Each value in the FTS is represented by the cluster center of the corresponding linguistic term. To illustrate the process, Table 2 shows the linguistic terms and their respective center values for TAIEX 2003 index.

Table 2. Crisp values for the representation of linguistic terms for TAIEX 2003 index

Linguistic Term	Value	Linguistic Term	Value	Linguistic Term	Value	Linguistic Term	Value
0	4439.08	13	5223.69	26	5488.22	39	5853.37
1	4537.30	14	5257.34	27	5513.87	40	5869.14
2	4590.80	15	5284.78	28	5522.88	41	5917.75
3	4648.07	16	5301.02	29	5553.36	42	5925.46
4	4691.68	17	5303.11	30	5582.89	43	5957.99
5	4827.69	18	5318.04	31	5620.80	44	6038.06
6	4893.06	19	5341.17	32	5645.91	45	6039.01
7	4939.72	20	5367.29	33	5678.97	46	6044.48
8	4970.38	21	5393.38	34	5694.98	47	6066.15
9	4997.74	22	5409.20	35	5721.49	48	6094.29
10	5075.14	23	5438.26	36	5750.26	-	-
11	5144.70	24	5448.49	37	5817.84	-	-
12	5203.78	25	5486.13	38	5818.87	-	-

The FTS is fuzzified using the linguistic terms defined on its domain. For example, the fuzzified training data set of TAIEX 2003 index using the linguistic terms presented in Table 2, is shown in Table 3.

Table 3. Training data set of fuzzy time series

$L_1, L_3, L_4, L_4, L_5, L_5, L_5, L_9, L_9, L_9, L_7, L_6, L_7, L_7, L_9, L_{10}, L_{10}, L_8, L_9, L_5, L_4, L_3, L_2, L_3, L_1, L_1,$
$L_4, L_2, L_1, L_1, L_1, L_2, L_0, L_0, L_0, L_1, L_1, L_0, L_0, L_0, L_0, L_0, L_0, L_0, L_0, L_1, L_1, L_2, L_2, L_2, L_1, L_1,$
$L_1, L_0, L_0, L_0, L_0, L_0, L_1, L_2, L_1, L_1, L_1, L_1, L_0, L_0, L_2, L_2, L_3, L_3, L_1, L_2, L_0, L_0, L_0, L_0, L_0, L_0, L_0,$
$L_0, L_0, L_0, L_0, L_0, L_0, L_0, L_0, L_0, L_0, L_0, L_0, L_0, L_0, L_0, L_0, L_0, L_1, L_1, L_4, L_4, L_4, L_4, L_5, L_5, L_5, L_6,$
$L_6, L_6, L_8, L_9, L_{10}, L_9, L_7, L_6, L_7, L_6, L_6, L_6, L_9, L_{10}, L_{10}, L_{11}, L_{18}, L_{20}, L_{20}, L_{15}, L_{13}, L_{19}, L_{19}, L_{22},$
$L_{16}, L_{15}, L_{13}, L_{14}, L_{15}, L_{22}, L_{21}, L_{24}, L_{19}, L_{17}, L_{18}, L_{21}, L_{20}, L_{14}, L_{13}, L_{14}, L_{13}, L_{13}, L_{14}, L_{23}, L_{23},$
$L_{26}, L_{27}, L_{27}, L_{29}, L_{31}, L_{32}, L_{33}, L_{29}, L_{29}, L_{28}, L_{32}, L_{34}, L_{35}, L_{33}, L_{31}, L_{32}, L_{35}, L_{33}, L_{31}, L_{32},$
$L_{31}, L_{34}, L_{36}, L_{36}, L_{36}, L_{33}, L_{33}, L_{35}, L_{34}, L_{32}, L_{32}, L_{31}, L_{30}, L_{34}, L_{36}, L_{39}, L_{39}, L_{38},$
$L_{40}, L_{43}, L_{42}, L_{42}, L_{44}, L_{46}, L_{47}, L_{47}, L_{46}, L_{43}, L_{41}, L_{43}, L_{47}, L_{48}, L_{48}.$

The next step is to derivate the fuzzy logical relationships from the FTS for, in the sequence, calculate the forecasted values. For instance, according to Table 3, the first second-order FLR with three consequents to be inserted in the FLR as proposed in this model is $L_1, L_3 \to L_4, L_4, L_5$, the second is $L_3, L_4 \to L_4, L_5, L_5$ and so on. After the FLR base has been defined, the forecasted values were calculated. The actual and forecasted TAIEX indexes for November and December 2003 are shown in Table 4.

Table 4. Actual and forecasted index for the months of November and December of 2003

Date	Actual	Forecasted	Date	Actual	Forecasted
2003/11/03	6087.45	6044.48	2003/12/03	5884.97	5917.75
2003/11/04	6108.99	6094.29	2003/12/04	5920.46	5869.14
2003/11/05	6142.32	6053.94	2003/12/05	5900.05	5917.75
2003/11/06	6013.40	6053.94	2003/12/08	5847.15	5917.75
2003/11/07	6056.83	6038.06	2003/12/09	5859.56	5853.37
2003/11/10	6059.03	6066.15	2003/12/10	5803.42	5799.73
2003/11/11	6022.08	6024.02	2003/12/11	5867.05	5817.84
2003/11/12	5982.75	6038.06	2003/12/12	5858.32	5869.14
2003/11/13	6035.44	5957.99	2003/12/15	5924.24	5853.37
2003/11/14	6044.77	6038.06	2003/12/16	5887.23	5925.46
2003/11/17	5952.32	6063.99	2003/12/17	5752.01	5818.87
2003/11/18	5939.47	5936.21	2003/12/18	5768.76	5750.26
2003/11/19	5865.51	5947.49	2003/12/19	5759.23	5791.74
2003/11/20	5834.24	5869.14	2003/12/22	5835.11	5791.74
2003/11/21	5830.06	5818.87	2003/12/23	5845.51	5818.87
2003/11/24	5821.58	5818.87	2003/12/24	5857.87	5833.78
2003/11/25	5861.18	5818.87	2003/12/25	5853.70	5812.87
2003/11/26	5860.61	5853.37	2003/12/26	5857.21	5812.87
2003/11/27	5740.57	5837.30	2003/12/29	5804.89	5812.87
2003/11/28	5771.77	5750.26	2003/12/30	5866.75	5873.35
2003/12/01	5870.17	5709.97	2003/12/31	5890.69	5861.44
2003/12/02	5911.45	5869.14	-	-	-

To illustrate the advantage of updating the FLR base and considering all the FLR with matching antecedent in the forecasting process, consider the forecasting for December 29, 2003. The two preceding actual values L_n and L_{n-1} in the time series are represented, respectively, by the linguistic terms L_{39} and L_{39}. In the FTS showed in Table 3, we can identify the FLR $L_{39}, L_{39} \rightarrow L_{38}, L_{40}, L_{43}$ to calculate the forecasted value S_0. If we consider, as usually is done in traditional forecasting, only this FLR and $\alpha = 0.1$ in Equation 10, the weight of each linguistic term in the FLR consequent would be 0.81, 0.09 and 0.1. Considering the linguistic terms in Table 2, and by the employment of Equation 11, the forecasted index would be 5837.30. However, before December 29, the FLR base was updated by the arrival of new samples after the initial training. With the samples of November 25 to 30 and December 1st, the FLR $L_{39}, L_{39} \rightarrow L_{36}, L_{36}, L_{40}$, was included in the FLR base. Similarly, the samples of December 08 to 12 generate the FLR $L_{39}, L_{39} \rightarrow L_{37}, L_{40}, L_{39}$.

Our method considers all the FLR whose antecedent matches the values used in the forecast. Thus, from the matching of the three FLR, we have $S_0 = 5837.30$, $S_1 = 5762.14$ and $S_2 = 5826.01$. Considering $\alpha = 0.5$ in Equation 11, the forecasted value is 5812.87, which is closer to the real value than the previous value. The graphics of actual index and forecasted index for TAIEX in the years 2001, 2002 and 2004, are shown in Figures 2, 3 and 4, respectively.

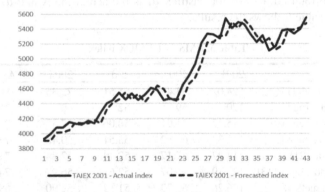

Fig. 2. Actual and forecasted indexes for November and December 2001

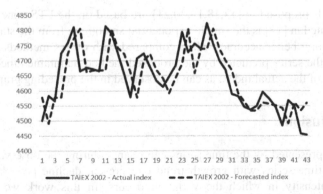

Fig. 3. Actual and forecasted indexes for November and December 2002

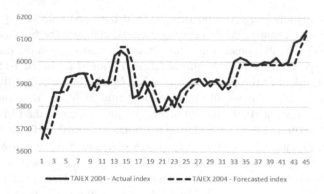

Fig. 4. Actual and forecasted indexes for November and December 2004

The obtained results were compared with six different methods by the Root Mean Square Error (RMSE) calculated from Equation 12.

$$RMSE = \sqrt{\frac{\sum_{i=1}^{n}(d_i - \bar{d_i})^2}{n}} \tag{12}$$

where n is the total number of forecasting, d_i is the actual index and $\bar{d_i}$ is the forecasted index. Table 5 shows the results.

Table 5. RMSE of TAIEX index

Method	2001	2002	2003	2004	Average
Huarng, et. al. [17]	124.02	93.48	65.51	72.35	88.84
Yu and Huarng [18]	120	69	52	60	75.25
Chen and Chen [19]	115.33	71.01	58.06	57.33	75.43
Chen and Chang [20]	113.33	66.82	53.51	60.48	73.53
Chen, et. al.[21]	114.47	67.17	52.49	52.84	71.74
Brown and Meyer [13]	123.19	66.07	52.68	56.97	74.73
Proposed method	106.26	66.73	51.12	52.90	69.25

The methods proposed in [17,18,19,20,21] are based on the FTS concepts and the method presented in [13] is the simple exponential smoothing from the statistical area. Besides obtaining better accuracy when compared with others methods available in the literature, the series predicted by the proposed method maintained the same behavior and trend of the actual index, as can be observed in the preceding graphics.

5   Conclusions

The behavior presented by the time series can change during the observation period. For instance, time series with growth trend can present decline periods, or yet, to change the intensity in which the variation occurs. In this work we proposed a forecasting method that aims at identifying and considering the chances in the series behavior in the forecasting process. The proposed method combines the concepts of the simple exponential smoothing with the fuzzy logical relationships. While in the traditional method the smoothing is applied in the past samples, in our work the smoothing is applied to the consequents of the FLR. Another important aspect of the method proposed is the constant update of FLR base toghether with the consideretion of all the FLR whose antecedent match the last two values in the series in the porecasting. Furthermore, the pre-processing has an essential role, given that the suitable linguistic representation of the data structure is fundamental for the proposed model. In this way, with the analysis of the obtained results is possible to assert that the proposed model is able to deal with different trends in the time series and to attain good results.

For future work will be considered the development of a method to analyze and classify the time series by means of clustering, where each time series will be considered an element in the cluster. The main purpose is to predict not only the time series values, but also changes in their behavior.

References

1. Song, Q., Chissom, B.S.: Fuzzy Time Series and its Models. Fuzzy Sets and Systems **54**, 269–277 (1993)
2. Song, Q., Chissom, B.S.: Forecasting Enrollments With Fuzzy Time Series – Part I. Fuzzy Sets and Systems **54**, 1–9 (1993)
3. Song, Q., Chissom, B.S.: Forecasting Enrollments With Fuzzy Time Series – Part II. Fuzzy Sets and Systems **62**, 1–8 (1994)
4. Uslu, V.R., Bas, E., Yolcu, U., Egrioglu, E.: A Fuzzy Time Series Approach Based on Weights Determined by the Number of Recurrences of Fuzzy Relations. Swarm and Evolutionary Computation **15**, 19–26 (2014)
5. Stepnicka, M., Cortez, P., Donate, J.P., Stepnicková, L.: Forecasting Seasonal Time Series With Computational Intelligence: On Recent Methods and the Potential of their Combinations. Expert Systems with Applications **40**, 1981–1992 (2013)
6. Chatterjee, S., Nigam, S., Singh, J.B., Upadhyaya, L.N.: Application of Fuzzy Time Series in Prediction of Time Between Failures & Faults in Software Reliability Assessment. Fuzzy Information and Engineering **3**, 293–309 (2011)
7. Kai, C., Fang-Ping, F., Wen-Gang,C.: A Novel Forecasting Model of Fuzzy Time Series Based on K-Means Clustering. In: Proc. Second International Workshop on Education Technology and Computer Science, pp. 223–225 (2010)
8. Joshi, B.P., Kumar, S.: A Computational Method for Fuzzy Time Series Forecasting Based on Difference Parameters. International Journal of Modeling, Simulation, and Scientific Computing **4**(1), 1250023-1–1250023-12 (2013)
9. Chu, H., Chen, T., Cheng, C., Huang, C.: Fuzzy Dual-Factor Time-Series for Stock Index Forecasting. Expert Systems With Applications **36**, 165–171 (2009)
10. Qiu, W., Liu, X., Li, H.: A Generalized Method for Forecasting Based on Fuzzy Time Series. Expert Systems With Applications **38**, 10446–10453 (2011)
11. Zadeh, L.A.: Fuzzy Set. Information and Control **8**, 338–353 (1965)
12. Zadeh, L.A.: The Concept of a Linguistic Variable and its Application to Approximate Reasoning - Part 1. Information Sciences **8**, 199–249 (1975)

13. Brown, R.G., Meyer, R.F.: The fundamental theory of exponential smoothing. Operations Research **9**, 673–685 (1961)
14. Santos, F.J.J., Camargo, H.A.: Preprocessing in Fuzzy Time Series to Improve the Forecasting Accuracy. In: 12th International Conference on Machine Learning and Applications, pp. 170–173 (2013)
15. Barnett, V., Lewis, T.: Outliers in Statistical Data, 3rd ed. John Wiley & Sons, NY (1994)
16. Bezdek, J.C., Tsao, E.C., Pal, N.R.: Fuzzy Kohonen Clustering Networks. In: IEEE International Conference on Fuzzy Systems, pp. 1035–1043 (1992)
17. Huarng, K., Yu, H.K., Hsu, Y.W.: A Multivariate Heuristic Model for Fuzzy Time-Series Forecasting. IEEE Trans. Syst. Man, Cybern. B, Cybern. **37**(4), 836–846 (2007)
18. Yu, T.H.K., Huarng, K.H.: A Bivariate Fuzzy Time Series Model to Forecast the TAIEX. Expert Systems With Applications **34**, 2945–2952 (2008)
19. Chen, S.M., Chen, C.D.: TAIEX Forecasting Based on Fuzzy Time Series and Fuzzy Variation Groups. IEEE Trans. Fuzzy Syst. **19**, 1–12 (2011)
20. Chen, S.M., Chang, Y.C.: Multi-Variable Fuzzy Forecasting Based on Fuzzy Clustering and Fuzzy Rule Interpolation Techniques. Information Sciences: an International Journal. **180**(24), 4772–4783 (2010)
21. Chen, S.M., Chu, H.P., Sheu, T.W.: TAIEX Forecasting Using Fuzzy Time Series and Automatically Generated Weights of Multiple Factors. IEEE Transactions on Systems, Man, and Cybernetics - Part A: Systems and Humans **42**, 1485–1495 (2012)

Online Evolving Fuzzy Clustering Algorithm Based on Maximum Likelihood Similarity Distance

Orlando Donato Rocha Filho[✉] and Ginalber Luiz de Oliveira Serra

Department of Electroelectronics, Laboratory of Computational Intelligence
Applied to Techonology, Federal Institute of Education, Science and Technology,
São Luís, MA, Brazil
{orlando.rocha,ginalber}@ifma.edu.br

Abstract. This paper proposes an online evolving fuzzy clustering algorithm based on maximum likelihood estimator. In this algorithm, the distance from a point to center of the cluster is computed by maximum likelihood similarity of data. The mathematical formulation is developed from the Takagi–Sugeno (TS) fuzzy inference system. In order to evaluate the applicability of the proposed algorithm, the prediction of the Box-Jenkins (Gas Furnace) time series, is performed. Computational results of comparative analysis with other methods widely cited in the literature illustrates the effectiveness of the proposed algorithm.

Keywords: Fuzzy clustering · Maximum likelihood · Recursive estimation · Takagi–Sugeno fuzzy model · Evolving fuzzy system · Prediction · Time series

1 Introduction

Engineering problems in different areas such as manufacturing, control and signal processing, motivate the development of modeling methodologies, specifically evolving algorithms as fundamentals for adaptive models [4]. In the literature, evolving intelligent systems are usually based on artificial neural networks and neuro-fuzzy artificial networks, which are able to change their structure and parameters [6], [8], [11] and [13].

Researches on evolving fuzzy clustering based on Mahalonobis distance, ie, Gustafson-Kessel fuzzy clustering algorithm and recursive Gath–Geva clustering algorithm have been developed in recent years [5], [4]. In this paper, an online evolving fuzzy clustering algorithm based on maximum likelihood criterion with recursive parameter estimation, is proposed. The performance of the proposed algorithm is validated through the prediction of the Box-Jenkins (Gas Furnace) time series, evaluated from Root Mean Square Error (RMSE) and compared with other efficient methods widely cited in the literature [6], [8], [11] and [13].

The main contribution of the proposed algorithm is the formulation of an online fuzzy inference system with Takagi–Sugeno evolving structure, which

© Springer International Publishing Switzerland 2014
A.L.C. Bazzan and K. Pichara (Eds.): IBERAMIA 2014, LNAI 8864, pp. 269–280, 2014.
DOI: 10.1007/978-3-319-12027-0_22

employs an adaptive distance norm based on the maximum likelihood criterion. Most of the clustering algorithms are based on idea of batch clustering, that is, the data set is assumed to be available before the clustering analysis is carried out, [4]. However, these algorithms require an initial condition from supervisor, that is, the number of initial clusters so the algorithm can be performed. The proposed algorithm is able to determine the new clusters as data are available, sequentially. The algorithm is based on adaptive distance measure, which can detect different shape and orientation of the clusters from data set.

This paper is organized as follows: in Section 2, the mathematical formulation for evolving fuzzy clustering algorithm based on maximum likelihood criterion from the fuzzy Takagi-Sugeno inference system is developed. The computational results for clustering of the EEG time series and for prediction of the Box-Jenkins (Gas Furnace) and Mackey–Glass time series, are presented in Section 3. The conclusions are discussed in Section 4.

2   Formulation of the Fuzzy Maximum Likelihood Clustering Algorithm

In this section the formulation of the fuzzy maximum likelihood clustering algorithm, is discussed. The algorithm is based on initial concept of fuzzy maximum likelihood estimator proposed by [1], cited by [2]. The implementation of the online evolving fuzzy clustering algorithm based on maximum likelihood criterion is performed in two stages named, respectively: batch algorithm (initial estimation), which is applied to N_{bt} data (**batch data number**) to perform the initial parametric estimation; after that, the recursive algorithm (evolution estimation) is applied to N_{rc} data (**recursive estimation**), so the recursive estimation of the evolving fuzzy model parameters is performed from each new point of the time series. A clustering algorithm partitions a data set

$$\mathbf{Z} = [\mathbf{X}, \mathbf{y}] = [\mathbf{z}_1, \mathbf{z}_2, \dots, \mathbf{z}_N]^T, \mathbf{z}_j \subset R^{p+1}, j = 1, 2, \dots, N, \tag{1}$$

where

$$\mathbf{X} = [\mathbf{x}_1, \mathbf{x}_2, \dots, \mathbf{x}_N], \mathbf{x}_j \subset R^p, j = 1, 2, \dots, N, \text{(input vector)} \tag{2}$$

$$\mathbf{y} = [y_1, y_2, \dots, y_N]^T, y_j \subset R, j = 1, 2, \dots, N, \text{(output vector)} \tag{3}$$

into c clusters so that members of the same group are considered similar according to distance measured. Let $2 \leq c \leq N$ be an integer; the c clusters may be represented by a set of c prototypes:

$$\mathbf{V} = [\mathbf{v}_1, \mathbf{v}_2, \dots, \mathbf{v}_c], \mathbf{v}_i \subset R^{p+1}, i = 1, 2, \dots, c \tag{4}$$

where N is the total of observations of some physical process and p is the dimensionality of the input vector [2], [5].

2.1   Batch Algorithm: Initial Estimation

In this section, the batch stage of the proposed algorithm is presented. The proposed algorithm corresponds to minimization of the function $\tilde{f}$, given by:

$$(\mathbf{U}_{bt}, \mathbf{V}_{bt}, \mathbf{A}_{\Sigma_{bt}}) = \tilde{f}(\mathbf{Z}_{bt}, c; \mathbf{U}_{FCM}, \mathbf{V}_{FCM}, \epsilon) \tag{5}$$

where

$\mathbf{X}_{bt} \in \Re^{N_{bt} \times p}$: input vector, defined in (2).

$\mathbf{y}_{bt} \in \Re^{N_{bt} \times 1}$: output vector, defined in (3).

$\mathbf{Z}_{bt} = [\mathbf{X}_{bt}, \mathbf{y}_{bt}], \in \Re^{N_{bt} \times p+1}$: matrix of regressors, defined in (1).

$\mathbf{U}_{bt} \in \Re^{c \times N_{bt}}$: fuzzy partition matrix from batch data series.

$\mathbf{U}_{FCM} \in \Re^{c \times N_{bt}}$: fuzzy partition matrix from fuzzy C-Means clustering algorithm.

$\mathbf{V}_{bt} \in \Re^{c \times p+1}$: prototypes of the clusters from batch data series.

$\mathbf{V}_{FCM} \in \Re^{c \times p+1}$: prototypes of the clusters from fuzzy C-Means clustering algorithm.

$\mathbf{A}_{\Sigma_{bt}} \in \Re^{c \cdot p \times p}$: covariance matrix from batch data series.

ϵ: tolerance, $\epsilon = 10^{-8}$.

The function $\tilde{f}$, represents the fuzzy maximum likelihood clustering algorithm, which emploies a distance norm based on maximum likelihood. The initial prototypes of the clusters, $\mathbf{V}_{FCM}$, and the initial fuzzy partition matrix, $\mathbf{U}_{FCM}$, are initial conditions to batch fuzzy c-means clustering algorithm; it is the initial step of the batch fuzzy clustering algorithm (initial estimation). After minimization of the function $\tilde{f}$, the following vectors are resulted: fuzzy partition matrix from batch data series ($\mathbf{U}_{bt}$), prototypes of the clusters from batch data series ($\mathbf{V}_{bt}$) and covariance matrix from batch data series ($\mathbf{A}_{\Sigma_{bt}}$). The batch fuzzy maximum likelihood clustering algorithm is implemented from the following steps:

Step 1: obtain N_{bt} elements of the time series, $\mathbf{Z}_{N_{bt}}$, for initial estimation.

Step 2: compute the initial partition matrix $\mathbf{U}_{FCM}$ and the prototypes of clustering vector $\mathbf{V}_{FCM}$, chosen for initial clustering, so that $1 \leq c \leq N_{bt}$ and tolerance $\epsilon > 0$, by fuzzy c-means algorithm (FCM):

$$(\mathbf{U}_{FCM}, \mathbf{V}_{FCM}) = FCM(\mathbf{Z}_{N_{bt}}, c, \mathbf{U}_0, \epsilon) \tag{6}$$

where

$$\mathbf{U}_0 \in \Re^{c \times N_{bt}} \Big| \mu_{0_{ik}} \in [0,1], \forall i, k; \sum_{i=1}^{c} \mu_{0_{ik}} = 1, \forall k; 0 < \sum_{k=1}^{N} \mu_{0_{ik}} < N, \forall i \tag{7}$$

Step 3: compute *a priori* probability to select the i–th cluster.

$$P_0(i) = \frac{1}{N_{bt}} \sum_{k=1}^{N_{bt}} \mu_{ik}^{(0)}, 1 \leq i \leq c \tag{8}$$

where, $\mu_{ik}^{(0)}$ is the initial membership degree from $\mathbf{U}_{FCM}$.

Repeat Steps (4,5 e 6) for the iterations $l = 1, 2, \ldots$

Step 4: determine the cluster covariance matrices

$$A_\Sigma = \frac{\sum_{k=1}^{N_{bt}} \mu_{ik}^{(l-1)} \left(z(k) - v_{FCM_i} \right) \left(z(k) - v_{FCM_i} \right)^T}{\sum_{k=1}^{N_{bt}} \mu_{ik}^{(l-1)}}, 1 \leq i \leq c \qquad (9)$$

Step 5: determine the maximum likelihood distances from member $z(k)$ of the same cluster with respect to the prototypes v_{FCM_i}

$$D_{ik}^2 = \frac{(2\pi)^{p/2}\sqrt{A_\Sigma}}{P_0(i)} \exp\left[\tfrac{1}{2}\left(z(k) - v_{FCM_i} \right) A_\Sigma^{-1} \left(z(k) - v_{FCM_i} \right)^T \right],$$

$$\text{for } 1 \leq i \leq c \text{ and } 1 \leq k \leq N_{bt} \qquad (10)$$

Step 6: update the partition matrix.

if $D_{ik} > 0$ for $1 \leq i \leq c$ and $1 \leq k \leq N_{bt}$,

$$\mu_{ik}^{(l)} = \frac{1}{\sum_{j=1}^{c} \left(\dfrac{D_{ik}}{D_{jk}} \right)^{-1}} \qquad (11)$$

else

$$\mu_{ik}^{(l)} = 0, \text{ if } D_{ik} > 0, \text{ and } \mu_{ik}^{(l)} \in [0,1] \text{ with } \sum_{i=1}^{c} \mu_{ik}^{(l)} = 1$$

end if

until $\left\| U^{(l)} - U^{(l-1)} \right\| < \epsilon.$

End Repeat.

Step 7: determine the memberships functions of the antecedent from maximum likelihood probabilistic method, for $1 \leq i \leq c$ and $1 \leq l \leq p$.

$$\beta_{il}(x_l) = \frac{1}{\sum_{j=1}^{c} \left(\dfrac{D_{ikA_\Sigma^\times(x_l, v_{0_i})}}{D_{jkA_\Sigma^\times(x_l, v_{0_j})}} \right)^{-1}} \qquad (12)$$

Step 8: compute the weighted matrix from the partition matrix, given by:

$$w_{ij} = \mu_{ij}, \text{ se } i = j,$$
$$w_{ij} = 0, \text{ se } i \neq j,$$
$$\text{para } i = 1, 2, \ldots, c;\, j = 1, 2, \ldots, N. \qquad (13)$$

where

$$\mathbf{W_i} = \begin{pmatrix} \mu_{i1} & 0 & \cdots & 0 \\ 0 & \mu_{i2} & \cdots & 0 \\ \vdots & \vdots & \vdots & \vdots \\ 0 & 0 & \cdots & \mu_{iN} \end{pmatrix} \tag{14}$$

Step 9: estimate the parameters of the consequent in batch mode.

$$\Theta_{bt} = \left(\mathbf{X}_e^T \mathbf{W}_i \mathbf{X}_e\right)^{-1} \mathbf{X}_e^T \mathbf{W}_i \mathbf{y}, \mathbf{X}_e = [\mathbf{X}_{N_{bt}} 1] \tag{15}$$

where $\mathbf{X}_{N_{bt}}$, is the data matrix for batch estimate and $\mathbf{X}_e$, is the data matrix for extended batch estimate.

2.2 Recursive Algorithm: Evolving Estimation

In this section, the recursive stage of the proposed algorithm is presented. Each new point, updates the matrix of regressors in the recursive stage. The si-milarity between the new point and each cluster is measured from maximum likelihood distance. The smallest distance from cluster to point is identified and called closest cluster. After closest cluster, the radius of this cluster is computed. The distance from the closest cluster in relation to radius of this cluster, is evaluated. If the distance from the closest cluster to point is smaller than radius of the closest cluster, the prototype of the centers and the covariance matrix according to rule of Kohonem [4] and [5], is updated. If distance from closest cluster is greater than radius, a new cluster is created, since the criterion of credibility of the closest clusters exceeds the minimum value defined as initial conditions of the algorithm. After update the membership functions of the antecedent from maximum likelihood probabilistic method and consequent parameters, the rules base of the Takagi–Sugeno fuzzy model, is updated. The recursive fuzzy maximum likelihood clustering algorithm is implemented from the following steps:

Step 1: compute the initial values of the matrices $\mathbf{V}_{bt}$, $\mathbf{U}_{bt}$ and $\mathbf{A}_{\Sigma_{bt}}$, for $i = 1, 2, \ldots, c$ from the batch algorithm, defined in section 2.1. Set values for μ_h, α and Pn_{tol}, where α: learning rate of online algorithm, $\alpha = [0,05 \ldots 0,3]$; μ_h: partition threshold and Pn_{tol}: dimensionality of the clusters.

Step 2: read the next point $\mathbf{z}(k)$.

Step 3: update the data matrix $\mathbf{Z}$.

$$\mathbf{Z}_{(N_{bt}+k)} = [\mathbf{Z}_{N_{bt}}, \mathbf{z}(k)] \tag{16}$$

where, $\mathbf{Z}_{(N_{bt}+k)} = [\mathbf{X}_{(N_{bt}+k)} \mathbf{Y}_{(N_{bt}+k)}] \in \Re^{N_{bt}+k \times p+1}$: matrix of regressors.

Step 4: compute the distances d_{ik} for $i = 1, 2, \ldots, c$

$$d_{ik} = \sqrt{\frac{(2\pi)^{p/2}\sqrt{A_\Sigma}}{P_0(i)}\exp\left[\frac{1}{2}(\mathbf{z}(k)-\mathbf{V}_{bt})A_\Sigma^{-1}(\mathbf{z}(k)-\mathbf{V}_{bt})^T\right]} \tag{17}$$

Step 5: determine the closest cluster g_{th} from $\mathbf{z}(k)$.

$$g_{th} = \arg \min (d_{ik}), i = 1, 2, \ldots, c \tag{18}$$

Step 6: compute the radius, $r_{g_{th}}$, of the closest cluster from $\mathbf{z}(k)$.

$$r_{g_{th}} = \max \|V_{g_{th}} - z_j\|_{A_{\Sigma g_{th}}} \tag{19}$$
$$\forall \mathbf{z}_j \in g_{th} \text{ and } \mu_{g_{th} j} > \mu h$$

Step 7: if $d_{gk} \leq r_g$
    Step 7.1: update the prototypes,V_g, and covariance matrix, A_{Σ}.

$$\mathbf{V}_{g_{new}} = \mathbf{V}_{g_{old}} + \alpha (\mathbf{z}(k) - \mathbf{V}_{g_{new}}) \tag{20}$$
$$\mathbf{A}_{\Sigma_{g_{new}}} = (1 - \alpha)\mathbf{A}_{\Sigma_{g_{old}}} + \alpha \left((\mathbf{z}(k) - \mathbf{V}_{g_{old}})^T (\mathbf{z}(k) - \mathbf{V}_{g_{old}})^T \right) \tag{21}$$

    Step 7.2: update the partition matrix, $\mathbf{U}$

$$\mu_{ik} = \frac{1}{\sum\limits_{j=1}^{c} \left(\dfrac{D_{ikA_{\Sigma}}}{D_{jkA_{\Sigma}}} \right)^{-1}} \tag{22}$$

Step 8: if $d_{gk} > r_g$
    Step 8.1: create a new cluster.

$$\mathbf{v}_{c+1} = \mathbf{z}(k) \tag{23}$$
$$\mathbf{A}_{\Sigma_{c+1}} = \mathbf{A}_{\Sigma_g} \tag{24}$$

    Step 8.2: recalculate the partition matrix, $\mathbf{U}_{(N_{bt}+k)}$

$$\left(\mathbf{U}_{(N_{bt}+k)} \right) = \tilde{f} \left(\mathbf{Z}_{(N_{bt}+k)}, \mathbf{U}_{(N_{bt}+k-1)}, \mathbf{V}, \mathbf{A}_{\Sigma}, \epsilon \right) \tag{25}$$

    Step 8.3: compute Pn_{c+1}.
    Step 8.4: if $Pn_{c+1} > Pn_{tol}$
        Step 8.4.1: accept the new cluster.

$$c = c + 1 \tag{26}$$

        Step 8.4.2: determine the memberships functions of the antecedent from maximum likelihood probabilistic method, for $1 \leq i \leq c$ and $1 \leq l \leq p$.

$$\beta_{il}(\mathbf{x}_l) = \frac{1}{\sum\limits_{j=1}^{c} \left(\dfrac{D_{ikA_{\Sigma}^{\times}(\mathbf{x}_l, v_{0_i})}}{D_{jkA_{\Sigma}^{\times}(\mathbf{x}_l, v_{0_j})}} \right)^{-1}}, 1 \leq i \leq c \tag{27}$$

    Step 8.5: if $Pn_{c+1} \leq Pn_{tol}$

Step 8.5.1: refuse the new cluster and keep the old structure.

Step 9: determine the best center that minimizes the cost function, $J_i, \forall i, i = 1, 2, \ldots, c$

$$J_i = \sum_{x_k \in v_i} \|\mathbf{x}_k - \mathbf{v}_i\| \tag{28}$$

Step 10: estimate the parameters in weighted recursive mode

$$w_{ij} = \begin{cases} \mu_{ij} & \text{if } i = j, \\ 0 & \text{if } i \neq j, \end{cases} \tag{29}$$

for $i = 1, 2, \ldots, c$ and $j = 1, 2, \ldots, N$.

$$\mathbf{P}_1 = w_{ij}^{(l+1)} \mathbf{P}^{(l)} \mathbf{X}^{(l+1)} \mathbf{X}^{T(l+1)} \mathbf{P}^{(l)}$$

$$P_2 = 1 + \mathbf{X}^{T(l+1)} \mathbf{P}^{(l)} \mathbf{X}^{(l+1)}$$

$$\mathbf{P}^{(l+1)} = \mathbf{P}^{(l)} - \frac{\mathbf{P}_1}{P_2}$$

$$\mathbf{P}_3 = \mathbf{P}^{(l+1)} \mathbf{X}^{(l+1)} w_{ij}^{(l+1)}$$

$$P_4 = \left(y^{(l+1)} - \mathbf{X}^{T(l+1)} \Theta^{i(l)} \right)$$

$$\Theta^{i(l+1)} = \Theta^{i(l)} + \mathbf{P}_3 P_4$$

$$l = 1, 2, 3, \ldots, N \tag{30}$$

Step 11: create the Takagi–Sugeno fuzzy model, described as follows:

$$R^i : \text{IF } y(k-1) \text{ is } F_1^i \text{ AND }, \ldots, \text{ AND } y(k - n_y) \text{ is } F_{n_y}^i \text{ AND}$$

$$u(k-1) \text{ is } F_1^i \text{ AND }, \ldots, \text{ AND } u(k - n_u) \text{ is } F_{n_u}^i$$

$$\text{THEN } y^i(k) = \sum_{j=1}^{n_y} \theta_{y_j}^i y(k - j) + \sum_{j=1}^{n_u} \theta_{u_j}^i u(k - j) + \theta_0^i$$

$$\tag{31}$$

where, θ_y, θ_u e θ_0 are the consequent parameters to be determined; n_y is the order of $y(k)$ and n_u is the order of $u(k)$, corresponding to the ARX models in the consequent proposition.

Step 12: go to step 2

3 Computational Results

In this section, computational results for analysis of the proposed algorithm, is presented.

3.1 Experimental Studies of Data Sets

In this subsection, computational results for clustering performance from proposed algorithm for artificial data sets (EEG data sets provided by UC Irvine Machine Learning Repository cited by [5]), is evaluated. The clustering procedure from evolving maximum likelihood (eML) clustering algorithm and the evolving Gustafson-Kessel (eGK) clustering algorithm is shown in Fig. 1. From statistical analysis of the distance from the cluster to the corresponding member, it is observed the better performance of the eML clustering algorithm (J = 197.33 for EEG data set) compared to eGK clustering algorithm performance (J = 218.07 for EEG data set), considering the same number of clusters obtained for both clustering algorithm equal to 14.

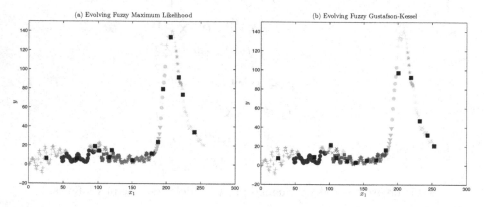

Fig. 1. Clustering performance for EEG cluster artificial data sets (a) proposed algorithm and (b) eGK algorithm

3.2 Prediction of Box–Jenkins (Gas Furnace) Time Series

In this subsection, computational results for prediction of the Box–Jenkins (Gas Furnace) time series are presented. The ARX Takagi-Sugeno fuzzy inference system, is given by:

$$R^i : \text{IF } y(k-1) \text{ is } F_1^i \text{ AND } u(k-4) \text{ is } F_2^i$$
$$\text{THEN } y^i(k) = \theta_2^i y(k-1) + \theta_1^i u(k-4) + \theta_0^i \tag{32}$$

The Box–Jenkins (Gas Furnace) time series presents two variables: an input variable, the flow of gas $u(k)$, and output variable, $y(k)$, which represents the concentration of CO_2. The normalized data set represents the concentration of CO_2 $y(k)$, from $y(k-1)$ and $u(k-4)$ values, [6], [8], [11] and [13]. The first 125 points were applied for model identification using the batch algorithm (initial estimation); and 120 final points were applied to validate the model using recursive algorithm (evolving estimation).

The Takagi-Sugeno fuzzy model after batch algorithm (initial estimation) is described by:

$$R^1 : \text{ IF } y(k-1) \text{ is } F_1^1 \text{ AND } u(k-4) \text{ is } F_2^1 \text{ THEN}$$
$$y(k)^1 = -0.497y(k-1) + 0.536u(k-4) + 0.469 \tag{33}$$
$$R^2 : \text{ IF } y(k-1) \text{ is } F_1^2 \text{ AND } u(k-4) \text{ is } F_2^2 \text{ THEN}$$
$$y(k)^2 = -0.513y(k-1) + 0.490u(k-4) + 0.523 \tag{34}$$

The fuzzy Takagi-Sugeno fuzzy model resulted from the recursive algorithm (evolving estimation) is described by:

$$R^1 : \text{ IF } y(k-1) \text{ is } F_1^1 \text{ AND } u(k-4) \text{ is } F_2^1 \text{ THEN}$$
$$y(k)^1 = -0.526y(k-1) + 0.,541u(k-4) + 0.488 \tag{35}$$
$$R^2 : \text{ IF } y(k-1) \text{ is } F_1^2 \text{ AND } u(k-4) \text{ is } F_2^2 \text{ THEN}$$
$$y(k)^2 = -0.431y(k-1) + 0.629u(k-4) + 0.396 \tag{36}$$
$$R^3 : \text{ IF } y(k-1) \text{ is } F_1^3 \text{ AND } u(k-4) \text{ is } F_2^3 \text{ THEN}$$
$$y(k)^i = -0.327y(k-1) + 0.743u(k-4) + 0.358 \tag{37}$$
$$R^4 : \text{ IF } y(k-1) \text{ is } F_1^4 \text{ AND } u(k-4) \text{ is } F_2^4 \text{ THEN}$$
$$y(k)^i = -0.403y(k-1) + +0.627u(k-4) + 0.398 \tag{38}$$

The performance of the online evolving fuzzy clustering algorithm based on maximum likelihood criterion, using the recursive algorithm (evolving estimation), for prediction of the Box-Jenkins (Gas Furnace) time series is shown in Fig. 2 and its comparative analysis with other methods widely cited in the literature is shown in Table 1. It is observed that the proposed algorithm presents better results compared to those efficient methods.

3.3 Preciction of Mackey–Glass Time Series

In this subsection, computational results for prediction of the Mackey–Glass time series, are presented. The Mackey–Glass time series, is given by:

$$\frac{dx(t)}{dt} = \frac{0.2x(t-\tau)}{1 + x^{10}(t-\tau)} \tag{39}$$

Table 1. Comparative analysis for prediction of the Box–Jenkins (Gas Furance) time series

Model	RMSE
Leite, [6]	0,0421
DENFis cited by [11]	0,0190
Bordignon, [13]	0,0327
Rosa, [11]	0,0232
Plamen, [5]	0,0188
Proposed Algorithm	**0,0181**

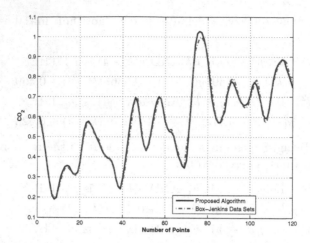

Fig. 2. Prediction of the Box–Jenkins (Gas Furnace) time series by proposed algorithm

where $\tau = 17$. The input vector is $\mathbf{X} = [x(k-13), x(k-7), x(k)]^T$ and the output is $y = x(k - 19)$. The ARX Takagi-Sugeno fuzzy inference system, is given by:

$$R^i : \text{IF } x(k - 1) \text{ is } F_1^i \text{ AND } x(k - 7) \text{ is } F_2^i \text{ AND } x(k - 13) \text{ is } F_3^i$$
$$\text{THEN } y^i(k) = x(k - 19) = \theta_3^i x(k - 1) + \theta_2^i x(k - 7) + \theta_1^i x(k - 13) + \theta_0^i \quad (40)$$

The first 4000 points were applied for model identification using the batch algorithm (initial estimation); and 8000 final points were applied to validate the model using recursive algorithm (evolving estimation). The Takagi-Sugeno fuzzy model after batch algorithm (initial estimation) is described by:

$$R^1 : \text{IF } x(k - 1) \text{ is } F_1^1 \text{ AND } x(k - 7) \text{ is } F_2^1 \text{ AND } x(k - 13) \text{ is } F_3^1$$
$$\text{THEN } y^i(k) = 0.939x(k - 1) - 2.865x(k - 7) + 2.9255x(k - 13) + 0.001 \quad (41)$$
$$R^2 : \text{IF } x(k - 1) \text{ is } F_1^2 \text{ AND } x(k - 7) \text{ is } F_2^2 \text{ AND } x(k - 13) \text{ is } F_3^2$$
$$\text{THEN } y^i(k) = 0.863x(k - 1) - 2.706x(k - 7) + 2.841x(k - 13) + 0.001 \quad (42)$$

The fuzzy Takagi-Sugeno fuzzy model resulted from the recursive algorithm (evolving estimation) is described by:

$$R^1 : \text{IF } x(k - 1) \text{ is } F_1^1 \text{ AND } x(k - 7) \text{ is } F_2^1 \text{ AND } x(k - 13) \text{ is } F_3^1$$
$$\text{THEN } y^i(k) = 0.945x(k - 1) - 2.876x(k - 7) + 2.930x(k - 13) + 0.001 \quad (43)$$
$$R^2 : \text{IF } x(k - 1) \text{ is } F_1^2 \text{ AND } x(k - 7) \text{ is } F_2^2 \text{ AND } x(k - 13) \text{ is } F_3^2$$
$$\text{THEN } y^i(k) = 0.936x(k - 1) - 2.853x(k - 7) + 2.917x(k - 13) + 0.0004 \quad (44)$$

The performance of the online evolving fuzzy clustering algorithm based on maximum likelihood criterion, using the recursive algorithm (evolving estimation), for prediction of the Mackey Glass time series is shown in Fig. 3 and its comparative analysis with other methods widely cited in the literature is shown in

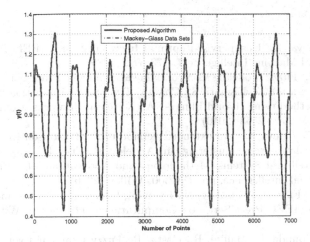

Fig. 3. Prediction of the Mackey–Glass time series by proposed algorithm

Table 2. Comparative analysis for prediction of the Mackey–Glass time series

Model	RMSE
Leite, [6]	0,0122
Neural Gas cited by [6]	0,0133
FBeM, cited by[6]	0,0642
IBeM, cited by[6]	0,0126
Plamen, [5]	0,0005
Proposed Algorithm	**0,0005**

Table 2. It is observed that the proposed algorithm presents better results compared to those efficient methods.

4 Conclusion

In this paper, an online evolving fuzzy clustering algorithm based on maximum likelihood estimator is proposed. The algorithm is an alternative to clustering problems whose learning data do not require additional tuning. The adjustments regarding the number of rules to be used and the metric of evaluation are based on maximum likelihood criterion. The results shown the efficiency of proposed algorithm as compared to others methods widely cited in the literature.

Acknowledgments. This work was supported by FAPEMA and encouraged by Ph.D. Program in Electrical Engineering of Federal University of Maranhao (PPGEE/UFMA).

References

1. Gath, I., Geva, A.: Unsupervised optimal fuzzy clustering. IEEE Trans. Pattern Analysis and Machine Intelligence **7**, 773–781 (1989)
2. Babuska, R.: Fuzzy Modeling Control. Kluwer Academic Publishers (1998)
3. Ardalani-Farsa, M., Zolfaghari, S.: Chaotic Time Series Prediction with Residual Analysis Method using Hybrid Elman-NARX Neural Networks. ELSEVIER: Neurocomputing, 2540–2553 (2010)
4. Filev, D., Georgieva, O.: An extended version of the Gustafson-Kessel algorithm for evolving data stream clustering. In: Angelov, P., Filev D., Kasabov, A. (eds.) Evolving Intelligent Systems: Methodology and Applications. IEE Press Series on Computational Intellegence, pp. 273–300. Willey (2010)
5. Angelov, P., Filev, D., Kasabov, N.: Evolving Intelligent Systems: methology and applications. IEEE Press Series on Computational Intelligence. Willey-Blackwell (2010)
6. Leite, D., Gomide, F., Ballini, R., Costa, P.: Fuzzy Granular Evolving Modeling for Time Series Prediction. In: IEEE: International Conference on Fuzzy Systems, pp. 2794–2801 (2011)
7. Samanta, B.: Prediction of Chaotic Time Series using Computational Intelligence. ELSEVIER: Expert Systems with Applications **38**, 11406–11411 (2011)
8. Melin, P., Soto, J., Castillo, O., Soria, J.: A new approach for time series prediction using ensembles of ANFis models. ELSEVIER: Expert Systems with Applications **39**, 3494–3506 (2012)
9. Ho, D.T., Garibaldi, J.M.: An Improved Optimisation Framework for Fuzzy Time-Series Prediction. In: Fuzzy Systems (FUZZ): IEEE International Conference, pp. 1–8 (2013)
10. Oysal, Y., Yilmaz, S.: Nonlinear System Identification Based on a Novel Adaptive Fuzzy Wavelet Neural Network. In: Electrical Engineering ICEE: 21st Iranian Conference, pp. 1–5 (2013)
11. Rosa, R., Gomide, F., Ballini, R.: Nonlinear System Identification Based on a Novel Adaptive Fuzzy Wavelet Neural Network. In: Machine Learning and Applications (ICMLA): 12th International Conference, vol. 2, pp. 378–383 (2013)
12. Soto, J., Melin, P., Castillo, O.: Time Series Prediction using Ensembles of Neuro-Fuzzy Models with Interval Type-2 and Type-1 Fuzzy Integrators. In: Neural Networks: The 2013 International Joint Conference, pp. 1–6 (2013)
13. Bordignon, F., Gomide, F.: Uninorm Based Evolving Neural Networks and Approximation Capabilities. ELSEVIER: Neurocomputing **127**, 13–20 (2014)

Knowledge Discovery
and Data Mining

The Grow-Shrink Strategy for Learning Markov Network Structures Constrained by Context-Specific Independences

Alejandro Edera[✉], Yanela Strappa, and Facundo Bromberg

Departamento de Sistemas de Información, Universidad Tecnológica Nacional,
Rodriguez 273, M5502 Mendoza, Argentina
{aedera,ystrappa,fbromberg}@frm.utn.edu.ar

Abstract. Markov networks are models for compactly representing complex probability distributions. They are composed by a *structure* and a set of numerical weights. The structure qualitatively describes independences in the distribution, which can be exploited to factorize the distribution into a set of compact functions. A key application for learning structures from data is to automatically discover knowledge. In practice, structure learning algorithms focused on *"knowledge discovery"* present a limitation: they use a coarse-grained representation of the structure. As a result, this representation cannot describe *context-specific independences*. Very recently, an algorithm called CSPC was designed to overcome this limitation, but it has a high computational complexity. This work tries to mitigate this downside presenting CSGS, an algorithm that uses the Grow-Shrink strategy for reducing unnecessary computations. On an empirical evaluation, the structures learned by CSGS achieve competitive accuracies and lower computational complexity with respect to those obtained by CSPC.

Keywords: Markov networks · Structure learning · Context-specific independences · Knowledge discovery · Canonical models

1 Introduction

Markov networks are parametric models for compactly representing complex probability distributions of a wide variety of domains. These models are composed by two elements: a *structure* and a set of *numerical weights*. The structure plays an important role, because it describes a set of independences that holds in the domain, thus making assumptions about the functional form or factorization of the distribution [5]. For this reason, the structure is an important source of knowledge discovery because it depicts intricate patterns of probabilistic (in)dependences between the domain variables. Usually, the structure of a Markov network can be constructed by algorithms using observations taken from an unknown distribution. Interestingly, the constructed structure can be used by human experts for discovering unknown knowledge [16]. For this reason, the problem of structure learning from data has received an increasing attention

© Springer International Publishing Switzerland 2014
A.L.C. Bazzan and K. Pichara (Eds.): IBERAMIA 2014, LNAI 8864, pp. 283–294, 2014.
DOI: 10.1007/978-3-319-12027-0_23

in machine learning [8,9,14]. However, Markov network structure learning from data is still challenging. One of the most important problems is that it requires weight learning that cannot be solved in closed-form, requiring to perform a convex optimization with inference as a subroutine. Unfortunately, inference in Markov networks is #P-complete [8].

As a result, structure learning algorithms seek the "best" approximation to the solution structure, making assumptions about the form of the solution space or the used objective function. The choice of these approximations depends on the *goal of learning* used for designing learning algorithms [8, Chapter 16]. In generative learning, we can find two goals of learning: *density estimation*, where a structure is "best" when the resulting Markov network is *accurate* for answering inference queries; and *knowledge discovery*, where a structure is "best" when it is *accurate* for qualitatively describing the independences that hold in the distribution. Depending on the goal of learning, we can categorize structure learning algorithms in: *density estimation algorithms* [4,11]; and *knowledge discovery algorithms* [1,15]. In this work, we are focusing in the knowledge discovery goal.

In practice, knowledge discovery algorithms exploit the fact that the structure can be viewed as a set of independences. Thus, for constructing a structure, such algorithms successively make *(in)dependence queries* to data in order to restrict the number of possible structures, converging toward the solution structure. To achieve a good performance in this procedure, knowledge discovery algorithms use a sound and complete *representation of the structure*: a single undirected graph. A graph can be viewed as an inference engine which efficiently represents and manipulates (in)dependences in polynomial time [14]. Unfortunately, this graph representation cannot capture a type of independences known as *context-specific independences* [6–8]. For these cases, knowledge discovery algorithms cannot achieve good results in their goal of learning, because a single graph cannot capture such independences, obscuring the acquisition of knowledge. To overcome this limitation, a novel knowledge discovery algorithm has recently been developed [3]. This algorithm, called CSPC, uses an alternative representation of the structure called *canonical models*, a particular class of *Context Specific Interaction models* (CSI models) [7]. Canonical models allow us to encode context-specific independences by using a set of mutually independent graphs. Using this representation, CSPC can learn more accurate structures than several state-of-the-art algorithms. However, despite the benefits in accuracy, CSPC presents an important downside: it has a high computational complexity, because it must perform a large number of independence queries in comparison to traditional algorithms.

Therefore, this paper focuses on reducing the number of independence queries required for learning canonical models. This reduction was thought in order to achieve competitive accuracies with respect to CSPC, but avoiding unnecessary queries. To achieve this, we present the CSGS algorithm, a knowledge discovery algorithm that learns canonical models by using the Grow-Shrink strategy [12] in a similar way to the GSMN algorithm, a Markov network structure learning algorithm [1]. Basically, under the assumption of bounded maximum degree, this

strategy constructs a structure in polynomial time by identifying local neighborhoods of each variable [12]. On an empirical evaluation, the canonical models
learned by CSGS achieve competitive accuracies and lower time complexity with
respect to those obtained by CSPC.

The remaining of this work is structured as follows: Section 2 reviews essential
concepts. Section 3 presents our contribution: CSGS. Next, Section 4 shows our
empirical evaluation of CSGS on synthetic datasets. Finally, Section 5 concludes
with directions for future work.

2   Background

We introduce our general notation. Hereon, we use the symbol V to denote a
finite set of indexes. Lowercase subscripts denote particular indexes, for instance
$a, b \in V$; in contrast, uppercase subscripts denote subsets of indexes, for instance
$W \subseteq V$. Let X_V be a set of random variables of a domain, where single variables
are denoted by single indexes in V, for instance $X_a, X_b \in X_V$ where $a, b \in V$.
We simply use X instead of X_V when V is clear from the context. We focus on
the case where X takes discrete values $x \in \text{Val}(V)$, that is, the values for any
$X_a \in X$ are discrete: $\text{Val}(a) = \{x_a^0, x_a^1, \ldots\}$. For instance, for boolean-valued
variables, that is $|\text{Val}(a)| = 2$, the symbols x_a^0 and x_a^1 denote the assignments
$X_a = 0$ and $X_a = 1$, respectively. Moreover, we overload the symbol V to also
denote the set of nodes of a graph. Finally, we use $\mathcal{X} \subseteq \text{Val}(V)$ for denoting an
arbitrary set of complete or *canonical assignments*, that is, all the variables take
a fixed value. For instance, $x_V^i \equiv x^i \in \text{Val}(V)$.

2.1   Conditional and Context-Specific Independences

A set of independence assumptions is commonly called the *structure* of a distribution because independences determine the factorization, or functional form,
of a distribution. Two of the most known types of independences are conditional
and context-specific independences. The latter has received an increased interest [2,3,6–8], because one conditional independence can be expressed as a set
of context-specific independences. Formally, context-specific independences are
defined as follows:

Definition 1. *Let $A, B, U, W \subseteq V$ be disjoint subsets of indexes, and let x_W be
some assignment in $\text{Val}(W)$. Let $p(X)$ be a probability distribution. We say that
variables X_A and X_B are* contextually independent *given X_U and the context
$X_W = x_W$, denoted by $I(X_A, X_B \mid X_U, x_W)$, iff $p(X)$ satisfies:*

$$p(x_A | x_B, x_U, x_W) = p(x_A | x_U, x_W),$$

for all assignments x_A, x_B, and x_U; whenever $p(x_B, x_U, x_W) > 0$.

As a consequence, if $I(X_A, X_B \mid X_U, x_W)$ holds in $p(X)$, then it logically
follows that $I(x_A, x_B \mid x_U, x_W)$ also holds in $p(X)$ for any assignment x_A, x_B,
x_U. Interestingly, if $I(X_A, X_B \mid X_U, x_W)$ holds for all $x_W \in \text{Val}(W)$, then we
say that the variables are conditionally independent. Formally,

Definition 2. *Let* $A, B, U, W \subseteq V$ *be disjoint subsets of indexes, and let* $p(X)$ *be a probability distribution. We say that variables* X_A *and* X_B *are conditionally independent given* X_U *and* X_W*, denoted by* $I(X_a, X_b \mid X_U, X_W)$*, iff* $p(X)$ *satisfies:*

$$p(x_A | x_B, x_U, x_W) = p(x_A | x_U, x_W),$$

for all assignments x_A*,* x_B*,* x_U*, and* x_W*; whenever* $p(x_B, x_U, x_W) > 0$*.*

Thus, a conditional independence $I(X_A, X_B \mid X_U, X_W)$ that holds in $p(X)$ can be seen as a conjunction of context-specific independences of the form $\bigwedge_{x_W} I(X_A, X_B \mid X_U, x_W)$ for all $x_W \in \mathrm{Val}(W)$. Moreover, each context-specific independence $I(X_A, X_B \mid X_U, x_W)$, that holds in $p(X)$, can be seen as a conditional independence $I(X_A, X_B \mid X_U)$ that holds in the conditional distribution $p(X_{V \setminus W} | x_W)$[2].

2.2 Representation of Structures

The independence relation $I(\cdot, \cdot \mid \cdot)$ commonly assumes *the Markov properties* [9, Section 3.1]; we also assume that probability distributions are *positive*[1]. Thus, an isomorphic mathematical object that conforms to the previous properties is an undirected graph [14]. An undirected graph G is a pair (V, E), where $E \subset V \times V$ is a set of edges which encodes conditional independences by using the graph-theoretic notion of *reachability*. As a result, the independence assertion $I(X_A, X_B \mid X_U)$ can be associated with the graphical condition: "every path from A to B is intercepted by the nodes U". Therefore, a graph G encodes knowledge in a readily accessible way, that is, the graph is highly interpretable. For instance, we can determine the adjacencies of a node $a \in V$, or its *Markov blanket* $\mathrm{MB}(a : G) \subseteq V \setminus \{a\}$[2], from its neighboring nodes in the graph G. Unfortunately, the use of a single graph as representation presents an issue when distributions hold context-specific independences, because it only encodes conditional independences, leading to excessively dense graphs [2,3].

In practice, for overcoming the previous limitation, an alternative representation of the structure consists in a set $\mathcal{F} = \{f_D^i\}$ of features, where each feature is commonly represented as an indicator function (Kronecker's delta), that is, a boolean-valued function $f_D : \mathrm{Val}(D) \mapsto \{0, 1\}$. Given an arbitrary assignment x, a feature $f_D^i(x)$ returns 1, if $x_D = x_D^i$; and 0 otherwise. A set of features is a more flexible representation than a graph, because the former can encode context-specific independences. For example, an independence of the form $I(X_a, X_b \mid x_W)$ is encoded in $\mathcal{F}$ iff for any feature $f_D^i \in \mathcal{F}' = \{f_D^i \in \mathcal{F} : x_W = x_W^i \land W \subseteq D\}$, the variables X_a and X_b do not appear simultaneously in the set D, that is, either $a \notin D$ or $b \notin D$. From a set $\mathcal{F}$ of features, we can induce a graph G by adding an edge between every pair of nodes whose variables appear together in some feature $f_D^i \in \mathcal{F}$ [3]. In a similar way, following our previous

---

[1] A distribution $p(X)$ is positive if $p(x) > 0$, for all $x \in \mathrm{Val}(V)$.

[2] We simply use $\mathrm{MB}(a)$ when the structure from which the Markov blanket is defined is clear from the context.

example, we can induce a graph from $\mathcal{F}' \subseteq \mathcal{F}$. This graph is known as an instantiated graph $G(x_W^i) = (V, E, x_W^i)$, namely, a graph $G = (V, E)$ whose nodes $W \subseteq V$ are associated to the assignment $x_W^i \in \text{Val}(W)$ [6]. Unfortunately, a set of features is not easily interpretable as a single graph, because we cannot efficiently verify independence assertions, since we are required to check all the features in $\mathcal{F}$.

A graph representation for overcoming the previous limitations is canonical models [3]. These models are a proper subset of the CSI models [6,7], which can capture context-specific independences in a more interpretable way than a set of features. A canonical model $\bar{\mathcal{G}}$ is a pair $(\mathcal{G}, \mathcal{X})$, where $\mathcal{G}$ is a collection of instantiated graphs of the form $\mathcal{G} = \{G(x^i) \in \mathcal{G} \ : \ x^i \in \mathcal{X} \subseteq \text{Val}(V)\}$, and $\mathcal{X}$ is a set of canonical assignments. These instantiated graphs are called *canonical graphs*, because every graph $G(x^i)$ is associated to a canonical assignment $x^i \in \text{Val}(V)$. In contrast to a single graph G, a canonical model requires several canonical graphs for capturing both conditional and context-specific independences. For instance, let us suppose that we want to encode the context-specific independence $I(X_a, X_b \mid x_w)$ in a canonical model $\bar{\mathcal{G}}$. By Definition 2.1, this independence implies a set of independences of the form $I(x_a, x_b \mid x_w)$, for all the assignments $x_a, x_b \in \text{Val}(a), \text{Val}(b)$. Then, each independence $I(x_a, x_b \mid x_w)$ is captured by a particular $G(x^i) \in \mathcal{G}$, one whose context x^i satisfies: $x_a^i = x_a$, $x_b^i = x_b$, and $x_w^i = x_w$.

2.3 Markov Networks

A Markov network is a parametric model for representing probability distributions in a compact way. This model is defined by a structure and a set of potential functions $\{\phi_k(X_{D_k})\}_k$, where $\phi_k : \text{Val}(D_k) \mapsto \mathbb{R}^+$, and $X_{D_k} \subseteq X$ is known as the *scope* of ϕ_k. For discrete domains, a usual representation of the potential functions is a table-based function. Markov networks can represent a very important class of probability distributions called *Gibbs distributions*, whose functional form is as follows: $p(X = x) = \frac{1}{Z} \prod_k \phi_k(x_{D_k})$, where Z is a global constant, called *partition function*, that guarantees the normalization of the product. A Gibbs distribution $p(X)$ *factorizes* over a graph G, if any scope X_{D_k} corresponds to a complete subgraph D_k (a.k.a. *clique*) of the graph G. Without loss of generality, the Gibbs distribution is often factorized by using the *maximum cliques* of the graph G. For positive distributions, one important theoretical result states the converse [5], that is, $p(X)$ can be represented as a Gibbs distribution (Markov network) that factorizes over G, if G is an *I-map*[3] for $p(X)$. As a result, given a positive Gibbs distribution $p(X)$, it can be shown that every influence on any variable $X_a \in X$ can be blocked by conditioning on its Markov blanket $\text{MB}(a : G)$, formally: $p(X_a | X_{V \setminus \{a\}}) = p(X_a | X_{\text{MB}(a)})$[4]. Interestingly, an extension of the previous property provides a criterion for

---

[3] A structure is an I-map for $p(X)$ if every independence described by the structure holds in $p(X)$.

[4] We further refer the readers to Section 3.2.1 in [9] and Section 4.3.2 in [8] for more details about Markov properties on undirected graphs.

determining the presence or absence of any edge (a, b) in an I-map graph G as follows [15, Theorem 1]:

Proposition 1. *Let $p(X)$ be a positive Gibbs distribution. Then, for any $a \in V$:*

1. *the set of assertions $\{I(X_a, X_b \mid X_{\mathrm{MB}(a) \setminus \{b\}}) : b \in \mathrm{MB}(a)\}$ is false in $p(X)$, presence of an edge (a, b), iff each assertion satisfies $p(X_a, X_b | X_{\mathrm{MB}(a)}) \neq p(X_a | X_{\mathrm{MB}(a)}) \cdot p(X_b | X_{\mathrm{MB}(a)})$.*
2. *the set of assertions $\{I(X_a, X_b \mid X_{\mathrm{MB}(a)}) : b \notin \mathrm{MB}(a)\}$ is true in $p(X)$, absence of an edge (a, b), iff each assertion satisfies $p(X_a, X_b | X_{\mathrm{MB}(a)}) = p(X_a | X_{\mathrm{MB}(a)}) \cdot p(X_b | X_{\mathrm{MB}(a)})$.*

Although a Gibbs distribution makes the structure explicit, it encodes the potential functions as a table-based function, obscuring finer-grained structures such as context-specific independences [8]. For this reason, a commonly used representation of a Markov network is the *log-linear model* defined as $p(x) = \frac{1}{Z} \exp \left\{ \sum_k \sum_i w_{i,k} f_k^i(x_{D_k}) \right\}$. A log-linear model can be constructed from a Gibbs distribution as follows: for the ith row of the table-based potential function ϕ_k, an indicator function $f_k^i(\cdot)$ is defined whose weight is $w_{i,k} = \log \phi_k(x_{D_k}^i)$.

3   Context-Specific Grow-Shrink Algorithm

In this section we present CSGS (Context-Specific Grow-Shrink), a knowledge discovery algorithm for learning the structure of Markov networks by using canonical models as structure representation. The design of CSGS was inspired by the search strategy used by CSPC for learning canonical models [3], and the GS search strategy for learning graphs [1,12]. Therefore, CSGS obtains a canonical model by learning a collection $\mathcal{G}$ of mutually independent canonical graphs, where each canonical graph $G(x^i) \in \mathcal{G}$ is learned by using the GS strategy. More precisely, GS obtains a graph in two steps: first, it *generalizes* an initial very specific graph (one that makes many independence assumptions) by adding edges. Then, the resulting graph is *specialized* by removing spurious edges. In sum, Algorithm 1 shows an overview of CSGS. In line 1 and 2, CSGS defines an initial specific canonical model from a set of canonical assignments $\mathcal{X}$. Subsequently, lines 3 and 4 construct each canonical graph $G(x^i) \in \mathcal{G}$ by using the GS strategy. For determining the presence or absence of an edge, CSGS uses Proposition 1 as criterion. The validation of this criterion is realized by eliciting context-specific independences from data in a similar way to CSPC [3, Section 4.3]. Finally, in a similar fashion to CSPC [3, Section 4.4], CSGS uses the resulting canonical model $\bar{\mathcal{G}}$ for generating a set $\mathcal{F}$ of features in order to enable us to use standard software packages for performing weight learning and inference. The remaining of this section is structured by using the key elements of CSGS: *i)* Section 3.1 describes how the initial canonical model is defined; *ii)* Section 3.2 presents the GS strategy for obtaining the canonical graphs; and *iii)* Section 3.3 concludes analyzing the time complexity of CSGS.

Algorithm 1. OVERVIEW OF CSGS

   Input: domain V, dataset $\mathcal{D}$

1 $\mathcal{X} \leftarrow$ Define the set of canonical assignments

2 $\mathcal{G} \leftarrow$ Define a set of initial graphs $\{G(x^i) \colon x^i \in \mathcal{X}\}$

3 **foreach** $G(x^i) \in \mathcal{G}$ **do**

4 | $G(x^i) \leftarrow$ GS$(G(x^i), \mathcal{D})$

5 $\mathcal{F} \leftarrow$ Feature generation from $\bar{\mathcal{G}} = (\mathcal{G}, \mathcal{X})$

3.1 Initial Canonical Model

The definition of the initial canonical model consists, firstly, in the set of canonical assignments $\mathcal{X}$. In a similar fashion to CSPC [3], this set is composed by the unique training examples in $\mathcal{D}$. This definition is the consequence of using the *data-driven approach*, that is, we use only contexts that appear in data, and for the remaining contexts which do not appear in the data, we assume that they are improbable due to the lack of other information. Lastly, once $\mathcal{X}$ is defined, we associate the most specific graph $G(x^i)$ to each context $x^i \in \mathcal{X}$, namely, the empty graph. As a result, in each initial canonical graph, every Markov blanket is empty. The idea behind the GS strategy is to add edges, thus adding nodes to each blanket.

3.2 Grow-Shrink Strategy for Learning Canonical Graphs

CSGS uses the GS strategy under the *local-to-global approach* [11,15]. In this approach, the structure is obtained by constructing each Markov blanket MB(a), $a \in V$ in turn. In this manner, for each node a, the strategy GS determines the Markov blanket MB(a) in two phases: the *grow phase* and the *shrink phase*. The grow phase adds a new edge (a, b) to E as long as Proposition 1.1 is satisfied in data. However, due to the node ordering used [1,12], the grow phase can add nodes that are outside of the blanket, resulting in spurious edges. For this reason, the shrink phase removes an edge $(a, b) \in E$ as long as Proposition 1.2 is satisfied in data. Algorithm 2 shows a more detailed description of the construction of the canonical graph $G(x^i)$. Initially, the canonical graph $G(x^i)$ is empty, then it is generalized by using the local-to-global approach shown in the loop of line 1. In this loop, the two steps of GS are performed: the grow phase, starting in line 2; and the shrink phase, starting in line 5. In each iteration of the main loop, line 4 and 7 change the Markov blanket by adding/removing new edges to the current set E of edges. Once the main loop has finished, the Markov blankets of each node are obtained and, in consequence, the resulting canonical graph encodes context-specific independences.

3.3 Asymptotic Complexity

As is usual in knowledge discovery algorithms, we analyze the complexity of CSGS by determining the number of independence tests performed for constructing a structure from data. Let m be the number of unique examples in the

---

Algorithm 2. GS STRATEGY

Input: graph $G(x^i) = (V, E, x^i)$, dataset $\mathcal{D}$

1 **foreach** *node* $a \in V$ **do**
2   **foreach** *node* $b \in V \setminus (\mathrm{MB}(a : G(x^i)) \cup \{a\})$ **do**
3   **if** $I(X_a, X_b \mid x^i_{\mathrm{MB}(a : G(x^i))})$ *is false in* $\mathcal{D}$ **then**
4             $E \leftarrow E \cup (a, b)$
5   **foreach** $b \in \mathrm{MB}(a)$ **do**
6   **if** $I(X_a, X_b \mid x^i_{\mathrm{MB}(a : G(x^i)) \setminus \{b\}})$ *is true in* $\mathcal{D}$ **then**
7             $E \leftarrow E \setminus (a, b)$
8 **return** $G(x^i)$

---

dataset, the complexity of performing a test is linear in m. However, this cost can be particularly high if m is large. In our implementation of CSGS, we reduce this cost by using ADTree [13]. We assume that nodes in line 1 in Algorithm 2 are taken in an unspecified but fixed order, and we bound the maximum degree of a node to $k = \mathrm{argmax}_{G(x^i) \in \mathcal{G}} \, \mathrm{argmax}_{a \in V}(|\mathrm{MB}(a : G(x^i))|)$. Let n be the number of variables, and let $G(x^i) = (V, E, x^i)$ be an empty canonical graph, we can decompose the analysis into the number of tests performed by grow and shrink phases. In the grow phase, a test is performed for each edge $(a, b) \notin E$, resulting in $O(n^2)$ tests. At the end of the grow phase, the size of a blanket is k at worst, thus shrink phase performs $O(nk)$ tests. Additionally, Algorithm 1 performs the GS strategy m times, one per each initial canonical graph. Therefore, the total complexity is $O(m(n^2 + nk))$ independence tests.

4   Empirical Evaluation

This section shows experimental results obtained from the structures learned by CSGS and several structure learning algorithms on synthetic datasets. Basically, the goals of our experiments remark the greatly practical utility of our algorithm in a two-fold manner. First, we compare the accuracy of the structures learned by CSGS and CSPC, as well as by other state-of-the-art structure learners. Second, we compare the computational complexity between CSGS and CSPC. For evaluating the accuracy of the learned structures, we use the underlying distributions that were sampled to generate the synthetic datasets; since there is a direct correlation between the correctness of the structure and the accuracy of the distribution[5], the accuracy of a structure can be measured by comparing the similarity between the learned and underlying distributions. On the other hand, for evaluating the computational complexity, we report the number of tests performed for constructing the structures[5]. Lastly, an open source implementation of CSGS algorithm as well as the synthetic datasets used in this section are publicly available[6].

---

[5] Additional empirical results are available in the online appendix http://dharma.frm. utn.edu.ar/papers/iberamia14/supplementary-information-on-csgs.pdf

[6] http://dharma.frm.utn.edu.ar/papers/iberamia14

4.1 Datasets

The datasets of our experiment are used in [2,3] and were sampled from Markov networks with context-specific independences for different n numbers of variables that range from 6 to 9, varying their sizes from 20 to 100k datapoints. For each n, 10 datasets were sampled from 10 different Markov networks with fixed structure but randomly choosing their weights. For more details, we refer the readers to [3, Appendix B]. Roughly speaking, the underlying structure of these models encodes independence assertions of the form $I(X_a, X_b \mid x_w^1)$ for all pairs $a, b \in V \setminus \{w\}$, becoming dependent when $X_w = x_w^0$. In this way, the underlying structure can be seen as two instantiated graphs: a fully connected graph $G(x_w^0)$, and a star graph $G(x_w^1)$ whose central node is x_w^1. Despite the simplicity of this structure, this cannot be correctly captured by using a single graph, yet it can be captured by sets of features or canonical models. On the other hand, as the maximum degree of the underlying structure is equal to n, learning the structure is a challenging problem [2,15]. The generated datasets are partitioned into: a *training set* (70%) and a *validation set* (30%). The validation set is used by density estimation algorithms to set their tuning parameters. Specifically, they use different tuning parameters for learning several structures from the training set, selecting one whose pseudo-likelihood on the validation set is maximum. In contrast, CSGS, CSPC, GSMN and IBMAP-HC algorithms do not use tuning parameters, thus they learn structures by using the whole dataset, i.e. the union of training and validation sets.

4.2 Methodology

In this subsection we explain the methodology used for evaluating our approach against several structure learning algorithms. First, we explain which structure learning algorithms are used as competitors and their configuration settings, and then we describe the method used for measuring the accuracies of the learned structures: *Kullback-Leibler divergence* (KL) [8, Appendix A].

CSGS is compared against CSPC (Context-Specific Parent and Children) algorithm and two representative algorithms for knowledge discovery and density estimation goals. The knowledge discovery algorithms are: GSMN (Grow-Shrink Markov Network learning algorithm) [1], and IBMAP-HC (IBMAP Hill-Climbing) [15]. For a fair comparison, we use the Pearson's χ^2 as the statistical independent test with a significance level of 0.05 for CSGS, CSPC and GSMN, but not for IBMAP-HC which only works with the Bayesian statistical test with a threshold equal to 0.5. On the other hand, the density estimation algorithms are: GSSL (Generate Select Structure Learning) [4], and DTSL (Decision Tree Structure Learner) [11]. For a fair comparison, we replicate the recommended tuning parameters for both algorithms detailed in [4], and [10], respectively. KL divergence is a "distance measure" widely used to evaluate how similar are two distributions. Thus, using the learned structures, we obtain Markov networks by

learning their weights with pseudo-likelihood[7], measuring their KL divergences
with respect to the underlying distribution. Lower values of KL divergence indicate better accuracy.

4.3 Results of Experimentation

Figure 1 presents the KL divergences computed from the structures learned by
the different algorithms. For comparison reasons, Figure 1 also shows the KL
divergence computed by using a Markov network whose structure is the underlying one, showing the best KL divergence that can be obtained. In these results,
we can see three important trends. First, the structures learned by CSGS reach
similar divergences in most cases to CSPC. Second, in most cases, the divergences
obtained by CSGS and CSPC are better than those obtained by the other structure learners. Finally, the divergences of CSGS and CSPC are closer to the divergences obtained by the underlying structure. These trends allow us to conclude
that the structures learned by CSGS and CSPC can encode the context-specific

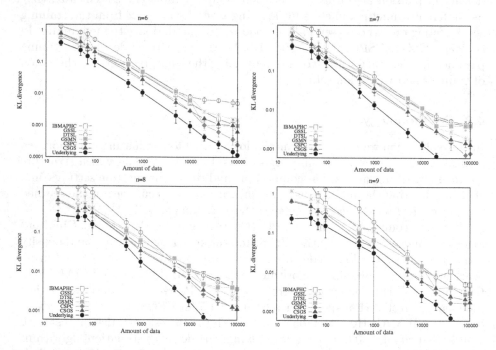

Fig. 1. KL divergences over increasing amounts of data for structures learned by several learning algorithms. For comparison reasons, the KL divergence of the underlying
structure is shown. Every point represents the average and standard deviation over ten
datasets with a fixed size. Lower values indicate better accuracy.

---

[7] Weight learning was performed using version 0.5.0 of the Libra toolkit (http://libra.
cs.uoregon.edu/).

independences present in data, resulting in Markov networks more accurate than those obtained by the remaining algorithms. Figure 2 presents the number of tests performed by CSGS and CSPC for learning the structures used previously for computing the KL divergences. As shown, the number of tests performed by CSGS is smaller than those performed by CSPC. The difference between both dramatically increases as data increases. These results show the great impact of using the GS strategy for learning canonical models. In conclusion, the results shown in both figures show that CSGS is an efficient alternative to CSPC for learning canonical models.

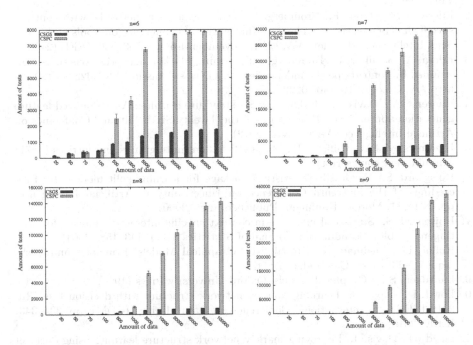

Fig. 2. Number of tests performed by CSGS and CSPC for learning structures over increasing amounts of data. Every bar represents the average and standard deviation over ten datasets with a fixed size.

5   Conclusions and Future Work

In this work we presented CSGS, a new knowledge discovery algorithm for learning Markov network structures by using canonical models. CSGS is similar to the CSPC algorithm [3], except that CSGS uses an alternative search strategy called Grow-Shrink [1,12], that avoids performing unnecessary independence tests. We evaluated our algorithm against CSPC and several state-of-the-art learning algorithms on synthetic datasets. In our results, CSGS learned structures with similar accuracy to CSPC but performing a reduced number of tests. The directions of future work are focused on further reducing the computational complexity and improving the quality of the learned structures using alternative search strategies. For instance, IBMAP-HC on the side of knowledge discovery algorithms [15], and GSSL on the side of density estimation algorithms [4].

References

1. Bromberg, F., Margaritis, D., Honavar, V.: Efficient Markov network structure discovery using independence tests. Journal of Artificial Intelligence Research 35(2), 449 (2009)
2. Edera, A., Schlüter, F., Bromberg, F.: Learning markov networks with context-specific independences. In: The 25th International Conference on Tools with Artificial Intelligence, Herndon, VA, USA, November 4-6, pp. 553–560. IEEE (2013)
3. Edera, A., Schlüter, F., Bromberg, F.: Learning Markov networks structures constrained by context-specific independences. viXra submission 1405.0222v1 (2014), http://viXra.org/abs/1405.0222
4. Haaren, J.V., Davis, J.: Markov network structure learning: A randomized feature generation approach. In: Proceedings of the Twenty-Sixth National Conference on Artificial Intelligence. AAAI Press (2012)
5. Hammersley, J.M., Clifford, P.: Markov fields on finite graphs and lattices (1971) (unpublished manuscript)
6. Højsgaard, S.: Yggdrasil: a statistical package for learning split models. In: Proceedings of the Sixteenth Conference on Uncertainty in Artificial Intelligence, pp. 274–281. Morgan Kaufmann Publishers Inc. (2000)
7. Højsgaard, S.: Statistical inference in context specific interaction models for contingency tables. Scandinavian Journal of Statistics 31(1), 143–158 (2004)
8. Koller, D., Friedman, N.: Probabilistic Graphical Models: Principles and Techniques. MIT Press, Cambridge (2009)
9. Lauritzen, S.L.: Graphical models. Oxford University Press (1996)
10. Lowd, D., Davis, J.: Learning Markov network structure with decision trees. In: 2010 IEEE 10th International Conference on Data Mining (ICDM), pp. 334–343. IEEE (2010)
11. Lowd, D., Davis, J.: Improving markov network structure learning using decision trees. Journal of Machine Learning Research 15, 501–532 (2014), http://jmlr.org/papers/v15/lowd14a.html
12. Margaritis, D., Thrun, S.: Bayesian network induction via local neighborhoods. Tech. rep., DTIC Document (2000)
13. Moore, A., Lee, M.S.: Cached Suficient Statistics for Efficient Machine Learning with Large Datasets. Journal of Artificial Intelligence Research 8, 67–91 (1998)
14. Pearl, J.: Probabilistic Reasoning in Intelligent Systems: Networks of Plausible Inference, 1st edn. Morgan Kaufmann Publishers Inc. (1988)
15. Schlüter, F., Bromberg, F., Edera, A.: The IBMAP approach for Markov network structure learning. Annals of Mathematics and Artificial Intelligence, 1–27 (2014), http://dx.doi.org/10.1007/s10472-014-9419-5
16. Smith, V.A., Yu, J., Smulders, T.V., Hartemink, A.J., Jarvis, E.D.: Computational inference of neural information flow networks. PLoS Computational Biology 2(11), e161 (2006)

An Evolutionary Methodology for Handling Data Scarcity and Noise in Monitoring Real Events from Social Media Data

Roberto C.S.N.P. Souza, Denise E.F. de Brito[✉], Rodrigo L. Cardoso,
Derick M. de Oliveira, Wagner Meira Jr., and Gisele L. Pappa

Computer Science Department, Universidade Federal de Minas
Gerais (UFMG), Belo Horizonte, Brazil
{nalon,denise.brit,rodrigolc,derickmath,meira,
glpappa}@dcc.ufmg.br

Abstract. Every day text-based social media channels are flooded with millions of messages that comprise the most diverse topics. These channels are being used as a rich data source for monitoring different real world events such as natural disasters and disease outbreaks, to name a few. However, depending on the event being investigated, this monitoring may be severely affected by data scarcity and noise, allowing just coarse grain analysis in terms of time and space, which lack the specificity necessary for supporting actions at the local level. In this context, we present a methodology to handle data scarcity and noise while monitoring real world events using social media data in a fine grain. We apply our methodology to dengue-related data from Brazil, and show how it could improve significantly the performance of event monitoring at a local scale almost doubling the correlation observed in some cases.

Keywords: Data mining · Dengue · Disease surveillance · Social media

1 Introduction

Every day text-based social media channels are flooded with millions of messages that comprise the most diverse topics. As these channels grow large, people are more committed to different subjects, discuss their personal lives, preferences in a manifold perspective and even health conditions. Flavored by the huge potential of such media, a large number of recent research have focused on the monitoring of social platforms using online data in order to detect real life events, such as natural disasters [17] and disease outbreaks [6,14], to name a few. The common approach is to consider people as sensors and their messages about an event (specified by a related set of keywords) as an indicator of its occurrence or intensity, that is, we predict the intensity of an event as a function of the number of messages posted about that event. Previous work have shown that text-based social media and other general mechanisms on the Web are very useful in the context of disease surveillance [10], [3], [6] and [14]. However, there is still

© Springer International Publishing Switzerland 2014
A.L.C. Bazzan and K. Pichara (Eds.): IBERAMIA 2014, LNAI 8864, pp. 295–306, 2014.
DOI: 10.1007/978-3-319-12027-0_24

significant room for improvement when we try to increase both the accuracy and the specificity of the predictions.

There are two key issues while using data from social networks for real-world event prediction:

1. Data availability: In order to make predictions, it is necessary to have enough data available about the event to be predicted. One important trade-off here is regarding the location specificity of the event. For instance, consider disease surveillance, which must be as accurate as possible regarding the location of the surges. The location grain should be a trade off between the area and the volume of messages. In practice, we should have enough messages for sake of prediction but they should be as restricted as possible w.r.t location.

2. Noisy data: Noisy data are inherent to social networks as a consequence of both language ambiguity and other related factors such as news and irony/sarcasm. Noisy data disturb our predictive ability because they may cause significant variations on the volume of messages that are not directly related to the event being predicted.

In this work we present a methodology for dealing with both issues and improving our ability to predict real events from social network data. Our methodology is based on determining more homogeneous domains for both data (social network and event), where the factors that must be used for sake of prediction are better determined. We demonstrate the effectiveness of our methodology in the context of dengue disease surveillance based on Twitter data as follows.

One basic premise from our approach is that every single message posted on a social platform and containing the related keywords should be taken into account as an event indicator, regardless the associated sentiment or opinion it carries. That is, we assume that people are expressing opinions about a specific event because the environment they live is somehow affected by that event and they are not randomly doing it. However, we also consider that different opinions or perspectives associated with each message represent a different level of public perception about an event. In this sense, our strategy consists of defining the weight of the various semantic categories that may be associated with a message in order to better correlate social media data and real world event.

In order to obtain such weights we employ an evolutionary strategy, more specifically a genetic algorithm (GA) that determines the coefficients that maximize the correlation between collected data and event-related statistics. We apply our methodology to dengue-related data from Brazil, from 2011 to 2013 and show that monitoring at a local scale, weighted sentiment categories improved our results.

2   Related work

In recent years, social media data and other Web-based mechanisms have been successfully used for disease surveillance. Most of these works are focused on the monitoring at global scale in the sense that one performs the analysis at state, region or even national level.

Global-scale: Global strategies may be divided into Web-based mechanisms and social media:

Web-based mechanisms: These approaches make use of different strategies, as, for instance, [12] crawled search queries submitted to a website in Sweden and found that certain web queries on influenza match data from traditional surveillance systems. Several works leveraged search engine queries, as follows. [3] observed that specific search keywords hold high correlation with dengue incidence in Singapore and Bangkok. In a similar fashion, [10] were able to accurately estimate the level of influenza activity at a regional-level in the United States (US) and [5] investigated the performance of such engines for surveillance, also in US during the type-A influenza pandemic. It is noteworthy that [16] used search engine queries for influenza surveillance and, even though part of real data was obtained at a city-level, the analysis was performed considering 9 US census regions.

Social media: A significant number of recent works rely on the real time nature of social media, specially Twitter, for disease monitoring. For example, [6] and [14] crawled Twitter messages to track influenza rates at the regional-level in UK and at the national-level in the US, respectively. In a more comprehensive perspective, [15] extended the analysis to the state-level for different ailments such as allergies, depression, and also flu, among others. In [1] and [2], a system was proposed to monitor messages posted on Twitter mentioning flu indicators to track the spread of an influenza epidemic at the regional-level. More recent work used social media data (and also web queries) for influenza prediction in Portugal [18].

Local-scale: Contrasting to the most of the other works, in [11], a city-level monitoring is performed based on dengue-related posts on Twitter. The strategy consists of analyzing content of collected messages to capture public perception. Based on that analysis, only messages expressing personal experience with the disease are used for dengue prediction.

Our work. This paper lies between the two approaches described above. We propose a methodology to work at a fine grain. The focus of our work is the monitoring of dengue disease in Brazil using Twitter messages. In Brazil the responsibility for taking public precautions regarding dengue surveillance belongs to each city hall. Hence, we are interested in a city-level analysis, different from most previous work. Besides, differently from [11], we assume that each Twitter message posted with different purposes should account as dengue epidemic indicator. Next section discusses in details the proposed methodology.

3 Proposed Methodology

This section proposes a new methodology to deal with data scarcity and noise when monitoring events using text-based social media. Recall that our strategy considers that every single message posted on a social media platform containing keywords related to the event of interest should de considered, regardless of the sentiment, opinion or fact it expresses.

The methodology is divided into four steps: (i) categorization of messages according to their sentiment or opinion; (ii) identification of data dimensions where the volume of messages better correlates to the intensity of the event; (iii) determination of weights to each message category and (iv) data correlation analysis.

Message categorization: The first step, which is to classify messages according to their sentiment, can follow a supervised or an unsupervised approach. In scenarios of disease surveillance, previous studies have already proposed sets of categories for that: Personal Experience, Ironic/Sarcastic, Information, Opinion, Campaign and Spam or non-related tweets [4]. In this case, manually labeled data is required to train a classifier. However, in scenarios where there is no set of predefined categories, clustering techniques can be used to generate preliminary groups. In the methodology proposed here we use all categories defined in [4] but the last, as we filter out spam and tweets not related to the dengue context.

Dimension identification: The second step identifies data characteristics that may be correlated to the number of messages and intensity of events. For example, in disease surveillance, these dimensions include the population size and the number of real cases of the disease. The bigger the population, the greater the number of messages. Similarly, the greater the number of cases the greater the number of messages. Identifying these dimensions is important because they will help creating different scenarios of analysis, where we know the volume of messages may vary significantly. For instance, in very populated cities, the number of messages posted in social media is bigger than in less populated cities. Hence, the importance of messages in different categories (and the number of messages in each category) will also vary.

Weight determination: The third step determines the contribution of each message category for predicting the event of interest, and this contribution is assessed according to the correlation between social media data and the real data. For the sake of simplicity, we first assume these message categories can be linearly combined to produce a good approximation of the real event. Consider a set of messages M_i posted along a time period, where i corresponds to one of the n available categories. Consider also the real series of events E. We want to find a set of n coefficients w_i that increase the correlation between $|E|$ and $\sum_{i=1}^{n} w_i \times |M_i|$.

These coefficients are estimated by a genetic algorithm [8]. Genetic algorithms are stochastic methods based on Darwin's theory of evolution and survival of the fittest. They evolve a population of individuals, where each individual represents a solution to the problem. The first population is randomly generated, and individuals are evaluated according to a fitness function, which is problem-dependent and assesses the quality of an individual to solve the problem being tackled. Fitter individuals have a higher probability of being selected to undergo crossover and mutation operations, according to user defined probabilities. The individuals produced by these operators form a new population, and the process is repeated again until a stopping criterion is met. Next we present the key characteristics of the genetic algorithm we proposed:

1.Individual Representation: Considering the problem of optimizing the n coefficients of different categories of messages, each individual represents a set of n real values. Before fitness calculation, these values are normalized within the [0,1] interval.

2.Fitness Function: The fitness function calculates the Pearson's correlation between the real series of events $|E|$ and $\sum_{i=1}^{n} w_i \times |M_i|$, where w_i are the coefficients evolved by the GA.

3.Operators: The individuals generated and evaluated are selected according to a tournament selection, which randomly chooses k individuals from the population, and elects the one with the best fitness value as the winner. The crossover operator used here is a bounded version of simulated binary crossover (SBX) [7]. SBX works with a parameter η, which represents a spread factor. The higher the spread factor, the more similar are the generated individuals to their parents. A simple mutation operator, which randomly shuffles the values within the positions of an individual, has been implemented.

Correlation Analysis The last step of our methodology aims to evaluate the correlation between the intensity of the events and the weighted volume of messages. First we should define the correlation metric to be used, in our case Pearson's correlation. We also define the comparison dimensions, that is, which data will be compared considering dimensions such as time period and location. We then design the set of experimental evaluations to be performed, that is, the set of experiments whose results will be compared. In our case we compare the performance of individual categories (in particular the personal experience category), all categories without weights and the weighted function we determined. This analysis will seek to understand the scenarios where our proposal worked better or no and the reasons behind the achieved performance.

4   Experimental Results

This section applies the methodology previously proposed to perform a local analysis of dengue cases based on messages posted on Twitter, and considers 298 different cities. Each of the phases of the proposed methodology are explored in the following sections.

4.1   Data Collecting and Preprocessing

In order to obtain dengue-related messages, we define as keywords the terms "dengue" and "Aedes". The dataset is composed by Twitter messages posted from January 2011 to December 2013. These messages are restricted to 140 characters, and the Twitter API also provides the user's geographic location when informed. User location can appear in three different forms: (i) a text field filled in by the user, which accepts any set of terms; (ii) a location suggested to the user according to his IP; (iii) geographic coordinates, in case of users tweeting from mobiles.

As we are interested in a city-level analysis, it is crucial all users are associated with a valid location. In this sense, we first removed from the data all tweets

Table 1. Number of tweets with respective location details

Location details	# tweets (% total crawled)
Total crawled with geographic location	2,164,450 (100%)
"Brazil" in location field	1,174,929 (54.28%)
After filtering other countries	1,174,676 (54.27%)
Location resolved	768,408 (35.50%)

coming from places different from Brazil, i.e. messages not presenting "Brazil" (or "Brasil", as in Portuguese) in the location field. In order to maximize recall, we verified the location fields very carefully, removing eventual tweets that had Brazil as another type of locality but country. After that, we assumed that all remaining messages were in Portuguese, and exhaustively seek for consistent and non-ambiguous names of Brazilian cities and their respective states. Tweets whose location were not resolved after these steps were discarded. Table 1 shows the number of messages after applying the filters aforementioned. Also, in the text pre-processing phase we filtered out URL's and accents. Bi-grams were created joining adjacent words with a separator, and then stop-words were filtered out as well as bi-grams composed of two stop-words.

4.2 Tweets Classification

With the dataset in hand, the first phase of the methodology was to classify tweets into different groups according to their sentiment or opinion. We do that in a supervised manner. In order to create a representative training dataset we used a selective sampling approach [13], and manually labeled 2,142 messages from 2010.

Similarly to [11], the tweets are classified into one out of five categories: Personal Experience, Ironic/Sarcastic, Information, Opinion and Campaign. The messages are classified using the Lazy Associative Classification Algorithm (LAC) [19]. The classifier uses association rules to assign textual patterns to the predefined categories. Each rule represents a vote with different weight depending on the rule confidence. A message is always assigned to the category with more votes.

As the confidence of a rule can change the category a tweet is assigned to, and we know that the bigger the size of a rule the higher its confidence, we performed a cross-validation on the training set varying the maximum rule size parameter. As the number of rules grow exponentially with rule size we fixed the values as 2, 3 or 4. We ran a 10-fold-cross-validation with 10 different seeds. Table 2 presents the results. As the results of accuracy obtained were very similar, we decided to use the lowest value, which demands less computational time.

4.3 Defining Different Scenarios of Analysis

Having categorized the messages, now we have to identify the data dimensions more correlated to the number of tweets posted, and guide this process according to the

Table 2. 10-fold-cross-validation results with 10 different seed for different maximum rule size

Rule size	Accuracy (all seeds)	Standard deviation (all seeds)
2	0.76504	0.00295
3	0.77012	0.00183
4	0.76755	0.00238

correlation of the generated model and the real data. In order to calculate data correlation, we first aggregate the number of tweets belonging to each category in a weekly basis, since official dengue reports provided by Brazilian Health Ministry is aggregated in the same way.

We start the analysis by all Brazilian cities with population higher than 100,000 inhabitants, which comprises 298 cities. These cities were grouped according to two dimensions: population size and dengue incidence rate. As each group tends to have homogeneous cities, this approach allow us to perform the analysis under different scenarios.

The dengue incidence rate follows the same scale that traditional surveillance system alarms do, defined by the Health Ministry and which comprises three ranges (always per 100 thousand inhabitants): under 100 cases – low incidence; 100 to 299 – medium incidence, from 300 cases on – high incidence. As this classification is punctual, we used the population estimates of 2013 to calculate the incidences along the three years, and the incidence rate considered for a city corresponds to the highest range the city reached within this time period.

Table 3 presents the characteristics of the groups of analysis and the number of cities within each group. Under our hypothesis of data scarcity, in Table 3 we signed the different scenarios to indicate our expectation of improvement on dengue cases prediction with the application of the proposed methodology. The symbol ▲indicates scenarios where we expect major improvement since it comprises the cities with lower number of sensors and also lower incidence rates. On the other hand, ●marks scenarios where we expect the methodology to obtain similar results since the total available information should be higher. Scenarios marked with both symbols are expect to present any of the two described behaviors. Table 4 shows detailed information about the number of messages per city in each scenario of analysis.

4.4   Weighted Messages and Correlation Analysis

The main objective of the proposed methodology is to improve the correlation between Twitter data and official dengue reports in scenarios of data scarcity (scenarios 0, 1 and 2 in Table 4) by taking into account all dengue-related messages. Therefore, this section compares the correlation between Twitter data and official statistics obtained in three different ways: considering only personal experience messages; considering all messages, regardless of their category, should have the same importance; considering the results obtained by the GA.

Table 3. Characteristics of population and dengue incidence per group of analysis. (·) represent the number of cities within that group.

Scenario 0 (131) ▲	Scenario 1 (52) ▲	Scenario 2 (23) ▲•
low incidence	medium incidence	high incidence
small population	small population	small population
Scenario 3 (45) ▲	Scenario 4 (20) ▲•	Scenario 5 (12) •
low incidence	medium incidence	high incidence
medium population	medium population	medium population
Scenario 6 (19) ▲•	Scenario 7 (8) •	Scenario 8 (6) •
low incidence	medium incidence	high incidence
large population	large population	large population

Table 4. Detailed number of tweets per city in each scenario. The first figure represents the total number of messages related to a specific category within a scenario. The number in parenthesis represents the rounded total number of messages belonging to that category divided by the number of cities within each scenario.

Scenario	# P.Exp.	# Ironic	# Opin.	# Info.	# Camp.
0	8309 (63)	10047 (76)	3901 (29)	11247 (85)	4058 (30)
1	7212 (138)	4481 (86)	2402 (46)	7659 (147)	2783 (53)
2	5481 (238)	2597 (112)	1545 (67)	4413 (191)	1815 (78)
3	12090 (268)	12425 (276)	4952 (110)	15165 (337)	5935 (5935)
4	12944 (647)	7634 (381)	4188 (209)	14337 (716)	4949 (247)
5	10348 (862)	4956 (413)	2750 (229)	7717 (643)	3186 (265)
6	43213 (2274)	41680 (2193)	17604 (926)	57799 (3042)	19308 (1016)
7	48794 (6099)	26024 (3253)	15995 (1999)	51558 (6444)	21017 (2627)
8	23690 (3948)	13712 (2285)	8352 (1392)	30523 (5087)	11450 (1908)
All	172081 (577)	123556 (414)	61689 (207)	200418 (672)	74501 (250)

In order to setup our methodology we used the DEAP tool [9], which is a framework that provides rapid prototype for evolutionary algorithms. For all cities we set the GA parameters as follows: 250 individuals evolved for 100 generations and tournament size of 3.

Due to space restrictions, Table 5 presents the correlation obtained by the three approaches aforementioned for 20 cities coming from different scenarios. Table 5 shows that for many cities the GA improves the correlation between social media data and the official dengue reports. Among the cities with the best results are smaller ones such as Sobral, Itabira, Angra dos Reis and Presidente Prudente, corroborating our initial hypothesis. On the other hand, for cities where the GA did not help significantly improving the results, two different scenarios were identified. The first scenario includes cities where personal experience messages are highly correlated with real cases, and adding other categories introduced no additional information to the model. The second scenario comprises cities where data are so scarce that even applying our methodology we could not obtain high correlations.

Table 5. Pearson's correlation measured between collected Twitter data and official dengue reports provided by Brazilian Health Ministry

City	Scenario	Pers. exp.	Complete data	GA
Americana	0	0.69849	0.66655	0.73856
Angra dos Reis	2	0.73787	0.78229	0.82366
Balneario Camboriu	0	0.06475	0.18414	0.18944
Belo Horizonte	8	0.97114	0.85872	0.97114
Cabo de Santo Agostinho	1	0.05335	0.00240	0.05335
Cuiaba	4	0.81636	0.76519	0.82048
Governador Valadares	4	0.64792	0.65170	0.69090
Itabira	1	0.36958	0.60337	0.69889
Jau	0	0.29092	0.19174	0.29092
Juazeiro do Norte	4	0.44257	0.70902	0.71369
Macapa	3	0.54160	0.64957	0.68035
Mossoro	0	0.81722	0.80474	0.84706
Parnamirim	7	0.42923	0.33175	0.58777
Petropolis	3	0.62612	0.72937	0.76548
Presidente Prudente	1	0.64152	0.69840	0.75159
Santana	1	0.07383	0.14538	0.21221
Sobral	0	0.50593	0.67816	0.71832
Sorocaba	7	0.79378	0.81262	0.83949
Taubate	4	0.91643	0.89527	0.92685
Tres Lagoas	2	0.15629	0.24186	0.25507

They include cities such as Cabo de Santo Agostinho, Santana and Tres Lagoas, which do not have enough tweets for any type, and cities with very low number of dengue cases, such as Balneario Camboriu and Jau.

Figure 1 shows the time series data for two cities, Sobral and Governador Valadares, two plots for each city. The blue lines represent the real dengue cases reported by the Health Ministry and are the same in both plots. The red lines are the numbers generated from the tweets. The top plot represents the time series after applying the GA, and weighting different message categories before aggregating them to generate the series. The bottom plot shows the time series considering only messages expressing personal experience. It is interesting to notice that our strategy smoothed the data. For instance, for Sobral, the second plot presents two sharp peaks near weeks 120 and 130. These same peaks seems to appear in the top plot, but they were smoothed after the weighting process. The same observation can be carried out for Governador Valadares. Notice that in week 60 the bottom plot has a peak reaching 20 tweets of personal experience. On the other hand, the weighted process leads to a value of 7 for the same week, for the same number of cases as we can see in the right-side axis. This shows that our strategy also plays an important role in reducing noise.

Figure 2 presents the message categories distribution per scenario. The left hand side was obtained by computing the proportion of each category relative to the total

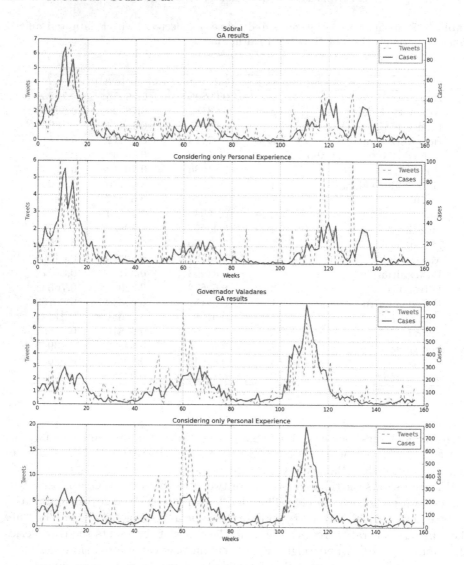

Fig. 1. Time series data for the cities of Sobral and Governador Valadares

number of messages. The right side was obtained by first weighting the number of tweets in each city and then aggregating the total per scenario to obtain the proportion. It is interesting to notice that the proportion of different message categories throughout the scenarios (left hand side) is almost constant, presenting a slightly variation. On the other hand, when we observe the weighted message categories distribution (right hand side) an interesting information appears. Observe that the scenarios are sorted in a different manner (by column) in order to better visualize the result. For the same level of dengue incidence, as the population increases the importance of messages expressing personal experiences also increases. In this sense, in low population cities our approach confirms our hypthesis that all messages should be considered as source of information for dengue surveillance.

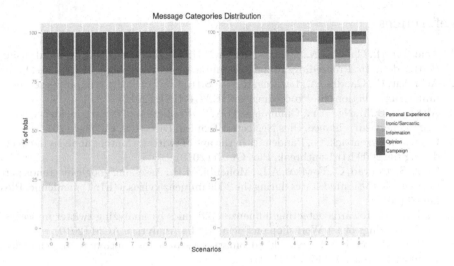

Fig. 2. Messages category distribution per scenario. The left hand side represents the percentage of each category relative to the total number of tweets per scenario. The right hand side represents the percentage of each weighted category relative to the total number of tweets per scenario.

5 Conclusion and Future Work

This paper presented a methodology for handling data scarcity and noise in event prediction based on text data coming from social media. The idea is to use every message containing the selected terms associated with the event of interest as event indicators.

The methodology classifies the messages according to their content; identifies dimensions that are highly correlated with the intensity of the event and generates different scenarios of analysis from these dimensions; finds different sets of weights for different message categories and finally analyses the correlations between real and social network indicators.

Results showed that, for dengue surveillance, defining different scenarios according to the population size and disease incidence helps understanding the impact of different sentiment categories in those scenarios. The methodology presented a good strategy to cope with data scarcity and also noise by assigning different weights to the messages.

As future work we plan to extend the methodology to consider temporal and spatial information. This could improve the monitoring at a local scale. Also, we will increase the scope of the application by analyzing cities with less inhabitants, making the problem of data scarcity even more prominent.

References

1. Achrekar, H., Gandhe, A., Lazarus, R., Yu, S.H., Liu, B.: Predicting flu trends using twitter data. In: Proceedings of the Communications Workshops. IEEE (2011)
2. Achrekar, H., Gandhe, A., Lazarus, R., Yu, S.H., Liu, B.: Twitter improves seasonal influenza prediction. In: Proceedings of HEALTHINF (2012)
3. Althouse, B.M., Ng, Y.Y., Cummings, D.A.T.: Prediction of dengue incidence using search query surveillance. Plos Neglected Tropical Disease 8, e1258–4 (2011)
4. Chew, C., Eysenback, G., Pandemics in the age of twitter: Content analysis of tweets during the 2009 h1n1 outbreak. Plos One 5 (2010)
5. Cook, S., Conrad, C., Fowlkes, A.L., Mohebbi, M.H.: Assessing google flu trends performance in the united states during the 2009 influenza virus a (h1n1) pandemic. Plos One 6 (2011)
6. Cullota, A.: Towards detecting influenza epidemics by analyzing twitter messages. In: Proceedings of 1st Workshop on Social Media Analytics. ACM (2010)
7. Deb, K., Agrawal, R.B.: Simulated binary crossover for continuous search space. Complex Systems 9, 115–148 (1995)
8. Einben, A.E., Smith, J.E.: Introduction to evolutionary computing. Springer (2003)
9. Fortin, F., De Rainville, F.M., Gardner, M., Parizeau, M., Gagne, C.: DEAP: Evolutionary algorithms made easy. Journal of Machine Learning Research 13, 2171–2175 (2012)
10. Ginsberg, J., Mohebbi, M.H., Patel, R.S., Brammer, L., Smolinski, M.S., Brilliant, L.: Detecting influenza epidemics using search engine query data. Nature 457, 1012–1015 (2009)
11. Gomide, J., Veloso, A., Meira Jr., W., Almeida, V., Benevenuto, F., Ferraz, F., Teixeira, M.: Dengue surveillance based on a computational model of spatio-temporal locality of twitter. In: Proceedings of the ACM WebSci Conference (2011)
12. Hulth, A., Ryvedik, G., Lindle, A.: Web queries as a source for syndromic surveillance. Plos One 4 (2009)
13. Kivinen, J., Mannila, H.: The power of sampling in knowledge discovery. In: Proceedings of the Symposium on Principles of Databases Systems, pp. 77–85 (1994)
14. Lampos, V., Cristianini, N.: Tracking the flu pandemic by monitoring the social web. In: Proceedings of 2nd Workshop on Cognitive Information Processing. IAPR (2010)
15. Paul, M.J., Dredze, M.: Analyzing twitter for public health. In: Proceedings ICWSM (2011)
16. Polgreen, P.M., Chen, Y., Pennock, D.M., Nelson, F.D., Weinstein, R.A.: Using internet searches for influenza surveillance. Clinical Infectious Diseases 47 (2008)
17. Sakaki, T., Okazaki, M., Matsuo, Y.: Earthquake shakes twitter users: real-time event detection by social sensors. In: Proceedings of International Conference on World Wide Web, pp. 851–860. ACM (2010)
18. Santos, J.C., Matos, S.: Analysing twitter and web queries for flu trend prediction. Theoretical Biology and Medical Modelling 11 (2014)
19. Veloso, A., Meira Jr., W., Zaki, M.J.: Lazy associative classification. In: Proceedings of the International Conference on Data Mining, pp. 645–654 (2006)

Opinion Search in Spanish Written Press

Rodrigo Stecanella[✉], Jairo Bonanata, Dina Wonsever, and Aiala Rosá

Facultad de Ingeniería, Udelar, Montevideo, Uruguay
{rodrigosteca,jbonanat}@gmail.com,
{wonsever,aialar}@fing.edu.uy

Abstract. We describe a press reading tool that focuses on sayings or opinions in the news about topics and sources of the reader's choice. This tool offers a graphical interface through which several sources can be linked given a certain topic and which allows readers to visualize opinions in a timeline and browse through them. This is done over a corpus that includes three Uruguayan written press media and integrates their current and previous editions. The opinion recognizer is mainly rule-based, with rules written in a formalism called Contextual Rules and machine learning methods and regular expressions rules were used during the different stages of the system. The accuracy of the system was evaluated with respect to the information retrieved, showing 76% precision.

Keywords: Information Retrieval · Online Newspapers · Natural Language Processing · Opinions Extraction · Data Mining · Machine Learning · Opinion Search

1   Introduction

In the last years, as more and more people have computers at hand and access information recorded in computer files which are accessible over the net, traditional newspapers are migrating to an online press paradigm. At present, most written media have an important presence on the net, thus making the reading of online news in web pages more frequent to the detriment of the paperback format. In response to this problem, having tools that allow us to quickly access the information we are looking for is of utmost importance.

One of the advantages of online press is the possibility of offering readers various reading materials that are geared towards different types of specific interests. Furthermore, it is possible for readers to browse several written media ordered by topics or other criteria and to consider current and previous editions of one or several media simultaneously. However, we are yet to encounter new functionalities in online editions of written media, maybe because these editions are quite recent and written media have not been able yet to integrate technological innovations. With this in mind, we have been working towards providing a service that gives information about the opinions expressed by well-known personalities of society. We thought such service could be of interest, for example, during election campaigns, when the general public is usually more eager to know what it is that each candidate thinks about the great many topics that are brought up for discussion during the campaign for office.

© Springer International Publishing Switzerland 2014
A.L.C. Bazzan and K. Pichara (Eds.): IBERAMIA 2014, LNAI 8864, pp. 307–318, 2014.
DOI: 10.1007/978-3-319-12027-0_25

This article describes a press reading tool that focuses on sayings or opinions of well-known personalities about topics of the reader's choice. This tool offers a graphical interface through which several sources can be linked given a certain topic and which allows readers to visualize opinions in a timeline and browse through them. This is done over a corpus that includes three Uruguayan written press media (El País[1], La República[2], El Observador[3]) and integrates their current and previous editions.

For the creation of the system, several tools and methods were integrated, some of them of general purpose and others that were specifically developed for either the extraction of opinions from written text or for the differentiation between informative content and other type of elements in the newspapers web pages. The opinion recognizer is mainly rule-based, with rules written in a formalism called Contextual Rules; in addition, machine learning methods and regular expressions rules were used during the different stages of the system.

The following components can be recognized:

- The creation of a corpus of newspaper articles in Spanish which were automatically extracted from online written media websites;
- The extraction of metadata about the newspaper articles, such as titles or dates of publication;
- The use of a search engine to correctly retrieve opinions from the source as well as key words about the topics expressed in the opinions;
- A user-friendly GUI for performing searches easily.

The accuracy of the system was evaluated with respect to the information retrieved, showing 76% precision while showing an average of around 8 on a scale from 1 to 10 with which users were proposed to rank the functionalities of the system.

In section 2 of this paper, some systems with which our system shares features are reviewed. In section 3, we present the methods used in the creation of the written press textual base, which works as the database that feeds the opinion finder. In section 4, the main components of the system, the system itself and its GUI are described, in section 5 we present different evaluations that have been carried on and in section 6 we discuss the obtained results and possible future work lines.

2   Related Work

To the best of our knowledge, there are no active press reading services such as the one described in this paper. Below is a description of two systems with some similarity to ours, namely Google News and News Explorer, and some background with respect to the extraction of opinions is presented.

---

[1] Available at http://www.elpais.com.uy/
[2] Available at http://www.republica.com.uy/
[3] Available at http://elobservador.com.uy/

2.1   Google News

Google News [1] is a feed reader and an automated news finder that constantly tracks the information of the most important online communication media (even though no Uruguayan version has been released yet). There are over 40 regional editions of Google News in many different languages, including German, Arabic, Chinese, Korean, Spanish, and French. Each of these editions is tailored to the readers from their corresponding countries. The articles are selected and classified by means of a computerized system which evaluates the frequency with and the websites in which a piece of news appears, among other things.

If one visits Google News homepage, one will see a series of news with a related image and a brief description. Besides, one can see several related articles and even links to Wikipedia articles on the topic. In addition, Google News allows visitors to perform searches about news and to use a variety of tools to filter results by date of publication and by the written media from which the articles were extracted.

In the past, Google explored a tool called Google in Quotes which allowed to compare sayings by different politicians on a given topic. This tool was released in its beta version due to the US presidential elections. However, this tool is no longer available.

2.2   News Explorer

This is a tool developed and administered by the European Union [2]. This tool is also a feed reader, but it is capable of dealing with a large number of media and people. For example, one can search for one person, for instance, Barack Obama, and the system will return a list of various entities (people) which are related to the search, such as the president's wife. For any search result one chooses, the tool returns a large amount of information about it, such as pieces of news in which the result is mentioned and the different ways in which it is being referred to. Furthermore, this tool also provides users with a short list of opinions expressed in the written press by the person being searched for and a list of opinions in which the person in question is mentioned.

Although this tool does not allow to perform searches which answer the question "What did X opine about Y?" we believe this tool to be related to our work given that it allows to answer the question "What opinions has X expressed lately?"

2.3   Related Work on Opinion Extraction

Regarding the identification of opinions, one of the most important references is the annotation schema for opinions and emotions presented in [3]. This model specifies the different kinds of expressions to be considered for the study of opinions: explicit mentions of private states (The U.S. fears a spill-over), speech events expressing private states ("The U.S. fears a spill-over," said Xirao-Nima), expressive subjective elements (The report is full of absurdities), and objective speech event (Sargeant O'Leary said the incident took place at 2:00pm). This work resulted in the creation of the corpus MPQA, annotated according to the diagram above, which was used in numerous proposals for identification of opinions. In particular, this corpus is the basis for Opinion Finder[4], a system developed by researchers from the University of Pittsburgh, Cornell University, and the University of Utah, available for download under the GNU General Public License. Opinion Finder processes documents and automatically identifies subjective sentences and different aspects of subjectivity in sentences, such as agentive sources of opinion, speech acts, and sentiment expressions.

Different works focus on source identification for English [4, 5, 6, 7, 8, 9, 10] and Chinese [11]. Almost all these authors apply machine-learning methods, only [11] and [10] have developed a rule-based system.

In addition, there are some works on reported speech identification, the typical mechanism for citation. Both studies analyzed [12, 13] propose rule systems. In the first case, the speech verb, the source and the reported clause are identified for each reported speech instance. In the second case, only direct speech is recognized.

3   Automatic Creation of a Written Press Textual Base

3.1   Alternatives to Web Crawling and Information Filtering

In order to perform searches, it was necessary to create a written press textual base based on the websites by the different written media by recognizing and keeping a record of the articles in full and the opinions found there. To solve this, the problem was broken down into another two problems, namely, downloading the web pages and processing them.

To tackle the problem of downloading the websites, a plugin for Nutch [14] was used. To tackle the problem of processing the web pages, a Java program called Scraper was created. The structure of the textual database –implemented in Lucene [15] and SolR [16, 17]- and the main processes related to its creation are described below.

3.2   Written Press Textual Database

The attributes the textual database comprises are the following:

- *Article*: This is the complete text of the newspaper article from which the opinion was extracted;
- *Title*: This is the title of the article;
- *Lead-in*: This is a brief description of the article;
- *Source*: This is the source of the opinion, extracted by the Opinion Identification Module;
- *Opinion*: This is the opinion itself, extracted by the Opinion Identification Module;
- *Date*: This is the date of publication of the article.

---

[4] Available in http://mpqa.cs.pitt.edu/opinionfinder/

3.3   Differentiation between Articles and the Boilerplate

The task of differentiating between web pages that correspond to articles and those that correspond to covers or other types of functionalities showed different degrees of difficulty for the different written media. In two cases, the task was fairly easy – namely, in the cases of La República and El Observador- since there were clear metadata to differentiate between articles and advertisements. However, the task was more complex in the case of El País and consequently, we chose to use a machine learning method for filtering articles with news content using a set of 224 web pages classified manually in order to train and test the algorithm. The features used for machine learning and the results obtained with different methods are described below.

Selection of Features

The features which seemed to best represent the data based on the HTML code were selected. For El País, the chosen features were the following: the HTML file size in bytes, the URL length, the number of H1, H2, H3, H4, and H5 tags, the number of TABLE tags, the number of DIV tags, the number of P tags, and the total number of tags, not counting B and P format tags. We chose these attributes for three reasons. Firstly, we determined by a manual inspection that, more often than not, pages that do not correspond to articles contain more data and are thus larger in size. Secondly, articles usually contain fewer highlight tags , such as H1, H2, etc. Finally, the total number of tags used in covers is different from the number of tags used in articles. Web page classification has two possible targets: true, if the web page corresponds to an article and false otherwise.

Results for the Different Algorithms

In this part, several supervised machine-learning algorithms were tested. Weka [18] was used to build the classifier and cross-validation was used to evaluate results. The classifiers we used were the following: C4.5, based on decision trees, an ID3 algorithm extension, a Simple Bayesian Classifier, and 1-NN –that is the k-nearest-neighbor algorithm with only the nearest neighbor being taken into account.

Table 1. Accuracy of the different algorithms

Algorithm	Accuracy
Bayes	82.5893 %
C4.5	95.5357 %
1NN	97.3214 %

A description of how these algorithms work can be found in [19]. Below, the results for the different classifiers are shown. These results were evaluated using a 10-step iterative cross-validation process.

Given the results shown above, the 1-NN classifier was chosen and since very good results were obtained for the classifiers mentioned above, more complex algorithms were not taken into consideration.

Table 2. Confusion matrix for the 1-NN classifier

	False	True
False	82	6
True	0	136

From the matrix above, it can be seen that 92.68% of web pages which do not correspond to articles were filtered out and that no article was discarded.

3.4   Opinion Recognition

In order to recognize opinions inside the extracted text, we used a previously developed tool [20, 21], mainly rule-based, with rules written in a formalism called Contextual Rules [22] that, given the sentence:

> Mujica respaldó importante inversión minera.
> [Mujica supports a major mining investment.]

produces the following output:

```
<opinion>
<source>Mujica</source>
<predicate>respaldó</predicate>
<topic>importante inversión minera</topic>
</opinion>
```

The concept of opinion in which the tool is based covers all the expressions attributed to different sources by the author of the text, including those in which the source transmits an objective content. We identify four relevant elements for the opinion:

- the predicate: expression that indicates the presence of an opinion (verbs like opinar/say, rechazar/reject; nouns like opinión/opinion, rechazo/rejection and source indicators like según, de acuerdo con/according to),
- the source: opinion holder,
- the topic: explicit subject on which the opinion is expressed,
- the message: content of the opinion.

In our analysis the predicate is the central element of the opinion and the remaining elements are its arguments.

In the following example we show the different elements of the opinion using the following notation: underlined source, predicate in bold, topic in italics and message shaded in gray.

> Consultado *sobre la lentitud de los procesos judiciales uruguayos*, <u>Carranza</u> **respondió**: "Hay una situación de un muy alto número de presos sin condena, hay que agilizar los procesos".

> [Consulted *about the slowness of the Uruguayan judicial processes*, <u>Carranza</u> **said**, "There is a situation of a very high number of unsentenced prisoners, we must speed up processes."]

Most instances of opinions in texts do not contain all the defined elements. The topic, for instance, is not very common. The source is sometimes absent, mainly when it can be recovered from context.

3.5   Date Extraction

Since regular expressions were used in date extraction, this task deserves special attention. For our system, accurate date extraction is crucial since opinions are sorted by the date in which they were expressed. Each written media uses a different way of recording the date in which a piece of news was published and even within a given written media, publication dates are recorded and displayed in many different ways. In addition, many dates can appear in any given web page not only in the piece of news itself, but also in the boilerplate, so special care should be taken to extract the correct dates. For example, the headers of El País's web pages include the current date, which is different from the date in which the pieces of news were published, and there are many pages that include the date in their URLs. In order to accomplish this task, 15 different regular expressions were used.

3.6   Article Extraction

The article itself was the only feature whose extraction was not based on regular expressions. Although we had thought about implementing article extraction based on regular expressions at the beginning of the project, we found out that there is an algorithm which can extract the main information in a web page –in this case the press article- while discarding all accessory information, that is, the boilerplate. This algorithm is described in [23, 24] by Christian Kohlschütter. In general terms, what this algorithm does is count those HTML tags that are opened and closed while determining which texts are more deeply nested within these tags. Both the title and the news are placed at the same level in the HTML tree, but the text in the article is longer, so this text is regarded as the main content.

4   Interface for Opinion Search

The textual base defined in the previous section is the repository which can be accessed from a GUI to execute the different functionalities of the system5. Figure 1 shows how a search for the source or the topic of opinions (that is Mujica and marihuana, respectively) can be performed. In the search results, opinions are highlighted and images are added when they are available. In addition, users can browse the complete articles from the search results.

Fig. 1. A search about the opinions of "Mujica" talking about "la legalización de la marihuana"

As it can be seen in figure 1, the search results include a timeline on which the different opinions expressed by the source about the topic being searched for are ordered chronologically. Opinions are displayed on this timeline and users can access the full articles where the opinions being displayed were expressed. Consequently, users can have an overview of the evolution of the opinions expressed by a person about a certain topic.

Finally, there is an interface which allows users to search for other sources of opinion on the topic being searched for. The system suggests other possible sources of opinion by using the faceted search option in Lucene.

5   Evaluation of the Results

The system we have developed has several components that should be evaluated. The local evaluations for the crawling and scraping components as well as the evaluation of searches are presented below.

---

[5] The system is available online at http://www.buscopiniones.com

5.1   Crawling of the Uruguayan Written Press

The evaluation measurement in this case was the system's recall. In other words, was the system able to access and download all the information available for each of the three written media we selected?

Knowing if all the web pages of a website have been downloaded is quite difficult since no website publishes a list of all the pages available in the site. What we did to estimate the system's recall was measuring the number of pages by each written media –by using Google- and then comparing that figure to the number of pages that had been downloaded. We then checked that these figures were more or less comparable. The evaluation of these results was done under the assumption that Google has all of the web pages for each of the three written media.

To date, 422,039 pages have been downloaded from El País, 86,156 from El Observador, and 64,351 for La República. Nevertheless, Google has 2,840,000 pages from El País, 284,000 from El Observador, and 66,400 for La República. These figures show that the number of pages we have downloaded from La República is almost identical to the number of pages Google shows for that written media. However, these figures also show that the number of pages we have downloaded from El País and El Observador is significantly smaller than the number of pages Google has retrieved from said websites. We believe this significant difference can be accounted for by the limited download capacity and computing power we had access to, so we believe it could be remedied in the future.

5.2   HTML Scraping

The evaluation of the scraping component assesses the accurate extraction of the titles, lead-ins, publication dates, and articles. To conduct the evaluation 25 pieces of news were randomly selected from each of the written media in our corpus and we manually verified whether their features had been extracted accurately or not.

In the case of El País, out of four incorrectly extracted dates , three of them were not present in the web pages. Those cases in which the articles were not extracted correctly can be accounted for by the addition of information pertaining to the page's boilerplate in spite of the articles' not being discarded. Therefore, this error can be considered barely significant.

We can conclude that the scraper showed a good performance, particularly with El Observador and La República, for which near 100% effectiveness was obtained. In the case of El País, errors can be accounted for by the many more web pages this written media has, if compared with the other two media, and by the many different formats it uses to render the web pages, making the extraction of features much more difficult.

5.3   Opinion Search

It is important to make clear that determining the number of documents from a corpus which are relevant to any given search is a difficult task not only because the corpus could contain millions of entries, but also because there is no measure for determining the relevance of a document to a given search before the search is performed. Therefore, only the precision measure, which determines whether a retrieved document is relevant or not, was used.

To measure the precision of our search engine, we defined searches for 20 different topics –all of which were relevant in 2013- and for the names of 5 politicians so as to be able to perform the opinion searches.

All of the 100 searches were performed and more than 400 results were obtained. Every result was analyzed aiming at determining whether it was relevant to the search we had performed or not. The overall precision obtained for all these searches was 76% in average. On another front, the average precision obtained for those searches in which more than 5 results were returned was 79% and for those searches in which more than 8 results were returned, average precision rose to 85%. In light of these results, we can claim that the more opinions a person has expressed on a certain topic, the lower the probability of the search engine's returning irrelevant results will be.

6   Discussion

The results obtained allow us to have a tool for searching for opinions in the Uruguayan written media. In the near future, this tool could be easily extended to encompass other written media from other Spanish-speaking countries. Our evaluation demonstrated that all users can make use of our system without any difficulty and actually find what they look for.

This system is part of a recent trend aiming to provide users with specialized online press reading services. In addition to being a general written press reading tool, we have observed that our system could aid journalists in their jobs. According to a journalist being interviewed, "As it is at present, I think the tool could be of help to journalists. If I were able to know everything Tabaré Vázquez has said about marihuana, for example… It seems very useful for writing an article on the topic."

From the results obtained in the evaluation, we concluded that errors are explained by two main reasons:

1. Problems when recognizing the topic about which an opinion is expressed;
2. Problems when recognizing the source of an opinion and when dealing with proper names in general.

The first problem relates to the wide scope of text over which the topic search is performed, that is, the whole article. We chose to perform these searches over the articles in full since limiting searches to opinions yielded very low levels of recall. There are two parallel ways in which this problem can be solved. First, recall could be increased by making use of external lexical resources, such as Wordnet, which allow improving searches by using synonyms or related expressions. Second, since any given article very often talks about more than one topic, we think a segmentation of articles in topics could be useful. At present, we are working on this line of research.

The second problem has also been regarded as one fundamental problem in News Explorer. In our case, this shows in two aspects. First, a co-reference solver between sources of opinions is needed since when there are several opinions about a given topic in a given text, the reference to the source is usually omitted or is expressed by the use of pronouns. Second, proper names do not univocally denote people. This shows when the names of people with ordinary last names are mixed in an article. For example, if one searches for "Malvinas" as a topic, one of the suggestions the system will return as a source of opinion will be "Fernández". However, if we search for that last name, we will find opinions by the President of Argentina, that is, Cristina Fernández, by the Uruguayan Minister of National Defense, that is, Fernández Huidobro. One possible solution to this problem could be developing or using a database which contains disambiguated names as well as possible referential expressions for them and which is able to handle temporal coordinates. This solution would let us point to the same entity, for example, when referring to "el Presidente", "Mujica", or "el mandatario".

References

1. Google News, https://news.google.com/
2. News Explorer, http://emm.newsexplorer.eu/
3. Wiebe, J., Wilson, T., Cardie, C.: Annotating expressions of opinions and emotions in language. Language Resources and Evaluation 39(2–3), 165–210 (2005)
4. Bethard, S., Yu, H., Thornton, A., Hatzivassiloglou, V., Jurafsky, D.: Automatic Extraction of Opinion Propositions and their Holders. In: AAAI Spring Symposium on Exploring Attitude and Affect in Text, pp. 20–27. The AAAI Press, Menlo Park (2004)
5. Bethard, S., Yu, H., Thornton, A., Hatzivassiloglou, V., Jurafsky, D.: Extracting opinion propositions and opinion holders using syntactic and lexical cues. In: Shanahan, J., Qu, Y., Wiebe, J. (eds.): Computing Attitude and Affect in Text: Theory and Applications. The Information Retrieval Series, vol. 20, pp. 125–141. Springer, Heidelberg (2006)
6. Choi, Y., Cardie, C., Riloff, E., Patwardhan, S.: Identifying Sources of Opinions with Conditional Random Fields and Extraction Patterns. In: HLT-EMNLP, pp. 355–362. Association for Computational Linguistics, Vancouver, Canada (2005)
7. Choi, Y., Breck, E., Cardie, C.: Joint Extraction of Entities and Relations for Opinion Recognition. In: EMNLP 2006, pp. 431–439. Association for Computational Linguistics, Sydney (2006)
8. Kim, S.-M., Hovy, E.: Extracting Opinions, Opinion Holders, and Topics Expressed in Online News Media Texts. In: Workshop on Sentiment and Subjectivity in Text (SST 2006), pp. 1–8. Association for Computational Linguistics, Stroudsburg (2006)
9. Wiegand, M., Klakow, D.: Convolution Kernels for Opinion Holder Extraction. In: NAACL HLT 2010, pp. 795–803. Association for Computational Linguistics, Los Angeles (2010)
10. Saurí, R., Pustejovsky, J.: Are You Sure That This Happened? Assessing the Factuality Degree of Events in Text. In COLI, 38(2), pp. 261–299. Association for Computational Linguistics (2012)
11. Lu, B.: Identifying Opinion Holders and Targets with Dependency Parser in Chinese News Texts. In: NAACL HLT 2010 Student Research Workshop, pp. 46–51. Association for Computational Linguistics, Los Angeles (2010)

12. Krestel, R., Bergler, S., Witte, R.: Minding the Source: Automatic Tagging of Reported Speech in Newspaper Articles. In: Sixth International Language Resources and Evaluation Conference (LREC 2008), pp. 2823–2828. ELRA, Marrakech (2008)
13. Pouliquen, B., Steinberger, R., Best, C.: Automatic Detection of Quotations in Multilingual News. In: Recent Advances in Natural Language Processing (RANLP 2007), Borovets, Bulgaria, pp. 487–492 (2007)
14. Apache Nutch, http://nutch.apache.org/
15. Apache Lucene, http://lucene.apache.org/
16. Smiley, D., Pugh, E.: Solr 1.4 Enterprise Search Server. Packt Publishing Ltd, Birmingham (2009)
17. Apache Solr, http://lucene.apache.org/solr/
18. Weka, http://www.cs.waikato.ac.nz/ml/weka/
19. Mitchell, T.: Machine Learning. McGraw Hill (1997)
20. Rosá, A., Wonsever D., Minel, J.-L.: Opinion Identification in Spanish Texts. In: Proceedings of the NAACL HLT 2010 Young Investigators Workshop on Computational Approaches to Languages of the Americas. Los Angeles (2010)
21. Rosá, A., Wonsever, D., Minel, J.-L.: Combining Rules and CRF Learning for Opinion Source Identification in Spanish Texts. In: Pavón, J., Duque-Méndez, N.D., Fuentes-Fernández, R. (eds.) IBERAMIA 2012. LNCS, vol. 7637, pp. 452–461. Springer, Heidelberg (2012)
22. Wonsever, D., Minel, J.-L.: Contextual Rules for Text Analysis. In: Gelbukh, A. (ed.) CICLing 2001. LNCS, vol. 2004, pp. 509–523. Springer, Heidelberg (2001)
23. Kohlschütter, C.: BoilerPipe, http://code.google.com/p/boilerpipe/
24. Kohlschütter, C., Fankhauser, P., Nejdl, W.: Boilerplate Detection using Shallow Text Features. Hannover - Germany : L3S Research Center/Leibniz Universität Hannover (2010)

Serendipitous Recommendation Based on Big Context

Andrew Koster[✉], Fernando Koch, and Yeun Bae Kim

Samsung Research Institute, Campinas, Brazil
{andrew.k,fernando.koch,kimybae}@samsung.com

Abstract. Context-awareness is an essential requirement in crafting recommender systems that provide serendipity, *i.e.* "pleasant surprises", independently of human command. These solutions must be able to infer interactions based on data from sensors and recognised activities in order to infer what is useful information and when to deliver it. For that, we are devising advanced models of context inference based on the analysis of users' signals during everyday activities. In this paper, we present a proof-of-concept platform that allows for the application of techniques of deep learning and context analytics to derive patterns in spatio-temporal context signals. We call this composition *Big Context*. We argue that by understanding how people and things are connected, one can devise novel forms of interactions that provide a more pleasant user experience. In this work, we introduce our method and platform, and illustrate some of the possible techniques using a prototype application that provides serendipitous recommendations.

1 Introduction

Serendipitous interfaces are an emerging paradigm in user experience. The idea is to create a self-governing recommender system that provides relevant information [18] as a "pleasant surprise" in the absence of intentional commands. Examples of such interfaces are: SAMSUNG S-Health[1], when it counts how many steps a user walked during the day and offers a congratulatory notification once a (supposedly healthy) threshold has been surpassed, and; Google Now[2], when it keeps track of your location and daily activities to provide contextualised advise. These sort of systems encompass: (i) sensors that collect multi-dimensional data; (ii) mechanisms of context inference in mobile computing; and (iii) a deliberation process to infer what is *useful information* and when to deliver it.

We hypothesise that it is possible to create inference models that classify and understand user behaviour based on analysis of events emitted by the handling of everyday things, such as smart phones, Smart TVs, fridges, and air conditioning. We investigate how to apply deep learning and context analytics

---

[1] http://www.samsung.com/global/microsite/galaxys4/lifecare.html#page=shealth

[2] http://www.google.com/landing/now

© Springer International Publishing Switzerland 2014
A.L.C. Bazzan and K. Pichara (Eds.): IBERAMIA 2014, LNAI 8864, pp. 319–330, 2014.
DOI: 10.1007/978-3-319-12027-0_26

to derive patterns and correlations in spatiotemporal context signals — we call this configuration *Big Context*. The leading questions in our investigation are:

- How to infer meaningful context events out of multi-dimension signals collected from a variety of sensors?
- How to reason explanation about facts or incidents with multi-aspectual proofs based on pre-classified events?
- How to design deliberation mechanisms aiming at context support and proactive interactions?

A brief illustration scenario is as follows. Let us assume that smart phones are instrumented to emit signals s_i containing information such as time, location, type of object, type of interaction and parameters of the interaction, which are captured and stored in repositories $\mathbf{S}_u$ for each user u. Then, sequences of signals $S \subseteq \mathbf{S}_u$ can be classified as context events e_i by applying techniques of sequence labelling algorithms, such as a Hidden Markov Model [4] and Conditional Random Fields (CRF) [12]. For instance, to classify sequences $s_1, \ldots, s_n$ as car parking signature, stored in a spatiotemporal repository $\mathbf{E}$. Moreover, techniques for learning probabilistic models for collections of discrete data (*e.g.* Latent Dirichlet Allocation [1]) are applied to identify patterns from the excess of spatiotemporal events that relate to salient contextual situations.

We expect to understand the context and deliberate to provide a "pleasant surprise". In this case, by informing that there is a high possibility that a parking space is to be freed up soon (around a area). The system infers this information by classifying the social behaviour upon historic context events from $\mathbf{E}$. Different scenarios may be drawn up, considering signals incoming from alternative objects and application domains, such as the provision of contextualised education material, introduced in [10].

In what follows, we introduce *Big Context* and related concepts, present the architecture of the "Sensible Lives Platform", and propose a proof-of-concept demonstration.

2   On Big Context and Related Concepts

Dey (2001) [3] characterises context in the following way: "Context is any information that can be used to characterise the situation of an entity. An entity is a person, place or object that is considered relevant to the interaction between a user and an application, including the user and the application themselves." Current approaches to context acquisition tend to focus on a bridge between the high-level context descriptions in applications and the low-level data that is collected from sensors [6,11,20]. We claim that current methods are insufficient to handle highly diversified views that can be derived from the multitude of sensors present on everyday devices. The ACE system [15] is nearest to our work in this sense, because it discovers the relations between contexts. We will discuss this further in Section 3.3, where we discuss our approach to the semantic modelling of contexts.

We are researching alternative techniques for multi-dimensional context analysis. We aim at new models to recognise patterns in data and then match these to contextual situations without previous understanding about these patterns or the configuration of analysis rules. We call this configuration *Big Context*.

This development seeks a new kind of context support mechanism that provides highly adaptive context inference, even to unanticipated situations where emerging patterns can be discovered. It will support real-time context-aware inference towards proactive deliberation and serendipity. Insofar as we know, there is only one similar platform, CQue [16], which aims at integrating information from various different classifiers in order to improve accuracy, reduce battery usage and provide better privacy. The main distinction is that CQue is intended to run on the mobile phone, and thus aims mainly at the detection of contexts that can be learned through analysis of a single user's information. By running the Big Context platform as a cloud-based service, we are able to leverage multiple users' contextual information to infer social context, as well as combine data from many users to better train classifiers, allowing us to recognise the occurence of rare events.

Figure 1 depicts the architecture of the Big Context platform. We integrate multiple different learning techniques, which we will describe in the next section, in an encompassing framework for collecting and reasoning upon multidimensional sensors. The composition includes interface support for deliberation mechanisms aiming at context support and pro-active interactions. It operates as follows:

- *Input Interface* receives signals captured by sensors in everyday life's devices.
- *Noise Filtering and Fusion* pre-processes this data eliminating entries that are either repetitive or not relevant; these signals are stored in a short-term repository for future reference.
- *Probabilistic Activity Recognition* analyses a sequence of signals, identifying the impact of each signal upon the sequence given the observations; recognised activity patterns are stored in a long-term repository for historic context analysis.
- *Probabilistic Situation Modelling* implements techniques of context modelling based on generative probabilistic models for collections of discrete data; recognised situation patterns are stored in a long-term repository for historic context analysis.
- *Semantic Context Classification* provides support to reason about facts or incidents with multi-aspectual proofs, using configurable *Context Analysis Rules* and *Semantic Rules*. The generated entries are stored in a long-term repository for historic context analysis.
- *Context Query Language* provides a query language to access the information stored in the four repositories being populated by the methods aforementioned.

The service can be executed in a combination between local- and server-based processing. For instance, in the prototype being presented in the next section,

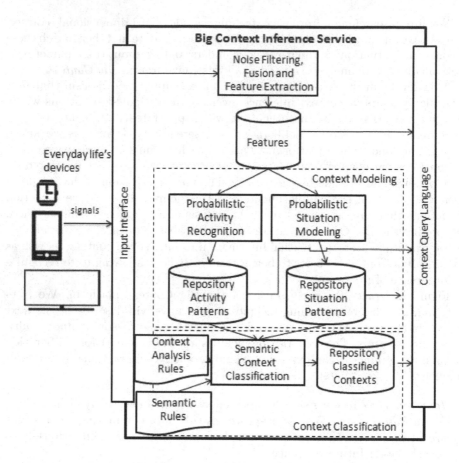

Fig. 1. Architecture of Big Context

we execute the methods for noise filtering and probabilistic activity recognition on the mobile device, whilst executing the information sharing services on the server.

This composition supports external applications to query for shared context information band intertwine local processing and global context. We claim that this setup greatly facilitates the implementation of serendipity, providing recognition of surrounding to support automatic processing.

Next we describe the main elements that compose this mechanism. Throughout this paper, we will demonstrate the concepts with an application that recognises parking spaces. We describe the algorithms we use for this specific situation, and briefly survey some of the other methods that can be used for the task at hand. The mobile app and its functioning is described in Section 4.

3   Context Recognition Methods

3.1   Activity Recognition

Activity features are not obvious when collecting data from multi-dimensional sensors. In order to categorise contextual patterns we need to identify powerful distinctive features out of data that is not easily explainable. Activity recognition is a temporal classification problem: the application must analyse a sequence of signals, identifying the impact of each signal upon the sequence given the observations [19].

For instance, let us consider the method for detecting car parking signatures from observed movements of user's device captured through sensors like accelerometer and gyroscope. The application collects and indexes timestamped signals $s_0, \ldots, s_t$ over a period of time t, and classifies discrete features to facilitate the machine learning. That is, features are considered together within a timeframe forming linear sequence of events $e_0, \ldots, e_t$, which represent discrete words w_i in a domain; for instance, distinct movements during car parking movement such as "reverse acceleration" (w_1), "slight right turn" (w_2), "slight left turn" (w_3), and so on.

Out of the various context modelling tasks, activity recognition is probably the one that has received the most attention so far. There are many different works focusing on recognising many different activities, using various different sensors. It is beyond the scope of this work to perform a sufficient survey, for which we refer to Mannini and Sabatini [14] regarding activity recognition using inertial sensors, and Poppe [17] for vision-based activity recognition.

A majority of the methods for recognising activity based on IMU sensor data, like the data we collect from drivers, use a method based on graphical models. We follow suit, and employ Conditional Random Fields (CRF) [12], one of the methods that places the least assumptions on the conditional independence relationship between variables. Nevertheless, an assumption underlying all graphical models is that the labels have the Markov property $Pr\{e_{t+1} = e', s_{t+1} = s | e_t, s_t\}$, that is the conditional probability distribution of future labels depends only upon the present labels, not on the sequence of events e_i and signals s_j that preceded it.

The aim of using CRF is to model the joint probability distribution for all the labels, given the observed features. It models this conditional probability distribution of the labels given the features as follows:

$$Pr(\mathbf{E}|\mathbf{S}) = \frac{1}{Z} \prod_{i=0}^{t} exp\big(\sum_{k=1}^{K} \theta_k f_k(e_{i-1}, e_i, s_i)\big),$$

where Z is a normalisation factor, $\theta_k \in \mathbb{R}$ are parameters of the model and f_k is a real-valued *feature function* for each of the K features we are interested in, such as w_1, w_2 and w_3 of the above example.

This technique yields the most likely explanation for the sequence of events. That is, it computes the joint probability of the entire sequence of hidden states that generated a particular sequence of observations within a distinct feature, such as "parking in signature", "parking out signature", or "non parking signature". Then, we can form a repository of historical activity patterns $\mathbf{E}$ where each record contains timestamp, location, user identification and distinct feature[3] by capturing the information from multiple users over time.

3.2   Situation Modelling

We expect that patterns also emerge at a global context level considering the relation between events across multiple users. These patterns constitute the situation a user is in, and situation modelling is generally approached in two ways: using a probabilistic method, or a rule-based semantic method. The latter is problematic, as it requires a prior description of the possible situations that we wish to model, whereas the former can be *generative* and discover novel situations. While the application of such methods to situation modelling is relatively new [5,13], similar methods have a rich history in understanding text. Examples of this type of method are Latent Dirichlet Allocation (LDA) [1,9], Topical N-gram Models [21] and Beta Process Hidden Markov Models [7,8].

These techniques allows us to classify and predict situations that involve subsets of context events and address questions like: (i) what is the probability that a frequency of context events over a period of time and region represents a situation x, such as a user looking for a parking space (x_1) or a user walking towards his car (x_2); or (ii) what is the probability of situation x being caused by a (subset of) context events E?

Currently, we do not have enough data to perform this kind of modelling in the parking place scenario, but when we gather more data we propose to use LDA, one of the most common generative probabilistic methods in topic modelling, to discern the various situations we are interested in. The LDA method operates as follows. The set $E_{R,T} \subseteq \mathbf{E}$ represents the spatiotemporal area of events to be considered, over a period of time T and within a spatial region R. We define the following notation:

K denotes the number of situational descriptors;

M specifies the number of areas being classified;

N is the number of events per area;

α is the parameter of the Dirichlet prior on the per-area distribution of situations;

β is the parameter of the Dirichlet prior on the per-situation distribution of events;

θ_m is the situation distribution for each area E_{R_m,T_m};

ϕ_x is the distribution of context events for situation x;

e_{mn} is the nth context event in the mth area, and;

x_{mn} is the situation that e_{mn} belongs to.

---

[3] Note: for privacy concerns, one can prevent to store user identification on $\mathbf{E}$; however, this approach limits the possibility of individual situation analysis at global context level.

Then the joint probability distribution we are interested in is (full explanation at [1]):

$$Pr(\mathbf{E}, \mathbf{X}, \theta | \alpha, \beta) = \prod_{k=1}^{K} Pr(\phi_k | \beta)$$

$$\times \prod_{m=1}^{M} Pr(\theta_m | \alpha) \prod_{n=1}^{N} Pr(x_{mn} | \theta_m) Pr(e_{mn} | \phi_{x_{mn}})$$

The method allows for the inference of various different probabilities, allowing us to answer questions like the ones above. For instance, an event might be the user driving slowly. In isolation, this activity could mean that he is lost, stuck in traffic, or searching for a parking space. However, in conjunction with other events the situation becomes clear. For instance, if many other users are driving slowly in the same area, the situation is most likely a traffic jam, while if this is a recurrent pattern for the user, in isolation, over various days, he is most likely to be searching for a parking space.

3.3 Semantic Context Classification

Patterns also emerge at a social level where people use their devices differently depending on their social environment. For that, rule-based classification methods provide a powerful tool to reason explanation about facts or incidents with multi-aspectual proofs based on pre-classified events. Moreover, these methods allow for the composition of *context intelligence* through the discovery of new facts and rules/patterns from networked context facts by exploring causality residing inside the relation between events, as presented in [2].

Consider the question: What is the possibility that a parking space is to be freed up soon around this area?. The reasoning implies the analysis of historical behaviour and other parameters of the social settings. For instance, let us assume the semantics rules in the knowledge space that represent the number of parking spaces available, such as:"parking at position", "leaving and entering parking", "startend of office hours", "parking spaces become available or unavailable", and so on. Then, we can compose logic formulae between the elements as:

who_am_I(?U)
local_query(current_location(?L))
server_query(parking_spaces(?Y, L))
possible_office_arrival_time(U, ?TO, ?Θ_x)
my_office_location(U, ?LO)
possible_parking_availability(LO, TO, ?Z, ?Θ_z)

Thus, the reasoning can infer the possibility of finding parking places at my office's location around the time I am about to arrive at my office. In this reasoning, it estimates the possible office arrival time TO with a certainty Θ_x e.g. based on historical information and/or driving information. it also infers the office location LO and thus is able to estimate the possible parking availability Z near that area with a certainty factor Θ_z. Intuitively, the more networked elements are being considered for the assertion, the more likely the prediction will align with observable features.

The use of a semantic layer in context-aware computing is not novel. As mentioned in the previous section, it is often used in situation modelling, but the use most similar to our proposal is found in ACE [15]. Their principal aim is to improve energy efficiency by recognising when sensors are needed, and when the context can be inferred through logical rules. For instance, if the user is driving (known because he is tethered to his hands-free set), then he is not at home, and thus there is no need to use the GPS to discover whether he is at home or not. These semantic relations are learned using a logical rule miner similar to the one we propose to use, however it learns Boolean rules. This is a problem, because everything else is based on probabilistic inference: they do not know the user is driving, they just infer it, possibly with a high probability. This is exacerbated, because the rules themselves are learned, there is a chance they are wrong, and thus come associated with some form of confidence value that the rule is correct. We thus learn probabilistic rules, which account for the inherent uncertainty in the domain.

4   Serendipitous Parking Recommendations

As a proof-of-concept implementation, we developed an application to find free parking spaces and also help the user locate his parked car. We intended to exploit concepts of non-intentional interactions, pro-active recommendations, and social connectedness. Figure 2 depicts the two screens in the wePark Application, and an overview of its classifier: (i) a widget that collects data (accelerometer, gyroscope, and GPS) on the background; (ii) the main screen that automatically presents free parking spaces around the user's location; and (iii) the classification process, explained below.

The application works as depicted in Figure 3. The widget operates autonomously collecting (a) data samples and pre-process locally for noise filtering and probabilistic activity recognition. Features are being extracted based on acceleration data in the XY plane divided into nine regions, turns around the Z-axis, clockwise or counter clockwise, movement speed, and movement duration. The application extracts the features using information fusion techniques, followed by discretisation, yielding (b) a sequence of movement features. We then apply a Conditional Random Fields (CRF) model to classify the sequence of features into (c) probabilities of parking movement events.

Once the application collects a sufficient amount of data, the information is grouped and labelled to know which clusters are movements corresponding parking movements. These events are communicated to a server-based application that: stores these events in repository of activity patterns, so that the server knows where the parking spaces are being freed up/occupied; and executes the probabilistic situation modelling to create the global context considering the relation between events across multiple users.

(a) Widget showing number of available spots.

(b) Map display of the available parking spots.

Fig. 2. Prototype wePark application

When the user taps on the wePark widget, it opens the (ii) main screen (Figure 2 (ii)) that queries the server-based component about free parking spaces around the current location. Moreover, the widget also detects walking patterns and when the user is wandering around the area where his car is parked, the application notifies the user, providing direction information where his car is parked.

5 Discussion

We seek a new kind of user experience, understanding user activities and delivering relevant information pro-actively. We expect that these developments will improve the quality of mobile applications with a new paradigm of user experience. In this paper, we present our work towards *Big Context* and support to serendipitous recommendations using our *Platform for Sensible Lives*. Nevertheless, these methods come at a cost. Firstly, it is necessary to collect and maintain the database of raw contextual data required to discover contextual patterns. Secondly, it requires local processing and continuous access to sensors, which in the case of mobile devices implies in battery utilisation. There are technical solutions to mitigate this problem, such as SAMSUNG Software Development Kits (SDKs) for the latest device technologies (*viz.* Galaxy S5 and Samsung Gear 2), which includes the "Motion package" with features for continuous sensor monitoring with low power technology.

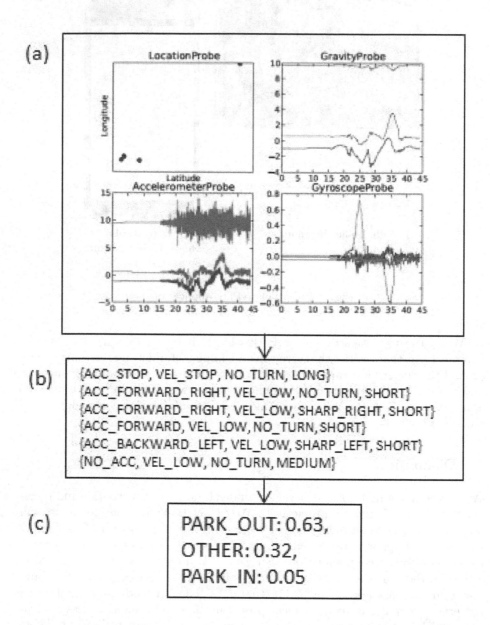

Fig. 3. Processing context signals for recognizing parking movements. (a) is a sample of sensor data, varying over time, collected from a 9DOF IMU, (b) shows the feature set that we extract from this data, and (c) the probability for each of the potential labels of this sample.

The development of Big Context and serendipitous interfaces is still experimental. We have ideas about initial applications, as described in this paper, and how to move forward with them. Nevertheless, the concept of Big Context is larger than the applications we can conceive of at this early stage. In future work we will refine the method of situation modelling, aiming to provide better support to group support in applications that relate context events across multiple users. Moreover, we will further develop the technology for semantic context classification, aiming at support to social connectedness by supporting applications that analyse patterns at a social level where people use their devices differently depending on their social environment.

References

1. Blei, D.M., Ng, A.Y., Jordan, M.I.: Latent dirichlet allocation. Journal of Machine Learning Research **3**, 993–1022 (2003)
2. Choi, K.-S., Kim, Y.-B.: Knowledge Seeking Activities for Content Intelligence. In: Sembok, T.M.T., Zaman, H.B., Chen, H., Urs, S.R., Myaeng, S.-H. (eds.) ICADL 2003. LNCS, vol. 2911, pp. 415–426. Springer, Heidelberg (2003)
3. Dey, A.: Understanding and Using Context. Personal Ubiquitous Computing **5**, 4–7 (2001)
4. Elliott, R.J., Aggoun, L., Moore, J.B.: Hidden Markov Models. Springer (1995)
5. Fischer, Y., Beyerer, J.: Defining dynamic bayesian networks for probabilistic situation assessment. In: Proc. of International Conference on Information Fusion (FUSION), pp. 888–895. IEEE (2012)
6. Fonteles, A.S., Neto, B.J.A., Maia, M., Viana, W., Andrade, R.M.C.: An Adaptive Context Acquisition Framework to Support Mobile Spatial and Context-Aware Applications. In: Liang, S.H.L., Wang, X., Claramunt, C. (eds.) W2GIS 2013. LNCS, vol. 7820, pp. 100–116. Springer, Heidelberg (2013)
7. Fox, E.B., Sudderth, E.B., Jordan, M.I., Willsky, A.S.: Sharing features among dynamical systems with beta processes. In: Conference on Neural Information Processing Systems (NIPS 2009), Vancouver BC, Canada, pp. 549–557 (2009)
8. Hughes, M., Suddereth, E.B.: Nonparametric discovery of activity patterns from video collections. In: IEEE Conference on Computer Vision and Pattern Recognition Workshops (CVPRW), Providence RI, USA, pp. 25–32 (2012)
9. Huỳnh, T., Fritz, M., Schiele, B.: Discovery of activity patterns using topic models. In: ACM International Joint Conference on Pervasive and Ubiquitous Computing (Ubicomp 2008), pp. 10–19. ACM, Seoul (2008)
10. Koch, F., Rao, C.: Towards massively personal education through performance evaluation analytics. International Journal of Information and Education Technology **4**(4), 297–301 (2014)
11. Kramer, D., Kocurova, A., Oussena, S., Clark, T., Komisarczuk, P.: An extensible, self contained, layered approach to context acquisition. In: Proceedings of the Third International Workshop on Middleware for Pervasive Mobile and Embedded Computing. ACM (2011)
12. Lafferty, J.D., McCallum, A., Pereira, F.C.N.: Conditional random fields: Probabilistic models for segmenting and labeling sequence data. In: Proceedings of the Eighteenth International Conference on Machine Learning (ICML), pp. 282–289. Morgan Kaufmann, San Francisco (2001)

13. López, G., Brena, R.: Probabilistic Situation Modeling from Ambient Sensors in a Health Condition Monitoring System. In: Urzaiz, G., Ochoa, S.F., Bravo, J., Chen, L.L., Oliveira, J. (eds.) UCAmI 2013. LNCS, vol. 8276, pp. 175–182. Springer, Heidelberg (2013)

14. Mannini, A., Sabatini, A.M.: Machine learning methods for classifying human physical activity from on-body accelerometers. Sensors **10**(2), 1154–1175 (2010)

15. Nath, S.: ACE: Exploiting correlation for energy-efficient and continuous context sensing. In: Proc. of MobiSys 2012, pp. 29–42. ACM (2012)

16. Parate, A., Chiu, M.C., Ganesan, D., Marlin, B.M.: Leveraging graphical models to improve accuracy and reduce privacy risks of mobile sensing. In: Proc. of MobiSys 2013, pp. 83–96. ACM (2013)

17. Poppe, R.: A survey on vision-based human action recognition. Image and vision computing **28**(6), 976–990 (2010)

18. Ricci, F., Rokach, L., Shapira, B.: Introduction to recommender systems handbook. In Ricci, F., Rokach, L., Shapira, B., Kantor, P.B. (eds.) Recommender Systems Handbook, pp. 1–29. Springer (2011)

19. Vail, D.L., Veloso, M.M., Lafferty, J.D.: Conditional random fields for activity recognition. In: Proceedings of the 6th International Joint Conference on Autonomous Agents and Multiagent Systems, pp. 1331–1338. ACM (2007)

20. Wang, A.I., Ahmad, Q.K.: CAMF - context-aware machine learning framework for android. In: Proceedings of the International Conference on Software Engineering and Applications (SEA 2010), IASTED, Article no. 725–003 (2010)

21. Wang, X., McCallum, A., Wei, X.: Topical n-grams: Phrase and topic discovery, with an application to information retrieval. In: IEEE International Conference on Data Mining (ICDM 2007), pp. 697–702. IEEE, Omaha (2007)

An Algorithm to Condense Social Networks and Identify Brokers

Luís Cavique[1(✉)], Nuno C. Marques[2], and Jorge M.A. Santos[3]

[1] LabMAg and Universidade Aberta, Lisboa, Portugal
lcavique@uab.pt
[2] CITI and FCT, Universidade Nova Lisboa, Lisbon, Portugal
nmm@fct.unl.pt
[3] Universidade de Évora, Évora, Portugal
jmas@uevora.pt

Abstract. In social network analysis the identification of communities and the discovery of brokers is a very important issue. Community detection typically uses partition techniques. In this work the information extracted from social networking goes beyond cohesive groups, enabling the discovery of brokers that interact between communities. The partition is found using a set covering formulation, which allows the identification of actors that link two or more dense groups. Our algorithm returns the needed information to create a good visualization of large networks, using a condensed graph with the identification of the brokers.

Keywords: Data mining · Graph mining · Social networks · Condensed network · Brokerage

1 Introduction

Social networks are usually represented with graph theory, where the set of vertices corresponds to the 'actors' (i.e. people, companies or social actors) and the set of edges corresponds to the 'ties' (i.e. relationships, associations or links).

The visualization of a small number of vertices can be easily mapped. However, when the number of vertices and edges increases, the visualization of the whole graph becomes incomprehensible as the large amount of available data in corporations and governments becomes incompatible with the complete drawing. There is a pressing need for new metrics and pattern recognition tools to explore and visualize large social networks.

Brokers can be defined as actors that work within communities. Although different methods are used to find network partitions [14], the specific discovery of brokers between partitions is scarce [21]. In this work we are interested in finding, not only the communities, but also the brokers. We also intend to show that the visualization of the brokers in a condensed graph undoubtedly simplifies the work of the social network analyst when dealing with large networks.

© Springer International Publishing Switzerland 2014
A.L.C. Bazzan and K. Pichara (Eds.): IBERAMIA 2014, LNAI 8864, pp. 331–343, 2014.
DOI: 10.1007/978-3-319-12027-0_27

In Figure 1, a small network is shown. A social network analyst should define the communities and the actors within them. The dense group {1,3,4,5} can be easily identified, but the rest of the network is more sparse. Three groups of nodes can also be recognized, although a formal definition of community is needed. In this work we define community as a k-clique [20].

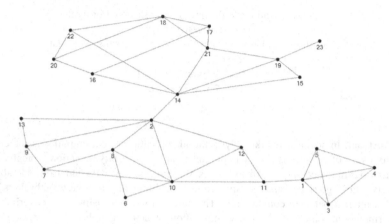

Fig. 1. Network for the running example

A strategy to condense the graph associated with the identification of brokers is presented in this work. The partition strategy is found using a set covering formulation with k-cliques [3], which allows over-covered nodes and isolated nodes.

In this study the words "network" and "graph" are used as synonyms. The terms "community", "dense group", "connected component", "clique" or "k-clique" are also equivalents.

In Section 2, we present the concept of brokerage in social networks and the two combinatorial problems related to the k-clique covering. In sub-section 2.1 structural holes, bridges and brokers in social networks are presented. In sub-section 2.2 the generation of cliques and k-cliques is introduced. And finally, in sub-section 2.3 the set covering problem is defined. In Section 3, we present the two phase algorithm to condense the graph and discover brokers in social networks. In Section 4, the computational results are presented. Finally, in Section 5 we draw some conclusions.

2   Related Work

The graph theory related work in this paper combines the areas of graph visualization, graph mining, social network concepts, sub-graphs and graph partition.

The aim of graph visualization techniques is to achieve the comprehension of the data by providing intuitive layouts associated with interactive functionalities. In Tarawneh et al. [25] five main areas in graph layout algorithms are referred: node-link layouts, tree layout, matrix visualization, 3D layout and nodes-and-edges clustering. The goal of clustering techniques is to reduce visual disorder in the final layout. Reducing the number of elements, edges and/or nodes, will increase the clarity of the visualization. Clustering algorithms can be divided into two groups: edge compression and nodes compression. The edge clustering approach [13] replaces individual edges with edges connected to groups of nodes. Modular decomposition and power-graph decomposition [22], are the most well-known edge clustering techniques. The second group, nodes clustering, based on a specified criteria divides the graph into different sets, and then reduces each set to a node. In Auber et al. [1] the clustering algorithms are applied to small-word networks.

The area of Graph Mining has seen significant growth in the last decade [7]. The use of cliques is also referred to in Du et al. [12]. A similar concept of brokerage is the communities overlapping in networks, when nodes belong to multiple dense groups [26].

In our work we use clustering techniques in order to find partition, but with an additional purpose – to find influential nodes that link two or more partition sets, the brokers. In order to condense the network and to discover brokers, three different concepts are combined: the brokerage in social networks and two combinatorial problems – the maximal k-clique generation and the set covering problem.

2.1   Social Network Concepts

In the late 1960s, while working on his Ph.D., Mark Granovetter interviewed people who had recently changed jobs, in order to come to a conclusion as to how they had found their new jobs. Surprisingly, he realized that the information about the new jobs had come from distant acquaintances instead of close friends. The concept of strong and weak ties [17] introduced a novel principle in social networks. Weak ties are valuable because they will more likely be the source of novel information, surprise and openness to new worlds. On the other hand, strong ties intensify group cohesion and the persistence of group identity. This resulted in the Triadic Closure property, which establishes that if the node has strong ties to two neighbors, these neighbors must have at least a weak tie between them. The property is based on the fact that if two people have a friend in common, it is probable that they will become friends in the future [14].

Following this issue, R.S. Burt [2] developed a complementary approach coined Structural Holes, referring to the absence of links in a connected organization. He also introduced the concept of brokerage, signifying nodes that connect two dense groups.

Figure 2 shows two ways of spanning structural holes, using a bridge or a broker. Structural hole, bridge and broker can be defined as follows:

1. structural hole refers to the lack of edges between components, or communities;
2. bridge is an edge whose removal increases the number of components in the network;
3. broker or cut-vertex is a vertex whose deletion increases the number of components in the network.

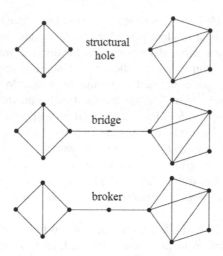

Fig. 2. Structural hole, bridge and broker

2.2   Generating k-Cliques

In order to find dense groups, components or communities, we are going to use the concept of k-clique.

Given an undirected graph G=(V, E), where V denotes the set of vertices (or nodes) and E, the set of edges (or arcs), graph $G_1= (V_1, E_1)$ is called a sub-graph of G, if $V_1 \subseteq V$, $E_1 \subseteq E$ and for every edge $(v_i, v_j) \in E_1$, the vertices $v_i, v_j \in V_1$. A sub-graph G_1 is said to be complete, if there is an edge for each pair of vertices. A complete graph is also called a clique.

A clique is maximal if it is not contained in another clique, while the maximum clique is the clique with maximum cardinality. The Maximum Clique is an NP-hard problem. In order to find a lower bound for the maximization problem, the heuristics proposed by Johnson [18] and the meta-heuristic that uses Tabu Search [16], developed by Soriano and Gendreau [24] can be used. Following works can be found in Cavique et al. [6] and Cavique and Luz [4].

The clique structure is very restrictive, since there must be an edge for each pair of vertices. More relaxed approaches were suggested in social sciences, such as k-cliques, k-clans, k-clubs and k-plexs [23].

In graph theory, the kth power of graph G returns a new graph G^k where each pair of vertices is adjacent when their distance in G is at most k. To find all the maximal k-cliques in the graph, we use the kth power of graph G in such a way that we can reuse an already well-known algorithm, the maximum clique algorithm. The transformation process adds edges to reach length k between every pair of nodes.

In Figure 2, each dense group is a 2-clique sub-graph, since the maximal distance between any pair of vertices is equal to 2.

Graph G^2 is equivalent to Granovetter's Triadic Closure, where a new edge is inserted because the distance between the pair of nodes is equal to 2. In this approach strong ties correspond to friends, and weak ties correspond to a friend's friend.

2.3   Network Partition

Community or dense group can be defined as a set of nodes with similarity. A partition is a sub-division of a graph into groups of vertices such that each vertex is assigned to one group.

One of the first studies is given by the Kernighan, Lin [19] algorithm, which finds a partition of the nodes by dividing the data into two disjoint subsets A and B of equal size, such that the sum of the weights of the edges between nodes in A and B is minimized.

Recent studies, based on physics, introduced the concept of clique percolation [11], where the network is viewed as a union of cliques.

The Girvan-Newman [15] method has been applied in recent years to social networks. This method successively deletes edges of high betweenness, and then recalculates all betweenness, breaking each component into smaller components [14].

A more relaxed problem that allows a node to share two components is the Set Covering problem. In the mathematical formulation the sign of the constraint is replaced for equal or greater instead of just equal, allowing the existence of over-covered nodes.

The optimization problem that finds the minimum number of columns that covers all the rows is the Set Covering problem. The matrix $[a_{i,j}]$ stores the information about the different communities and for each attribute x, a cost can be associated by using a vector c_j. The matrix and the cost vector are then used in the set covering problem, defined as:

minimize $f = \sum c_j.x_j$
subject to $\sum a_{i,j}.x_j \geq 1$
and $x_j \in \{0,1\}$ $j=1,\ldots,n$

The Set Covering problem is a widely studied problem in Combinatorial Optimization, with many computational resources which implement quasi-exact algorithms and heuristic approaches.

The set covering heuristic, proposed by Chvatal [8], repeats the process by choosing the line with fewer elements, followed by the choice of the column with the best ratio considering the cost of the column and the number of lines covered. This constructive heuristic is improved by using a Tabu Search heuristic that removes the most redundant columns and re-builds a new solution [5].

3   The Two-Phase Algorithm

In order to simply the visualization of the network, a condensed network is a graph where some of the nodes represent communities. In this condensed network the nodes that correspond to k-cliques are shrunk.

Although there are several partition algorithms, there are few studies about the linkage between them, namely concerning issues related to brokerage. In this paper we present a new approach that takes into account the common elements between partitions (over-covered) and elements that do not belong to any partition (isolated nodes), formulated as the set covering problem with k-cliques.

The Two-phase Algorithm, firstly, generates several k-cliques ([$a_{i,j}$]columns) from the network and secondly, runs the set covering problem in order to find the minimum number of k-cliques which cover all the vertices. The algorithm can be specified as follows.

Algorithm 1: The Two-phase Algorithm
Input: network/graph G, distance k
Output: condensed network/graph G_C^k
1) Generate maximal k-cliques columns
2) Run the set covering problem

This work is an extension of the work presented by Cavique et al. [3]. The novelty of this work is the identification of brokers and the generation of condensed networks which allows a clear visualization in large networks.

3.1   The Set Covering Problem with k-Cliques

In this work, to generate a large set of maximal k-cliques a multi-start algorithm is used, which calls for the Tabu Heuristic for the Maximum Clique Problem. To each generated k-clique will correspond a column of the matrix [$a_{i,j}$] referred in the partition and Set Covering problem formulations.

To implement the first step of Algorithm 1, the generation of several k-cliques, we use some previous work. Finding a maximal clique in a k-graph is the same as finding a maximal k-clique in a graph. Part of the described work in this sub-section can also be found in Cavique et al. [6] and Cavique and Luz [4].

We define A(S) as the set of vertices which are adjacent to vertices of a current solution S. Let $n=|S|$ be the cardinality of clique S and $A^k(S)$ the subset of vertices with k arcs incident in S. A(S) can be divided into subgroups $A(S) = \cup A^k(S)$, $k=1,...,n$. The cardinality of the vertex set $|V|$ is equal to the sum of the adjacent vertices A(S) and the non-adjacent ones $A^0(S)$, plus $|S|$, resulting in $|V| = \Sigma |A^k(S)|+n$, $k= 0,...,n$. For a given solution S, we define a neighborhood N(S) if it generates a feasible solution S'. In this work we are going to use three neighborhood structures. We consider the following notation:

$N^+ (S) = \{S': S'= S \cup \{v^i\}, v^i \in A^n(S)\}$
$N^- (S) = \{S': S'= S \setminus \{v^i\}, v^i \in S\}$
$N^0 (S) = \{S': S'= S \cup \{v^i\} \setminus \{v^k\}, v^i \in A^{n-1}(S), v^k \in S\}$
S – the current solution
S*– the highest cardinality maximal clique found so far
T– the tabu list
N(S) – neighborhood structures

Algorithm 2: Tabu Heuristic for the Maximum Clique Problem
Input: k-Graph; start sub-graph S;
Output: maximal clique S*;
1. T=∅; S*=S;
2. while not end condition
2.1.   if (N$^+$(S)\T ≠ null) choose the maximum S';
2.2.   else if (N^0(S)\T ≠ null) choose the maximum S'; update T;
2.2.1.   else choose the maximum S' in N$^-$(S); update T;
2.3.   update S=S';
2.4.   if (|S|>|S*|) S*=S;
3. end while;
4. return S*;

To implement the second step of Algorithm 1, the input for the k-clique cover is a matrix where the lines correspond to the vertices of the graph and each column is a k-clique that covers a certain number of vertices. We consider the following notation:

$[a_{i,j}]$ – input matrix with j columns
$[c_j]$ – vector of the cost of each column
T– the tabu list
R – remaining columns
S – the current solution
S*– the best solution

Algorithm 3: Tabu Heuristic for the k-Clique Covering
Input: [a(i,j)], [c(j)]
Output: the cover S*
1. T=∅; S*=∅;
2. while not end condition
2.1.   R=[a(i,j)]\T; S=∅;
2.2.   while R ≠ ∅ do
2.2.1.   choose the best line i*∈ R such as |a(i*,j)|=min |a(i,j)| ∀j;
2.2.2.   choose the best column j* that covers line i*;
2.2.3.   update R,S,T: R=R\a(i,j*) ∀i; S=S∪{j*}; update T;
2.3.   end while;
2.4.   sort the cover S by descending order of costs;
2.5.   for each Si do if (S\Si is still a cover) then S=S\Si;
2.6.   if (cost(S)< cost(S*)) S*=S;
3. end while;
4. return S*;

Each iteration of the inner cycle of the heuristic chooses a line to be covered. The best column which covers the line, updates solution S and the remaining R columns. The chosen line is usually the line that is more difficult to cover, i.e. the line which corresponds to fewer columns. After reaching the cover set, the second step is to remove redundancy, by sorting the cover in descending order of cost and checking if each k-clique is really essential. The outer cycle improves the constructive heuristic using a Tabu Search strategy that removes some already used columns and re-builds a new solution.

3.2   Numeric Example

In this sub-section the running example, initialized in section 1, is presented, in order to show the condensed graph and the brokers.

Following the rule of three degrees of influence, i.e., our friends' friends' friends affect us, proposed by Christakis and Fowler [9], we are going to use the 3-cliques, equivalent to a power graph G^3. In Figure 3, three 3-cliques partially cover the given graph. We can verify that in each k-clique the maximum distance between two nodes is equal to 3, the value of k.

In Figure 4, on the left, matrix [ai,j] shows that nodes 2,10,12 and 14 are over-covered and node 23 is an isolated node. Also in Figure 4, on the right, the condensed graph is composed by three communities: A, B and C.

In the condensed graph, the communities are represented by squares, and the brokers, represented by dots.

Table 1 shows the data extracted from the figures:

- the cost of the solution is equal to the number of columns, and is also equal to the number of communities in the social network, i.e., equal 3;
- in the solution, 22 covered nodes can be found;
- the over-covered nodes are 4 and they represent the brokers in the network;
- one node is isolated, which is a node in the periphery of the social network;

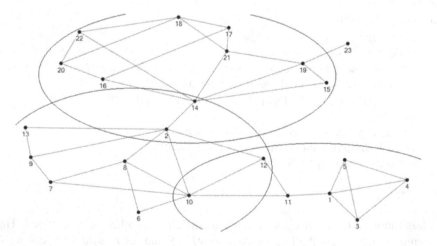

Fig. 3. Three k-cliques, with k=3, covers the graph partially

	A	B	C	isolated
1			1	
2	1	1		
3			1	
4			1	
5			1	
6		1		
7		1		
8		1		
9		1		
10		1	1	
11			1	
12		1	1	
13		1		
14	1	1		
15	1			
16	1			
17	1			
18	1			
19	1			
20	1			
21	1			
22	1			
23				1

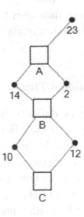

Fig. 4. The problem solution and the respective condensed graph G_C

Table 1. Information Extracted from Figures 3 and 4

$|x|$ = number communities	covered nodes	over-covered = brokers	isolated nodes
3 (A,B,C)	22	4	1

In this paper, the network is shrunk into a condensed network, where each community is reduced to a single node and the over-covered nodes are called brokers, as shown in Figure 4.

4 Computational Results

To implement the computational results of this algorithm some choices such as the computational environment, the datasets and the performance measures must be made. The computer programs were written in C language and the Dev-C++ compiler was used. The computational results were obtained from an AMD 1.90 GHz processor with 8.00 GB of main memory running under the Windows 7 Home Premium operating system.

To validate the proposed method, two groups of datasets were used, the Erdös graphs and some cliques from the DIMACS [10] benchmark instances. In the Erdös graphs, each node corresponds to a researcher, and two nodes are adjacent if the researchers published together. The graphs are named "erdos-x-y", where "x" represents the last two digits of the year the graphs were created, and "y", the maximum distance from Erdös to each vertex in the graph. The second group of graphs contains some clique instances from the second DIMACS challenge. These include the "brock" graphs, which contain cliques "hidden" within much smaller cliques, increasing the difficulty of discovering cliques in these graphs. The "c-fat" graphs are a result of fault diagnosis data.

The performance measures taken into account are the computational time and the quality of the solution, namely the quality of the visualization of the condensed network.

4.1   Computational Time

We selected 4 brock datasets, 3 c-fat datasets and 3 erdos datasets. For each dataset we tested from k=1 to k=7. For large k values, only one community was found and there were no brokers. In table 2, the chosen instances with the number of nodes, the diameter and the computational time are shown.

Although both algorithms are NP-hard, the less than 120 seconds computational time seems acceptable. The polynomial time complexity of the heuristics and the reduction of the optimization parameters insure the presented results.

Table 2. Datasets and Run Time for Kmax=7

Graph	nr nodes	diameter	time (seconds)
brock200-1	200	2	18
brock200-2	200	2	19
brock400-1	400	2	61
brock400-2	400	2	60
c-fat200-1	200	18	14
c-fat200-2	200	9	15
c-fat500-1	500	40	29
erdos-97-1	472	6	71
erdos-98-1	485	7	65
erdos-99-1	492	7	70

4.2   Quality of the Solutions

To test the visualization of the dataset erdos-97-1dataset was chosen. In Table 3, the k variable, number of communities |x|, the total number of covered nodes and the isolated nodes can be found.

Table 3. Solutions for erdos-97-1

k	|x| = number communities	covered	over-covered = brokers	isolated nodes
k1	49	204	27	90
k2	12	170	26	137
k3	4	164	20	143
k4	3	277	0	30
k5	1	305	0	2

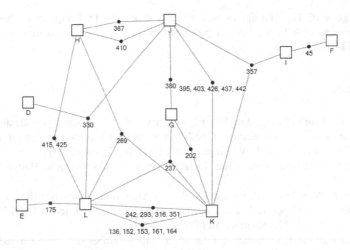

Fig. 5. Condensed erdos-97-1-k2 graph

Solution k2 was chosen with 12 communities allowing a good visualization of the network. In Figure 5, the condensed erdos-97-1-k2 graph is presented, where, the bridges were purposely omitted to simplify the visualization. Only 9 of the 12 communities are shown, the other three communities are connected by bridges.

The purpose of this experiment is not to highlight the exact solution, but rather to provide a good visualization of the network. The shrinking of the communities allows a general visualization of the network, the identification of the dense groups and the finding of the brokers. The analysis of the condensed networks also allows discovering the structural holes between communities.

5   Conclusions

The social networks' analysts have often referred the problematic of structural holes and brokerage. Automatic procedures are limited in finding, not only the communities but also the actors that play within them. The data extracted from social networking goes beyond the structure of communities, allowing the finding of the brokers that interact between groups. In this paper the finding of communities and the identification of their related brokers is shown.

The community partition can be relaxed for the set covering problem allowing brokers, i.e. over-covered actors. With this purpose in mind we defined community as a k-clique and the community partition as a set covering problem with k-cliques allowing over-covered and existence of isolated nodes.

The algorithm returns a condensed graph, which allows a new visualization of large networks. The communities and brokers in a condensed graph undoubtedly simplify the work of the social network analyst. The proposed visualization of the condensed network not only clearly shows the brokers, but also allows the social network analyst to detect structural holes, in order to enhance the hidden structures of the network.

Acknowledgement. The first author would like to thank the FCT support in the Funding of Strategic Projects with Public Interest promoted by Associated Laboratories and RD Units, PEst-OE/EEI/UI0434/2011.

References

1. Auber, D., Chiricota, Y., Jourdan, F., Melançon, G.: Multiscale visualization of small world networks. In: Proceedings of the Ninth annual IEEE conference on Information visualization, INFOVIS 2003, Washington, DC, USA, pp. 75–81 (2003)
2. Burt, R.S.: Structural Holes: The Social Structure of Competition. Harvard University Press (1992)
3. Cavique, L., Mendes, A.B., Santos, J.M.A.: An Algorithm to Discover the k-Clique Cover in Networks. In: Lopes, L.S., Lau, N., Mariano, P., Rocha, L.M. (eds.) EPIA 2009. LNCS, vol. 5816, pp. 363–373. Springer, Heidelberg (2009)
4. Cavique, L., Luz, C.J.: A heuristic for the stability number of a graph based on convex quadratic programming and tabu search. Journal of Mathematical Sciences **161**(6), 944–955 (2009)
5. Cavique, L., Rego, C., Themido, I.: Subgraph Ejection Chains and Tabu Search for the Crew Scheduling Problem. Journal of Operational Research Society **50**(6), 608–616 (1999)
6. Cavique, L., Rego, C., Themido, I.: A scatter search algorithm for the maximum clique problem. In: Ribeiro, C., Hansen, P. (eds.) Essays and Surveys in Meta-Heuristics, pp. 227–244. Kluwer Academic Pubs., Dordrecht (2002)
7. Chakrabarti, D., Faloutsos, C.: Graph mining: Laws, generators, and algorithms. ACM Computing Surveys **38**(1), 1–69 (2006)
8. Chvatal, V.: A greedy heuristic for the set-covering problem. Mathematics of Operations Research **4**, 233–235 (1979)
9. Christakis, N., Fowler, J.: Connected: The surprising power of networks and how they shape our lives, Back Bay Books/Little, Brown and Company. Hachette Book Group (2011)
10. DIMACS: Maximum clique, graph coloring, and satisfiability. Second DIMACS implementation challenge (1995), http://dimacs.rutgers.edu/Challenges/
11. Derenyi, I., Palla, G., Vicsek, T.: Clique Percolation in Random Networks. Physical Review Letters **94**(16), 160202 (2005)
12. Du, N., Faloutsos, C., Wang, B., Akoglu, L.: Large human communication networks: patterns and a utility-driven generator. In: Proceedings of the 15th ACM SIGKDD International Conference on Knowledge Discovery and Data Mining (KDD), pp. 269–278 (2009)
13. Dwyer, T., Riche, N.H., Marriott, K., Mears, C.: Edge Compression Techniques for Visualization of Dense Directed Graphs. IEEE Transactions on Visualization and Computer Graphics **19**, 2596–2605 (2013)
14. Easley, D., Kleinberg, J.: Networks, Crowds and Markets: Reasoning About a Highly Connected World. Cambridge University Press (2010)
15. Girvan, M., Newman, M.E.J.: Community structure in social and biological networks. Proc. Natl. Acad. Sci. USA **99**(12), 7821–7826 (2002)
16. Glover, F., Laguna, M.: Tabu Search. Kluwer Academic Publishers, Boston (1997)
17. Granovetter, M.: The strength of weak ties. American Journal of Sociology **78**, 1360–1380 (1973)

18. Johnson, D.S.: Approximation algorithms for combinatorial problems. Journal of Computer and Systems Sciences **9**(9), 256–278 (1974)
19. Kernighan, B.W., Lin, S.: An efficient heuristic procedure for partitioning graphs. Bell Systems Technical Journal **49**, 291–307 (1970)
20. Luce, R.D.: Connectivity and generalized cliques in sociometric group structure. Psychometrika **15**, 159–190 (1950)
21. Nooy, W., Mrvar, A., Batagelj, V.: Exploratory Social Network Analysis with Pajek. Cambridge University Press (2005)
22. Royer, L., Reimann, M., Andreopoulos, B., Schroeder, M.: Unraveling Protein Networks with Power Graph Analysis, in Berg, Johannes. PLoS Computational Biology **4**(7), e1000108 (2008), doi:10.1371/journal.pcbi.1000108
23. Scott, J.: Social Network Analysis: A Handbook. SAGE Publications Ltd. (2000)
24. Soriano, P., Gendreau, M.: Tabu search algorithms for the maximum clique. In: Johnson, D.S., Trick, M.A. (eds.) Clique, Coloring and Satisfiability, Second Implementation Challenge DIMACS, pp. 221–242. American Mathematical Society (1996)
25. Tarawneh, R.M., Keller, P., Ebert, A.: A General Introduction To Graph Visualization Techniques. In: Garth, C., Middel, A., Hagen, H. (eds.) Proceedings of IRTG 1131, Visualization of Large and Unstructured Data Sets Workshop, pp. 151–164 (2011)
26. Yang, J., Leskovec, J.: Overlapping Community Detection at Scale: A Nonnegative Matrix Factorization. In: ACM International Conference on Web Search and Data Mining (WSDM), pp. 587–596 (2013)

Relevance Measures for Multivalued Attributes in Multiclass Datasets

Mariana Tasca[1]([✉]), Bianca Zadrozny[2], and Alexandre Plastino[1]

[1] Instituto de Computação, Universidade Federal Fluminense, Niterói, Brazil
{mlobo,plastino}@ic.uff.br
[2] IBM Research, Rio de Janeiro, Brazil
biancaz@br.ibm.com

Abstract. An important step in the knowledge discovery in databases (KDD) process is the attribute selection procedure, which aims at choosing a subset of attributes that can represent the important information within the data. Most of the existing attribute selection methods can only handle simple attribute types, such as categorical and numerical. In particular, these methods cannot be applied to multivalued attributes, which are attributes that take multiple values simultaneously for the same instance in the dataset. This article proposes two relevance measures for multivalued attributes, which aim at measuring their importance for classification. The proposed measures are adaptations of two widely used relevance measures for categorical attributes: information gain and gain ratio. In order to evaluate the proposed measures, experiments were conducted with multiclass datasets submitted to multi-relational classifiers. The experiments show that the proposed measures are good indicators of the relevance of multivalued attributes for multiclass classification.

Keywords: Attribute selection · Classification · Multi-relational data mining · Multivalued attributes · Relevance measures

1 Introduction

One of the most studied and applied tasks in data mining is the classification task, which aims at estimating the class of an instance based on the available set of attributes. One method to improve the performance of the classification process is to perform an attribute selection procedure, an important step in the data mining process, which aims at choosing a subset of attributes that can represent the important information within the data, based on some criteria [20]. The use of this procedure is strongly recommended, especially if the dataset has a huge dimensionality, because most of the data mining algorithms may require a large computational effort if a large number of attributes is used. The use of an attribute selection procedure can provide: (a) improvement in the performance of the classifiers, eliminating useless attributes and those that can deteriorate the results, (b) simpler classification models, reducing the computational cost

© Springer International Publishing Switzerland 2014
A.L.C. Bazzan and K. Pichara (Eds.): IBERAMIA 2014, LNAI 8864, pp. 344–355, 2014.
DOI: 10.1007/978-3-319-12027-0_28

of executing this models and providing a better understanding of the obtained results, (c) smaller datasets.

Given the context of conventional data mining, where the dataset under investigation is represented by a single table or a sequential file, the feature selection algorithms and relevance measures available in the literature take into consideration only simple attributes, such as categorical and numerical. However, many real datasets have multivalued attributes, which are characterized by being able to assume multiple values simultaneously. Example: the types of books a person reads (which could be "children's" and "romance" or "comedy" and "mystery"), the research areas of a professor, etc.

This type of attribute may contribute or not to the classification task, depending on the target application domain. For example, knowing which types of books a person buys (multivalued attribute) can be important to find out if this person has children or not, but it may not bring any useful information about the usage of a credit card. Thus, it is important to deal with this type of attribute so one can assess its relevance for classification.

To avoid confusion, we note that there is work in the literature which uses the term "multivalued attributes" with a different meaning than what we use here. They address attribute selection when different attributes have very different domain sizes [4] and not when attributes can take multiple values simultaneously, which is the meaning of the term here and in most of the database and data mining literature.

The research area which develops methods that can deal with databases composed of multiple tables is known as Relational Mining (also called multi-relational just to emphasize the use of multiple tables) [7]. Several algorithms have been proposed in the relational mining literature [3,11,12,18,19,21,24,25]. Since the representation of multivalued attributes in databases is usually accomplished through a separate table to avoid redundancy within the main table [9], research about this type of attribute, which is the object of the present study, is therefore placed in the context of multi-relational mining.

Although there are many methods that deal directly with multivalued attributes, we did not find any work in the literature which specifically addresses multivalued attribute selection or any measure to determine their importance. In [13], a technique that transforms the k possible values of a multivalued attribute in k binary attributes is used, allowing the application of conventional attribute selection algorithms. However, this technique has the disadvantage of increasing the dimensionality of the original data, which can be problematic when k is large. Trying to fill this gap, in [26], we presented a relevance measure for multivalued attributes based on a weighted average of the differences in the conditional probability of the two classes, given each attribute value. However, this relevance measure has the limitation that it cannot be easily extended to datasets with more than two class labels (multiclass datasets). To address this limitation, here we present two new relevance measures for multivalued attributes, based on two well known measures for monovalued attribute, which can be used on datasets with more than two class labels.

This article is organized as follows. Section 2 contains a literature review on multi-relational classification, mainly about the k-NN algorithm and the distance measures used in this context. In Section 3, we present our proposed multivalued attribute relevance measures. In Section 4, we present the results obtained in the experiments and the evaluation of the proposed relevance measures. Finally, Section 5 presents the conclusions of this work and proposals for future work.

2   Classification Using Multivalued Attributes

Traditionally, data mining research addresses algorithms which extract information from datasets stored on a single table or a sequential file. However, the relational model, most commonly used, is composed of multiple tables referenced through foreign keys [9]. To allow data mining in these relational databases, the research area named relational mining emerged.

Multivalued attributes – which can assume multiple values simultaneously for the same instance – are represented in the relational model as separate tables referenced through foreign keys. So, the use of this type of attribute in data mining tasks requires the use of multi-relational techniques.

2.1   Multi-Relational Data Mining

Most common learning processes deal with flat files, composed by a set of instances, where each instance is represented by a fixed set of attributes and each attribute has a unique value for a given instance. However, real datasets are usually organized using the relational data model, where multiple tables store information in a normalized form and are related through foreign keys. There are two ways to extract information from relational databases through data mining techniques: using multi-relational data mining algorithms, which can deal directly with multiple tables, or performing a propositionalization, i.e., transforming the multi-relational problem into a propositional problem [19]. This transformation, in turn, can be done in two ways: (a) joining the target tables, grouping all attributes in a single table [12, 24], or (b) transforming the relational model into a single table by creating new attributes in the main table which summarize or aggregate information from the other tables.

Both of these alternatives may lead to problems: joining all tables may result in an extremely large table, which makes it difficult to deal with it. Furthermore, the table joints will generate a great number of redundant information, which may cause statistical problems [10]. Creating attributes in the main table with aggregated information from other tables, through operations such as sum, average or count, can lead to a significant loss of information. There is some work in the literature about categorical attribute aggregation generating less loss of information. In [22], a framework that performs propositionalization in relational databases using conventional numerical attribute aggregation operations (sum, average, count) and more sophisticated aggregation operations on categorical attributes has been presented.

There are also several proposals in the multi-relational data mining area which can deal with tables represented in their original data model. Most of them are related with Inductive Logic Programming (ILP) [8], which combine induction and logic programming [19]. In [3], a framework illustrated by the Warmr algorithm, a generalization of the Apriori algorithm for relational models has been presented. In [11] the problem of mining closed sets in multi-relational databases has been addressed. In [19], a framework for multi-relational decision trees has been presented. In [17], an approach based on Bayesian networks has been explored. The work presented in [21] proposes a new framework for constraint-based pattern mining in multi-relational databases. In [25], the authors introduce a novel approach to mining patterns in multi-relational data, proposing a new syntax for multi-relational patterns as complete connected subsets of database entities.

2.2 Classification Task Using Multivalued Attributes

One of the most important tasks in data mining is the classification task, which aims at estimating the class of an instance based on its attributes. The k-NN algorithm (k Nearest Neighbors) is a well known lazy classification technique, which has been used in the multi-relational data mining context [6,7]. It was proposed in the '50s, but it only became popular in the data mining and relational learning areas in the beginning of the '90s [1].

The main idea of this algorithm is to classify a new instance by comparing it with the instances in the dataset to identify the k most similar. The label of the new instance is determined by the most frequent label among the k instances which are most similar to the instance being classified. The value of k is an input parameter of the algorithm.

To compare the similarity between the instances of the dataset, distance measures are used. A popular distance measure usually used with this type of classifier when the attributes are numeric is the Euclidean distance measure [5]. When the attributes are categorical, a simple way to calculate the distance between them is to consider the difference equal to 1 (one), when the values are different, and equal to 0 (zero), when the values are the same.

In cases where one or more attributes to be considered in the classification represent a set of objects (multivalued attribute), a special kind of distance measure must be used, which can deal with set comparison. Different measures have been proposed in the literature for defining distances between sets of objects. Among them, we can cite Average Linking [16], Tanimoto [6] and RIBL [7], which were used in our experiments to calculate the distances for multivalued attributes. Since the results for these distances measures were very similar, to simplify the analysis we present only the results with Tanimoto distance.

The Tanimoto distance between sets A and B [6], represented by $D_T(A, B)$, is defined as: $D_T(A, B) = \frac{|A|+|B|-2|A \cap B|}{|A|+|B|-|A \cap B|}$. This measure is based on the size of the intersection between the two sets. Therefore, this distance measure is directly applicable to sets of discrete elements. For continuous elements, two elements a_i

and b_j are considered the same if the difference $d(a_i, b_j) = \frac{|a_i - b_j|}{|a_i + b_j|}$ is lower than a threshold defined by the user.

3   The Proposed Relevance Measures

With the aim of extending the previous work presented in [26], this work proposes two new relevance measures for multivalued attributes, $IGMv$ and $GRMv$, based respectively on two well known measures [23]: Information Gain (IG) and Gain Ratio (GR), widely used in practice with monovalued attributes. These new measures enable the evaluation of the relevance of multivalued attributes on multiclass datasets, i.e., datasets where the class label has two or more values. The next sections describe these two new measures.

3.1 $IGMv$ - Information Gain for Multivalued Attributes

Our proposed $IGMv$ measure is based on the information gain measure, which is defined as the change in class entropy from a prior state to a state where an attribute value is known. Let A be an attribute and C be the class. The Formulas (1) and (2) define the entropy before and after the observation of attribute A, respectively.

$$H(C) = -\sum_{c \in C} p(c) log_2 p(c). \tag{1}$$

$$H(C|A) = -\sum_{a \in A} p(a) \sum_{c \in C} p(c|a) log_2 p(c|a). \tag{2}$$

The information gain of an attribute A, $IG(A)$, is obtained from the difference between the class entropy before and after knowing A: $IG(A) = H(C) - H(C|A)$.

In Formula (2) the value $p(a)$ is obtained as the ratio between the number of instances for which A assumes the value a and the total number of instances. This is in agreement with the second axiom of probability theory, i.e., $\sum_{a \in A} p(a) = 1$, because the attribute values are mutually exclusive and cover all the cases. However, using this ratio for multivalued attributes would lead to a violation of the second axiom, because the sum of the number of occurrences of all the attributes values could be higher than the total number of instances and thus $\sum_{a \in A} p(a) > 1$. In that case, (2) would not be a valid entropy and the information gain value could be out of the $[0, 1]$ range.

To adapt the information gain measure to multivalued attributes respecting the axioms of probability, we propose replacing $p(a)$ by $w(a)$ in Formula (2), where $w(a)$ is the ratio between the total number of occurrences of a and the total number of occurrences of all values in the domain of A. This effectively changes the weighting factor which represents the contribution of the value a when calculating $H(C|A)$.

Thus, the information gain for multivalued attributes is defined as follows:

$$IGMv(A) = H(C) - H'(C|A), \tag{3}$$

where

$$H'(C|A) = -\sum_{a \in A} w(a) \sum_{c \in C} p(c|a) log_2 p(c|a). \qquad (4)$$

Previous research [14] has identified a problem with the information gain measure when the attribute entropy is very high (i.e., when the number of attribute values is very large), which raises the measure value even when there is not a clear dependency between the attribute and the class. The gain ratio measure has been proposed to address this problem. In the next section, we propose an adaptation of the GR to multivalued attributes.

3.2 $GRMv$ - Gain Ratio for Multivalued Attributes

The idea of the GR measure is to normalize the information gain value with the attribute entropy value. Thus, the GR value of an attribute A, $GR(A)$, is calculated as $GR(A) = IG(A)/H(A)$. In the same way as in the adaptation of information gain, we replace $p(a)$ by $w(a)$ in $H(A)$ to obtain $H'(A)$, and the gain ratio for multivalued attributes is defined as:

$$GRMv(A) = IGMv(A)/H'(A). \qquad (5)$$

Table 1 shows a toy example dataset used to explain how to calculate $IGMv$ and $GRMv$. The dataset is composed of five instances separated into three class labels. Each instance represents a person and the multivalued attribute A represents the types of movies watched by them. The domain of A is {mystery, romance, comedy}.

Table 1. A dataset toy example

Id	Class label	Multivalued attribute A
P1	1	mystery
P2	1	mystery, romance
P3	2	mystery, comedy
P4	3	romance
P5	3	comedy, romance

Using the example of Table 1, $p(c)$ values are calculated in the same way as for monovalued attributes, that is, $p(1) = 2/5$, $p(2) = 1/5$ and $p(3) = 2/5$. Similarly, $p(c|a)$ values are calculated, for each value a, independently, in the same manner as done for monovalued attributes. For example, $p(1|mystery) = 2/3$, $p(2|mystery) = 1/3$ and $p(3|mystery) = 0$.

Applying the $w(a)$ factor, we have $w(mystery) = 3/8$, $w(romance) = 3/8$ and $w(comedy) = 2/8$. Note that the denominator of the ratio is the total number of occurrences of all values from the domain of A, which in this case is 8.

4   Experiments and Results

To validate the proposed relevance measures, we conducted experiments on seven real datasets, composed of monovalued and multivalued attributes. KDD and EBook datasets were used previously on some work about multi-relational data mining [22]. Pnad88 and Censo2010 were obtained from IBGE [15]. Hypothyroid2 was adapted from the original Hypothyroid dataset, obtained from public UCI repository [2]. Details about these datasets can be seen in Table 2.

Table 2. Datasets used on the experiments

Datasets (Class: % of class distribution)	Number of instances	Number of monovalued attributes	Multivalued attributes (domain size)
EBook (Sex: 51.4 / 17.1 / 31.5)	1180	3	Book (6852) Categ (5)
Pnad88-5 (Sewer: 26.2 / 26.1 / 13.7 / 21.2 / 12.8)	1023	7	Mv1 (5) Mv2 (5)
Pnad88-6 (Garbage: 48.6 / 28.7 / 22.5)	984	7	Mv1 (5) Mv2 (5)
Hypothyroid2 (Class: 49.7 / 16.6 / 33.7)	513	3	Mv1 (9) Mv2 (9)
KDD (Wear: 17.7 / 22.9 / 37.8 / 21.6)	564	10	Prod (159) Coll (58)
KDD2A (Dress: 17.1 / 46.1 / 16.8 / 36.0)	542	10	Prod (124) Coll (58)
Censo2010 (Radio: 60.6 / 39.4)	17835	16	Activ (200) Occup (363)

Accuracy values obtained with relational classifiers were observed in conjunction with the relevance measure values of the multivalued attributes. Higher values for the relevance measure should generally lead to better accuracy values and vice-versa.

The relational classifiers were obtained with the relational k-NN (RelIbk) algorithm, which is publicly available within a relational data mining tool (RelWeka). The k-NN k parameter was fixed in 3. We experimented with three distance measures within the k-NN algorithm: Average Linking, Tanimoto and RIBL, but for the reasons already mentioned before, only the results with Tanimoto distance are presented. Both the relevance measures and accuracy values were calculated using a 10-fold cross validation.

A t-test (confidence level $\alpha = 0.05$) was used to decide if the difference of accuracy values between each pair of multivalued attributes was significant, i.e., if the classification result using one of the attributes is significantly better compared with the other one.

4.1   Analyzing Multivalued Attributes by Themselves

In the first experiment, we analyze if each of the relevance measure values ($IGMv$ and $GRMv$), for each attribute, is compatible with the accuracy value obtained as a result of using this single attribute in the classifier. We expect that higher relevance measure values are associated with higher accuracy values and vice-versa. Comparing two multivalued attributes A and B, where A has a higher relevance measure than B, we expect that the accuracy value obtained when A is submitted to the classifier is higher than the accuracy value associated to B.

Table 3 shows the results of this experiment. Each row represents the relevance measure and accuracy values for each pair of multivalued attribute of each analyzed dataset. Only for KDD, KDD2A and Censo2010 there is no statistical significance on the difference between accuracies obtained with the two multivalued attributes evaluated. For these three cases, we cannot be sure that one of the attributes generates a higher accuracy than the other one when they are used in the classifier. Thus, we do not analyze their relevance measure values. For all other datasets, there is a statistical significant difference between the accuracy values obtained with the evaluated attributes. And in all these cases, the relevance measures were consistent, indicating with a higher value the attribute which presented a better accuracy for classification.

It is important to highlight that in all cases the behaviors of both $IGMv$ (third column) and $GRMv$ (fourth column) were coherent, that is, if attribute A was considered better than B by $IGMv$, this was also true for $GRMv$.

The first four rows of Table 3 present the accuracy and relevance measures values for the datasets where the accuracy difference between evaluated attributes has statistical significance. Just for the sake of completeness, the three last rows represent the datasets where the accuracy difference between evaluated attributes has no statistical significance. The fifth column shows the accuracy values obtained from k-NN classifier with $k = 3$ and Tanimoto distance. And the last column presents an analysis about the relevance measures and accuracy values comparison. As we can observe, in all cases where we have statistical significance on the difference between accuracies, the higher rated attribute with respect to the relevance measures, also obtained a better accuracy value.

4.2   Analyzing the Contribution of Multivalued Attributes to a Initial Set of Monovalued Attributes

The experiment presented in Table 4 shows the analysis of accuracy values obtained when the set of attributes submitted to the classifier were a combination of some monovalued attributes and one multivalued attribute. Let A and B be two multivalued attributes where A has a higher relevance measure value than B. Let S be a set of monovalued attributes with some accuracy value associated to them. We want to verify if the contribution of attribute A to S in terms of accuracy is higher than the contribution of attribute B. In other words, we expect that the accuracy obtained with $A \cup S$ is higher than the accuracy obtained with $B \cup S$, since A is highly-rated. This is considered a coherent result.

Table 3. Relevance measures values for multivalued attributes and accuracies obtained

Dataset	Multivalued Attribute	IgMv	GrMv	Accuracy (Acc)	Result
EBook	Book	0.752	0.064	60.17	Book>Categ
	Categ	0.071	0.048	51.78	and Acc(Book)>Acc(Categ)
Pnad88-5	Mv1	0.145	0.063	40.76	Mv1>Mv2
	Mv2	0.045	0.020	30.89	and Acc(Mv1)>Acc(Mv2)
Pnad88-6	Mv1	0.100	0.043	60.67	Mv1>Mv2
	Mv2	0.019	0.008	55.18	and Acc(Mv1)>Acc(Mv2)
Hypothyroid2	Mv1	0.032	0.016	54.77	Mv1>Mv2
	Mv2	0.011	0.008	47.37	and Acc(Mv1)>Acc(Mv2)
KDD	Prod	0.668	0.102	39.00	Prod>Coll
	Coll	0.383	0.076	42.02	but Acc(Prod)<Acc(Coll)
KDD2A	Prod	0.540	0.085	42.43	Prod>Coll
	Coll	0.329	0.066	40.59	but Acc(Prod)<Acc(Coll)
Censo2010	Activ	0.017	0.003	58.82	Activ<Occup
	Occup	0.023	0.004	58.87	and Acc(Activ)<Acc(Occup)

One more time, KDD, KDD2A and Censo2010 datasets have no statistical significance on the accuracy difference between the two evaluated attributes. Thus, it makes no sense to analyze the behavior of the relevance measures, as we cannot be sure that the contribution of one of the attributes was better than the other one. For this reason and for the sake of simplicity, results for these datasets are not presented.

Table 4 presents the accuracy and relevance measures values for the datasets where the accuracy difference between evaluated attributes has statistical significance. The column identified by "TA" presents the accuracy values obtained by the RelIbk classifier. The "MN" label represents the set of monovalued attributes.

As we can observe, not always the inclusion of an attribute to the initial set of attributes represents an improvement in terms of accuracy. For all datasets, the inclusion of the worst-rated attribute represent a short decrease in the accuracy value (comparing the first and third "TA" values of each dataset). On the other hand, the inclusion of higher-rated attributes on the initial set of attributes represent an accuracy improvement (comparing the first and second "TA" values of each dataset). The results were coherent for all datasets. Highly-rated attributes generated a higher accuracy when they were inserted on the initial set of monovalued attributes.

From the results presented previously, we can conclude that $IGMv$ and $GRMv$ may be valid and useful relevance measures for attribute selection when multivalued attributes are considered in the evaluated context.

Despite the objective of GR is to address the problem of IG when the attribute entropy is very high, we do not verify any incompatibility between these two relevance measures when they were adapted to be applied on multivalued attributes. That is, both $IGMv$ and $GRMv$ relevance measures have

Table 4. Contribution of multivalued attributes when they are combined with mono-valued (MN) ones

EBook - Sex - Accuracy values		EBook - Sex - Relevance Measures		
Attributes used on classifier	TA	Attributes	IgMv	GrMv
MN	71.19			
MN + Book	75.25	Book	0.752	0.064
MN + Categ	70.59	Categ	0.071	0.048
Pnad88-5 - Sewer - Accuracy values		**Pnad88-5 - Sewer - Relevance Measures**		
Attributes used on classifier	TA	Attributes	IgMv	GrMv
MN	52.69			
MN + Mv1	53.76	Mv1	0.145	0.063
MN + Mv2	51.91	Mv2	0.045	0.020
Pnad88-6 - Garbage - Accuracy values		**Pnad88-6 - Garbage** - Relevance Measures		
Attributes used on classifier	TA	Attributes	IgMv	GrMv
MN	55.59			
MN + Mv1	56.20	Mv1	0.100	0.043
MN + Mv2	55.28	Mv2	0.019	0.008
Hypothyroid2 - Class - Accuracy values		**Hypothyroid2 - Class** - Relevance Measures		
Attributes used on classifier	TA	Attributes	IgMv	GrMv
MN	42.89			
MN + Mv1	43.66	Mv1	0.032	0.016
MN + Mv2	41.13	Mv2	0.011	0.008

the same behavior, so it was not possible to identify, based on the conducted experiments, if one of the measures is better than the other one.

5   Conclusions

This work proposes two relevance measures for multivalued attributes, which aim at measuring their importance for classification.

As we could not find in the literature any other relevance measure suitable for multivalued attributes in multiclass datasets, it was not possible to compare our proposed measures with other ones. However, we were able to verify that these measures are useful for selecting good attributes for the classification task. To perform this analysis we used some relational classifiers, but as the results were similar, we presented only results from k-NN with Tanimoto distance.

We performed this analysis using real datasets, and we were able to show that in most cases the proposed relevance measures can be a good indicator of the quality of multivalued attributes to the classification task. These measures could be quite useful in conjunction with algorithms for attribute selection which use the filter approach.

For each pair of evaluated multivalued attributes, we could verify that the relevance measure values were coherent with the accuracy values generated by the classifier when these attributes were used by itself, as the single attribute used for classification. Highly-rated attributes by relevance measure generated better accuracies and vice-versa.

We also evaluated these two distinct situations for each pair of evaluated multivalued attributes: (a) submitting to the classifier a set of monovalued attributes and (b) submitting to the classifier the same initial set in conjunction with one multivalued attribute. The relevance measure values for the multivalued attributes were consistent: the inclusion of a multivalued attribute in the initial set of monovalued attributes resulted on a higher contribution in terms of accuracy for that attribute related to a higher relevance measure and vice-versa.

The relevance measures proposed in this work take into account the quality of multivalued attributes by themselves. A future research could be performed to study some kind of relevance measure which could take into account the influence of sets of monovalued and multivalued attributes on predicting the class label.

Acknowledgments. This work was supported by CNPq and CAPES research grants.

References

1. Aha, D.W.: Tolerating noisy, irrelevant and novel attributes in instance-based learning algorithms. International Journal of Man-Machine Studies **36**(2), 267–287 (1992)
2. Bache, K., Lichman, M.: UCI machine learning repository (2013), http://archive.ics.uci.edu/ml
3. Dehaspe, L., Toivonen, H.: Discovery of relational association rules. In: Dězeroski, S. (ed.) Relational Data Mining, pp. 189–208. Springer, New York (2001)
4. Deng, H., Runger, G., Tuv, E.: Bias of Importance Measures for Multi-valued Attributes and Solutions. In: Honkela, T. (ed.) ICANN 2011, Part II. LNCS, vol. 6792, pp. 293–300. Springer, Heidelberg (2011)
5. Deza, M.M., Deza, E.: Encyclopedia of Distances. Springer, Heidelberg (2009)
6. Duda, R., Hart, P., Stork, D.: Pattern Classification and Scene Analysis. John Willey and Sons, New York (2001)
7. Dzeroski, S.: Multi-relational data mining: an introduction. SIGKDD Explorations Newsletter **5**(1), 1–16 (2003)
8. Dzeroski, S., Lavrac, N.: Relational Data Mining, 1st edn. Springer, Secaucus (2001)
9. Elmasri, R., Navathe, S.B.: Fundamentals of Database System, 6th edn. Addison-Wesley, USA (2010)
10. Emde, W., Wettschereck, D.: Multi-relational data mining using probabilistic relational models: research summary. In: Proceedings of the Workshop in Multi-relational Data Mining, Freiburg (2001)
11. Garriga, G.C., Khardon, R., De Raedt, L.: On mining closed sets in multi-relational data. In: Proceedings of the 20th International Joint Conference on Artifical Intelligence, pp. 804–809. Morgan Kaufmann Publishers Inc., San Francisco (2007)
12. Goethals, B., Page, W., Mampaey, M.: Mining interesting sets and rules in relational databases. In: Proceedings of the ACM Symposium on Applied Computing, pp. 997–1001. ACM, New York (2010)
13. Hall, M.A., Holmes, G.: Benchmarking attribute selection techniques for discrete class data mining. IEEE Transactions on Knowledge and Data Engineering **15**(3), 1437–1447 (2003)
14. Harris, E.: Information gain versus gain ratio: a study of split method biases. In: Proceedings of International Symposium on Artificial Intelligence and Mathematics (2002)
15. IBGE: Instituto Brasileiro de Geografia e Estatística (2008), http://loja.ibge.gov.br/

16. Kalousis, A., Woznica, A., Hilario, M.: A unifying framework for relational distance-based learning. Tech. rep., University of Geneva, Switzerland, (2005)
17. Kersting, K., De Raedt, L.: Interpreting bayesian logic programs. In: Proceedings of the Work-in-Progress Track at the International Conference on Inductive Logic Programming, Szeged, Hungary, pp. 138–155 (2001)
18. Kramer, S., Lavrac, N., Flach, P.: Propositionalization approaches to relational data mining. In: Dězeroski, S. (ed.) Relational Data Mining, pp. 262–286. Springer, New York (2001)
19. Leiva, H.: MRDTL: a Multi-Relational Decision Tree Learning Algorithm. Master's thesis, Iowa State University, Ames, USA (2002)
20. Liu, H., Motoda, H.: Feature Selection for Knowledge Discovery and Data Mining. Kluwer Academic Publishers, Norwell (1998)
21. Nijssen, S., Jimenez, A., Guns, T.: Constraint-based pattern mining in multi-relational databases. In: Proceedings of the 11th IEEE International Conference on Data Mining Workshops, pp. 1120–1127 (2011)
22. Perlich, C., Provost, F.: Distribution-based aggregation for relational learning from identifier attributes. Machine Learning 62(1–2), 65–105 (2006)
23. Quinlan, J.R.: C4.5: Programs for Machine Learning. Morgan Kaufmann Publishers Inc., San Francisco (1993)
24. Siebes, A., Koopman, A.: Discovering relational item sets efficiently. In: Proceedings of the SIAM International Conference on Data Mining, pp. 108–119 (2008)
25. Spyropoulou, E., De Bie, T., Boley, M.: Interesting pattern mining in multi-relational data. Data Mining and Knowledge Discovery 28(3), 808–849 (2014)
26. Tasca, M., Zadrozny, B., Plastino, A.: A relevance measure for multivalued attributes. Journal of Information and Data Management 4(3), 421–436 (2013)

Bio-inspired computing

Understanding the Treatment of Outliers in Multi-Objective Estimation of Distribution Algorithms

Luis Martí[1]([✉]), Nayat Sanchez-Pi[2], and Marley Vellasco[1]

[1] Department of Electrical Engineering,
Pontifícia Universidade Católica do Rio de Janeiro, Rio de Janeiro, RJ, Brazil
{lmarti,marley}@ele.puc-rio.br
[2] Instituto de Lógica, Filosofia e Teoria da Ciéncia (ILTC), Niterói, RJ, Brazil
nayat@iltc.br

Abstract. It has been already documented the fact that estimation of distribution algorithms suffer from loss of population diversity and improper treatment of isolated solutions. This situation is particularly severe in the case of multi-objective optimization, as the loss of solution diversity limits the capacity of an algorithm to explore the Pareto-optimal front at full extent.

A set of approaches has been proposed to deal with this problem but —to the best of our knowledge— there has not been a comprehensive comparative study on the outcome of those solutions and at what degree they actually solve the issue.

This paper puts forward such study by comparing how current approaches handle diversity loss when confronted to different multi-objective problems.

Keywords: Multi-objective optimization · Estimation of distribution algorithms · Model building · Outlier detection

1 Introduction

Multi-objective optimization problems (MOPs) are problems involving more than one goal that must be simultaneously optimized. Most real-world optimization problems are solved using MOPs. Methods that address this problems In these problems the optimizer must find one or more feasible solutions that conjointly find the extremal values (either maximum or minimum) of two or more functions subject to a set of constraints. Consequently, the solution to that problem is a set of equally valid, trade-off solutions. MOPs have been addressed using evolutionary computation (EC). This fact has prompted the creation of multi–objective optimization evolutionary algorithms (MOEAs) [1].

The inclusion of learning as part of the search process has been pointed out as a relevant alternative to "traditional" MOEAs [2]. Estimation of distribution algorithms (EDAs) [3] are one of those alternatives, as they are capable

© Springer International Publishing Switzerland 2014
A.L.C. Bazzan and K. Pichara (Eds.): IBERAMIA 2014, LNAI 8864, pp. 359–370, 2014.
DOI: 10.1007/978-3-319-12027-0_29

of learning the problem structure. EDAs replace the application of evolutionary operators with the creation of a statistical model of the fittest elements of the population in a process known as *model building*. This model is then sampled to produce new elements.

However, multi-objective EDAs (MOEDAs) have not yielded the anticipated results. Most of them have limitations transforming single-objective EDAs into a multi-objective formulation by including an existing multi-objective fitness assignment function.

It can be stated that this straightforward extrapolation might had lead to skip the fact that most current EDAs have some characteristics that interferes their capacity of handling some of the requirements of multi-objective optimization.

These matters have been already pointed out in some previous works [4]. It has been said that some of them are derived from the incorrect treatment of the isolated elements of the model-building dataset (outliers); the loss of population diversity, and that too much computational effort is being spent on model construction.

In particular, previous experimental evidence [5–7] has raised the hypothesis that those model-building algorithms that are more sensitive to outliers frequently yield better results than those who don't. However, this fact must be studied in a more formal manner, paying attention to what is actually happening during the optimization process.

The purpose of this paper is to present an in-depth study regarding outliers and diversity loss issues in MOEDAs from both theoretical and experimental points of view. We carry out an experimental study measuring the diversity of populations that, to the best of our knowledge, has not been yet been carried out. This is a key assessment as its outcome is a key step towards the solution of what constitutes one of the current main problems of multi-objective EDAs.

The rest of the paper is structured as follows. Section 2 briefly discusses the theoretical foundations of the work. After that, the outliers issue is presented in Section 3. Subsequently, in Section 4, an experimental study focused on measuring the diversity of the population is debated. Finally, Section 5 contains some final remarks.

2   Foundations

Multi-objective optimization has received lot of attention by the evolutionary computation community leading to *multi-objective evolutionary algorithms* (MOEAs) (cf. [1]). A *multi-objective optimization problem* (MOP) could be expressed as the problem in which a set of M *objective functions* $f_1(\boldsymbol{x}), \ldots,$ $f_M(\boldsymbol{x})$ with should be jointly optimized;

$$\min \boldsymbol{F}(\boldsymbol{x}) = \langle f_1(\boldsymbol{x}), \ldots, f_M(\boldsymbol{x}) \rangle \, ; \; \boldsymbol{x} \in \mathcal{D} \, ; \tag{1}$$

where $\mathcal{D} \subseteq \mathbb{R}^n$ is known as the *feasible set* and could be expressed as a set of restrictions over the *decision set*, that is usually $\mathbb{R}^n$. The image set of $\mathcal{D}$

produced by function vector $\mathbf{F}(\cdot)$, $\mathcal{O} \subseteq \mathbb{R}^M$, is called *feasible objective set* or *criterion set*.

The solution of (1) is a set of trade-off points. The adequacy of a solution can be expressed in terms of the *Pareto dominance relation*. The solution of (1) is the Pareto-optimal set, $\mathcal{D}^*$; which is the subset of $\mathcal{D}$ that contains all elements of $\mathcal{D}$ that are not dominated by other elements of $\mathcal{D}$. Its image in objective space is called Pareto-optimal front, $\mathcal{O}^*$.

If an MOP has certain characteristics, e. g., linearity or convexity of the objective functions or convexity of $\mathcal{S}$, the efficient set can be determined by mathematical programming approaches [8]. However, in the general case, finding the solution of (1) is an *NP*–complete problem. In this case, heuristic or metaheuristic methods can be applied in order to have solutions of practical value at an admissible computational cost.

Generally, an heuristic algorithm solving an MOP yields a discrete local Pareto-optimal set, $\mathcal{P}^*$, that attempts to represent $\mathcal{S}^*$ as best as possible, although, in the general case, optimality can not be guarantied. The image of $\mathcal{P}^*$ in objective space, $\mathcal{PF}^*$, is known as the local Pareto-optimal front.

2.1   Multi-Objective Estimation of Distribution Algorithms

EDAs are population-based optimization algorithms like other "traditional" evolutionary approaches. However, in EDAs, the variation step where the evolutionary operators are applied to the population is substituted by construction of a statistical model of the most promising subset of the population. This model is then sampled to produce new individuals that are merged with the parent population following a given substitution policy. Therefore, it has been stated that an additional benefit of EDAs is that not only do they return a solution to a problem, but a model representing the solutions is presented as well.

Multi-objective EDAs (MOEDAs) [9] are the extensions of EDAs to the multi-objective domain. Most MOEDAs are built by modifying an existing EDAs by substituting it fitness assignment function by one taken from an existing MOEA.

A very popular foundation for MOEDAs is a range of EDAs that builds the population model using a Bayesian network, leading to what has been called Bayesian optimization algorithms (BOA) [9].

Multi-objective real BOA (MrBOA) [10] is a multi-objective EDA based on a variant of single-objective BOA, in this case the real BOA (rBOA) [11]. RBOA performs a proper problem decomposition by means of a Bayesian factorization and probabilistic building-block crossover. To do this, it employs mixture models at the level of subproblems. MrBOA combines the fitness assignment of NSGA–II [1] with rBOA.

Another approach to modeling the subset with the best population elements is to apply a distribution mixture approach. Bosman and Thierens [12] proposed several variants of their multi-objective mixture-based iterated density estimation algorithm (MIDEA). They also proposed a novel Pareto-based and diversity-preserving fitness assignment function. MIDEA considered several types of probabilistic models for both discrete and continuous problems. A mixture of univariate distributions and a mixture of tree distributions were used for discrete variables. A mixture of univariate Gaussian models and a mixture of multivariate Gaussian factorizations were applied for continuous variables. An adaptive clustering method was used to determine the capacity required to model a population.

The MIDEA family has been progressively improved. One of such enhancements is the introduction of the adaptive variance scaling (AVS) and the standard–deviation ratio (SDR) [13]. The AVS and SDR combination helps fight the early reduction of the mixture densities variances and therefore the premature convergence and diversity loss. Another important milestone has been the introduction of the anticipated mean shift (AMS) that takes into account the previous values of the means of the distribution to "push" solutions towards the Pareto-optimal front. AMS has been conjointly used with AVS in the multi-objective adapted maximum-likelihood Gaussian mixture model (MAMaLGaM-X) [14].

3   Outliers and Model-Building in MOEDAs

There are many data analysis or machine learning tasks in which a large number of variables are being recorded or sampled. One of the first steps towards obtaining a coherent analysis is the detection of outlaying observations. Detected data outliers are likely to be treated as abnormal data that may adversely lead to an invalid modelling, biased parameter estimation and incorrect results. Hence, it has always been of fundamental importance for practitioners to identify and handle with them prior to modeling and analysis.

However, an exact definition of an outlier often depends on hidden assumptions regarding the data structure and the applied detection method. Some intuitive definitions can be regarded general enough to cope with various types of data and methods. For example, it can be said that an outlier is an observation that deviates so much from other observations as to arouse suspicion that it was generated by a different mechanism [15].

In spite of the intangibility of a proper definition of outliers, there are many real-world world problems, like fraud detection, weather prediction, network intrusion detection, anomaly detection, etc., that have prompted the development of different methods for outlier detection (see [16] for further reading). Different scientific communities define outliers differently, and such criteria can include outliers based on distribution, distance, density, etc. Therefore, several approaches have been proposed to deal with them.

The outliers issue is a good example of insufficient comprehension of the nature of the model-building problem. In machine-learning practice, outliers are handled as noisy, inconsistent or irrelevant data. Therefore, outlying data is expected to have little influence on the model or just to be disregarded.

However, that behavior is not adequate for model-building. In this case, is known beforehand that all elements in the data set should be take into account as they represent newly discovered or candidate regions of the search space and therefore must be explored. Therefore, these instances should be at least equally represented by the model and perhaps even reinforced.

As model-building strategies varies from EDA to EDA, it is hard to back the previous statement with a general theoretical support. In order to do so, we must define an individual z_i as the pair representing values in decision and objective sets,

$$z_i = \langle x_i, F(x_i) \rangle . \tag{2}$$

In a simplified case, we can state that model building is an unsupervised machine learning problem with learning dataset,

$$\Psi = \{x_i\} \, ; \forall z_i = \langle x_i, F(x_i) \rangle \in \hat{\mathcal{P}}_t \, , \tag{3}$$

where $\hat{\mathcal{P}}_t$ is the model-building dataset which is a subset of the algorithm population at iteration t.

A regular machine learning algorithm tunes the model $\mathfrak{M}(x, \theta, \phi)$ by adjusting its topology θ and parameters ϕ. In error-based learning this process involves the calculation of a set-wise error to which each element-wise error contribute to a different degree,

$$E_{\text{tot}} = \sum_{x_i \in \Psi} E\left(\mathfrak{M}(x_i, \theta, \phi)\right) . \tag{4}$$

There are many different forms of the set-wise and element-wise errors, E_{tot} and $E(\cdot)$ respectively, but they can be formulated in a more or less similar fashion as above.

If E_{tot} is to be minimized, then θ and ϕ will be set in such way that the aggregation of element-wise contributions is as minimal as possible. As outliers, by their own definition, are rare and infrequent, their element-wise contribution to E_{tot} could be left to be relatively large as it is more convenient to focus on those that by being more popular, have a larger contribution to E_{tot}.

Therefore, model $\mathfrak{M}(x, \theta, \phi)$ would end up representing more accurately elements more densely grouped than those isolated. However, as we already mentioned, in the model-building case, all elements of Ψ are important, and, perhaps, the isolated ones might be even more important than the clustered ones, as they represent locally optimal zones of the objective set that have not been properly explored.

Some EDAs have been proposed with the objective of dealing with the outliers issue and as an outlier-sensitive option. That is the case of the multi-objective neural EDA (MONEDA) [6] which uses a particular model-building growing neural gas (MB-GNG) [5]. MB-GNG relies on GNG, which has been shown to be an outlier-sensitive algorithm.

4   Measuring Outliers in MOEDAs

As already discussed earlier in this work, there are already some indirect experimental evidences that had lead to the conclusion that improper handling of outliers, loss of population diversity and low performance are related [4].

However, a comprehensive experiment is required to assess at what degree different model-building algorithms tend to disregard outliers.

For this task two elements are necessary: a shared EDA framework in that will be used to embed the different model-building algorithms and to define a measure of "outlierness" of population individuals.

4.1   Determining Outliers Using LOCI

The local correlation integral (LOCI) method [17], and its outlier metric, the multi-granularity deviation factor (MDEF), were proposed with the purpose of correctly dealing with multi-density and multi-granularity. That is why we have chosen to use MDEF as the outlier metric in this paper.

Let the r-neighborhood of an element x of $\mathcal{S}$ be the set of objects within distance r of x,

$$\mathcal{N}(x, r) = \{x' \in \mathcal{S} \,|\, \|x - x'\| \leq r\}. \tag{5}$$

Then, having $n(x, \alpha r)$ and $n(x, r)$, that count the number of elements in the αr- and r-neighborhoods of x, denominated local and sampling neighborhoods, respectively, with $\alpha \in [0, 1]$. Relying of $n(\cdot)$ average over all elements x' in the r-neighborhood of x of their $n(x', \alpha r)$ is constructed as

$$\hat{n}(x, \alpha, r) = \frac{\sum_{x' \in \mathcal{N}(x, f)} n(x', \alpha r)}{n(x', r)} \tag{6}$$

The degree of 'outlierness' of a given element x of the dataset is computed as the *multi-granularity deviation factor* (MDEF) at radius $r \in \mathbb{R}$,

$$\mathrm{MDEF}(x, \alpha, r) = \frac{\hat{n}(x, \alpha, r) - n(x, \alpha r)}{\hat{n}(x, \alpha, r)}, \tag{7}$$

given $x \in \mathcal{S}$ and α,

The MDEF at radius r for a x is the relative deviation of its local neighborhood density from the average local neighborhood density in its r-neighborhood. Therefore, an element whose neighborhood density is equals the average local neighborhood density will have an MDEF of 0. On the other hand, outliers will have MDEFs larger than 0.

Following the recommendations and results from [17], we have set r as to make $n(x, r) \geq 20$ and $\alpha = 0.05$ in order to have sufficient data as to make MDEF statistically valid.

4.2   Shared EDA Framework

In order to assess different model-building algorithms, a general EDA framework is necessary. The model-building algorithms will share this framework. Therefore, it will provide a testing ground common to all approaches and allows us to concentrate only on the topic of interest: measuring the degree at which each model-building algorithm is able to retain or loose outliers.

The shared EDA workflow maintains a population of individuals, $\mathcal{P}_t$, where t is the current iteration. It starts from a random initial population $\mathcal{P}_0$ of n_{max} individuals. A $\hat{\mathcal{P}}_t$ is constructed by determining the elements of $\mathcal{P}_t$ that produce the larger value of the hypervolume indicator, as in the HypE algorithm [18]. For problems of two and three objectives —like the ones used in our experiments— this task is carried out by calculating it exactly. For cases of more objectives the Monte Carlo sampling alternative is used, as it is more computational cost-effective.

A set $\hat{\mathcal{P}}_t$ containing the best $\lceil \alpha |\mathcal{P}_t| \rceil$ elements in terms of hypervolume contribution is extracted from the sorted version of $\mathcal{P}_t$.

The model builder under study is then trained using $\hat{\mathcal{P}}_t$ as training data set. An amount of $\lfloor \omega |\mathcal{P}_t| \rfloor$ new individuals are sampled from the model. Each one of these individuals substitute a randomly selected one from $\mathcal{P}_t \setminus \hat{\mathcal{P}}_t$, the section of the population not used for model–building. The set obtained is then united with the best elements, $\hat{\mathcal{P}}_t$, to form the population of the next iteration $\mathcal{P}_{t+1}$.

Iterations are repeated until the given stopping criterion is met. The output of the algorithm is the set of non-dominated solutions obtained from the final iteration, $\mathcal{P}_t^*$.

4.3   Experimental Setup

In these experiments will be focusing of a set of problems previously proposed for the CEC 2009 MOP competition [19]. From the set of problems proposed there we selected the unconstrained optimization problems UF1 to UF6. These are two-objective problems that can be configured to have any desired number of variables —60 variables in our experiments. These problems are well-known for the complexity of their Pareto-optimal sets and fronts.

Five model-building algorithm —MrBOA [10], Naive MIDEA [12], SDR-AVS MIDEA [13], MAMaLGaM-X$^+$ [14] and MB-GNG [5]— are tested under this scheme. The HypE [18] hypervolume estimation algorithm for multi-objective optimization algorithm was also included in the analysis to provide a ground for comparison with 'traditional' evolutionary multi-objective algorithms. For the experiments we have used $\alpha = 0.3$ and $\omega = 0.3$ for all cases.

4.4   Results

Figures 1 and 2 summarize the average results of 30 runs for every algorithm and problem combination. From them it is noticeable that there is a substantial difference on MDEF scores between the 'pure' machine learning model-building algorithms, in particular MrBOA. Results from more advanced algorithms like SDR-AVS MIDEA and MAMaLGaM-X$^+$ yield a better performance and also better MDEF scores, something that supports their leitmotif. Finally, and in our opinion most importantly, it is observable how MB-GNG —an algorithm that was devised with the particular objective of solving the outliers issue— is not

Table 1. Results Mann-Whitney-Wilcoxon U tests comparing the MDEF values of HypE (H), MrBOA (M), naive MIDEA (N), SDR-AVS MIDEA (S), MAMaLGaM-X$^+$ (A) and MB-GNG (G) as the optimization progressed. When the algorithm in the row yielded larger MDEF than one in the column is marked with a +, if smaller with a −. If there is not a significant difference in results a ~ is used.

— **Problem UF1** —

	$t=200$					$t=500$					$t=$end				
	M	N	S	A	G	M	N	S	A	G	M	N	S	A	G
H	+	+	+	+	~	+	+	+	+	~	+	+	~	+	−
M	·	−	−	−	−	·	−	−	−	−	·	−	−	−	−
N		·	−	−	−		·	−	−	−		·	−	−	−
S			·	~	−			·	+	−			·	+	−
A				·	−				·	−				·	−

— **Problem UF2** —

	$t=200$					$t=500$					$t=$end				
	M	N	S	A	G	M	N	S	A	G	M	N	S	A	G
H	+	+	+	+	+	+	+	+	+	+	~	+	+	+	+	~
M	·	−	−	−	−	·	−	−	−	−	·	−	−	−	−
N		·	−	−	−		·	−	−	−		·	−	~	−
S			·	~	−			·	~	−			·	~	−
A				·	−				·	−				·	−

— **Problem UF3** —

	$t=200$					$t=500$					$t=$end				
	M	N	S	A	G	M	N	S	A	G	M	N	S	A	G
H	+	+	+	+	~	+	+	+	+	~	+	+	+	+	~
M	·	−	−	−	−	·	−	−	−	−	·	−	−	−	−
N		·	~	~	−		·	~	~	−		·	−	−	−
S			·	~	−			·	~	−			·	+	−
A				·	−				·	−				·	−

— **Problem UF4** —

	$t=200$					$t=500$					$t=$end				
	M	N	S	A	G	M	N	S	A	G	M	N	S	A	G
H	+	+	+	~	+	+	+	+	~	+	+	+	+	−
M	·	−	−	−	−	·	−	−	−	−	·	−	−	−	−
N		·	−	−	−		·	−	−	−		·	−	−	−
S			·	~	−			·	~	−			·	~	−
A				·	−				·	−				·	−

— **Problem UF5** —

	$t=200$					$t=500$					$t=$end				
	M	N	S	A	G	M	N	S	A	G	M	N	S	A	G
H	+	+	+	+	~	+	+	+	+	~	+	+	+	+	~
M	·	−	−	−	−	·	−	−	−	−	·	−	−	−	−
N		·	−	~	−		·	−	~	−		·	−	−	−
S			·	+	−			·	~	−			·	+	−
A				·	−				·	−				·	−

— **Problem UF6** —

	$t=200$					$t=500$					$t=$end				
	M	N	S	A	G	M	N	S	A	G	M	N	S	A	G
H	+	+	+	+	+	+	+	+	+	+	~	+	+	+	−
M	·	~	−	−	−	·	−	−	−	−	·	−	−	−	−
N		·	−	−	−		·	−	−	−		·	−	−	−
S			·	~	−			·	~	−			·	+	−
A				·	−				·	−				·	−

only capable of producing good results in terms of convergence to the Pareto-optimal front, but also is the algorithm that is able to maintain a higher diversity on its population.

The statistical validity of the judgment of these results calls for the application of statistical hypothesis tests. It has been previously remarked by different authors that the Mann-Whitney-Wilcoxon U test is particularly suited for experiments in the context of multi-objective evolutionary optimization [20]. This test is commonly used as a non-parametric method for testing equality of population medians. In our case we performed pair-wise tests on the significance of the difference of the indicator values yielded by the executions of the algorithms. A significance level, α, of 0.05 was used for all tests.

The results of these tests applied to the MDEF values yielded at the end of each run are summarized in Table 1. That table reflects when an algorithm produced significantly larger or smaller values of MDEF and when the results are indistinguishable from one another. This condensed representation prompts some interesting and relevant conclusions. First, and most importantly,

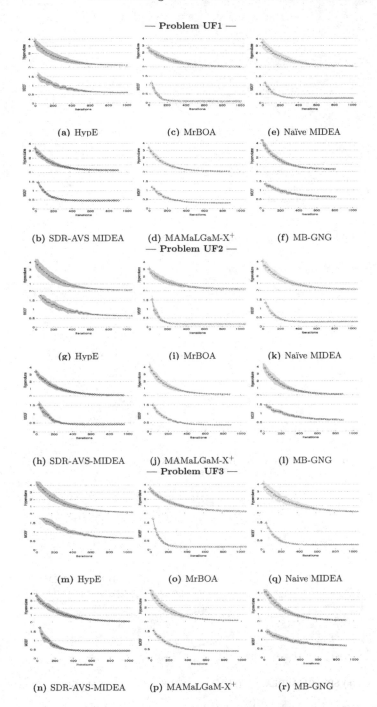

Fig. 1. Progress, expressed as the relative hypervolume indicator, and mean outliers index as calculated by MDEF for the different algorithms under study when solving problems UF1, UF2 and UF3

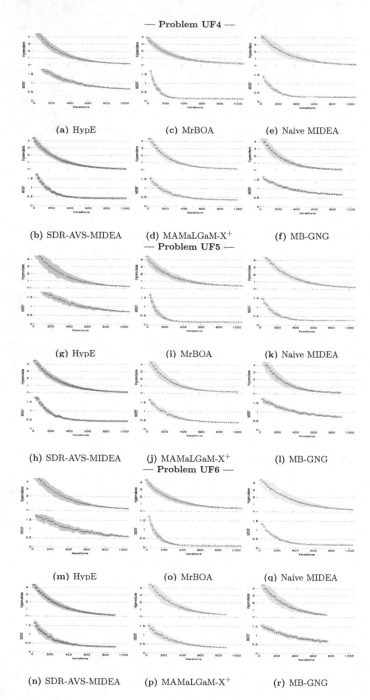

Fig. 2. Progress, expressed as the relative hypervolume indicator, and mean outliers index as calculated by MDEF for the different algorithms in study when solving problem UF4, UF5 and UF6

MG-GNG was the only algorithm capable to maintain a population diversity similar to that of a regular evolutionary algorithm, and correspondingly, larger than the rest of the algorithms. The rest of the algorithms consistently exhibited a lower diversity with regard to the EA and to MB-GNG. It is also very interesting how SDR-AVS MIDEA and MAMaLGaM-X frequently had similar MDEF scores.

5   Final Remarks

In this work we have taken the first steps towards the understanding and verification of the nature of the model-building problem of MOEDAs with an especial emphasis on the outliers issue. We have found that approaches based on traditional machine-learning techniques performed worst than better than less robust ones, a fact that we have shown to be related to their inability to maintain a proper population diversity. Although the outliers and diversity loss issues have been receiving some attention in recent years, this paper is the first study that exposes at what degree its situation is actually taking place, how it might impact the quality of results and how different algorithms behave with regard to it.

However, in order to gain a better comprehension more experiments are necessary. In one hand, different test problems must be addressed to realize if the results obtained here can be generalized. On the other hand, it is also of interest to further scale the problems to more objective functions. The analysis of the behavior of the algorithms in those situations might lead to their adaptation to the problem.

The experiences gained here can be used to sketch the requirements for a new model-building algorithm capable of inducing a quantum leap in the performance of MOEDAs and EDAs, for that matter.

References

1. Coello Coello, C.A., Lamont, G.B., Van Veldhuizen, D.A.: Evolutionary Algorithms for Solving Multi-Objective Problems. In: Genetic and Evolutionary Computation, 2 edn. Springer, New York (2007)
2. Corne, D.W.: Single objective = past, multiobjective = present, ??? = future. In: Michalewicz, Z. (ed.) 2008 IEEE Conference on Evolutionary Computation (CEC), part of 2008 IEEE World Congress on Computational Intelligence (WCCI 2008). IEEE Press, Piscataway (2008)
3. Lozano, J.A., Larrañaga, P., Inza, I., Bengoetxea, E., eds.: Towards a New Evolutionary Computation: Advances on Estimation of Distribution Algorithms. Springer (2006)
4. Martí, L.: Scalable Multi-Objective Optimization. PhD thesis, Departmento de Informática, Universidad Carlos III de Madrid, Colmenarejo, Spain (2011)
5. Martí, L., García, J., Berlanga, A., Coello Coello, C.A., Molina, J.M.: MB-GNG: Addressing drawbacks in multi-objective optimization estimation of distribution algorithms. Operations Research Letters 39(2), 150–154 (2011)

6. Martí, L., García, J., Berlanga, A., Molina, J.M.: Introducing MONEDA: Scalable multiobjective optimization with a neural estimation of distribution algorithm. In: GECCO 2008: 10th Annual Conference on Genetic and Evolutionary Computation, pp. 689–696. ACM Press, New York (2008)
7. Martí, L., García, J., Berlanga, A., Molina, J.M.: Multi-objective optimization with an adaptive resonance theory-based estimation of distribution algorithm. Annals of Mathematics and Artificial Intelligence **68**(4), 247–273 (2013)
8. Branke, J., Miettinen, K., Deb, K., Słowiński, R., eds.: Multiobjective Optimization. LNCS. vol. 5252 Springer, Heidelberg (2008)
9. Pelikan, M., Sastry, K., Goldberg, D.E.: Multiobjective estimation of distribution algorithms. In: Pelikan, M., Sastry, K., Cantú-Paz, E. (eds.) Scalable Optimization via Probabilistic Modeling: From Algorithms to Applications. SCI, pp. 223–248. Springer (2006)
10. Ahn, C.W.: Advances in Evolutionary Algorithms. Design and Practice. Springer (2006). ISBN: 3-540-31758-9
11. Ahn, C.W., Ramakrishna, R.S., Goldberg, D.E.: Real-Coded Bayesian Optimization Algorithm: Bringing the Strength of BOA into the Continuous World. In: Deb, K., Tari, Z. (eds.) GECCO 2004. LNCS, vol. 3102, pp. 840–851. Springer, Heidelberg (2004)
12. Bosman, P.A.N., Thierens, D.: The Naive MIDEA: A Baseline Multi–objective EA. In: Coello Coello, C.A., Hernández Aguirre, A., Zitzler, E. (eds.) EMO 2005. LNCS, vol. 3410, pp. 428–442. Springer, Heidelberg (2005)
13. Bosman, P.A., Thierens, D.: Adaptive variance scaling in continuous multi-objective estimation-of-distribution algorithms. In: Proceedings of the 9th Annual Conference on Genetic and Evolutionary Computation, GECCO 2007, p. 500. ACM Press, New York (2007)
14. Bosman, P.A.N.: The anticipated mean shift and cluster registration in mixture-based EDAs for multi-objective optimization. Proceedings of the 12th Annual Conference on Genetic and Evolutionary Computation, GECCO 2010, p. 351. ACM Press, New York (2010)
15. Hawkins, D.: Identification of Outliers. Chapman and Hall (1980)
16. Hodge, V.: A survey of outlier detection methodologies. Artificial Intelligence Review, 1–43 (2004)
17. Papadimitriou, S., Kitagawa, H., Gibbons, P., Faloutsos, C.: LOCI: Fast outlier detection using the local correlation integral. In: Proceedings 19th International Conference on Data Engineering (ICDE 2003), pp. 315–326. IEEE Press (2003)
18. Bader, J.: Hypervolume-Based Search for Multiobjective Optimization: Theory and Methods. PhD thesis, ETH Zurich, Switzerland (2010)
19. Zhang, Q., Zhou, A., Zhao, S., Suganthan, P., Liu, W., Tiwari, S.: Multiobjective optimization test instances for the CEC 2009 special session and competition. Technical report, University of Essex, Colchester, UK and Nanyang Technological University, Singapore (2009)
20. Knowles, J., Thiele, L., Zitzler, E.: A tutorial on the performance assessment of stochastic multiobjective optimizers. TIK Report 214, Computer Engineering and Networks Laboratory (TIK), ETH Zurich (2006)

A More Efficient Selection Scheme in iSMS-EMOA

Adriana Menchaca-Mendez[2], Elizabeth Montero[1]([⊠]), María-Cristina Riff[1], and Carlos A. Coello Coello[2]

[1] Department of Computer Science, Universidad Técnica Federico Santa María, Valparaíso, Chile
{Elizabeth.Montero,Maria-Cristina.Riff}@inf.utfsm.cl
[2] CINVESTAV-IPN, Departamento de Computación, Mexico, DF, Mexico
adriana.menchacamendez@gmail.com, ccoello@cs.cinvestav.mx

Abstract. In this paper, we study iSMS-EMOA, a recently proposed approach that improves the well-known *S metric selection Evolutionary Multi-Objective Algorithm* (SMS-EMOA). These two indicator-based multi-objective evolutionary algorithms rely on hypervolume contributions to select individuals. Here, we propose to define a probability of using a randomly selected individual within the iSMS-EMOA's selection scheme. In order to calibrate the value of such probability, we use the EVOCA tuner. Our preliminary results indicate that we are able to save up to 33% of computations of the contribution to hypervolume with respect to the original iSMS-EMOA, without any significant quality degradation in the solutions obtained. In fact, in some cases, the approach proposed here was even able to improve the quality of the solutions obtained by the original iSMS-EMOA.

Keywords: Multi-objective evolutionary algorithms · Tuning · Hypervolume contribution

1 Introduction

Many optimization problems involve the simultaneous optimization of several objectives. They are known as *multi-objective optimization problems (MOPs)* and in them, the notion of optimality refers to the best possible trade-offs among the objectives. Consequently, there is no single optimal solution but a set of solutions (the so-called *Pareto optimal set* whose image is called the *Pareto front*). The use of *Multi-Objective Evolutionary Algorithms (MOEAs)* to solve MOPs has become increasingly popular. In recent years, MOEAs based on the hypervolume indicator (I_H) have become relatively popular. This is due to two main reasons: first, the use of Pareto-based selection has several limitations[1]. And, second, I_H has interesting mathematical properties. For example, it is

---

This work is supported by the collaboration project Conacyt-Conicyt 2010-199. The last author acknowledges support from project B330.261.

[1] The number of non-dominated solutions grows exponentially as we increase the number of objective functions, and this rapidly dilutes the selection pressure of a MOEA [4].

A.L.C. Bazzan and K. Pichara (Eds.): IBERAMIA 2014, LNAI 8864, pp. 371–380, 2014.
DOI: 10.1007/978-3-319-12027-0_30

the only unary indicator which is known to be "Pareto compliant" [10]. I_H was originally proposed by Zitzler and Thiele in [9], and it is defined as the size of the space covered by the Pareto optimal solutions. I_H rewards convergence towards the Pareto front as well as the maximum spread of the solutions obtained. Fleischer proved in [5] that, given a finite search space and a reference point, *maximizing the hypervolume indicator is equivalent to finding the Pareto optimal set*. However, I_H has one important disadvantage: its high computational cost. The "S metric selection Evolutionary Multi-Objective Algorithm (SMS-EMOA)" [3] is currently, the most popular MOEA based on I_H and it works as follows: it creates only one individual by iteration. After that, it applies Pareto ranking. If the last front has more than one individual, SMS-EMOA deletes the individual with the worst contribution to I_H. SMS-EMOA is impractical when we want to solve MOPs with many objectives because if all individuals are non-dominated, it needs to compute the contribution to I_H of all individuals and we know that this task is computational expensive (the calculation of the minimal contribution to I_H is an **NP-hard** [1] problem). Recently, in [7] authors proposed a selection scheme based on I_H and its locality property giving rise to an improved version of SMS-EMOA called iSMS-EMOA. With this scheme, the new individual only competes with two other individuals of the population: its nearest neighbor and a randomly selected individual. This scheme allows a significant reduction in the running time. However, in [7], it was noted that the use of the randomly selected individual is not necessary in all iterations and it was left as future work to identify the cases in which it is required. In this paper, we propose to define a probability of use of the randomly selected individual which is automatically adjusted using the EVOCA tuner [8] with the two following aims: to maximize I_H and to minimize the running time (reducing the number of computations of the contribution to I_H). This is clearly a MOP, but with a clear order of preference: we aim to reduce the number of computations of the contribution to I_H without affecting the quality of the solutions. Thus, we decided to solve it using the ϵ-constraint method. Let $\mathcal{A}$ be the approximation of the Pareto optimal set obtained by the iSMS-EMOA algorithm and p_{rsi} be the probability of use of the randomly selected individual. First, we calibrate p_{rsi}, maximizing $I_H(\mathcal{A})$. After that, we calibrate p_{rsi}, minimizing the running time required by the iSMS-EMOA algorithm in order to obtain $\mathcal{A}$, having as a constraint: $I_H(\mathcal{A}) > maxI_H - \epsilon$, where $maxI_H$ is the maximum hypervolume found in the previous step and ϵ is a tolerance. We will show how this scheme produces savings of up to 33% of computations of the contribution to I_H (with respect to the original iSMS-EMOA) without losing quality in the solutions obtained. In fact, we will see how, in some cases, we can even improve the quality of $\mathcal{A}$ with respect to I_H when using our proposed approach.

The remainder of this paper is organized as follows: Section 2 states the problem of our interest and provides some basic definitions. The original iSMS-EMOA is described in Section 3. Our proposal is discussed in Section 4 and it is validated in Section 5. Finally, we provide our conclusions and some possible paths for future work in Section 6.

2 Basic Definitions and Problem Statement

We are interested in the general MOP, which is defined as follows: Find $\boldsymbol{x}^* = [x_1^*, x_2^*, \ldots, x_n^*]^T$ which optimizes

$$\boldsymbol{f}(\boldsymbol{x}) = [f_1(\boldsymbol{x}), f_2(\boldsymbol{x}), \ldots, f_k(\boldsymbol{x})]^T \tag{1}$$

such that $\boldsymbol{x}^* \in \Omega$, where $\Omega \subset \mathbb{R}^n$ defines the feasible region of the problem. Assuming minimization problems, we have the following definitions.

Definition 1. *We say that a vector* $\boldsymbol{x} = [x_1, \ldots, x_n]^T$ *dominates vector* $\boldsymbol{y} = [y_1, \ldots, y_n]^T$*, denoted by* $\boldsymbol{x} \prec \boldsymbol{y}$*, if and only if* $f_i(\boldsymbol{x}) \leq f_i(\boldsymbol{y})$ *for all* $i \in \{1, \ldots, k\}$ *and there exists an* $i \in \{1, \ldots, k\}$ *such that* $f_i(\boldsymbol{x}) < f_i(\boldsymbol{y})$*.*

Definition 2. *For a given MOP,* $\boldsymbol{f}(\boldsymbol{x})$*, the Pareto optimal set is defined as:* $\mathcal{P}^* = \{\boldsymbol{x} \in \Omega | \neg \exists \boldsymbol{y} \in \Omega : \boldsymbol{y} \prec \boldsymbol{x}\}$*.*

Definition 3. *Let* $\boldsymbol{f}(\boldsymbol{x})$ *be a given MOP and* $\mathcal{P}^*$ *the Pareto optimal set. Then, the Pareto Front is defined as:* $\mathcal{PF}^* = \{\boldsymbol{f}(\boldsymbol{x}) \mid \boldsymbol{x} \in \mathcal{P}^*\}$*.*

Definition 4. *If* Λ *denotes the Lebesgue measure, the hypervolume indicator* (I_H) *is defined as:*

$$I_H(\mathcal{A}, \boldsymbol{y}_{ref}) = \Lambda \left(\bigcup_{y \in \mathcal{A}} \{\boldsymbol{y}' \mid \boldsymbol{y} < \boldsymbol{y}' < \boldsymbol{y}_{ref}\} \right) \tag{2}$$

where $\boldsymbol{y}_{ref} \in \mathbb{R}^k$ *denotes a reference point that should be dominated by all the Pareto optimal points.*

Definition 5. *The contribution to* I_H *of a solution* $\boldsymbol{x}$ *is defined as:*

$$C_H(\boldsymbol{x}, \mathcal{A}) = I_H(\mathcal{A}, \boldsymbol{y}_{ref}) - I_H(\mathcal{A} \setminus \boldsymbol{x}, \boldsymbol{y}_{ref}) \tag{3}$$

where $\boldsymbol{x} \in \mathcal{A}$*. Then, the contribution of* $\boldsymbol{x}$ *is the space that is only covered by* $\boldsymbol{x}$*.*

3 iSMS-EMOA

The Improved S Metric Selection Evolutionary Multi-Objective Algorithm (iSMS-EMOA) [7] works as follows: First, it creates an initial population. After that, only one individual is created at each iteration using the operators of the NSGA-II (crossover and mutation). Let $\boldsymbol{x}_{new}$ be the new individual and $\mathcal{A}$ be the current population. We calculate the Euclidean distance of $\boldsymbol{x}_{new}$ to each solution in $\mathcal{A}$ and, we choose the nearest solution $\boldsymbol{x}_{near}$. These two solutions ($\boldsymbol{x}_{new}$ and $\boldsymbol{x}_{near}$) compete to survive. The core idea is to move a solution within its neighborhood with the aim of improving its contribution to I_H (locality property). It is important to consider the case in which $\boldsymbol{x}_{new}$ is located in an unexplored region. In this case, it is not a good idea to remove $\boldsymbol{x}_{new}$ or $\boldsymbol{x}_{near}$. To address this problem, the authors proposed to choose (randomly) another solution, $\boldsymbol{x}_{rand}$, such that $\boldsymbol{x}_{rand} \in \mathcal{A}$ and $\boldsymbol{x}_{rand} \neq \boldsymbol{x}_{near}$. This is considering that the probability of choosing a solution in a crowded region is high and the probability of choosing a solution in an unexplored region is low. Then, $\boldsymbol{x}_{rand}$, $\boldsymbol{x}_{new}$ and $\boldsymbol{x}_{near}$ will compete to survive.

4 Our Proposed Approach

We propose here to use a probability which enables us to decide when to incorporate the randomly selected individual into iSMS-EMOA. The new algorithm is called "improved S metric selection Evolutionary Multi-Objective Algorithm II (iSMS-EMOA II)", see Algorithm 1. The only difference between iSMS-EMOA and iSMS-EMOA II is that now, we flip a coin to decide if we use the randomly selected individual at each iteration, see Algorithm 1, line 6. Setting the value of p_{rsi} is not trivial: large values will lead to a waste of computational effort for calculating hypervolume contribution of solutions that won't be eliminated. On the other side, small values of p_{rsi} can decrease the diversification ability of the algorithm, reducing its capacity to generate solutions in specific zones of Pareto front.

For calibrating p_{rsi}, we used the EVOCA [8] tuner. This is an evolutionary algorithm that works with a population of parameter calibrations. The population size is computed considering the number of parameters and their domain sizes. The key idea is to include all the values allowed for each parameter, in an independent way, on the first population. EVOCA uses two transformation operators. First, it adopts a crossover operator (wheel-crossover) that constructs one calibration from the whole population. The child calibration generated replaces the worst calibration on the current population. Second, it adopts a mutation operator which is a hill climbing first improvement procedure that takes a copy of the child generated by the crossover operator and tries to improve it by modifying one of its parameter values. In case of a numerical parameter, it will try to randomly take a new value from the parameter interval, regarding it as a continuous range. The calibration generated by applying mutation replaces the second worst calibration on the current population, when a better individual is found. Algorithm 2 shows the EVOCA structure. We have considered two scenarios to calibrate p_{rsi}: first, we maximize the hypervolume of the approximation of the Pareto optimal set obtained by iSMS-EMOA II for a given MOP. And, second, we minimize the number of computations of the contribution to I_H required by iSMS-EMOA II to obtain the approximation of the Pareto optimal set of that MOP, avoiding to affect the value of the hypervolume obtained before.

4.1 Scenario 1: Maximizing the Hypervolume Indicator

In this part, we calibrate the probability p_{rsi}, solving the following problem:

$$\max I_H(\mathcal{A}) \tag{4}$$

where $\mathcal{A}$ is the approximation of the Pareto optimal set obtained by iSMS-EMOA II for a given MOP.

Setting EVOCA for iSMS-EMOA II in Scenario 1. For applying EVOCA in this scenario, we need to define the following criteria:

Algorithm 1. iSMS-EMOA II

Input : MOP to be solved.
Output: The approximation of the Pareto optimal set ($\mathcal{A}$).
1 Generate a random initial population ($\mathcal{A}$);
2 **while** *Stopping criterion is not met* **do**
3   Select randomly two individuals from $\mathcal{A}$ (x_1 and x_2);
4   Obtain an offspring (x_{new}) from x_1 and x_2, applying the operators of NSGA-II (crossover and mutation);
5     $near \leftarrow$ Index of the nearest neighbor to x_{new} in $\mathcal{A}$;
6   **if** $random(0,1) < p_{rsi}$ **then**
7        $rand \leftarrow$ Integer random number between 1 and $|\mathcal{A}|$ (such that $near \neq rand$);
8   Calculate the contribution to I_H of x_{new}, x_{near} and x_{rand};
9   **if** $C_H(x_{new}, \mathcal{A})$ *is better than* $C_H(x_{near}, \mathcal{A})$ *or* $C_H(x_{rand}, \mathcal{A})$ **then**
10   **if** $C_H(x_{near}, \mathcal{A}) < C_H(x_{rand}, \mathcal{A})$ **then**
11   Replace x_{near} with x_{new};
12   **else**
13   Replace x_{rand} with x_{new};
14   **end**
15   **end**
16   **else**
17   Compute the contribution to I_H of x_{new} and x_{near};
18   **if** $C_H(x_{new}, \mathcal{A}) > C_H(x_{near}, \mathcal{A})$ **then**
19   Replace x_{near} with x_{new};
20   **end**
21   **end**
22 **end**
23 **return** $\mathcal{A}$;

Algorithm 2. EVOCA

Input : Definition of parameters for target algorithm $\mathcal{M}$
Output: Set of best performing parameter calibrations for $\mathcal{M}$
1 Generate initial population ($\mathcal{P}$);
2 **while** *Stopping criterion is not met* **do**
3     $child \leftarrow$ wheel-crossover(P);
4   Evaluate $child$ using R random seeds ;
5   Replace worst calibration in $\mathcal{P}$ by $child$;
6     $mutated\_child \leftarrow$ mutation($child$) ;
7   Evaluate $mutated\_child$ using R random seeds;
8   **if** $mutated\_child$ *is* **better** *than* $child$ **then**
9   Replace the second worst calibration in $\mathcal{P}$ by $mutated\_child$;
10   **end**
11 **end**
12 **return** $\mathcal{P}$;

- When do we consider a parameter calibration to be better than another one? In this case, EVOCA takes into account one criterion to evaluate each parameter calibration for iSMS-EMOA II. One calibration c' is considered better than another c, in the case in which the use of c' in iSMS-EMOA II provides a higher hypervolume than the use of c.
- A parameter precision level for the initial population: Here, the initial precision must be defined for parameter p_{rsi}. It is important to remark that EVOCA is able to increase this precision during the calibration process using the mutation operator, which selects values from an interval. Thus, this precision is only considered to generate the initial EVOCA's population.
- Which is the result of the calibration? The best calibration that belongs to the final EVOCA's population is the one with the best hypervolume value.

4.2   Scenario 2: Minimizing the Number of Calculations of the Contribution to I_H

In this part, we are interested in minimizing the number of calculations of the contribution to I_H required by iSMS-EMOA II without losing too much quality in the solutions. For this, we calibrate p_{rsi}, solving the following problem:

$$\min(\text{Time required to obtain } \mathcal{A}) \text{ such that } I_H(\mathcal{A}) > maxI_H - \epsilon \qquad (5)$$

where $\mathcal{A}$ is the approximation of the Pareto optimal set obtained by iSMS-EMOA II for a given MOP; $maxI_H$ is the maximum hypervolume obtained when we solve eq. (4) and ϵ is a tolerance.

Setting EVOCA for iSMS-EMOA II in Scenario 2. For applying EVOCA in this scenario, we need to define the following criteria:

- When do we consider a parameter calibration to be better than another one? In this case, EVOCA takes into account two criteria to evaluate each parameter calibration for iSMS-EMOA II. One calibration c' is considered to be better than another one c, using two objectives: when the use of c' allows iSMS-EMOA II to achieve both, that the hypervolume value is higher than the tolerance level ϵ and that a lower running time than when using c is achieved.
- A parameter precision level for the initial population: Here, the initial precision must be defined for parameter p_{rsi}.
- Which is the result of the calibration? The best calibration that belongs to the final EVOCA's population is the one with the best hypervolume value.

We note that the tolerance value is used to define a minimum quality of the calibrations, in terms of hypervolume respect to the quality obtained with the iSMS-EMOA II when solving eq. 4. For our experiments, we considered a tolerance of 1%.

5   Experimental Results

To measure the performance of iSMS-EMOA II, we compare it with respect to the original iSMS-EMOA[2]. For our experiments, we used four problems with 3, 4 and 5 objective functions taken from the Deb-Thiele-Laumanns-Zitzler (DTLZ) test suite [2]. We used $k = 5$ for DTLZ1 and $k = 10$ for the remaining test problems. Also, we used two problems with 3, 4 and 5 objective functions, taken from the WFG toolkit [6], with $k\_factor = 2$ and $l\_factor = 10$. We chose these problems because each of them has a Pareto front with distinct features; and also, they are scalables with respect to the number of objective functions. For each test problem, we performed 30 independent runs. For both algorithms, we adopted the parameters suggested by the authors of NSGA-II: $p_c = 0.9$ (crossover probability), $p_m = 1/n$ (mutation probability), where n is the number of decision variables. Both for the crossover and mutation operators, we adopted $\eta_c = 15$ and $\eta_m = 20$, respectively. We performed a maximum of 50,000 fitness function evaluations (we used a population size of 100 individuals and we iterated for 500 generations). We adopted only I_H to validate our results because it rewards both convergence towards the Pareto front as well as the maximum spread of the solutions obtained. Also, iSMS-EMOA and iSMS-EMOA II, have as their aim to maximize the hypervolume and, therefore, it makes sense to use this indicator to assess their performance. To calculate I_H, we used the following reference points: $y_{ref} = [y_1, \cdots, y_M]$ such that $y_i = 0.7$ for DTLZ1, $y_i = 1.1$ for DTLZ2 and DTLZ5, $y_M = 6.1$ and $y_{i \neq M} = 1.1$ for DTLZ7. In the case of the WFG test problems, we generated the reference point using the highest value found for each objective function taking into account all the outputs of both algorithms.

5.1   Results in Scenario 1

In Table 1(a), we can observe that if the randomly generated individual is always selected (original iSMS-EMOA), we get better results in most cases. In fact, in most problems, EVOCA calibrates p_{rsi} with high values, e.g., it sets $p_{rsi} = 1.0$ for DTLZ1 with three objective functions and DTLZ1, DTLZ2, DTLZ5 and WFG1 with four objective functions. This means that in these problems EVOCA suggests to use all the time the randomly selected individual, as in the original iSMS-EMOA, to maximize I_H. For this reason, in these problems, iSMS-EMOA II does not save computations of the contribution to I_H. However, an interesting aspect is that in some problems this randomly selected individual is not necessary. In such cases, iSMS-EMOA results can be improved by selecting the randomly generated individual with a low probability. For example, in DTLZ7 and WFG4 with three objective functions, a probability $p_{rsi} = 0.127$ and $p_{rsi} = 0.1$, were calibrated respectively, which allowed us to save up to 30% of computations of the contribution to I_H. In the case of DTLZ7, we can note that iSMS-EMOA II significantly outperformed iSMS-EMOA, because it obtained better results, and the null

---

[2] iSMS-EMOA is compared to the original SMS-EMOA in [7], but such comparison was omitted here due to space limitations.

Table 1. We show average values over 30 independent runs. Values in parentheses correspond to the standard deviations. $P(H)$ shows the results of statistical analysis applied to our experiments using Wilcoxons rank sum considering I_H. P is the probability of observing the given result (the null hypothesis is true). Small values of P cast doubt on the validity of the null hypothesis. $H = 1$ indicates that the null hypothesis can be rejected at the 5% level. Both iSMS-EMOA and iSMS-EMOA II were compiled using the GNU C compiler and they were executed on a computer with a 2.66GHz processor and 4GB in RAM. (a) shows the results for scenario 1 and in (b) shows the results for scenario 2.

f	P_{rsi}	isms-emoa I_H	isms-emoa-ii I_H	isms-emoa Eval C_H	Savings	time	isms-emoa-ii Eval C_H	Savings	time	$P(H)$
DTLZ1(3)	1.0	0.316985 (0.000066)	0.316998 (0.000046)	150000 (0.00)	-0.00%	≈7s	150000 (0.00)	-0.00%	≈7s	0.450(0)
DTLZ2(3)	0.7	0.757890 (0.000100)	0.757863 (0.000075)	150000 (0.00)	-0.00%	≈7s	135022 (95.82)	-9.99%	≈6s	0.251(0)
DTLZ5(3)	0.8	0.439350 (0.000017)	0.439342 (0.000020)	150000 (0.00)	-0.00%	≈8s	140009 (96.04)	-6.66%	≈7s	0.062(0)
DTLZ7(3)	0.127	1.908824 (0.200002)	2.019564 (0.000926)	150000 (0.00)	-0.00%	≈7s	106353 (68.35)	-29.10%	≈5s	0.002(1)
DTLZ1(4)	1.0	0.234451 (0.000018)	0.234446 (0.000019)	150000 (0.00)	-0.00%	≈76s	150000 (0.00)	-0.00%	≈76s	0.314(0)
DTLZ2(4)	1.0	1.044211 (0.000159)	1.044281 (0.000159)	150000 (0.00)	-0.00%	≈80s	150000 (0.00)	-0.00%	≈80s	0.183(0)
DTLZ5(4)	1.0	0.437073 (0.000308)	0.437056 (0.000318)	150000 (0.00)	-0.00%	≈70s	150000 (0.00)	-0.00%	≈70s	0.801(0)
DTLZ7(4)	0.3	0.678273 (0.198672)	0.797852 (0.001903)	150000 (0.00)	-0.00%	≈49s	114974 (86.30)	-23.35%	≈39s	0.379(0)
DTLZ1(5)	0.8	0.166731 (0.000011)	0.166733 (0.000000)	150000 (0.00)	-0.00%	≈1254s	139258 (1773.08)	-7.16%	≈1110s	0.378(0)
DTLZ2(5)	0.8	1.295672 (0.000166)	1.295508 (0.000201)	150000 (0.00)	-0.00%	≈1413s	133891 (6474.89)	-10.74%	≈1167s	0.004(1)
DTLZ5(5)	0.8	0.446086 (0.000612)	0.445896 (0.000756)	150000 (0.00)	-0.00%	≈1411s	139122 (3351.63)	-7.25%	≈1258s	0.355(0)
DTLZ7(5)	0.4	0.158271 (0.058981)	0.187287 (0.031902)	150000 (0.00)	-0.00%	≈518s	120001 (125.76)	-20.00%	≈363s	0.325(0)
WFG1(3)	0.8	21.205641 (0.177134)	21.174222 (0.358121)	150000 (0.00)	-0.00%	≈8s	140003 (88.75)	-6.66%	≈7s	0.773(0)
WFG4(3)	0.1	29.346993 (0.095911)	29.328283 (0.081647)	150000 (0.00)	-0.00%	≈8s	104995 (74.26)	-30.00%	≈6s	0.363(0)
WFG1(4)	1.0	88.573606 (0.541177)	88.502834 (0.505897)	150000 (0.00)	-0.00%	≈95s	150000 (0.00)	-0.00%	≈95s	0.652(0)
WFG4(4)	0.7	301.253225 (1.155539)	301.415556 (1.056422)	150000 (0.00)	-0.00%	≈79s	135003 (94.41)	-10.00%	≈71s	0.695(0)
WFG1(5)	0.8	114.187823 (0.723549)	114.290414 (0.646247)	150000 (0.00)	-0.00%	≈1411s	119253 (7811.77)	-20.50%	≈1268s	0.970(0)
WFG4(5)	0.529	3465.333620 (17.840209)	3466.819998 (13.297479)	150000 (0.00)	-0.00%	≈1305s	126362 (431.92)	-15.76%	≈1164s	0.784(0)

(a)

f	P_{rsi}	isms-emoa I_H	isms-emoa-ii I_H	isms-emoa Eval C_H	Savings	time	isms-emoa-ii Eval C_H	Savings	time	$P(H)$
DTLZ1(3)	0.222	0.316985 (0.000066)	0.296946 (0.053188)	150000 (0.00)	-0.00%	≈7s	111095 (85.53)	-25.94%	≈6s	0.000(1)
DTLZ2(3)	0.193	0.757890 (0.000100)	0.757819 (0.000099)	150000 (0.00)	-0.00%	≈7s	109632 (99.38)	-26.91%	≈6s	0.011(1)
DTLZ5(3)	0.148	0.439350 (0.000017)	0.439266 (0.000029)	150000 (0.00)	-0.00%	≈8s	107403 (96.41)	-28.40%	≈5s	0.000(1)
DTLZ7(3)	0.1	1.908824 (0.200002)	2.019672 (0.000753)	150000 (0.00)	-0.00%	≈7s	104981 (49.98)	-30.01%	≈5s	0.000(1)
DTLZ1(4)	0.144	0.234451 (0.000018)	0.229403 (0.015504)	150000 (0.00)	-0.00%	≈76s	107183 (97.41)	-28.54%	≈37s	0.000(1)
DTLZ2(4)	0.075	1.044211 (0.000159)	1.043808 (0.000237)	150000 (0.00)	-0.00%	≈80s	103732 (53.76)	-30.85%	≈51s	0.000(1)
DTLZ5(4)	0.184	0.437073 (0.000308)	0.436148 (0.000376)	150000 (0.00)	-0.00%	≈70s	109197 (79.72)	-27.20%	≈51s	0.000(1)
DTLZ7(4)	0.107	0.678273 (0.198672)	0.797284 (0.002003)	150000 (0.00)	-0.00%	≈49s	105345 (75.00)	-29.77%	≈35s	0.830(0)
DTLZ1(5)	0.24	0.166731 (0.000011)	0.166415 (0.000599)	150000 (0.00)	-0.00%	≈1254s	112014 (110.94)	-25.32%	≈657s	0.000(1)
DTLZ2(5)	0.088	1.295672 (0.000166)	1.294868 (0.000348)	150000 (0.00)	-0.00%	≈1413s	104408 (66.34)	-30.39%	≈947s	0.000(1)
DTLZ5(5)	0.088	0.446086 (0.000612)	0.441584 (0.001664)	150000 (0.00)	-0.00%	≈1411s	104400 (55.24)	-30.40%	≈941s	0.000(1)
DTLZ7(5)	0.1	0.158271 (0.058981)	0.188343 (0.025764)	150000 (0.00)	-0.00%	≈518s	104995 (84.41)	-30.00%	≈324s	0.059(0)
WFG1(3)	0.4	21.205641 (0.177134)	20.718664 (0.794370)	150000 (0.00)	-0.00%	≈8s	120003 (123.57)	-20.00%	≈7s	0.005(1)
WFG4(3)	0.1	29.346993 (0.095911)	29.332057 (0.085921)	150000 (0.00)	-0.00%	≈8s	109207 (79.77)	-27.20%	≈6s	0.684(0)
WFG1(4)	0.149	88.573606 (0.541177)	87.677943 (1.065401)	150000 (0.00)	-0.00%	≈95s	107450 (66.60)	-28.37%	≈73s	0.000(1)
WFG4(4)	0	301.253225 (1.155539)	300.667942 (1.016813)	150000 (0.00)	-0.00%	≈79s	99999 (0.00)	-33.33%	≈48s	0.013(1)
WFG1(5)	0.124	114.187823 (0.723549)	114.272000 (0.955455)	150000 (0.00)	-0.00%	≈1411s	106165 (156.71)	-29.22%	≈935s	0.290(0)
WFG4(5)	0.127	3465.333620 (17.840209)	3457.761494 (14.631125)	150000 (0.00)	-0.00%	≈1305s	106336 (87.78)	-29.11%	≈898s	0.185(0)

(b)

hypothesis "medians are equal" in the statistical analysis (see column $P(H)$) can be rejected. In the remaining problems, the "null hypothesis" cannot be rejected, and then, both algorithms have a similar behavior. However, it is important to note that iSMS-EMOA II saved computations of the contribution to I_H in many problems without losing quality in their solutions.

5.2   Results in Scenario 2

In Table 1(b), we can observe that iSMS-EMOA II was able to save from 20% to 33% of computations of the contribution to I_H in all test problems and as the number of objective functions increases, a bigger impact in the running time can be observed (e.g., in DTLZ1 with five objective functions iSMS-EMOA-II decreases the running time in 9.9 minutes). Regarding the quality of the solutions, we can note that in five test problems both algorithms have a similar behavior because the null hypothesis "medians are equal" cannot be rejected. In one test problem, iSMS-EMOA II outperformed the original iSMS-EMOA and it saved 30% of computations of the contribution to I_H. In twelve cases, the original iSMS-EMOA outperformed iSMS-EMOA II. However, in this scenario the main objective is to minimize the computations of the contribution to I_H without losing more than an epsilon (ϵ) of quality in the solutions regarding I_H.

6   Conclusions and Future Work

We have proposed to define a probability of use for the randomly selected individual adopted by iSMS-EMOA, with the aim of saving calculations of the contribution to I_H. To set this probability, we used the ϵ-constraint method and the EVOCA tuner. Our preliminary results show that savings of up to 33% of computations of the contribution to I_H can be obtained. From the point of view of the tuner algorithm, it was able to successfully deal with two different objectives in the process of selecting good performing calibrations. This indicates the suitability of this tuner for calibrating an indicator-based multi-objective evolutionary algorithm and motivates the incorporation of this approach on other MOEAs that use indicator-based selection or decomposition schemes.

References

1. Bringmann, K., Friedrich, T.: Approximating the least hypervolume contributor: NP-hard in general, but fast in practice. Theoretical Computer Science **425**, 104–116 (2012)
2. Deb, K., Thiele, L., Laumanns, M., Zitzler, E.: Scalable Test Problems for Evolutionary Multiobjective Optimization. In: Abraham, A., Jain, L., Goldberg, R. (eds.) Evolutionary Multiobjective Optimization. Theoretical Advances and Applications, pp. 105–145. Springer, USA (2005)
3. Emmerich, M., Beume, N., Naujoks, B.: An EMO Algorithm Using the Hypervolume Measure as Selection Criterion. In: Coello, C.A.C., Hernández Aguirre, A., Zitzler, E. (eds.) EMO 2005. LNCS, vol. 3410, pp. 62–76. Springer, Heidelberg (2005)

4. Farina, M., Amato, P.: On the Optimal Solution Definition for Many-criteria Optimization Problems. In: Proceedings of the NAFIPS-FLINT International Conference 2002, Piscataway, New Jersey, pp. 233–238. IEEE Service Center (June 2002)
5. Fleischer, M.: The Measure of Pareto Optima Applications to Multi-objective Metaheuristics. In: Fonseca, C.M., Fleming, P.J., Zitzler, E., Deb, K., Thiele, L. (eds.) EMO 2003. LNCS, vol. 2632, pp. 519–533. Springer, Heidelberg (2003)
6. Huband, S., Hingston, P., Barone, L., While, L.: A Review of Multiobjective Test Problems and a Scalable Test Problem Toolkit. IEEE Transaction on Evolutionary Computation 10(5), 477–506 (2006)
7. Menchaca-Mendez, A., Coello, C.A.C.: A New Selection Mechanism Based on Hypervolume and its Locality Property. In: 2013 IEEE Congress on Evolutionary Computation (CEC 2013), Cancún, México, June 20-23, pp. 924–931. IEEE Press (2013)
8. Riff, M.-C., Montero, E.: A new algorithm for reducing metaheuristic design effort. In: IEEE Congress on Evolutionary Computation (CEC 2013), Cancún, México, pp. 3283–3290 (June 2013)
9. Zitzler, E., Thiele, L.: Multiobjective Optimization Using Evolutionary Algorithms - A Comparative Case Study. In: Eiben, A.E., Bäck, T., Schoenauer, M., Schwefel, H.-P. (eds.) PPSN 1998. LNCS, vol. 1498, pp. 292–301. Springer, Heidelberg (1998)
10. Zitzler, E., Thiele, L., Laumanns, M., Fonseca, C.M., da Fonseca, V.G.: Performance Assessment of Multiobjective Optimizers: An Analysis and Review. IEEE Transactions on Evolutionary Computation 7(2), 117–132 (2003)

Continuous Optimization Based on a Hybridization of Differential Evolution with K-means

Luz-Marina Sierra, Carlos Cobos$^{(\boxtimes)}$, and Juan-Carlos Corrales

Universidad del Cauca, Popayán, Colombia
{lsierra,ccobos,jcorral}@unicauca.edu.co

Abstract. This paper presents a hybrid algorithm between Differential Evolution (DE) and K-means for continuous optimization. This algorithm includes the same operators of the original version of DE but works over groups previously created by the k-means algorithm, which helps to obtain more diversity in the population and skip local optimum values. Results over a large set of test functions were compared with results of the original version of Differential Evolution (DE/rand/1/bin strategy) and the Particle Swarm Optimization algorithm. The results shows that the average performance of the proposed algorithm is better than the other algorithms in terms of the minimum fitness function value reached and the average number of fitness function evaluations required to reach the optimal value. These results are supported by Friedman and Wilcoxon signed test, with a 95% significance.

Keywords: continuous optimization · differential evolution · particle swarm optimization · K-means

1   Introduction

The word "metaheuristic" is broadly used to refer to a stochastic algorithm that guide the search process toward finding solutions very close to the optimum [1]. There are many algorithms for carrying out this type of task - for example, Random Search, Tabu Search, Simulated Annealing, Harmony Search, and Differential Evolution, among others [1, 2]. In this paper we center on Differential Evolution, which showed good performance in solving many theoretic and real optimization problems.

Differential Evolution was proposed by Rainer Storn and Kenneth Price [2] in 1997. Many implementations and changes have since been proposed. In [3] a hybrid particle swarm differential evolution (HPSDE) is presented, this algorithm outperforms both DE and PSO algorithms. In [4], the authors propose two hybrids with PSO: one uses DE operator to replace the standard PSO method for updating a particle's position; and the other integrates both the DE operator and a simple local search; these perform well in quickly finding global solutions. In [5] a hybrid algorithm named CDEPSO is proposed, which combines PSO with DE and a new chaotic local search. The study in [6] presents a performance comparison and analysis of fourteen variants of DE and Multiple Trial Vectors DE algorithms to solve unconstrained

© Springer International Publishing Switzerland 2014
A.L.C. Bazzan and K. Pichara (Eds.): IBERAMIA 2014, LNAI 8864, pp. 381–392, 2014.
DOI: 10.1007/978-3-319-12027-0_31

global optimization problems. In [7] a new DE is empowered with a clustering technique to improve its efficiency over multimodal landscapes (25 test functions were used), the population is initialized randomly and divided into a specific number of clusters (a minimum and maximum number of clusters is defined), after much iterations each cluster exchanges information (in each cluster a best local solution is searched for and the global solution determined), the number of clusters is self-adaptive (when the algorithm is performing well, the cluster number is decreased; otherwise it is increased), a rule is defined for the number of exploiters based on the fitness of each vector solution in each cluster. In [8] the ACDE-k-means algorithm is proposed, which improves the performance of the DE algorithm using a more balanced evolution process through automatic adjustment of the parameter F [0.5; 1] and a dynamic number of clusters between 2 and $\sqrt{NPop}$. In [9], the SaCoCDE algorithm improves the efficiency of DE by means of: 1) the cluster neighborhood mutation operator, through the auto-adaptation of Cr and F parameters; 2) the overall mutation operator, which uses the centers of each cluster to generate three test vectors using equations presented there, and selects from these three generated vectors the new vector solution for the next generation.

The main contributions of this paper are: 1) a new version of the DE algorithm that improves results of optimal values founded on 50 test functions against original version of DE and PSO. 2) Feasible way of hybridizing DE with k-means in order to provide a new operator to escape from the local optimum. 3) The definition of a new selection strategy that combines the original operator of DE with the results of the k-means algorithm (groups of solutions), providing more diversity and also increasing the ability of the algorithm to work with multimodal test functions.

In section 2 that now follows, DE and K-means algorithms are briefly described. The proposed hybrid algorithm is then presented in section 3. Later in section 4, the results of the experiments are presented and analyzed. Finally, section 5 presents conclusions, remarks and future work.

2   Strategies

This section gives a brief description of the Differential Evolution algorithm, the K-means algorithm, and the rank selection strategy used in genetic algorithms (the strategy used in the proposed algorithm).

2.1   Differential Evolution

Differential Evolution (DE) is an algorithm that works for optimization problems with non-linear and non-differentiable continuous functions [1]. DE looks to optimize functions from a set of randomly generated solutions using specific operators of recombination, selection and replacement. Broadly speaking, the steps of the algorithm are [10]:

- Step 1: An initial random population is generated taking into account the limits of each test function.
- Step 2: The objective function value for all solution vectors ($X_{i,G}$) of the initial population is calculated.
- Step 3: Three vectors solution are randomly selected from the current population, in this research the DE/rand/1/bin strategy was used. Then the mutation operator is applied to each of these vectors in order to generate a disturbed vector, using the Equation (1) [2], where i=1,...,*PopulationSize*, $r_1, r_2, r_3 \in$ *{1,...,PopulationSize}*, $r_1 \neq r_2 \neq r_3 \neq i$; F$\in$ [0,1] is a parameter to control the amplitude of the differential variation at the time of disturbing the vector [1].

$$DE|rand|1: V_{i,G+1} = X_{r1,G} + F * (X_{r2,G} - x_{r3,G}) \qquad (1)$$

- Step 4: The process of crossover starts, so each vector solution in the population is recombined using the Equation (2) [2], where j=1...*Dimension, Crossover rate* [1], Cr, is a parameter to control the crossover operation and has to be determined by the user, rnbr(i) is chosen randomly at the time of the crossover process [1], and *rand* is the jth evaluation of a uniform random number generator with outcome $\in$ [0; 1].

$$U_{j,i,G+1} = \begin{cases} V_{j,i,G+1} & if \ rand \leq Cr \ or \ j = rnbr(i) \\ X_{j,i,G} & otherwise \end{cases} \qquad (2)$$

- Step 5: Is related to the selection operator. This operation includes a vector in the new population of DE, in order to decide which the best is. DE compares the fitness of the vector resulting from the crossover operation with the fitness of the vector target in the current population. Equation (3) [2] summarizes the operation.

$$X_{i,G+1} = \begin{cases} U_{i,G+1} & if \ f(U_{i,G+1}) \leq f(X_{i,G}) \\ X_{i,G} & otherwise \end{cases} \qquad (3)$$

- Step 6: steps 3-5 are repeated for each element of the current population. The algorithm stop based on a specific number of generations defined by user. **Fig. 1** summarizes the algorithm.

01	Generate the initial population
02	Calculate the fitness value for each element of the population
03	**Repeat**
04	**For each** agent $X_{i,G}$ in the population **do**
05	Select parents vectors ($X_{r1,G}$, $X_{r2,G}$ and $X_{r3,G}$ where $r_1 \neq r_2 \neq r_3 \neq i$)
06	Generate the perturbed vector ($V_{i,G+1}$, using the equation (1)).
07	Build the Crossover vector ($U_{i,G+1}$, using the equation (2))
08	Get a new element for the population ($X_{i,G+1}$, using the equation (3))
09	**End for each**
10	**Until** (Stop conditions are reached)

Fig. 1. Pseudo code of Differential Evolution

Authors of DE algorithm [2] present three simple rules for setting DE parameters: "1) NP (Population size) is between 5*D and 10*D but NP must be at least 4 to ensure that DE will have enough mutually different vectors with which to work. 2) F = 0.5 is usually a good initial choice, but if the population converges prematurely, then F and/or NP should be increased. 3) A large Cr often speeds convergence, to first try Cr = 0.9 or Cr = 1.0 is appropriate". For this work, the Cr and F values were taken from those used in other experiments in order to have reference values to use for comparison and the analysis of the algorithm performance.

2.2   K-means Algorithm

K-means is a clustering algorithm that looks to find clusters among a set of individuals by calculating the distances between each individual and the centroid of the nearest group (cluster) [11]. Fig. 2 summarizes the k-means algorithm [12]. Below, a list of some specific considerations of the k-means algorithm for the proposed algorithm is presented:

- The data to be processed by the k-means algorithm are all vector solutions in the population of DE.
- The number of desired groups (k) is previously defined and constant during the execution of the entire hybrid algorithm; in this case, this value is equal to the greater integer of the population size divided by 4. Preliminary tests show that higher values of this parameter allow obtaining better results.
- The centroids of every cluster are initially randomly selected.
- The Euclidean distance (see Equation (4)) is used for finding the similarities between vector solutions and centroids of each cluster (group), then the centroids are re-calculate for each cluster.

$$d(x,y) = \sqrt{\sum_{i=1}^{n}(x_i - y_i)^2} \tag{4}$$

- The set of data (vector solutions in population) is organized into the numbers of clusters previously defined.

01	Define the number of clusters (groups)
02	Randomly select a set of initial centroids
03	**Repeat**
04	Assign every data in a specific cluster based on Euclidian distance
05	Re-Calculate the centroids of each cluster
06	**Until** (there no more changes in centroids or iterations max are achieved)
07	**Return** groups

Fig. 2. Pseudo code of the K-means algorithm

2.3   Rank Selection

Rank selection was initially proposed by Baker to eliminate the high convergence of genetic algorithms when using proportional selection methods. This selection method chooses a new vector solution from the population, based on a ranking table. This table lists in order all the solutions based on the fitness function of solutions. Values in the ranking table are calculated based on formula (5), where n is the total number of vector solutions in the population (population size) and i (between 0 and n-1) is the order number of each specific vector solution [13].

$$\frac{0.25 - 1.5*(i*\frac{1.0}{n} - 1)}{n} \tag{5}$$

3   The Proposed Algorithm

In this section, the proposed hybrid algorithm is presented, called DEKmeans. DEKmeans is the result of combining the original version of Differential Evolution with K-means. The main motivation for the development of this proposal is the change of the selection operator in DE based on groups formed by the k-means algorithm, so that the algorithm gets more exploration, in order to seek more diversity and skip the local optimum.

This proposed algorithm includes some improvements, such as adapting a version of k-means strategy to operate sometimes on the population in order to organize the vector solutions in groups and then use the DE mutation operator (See Eq. 1) as a step to create the new vector solution. In DEKmeans, the rand/1/bin strategy of the original DE is also used. The computational steps of this hybrid algorithm are described as follows:

- The initial population is generated in the same way described above in the differential evolution section.
- The fitness of every vector solution is calculated according to each function.
- In the generation of the following populations, a variation was proposed that includes two ways to generate every new population:

  — The first way, given the PEOA - percentage of execution of the original algorithm - parameter, involves using the method described above for differential evolution 95% of the time (this parameter can be defined by the user,) when a new population is generated.
  — The second way, the remaining 5% (1 - PEOA) of the time, the parent selection operator uses a version that includes the adaptation of k-means algorithm. Parents vectors are selected in a special way: first they are taken from the different groups and special probabilities (Rank Selection, see Section 2.3) assigned to them in order to increase the probability for selecting registers with best fitness on each group.

— Following application of the mutation, crossover, and replace operators, the algorithm carries out a review of the elements of the new population, to avoid including a vector solution that already exists in the new population generated. If the resulting vector solution exits in the population a new randomly vector solution is generated. This approach avoids premature converged.

Comparing our proposed algorithm (DEKmeans) with other work presented above: 1) In reference to [3, 4, 5, 6] our proposal introduces a new version of the DE algorithm (DE/rand/1/bin strategy), which hybridizes to DE with the K-means algorithm and uses Rank Selection, so that it not only generates a hybrid algorithm but a whole strategy that improves its performance by helping it out of local optima, making it more effective, comparing it with the original version of DE and PSO using 50 test functions (which include a variety of problems), in contrast with the others that use some aspects of DE or PSO for use within each. 2) In reference to [7, 8, 9], DEKmeans presents a simple and robust solution comparable with those that have a greater complexity and also implement K-means, but applied from different points of view and even redefining the operators of the DE algorithm, in contrast with DEKmeans that retains the advantages of the original DE version but improving the evolution process of DE in the selection of the vectors to be used in the mutation operator (see Equation (1)) (applying Rank Selection to the groups obtained by the k-means algorithm) and to improve in a simple way the process of selection of the population, avoiding that the algorithm converges quickly and becomes trapped in local minima.

A summary of the proposed algorithm can be seen in Fig. 3. Lines 5, 8, 9, 14 and 15 are new; the other lines correspond to the original version of DE.

4   Experiments: DEKmeans vs DE and PSO

DEKmeans was compared against DE and Particle Swarm Optimization (PSO). To do this, a set of fifty (50) test functions was used. This set of functions includes many different kinds of problems - unimodal, multimodal, separable, regular, irregular, non-separable and multidimensional. For every test function we ensured that the solution vectors always are between the lower and upper limit in each dimension (D). Unconstrained problems were not taken into account in this proposal.

4.1   Settings

Test function: the definitions, parameters and ranges used for the implementation of the test function are the same as described in [14], because this test functions are used in several recent papers where new continuous optimization algorithms have been proposed.

For the experiments, the values of the common parameters used in each algorithm such as population size and total evaluation number were the same. Population size (or swarm size in PSO) was set to 50 and the maximum evaluation number was set to 500.000 for all functions. The other specific algorithm parameters are summarized below.

In DE, F is 0.5 and Cr is 0.9, similar to [10] [14].

In PSO, maximum speed (Vmax) is 5, minimum speed (Vmin) is -5, Cognitive and social component varies between 0.5 and 1, and moment varies between 0.4 and 0.9, Global Optimum in false is similar to [15], where the values of these parameters are taken adaptively on each generation.

In DEKmeans, the execution frequency of the original DE operators against those based on K-means is 95% of the time.

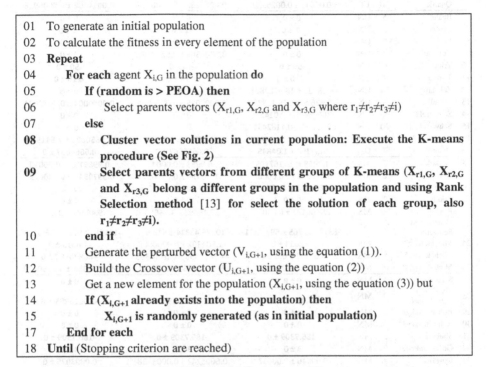

Fig. 3. Hybrid algorithm Differential Evolution and K-means pseudo code

4.2   Results

All algorithms were executed 30 times for each test function and the average fitness and standard deviation calculated. The average results obtained in the experiments are summarized in Table 1.

DEKmeans reaches the optimum (minimum) value of thirty eight (38) functions before completing the 500,000 evaluations of the fitness function, meanwhile DE reaches thirty seven (37) and PSO only twenty seven (27).

Taking as a reference the PSO algorithm (baseline, line with value equal to cero), Fig 4 shows that DE and DEKmeans required less evaluations of the fitness function in order to reach the optimum, e.g. in test function 9 (Colville), PSO required on average 498081 evaluations, DE 124951 and DEKmeans only 30126, therefore, DE required on average 373130 evaluations less than PSO, and DEKmeans required on average 467955 evaluations less than PSO.

Table 1. General Results (Mean ± Standard Deviation) of PSO, DE And DEKmeans Over Each Test Function. D: Dimension, T: Type, U: Unimodal, M: Multimodal, S: Separable, N: Non-Separable

Id	Function	D	Type	PSO	DE	DEKMEANS
1	StepInt	5	US	0 ± 0	0 ± 0	0 ± 0
2	Step	30	US	0 ± 0	0.0333333 ± 0.1825742	0 ± 0
3	Sphere	30	US	0.00044 ± 0.0010574	0 ± 0	0 ± 0
4	SumSquares	30	US	0.00201 ± 0.0029216	0 ± 0	0 ± 0
5	Quartic	30	US	0.00642 ± 0.0026019	0.0016232 ± 0.0006038	**0.0014402 ± 0.0005918**
6	Beale	5	UN	0 ± 0	0 ± 0	0 ± 0
7	Easom	2	UN	-1 ± 0	-1 ± 0	-1 ± 0
8	Matyas	2	UN	0 ± 0	0 ± 0	0 ± 0
9	Colville	4	UN	0 ± 0	0.1206508 ± 0.5217277	0 ± 0
10	Trid6	6	UN	-50 ± 0	-50 ± 0	-50 ± 0
11	Trid10	10	UN	-210 ± 0	-210 ± 0	-210 ± 0
12	Zakharov	24	UN	4.98533 ± 18.9722821	0 ± 0	0 ± 0
13	Powell	30	UN	56.26736 ± 75.19882	0.0000005 ± 0.0000004	**0.0000004 ± 0.0000004**
14	Schwefel2	30	UN	0.006425 ± 0.01428	0 ± 0	0 ± 0
15	Schwefel	30	UN	0.99335 ± 0.4182441	0 ± 0	0 ± 0
16	Rosenbrock	30	UN	51.596532 ± 34.24415	15.56863 ± 7.76282	**15.5650881 ± 7.5419387**
17	DixonPrice	30	UN	1.37192 ± 1.04845	0.6666667 ± 0	**0.6666667 ± 0**
18	Foxholes	2	MS	1.3958 ± 0.6167405	0.9983 ± 0.0004	**0.9985195 ± 0.00058**
19	Branin	2	MS	0.3979313 ± 0.00003	0.39794 ± 0.00003	**0.3979349 ± 0.0000297**
20	Bohachevsky1	2	MS	-0.2690782 ± 0.2067532	0 ± 0	0 ± 0
21	Booth	2	MS	0 ± 0	0 ± 0	0 ± 0
22	Rastrigin	30	MS	127.06191 ± 64.4077	12.46682 ± 3.55653	**9.48422 ± 3.5301**
23	Generalized Schwefel	30	MS	-6373.901205 ± 697.3241	-10275.43814 ± 512.582	**-11179.76933 ± 506.52748**
24	Michalewicz2	2	MS	-1.8013 ± 0	-1.801302 ± 0.0000009	**-1.8013 ± 0**
25	Michalewicz5	5	MS	-4.67431 ± 0.03721	-4.6820898 ± 0.0144393	**-4.6876582 ± 0**
26	Michalewicz10	10	MS	-9.34212 ± 0.43607	-9.6185266 ± 0.037151	**-9.6525355 ± 0.0160679**
27	Schaffer	2	MN	0 ± 0	0 ± 0	0 ± 0
28	Six-Hump Camel-Back	2	MN	-1.03163 ± 0	-1.0316285 ± 0	-1.0316285 ± 0
29	Bohachevsky2	2	MN	0 ± 0	0 ± 0	0 ± 0
30	Bohachevsky3	2	MN	0 ± 0	0 ± 0	0 ± 0
31	Shubert	2	MN	-186.7309 ± 0	-186.7309 ± 0	-186.7309 ± 0
32	GoldsteinPrice	2	MN	3 ± 0	3 ± 0	3 ± 0
33	Kowalik	4	MN	0.00046 ± 0.00032	0.0005242 ± 0.0003738	**0.0003075 ± 0**
34	Shekel5	4	MN	-10.05353 ± 0	-10.0535269 ± 0	-10.0535269 ± 0
35	Shekel7	4	MN	-10.06371 ± 0	-10.0637085 ± 0	-10.0637085 ± 0
36	Shekel10	4	MN	-10.07505 ± 0	-10.0750459 ± 0	-10.0750459 ± 0
37	Perm	4	MN	0.00291 ± 0.0020308	0.05509 ± 0.1436	**0.0002862 ± 0.0004535**
38	PowerSum	4	MN	0.00781 ± 0.0053186	0.00012 ± 0.000133	**0.0001066 ± 0.0001298**
39	Hartman3	3	MN	-3.90511 ± 0.0232529	-3.89989 ± 0.0248041	**-3.8978425 ± 0.0240514**
40	Hartman	6	MN	-3.1916115 ± 0.0725006	-3.23495 ± 0.0536161	**-3.3183945 ± 0.021764**
41	Griewank	30	MN	**0.0000324 ± 0.0000783**	0.00156 ± 0.0036878	0.0004927 ± 0.0026984
42	Ackley	30	MN	0.0106014 ± 0.0129442	0 ± 0	0 ± 0
43	Penalized	30	MN	0 ± 0	0 ± 0	0 ± 0
44	Penalized2	30	MN	8.00602 ± 43.85012	0.0030181 ± 0.0165308	0 ± 0
45	Langerman2	2	MN	-1.08052 ± 0.00022	-1.080499 ± 0.0002486	**-1.0805055 ± 0.0002397**
46	Langerman5	5	MN	**-1.83903 ± 0.13651**	-1.9217559 ± 0.0734335	-1.9372483 ± 0.0687818
47	Langerman10	10	MN	-2.44412 ± 0.22349	-2.5296588 ± 0.0407439	-2.5354428 ± 0.0320827
48	FletcherPowell2	2	MN	129.16175 ± 262.73961	0 ± 0	0 ± 0
49	FletcherPowell5	5	MN	432.89501 ± 616.72146	321.88845 ± 668.95475	0 ± 0
50	FletcherPowell10	10	MN	1385.35261 ± 1676.62682	869.99811 ± 2320.78567	**179.35054 ± 220.58321**

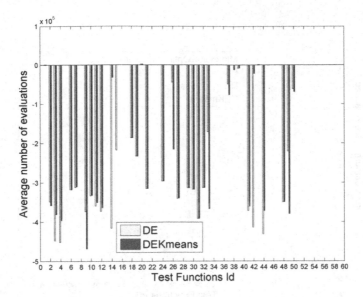

Fig. 4. Average number of evaluations of fitness function in DE and DEKmeans, with PSO as reference

Fig. 5 presents the worst performance of the PSO, DE, and DEKmeans algorithms in contrast with the minimum (optimum) value of each test function. It can be seen that the worst performance of DEKmeans is extremely close to the optimum value of each function. Only in function 23 (Generalized Schwefel) is the result of DEKmeans a little far from the optimum, but nearest than the other algorithms. In functions, 49 (FletcherPowell5) and 50 (FletcherPowell10) DEKmeans improves the results of the other two algorithms.

Fig. 6 presents the best performance of the DE, DEKmeans and PSO algorithms compared to the minimum (optimum) value of each test function. DEKmeans results match almost exactly the optimal solution of each test function. Only in function 23 (Generalized Schwefel) there is a significance difference between the algorithm results and the minimum value for these function, but DEKmeans is nearest than the other algorithms.

Average rankings of optimum values reached in each test function using the Friedman test show that DEKmeans is the best algorithm, with a Friedman statistic (distributed according to chi-square with 2 degrees of freedom) equal to 15.61 and p-value equal to 4.07691E-4 (see Table 2). Additionally, in Wilcoxon test results, DEKmeans was an improvement on the other two algorithms, and DE was an improvement on PSO with a level of significance equal to 0.95.

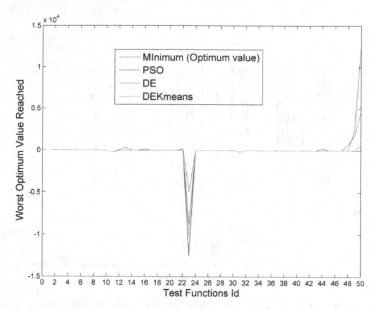

Fig. 5. Worst performance of DE, PSO and DEKmeans algorithms compared against the minimum value for each test function

Table 2. Friedman Test Rankings

Algorithm	Optimum Value Reached	
	Ranking	Position
DEKmeans	1.6	1
DE	2.01	2
PSO	2.39	3

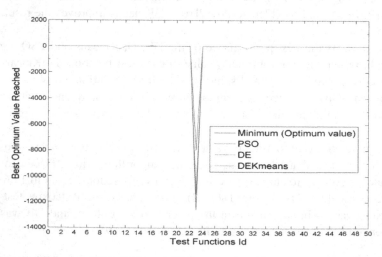

Fig. 6. Best performance of DE, PSO and DEKmeans algorithms compared against the minimum value for each test function

5   Conclusion and Future Work

Three metaheuristics for continuous optimization were compared, namely: 1) Differential Evolution (DE/rand/1/bin), 2) Particle Swarm Optimization, and 3) DEKmeans, a hybrid algorithm between Differential Evolution and K-means. The three algorithms were tested using 50 test functions of different types (Unimodal, Multimodal, Separables, and Non-Separables).

Performing thirty test runs of each algorithm in all test functions, DEKmeans shows better results than the original DE and PSO algorithms. DEKmeans shows that:

- It can achieve an optimal solution with far fewer iterations, as shown in Fig 4.
- The best and worst performances of DEKmeans are better in some functions and similar to the other algorithms, DE and PSO, but approximate very closely to the optimal values of the test functions.

For these reasons, we can say that the DEKmeans algorithm has practical advantages for solving unimodal, multimodal, separable, and non-separables continuous optimization problems.

As regards future work, it is hoped to compare DEKmeans with other metaheuristics and make further improvements to this hybrid algorithm, for example some of the algorithms presented in the introduction section of this paper. Adjustments are required to be made to the DE parameters in order get the best performance from the proposed algorithm.

Acknowledgements. We are grateful to Universidad of Cauca and its research groups GTI and GIT of the Computer Science and Telematics departments. We are especially grateful to Colin McLachlan for suggestions relating to the English text.

References

1. Brownlee, J.: Clever Algorithms Nature-Inspired Programming Recipes, Melbourne: lulu.com (2011)
2. Storn, R., Price, K.: Differential Evolution – A Simple and Efficient Heuristic for Global Optimization over Continuous Spaces. Journal of Global Optimization (1997)
3. Nwankwor, E., Nagar, A.K., Reid, D.C.: Hybrid differential evolution and particle swarm optimization for optimal well placement. Computational Geosciences **17**(2), 249–268 (2013)
4. Fu, W., Johnston, M., Zhang, M.: Hybrid Particle Swarm Optimisation Algorithms Based on Differential Evolution and Local Search. In: Li, J. (ed.) AI 2010. LNCS, vol. 6464, pp. 313–322. Springer, Heidelberg (2010)
5. Tan, Y., Tan, G.-Z., Deng, S.-G.: Hybrid Particle Swarm Optimization with Differential Evolution and Chaotic Local Search to Solve Reliability-redundancy Allocation Problems. Journal of Central South University **20**(6), 1572–1581 (2013)
6. Jeyakumar, G., Velayutham, C.: A Comparative Performance Analysis of Multiple Trial Vectors Differential Evolution and Classical Differential Evolution Variants. In: Sakai, H., Chakraborty, M.K., Hassanien, A.E., Ślęzak, D., Zhu, W. (eds.) RSFDGrC 2009. LNCS, vol. 5908, pp. 470–477. Springer, Heidelberg (2009)

7. Maity, D., Halder, U., Dasgupta, P.: An Informative Differential Evolution with Self Adaptive Re-clustering Technique. In: Panigrahi, B.K., Suganthan, P.N., Das, S., Satapathy, S.C. (eds.) SEMCCO 2011, Part I. LNCS, vol. 7076, pp. 27–34. Springer, Heidelberg (2011)

8. Kuo, R.J., Suryani, E., Yasid, A.: Automatic Clustering Combinign Differenctial Evolution Algorithm and K-means Algorithm. In :Proceedings of the Institute of Industrial Engineers Asian Conference 2013, pp. 1207–215 (2013)

9. Yang, X., Liu, G.: Self-adaptive Clustering-Based Differential Evolution with New Composite Trial Vector Generation Strategies. In: Gaol, F.L., Nguyen, Q.V. (eds.) Proc. of the 2011 2nd International Congress on CACS. AISC, vol. 144, pp. 261–267. Springer, Heidelberg (2012)

10. Ali, M., Pant, M., Abraham, A.: A simplex differential evolution algoritm: development and applications. Transactions of the Institute of Measurement and Control **34**(6), 691–704 (2012)

11. Hernández O., J., Ramírez Q., M. J., Ferri R., C.: Introducción a la Mineria de Datos. Pearson - Prentice Hall, España (2004)

12. Zu-Feng, W., Xiao-Fan, M., Qiao, L., Zhi-guang, Q.: Logical Symmetry Based K-means Algorithm with Self-adaptive Distance Metric. In: S. Obaidat, M. (ed.) Advanced in Computer Science and Its Applications. LNEE, vol. 279, pp. 929–936. Springer, Heidelberg (2014)

13. Jiang, H., Liu, Y., Zheng, L.: Design and Simulation of Simulated Annealing Algorithm with Harmony Search. In: Tan, Y., Shi, Y., Tan, K.C. (eds.) ICSI 2010, Part II. LNCS, vol. 6146, pp. 454–460. Springer, Heidelberg (2010)

14. Karaboga, D., Akay, B.: A comparative study of Artificial Bee Colony algorithm. Applied Mathematics and Computation **214**(1), 198–132 (2009)

15. Poli, R., Kennedy, J., Blackwell, T.: Particle swarm optimization. Swarm Intelligence **1**(1), 33–57 (2007)

16. Alcalá-Fdez, J., Sánchez, L., García, S., Del Jesus, M., Ventura, S., Garrell, J., Otero, J., Romero, C., Bacardit, J., Rivas, V., Fernández, C., Herrera, F.: KEEL: A Software Tool to Assess Evolutionary Algorithms to Data Mining Problems. Soft Computing **13**(3), 307–318 (2009)

Automatic Step Evolution

Tiago Baptista[✉] and Ernesto Costa

CISUC, Department of Informatics Engineering,
University of Coimbra, Coimbra, Portugal
baptista@dei.uc.pt
http://baptista.dei.us.pt

Abstract. A common issue in Artificial Life research, and mainly in
open-ended evolution simulations, is that of defining the bootstrap conditions of the simulations. One usual technique employed is the random
initialization of individuals at the start of each simulation. However, by
using this initialization method, we force the evolutionary process to
always *start from scratch*, and thus require more time to accomplish the
objective. Artificial Life simulations, being typically, very time consuming, suffer particularly when applying this method. In a previous paper
we described a technique we call step evolution, analogous to incremental evolution techniques, that can be used to shorten the time needed
to evolve complex behaviors in open-ended evolutionary simulations. In
this paper we further extend this technique by automating the process
of stepping the simulation. We provide results from experiments done
on an open-ended evolution of foraging scenario, where agents evolve,
adapting to a world with a day and night cycle. The results show that
we can indeed automate this process and achieve a performance at least
as good as on the best performant non-automated version.

Keywords: Artificial life · Multi-agent systems · Open-ended evolution · Incremental evolution

1 Introduction

In most Artificial Life research, populations of artificial organisms are evolved
throughout several generations. An issue that needs attention when first designing these systems is the creation of the seed population. The choice on how to
generate this initial population will have, naturally, a considerable effect on the
evolutionary process. Also known as the bootstrap problem, this same issue is
also typically addressed in evolutionary robotics [9].

One usual solution to this issue is to randomly initialize the seed population
[18][4]. This solution has, however, at least one drawback. As the initial population of organisms is always randomly initialized on every simulation run, the
evolutionary process will always have to *start from scratch*. These systems are
typically very time consuming, having simulation runs easily last several hours
to several days or weeks. The random initialization of the seed population will
only add to this time requirement.

© Springer International Publishing Switzerland 2014
A.L.C. Bazzan and K. Pichara (Eds.): IBERAMIA 2014, LNAI 8864, pp. 393–404, 2014.
DOI: 10.1007/978-3-319-12027-0_32

Another usual solution to the issue is to initialize the seed population with hand-crafted simple organisms [11][5]. Again, this technique is not without its disadvantages. Although it may shorten the time needed to evolve the population, the definition of an initial seed organism will place the burden of choosing a known good solution to the problem at hand on the researcher, instead of leaving it to evolution to find that solution. To some extent, this technique defeats some of the founding principles of Artificial Life.

One specific area of Artificial Life research where the issue of the seed population is particularly important is in open-ended evolution. Although a formal definition of open-ended evolution has not yet gathered consensus, it can be broadly defined as the ability of an evolutionary system to continually produce novel forms [14].

To achieve open-ended evolution, a number of authors consider that a major requirement is the absence of an explicitly defined goal or notion of "better" individual [3]. In most evolutionary computation and artificial life research, this notion of "better" individual is implemented via fitness functions. However, in the real world, there are clearly no explicit fitness functions governing the evolution of organisms. In the work described here, we look into the issue of open-ended evolution, considering that simulations don't employ fitness functions or any other kind of artificial selection mechanism.

The requirement of not enforcing a notion of "better" individual makes the solution of randomly initializing the population, better suited to open-ended evolution, than hand-coding the initial organisms. By creating an initial solution to seed the population, be it a known-good or only a viable solution, would introduce into the simulation, even if inadvertently, a bias into what is expected of evolution. Conversely, as open-ended evolution seems harder to model [7], and heavier on computational resources, randomly initializing the population will show its toll on the time requirements of the simulations.

In a previous paper [2], we described a technique we call *step evolution*, that can be used to shorten the time requirements for open-ended evolution simulations. Using it, we are able to use the solution of randomly initializing the population, whilst reducing the computational effort required. In this paper we further extend the technique in an effort to better automate the process. We will start by describing the step evolution conceptual model, and its automatic extension. Next we will detail the experimental setup used to test the technique, and follow with the results from the experiments. We will end with some conclusions and future work.

2   Step Evolution

In complexity science, it is generally accepted that complex systems can be structured hierarchically, where each system is composed of subsystems, these subsystems are themselves composed of subsystems, and going on until we reach the most basic components (e.g. sub-atomic particles). It can also be considered that emergent properties frequently appear across levels. That is, an emergent property observed at a given level, is the product of interactions of components on the level below. On another note, in biology, an important theory that gathers some consensus is that evolution is not continuous, but happens mostly in large transitions [13]. Smith and Szathmáry's theory states that, although small changes can occur and propagate in a population, the big changes are the ones that drive the evolutionary process.

We combine aspects from the two aforementioned theories to create the step evolution technique. Essentially, it consists of identifying the perceived complexity levels, and dividing the problem accordingly. We first simulate a scaled down version of the problem, and when the agents evolve to solve this simpler problem, we change the simulation by adding the features removed earlier, and continue the evolution. In other words, if a problem with a very large search space, has an extremely small number of viable solutions, we can simplify the problem, increasing the number of viable solutions, eventually maintaining the search space. When the simpler version of the problem is solved, we then try to solve the initial problem, starting from the solutions already found. Obviously, not all problems are prone to this kind of decomposition. Nonetheless, we believe that evolutionary processes, especially when open-ended, are ideal candidates to apply this technique.

We can find some examples of similar techniques being applied in different settings. One of the early examples is the incremental evolution of neural networks in a prey capture task [6]. In this paper the authors describe a method of transforming the final task to evolve into a series of progressively more demanding sub-tasks. All these tasks translate into the fitness functions used at each stage of the evolutionary process. In evolutionary robotics we can also find the use of incremental fitness functions, or incremental evolution [10][9]. In [9], the authors define four sub-categories of incremental evolution: *staged evolution*, *environmental complexification*, *fitness shaping* and *behavioral decomposition*. To some extent, in cartesian genetic programming [8], the use of incremental fitness functions can also be considered a similar technique, as is the case in an application of genetic algorithms to multiprocessor scheduling [17], where incremental fitness is also used. In [15], the authors use *environmental complexification* in an effort to compare the use of homogeneous of heterogeneous strategies to decompose the problem domain into increasing complexity objective functions. In all these works, the usage of these techniques is applied to fitness functions. We are however interested in open-ended evolution scenarios, without any explicit fitness functions, or other artificial selection mechanisms.

This concept of decomposing a given problem into simple sub-problems has been the focus of study in several areas within artificial intelligence. One such example is the layered learning machine learning technique [16], having been used mainly in robotics, and more specifically in robotic soccer. In this technique, the same principals of task decomposition, and of relating a low-level task learnt with the next level task, are also used. However, in our work we are mainly interested in evolutionary scenarios, and in layered learning works no evolution—as in evolutionary computation—is employed.

To better define the step evolution technique, we use a multi-agent simulation framework as our modeling mindset. This type of framework is extensively used in artificial life, as it easily mimics the Natural World. Making use of the concepts of agent (which are subject to evolution), and environment, we can better explain the technique.

The step evolution technique consists of allowing the agents to evolve in steps, by gradually building up the environment, analogous to what was described for *environmental complexification*, and/or the agents' structure (perceptions, actions, features). For example, if an agent is in an environment where the possible survival behaviors are very few, the evolutionary search process will effectively be almost like a random search. We thus, initially setup the environment in such a way that widens the space of viable behaviors, for example by removing constraints. We then let the agents evolve in this simpler environment, and later reintroduce the removed constraints. The agents will then continue to evolve in the new environment, but now from solutions that were already viable in the previous one.

In our first implementation of step evolution [2], the time in the simulation when the step is applied is configured as a parameter of the simulation run. Several possible values for this parameter were experimentally tested. In the present paper, we now propose to automatically determine the time at which this change should occur for each run of the simulation. By monitoring the population as it evolves, we make the choice based on the capability of the population to survive and prosper in the current environment. This technique is similar to the one proposed by Gomez et al. in [6], where the increase in task complexity is only applied when a given performance level for the current task is achieved.

A number of different population metrics can then be used to determine the time at which to apply the steps. The choice on what to use will be highly dependent on the specific simulation or artificial life framework used. The experimental setup described in this paper uses a specific alife framework, and a specific simulation scenario. However, the technique can be easily applied to other frameworks and scenarios.

3   Experimental Setup

The simulations described in this paper were implemented using the BitBang framework [1]. Implementing a modern autonomous agent model [12], this framework has roots in Artificial Life systems and Complexity Science. The simulated world is composed of entities. These can either be inanimate objects that are designated as *things*, or entities that have reasoning capabilities and power to perceive and affect the world—the *agents*. Both have traits that characterize them, such as color, size, or energy—the *features*. The agents communicate with, and change the environment using *perceptions* and *actions*, taking decisions using the *brain*.

Although the framework is agnostic regarding the algorithm used for the agents' brains, in the experiments shown in this paper, we used an ordered rule list. This algorithm uses a list of rules where each one is composed of a conjunction of conditions. The decision process is straightforward. The rule list is ordered, and rules are evaluated in order. The first rule that evaluates to true is chosen, and its corresponding action is selected.

To test the step evolution technique, we implemented a world where agents need to evolve foraging capabilities and adapt to an environment with day and night. We follow the same experimental setup as the one from a previous open-ended evolution experiment described in [1].

In those simulations we implement a world where both agents and resource items are placed. To survive, the agents need to search for and eat the resource items. The terrain is a square. This area restricts the placement of agents, and resources, but does not restrict the movement of the agents. The world is infinite, i.e., an agent can move past the boundaries of the populated terrain. At startup, the field is populated with a configured amount of randomly placed food items. These are periodically replenished so that the total food count is maintained.

To differentiate the day from the night, the environment has a light level that oscillates between a configurable maximum and minimum. For each day the maximum light level is randomly calculated as the overall maximum minus a random value between zero and the delta. The same applies for the day's minimum. For example, if the maximum light level is 100, the minimum light level is 0, and the delta is 10, each day's maximum light level will be a random value between 90 and 100, and each day's minimum light level will be a random value between 0 and 10. Additionally, the light level does not rise or fall abruptly, but rather changes linearly during a specified time interval, simulating dusk and dawn.

In this environment, the agents will need to evolve the capabilities to find and eat food, to reproduce, and to synchronize with the day and night cycle, sleeping during the night, moving and eating during the day.

The agents have a set of features, perceptions and actions, that define their structure. In this world the agents have the following structure:

- Features:
    - *Energy:* This feature represents the current energy level of the agent. When this feature reaches zero, the agent dies.
    - *Metabolic Rate:* The metabolic rate is the amount of energy the agent consumes per time unit. This rate is initialized to its configured base value, and changes as the agent moves (increases) or sleeps (decreases).
    - *Birth Date:* This feature is set to the current time at birth. It is used to calculate the agent's age. When the agent reaches a given age, it dies.
- Perceptions:
    - *Energy:* This is a self-referencing perception on the agent's current energy level.
    - *Resource Location:* This is the agent's perception of vision, representing the position of the nearest resource, relative to the agent's position and orientation. The agent's vision field is defined by a given range and angle. An object is within the vision field of an agent if its distance to the agent

is less than or equal to the vision range, and the relative angle to the agent is within the defined vision angle. This perception is influenced by the light level of the environment. As the light level drops, so does the range of vision for the agent.

- *Reach Resource:* This is a boolean perception that evaluates to true whenever the agent has a resource within its reach.
- *Light Level:* This perception gives the agent the power of sensing the brightness of the environment.

– Actions:
  - Movement: We define three actions for movement. One to walk forward, one to turn left, and one to turn right.
  - Eat: This action enables the agent to eat a resource within its reach. If no resource is within reach when the action is executed, nothing happens.
  - Sleep: The agent can use this action to sleep. In this simulation, when an agent is sleeping, it will stand still and its metabolic rate will decrease.
  - Reproduce: This action allows the agent to reproduce itself. The reproduction implemented is asexual. When the action is executed, a new agent is created and placed in the world. The new agent will be given a brain that is a mutated version of its parent's brain. The action will also transfer energy from the parent to the offspring. The amount of energy consumed in the action is the sum of the initial energy for the new agent and a configurable fixed cost for the action.

As mentioned before, we randomly initialize the population when we start the simulation. That means that initially the agents will most likely not be able to search for food, eat, or even reproduce. To prevent the population from dying out right from the start of the simulation, we keep introducing new agents into the population until they evolve to be self-sustained, i.e. when they are capable of searching for food, eating, and reproducing. When the global number of agents falls bellow a given threshold, we randomly pick an agent from the live ones, and force the reproduction of that agent. If there are no live agents, a completely random new one is generated. Once the population can self-sustain, no new agents are forcedly introduced.

In the previous experiments, to implement the step evolution technique in this world, we setup two different options. First, we implemented a version where we remove the light level variation from the environment for the first step, and then reintroduce it later in the simulation, as a second step. This way, the evolution of foraging will happen in an environment that is less challenging. The other option implemented was to also scale down the agent structure for the first step of the simulation. In this case, we removed from the agent the perception of the light level, and the action of sleeping, re-adding them on the second step of the simulation. With these two variants we tested the step evolution concept to the environment and to the structure of the agents. We showed that, with both environmental and structural step evolution, the time required to evolve the adaptation to the light level, significantly reduces.

To implement automatic step evolution, we monitor the size of the population, as a measure of adaptation to the current step in the evolution. When the population size increases above a given threshold, we advance to the next step. In these experiments we always use the version with both environmental and structural step evolution.

Simulations were configured following the previous experiments on step evolution. As previously, we are mainly interested in the time it takes to evolve behaviors adapted to this environment. We thus created several experiments to compare the step evolution using a fixed time step, and the automatic step evolution. For each experiment we ran thirty independent simulations. For the automatic step evolution technique, we tested different methods to monitor the population size, and apply the threshold. We first tried to simply test the population size and compare it to the threshold. However, to prevent a premature change due to a non-stable rise in population above the threshold, we tested the averaging of the population size over a given time interval. We were also interested in finding if the use of this automatic step would allow the time limit of the experiments to decrease, and still allow for mostly successful runs. In table 1 we show the various experimental configurations tested.

The value of the threshold tested is set to 100 agents, for any of the automatic step evolution experiments. The choice of this threshold was based on the previous experiments. If we were to apply the technique to a completely new scenario, we would not be able to base our decision on previous knowledge. As a general rule-of-thumb, this threshold should always be higher than the minimum number of agents configured for the given experiment. However, as stated earlier, the choice of monitoring parameter and threshold will be highly dependent on the specific simulation scenario that is implemented.

To analyze the results from the various parameter configuration variations, we determined the statistical significance of the null hypothesis of no difference for each set of experiments using Kruskal-Wallis ANOVAs with $\alpha = 0.05$. If a significant difference in one of these sets of experiments was found, further pairwise Mann-Whitney U tests with Holm's p-value adjustment were conducted.

Table 1. Configuration values for the several experiments

Step Evolution	Time Limit	Chg. Time	Interval
None	100k	N/A	N/A
Manual	100k	20k	N/A
		50k	N/A
		70k	N/A
	50k	20k	N/A
Automatic	100k	N/A	0
		N/A	1000
		N/A	5000
	50k	N/A	1000
		N/A	5000

These non-parametric tests were chosen because the data is not guaranteed to follow a normal distribution, and runs are independent and non-related.

4   Results

In this section we show and analyze the results from the experiments conducted. As we are mainly interested in finding if the technique allows for lower time requirements, we look at the time when important behavioral features emerge in the population. Namely, we will analyze the time when agents start having a good foraging behavior, the time when the population starts to have self-sustained reproduction behaviors, and the time when the population adapts to the daily cycle, sleeping during the night, and being active during the day. To better illustrate, we show in Fig. 1 an evolutionary plot from a typical run of an experiment without step evolution. We can clearly pinpoint the time when the agents start gathering food (about 16 000), the time when they start to reproduce (about 34 000), and the time when they synchronize (about 36 000).

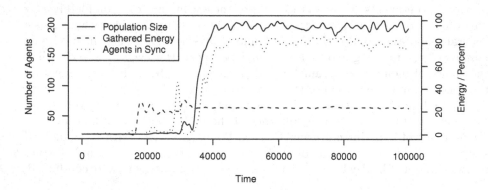

Fig. 1. Plot of the evolution of the number of agents, their average gathered energy, and percentage of agents in sync, over the course of one simulation run

Although it is easy to pinpoint the time at which these behaviors emerge by analyzing the evolutionary plots, we needed to do it programmatically. To that end, scripts were created to analyze the simulation logs, and determine these performance metrics. To determine both the time for evolution of foraging and for evolution of synchronization, we go through the whole simulation, starting from the end of the simulation to the beginning, calculating the average of all agents, alive at that time, for the given metric. When this average drops below a given threshold, that is the time when the behavior evolved. The thresholds used for these experiments where 6 for the gathered energy, and 0.3 for the ratio of agents in sync over all agents with known sync. To determine the time when the population starts to have self-sustained reproduction, we again go through the simulation starting from the end, and find the last agent that was forcibly reproduced.

4.1   Experiments with 100k Time Limit

First we ran the set of experiments with a time limit of 100k, both for manual step evolution and automatic step evolution. In Figure 2 we compare the results from this set of experiments. Examining the boxplots, we can see that there is a clear improvement when using step evolution, when compared to not using it, regarding all tested performance values. When comparing the manual to the automatic step evolution, the performance seems to be identical to that of the 20k change time experiment. In fact, performing the statistical tests, we found that to be the case.

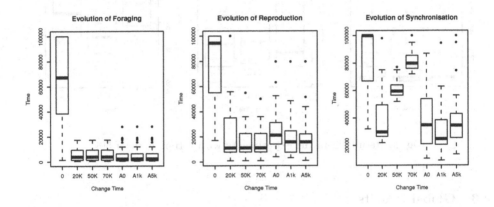

Fig. 2. Results from the experiments with a time limit of 100k

Considering the results from Figure 2, we found that in all the performance values there are significant differences in the results, with a p-value of 7.516×10^{-12} for the evolution of foraging, 3.128×10^{-13} for the evolution of reproduction, and 8.276×10^{-26} for the evolution of synchronization. Further pairwise tests revealed that those differences are mainly due to the poor performance of the experiment without step evolution. Comparing the two step evolution variations, we only find significant differences when comparing the evolution of synchronization for the 50k and 70k experiments, and the automatic step experiments, where the latter perform better. In fact, we can see that all the automatic step evolution experiments have a similar performance to the 20k experiments. It thus seems that the automatic technique can produce results at least as good as the best tested manual setting.

4.2   Experiments with 50k Time Limit

We then ran the experiments with a time limit of 50k, in an attempt to see if we can further reduce the time limit of these experiments and still evolve the behavior adapted to the changing light level. Those results are shown in Fig. 3. Analyzing the boxplots, we get an indication that the use of automatic step evolution had no impact in the evolution of foraging or reproduction. However, when analyzing the evolution of synchronization, there seems to be a better performance of the automatic evolution with 1000 time interval experiment. The statistical tests do verify that indeed the Auto1k experiment has a better performance than the 20k experiment, with a p-value of 0.0240.

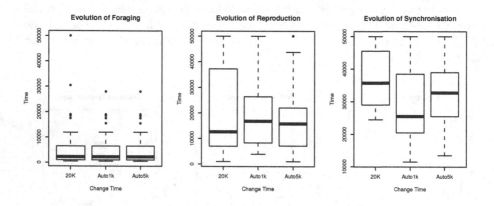

Fig. 3. Results from the experiments with a time limit of 50k

4.3   Global Results

Another important performance metric is the number of runs from each experiment that are successful. We say that a run is successful if, in the time limit assigned, the agents evolve the behaviors adapted to the environment and have a self-sustained population. In this case, we are looking to see, from the thirty runs, how many are successful in first evolving foraging and reproduction, but mainly in evolving synchronization. One important thing to note is that, if in a run, the agents don't evolve a foraging behavior, they will obviously not be able to evolve any other behavior. In table 2 we show these results for all the experiments.

Again, when looking at this performance metric, we can see that using step evolution does allow a higher number of runs to be successful in evolving synchronization. Especially in the experiments with a time limit of 100k, we can go from having 13 successful runs without step evolution, to 30 successful runs with step evolution. Again, comparing manual to automatic step evolution, we can see that we are able to at least maintain performance in the 100k time limit simulations. When considering the 50k time limit experiments, in the case of this performance metric, we did not find a pronounced difference in the number of successful runs when using automatic step evolution.

Table 2. Number of successful runs for each experimental configuration

Step Evolution	Time Limit	Change Time	Runs	Foraging	Sync
None	100k	0	30	16	13
Manual	100k	20k	30	29	29
	100k	50k	30	30	30
	100k	70k	30	30	29
	50k	20k	30	26	25
Automatic	100k	Auto0	30	30	30
	100k	Auto1k	30	30	30
	100k	Auto5k	30	30	29
	50k	Auto1k	30	27	24
	50k	Auto5k	30	28	25

5   Conclusions

We set out to extend the step evolution technique by automating the process of choosing the time when the change in step occurs in a simulation. The results show that we can indeed automate this process, and still maintain the same performance levels as the previously best tested parameter values. We did not, however, see a clear improvement in the performance when comparing the manual to the automatic step evolution. Nevertheless, as the main contribution is the automation of the process, we feel that achieving the same level of performance is an important achievement.

Also, by automating this process, we are to some extent removing the burden of specifying the time steps from the simulation designer. This can contribute to the overall objective of achieving open-ended evolution. There are still parameters and thresholds to set for the automated process. And thus, there might still be room for further improvement in this regard.

We evaluated the effects of using automatic step evolution on the time requirements of the simulations, as that was our primary goal in developing this technique. However, it would also be important to verify if by using it, other aspects of the simulation are maintained (e.g. diversity).

In terms of future work, having tested the technique in one simulation scenario, it is now important to also test in other scenarios. In the experiments presented we tested the technique with two steps. A larger number of steps should be tested as well. Furthermore, it would also be interesting to test the technique using a different artificial life framework.

References

1. Baptista, T.: Complexity and Emergence in Societies of Agents. Ph.D. thesis, University of Coimbra, Coimbra (July 2012)

2. Baptista, T., Costa, E.: Step Evolution: Improving the Performance of Open-Ended Evolution Simulations. In: 2013 IEEE Symposium on Artificial Life (ALIFE), pp. 52–59 (2013)
3. Channon, A.: Three evolvability requirements for open-ended evolution. In: Maley, C.C., Boudreau, E. (eds.) Artificial Life VII Workshop Proceedings, Portland, OR, pp. 39–40 (2000)
4. Channon, A.: Evolutionary Emergence: The Struggle for Existence in Artificial Biota. Ph.D. thesis, University of Southampton (November 2001)
5. Eiben, A., Griffioen, A.R., Haasdijk, E.: Population-based Adaptive Systems: an Implementation in NEWTIES. In: ECCS 2007: European Conference on Complex Systems, Dresden, Germany (July 2007)
6. Gomez, F., Miikkulainen, R.: Incremental evolution of complex general behavior. Adaptive Behavior 5(3–4), 317–342 (1997)
7. Maley, C.: Four steps toward open-ended evolution. In: GECCO 1999: Proceedings of the Genetic and ... (1999)
8. Miller, J.F. (ed.): Cartesian Genetic Programming. Natural Computing Series, 1st edn. Springer (September 2011)
9. Mouret, J., Doncieux, S.: Overcoming the bootstrap problem in evolutionary robotics using behavioral diversity. In: IEEE Congress on Evolutionary Computation, CEC 2009, pp. 1161–1168 (2009)
10. Nelson, A.L., Barlow, G.J., Doitsidis, L.: Fitness functions in evolutionary robotics: A survey and analysis. Robotics and Autonomous Systems 57(4), 345–370 (2009)
11. Ray, T.S.: Evolution, Ecology and Optimization of Digital Organisms. Tech. Rep. 92-08-042, Santa Fe Institute (1992)
12. Russell, S., Norvig, P.: Artificial Intelligence: A Modern Approach, 2nd edn. Prentice Hall (December 2002)
13. Smith, J.M., Szathmáry, E.: The Major Transitions in Evolution. Oxford University Press, Oxford (1985)
14. Standish, R.K.: Open-ended artificial evolution. Int. J. Comput. Intell. Appl. 3(2), 167–175 (2003)
15. Stanton, A., Channon, A.: Heterogeneous complexification strategies robustly outperform homogeneous strategies for incremental evolution. In: Proceedings of the Twelfth European Conference on the Synthesis and Simulation of Living Systems, pp. 973–980. MIT Press, Taormina (2013)
16. Stone, P., Veloso, M.M.: Layered Learning. In: Lopez de Mantaras, R., Plaza, E. (eds.) ECML 2000. LNCS (LNAI), vol. 1810, pp. 369–381. Springer, Heidelberg (2000)
17. Wu, A.S., Yu, H., Jin, S., Lin, K.C., Schiavone, G.: An Incremental Genetic Algorithm Approach to Multiprocessor Scheduling. IEEE Transactions on Parallel and Distributed Systems 15(9) (September 2004)
18. Yaeger, L.: Computational genetics, physiology, metabolism, neural systems, learning, vision, and behavior or Poly World: Life in a new context. In: Langton, C.G. (ed.) Artificial Life III: Proceedings of the Workshop on Artificial Life, pp. 263–298. Addison-Wesley (1994)

Parallel MOEA/D-ACO on GPU

Murilo Zangari de Souza[(✉)] and Aurora Trinidad Ramirez Pozo

DInf, Federal University of Parana, CP: 19081, Curitiba 19031-970, Brazil
{murilo.zangari,auroratrinidad}@gmail.com.br

Abstract. This paper describes the idea of MOEA/D-ACO (Multiobjective Evolutionary Algorithm based on Decomposition and Ant Colony Optimization) and proposes a Graphics Processing Unit (GPU) implementation of MOEA/D-ACO using NVIDIA CUDA (Compute Unified Device Architecture) in order to improve the execution time. ACO is well-suited to GPU implementation, and both the solution construction and pheromone update phase are implemented using a data parallel approach. The parallel implementation is applied on the Multiobjective 0-1 Knapsack Problem and the Multiobjective Traveling Salesman Problem and reports speedups up to 19x and 11x respectively from the sequential counterpart with similar quality results. Moreover, the results show that the size of test instances, the number of objectives and the number of subproblems directly affect the speedup.

Keywords: MOEA/D-ACO · GPU · NVIDIA CUDA · Multiobjective 0-1 knapsack problem · Multiobjective traveling salesman problem

1 Introduction

Ant colony optimization (ACO) [1] is one of the most successful swarm intelligence techniques. Its initial application was to single objective combinatorial problems. However, ACO was soon extended to tackle multiobjective optimization problems (MOPs) using the Pareto dominance concepts, called Multiobjective ACO (MOACO) algorithms [2] [3].

MOEA/D [4] (Multiobjective Evolutionary Algorithm based on Decomposition) is a recent evolutionary algorithm for multiobjective optimization using the decomposition idea. MOEA/D outperforms Multiobjective Genetic Local Search (MOGLS) and Non-dominated Sorting Genetic Algorithm II (NSGA-II). Extensions of MOEA/D have been applied for solving a number of MOPs. Recently in [5] an extension, called MOEA/D-ACO was proposed where each ant is responsible for solving one subproblem. The algorithm was applied on the multiobjective 0-1 knapsack problem (MOKP) and on the bi-objective traveling salesman problem (b-TSP) and achieved better results than MOEA/D and BicriterionAnt [6] respectively.

ACO algorithms are population-based, that is, a collection of agents contribute to find optimal (or satisfactory) solutions, and such approaches are suited

© Springer International Publishing Switzerland 2014
A.L.C. Bazzan and K. Pichara (Eds.): IBERAMIA 2014, LNAI 8864, pp. 405–417, 2014.
DOI: 10.1007/978-3-319-12027-0_33

to parallel processing. Several GPU (Graphics Processing Unit) parallelization approaches have been proposed for the ACO to solve single-objective problems [7] [8] [9] [10]. These researches improve the performance achieving high quality results in a reasonable execution time. Some studies proposed a CPU-based approach to parallel MOACOs [11] [12] applied on bi-TSP, and also a CPU-based to parallel MOEA/D [13] applied on continuous MOPs. These studies did not achieve a high speedup due to target hardware. In [14] the author proposed a parallel MOEA on GPU applied on continuous MOPs and achieved speedups range from 5.62x to 10.75x. Parallel MOACO algorithm on GPU is a recent and open research field.

NVIDIA introduced CUDA (Compute Unified Device Architecture), a general purpose parallel computing platform and programming model for direct execution on GPUs to solve many complex computational problems in a more efficient way than on a CPU. CUDA exposes the GPU's massively parallel architecture so parallel code can be written to execute faster than its optimized sequential counterpart [15]. The success of a GPU approach depends on the nature of the particular problem and the underlying hardware available.

This paper describes a parallel implementation of MOEA/D-ACO on GPU with CUDA where both stages *solution construction* and the *pheromone update* are parallelized. The paper presents results from two benchmarks: on the Multiobjective 0-1 Knapsack Problem (MOKP) and on the Multiobjective Traveling Salesman Problem (MOTSP). The solution quality and the speedups are compared to the sequential counterpart with different number of objectives and subproblems.

The remainder of this paper is organized as follows. Section 2 introduces MOP and describes the MOEA/D-ACO proposed by [5]. Section 3 describes the parallel implementation of MOEA/D-ACO. Section 4 reports the experimental results. The conclusion and future work are presented in Section 5.

2 MOEA/D-ACO

This section reviews concepts of MOP and the MOEA/D-ACO [5] algorithm.

MOP Definition: A general MOP can be state:

$$minimize \ (or \ maximize) \ F(x) = (f_1(x), ..., f_m(x)) \ subject \ to \ x \in \Omega \qquad (1)$$

where $x = [x_1, x_2, x_n]^T$ is the decision variable vector, Ω is the decision (variable) space, $F : \Omega \rightarrow R^m$ consist of m real-valued objective functions, and R^m is called the *objective space*. The *attainable objective set* is defined as set $\{F(x)|x \in \Omega\}$.

Let the vectors $u, v \in R^m$, u is said to *dominate* v if and only if $u_i \leq v_i$ for every $i \in \{1, ..., m\}$ and $u_j < v_j$ for at least one index $j \in \{1, ..., m\}$[1]. Point $x^* \in \Omega$ is *Pareto optimal* if there is no point $x \in \Omega$ so that $F(x)$ dominates $F(x^*)$.

---

[1] This definition of domination is for minimization. For maximization the inequalities should be reversed.

$F(x^*)$ is then called a *Pareto optimal (objective) vector*. So, any improvement in the one objective of a Pareto optimal point must lead to deterioration to at least another objective. The set of all the Pareto optimal is called the *PS*, and the set of all the Pareto optimal objective vectors is called the *PF*.

2.1 The Algorithm MOEA/D-ACO

MOEA/D-ACO algorithm decomposes a MOP into N single-objective subproblems by choosing N weight vectors $\lambda^1, ..., \lambda^N$. Subproblem i is associated with weight vector λ^i and its objective function is denoted as $g(x|\lambda^i)$. The algorithm employs N ants for solving these single-objective subproblems. Ant i represents the subproblem i. The algorithm has two concepts: **(1) Neighborhood:** $B(i)$ of ant i contains T ants, where T is the size of the neighborhood. The neighbors of ant i are T closest to λ^i among all the N weight vectors; **(2) Groups:** where N ants are divided into K groups by clustering their corresponding weight vectors. The ants in the same group share one pheromone matrix which contains learned information about the position of their Pareto, each group is intended to approximate a small range of the PF.

The algorithm maintains: (I) $\tau^1, ..., \tau^K$, where τ^j is the current pheromone matrix for group j, storing its learned knowledge about the sub-region of PF that it aims at approximating; (II) $\eta^1, ..., \eta^N$, where η^i is the heuristic information matrix for subproblem i, which is predetermined before the construction solution starts; (III) EP, which is the external archive containing all the non-dominated solutions found so far. First, the algorithm generate the N initial solutions, the heuristic information matrix and the pheromone information matrix. Then, at each iteration the MOEA/D-ACO executes the following steps:

1. Generate N solutions according a probabilistic rule;
2. Update EP;
3. Update the pheromone matrices according with the new solutions that were constructed by ants in group j and have just been added to EP;
4. Check the solutions on the neighborhood and updates the solutions if there is a solution that: 1) is better than its current solutions; 2) has not been used for updating other old solutions. This mechanism makes collaboration among different ant groups (sharing information).
5. The algorithm stops if a criterion is met.

Other details of the projects are problem specific and are described next [5].

2.2 Project of MOKP

Data Structure of Pheromone Matrices: Each candidate solution is a 0-1 *n-Dimensional* vector, where n is the number of items. So, the pheromone matrix for group j is $\tau^j = (\tau_1^j, ..., \tau_n^j)$. The approach *Max-Min* [16] is used, so there are boundaries to maximum and the minimum value of τ. All the τ_k^j is initially with $\tau_{max} = 1$ for all $j = 1, ..., K$ and $k = 1, ..., n$.

Heuristic Information Matrices: The heuristic information matrix for ant i is $\eta^i = (\eta^i_1, ..., \eta^i_n)$, where η^i_k is to measure the desirability, learned from the domain knowledge before the search. The value of kth in η^i for ant i is

$$\eta^i_k = \frac{\sum_{l=1}^{m} \lambda^i_l p_{l,k}}{\sum_{l=1}^{m} w_{l,k}} \tag{2}$$

where $p_{l,k}$ is the profit of item k with the objective l, $w_{l,k}$ is the weight of item k with the objective l. **EP** is initialized empty.

Solution Construction: At each subproblem N, the probability of each $item_k$ is denoted as ϕ_k calculated by Equation 3. The solution vector starts empty, which means that the n-*Dimensional* vector starts with 0 in all dimensions. The items are randomly (using roulette wheel selection) added to the solution one by one, respecting the constraints. The probability is calculated as follows:

$$\phi_k = \frac{(\tau^i_k + \Delta \times x^i_k)^\alpha \times (\eta^i_k)^\beta}{\sum_{k \in I} \phi_k} \tag{3}$$

where I is the feasible items; τ^i_k is the pheromone of item k in the subproblem i; $\Delta \times x^i_k$ is a private knowledge; η^i_k is the heuristic value of item k in the subproblem i; α, β and Δ are control parameters. After all ants have constructed their solutions the EP is updated with the new solutions. Solutions that are dominated by the new solutions are removed.

Update the Pheromone Matrices: Let Π be the set of all the new solutions that satisfy: (a) they were constructed by the ants in group j of the current iteration; (b) they were just added to EP and (c) in which $item_k = 1$ in n-*Dimensional* vector . Then, τ^j_k, i.e., the pheromone trail value of item k for group j, is updated as follows:

$$\tau^j_k := \rho\tau^j_k + \sum_{x \in \Pi} \frac{1}{\sum_{l=1}^{m} \sum_{k=1}^{n} p_{lk} - g(x|\lambda^j)} \tag{4}$$

where ρ is the persistence rate of the old pheromone trails; p_{lk} is the profit of item k on the knapsack l and $g(x|\lambda^j)$ is the objective function to subproblem λ^j. According to [5], in this update scheme, pheromone matrix τ^j stores some statistical information of good solutions found so far for the task of group j.

2.3   Project of MOTSP

Data Structure of Pheromone Matrices: Each group j has pheromone trail $\tau^j_{k,l}$ for a link between two different cities k and l. The approach *Max-Min* is also used. All the $\tau^k_{k,l}$ is initialized to $\tau_{max} = 1$.

Heuristic Information Matrices: Each ant i has an heuristic information value $\eta^i_{k,l}$ for a link between cities k and l. The value of heuristic information are initialized as

$$\eta^i_{k,l} = \frac{1}{\sum_{j=1}^{m} \lambda^i_j c^j_{k,l}} \tag{5}$$

where m is the number of objectives, $c_{k,l}^j$ is the cost between k and l with respect the objective j.

Solution Construction: Assume that ant i is in group j, and its full-scale current solution $x^i = (x_1^i, ..., x_n^i)$. Ant i constructs its new solution following the steps:

1) First, the probability of choosing a link is set. For $k, l = 1, ..., n$ set

$$\phi_{k,l} = [\tau_{k,l}^i \times In(x^i, (k,l)]^\alpha (\eta_{k,l}^i)^\beta \tag{6}$$

where α and β are control parameters. ϕ represents the attractiveness of the link between cities k and l to ant i. The indicator function $In(x^i, (k,l))$ is equal to 0 if link (k,l) is already in tour x^i or 1 otherwise.

2) Ant i first randomly selects a city to start the tour. After, each city is chosen using the roulette wheel selection. Suppose that its current position is k and it has not completed its tour. It is chosen city l to visit from C (cities not visited so far), according to the following probability by the roulette wheel selection:

$$\frac{\phi_{k,l}}{\sum_{s \in C} \phi_{s,l}} \tag{7}$$

3) If the ant has visited all the cities, return its tour.

Pheromone Update: Let Π be the set of all the new solutions that satisfy: (a) were constructed by the ants in group j in the current iteration; (b) were just added to EP; (c) contain the link between cities k and l.

The pheromone trail value of link (k,l) for group j, is updated as follows:

$$\tau_{k,l}^j := \rho \tau_{k,l}^j + \sum_{x \in \Pi} \frac{1}{g(x|\lambda^i)} \tag{8}$$

where ρ is the persistence rate of the old pheromone trail. As mentioned, τ_{max} and τ_{min} are used to limit the range of the pheromone.

3   Parallel Implementation of MOEA/D-ACO

This section briefly describes the CUDA architecture and then reports the decisions made to implement a parallel version of MOEA/D-ACO.

CUDA allows developers to run blocks of code, known as *kernels*, directly on the GPU using a parallel programming interface and using familiar programming languages. CUDA parallel programming model has a hierarchy of thread groups called *grid*, *thread blocks* and *threads*. When a *kernel* function is invoked, it is executed N times in parallel by N different *CUDA threads*. A single grid is organized by multiple blocks, each of which has equal number of threads [15].

CUDA threads may access data from multiple memory spaces during their execution. All threads have access to the same *global memory*, which is implemented as an off-chip DRAM of the GPU, and has large capacity, say, 1.5-6

Gigabytes, but its access latency is very long. Each thread block has *shared memory* visible to all threads into a block and with the same lifetime as the thread block. The *shared memory* is an extremely fast on-chip memory with lower capacity, say, 16-48 Kbytes. Each thread has its local (private) memory on-chip, called *register memory*. Registers are the fastest form of storage and each thread within a block has access to a set of fast local registers that are placed on-chip. Each thread can only access its own registers; moreover the number of registers is limited per block, so blocks with many threads will have fewer registers per thread. The efficient usage of the memory types is a key for CUDA developers to accelerate applications using GPU [15]. When threads accesses to continuous locations in a row of a 2-dimensional array *(horizontal access)*, the continuous locations in address space of the global memory are accessed in the same time *(coalesced access)*. From the structure of the global memory, the coalesced access maximizes the bandwidth of memory access. On the other hand, the stride access *(vertical access)* needs a lot of clock cycles [10].

Cecilia et al. [9] noted that the existing task-based approach of mapping one ant per thread is not suited to the GPU, because each thread must store each ant's memory (data structures of a solution) and this approach works only for small solutions but quickly becomes problematic with larger solutions, as there is limited shared memory and registers available for each block. Based on this issue, the studies [7] [8] [9] adopted a novel data parallel approach that maps each ant to a block. All threads within the thread block then work in cooperation to perform a common task such as tour construction.

The performance on GPU can be drastically affected by the use of a costly math function like *powf()* see Eq.(3). Fortunately, there are analogous CUDA functions which map directly to the hardware level (like *__powf()*) [15], although this comes at the expense of some loss of accuracy. [9] shown a comparison using *__powf()* on an equation which improve the execution time.

First, the algorithm was implemented sequentially and the parallel implementation was made based on it. We base our parallelization strategy on the works [7] [8] [9] and adopt a data-parallel approach mapping each ant to a thread block. The parallel implementation consists of three CUDA parts (initialization, tour construction and pheromone update) and one CPU part (*EP* updated). The *EP* is updated in host (sequential) because each new solution needs to be analyzed at time to update the *EP*. In parallel, it would be hard to guarantee correctness even using atomic functions. The details of the three GPU parts for the MOKP and MOTSP are described as follows.

3.1   Parallel Approach for the MOKP

Initialization: The algorithm allocates memory and the relevant data structures: *N-Dimensional* ants vector (which contains the partial solution, the accumulated profit and its group), *n-Dimensional* items vector (which contains the profit and weight of each item) and the *m-Dimensional* knapsack vector (which contains the capacity of each knapsack).

The ants need to choose items in probabilistic way using the roulette wheel selection. The algorithm initializes the random seeds using the CURAND, which is a library that provides a pseudorandom number generator on the GPU by NVIDIA [17].

Solution Construction: Each subproblem i is associated with a thread block. So the N ants (subproblems) construct their solution in parallel. To improve the performance, the number of access to global memory is decreased, allocating some structures on shared memory and register memory. So, the data structure of an ant (solution) is saved on its respective thread register memory; the items vector is also copied to each thread register memory because they are accessed many times; and the data structure of m knapsacks are placed on the shared memory because they are accessed few times. When an ant ends its solution construction the ant is copied to the *N-Dimensional* vector allocated on the global memory. In [8], the authors report that using the shared memory and registers for these structures would restrict the algorithm to limited number of ants and this restriction would grow linearly with the problem size. The *N-Dimensional* ants vector is copied to host to update the *EP*.

Pheromone Update: A new *kernel* is invoked, now each block corresponds to a group and each thread corresponds to an ant that satisfies Π (see Section 2.2). The data structure of items is copied to device again, and placed in shared memory. The first step of the update is the pheromone evaporation, which is trivial to parallelize as all pheromone matrices are evaporated by a constant factor ρ. In the second step, each group updates its pheromone matrix in parallel. For each ant in group j that was added to *EP* and in which $item_k = 1$ in n-*Dimensional* vector updates the pheromone trail τ_k^j following Equation 4, so we do not need to use atomic operations to guarantee correctness.

3.2   Parallel Approach for the MOTSP

Initialization: Give n cities, the city-to-city distances are loaded in an $(n \times n)$ matrix for each objective (recall, $d_{k,l} = d_{l,k}$). The N ants are loaded to store each ant current tour and tour length. A kernel is invoked to calculate the distance between the cities and set the pheromone matrix initialization. The heuristic value and probability to be chosen is executed during the tour construction, so we do not need to allocate a vector with size N (number of subproblems) to store the N heuristic values for each link *(k,l)*. Also, the algorithm initializes the random seeds using the CURAND [17].

Tour Construction: Each subproblem i is associated with a thread block. So the N ants (subproblems) construct their tour in parallel. The weigh vectors are allocated on shared memory because they are accessed few times. Each ant stores its structure (current tour, tour length, cities not visited, and its group) on the local memory (registers) of a thread. The matrix of cities $(n \times n)$ is stored on the global memory, however, the treads access only continuous location in a row of the matrix $(n \times n)$, i.e., when the current city of a tour is k, the threads access only the k row of the matrix (k,l), where $l = (1,...,n)$. As we mentioned the coalesced access to the global memory is a key issue to accelerate the computation. When an ant ends its tour construction the ant is copied to the vector N-dimensional allocated on the global memory. When all N ants end their tour construction, the N-Dimensional vector of ants is copied back to host to update EP.

Pheromone Update: A new kernel is called to update the pheromone. Now each thread block corresponds to a group and each thread corresponds to an ant that satisfies Π (see Section 2.3). The matrix $(n \times n)$ is allocated on the global memory. The pheromone update uses the same approach that the MOKP.

4   Experiments

Our sequential algorithm achieves similar results to original MOEA/D-ACO [5] in terms of solution quality. In this section we attained the comparison between the implementations (sequential and parallel) in terms of solution qualtity and execution time. In the comparison we use twelve instances from [18] for the MOKP (which is a benchmark for many-objectives problems) and nine different combinations of instances from [19] for the MOTSP (with a large number of cities compared with studies [11] [12]). The metric to evaluate the quality of the solutions is the *Hypervolume* [20]. To evaluate the execution time we show the speedup of the parallel implementation against the sequential counterpart.

The implementations were made using an NVIDIA GeForce GTX680 that contains 1536 CUDA cores and has a processor speed of 1058 MHz. It uses 32 threads per warp and up to 1024 threads per thread block with maximum shared memory size of 64 Kb. The CPU is an Intel i7-380QM and has 4 cores with support 8 threads with a clock speed of 3.60 GHz. The implementation was written and compiled using the CUDA toolkit 5.0 for C with the Nsight Eclipse environment executed under Ubuntu 12.04.

All the statistics are based on 30 independents runs. For the decomposition approach it was used only *Weighted sum*, because *Weighted sum* outperform the *Tcheby-cheff* approach as cited in [5].

4.1   Results from MOKP

The ACO parameters setting was the same used in [5]: $\alpha = 1, \beta = 10, \rho = 0.95$. The algorithms stop after 300 generations. The test instance with 750 items and 4 objectives was infeasible due to registers constraints.

Solution Quality: Also based on [5], we set the number of subproblems to $N=300$ and number of groups to $K=10$. The average and standard deviation of hypervolume for the 30 runs are summarized in Table 1. The name of the test instances are abbreviated, for example, the instance with 500 items and 2 knapsacks is called 500-2. The highest hypervolume value for each instance is highlighted in bold face. The Wilcoxon statistic test [21] was applied and showed that the results do not have significant difference at 0.99 level of confidence, i.e.,

Table 1. Average hypervolume and standard deviation obtained

Instance	Sequential		Parallel	
	Average	Stand. Dev.	Average	Stand. Dev.
100-2	**6.711E+05**	6.213E+02	6.709E+05	3.643E+02
250-2	5.651E+06	4.127E+03	5.651E+06	5.972E+03
500-2	**1.476E+07**	1.002E+04	1.475E+07	7.016E+03
750-2	**3.915E+07**	4.521E+04	3.908E+07	4.123E+04
100-3	**9.240E+08**	1.256E+06	9.232E+08	1.484E+06
250-3	1.199E+10	1.050E+07	**1.200E+10**	8.038E+06
500-3	7.381E+10	1.249E+08	**7.401E+10**	1.656E+08
750-3	**1.896E+11**	2.295E+08	1.881E+11	2.564E+08
100-4	**8.089E+11**	4.409E+09	8.058E+11	2.618E+09
250-4	1.986E+15	1.601E+13	**2.013E+15**	1.725E+13
500-4	**6.173E+16**	7.504E+14	6.081E+16	4.521E+14

Table 2. Average execution times in seconds (s)

Instance	Sequential (CPU)	Parallel (GPU)	Speedup x
100-2	62.92	5.69	11.065
250-2	431.68	27.75	15.55
500-2	1952.95	105.74	18.47
750-2	4574.43	233.68	19.58
100-3	76.58	9.53	8.03
250-3	447.85	38.49	11.63
500-3	1692.39	123.62	13.69
750-3	3582.08	245.44	16.6
100-4	96.47	23.65	4.08
250-4	368.725	39.13	9.42
500-4	1306.98	137.43	9.51

the results show that to parallelize the MOEA/D-ACO does not decrease the solutions quality.

Execution Time: The parameters number of subproblems and the number of groups are set to $N = 300$ and $K = 10$ respectively and the execution time is analyzed on the different test instances. Table 2 presents the average execution time (in seconds) for eleven test instances and the speed up of the parallel against the sequential. The results show a speedup up to 19x faster than the sequential implementation.

As reported in Table 2, the number of items affects the execution time. When the number of items increases (see test instances: 100-2, 250-2, 500-2, 750-2), the speedup increases, because the number of items affects the solution construction phase which is executed in the parallel stage. Thus, when the algorithm consumes more time in the parallel stage the speedup increases.

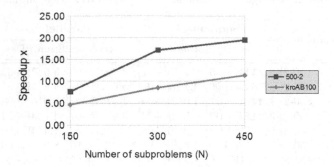

Fig. 1. Speedup of parallel vs. sequential algorithm on 500-2 (MOKP) and kroAB100 (MOTSP) test instances with number of subproblems $N = \{150, 300, 450\}$. The number of groups is fixed $K=10$ to 500-2 and $K=3$ to kroAB100.

In addition, as shown in Table 2, the number of objectives also affects the execution time. When the number of objectives increases (see test instances: 500-2, 500-3, 500-4), the speedup decreases because with more objectives more solutions become non-dominated with each other on the objective space, consequently, the size of EP increases at each generation consuming more time of the algorithm in the sequential part. For example, with 500-2 test instance, one generation found 58 non-dominated solutions (19% of the solutions) with final size of $|EP|=190$; with 500-4 test instance, one generation found 255 non-dominated solutions (85% of the solutions) with the final size higher than 4000 solutions. The number of non-dominated solutions is an issue on many-objective optimization problem.

The number of subproblems also affects the speedup. Figure 1 shows the speedup with $N = \{150, 300, 450\}$ on the 500-2 test instance. Each subproblem corresponds to a thread block in the parallel solution construction phase, so higher the number of subproblems higher the number of thread blocks will be executing in parallel which increases the speedup. However, because of the limited size of CUDA memories (shared memory and registers) a higher number of subproblems can be infeasible.

4.2   Results from MOTSP

The ACO parameters setting was the same used in [5]: $\alpha = 1, \beta = 2, \rho = 0.95$. The algorithms stop after 1000 generations. The test instance with 500 cities and 4 objectives was infeasible due to CUDA memory constraints.

Solution Quality: We set the number of subproblems and number of groups to $N=300$ and $K=3$ respectively. The average and standard deviation of hypervolume for the 30 independent runs are summarized in Table 3. The highest hypervolume value for each instance is highlighted in bold face. The Wilcoxon

Table 3. Average hypervolume and standard deviation obtained

Instance	Sequential		Parallel	
	Average	Stand. Dev.	Average	Stand. Dev.
kroAB100	1.860E+10	2.439E+07	**1.861E+10**	1.938E+07
euclidAB300	1.654E+11	4.820E+07	**1.654E+11**	6.680E+07
euclidAB500	**5.162E+11**	7.569E+07	5.162E+11	6.367E+07
kroABC100	**2.618E+15**	1.616E+12	2.596E+15	2.488E+12
euclidABC300	5.461E+16	4.415E+13	**5.446E+16**	4.830E+13
euclidABC500	**3.148E+17**	2.802E+14	3.129E+17	2.213E+14
kroABCD100	2.156E+20	1.229E+19	**2.551E+20**	5.244E+17
euclidABCD300	1.307E+22	1.218E+20	**1.337E+22**	9.224E+19

Table 4. Average execution times in seconds (s)

Instance	Sequential (CPU)	Parallel (GPU)	Speedup x
kroAB100	172.02	20.14	8.54
euclidAB300	1327.92	169.10	7.85
euclidAB500	2870.92	459.00	6.25
kroABC100	491.46	186.18	2.64
euclidABC300	1617.44	474.19	3.41
euclidABC500	3726.14	798.40	4.67
kroABCD100	909.85	430.93	2.11
euclidABCD300	1895.88	582.07	3.26

statistic test [21] was applied and showed that the results do not have significant difference at 0.99 level of confidence as the same in MOKP.

Execution Time: Table 4 presents the average execution time (in seconds) for eight test instances and the speed up of the parallel against the sequential. The results with 300 subproblems and 3 groups show a speedup up to 8x faster than the sequential counterpart.

As showed in Table 4 the number of objectives affects the execution time for the same reason on the MOKP. When the number of objectives increases (see test instances: *kroAB100*, *kroABC100* and *kroABCD100*) the speedup decreases.

As on the MOKP, the number of subproblems affects the speedup. Figure 1 shows the speedup with $N = \{150, 300, 450\}$ on the kroAB100 test instance. With 450 subproblems the parallel algorithm achieves a speedup up to 11x faster than the sequential counterpart. However, because of the limited size of CUDA memories a higher number of subproblems can be infeasible.

5   Conclusion and Future Work

This paper proposed a parallel implementation of the MOEA/D-ACO on GPU with CUDA where both solution construction and pheromone update stages are executed on GPU. We achieve similar and sometimes higher speedup than [14]. Our results show a speedup up to 19x faster for the MOKP and 11x faster for the MOTSP using a reasonable number of subproblems and groups. The algorithm achieves a higher speedup for the MOKP because the algorithm makes fewer accesses to global memory when compared with the MOTSP. On the MOTSP the data structure for the $n \times n$ matrix of cities was infeasible to allocate on the shared memory or registers.

Other aspects that affects the execution time: (1) A high number of objectives degrades the speedup because it affects the size of the *EP*, which the *EP* update stage is implemented on host (CPU); (2) A high number of subproblems increases the performance, because each subproblem executes its solution construction in parallel, but a high number can be an issue due to the memory limits.

Some aspects to consider for future work: (1) How to deal with the memory limits for work with largest test instances and a higher number of subproblems; (2) Improving the execution time using other parallelization approaches, e.g., a parallel version of the roulette wheel selection as in [9] (not implemented due the architecture of the GPU available); (3) Parallelizing the *EP* update stage which is the main reason that we do not achieve highest speedup.

References

1. Dorigo, M., Caro, G.D.: The ant colony optimization meta-heuristic. In: New Ideas in Optimization, pp. 11–32. McGraw-Hill (1999)
2. Lopez-Ibanez, M., Stutzlee, T.: The automatic design of multi-objective ant colony optimization algorithms. IEEE Trans. on Evol. Comp. **16**(6), 861–875 (2012)
3. Lopez-Ibanez, M., Stutzle, T.: The impact of design choices of multi-objective ant colony optimization algorithms on performance: An experimental study on the biobjective TSP. In: GECCO 2010, pp. 71–78 (2010)
4. Zhang, Q., Li, H.: Moea/d: A multiobjective evolutionary algorithm based on decomposition. IEEE Trans. Evolutionary Computation **11**(6), 712–731 (2007)
5. Ke, L., Zhang, Q., Battiti, R.: Moea/d-aco: A multiobjective evolutionary algorithm using decomposition and ant colony. IEEE Trans. Cybern. **43**(6), 1845–1859 (2013)
6. Iredi, S., Merkle, D., Middendorf, M.: Bi-Criterion Optimization with Multi Colony Ant Algorithms. In: Zitzler, E., Deb, K., Thiele, L., Coello, C.A.C., Corne, D.W. (eds.) EMO 2001. LNCS, vol. 1993, pp. 359–372. Springer, Heidelberg (2001)
7. Dawson, L., Stewart, I.A.: Improving ant colony optimization performance on the gpu using cuda. In: IEEE Congress on Evol. Comp., pp. 1901–1908 (2013)
8. Delevacq, A., Delisle, P., Gravel, M., Krajecki, M.: Parallel ant colony optimization on graphics processing units. J. Parallel Distrib. Comput. **73**(1), 52–61 (2013)
9. Cecilia, J.M., Garcia, J.M.: Nisbet: Enhancing data parallelism for ant colony optimization on gpus. J. Parallel Distrib. Comput. **73**(1), 42–51 (2013)
10. Uchida, A., Ito, Y., Nakano, K.: An efficient gpu implementation of ant colony optimization for the traveling salesman problem. In: Third International Conference on Networking and Computing, pp. 94–102 (2012)
11. Mora, A.M., Garcia-Sanchez, P., Castillo, P.A.: Pareto-based multi-colony multi-objective ant colony optimization algorithms: an island model proposal. In: Soft Computing. LNCS, vol. 17, 1175–1207. Springer, Heidelberg (2013)

12. Mora, A.M., Merelo, J.J., Castillo, P.A., Arenas, M.G., García-Sánchez, P., Laredo, J.L.J., Romero, G.: A Study of Parallel Approaches in MOACOs for Solving the Bicriteria TSP. In: Cabestany, J., Rojas, I., Joya, G. (eds.) IWANN 2011, Part II. LNCS, vol. 6692, pp. 316–324. Springer, Heidelberg (2011)
13. Nebro, A.J., Durillo, J.J.: A Study of the Parallelization of the Multi-Objective Metaheuristic MOEA/D. In: Blum, C., Battiti, R. (eds.) LION 4. LNCS, vol. 6073, pp. 303–317. Springer, Heidelberg (2010)
14. Wong, M.L.: Parallel multi-objective evolutionary algorithms on graphics processing units. In: GECCO 2009, pp. 2515–2522 (2009)
15. NVIDIA: Cuda c programing guide v5.5 (2014)
16. Stutzle, T., Hoos, H.: Max-min antsystem. Fut. Gen. Comp. Syst. 16(8) (2000)
17. NVIDIA: Cuda toolkit guide v4.1 curand (2014)
18. Zitzler, E., Thiele, L.: Multiobjective evolutionary algorithms:a comparative case study and the strength pareto approach. IEEE Trans. Evol. Comp. 3(4), 257–271 (1999)
19. http://eden.dei.uc.pt/paquete/tsp/
20. Yan, J., Li, C., Wang, Z., Deng, L., Demin, S.: Diversity metrics in multi-objective optimization: Review and perspective. In: IEEE International Conference on Integration Technology, ICIT 2007, pp. 553–557 (2007)
21. Derrac, J., Garcia, S.: A practical tutorial on the use of nonparametric statistical tests as a methodology for comparing evolutionary and swarm intelligence algorithms. Swarm and Evol. Comp. 1(1), 3–18 (2011)

Function Optimization in Conformal Space by Using Spherical Inversions and Reflections

Juan Pablo Serrano Rubio[1]([✉]), Arturo Hernández Aguirre[2],
and Rafael Herrera Guzmán[2]

[1] ITESI, Information Technologies Laboratory, Irapuato, Guanajuato, Mexico
juserrano@itesi.edu.mx
[2] Center for Research in Mathematics, Computer Science
Department, Guanajuato, Mexico
{artha,rherrera}@cimat.mx

Abstract. This paper introduces an Evolutionary Algorithm in Conformal Space (EACS) for global continuous optimization and its implementation by using Conformal Geometric Algebra (CGA). Two new geometric search operators are included in the design of the EACS: Inversion Search Operator (ISO) and Reflection Search Operator (RSO). The ISO computes the inverse points with respect to hyper-spheres, and the RSO redistributes the individuals on the surface of the hyper-sphere. The nonlinear geometric nature of the ISO furnishes and enhances the search capability of the algorithm. The reproduction operators are described in the framework of the CGA. CGA provides a concise way to perform rigid euclidean transformations(rotations, translations, reflections) and inversions on hyper-spheres. These transformations are easily computed by using the products of the CGA. The performance of the EACS is analyzed through a benchmark of 28 functions. Statistical tests show the competitive performance of EACS in comparison with current leading algorithms (PSO and DE).

Keywords: Evolutionary algorithm · Geometric search operators · Conformal geometric algebra

1 Introduction

An evolutionary algorithm (EA) is inspired by the process of natural evolution. In general an evolutionary algorithm is defined by the operators which are used to create new individuals such as a recombination or mutation. The reproduction and mutation operators define the mechanism of search for each algorithm. For instance, Particle Swarm Optimization (PSO) generates new individuals by the linear combination of vectors or particles (individuals) of the swarm. Another example is Differential Evolution (DE) which creates new individuals by adding a mutation vector (computed as the difference of two random vectors) to a third vector. The analysis of the search performed by evolutionary algorithms may be approached through the geometric properties of the operators and the

© Springer International Publishing Switzerland 2014
A.L.C. Bazzan and K. Pichara (Eds.): IBERAMIA 2014, LNAI 8864, pp. 418–429, 2014.
DOI: 10.1007/978-3-319-12027-0_34

space itself. Recently, the search space has been described as a geometric space with a notion of distances between points, and candidate solutions in the space. The Geometric Search Operators, introduced by Moraglio [1,2], are defined upon geometric shapes which delimit a region of the search space that will be occupied by the new offsprings. Thus, the offsprings are placed in some predicted region of the space which is geometrically related to the position of the parents. In 2007, Moraglio [3] proposed a new operator called product geometric crossover in order to generate new individuals by using a convex linear combinations of vectors. In 2009, Moraglio [4] generalized the DE algorithm to combinatorial search spaces extending its geometric interpretation to those spaces.

The goal of this paper is to introduce two new geometric search (reproduction) operators which are called the Inversion Search Operator (ISO), and the Reflection Search Operator (RSO). ISO and RSO operators are designed with the help of the Geometric Algebra (GA) and Conformal Geometric Algebra (CGA). The development of the CGA has made possible a large number of applications in areas such as computer vision, robotics and pattern recognition [5,6]. The advantage of these algebras are two fold: 1) their potential to model and manipulate objects defined in their space is larger than that of the common linear algebra; 2) every Euclidean transformation can be reproduced in the conformal space using the conformal geometric product. Furthermore, it also allows the compact representation and manipulation of a greater number of geometric objects such as hyperplanes and hyper-spheres. The inner and outer products in the conformal space can be used to measure the distance between pairs of points, a plane and a point, as well as to determine whether a point is inside or outside a hyper-sphere. Therefore, in our Evolutionary Algorithm in Conformal Space (EACS), the population is created in the usual way, however, it is mapped into the conformal space where all the computations are performed.

The rest of this paper is organized as follows: for the convenience of the reader, in Section 2, the proposed EACS and its implementation are presented. Experimental and numerical results are presented in Section 3. Future work and conclusions are given in Section 4.

2   EACS: An Evolutionary Algorithm in Conformal Space

The pseudo-code for EACS is shown in Algorithm (1). It is written in terms of the CGA expressions, however, the equivalent to vector calculus expressions are given with smaller font. The individuals of the population are points $x \in \mathbb{R}^n$, which are initialized in the domain in the function to be optimized. In the EACS, the individuals (vectors in Euclidean space) are mapped into the Conformal Space where the evolutionary (inversion and reflection) operators and the actual search is performed. Equation(1) defines the required mapping.

$$\mathbb{P}(x) = x_1 e_1 + x_2 e_2 + \ldots + x_n e_n + \frac{1}{2} x^2 e_\infty + e_0, \qquad (1)$$

Therefore, an individual (Euclidean vector) $x = x_1 e_1 + x_2 e_2 +, \ldots . x_n e_n$ in $\mathbb{R}^n$ is mapped to $\mathbb{R}^{n+1,1}$ as a $(n+2)$-dimensional real vector space that includes the

Euclidean space $\mathbb{R}^n$ and two more independent directions generated by two basic vectors e_0 and e_∞ [7]. Furthermore, $\mathbb{R}^{n+1,1}$ is endowed with a scalar product (denoted by $\bullet$) of vectors satisfying: $e_i \bullet e_i = 1$, $e_i \bullet e_j = 0$, $e_i \bullet e_\infty = 0$, $e_i \bullet e_0 = 0$, $e_\infty \bullet e_0 = -1$, $e_\infty \bullet e_\infty = 0$, $e_0 \bullet e_0 = 0$, where $1 \leq i, j \leq n$. The vectors e_0 and e_∞ represent the origin and a point at infinity, respectively. The number x^2 is the scalar product of x with itself. The inner product between such point $\mathbb{P}(x)$ and $\mathbb{P}(y)$ is directly proportional to the square of the Euclidean distance between the points x and y multiplied by -2,

$$- 2(\mathbb{P}(x) \bullet \mathbb{P}(y)) = -2 \left(x \cdot y - \frac{1}{2}y^2 - \frac{1}{2}x^2 \right) = (x - y)^2 \qquad (2)$$

A hyper-sphere in $\mathbb{R}^n$ is determined by its center $c \in \mathbb{R}^n$ and its radius $r \in \mathbb{R}$. Its conformal model representation is the point:

$$\mathbb{S}(c, r) = \mathbb{P}(c) - \frac{1}{2}r^2 e_\infty. \qquad (3)$$

The inner product between a point $\mathbb{P}(x)$ and a hyper-sphere $\mathbb{S}(c, r)$

$$\mathbb{P}(x) \bullet \mathbb{S}(c, r) = \frac{1}{2}r^2 - \frac{1}{2}(c - x)^2 \qquad (4)$$

can be used to decide whether a point is inside or outside of the hyper-sphere [7]:

- $\text{Sign}(\mathbb{P}(x) \bullet \mathbb{S}(c, r)) > 0$: x is inside the hyper-sphere.
- $\text{Sign}(\mathbb{P}(x) \bullet \mathbb{S}(c, r)) < 0$: x is outside the hyper-sphere.
- $\mathbb{P}(x) \bullet \mathbb{S}(c, r) = 0$: x is on the hyper-sphere.

Equation (5) presents the result of the scalar/inner product between two conformal vectors.

$$\mathbb{P}(c) \bullet \mathbb{P}(x) = \left(\sum_{i=1}^{n} c_i e_i + c_\infty e_\infty + c_0 e_0 \right) \bullet \left(\sum_{i=1}^{n} x_i e_i + x_\infty e_\infty + x_0 e_0 \right)$$
$$= \underbrace{c \cdot x}_{\text{Euclidean scalar product}} -c_0 x_\infty - c_\infty x_0 \qquad (5)$$

The EACS performs either the Inversion Search Operator (ISO) or the Reflection Search Operator (RSO) with a probability of 0.5. These operators need an individual as a center of the hyper-sphere. The individual is randomly chosen from the set $\mathcal{P}$ of the best individuals in the population. These geometric search operators produce a candidate individual y. The current individual x_i is replaced by y, when y has a better fitness than x_i.

The pseudo-code for RSO is shown in Algorithm (2). RSO redistributes the individuals on the surface of a hyper-sphere by using reflections. Figure 1(a) shows three possible reflections of an individual x in the search space, however only one reflection is randomly selected to produce a new individual. The radius r

---

Algorithm 1. Pseudo-code of the EACS

---

procedure EACS
    /* d: dimension of the problem
      ps: population size
      η: Number of hyper-spheres for inverse points */
    /*1. **Initialize a population** */
    $Pop \leftarrow \{x^{(1)}, x^{(2)}, ..., x^{(ps)}\}$ where the individual $x^{(i)} \in \mathbb{R}^d$
    $t \leftarrow 0$
    while not stopping condition **do**
        $\mathcal{P} \leftarrow$ Select the best η individuals.
        for $i \leftarrow 1$ to ps **do**
            /*2. **Select a center of the hyper-sphere** */
            repeat
                $c \leftarrow$ select randomly one from $\mathcal{P}$
            until $c \neq x^{(i)}$
            if $U(0,1) \geq 0.5$ **then**
                /*3. **Inversion Search Operator** */
                $y \leftarrow$ INVERSIONSEARCHOPERATOR$(c, x^{(i)})$
            else
                /*4. **Reflection Search Operator** */
                $y \leftarrow$ REFLECTIONSEARCHOPERATOR$(c, x^{(i)})$
            end if
            /*5. **Replace the individual** */
            if $fitness(x^{(i)}) > fitness(y)$ **then**
                $x^{(i)} \leftarrow y$
            end if
        end for
        $t \leftarrow t + 1$
    end while
end procedure

---

of the hyper-sphere is set to be equal to the Euclidean distance between the center c and the current individual x. The reflection of the individual with respect to the center is carried out by using the Clifford product, as shown in Figure 1(b). A canonical vector e_k is selected randomly according to the problem dimensionality to perform the reflection y. Equation (6) is defined by using the Clifford product to perform a reflection of a vector x with respect to a vector e_k.

$$y = e_k x e_k^{-1} \equiv e_k \mathbb{P}(x) e_k^{-1}, \tag{6}$$

Figure 2(a) presents an example of the calculation to obtain three possible reflections of a vector $x \in \mathbb{R}^3$ by using the Clifford product. Figure 2(b) shows the multiplication table of the Clifford product.

The ISO is based on the inversion of a vector with respect to a hyper-sphere. The individuals outside the hyper-sphere are mapped inside the hyper-sphere and viceversa. The hyper-sphere determines a region in space where we can

Algorithm 2. Pseudo-code of the Reflection Search Operator

procedure REFLECTIONSEARCHOPERATOR(c,x)
    $y \leftarrow c - x$
    $e_k \leftarrow$ Select randomly one canonical component according to the problem
        dimensionality.
    return $x^R \leftarrow e_k y e_k + c$
end procedure

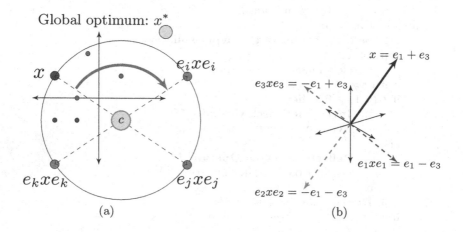

(a)   (b)

Fig. 1. (a) Mutation of an individual by using RSO. (b)After the reflection operation is applied to the point (individual) x, one of the three possible positions is chosen.

vector	Reflections				**1**	e_1	e_2	e_3
	$e_1 x e_1$	$e_2 x e_2$	$e_3 x e_3$	**1**	1	e_1	e_2	$e_2 e_3$
	$e_1(e_1+e_3)e_1$	$e_2(e_1+e_3)e_2$	$e_3(e_1+e_3)e_3$	e_1	e_1	1	$e_1 e_2$	$e_1 e_3$
$x = e_1 + e_3$	$(1+e_1 e_3)e_1$	$(e_2 e_1 + e_2 e_3)e_2$	$(e_3 e_1 + 1)e_3$	e_2	e_2	$-e_1 e_2$	1	$e_2 e_3$
	$e_1 - e_3$	$-e_1 - e_3$	$-e_1 + e_3$	e_3	e_3	$-e_1 e_3$	$-e_2 e_3$	1

(a)   (b)

Fig. 2. (a)Reflections of a vector x in $\mathbb{R}^3$ by using the Clifford product. As shown in Figure 1(b), the reflection operator applied to a vector x produces new positions of x that can be replicated with standard rotations (of the linear algebra) about the coordinate axis. (b) Multiplication table of the Clifford product in $\mathbb{R}^3$.

potentially find a global minimum. The main steps of ISO which furnish and enhance the search capability of the EACS are listed in the next paragraphs.

Mutation for the Center of Hyper-Sphere. A mutation is applied to the center of hyper-sphere with a probability of 0.5. This mutation consists in adding a normal random number to one the components of the Euclidean vector representing the center.

Calculation of the Radius of Hyper-Sphere. The radius r of the hyper-sphere is set to be equal to the square of Euclidean distance between the center c and the individual x multiplied by a uniform random variable defined on the interval $(0,2)$. In this way, when the radius is higher than the Euclidean distance, the inverse point is inside of the hyper-sphere and vice versa.

Calculation of the Inverse Individual in the Acceptable Region. In CGA, the inversion of point $\mathbb{P}(x)$ with respect to a hyper-sphere $\mathbb{S}(c,r)$ is also performed as a conjugation as follows

$$\mathbb{P}(x) \mapsto \mathbb{P}(x)^\wedge = \mathbb{S}(c,r)\mathbb{P}(x)\mathbb{S}(c,r)^{-1}, \tag{7}$$

where $\mathbb{S}(c,r)^{-1} = \frac{1}{r^2}\mathbb{S}(c,r)$. Equation (8) is the formula of the inversion of a point with respect to a hyper-sphere in Euclidean notation.

$$x^\wedge = \frac{r^2}{\|c-x\|}\frac{(c-x)}{\|c-x\|} + c. \tag{8}$$

Figure 3 shows the graph of the inversion function $f(x) = x^\wedge$. Notice that the individuals near the center are sent very far from our region of interest ("near infinity"), and the individuals located far from the center are sent to a position near the center. In order to restrict the inversion to an acceptable region (close to the inversion hyper-sphere), we use two more hyper-spheres. These two hyper-spheres have the same center but different radii

$$\alpha = re^{\frac{-1}{r}} \quad \text{and} \quad \beta = re^{\frac{1}{r}},$$

which result from an intrinsic choice as follows. We find the radii of the two hyper-spheres by setting the area A of the figure to be equal to r, which determines a point y along the line:

$$r = \underbrace{\left| \int_{c+r}^{y} \left(c + \frac{r^2}{x-c} \right) \mathrm{d}x - \int_{c+r}^{y} c\,\mathrm{d}x \right|}_{area\ A} \tag{9}$$

$$y = c + re^{\frac{1}{r}}.$$

The calculation for the left bound is similar. Therefore, the acceptable region is given as follows

$$\underbrace{re^{-\frac{1}{r}}}_{\alpha} \leq \| x - c \| \leq \underbrace{re^{\frac{1}{r}}}_{\beta}. \tag{10}$$

Figure 4 shows the acceptable region determined by the hyper-spheres $\mathbb{S}(c,\alpha)$ and $\mathbb{S}(c,\beta)$. In addition, it presents an example of the inversion of two vectors with respect to hyper-sphere.

3 Experiments

The EACS is compared with the Differential Evolution Algorithm (DE) and Particle Swarm Optimization (PSO). A benchmark of 28 functions is listed in

Algorithm 3. Pseudo-code of the Inverse Search Operator

procedure INVERSIONSEARCHOPERATOR(c, x)

　/*1. Mutation for the center*/
　if $U(0,1) \geq 0.5$ **then**
　　$k \leftarrow$ Select randomly one component of the vector which corresponds to
　　　the center of the hyper-sphere.
　　$c_k \leftarrow c_k + N(0,1)$ //Add a normal random number.
　end if
　/*2. Calculate the radius of the hyper-sphere*/
　$rand \leftarrow U(0,2)$ //Uniform random variable in the interval (0,2).
　$r \leftarrow (rand)\underbrace{(-2(\mathbb{P}(c) \bullet \mathbb{P}(x)))}_{\|c-x\|^2}$

　if $\mathbb{P}(c) \bullet \mathbb{P}(x) > 0$ **then**
　　/*3. Compute the inverse point*/
　　//Function $\mathbb{E}(\cdot)$ returns the Euclidean vector x from the vector in $\mathbb{R}^{n+2}$.
　　$x^\wedge \leftarrow \underbrace{\mathbb{E}(\mathbb{S}(c,r)\mathbb{P}(x)\mathbb{S}(c,r)^{-1})}_{\left(\frac{r^2}{\|c-x\|}\right)\left(\frac{c-x}{\|c-x\|}\right)+c}$

　　/*4. Calculate the acceptable regions and identify when inverse
　　　individual is inside or outside of the acceptable region*/
　　$\alpha \leftarrow r\left(e^{\frac{-1}{r}}\right); \beta \leftarrow r\left(e^{\frac{1}{r}}\right)$
　　if $\mathbb{P}(x^\wedge) \bullet \mathbb{S}(c,\alpha) < 0$ **then**
　　　$x^\wedge \leftarrow \alpha\left(\frac{c-x^\wedge}{\|c-x^\wedge\|}\right) + c$
　　else if $\mathbb{P}(x^\wedge) \bullet \mathbb{S}(c,\beta) > 0$ **then**
　　　$x^\wedge \leftarrow \beta\left(\frac{c-x^\wedge}{\|c-x^\wedge\|}\right) + c$
　　end if
　else
　　$x^\wedge \leftarrow x$ //The center of the hyper-sphere is the same individual.
　end if
　return $x^\wedge$
end procedure

Table 1. Functions 1-20 and 21-28 have been solved in [8–10] and [11] respectively. The parameter used by the EACS, DE and PSO are the following:

- For the DE and PSO algorithms the population size (ps) is set to 100 [9,12]. For the EACS algorithm the population size is set to 129 and the number of hyper-spheres is set to $\eta = 9$.
- For DE the scale factor F is set to 0.5, the crossover probability is set to 0.9 and the crossover scheme is binomial. [9].
- For PSO the inertia weight is set to 0.7298, and both c_1 and c_2 factors are set to 1.49618 [13].
- The problem dimensionality is set to 30 dimensions (d) for the 1-13 and 21-28 benchmark functions. The 14-20 benchmark functions are tested in small dimensions according to the Table 1.

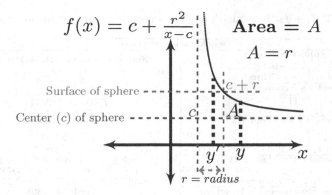

Fig. 3. The figure presents the distances between the center c with respect to the inverse points in one dimension. The acceptable region is defined by the interval from y' to y. $f(x)$ is the curve that describes the distance between the center and the inverse points in the domain of x.

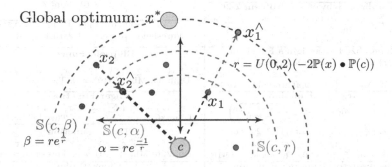

Fig. 4. The ISO produces a new point by using the inversion of a vector with respect to hyper-sphere. The point x_i which is inside of hyper-sphere $\mathbb{S}(x, r)$ is mapped outside of hypersphere. The point x_j which is outside of hyper-sphere $\mathbb{S}(x, r)$ is mapped inside of hypersphere. Two hyper-spheres have the same center but different radii to restrict the inversion in an acceptable region. The hyper-sphere $\mathbb{S}(c, \alpha)$ has a radius lower than the hyper-sphere $\mathbb{S}(c, r)$. The hyper-sphere $\mathbb{S}(c, \beta)$ has radius greater than the hyper-sphere $\mathbb{S}(c, r)$.

- The stop criteria is given true when the Fitness Functions Evaluations (FFE) reach the MaxFEs or the Best Fitness Value (BFV) found so far is below the objective threshold. The MaxFes is set to 1e+06. The threshold value is reported in Table 1.
- Each algorithm is run 50 times on each function.

Table 1. $f_1 - f_{28}$ benchmark functions used in this experimental study

Benchmark functions	
Sphere Model $f_1(x) = \sum_{i=1}^{d} x_i^2$, $-100 \leq x_i \leq 100$ Dim: 30, Min: $f_1(0) = 0$, Threshold = 1e-10	**Six-Hump Camel-Back Function** $f_{15}(x) = 4x_1^2 - 2.1x_1^4 + \frac{1}{3}x_1^6 + x_1 x_2 - 4x_2^2 + 4x_2^4$ $-5 \leq x_i \leq 5$, Dim: 2, Min: $f_{15}(0.08983,-0.7126) = -1.0316285$ $f_{15}(-0.08983,0.7126) = -1.0316285$ Threshold = -1.0316
Schwefel's Problem 2.22 $f_2(x) = \sum_{i=1}^{d} |x_i| + \prod_{i=1}^{d} x_i$, $-10 \leq x_i \leq 10$ Dim: 30, Min: $f_2(0) = 0$, Threshold = 1e-10	
Schwefel's Problem 1.2 $f_3(x) = \sum_{i=1}^{d} \left(\sum_{j=1}^{d} x_j \right)^2$, $-100 \leq x_i \leq 100$ Dim: 30, Min: $f_3(0) = 0$, Threshold= 1e-10	**Branin Function** $f_{16}(x) = \left(x_2 - \frac{5.1}{4\pi^2}x_1^2 + \frac{5}{\pi}x_1 - 6 \right)^2 +$ $10 \left(1 - \frac{1}{8\pi} \right) cos(x_1) + 10$ $-5 \leq x_1 \leq 10$ and $0 \leq x_2 \leq 15$ Dim: 2, Min: $f_{16}(x) = 0.397887$ $x = (-\pi, 12.275), (\pi, 2.275)$ and $(9.42478, 2.475)$ Threshold: 0.398
Schwefel's Problem 2.21 $f_4(x) = max\{|x_i|, 1 \leq i \leq d\}$, $-100 \leq x_i \leq 100$ Dim: 30, Min: $f_4(0) = 0$, Threshold= 1e-10	
Generalized Rosenbrock's Function $f_5(x) = \sum_{i=1}^{d} \left[100(x_{i+1} - x_i^2)^2 + (1 - x_i^2)^2 \right]$ $-30 \leq x_i \leq 30$ Dim: 30, Min: $f_5(1) = 0$, Threshold= 1e-10	**Goldstein-Price Function** $f_{17}(x) = [1 + (x_1 + x_2 + 1)^2(19 - 14x_1 + 3x_1^2$ $-14x_2 + 6x_1 x_2 + 3x_2^2)][30 + (2x_1 - 3x_2)^2$ $(18 - 32x_1 + 12x_1^2 + 48x_2 - 36x_1 x_2 + 27x_2^2)]$ $-2 \leq x_i \leq 2$ Dim: 2, Min: $f_{17}(0,1) = 3$ Threshold: 3 + 1e-10
Step Function $f_6(x) = \sum_{j=1}^{d} \lfloor x_i + 0.5 \rfloor$, $-100 \leq x_i \leq 100$ Dim: 30, Min: $f_6(0) = 0$, Threshold= 1e-10	
Quartic Function i.e. Noise $f_7(x) = \sum_{j=1}^{d} i(x_i^4) + random[0,1)$ $-1.28 \leq x_i \leq 1.28$ Dim: 30, Min: $f_7(0) = 0$, Threshold = 1e-10	**Shekel Family** $f_{18,19,20} = -\sum_{i=1}^{m} \left[(x - a_i)(x - a_i)^T + c_i \right]^{-1}$ $0 \leq x_i \leq 10$, Dim: 2
Generalized Schwefel's Problem 2.26 $f_8(x) = \sum_{j=1}^{d} -x_i sin(\sqrt{|x_i|})$, $-500 \leq x_i \leq 500$ Dim: 30, Min: $f_8(420.9687) = -12569.5$ Threshold= -1.25e+04	Min: | $m = 5$ | $m = 7$ | $m = 10$ $f_{18,19,20}(x)$ -10.1532 | -10.4029 | -10.5364 Threshold | -10.15 | -10.4 | -10.53
Generalized Rastrigin's Function $f_9(x) = \sum_{j=1}^{d} \left[x_i^2 - 10cos(2\pi x_i) + 10 \right]$ $-5.12 \leq x_i \leq 5.12$ Dim: 30, Min: $f_9(0) = 0$, Threshold = 1e-10	**Ellipsoid Function** $f_{21}(x) = \sum_{i=1}^{d} 10^{6\left(\frac{i}{d-1}\right)} x_i^2$, $-10 \leq x_i \leq 5$ Dim: 30, Min: $f_{21}(0) = 0$, Threshold= 1e-10
Ackley's Function $f_{10}(x) = -20exp\left(-0.2\sqrt{\frac{1}{d}\sum_{i=1}^{d} x_i^2} \right)$ $-exp\left(\frac{1}{d}\sum_{i=1}^{d} cos(2\pi x_i) \right) + 20 + e$ $-32 \leq x_i \leq 32$ Dim: 30, Min: $f_{10}(0) = 0$, Threshold = 1e-10	**Cigar Function** $f_{22}(x) = x_1^2 + \sum_{i=2}^{d} 10^6 x_i^2$, $-10 \leq x_i \leq 5$ Dim: 30, Min: $f_{22}(0) = 0$, Threshold= 1e-10
	Tablet Function $f_{23}(x) = 10^6 x_1^2 + \sum_{i=2}^{d} x_i^2$, $-10 \leq x_i \leq 5$ Dim: 30, Min: $f_{23}(0) = 0$, Threshold= 1e-10
Generalized Griewank Function $f_{11}(x) = \frac{1}{4000} \sum_{i=1}^{d} x_i^2 - \prod_{i=1}^{d} cos\left(\frac{x_i}{\sqrt{i}} \right) + 1$ $-600 \leq x_i \leq 600$ Dim: 30, Min: $f_{11}(0) = 0$, Threshold = 1e-10	**Cigar Tablet** $f_{24}(x) = x_1^2 + \sum_{i=1}^{d-1} 10^4 x_i^2 + 10^8 x_d^2$ $-10 \leq x_i \leq 5$ Dim: 30, Min: $f_{24}(0) = 0$, Threshold: 1e-10
Generalized Penalized Functions $f_{12}(x) = \frac{\pi}{d}\{10sin^2(\pi y_1) + \sum_{i=1}^{d-1}(y_i - 1)^2$ $[1 + 10sin^2(\pi y_{i+1})] + (y_d - 1)^2)\}$ $+ \sum_{i=1}^{d} u(x_i, 10, 100, 4)$, $f_{13}(x) = 0.1\{sin^2(3\pi x_1) + \sum_{i=1}^{d-1}(x_i - 1)^2$ $[1 + sin^2(3\pi x_{i+1})] + (x_d - 1)$ $[1 + sin^2(2\pi x_d)]\} + \sum_{i=1}^{d} u(x_i, 5, 100, 4)$, Dim: 30, Min: $f_{12}(-1) = f_{13}(1) = 0$ Threshold = 1e-10, Constraints functions: $y_i = 1 + \frac{x_i+1}{4}$, $-50 \leq x_i \leq 50$ $u(x_i, a, k, m) = \begin{cases} k(x_i - a)^m, & x_i > a. \\ 0, & -a \leq x_i \leq a, \\ k(-x_i - a)^m, & x_i < -a \end{cases}$	**Different Powers** $f_{25}(x) = \sum_{i=1}^{d} |x_i|^{2+10\frac{i}{d}}$, $-10 \leq x_i \leq 5$ Dim: 30, Min: $f_{25}(0) = 0$, Threshold: 1e-10
	Parabolic Ridge $f_{26}(x) = -x_1 + 100\sum_{i=2}^{d} x_i^2$ $-10 \leq x_i \leq 5$ Dim: 30, Min: $f_{26}(5, 0, 0, ..., 0) = -5$, Threshold: 5 + 1e-10
	Sharp Ridge $f_{27}(x) = -x_1 + 100\sqrt{\sum_{i=2}^{d} x_i^2}$, $-10 \leq x_i \leq 5$ Dim: 30, Min: $f_{27}(0) = 0$, Threshold: 1e-10
Shekel's Foxholes Function $f_{14}(x) = \left[\frac{1}{500} + \sum_{j=1}^{25} \frac{1}{j+\sum_{i=1}^{2}(x_i - a_{ij})^6} \right]^{-1}$ $-65.536 \leq x_i \leq 65.536$ Dim: 2, Min: $f_{14}(-32) \approx 1$, Threshold = 0.9981	**Two Axes** $f_{28}(x) = \sum_{i=1}^{d/2} 10^6 x_i^2 + \sum_{i=D/2+1}^{d} x_i^2$ $-10 \leq x_i \leq 5$ Dim: 30, Min: $f_{28}(0) = 0$, Threshold: 1e-10

Table 2. Descriptive Best Fitness Value (BFV) and number of Fitness Function Evaluations (FFEs) for the 28 benchmark functions by using EACS, DE and PSO algorithms. In addition the best fitness value means and fitness functions evaluation means differences for each function. The p-values are obtained through a Bootstrap technique. (The best values and the p-values below 0.05 (the significant level) are typed in boldface).

f	EACS BFV / FFE	EACS Std Dev / StdDev	EACS SR %	DE BFV / FFE	DE Std Dev / StdDev	DE SR %	PSO BFV / FFE	PSO Std Dev / Std Dev	PSO SR %	95% interval confidence p-value EACS vs DE	EACS vs PSO
f_1	8.85e-11	7.13e-12	100	**8.33e-11**	**1.09e-11**	100	9.28e-11	5.71e-12	100	**6.29e-03**	**1.79e-03**
	5.37e+04	1.36e+03		8.31e+04	1.68e+03		5.59e+04	2.35e+03		9.99e-05	9.99e-05
f_2	**8.70e-11**	**1.95e-11**	100	9.28e-11	6.58e-12	100	9.29e-11	8.93e-12	100	5.26e-02	5.47e-02
	1.07e+05	1.10e+04		1.38e+05	2.21e+03		**9.61e+04**	**1.10e+04**		9.99e-05	9.99e-05
f_3	**9.23e-11**	**9.03e-12**	100	9.34e-11	5.55e-12	100	9.76e-11	2.76e-12	100	4.51e-01	**2.99e-04**
	5.50e+05	7.14e+04		**3.69e+05**	**1.41e+04**		3.84e+05	1.81e+04		9.99e-05	9.99e-05
f_4	1.88e-08	2.84e-08	4	1.87e+00	1.45e+00	0	**9.82e-11**	**1.64e-12**	100	**9.99e-05**	**9.99e-05**
	9.97e+05	1.84e+04		1.00e+06	0.00e+00		4.47e+05	2.38e+04		1.83e-01	9.99e-05
f_5	**9.45e-11**	**6.72e-12**	100	3.18e-01	1.09e+00	92	3.50e+00	1.03e+01	0	6.65e-02	**2.66e-02**
	6.15e+05	5.90e+04		**5.09e+05**	**1.48e+05**		1.00e+06	0.00e+00		9.99e-05	9.99e-05
f_6	0.00e+00	0.00e+00	100	0.00e+00	0.00e+00	100	0.00e+00	0.00e+00	100	1.00e+00	1.00e+00
	1.59e+04	2.42e+03		2.64e+04	1.03e+03		3.43e+04	4.06e+04		9.99e-05	**3.69e-03**
f_7	5.19e-02	2.46e-02	100	1.24e+03	1.12e-02	0	1.24e+03	2.71e-01	0	**9.99e-05**	**9.99e-05**
	3.93e+04	1.01e+04		1.00e+06	0.00e+00		1.00e+06	0.00e+00		9.99e-05	9.99e-05
f_8	-8.79e+03	7.47e+02	0	-1.23e+04	1.60e+02	22	-9.88e+03	5.65e+02	0	**9.99e-05**	**9.99e-05**
	1.00e+06	0.00e+00		8.02e+05	3.76e+05		1.00e+06	0.00e+00		1.00e+00	1.00e+00
f_9	8.81e-11	9.24e-12	100	1.46e+01	4.35e+00	0	4.86e+01	1.29e+01	0	**9.99e-05**	**9.99e-05**
	1.85e+05	2.03e+04		1.00e+06	0.00e+00		1.00e+06	0.00e+00		9.99e-05	9.99e-05
f_{10}	9.38e-11	4.27e-12	100	**9.33e-11**	**5.80e-12**	100	3.51e-01	6.57e-01	76	6.16e-01	**6.99e-04**
	9.45e+04	3.95e+03		1.33e+05	1.70e+03		3.10e+05	3.91e+05		9.99e-05	9.99e-05
f_{11}	6.59e-03	9.83e-03	54	**8.64e-11**	**1.11e-11**	100	1.29e-02	1.99e-02	46	**9.99e-05**	**4.52e-02**
	4.89e+05	4.76e+05		**8.53e+04**	**1.56e+03**		5.66e+05	4.74e+05		8.91e-01	3.64e-01
f_{12}	1.01e-01	1.58e-01	58	**2.07e-03**	**1.46e-02**	98	6.63e-02	1.10e-01	60	**2.99e-04**	1.88e-01
	4.56e+05	4.70e+05		**9.28e+04**	**1.30e+05**		4.35e+05	4.65e+05		7.88e-01	8.04e-01
f_{13}	8.73e-11	7.86e-12	100	**8.43e-11**	**1.04e-11**	100	4.80e-03	1.58e-02	80	1.08e-01	**3.61e-02**
	5.66e+04	5.17e+03		8.06e+04	2.33e+03		2.47e+05	3.80e+05		9.99e-05	9.99e-04
f_{14}	9.98e-01	2.64e-05	100	9.98e-01	2.68e-05	100	**9.98e-01**	**2.56e-05**	100	7.92e-01	8.73e-01
	3.31e+03	8.43e+02		3.80e+03	7.31e+02		**2.63e+03**	**1.08e+03**		2.59e-03	1.09e-03
f_{15}	-1.03e+00	7.54e-06	100	-1.03e+00	7.93e-06	100	-1.03e+00	8.15e-06	100	7.29e-01	6.37e-01
	2.79e+03	6.40e+02		2.90e+03	4.50e+02		**2.75e+03**	**6.83e+02**		3.33e-01	7.50e-01
f_{16}	3.97e-01	2.56e-06	100	3.97e-01	1.92e-07	100	**3.97e-01**	**2.07e-07**	100	**9.99e-05**	**9.99e-05**
	2.78e+03	**5.64e+02**		5.55e+03	9.51e+02		4.42e+03	5.56e+02		9.99e-05	9.99e-05
f_{17}	3.00e+00	3.13e-11	100	**3.00e+00**	**2.78e-11**	100	3.00e+00	3.15e-11	100	3.34e-01	4.81e-01
	8.19e+04	8.08e+02		**5.27e+03**	**3.30e+02**		9.07e+03	8.28e+02		9.99e-05	9.99e-05
f_{18}	-9.79e+00	1.43e+00	94	-1.01e+01	8.38e-04	100	-7.08e+00	3.21e+00	50	8.51e-02	**9.99e-05**
	6.46e+04	2.38e+05		**6.81e+03**	**6.19e+02**		5.10e+05	4.96e+05		8.28e-01	9.99e-05
f_{19}	-1.02e+01	7.51e-01	98	**-1.04e+01**	**8.36e-04**	100	-8.14e+00	3.24e+00	66	3.12e-01	**9.99e-05**
	2.48e+04	1.40e+05		**6.25e+03**	**6.04e+02**		3.49e+05	4.71e+05		6.93e-01	9.99e-05
f_{20}	-1.04e+01	7.64e-01	98	**-1.05e+01**	**1.77e-03**	100	-8.52e+00	3.15e+00	70	2.30e-01	**9.99e-05**
	2.46e+04	1.40e+05		**5.94e+03**	**4.46e+02**		3.07e+05	4.58e+05		6.85e-01	2.99e-04
f_{21}	8.78e-11	7.81e-12	100	**8.65e-11**	**9.47e-12**	100	9.11e-11	6.84e-12	100	4.33e-01	**2.67e-02**
	6.44e+04	1.80e+03		9.18e+04	1.80e+03		**6.27e+04**	**2.55e+03**		9.99e-05	4.99e-04
f_{22}	9.02e-11	6.83e-12	100	**8.81e-11**	**9.49e-12**	100	9.22e-11	5.88e-12	100	2.05e-01	1.23e-01
	7.28e+04	1.81e+03		1.04e+05	1.81e+03		**7.12e+04**	**2.91e+03**		9.99e-05	1.59e-03
f_{23}	**8.63e-12**	**6.96e-12**	100	8.80e-11	9.05e-12	100	9.27e-11	6.00e-12	100	2.92e-01	**9.99e-05**
	5.33e+04	1.48e+03		7.48e+04	1.35e+03		**5.21e+04**	**2.34e+03**		9.99e-05	4.89e-03
f_{24}	8.70e-11	7.83e-12	100	**8.41e-11**	**9.54e-12**	100	9.26e-11	7.15e-12	100	9.29e-02	**6.99e-04**
	6.77e+04	1.83e+03		9.54e+04	1.65e+03		**6.46e+04**	**2.49e+03**		9.99e-05	9.99e-05
f_{25}	8.11e-11	1.16e-11	100	**7.76e-11**	**1.57e-11**	100	8.79e-11	1.27e-11	100	2.00e-01	**8.69e-03**
	3.08e+04	1.64e+03		5.00e+04	7.81e+03		3.49e+04	2.19e+03		9.99e-05	9.99e-05
f_{26}	**-5.00e+00**	**1.10e-11**	100	-5.00e+00	7.66e-12	100	-4.99e+00	6.01e-03	0	3.76e-01	**1.49e-03**
	6.17e+04	1.88e+03		8.64e+04	1.49e+03		1.00e+06	0.00e+00		9.99e-05	9.99e-05
f_{27}	-5.00e+00	3.22e-12	100	**-5.00e+00**	**7.03e-12**	100	-4.98e+00	4.12e-02	0	**4.07e-02**	**2.39e-03**
	1.08e+05	2.45e+03		1.50e+05	1.81e+03		1.00e+06	0.00e+00		9.99e-05	9.99e-05
f_{28}	8.66e-11	1.06e-11	100	**8.54e-11**	**1.15e-11**	100	9.30e-11	6.24e-12	100	5.86e-01	**1.19e-03**
	6.29e+04	1.64e+03		9.44e+04	1.60e+03		6.65e+04	2.73e+03		9.99e-05	9.99e-05

3.1   Numerical Results and Discussion

Table 2 presents all experimental results for the three algorithms and the 28 functions. The mean and the standard deviation of the Best Fitness Value (BFV) are presented in the first line for each function. The second line shows the mean and standard deviation of Fitness Function Evaluations (FFE). The column SR is the Success Rate. To properly compare the performance of the algorithms, the p-values of two hypothesis tests for the difference of the means of the BFV is given in the first line. The second line shows the p-values of two hypothesis tests for the difference of the means of the FFE. For comparison purposes, the functions test are classified according to the success rate for the EACS, DE and PSO algorithms.

- The algorithms obtain a success rate of 100% in the functions 1-3, 6,14-17,21-25 and 28. Function f_{15} the p-value supports there is no significative difference between the three algorithms. There is statistical evidence that EACS is better than DE in the number of FFEs for functions 1, 2, 6, 14, 16, 21, 22, 23, 24, 25, 28. Similarly, EACS is better than PSO in the number FFEs for functions 1, 6, 16, 17, 25, 28.
- EACS has a success rate of 100% in functions 7 and 9. DE and PSO have a success rate of 0%.
- EACS and DE have a success rate of 100% in functions 26 and 27; the success rate of PSO is 0%.
- DE has a better success rate than EACS, however, the p-value does not support that DE is better than EACS for functions 18, 19 and 20.
- EACS has a better success rate than PSO in functions 5,10,11,13,18,19 and 20.
- EACS has a success rate of 100% in function 5, where DE only gets 92%. However, the p-value does not support the statistical evidence to confirm that EACS is the best. Furthermore, the p-value provides the statistical evidence to support that DE has better FFEs than EACS.

Acknowledgments. The authors gratefully acknowledge the financial support from the National Council for Science and Technology of Mexico (CONACyT), from the Technological Institute of Irapuato (ITESI) and from the Center for Research in Mathematics (CIMAT). The third author would like to thank the International Centre for Theoretical Physics (ICTP) for its hospitality and support.

References

1. Moraglio, A., Togelius, J.: Inertial geometric particle swarm optimization. In: IEEE Congress on Evolutionary Computation, CEC 2009, pp. 1973–1980. IEEE (2009)
2. Moraglio, A., Togelius, J., Lucas, S.: Product geometric crossover for the sudoku puzzle. In: IEEE Congress on Evolutionary Computation, CEC 2006, pp. 470–476 (2006)
3. Moraglio, A., Di Chio, C., Poli, R.: Geometric particle swarm optimisation. In: Ebner, M., O'Neill, M., Ekárt, A., Vanneschi, L., Esparcia-Alcázar, A.I. (eds.) EuroGP 2007. LNCS, vol. 4445, pp. 125–136. Springer, Heidelberg (2007)

4. Moraglio, A., Togelius, J.: Geometric differential evolution. In: Proceedings of the 11th Annual Conference on Genetic and Evolutionary Computation, GECCO 2009, pp. 1705–1712. ACM, New York (2009)
5. Bayro-Corrochano, E., Reyes-Lozano, L., Zamora-Esquivel, J.: Conformal geometric algebra for robotic vision. Journal of Mathematical Imaging and Vision **24**(1), 55–81 (2006)
6. Hiroyuki, I., Jun-Ichi, M., Yoshiko, K., Takashi, N.: 3D road boundary detection using conformal geometric algebra. IPSJ Transactions on Computer Vision and Applications **5**, 176–182 (2013)
7. Dorst, L., Fontijne, D., Mann, S.: Geometric Algebra for Computer Science: An Object-Oriented Approach to Geometry. The Morgan Kaufmann Series in Computer Graphics. Morgan Kaufmann Publishers Inc., San Francisco (2007)
8. Brest, J., Greiner, S., Boskovic, B., Mernik, M., Zumer, V.: Self-adapting control parameters in differential evolution: A comparative study on numerical benchmark problems. IEEE Transactions on Evolutionary Computation **10**(6), 646–657 (2006)
9. Hui, W., Rahnamayan, S., Hui, S., Omran, M.: Gaussian bare-bones differential evolution. IEEE Transactions on Cybernetics **43**(2), 634–647 (2013)
10. Xin, Y., Yong, L., Guangming, L.: Evolutionary programming made faster. IEEE Transactions on Evolutionary Computation **3**(2), 82–102 (1999)
11. Bosman, P., Grahl, J., Thierens, D.: Adapted maximum-likelihood gaussian models for numerical optimization with continuous edas. Technical report. CWI, Amsterdam (2007)
12. Jin, W.: Particle swarm optimization with adaptive parameter control and opposition. Journal of Computational Information Systems **7**(12), 4463–4470 (2011)
13. van den Bergh, F., Engelbrecht, A.: A study of particle swarm optimization particle trajectories. Information Sciences **176**(8), 937–971 (2006)

A Hyper-Heuristic Evolutionary Algorithm for Learning Bayesian Network Classifiers

Alex G.C. de Sá[✉] and Gisele L. Pappa

Computer Science Department, Universidade Federal de Minas Gerais,
Belo Horizonte, Brazil
{alexgcsa,glpappa}@dcc.ufmg.br

Abstract. Hyper-heuristic evolutionary algorithms (HHEA) are successful methods for selecting and building new heuristics or algorithms to solve optimization or machine learning problems. They were conceived to help answer questions such as given a new classification dataset, which of the solutions already proposed in the literature is the most appropriate to solve this new problem? In this direction, we propose a HHEA to automatically build Bayesian Network Classifier (BNC) tailored to a specific dataset. BNCs are powerful classification models that can deal with missing data, uncertainty and generate interpretable models. The method receives an input a set of components already present in current BNC algorithms and a specific dataset. The HHEA then searches for the best combination of components according to the input dataset. Results show the customized algorithms generated obtain results of F-measure equivalent or better than other state of the art BNC algorithms.

Keywords: Hyper-heuristics · Automatic algorithm design · Bayesian network classifiers

1 Introduction

Hyper-heuristic evolutionary algorithms are successful methods for selecting and building new heuristics or algorithms to solve optimization or machine learning problems [13]. They were conceived to help experts and practitioners in the following task: given a new classification data set or a new instance of the traveling salesman problem, which of the solutions already proposed in the literature is the most appropriate to solve this new problem?

The answer to this question can be given in two different levels: (i) by selecting existing heuristics/algorithms [3] or (ii) by building new heuristics/algorithms using components from different existing algorithms [14]. In the context of machine learning, the first level can be solved using meta-learning algorithms [5]. However, in this work we are in interested in a different approach: selecting components from existing classification algorithms to produce a potentially better and customized one. Given a new dataset, we build (novel) algorithms by selecting the most promising components previously proposed. We do that by using a

© Springer International Publishing Switzerland 2014
A.L.C. Bazzan and K. Pichara (Eds.): IBERAMIA 2014, LNAI 8864, pp. 430–442, 2014.
DOI: 10.1007/978-3-319-12027-0_35

hyper-heuristic evolutionary algorithm (HHEA), which is used to automatically build a specific type of classification algorithms: Bayesian Networks Classifiers.

Bayesian Networks Classifiers (BNCs) [11] are robust and precise statistical methods for data classification based on the theoretical foundations of Bayesian networks [6]. They produce a classification model that assumes cause-effect relations among all data attributes (including the class). They represent data using a directed acyclic graph, where each node maps an attribute and edges define probabilistic dependencies among them. Furthermore, each node is associated with a conditional probability table, which represents the network parameters.

BNCs are interesting methods for classification because (i) they encode the dependencies among all variables of the problem, and are ready to deal with lack of data; (ii) they learn causal relationships and, therefore, can be used to gain understanding about a problem domain and to predict the consequences of events; (iii) they can be interpreted by domain specialists.

The most well-known and simplest BNC approach is the Naïve Bayes algorithm [21]. In this case, the network considers independence among all predictive attributes (they are no edges connecting them) and all of them depend on the class attribute. The first graph-based BNC, in turn, was presented in the early nineties [7], and since then many others were proposed. However, determining which algorithm should be used in a specific dataset is an open problem [5]. In this direction, the proposed HHEA can help finding an appropriate algorithm to any given dataset.

BNCs are usually built in two phases: structure learning and parameters learning. The first phase is more tricky than the second, as after having the network structure, learning the parameters in a more straightforward process [17]. Hence, the proposed HHEA focus on the first phase, where different search methods, attribute selection and evaluation metrics, among other components, are combined to produce new, customized BNC algorithms.

The proposed method works as follows. It receives a list of the main components of BNC algorithms, and uses an HHEA to encode these components. Given an input dataset, the method tests different combinations of components to that specific dataset. In order to evaluate the performance of the BNC generated, the algorithm is trained with a subset of the domain data available, and its accuracy assessed in a validation set. At the end of the evolutionary process, the best algorithm found is tested in data from the same application domain.

A preliminary version of this work was presented in Sá & Pappa [15], where the algorithm dealt with fewer BNC components (the search space of the evolutionary algorithm was very restricted), was tested in a limited number of datasets and used a different individual-components mapping scheme. The new individual representation proposed here is more robust and considers the dynamic nature of the components of BNC algorithms by using a real-coded mapping (in contrast with the previous static integer-coded representation). It is also important to emphasize that this work is one of the first efforts to consider the problem of generating a customized classification algorithm to a given dataset.

The algorithm was tested in 15 different datasets from different domains extracted from the UCI Repository [2], and compared to three popular BNCs: Naïve Bayes [21], Tree-Augmented Naïve Bayes (TAN) [11] and K2 [7]. Results showed that, in average, the values of F-measure obtained by HHEA are equivalent to those obtained by the algorithms already proposed in the literature. However, looking carefully at each evolved algorithm in isolation, we observe they can produce BNC algorithms very different from the state of the art, and with F-measures equivalent or better.

The reminder of this paper is organized as follows. Section 2 reviews related work in the automatic evolution of algorithms with hyper-heuristics. Section 3 details the proposed method, while Section 4 presents and discusses the results obtained. Finally, Section 5 draws some conclusions and discusses directions of future work.

2   Related Work

The use of HHEAs to generate machine learning algorithms customized to datasets is an outgrowing research field. We focus on works which dealt with this problem with three different classification models: decision trees [3], artificial neural networks[18,22] and rule induction algorithms [14]. Besides, we review the work of Thornton et al. [19], where a different search method was used and considered different types of classification algorithms simultaneously.

Artificial neural networks were the first methods to be automatically evolved using evolutionary algorithms. As discussed by Yao [22], the methods can evolve new neural networks considering three levels of abstraction: (i) synaptic weights, (ii) topology design or (iii) selection of the learning rule. One work that combines the three aspects aforementioned in different ways is Floreano et al. [10], which proposed neuroevolution. One specific example of neuroevolution is NEAT (Neuroevolution of Augmentative Topologies) [18], which evolves simultaneously the topology and weights of the network.

Pappa & Freitas [14], in turn, proposed a grammar-based evolutionary algorithm to guide the process of automatically evolving a rule induction algorithm. They considered three different components: search method, rule evaluation and pruning. Different from previous work, a genetic programming algorithms was used to allow creating completely new algorithms, considering programming primitives such as loops and conditionals. The results showed the HHEA generated new algorithms competitive with the state of the art.

Regarding decision trees, Barros et al. [3] proposed HEAD-DT (Hyper-heuristic Evolutionary Algorithm for Automatically Designing Decision-Tree algorithms). The authors identified four components that can change significantly the results of decision tree algorithms: splitting criterion, stop criterion, pruning and the way missing values are treated. The evolutionary algorithms was then evolved to consider variations of these four main components, and results showed the automatically generated algorithms obtain better results of accuracy than other state of the art decision tree algorithms. Following this line, the work

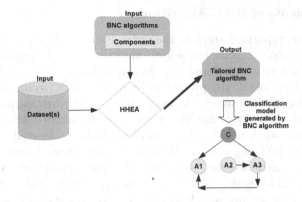

Fig. 1. HHEA scheme for evolving BNC algorithms

proposed here automatically evolves customized Bayesian Network algorithms for a given dataset.

Concerning methods not based on HHEAs, Thornton *et al.* [19] recently proposed Auto-WEKA to consider the problem of automatically selecting a learning algorithm and tuning its hyper-parameters. Auto-WEKA uses as input the feature selection algorithms and all classification algorithms implemented in WEKA [21], being more generic than the aforementioned algorithms. The searching process used by Auto-WEKA is based on sequential model-based optimization.

3 Evolving Algorithms for Learning Bayesian Network Classifiers

This section presents the proposed approach to automatically evolve algorithms for learning BNCs, illustrated in Figure 1. The method receives as input a dataset and a set of components identified from previously proposed BNC algorithms. Then, a HHEA is used to combine this components, outputting a BNC algorithm tailored to the domain of the input data.

In the HHEA, each individual represents a BNC algorithm (see Section 3.2), randomly generated from a combination of the available components (described in Section 3.1). During the evaluation of the individuals, a mapping between the individual and a BNC algorithm is performed (see Section 3.3).

Following, the individuals undergo uniform crossover and one-point mutation operations to generate a new population, and a elitist process copies the best individual to the next population. After a predefined number of generations, the best BNC algorithm generated is returned, and its associated model tested using a new set of data coming from the same domain used for training.

3.1 Components of BNC Algorithms

One of the most important steps in the conception of the HHEA is to identify a set of relevant components the search algorithm should explore to build a solution (BNC algorithm) tailored to a specific dataset.

As already mentioned, the process of learning BNCs occurs in two phases: structure learning and parameter learning. In the structure learning phase, the idea is to learn the causal relationships among the attributes of the input dataset, i.e. which nodes (attributes) in the graph should be connected to each other. Different types of BNC algorithms will work in different ways here, and they can be score-based, constraint-based or hybrids [8]. Score-based methods use a score metric, such as the Entropy criterion, to guide the search process, which can be performed by virtually any search algorithm. Constraint-based approaches, in contrast, use a conditional independence test, such as the χ^2, to guide the graph construction. Hybrid method combine the two previous approaches.

The parameters learning phase, in turn, learns the Conditional Probability Tables (CPTs) for each node of the BNC. These tables are used to make estimations about the data. However, learning the parameters of a BNC is a relatively straightforward procedure when the network structure is defined with specific dependencies among the variables [17]. For this reason, this paper will focus on the structure learning phase, and will always consider the same parameter estimation method. It uses a simple estimator tuned according to a parameter α, which represents the initial count on each probability value and is used to estimate the probability tables. The value of α is also tuned by HHEA.

When learning the structure of the network, we can generate Naïve Bayes like structures, which assume all attributes are independent, or generate networks represented by graphs or trees. According to the first component choice, we determine the type of algorithm being generated (Naïve Bayes, score-based, constraint-base or hybrid) and, consequently, the type of model being generated (i.e. tree, graph, none).

Concerning this search algorithm, 12 different options can be performed: Naïve Bayes [21] (NB), *Tree Augmented Naïve Bayes (TAN) using Conditional Independence Tests* [11], *Inductive Causation Search* (ICS) [20], Hybrid ICS (ICS-H), *General Augmented Naïve Bayes* (GAN) [16], Hybrid GAN (GAN-H) Greedy Search of K2 algorithm (GSK2) [7], *Hill Climbing* (HC) [12], *Look Ahead in Good Directions Hill Climbing* (LAGDHC) [1], *Repeated Hill Climbing* (RHC) [12], Tabu Search (Tabu) [4] and *Simulated Annealing* (SA) [4].

Depending on the choice performed in the first level, a new set of parameters is chosen. Table 1 shows which components the search methods depend on. Note that here, due to lack of space, we do not specify all the values they can assume, but the search space of BNC algorithms is bounded to 4,960,000 possible solutions. For details about these components, see the works of Bouckaert et al. [4], Witten et al. [21] and Sacha [16].

In Table 1, each column represents the template of a different search algorithm, which is the first gene of the individual. Each line shows a different component, which might suit or not the chosen search procedure, which will describe

Table 1. Dependency relationship between search method and other components

Components	Structure Learning											
	NB	TAN	ICS	ICS-H	GAN	GAN-H	GSK2	HC	LAGDHC	RHC	Tabu	SA
NB as initial structure	X						X	X	X	X	X	
Structure complexity					X	X						
Use arc reversal							X	X	X	X	X	
Markov Blanket Classifier		X	X	X	X	X	X	X	X	X	X	X
Feature selection	X		X	X	X	X	X	X	X	X	X	X
Scoring metrics				X	X	X	X	X	X	X	X	X
Accuracy estimation					X	X	X	X		X	X	X
Independence test		X	X	X		X						
Maximal cardinality			X	X								
Number of Parents							X	X	X	X	X	
# of look ahead steps									X			
# of operations									X			
Tabu list length											X	
Initial temperature and Δ												X
Iterations										X	X	X
Parameters Learning												
α from estimator	X	X	X	X	X	X	X	X	X	X	X	X

now. The first line, *NB as initial structure*, says that the search starts considering no dependencies among predictive attributes. *Structure complexity*, in turn, defines whether a tree or a forest can be generated by an algorithm. *Arc reversal* says whether this operation should be used during the search. The *Markov Blanket Classifier (MBC)*, in turn, applies a correction on the BNC structure that excludes nodes outside the Markov Blanket of the class node [8]. *Feature selection* chooses the most appropriate subset of attributes that should be class-dependent.

In scoring-based methods, the *scoring metric* guides the search for the structure, and can be composed of local or global metrics. Global metrics can define different ways of model *accuracy estimation*. In constraint-based approaches, the *independence test* defines which test will be used, and *maximum cardinality* restricts the breadth of the search in methods based on conditional independence tests. The *number of parents* determines the maximum number of parents (dependencies) a node can have. The last five lines in the structure learning part of the table show parameters of different search methods: *# of look ahead steps* and *# of operations* are parameters of the LAGD search method, where at each lookahead step the best n operations are considered, and the number of operations defines n. We also have parameters for the *length of the Tabu* list and the *initial temperature* and Δ factor used to update the temperature during Simulated Annealing algorithms. Finally, *iterations* defines the number of executions of iterative search methods.

3.2 Individual Representation and Genetic Operators

After identifying the main components of BNCs, we created an appropriate representation for them. An individual is a real vector with 11 positions, and its values are within the $[0, 1]$ interval. Each individual position represent an algorithm component, and different algorithms might vary significantly in their number of components. Because of that, the individual representation is dynamic, and some individual positions might be non-functional.

The smallest individual is encoded when a Naïve Bayes search is chosen, when we have three active positions in the genome and the others are non-functional (according to Table 1, when a NB search is chosen (gene 1), we use a NB structure (gene 2) and optimize α (gene 3)). The biggest individual is generated by the Tabu Search, when the 11 positions are mapped to different components (see Table 1, column Tabu, for details).

It is important to mention that although the individual phenotype is dynamic, crossover and mutation operations are applied to the individual genotype (real-coded representation) to avoid problems of individuals with different sizes. The uniform crossover builds a uniformly distributed binary mask the size of the individual genotype. A mask value of one (1) means that exchanges will occur in that gene position while a value zero (0) does not modify the content of the corresponding gene. The one-point mutation is applied into one of the 11 possible genes. Each gene has the same probability of being selected, and the value of the selected gene is replaced by a value randomly chosen within its domain (which here varies from zero to one).

3.3   Mapping and Fitness Function

In order to evaluate how effective the generated algorithms are, the classifiers represented by each individual need to be built and run in a dataset to generate a BNC model. Figure 2 shows the whole process of evaluation of a given individual.

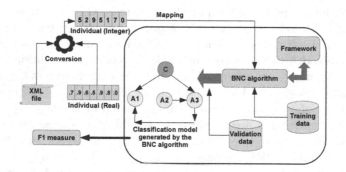

Fig. 2. Evaluation process of one individual

Initially, all individuals have a real-coded representation, where each chromosome position determines the use of a specific component option. We want to map each position of the individual to a BNC component, using an *XML* file that describes components and their dependencies. For that, the real-coded chromosome is converted into an integer-coded chromosome of the same size. In this conversion, the real number of a gene is multiplied by the maximum number of choices associated with that component, resulting in a rounded integer that indicates a component option in the *XML* file. For example, suppose the real value of the gene representing the search method is 0.35, and we know the number of components for search is equals to 12. In this case, the rounded integer resulting from this combination will be 4, which means the fourth component in the search method components list in the XML file will be selected. When the mapping process finishes, genes not used receive value -1. This process ensures that HHEA will not generate infeasible individuals.

Given the integer-coded individual, its chromosome is mapped to a BNC algorithm. To define the BNC algorithm according to the individual, the frameworks jBNC [16] and WEKA [21] were used. It is noteworthy the jBNC features and algorithms (inducers) were included in WEKA, generating a robust framework for generating the algorithm.

In the next step, the algorithms built are run in a training set to induce a BNC model, which is then evaluated using a validation set. The fitness function is generated from the validation set, using the F-measure [21].

F-measure is the harmonic mean between precision and recall and is defined in Equation 1. It is an interesting metric because it accounts for different levels of class imbalance, and considers both the precision (which is the number of correctly classified examples over the total number of examples) and recall (which is the number of correctly classified examples in class c over all examples classified as belonging to c, regardless of their real class). In order to prevent overfitting, the training and validation sets are resampled every n generations.

$$F\text{-}measure = \frac{2 \cdot (Precision \cdot Recall)}{(Precision + Recall)} \tag{1}$$

4 Experimental Results

This section presents results obtained when testing HHEA in 15 datasets from the UCI (University of California Irvine) repository [2]. Table 2 shows the datasets and their main characteristics, including number of instances, attributes, classes and missing values.

All experiments were executed five times using a 5-fold cross-validation, and two types of experiments were performed. The first compares HHEA with a greedy local search (GS) method to evaluate whether it is a good method to evolve BNC algorithms. GS is a simple method that performs a local search, and works as follows. Taking into account the same BNC components considered by the HHEA, an initial random solution is generated, and for each component choice, all possible values for that component are tested, and the best one chosen as the most appropriate. In the next iteration, having fixed the previous component, the same procedure is performed for the next one, until a complete solution (BNC) is generated.

The second experiments compare HHEA to three popular BNCs, namely Naïve Bayes (NB), Tree Augmented Naïve Bayes (TAN) and K2. The aforementioned

Table 2. Datasets used in the experiments

Datasets	#Instances	#Attributes	#Classes	Missing?
Balance Scale	625	4	3	No
Breast Cancer (W)	286	9	2	Yes
Car	1,728	6	4	No
CMC	1,473	9	3	No
Credit (A)	690	14	2	Sim
Diabetes	768	8	2	No
Ecoli	336	7	8	No
Glass	214	9	7	No
Haberman	306	4	2	Não
Heart (C)	303	12	3	Sim
Iris	150	5	3	No
Led Diplay Domain	2,880	7	10	No
Liver Disorders	345	7	2	No
Monks	432	6	2	No
Tic Tac Toe	958	10	2	No

classifiers were chosen because they assume different premises when building the BNC. While Naïve Bayes assumes independence between the attributes (the only relationship considered is among a single attribute and the class attribute), TAN builds a tree to represent relationships between them. K2, in turn, uses a graph to represent the attributes relationships, with no restrictions regarding the BNC structure. For all algorithms, the value of the parameter α was set to 0.5. K2 was configured to use a Bayesian scoring metric and, at most, three parents for each node on the generated BNC.

The parameters of the genetic algorithms were set in preliminary experiments performed using a grid search. The best configuration resulted in the following parameters: 35 individuals evolved for 35 generations, tournament size 2 and crossover and mutation probabilities of 0.9 and 0.1, respectively. The relatively low number of individuals and generations are due to the complexity of the solutions generated. Recall that each individual represents a full BNC algorithm, which will be trained and tested in a given dataset. The training and validation sets were resampled every five generations in order to avoid overfitting. These two sets are merged to form a complete training set when we compared the HHEA to other methods.

We use the statistical approach proposed by Demvšar [9] to compare the results. This approach aims to compare various algorithms in various datasets, relying on the adaptation of the Friedman test with a corresponding (Nemenyi) *post-hoc* test.

Table 3 shows the results of F-measure followed by standard deviations in the 15 selected datasets. Two versions of the HHEA are presented: HHEA represents the method described in Section 3, and HHEA-I (Initialized HHEA) introduces a simple modification to HHEA. In this version, the three state-of-art algorithms (NB, TAN and K2) are included into the initial population of the algorithm, to test whether it can faster improve over these three popular algorithms. Results in bold show the best absolute values obtained for each dataset.

Table 3. Results of F-measure for HHEA, HHEA-I, GS and selected state-of-art algorithms

Datasets	HHEA	HHEA-I	GS	NB	TAN	K2
Balance Scale	0.715 (0.046)	0.693 (0.101)	0.691 (0.109)	**0.719 (0.048)**	0.703 (0.055)	0.710 (0.053)
Breast Cancer	0.701 (0.066)	0.701 (0.076)	0.701 (0.090)	**0.733 (0.038)**	0.670 (0.053)	0.719 (0.054)
Car	0.930 (0.086)	**0.972 (0.016)**	0.914 (0.067)	0.849 (0.030)	0.945 (0.019)	0.906 (0.020)
CMC	0.499 (0.041)	0.492 (0.046)	0.475 (0.063)	0.504 (0.044)	**0.507 (0.034)**	0.493 (0.038)
Credit (A)	0.853 (0.021)	0.859 (0.025)	0.847 (0.039)	**0.862 (0.036)**	0.842 (0.025)	0.845 (0.017)
Diabetes	0.733 (0.050)	0.723 (0.069)	0.740 (0.028)	0.737 (0.030)	**0.747 (0.020)**	0.741 (0.024)
Ecoli	0.777 (0.045)	0.801 (0.022)	0.782 (0.026)	**0.812 (0.014)**	0.798 (0.019)	0.807 (0.014)
Glass	0.599 (0.101)	0.636 (0.122)	0.600 (0.104)	**0.685 (0.040)**	0.658 (0.084)	0.682 (0.034)
Haberman	0.642 (0.087)	0.664 (0.092)	0.660 (0.091)	**0.679 (0.080)**	0.678 (0.122)	**0.679 (0.080)**
Heart (C)	0.823 (0.032)	0.824 (0.031)	0.817 (0.067)	**0.836 (0.038)**	0.835 (0.020)	**0.836 (0.024)**
Iris	0.921 (0.050)	0.932 (0.052)	**0.939 (0.033)**	0.932 (0.030)	0.926 (0.031)	0.926 (0.031)
Led	**0.735 (0.022)**	0.703 (0.145)	0.732 (0.023)	0.732 (0.023)	**0.735 (0.026)**	0.732 (0.023)
Liver Disorders	0.447 (0.103)	0.447 (0.103)	0.442 (0.101)	0.447 (0.113)	0.447 (0.113)	0.447 (0.113)
Monks	**0.352 (0.039)**	0.351 (0.040)	0.344 (0.046)	0.254 (0.051)	0.337 (0.024)	**0.352 (0.039)**
Tic Tac Toe	0.700 (0.020)	0.692 (0.045)	0.700 (0.020)	0.700 (0.022)	0.700 (0.022)	0.700 (0.022)

First, the *Demvšar* test [9] was performed considering the F-measure obtained by the two versions of HHEA and GS. The critical value of $F(k-1;(k-1)(N-1)) = F(2;28)$ for $\alpha = 0.05$ is 3.340. Since $F_F = 1.809$ and $F_F < F_{0.05}(2,28)$, the null hypothesis of similarity between classifiers is accepted, meaning there is no statistical evidence to show HHEA and GS present different results in terms of F-measure.

We applied the same statistical test to compare the versions of HHEA and the state-of-art methods. The critical value of $F(k-1;(k-1)(N-1)) = F(4;56)$ for $\alpha = 0.05$ is 2.537. Since $F_F = 4.650$ and, consequently, $F_F > F_{0.05}(4;56)$, the null hypothesis is rejected. In this case, we proceed with the Nemenyi *post hoc* test, and conclude that both versions of HHEA and state-of-art methods have similar classification behavior within the 15 datasets and the F-measure for statistical evaluation. Note that the data resampling applied every five generations can affect HHEA-I results, despite the use of elitism.

The comparisons made so far consider the average results of 25 different algorithms (5 executions x 5 folds) tested over 15 different datasets. Next, we compare results produced by a single BNC algorithm, which should selected among the 25 to be used in a practical situation. We selected the algorithm with the best fitness value found in the validation set, used during the fitness calculation process, and the results are presented in Table 4.

The results are again compared using the same methodology described above. The critical value of $F(k-1;(k-1)(N-1)) = F(4;56)$ for $\alpha = 0.05$ is 2.537. With $F_F > F_{0.05}(4;56)$, the null hypothesis is rejected, and the Nemenyi test performed. The critical difference for this test is given by 1.575. Comparing the results by pairs, we conclude that HHEA is statistically better then TAN and no statistical difference between NB and K2 is found. HHEA-I, in turn, is statistically better than TAN and K2, but no evidence of difference between NB is found. As the methods generated vary a lot among each other, and the search space is huge, isolated analysis of the algorithms is essential, and there are always solution better than those state of the art.

We evaluated the components present in the BNC algorithms produced for the *Car* dataset (Table 3). The generated BNCs use, in their majority, a Hill

Table 4. Solutions found by one algorithm produced by HHEA and HHEA-I when compared to three state of the art methods

Base de Dados	HHEA	HHEA-I	NB	TAN	K2
Balance Scale	**0.729 (0.051)**	0.724 (0.046)	0.719 (0.048)	0.703 (0.055)	0.710 (0.053)
Breast Cancer	0.730 (0.051)	**0.733 (0.053)**	0.733 (0.038)	0.670 (0.053)	0.719 (0.054)
Car	0.979 (0.009)	**0.983 (0.009)**	0.849 (0.030)	0.945 (0.019)	0.906 (0.020)
CMC	**0.521 (0.038)**	0.517 (0.037)	0.504 (0.044)	0.507 (0.034)	0.493 (0.038)
Credit (A)	0.875 (0.012)	**0.879 (0.017)**	0.862 (0.036)	0.842 (0.025)	0.845 (0.017)
Diabetes	0.754 (0.020)	**0.759 (0.032)**	0.737 (0.030)	0.747 (0.020)	0.741 (0.024)
Ecoli	0.809 (0.041)	**0.821 (0.004)**	0.812 (0.014)	0.798 (0.019)	0.807 (0.014)
Glass	0.665 (0.107)	**0.724 (0.030)**	0.685 (0.040)	0.658 (0.084)	0.682 (0.034)
Haberman	0.676 (0.066)	**0.694 (0.095)**	0.679 (0.080)	0.678 (0.122)	0.679 (0.080)
Heart (C)	**0.854 (0.019)**	0.848 (0.023)	0.836 (0.038)	0.835 (0.020)	0.836 (0.024)
Iris	0.955 (0.017)	**0.962 (0.027)**	0.932 (0.030)	0.926 (0.031)	0.926 (0.031)
Led	**0.741 (0.021)**	0.740 (0.026)	0.732 (0.023)	0.735 (0.026)	0.732 (0.023)
Liver Disorders	0.447 (0.113)	0.447 (0.113)	0.447 (0.113)	0.447 (0.113)	0.447 (0.113)
Monks	0.386 (0.049)	**0.400 (0.021)**	0.254 (0.051)	0.337 (0.024)	0.352 (0.039)
Tic Tac Toe	0.700 (0.022)	0.700 (0.022)	0.700 (0.022)	0.700 (0.022)	0.700 (0.022)

Climbing or Repeated Hill Climbing search method, combined with a global score function. Furthermore, we observed that the algorithms that impose fewer restrictions to the BNC (allowing, for example, a greater number of parents), perform feature selection and use lower α values for the parameter estimator (between 0.0 and 2.0) have better classification performance. This is an evidence that certain components should be prioritized during the search.

Regarding computational time, we cannot forget each individual is a classification algorithm, executed in a dataset to assess its fitness value. Some of the algorithms might execute a simulated annealing algorithm to find the BNC structure, while others might perform a greedy search. Hence, the running time of the HHEA depends on the BNC algorithms generated. In order to give the reader an idea of the real execution time, the fastest HHEA execution was in the *Haberman* dataset, where it took 118.5 seconds to run for all partitions of the 5-fold cross-validation. On the other hand, *Credit (A)* took the longest to run, with an average time of 16,114 seconds to execute in all folds.

5   Conclusions and Future Work

This work proposed a hyper-heuristic evolutionary algorithm to automatically evolve BNCs. The algorithm receives as input a dataset, and outputs a BNC tailored to that dataset. BNC algorithms are generated from a predefined set of components, which were identified analysing a set of BNC algorithms. By producing algorithms personalized to a dataset, we automate the process of choosing which algorithm is more suitable for that domain.

The method was tested in 15 UCI datasets, and the results showed that, in average, the values of F-measure obtained by HHEA are equivalent to those obtained by the algorithms already proposed in the literature. However, looking carefully at each evolved algorithm in isolation, we observe they can produce BNC algorithms very different from the state of the art, and with F-measures equivalent or better.

The next step for this work is to test the algorithm in other real world datasets. We known the UCI datasets are a great first testbed, but as many algorithm already proposed were fine tuned over them, improving their results with automatically generated algorithms might prove difficult. The use of the algorithm is much more productive in unknown scenarios. Furthermore, it would be interesting to look not only at the accuracy of the algorithms evolved, but also to the simplicity of the models they generate, as to a specialist simple models are more valuable than complex ones.

Acknowledgments. This work was partially supported by the following Brazilian Research Support Agencies: CNPq, CAPES and FAPEMIG.

References

1. Abramovici, M., Neubach, M., Fathi, M., Holland, A.: Competing fusion for Bayesian applications. In: Proc. of Information Processing and Management of Uncertainty inKnowledge-Based Systems, pp. 378–385 (2008)
2. Asuncion, A., Newman, D.: UCI machine learning repository (2007)
3. Barros, R.C., Basgalupp, M.P., de Carvalho, A.C.P.L.F., Freitas, A.A.: Automatic design of decision-tree algorithms with evolutionary algorithms. Evolutionary Computation (MIT) **21**(4), 659–684 (2013)
4. Bouckaert, V.: Bayesian Belief Networks: From Construction to Inference. PhD thesis (1995)
5. Brazdil, P., Giraud-Carrier, C., Soares, Vilalta, R.: Metalearning: Applications to Data Mining. Springer (2008)
6. Cheng, J., Greiner, R.: Learning Bayesian belief network classifiers: Algorithms and system. In: Stroulia, E., Matwin, S. (eds.) AI 2001. LNCS (LNAI), vol. 2056, pp. 141–151. Springer, Heidelberg (2001)
7. Cooper, G.F., Herskovits, E.: A Bayesian method for the induction of probabilistic networks from data. Machine Learning **9**(4), 309–347 (1992)
8. Daly, R., Shen, Q., Aitken, S.: Learning Bayesian networks: approaches and issues. The Knowledge Engineering Review **26**(2), 99–157 (2011)
9. Demšar, J.: Statistical comparisons of classifiers over multiple data sets. The Journal of Machine Learning Research **7**, 1–30 (2006)
10. Floreano, D., Durr, P., Mattiussi, C.: Neuroevolution: from architectures to learning. Evolutionary Intelligence **1**(1), 47–62 (2008)
11. Friedman, N., Geiger, D., Goldszmidt, M.: Bayesian network classifiers. Machine **29**(2–3), 131–163 (1997)
12. Hesar, A.S., Tabatabaee, H., Jalali, M.: Structure learning of Bayesian networks using heuristic methods. In: Proc. of International Conference on Information and Knowledge Management (ICIKM 2012) (2012)
13. Pappa, G., Ochoa, G., Hyde, M., Freitas, A., Woodward, J., Swan, J.: Contrasting meta-learning and hyper-heuristic research: the role of evolutionary algorithms. Genetic Programming and Evolvable Machines **15**(1), 3–35 (2014)
14. Pappa, G.L., Freitas, A.A.: Automating the Design of Data Mining Algorithms: An Evolutionary Computation Approach. Springer (2009)
15. Sá, A.G.C., Pappa, G.L.: Towards a method for automatically evolving bayesian network classifiers. In: Proc. of the Conference Companion on Genetic and Evolutionary Computation Conference Companion, pp. 1505–1512 (2013)
16. Sacha, J.P.: New synthesis of bayesian network classifiers and cardiac spect image interpretation. PhD thesis (1999)

17. Salama, K.M., Freitas, A.A.: Extending the ABC-Miner Bayesian classification algorithm. In: Terrazas, G., Otero, F.E.B., Masegosa, A.D. (eds.) NICSO 2013. SCI, vol. 512, pp. 1–12. Springer, Heidelberg (2014)
18. Stanley, K.O., Miikkulainen, R.: Evolving neural networks through augmenting topologies. Evolutionary Computation **10**(2), 99–127 (2002)
19. Thornton, C., Hutter, F., Hoos, H.H., Leyton-Brown, K.: Auto-WEKA: Combined selection and hyperparameter optimization of classification algorithms. In: Proc. of KDD, pp. 847–855, (2013)
20. Verma, T., Pearl, J.: An algorithm for deciding if a set of observed independencies has a causal explanation. In: Proc. of the Eighth Conference on Uncertainty in Artificial Intelligence, pp. 323–330 (1992)
21. Witten, I.H., Frank, E., Hall, M.A.: Data Mining: Practical Machine Learning Tools and Techniques. Morgan Kaufmann Publishers Inc. (2011)
22. Yao, X.: Evolving artificial neural networks. Proc. IEEE **87**(9), 1423–1447 (1999)

Robotics

Live Robot Programming

Johan Fabry[(✉)] and Miguel Campusano

PLEIAD and RyCh Labs, Computer Science Department (DCC),
University of Chile, Santiago, Chile
{jfabry,mcampusa}@dcc.uchile.cl

Abstract. Typically, development of robot behavior entails writing the
code, deploying it on a simulator or robot and running it for testing. If
this feedback reveals errors, the programmer mentally needs to map the
error in behavior back to the source code that caused it before being able
to fix it. This process suffers from a large cognitive distance between the
code and the resulting behavior, which slows down development and can
make experimentation with different behaviors prohibitively expensive.
In contrast, Live Programming tightens the feedback loop, minimizing
cognitive distance. As a result, programmers benefit from an immediate
connection with the program that they are making thanks to an immediate, 'live' feedback on program behavior. This allows for extremely rapid
creation, or variation, of robot behavior and for dramatically increased
debugging speed. To enable such Live Robot Programming, in this article we propose a language that provides for live programming of nested
state machines and integrates in the Robot Operating System (ROS).
We detail the language, named LRP, illustrate how it can be used to
rapidly implement a behavior on a running robot and discuss the key
points of the language that enables its liveness.

1 Introduction

Live programming has recently come under the attention thanks to the widely
commented talk by Bret Victor at CUSEC'12 [9]. Its origins can however be
traced back to the early work of Tanimoto on Viva [7]. In this work an argument
is made for maximizing feedback to the programmer through a 'continuously
active' system: every edit action triggers computation of the program and the
display of computed values is updated live, as inputs vary.

In a nutshell, Live Programming postulates that programmers benefit from
an immediate connection with the program that they are making. Languages for
live programming therefore provide for an immediate, 'live' feedback on program
behavior. Such tightening of the feedback loop lightens the cognitive load of
building accurate mental models of the system when its execution is observed.
This permits, on the one hand, for extremely rapid creation of program behavior
as the effects of variations in the behavior are immediately visible. On the other
hand, it immediately reveals bugs that are due the programmers' mental model
of the executing program differing from the actual behavior.

© Springer International Publishing Switzerland 2014
A.L.C. Bazzan and K. Pichara (Eds.): IBERAMIA 2014, LNAI 8864, pp. 445–456, 2014.
DOI: 10.1007/978-3-319-12027-0_36

Putting this in a robotics context, programming of robot behaviors is however currently far from 'live'. Typically, the robot behavior is written, compiled and then deployed on a simulator (or the robot itself) for testing. The feedback loop between writing code and seeing the results is not tight at all. This wide gap between writing and observing slows down development and can make experimentation with different behaviors prohibitively expensive.

Considering the languages used for programming robot behavior, arguably the most successful are those based on hierarchical state machines, e.g. XABSL [4] or the Kouretes Statechart Editor [8]. Such machines are said to naturally map to the problem domain, and multiple RoboCup teams have won the competition using these languages. Live programming in such languages would enable — while the program is running in a simulator, or on the robot itself — to add behavior by adding extra states or machines, or to debug behavior by changing the program on the fly. An example of the latter is a bug in the activation condition of a transition: It should trigger with the current inputs but does not. While the program is running, the condition is edited such that it does trigger, which is immediately observed, confirming that the bug is fixed.

In this text, we introduce a language and associated interpreter for live programming of robot behaviors, called LRP. LRP is a language for nested state machines that provides for a custom visualisation of the program while it runs and notably has the ability to change the program *while it is running*. LRP has an integration with the Robot Operating System (ROS), yet can also be integrated in any robot software for which an API is available.

This paper presents the following contributions:

- It introduces the concept of live programming for robot behaviors.
- It presents a live programming language for nested state machines, with an associated interpreter and integration in ROS.
- It defines which code changes allow the interpreter to continue seamlessly.
- It states which program errors needs to be ignored to ensure that the interpreter keeps operating in the face of errors.

This paper is structured as follows: The next section introduces the LRP language, using a simple line follower program as example. Section 3 then illustrates how Live Programming in LRP aids in programming the behavior of looking for the line. This is followed in Section 4 by a discussion on how to ensure liveness. The paper then presents related work before concluding.

2   The LRP Language

LRP (Live Robot Programming) is a language for nested state machines, which is arguably a natural paradigm for designing and programming robot behaviors. The design of the language is inspired by existing languages for robot behavior programming based on the same paradigm, e.g. XABSL [4], Kouretes State Charts [8], and the Lua behavior engine [6]. As such, the language is not intended for computationally intensive applications such as image recognition and the like.

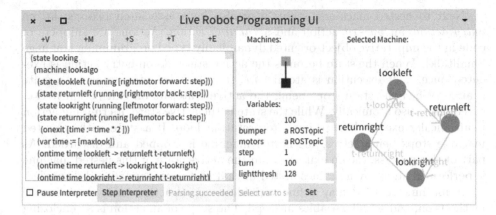

Fig. 1. The LRP editor showing part of the running example of this text

Instead the goal of the language is to enable the straightforward expression of complex behaviors based on already processed sensor inputs.

The core difference of LRP with respect to previous work is the focus on live programming. The editor, shown in Figure 1, includes the integration of an always-on state machine interpreter whose machines change in sync with the code as it is being edited, and is coupled to a custom interactive visualization. In one pane, the tree of nested machines is shown. The programmer selects which machine to visualize, in another pane, by clicking on a node of the tree. The machine visualization shows active states and last triggered transitions as well as the values of variables in scope, all of this updated as the interpreter runs. Furthermore, the editor also allows for the interpreter to be paused and stepped as well as the current values of variables to be modified by the programmer.

Considering the UI, there is no inherent requirement for the visualization to be present, nor even the UI for code editing. Indeed, LRP programs can be deployed on a 'bare' interpreter, which would have no user interface and hence consume fewer resources. Also, it is not the goal of the LRP UI to give all possible visualizations for robot sensors, *e.g.* also showing an image that is being captured by a camera. Instead we expect that during development the LRP UI is complemented with other, existing, visualizations that show camera images or a visualization of the robot's world model, for example.

2.1 Language Design

LRP is a language that allows for the description of nested *state machines*. Nesting in LRP means that a given *state* may contain a complete state machine (whose states may again contain a machine, and so on). The language is tightly coupled with its interpreter, due to its live programming nature and the need to interface to 'the outside world', *i.e.* the parts of the robot software on which the behavioral layer relies.

Next to nested machines, states may also have associated *actions*: an *on entry action*, an *on exit* action and a *running* action. Actions are snippets of code in the imperative object-oriented dynamically typed programming language Smalltalk[1]. When the state becomes the active state, its on entry action is executed once. This execution is atomic, *i.e.* it cannot be interrupted by a state change. When the state stops being the active state, its on exit action is executed once, also atomically. While the state is the active state, its running action is atomically executed, once per interpretation loop. If a state with a nested machine stops being active, the nested machine is stopped and discarded. As part of this process, the on exit action in the active state of this nested machine is performed after any machines nested in that state are stopped and discarded.

A machine in LRP may define variables and all actions may read, invoke methods on, and set all variables in scope. The scope of an action is its enclosing machine plus the machine that encloses it, and this up to the root of the hierarchy. Global variables may also be defined, outside of the root machine. Variables and actions act as the link from the interpreter to the outside world, allowing it to be connected to ROS, or indeed any piece of software for which a suitable API is available.

Machines may also define *events*: named actions that are the conditions for transitions. If the result of the evaluation of the action is the boolean `true`, the event is said to *occur*.

Transitions are also declared inside a machine. When an event occurs, transitions outgoing from the currently active state are inspected to see if they are stated to *trigger* on this event. This inspection happens from the root machine down the tree to the most deeply nested active machine, as executing a nested machine implies that its enclosing state is active. The direction of inspection from the root down to the leaves of the tree prioritizes leaving states that are at a higher level in the tree of machines. Note that this means that the interpretation of a currently executing machine stops when its enclosing state has become inactive due to one of its transitions being triggered. Also, in case multiple transitions may trigger in one machine, the first transition in lexical program order is triggered.

There are four kinds of transitions: normal transitions, epsilon transitions, timeout transitions and wildcard transitions. Normal transitions are the usual transitions we described above, epsilon transitions trigger automatically when the state is active, *i.e.* after their on entry action is executed. Timeout transitions specify a timeout in milliseconds, either as a literal or a variable reference, and trigger after this timeout. Wildcard transitions have no specific source state, instead they consider all of the states in their machine as the source state.

A last construct is the bootstrapping construct that specifies the machine to *spawn* and which is the start state of that machine. One spawn construct can be placed at top-level, and the on entry actions of states may spawn all machines that are lexically in scope.

---

[1] This because the interpreter and its connection to ROS is written in Smalltalk. Fundamentally this may be any other imperative programming language.

2.2   LRP By Example

To show the concrete syntax of the language and illustrate how it can be used to provide the behavior logic for a robot, we now present the program for a line following robot. This program was chosen as it illustrates almost all of the language features while remaining a conceptually simple task. The robot is a differential drive robot with a front mounted ground pointing light sensor and a front bumper. Its task is to first follow a black line painted on the ground until it bumps an obstacle. It then needs to turn around and follow the line back, until it again bumps an obstacle.

The code for this behavior is given below, and we will discuss it step by step.

```
1  (var lightthresh := [128]) (var maxlook := [100])
2  (var step := [1]) (var back := [10]) (var turn := [100])
```

The first two lines of code show the declaration of variables, declaring five different variables: lightthresh, maxlook, step, back, turn. Each is initialized with their specific value, given between square brackets. These variables are defined at top-level and are hence global variables. In this code they are mainly used as calibration constants, *e.g.* lightthresh establishes the threshold between black and white for the light sensor.

For clarity we do not include here the code that creates the connection to ROS, nor the full code of how commands are published, as this is not key to the example. In a nutshell, we represent sensors and motors as variables: respectively bumper, light and leftmotor, rightmotor, motors. These can later be used inside actions. The initialization of these variables consists of code that connects to the appropriate ROS topics. For example, to be able to publish on the teleoperation topic of a command velocity multiplexer the code is as follows: ROSbridge publish:'/cmd_vel_mux/input/teleop' typedAs: 'geometry_msgs/Twist'. This code results in a Smalltalk object that can be assigned to a variable, *e.g.* control. This object can be used to publish messages of the Twist type on the teleop topic. For example, code to go forward could be: control send: [:message | message linear x: 10] sends a Twist message where the x value of the linear part is 10, and all other values are 0.

Note that in the remainder of this text code between square brackets is in effect Smalltalk code. The result of this code is the result of the evaluation of the last statement. For example in the variable initialization cases shown above, these numbers simply evaluate to themselves. As the code that will be presented in this text is quite simple and can be read more or less like natural language, we do not discuss the syntax of Smalltalk in detail here.

```
3  (machine follower
4    (state moving (running [motors forward: step]))
5    (on outofline moving -> looking t-looking)
6    (on intheline looking -> moving t-moving)
7    (event outofline [light read > lightthresh + 10])
8    (event intheline [light read < lightthresh - 10])
```

Line three starts with the definition of a state machine, named `follower`. On line four, a state is specified, named `moving`. This state represents the machine moving straight, as it is located on top of the line. While this state is active, the interpreter will send commands on the `motors` topic, instructing to move forward for a `step` distance. Sending the message will happen once per interpretation loop. Note that between each iteration of this loop a user-specified delay takes place (which may be set to zero).

Lines 5 and 6 define two transitions. The first triggers on occurrence of the event `outofline`, defined in line 7, and causes a transition from the `moving` to the `looking` state. It has as name `t-looking`. The second is responsible for transiting back from the `looking` to the `moving` state.

Lines 7 and 8 define the events of interest for the above two transitions. Both use the light sensor, which returns an integer value that is higher as the measured luminosity is higher. The `outofline` event on line 7 is triggered when reading the light sensor produces a value that is higher than the light threshold plus ten[2]. The `intheline` event lowers the threshold by ten and verifies the inverse.

```
9      (state looking
10        (machine lookalgo
11           (state lookleft (running [rightmotor forward: step]))
12           (state returnleft (running [rightmotor back: step]))
13           (state lookright (running [leftmotor forward: step]))
14           (state returnright (running [leftmotor back: step])
15             (onexit [time := time * 2 ]))
16           (var time := [maxlook])
17           (ontime time lookleft -> returnleft t-returnleft)
18           (ontime time returnleft -> lookright t-lookright)
19           (ontime time lookright -> returnright t-returnright)
20           (ontime time returnright -> lookleft t-lookleft))
21        (onentry (spawn lookalgo lookleft)))
```

The `looking` state defines a nested state machine, its definition spans the lines 10 through 20 above. Note that the rightmost column of Figure 1 shows a diagram of this nested machine. The looking algorithm is an iterative left to right sweeping motion. Line 10 specifies the name of the nested machine: `lookalgo`. The four states (lines 11 through 15) respectively represent looking to the left, returning back to center from the left, looking to the right, and returning from the right. The sweeping behavior is orchestrated by the four timeout transitions of lines 17 to 20. Each times out after the time contained in the `time` variable. This initially contains the value of `maxlook`, but is multiplied by two at the end of each sweep, when leaving the `returnright` state (line 15). As a result, the size of the sweeping motion doubles at the end of each sweep.

Line 21 declares that on entering the looking state, the algorithm is spawned and the machine starts in the `lookleft` state. Note that exiting this state happens whenever the `intheline` event of line 8 occurs, causing the `t-moving`

---

[2] This statement is evaluated by obtaining the `light read` value, summing the light threshold with ten, and testing the given inequality. This results in a boolean value.

transition of line 6 to trigger. When this happens the `lookalgo` machine is discarded.

```
22    (var nobump := [true])
23    (event bumping [bumper isPressed & nobump])
24    (event ending [bumper isPressed & nobump not])
25    (on bumping *-> bumpturn t-bumpturn)
26    (on ending *-> end t-end)
27    (state bumpturn
28       (onentry [motors backward: back .
29                 rightmotor backward: turn .
30                 leftmotor forward: turn .
31                 nobump := false .
32                 LRP delaySec: 2]))
33    (eps bumpturn -> looking t-bumplook)
34    (state end)
35  )
36  (spawn follower looking)
```

The last piece of code is responsible for the bumping and stopping behavior. Recall that on the first bump the robot turns around and follows the line back and on second bump it should stop. The `nobump` variable of line 22 records if the robot has not yet bumped. The events at lines 23 and 24 occur on a bump sensor press combined with a logical **and** operation on the variable, in line 23, and the negation of this variable in line 24.

Lines 25 and 26 are wildcard transitions that trigger on these events. Note that these have no origin state and the arrow notation is different: including the asterisk to highlight the 'wildcard' nature of these transitions. For example, the `bumping` transition takes the machine from all `moving`, `looking`, `bumpturn` and `end` states to the `bumpturn` state.

The `bumpturn` has a rather complex on entry action: Line 28 instructs both motors to move back for a distance of `back` (of line 2). Lines 29 and 30 turn the robot around, each motor traveling a distance `turn` (of line 2). Line 31 records the bump, and line 32 pauses the interpreter for two seconds. The latter is to allow enough time for all these actions to be exectued by the robot. Note that pausing the intepreter is possible because the on entry action happens atomically, *i.e.* no events are evaluated during this time and no actions are triggered. The pause also ensures that if the bumper is pressed during this maneuver, the state is not exited and entered again due to the `t-bumpturn` transition triggering. Exit from the state is instead provided by the epsilon transition on line 33. It executes after the on entry action completes and goes to the `looking` state.

The state in line 34 does nothing. Note that the state name `end` has no special status within the language. The last line of the program: 36, instructs the interpreter to run the program by spawning the `follower` machine and making the `looking` state the active state. This makes the robot start by looking for the line.

3   Using LRP: Live Programming of the Looking Behavior

It is difficult to capture the experience of live programming in a piece of text. The most convincing argument for how it dramatically shortens development time is seeing it in action, which is arguably why Bret Victor's keynote [9] sparked wide interest, and pioneering work [7] has received little attention. As a textual attempt to convey how live programming with LRP enables rapid development of a behavior, we now present one scenario of use: developing the nested machine for the looking algorithm in Section 2.2 (lines 10 to 20). Recall that the interpreter and visualization of LRP are updated as each character of code is being edited, *e.g.* showing new states immediately when their definition is complete, and highlighting them as soon as they become active.

Consider the setting where the LRP development environment is deployed, on a simulator of the robot or even the robot itself. The states and values in the environment reflect the states and values of the robot. The robot starts on the line, and goes forward until it leaves the line, suppose having the line on its left hand side. This triggers a transition to the looking state, stopping the robot. As the state has no behavior defined, the robot is frozen and the LRP interpreter visualization shows that no further state changes occur. Development of the looking algorithm may now start.

First, an empty nested machine lookalgo is added. In lookalgo, the states lookleft and returnleft and their timeout transitions are added (lines 11, 12, 17, 18). In the looking state the on entry spawn statement is added. This last edit changes the currently active state, which requires the interpreter to be reset (details on why are in Section 4.1). Interpretation starts in the moving state, causing the robot to move briefly forward before the interpreter goes to the looking state, as the robot is still out of the line. The robot makes a left sweep, detects the line and goes back to moving, again following the line.

All goes well whenever the robot keeps the line to its left hand side. When it leaves the line to the other side, it however starts looking left, and does not find it before the timeout occurs. This causes it to move back to the center. The visualization shows that first the lookleft state is active and after the timeout a transition is made to the returnleft state. There is however no outgoing transition from that state shown, because the code in line 18 referes to a state that does not exist yet! (Details on handling of incorrect code is given in Section 4.2). This means that the robot will never stop its returning motion. Seeing this, the programmer pauses the interpeter, which stops the robot as motor commands are no longer published. The programmer then adds the lookright and returnright states, let us suppose without the code of line 15. The interpreter is unpaused, the robot looks to the right and finds the line.

All goes well until the line curves so much that it cannot be found by looking left or right in the specified timeframe. The robot endlessly sweeps left to right. The programmer can then, *e.g.* increase the value of maxlook, immediately increasing the breadth of the sweeps. Experimenting with this value will, in time, yield the right timeout for this specific case. Alternatively, the programmer may provide a general solution in the form of the time := time * 2 on exit action of line 15 omitted above. In that case the sweeps of the robot will progressively get larger, which is visible immediately after exiting the `returnright` state.

4 How the LRP Interpreter Ensures Liveness

Running an existing program is not the essence of live programming. The essence is running a program *while it is being changed by the programmer*. For example, adding a new state to a machine should not cause its interpretation to start afresh. Instead, the currently active state should remain the same and values of variables should not change *as these parts of the code were not changed*. Correctly dealing with program changes allows the program to be adapted while it is running: adding new behavior, or modifying existing behavior 'live'. We present here how this is achieved in LRP.

4.1 Dealing with Program Changes

To deal with program changes, the LRP interpreter briefly pauses when they occur, to analyze each change and determine in what way it affects the program being executed. These changes are then applied to the copy of the program used by the interpreter, before resuming interpretation. This process is described next.

A change in the code is first analysed for syntactical correctness. While a program text has syntax errors, no changes are considered. Consequently, program changes are seen from one syntactically correct program to another syntactically correct program. They are therefore analyzed at the higher level of machines, states, transitions and variables. Regarding a program as a group of all these elements, we consider that a program change results in either elements being added or removed from this group. For example, when a new machine has been added to the program, the machine is added to the group, and when a transition has been deleted from the program, it is removed from the group.

Adding an element to the group never leaves the program in an undefined situation. The values of existing variables are unmodified, active states will remain active, hence running machines may keep running. When interpretation resumes, it only needs to take the added elements into account. Removing elements only leaves the program in an undefined situation in one particular case: when the active state or active machine is removed. In any other case, when interpretation resumes it simply needs to be without the removed elements.

Regarding the case of an active state or machine being removed, it is clear that the program can no longer be in that state or machine since it no longer exists. For the active state case, there is no transition that triggers, so no on exit action to execute, nor another state to make active. Hence the machine that contains this state is invalid, which means that the state that contains that machine is invalid, and so on up to the root machine. Similarly, if an active machine is removed, the state that contains it is in an undefined situation as well. As a result, in both cases of the active state or active machine being removed, the entire program is in an undefined condition. In this case, interpretation of the program needs to be restarted from scratch.

Note that changing an element, *e.g.* changing the name of a state, is equivalent to a removal and an addition operation on this group. A straightforward case of this is changing the name of a transition: the old transition is removed and the new one is added, going from the same state as the old one and to the same state as the new one. The effects of other changes are not so straightforward, yet still sensible: Changing the name of an event causes all transitions using it to no longer trigger, as these refer to the event name of an event that no longer exists. Changing the name of a state causes its incoming and outgoing transitions to no longer be valid, as these use the name of a state that no longer exists. Lastly, and most significantly, changing the initialization value of a variable causes the old variable to be removed and a new one with the same name to be added. This is essentially equivalent to resetting the variable used by the interpreter to the new initial value.

To conclude: our analysis reveals that nested state machines are actually quite robust in the context of live programming. The only case where a program ends up in an undefined condition is when an active state or an active machine is removed. In this case, and only this case, interpretation of the program needs to resume from scratch. All other changes allow interpretation of the program to seamlessly continue.

4.2 Dealing with Program Errors

Code that is syntactically correct, and hence ran by the interpreter, may however still contain errors. For example, in Section 2.2 we have seen a transition that specifies the name of a destination state that does not exist yet. The interpreter should nonetheless keep running, allowing the programmer to keep entering code, supposing that the missing state will be added at some point. Another example is actions referring to variables that are not present. Again, the interpreter needs to keep running, or otherwise the 'liveness' aspect of LRP is lost. In general, the interpreter needs to deal with errors in the program in the most relaxed way possible, prioritizing keeping itself running in a consistent fashion over stopping and throwing an error.

To allow this to happen, the LRP interpreter ignores the following errors:

- A transition makes a reference to an event or state that does not exist.
- A spawn statement refers to a machine or state that does not exist.
- A reference is made to a variable that does not exist.
- The execution of an action causes an exception.

Currently, the interpreter ignores the entity that produced the error in the interpretation loop, *e.g.* in the first case the transition never triggers. It does notify when it encounters such errors, using a minimally intrusive error window that auto-closes after a timeout, in the style of MacOS notification banners.

5   Related Work

The Kouretes Statechart Editor [8] is a visual tool that forms part of a model-driven process for robot behavior development. In it, state machines are graphically edited, optionally starting from a text-based description, and the model-driven process then generates the executable code for these machines. There is however no visualization of execution of the state machine, prohibiting any form of live programming, nor is there integration with a simulator or robot.

XABSL [4] is a text-based approach to define nested state machines that features a variety of support tools. For example, it allows for the automatic creation of diagrams of the state machine, but however does not include any simulation support or simulator integration. As a result it has the same drawbacks as the Kouretes Statechart Editor when compared to LRP.

Niemüller et al. [6] propose the implementation of behaviors in a general-purpose scripting language. It is however unclear from the text what the concrete syntax for state machine description is, nor what features the system supports. Their tools do provide support for visualization of the state machines, including showing the current state and last taken transitions as the program runs. There is however no support for updating the state machine while it runs, which is fundamental to live programming.

Live programming was first proposed by Tanimoto [7], where the goal was set to provide a maximum of feedback to the programmer while a program is being constructed. The language presented in that work is VIVA, a visual programming language for image manipulation. Another, well-known, example of a live visual programming language is VVVV [2].

Outside of visual programming, the SuperGlue language [5] is a textual language that is also based on dataflow programming and extended with object-oriented constructs. Burckhard et al. add live programming features for UI construction to an existing live programming language [1]. The work of Victor [9] showcases various examples of live programming in Javascript that produce pictures, animations and games. It can be credited for sparking wide-scale interest in Live Programming, which helped the crowdfunding of Light Table [3]: an editor that adds live programming features to a number of general-purpose languages.

None of these languages however consider state machines as their computational model, which is why we consider them radically different of LRP.

6   Conclusion and Future Work

In this paper we presented LRP: a live programming nested state machine language, with a connection to ROS. As a result, it permits live programming of robot behaviors. We have given an overview of the language, shown how it helps development, and discussed how its state machine interpreter achieves liveness.

An interesting observation resulting from this work is that nested state machines are actually quite robust in the context of live programming. The only cases where program interpretation has to be resumed from scratch is when an active state is changed or removed, or when an active machine is removed. It is also worthwhile to notice that LRP is not necessarily limited to the field of robotics. Since its action blocks can interface with any piece of software, it is feasible to use LRP as a general nested state machine language.

Immediate future work is the implementation of refactorings that allow renaming, *e.g.* of states, allowing some interpreter restarts to be avoided. Longer term goals include testing the limits of expressibility of the language by building a wide variety of behaviors, and adding new language features as required.

Acknowledgments. We would like to thank the following colleagues for fruitful discussions on a precursor of the LRP language that helped shape LRP itself: Wolfgang De Meuter, Pablo Guerrero, Andoni Lombide, Serge Stinkwich and Éric Tanter. We thank ESUG (http://esug.org) for providing sponsoring for this article.

References

1. Burckhardt, S., Fahndrich, M., de Halleux, P., McDirmid, S., Moskal, M., Tillmann, N., Kato, J.: It's alive! continuous feedback in UI programming. In: Proceedings of the 34th ACM SIGPLAN Conference on Programming Language Design and Implementation, PLDI 2013, pp. 95–104. ACM, New York (2013), http://doi.acm.org/10.1145/2491956.2462170
2. vvvv group: vvvv - a multipurpose toolkit, http://www.vvvv.org/
3. Kodowa Inc.: Light table - the next generation code editor, http://www.lighttable.com/
4. Lötzsch, M., Risler, M., Jüngel, M.: XABSL - A pragmatic approach to behavior engineering. In: Proceedings of IEEE/RSJ International Conference of Intelligent Robots and Systems (IROS), Beijing, China, pp. 5124–5129 (2006)
5. McDirmid, S.: Living it up with a live programming language. In: Proceedings of the 22nd Annual ACM SIGPLAN Conference on Object-oriented Programming Systems and Applications, OOPSLA 2007, pp. 623–638. ACM, New York (2007), http://doi.acm.org/10.1145/1297027.1297073
6. Niemüller, T., Ferrein, A., Lakemeyer, G.: A lua-based behavior engine for controlling the humanoid robot Nao. In: Baltes, J., Lagoudakis, M.G., Naruse, T., Ghidary, S.S. (eds.) RoboCup 2009. LNCS, vol. 5949, pp. 240–251. Springer, Heidelberg (2010). http://dx.doi.org/10.1007/978-3-642-11876-0_21
7. Tanimoto, S.: VIVA: A visual language for image processing. Journal of Visual Languages & Computing 1(2), 127–139 (1990). http://dx.doi.org/10.1016/S1045-926X(05)80012-6
8. Topalidou-Kyniazopoulou, A., Spanoudakis, N.I., Lagoudakis, M.G.: A case tool for robot behavior development. In: Chen, X., Stone, P., Sucar, L.E., van der Zant, T. (eds.) RoboCup 2012. LNCS, vol. 7500, pp. 225–236. Springer, Heidelberg (2013). http://dx.doi.org/10.1007/978-3-642-39250-4_21
9. Victor, B.: Inventing on principle. Invited Talk at CUSEC 2012, video recording available at http://vimeo.com/36579366

An Orientation Assignment Heuristic to the Dubins Traveling Salesman Problem

Douglas G. Macharet$^{(\boxtimes)}$ and Mario F.M. Campos

Computer Vision and Robotics Laboratory, Computer Science Department,
Universidade Federal de Minas Gerais, Belo Horizonte, MG, Brasil
{doug,mario}@dcc.ufmg.br

Abstract. In this paper we deal with the DTSP, which is the optimization problem where a path that goes through a set of two-dimensional points must be calculated considering the use of robots modeled as Dubins vehicles. Assuming that the sequence of visits is initially obtained accordingly to the ETSP, we propose an heuristic to assign orientations for each point in order to achieve a path which is length minimized and respects the vehicle's nonholonomic constraints. The heuristic takes into account the vehicle's minimum turning radius and distance between neighbors points to proportionally adjust the orientation on each point, allowing the definition of shorter Dubins curves connecting them. The methodology was horoughly evaluated through numerous trials in different simulated scenarios, providing statistical examination of the final results.

1 Introduction

Among the several challenges involved in mobile robotics, a well known problem can be posed by a basic question related to navigation: *"How can a robot get to a given goal?"*. The question is directly related to the strategy being used by the robot to safely achieve a goal position in the environment.

A major issue concerning path planning problems is related to the mobility constraints of the robotic platforms. Ackerman geometry vehicles (e.g. automobiles), for example, present curvature constraints and cannot perform lateral movements, i.e., move orthogonally in relation to the plane of its wheels. By definition, such restrictions (e.g. on sliding and rolling moments) are known as nonholonomic constraints [17], and they affect almost all real world platforms.

Nevertheless, the most fundamental requirement for a path is termed *feasibility*, that is, the planned path must be able to be executed by the proposed vehicle. During navigation, for example, we have to ensure that the vehicle's nonholonomic constraints will be correctly taken into account.

Another relevant characteristic of the path that must be considered is its length, which is directly related to the energy consumption. Therefore, the path must also be as short and smooth as possible in order to increase the vehicle's

© Springer International Publishing Switzerland 2014
A.L.C. Bazzan and K. Pichara (Eds.): IBERAMIA 2014, LNAI 8864, pp. 457–468, 2014.
DOI: 10.1007/978-3-319-12027-0_37

endurance. Several optimization issues lurk inside path planning problems which need to be adequately tackled so to enable mobile robots to efficient traverse the environment and fulfill their designated tasks.

In this paper we deal with the Dubins Traveling Salesman Problem (DTSP), which poses that the planned path through a set of points must conform to the vehicle's minimum turning radius. We propose an orientation assignment heuristic which takes into account the vehicle's characteristics and the distance between neighbors points, allowing the definition of shorter Dubins curves connecting them.

The remainder of this paper is structured as follows. A review of the literature is presented in Section 2; in Section 3, initially we provide the problem formalization, next we propose an heuristic to assign orientations to a set of points focusing on length optimized paths and present a formal analysis regarding time and length complexity; numerical results for different scenarios and statistical analysis are shown in Section 4. Finally, in Section 5 we draw the conclusions and discuss avenues for future investigation.

2   Related Work

The Traveling Salesman Problem (TSP) is a fundamental combinatorial optimization problem which is widely studied [2]. One of the main shortcomings when using the model proposed by TSP in robotic systems is the fact that this model does not incorporate the characteristics of the vehicle which should execute the path. Therefore, the generation of paths for nonholonomic vehicles, i.e. those with movements retrictions, is a topic of great importance [6,17]. The literature reports on several methods that address this, which is one of the central problems in robotics.

Many different works dealing with this problem are based on probabilistic algorithms. This type of algorithms relies on its majority on sampling-based methods [5,12] or Evolutionary Algorithms [3,11]. The main advantage of such algorithms is the possibility to use a more simplified representation of the constraints involved in the problem, for example, the curvature of the vehicle.

The aforementioned methodologies allow for a feasible path to be established, however, most of the time there is little concern as to providing solutions regarding the path length, giving priority to feasibility over optimality.

Dubins, in his classical work [4], presented a method to calculate the shortest path in the two-dimensional space, respecting curvature motion constraints between two points with orientations. The generated path is composed of straight line segments and arcs with radius bounded to the maximum curvature executable by the vehicle.

The problem of generating a minimum length path through a set of points, considering a single vehicle subject to a minimum turning radius constraint, and making use of Dubins curves, was initially introduced in [14], and was called Dubins Traveling Salesman Problem (DTSP).

A fundamental difference between methods dealing with the DTSP is the determination of the sequence of visits. The sequence can be initially determined based on the Euclidean [8,14] or angular [13] metric, while the orientations and Dubins curves are calculated in a second step. Another approach is to first determine the orientations and then obtain the best sequence considering these configurations [7,18].

In this work, the methodology is based on a preliminary solution obtained for the Euclidean Traveling Salesman Problem (ETSP). Given the sequence of visit, we propose an heuristic to assign orientations to the points in order to achieve a path which is length minimized and formed by Dubins curves.

3   Methodology

3.1   Theoretical Formalization

As for the nonholonomic motion constraints, in this work we adopt the classical Dubins vehicle model [4]. This model encompasses a large class of nonholonomic vehicles, such as Ackerman steering cars and fixed-wing airplanes flying at constant altitude. Under this model, the path is restricted to a maximum curvature κ. This value is inversely proportional to the minimum turning radius (ρ) of the curve that the vehicle is capable to execute.

The DTSP is a generalization of the TSP in which the path is composed by Dubins curves. This implies two requirements: (i) between any two points, the path is a Dubins curve and (ii) orientations of two Dubins curves that meet at the same point are equal.

In the kinematic of a Dubins vehicle, not only position $\mathbf{p}$, but also the orientation ψ of the robot is important to the problem. We use a configuration vector $\mathbf{q}_i = \langle \mathbf{p}_i, \psi_i \rangle$ to represent the complete state of the vehicle in the SE(2) domain.

With this approach, we can define the problem at hand as finding the shortest Hamiltonian path through a set of points for a robot with Dubins kinematic constraints. Formally:

Problem 1 *Dubins Traveling Salesman Problem (DTSP): Given a set of points $\mathcal{P}$, the DTSP is the optimization problem whose solution is a feasible path over $\mathcal{P}$ that minimizes $\mathcal{L}_\rho(\mathcal{Q})$, i.e.:*

$$\mathcal{Q}_{\text{DTSP}} = \underset{\mathcal{Q}}{\text{minimize}}\, \mathcal{L}_\rho(\mathcal{Q}), \tag{1}$$

where $\mathcal{Q}$ is the set of configurations (positions+orientations). The length of a Dubins curve $\mathcal{D}_\rho(\mathbf{q}_i, \mathbf{q}_j)$ is the length between two configurations $\mathbf{q}_i$ and $\mathbf{q}_j$ that satisfies the minimum curvature radius ρ, i.e., $\mathcal{D}_\rho : SE(2) \times SE(2) \to \mathbb{R}_0^+$. The length of a Dubins circuit over a given configuration sequence $\mathcal{Q}$ is the sum of the lengths of the curves defined by each pair of consecutive configurations:

$$\mathcal{L}_\rho(\mathcal{Q}) = \sum_{i=1}^{P-1} \mathcal{D}_\rho(\mathbf{q}_i, \mathbf{q}_{i+1}) + \mathcal{D}_\rho(\mathbf{q}_P, \mathbf{q}_1), \tag{2}$$

where P is the number of configurations in $\mathcal{Q}$.

3.2   Orientation Assignment Heuristic

Many different works in the literature assume that the sequence of visits can be initially determined based on the Euclidean distance between the points [8,14], leaving the important problem of determining the orientation in each point for a second stage.

The first technique to tackle this problem is called Alternating Algorithm (AA) [14], which is a very simple heuristic. It builds the circuit in such a way that consecutive pairs of waypoints are linked together with straight line segments, and the remaining (non-straight line) links are built using Dubins curves based on the orientations previously assigned to the waypoints.

Also considering the benefits of connecting close points with straight line segments, an heuristic called Mean Angle Algorithm (MA) was presented in [10]. Dubins curves known as the short case (i.e. composed by three arcs) may only occur when the distance between the two adjacent waypoints is less than 2ρ. Therefore, the MA states that adjacent waypoints, whose distance is less than 2ρ, must be linked together by straight line segments, starting from the closest pair. The orientation of the remaining waypoints are set to the mean angle based on the vertex formed with the previous and the following neighbors.

Although both techniques can produce good results, they may produce paths much longer than the expected accordingly to the displacement of the points on the environment. Figure 1(c) presents the path obtained by the AA and MA for points placed on the the vertices of a square whose edges are smaller than 2ρ. As can be seen, without the need to connect neighboring points with straight line segments, it may be possible to obtain better solutions.

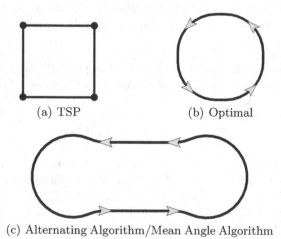

(a) TSP   (b) Optimal

(c) Alternating Algorithm/Mean Angle Algorithm

Fig. 1. Example where the solution given by Alternating Algorithm [14] and Mean Angle Algorithm [10] are much longer than the optimal. The yellow arrows represent the orientation of the vehicle at that point. (a) TSP result. (b) Optimal path. (c) Path obtained by AA and MA.

Therefore, we propose an heuristic where initially all orientations are set accordingly to the position of the point in relation to its neighbors. Next, the orientation of each point is adjusted proportionally to the minimum turning radius and the distance to its neighbors. The entire technique is detailed in Algorithm 1.

Algorithm 1. Dubins Traveling Salesman Problem $(\mathcal{P})$

1. $\mathcal{Q} \leftarrow \emptyset$
2. $\mathcal{P}_\Sigma \leftarrow \text{ETSP}(\mathcal{P})$
3. **for** $i = 1$ **to** P **do**
4. $\psi_i \leftarrow \frac{\mathbf{v}_1 + \mathbf{v}_2}{\|\mathbf{v}_1 + \mathbf{v}_2\|}$
5. $\eta_1 \leftarrow \exp(-\frac{\|\mathbf{p}_i - \mathbf{p}_{i-1}\| - 2\rho}{\rho/2})$
6. $\eta_2 \leftarrow \exp(-\frac{\|\mathbf{p}_{i+1} - \mathbf{p}_i\| - 2\rho}{\rho/2})$
7.   **if** $\eta_1 > \eta_2$ **then**
8. $\hat{\psi}_i \leftarrow \mathbf{v}_1 - \psi_i$
9.   **else**
10. $\hat{\psi}_i \leftarrow \mathbf{v}_2 - \psi_i$
11.   **end if**
12. $\lambda \leftarrow |\eta_1 - \eta_2|$
13. $\psi_i = \psi_i + \lambda \cdot \hat{\psi}_i$
14. $\mathbf{q}_i \leftarrow \langle \mathbf{p}_i, \psi_i \rangle$
15. $\mathcal{Q} \leftarrow \mathcal{Q} \cup \{\mathbf{q}_i\}$
16. **end for**
17. **return** $\mathcal{Q}$

The proposed algorithm receives as input a set of points $\mathcal{P}$ that needs to be visited, and returns a set of configurations $\mathcal{Q}$, which can be used to calculate the Dubins curves. The sequence of visits is initially determined by finding a solution to an instance of the ETSP.

Given the sequence, we must traverse the entire set of ordered points $\mathcal{P}_\Sigma$ assigning an orientation angle ψ at each point. For the sake of notational simplicity, since the sequence of points forms a cyclic group, we assume that $\mathbf{p}_i \equiv \mathbf{p}_j$ if $i \equiv j \pmod P$.

Each orientation is first initialized with the value of the mean angle of the orientation of the unit vectors (Line 4), accordingly to the previous and the following neighbors, given by

$$\mathbf{v}_1 \leftarrow \frac{\mathbf{p}_i - \mathbf{p}_{i-1}}{\|\mathbf{p}_i - \mathbf{p}_{i-1}\|} \quad \text{and} \quad \mathbf{v}_2 \leftarrow \frac{\mathbf{p}_{i+1} - \mathbf{p}_i}{\|\mathbf{p}_{i+1} - \mathbf{p}_i\|}, \tag{3}$$

where $\|\cdot\|$ denotes the Euclidean norm.

Figure 2 exemplifies the assignment of an orientation ψ_i for a given point $\mathbf{p}_i$ based on the positions of neighbor points.

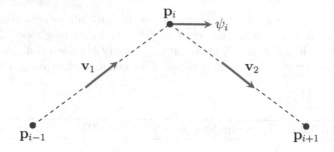

Fig. 2. Given a point $\mathbf{p}_i$, initially assign its orientation based on the positions of neighbor points. Red arrows are unit vectors representing the direction from the previous point ($\mathbf{v}_1$) and to the next point ($\mathbf{v}_2$). The green arrow is the resulting orientation $\mathbf{p}_i$ (Algorithm 1, Line 1).

Next, a proportional factor (η) for each of the neighbors points must be defined (Line 5 and Line 6). This factor represents which neighbor has the highest priority to be aligned with the orientation of the point.

The proportional factor increases exponentially accordingly to the distance between the point and the neighbor and also considering twice the value of the vehicle's minimum turning radius, i.e. CCC^1 curves (as defined in [4]) should be avoided. The proportional factor of a point $\mathbf{p}_i$ in relation to another point $\mathbf{p}_j$ in the sequence can be obtained by

$$\eta = \exp\left(-\frac{\|\mathbf{p}_i - \mathbf{p}_j\| - 2\rho}{\rho/2}\right), \tag{4}$$

where $\|\cdot\|$ denotes the Euclidean norm.

Finally, we calculate the necessary angular deviation ($\hat{\psi}_i$) to align the orientation of point $\mathbf{p}_i$ with the orientation of the unit vectors of one of its neighbors (Line 7 to Line 11). The proportional factor is used to determine in which direction the orientation must be rotated (Line 7) and also to give a weight to this rotation based on both proportional factors (Line 12 and Line 13).

This proportional factor tends to align the orientations of points that are closer than 2ρ, however, if both neighbors are closer than 2ρ and at the same distance, it will not give priority to neither of them, remaining with the same value.

3.3   Complexity Analysis

In this section, we present a brief analysis of the overall computational complexity of the proposed methodology, as well as bounds regarding both the execution time and the path's length.

---

[1] A Dubins curve is composed of line segments (S) and arcs (C). A CCC path is a composition of three arcs with the minimum curvature radius (short case).

The complete methodology runs in exponential time, due to the need of finding a solution to an ETSP instance. Considering that the sequence of visit is initially known, the proposed orientation assignment heuristic runs in $O(n)$, where n is related to the number of waypoints (P).

Theorem 3.4 from [15] demonstrates that the Dubins distance between two configurations is bounded by

$$\mathcal{D}_\rho(\mathbf{q}_i, \mathbf{q}_j) \leq \|\mathbf{p}_i - \mathbf{p}_j\| + \tau\rho\pi, \tag{5}$$

where $\tau \in [2.657, 2.658]$. Then, one may directly observe that a not tight upper bound for the length of the path is

$$\mathcal{L}_\rho \leq \mathrm{ETSP}(\mathcal{P}) + P\tau\rho\pi, \tag{6}$$

with $P > 2$ and $\rho > 0$, since we can consider an optimal ETSP solver and all connecting links are are Dubins curves.

The proposed methodology presents an upper bound worse than the classical Alternating Algorithm [14], since there are no guarantees that alternating pairs of adjacent points will necessarily be connected by a line segment, and all connecting segments can be Dubins curves. However, it is important to observe that in practice the results have a good chance of being better than this limit, since closer points have a high probability of being connected by straight lines.

4   Numerical Evaluation

In this section, we describe our simulations and the corresponding statistical analysis. All ETSP problems instances were solved to optimality using the well-known TSP solver *Concorde* [1].

Initially, we present an example of the results given by the compared techniques for a small instance. In this first example we have 10 points randomly distributed in an environment with dimensions $200\,\mathrm{m} \times 200\,\mathrm{m}$, and the vehicle has a minimum turning radius $\rho = 20\,\mathrm{m}$.

We compare the results given by the proposed methodology with the ones obtained by the Best Alternating Algorithm (BAA) [9] and the Mean Angle Algorithm (MA) [10]. The BAA is a simple generalization made over the classical Alternating Algorithm [14]. The resulting circuit (and its total length) given by the AA depends on the arbitrary selection of the first waypoint, hence, the BAA proposes that all possible solutions must be analyzed and the shortest one picked. The MA, as stated before, connects with straight line segments all adjacent waypoints whose distance is less than 2ρ, starting from the closest pair, and the remaining waypoints are set to the mean angle based on the vertex formed with the previous and the following neighbors.

Figure 3 presents the results for each one of the techniques. Figure 3(a) presents a path obtained by the classical TSP solution. Figures 3(b) and 3(c) present the resulting paths obtained by BAA and Mean Angle, respectively. Finally, Figure 3(d) is the result produced by the proposed methodology.

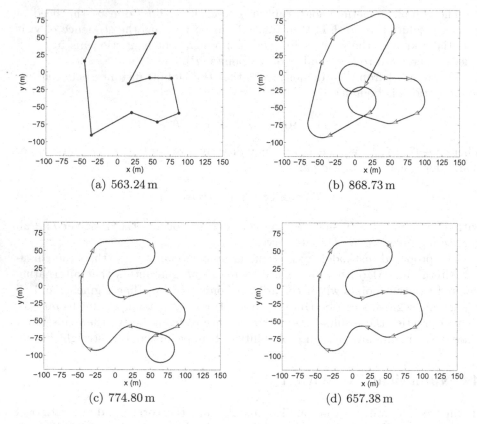

(a) 563.24 m

(b) 868.73 m

(c) 774.80 m

(d) 657.38 m

Fig. 3. Example solutions obtained by (a) TSP, (b) BAA [9], (c) Mean Angle [10] and (d) Methodology. The yellow arrows represent the orientation the vehicle must assume at that certain point.

One may clearly observe in Figure 3(d), the main effect of the proposed methodology. Both BAA and MA produce at least one CCC curve to connect a pair of the three points at the bottom right corner of the environment, since these points are less than 2ρ distant from each other. However, the proposed orientation assignment heuristic is able to handle this case, slightly rotating the orientation of the middle point towards the next point of the sequence of visits (since the next point is closer than the previous one), and by that producing a much shorter Dubins curve connecting them.

In order to perform a thorough statistical analysis we present next the results of a Monte Carlo Simulation. In this experiment we considered an environment with dimensions $500\,\text{m} \times 500\,\text{m}$, the number of points varied in the interval $\{10, 20, ..., 100\}$, and the vehicle's minimum turning radius varied in the interval $\{10\,\text{m}, 20\,\text{m}, ..., 50\,\text{m}\}$. For each specified value, 30 random instances were used to obtain the paths. The points are placed in the environment according to an uniform random distribution.

Figure 4(a) and Figure 4(b) present the results for the comparisons against the BAA and MA, respectively.

The color represents the ratio between the average tour length obtained by the proposed methodology and the technique being used for comparison. Dark blue regions indicate scenarios where the methodology obtained better results and light blue regions indicate similar performance, while red regions indicate scenarios where the methodology produced worse results.

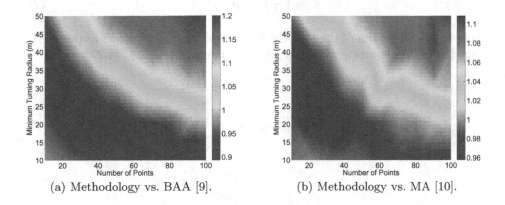

(a) Methodology vs. BAA [9].   (b) Methodology vs. MA [10].

Fig. 4. Experimental results for the comparisons against the BAA and MA, respectively. The color represents the ratio between the average tour length obtained by the proposed methodology and the technique being compared.

One may clearly observe that the proposed methodology produces better results in scenarios where there is a tradeoff between the density of points in the environment and the minimum turning radius of the vehicle.

In scenarios with a small number of points and a high value of minimum turning radius the methodology produces better results than the BAA and MA, since the orientation in the middle of the curves may result in shorter paths. The same fact applies for high density scenarios and a vehicle with a low value minimum turning radius, where the characteristic of the vehicle can be better treated by the methodology.

Although connecting pairs of points may not be the best approach for instances with a small number of points (considering both vehicles with a low or high value of minimum turning radius), this solution becomes important in high density scenarios, since points will be closer to each other, and consequently increasing the chance of resulting in CCC curves.

Enforcing the connection of pair of points with straight line segments may also be a better form to guarantee that at least part of the circuit will have a bounded length. The proposed orientation assignment heuristic does not present such guarantee, since all links between points can assume any form of a Dubins curve.

It is also possible to empirically evaluate the asymptotic behavior of the algorithms accordingly to the number of points, and compare them with the known DTSP asymptotic lower bound. We considered a median case, where the vehicle has a minimum turning radius $\rho = 30$ m.

Figure 5 presents the results comparing the performance of the three different algorithms. The DTSP asymptotic lower bound shown was taken from [15] and is given by $Cn^{2/3}$ for any $\rho > 0$, with

$$C = \left(\frac{3}{4}\right) \sqrt[3]{3\rho W H}, \tag{7}$$

where W and H represent the width and height of the environment, respectively. Considering the parameters used in our experiment, we have $C \approx 200$.

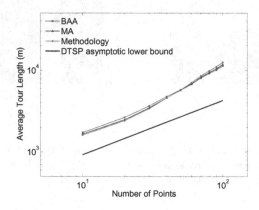

Fig. 5. Average tour length behavior accordingly to the number of points, plot on a log-log scale.

Table 1 presents the empirical growth rates for the different algorithms obtained by a linear regression based on the simulation results presented in Figure 5.

Table 1. Experimental growth rate of the average tour length, with randomly distributed points in a 500x500 environment

Algorithm	Average Tour Length
BAA	$5.4 \times n^{0.84}$
MA	$5.3 \times n^{0.88}$
Methodology	$5.1 \times n^{0.93}$
Lower bound	$5.3 \times n^{0.67}$

In a similar manner, it is also possible to observe that the proposed methodology gives better results than the BAA and MA for small instances, however getting a worse asymptotic performance with the increase of the number of points in the environment.

5 Conclusion and Future Work

In this paper we have proposed an orientation assignment heuristic which takes into account the vehicle's minimum turning radius and the distance between neighboring points, allowing the definition of shorter Dubins curves connecting them. Initially, all orientations are set accordingly to the position of the point in relation to its neighbors. Next, the orientation of each point is adjusted proportionally to the minimum turning radius and the distance to its neighbors.

The proposed methodology obtained better results in scenarios where there is a tradeoff between the number of points in the environment and the minimum turning radius of the vehicle. In scenarios with a high density of points and a high value of minimum turning radius both BAA [9] and MA [10] produced better result, primarily due to the mandatory connection of points with straight line segments.

Regardless of the good results obtained, the methodology presented the worst asymptotic performance among the compared techniques. Therefore, we intend in the future to focus on the development of methods with constant growth rates.

Future directions also include the extension of the proposed methodology to deal with the DTSP for multirobot ensambles. The methodology must also be extended to deal with environments containing obstacles, which is a better representation of real world scenarios.

A known problem concerning the use of Dubins curves is the discontinuity of the curvature derivative, leading to abrupt lateral accelerations. Consequently, that can result in paths that are not actually feasible by real robots. Therefore, we intend to investigate possible techniques for generating smoother variations of acceleration, e.g., the use of other types of curves such as clothoids [16].

Acknowledgments. This work was developed with the support of the Conselho Nacional de Desenvolvimento Científico e Tecnológico (CNPq), Coordenação de Aperfeiçoamento de Pessoal de Nível Superior (CAPES) and Fundação de Amparo à Pesquisa do Estado de Minas Gerais (FAPEMIG).

References

1. Concorde TSP solver, http://www.tsp.gatech.edu/concorde/index.html (2013) (Online; accessed December 12, 2013)
2. Applegate, D.L., Bixby, R.E., Chvatal, V., Cook, W.J.: The Traveling Salesman Problem: A Computational Study (Princeton Series in Applied Mathematics). Princeton University Press, Princeton (2007)
3. Cobano, J., Conde, R., Alejo, D., Ollero, A.: Path planning based on Genetic Algorithms and the Monte-Carlo method to avoid aerial vehicle collisions under uncertainties. In: Proceedings of the IEEE International Conference on Robotics and Automation (ICRA), pp. 4429–4434 (May 2011)

4. Dubins, L.E.: On Curves of Minimal Length with a Constraint on Average Curvature, and with Prescribed Initial and Terminal Positions and Tangents. American Journal of Mathematics **79**(3), 497–516 (1957)
5. Kuwata, Y., Fiore, G., Teo, J., Frazzoli, E., How, J.: Motion planning for urban driving using RRT. In: Proceedings of the IEEE/RSJ International Conference on Intelligent Robots and Systems (IROS), pp. 1681–1686 (September 2008)
6. LaValle, S.M.: Planning Algorithms. Cambridge University Press, New York (2006)
7. Le Ny, J., Feron, E.: An Approximation Algorithm for the Curvature-Constrained Traveling Salesman Problem. In: Proceedings of the 43rd Annual Allerton Conference on Communications, Control and Computing (2005)
8. Ma, X., Castañón, D.A.: Receding Horizon Planning for Dubins Traveling Salesman Problems. In: Proceedings of the 45th IEEE Conference on Decision and Control (CDC), pp. 5453–5458 (December 2006)
9. Macharet, D.G., Alves Neto, A., da Camara Neto, V.F., Campos, M.F.M.: Nonholonomic path planning optimization for Dubins' vehicles. In: Proceedings of the IEEE International Conference on Robotics and Automation (ICRA 2011), pp. 4208–4213 (May 2011)
10. Macharet, D.G., Alves Neto, A., da Camara Neto, V.F., Campos, M.F.M.: Data gathering tour optimization for Dubins' vehicles. In: IEEE Congress on Evolutionary Computation (CEC), pp. 1–8 (June 2012)
11. Macharet, D.G., Neto, A.A., Campos, M.F.M.: Feasible UAV path planning using genetic algorithms and Bézier curves. In: da Rocha Costa, A.C., Vicari, R.M., Tonidandel, F. (eds.) SBIA 2010. LNCS, vol. 6404, pp. 223–232. Springer, Heidelberg (2010)
12. Marble, J.D., Bekris, K.: Towards small asymptotically near-optimal roadmaps. In: Proceedings of the IEEE International Conference on Robotics and Automation (ICRA), pp. 2557–2562 (2012)
13. Medeiros, A., Urrutia, S.: Discrete optimization methods to determine trajectories for Dubins' vehicles. Electronic Notes in Discrete Mathematics **36**, 17–24 (2010), International Symposium on Combinatorial Optimization (ISCO)
14. Savla, K., Frazzoli, E., Bullo, F.: On the point-to-point and traveling salesperson problems for Dubins' vehicle. In: Proceedings of the IEEE American Control Conference (ACC), vol. 2, pp. 786–791 (June 2005)
15. Savla, K., Frazzoli, E., Bullo, F.: Traveling Salesperson Problems for the Dubins Vehicle. IEEE Transactions on Automatic Control **53**(6), 1378–1391 (2008)
16. Shanmugavel, M., Tsourdos, A., White, B., Żbikowski, R.: Co-operative path planning of multiple UAVs using Dubins paths with clothoid arcs. Control Engineering Practice **18**(9), 1084–1092 (2010)
17. Siegwart, R., Nourbakhsh, I.R., Scaramuzza, D.: Introduction to Autonomous Mobile Robots, 2nd edn. MIT Press, Cambridge (2011)
18. Tang, Z., Özgüner, Ü.: Motion planning for multitarget surveillance with mobile sensor agents. IEEE Transactions on Robotics **21**(5), 898–908 (2005)

A Motion Planner for Car-Like Robots Based on Rapidly-Exploring Random Trees

Rômulo Ramos Radaelli, Claudine Badue(✉), Michael André Gonçalves,
Thiago Oliveira-Santos, and Alberto F. De Souza

Departamento de Informática, Universidade Federal do Espírito Santo, Vitória, ES, Brazil
{rmradaelli,es.michael}@gmail.com,
{claudine,alberto}@lcad.inf.ufes.br, todsantos@inf.ufes.br

Abstract. We propose a motion planner for car-like robots based on the rapidly-exploring random tree (RRT) method. Our motion planner was designed especially for cars driving on roads. So, its goal is to build trajectories from the car's initial state to the goal state in real time, which stay within the desired lane bounds and keep a safe distance from obstacles. For that, our motion planner combines several variants of the standard RRT algorithm. We evaluated the performance of our motion planner using an experimental robotic platform based on a Ford Escape Hybrid. Our experimental results showed that our motion planner is capable of planning trajectories in real time, which follow the lane and avoid collision with obstacles.

Keywords: Motion planning · Car-like robots · Rapidly-exploring random trees

1 Introduction

Mapping, localization and control are very important tasks in autonomous robotics. Mapping involves the creation of a map of the environment around the robot, that may contain information pertaining to the places that the robot may or may not be able to navigate, localization involves the estimation of the robot's state relative to the map, and control involves the translation of control commands of velocity and steering wheel angle into acceleration, brake and wheel efforts. Another very important task in autonomous robotics, and the focus of this paper, is motion planning. To perform this task, a software module receives as input the map of the environment, the initial robot's state relative to the map, and the goal state; and produces as output a trajectory from the initial robot's state to the goal state. The trajectory might be represented in several ways. For a car-like robot, we represent it using a list of commands of velocity and steering wheel angle, along with the respective execution durations (a list of triplets $(v, \varphi, \Delta t)$). A proper trajectory leads the robot from its initial state to the goal state, while avoiding collision with known obstacles.

Different methods can be found in the literature to address the problem of motion planning for car-like robots. This type of robots is subject to both kinodynamic constraints (arising from kinematic and dynamic constraints) and environmental constraints (arising from obstacles). A possible approach is to reduce and discretize the

© Springer International Publishing Switzerland 2014
A.L.C. Bazzan and K. Pichara (Eds.): IBERAMIA 2014, LNAI 8864, pp. 469–480, 2014.
DOI: 10.1007/978-3-319-12027-0_38

state space so that classical search methods like A* [1] or D* [2] can find a collision-free trajectory from the car's initial state to the goal state in the constrained space. This approach usually converges very fast and provides good results. Nevertheless, the trajectory found with those methods might not be followed exactly by the car, because, in its building, not all the constraints of the movement of the car can be properly considered. Thus, the solution has to be further processed to generate an improved version that can be followed by the car. Another possible approach is to employ a more accurate model of the car motion and use sampling based search methods that can deal with the high-dimensional state space to find a feasible solution. An example of this type of method is the Rapidly-Exploring Random Tree (RRT), which was first introduced by LaValle [3]. RRT has been successfully used in the motion planning of car-like robots–the motion planning subsystem of the fourth placed winner of the DARPA Urban Challenge, the MIT robot "Talos", is based on the RRT [4].

In this paper, we propose a motion planner based on RRT for car-like robots that are subject to both kinodynamic and environmental constraints. Our motion planner was designed especially for cars driving on roads. So, its goal is to build trajectories from the car's initial state to the goal state in real time, which stay within the desired lane bounds and keep a safe distance from obstacles. For that, our motion planner combines two previous variants of the standard RRT to (i) reduce its sensitivity to the distance metric [5] and (ii) attempt to quickly grow the tree toward the goal state [6]. Our motion planner also incorporates five unique RRT variants to: (i) bias the location of sampling random states toward the lane region, (ii) select the most promising control commands for extending states, (iii) choose the best trajectories, (iv) discard non-promising states, and (v) reuse part of the trajectory built in the previous planning cycle. Although, in the form we have design them, they are unique to our work, the main ideas behind these last five RRT variants are similar to those proposed by Kuwata et al. [4] (first and third ones), Powers et al. [7] (second one), Frazzoli et al. [8] (fourth one), and Bekris and Kavraki [9] (fifth one).

We evaluated the performance of our motion planner using an experimental robotic platform based on a Ford Escape Hybrid. Our experimental results showed that our motion planner is capable of planning trajectories in real time, which follow the lane and avoid collision with obstacles. To the best of our knowledge, the combination of techniques we have employed to solve the motion planning problem is unique and the results we have obtained are satisfactory.

This paper is organized as follows. After this introduction, in Section 2, we present the motion model of car-like robots we have used and the standard RRT algorithm. In Section 3, we describe our approach for motion planning for car-like robots. In Section 4, we describe our experimental methodology and, in Section 5, we analyze our experimental results. Our conclusions and directions for future work follow in Section 6.

2   Background

The motion model for car-like robots can be described as follows. Let x and y be the car's location, given by the midway of the two rear wheels; θ the car's orientation;

L the distance between the front and rear wheels' axles; v the car's velocity; a the car's acceleration; φ the steering wheel angle, given by the average of the angle of the right and left front wheels; and r the rate of change of the steering wheel angle. Also, let $x_t = (x, y, \theta, v, \varphi)$ be the state of the car at time t and $u_t = (v', \varphi', \Delta t)$ the control command at time t. So, after the small Δt time interval, the car will be at state $x_{t+1} = (x', y', \theta', v', \varphi')$ given by $x' = x + \Delta t\, v' \cos\theta$, $y' = y + \Delta t\, v' \operatorname{sen}\theta$, and $\theta' = \theta + \Delta t\, v'\frac{\tan\varphi'}{L}$, where $v' = v + \Delta t\, a$ and $\varphi' = \varphi + \Delta t\, r$.

A high-level description of the standard RRT algorithm [10] is given in the following. The initial car's state, x_{init}, is added to an initially empty tree, T. At each iteration, a random state, x_{rand}, is firstly taken from the collision-free state space, X_{free}. Secondly, the state closest to x_{rand} already present in T, x_{near}, is identified according to a distance metric. Thirdly, x_{near} is extended to a new state, x_{new}, as follows. A control command is selected either randomly or according to a specific criterion. A possible criterion is to choose the command that yields a x_{new} as close as possible to x_{rand}. The command is then applied to x_{near} over a small time interval, which creates x_{new}. If x_{new} lies in X_{free}, then a vertex representing x_{new} and a directed edge representing the command that takes x_{near} to x_{new} are added to T. A trajectory is found when x_{new} reaches the goal state, x_{goal}. The iterative procedure is executed until a stop criterion is satisfied (e.g., x_{goal} is reached or a maximum number of iterations is achieved).

3   Our Approach for Motion Planning

Our motion planner incrementally builds T from x_{init} using random states biased toward the lane region, and plans a trajectory from x_{init} to x_{goal} in real time, which stays within the desired lane bounds and keeps a safe distance from obstacles. At each planning cycle, our motion planner receives as input: (i) an updated map of the environment around the car; (ii) the initial car's state relative to the map; (iii) the location of the lane center relative to the map; (iv) an updated list of goal states, comprising intermediate goal states and the final goal state; and (v) the trajectory built in the previous planning cycle. Our motion planner then produces as output a trajectory from the initial car's state, x_{init}, to the first goal state, x_{goal}, of the updated list of goal states. The trajectory is represented by a list of control commands (triplets $(v, \varphi, \Delta t)$) that leads the car from x_{init} to x_{goal} and is planned at a fixed frequency (12.5 hz in our experiments).

It is important to note that, in spite of being ready to, our motion planner does not handle movable obstacles yet. For this, it would be enough to add a system for tracking the movable obstacles states in the present and estimating their states in the future. The movable obstacle state would comprise obstacle's geometry, pose, and velocity. When selecting x_{near} or control commands to extend x_{near}, given the future states of movable objects, our motion planner would discard states or commands which would lead to a collision with a movable obstacle.

3.1   Reducing Metric Sensitivity

Our motion planner incorporates the RC-RRT [5], a variant of the standard RRT designed for reducing its sensitivity to the distance metric. The RC-RRT collects information during the exploration of the state space and extends T according to both the distance metric and exploration information, which can make it less sensitive to the distance metric. For each state in T, the RC-RRT records whether a control command has already been applied to the state. If a command has already been applied to the state, it is *discarded*, i.e., it is not considered for the state anymore. If all possible commands have already been applied to the state, it is *discarded*, i.e., it is not considered as a x_{near} anymore. For each state in T, RC-RRT also computes a constraint violation frequency (CVF). For each x_{new} inserted to T, its CVF is initialized to zero. When a control command applied to the state leads to a collision, the CVF of the state is increased by $\frac{1}{m}$, the CVF of the parent state is increased by $\frac{1}{m^2}$, and the CVF of the k-th parent state is increased by $\frac{1}{m^{k+1}}$, where m is the number of possible commands. So, each state's CVF is bounded to the $[0, 1]$ interval. When selecting a state to be extended, RC-RRT verifies if the commands for the state are exhausted. If so, the state is discarded; otherwise, the state is discarded with a probability equal to its CVF.

3.2   Biasing the Location of Random States toward the Lane Region

Another variant of the standard RRT is employed to bias the location of random states toward the lane region. For that, with a given probability, x_{rand} is taken from the lane region instead of from the whole state space as follows. A first sample is taken randomly from the lane center between x_{init} and x_{goal}, and a second sample is taken randomly from a circle with a small radius centered in the first sample. The second sample is then considered as x_{rand}.

3.3   Selecting the Most Promising Control Commands

Another variant of the standard RRT is employed to select the most promising control commands for extending states. It considers not only the proximity to x_{rand}, but also other criteria associated with environmental and traffic-law constraints, namely distance from obstacles, proximity to the lane center, maintenance of velocity limits, and execution of authorized maneuvers. The space of control commands is discretized and each possible command, u, receives a cost calculated according to the following equation:

$$u.cost = \sum_i cost(u, c_i) * weight(c_i), \tag{1}$$

where c_i is a command selection criterion, $cost(u, c_i)$ is the cost assigned to u with regard to c_i, and $weight(c_i)$ is the weight assigned to c_i. Both $cost(u, c_i)$ and $weight(c_i)$ are bounded to $[0, 1]$. The sum of the weights of all criteria is equal to one, i.e., $\sum_i weight(c_i) = 1$. When selecting a control command for extending a state, for each possible command, our motion planner verifies if the command has already been applied to the state. If so, the command is discarded; otherwise, it is applied to the state to check if x_{new} lies in X_{free}. If not, the command is discarded, and the CVF of the state and the parent states are increased. The non-discarded command with smallest cost is selected. Our motion planning considers the five criteria described below to select a control command.

1. Proximity to x_{rand}. Higher costs are attributed to commands that take x_{new} farther from x_{rand}, while lower ones are assigned to commands that bring x_{new} closer to x_{rand}.

2. Distance from obstacles. An occupancy grid map is used to represent the probability of occupancy by obstacles. An obstacle distance grid map is used to represent the proximity to obstacles. The obstacle distance map is derived from the occupancy map as follows. If the value of an occupancy map cell is higher than a given threshold, then it is considered to be occupied and the corresponding cell of the obstacle distance map is set to one. Otherwise, it is considered free and the corresponding cell of the obstacle distance map is made equal to the corresponding cell of the occupancy map. The obstacle distance map is used to attribute costs to control commands according to the distance from obstacles. Higher costs are attributed to commands that bring x_{new} closer to an obstacle, while lower ones are assigned to those that take x_{new} farther from an obstacle.

3. Proximity to the lane center. A lane distance grid map is used to represent the proximity to the lane center. In the lane distance map, a value in the $[0, 1]$ interval indicates the distance to the lane center: the closer to 1 a grid cell, the farther it is to the lane center. The lane distance map is used to attribute costs to control commands according to the proximity to the lane center. Higher costs are attributed to commands that extend a state to another farther from the lane center, while lower ones are assigned to those that extend a state to another closer to the lane center.

4. Maintenance of velocity limits. A minimum cost is attributed to velocity commands equal to the maximum limit; the cost increases as the difference between the velocity command and the desired limits increases.

5. Execution of authorized maneuvers. A maximum cost is attributed to control commands that move the car backwards, while a minimum one is assigned to those that move it forward.

3.4   Selecting the Best Trajectories

Another variant of the standard RRT is employed to select the best trajectories. It takes into account not only the time to achieve x_{goal}, but also other criteria associated with environmental constraints, namely distance from obstacles and proximity to the lane center (second and third criteria described above in Section 3.3). The trajectory cost is defined by the cost of its last state, i.e., the state that reaches x_{goal}. The initial state, x_{init}, receives a cost equals to zero. Each of the other states, x, receives a cost computed according to the following equation:

$$x.cost = x_{parent}.cost + time(x_{parent}, x, u) + \sum_i cost(x, c_i) * weight(c_i), \qquad (2)$$

where x_{parent} is the parent state; $time(x_{parent}, x, u)$ is the time taken by the control command, u, to bring x_{parent} to x; $cost(x, c_i)$ is the cost assigned to x with regard to c_i; and $weight(c_i)$ is the weight assigned to c_i. Both $cost(x, c_i)$ and $weight(c_i)$ are bounded to $[0, 1]$. The sum of the weights of all criteria is equal to one, i.e., $\sum_i weight(c_i) = 1$.

At each planning cycle, T is made empty and the cost of the best trajectory, P_{best}, is initialized to infinity. Every time a new trajectory, P_{new}, is found, the cost of the best trajectory is updated to $P_{best}.cost = \min(P_{best}.cost, P_{new}.cost)$.

3.5 Growing the Tree toward the Goal State

The Connect heuristic [6] is employed to attempt to quickly grow T toward x_{goal} after each successful extension (x_{new} addition). Instead of attempting to extend T by a single step, the Connect heuristic repeats the extension step until x_{goal} or an obstacle is reached. In this way, if x_{goal} is in the car's direction and there is no obstacle between the car and x_{goal}, a trajectory may be generated with a smaller number of iterations.

3.6 Discarding Non-promising States

Another variant of the standard RRT is employed to discard non-promising states. For that, a state, x, has its lower bound on the cost-to-go to x_{goal} estimated as:

$$x.cost\_to\_go = \frac{\|x - x_{goal}\|}{v_{max}}, \qquad (3)$$

where $\|x - x_{goal}\|$ is the Euclidean distance between x and x_{goal}, and v_{max} is the maximum velocity. Every time a new trajectory is found, for each state, x, if $x.cost + x.cost\_to\_go \geq P_{best}.cost$, then x can be safely discarded from T, as it cannot provide a better solution than the one that has just been found. Additionally, whenever x_{new} is created, if $x_{new}.cost + x_{new}.cost\_to\_go \geq P_{best}.cost$, then x_{new} is discarded.

3.7 Reusing Part of the Previous Trajectory

Another variant of the standard RRT is employed to reuse part of the trajectory built in the previous planning cycle. A large part of the trajectory built in the previous planning cycle might still be valid and can be used to speed up the search for a new solution. The valid states – those that lie in X_{free} and have not been followed by the car yet – are added to T.

3.8   Our Motion Planner Algorithm

A high-level description of our motion planner algorithm is given in the following. The initial car's state, x_{init}, and the valid states of the previous trajectory are added to T. At each iteration, the random state, x_{rand}, is firstly taken from the lane region with a given probability. Secondly, x_{new} is identified using the Euclidean distance and the CVF information as follows. For each state in T, x, the motion planner checks if all possible commands have already been applied to x. If so, x is discarded; otherwise, the probability of discarding x is equal to the value of its CVF. The non-discarded x with least distance to x_{rand} is selected as x_{near}. Thirdly, x_{near} is extended as follows. For each possible command, u, the motion planner verifies if u has already been applied to x_{near}. If so, u is discarded; otherwise, u is applied to x_{near} to check if x_{new} lies in X_{free}. If not, u is discarded, and the CVF of x_{near} and the parent states are increased. The non-discarded u with smallest cost is applied to x_{near} to verify if $x_{new}.cost + x_{new}.cost\_to\_go \geq P_{best}.cost$. If so, x_{new} is discarded; otherwise, a vertex representing x_{new} and a directed edge representing the command that takes x_{near} to x_{new} are added to T. Fourthly, if the extension is successful, the Connect heuristic repeats the extension step until x_{goal} or an obstacle is reached. Fifthly, if x_{goal} is reached and $P_{new}.cost = x_{new}.cost < P_{best}.cost$, then the best trajectory is updated and T is *pruned*, i.e., for all states, x, in T, if $x.cost + x.cost\_to\_go \geq P_{best}.cost$, then x is discarded from T.

The iterative procedure is executed until the minimum planning time is reached. However, if no trajectory is found during the minimum planning time, the iterative procedure is executed until the maximum planning time (or timeout). In case of timeout, the car is stopped.

4   Experimental Methodology

Our Intelligent and Autonomous Robotic Automobile (IARA) is based on a Ford Escape Hybrid (Fig. 2(a)). It has several high-end sensors, including: two Point Grey Bumblebee XB3 stereo cameras and two Point Grey Bumblebee 2 stereo cameras, one Light Detection and Ranging (LIDAR) Velodyne HDL 32-E, and one GPS-aided Attitude and Heading Reference System (AHRS/GPS) Xsens MTiG. To process the data coming from the sensors, the platform can hold up to four Dell Precision R5500. We implemented many software modules for IARA that currently allows for its autonomous operation, such as modules for mapping, localization, behavior selection, path following, control, and motion planning (that is the focus of this paper). We also implemented a software module for autonomous vehicle simulation to help in the development and testing of all the other IARA's modules (that was also used to evaluate the performance of the motion planner presented in this paper).

The main parameters of our motion planner are: maximum car's velocity, v_{max}; maximum steering wheel angle, φ_{max}; minimum planning time, t_{min}; maximum planning time (or timeout), t_{max}; maximum distance between states, d_{max}, given by the maximum distance x_{near} and x_{new}; and the probability of taking x_{rand} from the lane region, p_{bias}. The values of the main parameters used in our simulation experiments were: $v_{max} = 2.5$ m/s, $\varphi_{max} = 26.4$ deg, $t_{min} = 120$ s, $t_{max} = 120$ s, $d_{max} = 3.5$ m, and $p_{bias} = 0.8$. The values of the parameters used in the experiments with IARA are the same as those used in the simulation experiments, except for $t_{min} = 0.08$ s and $t_{max} = 0.8$ s.

The experiments with our autonomous vehicle simulator were carried out on maps and other data computed using sensor logs captured by IARA while manually driven on a part of the road that surrounds the main campus of our university. For defining the location of the lane center, IARA was driven along the center of the desired lane segment of the road. During the course, estimated car's locations were acquired. These locations are considered as lane center estimates and provided as input to our motion planner.

The experiments with IARA were conducted on a parking lot of the campus of our university. We defined a fake lane in the parking lot and driven IARA along the center of the fake lane for acquiring car's locations to be provided as lane center estimates.

5   Experimental Results and Discussion

5.1   Experiments with the Autonomous Vehicle Simulator

To evaluate the contributions of each RRT variant considered in this paper, we examined the performance of our motion planner in the simulator using five different configurations. The Configuration 1 incorporates only the standard RRT. The Configuration 2 incorporates only the RC-RRT [5]. The Configuration 3 incorporates (a) the Configuration 2 and (b) discarding of non-promising states using only the time criteria. The Configuration 4 incorporates (a) the Configuration 2 and (b) selection of the most promising control commands for extending states, discarding of non-promising states, and selection of the best trajectory using various criteria associated with environmental and traffic-law constraints. The Configuration 5 incorporates (a) the Configuration 2, (b) the Configuration 4, and (c) biasing of the location of random states toward the lane region and the Connect heuristic [6].

In the simulation experiments, the list of goals was composed of only the final x_{goal}. Thus, the motion planner executed only a single planning cycle. Consequently, the reuse of previous trajectories was not evaluated. Finally, it was used the same x_{init} and final x_{goal}.

Fig. 1 shows the results of our simulation experiments. In each of these figures, the blue rectangle denote x_{init}, the yellow rectangle the final x_{goal}, yellow lines T edges, grey lines edges leaving states with a high CVF (equal to 1), red lines edges leaving discarded states, green lines trajectories found, and the blue line the best trajectory found.

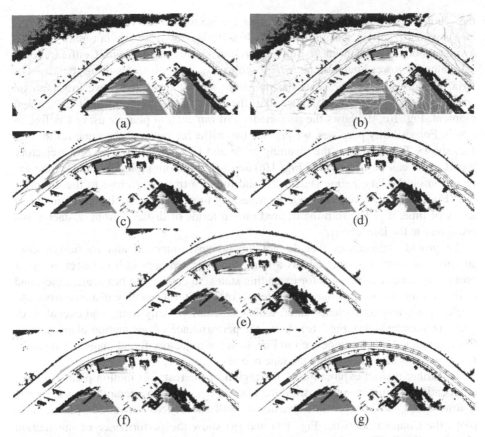

Fig. 1. Performance of our motion planner using: (a) Configuration 1, (b) Configuration 2, (c, d) Configuration 3, (e) Configuration 4, and (f, g) Configuration 5. For visibility purposes, we provide two different views of the same result: views (c) and (d) show T and the best trajectory found for Configuration 3, and views (f) and (g) show T and the best trajectory found for Configuration 5.

Fig. 1(a) shows the performance of our motion planner using Configuration 1. As it can be observed in Fig. 1(a), the state space was sparsely explored. Also, the final trajectory (blue line) passes close to obstacles and far from the lane center.

Fig. 1(b) shows the performance of our motion planner using Configuration 2. Our motion planner with the RC-RRT explored the state space much better than with the standard RRT. The reason is that the RC-RRT avoids similar expansions by applying a control command to a state only once. This guarantees that new T expansions will always explore new regions. The RC-RRT also penalizes states whose expansion attempts are likely to fail based on the CVF. As it can be seen in Fig. 1(b), states with a high CVF (grey lines) are those close to obstacles that, most of the time, extend to obstacles.

Despite the fact that the RC-RRT explored the state space better than the standard RRT, the solutions found by both algorithms are equivalent. Both algorithms explore the whole state space, instead of focusing the search on the region of interest (the lane), which result in feasible solutions but clearly far from the optimum one. To avoid exploration of non-interesting regions, our motion planner with Configuration 3 estimates the lower bound on the cost-to-go to x_{goal} for all states using the time criteria, and discards and prevents the insertion in T of those that have lower bound costs (plus their own costs) higher than the best trajectory found until the current moment. Fig. 1(c, d) shows the performance of our motion planner using Configuration 3. For visibility purposes, we provide two different views of the same result: Fig. 1(c) shows T built during the planning cycle and Fig. 1(d) shows the best trajectory found. As it can be observed in Fig. 1(c) and (d), the motion planner focused the exploration on the lane region (Fig. 1(c)) and found a trajectory close to the optimum one (Fig. 1(d)). However, although the trajectory found is close to the optimum one in terms of time, it is far from the desired one in terms of distance from obstacles and proximity to the lane center.

To provide trajectories that do not violate environmental and traffic-law constraints, our motion planner adopts a more sophisticated approach to select the most promising control commands for extending states, to choose the best trajectories, and to discard non-promising states considering other criteria (namely distance from obstacles, proximity to the lane center, maintenance of velocity limits and execution of authorized maneuvers). Fig. 1(e) shows the performance of our motion planner using Configuration 4. As it can be seen in Fig. 1(e), the trajectory found maintains distance from the curbs and stays within the lane bounds.

To further restrict exploration to the region of interest, our motion planner biases the location of random states toward the lane region. Also, to attempt to quickly grow T toward x_{goal}, whenever an expansion is well succeeded, our motion planner employs the Connect heuristic. Fig. 1(f) and (g) show the performance of our motion planner using Configuration 5. For visibility purposes, we provide two different views of the same result: Fig. 1(f) shows T built during the planning cycle and Fig. 1(g) shows the best trajectory found. As it can be observed in Fig. 1(f) and (g), the motion planner restricted the exploration on the lane region even further (Fig. 1(f)) and built a trajectory from a safe distance from the curbs and within the lane bounds (Fig. 1(g)).

5.2   Experiments with IARA

Different from the simulation experiments, in the experiments with IARA the list of goals was composed of several goal states. Thus, the motion planner executed several planning cycles and, consequently, reused part of previous trajectories. Also, it was used approximately the same x_{init} (in the real world it is impossible to pose the car in the same state more than once) and the same final x_{goal}.

We executed the same experiment with IARA ten times. The experiments were executed with a safety driver and a computer operator inside the car. The former was responsible for stopping the car if any problem occurred, and the later for operating and observing the progress of the IARA's autonomous operating system.

Fig. 2(b) shows the estimated IARA's locations acquired during each of the ten runs. In this figure, different-colored lines denote the estimated IARA's locations in distinct runs. In all runs, the motion planner built trajectories within the fake lane around the parking lot. The whole trajectory length (from x_{init} to x_{goal}) was 145.82 m long on average and the whole trajectory time was of 60.18 s on average. Also, although T is built randomly, in all runs our motion planner built very similar trajectories. The reason is that the search of the state space was biased toward the lane region, which constrained the possible solutions. Finally, the motion planner was capable of planning trajectories in only 0.08 s (12.5 hz).

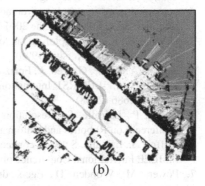

(a)   (b)

Fig. 2. (a) Intelligent and Autonomous Robotic Automobile (IARA); (b) Estimated locations of IARA acquired during each one of the ten runs

6   Conclusions and Future Work

We presented a motion planner for car-like robots driving on roads based on RRT. Our motion planner combines several variants of the standard RRT algorithm to reduce its sensitivity to the distance metric, build trajectories within the desired lane bounds, and speed up its convergence.

We evaluated the performance of our motion planner using an autonomous vehicle simulator. To evaluate the contributions of each RRT variant considered in this paper, we examined the performance of our motion planner using several combinations of them, ranging from the most naïve (that includes only the standard RRT) to the most sophisticated one (that includes all the RRT variants considered). The results of the simulation experiments showed that the most sophisticated configuration outperforms the others in terms of distance from obstacles and proximity to the lane center. We also analyzed the performance of our motion planner using the Intelligent and Autonomous Robotic Automobile (IARA) based on a modified Ford Escape Hybrid. The results of the experiments with IARA showed that our motion planner is capable of planning trajectories in real time, which stay close to the lane center and keep a safe distance from obstacles.

Directions for future work include: (i) smoothing of the trajectory to make it more close to that generated by a human driver; (ii) interaction with other environmental structures, such as movable obstacles and traffic signs; (iii) motion planning on unstructured parking lots; and (iv) comparison of the performance of our motion planner and human drivers using IARA.

References

1. Dolgov, D., Thrun, S., Montemerlo, M., Diebel, J.: Path Planning for Autonomous Driving in Unknown Environments. In: Khatib, O., Kumar, V., Pappas, G.J. (eds.) Experimental Robotics. STAR, vol. 54, pp. 55–64. Springer, Heidelberg (2009)
2. Urmson, C., Anhalt, J., Bagnel, D., Baker, C., Bittner, R., Clark, M., Dolan, J., Duggins, D., Gittleman, M., Harbaugh, S., Wolkowicki, Z., Ziglar, J., Bae, H., Brown, T., Demitrish, D., Sadekar, V., Zhang, W., Struble, J., Taylor, M., Darms, M., Ferguson, D.: Autonomous driving in urban environments: Boss and the urban challenge. Journal of Field Robotics: Special Issues on the 2007 DARPA Urban Challenge **25**(8), 425–466 (2008)
3. LaValle, S.: Rapidly-exploring random trees: a new tool for path planning. Technical Report, Iowa State University (1998)
4. Kuwata, Y., Fiore, G., Teo, J., Frazzoli, E., How, J.: Motion planning for urban driving using RRT. In: IEEE/RSJ International Conference on Intelligent Robots and Systems, pp.1681–1686 (2008)
5. Cheng, P., LaValle, S.: Resolution complete rapidly-exploring. In: IEEE International Conference on Robotics and Automation, pp. 267–272 (2002)
6. Kuffner, J., LaValle, S.: RRT-connect: an efficient approach to single-query path planning. In: IEEE International Conference on Robotics and Automation, pp. 995–1001 (2000)
7. Powers, M., Wooden, D., Egerstedt, M., Christensen, H., Balch, T.: The sting racing team's entry to the urban challenge. In: Rouff, C., Hinchey, M. (eds.) Experience from the DARPA Urban Challenge, pp. 43–66. Springer, London (2012)
8. Frazzoli, E., Dahleh, M., Feron, E.: Real-time motion planning for agile autonomous vehicles. In: American Control Conference, pp. 43–49 (2001)
9. Bekris, K., Kavraki, L.: Greedy but safe replanning under kinodynamic constraints. In: IEEE International Conference on Robotics and Automation, pp. 704–710 (2007)
10. LaValle, S., Kuffner, J.: Rapidly-exploring random trees: progress and prospects. In: Donald, B., Lynch, K., Rus, D. (eds.) Algorithmic and Computational Robotics: New Directions, pp. 293–308. A. K. Peters, Welessley (2001)
11. Macek, K., Becked, M., Siegwart, R.: Motion planning for car-like vehicles in dynamic urban scenarios. In: IEEE/RSJ International Conference on Intelligent Robots and Systems, pp. 4375–4380 (2006)
12. Franchi, A., Freda, L., Oriolo, G., Vendittelli, M.: A Randomized Strategy for Cooperative Robot Exploration. In: International Conference on Robotics and Automation, pp. 768–774 (2007)
13. Chang-an, L., Jin-gang, C., Guo-dong, L., Chun-Yang, L.: Mobile robot path planning based on an improved rapidly-exploring random tree in unknown environment. In: International Conference on Automation and Logistics, pp. 2375–2379 (2008)
14. LaValle, S.M., Kuffner, J.J..: Randomized kinodynamic planning. In: IEEE International Conference on Robotics and Automation, pp. 473–479 (1999)
15. Ju, T., Liu, S., Yang, J., Sun, D.: Rapidly exploring random tree algorithm-based path planning for robot-aided optical manipulation of biological cells. Transactions on Automation Science and Engineering **11**(3), 649–657 (2014)

Omnidirectional Walking with a Compliant Inverted Pendulum Model

Abbas Abdolmaleki[1,2,3(✉)], Nima Shafii[1,2], Luis Paulo Reis[2,3], Nuno Lau[1], Jan Peters[4,5], and Gerhard Neumann[4]

[1] Instituto de Engenharia Eletrónica e Telemática de Aveiro, Universidade de Aveiro, Aveiro, Portugal
abbas.abdolmaleki@yahoo.com
[2] Laboratório de Inteligência Artificial e Ciência de Computadores, Universidade do Porto, Porto, Portugal
[3] Departamento de Sistemas de Informação, Escola de Engenharia da Universidade do Minho, Braga, Portugal
[4] Intelligent Autonomous Systems, TU Darmstadt, Darmstadt, Germany
[5] Max Planck Institute for Intelligent Systems, Stuttgart, Germany

Abstract. In this paper, we propose a novel omnidirectional walking engine that achieves energy efficient, human like, stable and fast walking. We augment the 3D inverted pendulum with a spring model to implement a height change in the robot's center of mass trajectory. This model is used as simplified model of the robot and the zero moment point (ZMP) criterion is used as the stability indicator. The presented walking engine consists of 5 main modules including the "next posture generator" module, the "foot trajectory generator" module, the "center of mass (CoM) trajectory generator" module, the "robot posture controller" module and "Inverse kinematics (IK) solver" module. The focus of the paper is the generation of the position of the next step and the CoM trajectory generation. For the trajectory generator, we extend the 3D-IPM with an undamped spring to implement height changes of the CoM. With this model we can implement active compliance for the robot's gait, resulting in a more energy efficient movement. We present a modified method for solving ZMP equations which derivation is based on the new proposed model for omnidirectional walking. The walk engine is tested on simulated and a real NAO robot. We use policy search to optimize the parameters of the walking engines for the standard 3D-LIPM and our proposed model to compare the performance of both models each with their optimal parameters. We optimize the policy parameters in terms of energy efficiency for a fixed walking speed. The experimental results show the advantages of our proposed model over 3D-LIPM.

Keywords: Humanoid Walking · Inverted Pendulum Model · Zero Moment Point

1 Introduction

Bipedal locomotion includes any type of omnidirectional walking or running. Humanoid robots must have the capability to adjust the speed and the direction of its walk to perform versatile omnidirectional locomotion. Due to the large continuous

© Springer International Publishing Switzerland 2014
A.L.C. Bazzan and K. Pichara (Eds.): IBERAMIA 2014, LNAI 8864, pp. 481–493, 2014.
DOI: 10.1007/978-3-319-12027-0_39

state and action space of the robot, as well as being an inherently nonlinear system, it is very difficult to control the balance of the humanoid robot during walking. There are different methods to synthesize walking motion. The most popular methods generate a pattern motion for CoM based on a simplified dynamic model of the robot given planned footsteps [1],[2]. The Omnidirectional footstep planner, plans the position of the feet and CoM based on desired speed in an obstacle free and flat surface. In [3] the authors present a heuristic footstep planner that constraints the position of the CoM at the end of the step to be always in the middle of feet. We propose a new heuristic method for omnidirectional footstep planning, we introduce a control parameter to define the position of the CoM between the feet at the end of the step. After planning the foot step, CoM motion pattern should be generated. There are many successful walking algorithms that model the robot as a linear inverted pendulum model(LIPM) and use the zero moment point (ZMP) as stability criterion [4] for CoM trajectory planning[1][2][3][5]. These LIPM based methods effectively achieve biped locomotion in legged robots with flat feet. Nevertheless, they assume a constant CoM height of the robot during walking, i.e. the CoM does not have any motion along z axis. Such a constant height of the CoM cancels out the natural dynamics of the system. The achieved gait pattern results in a typical 'bent-knee' posture in order to avoid singularities of inverse kinematics. For this reason, these methods are not efficient, since torque must be continuously applied to the knee joint to keep a bent-knee posture. Moreover, biomechanical studies show that the CoM height is variant during human walking [6]. Hence the shape of CoM height trajectory and the vertical CoM trajectory is very important for energy consumption [7]. There are studies to achieve ZMP-based walking with CoM height change [8], but they do not offer principled models for CoM height change. In this paper, we augment the Inverted Pendulum Model with a spring to model the dynamics of the CoM along x and y axis as well as along z axis. We use our proposed model for omnidirectional walking and show that our proposed model can generate more energy efficient gaits than the standard LIPM. Moreover, we propose a new heuristic method for footstep planning which does not constrained the position of the CoM in a specified position between feet, and finally we show the efficiency of our method for omnidirectional walking.

2   Overview of Walking Engine

The walking engine is omnidirectional in the sense that the robot can walk toward any desired direction and rotate simultaneously. The walking engine gets the desired velocity of the COM along the x-axis and y-axis, and the angular velocity of the orientation of the body around the z-axis in the robot base-frame and outputs the joint positions for the leg servo motors. The origin of the robot base-frame is on the torso of the robot, with the x-axis pointing forward, y-axis pointing to the left, and z-axis pointing up. We generate walking trajectories by a parametric controller that is based on the inverted pendulum model and a ZMP stability criterion. The walk engine uses an inverted pendulum model augmented with an undamped spring and a ZMP stability criterion to generate the torso trajectories, which we assume is identical to the COM trajectory. We use Bezier curves to generate the trajectory of the swing foot.

The feedback controller uses an error signal from the tilt and the roll of the torso to adapt the position and orientation of the feet at each time step in order to keep the trunk of the robot upright. Given the CoM position and the swing foot trajectory we use inverse kinematics to compute the desired joint positions. Finally, we use a PD controller to convert these joint positions to proper motor commands.

We decomposed the walk engine in several modules and addressed each module independently. Figure 1 depicts the role of each module and their interactions. In following a description of each module is given.

Next-Step Position Generator, Based on the desired input COM speed along x-axis and y-axis and which foot is support and which is swing, it calculates where the torso and swing foot should be at the end of the step with taking to account foot reachability and feet collision, please find the details in Section 3.

Swing Foot Trajectory Generator, This module is responsible to generate a trajectory for the swing foot to reach to its next position given by Next-Step-Posture Generator module. The idea is that swing foot should smoothly move from current position to next foot step position with almost zero lifting and landing speed. The cubic Bézier Curve is used to generate such a desired smooth trajectory.

COM Trajectory Generator, in this module COM trajectories in 3 dimensions are generated. It utilizes a 3D-IPM model augmented with springs as a simplified model of the robot with the ZMP criterion as stability indicator. This module will be explained in the Section 4.

COM Rotation Controller, Based on the desired input angular velocity of the orientation of the COM around the z-axis, this module controls the orientation of both feet relative to the desired COM orientation. In order to rotate CoM θ degrees, we simply rotate the swing foot, θ degrees relative to the CoM frame.

Robot Posture Controller, This module maintains the stability of the robot by keeping the posture of the robot upright. Please refer to [3] for details.

Inverse Kinematics Solver, This module computes the reference joint angles based on the relative position of feet to torso frame. Please refer to [10] for details.

In this paper we will explain Next-Step Position Generator and COM Trajectory Generator modules where we have contribution.

3   Next-Step Position Generator

After receiving the desired CoM speed command, the first job of the walking engine is to calculate where to take the next step. The next-step position generator, gets (v_x, v_y, ω_z), current position of CoM and current configuration of feet and calculates the position of swing foot and CoM at the end of the step considering foot reachability and avoiding feet collision. Figure 2 shows top-down view of how to generate the next position of foot and CoM in the XY plane. We first simply compute the next position of CoM by multiplying the period of the current step by the input velocity (v_x, v_y) to obtain the displacements along x and y denoted as d_x and d_y. Then, we compute predicted CoM position $(d_x + \beta \times d_x, d_y + \beta \times d_y)$ where $\beta \epsilon [0,1]$ and we place the next foot step beside the predicted CoM position. By changing the parameter β from 0 to 1 we can control the position of the CoM between feet. For example if we set the $\beta = 0.5$, CoM always will be in middle of feet. It is different from our previous works that that assume the CoM is always in the middle of feet.

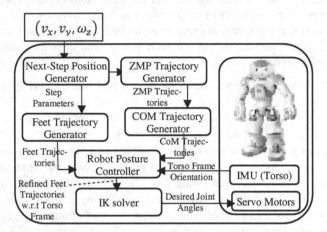

Fig. 1. This sketch shows the modules of omnidirectional walking engine and their relation

We also take into consideration two constraints, foot reachability and self-collision of feet when calculating target foot. Based on the predefined constraints on position of feet relative to each other, we use a "MinMax" operation to correct the position of computed foot step to avoid violation of these constraints.

4   CoM Trajectory Generator

ZMP criterion is a well-known stability indicator for humanoid robots. Biped walking robot can keep its dynamic balance by placing its foot on its ZMP. In other word we can maintain the stability of the biped robot by controlling its ZMP to be on the supporting foot. We choose the reference ZMP to be at the center of the supporting foot during the single support phase and linearly move towards to the center of the other foot during double support phase. Given the calculated next position of foot and CoM from last section, the desired ZMP trajectory is generated as follows:

$$
\begin{bmatrix} x_{ZMP}(t) \\ y_{ZMP}(t) \end{bmatrix} = \begin{cases} \boldsymbol{CoM}_{t_0} + \left(\frac{\boldsymbol{R}_{t_0} - \boldsymbol{CoM}_{t_0}}{t_1 - t_0}\right) \times (t - t_0) & t_0 \le t < t_1 \\ \boldsymbol{R}_{t_0} & t_1 \le t < t_2 \\ \boldsymbol{R}_{t_0} + \left(\frac{\boldsymbol{CoM}_T - \boldsymbol{R}_{t_0}}{T - t_2}\right) \times (t - t_2) & t_2 \le t < T \end{cases} \tag{1}
$$

Where x_{ZMP} and y_{ZMP} are desired ZMP position along x and y axis, $\boldsymbol{CoM}_{t_0}$ and $\boldsymbol{CoM}_T$ are initial and terminal positions of the CoM and $\boldsymbol{R}_{t_0}$ denotes the position of the support foot. Please note that in $[t_0, t_1]$ and $[t_2, T]$ intervals we have double support phase and in $[t_1, t_2]$ interval we have single support phase.

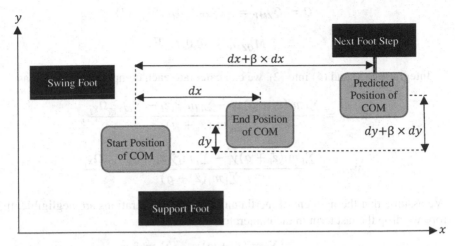

Fig. 2. Calculation of next foot and CoM position for input walk vector (x, y)

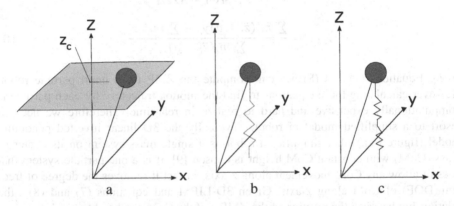

Fig. 3. a: shows a LIPM which has constrained movement along x-y plane with constant height z_c. b: It is an IPM augmented with a spring which has spring movements in both x-z and y-z freely. c: it is an IPM which it's movement along z axis is modeled by 2 coupled springs.

We use D'Alambert's principle to drive ZMP equations which states that the following equation holds for any arbitrary point Q when there are no external moments and forces exerted on system

$$\Sigma_i(q_i - q) \times m_i \left(\ddot{q}_i + \begin{bmatrix} 0 \\ 0 \\ g \end{bmatrix} \right) + \Sigma_i J_i . \ddot{\Omega}_i = M_Q, \qquad (2)$$

Where q_i denotes position vector of the i-th link and m_i is the mass of the i-th link, g is gravity, J_i and $\ddot{\Omega}_i$ are the moments of inertia matrix and the angular acceleration vector of i-th link, and q and M_Q are the position vector and the moment of point **Q**.

ZMP is the point on the ground where the net moment along x-axis and y-axis is zero. By this definition

$$Q = Q_{ZMP} = [x_{ZMP}, y_{ZMP}, 0]^T, \quad (3)$$

$$M_{QZMP} = [0, 0, M_Z]^T, \tag{4}$$

Integrating (3) and (4) into (2), we can calculate each component of Q_{ZMP} as

$$x_{ZMP} = \frac{\sum_i m_i(\ddot{z}_i + g)x_i - \sum_i m_i \ddot{x}_i z_i - \sum_i J_{Y_i} \cdot \ddot{\Omega}_{Y_i}}{\sum_i m_i(\ddot{z}_i + g)}, \tag{5}$$

$$y_{ZMP} = \frac{\sum_i m_i(\ddot{z}_i + g)y_i - \sum_i m_i \ddot{y}_i z_i - \sum_i J_{X_i} \cdot \ddot{\Omega}_{X_i}}{\sum_i m_i(\ddot{z}_i + g)}, \tag{6}$$

We assume that the moment of inertia and angular accelerations are negligible, therefore we drop the last term in the numerator and we obtain

$$x_{ZMP} = \frac{\sum_i m_i(\ddot{z}_i + g)x_i - \sum_i m_i \ddot{x}_i z_i}{\sum_i m_i(\ddot{z}_i + g)}, \tag{7}$$

$$y_{ZMP} = \frac{\sum_i m_i(\ddot{z}_i + g)y_i - \sum_i m_i \ddot{y}_i z_i}{\sum_i m_i(\ddot{z}_i + g)}, \tag{8}$$

Using Equations (7) and (8), we can compute the ZMP for a multi particle robot. However calculating these equations to find the motion trajectory for each particle is computationally expensive and hard to realize in real-time. Therefore we need to resort to a simplified model of robot. Typically the 3D linear inverted pendulum model (figure (3.a)) that simplifies a robot as a single mass system on its center of mass (CoM) with constant CoM height is chosen [9]. It is a one particle system that doesn't allow any CoM movement along z-axis, in fact it removes the degree of freedom(DOF) of CoM along z-axis. Given 3D-LIPM and equations (7) and (8) , the relationship between the position of the ZMP and the CoM can be obtained by:

$$x_{ZMP} = x_{CoM} - \frac{\ddot{x}_{CoM} \cdot z_c}{g}, \quad (9) \qquad y_{ZMP} = y_{CoM} - \frac{\ddot{y}_{CoM} \cdot z_c}{g}, \quad (10)$$

Here $(x_{ZMP}, y_{ZMP}, 0)$ and (x_{CoM}, y_{CoM}, z_c) are the position of ZMP and position of CoM respectively and g is gravitational acceleration. Note that z_c is a constant.

Constrained CoM height assumed by LIPM has some advantages and disadvantages. One of the advantage is that, LIPM offers linear ZMP equations in x_{CoM} and y_{CoM} which makes it easier to compute the x_{CoM} and y_{CoM} trajectories. The other advantage is that, it is easier to implement. Because height of the CoM is assumed constant during the walking, we will not be worry about generating the trajectory along z-axis. In the other hand, the disadvantage of height constrained is that, the walk will not be energy efficient because robot always needs to have bent knee to avoid inverse kinematics singularities and continuously apply torque to knee and ankle joints. Also it is not human-like, because studies show that human being has variant CoM height while walking [4]. Figure (4.b) shows the walking motion using the 3D-LIPM.

In order to release height constraint and achieve more human-like and energy efficient walk, we propose an inverted pendulum model augmented with a spring as explained by figure (3.b ,3.c). Our goal is to use the degree of freedom of CoM along z-axis to achieve active compliant, human-like and energy efficient motion, Therefore it is intuitive to choose an undamped spring to model the dynamics of CoM along z-axis.

Assuming our new model and Equations (7) and (8) the relationship between the position of the ZMP and the CoM can be obtained by:

$$x_{ZMP} = x_{CoM} - \frac{\ddot{x}_{CoM} \cdot z_{CoM}}{\ddot{z}_{CoM} + g}, \quad (11) \qquad\qquad y_{ZMP} = y_{CoM} - \frac{\ddot{y}_{CoM} \cdot z_{CoM}}{\ddot{z}_{CoM} + g}, \quad (12)$$

z_{CoM} and $\ddot{z}_{CoM}$ are the position and acceleration along z-axis. In fact the z_{CoM} and $\ddot{z}_{CoM}$ trajectories are already determined by the dynamics of the spring. According to hook's law when a spring is displaced from its equilibrium state, the force F exerted by the spring on any object it is pulling its free end is proportional to the displacement x. That is $F = -kx$, where k is a constant factor of the spring that explains its stiffness. Using Newton's second law we obtain:

$$F = ma = m\frac{d^2x}{dt^2} = -kx, \qquad\qquad\qquad (13)$$

Solving this differential equation we obtain the motion of CoM along z-axis as follows:

$$z_{CoM}(t) = x_0 + A\cos(\omega t + \phi) ; \; \omega = \frac{2\pi}{T}, \qquad (14)$$

Like walking it is a periodic motion with amplitude A which determines the desired amount of CoM displacement along z-axis around spring rest position x_0 , the period T is the amount of time for a single oscillation which is same as the period of one walk step and ϕ is phase of the motion which determines the starting position of z_{CoM} at the beginning of the step. Calculating the second derivative of equation, we obtain $\ddot{z}_{CoM}$

$$\ddot{z}_{CoM}(t) = -A\omega^2\cos(\omega t + \phi); \; \omega = \frac{2\pi}{T} \qquad (15)$$

Figure (4.a) shows the walk motion using our proposed model.

The problem now is how to generate the x_{CoM} and y_{CoM} trajectories online for one step given z_{CoM} , $\ddot{z}_{CoM}$, x_{ZMP}, y_{ZMP} trajectories and initial, terminal position of CoM for one step. In fact it is the inverse problem of (11) and (12). Generating the CoM trajectories with constant height using preview control [1] and analytically solving the linear differential equation [5] has been proposed. These methods by assuming z_{CoM} as a constant, enjoy the linearity of equations (1) and (2) with respect to (x_{CoM}, y_{CoM})

and employ existing methods for controlling linear dynamical systems [1] or existing methods for solving the linear differential equations analytically[5]. However, in our proposed model we have variant CoM height assumption, therefore we extend the resolution method proposed in [6] for solving the differential equations (11) and (12).We only explain the method for finding x_{CoM} motion trajectory and same method can be used to find the y_{CoM}. Using central difference approximation of the second derivative of x_{CoM} , (11) is discretized as follows:

$$\ddot{x}_{CoM}(t) = \frac{x_{CoM}(t+T) - 2x_{CoM}(t) + x_{CoM}(t-T)}{T^2}$$

$$= \frac{x_{CoM}(k+1) - 2x_{CoM}(k) + x_{CoM}(k-1)}{T^2}$$

(16)

Where T is the sampling period and k = 1...n is the index of the discretized samples with n total number of samples which depends on sampling period T. Note that we use the same sampling period T to discretize the given z_{CoM} , $\ddot{z}_{CoM}$, x_{ZMP}, y_{ZMP} trajectories.

Incorporating (16) into (11) we obtain

$$a(k)x_{CoM}(k-1) + b(k)x_{CoM}(k) + c(k)x_{CoM}(k+1) = x_{ZMP}(k) \ , k = 1 \dots n$$

Where $a(k) = -\frac{z_{CoM}(k)}{(-\ddot{z}_{CoM}(k)+g)T^2}$, $a(1) = 0$, $b(k) = 1 - 2a(k)$, (17)

$$c(k) = -\frac{z_{CoM}(k)}{(-\ddot{z}_{CoM}(k)+g)T^2} \ , c(n) = 0$$

This system of equations is a tridiagonal system for n unknowns x_{CoM}(k) k=1...n. For such a system, Thomas algorithm [6] can find the solutions efficiently in $O(n)$ operations so it can be used for real-time gait generation. In order to get this method applicable for omnidirectional walking we need slightly modify the original Thomas algorithm to incorporate initial position of the CoM at the beginning of the step denoted as x_0 and the final position of the CoM at end of the step denoted as x_n into the formulation. The intuition behind it is that if we can set initial and terminal positions of the CoM in formulation then easily we can connect the trajectories together and obtain an omnidirectional walk. The modified method to incorporate x_0 and x_n is as follows. First we rearrange the coefficients. New coefficients are denoted with primes

$$c(k)' = \begin{cases} 0 & k = 1 \\ \dfrac{c(k)}{b(k) - a(k-1)c(k-1)'} & k = 2,3,..,n-1 \end{cases}$$

(18)

$$x_{ZMP}(k)' = \begin{cases} x_0 & k = 1 \\ \dfrac{x_{ZMP}(k) - a(k)x_{ZMP}(k-1)'}{b(k) - a(k)c(k-1)'} & k = 2,3,..,n \end{cases}$$

(19)

The solution is then obtained by back substitution

$$x_{CoM}(k) = \begin{cases} x_n & k = n \\ x_{ZMP}(k)' - c(k)'x_{CoM}(k+1) & k = n-1, n-2, \dots, 1 \end{cases} \quad (20)$$

Now we have both x_0 and x_n into the x_{CoM} trajectory calculator formulation. Using the same method we can obtain the y_{CoM} trajectory. Figure (5) shows the output of step Generator and CoM generator for walk engine parameters ($v_x = 0.2$, $v_y = 0.2$, $\beta = 0.5$, $T = 1$, $DSP = 0.2$, $x_0 = 0.19$, $A = 0.02$, $\phi = 0$), figure (5.a) and (5.b) shows the generated footsteps and CoM positions for 10 steps. Figure (5.c) and (5.d) shows ZMP trajectories CoM trajectories along y and x axis.

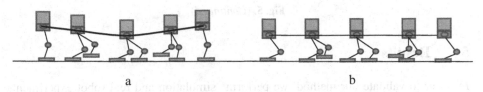

a   b

Fig. 4. a: walking offered by our method which has variant CoM height while walking, b: Walking offered by LIPM which has fixed CoM height during walk

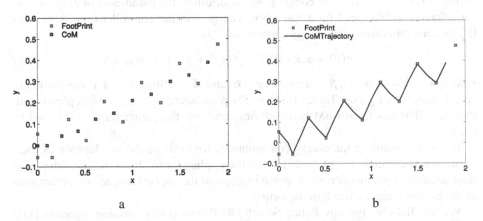

a   b

Fig. 5. a:Top-Down view of generated footsteps and CoM positions in x-y plane for 10 steps, b: Top-Down view of generated footsteps and CoM trajectory in x-y plane for 10 steps, c: ZMP and CoM trajectory along y axis for 5 step d:ZMP and CoM trajectories along x axis for 5 steps.

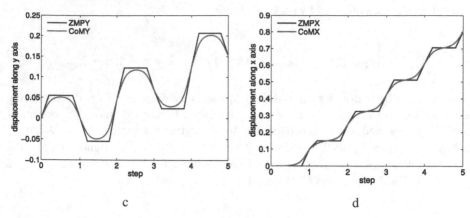

c   d

Fig. 5. (*Continued*)

5   Results

In order to validate our method, we perform simulation and real robot experiments
using a simulated and real NAO humanoid robot (figure 6). The 3d simulator for the
Robocup domain is used as simulator of the NaO robot . We compare our proposed
model with LIMP in terms of energy efficiency and generating human like movements. In order to have a fair comparison, we optimize the parameters of both models
for a fixed feasible speed for a real robot. The goal of the controller is walking with
0.2 m/s and minimizing the energy consumption ,i.e.,

$$R(\theta) = \alpha(\dot{x} - 0.2)^2 + \beta(\dot{y})^2 + \gamma(E)^2 + \delta(1_{Fall}), \tag{21}$$

where we choose $\alpha=10$, $\beta = 1$, $\gamma = 1e - 6$ and $\delta = 100$, . $\dot{x}$ and $\dot{y}$ represent the
speed along x and y axis. Table (1) shows the parameters to be optimized, please note
that, as LIPM has fixed CoM height during walking, the parameter A will be set to
zero.

In order to estimate the energy consumption, we measure the acceleration of each
joint, as it is currently not possible to read the applied torque from the simulator. The
joint acceleration value is a good approximation of the applied torque, as acceleration
of the joint is mainly a result of the torque.

We use Relative Entropy Policy Search (REPS) as policy learning algorithm[11].
REPS is an information theoretic policy search method. The main insight of using
information theory is to bound the relative entropy, also called Kullback-Leibler divergence, between two subsequent policies. By limiting the relative entropy, we can control the information loss of the policy update and the policy will keep the information
about what areas of the parameter space still need to be explored. REPS directly
searches in the parameter space of the our controller. It aims at finding a good upper
level policy $\pi(\theta)$ that maximizes the expected performance $J(\pi)$ of the controller, i.e.,

$$J(\pi) = \int \pi(\theta)R(\theta) \, d\theta, \tag{22}$$

where $R(\theta)$ denotes the reward of executing the walk controller with parameters θ. The policy update in REPS is implemented as a weighted maximum likelihood estimate. To do so, we generate parameter samples from the current policy and estimate the quality of the sample by REPS. Please refer to the paper [11] for more details on the quality estimate of the samples obtained from REPS. This quality estimate results in a weight for each sample, that we can use to estimate a new search policy $\pi(\theta)$ by using a weighted maximum likelihood estimate. In standard REPS, $\pi(\theta)$ is modelled as Gaussian policy, i.e., $\pi(\theta) = \mathcal{N}(\theta|a, \Sigma)$. In this case, the parameters a and Σ can be obtained by a weighted linear regression.

5.1   Simulation and Real Robot Results

The optimization starts from complete stop and runs for 10 seconds, we optimize the parameters of each controller for 150 iterations where each iteration consists of sampling 10 new parameter vectors. for 10 trials which each trial has 150 episodes and in each episode the algorithm tries 10 new parameters on the robot.

Figure (6) shows the average reward for both controllers. The results show that our proposed model achieves a better final reward than LIPM.

After the optimization in simulation, we tested the optimum parameters in the simulation with minor tuning on the real robot and we successfully achieved a more

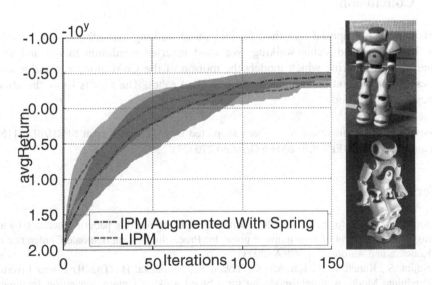

Fig. 6. The learning curves for controller based on LIPM and our proposed model, on the right side you can see the simulated and real NAO robots

Table 1. Parameters of the walk controllers

Notation	Description
x_0	Height of the CoM from ground
z_{step}	Maximum height of the swing foot from the ground
T	Duration of the step
A	Spring parameter (equation 4),Zero for LIPM
v_x	The step size along x axis
Φ_{DSP}	Duration of double support phase

human-like walk than the LIPM on real robot. Please refer to https://www. dropbox.com/sh/uzbhqma78ec69fe/AAD3Gh20J5P4440lHnUBd-mYa to watch the movies of both controller with optimized parameters. The first video is walking with optimized parameters using our proposed model and second video is walking with optimized parameters using LIPM.

We also did an omnidirectional experiment which robot walk in different direction and rotates simultaneously. Please watch the third video of mentioned link above for omnidirectional walking.

6   Conclusion

In this paper we proposed a method for humanoid walking that achieves energy efficient, humanlike and stable walking. We used inverted pendulum model and augmented it with a spring which models the motion of the CoM along x,y and z axis. We tested our method on simulated and real NaO robot. The results show the effectiveness of our method.

Acknowledgment. This research has been supported by FCT under grant SFRH/BD/81155/ 2011 and CompLACS(FP7-ICT-2009-6 Grant.no.270327).

References

1. Kajita, S., Kanehiro, F., Kaneko, K., Fujiwara, K.: Biped walking pattern generation by using preview control of zero-moment point. In: Proceeding of International Conference on Robotics and Automation, ICRA (2003)
2. Kajita, S., Kanehiro, F., Kaneko, K., Yokoi, K., Hirukawa, H.: The 3D Linear Inverted Pendulum Mode: A simple modeling for a biped walking pattern generation. Intelligent Robots and Systems (2001)
3. Shafii, N., Abdolmaleki, A., Ferreira, R., Lau, N., Reis, L.P.: Omnidirectional Walking and Active Balance for Soccer Humanoid Robot. In: Proceeding of 16th Portuguese Conference on Artificial Intelligence (2013)
4. Vukobratovic, M., Stokic, D., Borovac, B., Surla, D.: Biped Locomotion: Dynamics, Stability, Control and Application. Springer (1990)

5. Harada, K., Kajita, S., Kaneko, K., Hirukawa, H.: An analytical method for real-time gait planning for humanoid robots. International Journal of Humanoid Robotics (2006)
6. Kuo, A.D., Donelan, J.M., Ruina, A.: Energetic consequences of walking like an inverted pendulum: step-to-step transitions. Exerc. Sport Sci. Rev. (2005)
7. Srinivasan, M., Ruina, A.: Computer optimization of a minimal biped model discovers walking and running. Nature 437(7057) (2005)
8. Kormushev, P., Ugurlu, B., Calinon, S., Tsagarakis, N.G., Caldwell, D.G.: Bipedal walking energy minimization by reinforcement learning with evolving policy parameterization. In: Proceedings of the International Conference on Robot Systems (2011)
9. Kagami, S., Nishivaki, K., Inaba, M., Inoue, H.: A Fast Dynamically Equilibrated Walking Trajectory Generation Method of Humanoid Robot. Auton. Robots 12(1) (2002)
10. Kofinas, N., Orfanoudakis, E., Lagoudakis, M.G.: Complete analytical inverse kinematics for NAO. In: Proceeding of 13th International Conference on Autonomous Robot Systems (Robotica) (2013)
11. Kupcsik, A.G., Deisenroth, M.P., Peters, J., Neumann, G.: Data-Efficient Generalization of Robot Skills with Contextual Policy Search. In: Proceedings of the National Conference on Artificial Intelligence (AAAI) (2013)

Analogical Generalization of Activities from Single Demonstration

Jason R. Wilson[✉] and Matthias Scheutz

Human-Robot Interaction Laboratory, Tufts University, 200 Boston Avenue,
Medford, MA, USA
wilson@cs.tufts.edu

Abstract. Learning new activities (i.e., sequences of actions possibly involving new objects) from single demonstrations is common for humans and would thus be very desirable for future robots as well. However, "one-shot activity learning" is currently still in its infancy and limited to just recording the observed objects and actions of the human demonstrator. In this paper, we introduce a process called "Mental Elaboration and Generalization by Analogy" to create a generalized representation of an activity that has been demonstrated only once. By abstracting over various dimensions of the learned activity, the obtained activity representation is applicable to a much wider range of objects and actions than would otherwise be possible.

Keywords: Learning generalization analogy robot

1 Introduction

Learning new activities on robots from human demonstration has been investigated for quite some time (e.g., see [1] for an overview). However, there are surprisingly few attempts to learn activities in a more natural, human-like way from a *single demonstration paired with natural language instructions* (e.g., see [5]). The challenges in such "one-shot activity learning" include the processing of fairly unconstrained task-based natural language instructions in real-time and the difficulty of integrating demonstrations and natural language instructions in a mutually synergistic way.

Determining the relevant features that constitute the activity is another problem. It is believed that human learners use their imagination invoking a mental simulation to construct variations of the scenario. They are then able to distinguish those features that are relevant to the activity from those that are not.

In this paper, we introduce our first attempts at using mental simulations to learn relevant features of single presentations of activities. Specifically, we describe a first set of algorithms that can generate novel, yet similar, situations from a given situation and use analogical reasoning to determine which of the different features in the new situation matter for the previously observed activity. From these simulations, we then generate a more abstract activity description that includes the most relevant relations and entities.

© Springer International Publishing Switzerland 2014
A.L.C. Bazzan and K. Pichara (Eds.): IBERAMIA 2014, LNAI 8864, pp. 494–505, 2014.
DOI: 10.1007/978-3-319-12027-0_40

2   Background

Human lives are filled with learned activities that are performed on a daily basis, from driving to the grocery store, selecting and fetching appropriate items from the shelves, packing them in grocery bags at the cash register, stacking the fridge at home, to preparing meals, cleaning the dishes, and so forth. Humans are particularly good at learning and executing such activities, which are often learned from one single demonstration by a teacher – we will call this "one-shot activity" learning. In *one-shot activity* learning, the teacher typically uses a mixture of natural language instructions, gestures, and action demonstrations to teach the activity, while the learner uses multi-modal cues to make sense of the demonstrated activity. This includes determining the relevant objects and actions, as well as the appropriate sequencing of actions and events. When successful, the learner will have formed an appropriate "activity representation" that removes irrelevant physical details (e.g., the distance of the target object from the hand before a grasp or the particular motion trajectories on the way to the grasp, etc.) while capturing relevant details (e.g., the target object needs to be picked up and placed in a particular location relative to another object).

Recent work in robotics has proposed solutions to different aspects of human activity learning. For example, [2] showed how to learn new (primitive) actions from natural language instructions. Beyond actions, [11] demonstrated how various additional properties of objects could be learned from one-shot natural language descriptions. [12] demonstrated how a robot could learn to follow recipes written in natural language on wikihow.com, also utilizing a variety of corpora (the WordNet lexical database. The KeJia project has also made progress in allowing robots to learn from written natural-language data [3] when gaps in the robot's knowledge base are detected. However, none of these projects allow for learning abstractions from single presentations that lead to generalized activity representations which include novel situations with new objects and features.

3   Architecture

The components and control flow of Mental Elaboration and Generalization by Analogy (MEGA) are shown in the gray box of Figure 1. Also in the figure is the control flow for a new scenario. The Measure Applicability of Novelty (MAN) component receives a new scenario and compares it to the generalization using the "structure mapping engine" (SME) [7]. If the generalized activity, which includes a partial description of the context in which it may be applied, and the new scenario are sufficiently similar, then the activity is applicable to the scenario and analogical inferences generated by SME are inspected to find the appropriate variable bindings. In the nest section, we will describe the two main components of MEGA, Mental Elaboration and Generalization by Analogy.

The components of MEGA and MAN are are designed to be easily integrated into the DIARC architecture [13]. We have defined the interface to the Action Manager component to receive the propositional description of the demonstrated

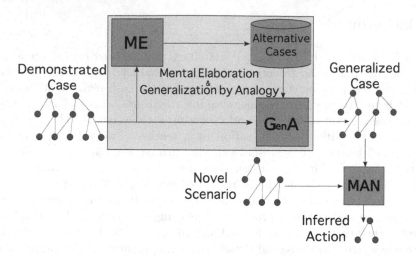

Fig. 1. MEGA process creates a generalized activity, which is later used to infer appropriate activities and variables in a novel situation

activity. MEGA then internally stores the generalized activity. Later, when the Action Manager is selecting the appropriate actions to complete an activity, it provides the new scenario to the MAN component, which will compare the scenario with the generalized activities and return the applicable action.

4   MEGA

We will tackle the generalization of activities from single demonstrations using SME. Similar to [9], we attempt to find correspondences between different cases (*activities* in our work) using structure mappings, but different from [9] we determine the generalization over all comparisons in parallel (instead of a pair-wise sequence). Moreover, because we are concerned with the generalization of a single activity, all comparisons are made to the demonstrated target activity. Our approach uses a two-phase process. In the first phase (ME in Figure 1) a single demonstration of an activity, e.g., "picking up a medical kit" as might be critical for a search-and-rescue robot – the situation encoded in a "propositional frame" is elaborated upon to develop alternatives cases. Each valid case is then compared to the original case in the second phase (GenA). Comparisons attempt to find an analogical mapping between the cases. Based on these mappings and an evaluation of the similarity between the cases, the most salient items in the case are identified and incorporated into a generalization of the activity.

4.1   Mental Elaboration

The Mental Elaboration (ME) phase of MEGA produces a set of alternative cases based on a single given case. This process is described in Algorithm 1. The case is altered along two dimensions, feature and object, to create combinations

---

Algorithm 1. Mental Elaboration

Require: *base* case - propositional frame describing demonstrated action
  $H \leftarrow \{base\}$
  $H \leftarrow H \cup objAlts(base)$
  $OUT \leftarrow \emptyset$
  for all $hcase \in H$ **do**
    $candidates \leftarrow featAlts(hcase)$
    for all $c \in candidates$ **do**
      if valid(c) **then**
        $OUT \leftarrow OUT \cup c$
      end if
    end for
  end for
  return OUT

---

of variations. We begin with generating the object alternatives (*objAlts*) for the base case, and then generating a set of feature alternatives (*featAlts*) for each object alternative. Together this creates a set of candidate cases that are varied along the feature and object dimensions. Candidates are filtered to check for validity and consistency before being accepted as an alternative case for generalization consideration.

Object Dimension. The object dimension represents different entities that are involved in the context on the activity. The intent of the object dimension is to identify the range of objects to which the activity can be applied. The mental elaboration process imagines other objects that may fit the scenario. To illustrate this process, we will use the example of a "medical kit" that is defined as "a white box with a red cross on it and a handle on top". The alternative cases will range over objects that have handles, some of which may be highly similar to the medical kit, such as toolboxes or a suitcase. Some objects, however, have handles in a different orientation, like a mug or a milk jug. Other objects have multiple handles, like a suitcase (one on the side, one on top) and a tote bag (two handles that come together to form a single handle). Additionally, objects that have handles but are not intended for lifting, like a door, are also included as alternative cases. Table 1 lists all considered objects, including the number of alternative cases used in the generalization phase. The total includes variations along the feature dimension and then checked to meet basic validation constraints. Each of these processes are discussed further below.

Each scenario - which includes the object to be lifted, the agent doing the lifting, and descriptions of the start and end states - is captured in a propositional frame called a "case". For each alternative object, a duplicate case is generated with the original object and its corresponding facts removed and the new object and its facts inserted in its place. The facts relating to the object are defined in the knowledge base and include features like the shape, color, and position and location of handle(s). Examples of facts from the knowledge base related to a a medical kit and those related to one alternative object are shown in Table 2.

Table 1. The objects considered vary in the number of handles, location of the handle, and the purpose of the handle. The alternative objects generated that pass the validation constraints are the source of the generalized action.

object	# handles	handle location(s)	lifting handle	alternatives
medical kit	1	top	yes	144
toolbox	1	top	yes	1512
suitcase	2	top/side	yes	5292
basket	1	top	yes	648
tote bag	2	top	yes	648
mug	1	side	yes	324
milk jug	1	side	yes	432
door	1	side	no	432

Feature Dimension. Exploring the relevant feature space is done through alterations along the feature dimension. We include amongst the features not only attributes like color and shape but also relations like spatial orientation. The intent of making alterations along this dimension is to identify which features are significant to the activity to be generalized. For example, in most cases the color of an object has no influence on how one manipulates the object. However, the orientation of the handle relative to the object is significant in many activities.

Only a small set of the features may be integral and necessary for the activity, and the challenge is to efficiently identify them. In analogical comparisons, greater contributions to the similarity of two cases originate from higher-order relations and enhance the systematicity of the case. Hence, we expect that the features that are less important contribute less to the overall structure of the representation of the context and should not be included in the generalization of the action. One example of the difference between significant and insignificant features is the color of the medical kit versus the force exerted on the handle of the medical kit. The color is only referenced in relation to the medical kit, and thus the color of the medical kit is irrelevant. The upward force exerted on the handle is referenced in three relations, thus it is a significant feature and is necessary for lifting the object by its handle.

Note that recognizing these differences is problematic for many statistical approaches that primarily rely on frequency of features. E.g., if the majority of the objects lifted are white, then it is inferred that the action requires the object to be white. Similarly, to teach a robot to place a yellow object on a higher platform requires a series of trials consistently demonstrating the proper placing of the yellow object [6]. The intent of our approach is to leverage mental simulation and analogy-based comparisons to enable the identification of the significant and influential features of the scenario from a single demonstration. If the color of the object is significant to the action, then this is captured in the representation of the scenario with the color being related to some other entity in the scenario. This information may originate from natural language instruction and then encoded as a proposition in the scenario.

Table 2. The facts on the left are related to a medical kit and are replaced by the facts about a mug on the right when generating the alternative case for the mug

medical kit	mug
| ```
(medical-kit ?instance (
   (medical-kit ?instance)
   (box ?instance)
   (rigid-object ?instance)
   (has-color ?instance white1)
   (white white1)
   (greater-than (width ?instance)
    (height ?instance))
   (handle handle0)
   (graspable handle0)
   (has-part ?instance handle0)
   (on-top-of handle0 ?instance)
   (connection c1)
   (end-of c1 ?instance)
   (end-of c1 handle0)
   (rigid-object c1)
   (left-of c1
      (center-of-mass ?instance))
   (connection c2)
   (end-of c2 ?instance)
   (end-of c2 handle0)
   (rigid-object c2)
   (right-of c2
    (center-of-mass ?instance))))
``` | ```
(mug ?instance (
   (mug ?instance)
   (cylinder ?instance)
   (rigid-object ?instance)
   (has-color ?instance white1)
   (white white1)
   (equal (width ?instance)
    (height ?instance))
   (handle handle0)
   (graspable handle0)
   (has-part ?instance handle0)
   (on-side-of handle0 ?instance)
   (connection c1)
   (end-of c1 ?instance)
   (end-of c1 handle0)
   (rigid-object c1)
   (right-of c1
      (center-of-mass ?instance))
   (connection c2)
   (end-of c2 ?instance)
   (end-of c2 handle0)
   (rigid-object c2)
   (right-of c2
    (center-of-mass ?instance))))
``` |

Modifying propositions and creating sets of modifications generates new alternative cases. Changes along the feature dimension consists of modifying classes, attributes, and relations. Table 3 lists the features of each type that are included in the demonstrated scenario. The knowledge base contains a range of possible values for each feature.

Each type of feature requires its own rules for finding alternative values. Each rule follows the pattern of verifying that the proposition is true in the scenario, identifies a value for that feature, and verifies that the new value is different than the original. A rule for changing the class of an entity is the following:

```
(<- (change-class (?type ?entity) (?new-type ?entity))
    (instanceof ?entity ?type)     ;; entity is an instance of type
    (isa ?type ?super)             ;; type is known to have a super class
    (isa ?new-type ?super)         ;; new-type is a member of the class
    (different ?type ?new-type))   ;; new-type and type are not the same
```

The *change-class* rule is applied to propositions in the case that define the class of an entity. Similar rules are used to change attribute values and relationship types. Combinations of these values produces the new cases along the

Table 3. Each feature and its set of valid values

type	feature	values
class	agent	human, robot
class	surface	table, floor, shelf
class	color	white, red, blue, gray, maroon, pink, yellow
attribute	shape	box, cylinder, cube, flat, spherical
relationship	spatial	left-of, right-of
relationship	inequality	equal, less-than, greater-than

feature dimension. For example, an alternative case for lifting the medical kit will have the agent modified to be a robot. Another case will have the robot as the agent and the color of the kit is yellow.

Validation of Features. Not all feature values or combinations of values are always valid for all objects (e.g., cubic or box-shaped mugs are invalid). The validation rules, which are based on knowledge of valid features of an object, verify that the combination of features is acceptable. For example, we require that any medical kit be either red or white. If no validation rules pass, then the case is rejected. Once a generated case has been determined to be valid, it is made available for the generalization process. The tally of valid cases generated for each object type is shown in Table 1.

MEGA requires a knowledge base of facts and rules that are assumed background knowledge needed to quickly learn. However, the whole MEGA process requires very little knowledge. The generation and validation of the alternative cases requires less than 250 facts and 50 rules. The majority of the facts are descriptions of objects, and the most of the rules define the Mental Elaboration (ME) process and are independent of the objects and features included in the knowledge base. Expanding the knowledge base to incorporate additional objects to be used in the ME process mostly requires an addition of roughly 20 facts (see examples in Table 2). Constraints on valid features of each object is currently defined as a set of rules, which also would need to be added to the knowledge base when including new objects.

4.2   Generalization by Analogy

Once all the alternative cases have been generated, we identify the similarities in the cases to construct the generalization. Using a computational model of analogy, we can select the items in the cases that are most significant. The structure mapping engine (SME) [7] is an analogical reasoning engine that adheres to the principles of structure mapping theory [8]. SME compares representations of the two cases by finding correspondences between items in each representation. This processes is governed by the constraints of *structural consistency*: *one-to-one mapping* and *parallel connectivity*. A one-to-one mapping means that a structurally consistent mapping between the base case and the target case does not include any item in the base case being mapped to more than one item in the target case, and vice versa. Parallel connectivity requires the arguments of a

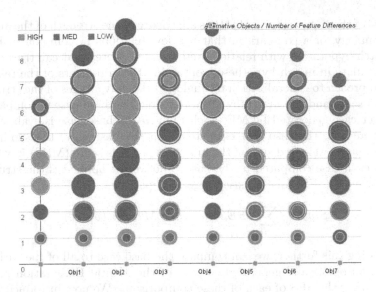

Fig. 2. The horizontal axis has the alternative objects considered, from left to right: medical kit, toolbox, suitcase, basket, tote bag, mug, milk jug, and door. The vertical axis is the number of feature differences. The size of the circle is how many cases were generated. The color of the circle shows how similar the case is to the original case of lifting a medical kit.

pair of statements to be mapped if the statements are in correspondence. Additionally, SME implements the *systematicity principle*, which requires relations that are included in the analogy to be part of a system of relations. It has been shown that people identify the key facts in an analogy as the one that are part of a system of connected relations [4].

These principles are key in identifying salient elements in a scenario where an action is used. For example, a one-to-one mapping associates the agent in the base case doing the lifting to the agent in the new case doing the lifting. Mapping it to multiple agents is not appropriate as a two agent lifting action has many differences compared to a single agent lifting. Systematicity is also crucial because it helps differentiate between elements that are essential in the scenario and those that are just surface features. Essential elements are likely to take part in multiple relations. For example, the hand is essential in the lifting action. It is part of the relations defining it as part of the agent, as part of the action, and as the thing grasping the object. It is not necessary that it be a hand, but some common entity must fill the role of being part of the agent, be involved in the lifting action, and grasping the object.

The analogical comparison process done by SME constructs proposed correspondences between an item in the base case and an item in the target. Each correspondence, called a *match hypothesis*, is assigned a score based on an initial value and some value inherited from a parent match hypotheses. The sum of all the match hypothesis scores produces the overall structural evaluation score (SES) for the whole comparison. This score is a measure of the structural soundness of the comparison and is thus a measure of the strength of the analogy. A poor analogy, or a comparison that has few relations in common, will have fewer match hypotheses with relations and thus less scores that can trickle down and accumulate in match hypotheses containing the arguments of the relation.

Our approach to generalization by analogy takes advantages of the structural evaluation score and the match hypothesis score. The base case is compared to each target case generated by ME. Each item in the base case is evaluated for its significance to the case. For each item i in the base case, the significance score (Sig) is the weighted sum of the match hypothesis score (MHS) in which it occurs in each case compared to the base. The weight applied is the structural evaluation score (SES) for the base/target comparison.

$$Sig_i = \sum_{c \in cases} SES(base, c) * MHS(i, base, c) \tag{1}$$

Extending this further, we can compare the base case to all of the variations that were automatically generated as part of the Mental Elaboration process. Figure 2 shows the SES of each of these comparisons. We now introduce GenA, an engine for automatically doing these comparisons, identifying the most significant elements of the cases, and producing a generalization of the base case. Algorithm 2 describes this process. It begins with the demonstrated cases and the alternative cases generated from it. For each of these generated cases, it is compared with the demonstrated case. This is an analogical comparison that produces a set of mappings between items in the cases. The mapping with the best score is further analyzed. For each match hypotheses (mh) in the mapping, the score of the mh is added to the score of the base item in the mh. At this point, each item has a a significance rating associated to it. If the item significance is greater than a threshold, it is included in the generalization.

Filtering all the expressions to include only those with a significance greater than some threshold ensures that the generalization includes only the most important expressions. If an expression has a valid mapping in each analogy then it is likely the expression is necessary for the generalization. If it has a mapping in the majority of the cases, then it is still likely to be an important expression. Given these assumptions, we calculate the threshold as the minimum score for an expression if it has a mapping in the majority of cases and each of these cases is a perfect analogy.

5   Measure Applicability of Novelty

When a new, and potentially novel, scenario is presented, a comparison of the scenario with the generalized action case reveals the applicability of the action to the new scenario. This process, called Measure Applicability of Novelty (MAN), uses SME to compare the new case to the generalized case. If the cases are sufficiently similar, then the inferences produced by SME are examined. The candidate inferences provides potential projections of the generalized case onto the novel case. The most important projections are the action and its parameters.

Algorithm 2. Generalization by Analogy

Require: *base* - demonstrated case
Require: *generatedCases* - generated alternative cases
   items ← items(*base*)
   for all *gencase* ∈ *generatedCases* **do**
      mappings ←compare(*base*, *gencase*)
      bm ←greatestSES(*mappings*)
      ses ←score(*bm*)
      for all *mh* ∈mhs(*bm*)) **do**
         baseItem ←base(*mh*)
         if *baseItem* ∈ *items* **then**
            sig(*baseItem*) ←score(*baseItem*) + score(*mh*)
         end if
      end for
   end for
   threshold ←computeThreshold(*base*)
   keeprItems ←filter(*items*, *threshold*)
   return expressions(*keeprItems*)

The comparison with the generalization and inferences made about the new situation is a similar process to that used in case-based reasoning [10]. However, SME is a domain-general engine for adapting the new scenario. Additionally, it provides a common mechanism across the MEGA and MAN components.

We evaluate the quality and utility of the generalized action by presenting a novel scenario to MAN. It is our hypothesis that the generalized action will be most similar to novel scenarios that have a handle for lifting on top of the object. It is also expected that the process will be resilient to feature variations that were not previously seen.

The novel scenario has a brown briefcase sitting on a desk. The goal is for the robot to be holding the briefcase above the desk. We also introduce additional features to the scenario to show that these are easily ignored. We add that the handle is black and, the briefcase is metallic, and the briefcase is heavy. The intent is for MAN to determine that the generalized action case for lift-up is similar to this novel scenario and that the parameters to the lift-up activity are the robot and its hand.

Comparing the generalized activity to a variety of other novel scenarios shows a consistent pattern. In all these novel cases, the surface is a desk, which was never seen in the original demonstration or the mental elaboration of it. We also introduce new objects: a hammer, a desk drawer, a cooking pan, and a soda can. It is important to note that a soda can clearly does not have a handle, and it would be anticipated that this scenario would be less similar. Additionally, we try objects that were included in the elaboration phase but with never seen before features (e.g., black handles, red cross on medical kit, and suitcase with a single handle). In keeping consistency with our intent to have the robot learn to perform these actions, all of these novel cases have the robot performing the action.

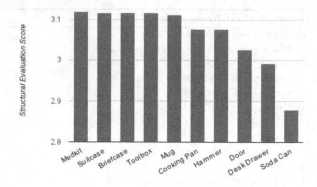

Fig. 3. The generalized action is most similar to objects with a handle on top. Other orientations and uses of handles result in even less similarity. Finally, an object without a handle is least similar.

Figure 3 shows that one class of scenarios (medical kit, suitcase, briefcase, tool-box, and mug) have nearly the same similarity score to the generalized case. This similarity drops off as the action becomes less applicable to the scenario. The cooking pan and hammer each have a handle, but the handle is attached to the object in a different manner, leading to the diminished similarity. The door and the desk drawer have handles, but they are not lifting handles. Finally, the least similar case is a soda can because it does not have a handle.

6   Discussion and Conclusion

Being able to quickly learn is not only a feature of human learning but is critical for developing natural interactions with robots. We have presented a system that learns to apply an activity to novel situations based on a single demonstration of the activity. Through a process of Mental Elaboration and Generalization by Analogy (MEGA), we are able to determine the most significant elements in the application of an action and create a generalized action. We demonstrated the quality of the generalization by comparing to new situations. In addition to the comparison results being as expected, the analogical comparison produces inferences that includes the action and the proper bindings of the action's variables.

While the solution proposed here bears great promise, there are some potential issues. The representation of the cases is important, but much of the information included is general world knowledge. The Mental Elaboration phase relies on a knowledge base that contains facts about the structure and features of objects and ontological relations of entities. However, rapid learning by humans is also greatly dependent on background knowledge. In addition to requiring a relatively small knowledge base, SME (which is at the core of our approach) does not require any background knowledge.

Future work will focus on integrating the algorithms introduced in this paper into a robotic architecture. This type of integration will bring various challenges such as extracting the symbolic expressions needed for MEGA from the perceptual components. However, it will also allow us to utilize other features of the architecture, namely the simulation components. Supplementing MEGA with a simulation of cases that are sufficiently similar will reveal which of the cases are physically impossible and thus can be ruled out. An additional future development is reducing the overall computational complexity of MEGA. The greatest efficiencies can be gained from limiting object alternatives to similar objects, a heuristic search on which features to vary, and only generating enough alternative cases to construct a cohesive generalization.

Acknowledgments. This work was supported by ONR BRC #N00014-11-1-0493.

References

1. Argall, B.D., Chernova, S., Veloso, M., Browning, B.: A survey of robot learning from demonstration. Robotics and Autonomous Systems **57**, 469–483 (2009)
2. Cantrell, R., Schermerhorn, P., Scheutz, M.: Learning actions from human-robot dialogues. In: Proc. 2011 IEEE Symp. Robot and Human Interactive Comm. (2011)
3. Chen, X., Xie, J., Ji, J., Sui, Z.: Toward open knowledge enabling for human-robot interaction. J. of Human-Robot Interaction **1**(2), 100–117 (2012)
4. Clement, C., Gentner, D.: Systematicity as a selection constraint in analogical mapping. Cognitive Science **132**, 89–132 (1991)
5. Dominey, P.F., Mallet, A., Yoshida, E.: Real-time spoken-language programming for cooperative interaction with a humanoid apprentice. Intl. J. of Humanoid Robotics **6**(2), 147–171 (2009)
6. Erlhagen, W., Mukovskiy, A., Bicho, E., Panin, G.: Goal-directed Imitation for Robots: A Bio-inspired Approach to Action Understanding and Skill Learning. Robotics and Autonomous Systems **54**(5), 353–360 (2006)
7. Falkenhainer, B., Forbus, K., Gentner, D.: The structure-mapping engine: Algorithm and examples. Artificial Intelligence **41**, 1–63 (1989)
8. Gentner, D.: Structure-mapping: A theoretical framework for analogy. Cognitive Science **7**, 155–170 (1983)
9. Kuehne, S., Forbus, K., Gentner, D., Quinn, B.: Category learning as progressive abstraction using structure mapping. In: Proc. 22nd Cognitive Sci. Conf. (2000)
10. Lopez De Mantaras, R., McSherry, D., Bridge, D., Leake, D., Smyth, B., Craw, S., Faltings, B., Maher, M.L., Cox, M.T., Forbus, K., et al.: Retrieval, reuse, revision and retention in case-based reasoning. Knowledge Eng. Review **20**(03), 215–240 (2005)
11. Mohan, S., Mininger, A., Kirk, J., Laird, J.E.: Learning grounded language through situated interactive instruction. AAAI Fall Symp. Series, pp. 30–37 (2012)
12. Nyga, D., Beetz, M.: Everything robots always wanted to know about housework (but were afraid to ask). In: 2012 IEEE/RSJ Intl. Conf. on Intelligent Robots and Systems (IROS), pp. 243–250. IEEE (2012)
13. Scheutz, M., Schermerhorn, P., Kramer, J., Anderson, D.: First steps toward natural human-like HRI. Autonomous Robots **22**(4), 411–423 (2007)

Vision

Feedback-Based Parameterized Strategies for Improving Performance of Video Surveillance Understanding Frameworks

Nuria Sánchez[✉], Noa García, and José Manuel Menéndez

Grupo de Aplicación de Telecomunicaciones Visuales. ETSI. Telecomunicación,
Universidad Politécnica de Madrid. Av Complutense, 30. Madrid – 28040, Spain
{nsa,ngd,jmm}@gatv.ssr.upm.es

Abstract. One of the most ambitious objectives for the Computer Vision research community is to achieve for machines similar capacities to the human's visual and cognitive system, and thus provide a trustworthy description of what is happening in the scene under surveillance. Most of hierarchic and intelligent video-based understanding frameworks proposed so far allow the development of systems with necessary perception, interpretation and learning capabilities to extract knowledge from a broad set of scenarios, having in common the one-way sequential structure of the functional processing units that compose the system. However, only in a limited number of works, once visual evidence is achieved, feedback is provided within the system to improve system's performance in any sense. With this motivation, a methodology for introducing feedback in perceptual systems is proposed. Experimental results demonstrate how different parameterized strategies let the system overcome limitations mainly due to sudden changes in the environmental conditions.

Keywords: Feedback · Scene understanding · Visual interpretation · Knowledge representation · Framework

1 Introduction

One of the most ambitious objectives for the computer vision and pattern recognition research community is to achieve for machines similar capacities to the human's visual and cognitive system, thus, allowing them to understand automatically what is happening in the scene. In the past years, several approaches for the automatic analysis, recognition and description of human-related behaviours have been proposed. As a result, a number of generic integrative frameworks for scenario understanding can be found in the literature.

In a typical Intelligent Transportation Systems scenario [1], where humans and/or vehicles are the usual target objects whose behaviours are analysed, effective and real-time sensor analysis has shown to be a key factor for establishing a reliable monitoring infrastructure [2]. In addition, intelligent capabilities have been proven

© Springer International Publishing Switzerland 2014
A.L.C. Bazzan and K. Pichara (Eds.): IBERAMIA 2014, LNAI 8864, pp. 509–520, 2014.
DOI: 10.1007/978-3-319-12027-0_41

necessary to let these systems reach their full potential [3]. Frameworks like the one proposed in [4] set the basis for developing systems with the necessary perception, interpretation and learning capabilities to understand what is happening in the scene under surveillance. However, there is a need for improving automated surveillance systems' performance, as the environments become more loosely controlled.

Accomplishing so ambitious task requires the incorporation in this kind of understanding frameworks of a feedback control module, like the one proposed in this paper, able to monitor the information processed at different levels of abstraction, control the interactions among independent processing modules and launch at each moment the most suitable feedback strategy so that detection and classification results can be improved.

Experiments will demonstrate, from a practical point of view, the flexibility and effectiveness of the proposed feedback-based parameterized strategies in two different video surveillance domains, having set up the basis for the improvement of existing applications that aim to understand human-related scenarios in other environments.

2   Related Work

In recent years, many automated video understanding systems have been proposed for monitoring human and/or vehicles activities in real scenarios [4]. PRISMATICA [2] and the IBM Smart Surveillance System [5] represent some of the most sophisticated video surveillance systems developed to detect relevant situations in complex real environments such as urban traffic or public transport. In these systems, once system goals are defined, information from a set of selected sensors uses to be analysed using state-of-the-art image processing algorithms and stochastic techniques for data analysis. The common goal consists of translating data in a set of low-level features that provide motion information in the scene as well as other visual cues, allowing the detection, classification and tracking of objects of interest. As a result, higher-level spatio-temporal reasoning modules are provided with the necessary knowledge about the objects and their context, which allows the system to make an inference about the activity being carried out and therefore to describe the scene.

All of them have in common the one-way sequential structure of the functional units that compose the system, i.e. only one module uses to be active at any time, and the communication between modules is unidirectional. Only in a limited number of works, once visual evidence is achieved, feedback is provided within the system to exploit the redundancy of processing enabled at different levels of abstraction in order to improve system's performance in any sense [6]. Feedback is usually introduced either to correct an error or to seek for more information that may help the system to resolve any uncertainty [7]. Focusing on Computer Vision-based applications, the possible strategies to be applied range from fine parameter tuning to overcome limitations due to change in the environmental conditions to the selection of a more suitable image processing algorithm according to the requirements of a particular moment [8].

At the same time, feedback strategies uses to be applied only on individual processing stages with the objective to enhance the results of each stage independently of the results obtained in the other [9]. However, from the authors' point of view, the real challenge consists of exploiting expectations derived from high-level analysis to improve the performance of lower levels of analysis in a more autonomous way, contributing thus to the development of more reliable and intelligent systems [10][11].

Among these solutions, it can be found, for instance, a self-adaptive real-time tracking system able to judge their own performance and to apply specific repair strategies on other low-level modules when needed; or a video surveillance system able to switch when the people density increases in the scene from an individual to a crowd tracking algorithm is found. In advanced solutions like these, a control module is usually in charge of managing information of completely different nature. In addition, agreement on data structures and reference models is needed to allow bidirectional exchanges of knowledge, so that the output from one module has direct influence on the other module before it finishes processing. But, while it is clear that the concrete implementation of these modules will be always application dependent, a more detailed description of the necessary steps to design a generic feedback control component is needed, so that these video understanding frameworks can be easily adapted to a wide range of domains.

With this motivation, a new methodology for introducing parameterized feedback in perceptual systems is presented in the next Section. The approach assumes that a modular and hierarchical framework for scenario understanding is available, so that different system routines can effectively work at different processing levels A global feedback-based analysis strategy can be thus exploited to combine top-down with bottom-up information in a closed feedback loop. One of the advantages of the proposed solution is that it contributes to simplify the design of this kind of systems considerably since all the required steps are well structured and formalized. It will be demonstrated how thanks to the suitable repair strategy, the performance of baseline systems used for the experiments can be iteratively improved.

3   Challenges of Video Surveillance in Transport Related Scenarios

Many efforts are being made by the scientific community to develop systems able to provide reliable outdoor surveillance at all times, with the capability to cope with changing light and climate conditions, from one minute to the next, and from brightest daylight to darkest night. However, while sensors being deployed already integrate the necessary capabilities to provide clear image quality regardless of weather, lighting or image complexity, processing algorithms which most of video surveillance systems rely on, require of a costly and continuous manual fine tuning in order to be able to adapt to any change in the environmental physical conditions. In order to let the reader understand better the benefits of the integration of feedback control strategies to design more reliable video surveillance systems, before presenting it, two different scenarios will be studied.

First video understanding framework of reference that will serve as baseline system for our experiments is the outdoor vacant parking space detector system proposed by authors in [12] which strongly relies on pyramid of histogram of gradients (PHOG descriptor) extracted from the region of interest to infer whether that region is really occupied or not. Main problems faced by this kind of systems are the low contrast of dark vehicles in shadowed areas in general, most challenging even in a cloudy or rainy day (Figure 1a), and the sudden changes in the illumination of a region when a shadow of any object in the surroundings is projected on the parking area (Figure 1b). The second video understanding framework of reference will be the system for the automatic detection of traffic incidents in highways proposed by authors in [13] which relies on a background subtraction method to warn about the possibilities of having a new stopped vehicle-related event registered by the system. Figure 1c shows the typical illumination challenge the system has to deal with due to shadow projected on the highway when the bridge crossing over is blocking the sun light source. This highway scenario will be also used to demonstrate the flexibility of the proposed approach to handle changes in the logical context and adapt to any new situations that may occur (e.g. after stopping, driver leaves the vehicle).

a   *b*   *c*

Fig. 1. Different captures from different scenarios under different environmental conditions. Figure *a* corresponds to a parking area in a rainy day in which low contrast images are usually acquired. Figures *b* shows an image from same scenario acquired in a sunny day when shadow cast associated to building in the proximity is projected over the parking area. Figure *c* shows similar problem found in a different scenario (M-12 highway in Spain).

4   Integration of Feedback Control Strategies in the Design of Self-adaptive Perceptual Systems

Feedback can be defined as the process by which a specific processing stage receives information about its success, or otherwise, its bad performance together with the corresponding decision on the most suitable strategy the system needs to launch for its self-improvement [7]. Based on a hypothesis generation-hypothesis verification approach, a general self-adaptive processing scheme to improve classical video understanding frameworks is proposed in this paper as shown in Figure 2.

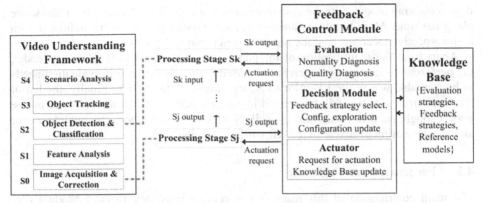

Fig. 2. General self-adaptive processing scheme proposed in this paper to improve performance of classical video understanding frameworks like the ones proposed in [12] and [13]

Unlike other feedback schemes, our approach allows the parameterization of the steps that support the feedback process, ensuring its applicability with independence of the domain, the specific task to be solved and the processing stage(s) which the system will act on. More details are provided in the following sections.

4.1   Knowledge-Based Reference Model, Evaluation and Feedback Strategies

According to authors in [14], a model of system objectives should be the first step in the formulation. Following the schema proposed in Figure 2, the relevant information that is necessary and sufficient for developing a convenient solution needs to be identified and stored in an independent module known as Knowledge Base (KB), contributing thus to favour reusability of developed modules. It is basically a structured database with the *reference model* that lets the Feedback Control Module start operating. Among the information of different nature the most representative is: the list of available algorithms for executing a specific task along with their corresponding identifiers and descriptions, with the input/output variables; configuration parameters with their individual range; and, finally, the contextual data linked to a particular video surveillance scenario integrating information about target objects and key events to be detected, and other logical, spatial or temporal constraints that support the analysis.

For instance, the reference model for the vacant space detector presented in [12] and described above would be composed of the corresponding well-known image-processing algorithms for vehicle modelling in 3D, object detection and target classification. Input/output variables would be image frames, low-level features relying on a set of PHOG descriptors and final target locations respectively. Different configuration parameters could be set as well, from image contrast c to the detection thresholds whose values may range from a minimum $th1$ to a maximum value $th2$. In the case of the highway incident detection system [13], the reference model would be defined by an adaptive background modelling module which provides information about motion in the image; followed by a shape-based object detection approach in which parameters such as motion detection threshold th or shape confidence coefficient sh can be adjusted to focus the detection on vehicles and people respectively. Finally, output from a tracking module lets the system supervise at high-level the activity in the scene along the time. Main output parameters are foreground pixels, blob candidates with their respective locations, and the semantic description of events.

Apart from the identification of the particular knowledge-based reference model, the *performance and quality criteria* to be used for the system's self-evaluation needs to be available within the KB prior to the execution of the system. Finally, the list of *feedback strategies* that will be applied in case the result after evaluation may not be good enough, need to be defined as well. Next section introduces the module where all the information available in the KB will be exploited.

4.2 Feedback Control Module

The main contribution of this paper is the generic Feedback Control Module presented in Figure 2, necessary for providing any perceptual system with the necessary self-adaptive capabilities to overcome the typical problems this kind of systems suffer from. This control module is composed of three main sub-modules, which are common to any particular implementation: Evaluation, Decision and Actuation. This basic structure allows the formalization of the general approach to let the system respectively: 1) perform its own diagnosis for self-assessment based on predefined performance or quality criteria; 2) autonomously make a decision on the most appropriate feedback strategy for corrective action or completeness; and, 3) make the corresponding request to a particular module within a processing stage Si with $i = 1, 2...N$, being $N \in Z$ the number of processing stages. The Actuation module is also in charge of keeping the KB continuously updated by tracking changes in the reference model. Specific actions to be carried out by the system during these steps need to be carefully defined. But, in order to ensure the independence of these modules, a good interface is first necessary.

Table 1. Generic communication interface for a self-adaptive processing scheme

Evaluation-related commands
negEval: Negative evaluation after applying performance or quality criteria
posEval: Positive evaluation after applying performance or quality criteria
Decision-related commands
initKB: Initializes the files and defaults necessary to start processing
updateKB: Asks the decision module to make the Knowledge Base up-to-date
getNewStrategy from <feedback_strategies>: New strategy can be still applied
Actuation-related commands
stateUpdate: Confirms the last state in which the processing stage is
selectAlgo from <algorithm_list>: Select algorithm to start processing with
selectParam from <config_param_list>: Select parameter for running algorithm
selectValue from <config_param><type><range_values>: Select value for a parameter
changeAlgo <algorithm_list>: Request for changing the algorithm currently used
changeParam <config_param>: Modify the configuration parameter to be used
changeValue <range_values>: Modify value of the configuration parameter used
infoRequest: Additional queries made by system to retrieve additional information.
responseToQuery: Binary response to additional queries made

For its design, we have taken into account basic semantic information that all modules within the framework should be able to understand in order to increase their knowledge and be able to react after first assessment is made. The most relevant functions used are the ones described in Table 1. Other commands not included allow the communication between the Feedback Control Module and the Knowledge Base.

Evaluation: Normality and Quality Diagnosis Based on Predefined Criteria

For a normality diagnosis, performance evaluation measures allow the Evaluation module automatically measure the 'error' or deviation with respect to the defined value of reference. Quality measures can be also defined as part of the quality diagnosis process inside this module. The performance evaluation and quality measures space is composed of: the list of performance and quality variables, its type and the acceptable response. A space within the KB is reserved for storing this information.

Most of performance measures applied in the literature consist of comparing findings with ground truth. This way, performance variables such as Precision, Recall or Accuracy can be calculated. For instance, in [12] the accuracy is based on the ratio of samples that the system has been able to classify correctly as vehicle among all samples. In the second case [13], authors calculate accuracy comparing the times a particular event ('stopped vehicle') are correctly detected during a video sequence. To let the system further assess on the quality of the results, other measures can be defined. As an example, local contrast or cast shadow probability could be computed for a particular zone within the parking area in [12]; while a shape confidence coefficient could be calculated at each iteration of the tracking module in [13].

Decision and Actuation: From Selection to Validation of Feedback Strategies

One of the most relevant contributions of the present work is the parameterization of the multiple feedback strategies that can be launched to improve the accuracy of this kind of systems. Following the approach in [15], two kinds of feedback strategies are considered: a *repair-oriented feedback* and a *focus-oriented feedback*. The first aims to eliminate errors due to the inconsistency of the new findings in level Sj and the knowledge of level Sk. The second aims to refine or increment the existing information at any abstraction level. A procedure for managing the interaction between such strategies is then required. Using as input the system evaluation response, a rule-based decision module is proposed as an appropriate solution to achieve this objective. Finally, an actuator is in charge of performing the corresponding decisions and assessing on the suitability of the feedback strategy followed.

First consideration as part of repair-oriented feedback strategies is that decision on the algorithm to be executed at any new iteration needs to be made. The algorithm does not need to be necessarily the same. Additionally, in case of the same algorithm is applied, an adjustment of the initial configuration parameters may be needed. However, sometimes, lack of detail at low level avoids the system being able to detect an object or event with high probability. Focus-oriented feedback strategies would be more suitable in this case to enhance the knowledge about the scenario the system has. Table 2 summarizes the different feedback strategies that would improve the accuracy of systems presented in [12] and [13], altogether with the conditions that must be met to launch the process.

Table 2. List of possible feedback strategies for the scenarios described in Section 3. Corresponding processing stages are identified by *Si* label following the representation in Fig 2. Activity within the Evaluation (E), Decision (D) and Actuator (A) is also identified.

	Outdoor vacant parking space detector system [12]	System for the automatic detection of incidents in highways [13]
Repair-oriented feedback strategies	**E** > Accuracy of vehicle detector (S2) below expected. Compute cast shadow probability in S0 to confirm illumination transition in the parking zone. **D** > If transition confirmed, ask S0 to increase image contrast locally. **A** > Actuate on processing stage S0 and continue (S1-S2) **E** > Check if accuracy is improved.	**E** > Accuracy of event detector (S4) below expected. Compute cast shadow probability in S0 to confirm illumination transition in the highway area. **D** > If transition confirmed, ask S1 to adjust motion detection threshold **A** > Actuate on S1 and continue **E** > Check if accuracy is improved.
Focus-oriented feedback strategies	**E** > Accuracy of vehicle detector (S2) below expected but no illumination transition confirmed by S0. **D** > Ask feature analysis module (S1) to change feature extraction strategy (local edge enhancement before PHOG) **A** > Actuate on processing stage S1 and continue (S2) **E** > Check if accuracy is improved.	**E** > After stop vehicle has been detected, S4 fails to describe event linked to new object detected by S2. **D** > Ask tracking module S3 to compute shape confidence coefficient and ask S2 launch people detector **A** > Actuate on processing stages S3 and S2 and continue **E** > Check if a person is now detected. High-level description achieved (S4)

5   Experimental Results

In this section, experiments carried out to demonstrate the applicability of the proposed approach on different types of computer vision scenarios and methodologies are described. The objective behind the integration of feedback approaches is to let systems like the proposed in [12] and [13] efficiently tackle problems linked to challenges already identified in Section 3 in an autonomous way, i.e. the impossibility for the system to keep on detecting correctly vehicles when the illumination conditions suddenly change; and the lack of information that can be extracted from the region of interest in the case of low contrast images. Different video sequences corresponding to different scenarios were acquired using an AXIS IP camera: 'Parking B_191112' corresponds to a rainy day and 'Parking B_020713' to sunny day in the same parking area ([12] reported errors in the event of sudden illumination transition and due to dark vehicles on shadowed areas); 'Highway_M12_270711' to sunny day ([13] reported difficulties to detect stopped vehicle during illumination transition, and to detect person leaving the car). Then, details of specific routines implemented within the Feedback Control Module are given below. Information already provided in previous sections may be omitted in order to avoid repetitions.

We will focus first on the outdoor vacant space detector system proposed by authors in [12]. In a training stage, a first normality diagnosis based on differences between vehicle detection results got for frame *f* and ground truth are computed, so that the system is able to assess whether the current detection results in some zones of the parking area are not satisfactory and if, therefore, the accuracy of the system could be likely improved. A quality diagnosis is then performed by the Evaluation module. In particular, a shadow detector module within the image acquisition stage is asked to confirm whether a sudden transition from occlusion shadow to direct lighting up is happening or not. In the event of sudden illumination transition, once the evaluation is carried out, the Decision module selects the most suitable feedback strategy among all available in the Knowledge Base, in particular a repair-oriented strategy recommends increasing image contrast locally. A diagram showing the complete information flow is presented in Figure 3.

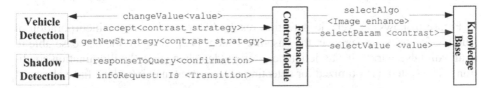

Fig. 3. Proposed repair-oriented feedback strategy for the system in [12]

As introduced in the previous section, objective behind focus-oriented feedback strategies is to let the system decide if the processing stage could provide additional information by executing an additional routine (e.g. multi-resolution analysis on ROI) or if there are elements that can be added to or excluded from the analysis (objects, events not included in the reference models) in order to maximize the information gathered at the same time noise is reduced. Feature analysis performed by system in [12] relies on the analysis of Pyramid Histogram of Oriented Gradients (PHOG) features which basically consists of a set of histograms of orientation gradients computed over an image region that is divided, at each resolution level, into a predetermined number of blocks. One of the problems faced by using these features is the lack of enough information in the presence of low illumination conditions. A focus-oriented feedback strategy is available, which allows the system in this case to have a more robust illumination insensitive image representation of dark vehicles in the image. The algorithm this feedback strategy relies on is the gradient-based pre-processing technique proposed in [16]. Pre-processing of region of interest is shown in Figure 4.

Fig. 4. For a low contrast vehicle sample (left) differences in the gradient image used by the detection stage in the baseline system (middle) and the one used by the same module after applying the focus-oriented feedback strategy (right)

A diagram showing the complete information flow in this case is presented in Figure 5.

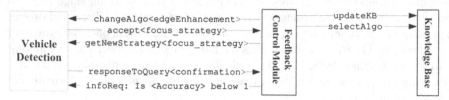

Fig. 5. Proposed focus-oriented feedback strategy for the system in [12]

Figure 6 shows the vehicle detection results before and after the incorporation of suitable feedback strategies in the baseline system [12], being in the last case able to deal with false alarms due to deficiencies or sudden changes in the illumination conditions. The system is optimized for detecting cars so vans may introduce false alarms.

Fig. 6. From left to right, figure shows respectively the improved results in the bottom and top regions after integrating feedback strategies in the baseline system [12]

We will finally show the flexibility of the proposed approach to cope with the requirements of the automatic incident detection system proposed in [13]. In this case, after illumination transition is detected by the Evaluation module, and once assessment on the list of possible feedback strategies is made by the Decision module, the Actuator requests the feature analysis module in charge of analysing motion to rerun the previous frame but with different configuration parameters to those using during the initialization. In this case, relying on the same algorithm (i.e. based on the well-known background subtraction approach) a different threshold is decided to be applied for the affected zone. The reference model available in the KB is updated accordingly with the new configuration parameter. Problems identified for this scenario are completely solved and performance, in terms of accuracy is increased.

Unlike other feedback related approaches which are focused on the improvement of single processing stages, our strategy covers the complete system so that a state-of-art comparison with such approaches is not possible. We will compare instead the results got by two video surveillance systems after applying both a repair-oriented and focus-oriented feedback strategies. Table 3 presents results on selected datasets corresponding to two different scenarios, showing the improvement of the initial system in terms of accuracy as defined before. Not all video sequences may be affected by the same problems. For instance, due to the constant illumination conditions, it may be the case of not registering sudden illumination transition so that the repair-oriented feedback strategy for the parking system proposed in this paper is never launched.

Table 3. Comparison of accuracy rates/final system response when feedback strategies are integrated in the operational workflow of the selected baseline systems [12] and [13]

Video sequence System tested	Vacant spaces detector [12]		Incident detect. [13]
	Parking B_191112	Parking B_ 020713	Highway_M12 _270711
Baseline system	0.937	0.821	No event detected
Baseline system + repair-oriented feedback strategy	N/A (no illumination transition)	0.873	Stopped vehicle detected
Baseline system + focus-oriented feedback strategy	0.972	0.886	Driver detected on hard shoulder

6   Conclusions and Future Work

Related work in the field serves to justify that, in addition to the emerging communication between two different processing stages which corresponds to a flow of bottom-up information from stage S-1 to its immediately higher level stage S, there is a clear need for a top-down information flow and a continuous updating process that allows the creation of more robust and reliable video surveillance systems. Thanks to the proposed parameterised approach, typical video understanding frameworks can be therefore extended to support the inclusion of the proposed feedback strategies. It has been shown that a well-structured knowledge base needs to be built to identify for each processing stage the reference models, evaluation criteria and the list of feedback analysis strategies to be applied. Once the Knowledge Base is ready, system can start operating in a more reliable and robust manner requiring little adjustment from the developers. The key advantages of the proposed feedback strategy over those integrated in other video understanding frameworks proposed so far are: (1) the global feedback control strategy is independent of the processing stage that triggers it; (2) a control module is in charge of dynamically orchestrating feedback data flow between two independent stages ensuring that information shared can be interpreted by any specific module at a particular abstraction level; (3) thanks to a common communication interface with the feedback control module, feedback not necessarily needs to flow from stage S to processing stage S-1, being possible the interaction between two modules of completely different semantic nature; finally, (4) such a well-structured approach allows the flexible implementation and integration of suitable feedback strategies in existing video understanding frameworks.

Experiments carried out on a baseline video surveillance system show the improvement in performance when different feedback strategies are integrated. In the future, other feedback strategies that exploit high temporal coherence among closer frames in the video sequence will be explored. In addition, additional tests combining multiple feedback strategies will be performed.

References

1. Kumar, P., Ranganath, S., Huang, W., Sengupta, K.: Framework for real-time behavior interpretation from traffic video. IEEE Transactions on Intelligent Transportation Systems **6**(1), 43–53 (2005)
2. Velastin, S.A., Boghossian, B.A., Lo, B.P.L., Sun, J., Vicencio-Silva, M.A.: PRISMATICA: toward ambient intelligence in public transport environments. IEEE Trans. Syst. Man Cybern. Part A **35**(1), 164–182 (2005)
3. Hu, W., Tan, T., Wang, L., Maybank, S.: A survey on visual surveillance of object motion and behaviors. IEEE Transactions on Systems, Man, and Cybernetics, Part C: Applications and Reviews **34**(3), 334–352 (2004)
4. Sánchez, N., Menéndez, J.M.: Video Analysis Architecture For Enhancing Pedestrian And Driver Safety In Public Environments. In: 10th International Workshop on Image Analysis for Multimedia Interactive Services (WIAMIS 2009), London (2009)
5. Tian, Y., Brown, L., Hampapur, A., Lu, M., Senior, A., Shu, C.: IBM smart surveillance system (S3): event based video surveillance system with an open and extensible framework. Machine Vision and Applications **19**(5), 315–327 (2008)
6. Oliver, N., Rosario, B., Pentland, A.P.: A Bayesian computer vision system for modelling human interactions. IEEE Transactions on Pattern Analysis and Machine Intelligence **22**(8), 831–843 (2000)
7. Mirmehdi, M., Palmer, P.L., Kittler, J., Dabis, H.: Complex feedback strategies for hypothesis generation and verification. In: BMVC, pp. 1–10 (1996)
8. Hall, D.: Automatic parameter regulation of perceptual systems. Image and Vision Computing **24**(8), 870–881 (2006)
9. Kim, J.: Improved Vehicle Detection Method Using Feedback-AdaBoost Learning. International Journal of Computer Theory & Engineering **5**(1) (2013)
10. Wang, J., Bebis, G., Nicolescu, M., Nicolescu, M., Miller, R.: Improving Target Detection by Coupling It with Tracking. Machine Vision and Applications **20**(4), 205–223 (2009)
11. García, A., Bescós, J.: Video Object Segmentation Based on Feedback Schemes Guided by a Low-Level Scene Ontology. In: Blanc-Talon, J., Bourennane, S., Philips, W., Popescu, D., Scheunders, P. (eds.) ACIVS 2008. LNCS, vol. 5259, pp. 322–333. Springer, Heidelberg (2008)
12. Bravo, C., Sánchez, N., García, N., Menéndez, J.M.: Outdoor Vacant Parking Space Detector for Improving Mobility in Smart Cities. In: Reis, L.P., Correia, L., Cascalho, J. (eds.) EPIA 2013. LNCS, vol. 8154, pp. 30–41. Springer, Heidelberg (2013)
13. Pecharromán, A., Sánchez, N., Torres, J., Menéndez, J.M.: Real-Time Incidents Detection in the Highways of the Future. In: 15th Portuguese Conference on Artificial Intelligence, EPIA 2011, pp. 108–121, Lisbon, Portugal, October 10-13 (2011)
14. Renouf, A., Clouard, R., Revenu, M.: A platform dedicated to knowledge engineering for the development of image processing applications In: AIDSS, pp. 271–276 (2007)
15. Carmona, E.J., Rincón, M., Bachiller, M., Martínez-Cantos, J., Martínez-Tomás, R., Mira, J.: On the effect of feedback in multilevel representation spaces for visual surveillance tasks. Neurocomputing **72**(4), 916–927 (2009)
16. Han, H., Shan, S., Chen, X., Gao, W.: A comparative study on illumination preprocessing in face recognition. Pattern Recognition **46**(6), 1691–1699 (2013)

Multi-Agent Systems

Imperfect Norm Enforcement in Stochastic Environments: An Analysis of Efficiency and Cost Tradeoffs

Moser Silva Fagundes[1]([✉]), Sascha Ossowski[2], and Felipe Meneguzzi[3]

[1] Federal Institute of Education, Science and Technology Sul-Rio-Grandense (IFSul),
Charqueadas, RS, Brazil
moserfagundes@charqueadas.ifsul.edu.br
[2] Centre for Intelligent Information Technologies (CETINIA),
University Rey Juan Carlos (URJC), Móstoles, Madrid, Spain
sascha.ossowski@urjc.es
[3] School of Informatics, Pontifical Catholic University of Rio
Grande do Sul (PUCRS), Porto Alegre, Brazil
felipe.meneguzzi@pucrs.br

Abstract. In heterogeneous multiagent systems, agents might interfere with each other either intentionally or unintentionally, as a side-effect of their activities. One approach to coordinating these agents is to restrict their activities by means of social norms whose compliance ensures certain system properties, or otherwise results in sanctions to violating agents. While most research on normative systems assumes a deterministic environment and norm enforcement mechanism, we formalize a normative system within an environment whereby agent actions have stochastic outcomes and norm enforcement follows a stochastic model in which stricter enforcement entails higher cost. Within this type of system, we analyze the tradeoff between norm enforcement efficiency (measured in number of norm violations) and its cost considering a population of norm-aware self-interested agents capable of building plans to maximize their expected utilities. Finally, we validate our analysis empirically through simulations in a representative scenario.

Keywords: NMDP · MDP · Stochastic · Norm · Enforcement

1 Introduction

Autonomous selfish agents in heterogenous societies must act in order to accomplish their individual objectives while taking into account potential disruption caused by other members of the society. The key challenge in designing these open societies is in ensuring that the agents are able to achieve their own goals while minimizing the impact of negative interference between their actions. When dealing with a small number of agents this problem is typically modeled using game theory, with algorithms designed to find strategies in some kind of equilibrium. However, finding a Nash equilibrium [11] with a lower bound on the

© Springer International Publishing Switzerland 2014
A.L.C. Bazzan and K. Pichara (Eds.): IBERAMIA 2014, LNAI 8864, pp. 523–535, 2014.
DOI: 10.1007/978-3-319-12027-0_42

expected payoff within a stochastic multiplayer game is undecidable in general, and typically contained in the PSPACE complexity class even with simplifications on the types of acceptable strategy in the equilibrium [16].

An alternative approach to achieve desirable properties within a multiagent society is to define societal norms [9] that regulate agent behavior. Norms use deontic concepts of obligations and prohibitions in the specification of soft-constraints on agent behavior, with failure to comply with the norms resulting in sanctions designed to restore a society to a desirable state. To ensure that a norm-regulated society operates as expected, it must provide enforcement mechanisms that monitor agent behavior and apply sanctions when transgressions are detected. As stated in [10], most existing work on norm-regulated agent societies assume a deterministic environment and disregard the norm enforcement cost, which limits the applicability of these techniques.

In this paper, we define the dynamics of the world and the norm enforcement mechanism in Section 2 without the assumption of determinism, and we formalize the decision making process of our agents with *Normative Markov Decision Processes* (NMDPs) [5–7] in Section 3. We consider a stochastic norm-based coordination mechanism aiming at ensuring that the multiagent system as a whole runs according to the properties specified in a set of social norms. Thus, agents are subjected to social norms, and failure to comply with these norms brings about some kind of sanction. Norms are enforced on the basis of the observation of the current world-state by a mechanism that detects violations with a certain probability. Within this model, we associate a cost such that stricter enforcement mechanisms incur a higher cost to the enforcement authority. Such an enforcement costing model mirrors the real world, where mechanisms with a higher probability of detecting (and sanctioning) violations are more expensive. We develop a simulation-based method to calculate this tradeoff (norm enforcement efficiency measured in number of norm violations and its cost), and show results for a representative scenario in Section 4. Finally, we conclude the paper pointing towards future developments in Section 5. In summary, this paper makes two major contributions. First, we define a rich stochastic norm enforcement mechanism in stochastic environments populated with self-interested rational agents, and second, we provide insights into the tradeoffs involved in norm enforcement.

2   Normative Stochastic Environment

2.1   World Model and Norms

Let $\mathcal{G} = \{a_1, \ldots, a_n\}$ be the set of agents operating in the multiagent system. The state space of an agent $a_i \in \mathcal{G}$ is defined as follows. Let $\mathcal{F}$ be the set of features that characterize different aspects of the states of the world. A feature $f_j \in \mathcal{F}$ can take on a finite number of values and $\mathcal{V}_{f_j}$ corresponds to the finite set of possible values of f_j. The state of an agent is a complete assignment of values to its features, and the state space $\mathcal{S}$ is the cross product of the value spaces for the features, i.e.: $\mathcal{S} = \times_{i=1}^{|\mathcal{F}|} \mathcal{V}_{f_j}$. The *current state* of the agents determines the system's current state and it is represented as a vector $\{s_1, \ldots, s_n\}$ in which s_i is the current state of the agent $a_i \in \mathcal{G}$. In our environment, the outcome of the actions is *stochastic*, that is, the intended resulting state of executing an action occurs with a given probability. For each state-transition, an agent receives an *immediate reward* and the sum of rewards received by this agent determines its *utility*. The current utility of the agents in $\mathcal{G}$ is represented as a vector $\mathcal{U} = \{u_1, \ldots, u_n\}$ in which u_i is the utility of $a_i \in \mathcal{G}$.

Although the various efforts to develop normative multiagent systems proposed in the literature differ on technical details, they all share the intuition that norms are constraints on the behaviour of agents, by means of which some global goals can be achieved [1]. Our approach is related to strands of research on governing environments [14] and coordination infrastructures [12], in that we assume the existence of coherent set of norms, allowing the agents to be fully compliant with the norms if they decide to do so. We assume that the norms are expressed in a sufficiently expressive language, but with associated mechanisms which are tractable, regulating the behavior of autonomous agents in an otherwise open multiagent system. In what follows, we formalize the key notions that characterize our model of norms.

Definition 1. (Norm). *A norm is a tuple* $\langle \delta, \mathcal{X}, \mathcal{E}, \sigma \rangle$ *where:* $\delta \in$ $\{$OBLIGATION, PROHI- BITION$\}$ *is the deontic modality;* $\mathcal{X} \subseteq \mathcal{S}$ *is the set of states (normative context) in which the norm applies;* $\mathcal{E} \subseteq \mathcal{X}$ *is the subset of states in the normative context which are obliged or prohibited (target states); and* σ *is a sanction represented by a tuple* $\langle \rho, \phi \rangle$:

- $\rho : \mathcal{S} \mapsto \mathbb{R}$ *is a function that gives the penalty for violating this norm in a given state* ($\rho(s)$ *yields the penalty to be paid in s*);
- $\phi : \mathcal{S} \mapsto \mathcal{S}$ *is a function that calculates the state resulting from an enforced state-transition in response to the violation of this norm* ($\phi(s)$ *yields the outcome of an enforced state-transition in s*).

Broadly speaking, the intended semantics of a norm is as follows: if the norm is a *prohibition*, in the set of states $\mathcal{X}$ where the norm applies, the agents are prohibited to be in any state in $\mathcal{E}$; if it is an *obligation*, in the set of states $\mathcal{X}$ where the norm applies, the agents are obliged to be in some state in $\mathcal{E}$. A *sanction* consists of a penalty and an enforced state-transition aimed at updating the current state of agents that have transgressed a norm. The underlying intent of the sanctions is to punish the transgressors by decreasing their utility, and moving them from violating states to states where the norms are obeyed and/or their capabilities are limited. A set of states is relevant to a norm $\langle \delta, \mathcal{X}, \mathcal{E}, \sigma \rangle$ if this set of states is a subset of $\mathcal{X}$, which indicates the context where the norm applies. Given a set of states that are relevant to a norm, we can determine which of them violate it. In Definition 2 we formalize the norm violating states.

Definition 2. (Violating states). *Let q be a norm* $\langle \delta, \mathcal{X}, \mathcal{E}, \sigma \rangle$, *the set of states that violate q, denoted as* $\mathcal{S}_q^\triangledown$, *is defined as:*

$$\mathcal{S}_q^\triangledown = \begin{cases} \mathcal{E} & \text{if } (\delta = \text{PROHIBITION}) \\ \mathcal{X} \setminus \mathcal{E} & \text{if } (\delta = \text{OBLIGATION}). \end{cases}$$

Previous research [3] has shown that *factored* representations can be used to design efficient MDP solution algorithms that exploit *structures* in the state space. Using this factored representation, the norm in Definition 1 can be expressed in a compact way as in [7] (an example is given in Section 4.1). In the systems that we envision, norms are assumed to be common knowledge, represented as the following set.

Definition 3. (Set of norms). *A set of norms $\mathcal{N}$ is a totally ordered set $\{q_1, q_2, \ldots q_m\}$ where each norm $q_k \in \mathcal{N}$ is defined according to Definition 1.*

2.2 Norm Enforcement Mechanism

The model of norm enforcement mechanism developed in this paper is based on the detection of violating states in terms of observations of the agents' current state in the world. Such observations are assumed to be imperfect[1], so that the mechanism only detects violations with a certain probability, as stated in Definition 4.

Definition 4. (Detection model). *Let $\mathcal{N}$ be the set of norms and $\mathcal{S}$ be the state space. A probabilistic detection model consists of a function $\mathcal{D} : \mathcal{N} \times \mathcal{S} \to [0,1]$ such that $\mathcal{D}(q, s)$ returns the detection probability of the violation of the norm $q \in \mathcal{N}$ in the state $s \in \mathcal{S}$.*

Besides being imperfect, the enforcement mechanism is *resource-bounded* so that monitoring the environment has an associated cost. This cost is a function of the accuracy of observations and the size of the population of agents. We formalize this function as $\mathcal{MK}(\mathcal{D}, \mu)$, which returns the cost per time step of detecting norm violations according to the model $\mathcal{D}$ in a multiagent system with population size μ. Note that at this point we do not provide a specific formulation for this function since the degree in which parameters affect the costs depends on the environment to be created or simulated.

If a norm violation is detected by the norm enforcement mechanism, the respective sanction is applied immediately. According to Definition 5, which formalizes the application of a single sanction, the mechanism has the power to change the current state s_i (enforced state-transition) and the utility u_i (penalization) of an agent a_i. Multiple sanctions can be applied where multiple norms have been violated – one sanction per norm violation that has been detected. This is formalized in Definition 6.

Definition 5. (Application of sanction). *Let $q \in \mathcal{N}$ be a norm violated by a given agent in a state $s \in \mathcal{S}$, and let $\sigma = \langle \rho, \phi \rangle$ be the sanction of q to be applied in this state. Then the application of σ in the state s results in a state-transition of the agent to the state $\phi(s)$ and a penalty of $\rho(s)$ utility units.*

---

[1] Given the number of state features of some complex domains (large state spaces), it can be computationally costly for the norm enforcer to keep track of all potentially relevant features. It happens in real life situations as well. For example, when a police district has to distribute a limited number of officers in a region. Some norm violations may not be detected given that the police cannot cover all public spaces of the region.

Definition 6. (Application of sanctions). *Let* $\{q_1, q_2, \ldots q_m\} \subseteq \mathcal{N}$ *be an ordered set of norms which violation has been detected in a given state* $s \in \mathcal{S}$. *Let* $\{\sigma_1, \sigma_2, \ldots \sigma_m\}$ *be the sanctions to be applied in this state, such that* $\sigma_k = \langle \rho_k, \phi_k \rangle$ *corresponds to the sanction of the norm* q_k. *The application of* $\{\sigma_1, \sigma_2, \ldots \sigma_m\}$ *in* s *results in a transition to* $\phi_1(\phi_2(\ldots(\phi_m(s))))$ *and a penalization of* $\rho_1(s) + \rho_2(s) + \ldots + \rho_m(s)$ *utility units.*

Our approach consists of merging multiple state-transitions into one in which the initial state is the violating state, and the outcome state is calculated by applying
the function ϕ of the sanctions sequentially. Similarly to detecting norm violations, the application of sanctions implies costs for the norm enforcement mechanism. Thus, the sanctioning cost $\mathcal{SK}(t)$ for a given time step t, is:

$$\mathcal{SK}(t) = \sum_{k=1}^{|\mathcal{N}|} \mathcal{I}(\sigma_k, t)\, \mathcal{SSK}(\sigma_k)$$

where the function $\mathcal{I}(\sigma_k, t)$ gives the number of times that the sanction σ_k has been applied in the time step t, and the function $\mathcal{SSK}(\sigma_k)$ returns the cost of applying the sanction σ_k. In summary, the total norm enforcement cost at a given time step t, denoted as $\mathcal{K}(t)$, is determined as follows:

$$\mathcal{K}(t) = \mathcal{MK}(\mathcal{D}, \mu) + \mathcal{SK}(t) \tag{1}$$

where $\mathcal{MK}(\mathcal{D}, \mu)$ is detection cost per time step employing the detection model $\mathcal{D}$ in a population μ, and $\mathcal{SK}(t)$ is the sanctioning cost in the time step t.

3   Normative Agent Reasoning

We use *Normative Markov Decision Processes* (NMDPs) to generate the policies followed by our selfish agents operating under the norm enforcement mechanism. An NMDP is a formal model that integrates the normative framework detailed in Section 2 with the widely known MDPs [2]. The result of such an integration is a framework to develop rational agents that comply with a norm only if the expected utility of doing so exceeds the expected utility of violating this norm (for details about NMDPs and a comparison with related work, including normative multi-agent systems and electronic institutions, see Fagundes [5]).

Definition 7. (Normative Markov Decision Process). *An NMDP is a tuple* $\langle \mathcal{S}, \mathcal{A}, \mathcal{C}, \mathcal{T}, \mathcal{R}, \mathcal{N}, \mathcal{D} \rangle$ *where:* $\mathcal{S}$ *is the finite set of states of the world;* $\mathcal{A}$ *is a finite set of actions;* $\mathcal{C} : \mathcal{S} \to \mathcal{A}$ *is a capability function that denotes the set of admissible actions in a given state* ($\mathcal{C}(s)$ *corresponds to the set of admissible actions in the state* s); $\mathcal{T} : \mathcal{S} \times \mathcal{A} \times \mathcal{S} \to \mathbb{R}$ *is a state-transition function* ($\mathcal{T}(s, a, s')$ *indicates the probability of executing* a *at* s *and ending at* s'); $\mathcal{R} : \mathcal{S} \times \mathcal{A} \times \mathcal{S} \to \mathbb{R}$ *is a reward function that determines the reward* ($\mathcal{R}(s, a, s')$ *corresponds to the one gained by the agent for executing* a *at* s *and ending at the state* s'), $\mathcal{N}$ *is a set of norms specified according to Definition 3; and* $\mathcal{D} : \mathcal{N} \times \mathcal{S} \to \mathbb{R}$ *is a detection function specified according to Definition 4.*

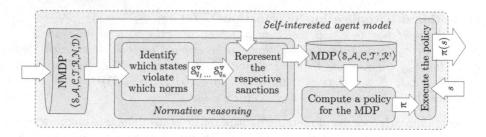

Fig. 1. Control flow of the self-interested agent model

In order to generate a behavior policy for an NDMP, agents use the control flow of Figure 1. In this model, agents perform *normative reasoning* to identify which states violate which norms and represent the respective sanctions within the violating states. The outcome of this process is a standard MDP, which can be solved by well known algorithms [2,8,13]. Finally, the agent executes the resulting policy π.

Hardwiring normative constraints into agent behavior [15] can be problematic since it constrains the agent's ability to adapt to changes in the system's norms [4]. In consequence, we develop a technique to generate an MDP at runtime that incorporates sanctions from an NMDP. This technique consists of identifying, for all states, which norms they violate (if any), following Definition 2. Then, for each violating state $s \in S_q^\triangledown$, the sanction of the norm q is represented with s by modifying the transition probabilities $\mathcal{T}$ and rewards $\mathcal{R}$ based on the norms $\mathcal{N}$ and detection probabilities $\mathcal{D}$. The result of the *normative reasoning*, as shown in Figure 1, is a standard MDP $\langle S, \mathcal{A}, \mathcal{C}, \mathcal{T}', \mathcal{R}' \rangle$ in which $\mathcal{T}'$ is the new state-transition function and $\mathcal{R}'$ is the new reward function. In what follows, we describe how $\mathcal{T}'$ and $\mathcal{R}'$ are computed.

Let $\mathcal{Q}_s$ be the set of norms violated in a given state $s \in S$. The combinations of sanctions in s are provided by the power set of $\mathcal{Q}_s$ denoted as $\mathsf{P}(\mathcal{Q}_s)$. For instance, if $\mathcal{Q}_s = \{q_1, q_2\}$ then $\mathsf{P}(\mathcal{Q}_s) = \{\emptyset, \{q_1\}, \{q_2\}, \{q_1, q_2\}\}$. The outcome resulting from a combination of sanctions $\mathcal{B} \in \mathsf{P}(\mathcal{Q}_s)$ in s is computed by the function below[2]:

$$\mathsf{Out}(s, \mathcal{B}) = \begin{cases} \mathsf{Head}(\mathcal{B}).\sigma.\phi(\mathsf{Out}(s, \mathcal{B} \setminus \mathsf{Head}(\mathcal{B}))) & \text{if } |\mathcal{B}| > 1 \\ \mathsf{Head}(\mathcal{B}).\sigma.\phi(s) & \text{if } |\mathcal{B}| = 1 \end{cases}$$

where $\mathsf{Head}(\mathcal{B})$ is a function that returns the first element in $\mathcal{B}$ and $\mathsf{Head}(\mathcal{B}).\sigma.\phi$ refers to the function ϕ of the sanction σ of the norm $\mathsf{Head}(\mathcal{B})$. Note that function $\mathsf{Out}(s, \mathcal{B})$ computes the outcome state resulting from a combination of sanctions $\mathcal{B}$ according to Definition 6, ensuring that norm enforcement mechanism and agents calculate the same outcome state for any combination of sanctions.

In order to represent the effect of sanctions in the transition and reward functions of the new MDP, we determine the set of all combinations of sanctioned norm violations $\mathsf{W}(s, s') \subseteq \mathsf{P}(\mathcal{Q}_s)$ which, if executed in $s \in S$, bring about $s' \in S$:

---

[2] In an abuse of notation, we refer to sub-components of tuples using an object-oriented programming idiom, so that $\sigma.\phi$ refers to the component ϕ of tuple σ.

$$W(s, s') = \{\mathcal{B} \in P(\mathcal{Q}_s) \mid (\mathcal{B} \neq \emptyset) \wedge \text{Out}(s, \mathcal{B}) = s'\}.$$

Using the detection probabilities from function $\mathcal{D}$, we compute the probability that a combination $\mathcal{B} \in P(\mathcal{Q}_s)$ occurs in $s \in \mathcal{S}$ as follows:

$$\text{Pro}(\mathcal{B}, s) = \prod_{q \in \mathcal{B}} \mathcal{D}(q, s) \prod_{q \in \mathcal{Q}_s \setminus \mathcal{B}} (1 - \mathcal{D}(q, s)).$$

Bringing it all together, Formula (2) calculates $\mathcal{T}'(s, a, s')$: the probability of executing action a at s and ending up at s' taking into account the sanctions to be applied in the initial state s. First, take the probability of a transition if no sanction takes place. This is determined by multiplying the transition probability $\mathcal{T}(s, a, s')$ by the probability $\text{Pro}(\emptyset, s)$ that no sanctioning happens. Then, we take the probability of occurrence for each combination of sanctions $\mathcal{B} \in W(s, s')$, which if executed in s ends in s'.

$$\mathcal{T}'(s, a, s') = \mathcal{T}(s, a, s') \text{Pro}(\emptyset, s) + \sum_{\mathcal{B} \in W(s,s')} \text{Pro}(\mathcal{B}, s) \tag{2}$$

Finally, Formula (3) describes how to calculate $\mathcal{R}'(s, a, s')$, the immediate reward of executing action a at the origin state s and ending at s' taking into account the sanctions to be applied at s. To calculate $\mathcal{R}'(s, a, s')$ we use $\mathcal{R}(s, a, s')$, the immediate reward for this state-transition if no sanction is applied, and $\text{Pen}(\mathcal{B}, s)$, the penalty of a combination of sanctions $\mathcal{B} \in W(s, s')$ at s. As these combinations of sanctions are mutually exclusive and happen with different probabilities, we calculate $\mathcal{R}'(s, a, s')$ as a weighted average reward on which the probabilities are the weights, where the penalty of $\mathcal{B} \in P(\mathcal{Q}_s)$ is :
$\text{Pen}(\mathcal{B}, s) = \sum_{q \in \mathcal{B}} q . \sigma . \rho(s).$

$$\mathcal{R}'(s, a, s') = \frac{\text{Pro}(\emptyset, s) \, \mathcal{T}(s, a, s') \, \mathcal{R}(s, a, s') + \sum_{\mathcal{B} \in W(s,s')} \text{Pro}(\mathcal{B}, s) \text{Pen}(\mathcal{B}, s)}{\mathcal{T}'(s, a, s')} \tag{3}$$

4   Experiments

We now turn our attention to evaluating stochastic norm-enforcement mechanisms. The goal of our evaluation is to determine effective norm enforcement intensities that balance the ability of the mechanism to self-support itself and at the same time to ensure that coordination problems do not exceed a maximum acceptable level.

4.1   Motion Environment

The motion environment, shown in Figure 2, is a stochastic environment as defined in Section 2.1, made up of discrete cells, where the agents (depicted as triangles indicating their moving direction) are able to move one cell at a time. There are 8 lanes and each lane contains 24 contiguous cells. There are also 8 gateways through which the agents enter and leave the environment. The position of each agent is determined by features LANE and CELL, its orientation is defined by DIRECTION, and STATUS indicates whether it is holding a position or moving through the cells.

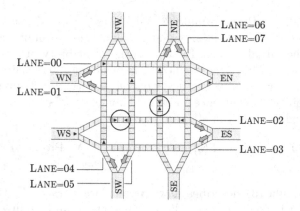

Fig. 2. Motion environment. Circles indicate imminent crashes.

Each norm-aware agent $a_i \in \mathcal{G}$ operating in the motion environment is modeled as an NMDP that computes its policy following the reasoning process described in Section 3. The agents' current state (c.f. Section 3) determines the system's current state and it is represented as a vector $\{s_1, \ldots, s_n\}$ in which s_i, the current state of the agent $a_i \in \mathcal{G}$, is a complete assignment of values to its features.

Once released in a gateway, an agent can choose between two adjoining lanes. Non-determinism is modeled by the fact the move action is "unreliable": its intended outcome occurs with probability 0.99, but with probability 0.01 the agent remains in the same position. With this we intend to model the fact that the "engine" of our agent can fail (i.e. out of gas, mechanical problems). The agents' actions are executed synchronously within the motion environment, that is, each agent executes one action per time-step. For every state-transition implied by an action, the agent receives a reward, which may be positive or negative. For this environment, the reward is $-0.01R_N$ for all transitions (R_N is the reward unit), except when the agent reaches the assigned destination gateway, which results in a reward of $+0.4R_N$ (an incentive to reach this gateway quickly). Note that leaving the environment via any other gateway gives $-0.01R_N$. These state-transition probabilities and rewards have been arbitrarily chosen. In this section, we focus on the experimental analysis in simulated environments, and our technique can be applied with different probabilities and reward levels.

In our experiments, the agents know the norms and the detection probabilities. That is, although they do not know whether individual norm violations will be detected, they are aware of the probability of violations being detected in general.

The agents' perception is incomplete, so while traveling across the environment, the agents always know their own position, but not the position of other agents. This assumption about the agents' perception may cause coordination problems: two agents that come from *opposite directions* crash into each other if they try to occupy the same cell or try to cross each other (two examples of imminent crashes are highlighted in Figure 2 with circles). When agents crash, they are removed from the environment. To cope with these coordination problems, we introduce a set of norms to regulate the traveling direction in each lane (see the arrows in Figure 2). If a violation is detected, the agent is driven to the obliged direction and loses $0.1R_N$. These norms are specified using the following template, where X is a particular lane and Y is the obliged moving direction:

$$\langle \text{OBLIGATION}, (\text{LANE}=X), (\text{DIRECTION}=Y),$$
$$\langle \{ \top \rightarrow -1.0R_N \}, \{ \top \rightarrow \{(\text{DIRECTION}=Y)\} \} \rangle \rangle$$

The main purpose of this environment is to serve as a testbed for studying the tradeoff between norm enforcement efficiency and its cost, taking into account a population of norm-aware self-interested agents capable of complex planning to maximize their expected utilities. Origin and destination gateways of each agent were randomly assigned using a uniform distribution. Each simulation ran for 10^6 time steps, resulting in a 95% confidence interval for the results shown in this section, allowing us to identify the parameters and value ranges in which the societal behavior changes significantly:

- β is the detection probability of violations. In our simulations, $\mathcal{D}(q, s) = \beta$ for all norms and all states, and β ranges from 0.01 to 0.13 in intervals of 0.01.
- μ is the population setting, corresponding to the number of agents in the environment at any given time throughout the entire simulation. In our simulations $\mu = 10$.

The norm enforcement cost is computed using Formula 1 where $\mathcal{MK}(\mathcal{D}, \mu)$ is the cost of monitoring violations, and $\mathcal{SK}(t)$ is the sanctioning cost. Here, the cost of monitoring norm violations is a function of the accuracy of observations and the number of agents. Monitoring and sanctioning cost in this environment are defined, respectively, as:

$$\mathcal{MK}(\mathcal{D}, \mu) = \mathcal{MK}(\beta, \mu) = 1.1^{10\mu\beta} \times 10^{-3}R_N$$

$$\mathcal{SK}(t) = \sum_{k=1}^{8} \mathcal{I}(\underset{k}{\sigma}, t)\, 0.05R_N$$

where $\mathcal{I}(\sigma_k, t)$ yields the number of times that the sanction σ_k has been imposed in the time step t, and $0.05R_N$ is the cost of applying any sanction in the motion environment. There are 8 norms in our normative system: one obligation per lane and the cost of sanctioning in each of them is the same. Using these functions, we can calculate the average norm enforcement cost per time step, denoted as $\overline{\mathcal{K}}$, in 10^6 time steps of simulation:

$$\overline{\mathcal{K}} = \frac{1}{10^6} \sum_{t=1}^{10^6} \mathcal{K}(t).$$

Note that each cost function is specific to the domain being simulated. For example, in simulated environment used in this paper, the monitoring cost increases exponentially with the detection probability β and the size of the population μ, and the cost of applying a sanction is fixed.

4.2   Results

In the absence of norms regulating the motion environment, the optimal choice would be taking the shortest path from the origin gateway to the destination gateway. However, in a norm regulated setting, agents adapt their behavior taking the sanctions into account. As the detection probability β rises, the agents tend to commit fewer violations. When β > 0.09, the agents start to comply with the norms because the expected utility gain of compliance outweighs that of violating them.

From the macro perspective, we estimate the effectiveness of various detection probabilities of norm violations β using the sum of penalties paid by the agents that violate norms (i.e. norm enforcement income). As we shall see, this income is used to fund the norm enforcement costs. For each β, Figure 3 shows the average norm enforcement income per time step (dotted line, left y-axis). We can see that high detection probabilities (β > 0.09) result in no income as these settings inhibit any violation of norms (starving the enforcement mechanism of funds). As the detection probability β decreases, the number of norm violations increases monotonically (solid line, right y-axis), whereas the enforcement income varies non-monotonically. This happens because the norm enforcement income is determined not only by β, but also by the number of norm violations, which in turn, is determined by the agents' policies.

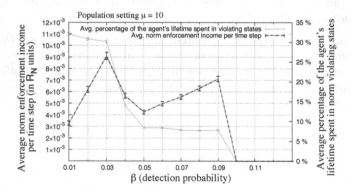

Fig. 3. Average norm enforcement income and percentage of time spent in violating states

We now look at an example of calculation of the norm enforcement income. Our experiments have shown that under detection probabilities {0.02, 0.03, 0.04}, agents stay on average 30.8%, 30.1% and 13.9% of their lifetime in violating states, respectively.

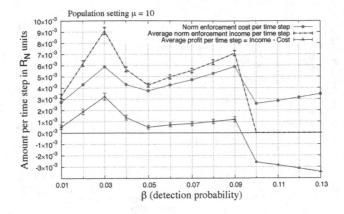

Fig. 4. Average norm enforcement cost, income and profit per time step

By multiplying these percentages by their respective β we find how many times, on average, the violations are detected: $\{0.00616, 0.00903, 0.00556\}$. Finally, if we multiply these values by the penalty value $(0.1R_N)$ and by the number of agents running simultaneously in the multiagent system $(\mu = 10)$, we obtain the respective average enforcement income values shown in Figure 3:

$$(\beta = 0.02, \ 6.16 \times 10^{-3} R_N), \quad (\beta = 0.03, \ 9.03 \times 10^{-3} R_N), \quad (\beta = 0.04, \ 5.56 \times 10^{-3} R_N).$$

If we increase the detection probability β from 0.02 to 0.03, the average income per time step increases from $6.16 \times 10^{-3} R_N$ to $9.03 \times 10^{-3} R_N$. However, if we increase β from 0.03 to 0.04, the agents change their policies (they perform less norm violations) and the income decreases to $5.56 \times 10^{-3} R_N$.

The norm enforcement cost per time step $\overline{\mathcal{K}}$ is drawn in Figure 4 as a solid line with circles. If we subtract this cost from the average enforcement income (dotted line), we have the average profit (solid line with triangles). In our experiments, the system profits when $\beta \lesssim 0.09$. Notice that the enforcement income increases as μ (number of agents simultaneously running in the environment) increases. Assuming that the detection cost does not depend on the value of μ, certain normative solutions may become profitable if we allow more agents to join the system.

Although Figure 4 shows that the highest profit occurs when $\beta = 0.03$, in multiagent systems with self-interested agents, such a low detection probability of norm violations may entail a significant amount of coordination problems, nullifying the effectiveness of the norms as a multiagent coordination device. For each detection probability β, Figure 5 shows the average percentage of agents that crash (dotted line, right y-axis) and the average profit of enforcing norms (solid line with triangles, left y-axis) when $\mu = 10$. In a system in which crashes (coordination problems) must not occur, any $\beta \geq 0.10$ can be employed, and $\beta = 0.10$ achieves norm compliance with the lowest cost (i.e. a larger enforcement intensity wastes resources).

If some coordination problems are acceptable, then the norm enforcement mechanism can consider a wider range of settings. For instance, any $\beta \geq 0.05$ can be used if a 20% maximum average percentage of crashes is acceptable, with the

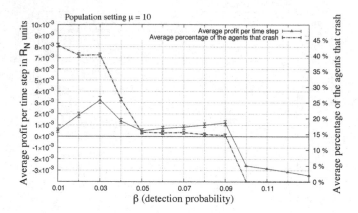

Fig. 5. Average percentage of agents that crash and average enforcement profit per time step

best option being $\beta = 0.09$ since it results in the highest income with a crash rate lower than 20%.

5   Conclusion and Future Work

In this paper we have defined a stochastic norm enforcement mechanism for agents operating in stochastic environments extending our earlier work and evaluated the tradeoffs involved when the effectiveness of the norm enforcement mechanism incurs a cost. Our evaluation led to a number of insights. From the agent's perspective, our experiments show that adequate norms can help shape the behavior of rational normative agents with an MDP-based world model, fostering coordination in a multiagent setting. From a macro perspective, we empirically show how our approach can estimate the global benefits of norms together with their enforcement cost in order to design economically viable norm enforcement mechanisms for systems populated by self-interested rational agents. In complex stochastic environments, our approach can be used to identify settings that make monitoring independent external funding (self-supporting).

We aim to extend this research in several promising ways. First, we can extend the agent model to account for the behavior of other agents or construct policies when the detection probabilities are unknown. Finally, although we have discussed insights in the context of one specific scenario, we aim to study ways to generalize the estimation of norm enforcement intensities.

Acknowledgments. This research is partially supported by the Spanish Ministry of Economy and Competitiveness through the projects AT (grant CSD2007-0022; CONSOLIDER-INGENIO 2010) and iHAS (TIN2012-36586-C03-02). The second and third authors acknowledge the support of the Brazilian National Council for Scientific and Technological Development (CNPq) under project Universal (grant 482156/2013-9), and PQ (grant 306864/2013-4).

References

1. Ågotnes, T., van der Hoek, W., Wooldridge, M.: Normative system games. In: Durfee, E.H., Yokoo, M., Huhns, M.N., Shehory, O. (eds.) AAMAS, pp. 881–888. IFAAMAS (2007)
2. Bellman, R.E.: Dynamic Programming. Dover Publications, Incorporated (2003)
3. Boutilier, C., Dean, T., Hanks, S.: Decision-Theoretic Planning: Structural Assumptions and Computational Leverage. J. Artif. Intell. Res. (JAIR) 11, 1–94 (1999)
4. Castelfranchi, C., Dignum, F., Jonker, C.M., Treur, J.: Deliberative Normative Agents: Principles and Architecture. In: Jennings, N.R., Lespérance, Y. (eds.) ATAL 1999. LNCS, vol. 1757, pp. 364–378. Springer, Heidelberg (2000)
5. Fagundes, M.S.: Sequential Decision Making in Normative Environments. Ph.D. thesis, Universidad Rey Juan Carlos (2012)
6. Fagundes, M.S., Billhardt, H., Ossowski, S.: Reasoning about Norm Compliance with Rational Agents. In: Coelho, H., Studer, R., Wooldridge, M. (eds.) ECAI. Frontiers in Artificial Intelligence and Applications, vol. 215, pp. 1027–1028. IOS Press (2010)
7. Fagundes, M.S., Ossowski, S., Luck, M., Miles, S.: Using Normative Markov Decision Processes for evaluating electronic contracts. AI Commun. 25(1), 1–17 (2012)
8. Howard, R.A.: Dynamic Programming and Markov Processes. The M.I.T. Press (1960)
9. Jones, A.J.I., Sergot, M.: On the characterisation of law and computer systems: the normative systems perspective. In: Deontic Logic in Computer Science: Normative System Specification. Wiley Professional Computing Series, pp. 275–307. Wiley (1993)
10. Modgil, S., Faci, N., Meneguzzi, F.R., Oren, N., Miles, S., Luck, M.: A framework for monitoring agent-based normative systems. In: Sierra, C., Castelfranchi, C., Decker, K.S., Sichman, J.S. (eds.) AAMAS (1), pp. 153–160. IFAAMAS (2009)
11. Nash Jr, J.F.: Equilibrium points in n-person games. Proceedings of the National Academy of Sciences 36, 48–49 (1950)
12. Omicini, A., Ossowski, S., Ricci, A.: Coordination infrastructures in the engineering of multiagent systems. In: Bergenti, F., Gleizes, M.P., Zambonelli, F. (eds.) Methodologies and Software Engineering for Agent Systems: The Agent-Oriented Software Engineering Handbook, Multiagent Systems, Artificial Societies, and Simulated Organizations, vol. 11, ch. 14, pp. 273–296. Kluwer Academic Publishers (2004)
13. Puterman, M.L., Shin, M.C.: Modified Policy Iteration Algorithms for Discounted Markov Decision Problems. Management Science 24, 1127–1137 (1978)
14. Schumacher, M., Ossowski, S.: The governing environment. In: Weyns, D., Van Dyke Parunak, H., Michel, F. (eds.) E4MAS 2005. LNCS (LNAI), vol. 3830, pp. 88–104. Springer, Heidelberg (2006)
15. Tennenholtz, M.: On social constraints for rational agents. Computational Intelligence 15(4), 367–383 (1999)
16. Ummels, M., Wojtczak, D.: The complexity of nash equilibria in stochastic multiplayer games. Logical Methods in Computer Science 7(3) (2011)

Using a Priori Information for Fast Learning Against Non-stationary Opponents

Pablo Hernandez-Leal[✉], Enrique Munoz de Cote,
and L. Enrique Sucar

Instituto Nacional de Astrofísica, Óptica y Electrónica,
Luis Enrique Erro #1, Sta. María Tonantzintla, Puebla, Mexico
{pablohl,jemc,esucar}@ccc.inaoep.mx

Abstract. For an agent to be successful in interacting against many different and unknown types of opponents it should excel at learning fast a model of the opponent and adapt online to non-stationary (changing) strategies. Recent works have tackled this problem by continuously learning models of the opponent while checking for switches in the opponent strategy. However, these approaches fail to use *a priori* information which can be useful for a faster detection of the opponent model. Moreover, if an opponent uses only a finite set of strategies, then maintaining a list of those strategies would also provide benefits for future interactions, in case of opponents who return to previous strategies (such as periodic opponents). Our contribution is twofold, first, we propose an algorithm that can use *a priori* information, in the form of a set of models, in order to promote a faster detection of the opponent model. The second is an algorithm that while learning new models keeps a record of them in case the opponent reuses one of those. Our approach outperforms the state of the art algorithms in the field (in terms of model quality and cumulative rewards) in the domain of the iterated prisoner's dilemma against a non-stationary opponent that switches among different strategies.

1 Introduction

Learning against humans is a difficult task because of the complexity that we convey, such as changes in behaviour, randomness and drifting.[1] This causes several problems since many real world applications (like medical and military systems) demand a human and a machine to work together.

Whether the agent is interacting with another (computer) agent or a human, and regardless of the task's nature (a cooperative team or competing against each other), it is reasonable to expect that its counterpart's behaviour will change eventually (more so if they interact for a long time). Competitive examples range from poker playing, where a common tactic is to change play style, negotiation tasks, where agents may change preferences or competitive-negotiation-coordination scenarios like the lemonade stand game tournament,[2] where the winning strategy has always been the fastest to adapt to how other agents act.

---

[1] Tendency to switch to a different behavioural pattern.
[2] http://martin.zinkevich.org/lemonade/

© Springer International Publishing Switzerland 2014
A.L.C. Bazzan and K. Pichara (Eds.): IBERAMIA 2014, LNAI 8864, pp. 536–547, 2014.
DOI: 10.1007/978-3-319-12027-0_43

Cooperative domains include settings where agents need to work together to complete a task like tutoring systems, robot football teams and human-machine interaction scenarios, like service robots aiding the elderly and autonomous car assistants. All these scenarios have one thing in common: agents should learn how its counterpart is acting and react quickly to changes in its behaviour.

Game theory provides the foundations for building strategies under similar scenarios. However, its classical assumptions: 1) full rationality, implying agents that have unlimited power to compute optimal strategies and 2) stationary strategies, implying no possible change in behaviours, are too restrictive to be useful in many real interactions. Recent approaches, such as behavioural game theory [5] try to deviate from these typical assumptions by taking into account human characteristics in strategic scenarios. Research in this area suggests that humans sometimes exhibit not fully rational behaviour [9]. Game theorists have recognised that repeated interaction may modify current behaviour [4] and when this change in behaviour happens (making the environment non-stationary) most machine learning algorithms to date fail. In this work we relax these strong assumptions since we focus on a special type of non-stationarity opponent, those that switch from one stationary strategy to another.

Dealing with not fully rational and non-stationary opponents involves three different tasks: 1) learning a model of the opponent,[3] 2) computing an optimal plan against the opponent and 3) detecting behavioural changes (i.e. strategy switches). Specifically, this work focus on two non homogeneous (different) agents that interact through an infinitely repeated normal form game. We care for designing one of the two agents, while the opponent uses a non stationary strategy, it is reasonable to assume that when dealing with not fully rational opponents, they switch between strategies by selecting one from a handful of possible strategies. Having a priori information (in the form of a set of possible opponent strategies) is possible in some cases and therefore could be exploited.

Our contribution is twofold, first, we propose an algorithm that can use a priori information, in the form of a set of models, in order to promote a faster detection of the opponent model. The second is an algorithm that while learning new models keeps a record of them in case the opponent reuses one of those. Our approach outperforms the state of the art algorithms in the field (in terms of model quality and cumulative rewards) in the domain of the iterated prisoner's dilemma against an non-stationary opponent that switches among different strategies.

The paper is organized as follows. Section 2 describes related work in the area of opponent modelling and fast learning against non-stationary opponents. Section 3 provides the formal setting we use in our problem and describes the MDP-CL (MDP-continuous learning) framework which is used as basis and comparison for our proposed algorithms. In Section 4 we present the two algorithms, the first one uses a priori information (A priori MDP-CL) and the second learns models while keeping them in memory for future use (Incremental MDP-CL). Section 5 presents the experimental results in the iterated prisoner's dilemma against non-stationary opponents. Finally Section 6 presents conclusions and future work.

---

[3] By model of the opponent we mean one that can predict future actions.

2   Related Work

General opponent modelling literature is spread among different areas. However, one common assumption across all is that the opponent to be modelled is stationary. Some works stand aside and have been designed for real-world problems such as poker, like the work in [2] where the authors use a particle filtering approach to address the problem of opponent modelling. This approach is not suitable for our setting as they do not detect switches.

A related problem in the reinforcement learning community is tackled in [6] where the authors use reward shaping [13] in order to accelerate the learning process in the presence of different *contexts*. They assume only two contexts based on how the agent behaves: a selfish context where it ignores the rest of the agents, and a second context where it fully models the interaction with others. The authors assume to know in which of these two situations the agent is, and therefore they can use different shaping functions for each context.

Fast Adaptive Learner (FAL) [8] is an algorithm that focuses on learning in two-person repeated games. To predict the next action of the opponent it maintains a set of hypotheses according to the history of observations. To obtain a strategy against the opponent they use a modified version of the Godfather strategy[4]. However, the Godfather strategy is not a general strategy that can be used against any opponent and in any game. Also FAL shows an exponential increase in the number of hypotheses (in the size of the observation history) which may limit its use in larger domains. Recently, a similar version of FAL designed for stochastic games [7] has been presented.

A similar work to FAL is [10], where the authors proposed MDP4.5, a framework for learning against switching opponents in repeated games. MDP4.5 uses decision trees to learn a model of the opponent. The learned tree, along with information from the environment are transformed into a Markov decision process (MDP) [14] in order to obtain an acting policy. Since decision trees are known to be unstable for small datasets this posses a problem for learning efficient models in a fast way. In order to avoid using decision trees, in [11], the authors proposed the MDP-CL (MDP-continuous learning) framework which is also designed to detect switches against non-stationary opponents, but opposed to MDP4.5, it makes use of MDPs for both learning and planning. Both these frameworks work against non-stationary opponents. However, prior information is not taken into account for fast learning, nor they keep a history of previous models to be used for future interactions.

3   Preliminaries

Consider two players (A and B) that face each other and repeatedly play a *bimatrix game*. A bimatrix game is a two player simultaneous-move game defined by the tuple $\langle \mathcal{A}, \mathcal{B}, R_A, R_B \rangle$, where $\mathcal{A}$ and $\mathcal{B}$ are the set of possible actions

---

[4] *Godfather* [12] offers the opponent a situation where it can obtain a high reward. If the opponent does not accept the offer, Godfather forces the opponent to obtain a low reward.

Table 1. A bimatrix game representing the prisoner's dilemma, two agents can chose between two actions cooperate (C) and defect (D)

	C	D
C	3,3	0,4
D	4,0	1,1

for player A and B, respectively. R_i is the reward matrix of size $|\mathcal{A}| \times |\mathcal{B}|$ for each agent $i \in \{A, B\}$, where the payoff to the ith agent for the joint action $(a, b) \in \mathcal{A} \times \mathcal{B}$ is given by the entry $R_i(a, b)$, $\forall (a, b) \in \mathcal{A} \times \mathcal{B}$, $\forall i \in \{A,B\}$. A *stage game* is a single bimatrix game and a series of rounds of the same stage game form a *repeated game*. A *strategy* of a player is a function that assigns an action for every history.

Prisoner's dilemma is a two person game where the interactions can be modelled as a symmetric two-player game defined by the payoff matrix in Table 1 using values $d = 4, c = 3, p = 1, s = 0$, where the following two conditions must hold $d > c > p > s$ and $2c > d + s$ (to prevent alternating C and D giving a higher payoff than full cooperation). When both players cooperate they both obtain the reward c. If both defect, they get a punishment reward p. If a player chooses to cooperate (C) with someone who defects (D) receives the sucker's payoff s, whereas the defecting player gains the temptation to defect, d. A common strategy which won a tournament of the iterated prisoner's dilemma (iPD) is called Tit-for-Tat (TFT) [1] it starts by cooperating, then does whatever the opponent did in the previous rounds (it will cooperate if the opponent cooperated, and will defect if the opponent defected). Another very successful strategy is called Pavlov and cooperates if both players coordinated with the same action and defects whenever they did not.

In this domain, if we knew (a model of) the opponent we could build a policy to act against it, i.e. the best action in each step of the interaction. Machine learning provides algorithms to learn models from experience and a way to obtain an optimal policy is with reinforcement learning (RL). In RL an agent must learn an optimal policy, in terms of maximising its expected long-term reward in an initially unknown environment modelled as a Markov decision process (MDP) [14]. An MDP is defined by $< S, A, T, R >$, where S is the set of states, $\mathcal{A}$ is the set of actions, T is the transition function and R is the reward function. A *policy* is function $\pi(s)$ that specifies an appropriate action a for each state s. The idea is that the interaction with the opponent generates Markovian observations which can be used to learn an MDP that represents the opponent strategy. Solving this MDP dictates a policy which prescribes the optimal plan against that opponent. An approach to detect strategy switches by learning opponent models (in the form of MDPs) is the MDP-CL framework.

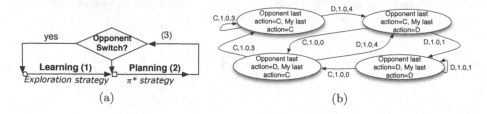

Fig. 1. (a) The three main parts of the approach: (1) learning, with an exploration strategy, (2) planning, to compute the optimal policy and (3) the switch detection process. (b) A model that represents the TFT strategy, states are ovals, each arrow has a corresponding triplet: action, transition probability and reward to the next state.

3.1 MDP-CL

The MDP-CL framework [11] is a state of the art framework whose objective is to enable a switch detection mechanism to any opponent modelling algorithm. The approach consists of three main parts:

1. *A learning phase* in which a model of the opponent in the form of a MDP is learned using the interaction history.
2. *A planning phase* that uses the learned model along with information from the environment in order to compute an optimal plan against the opponent.
3. *A change detection process*, that embeds the learning and planning phases to identify switches in the opponent strategy.

In Figure 1 (a) the three parts of the approach are depicted. Learning is the initial phase and uses a random strategy in order to learn the opponent's model. The next phase is planning, where an optimal policy π^* is computed to play against the opponent. To solve the learned MDP, any off-the-shelf technique like value iteration [3] can be used. Then, the switch detection process starts: if the opponent switches strategies then restart the learning phase, if not, continue using the same policy.

Formally, the MDP representing the opponent strategy is composed of:

- The set of states $S := \times_{o_i \in O} o_i$, i.e. each state is formed by the cross product of the set of attributes O.
- The set of actions, $\mathcal{A}$ is heritage from the game matrix,
- The transition function, $T : S \times \mathcal{A} \to S$ is learned using counts $\hat{T}(s, a, s') = \frac{n(s,a,s')}{n(s,a)}$ where $n(s, a, s')$ is the number of times the agent was in state s, used action a and arrived at state s', $n(s, a)$ is defined as the number of times the agent was in state s and used action a.
- The reward function R is learned in a similar way $\hat{R}(s, a) = \frac{\sum r(s,a)}{n(s,a)}$ where $\sum r(s, a)$ is the cumulative reward obtained by the agent when being in state s and performing action a.

The set of attributes O used to construct the states is assumed to be given by an expert. For example, in the iPD case, we used as attributes the previous action of both players. An example of the MDP induced by the strategy TFT using the attributse just described is depicted in Figure 1 (b). These learned models are used in the next phase, the change detection process.

MDP-CL learns a different model every kw steps ($k = 2, 3, \ldots$), where w is a parameter represeting the interaction window, and compares it to the current model to evaluate their similarity. If the *distance* between models is greater than a given threshold, δ, it means the opponent has changed strategy and the modelling agent must restart the learning phase, resetting the learned model and starting from scratch with a random (exploration) strategy. Otherwise, the opponent has not switched strategies and k is incremented. The total variation distance (TVD) is used to compare MDPs

$$TVD(\mu, v) = \frac{1}{2} \sum_{x \in \Omega} |\mu(x) - v(x)| \tag{1}$$

where μ and v are the transition functions of the compared MDPs.

Even when MDP-CL detects strategy switches it fails to exploit prior information therefore we proposed two different extensions.

4   MDP-CL Extensions

In this section we present two algorithms that extend MDP-CL. The first one (a priori MDP-CL) uses prior information to quickly detect the opponent model. The second approach (incremental MDP-CL) learns new models from history of interactions but it will not discard them once it detects a switch. In this way it keeps a record in case the opponent reuses a previous strategy.

A priori MDP-CL assumes *a priori* information in the form of a set of possible strategies used by the opponent $\mathcal{M}$ (represented by MDPs, similar to the one depicted in Figure 1 (b)). However, there is still the problem to detect in fast way which of these strategies is the one used by the opponent. In the original version of MDP-CL, this was not a problem since there were no prior models to compare. The problem we face is the one of model selection. At each round of the repeated game we have an experience tuple in the form (s, a, r, s'). In a similar fashion to MDP-CL we learn models as if there were no prior information, with the difference that in a priori MDP-CL we learn a model in each round of the repeated game. This learned model is compared (at each round) with each $m \in \mathcal{M}$ using the TVD (equation 1). Thus we assume that the strategy used by the opponent belongs to the set of models and we can guarantee that with enough experience tuples, the correct model will have a perfect similarity ($TVD = 0.0$) with at least one of the models in $\mathcal{M}$. When this happens we stop the exploration phase and we change to planning phase, setting the opponent model to compute a policy against it. The rest of the algorithm behaves as MDP-CL.

A priori MDP-CL make use of an initial set of models, but with incremental MDP-CL we relax the assumption of having the complete set of models $\mathcal{M}$

Algorithm 1. Incremental MDP-CL

```
1   M = ∅, currentModel = null
2   for each round of repeated game do
3       currentModel = learnModel()
4       if w interactions then
5           m' = newModel()
6           M = M ∪ m'
7           currentModel = m'
8       else
9           for each m ∈ M do
10              if TVD(currentModel, m) ≤ ρ then
11                  currentModel = m
12                  π* = planWithModel(currentModel)
```

---

from the beginning, assuming only there is finite set of strategies used by the opponent and that these strategies will be used repeatedly during the interaction. We adapt MDP-CL in order to both, learn new models if the opponent uses a different strategy and maintain a history of learned models in case the opponent switches to a previous one.

A high level view of incremental MDP-CL is described in Algorithm 1. It starts by initializing the set of learned model $M = \emptyset$ and setting the current model variable to *null*. Then, for every round of the repeated game it learns an opponent model *currentModel*. Then it compares this *currentModel* with those in M. If the TVD is lower than a threshold ρ then it means the model has been previously used and it computes a policy to act. Otherwise, we need w interactions to learn a new model and add it to the set M.

5 Experiments

In this section we present experiments comparing a priori and incremental versions against the original MDP-CL in terms of *performance* (average utility over the repeated game) and *quality* (predictions about the opponent's next action at each round) of the learned models. Experiments were performed on the iPD with values $d = 4, c = 3, p = 1, s = 0$ (as shown in Table 1). We used the three most successful and known human crafted strategies that the literature has proposed: Tit-For-Tat (TFT), Pavlov and Bully [12] as opponent strategies. These three strategies have different behaviours in the iPD and the optimal policy differs across them.

First, we present how the total variation distance (TVD) behaves under nonstationary opponents showing that it can be used to efficiently compare models. Second, we present empirical results showing that prior information increases the cumulative rewards and provides a better prediction for the opponent model. Third, we show the advantages of incremental MDP-CL in case the opponent reuses a previous strategy. Finally, we relax the assumption of having the complete set of models used by the opponent and instead assume a set of noisy models that are an approximation of the real ones. We first provide qualitative results showing one simple example and then quantitative results with comparative data.

5.1   Model Selection in a Priori MDP-CL

First we present an example how the TVD behaves against a switching opponent (TFT-Bully) which switches from strategy (TFT) to another (Bully) in the middle of the game. The game consisted of 300 rounds and our agent is given as prior information the set of strategies {Bully, TFT, Pavlov}.

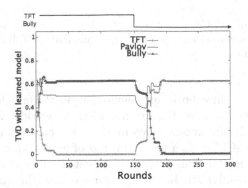

Fig. 2. Total variation distance of the current learned model compared with each strategy given as prior information using a priori MDP-CL. The opponent is TFT-Bully switching at the middle of the game.

In Figure 2 we depict the TVD of each strategy compared to the currently learned model for each round of the repeated game. From the figure we can observe that from round 5 the most similar model is TFT, which is in fact the one used by the opponent. At round 150 the opponent changes its strategy to Bully and two things happen: the TVD with respect to Bully decreases and the TVD with respect to TFT increases. Before round 200 the learned model has a perfect similarity (with the correct model). This figure shows how the TVD is able to efficiently provide a score useful to identify which model is the one used by the opponent. The next section shows the improvement of using *a priori* models on quantitative terms.

5.2   Rewards and Quality in a Priori MDP-CL

In this section we compare MDP-CL and a priori MDP-CL in terms of cumulative rewards and quality of the current model. We use the same opponent as in the previous section.

In Figure 3 we depict the (a) immediate and (b) cumulative rewards (average of 10 iterations) for MDP-CL and a priori MDP-CL against the TFT-Bully opponent. In (a) we note that the first 15 rounds of the interaction there is not much

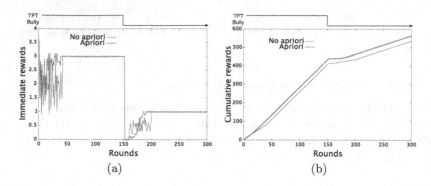

(a)   (b)

Fig. 3. Comparison of MDP-CL and a priori MDP-CL in terms of (a) Immediate rewards and (b) cumulative rewards against the opponent TFT-Bully that switches at the middle of the game

difference in rewards, since both approaches are exploring (learning/detecting the opponent model). However, from round 15 to 40 a priori MDP-CL increases its rewards since it already knows which model is the correct one and can exploit it. In contrast, MDP-CL needs a longer period of exploration to determine correctly the opponent model. This pattern is repeated when a switch is performed by the opponent (round 150). In (b) we can see how the cumulative rewards increase each time there is a switch in the opponent because of the faster detection of a priori MDP-CL.

Now with respect to quality of the model, in Figure 4 we depict the quality of the predictions made by MDP-CL and a priori MDP-CL (average of 10 iterations) against the TFT-Bully opponent. Here it is easy to note that since MDP-CL needs to complete an exploration phase of certain size (in this case 40) it does not have a correct model until that round. In contrast to a priori MDP-CL which always achieve a better quality in fewer interactions.

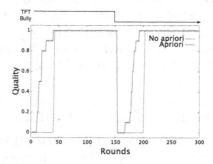

Fig. 4. Model quality of MDP-CL and a priori MDP-CL against the switching opponent TFT-Bully

Table 2. Comparison in terms of average rewards of MDP-CL and a priori MDP-CL of the learning agent $R(Agent)$ and the opponent $R(Opp)$ against non-stationary opponents. The symbol * indicate statistical significance

	MDP-CL		A priori MDP-CL	
Opponent	$R(Agent)$	$R(Opp)$	$R(Agent)$	$R(Opp)$
Bully-Pavlov	1.74	2.03	1.89*	1.88
Bully-TFT	0.93	1.20	0.99*	1.03
Pavlov-Bully	1.79	2.12	1.89*	2.11
Pavlov-TFT	2.88	2.86	2.96*	2.95
TFT-Bully	1.76	2.17	1.86*	2.23
TFT-Pavlov	2.87	2.87	2.94*	2.94
Average	2.00	2.21	**2.09**	2.19

As final experiment, we compare MDP-CL and a priori MDP-CL in terms of average rewards against switching opponents (switch in the middle of a repeated game of 300 rounds). Results are shown in Table 2 where $R(Agent)$ represent the rewards of the learning agent and $R(Opp)$ of the opponent. Each row is average of 50 repetitions. From the table we can observe that for all opponents, a priori MDP-CL obtained statistical significant better results (using t-test), which means a faster detection and an earlier exploitation of the opponent model.

5.3   Incremental Models

Now we relax the assumption of starting the interaction with a set of known models. Thus, the algorithm needs to learn these models trough interaction. In Figure 5 (a) we depict the difference between cumulative rewards of incremental MDP-CL and MDP-CL against the opponent TFT-Bully-Pavlov-Bully (that changes from one strategy to another every 150 rounds) in a game of 600 rounds. We selected this opponent since it uses the Bully strategy two occasions during the interaction. From the figure we can observe that from round 0 to 470 the score moves around 0, this means there is no difference in rewards between the approaches since both are learning new models (TFT, Bully and Pavlov). However starting from round 470 there is an increase of rewards. This happens because the strategy used by the opponent (from round 450) is Bully, which has been previously used (rounds 0 to 150), therefore incremental MDP-CL has this model in its memory which is faster to detect than to relearn it (as the original MDP-CL does). This example shows how keeping a history of models increases the rewards when the opponent reuses one of those previous models.

5.4   A Priori Noisy Models

As final experiment we assume now a set of approximately similar strategies with respect to the real ones. This aims to analyze when given models are not perfect, which may happen due to error (noise), because the opponent is human or a hybrid (mixed) strategy. In order to emulate noise in the models, we changed two transitions of the MDPs to random values. Now, a priori MDP-CL will start with a set of *a priori* noisy models of {TFT, Pavlov, and Bully}.

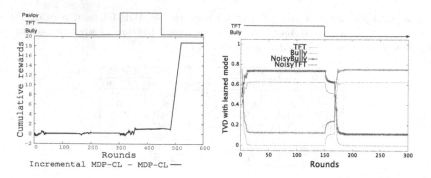

Fig. 5. (a) Difference of cumulative rewards between incremental MDP-CL and MDP-CL against the opponent TFT-Bully-Pavlov-Bully. (b) Total variation distance of the learned model and the noisy representations of TFT and Bully while using a priori MDP-CL.

In Figure 5 (b) we depict the TVD of a priori MDP-CL against the TFT-Bully opponent. The TVD of the real models and the noisy ones is depicted in the figure. We can observe that the TVD is still capable of detecting which model is the correct even in the presence of noisy models. The difference is that in this case, the TVD will not reach the perfect score since our models are not exact, in this case, the best score is close to 0.2 (instead of 0.0).

In order to use the previous algorithms while starting from a set of noisy models, we need only to adjust the ρ parameter in Algorithm 1 to the desired value.

6 Conclusions and Future Work

In real world scenarios especially in human-machine interaction, agents must learn models of people whose behaviour is not fully rational. Humans, and in general agents often use a set of strategies or behaviours for different scenarios which eventually change during the interaction. In some cases, knowing this set of models is possible and therefore using this *a priori* information for detecting the correct model is important. For this situation we propose an algorithm which uses prior information to perform model selection against non-stationary opponents in repeated games. Then, we relax the assumption of knowing the set of behaviours and propose a second algorithm which learns opponent models and keeps them in memory in case the opponent returns to a previous strategy. Experiments were performed on the well known setting of the iterated prisoner's dilemma showing that using both *a priori* information and keeping a history of previously learned models is beneficial in terms of cumulative rewards and quality of the learned model. As future work we would like to use this algorithms in a larger domain such as negotiation and continue analyzing the presence of noise in the models in order to use transfer learning ideas.

References

1. Axelrod, R., Hamilton, W.D.: The evolution of cooperation. Science **211**(27), 1390–1396 (1981)
2. Bard, N., Bowling, M.: Particle filtering for dynamic agent modelling in simplified poker. In: Proceedings of the 22nd Conference on Artificial Intelligence, pp. 515–521. AAAI Press, MIT Press, Menlo Park, Cambridge (1999, 2007)
3. Bellman, R.: A Markovian decision process. Journal of Mathematics and Mechanics 6(5) (1957)
4. Bó, P.D.: Cooperation under the shadow of the future: experimental evidence from infinitely repeated games. American Economic Review, 1591–1604 (2005)
5. Camerer, C.F.: Behavioral Game Theory: Experiments in Strategic Interaction. Roundtable Series in Behavioral Economics. Princeton University Press (February 2003)
6. De Hauwere, Y.M., Devlinb, S., Kudenko, D., Nowé, A.: Context-sensitive reward shaping for sparse interaction MAS. In: 25th Benelux Conference on Artificial Intelligence, Delft, Netherlands (2013)
7. Elidrisi, M., Johnson, N., Gini, M., Crandall, J.: Fast adaptive learning in repeated stochastic games by game abstraction. In: Proceedings of the Autonomous Agents and Multiagent Systems, Paris, France (2014)
8. Elidrisi, M., Johnson, N., Gini, M.: Fast Learning against Adaptive Adversarial Opponents. In: Proceedings of the 11th International Conference on Autonomous Agents and Multiagent Systems, Valencia, Spain (November 2012)
9. Goeree, J., Holt, C.: Ten little treasures of game theory and ten intuitive contradictions. American Economic Review, 1402–1422 (2001)
10. Hernandez-Leal, P., Munoz de Cote, E., Sucar, L.E.: Modeling Non-Stationary Opponents. In: Proceedings of the 12th International Conference on Autonomous Agents and Multiagent Systems (AAMAS 2013), pp. 1135–1136 (May 2013)
11. Hernandez-Leal, P., Munoz de Cote, E., Sucar, L.E.: A framework for learning and planning against swithching strategies in repeated games. Connection Science **26**(2), 103–122 (2014)
12. Littman, M.L., Stone, P.: Implicit Negotiation in Repeated Games. In: Meyer, J.-J.C., Tambe, M. (eds.) ATAL 2001. LNCS (LNAI), vol. 2333, pp. 393–404. Springer, Heidelberg (2002)
13. Ng, A.Y., Harada, D., Russell, S.: Policy invariance under reward transformations: Theory and application to reward shaping. In: Proceedings of the Sixteenth International Conference on Machine Learning, Bled, Slovenia, pp. 278–287 (1999)
14. Puterman, M.: Markov decision processes: Discrete stochastic dynamic programming. John Wiley & Sons, Inc. (1994)

The Double Knapsack Negotiation Problem: Modeling Cooperative Agents and Experimenting Negotiation Strategies

Pablo Pilotti[1]([✉]), Ana Casali[1,2], and Carlos Chesñevar[3]

[1] Centro Internacional Franco Argentino de Ciencias de la Información y de Sistemas (CIFASIS), Rosario, Argentina
pilotti@cifasis-conicet.gov.ar
[2] Facultad de Cs. Exactas, Ingeniería y Agrimensura,
Universidad Nacional de Rosario (UNR), Rosario, Argentina
acasali@fceia.unr.edu.ar
[3] Depto. de Cs. e Ingeniería de la Computación,
Universidad Nacional del Sur (UNS) - CONICET, Bahía Blanca, Argentina
cic@cs.uns.edu.ar

Abstract. This paper presents a novel approach to the well-known Knapsack problem, extending it as a bilateral negotiating problem with default information where each of the two agents has a knapsack and there is a set of items distributed between them. The agents can exchange items in order to reach their goal: fill their knapsacks with items without exceeding their capacity with the aim of maximizing their utility function. Initially the agents do not have any information about their counterpart, e.g. the exact weight of their items and their associated values, so that they consider default assignments for them. This default information can change as the negotiation progresses. A sequential negotiation protocol is proposed, along with different strategies of information exchange and the results obtained when the agents negotiate using them. Information transfer efficiency is assessed in terms of the overall usefulness, quantity of information disclosed and negotiation duration.

Keywords: Automatic negotiation · Bilateral negotiation · Knapsack problem · Default knowledge · Negotiation strategies

1 Introduction

Negotiation is an interaction that happens in multi-agent systems when agents have conflicting objectives and must look for an acceptable agreement. A typical negotiating situation involves two agents that have items to exchange and they are willing to cooperate in order to improve their situations. Therefore, they must start a negotiation dialogue taking into account that they might have incomplete or wrong information about the other agent's goals and items.

Different approaches can be used to model negotiation in multiagent systems. Rahwan et al. [1] distinguish three different kinds of such approaches: those

© Springer International Publishing Switzerland 2014
A.L.C. Bazzan and K. Pichara (Eds.): IBERAMIA 2014, LNAI 8864, pp. 548–559, 2014.
DOI: 10.1007/978-3-319-12027-0_44

which are *game-theoretic*, those which are *heuristic-based*, and finally those based on *argumentation* (*argumentation-based negotiation* or ABN). Game-theoretic approaches are based on studying and developing strategic negotiation models using game-theory precedents [2]. At present, there is no agreed approach to characterize all negotiation frameworks. However, in [3] it has been argued that automated negotiation research can be considered to deal with three broad topics: *a) Negotiation Protocols* (the set of rules that govern the interaction); *b) Negotiation Objects* (the range of issues over which agreement must be reached) and *c) Agents' Decision Making Model* (which accounts for the decision making apparatus the participants employ to act in line with the negotiation protocol in order to achieve their objectives). ABN approaches emphasize the impact of the information exchanged with the proposals in the negotiating process [4]. In this work we address how negotiating agents can select the information exchanged and the impact each selection has in the negotiation process. For this analysis we formalize an extended version of the well-known Knapsack problem.

In the classical Knapsack problem an agent Ag has a knapsack and a set N of items, so that each item $r_i \in N$ has an associated weight ω_i given by the problem definition and a value v_i, representing the benefit the item means for the agent. The problem that the agent faces is to fill *his knapsack* (that supports a maximum weight c, i.e. its capacity) so that the sum of the values of the objects he chooses is maximal. We present a novel, extended version of this problem, modeling it as a bilateral negotiation problem with incomplete information, providing a negotiation model for the analysis and comparison of different strategies. We will assume a scenario with two agents; each of them has a knapsack and a finite set of items. The capacities of their respective knapsacks are known by both agents. The agents can negotiate some exchange of items in order to maximize their own utility function, given by the sum of the values of the items to be put into each knapsack. We assume that initially the agents do not know the weight of the items of their counterpart and the value he has assigned to all the items involved in the problem. Consequently, the agents can compensate this lack of information with default knowledge (possibly inaccurate) about their counterpart. During the dialog, an agent may give an argument to support a claim associated with what he has to offer, revealing some private information which is made available to the other agent.

In this work we propose a negotiation model and a sequential protocol for the agents involved, and we analyze different negotiation strategies, focusing on the selection of the information items the agents reveal in their messages. To compare the proposed strategies we carried out some experiments on different problem instances of the extended version of the Knapsack problem. Then, the information transfer efficiency is empirically assessed in terms of the overall utility, the amount of information disclosed and the negotiation duration. The rest of this paper is structured as follows: next, in Section 2 we provide a generic description of the problem and its underlying formalization. In Section 3 we define the negotiation protocol, and in Section 4 different information concession strategies were proposed. Section 5 summarizes the empirical results obtained, analyzed according to different dimensions. Finally, Section 6 discusses related and future work, and summarizes the main conclusions that have been obtained.

2   Problem Definition and Modeling

We assume that two agents Ag^0 and Ag^1 have knapsacks with capacities c^0 and c^1, resp. This information is known by both agents. They also know that there is a set of N items distributed between them, such that N^j is the set of items that initially the agent Ag^j has, and that all items are distributed between the two agents, i.e. $N = N^0 \cup N^1$ and $N^0 \cap N^1 = \emptyset$. Each item $r_i \in N^j$ has a weight ω_i; this information is initially known only by the agent Ag^j who owns the item and is estimated with $\widehat{\omega}_i$ by the other agent. Besides, we assume that the item r_i will produce a profit of v_i^j to Ag^j, and he can also estimate that this item produces a profit of $\widehat{v}_i^j$ to its counterpart Ag^{1-j}. These default values are part of an agent's beliefs, and may be updated during the negotiation dialog.

2.1   Agent Model

In what follows, for the sake of simplicity we will only refer to Ag^j (one of the two agents involved). The elements identified can be made extensible to the other agent as well. Let Ag^j be one of the negotiating agents. The mental state of Ag^j represents all the information he has about the knapsack problem: the items he initially has and his beliefs about his counterpart i.e.: Ag^j's mental state will take into account the weight of his items (W^j), his items values (V^j) and his beliefs about his opponent's items values ($\widehat{V}^j$) and weights ($\widehat{W}^j$). Formally:

$$W^j = (\omega_1^j, ..., \omega_{|N^j|}^j) \qquad V^j = (v_1^j, ..., v_{|N|}^j)$$

$$\widehat{W}^j = (\widehat{\omega}_1^j, ..., \widehat{\omega}_{|N^{1-j}|}^j) \qquad \widehat{V}^j = (\widehat{v}_1^j, ..., \widehat{v}_{|N|}^j)$$

Notice that V^j and W^j do not change during the negotiation, whereas $\widehat{V}^j$ and $\widehat{W}^j$ contain default information that may change during an agent's updating belief process as the negotiation dialog occurs.

The following sets characterize the agents belief: *Private Information* (I^j), which accounts for that personal information that was not informed yet in the negotiation dialogue; *Public Information* (P^j), which accounts for personal information that has been given out in the negotiation dialogue and *Default Information* ($\widehat{I}^j$), which accounts for information that is unknown, but tentatively assumed. Initially $P^j = \{c^j, c^{1-j}, N^j, N^{1-j}\}$, $I^j = \{\omega_i | r_i \in N^j\} \cup \{v_i^j | r_i \in N\}$ and $\widehat{I}^j = \{\widehat{\omega}_i | r_i \in N^{1-j}\} \cup \{\widehat{v}_i^{1-j} | r_i \in N\}$.

The decision making apparatus an agent employs to decide his negotiation actions depends on his mental state. This apparatus will be in charge of computing those messages the agent will send to the other agent.

The first dialogue message associated with the initial proposal will be singled out by using an initialization function *Init*. A belief revision process and further proposals are computed by another function *Response*. In the following definition we formalize these concepts.

Definition 1 (Agent Model). *An agent Ag^j is defined as*
$$Ag^j := \langle Ms^j, Init^j, Response^j \rangle, \text{ where } Ms^j = \langle W, \widehat{W}, V, \widehat{V}, P, I, \widehat{I} \rangle^1 \text{ is the}$$
agent mental state, $Init^j : Ms^j \rightarrow Message$ is the function associated with starting the negotiation and $Response^j : Ms^j \times Message \rightarrow Ms^j \times Message$ is the function associated with generating new message.

For every agent, his aim is to maximize the total utility of their respective knapsacks. In order to do so, they proceed in a negotiation dialogue, exchanging proposals of possible exchanges (which are the items the agent is asking for and what he is willing to offer in return) and some private information they decide to share.

A dialogue between the two agents will be defined as a finite sequence of messages performed alternatively by each of the agents involved in the dialogue, ending with *accept* (there is a deal) or *withdraw* (no deal is possible).

Definition 2 (Message). *A message is defined as:*

$$Message := (x, \Lambda) \mid Accept \mid Withdraw$$

where x is a proposal to exchange and reallocate items, Λ is private information the sender reveals. The Accept and Withdraw messages are used to indicate the end of the dialogue.

A proposal of items exchange and allocation is defined as a tuple where Ag^j proposes the items to be exchanged (X_e^j, X_e^{1-j}) together with its support (X_s^j, X_s^{1-j}). Formally:

Definition 3 (Proposal). *Let $m^j = (x, \Lambda)$ be a message sent by Ag^j,*

- *A proposal x to exchange and reallocate items is defined as*
  $x = (X_s^j, X_e^j, X_e^{1-j}, X_s^{1-j})$ *where:*

  1. $X_s^j \cup X_e^j \subseteq N^j$
  2. $\sum_{r_i \in X_s^j} W_i^j + \sum_{r_i \in X_e^{1-j}} \widehat{W}_i^j \leq c^j$

  3. $X_s^{1-j} \cup X_e^{1-j} \subseteq N^{1-j}$
  4. $\sum_{r_i \in X_e^j} W_i^j + \sum_{r_i \in X_s^{1-j}} \widehat{W}_i^j \leq c^{1-j}$

  this proposal suggests to exchange the set of items X_e^j for X_e^{1-j} and also suggests to fill Ag^j's knapsack with $X_s^j \cup X_e^j$, where X_s^j represents the items he already has (i.e the exchange support) and X_e^j the items he is asking for exchange.

- *$\Lambda \subseteq I^j$ stands for the private information that the agent Ag^j chooses to disclose.*

---

[1] Notice that these sets include redundant information; however this representation helps to make clearer the different negotiation processes involved in our model. When it is understood which is the agent Ag^j the superscript j is omitted.

As the agents initially may have wrong information about their counterpart (i.e. items weight and values), during the negotiation dialog they update their beliefs (and consequently their mental state) according the messages exchanged. Thus, in the context of the ABN framework [5] we will use a belief update approach for the argument interpretation.

Definition 4 (Belief Update). *Let Ms_t^0 and Ms_t^1 the agents mental state at time t, and $m_{t+1}^0 = (x, \Lambda)$ a message sent by Ag^0. Then the agent Ag^0 updates his beliefs transferring the information he has revealed from private to public information set as follows[2]:*

1. $Ms_{t+1}^0.P = Ms_t^0.P \cup \Lambda$ 2. $Ms_{t+1}^0.I = Ms_t^0.I - \Lambda$

On the other hand, the agent Ag^1 updates his beliefs replacing the assumed values by the ones revealed in the message, making as well this information part of the public information set. Formally:

1. $Ms_{t+1}^1.\widehat{W_i} = \begin{cases} \omega_i & if\ \omega_i^0 \in \Lambda \\ Ms_t^1.\widehat{W_i} & if\ \omega_i^0 \notin \Lambda \end{cases}$ 3. $Ms_{t+1}^1.\widehat{V} = \begin{cases} v_i^0 & if\ v_i^0 \in \Lambda \\ Ms_t^1.\widehat{V_i} & if\ v_i^0 \notin \Lambda \end{cases}$

2. $Ms_{t+1}^1.P = Ms_t^1.P \cup \Lambda$ 4. $Ms_{t+1}^1.\widehat{I} = Ms_t^1.\widehat{I} - \Lambda$

When an agent receives a proposal, he computes its expected utility as the maximum of the utility that can be obtained if the exchange is made, considering the different possibilities to fill his backpack according to that proposal.

Definition 5 (Utility). *Given a proposal $x = (X_s^j, X_e^j, X_e^{1-j}, X_s^{1-j})$, the utility expected for an agent Ag^j is defined as:*

$$U^j(x) = \max \sum_{r_i \in X_s^j \cup X_e^{1-j}} V_i^j$$

$$s.t. \sum_{r_i \in X_s^j} W_i^j + \sum_{r_i \in X_e^{1-j}} \widehat{W_i^j} \le c^j$$

whereas Ag^j's expected utility wrt his counterpart will be defined as:

$$\widehat{U}^j(x) = \max \sum_{r_i \in X_e^j \cup X_s^{1-j}} \widehat{V_i^j}$$

$$s.t. \sum_{r_i \in X_e^j} W_i^j + \sum_{r_i \in X_s^{1-j}} \widehat{W_i^j} \le c^{1-j}$$

In negotiation theory, the *Best Alternative to a Negotiated Agreement* (or BATNA for short) is the course of action that will be taken by a party if the current negotiations fail and an agreement cannot be reached [6]. In our scenario, the BATNA is the proposal that maximizes the utility of the agents without exchanging items.

---

[2] We use dot notation in order to represent the agent's mental state components, e.g. $Ms^j.P$ represents the private information of Ag^j.

Definition 6 (BATNA). *Each Ag^j believes that the Best Alternative to a Negotiated Agreement is defined as:*

$$bat^j = (X_s^j, X_e^j, X_e^{1-j}, X_s^{1-j}) = \arg\max\{U^j(x) + \widehat{U}^j(x) \mid X_e^j = X_e^{1-j} = \emptyset\}$$

If the negotiation break down the agent Ag^j expect to receive $U^j(bat^j)$, and he expect that his counterpart receives $\widehat{U}^j(bat^j)$. Therefore agents will try to suggest proposal with benefit greater than the BATNA benefit.

3 Negotiation Protocol

The Monotonic Concession Protocol is used in problems with complete information [2] where it is assumed that each agent is fully aware of the utility function of its counterpart. This protocol is performed in rounds such that in each round both agents make simultaneously a proposal; in the first round each agent is free to make any proposal, whereas in the following rounds each agent can make an utility concession, i.e. make the new proposal to improve the usefulness of the counterpart about the latest proposal or stay in the previous proposal.

3.1 Protocol Based on Disclosure of Information/Utility

We focus on incomplete information problems where the negotiating agents have beliefs (probably erroneous) about each other. Based on the Monotonic Concession Protocol, we propose a novel protocol where agents can make a concession either regarding *utility* (making a new proposal that improves the expected usefulness of the counterpart compared to the last proposal made) or regarding *information* (revealing private information not disclosed earlier).

The protocol between the two agents is determined by a finite sequence of messages $[m_1^0, m_2^1, m_3^0, m_4^1, ...]$ sent alternately by each agent[3], where each message m_t^j has the form according to Definition 2, we will say that an agent concedes information if a message $m_{t+1}^0 = (x, \Lambda)$ is sent, such that Λ contains information that was not disclosed previously. Formally:

Definition 7 (Concession of Information). *We will say that Ag^0 concedes information in the message $m_{t+1}^0 = (x, \Lambda)$ iff $\Lambda \nsubseteq \Lambda_{t-1} \cup \Lambda_{t-3}..\Lambda_0$. This is denoted as $C_I^0(m_{t+1}^0)$*

Similarly, we will say that an agent concedes utility whenever he believes that the proposal sent in message $m = (x, \Lambda)$ is such that the expected utility for its counterpart represents an improvement compared to the last proposal made. Formally :

Definition 8 (Concession of Utility)

1. Ag^1 concedes utility to Ag^0 in message m_t^1 iff $U^0(m_t^1.x) > U^0(m_{t-2}^1.x)$. This is denoted as $C_U^0(m_t^1)$

---

[3] Without loss of generality we assume that Ag^0 initiates the negotiation.

2. Ag^1 believes that he has conceded utility to Ag^0 in message m_t^1 iff
$\widehat{U}^1(m_t^1.x) > \widehat{U}^1(m_{t-2}^1.x)$ This is denoted as $\widehat{C}_U^1(m_t^1)$

We will define a protocol based on concession of information and concession of utility as follows:

Definition 9 (Protocol). Let $[...m_{t-3}^0, m_{t-2}^1, m_{t-1}^0, m_t^1, m_{t+1}^0]$ be the last part of a dialogue between the two agents. Then m_{t+1}^0 is defined as follows:

1. accept iff $U_t^0(m_t^1.x) \geq U_t^0(m_{t-1}^0.x)$.
2. withdraw iff
$\neg C_I^0(m_{t-3}^0) \wedge \neg C_I^1(m_{t-2}^1) \wedge \neg C_I^0(m_{t-1}^0) \wedge \neg C_I^1(m_t^1) \wedge \neg\widehat{C}_U^0(m_{t-1}^0) \wedge \neg C_U^0(m_t^1)$
3. (x, Λ) such that $U^j(x) \geq U^j(bat^j)$ and $\widehat{U}^j(x) \geq \widehat{U}^j(bat^j)$ Otherwise.

Note that (1) indicates that Ag^j will accept those proposals whose utility is the same or better than the last proposal advanced by the agent itself; (2) indicates that the agent will abandon the negotiation if there was no information concession in the last four messages, nor utility concession in the last two messages; and (3) another proposal will be presented if the previous cases do not hold. Such proposal must better than the BATNA.

4   Negotiation Strategies Based on Information Concession

In this paper, we explore the results of the bilateral negotiation in the Knapsack problem according to different strategies the agents use to disclose information in their messages. Thus, the information that an agent reveals with a proposed exchange can be considered as a *justification* of the current proposal or a *critique* to the last received proposal. An agent can also give private information on items that are considered more or less valuable for him, or information about a random item, among other alternatives. Below, we formalize some of these strategies, analyzing then the results obtained in different experiments we conducted with negotiating agents. For the The Double Knapsack Negotiation Problem, we propose different negotiation strategies in which the agents choose a set Λ containing information's items to reveal.

We assume that in all the alternatives the information an agent communicates is private (i.e. it is fully accurate and associated with his own beliefs) and has not been made public previously in the negotiation process. In our context, the following information concession strategies are defined:

1. **Random:** the agent selects a random item r_i. If $r_i \in N^j$ then he reveals v_i^j and ω_i; otherwise he only communicates v_i^j.
2. **Max:** the intuition behind the Max strategy is that the agent reveals the information of the item that has *the maximum relative value* for him. He first selects $r_i \in N$ such that it maximizes v_i^j/ω_i and reveals v_i^j. Then, he chooses $r_i \in N^j$, maximizing v_i^j/ω_i, and reveals ω_i.

3. **Min:** in analogous way than in the previous strategy, the agent communicates the information of the item that has *the minimum relative value*. Firstly, he selects $r_i \in N$ such that he minimizes v_i^j/ω_i and reveals v_i^j. Then, he chooses $r_i \in N^j$, minimizing v_i^j/ω_i, and communicates ω_i.

4. **Dissimilar:** in this strategy the agent communicates the information related to items r_i such that his current proposal differs from the last received proposal. It can be seen as a justification of his counterproposal based on the differences. Formally, let $x = (X_s^0, X_e^0, X_e^1, X_s^1)$ be the proposal made by Ag^{1-j} and $Y = (Y_s^0, Y_e^0, Y_e^1, Y_s^1)$ the current proposal of Ag^j then, Ag^j does not reveal ω_i, v_i^j if $r_i \in (X_s^0 \cap Y_s^0) \cup (X_e^0 \cap Y_e^0) \cup (X_e^1 \cap Y_e^1) \cup (X_s^1 \cap Y_s^1)$

5. **Similar:** this approach is complementary to the previous one, since it communicates all items where there is an overlap between the counterproposal and the last received proposal. Formally let $x = (X_s^0, X_e^0, X_e^1, X_s^1)$ be the proposal made by Ag^{1-j} and $Y = (Y_s^0, Y_e^0, Y_e^1, Y_s^1)$ the Ag^j current proposal then, Ag^j revels ω_i, v_i^j if $r_i \in (X_s^0 \cap Y_s^0) \cup (X_e^0 \cap Y_e^0) \cup (X_e^1 \cap Y_e^1) \cup (X_s^1 \cap Y_s^1)$

It must be remarked that every negotiation process using some of the above strategies concedes information, since agents are allowed to concede pieces of knowledge until all possible individual knowledge has been disclosed. If such is the case, then both agents will accept the resulting solution to the problem.

5   Experiments and Results

We have implemented different kinds of negotiating agents following the proposed model and selecting –in each case– one of the five strategies we have defined in the previous Section 4. We have conducted a number of experiments, where both agents use the same strategy, with the aim of comparing the results of the negotiation process in terms of the total utility gained, information revealed and duration of the negotiation. Next, we present the experiments that were carried out and the results obtained.

Experiments Design: We have run 30 negotiating simulations for problems of size N (i.e. number of items), experimenting with $N = 6 \ldots 40$. In all the negotiation problems the two agents have been assigned $N/2$ items and each knapsack was assumed to support a maximum weight of 550. The items weight ω_i were generated randomly in the range [50..100] and the items value v_i^j were also random values in the range [30..80]. The default knowledge each agent initially was also set randomly with an accuracy of ±30.

We assume as well that both agents are trustworthy (no false information is communicated on purpose). The agents send messages (x, Λ) where x is the proposal for exchanging items and Λ accounts for information that the agent is willing to reveal according to the strategy selected.

The generated proposal x corresponds to the assignment that maximizes $\lambda U^j(x) + (1 - \lambda)\widehat{U}^j(x)$, where $\lambda \in [0,1]$ is a parameter that allows to weigh his own estimated utility and the estimated utility for its counterpart. Different values for λ can represent how "collaborative" the agent is when generating proposals (i.e. different agent personalities). If $\lambda = 1$ then, the agent is assessing only his own utility (selfish agent), whereas $\lambda = 0$ stands for a totally generous agent. An intermediate value, i.e. $\lambda = 0.5$, can be assumed to represent equitable agents which combine both utilities with the same weight. For our experiments we have considered that both agents are equitable ($\lambda = 0.5$).

The aim of the experiments is to analyze the outcomes of the negotiating agents using the five strategies. The results to be analyzed are:

- *The negotiation length:* number of messages exchanged during the negotiating process.
- *The hiding of information:* the ratio of information items that were not revealed in the negotiation process respect to the total of private items in the problem.
- *Expected-Real Efficiency ratio:* the rate of the expected utility value of the reached agreement, with respect to the utility obtained after carrying out the exchange of items.
- *Expected-Optimal Efficiency ratio:* the rate of the expected utility value of the reached agreement, with respect to the utility obtained in the outcome of the same negotiation problem under complete information.

Results: Figure 1a shows the average over the number of messages per negotiation for different sizes of negotiating problems. As the strategies *Dissimilar* and *Similar* can exchange more information items in each message, they tend to reach faster a negotiation agreement than the other ones, requiring consequently less duration. From both of them, *Dissimilar* has the best performance concerning duration.

Figure 1b shows the percentage of private information non disclosed during the negotiation processes. We can observe that the strategy that allows agents to share less private information is the *Dissimilar*. The results of the rest of the strategies have a similar behavior. They are under the 10% of concealment for problems of size 10 or greater, i.e. reveal almost all the information until the negotiation process concludes. We can notice the behavior change in the graphics around problems size 15. In our experiments, the item's weights and the knapsacks capacities used allow a maximum amount of items for each knapsack closer to 7 items in average, thus we consider that it is the reason the strategies behave differently when the problem's size is less than 15.

In Figure 1c we present the average results of the *Expected-Optimal Efficiency* (i.e the ratio of the total expected utility obtained respect to the utility associated with the problem under complete information). We can observe that the performance obtained with the strategy *Dissimilar* has a ratio between 96% and 100%. This percentage is less than the one obtained with the other ones because this is the strategy that allow the agents to reach an agreement with less information exchange. Even so, we notice that for problems size greater than 15, the obtained ratio is over 99.5%. Thus, we can conclude that the *Dissimilar* strategy allows the agents to obtain total utility results closer to the ones

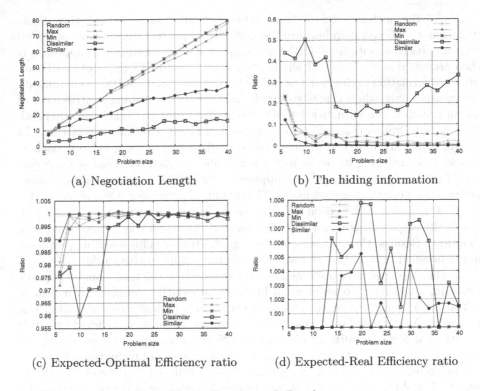

(a) Negotiation Length

(b) The hiding information

(c) Expected-Optimal Efficiency ratio

(d) Expected-Real Efficiency ratio

Fig. 1. Experiment's Results

obtained in the problems under complete information, but with less information exchange and in fewer iterations.

Because the negotiating agents may reach an agreement with incomplete information, after carrying out the exchange of items, the accepted proposal expected utility may be not equal to the utility received after exchanging the items, we call this the "real" utility. Figure 1d shows the *Expected-Real Efficiency ratio* obtained after the negotiation wrt the expected one. The strategies that reveal more information are the ones with ratio nearest to 1.

6 Related Work and Conclusions

In recent years, there have been several approaches concerned with formalizing negotiation in multiagent environments. ABN-based approaches emphasize the impact of the information exchanged with the proposals in the negotiating process [4]. To the best of our knowledge, there are no previous studies addressing how negotiating agents can select the information to exchange and the impact the different strategies have in the negotiation process. Next, we will briefly discuss some recent research related to our proposal.

In [7] the authors explore how exchanging information about the agents underlying goals can help improve the negotiation process, formalizing so-called "interest-based negotiation" (IBN). An empirical assessment of this approach is then presented in [8]. Our work shares some aspects with IBN (e.g. notion of deal, utility, information exchange), but differs in that the agents in IBN communicate information only when this is required. Another distinguishing contribution of our approach is the formalization of a "cannonical problem" (Double Knapsack Negotiation Problem) in order to compare and assess alternative strategies. In [9], an algorithm based on Branch and Bound to search for good proposals is introduced, analyzing its performance in a problem called the *Negotiating Salesmen Problem*. In contrast with our approach, the Salesmen agents have complete information about the environment. Pilotti et al. in [5] present a formalization for bilateral negotiation based on belief revision. In contrast with the present proposal, this approach is based on belief revision operators (including an incision function). Besides, they neither consider agents strategies for selecting proposals nor concession information strategies, as we have done in this work.

In this paper we have presented a novel approach to the traditional Knapsack problem, adapting it to represent a bilateral negotiating problem with default information. Also, a protocol based on utility and information concession was proposed. As discussed in the introduction, the focus of our work was to provide a suitable model for capturing different negotiation strategies in agent dialogues. We have implemented this negotiation model in C++ and using the solver Scip (http://scip.zib.de/). The agents using this solver are capable to deal with big knapsack problems. As the illocutions the agents exchange in the proposed model are very simple, we did not consider it necessary to use an agent communication platform (e.g. JADE).

Besides, we have developed different kinds of negotiating agents following the proposed model and selecting –in each case– one of the five strategies we have defined. The experiments allow us to compare the results of the negotiation process in terms of the total utility gained, information revealed and duration of the negotiation. As result, we can conclude that *Dissimilar* gives good results considering a balance between the three analyzed aspects. The intuition behind this strategy is that the agent reveals information supporting a counter-proposal from the point of view of the differences with the previous proposal.

Part of our future work involves the study and analysis of alternative strategies and their impact for reaching agreements. Also, we want to compare the individual results of negotiating agents modeled using different strategies and varying the accuracy level of their initial beliefs. The resulting protocol can be enriched by including additional considerations (e.g. costs associated with making some particular proposal, etc.) and moreover, another protocol can be experienced. Another issue which deserves particular consideration is a full-fledged model with a group of different agents, where two or more agents can get involved in a negotiation dialogue using extended notions of information and utility (e.g. some information or utility could be disclosed only for the other agent in the dialogue, or to all the other agents in the group). Research in these directions is currently underway.

Acknowledgments. The authors thank the anonymous reviewers for many useful comments that have helped to significantly improve the paper and acknowledge the partial support of the Research Projects PICT-ANPCyT 2009-0015, PID-UNR ING 466, PIP-Conicet 112-200801-02798 and LACCIR Project R1211LAC004.

References

1. Rahwan, I., Ramchurn, S.D., Jennings, N.R., Mcburney, P., Parsons, S., Sonenberg, L.: Argumentation-based negotiation. Knowl. Eng. Rev. **18**, 343–375 (2003)
2. Rosenschein, J.S., Zlotkin, G.: Rules of Encounter - Designing Conventions for Automated Negotiation among Computers. MIT Press (1994)
3. Jennings, N.R., Faratin, P., Lomuscio, A.R., Parsons, S., Sierra, C., Wooldridge, M.: Automated negotiation: Prospects, methods and challenges. International Journal of Group Decision and Negotiation **10**(2), 199–215 (2001)
4. Amgoud, L., Dimopoulos, Y., Moraitis, P.: A unified and general framework for argumentation-based negotiation. In: Proceedings of the 6th International Joint Conference on Autonomous Agents and Multiagent Systems, AAMAS 2007 (2007)
5. Pilotti, P., Casali, A., Chesñevar, C.: A belief revision approach for argumentation-based negotiation with cooperative agents. In: McBurney, P., Parsons, S., Rahwan, I., (eds.) Post-Proceedings of the 9th International Workshop on Argumentation in Multi-Agent Systems (ArgMAS 2013) (2013)
6. Fisher, R., Ury, W.L.: Getting to Yes: Negotiating Agreement Without Giving, 2nd edn. Penguin (Non-Classics) (December 1991)
7. Rahwan, I., Pasquier, P., Sonenberg, L., Dignum, F.: On the benefits of exploiting underlying goals in argument-based negotiation. In: Twenty-Second Conference on Artificial Intelligence (AAAI), Vancouver, pp. 116–121 (2007)
8. Pasquier, P., Hollands, R., Rahwan, I., Dignum, F., Sonenberg, L.: An empirical study of interest-based negotiation. Autonomous Agents and Multi-Agent Systems **22**(2), 249–288 (2011)
9. Jonge, D.D., Sierra, C.: Branch and bound for negotiations in large agreement spaces. In: van der Hoek, W., Padgham, L., Conitzer, V., Winikoff, M., (eds.) AAMAS, IFAAMAS, pp. 1415–1416 (2012)

Institutional Environments: A Framework for the Development of Open Multiagent Systems

Marcos de Oliveira[1($\boxtimes$)], Enyo Golçalves[1], and Martin Purvis[2]

[1] Universidade Federal do Ceará, Quixadá, Brazil
{marcos.oliveira,enyo}@ufc.br
[2] University of Otago, Dunedin, New Zealand
martin.purvis@otago.ac.nz

Abstract. This paper focuses on the development of open Multiagent Systems. It is argued here that this kind of system can be designed and implemented as institutional environments, where heterogeneous agents can participate by playing roles, and interact by means of institutional acts. To have that set up an institutional model was designed and implemented in a framework where are employed technologies such as Coloured Petri Nets, for the Agent's Role design and implementation, commitments among agents and agent's reputation, for norm enforcement and social order management.

Keywords: Institution of Agents · Commitments · Reputation · Colored Petri Nets

1 Introduction

This paper explores the ideas behind an approach to design and develop open Multiagent Systems (MAS). It is defined here Institutional Environments where heterogeneous agents can participate by playing roles and interact by means of institutional acts. To have that set up a distributed architecture was designed and implemented as a framework using technologies such as Coloured Petri Nets (CPN) [1,2], commitments [3], reputation [4,5], model checking [6,7], object-oriented language, functional language, temporal logic formulas, and an environment for development of FIPA-based agents and FIPA-ACL-based message exchange [8].

Those technologies are employed in this work to approach the following problems:

- Concurrent conversation management and representation (using CPN);
- Institutional norm representation and enforcement (using commitments);
- Implementation of social control, i.e. the imposition of constraints on the behavior of agents that agree to become members of the MAS (using reputation).

This work explores various approaches to designing and implementing novel open MAS, where a common architecture for organizational infrastructures is employed. We claim to have developed a distributed architecture, which leaves out a middleware layer and organizational proxy agents [9].

© Springer International Publishing Switzerland 2014
A.L.C. Bazzan and K. Pichara (Eds.): IBERAMIA 2014, LNAI 8864, pp. 560–571, 2014.
DOI: 10.1007/978-3-319-12027-0_45

The institutional environment is built upon an architecture, that gives more autonomy to the agents in the sense that there are no strict interface agents involved in the process of interoperation as in other approaches [10,11,12,13], but instead we have a normative workflow that guides the agents in their interactions in the environment. The normative space has implemented in it mechanisms to contemplate interactions unpredicted at design time, allowing for more flexibility to the agents' behavior in the institutions. The reputation of the agents is built upon their behavior, and it associates with the agents a label that can be verified before others start interacting with them implementing social control [4].

1.1   Research Contributions

Institutional Environments bring the following benefits:

- External agents can participate in both audited and non-audited interactions, and our institutional environments provide auditing and reputation management services so that the developers of external agents do not need to write code for that.
- In our approach we implement elements that aim to make the institutional environment more distributed. This is different from the majority of approaches present in the current research where there is a great use of middleware to provide a controlled environment for the implementation of organizational infrastructures. We provide a way to develop institutional environments where the external agents do not need to worry about how the services provided by the system agents from the environment are implemented.
- Agents present in the institutional environment implement behaviors in the form of workflows defined as Coloured Petri Nets. This allows for the modeling and implementation of conversations with a tool made to handle concurrent processes.
- The organizational control of the institutional environment is distributed in the agents that are part of it. With that we aim to have a more scalable environment suitable to manage concurrent and asynchronous conversations.
- In our approach we had the concern to separate system level concepts from the domain level concepts. Applying counts-as rules to manipulate low level concerns of the Institutional Environment addresses issues that would influence higher level concerns of the agents involved in the Institutional Environment.
- We use commitment objects for the implementation of norms in an Institutional Environment. This choice fits well with our proposal to implement norms that regulate the environment and norms that regulate agreements unpredicted at design time among agents present in the institutional environment.
- Our approach uses a model checker for the manipulation of a history of facts, relevant for the change of state of the commitment objects. These commitments represent the social norms in our Institutional Environments. The model checker verifies temporal propositions used to define the condition and content of commitments, allowing for the management of the temporal characteristics of these commitments' attributes.

1.2   Structure

The next section describes the specification of Institutional Environments.. After that, the Institution Agent system role is described, the empirical evaluation is analyzed, and some conclusions are made.

2   Specification of the IE

A significant characteristic of our approach is its open and distributed nature. Elements are organized in such a way that they are not compelled to report their actions to any other participating agent in the structure. We define our Institutional Environment (IE) as:

$$IE = (O_s, N_s, I_a) \tag{1}$$

Where:

- O_s stands for system ontology;
- N_s stands for normative space;
- I_a stands for institutional actions.

The N_s is defined as:

$$N_s = (R_s, R_e, O_c, L, C) \tag{2}$$

Where:

- R_s stands for system roles;
- R_e stands for external roles and corresponds to roles available to be played by external agents that register to the institutional environment; they are made available in the form of Deputy Agents that are allocated to external agents fulfilling some role in the institutional environment;
- O_c stands for context ontology;
- L stands for content language and represents the language expressed in the content attribute of the FIPA ACL messages exchanged among agents in the N_s;
- C stands for commitments. These can be social commitments when an external agent commits with the institutional environment represented by the Institution Agent, or compulsory commitments embedded in the interaction protocols used by the external agents. Regular commitments that are made necessary through the request of monitored interactions not predicted in the interaction protocols are not listed here but most definitely can appear in the institutional environment.

We identify three types of commitments:

- The **Social Commitment** is defined with an external agent as debtor and the Institution Agent as creditor.

- The Institution Agent represents the entity in charge of managing the IE, and therefore rules from the society are enforced through the creation of the social commitments, and their observation when defining the reputation of the agents that are registered in the IE. **Compulsory Commitments** are defined by the context of the application domain, and their creation is embedded in the CPNs of the Deputy Agents. Deputy Agents enact the roles that external agents can play in the IE, and the compulsory commitments are defined among external agents.
- **Regular Commitments** are the ones that are not defined at design time but that can become necessary in some conversations at run time. As the external agents have the option of developing conversations that are not pre-defined by the IE, they might find it necessary to create a commitment that was not predicted at design time.

The O_s and O_c are defined separately because they represent concepts related to the management of the IE, in the first case, and concepts related with the application domain where the IE is found in the second case. These represent separate concerns.

The content language L is used to construct expressions that contain elements from O_s and O_c, and represent statements exchanged among agents in the IE through FIPA ACL messages.

The system level infrastructure identifies system agents that assume roles from R_s and are deployed to manage the interactions in the N_s.

The following describes such agents:

- Institution Agent: This agent is responsible for the registration of external agents in the system and management of the facts that trigger the change o state of he commitments managed by the Monitor Agent.
- Monitor Agent: This system agent represents a monitoring authority in the institutional environment. It monitors certain activities, defined as institutional actions, according to the norms represented by commitments that are defined in the normative space.
- Reputation Agent: This agent stores and updates the reputation of the external agents that play a role in the system.

3   Institutional Agent Workflow

The Institution Agent is the system agent responsible for the registration, unregistration and change of role of agents external to the institutional environment. All the interactions between the external agent and the agents in the institutional environment are made upon the exchange of FIPA ACL messages. The FIPA ACL messages will have, in their content, reference to institutional acts identified in the institutional environment application domain when it was modeled. For example, in an auction institutional environment we could have the following contents: (register (role auctioneer)), (bid (value 1000)) or (declare_winner (agent_name buyer01@auctionhouse).

Like the other system agents and all the deputies modeled, the Institution Agent has its role represented by a CPN, shown in Figure 1 above. One can identify the In places, where incoming messages from different agents arrive represented as CPN tokens of type message, and Out places where messages are put to be sent to other agents. It is important to mention that the CPNs are connected through FIPA message passing; therefore there is no problem to have all the CPNs that represent the agents' roles with these special places named In and Out.

The routing of messages is made through Opal and, for example, all the messages addressed to the Institutional Agent will be delivered to its In place without causing any confusion with the other In places from other roles. The Out place, likewise, is always checked for the arrival of tokens every time a run in the JFern CPN simulator is made; if there are tokens available they are taken out of the Out places and delivered to the In places of the other agent through Opal FIPA message passing layer. The workflows are therefore connected through Opal´s FIPA message passing layer

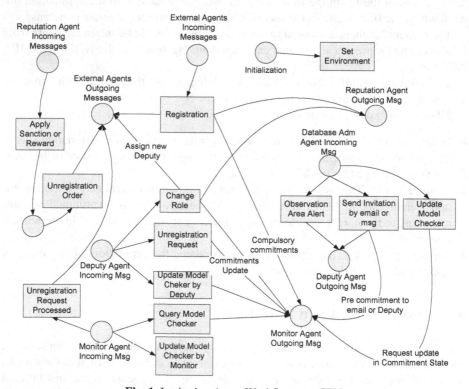

Fig. 1. Institution Agent Workflow as a CPN

4   Empirical Evaluation

To evaluate our model we have developed a prototype of a Institutional Environment based in the WikiCrimes Collaborative System (www.wikicrimes.org) [16]. In the

WikiCrimes system users can interact with the system do add information about crime occurrences as well as, consult information and corroborate with the veracity of it. The WikiCrimes Institutional Environment prototype simulates the interaction from real users with the modeling of agent roles that makes external agents able to behave as real users would in the real system. In the next subsections we explore empirically the creation of the prototype developed.

4.1   Roles

- **Browser User:** the user that browses the institutional environment basically seeks information in the system. The institution will try to make this kind of user assume the Registered User Role.
- **Registered User:** in this role the agent will be a typical user of a collaborative system. In the case of the WikiCrimes Institutional Environment, it will be able to register crimes, browse the environment, confirm crimes, denounce abuse, disconfirm crimes and invite other agents to confirm crimes. These invited agents can be a Registered User or external agents that are not registered yet in the institutional environment but can become an Invited User only to confirm the crime and decide if they want to become Registered Uscrs.
- **Invited User:** this role is played by the agent that is indicated to confirm a crime. The indication is done by an agent playing the Registered User role. This agent is one step closer to playing the Registered User role rather than the Browser User.
- **Certifier Entity:** this is a special kind of role played by agents that own a respected position in the WikiCrimes Institutional Environment. This agent has the reputation of a System Agent; the difference is that the Registered Users should not denounce abuses or disconfirm crimes registered by this category of agent. If this situation arises it could be an indication that the Certifier Entity can have their position in the WikiCrimes Institutional Environment reviewed or possibly that they have made a mistake.

4.2   Institutional Acts

Apart from the generic institutional acts that are defined for any institutional environment implemented using our approach, there are the specific institutional acts that relate to the application domain of the WikiCrimes System [16]. Below we list the institutional acts that initiate interaction protocols in the agents' workflows, and the respective agents that participate in the interaction. The agents that use the institutional act are specified in parentheses, where 'generic' means that all the external agents can use the act and 'specific' means that only the listed roles use the act:

- Registration (generic)
- Deregistration (generic)
- Change Role (specific, an Invited User requests to be Registered User; a Browser User requests to be Registered User; a Registered User requests to be Certifier Entity)
- Register a Criminal Fact (specific, Registered User, Certifier Entity)

- Invite to Confirm a Crime (specific, Database Administrator Agent)
- Commitment Proposal (specific, Monitor Agent)
- Confirm a Crime (specific, Registered User, Invited User)
- Denouncing Abuse (specific, Registered User)
- Commenting on a Criminal Fact (specific, Registered User)
- Commenting on the Institutional Environment (specific, Registered User, Browser User, Invited User)
- Registering an Observation Area (specific, Registered User)
- Deregistering an Observation Area (specific, Registered User)
- Ask for a safe route (Generic)
- Query the Criminal Database (Generic)
- Query the Reputation Database (Specific, Registered User):
- Ask another Agent to be part of a group (Specific, Registered User)

4.3 Workflows

The workflows developed in the Institutional Environment are managed by the JFern CPN Tool Box [15]. For each workflow, an instance of the tool is created for the visualization of the message-passing among the agents that are registered with the institutional environment. Of course the number of visual instances of the tool can be managed to avoid overload of the system or visual confusion on the screen.

The Database Administrator Agent workflow manages the Institutional Acts that are related to the storage or retrieval of information from a Database Management System. In the Case of the WikiCrimes Institutional Environment there are the general Institutional Acts, present to all the institutional environments that require this type of system agent.

All the negotiation with the Database Management System, which manages the criminal database, is made by side effects implemented in the transitions of the Database Administrator Agent.

The Deputy Agents have a generic workflow, depicted in Figure 2. This workflow manages all the institutional acts that are used in any institutional environment. The specification of the institutional acts that are specific to a role identified in the institutional environment is done by the expansion of the subnet "Process specific institutional actions". The subnet has all the input places connected to new transitions that form the particulars of the behaviour of the role and leads to output places drawn in the Deputy Agent Generic Workflow bellow.

The Deputy Registered User and the Deputy Certifier Entity have the same specific behaviour implemented. These two roles basically deal with the Database Management Agent to register a criminal fact, comment on a criminal fact, confirm a criminal fact and denounce abuses in the WikiCrimes Institutional Environment. They can also invite another deputy agent to be part of a group, for example, to join people from a neighbourhood or that have other particular interests in registering criminal facts in that region or evaluating if the information registered in the criminal database can be confirmed positively or negatively. The distinction between these two roles is only in relation to the reputation model implemented in the WikiCrimes Institutional Environment.

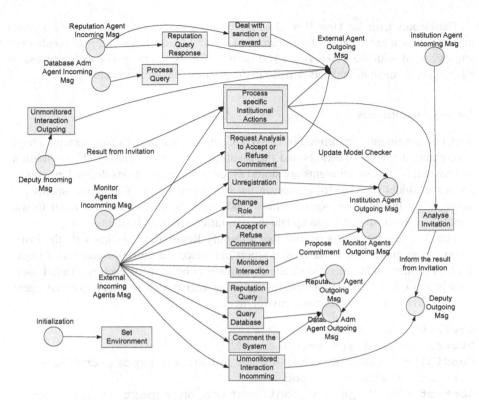

Fig. 2. Deputy Agent generic workflow as a CPN

A Certifier Entity is a special kind of agent that represents a person or group of persons that have a high level of reputation that cannot be changed and should not be complained about. If this happens it might be an indication that the Certifier Entity has committed a mistake or that a Registered User is trying to change the image of this agent in the Institutional Environment. Examples of this kind of institution are the police department or a well-established newspaper. The Deputy Registered User does not have the same treatment in relation to its reputation in the WikiCrimes Institutional Environment. It has its reputation evaluated all the time by the observation of the commitments that it assumes in the institutional environment.

The Registered User and Certifier Entity roles can as well invite other external agents to confirm a crime. This invitation is sent to the Institution Agent because it will check if the agent is already registered with the WikiCrimes Institutional Environment, or not. If the agent is registered it is proposed for the Institutional agent to assume the commitment of confirming a crime within a maximum of 15 days from the invitation, or, if the agent is not registered, an email is sent to the External Agent inviting it to join the institutional environment to confirm a crime. A pre-commitment is generated in this last case, and it becomes active if the external agent joins the WikiCrimes Institutional Environment and accepts the invitation to confirm the crime within a maximum of 15 days past the registration.

The Deputy Browser User Workflow represents a random user that is only browsing the criminal environment for information trying to meet other external agents that are registered with the WikiCrimes Institutional Environment. It is capable of using all the generic institutional acts defined in the institutional environment.

4.4   Commitments

Social commitments are defined in the WikiCrimes Institutional Environment. These have external agents as debtors and the Institution Agent as creditor. The condition and content of the commitments are stored as temporal propositions defined as formulas in the Model Checker [6] present in the Institution Agent. The commitments are managed by the Monitor Agent, which sends updates on the state of them to the Reputation Agent so that it can update the reputation score of the debtors.

This first commitment is the one that a Deputy Registered User has with the Institution Agent that it will never have a report denounced as abuse or confirmed negatively. For this commitment, a standard template is offered for each registered user. This is a compulsory commitment that is set at registration to every external agent that registers with the institutional environment.

Creditor InstitutionAgent
Debtor DeputyRegisteredUser_001
Condition DeputyRegisteredUser_submited_report **and** Report_has_status_accepted
Content not (Negative_confirmation_on_report_is_made **or** Abuse_denouce_on_report_is_made)

Related to this commitment there is a set of three counts-as rules that refers to institutional facts that may result from them (listed below). Those rules express the necessary infrastructure for the institutional environment to carry on with the evaluation of the commitments. The counts-as rules are defined here to separate low-level concerns related to the functioning of the institutional environment from the high-level concerns that relate to the application domains of the institutional environment.

The counts-as rules are verified by the Institution Agent, which inserts new states in the model checker where the counts-as part of the rule is asserted as true or false. The history of the model checker will determine if the propositions that represent the condition and content of the commitments are true or false in the moment of its evaluation. The three counts-as rules are listed as follows:

InstitutionAgent_is_Online
and MonitorAgent_is_Online
and ReputationAgent_is_Online
and DatabaseAdministratorAgent_is_Online
and DeputyRegisteredUser_is_Online
and
DatabaseAdministratorAgent_receives_RegisterCriminalFactMessage

counts as `Report_has_status_accepted`

`InstitutionAgent_receives_Negative_Confirmation_Informati`
`on_from_DatabaseAdmAgent`
counts as `Negative_confirmation_on_report_is_made`

`InstitutionAgent_receives_AbuseDenounce_from_RegisteredUs`
`er`
or
`InstitutionAgent_receives_AbuseDenounce_from_InvitedUser`
or `InstitutionAgent_receives_AbuseDenounce_ from_Browser`
`User`
counts as `Abuse_denouce_on_report_is_made`

For the evaluation of the counts-as rules, the reports are identified by an ID that is added to the institutional fact when the model present in the model checker is updated.

The next commitment is the one that the Deputy Invited User has with the Institution Agent that it will confirm a crime positively or negatively within 15 days from the invitation to confirm a crime.

Creditor `InstitutionAgent`
Debtor `DeputyInvitedUser`
Condition `Invitation_has_status_accepted`
Content `Confirmation_on_report_is_made_within_15_days`

In that commitment:

`InstitutionAgent_is_Online`
and `MonitorAgent_is_Online`
and `ReputationAgent_is_Online`
and `DatabaseAdministratorAgent_is_Online`
and `DeputyInvitedUser_is_Online`
and `InstitutionAgent_received_InvitationAcceptanceMessage`
counts as `Invitation_has_status_accepted`

In the last commitment if Invitation_has_status_accepted, the Deputy Invited User can change his role with the Institution Agent to Deputy Registered User and the Monitor Agent reassigns the commitment to the Deputy Registered User.

The Deputy Registered Agents can check the reputation of agents that have registered crimes in the area where it has registered crimes and ask them to form a group of agents that register crime together in a specific area. If the agent does not check the reputation, before sending the invitation to form a group, they may get partners with bad behaviour in the group. But it is an option for the agent that is inviting others to participate in the group. It may have it own history about the behaviour of a specific external agent that has not yet developed a good reputation in the institutional environment and, decide to send the invitation anyway.

Another policy that can be employed could be for the Institution Agent to check from time to time the reputation database to identify agents with a bad reputation score. These agents can then be asked to perform better or leave the institutional environment.

5   Conclusions

An important aspect of our approach is that we do not use finite state machines to represent an electronic institution and the conversations in the institution. Our approach is the use of CPNs to represent the institution's normative space and conversation space, which includes the roles played by agents in the institution. By that we seek the use of a formalism defined over concurrency concepts and powerful semantics relating states and actions. In our workflows we can accommodate concurrent interactions, a feature that is not possible through the use of finite state machines.

Our aim has been to enable real distributed environments to be built observing institutional norms. The strict control associated with conventional interface agents of other approaches is too restrictive and more middleware-like than agent-like. That approach was taken to allow more autonomy for the agents registered in the institutional environment, since they may not behave as predicted at the design time of the Institutional Environment. Embedded in the Institutional Environment model is the capacity of developing unpredicted behavior that may be very pertinent to more autonomous agents with a higher capacity for reasoning.

The empirical evaluation, with the development of the WikiCrimes Institutional Environment, has demonstrated the suitability of our model for the development of true open SMAs, making possible as well the construction of a more scalable environment where heterogeneous agents can join the artificial institution at any time and pursue its goals being the system agents responsible to establish the social order in the system.

References

1. Jensen, K.: Coloured Petri Nets - Basic Concepts, Analysis, Methods and Pratical Use. In: EATCS Monographs on Theoretical Computer Science, vol. I (1992)
2. Cost, R., Chen, Y., Finin, T., Labrou, Y., Peng, Y.: Using Coloured Petri Nets for Conversation Modelling. In: Dignum, F.P., Greaves, M. (eds.) Issues in Agent Communication. LNCS, vol. 1916, pp. 178–192. Springer, Heidelberg (2000)
3. Fornara, N., Colombetti, M.: Operational specification of a commitment-based agent communication language. In: First International Joint Conference on Autonomous Agents and Multiagent Systems, pp. 536–542 (2002)
4. Castelfranchi, C.: Engineering Social Order. In: Omicini, A., Tolksdorf, R., Zambonelli, F. (eds.) ESAW 2000. LNCS (LNAI), vol. 1972, pp. 1–18. Springer, Heidelberg (2000)
5. Conte, R., Paolucci, M.: Reputation in Artificial Societies. Social Beliefs for Social Order. Kluwer Academic Publishers, Dordrecht (2002)

6. Cranefield, S., Winikoff, M.: Verifying Social Expectations by Model Checking Truncated Paths. In: Hübner, J.F., Matson, E., Boissier, O., Dignum, V. (eds.) COIN@AAMAS 2008. LNCS, vol. 5428, pp. 204–219. Springer, Heidelberg (2009)
7. Markey, N., Schnoebelen, P.: Model Checking a Path. In: Amadio, R.M., Lugiez, D. (eds.) CONCUR 2003. LNCS, vol. 2761, pp. 251–265. Springer, Heidelberg (2003)
8. FIPA, FIPA ACL Message Structure Specification (SC00061) (2002)
9. Hübner, J., Boissier, O., Kitio, R., Ricci, A.: Instrumenting multi-agent organisations with organisational artifacts and agents Giving the organisational power back to the agents. In: Autonomous Agents and Multi-Agent Systems Conference (AAMAS), pp. 369–400 (2010)
10. Esteva, M.: Electronic Institutions: from specification to development (2003)
11. Esteva, M., Rodríguez-Aguilar, J.A., Rosell, B., Arcos, J.L.: AMELI: An agent-based middleware for electronic institutions. In: Proceedings of the Third International Joint Conference on Autonomous Agents and Multi-Agent Systems (AAMAS 2004), New York, pp. 236–243 (2004)
12. Boissier, O., Hübner, J.F., Sichman, J.S.: Organization oriented programming: from closed to open organizations. In: O'Hare, G.M., Ricci, A., O'Grady, M.J., Dikenelli, O. (eds.) ESAW 2006. LNCS (LNAI), vol. 4457, pp. 86–105. Springer, Heidelberg (2007)
13. Minsky, N., Ungureanu, V.: Law-Governed Interaction: a Coordination and Control Mechanism for Heterogeneous Distributed Systems. ACM Transactions on Software Engineering and Methodology 9(3), 273–305 (2000)
14. Nowostawski, M., Purvis, M., Cranefield, S.: OPAL - A Multi-level Infractructure for Agent-Oriented Development. In: International Joint Conference on Autonomous Agents and Multi-Agent Systems, pp. 88–89 (2002)
15. Nowostawski, M., Fern, J.: Manual (2009)
16. Furtado, V., et al.: Collective intelligence in law enforcement – The WikiCrimes system. Information Sciences - Informatics and Computer Science Intelligent System Applications 180(1), 4–17 (2010)

Huginn: Normative Reasoning Based on Mood

Tiago Luiz Schmitz[✉] and Jomi Fred Hübner

Federal University of Santa Catarina, CP 476, Florianópolis, SC 88040-900, Brazil
tiagolschmitz@gmail.com, jomi@das.ufsc.br

Abstract. A multi-agent system can be helped by a normative system that guides its (autonomous) agents towards an expected behavior. The agents on their side have to reason about the impact of those norms in its personal goals. Considering that agents have limited resources, it is necessary to reason also about available resources and whether they are enough to reach goals related to obligations. A proposal for this kind of reasoning is relevant in some applications, however current proposals for normative reasoning do not consider the limited resources. This paper proposes a deliberation process that uses the concept of mood to reason about norms, desires and resources. The proposed deliberation process translates the norms, desires and resources to an optimization problem known as multidimensional knapsack problem with multiple-choice.

Keywords: Norms · Reasoning · Limited resources

1 Introduction

MAS is a suitable approach to develop open systems where unknown agents can enter and leave freely. To protect these systems against malicious agents, a normative system can be used to control the agents behavior [1]. From the agent side, the ability to understand and interpret the normative system is a desirable feature.

A normative agent likely needs to solve conflicts between desires and norms. Sometimes these agents have a desire to reach a specific goal, but a norm prohibits it to reach this goal. For example, while an agent wants to reach the top of the hill, a norm forbids to reach the top. These agents need thus to balance what is best for them and for the group, then they can decide whether to commit a goal.

In the specific case where normative agents have limited resources they need to reason also about available resources. Sometimes, an agent can agree with the norm, but it does not have enough resources to reach the goal related to the norm. Or, the norm's reward does not justify the required resource.

An agent that is capable to reason about norms and manage resources can get better results for the system and for itself within its contexts. Mobile robots are an application for this proposal, because they work with limited resources and in some cases they need to choose between the norm and the desire. For example, a robot in mars has accepted a norm that obliges it to gather rocks

© Springer International Publishing Switzerland 2014
A.L.C. Bazzan and K. Pichara (Eds.): IBERAMIA 2014, LNAI 8864, pp. 572–584, 2014.
DOI: 10.1007/978-3-319-12027-0_46

and it also has the desire to say in the safety zone. The rocks however are out of the safety zone. The agent also has only 5 units of fuel. Therefore the agent needs to solve the conflict between the norm and the desire (to gather rocks or to stay in the safety zone) and do not spend more fuel than it has.

This paper proposes a reasoning model inspired in the mood concept [2] capable to deliberate about desires and norms, considering available resources. The proposed model is called Huggin and is conceived to be an extension of BDI architecture.

This paper is divided in 7 sections. The section 2 presents the background concepts of norms, desires and mood. The section 3 presents the model proposed in this paper. The section 4 presents a problem instance to exemplify the proposed model. The section 5 presents some preliminaries results about the time response. The section 6 presents a short descriptions about related works and a comparison among the related works and the proposed model. At last, the section 7 presents a consideration about the model features, and perspectives of future works.

2   Preliminaries

2.1   Norms

Norms are representations of ideal behaviors. Many studies [3–5] in the sociology field describe different norms types in the same normative system. In this paper we dealt with deontic norms. These norms usually define obligations, prohibitions, and permissions for the agents. Obligations can be used to define states of the world that agents have to achieve. Prohibitions can be used to define states of the world that agents have to not achieve. Permissions are not explicitly considered in this paper, but can be seen as the negation of a prohibition.

Normally norms are not applied all the time. Their specifications have thus activation and expiration conditions. The activation condition defines when the norm is active. The agent knows that when the activation condition is true, it needs to accomplish the norm. The expiration condition defines when the norm is inactive. The sanction is the negative reinforcement for an agent who does not accomplish a norm. The reward is the positive reinforcement for an agent that accomplish a norm. In this paper, we adopt the norm [6] as represented by the tuple 1:

$$\langle D, C, T, A, E, S, R \rangle \tag{1}$$

Where $D \in \{O, F\}$ is the deontic norm's type, obligation (O) or prohibition (F); C is the goal related to the norm; T is the agent target; A is the activation condition; E is the expiration condition; S is the sanction; R is the reward. The sanction and reward values are numbers between 0 and 1. For the norm "the driver is prohibited to run faster than 40Km/h in urban area", the target is the driver; the norm is activated when the driver enters an urban area; is inactive when it leaves the urban area. The driver receives a sanction if he disobeys this norm. If the driver obeys the norm he receives a reward. This norm is represented by the tuple (2).

$$\langle P, \neg run\_fast\_than\_40Kmh, driver, urban\_area, \neg urban\_area, 1.0, 0.1 \rangle \qquad (2)$$

2.2 Desires

Desires are the agent's wishes and their origin are in the agent's mind, representing the agent's nature. We propose that a desire is composed of: a state that the agent wants to reach (C), a necessity (N) and an intensity (I). Necessity and intensity are scalar values. The necessity represents how much it is essential to satisfy the desire. If the agent does not satisfy the desire, it will suffer by the necessity to satisfy it. The intensity represents how much it is desirable to reach a goal. If the agent satisfies the desire, it will be rewarded by the intensity to satisfy it. In this paper, we consider that necessity and intensity values are numbers between 0 and 1. This work considers a desire as a tuple as in (3).

$$\langle C, N, I \rangle \qquad (3)$$

For example, a glutton agent has a desire with intensity 1 of be fed. However the agent has a high fat percentage, thus, in this moment, the agent has a necessity 0.2 of being fed. This desire is represented by a tuple like (4).

$$\langle fed, 0.2, 1 \rangle \qquad (4)$$

2.3 Mood Concept

This paper uses a mood psychological concept [2] as the main inspiration for a deliberation process that considers norms, desires and resources. Thayer considers that the mood is a relation between *energy* and *tension* to gain *benefits* [7]. A person can be energetic or tired while also being tense or calm. The energy is the state of being (tired or energetic) and the tension is the psychic state of being (tense or calm). According to Thayer, people feel better when they are in a calm-energy mood. They feel worse when in a tense-tired state.

Different elements can regulate the mood. These elements can change the mood because they provide a gain of *benefit*. This gain provides a satisfaction, relaxing the being's tension. For example, people often use food to regulate mood. Thayer identifies a fundamental food-mood connection, and advises against the reliance on food as a mood regulator. Another element that can regulate the mood is the physical activity. For example, great quantities of hormones are produced during a walk. On the other hand, the walk consumes energy and generates tension during the process. However, the hormones it produces can counteract the tension, as experienced in a bad mood.

The "being" needs to find the middle term among regulatory elements (food, physical activity, and others) to reach the best mood state. Therefore, *the "being" needs to choose goals that avoid tension and give more benefit, counterattacking the bad mood.*

3   Normative Reasoning Based on Mood

The normative reasoning based on mood enables the agent to reasoning about norms and desires considering the available resources. The figure 1 represents this context. The agent recognizes his desires and obtains the environmental resources and norms. Hereafter, the agent deliberates about the desires, norms and resources and it changes its behavior to reach a better mood. The mood concept [2] allows us to conceive a deliberation process to choose the best set of goals (decreasing the tensions and increasing the benefit).

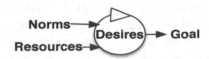

Fig. 1. Model overview

In the proposed model, the energy of the agents is the amount of resources they need to have to accomplish the goals related to norms and desires. The agent's tension represents how much it costs to do not accomplish a goal. The agent's benefit represents how much it receives to accomplish a goal.

The agent's energy state is a n-dimensional space, whose each dimension represents one limited resource. For example, an agent has two resources, tires and fuel. Thus the mood space is two-dimensional and it uses these resources to minimize the tension and maximize the benefit (best mood).

We proposed to model the energies, tension and benefit as an optimization problem for the agent to find the best mood (less tension and more benefit). Therefore it is possible to use an optimization solver to find the best set of goals to achieve with the available resources.

In this paper the deliberation process has as inputs the desires, norms and resources and it has as output the best set of goals. Therefore, the deliberation process is triggered when it occurs some events in that input data. The first trigger is the norm expiration. When the norm has the expiration condition true, the goal related to it is not more relevant. This situation triggers a deliberation process to produce a new set of goals related to norms and desires.

The second trigger is the perception of a new norm, desire, or resource. In these situations the deliberation process is triggered because it is possible to produce a new set with a better mood than the current set.

The figure 2 illustrates the proposed deliberation process. The hexagon represents the process of goals selection, the rectangles represent sets, and the dashed box represents the definition of energies, tension and benefit. This paper focuses on the gray elements of the figure. The first element is the definition of energies, tension and benefit of the goals related to desires and norms. The second

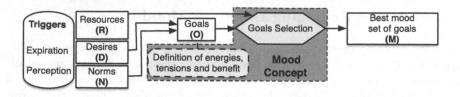

Fig. 2. Deliberation process flowchart

focused element is the selection of goals that will be committed. These elements are described in sections 3.1 and 3.2.

The figure 2 presents five sets (R, D, N, O, M). Where R is composed of all kind of available resources to the agent, D is the set of all desires, N is composed of all active norms, O is the set of goals related to the desires and norms in the D and N, and M is the set of goals that maximizes the agent gains.

3.1 Definition of Energies, Tension and Benefit

For each goal in O it is defined: how much *tension* would be generated by not reaching the goal, how much *benefit* would be generated if the goal is reached and how much *resources* would be consumed to reach the goal.

In this paper the tension is represented by the *loss* that the agent suffers by not fulfilling a goal. The tension is represented by a function which returns a value between 0 and 1 as defined in (5).

$$tension : O \rightarrow [0..1] \tag{5}$$

The tension has two origins. The tension is based on the norm's sanction for goals related to norms. The tension is based on the desires's necessity for goals related to desires. The tension is defined in (6), where $sanction(o)$ returns the norm's sanction value (the S value represented in (1)) and $necessity(o)$ returns the desire necessity value (the N value represented in (3)).

$$tension(o) = \begin{cases} sanction(o) & \text{if } o \text{ is related to a norm} \\ necessity(o) & \text{if } o \text{ is related to a desire} \end{cases} \tag{6}$$

The *benefit* is the reward for the agent to fulfill a goal. This benefit is a function that returns a value between 0 and 1 corresponding to the agent's gain when reaching the goal. This function type is defined in (7).

$$benefit : O \rightarrow [0..1] \tag{7}$$

The benefit, as well as tension, has two origins. The benefit is based on the norm's reward for goals related to norms. The benefit is based on the desire's intensity for goals related to desires. A generic form of the benefit is defined in (8), where $reward(o)$ returns the norm reward value (the R value represented in

(1)) and *intensity(o)* returns the desire intensity value (the *I* value represented in (3).

$$benefit(o) = \begin{cases} reward(o) & \text{if } o \text{ is related to a norm} \\ intensity(o) & \text{if } o \text{ is related to a desire} \end{cases} \tag{8}$$

Sometimes, the set O can contains goals with the same meaning but different sources (norm or desire). When this occurs, these goals are merged in only one goal (*mgoal*). The *mgoal* benefit is equal to the sum of these goals benefits. The same occurs with the tension where the *mgoal* tension is equal to the sum of these goals tensions. The energy required to accomplish the *mgoal* is equal to the energy required to accomplish one of the merged goals. For example, one goal g is related to a norm, with benefit 0.5, tension 0.3 and it needs 5 liters of fuel. The same goal g is related to a desire with benefit 0.3, tension 0.6 and it needs the same 5 liters of fuel. These two benefits and tensions are merged. Thus the goal g has the benefit 0.8, the tension 0.9 and to be accomplish it needs 5 liters of fuel.

As previously presented, the available resources are the agent's energies. These represents a $|R|$ - dimensional space where each dimension corresponds to a resource type r, where $r \in R$ and R is the set of all resources. In this way the function $energy_{req}$ returns a real value corresponding to the required resource quantity to reach the goal. This function is in definition (9) and $energy_{req}(o, r)$ returns how much of resource r is necessary to reach the goal o.

$$energy_{req} : O \times R \to \mathbb{R}^+ \tag{9}$$

For example, consider a norm n that obliges the agent to reach the goal o, has a sanction 0.5, a reward 0.7 and to reach o it is necessary do spend 5 fuel units. Therefore $tension(o) = 0.5$, $benefit(o) = 0.7$, and $energy_{req}(o, fuel) = 5$.

The energy dynamics considers that agents can receive more resources during their life cycle. When this occurs, the available amount of energy is updated and the deliberation process is started to find the best mood. The model do not considers the energy consumed by the deliberation process.

3.2   Goals Selection

In the goal selection process the agent deliberates about which goals from the set O will be adopted to reach the best mood (set M). To do this, it needs to treat goal's conflicts and resource's conflicts that may happen.

The majority of the related work [6,8,9] treats the goal's conflicts using preference systems. Therefore, a norm or desire with high-priority will be fulfilled even if it underutilized the agent's capacity. For example, a goal with high-priority consumes 5 liters of fuel to grant a benefit. On the other hand, the agent has other two goals with low-priority that together consume the same 5 liters of fuel, and they grant a better benefit. Therefore to fulfill the high-priority goal the agent's capacity will be underutilized. To avoid this, we propose to maximize the agent's benefit, choosing non-conflicting goals that compose the best benefit using the available resources.

We model the choice of a set of non-conflicting goals as a multiple - choice knapsack problem [10]. This problem has an additional constraint in relation to the traditional knapsack problem. The items are divided into classes. To solve the problem, at most one item can be chosen per class. For example the items torch, lantern, candle, penknife, and tent are divided in three classes: light (torch, lantern, candle), cut (penknife), and shelter (tent). Therefore, a feasible solution of this problem does not contain in the knapsack a torch, a lantern or a candle simultaneously.

To solve the goal's conflicts problem, each class c is a set of conflicting goals and all goals in conflict belong a same class. Otherwise, if the goal does not have conflict it belongs a class with just itself. With these classes and the constraint (10) we grant that at most one goal of each class will be chosen. In the constraint (10), m_o is the binary decision variable of goal o. When the m_o value is 1 the goal o is selected and when m_o is 0 the goal is not selected. C is a subset of the power set of O (11) that contains all classes (C) mutually exclusive (12) and collective exhaustive (13).

$$\sum_{o \in c} m_o \leq 1, c \in C \tag{10}$$

$$C \subseteq 2^O \tag{11}$$

$$c_i \cap c_j = \emptyset, i \neq j, 0 < i < |C|, 0 < j < |C| \tag{12}$$

$$\bigcup_{c \in C} c = O \tag{13}$$

For example, the goals $\neg p$, p, and q are divided in two classes, represented in (14). $\neg p$ and p are in the same class because they are obviously in conflict.

$$c_1 = \{\neg p, p\}, c_2 = \{q\} \tag{14}$$

We model the choice of a set of goals respecting the available resources as a multidimensional knapsack problem [10]. To solve the resources conflicts problem, each resource $r \in R$ is a constraint in the problem. Thus, a solution for the problem shall not pass the available resources limit. The inequality (15) is the optimization problem constraint that represents this condition. Where E_r is how much resource r the agent has.

$$\sum_{c \in C} \sum_{o \in c} (m_o energy_{req}(o, r)) \leq E_r, \quad r \in R \tag{15}$$

The problem definition is thus presented in (16). In this problem formulation it is possible to see that the maximization function proposed to choose the goals considers their benefits and tensions. This function shows mood generated by the goal as the *benefit* to reach the goal plus the *tension*. If the agent fulfills the goal it receives the benefit and avoid the tension. For example, when some goal

o is fulfilled the agent benefit is 0.5 and when the goal is not fulfilled it loses (tension) 0.4. Therefore when the agent fulfills o, it gains 0.5 and *does not lose* 0.4. Thus mood generated by the goal is 0.9.

$$Maximize \sum_{c \in C} \sum_{o \in c} (m_o(benefit(o) + tension(o))) \tag{16}$$

Subject to

$$\sum_{c \in C} \sum_{o \in c} (m_o energy_{req}(o, r)) \leq E_r, r \in R$$

$$\sum_{o \in c} m_o \leq 1, c \in C$$

4   Example

This section presents an example of how the deliberation process works. We consider an agent with 10 liters of fuel. Thus, the energetic limit is 10 ($E_{fuel} = 10$). The agent needs to handle the set of norms represented in Table 1. Also the agent has a desire as represented in Table 2.

In this example we consider that all norms have the activation condition true. Thus the agent has one goal related to each norm and one goal related to the desire. The values returned by the functions for this set of goals are in Table 3 with all the components used in the deliberation process. We consider that the initial state of the world is $\{\neg x, \neg y, \neg q\}$. Therefore, the goals x, y and q are not reached and the goal $\neg x$ is fulfilled. The agent does not have an energy associated to $\neg x$.

Table 1. Norms perceives

Norm	Type	Goal	Sanction	Reward
N_1	Prohibition	$\neg x$	0.2	0.0
N_2	Obligation	x	0.2	0.7
N_3	Obligation	y	0.1	0.7

Table 3. Goal values

o	$tension(o)$	$benefit(o)$	$energy_{req}(o, fuel)$
$\neg x$	0.2	0.0	0
x	0.2	0.7	10
y	0.1	0.7	7
q	0.2	0.3	3

Table 2. Desires

Desire	Goal	Intensity	Necessity
D_1	q	0.2	0.3

The set $O = \{\neg x, x, y, q\}$ related to the norms (N) and desires (D) has three conflicts classes: $c_1 = \{\neg x, x\}$ $c_2 = \{y\}$ $c_3 = \{q\}$. An optimization problem instance is created with the information of the sets O and C. This instance is the input to a linear programming solver. The solver used in this case adopts a branch-and-bound algorithm together with Gomory's mixed integer cuts to find the optimal set of goals [11]. In this example, the result is: $m_{\neg x} = 1, m_x = 0, m_y = 1, m_q = 1$.

Therefore, the current set M of goals for a better mood is $\{\neg x, y, q\}$. We highlight this situation where the goal (x) with the highest gain will not be fulfilled because the composition of others goals produces a better gain.

Table 4. New goal values

o	$tension(o)$	$benefit(o)$	$energy_{req}(o, fuel)$
$\neg x$	0.2	0.0	0
x	0.2	0.7	10
y	0.1	0.7	6
q	0.2	0.3	1
z	0.2	0.6	1

Suppose that, after some execution cycles the agent perceives a new norm (N_4) that obliges a goal z where: tension is 0.2, reward is 0.6, and energy is 1. This new norm triggers the deliberation process. In this point, some resources were already consumed by the goals y and q. The goal y consumed 1 liter and q consumed 2 liters. Therefore, the energy necessary to fulfill y and q decreased respectively to 6 and 1. This generate a new state represented in Table 4.

After running the goal selection again the solution produced is $M = \{\neg x, y, z\}$. We highlight that despite of consumed resources to fulfill q the agent drops it, because the goal z generates more gain with the same energy.

5   Preliminary Evaluation

The response time of the deliberation process is relevant for several MAS applications. It is not appropriate that the reasoning of the agent stays blocked for a long time causing problems like the user's discomfort (freeze sensation). Since our proposal to deliberation process is a knapsack problem variation, known as a complex problem with a high cost of processing, this performance issue was an initial concern.

We made a set of 90000 random instances to the set R, O and C to create a set of problems to make a preliminary test. The instances generated have 100 goals and 4 resources. The number of conflicts between goals has varied among 0, 25 and 50. The energy available has varied among 100, 600, 1100. The energy cost of a goal has varied in the interval of 0 until 50.

We used a linear solver, the GLPK (GNU Linear Programming Kit), to solve this problem set. We used a machine with a processor Intel Core 2 Duo 3.06 GHz and 4 GB 1067 MHz DDR3 of memory to run the tests. The operational system was Mac OS X 10.6.8 and the GLPK version was 4.48.

The average response time to obtain the current set M was 25.94 ms with a standard deviation of 27.96 ms. Using these data the time average is under 90.99

ms with confidence degree 99%[1]. The worst case analyzed has spent 324 ms. This preliminary result give us evidences that the approach proposed is suitable for the process of deliberation once the average response time is acceptable.

6 Related Work

There has been considerable work on normative programming frameworks and middleware to support the development of normative multi-agent organizations, and such frameworks are often designed to interoperate with existing agent's languages programs. Some of agent's architectures allow the agent deliberating about whether to comply with norms.

For example, the *BOID* model proposes a BDI extension with the explicit obligation notion. Agents of type BOID [9] are composed of four components: beliefs, obligations, intentions and desires. This is one of the first models that works with obligations (a kind of norm). This model uses static preferences to identify the component's this preference and the agent uses the relevance to deliberate about the norm compliment.

In contrast, the *Carabelea's* model [12] works before the agent joins the organization. This model proposes to use the social power theory [13,14] for the agent to deliberate about joining a group. The Carabelea's objective is to use this theory for the agent understand its powers and the powers of the other agents to deliberate about the entrance in the organization. Carabelea's model enables the agent to reasoning about dependencies among agents. On the other hand, after the agent has joined the organization, it will obey all the norms.

Kollingbaum model [8] is another model where the agent try to fulfill all norms. But, if there are conflicts between norms the agent detects and solves them. Kollingbaum defines algorithms to detect and to solve the norms conflict. They use seven strategies: Arbitrary decision, recency, seniority, cautions, bold, renegotiate and social power.

Criado model presents an architecture called n-BDI (normative BDI). The deliberation process about norms uses utility functions. Thus, the agent uses the rewards and sanctions to define which norms will be accepted [15]. Other relevant model is the *N-2APL* [16]. This model allows the creation of agents capable to deliberate about norms. The N-2APL adds to 2APL language [17] the support to normative concepts as obligations, prohibitions, sanctions and deadlines. The deliberation process considers deadlines and priority criteria to choose the norms.

The deliberation process proposed in this paper has some similarities with related studies like the use of N-BDI architecture. Our deliberation process has a singular feature when compared with the related studies: we worked with limited resources to deliberate about norms and desires. In addition, the process uses another elements like rewards, sanctions, intensities and necessities to deliberate.

The proposed model also does not use a preference system. Thus, our proposal cannot directly prioritize a goal against others. For the goal to be prioritized it

---

[1] Using an approximation to a normal distribution.

needs a high benefit, because as higher is the benefit the higher are the chances to select it. However is not possible to guarantee that goal will be fulfilled. The model selects a set of goals that provides the best mood for the agent. The goals are not evaluated one by one, but evaluated by the mood generated by the set of selected goals. Therefore a goal with a high benefit is not guaranteed in the set of goals, because eventually a set without this goal can provide a better mood.

Deadlines are out of the scope of our initial proposal, as done, for instance, in [16] they do this treatment. In our proposal, it is possible to represent the time like a limited resource. Therefore it is possible to choose a set of goals that will be fulfilled before a maximum time. However, the proposal does not grant that the goal will be fulfilled before the deadline.

7 Conclusions

This paper has presented some initial results for a normative reasoning with limited resources. The main feature of the proposal is the agent's ability to understand the limited resources and to reason about the norms and desires, to find out the best set of goals which will give more benefit for the agent. To create this normative reasoning model we need make a process able to:

- reason about the accomplishment and relevance of desires and norms;
- solve conflicts between desires and norms;
- solve resources conflicts.

To solve these problems we propose:

- a model based on mood where it is possible to define the tension (negative feedback), benefit (positive feedback) and energies (limited resources) to reason about the accomplishment and relevance of desires and norms;
- to use the Multiple-Choice Knapsack Problem to reduce the problem of conflicts between desires and norms, where, at the most, one goal can be chosen by each conflict class;
- to use the Multidimensional Knapsack Problem to reduce the resources conflict problem, where each dimension constraint represents a limited resource.

We have some possible future works in the actual state of this research. The first one is to include the deliberation process in a N-BDI architecture. Therefore, we will extend and agent architecture, like JaCaMo [18], that already has the representation of norms and desires as assumed in this paper. This new architecture should be capable of reasoning about limited resources. This implementation will be the instrument to evaluate the proposed deliberation process in a real setting.

The second work is to define goal's commitment for the agent. This feature makes the agent to have a more stable behavior, avoiding unnecessary change of goals, which may prevent it to spend resources unnecessarily.

The third work is to better identify conflicts between norms. This paper proposes a very simple way to solve the conflicts, however a more realistic procedure should be conceived. Cases like presented in the section 4, where there are a goal r and $\neg r$, are easy to solve. But, there are some cases where it is not easy to detect the conflict. For example, two goals need to move the agent in opposite directions. In this case, the agent needs to understand all the consequences involved in reaching the goals to discover the conflict.

The last future work is to define a way for the agent to interact with the other agents, because in the actual state, the agent does not handle goals received from the other agents. In order to reason about these goals, it is necessary to define how important the agent that request the goal is. Some studies like [12] use the social power to define this kind of power relation.

References

1. Boella, G., Torre, L., Verhagen, H.: Introduction to normative multiagent systems. Computational & Mathematical Organization Theory **12**(2–3), 71–79 (2006)
2. Thayer, R.E.: The biopsychology of mood and arousal, 1st edn. Oxford University Press (1989)
3. Rawls, J.: Two Concepts of Rules. Bobbs-Merrill reprint series in philosophy. Ardent Media, Incorporated (1955)
4. Searle, J.: Speech Acts: An Essay in the Philosophy of Language. Cam: [Verschiedene Aufl.]. Cambridge University Press (1969)
5. Searle, J.R.: The Construction of Social Reality. Free Press (1997)
6. Pacheco, N.C.: Using Norms to Control Open Multi-Agent Systems. Tesis doctoral en informática, Departamento de Sistemas Informáticos y Computación, Universidad Politécnica de Valencia (2012)
7. Thayer, R.E.: The origin of everyday moods: Managing energy, tension and stress, 1st edn. Oxford University Press (1996)
8. Kollingbaum, M.J., Norman, T.J.: Informed Deliberation During Norm-Governed Practical Reasoning. In: Boissier, O., Padget, J., Dignum, V., Lindemann, G., Matson, E., Ossowski, S., Sichman, J.S., Vázquez-Salceda, J. (eds.) ANIREM 2005 and OOOP 2005. LNCS (LNAI), vol. 3913, pp. 183–197. Springer, Heidelberg (2006)
9. Broersen, J., Dastani, M., Hulstijn, J., Huang, Z., van der Torre, L.: The BOID architecture: conflicts between beliefs, obligations, intentions and desires. In: Proceedings of the Fifth International Conference on Autonomous Agents, AGENTS 2001, pp. 9–16. ACM, New York (2001)
10. Kellerer, H., Pferschy, U., Pisinger, D.: Knapsack Problems. Springer (2004)
11. Balas, E., Ceria, S.: Cornuéjols, G., Natraj, N.: Gomory cuts revisited. Operations Research Letters **19**(1), 1–9 (1996)
12. Carabelea, C., Boissier, O., Castelfranchi, C.: Using Social Power to Enable Agents to Reason About Being Part of a Group. In: Gleizes, M.-P., Omicini, A., Zambonelli, F. (eds.) ESAW 2004. LNCS (LNAI), vol. 3451, pp. 166–177. Springer, Heidelberg (2005)
13. Castelfranchi, C.: A micro and macro definition of power. ProtoSociology - An International Journal of Interdisciplinary Research, 208–268 (2002)
14. Jones, A., Sergot, M.: A formal characterisation of institutionalised power (1996)
15. Criado, N., Argente, E., Botti, V.: Rational Strategies for Norm Compliance in the n-BDI Proposal. In: De Vos, M., Fornara, N., Pitt, J.V., Vouros, G. (eds.) COIN 2010. LNCS, vol. 6541, pp. 1–20. Springer, Heidelberg (2011)

16. Alechina, N., Dastani, M., Logan, B.: Programming norm-aware agents. In: Conitzer, V., Winikoff, M., Padgham, L., van der Hoek, W. (eds.) Proceedings of the 11th International Conference on Autonomous Agents and Multiagent Systems (AAMAS 2012), Valencia, Spain (June 2012)
17. Dastani, M.: 2APL: a practical agent programming language. Autonomous Agents and Multi-Agent System **16**(3), 214–248 (2008)
18. Boissier, O., Bordini, R.H., Hübner, J.F., Ricci, A., Santi, A.: Multi-agent oriented programming with jacamo. Science of Computer Programming **78**(6), 747–761 (2013)

Agent-based Modelling
and Simulation

Krowdix: Agent-Based Simulation
of Online Social Networks

Diego Blanco-Moreno, Marlon Cárdenas, Rubén Fuentes-Fernández,
and Juan Pavón⁽✉⁾

Dep. Ingeniería del Software e Inteligencia Artificial, Universidad Complutense de Madrid,
Profesor José García Santesmases, s/n,
28040, Madrid, Spain
{diego.blanco,ruben,jpavon}@fdi.ucm.es,
marlon.cb@gmail.com

Abstract. Simulations can be used for the study of Online Social Networks
(OSNs) as a means to harness their size and complexity, and to overcome the
difficulties to set up experiments in real environments. Most existing tools for
the analysis of OSNs focus on the graph structure of networks and emulate
changes only from statistical data. This approach is unsuitable to study the evolution of OSNs as a consequence of the personal attributes and behaviours of
their members. Our work addresses this issue with an agent-based simulation
framework for OSNs called Krowdix. It provides support to specify discrete
time simulations, where agents represent members of OSNs acting according to
their profiles and context. This context comprehends the environment, other
agents, groups of agents, and the whole network. *Agent actions* are responsible
of network changes. Additionally, *system actions* can represent unexpected
events external to agents. This agent-based approach facilitates the translation
of actual observations to simulation models, and explaining networks in terms
of their members.

Keywords: Krowdix · Twitter · Online Social Network · Agent-Based Modelling · Simulation · Tool

1   Introduction

Online Social Networks (OSNs) allow people to establish relationships with other
members and share information with them. Research interest in OSNs has grown at
the same pace as they increased their scope and visibility. Offline networks have been
profusely analysed for many decades, but scaling analysis to OSNs is complex, difficult, and expensive [1]. Among other reasons for this, there is the need to process big
volumes of information with heterogeneous data, in complex environments and situations. Besides, experiments involving real subjects are always hard to set up and control, but for very constrained settings. Different research fields are applicable in this
context to study the distinct aspects of OSNs, from the perspective of the social structure of communities to the socio-psychological aspects involving their members.

Simulation can be considered as a tool to analyse OSNs by developing models that
intend to mimic actual OSNs. Changing the configuration of these models is possible

© Springer International Publishing Switzerland 2014
A.L.C. Bazzan and K. Pichara (Eds.): IBERAMIA 2014, LNAI 8864, pp. 587–598, 2014.
DOI: 10.1007/978-3-319-12027-0_47

to control the influence of different aspects of the network, gaining a deeper understanding of the underlying phenomena [2].

Despite its advantages, the current application of simulation to OSNs presents some issues. First, most existing models and tools are too focused only on the structure of the network [3]. This disregards the influence of individual components in the evolution of the OSN, for instance, to analyse the influence of user profiles and behaviours [4]. Second, models usually rely on some statistical data that abstract real observations [5]. This approach can be suitable to study trends, but it makes difficult to consider unexpected real-time events, changes in context variables, and the influence of individuals. Third, tools for OSN simulation frequently fall in one of two extremes that make them unsuitable in certain settings. Either they offer a predefined set of models and examples to consider in the generation of the network, or they are general-purpose simulation frameworks [6]. In the first case, they are hard to adapt to specific characteristics of real OSNs that are different from those originally intended, and impose certain assumptions on the analysis. In the second case, researchers need to implement almost from scratch most of the elements.

Our research addresses these issues with Krowdix, a tool to simulate OSNs that follows an Agent-Based Modelling (ABM) approach [7]. ABM focuses on the intentional and knowledge features of agents, and regards interactions as the core of social modelling. It provides techniques for simulating social phenomena with flexibility to consider both the macro (e.g. complete OSNs, communities, or groups) and micro (i.e. agents) levels. ABM is also intrinsically appropriate for domains where components are situated and distributed. With respect to more general ABM tools, Krowdix offers a good balance between a rich library of predefined components to build models of OSNs, and extension points to create new and customised components when needed.

Krowdix models OSNs in terms of their users, which are represented as agents, and certain shared environment (e.g. the external society). Users are defined by their attributes and their actions (called *common actions*). There are also environment actions (called *system actions*) to represent environment events or management actions in an OSN. A simulation has a state that is the combination of the states of all its agents and the environment. This state evolves because of the execution of actions.

Actions can depend on the user and environment states for their triggering and results. They are executed under discrete time, i.e. at each simulation step their execution advances a given percentage. Systems actions are instantaneous, but common actions have duration and consume part of the execution time assigned to each agent.

A methodology to model OSNs with an initial version of Krowdix has been reported in [7]. The platform has evolved in the last year towards a more robust and functional tool, while it has been validated through different case studies such as modelling Twitter[1] and Facebook[2]. This paper presents the Krowdix architecture, its main components, and how it supports simulations based on the previous concepts. Besides its library of components, it offers a structure of plug-ins for actions and simulation visualizations in order to facilitate researchers customising new components.

The rest of the paper is organised as follows. Section 2 introduces the simulation model of Krowdix for OSNs. Section 3 presents the architecture of the simulation tool

---

[1] http://www.twitter.com   (retrieved 01/07/2014)
[2] http://www.facebook.com (retrieved 01/07/2014)

that implements the previous model. Section 4 illustrates the application of Krowdix to build the model and components required to study a typical OSN, Twitter. Section 5 compares Krowdix with other ABM tools. Finally, Section 6 discusses some conclusions and future lines of research.

2   Modelling OSNs in Krowdix

Although there are multiple types of OSNs (e.g. blogging, content sharing, dating, or professional), all of them share some common features. Participants relate to others directly by means of some kind of friendship relationship with acknowledgement of mutual information access, or indirectly using shared groups or publishing/consuming public content accessible/created by other participants. Most OSNs only support some of these mechanisms, and use some permission system to limit who can do what. For instance, not everybody can tag other users in Facebook, and friendship cannot be established with a user with a private profile in Twitter. Within these constraints, users shape their own use of OSNs according to their preferences and state. For instance, users can publish personal information following their preferences, have privacy concerns, establish relationships with others with different degrees of affinity, and share contents with different accessibility constraints.

In Krowdix, an OSN is characterized by a Social Network Model (SNM), whose main components are Social Network Users (SNUs) that represent the members of the OSN. SNUs manage information and perform actions within the simulation to alter the state of the network. Links among them take the form of binary unidirectional *relationships*. SNMs also include *groups* to define shared features among populations of SNUs (e.g. interests and contents).

SNUs create and manipulate *content*, i.e. any kind of information present in OSNs. Each piece of content is created by only one SNU, but can be processed, shared, or distributed by multiple SNUs or groups. Permissions can be established based on *relationships* and *attributes* of the participating components.

Attributes represent semantic information of any of the previous elements. They are key-value pairs of a given type. Common uses of attributes are the calculation of semantic distances among elements in the SNMs (e.g. finding people and groups sharing some common interest, or relevant contents for a user), or controlling privacy.

Actions guide changes in OSNs. There are two types of actions: *common* and *system* ones. SNUs carry out *common actions* according to their state and context. Finding new friends, searching for interest groups for the user, or commenting on reachable contents, are typical *common actions*. In addition, actions can change SNU attributes. This supports complex evaluation and evolution of SNUs, and therefore of the overall SNM. *System actions* are defined to force unexpected events in the normal flow of the simulation, by modifying elements that channel evolution to arbitrary new simulation states. They are used to represent environment events or management activities in OSNs.

Using the previous elements, SNUs are defined by means of *profiles*. A *profile* consists of a set of *attributes*, maybe with some initial or default values for them, and a set of *actions*. *Actions* are distributed assigning them the percentage of time a SNU with that *profile* will devote to execute each of them.

A Krowdix simulation executes at each step the programmed *system actions*. If there is no *system action* to perform, it executes the queued *common actions* for each SNU in the time they have assigned. These executions change the state of the simulation, and start a new simulation cycle.

3   Krowdix Environment Architecture

The Krowdix environment supports the specification, development, and execution of simulations following the Krowdix model (see Section 2). It provides proper Application Programming Interfaces (APIs) to reuse and extend components, both at design and runtime, and build component libraries for reuse.

The Krowdix Integrated Development Environment (IDE) is a graphical web-based editor to manage components and repositories. For the different elements of the architecture, researchers have basic types ready to use in a repository. They can create additional components as combinations of other components and add them to the repository, although for specific aspects it can require some programming. In this way, efforts in creating OSN simulation elements can be reused in subsequent OSN simulations. This allows creating a growing ecosystem of simulation components that simplifies the task of transforming OSNs into simulation models, or improving existing simulations adapting them to new changes in the OSNs analysed.

The architecture is organized around three basic sub-systems (see Fig. 1): the *Structural Architecture,* for manipulating the OSN types needed to define the model to simulate; the *Dynamic Architecture,* which manages the execution elements of SNUs, i.e. *Actions* and *Visualizations*; and the *Simulation Architecture,* to manage the definition and execution of simulations. Table 1 summarises the main public APIs of the Krowdix architecture. Next sub-sections discuss these elements in more detail.

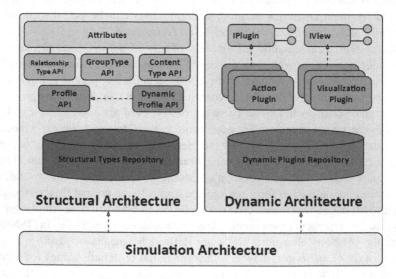

Fig. 1. Krowdix environment architecture

Table 1. Krowdix Architecture APIs

Krowdix APIs	Functionality
Attribute	Manages *attributes* for SNU and simulation instances.
Content	Manages *content* and its types in simulation.
Engine	Add new SNUs to the simulation and retrieves time information during simulation.
Group	Manages *group* instances and participation of SNUs in *groups*.
Relationship	Manages *relationships* between SNUs.
SNU	Manages the SNU information, *profile*, and *actions*. SNUs can be traversed to reach other SNUs related to them according to different filters (e.g. *Friends* and *Friends of Friends*)

3.1   Structural Architecture

The *Structural Architecture* supports the definition and manipulation of elements for modelling OSNs. It includes *Relationship Types, Group Types, Content Types, Attributes,* and *Static* and *Dynamic Profiles*.

User *profiles* are one of the core elements of this architecture, as they define the kind of behaviours that SNUs can execute during simulations. *Static Profiles* are the basic ones. They are sets of *common actions* that have assigned percentages of execution time of the corresponding SNUs. In order to represent the potential evolutions of behaviour over time, *Static Profiles* can be grouped into *Dynamic Profiles*. A *Dynamic Profile* establishes potential changes in the behaviour of SNUs (i.e. adopting another *Static Profile*) based on their attributes or time. This facilitates, for instance, representing how users posting activity frequently declines over time when compared with their initial participation in an OSN.

All these elements are created using the Krowdix IDE and can be accessed for simulations using their APIs. For instance, to create a *Content Type* "Tweet" for a model of Twitter, developers use the `ContentAPI` to generate and assign a Tweet to the executing SNU:

```
int idContent = ContentAPI.createContent(conn, oneSNU, "Tweet",
simulationTime).getIdContent();
```

3.2   Dynamic Architecture

The *Dynamic Architecture* is responsible for manipulating the structural aspects of SNUs during simulations. For every discrete time simulation step, it applies *Actions* to change the state and *Visualizations* to define the presentation of the results.

Actions and visualizations respectively implement the `IPlugin` and `IVisualization` interfaces. They consult and alter the simulation status adding new elements, or modifying and deleting existing ones using the APIs of the *Structural Architecture* (see Section 3.1) or the set of utility APIs for manipulating OSN simulation elements (e.g. SNUs, *Contents, Groups,* and *Relationships*) shown in Fig. 2.

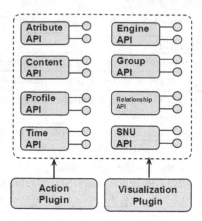

Fig. 2. Dynamic APIs for *Action* and *Visualization* implementations

3.3   Simulation Architecture

The *Simulation Architecture* manages the overall simulation and its evolution over time. It includes mechanisms to define the *profiles* in the simulation and the initial configurations, the number of SNUs to start for each profile, and the *action points* to be consumed at each iteration (i.e. ticks of time). During the execution of a simulation, the engine examines the state of structural and dynamic elements. According to this, it executes *actions*. A detailed discussion of action execution can be seen in [7].

Common actions are executed in a non-linear way according to their distribution in the profile. When all of them have been executed, and if the SNU has not finished its life, they are rearranged and executed again.

System actions can also be executed at each simulation step as instantaneous actions. They represent external events to the simulation. When executed, the Krowdix engine splits the execution in two branches: one for the simulation after executing the actions and another for the simulation without executing them. This facilitates the comparison of alternative evolutions.

4   Architecting Twitter with Krowdix

Twitter is a popular but atypical OSN. It is based on open information flows whose basic unit are the "tweets" or "micro-messages" that users send, share, discuss, track, and rank. Both users and messages are associated under common interests. The dissemination of information instantly has become the main feature of this network, which focuses on the relationship between the issuer of the information and the receiver or group of receivers that can consume such information.

4.1   Structural Elements for the Twitter Model

The analysis of a network like Twitter begins with the specification of the structure, definition, and relationships of its components. In Krowdix, this means the static analysis of the network elements from the typical interactions.

The basic interactions in Twitter can be summarised as follows:

- An account is created and a basic configuration is defined.
- Users post their first "tweets".
- Users search accounts to "follow" and "be followed" by others.
- Users can generate direct communications to other users.
- Users share information of their interest using "Retweets" (RTs).

Given these interactions, the main static elements to consider for a model of Twitter are: *Configuration content, Tweets content, Retweets content, Following relationship, Followers relationship,* and *Direct Messages content.*

Static elements in Krowdix are defined as *types*, which are aggregations of *attributes*. There are multiple primitive types for attributes, e.g. Integers, Strings, and Lists of Values. Designers can reuse available types or create new ones. After defining a new type, designers can add it to the repository. In this case, types will be defined for each type of interaction. Twitter static elements are created (see Fig. 3) and aggregated to the repository.

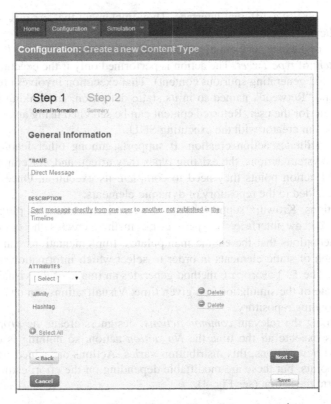

Fig. 3. Content Type creation with attribute aggregation

4.2   Dynamic Elements for the Twitter Model

The dynamic analysis identifies the profiles. There are multiple sources for Twitter on this aspect. The most widely available are the analysis on user's profiles performed by different web sites, such as Social Media Today[3]. Profiles are defined in terms of actions that SNUs perform over time following some patterns.

Common actions reflect the user behaviour and manipulate the static components. They are programmed in Java using the Krowdix APIs (see Table 1). Every new action has to implement the `IPlugin` interface. Its main methods are the following:

```
public interface IPlugin extends Serializable {
    // Default method for system action execution
    public int executeAction();
    // Main execution method
    public int executeAction(Connection conn, SNU pSNU);
    // Condition to decide if a SNU is able to execute the action
    public boolean feasible(Connection conn, SNU pSNU);
}
```

System actions use a different interface. They implement the `executeAction()` method, as they affect the overall simulation status.

In the case of Twitter, an example of *common action* is *publishing a Retweet* for an existing *content* of *type Tweet*. The action is performed only if the executing SNU has friends (to avoid generating spurious content). That execution involves creating a new content of type "Retweet", named so in its static definition, and linking it to another existing content for the user. Referred content can be searched using any attribute, e.g. affinity of content creator with the executing SNU.

The IDE facilitates action creation. It supports, among other features, defining common and system actions, the existing types they affect, and, for common actions, the amount of action points they need to complete its execution. Once defined, the action can be added to the repository of dynamic elements.

As for actions, Krowdix supports creating new visualizations as plugins that implement the `IView` interface. Its `generate` method creates the components for visual representations that the engine manipulates. Implementations can traverse the complete graph of static elements in order to select which information is relevant to be displayed. The `fileExport` method generates an image of the visual representation of the state of the simulation in a given time. Visualizations can also be added to their corresponding repository.

After defining the relevant *common actions*, designers create the *profiles*. By default, profiles execute all the time the *No_action* action, so nothing is done. When designers add new actions, this distribution varies. Actions are added with their default action points, but these are modifiable depending on the effort estimated for the user to perform the action (see Fig. 3).

---

[3]   http://socialmediatoday.com/minterdial/1781106/who-follow-twitter-cartography-types-twitter-profiles-and-users (retrieved 01/07/2014)

Dynamic Profiles are composed of several simple *Static Profiles*. *Dynamic Profiles* define triggering conditions to adopt a new *Static Profile*. Both, *Dynamic* and *Static Profiles*, and triggering conditions are in the repository to be used or reconfigured. New triggering conditions can be added using a wizard similar to that for actions. Conditions can be defined over any attribute available in the repository. They also require uploading the code to evaluate the condition.

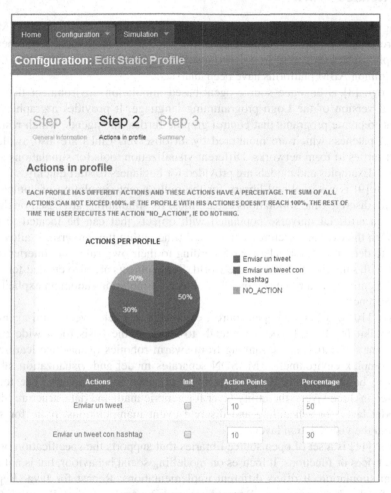

Fig. 4. Static Profile creation

4.3 Configuration of the Simulation

The final step to define the simulation is the configuration of its global settings. First, designers indicate the number of SNUs that constitute the initial population. Then, they select the profiles of that population, the action points assigned to each one per simulation step, and their percentage of the initial population. Profiles can be active as eligible for newly created SNUs only after certain simulation time. Finally, visualization plugins for evolutionary snapshots are selected. Every node in the time tree will have its own simulation image depending on the selected plugin. After this configuration, simulation is ready for execution.

5   Related Work

Existing ABM software toolkits can be used to simulate social networks. Most of them are general purpose, because they can be used to simulate models of other kinds of complex systems as well. In order to justify the interest of a specific OSN tool, the most common ABM platforms have been analysed.

NetLogo [8] is an open source agent-based simulation environment that uses a modified version of the Logo programming language. It provides a graphical environment to create programs that control graphic turtles, the agents, which reside in a world of patches, which are monitored by an observer. Links are also available to connect turtles to form networks. Different visualization tools for simulations are also available. Examples and models are provided for beginners to start quickly.

Swarm [9] is a kernel and library for the multi-agent simulation of complex systems with discrete time simulations capabilities. Its simulations are based on the creation of an artificial universe populated with objects that can be located to certain "points" in the overall structure of space and time within the universe. It allows these objects to determine their behaviour according to their own rules and internal state in concert with sampling the state of the world. Some objects are also created for observing and recording data produced by other objects. Simulations adopt an explicit model of concurrency.

Mason [10] is a free and open source, extensible, discrete-event multi-agent simulation toolkit for Java. Its design intends to serve as the basis for a wide range of multi-agent simulation tasks, ranging from swarm robotics to machine learning, and social complex environments. MASON separates model and visualization, allowing models to be dynamically detached from or attached to visualizers. The toolkit is organized in three layers: the utility layer for generic math and data structure libraries; the model layer for scheduling and discrete event manipulations, basic for simulations; and the visualization layer.

Repast [11] is a set of open source libraries that supports the specification of agent-based services or functions. It focuses on modelling social behaviour, but is not limited to social simulation. It offers different implementations: Repast for Java (Repast J), Repast for the .Net framework (Repast.Net), and Repast for Python Scripting (Repast Py). Repast includes examples and templates of agents, allowing for the flexible specification of properties and behaviours. Repast is based on a concurrent discrete event scheduler for sequential and parallel operations. It also supports access and modification of agent properties, behavioural equations, and model properties, at run time.

Krowdix emerged from the need of generating a shared repository of behaviours for OSN investigators from different fields. It provides a declarative configuration of simulations that can serve as the basis for creating more complex simulations based on prebuilt and shared agents or visualizations, accessed and managed online.

With ABM tools, OSN analysis can be performed by creating from scratch or adapting some existing models to the behavioural and structural needs of these. On the other hand, Krowdix is fully oriented to OSN simulations, searching for flexibility in supporting OSN user behaviour functions, with a general-purpose time-discrete scheduler and with a repository of directly reusable tools adapted for simulation needs. For OSN simulations that need to create more tailored behaviours, extension of existing elements or creation of new ones is possible using predefined utility APIs, reducing the implementation learning curve. Differently to Swarm or NetLogo, Krowdix uses Java, a general and widely used language to ease the adoption and addition of new elements to the existing repository. Besides, interpreted languages as Logo in NetLogo, while suitable for experimenting in rapid prototyping simulations, are not suitable for long-time running simulation because of the overhead generated by interpretation when running simulations.

Similarly to Mason, Krowdix isolates the visualization requirements from the existing model by extending the capabilities with user-defined plugins or reusing the repository for OSN simulation visualization, allowing the integration of specific purpose visualization tools such as Gephi[4], or libraries such as Jung[5].

All the described platforms allow some kind of time management. Repast, for example, manages modification of agents during simulation and Mason allows for pause and resuming simulations. A particularity of Krowdix is the capability of analysing different time branches during the same simulation. This is achieved by allowing the creation of different simulation evolutions from a certain state after a certain system action is executed to modify the simulation state at any level of detail. This opens the possibility to evaluate the impact of change without repeating and configuring from the beginning, by just modifying any state at any moment of simulation and travelling back and forth in time.

6   Conclusions

This paper has presented the architecture, mechanisms, and editors incorporated in Krowdix to support the OSN simulation. In Krowdix, OSN elements are analysed and transformed into structural or dynamic elements for capturing declarative and dynamic aspects of OSN simulations.

Krowdix differs from general purpose ABM tools in its focus on OSN simulation versus more generic approaches to agent-based simulations. Moreover, its mechanisms for time management of simulation give researchers the possibility of navigating the tree time of the simulation in order to evaluate what would happen from a certain point under given conditions.

It also promotes reutilization of pieces for creating new simulations without programming. As OSNs share comparable elements and behaviours, researchers can incorporate their components into the repository of the tool. This allows expanding the range of OSNs that can be easily studied using the proposed mechanisms of model composition and parameterization to reuse already available elements.

---

[4] https://gephi.org (retrieved 01/07/2014)
[5] http://jung.sourceforge.net (retrieved 01/07/2014)

Twitter OSN is selected as the case study for showing the modelling process of a Krowdix simulation. Although initially it requires the creation of the different elements, reutilization for further simulation processes is simple and direct.

There are several open issues around Krowdix. First, OSN evolution, in the form of new functionalities or characteristics appears frequently. Krowdix elements cover a great deal of new needs, but the addition or modification of existing elements is necessary to keep it updated. Second, dynamic profiles in the simulation are currently based on attribute changes, which trigger the evolution. They need to evolve to capture more complex dynamic changes in agents, which are closer to those of real users. For instance, attributes of a SNU can also evolve over time and dynamic profiles should support this. Finally, researchers need to evaluate the methodology to analyse and describe OSNs in terms of Krowdix models. The identification and parameterization of the different elements of a model requires some expertise on the available resources, how to combine them, and the way to examine the actual output of the simulation to tune the model.

Acknowledgements. This work has been done in the context of the project "Social Ambient Assisting Living – Methods (SociAAL)", supported by the Spanish Ministry for Economy and Competitiviness, with grant TIN2011-28335-C02-01.

References

1. Boyd, D.M., Ellison, N.B.: Social Network Sites – Definition, History, and Scholarship. Journal of Computer Mediated Communication 13(1), 210–230 (2007)
2. Davidsson, P.: Agent Based Social Simulation – A Computer Science View. Journal of Artificial Societies and Social Simulation 5(1), 7 (2002)
3. Wasserman, S., Faust, K.: Social Network Analysis – Methods and Applications. Cambridge University Press (1994)
4. Thelwall, M.: Social networks, gender, and friending: An analysis of MySpace member profiles. Journal of the American Society for Information Science and Technology 59(8), 1321–1330 (2008)
5. Snijders, T.A.B.: The Statistical Evaluation of Social Network Dynamics. Sociological Methodology 31(1), 361–395 (2001)
6. Railsback, S.F., Lytinen, S.L., Jackson, S.K.: Agent-Based Simulation Platforms – Review and Development Recommendations. Simulation 82(9), 609–623 (2006)
7. Blanco-Moreno, D., Fuentes-Fernández, R., Pavón, J.: Simulation of Online Social Networks with Krowdix. In: 2011 Int. Conf. on Computational Aspects of Social Networks (CASoN 2011), pp. 13–18 (2011)
8. Sklar, E.: Netlogo – A Multi-Agent Simulation Environment. Artificial Life 13(3), 303–311 (2007)
9. Minar, N., Burkhart, R., Langton, C., Askenazy, M.: The Swarm Simulation System – A Toolkit for Building Multi-agent Simulations. Santa Fe Institute (1996)
10. Luke, S., Cioffi-Revilla, C., Panait, L., Sullivan, K., Balan, G.: MASON: A Multiagent Simulation Environment. Simulation – Transactions of the Society for Modeling and Simulation International 81(7), 517–527 (2005)
11. North, M.J., Collier, N.T., Vos, J.R.: Experiences Creating Three Implementations of the Repast Agent Modeling Toolkit. ACM Transactions on Modeling and Computer Simulation 16(1), 1–25 (2006)

Estimation of Parameters of *Mycobacterium tuberculosis* Growth: A Multi-Agent-Based Simulation Approach

Pablo Werlang, Michel Q. Fagundes, Diana Francisca Adamatti, Karina Santos Machado, Andrea von Groll, Pedro E.A. da Silva, and Adriano Velasque Werhli[✉]

Grupo de Pesquisa em Biologia Computacional, Centro de Ciências Computacionais Núcleo de Pesquisa em Microbiologia Médica, Faculdade de Medicina, Universidade Federal do Rio Grande, Rio Grande, Brazil
{pswerlang,michelqf,dianaada,karinaecomp,pedrefurg, werhli}@gmail.com,avongrol@hotmail.com

Abstract. The infectious disease Tuberculosis still causes many death around the world nowadays. The study of the bacillus that causes Tuberculosis, *M. tuberculosis*, is therefore very important. One special aspect to be studied is its growth. In this work we try a first attempt in estimating the parameters of a Multi-Agent-Based Simulation that can reproduce the growth of the real bacteria. In a previous work we have developed a Multi-Agent-Based Simulation and observed that the proper setting of parameters in order to reproduce the real behaviour of the growth is not a trivial task. Moreover, it is hard to tell if the adjustment of parameters is incorrect or if the model needs to be more detailed. Hence, in this work, we proceeded with the estimation of the parameters using a numerical method. The results are promising and show a very interesting venue for further research, both in terms of the growth behaviour as in the general aspects of modelling with Multi-Agent-Based Simulation.

Keywords: Multi-Agent-Based Simulation · Tuberculosis · Bacterial growth curve · Estimation of parameters

1 Introduction

Determination of mycobacterial growth is relevant specially due to its implications in tuberculosis (TB) research. Recently, a new method for determination of mycobacterium growth has been proposed [8]. In this work we propose a method for estimating the parameters of a Multi-Agent Based Simulation (MABS) model of mycobacterial growth. In a previous work we proposed a MABS model of bacterial growth [20] specially because MABS are flexible and allow the representation of each individual present in the system being simulated. These characteristics are very important particularly when dealing with

© Springer International Publishing Switzerland 2014
A.L.C. Bazzan and K. Pichara (Eds.): IBERAMIA 2014, LNAI 8864, pp. 599–610, 2014.
DOI: 10.1007/978-3-319-12027-0_48

biological systems. Unfortunately these characteristics are not present in classical deterministic models of bacterial growth e.g. Baranyi and Gompertz [12].

The main reason of proposing a MABS model of bacterial growth is because the golden goal of using biological computer simulations is to have a computational system in which a biological behaviour can be exactly reproduced. This type of model would allow new biological hypothesis to be tested cheaper, faster and without using living organisms. After the simulations phase, only those tests that showed some interesting results *in silico* will be carried out *in vitro*.

One problem with the MABS model is that after building the model an specialist has to test sets of parameters so that the simulated model can mimic the real behaviour of the system under scrutiny. In general the task of finding the correct parameters, or parametrizing, the MABS is not an easy one. For instance, if the setting of the parameters is not trivial it can lead the specialist to adapt the MABS by including unnecessary parameters thus making it easier to parametrize. These MABS with unneeded parameters are more difficult to interpret, not elegant, less general and thus unwanted.

Therefore, in this paper we propose a first approach to try to estimate the parameters of a MABS model using a numerical method to estimate them. The results are promising as they show potential to avoid that the specialist decides to over-parametrize the MABS model.

This paper is organized as follows. Section 2 presents Tuberculosis and the growth curve of the *Mycobacterium tuberculosis* as well as Multi-Agent-Based Simulations. In Section 3 the proposed model is described. Section 4 presents the methodology for the estimation of the parameters. Section 5 brings the simulation set up and the results. Finally, in Section 6, a discussion and conclusions about the results is presented.

2   Background

2.1   Tuberculosis

TB is an infectious disease caused by the *M. tuberculosis* bacillus. The World Health Organization (WHO) in the last Global Tuberculosis Report in 2012 estimates that there were almost 9 million new cases in 2011 and 1.4 million TB deaths remaining a major global health problem and being the second leading cause of death from an infectious disease [10].

The multidrug-resistant and extensively drug-resistant TB are two forms of highly drug-resistant TB that can convert this disease untreatable and fatal, specially in poor countries with a high incidence of AIDS [2]. Due to these reasons it is necessary to investigate rapid diagnostic of drug-resistant TB and the development of new drugs to effectively treat all forms of TB.

2.2   Growth Curve of *Mycobacterium tuberculosis*

Determination of growth curve of *M. tuberculosis* has wide applications in tuberculosis research. It has been useful in assessing the viability of the bacteria in cases of: environmental stress [18], alterations in gene regulation [17], response to different physic-chemical conditions [1], presence of gene mutations associated with drug resistance [8] and deciphering the function of unknown genes revealed by genome sequencing [14].

The fact that *M. tuberculosis* has a slow growth rate and the tendency to form clumps when grown in liquid media, makes it more difficult to study mycobacterial growth by methods commonly used for other bacteria [9]. The standard plate count method of viable cells is laborious, time consuming and requires at least 3 weeks to give results and frequently fails due to either contamination or dehydratation of the medium during the long incubation period [5].

Recently, von Groll et al. [8] standardized a new method to determine the growth curve based on MGIT960^{TM} system which assesses mycobacterial growth by the consumption of oxygen in the liquid medium [11]. This method allows closely monitoring the metabolic activity of the bacteria, which is measured automatically every hour by the apparatus. Unlike counting of viable cells, the main classical method to determine a growth curve, it does not require the use of detergents to disperse the bacterial cells in the medium. It is less time consuming, and the turnaround time is between 12-20 days. Besides, this system measures automatically and stores the data, which is an advantage to any current method to determine growth curve. Furthermore, it can be easily set up by any person having the Epicenter® [15] software. On the other hand, this method requires expensive equipment and they are inflexible since they depend on a single pre-packaged growth media [3,19].

The normal bacterial growth curve *in vitro* has four stages (see Figure 1):

1. *Lag phase:* is the adaptation period of the bacteria to the culture medium. Although bacteria have metabolic activity, there is no population growth. This phase may be affected by differences in the environment prior to the bacteria was growing and also the growth phase which the bacteria was in the moment of the inoculums. Another factor that influences is the concentration of the inoculums which smaller concentration, the longer it takes to reach the minimum population that can be quantified by the method used.

2. *Log phase:* the exponential growth phase of the bacterium. Bacterial biomass increases linearly, with the number of bacterial cells doubling with every generation time. This growth occurs until reach a high population density, an increase of toxic metabolites and reduction of nutrients. During the growth phase, the bacterial cells can release chemical molecules (quorum sensing), which may stimulate reducing the bacterial growth rate at high population density.

3. *Stationary phase:* this occurs when there is a stable bacterial population growth. The number of cells which die is similar to the number of new cells. Furthermore, part of the bacterial cells stop to multiply, however, through the dormancy factor, they remain viable. The better the ability of the bacterium to survive in dormancy longer the stationary phase it.

4. *Decline phase (death):* eventually, death phase is reached where bacterial cells are broken down (cell lysis) due to the additional accumulation of inhibitory byproducts, depletion of cellular energy, reduction of O_2 and pH changes.

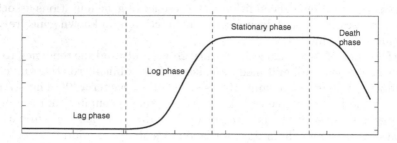

Fig. 1. Phases of a typical bacterial growth curve. See the main text for a detailed description of each phase.

2.3   Experimental Data: The *Mycobacterium tuberculosis* Strains and Growth Curve

In our studies, we consider experimental data about real *M. tuberculosis* growth curves. These experimental results are detailed in [8]. In this work we are considering four *M. tuberculosis* clinical isolates from Bangladesh or Georgia countries and the reference one (H37Rv). The susceptibility profiles of the strains are in the table 1. The strains 01-2522, 02-2761 and H37Rv were susceptible to Isoniazid (INH), Rifampicin (RIF), Ethambutol (EMB) and Streptomycin (SM). The strain 03-2922 was resistant to INH and SM and the strain 03-0850 was resistant to INH, RIF, EMB and SM, being classified as a multidrug resistant (MDR) strain.

Table 1. The *M. tuberculosis* strains

Strain Identification	Origin of isolates	Susceptibility			
		INH	RIF	EMB	STM
GC 02-2761	Bangladesh	S	S	S	S
GC 03-0850	Bangladesh	R	R	R	R
GC 01-2522	Georgia	S	S	S	S
GC 03-2922	Georgia	R	S	S	R
H37Rv	ATCC	S	S	S	S

The growth curve determined by MGIT960^{TM}: all strains were freshly subcultured on Lowenstein Jensen medium and incubated at 37°C for exactly 3 weeks. The inoculum was prepared by suspending bacilli in 4 ml ultra-pure water containing glass beads. The suspension was vortexed for 30s and allowed to sediment for 15 min. The supernatant was transferred to another tube, diluted to match the turbidity of a McFarland tube No. 0.5 and adjusted at 595 nm to an OD of 0.01-0.03. A dilution 1:1000 was prepared in ultra-pure water. One hundred

μl of this dilution was added in triplicate to MGIT960^{TM} Mycobacteria Growth Indicator Tubes (Becton Dickinson Diagnostic Systems, Sparks, MD, USA) supplemented with 10 % MGIT960^{TM} SIRE Supplement (Becton Dickinson, USA). The tubes were entered into the MGIT960^{TM} system and incubated at 37°C. Growth curves were obtained by monitoring the fluorescence and recording the growth units (GU) every hour using the BD EpiCente software.

2.4   Multi-Agent-Based Simulation (MABS)

Multiagent Systems (MAS) study the behaviour of sets of independent agents with different characteristics, which evolve in a common environment. These agents interact with each other, and try to execute their tasks in a cooperative way by sharing information, preventing conflicts and coordinating the execution of their own activities [21].

The combination of both, multiagent systems and simulation, generates a new research area called Multi-Agent-Based Simulation (MABS), that deals with problems that involve multiple domains [7]. An example of a MABS application domain is medicine and how the diseases are disseminated.

MABS has provided architectures and platforms for the implementation and simulation of relatively autonomous agents and it has contributed to the establishment of the agent-based computer simulation paradigm. The agent-based approach enhances the potentialities of computer simulation as a tool for theorizing about social scientific issues. In particular, the notion of an extended computational agent, implementing cognitive capabilities, is giving encouragement to the construction and exploration of artificial societies, since it facilitates the modeling of artificial societies of autonomous intelligent agents [4]. According to Drogoul and Ferber [6], MABS goals are:

1. Testing hypotheses about the emergence of social structures from the behaviours and interactions of each individual. This is done by testing the minimal conditions given at the micro-level that are necessary to observe these structures at the macro-level;
2. Building theories that contribute to the development of a general understanding of ethological, sociological and psycho-sociological systems, by relating behaviours to structural and organizational properties; and
3. Integrating different partial theories coming from various disciplines, as sociology, ethnology or cognitive psychology, into a general framework, by providing tools that allow the integration of different studies.

In this work, our ideas are to test the goal (1), searching the global variables to help in the understanding of the mycobacterial growth.

3   Proposed Model

The model uses agents analog to the *M. tuberculosis* bacteria. Each of these agents has features that allow them to perform their role in the model, mimicking features of the real world. The agents' features are:

- **Energy**: Describes how healthy is the agent.
- **Consumption**: Determines how much nutrients the agent is consuming from the environment at each time interval. It also determines the rate at which it consumes their energy.
- **Adaptation**: Determines the time needed to the agent to make the transition between lag and log phase.
- **Sense**: Determines if the agent detected enough signalling molecules in the environment. Once this detection is positive the agent enters a reduced power state.

The model is also composed by the environment, which is the space where the agents can move. Every patch of this environment has its own characteristics. In the present model these characteristics are *nutrients* and *waste*. *Nutrients* represents the resource that agents consume to produce energy and *waste* is related to the waste that agents produce and dispose into the environment after metabolising nutrients.

Initially the agents need time to adapt to the environment where they live until they start replicating. This is the *Lag phase* in the bacterial growth.

After this period agents starts to reproduce in a process analogous to cell division in which a new agent is an exact copy of the agent that gave birth to it. However, in order for this reproduction to occur, agents need to have a certain amount of energy, due to the fact that this resource is divided between the two agents in the process. Therefore, the limiting factor for reproduction of the agents is the amount of energy that they can acquire from the environment by metabolising nutrients. This represents the *Log phase*.

At each time interval the agents consume from the environment a certain amount of nutrients. After metabolising these nutrients the agent acquires energy and produces waste. The higher the concentration of waste in the environment, less energy the agent can extract from it.

4   Estimation of Parameters

In the model created there are three parameters that are likely to permit that any growth curve can be obtained. These parameters are *loglim*, *decaiconsumo* and *enconsumo*. The *loglim* parameter influences in the maximum population of the curve (the larger it is, the bigger is the population). The *decaiconsumo* parameter defines the population growth decrease, according to the proportion of agents indicated by signaling molecules defined by *loglim*. The *enconsumo* parameter influences the growth rate the higher it is the faster the agents will reproduce.

However, it is hard to define the correct values to these parameters in order to produce the desired growth behaviour. In this way we resort to the estimation of the parameters using a numerical method. In fact, the literature presents many examples where the combination of evolutionary algorithms and multiagent models are used [16]. However, in this work we chose to use a numerical method to solve the present problem. This choice is based in two important factors: (i) Our problem has a well-defined objective function and it can be expressed mathematically by a curve where the changes in values of the parameters have predictable changes in the resulting curve and (ii) A numerical method requires a smaller computational effort compared with an evolutionary algorithm and in our study this is an important feature due to the large number of agents.

4.1 The Bisection Method

The bisection method is able to find a root of a function, $f(x) = 0$, or any specific value of a function, $f(x) = m$, in a given interval $[a, b]$ [13]. The method is depicted in the algorithm 1. Considering as inputs of the algorithm a function f, the limits a and b, error ε and respecting the conditions $a < b$, either $f(a) < m$ and $f(b) > m$ or $f(a) > m$ and $f(b) < m$.

Also, considering N_{max} as the maximum number of steps to prevent an infinite loop, the algorithm 1 will output a value which differs from the desired value x_0 of $f(x_0) = m$ by less than ε.

Algorithm 1. Bisection Method

---

  function BISECTION(f, a, b, ε)
    $N \leftarrow 1$
    while $N \leq N_{max}$ **do**
      $x_0 = (a + b)/2$
      if $f(x_0) = m$ or $(b - a)/2 < \varepsilon$ **then**
        return x_0
        Stop
      end if
      $N \leftarrow N + 1$
      if $f(x_0) < m$ **then**
        $a \leftarrow x_0$
      else
        $b \leftarrow x_0$
      end if
    end while
    Output "Method failed, maximum number of steps exceeded"
  end function

In our problem we used the bisection method to infer the three parameters of interest. We proceed by inferring one parameter while keeping fixed the other two. In this way we cycle over the three parameters until a convergence criterion is met.

5   Results and Analysis

5.1   Simulation Set Up

In order to adjust the simulated growth curve with the experimental results by inferring the parameters we use the five real strains described in Table 1. For each one of the five strains we performed 50 estimation of parameters as a way to compare them with real curves. The comparison is accomplished using the average and standard deviation over the 50 estimation of parameters. The stop criteria for the bisection method is $\varepsilon < 3\%$ or 10 iterations whichever occurs first. The following parameters were set for all simulations as follows:

- Number of agents: 30
- Nutrients from each patch: 100
- Adaptation time: 250
- Minimum consumption: 0.1
- Chance of the agent to produce a signalling molecule: 0.05
- Gradual rate of decay of consumption upon entering the reduced power state: 0.3

The real curves do not measure the number of bacteria directly, instead they measure bacteria's fluorescence. Due to this fact we had to choose an arbitrarily low number of initial agents, 30, to imitate the initial value of fluorescence which is very low. Also, a higher number of initial agents may have had a negative impact in the computational performance of the simulations. The variable "Gradual rate of decay of consumption upon entering the reduced power state" causes the more or less abrupt end of the curve. It happens because once the population enter this state, they will begin to gradually reduce their consumption, which will lead them to reproduce less and therefore stabilize the curve. The intensity of this gradual reduction in consumption will dictate how quickly the curve will stabilize.

The variable "Threshold where agents will enter the reduced power state" determines the final size of the population. This is because the variable associated with this threshold is obtained by calculating the proportion of signalling molecules in the environment compared to the total space. Therefore, for larger thresholds more signalling molecules will be allowed to populate the environment, thus more agents will be produced until the population reaches the reduced power state.

The variable "Amount of energy expended per unit time to maintain the vital functions of the agent" is associated with the inclination of the log phase of the growth curve. This is due to the fact that the more energy is required to maintain a live agent, less energy is left for him to reproduce, and therefore the reproduction speed of the population is affected.

Real growth curves are obtained with the MGIT960^{TM} system which assesses mycobacterial growth by the consumption of oxygen in the liquid medium [11]. In this method bacteria are not directly counted, instead its growth is monitored by means of measuring the fluorescence resulting from its metabolic activity. Moreover, the time in the real growth curves is measured in days.

Simulated curves are obtained from MABS in which the time is represented by "ticks" and each agent corresponds to one bacteria, therefore, bacteria is directly counted. In order to establish a correspondence among the variables in the real curves and the ones in the MABS system, and therefore be able to compare them, we set one agent to be equivalent to four metabolic activity units and 41.88 ticks to represent one day. Note that these factors are arbitrary and determined by the choice of constants defined in the MABS system.

Having described all the variables that are fixed in the MABS system we define the limits for the estimated variables. These limits are $[0.1, 0.9]$ for *enconsumo*, $[0.001, 0.02]$ for *decaiconsumo* and $[0.001, 0.05]$ for *loglim*.

5.2   Results

In order to evaluate the estimation of parameters the results are presented in Figure 2. Each panel presents real and simulated growth curves for the strain indicated at the top of the panel. Dotted line is the real (measured) curve. The dashed line and the gray region are respectively the mean and one standard deviation obtained from 50 different parameter estimation simulations.

From the resulting curves it is possible to see that the estimation of parameters produced curves of distinct quality. The method appear to be able to reproduce with fidelity some of the characteristics of the real curve but not all of them at the same time. For instance, the maximum number of bacteria, or metabolic activity, is always very close to the target in the real experimental data.

On the other hand the growing rate and the point where the growth starts is not perfect in all simulations. This is very likely to be an effect of the estimation method utilized. Because the bisection method cannot estimate all the parameters at once it may be that by adjusting one parameter at a time the other two are not correctly adjusted. It is also possible that the number of iterations which was set to 10 is too low and the error admissible (3%) is to high leading to small deviations in the estimation that in turn produce a great effect in the final curve.

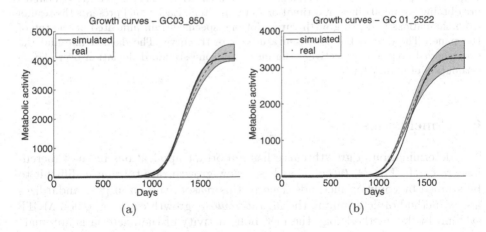

Fig. 2. *(Continued)*

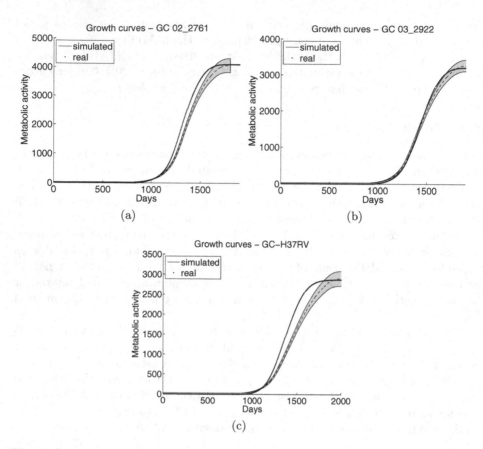

Fig. 2. Comparison of real and simulated growth curves. The simulated growth curves are obtained from 50 different estimation of parameters. Each panel presents the results from simulations and real growth curves for one specific strain indicated at the top of the panel. The dotted line is the measured growth curve. The dashed line and the grey shaded area are respectively the mean and one standard deviation over the 50 estimation of parameters.

6   Conclusions

The determination of growth curve has important applications in the tuberculosis research. The *M. tuberculosis* has a slow growth rate turning it difficult to be studied by common methods. Due to this reason, von Groll [8] standardizes a new method of determining the *M. tuberculosis* growth curve based on MGIT system. In this methodology the metabolic activity of the bacteria is automatically measured by the apparatus during 12-20 days. Despite the advantages of this methodology, it still time consuming and requires an expensive equipment. Due to these reasons in this work we proposed a method to estimate parameters of MABS that mimics the mycobacterium growth.

The main goal of having a MABS simulator of the growth curve of *M. tuberculosis* is to study the biological mechanisms of growth in a manner which is faster, safer and cheaper than doing it with the real bacteria. In order to achieve this goal we have first to be sure that the MABS system can behave as close as possible to the real system. In a previous work we have presented a MABS system to simulate the growth behaviour of the mycobacterium. One of the problems in this previous work was the correct setting of the parameters which was not trivial to obtain. In the present work we presented a first effort in trying to estimate the MABS parameters so that it can reproduce correctly the real behaviour of the system.

Another interesting fact is that by having the real curves and the MABS system that can reproduce these curves one can have new insights about the biological mechanisms of growth. By estimating the parameters to adjust different curves or by having to elaborate more in the MABS biologists have the opportunity of hypothesizing about new mechanisms of growth and test them both in vitro and in silico.

From the results obtained we can see that this method is promising but there are still some questions to be answered. It is clear that the simulated curves are not yet exactly matching the real curves. This can be due to various reasons. The most likely reason is that the MABS system is lacking some mechanism which is present in the real system and which has great influence in the shape of the curve. For instance, in our simulator all the bacteria start to reproduce at the same time. In the real system it is reasonable to admit that the bacteria starts to reproduce following a distribution over time. The same lack of "distribution over time" in other phases of growing in the MABS can be a limiting factor for obtaining better matching between simulated and real growth curves. The other possible reason is that the numerical method as it was set up for this experiment may not be able to find the parameters with the accuracy necessary for the exact reproduction of the real curves.

In future work we will investigate the inclusion of more realistic behaviour of bacteria in the MABS. We will also investigate the use of more robust methods for the estimation of parameters. These two venues of research will be carried out together as they are highly dependent to each other.

References

1. Barkan, D., Liu, Z., Sacchettini, J., Glickman, M.: Mycolic acid cyclopropanation is essential for viability, drug resistance, and cell wall integrity of mycobacterium tuberculosis. Chem. Biol. **16**, 499–509 (2009)
2. Chan, E.D., Iseman, M.D.: Multidrug-resistant and extensively drug-resistant tuberculosis: a review. Curr. Opin. Infect. Dis. **21**(6), 587–595 (2008)
3. Chien, H., Yu, M., Wu, M., Lin, T., Luh, K.: Comparison of the bactec mgit 960 with lwenstein-jensen medium for recovery of mycobacteria from clinical specimens. Int. J. Tuberc. Lung. Dis. **4**(9), 866–870 (2000)
4. Conte, R., Gilbert, N., Sichman, J.S.: MAS and Social Simulation: A Suitable Commitment. In: Sichman, J.S., Conte, R., Gilbert, N. (eds.) MABS 1998. LNCS (LNAI), vol. 1534, pp. 1–9. Springer, Heidelberg (1998)

5. Damato, J.J., Collins, M.T., Rothlauf, M.V., McClatchy, J.K.: Detection of mycobacteria by radiometric and standard plate procedures. J. Clin. Microbiol. **17**, 1066–1073 (1983)
6. Drogoul, A., Ferber, J.: Multi-agent simulation as a tool for modeling societies: Application to social diferentiation in ant colonies. In: Proceedings of Workshop on Modelling Autonomous Agents in a Multi-Agent World (1992)
7. Gilbert, N., Troitzsch, K.G.: Simulation for the Social Scientist. Buckingham and Philadelphi (2005)
8. von Groll, A., Martin, A., Stehr, M., Singh, M., Portaels, F., da Silva, P.E.A., Palomino, J.C.: Fitness of mycobacterium tuberculosisstrains of the w-beijing and non-w-beijing genotype. PLoS ONE **5**(4), e10191 (2010)
9. Lambrecht, R.S., Carriere, J.F., Collins, M.T.: A model for analyzing growth kinetics of a slowly growing mycobacterium sp. Appl. Environ. Microbiol. **54**, 910–916 (1988)
10. Organization, W.H.: Global tuberculosis report (2012), http://www.who.int/tb/publications/global_report/
11. Pheiffer, C., Carroll, N., Beyers, N., Donald, P., Duncan, K., Uys, P., van Helden, P.: Time to detection of mycobacterium tuberculosis in bactec systems as a viable alternative to colony counting. Int. J. Tuberc. Lung. Dis. **12**(7), 792–798 (2008)
12. Buchanan, R.L., Whiting, R.C., Damert, W.C.: When is simple good enough: a comparison of the gompertz, baranyi, and three-phase linear models for fitting bacterial growth curves. Food Microbiology **14**, 313–326 (1997)
13. Ruggiero, M.A.G., Lopes, V.L.D.R.: Cálculo Numérico: Aspectos teóricos e Computacionais. Pearson (1997)
14. Sassetti, C., Boyd, D., Rubin, E.: Genes required for mycobacterial growth defined by high density mutagenesis. Mol. Microbiol. **48**(1), 77–84 (2003)
15. Technologies, B.: The bd epicenter microbiology data management system, http://www.bd.com/ds/technicalCenter/brochures/br_1_2704.pdf (January 2013)
16. Terano, T.: Exploring the Vast Parameter Space of Multi-Agent Based Simulation. In: Antunes, L., Takadama, K. (eds.) MABS 2006. LNCS (LNAI), vol. 4442, pp. 1–14. Springer, Heidelberg (2007)
17. Verma, A., Sampla, A., Tyagi, J.: Mycobacterium tuberculosis rrn promoters: differential usage and growth rate-dependent control. J. Bacteriol. **181**(14), 4326–4333 (1999)
18. Voskuil, M., Visconti, K., Schoolnik, G.: Mycobacterium tuberculosis gene expression during adaptation to stationary phase and low-oxygen dormancy. Tuberculosis (Edinb) **84**(3-4), 218–227 (2004)
19. Walters, S.B., Hanna, B.A.: Testing of susceptibility of mycobacterium tuberculosis to isoniazid and rifampin by mycobacterium growth indicator tube method. J. Clin. Microbiol. **34**, 1565–1567 (1996)
20. Werlang, P., Fagundes, M.Q., Adamatti, D.F., Machado, K.S., von Groll, A., da Silva, P.E.A., Werhli, A.V.: Multi-agent-based simulation of mycobacterium tuberculosis growth. In: Alam, S.J., Van Dyke Parunak, H. (eds.) MABS 2013, LNAI 8235, pp. 131–142. Springer, Heidelberg (2014)
21. Wooldridge, M.: An Introduction to MultiAgent Systems. John Wiley & Sons (2009)

AI in Education, Affective Computing, and Human-Computer Interaction

Effect of Emotional Feedback
in a Decision-Making System
for an Autonomous Agent

Javier Guerrero Rázuri^(✉), David Sundgren, Rahim Rahmani,
and Aron Larsson

Department of Computer and Systems Sciences,
Stockholm University, Stockholm, Sweden
{javier,dsn,rahim,aron}@dsv.su.se
http://dsv.su.se/en/

Abstract. The main purpose of this research is the implementation of a decision model affected by emotional feedback in a cognitive robotic assistant that can capture information about the world around it. The robot will use multi-modal communication to assist the societal participation of persons deprived of conventional modes of communication. The aim is a machine that can predict what the user will do next and be ready to give the best possible assistance, taking in account the emotional factor. The results indicate the benefits and importance of emotional feedback in the closed loop human-robot interaction framework. Cognitive agents are shown to be capable of adapting to emotional information from humans.

Keywords: Affective computing · Artificial neural network · Facial expression recognition · Detection of emotional information · Adversarial risk analysis · Broaden and Build theory

1 Introduction

Over the years machines have incorporated emotional acquisition into their architectures [1], [2], [3], [4], [5], which makes it possible to solve tasks that go further than performing accurate and quick calculations with rational, rigorous and logical behavior. Looking forward, humans might be partakers of a new Human-Machine Interaction with entities that can develop human emotions, such as kindness, loyalty, friendship and even love. It is possible to think, that future generations of machines must have some skills to understand human emotions and these emotions can serve as a guide for their actions. The new machines could have some kind of functionalities to respond more flexibly, foretelling and adjusting to what humans want. In the present article, we address the problem of designing a model which supports making decisions affected by human's emotions in an autonomous agent, capable of interacting with an individual. We

This work is supported by VINNOVA - Swedish Governmental Agency for Innovation Systems through the ICT project "The Next Generation (TNG)".

© Springer International Publishing Switzerland 2014
A.L.C. Bazzan and K. Pichara (Eds.): IBERAMIA 2014, LNAI 8864, pp. 613–624, 2014.
DOI: 10.1007/978-3-319-12027-0_49

thus aim at supporting the decision making of an autonomous agent so as to improve the human-machine interaction, that it still is far from be fluent [6]. We tackle the problem with the proposal of combining two models: an emotional model and a decision-making model for an agent. The combination will give rise to an evolution of the agent's behavior that can lead to closer social interrelation with humans. In light of this remark, the decision agent will be able to make decisions influenced by the emotional information conveyed through the human face, using the framework of Adversarial Risk Analysis (ARA) [7] and neural network based methods in facial emotion recognition [8], [9]. We illustrate the implementation of the model with a robot endowed with several sensors to infer the user's actions and environment's states.

This paper is organized as follows. Section 2 describes the general scenario where the interactions between the agent and human are performed. Subsections 2.1 and 2.2 describe the proposed models that allow an agent to make choices and to capture human's emotions. Section 3 presents a literature review related to emotions in machines. Section 4 describes a rule-based design of emotional feedback for self-regulation of positive behavior. Section 5 describes the experimental results of simulations examining the effects of emotional feedback in the behavioral model of the autonomous agent are shown. Discussion and future work are presented in Section 6.

2   Interaction Model

As we can see in Fig. 1, within the scenario the interaction between an agent and human is being carried out. The arrows show the direction of the input and output data that the agent will use. The emotional input will comprise the current emotion provided by the facial expression. The agent will behave taking into account the information of the human adversary and the information of the environment in which the agent evolves. The next action selected by the agent will be affected by the perceived emotion of the adversary. This will change behavior of the agent in a manner that can be suitable for a future learning process in a social context. Part of the model is essentially multiattribute decision analytic, [10], [11], but the agent manages also forecasts models of the evolution of its adversary taking into account the emotional feedback and the environment surrounding all of them.

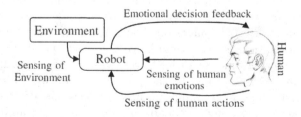

Fig. 1. Interaction general model

2.1 Emotion Detection Model

The agent constantly stores the information provided by the opponent's face, this information will be the emotional feedback input that will support the final decision. The model is based on two modules: facial image treatment and a feed-forward neural network algorithm trained by back-propagation to recognize facial expressions. Basically, this facial emotion detection loop starts when the agent recognizes the face of the opponent. The algorithm starts with images of the eyes and the mouth, merging the two extractions into a single new image. The Artificial neural network has trained previously with a series of images that the agent has stored in the memory. The group of images, connected with six different facial expressions (six for each individual), are the training set with the same treatment of the input image. Finally, once the group to which the image belongs is found, the system reports about the emotional state of the opponent's face. The output layer of the Artificial neural network contains six nodes representing the output variable to the problem. The number of neurons that has to be in the output layer is fixed to the number of emotions that we are going to consider. The set of emotions is: Anger, Disgust, Surprise, Happiness, Sadness and Fear, each of which is represented by each person in the training set. Fig. 2 shows a sample of images from the Cohn-Kanade database that belong to the training data set and an example of the facial image treatment. In [12] results of the algorithm are shown, along with the structure of the Artificial neural network and the percentage of accuracy from the system.

Fig. 2. Cohn-Kanade (CK) database samples and facial image treatment

2.2 Interactive Decision Model

The agent maintains *Interaction prediction modules* that assess probabilities when the opponent has performed an action that triggers surrounding reactions, given the past history of agent's actions, opponent's actions and the evolution of the surroundings state, as was the case in [13]. The surrounding states are under the control of the opponent and are influenced by the latest of the opponent's action, e.g., the individual can control the heating or tenuity of light. The simulation is implemented with four surrounding states (Energy, Temperature, Position and Detection). Furthermore, the model allows for evolution of the behavior of the opponent, affected by how he reacts to the agent's actions, thus incorporating the adversarial risk analysis principle, where risks stem from deliberate actions of intelligent adversaries. Related with ARA principle we have two modules, one represents the opponent's own evolution and is called *opponent's evolution module* and the other represents the opponent's reactions to the agent's actions and is called *classical conditioning module*. The actualization of the data in these modules takes place in the model based on the average of the posterior distributions, using the opponent's evolution module and the classical conditioning module, [14]. Assuming that $p(M_i)$ designates the probability that the agent follow the model i, with $p(M_1) + p(M_2) = 1$, $p(M_i) \geq 0$, this model captures the agent's reactive behavior facing the opponent actions that will be modified through the emotional feedback, for more detail see, [13].

The agent's behavior provides utilities and probabilities, on which we can apply the Maximum Expected Utility (MEU) criterion [15], [16], to select the optimal action based on all current information. The agent constantly faces multiple synergy states. The consequences are provided by the synergy states that depend on the agent's actions, the opponent's actions and the future surrounding state. The future surrounding state happens just after the agent's and opponent's actions. Through a multi-attribute utility function [10], we will evaluate the synergy states without much loss of generality [17]. In order to compute the maximum expected utility, we plan one period ahead assuming additive utilities over time, as reflected in the results of the simulations, see Section 5. The decision is probabilistic, based on a probability model that randomly generates alternatives with probability proportional to the expected utility [18], therefore, it increases unpredictability of the agent's decisions under similar circumstances.

The agent aims at satisfying some hierarchically ordered self-objectives in order to support its own evolution. This hierarchy entails that the agent will invest most resources in achieving a sufficient level in the lowest self-objective, because of its higher weight, see [19]. Once it has attained a sufficient value in that level, it will redistribute its own resources to achieve the next level, and so on, e.g., if the agent needs to socialize with the opponent he will probably tend to draw his attention with a salutary action. The hierarchy levels can grow and be constructed depending of the autonomous adaptation that we want to project in the agent, e.g., a caregiver agent will probably show a highly sophisticated hierarchy of levels, with socialization components. If the agent is based on biological entities like humans, it will be imperative to satisfy its security in order to survive and energy that will provide self-health. *Self-objective* as Energy and Security are the requirements for agent survival. In the case of the *Self-objective of Security*, it will that the agent takes into account the risk of injury when it is attacked (Atk) by a human. At the same time, the agent needs to remain at an appropriate level of temperature (Tp) for its proper operation. If the agent does not have enough levels of energy to satisfy *Self-objective of Energy*, it will probably not continue with the normal course of its activities. All self-objectives are constructed based on component utility functions that will evaluate in a *Global utility function*. The global utility function will be the weighted sum of the utilities of the lowest level objectives energy, security and temperature.

3   Related Work

Through the procedure described above the agent has the capability to evolve with a positive behavior facing the opponent by implicit communication, e.g., in case of a robot caregiver as an intelligent agent, its positive actions can influence the patients that in turn would be more inclined to engage in a closed loop human-robot emotional interaction [20]. The idea is that the agent can recognize the affective state of the human captured by the facial expression implicitly and adapt to it modifying its actions appropriately, reflecting some degree of emotional intelligence [21]. Authors such as those of [22] and [23] have raised doubts on whether machines can exhibit intelligent behavior without sign of emotion. In human communication, emotions play an important role, and the ability to display and understand the human emotions and affective states are essential for effective communication [6]. A machine that expresses, recognizes and understands emotions similar to human ones could be a good collaborator. This is indeed an area of growing interest [24], and many designs have demonstrated how human-robot interaction in cognitive robotics can be augmented by a closed loop that implies an implicit emotional communication, [25], [26], [27], [28], [29]. The connection between decision making and emotions is very thin [30]. In this case, emotions must be seen as features that can influence the decision level. Some emotion models take into account theories which connect decision making and emotions using weighing criteria and evaluation of alternatives, [31], the mood congruency of memories that affect predictions [32], a model of intensity from the visceral factors involved in decision making [33], the weighted average of decayed base emotion [34] and numerous descriptive findings on such relations [35]. In the future we would like to extend the capabilities of the model presented in this paper using weight categorization from the integration of two or more emotions; it could be an internal emotional model that will use secondary emotions. The acquisition of emotions by a machine is a promising paradigm that allows human-like social interaction due to their ability to give emotional feedback. The appropriate responses to the emotions of others is a contextually sensitive ability that humans are particularly skilled at, given this advantage, machines could learn how to modify actions and behaviors based on emotional feedback from our system of emotional signals, [36], [37], [38]. In humans emotions motivate future behavior, the connection of actions to specific emotions is often hard-wired. Emotions help humans to overcome obstacles, and in fact pave the way to select the most appropriate behavior.

4   Rule-Based Design of Emotional Feedback

Our agent will show increasingly positive behavior and will keep a self-regulation between actions and emotions. To achieve this goal, we will base the rules on principles of the *broaden and build theory*, [39], [40]. In this case, the agent's reactions when it is facing the opponent's positive behavior, could trigger a cycle of positive emotions connected to the relevant action. Through positive emotions humans can develop various types of skills and capacities which negative emotions are not able to support. Negative emotions tend to favour some preferences [41], [42], [43], e.g., anger tends to maintain a course of action or in the most extreme case attack, while fear can evade the immediate context or the course of action. Disgust is associated as a specific reaction to something that is offensive, and the action that it will generate pursues to expel the trigger stimulus. As opposed to negative emotions, positive emotions help the body move from a narrow set of actions to a broader one, allowing pursuit of a wider array of thoughts and alternatives. Table 1 shows six basic emotions [44], [45], represented in a set of rule-based action/response-pairs. The categorization that we assumed was arbitrarily chosen, taking into account that it is possible to modify the model with another order of emotions. For this first scheme, we have ordered the emotions according to the "Basic emotion theories", where we can differentiate two groups "positive" and "negative" based on the emotional stimuli organized in a categorical manner, with innate categories found in humans [46], [47]. This table shows the possibility of deciding the agent's behavior by mixing the emotional feedback and the outputs of the decision system using a rule-based algorithm. The algorithm simply corrects the agent's behavior using the human biological emotions; in this case the human-machine emotional loop will be the closest connection. The reactive response between the emotion and action is dependent on the positive or negative influence that is shown, and will be the trigger of the corrective emotional output. In other words, we hold that priority should be attached to the opponent's emotions. For practical purposes, we need to define a hierarchy of levels according to the signs of the emotions and agent's actions, showing the relative importance of these signs, see Fig. 3. A pertinent focus for future research would be to examine the inclusion of different levels of precision in the emotional hierarchy into the "Rule-based design of emotional feedback", that could be the setting of intervals related to primary and secondary emotions [30].

Table 1. Emotions, Actions, and Modified Actions

OS_{em}	R_1	R_2	NR_1	NR_2
Anger (-)	(+)	(-)	R_{upL}	R_{upL}
Sadness (-)	(+)	(-)	R_{upL}	R_{upL}
Fear (-)	(+)	(-)	R_{upL}	R_{upL}
Disgust (-)	(+)	(-)	R_{upL}	R_{upL}
Happiness (+)	(+)	(-)	R_{upL}	M_L
Surprised (+)	(+)	(-)	R_{upL}	M_L

Note: $R_a \{R_1, R_2\}$, $R_a \{(+), (-)\}$ are signs of the agent's actions before the emotional feedback. NR_1 and NR_2 are the modified actions of the agent taking into account the emotional feedback. R_{upL}: Reject and change the hierarchy level of agent's action (to positive action); M_L: Maintain the current hierarchy level of agent's action (maintain the negative action); OS_{em} : Signs of the opponent's emotion.

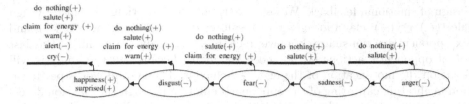

Fig. 3. Hierarchy of levels

If the opponent shows positive emotional behavior he will be willing to accept a negative behavior from outside, in this case provided by the agent's actions. Only emotions like surprise and happiness will preserve the current hierarchy level of the agent's action, e.g., "When the opponent's emotion is happiness (+) and the agent's action is cry(-), the agent preserves the negative action, in other case the agent rejects the action and increases the hierarchy level" (In real life, we are willing to manage difficult situations when we have positive emotional charge). Positive emotions may influence the generation of resources and flexible thoughts in order to choose the right action [48]. The flow chart of the agent's action modified by the positive emotion is shown in Fig. 4.

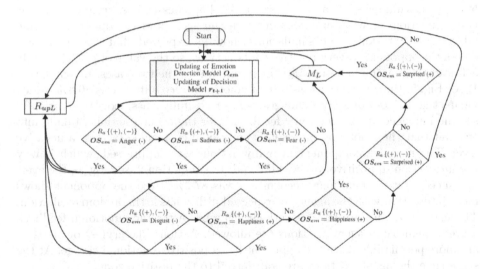

Fig. 4. Flow chart from correction of agent's action through emotional feedback

5   Experimental Results

The simulations cover the evolution of the expected utility just one period ahead, the agent's reactive behavior facing the opponent's actions through the weighting of posterior model probability, the evolution of the emotional feedback provided by the opponent's face and evolution of the agent's behavior using the rule-based design of emotional feedback. We select only six agent's actions classified by sign [alert($-$), cry($-$), claim for energy($+$), salute($+$), warn($+$), do nothing($+$)] and six opponent's actions [attack, move, recharge, stroke and do nothing], this last set of opponent's actions do not need the signs, because all the analysis will focus on the modification of the agent's behavior. The system works per iteration facilitating capturing of the opponent's emotion through the emotion detection model. In the simulation 250 iterations were fixed, related to the training set and test set used in the Artificial neural network propagation algorithm to recognize the opponent's emotions. We used the Cohn-Kanade (CK) database [49] to construct the training set and test set. This database contains 97 individuals showing different expressions. We selected only 50 individuals from the 97 in order to capture the set of more pronounced facial emotions. We collected 6 images per individual coming to have a total of 300 images. We trained the Artificial neural network with 50 images. The rest is comprised of 250 images and it has been used as test set. Every time that the emotion detection model has reported a misclassification, the inaccurate emotional output is replaced by the most positive agent's action, in this case do nothing($+$), for the purpose of developing a positive behavior in the agent. Finally, in order to correct the agent's behavior using the emotional feedback provided by the opponent, we determine a hierarchy level of the agent's action from negative to positive; [anger($-$), sadness($-$), fear($-$), disgust($-$), happiness($+$), surprised($+$)]. The two simulations show interactions between the agent and the opponent during all the 250 iterations. The simulations show as expected that the agent perceives the opponent as very reactive to its actions, so the value of $p(M_1)$ rapidly achieves the maximum and $p(M_2)$ the minimum for the two cases. In simulation 1, see Fig. 5, the average success rate of emotional recognition was 86.8%, which means that 217 out of 250 test images were successfully classified. We can clearly see the influence of the emotional feedback over the agent's actions, taking into account that the emotional opponent's emotional evolution starts at a negative level. The negative component in many actions was suppressed, which is why the interaction in positive way was favored. In simulation 2, see Fig. 6, the average success rate of emotional recognition was 87.2%. Here the opponent shows more interaction with the agent, its expected utility has little random oscillation. The agent's actions are more negatively charged. After the emotional feedback a great quantity of agent's actions are allowed. Actions like cry($-$) or alert($-$) are more permissible when the opponent has a positive emotional charge. At the same time the agent's actions are transferred to the positive zone.

6   Discussion and Future Work

We have described a behavioral model for an autonomous agent, capable of reading information from its sensors and selecting appropriate actions based on the emotional signals expressed by a human opponent. The model uses multi-attribute decision analysis, forecasting models of the adversary and emotional feedback provided by the opponent, all supporting the final decision of the agent.

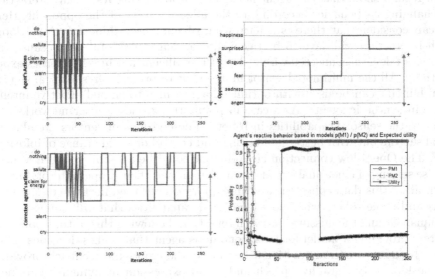

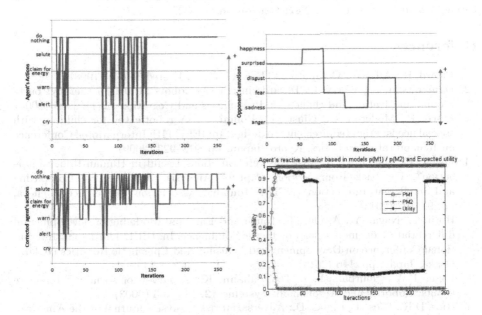

Fig. 5. Simulation 1

Fig. 6. Simulation 2

The results show that the agent is capable of improving its social interaction by changing its behavior according to the affective state of the opponent. Here we can consider that there is a narrowing of human-machine emotional loop. Such interaction will have to be taken into account in the future, because the number of devices connected wirelessly with intelligent machines increases exponentially. All the multimodal sensor inputs that recover biophysiological signals from humans can be used with optimized algorithms to embed affective intelligence in synthetic agents. As a case in point, the wireless sensor networks can improve the sensory capabilities in robots. These groups of sensors are akin to usual sensors but with better monitoring and control of a wide range of information. The OpenFlow connection environment could be the link between a more precise sensing of emotional signals from humans and their proper interpretation. With all of this data collected, we can explore deeper the affective communications and make robots with more emotional capabilities that will connect with humans, offering the missing natural interaction. Following this, future work will address providing a model for an autonomous agent that makes decisions influenced by more accurate emotional factors as the emotional feedback provided by the kinetic typography, speech and facial expression in humans. This new approach could make interaction between humans and agents more fluent and natural.

Acknowledgments. The authors greatly appreciate the financial support provided by the institution VINNOVA - Swedish Governmental Agency for Innovation Systems through the ICT project "The Next Generation (TNG)".

References

1. Picard, R.: Affective Computing. The MIT Press, United States (1998)
2. Dautenhahn, K., Werry, I.: Towards interactive robots in autism therapy: background, motivation and challenges. Pragmatics and Cognition 12(1), 1–35 (2004)
3. Marti, P., Moderini, C., Giusti, L., Pollini, A.: A robotic toy for children with special needs: From requirements to design. In: IEEE 11th International Conference on Rehabilitation Robotics, Kyoto, Japan, pp. 918–923 (2009)
4. Lewis, M., Cañamero, L.: Are Discrete Emotions Useful in Human-Robot Interaction?, Feedback from Motion Capture Analysis. In: Affective Computing and Intelligent Interaction (ACII), Humaine Association Conference, Geneva, pp. 97–102 (2013)
5. Horii, T., Nagai, Y., Asada, M.: Touch and Emotion: Modeling of developmental differentiation of emotion lead by tactile dominance. In: IEEE Third Joint International Conference on Development and Learning and Epigenetic Robotics (ICDL), Osaka, Japan, pp. 1–6 (2013)
6. Fong, T.W., Nourbakhsh, I., Dautenhahn, K.: A survey of socially interactive robots. Robotics and Autonomous Systems 42, 143–166 (2003)
7. Ríos, D.R., Ríos, J., Banks, D.: Adversarial risk analysis. Journal of the American Statistical Association 104(486), 841–854 (2009)
8. Kobayashi, H., Hara, F.: Facial Interaction between Animated 3D Face Robot and Human Beings. In: Proceedings of International Conference on Systems, Man, Cybernetics, vol. 3, pp. 732–737 (1997)

9. Pantic, M.: Automatic analysis of facial expressions: The state of the art. IEEE Transactions on Pattern Analysis and Machine Intelligence **22**(12), 1424–1445 (2000)

10. Clemen, R.T., Reilly, T.: Making Hard Decisions with Decision Tools. Duxbury, Pacific Grove (2001)

11. Hwang, C.L., Yoon, K.: Multiple Attribute Decision Making Methods and Applications: A State of the Art Survey. Springer, Heidelberg (1981)

12. Rázuri, J.G., Sundgren, D., Rahmani, R., Cardenas, A.M.: Automatic Emotion Recognition through Facial Expression Analysis in Merged Images Based on an Artificial Neural Network. In: Proceedings of 12th Mexican International Conference on Artificial Intelligence (MICAI), Mexico City, Mexico, pp. 85–96 (2013)

13. Rázuri, J.G., Esteban, P.G., Insua, D.R.: An adversarial risk analysis model for an autonomous imperfect decision agent. In: Guy, T.V., Kárný, M., Wolpert, D.H. (eds.) Decision Making and Imperfection. SCI, vol. 474, pp. 165–190. Springer, Heidelberg (2013)

14. Hoeting, J., Madigan, D., Raftery, A., Volinsky, C.: Bayesian model averaging: A tutorial. Statistical Science **4**, 382–417 (1999)

15. Pearl, J.: Probabilistic Reasoning in Intelligent Systems: Networks of Plausible Inference. Morgan Kaufmann Publishers, San Mateo (1988)

16. French, S., Ríos, D.R.: Statistical Decision Theory. Oxford University Press, New York (2000)

17. Von Winterfeldt, D., Edwards, W.: Decision Analysis and Behavioral Research. Cambridge University Press, New York (1986)

18. Bielza, C., Müller, P., Ríos, D.R.: Monte Carlo Methods for Decision Analysis with Applications to Influence Diagrams. Management Science **45**(7), 995–1007 (1999)

19. Maslow, A.H.: A theory of human motivation. Psychological Review **50**(4), 370–396 (1943)

20. Leite, I., Castellano, G., Pereira, A., Martinho, C., Paiva, A.: Long-Term Interactions with Empathic Robots: Evaluating Perceived Support in Children. In: Ge, S.S., Khatib, O., Cabibihan, J.-J., Simmons, R., Williams, M.-A. (eds.) ICSR 2012. LNCS, vol. 7621, pp. 298–307. Springer, Heidelberg (2012)

21. Kuremoto, T., Tsurusaki, T., Kobayashi, K., Mabu, S., Obayashi, M.: A Model of Emotional Intelligent Agent for Cooperative Goal Exploration. In: Huang, D.-S., Bevilacqua, V., Figueroa, J.C., Premaratne, P. (eds.) ICIC 2013. LNCS, vol. 7995, pp. 21–30. Springer, Heidelberg (2013)

22. Minsky, M.: The Society of Mind. Simon and Schuster (1985)

23. Charland, L.C.: Emotion as a natural kind: Towards a computational foundation for emotion theory. Philosophical Psychology **8**(1), 59–85 (1995)

24. Ziemke, T., Lowe, R.: On the role of emotion in embodied cognitive architectures: From organisms to robots. Cognitive Computation **1**(1), 104–117 (2009)

25. El-Nasr, M.S., Yen, J., Ioerger, T.R.: FLAME Fuzzy logic adaptive model of emotions. Autonomous Agents and Multi-Agent Systems **3**(3), 219–257 (2000)

26. Velasquez, J.: From affect programs to higher cognitive emotions: an emotion-based control approach. In: Proceedings Emotion-Based Agent Architecture Workshop at the International Conf. Autonomous Agents, pp. 114–120 (1999)

27. Kirby, R., Forlizzi, J., Simmons, R.: Affective social robots. Robotics and Autonomous Systems **58**, 322–332 (2010)

28. Hanson, D., Baurmann, S., Riccio, T., Margolin, R., Dockins, T., Tavares, M., Carpenter, K.: Zeno: a Cognitive Character. In: AI Magazine, and special Proc. of AAAI National Conference, Chicago (2009)

29. Pioggia, G., Sica, M.L., Ferro, M., Igliozzi, R., Muratori, F., Ahluwalia, A., De Rossi, D.: Human-robot interaction in autism: FACE, an android-based social therapy. In: The 16th IEEE International Symposium on Robot and Human interactive Communication, pp. 605–612 (2007)

30. Damasio, A.: Descartes' error: Emotion, reason, and the human brain. Putmam, New York (1994)

31. Lerner, J.S., Keltner, D.: Fear, anger, and risk. Journal of Personality and Social Psychology 81(1), 146–159 (2001)

32. Rusting, C.L., DeHart, T.: Retrieving positive memories to regulate negative mood: Consequences for mood-congruent memory. Journal of Personality and Social Psychology 78, 737–752 (2000)

33. Loewenstein, G., Lerner, J.S.: The role of affect in decision making. In: Davidson, R., Scherer, K., Goldsmith, H. (eds.) Handbook of Affective Science, pp. 619–642. Oxford University Press, New York (2003)

34. Moshkina, L.: An integrative framework for affective agent behavior. In: IASTED Int. Conf. on Intelligent Systems and Control (2006)

35. Mellers, B.A., Schwartz, A., Ho, K., Ritov, I.: Decision affect theory: Emotional reactions to the outcomes of risky options. Psychological Science 8, 423–429 (1997)

36. Johnson, W., Rickel, J., Lester, J.: Animated pedagogical agents: Face-to-face interaction in interactive learning environments. International Journal of Artificial Intelligence in Education 11(1), 47–78 (2000)

37. Leite, I., Martinho, C., Pereira, A., Paiva, A.: iCat: an affective game buddy based on anticipatory mechanisms. In: Proc. 7th Intl. Joint Conf. on Autonomous Agents and Multiagent Systems, vol. 3, pp. 1229–1232 (2008)

38. Becker-Asano, C., Stahl, P., Ragni, M., Courgeon, M., Martin, J.-C., Nebel, B.: An affective virtual agent providing embodied feedback in the paired associate task: system design and evaluation. In: Aylett, R., Krenn, B., Pelachaud, C., Shimodaira, H. (eds.) IVA 2013. LNCS, vol. 8108, pp. 406–415. Springer, Heidelberg (2013)

39. Fredrickson, B.L., Levenson, R.W.: Positive emotions speed recovery from the cardiovascular sequelae of negative emotions. Cognition and Emotion 12, 191–220 (1998)

40. Levenson, R.W.: Emotion and the autonomic nervous system: A prospectus for research on autonomic specificity. In: Wagner, H.L. (ed.) Social Psychophysiology and Emotion: Theory and Clinical Applications, pp. 17–42. Wiley, London (1988)

41. Frijda, N.H.: The emotions. Cambridge University Press, Cambridge (1986)

42. Frijda, N.H., Kuipers, P., Schure, E.: Relations among emotion, appraisal, and emotional action readiness. Journal of Personality and Social Psychology 57, 212–228 (1989)

43. Lazarus, R.S.: Emotion and adaptation. Oxford University Press, New York (1991)

44. Ekman, P.: An argument for basic emotions. Cognition and Emotion 6, 169–200 (1992)

45. Plutchik, R.: The nature of emotions. American Scientist 89(4), 344–350 (2001)

46. Öhman, A., Mineka, S.: Fears, phobias, and preparedness: Toward an evolved module of fear and fear learning. Psychological Review 108, 483–522 (2001)

47. Panksepp, J.: Affective neuroscience: The foundations of human and animal emotions. Oxford University Press, New York (1998)

48. Fredrickson, B.L.: What Good Are Positive Emotions? Review of General Psychology 2(3), 300–319 (1998)

49. Kanade, T., Cohn J.F., Yingli, T.: Comprehensive database for facial expression analysis. In: Proceedings of Fourth IEEE Int. Conf. Automatic Face and Gesture Recognition, pp. 46–53 (2000)

Using Agents and Open Learner Model Ontology for Providing Constructive Adaptive Techniques in Virtual Learning Environments

Vitor Bremgartner[1(✉)], José M. Netto[1], and Crediné Menezes[2]

[1] Federal University of Amazonas, Manaus, Brazil
vitorbref@gmail.com
[2] Federal University of Rio Grande do Sul, Porto Alegre, Brazil

Abstract. Typically, the existing resources in Virtual Learning Environments (VLEs), used in distance education courses and blended, are presented in the same way for all students. This may not be useful for effective learning of each learner. Faced with this problem, this paper presents a strategy that allows content adaptation to students in VLEs based on a constructivist approach, using multi-agent system technology manipulating an open learner model ontology comprised of several learner characteristics, such as their competencies, skills, equipment which the learner uses, performance on activities, frequency and learning styles. The leaner model is dynamically changed during the course, through the interactions of the student with VLE. Moreover, this model is shown to the student, with the aim of student to know their current status in the course. Results obtained in a Numerical Analysis discipline show the feasibility of the proposal.

Keywords: Open Learner Model · Virtual Learning Environments · Multi-Agent System · Ontology · Adaptive Techniques

1 Introduction

Distance Education is a modality widely used in the teaching-learning processes. To support the Distance Education or blended there are educational environments called Virtual Learning Environments (VLEs) or Learning Management Systems (LMSs). These environments support the process of communication between students, teachers, tutors, and the community, allowing everyone to participate in an interactive mode and with availability of teaching materials.

In addition, there are VLEs that use smart characteristics, especially with regard to the possibility of the flexible education for students, called Intelligent Tutoring Systems (ITSs), where the learning environment is able to adapt and display contents in order to achieve a more effective learning, according to the needs of the student. Tools in the field of Artificial Intelligence such as ontologies and software agents can act integrated into the ITSs or VLEs being responsible for the layer of intelligence making use of the learner model [1].

© Springer International Publishing Switzerland 2014
A.L.C. Bazzan and K. Pichara (Eds.): IBERAMIA 2014, LNAI 8864, pp. 625–636, 2014.
DOI: 10.1007/978-3-319-12027-0_50

The learner model can be obtained through the learner profile. This model is a record of student actions as well as his useful information in the learning environment. As the learner profile is raw data of the students in the system [2], the learner model is made up of information considered most important in the learner profile for the adaptation and customization processes of a VLE in order to achieve a more effective learning by students. This data can be personal information, preferences, and academic information. Institutions and international organizations have been working on the standardization of learner model used in VLEs or ITSs, and the most currently known standard is the Instructional Management Systems Learning Information Package (IMS LIP) [3].

However, despite the increasing use of educational environments, they usually offer learning resources in the same way for all students, resulting that the learning cannot become effective for all because of several cognitive characteristics that each student has and due to different characteristics of equipment that are used by students. This therefore creates difficulties of knowledge acquisition for some students or even lack of interest by the students in the use of learning environment. Moreover, although there are several techniques for content adaptation for students in literature as context-awareness [4], group support [5], personalization with agents [6], and adaptable m-learning services [7], not all have been proven effective, and many not ceased to be mere technological innovations, without being supported by an educational theory. In this paper, we considered the term "content adaptation in VLEs" as the action of changing content (e. g., activities passed, learning objects delivered, and interface changing) in VLEs to adapt according to the students' characteristics.

As an example scenario, we have especially in the Numerical Analysis discipline, curricular component of Engineering and some Science courses, activities to solve numerical problems (linear systems, interpolation, and regression). These numerical problems can be solved with the aid of a computer, allowing the student to develop scripts in programming languages to perform their calculations that manually it is more complicated to do. However, many students of Numerical Analysis lack a basic prior knowledge of computer programming often lacking this skill for good student performance in the course. A student may have a good knowledge in mathematical modeling to solve an activity, but not able to transcribe this model in a programming language.

As a strategy to solve this problem, in this paper we propose a multi-characteristic learner model that can encompass four items to describe the student: (a) performance on activities and frequency in the educational environment; (b) learning styles; (c) equipment that the student uses, e.g. a PC, a mobile device, and (d) competencies and skills. We extended the LIP standard to integrate all these four characteristics. Therefore, the central idea of this work is focused on the development of a learner model from this extension of the LIP standard, consisting of an ontology that describes such model used by a multi-agent system. The multi-agent system tests the effectiveness of the learner model applied, with the aim of providing constructivist adaptations in VLEs. With agents and learner model ontology integrated, the VLE will have characteristics of ITS from the customization promoted by these technologies. The student model is also presented to the learner, being an Open Learner Model (OLM).

OLM refers to making a student's learner model explicit, externalizing the learner model contents to the learner, so as to provide an additional resource through self-awareness and possible self-regulation of the learning process that is believed to enhance learning and learner autonomy. The aims of OLM are to encourage reflection, independent learning and formative assessment/progress monitoring [8]. Through the OLM, learners may access information about their current state of knowledge, difficulties in the subject area and any possible misconceptions where this information is modeled. Primary aims of OLMs include prompting metacognitive activities such as reflection, planning and self-assessment; supporting navigation; and facilitating collaboration [9]. Therefore, in this work was chosen to use OLM.

Thus, besides providing OLM, other teaching resources such as: forming groups of students; provision of learning objects according to students' needs; recommendation of students to support others with questions; constructivist and collaborative activities such as thesis debate [10]; collaborative correction (peer review among colleagues, providing feedback); provision of open challenges with continuous dialogue with the student and other teaching resources will be performed with greater ease. It is believed that in this way the VLE will have a better context-awareness course and will be able to react according to the students' interactions.

Besides this Introduction, the paper is structured as follows: Section 2 discusses the use of constructivist practices and learner model in VLEs. Section 3 presents an overview of the proposed system and its architecture, describing the learner model. Section 4 reports tests showing OLM students and providing content adaptation in a discipline of Numerical Analysis in a VLE. Section 5 presents the conclusions and future work.

2   Using Constructivist Practices and Learner Modeling in VLEs

Using constructivist practices related with learner model in VLEs has been an alternative used to support decision making in the teaching and learning processes mediated by technology. As way to overcome the general feeling of isolation and consequent high dropout of students in VLEs, [11] presents the results of an experiment with the model called i-Collaboration that promotes collaboration between users in VLE. The i-Collaboration is based on the use of Virtual Learning Companions (VLC) agents as collaboration monitors based on constructivist theory. The VLC agents are integrated with collaborative tools of VLE and know each student profile and his behavior in the learning environment. The Intelligent Open Challenges System (IOCS) [12] is a proposal for a multi-agent system to adapt some patterns of Piaget's Clinical Method. It consists of a system and the strategist agent, performing mediation between the system and the user. The system has the proposal to work learning through the application of challenges consisting by logical-mathematical proofs of open conception, worrying to acknowledge and document the reasons for the user compared to the solution, as well giving visibility to ongoing cognitive processes.

The Oscar Conversational ITS (CITS) in [13] is a sophisticated ITS which uses a natural language interface to enable learners to construct their own knowledge through discussion. Oscar CITS aims to mimic a human tutor by dynamically detecting and adapting to an individual's learning styles whilst directing the conversational tutorial. Using mobile technology, the educational paradigm considered in COMTEXT project [4] is interactionist-constructivist. The tools within the learning environment COMTEXT aims to support the development of competencies, promoting interaction among a community of learners, focused on knowledge sharing and the development of skills and attitudes.

Using learner modeling, the work in [14] introduces an adaptive mechanism which enables LMSs to provide students with courses that fit their individual learning styles. The adaptive mechanism is based on an advanced student modeling approach which identifies learning styles by automatic, dynamic, and global student modeling. Based on the identified learning styles, the adaptive mechanism composes courses that match the students' learning styles, aiming at making learning easier for students. They use Felder-Silverman learning style model. Dealing with OLM, [15] uses the simple independent Open Learner Model, presenting students' interest in viewing their learner model and considers the potential for open learner models as an approach to encourage self-directed and long life learning amongst students in institutes of higher learning.

We can thus see that there are several studies in literature that deal with constructivists features and learner model applied to VLEs. However, we can note with these works described above, that although there are many publications in the literature about adaptation of VLEs using Constructivism and learner modeling, many of these studies use specific student characteristics separately. In other words, some studies deal only with learning styles, others with students' competencies; others just depending on the equipment. So, the learner model is not be able to inform the e-learning system the global profile of the student and his current situation more accurately on the learning environment. Consequently, the VLE can be more vulnerable to take wrong decisions in helping the student in his real needs.

This work differs because we consider several characteristics of the students at a same time, changing according to the students interaction with the VLE and then showing the learner model to the learner itself in courses or disciplines, in order to obtain a more accurate diagnosis of the students' situation in the educational environment and stimulating them to obtain more knowledge, besides providing content adaptation depending of their OLMs using a constructivist approach. The next section describes our proposal detailed.

3   Our Proposal

3.1   An Overview of the Project

An overall system architecture is shown in Fig. 1. The teacher prepares activities, registers students and accesses the VLE. The student, in turn, interacts with the system, either by registration of his personal data, posting something in the forum or resolution of proposed activities in the environment. For this work we used the Moodle VLE [16].

Furthermore, in VLE were created 3 questionnaires for students answer at the beginning of the course, with the aim of obtaining the initial learner model, because these are the first information that forms the knowledge base about students in the VLE DataBase. The questionnaires are: 1) Index of Learning Styles, seeking to know the Felder-Silvernam learning styles [17] of students; 2) Honey-Alonso Learning Styles Questionnaire, adapted from Honey-Mumford [18]; 3) Questionnaire about computer programming, where students will answer questions about their level of knowledge in programming concepts (conditional structures; repetition; data structures; level of expertise in using a programming language, chosen for this discipline Scilab [19]; and experience of using the computer in Numerical Analysis) related to Numerical Analysis. The links to these questionnaires in the VLE can be seen in Fig. 2, as well as the link to the student see his OLM.

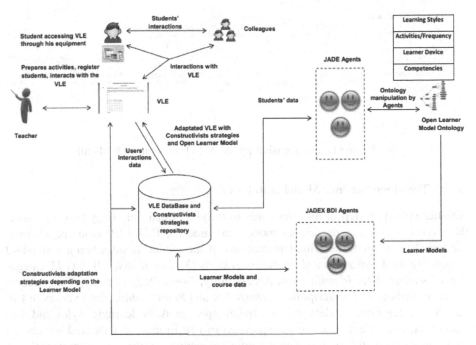

Fig. 1. System Architecture

The agents were developed in JADE [20] and JADEX [21] frameworks. The JADE agents manipulate students' data in VLE DataBase, allowing updates in their model. The learner model is described by its ontology, which contains the model data as learning styles, learner device (equipment), the student competencies, the activities that the student does and the frequency of the student in the environment. The ontology is also useful for the correct handling of message exchanges between agents. In turn, the JADEX agents, from the learner model data obtained, using the Beliefs-Desires-Intentions (BDI) model [22] will select constructivist strategies contained in the Repository Strategies (staying on the VLE DataBase) which will be used by VLE so that the environment can be adapted to these strategies.

Finally, the student accesses VLE with its adapted content, and the student can access his OLM. Students can also interact with each other, doing collaborative activities in VLE.

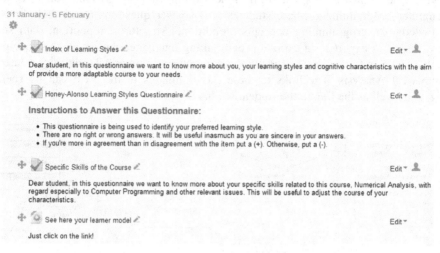

Fig. 2. Links to questionnaires presented to learners in VLE Moodle

3.2   The Open Learner Model Ontology

Another important step of this work was to build a domain ontology that represents the learner model. For the learner model was used the IMS LIP standard, which is supported by examples and implementations of the model, besides being a standard commonly used nowadays and allows extensions [3]. Originally, LIP has 11 categories of student data: *Identification*, *Accessibility*, *Goal*, *QCL*, *Activity*, *Competency*, *Interest*, *Affiliation*, *Transcription*, *Security key* and *Relationship*. However, even LIP has these categories, the data such as student specific skills, learning styles and data about their equipment used are not specified in LIP in more details, and for certain disciplines or specific courses, may not reflect directly what the core characteristics of student really are. Thus, although using LIP categories, this standard has been extended to the needs of this project, emphasizing the competencies of the student, equipment that he uses (desktop, smartphone, tablet), activities answered, frequency of the accesses in the VLE, and the learning styles of the student.

In the category *Activity* are given the activities proposed by the teacher. The learner model ontology in class *Competency* also describes the skill level of each student, which it is useful to identify the students that have a higher level of competency in a discipline or course. In our proposal, each student's competency is composed of a set of specific skills. For example, in the Numerical Analysis discipline, the competency "Finding roots of functions by the bisection method" consists on the following skills: "Handling the calculating machine", "Understanding of functions (continuity, the

Intermediate Value Theorem, plotting graphs, convergence and divergence)" and "Understanding the bisection method operations (choice of the initial interval, the formula and criteria for selecting the new range)" [23]. The agents may make frequent assessments of students' activities, being a formative assessment, obtaining their performance and upgrading the skills levels of the students.

Other categories used are *Identification* (for the student personal data), *Accessibility* (accessibility data of user, credentials in the e-learning system) and *Interest* (containing the students' interests). The other categories were not used because they don't make part in the scope of this work or are already replaced by categories that were used, avoiding any conflict of information with similar elements. However, the LIP standard was extended in three other categories (or classes): *CCPP_Device*, *Learning_Styles,* and *Frequency*.

The *CCPP_Device* category describes the devices used by students. As there is standards for learner model allowing content adaptation, there are standards for the characterization of mobile devices, with their features like screen size, CPU performance, memory, among others. One of the most used today and used in this work is the Composite Capabilities/Preference Profile (CC/PP) [24]. The characterization of mobile devices can be considered as the device profile and it is useful for content adaptation in different formats to be presented to students depending on the device.

Using *Frequency* category, it describes the frequency of students in VLE, which is verified in a continuous 20-day period whether the student has not accessed the VLE and also it is checked whether or not the student has finished its activities. Finally, *Learning_Styles* category contains information about the Felder-Silvernam and Honey-Mumford student learning styles.

The learner model ontology was built in the Protégé [25] editor and has three main classes: *Concept,* whose daughters are subclasses *AID* (describing the agents that constitute the multi-agent system) and *Learner_LIP* (containing the LIP categories used in this work plus the *CCPP_Device, Learning_Styles* and *Frequency*); *Predicate,* responsible for the facts about the environment where the agents act; and *AgentAction* (containing the actions that agents perform on the VLE). All three classes are useful allowing the ontology to be integrated into the multi-agent system. Fig. 3 shows a summarized graphical representation of the Open Learner Model Ontology, only the subclass *Learner_LIP,* describing the extended LIP standard, presenting the slots (properties) of the classes. For example, in the *Learning_Styles* class, a property is *ls_fs_active_reflective,* indicating if the learner tends to be more active or reflective in the Felder-Silvernam learning styles. The single *AID* presented in Fig. 3 is the *Update Profile Agent,* implemented in JADE and responsible for updating the learner model data by interactions with the environment. The relationships between classes describe the facets of ontology, represented by blue and black arrows (the latter indicating only the relationship "isa", subclass to superclass). As some examples of facets (in this case, rules) in blue arrows, the student *doesActivity* and *hasDoubts_Errors* (connecting *Identification* and *Activity* classes), *hasSkillsCompetencies* (connecting *Identification* and *Competency* classes).

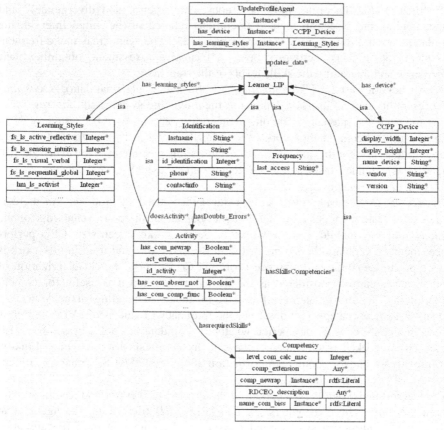

Fig. 3. Graphical representation of the Open Learner Model LIP ontology summarized

4   Experiments

4.1   Presenting the Open Learner Model to Students

The student can access his model via the link "See here your learner model" in VLE, as shown in Fig. 2. It is important that the OLM be easily understood by the student. Thus, Fig. 4 shows an example of OLM presented to students composed of three graphs, which is the result of students' responses to the questionnaires. In the first graph is presented the learning styles according to the Honey-Alonso questionnaire, in percentage of *Activist, Reflector, Theorist* and *Pragmatist* styles. In the second, the Felder-Silvernam styles (*Active/Reflective, Sensing/Intuitive, Visual/Verbal*, and *Sequential/Global*) are presented in odd values ranging from -11 to +11. For example, if a student has in the field *Visual/Verbal* value +7, it means that he is more *Visual*. If it was -7, he would be more *Verbal*. Finally, the third graph shows the skills of the student in a specific course, in our case study, the Numerical Analysis.

Moreover, in Fig. 4 is shown if the student uses or not mobile devices to access the VLE, and this information is dynamically changed (depending on whether a student is using or not mobile at a given time) and a link to situations in which the student disagrees with this learner model, who can send this information to his teacher. It is believed that this is useful to detect if there are students who agree or disagree with the model, because it is possible that a student be judged to be very able in the course himself, but not by the system.

4.2   Adaptation Techniques Tested

In VLE two constructivists techniques were tested, used in a real class comprised of 33 students of the Numerical Analysis discipline at Federal University of Amazonas, delivered in a blended learning using the Moodle VLE. These two techniques are monitoring and recommendation of colleagues to help students who had questions in activities.

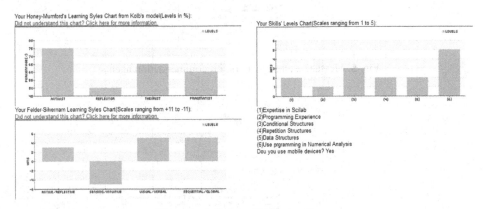

Fig. 4. Presenting OLM to students

The process occurs as follows: students accessing the VLE execute the activities proposed by the teacher and doubts/errors may arise, detected by monitoring. Simultaneously, as the students will interact with VLE, their learner models are updated in the VLE database through the multi-agent system, which is also responsible, along with the ontology, by searching the students with best specific competency levels able to help the one student who is in doubt with activities. Thus, students with appropriate profiles found by the multi-agent system will be recommended in the VLE to that student who has doubts/errors. Fig. 5 shows the messages exchanging between two agents implemented on framework JADE. One of them is *Doubt & Error Profile Agent*, responsible for finding students with problems in activities, doing requests to *Recommended Profile Agent*, in order to the latter select students who will assist his colleagues with questions. A detailed list of the agents used in this work can be found in [26].

Fig. 6 shows a notification through the *Help Tutor Agent* to the student who has failed to finish the activity at the time specified by teacher. In this notification message there is a link to the student clicks to get a screen of recommended colleagues by system that can help the one with questions or other problems. This screen is shown in Fig. 7, showing the activity name, students recommended for that activity, and the interests of recommended students. These information may be useful to encourage interaction among students. At the end of these two tests we could see an improvement by 180% of correct answers of the students. From 33 students, only four initially answered correctly all proposed activities. After the application of recommendation resource, 12 students answered correctly the same activities.

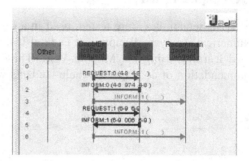

Fig. 5. Message exchange among recommendation agents

Fig. 6. Message sent by Help Tutor Agent

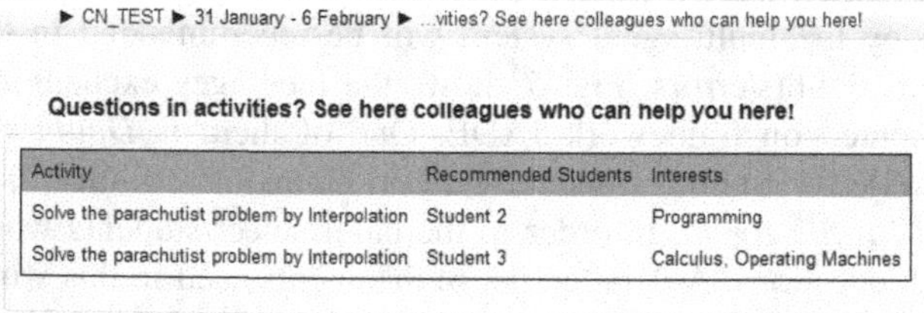

▶ CN_TEST ▶ 31 January - 6 February ▶ ...vities? See here colleagues who can help you here!

Questions in activities? See here colleagues who can help you here!

Activity	Recommended Students	Interests
Solve the parachutist problem by Interpolation	Student 2	Programming
Solve the parachutist problem by Interpolation	Student 3	Calculus, Operating Machines

Fig. 7. Recommended Students screen

We could note with these tests that notification to students with problems in activities and the suggestion of colleagues to help students with questions are constructivist techniques useful for student learning, encouraging the practice of collaborative activities in VLEs.

5   Conclusions and Future Work

This paper showed a proposal containing content adaptation strategies in VLEs based on the constructivist approach. We developed a multi-agent system and Open Learner Model ontology, characterizing a learner in the IMS LIP standard able to select strategies that allow content adaptation in the VLE Moodle. This proposal allows greater customization of content presented by means of the characteristics of the students. The adaptation process described in the system architecture increases the interaction among students of the same course or discipline, thus increasing the knowledge level of learners as a whole and greater correctness in the tasks performed.

The tests showed that the recommendation of students to assist others with questions through collaborative learning is a useful and effective constructivist solution to the problem of aid to students with questions in VLEs, improving student learning. This strategy can be a way to improve the teaching of students using VLEs. The approach of the multi-agent system together with the OLM can be applied to other VLEs, since the agents and the e-learning environment share the same database.

Expanding this work in future, the idea is to test the system for adaptation in mobile devices, because the ontology already describes the features of the mobile device in the CC/PP standard. Also, whereas the ontology and multi-agent system work to provide content adaptation, the next step is also recommend several types of collaborative activities based on the learner model, as simulated jury, virtual diary, and other learning projects.

References

1. Viccari, R.M., Giraffa, L.M.M.: Foundations of Intelligent Tutoring Systems (In original Portuguese name: Fundamentos dos Sistemas Tutores Inteligentes). In: Barone, D. (Org). Artificial Societies: A New Frontier of Machine Intelligence (In original Portuguese name: Sociedades Artificiais: A Nova Fronteira da Inteligência das Máquinas). Bookman, Porto Alegre (2003)
2. Fröschl, C.: User Modeling and User Profiling in Adaptive E-learning Systems. Master's Thesis. Institute for Information Systems and Computer Media, Graz University of Technology, Graz, Austria (2005)
3. LIP. Learner Information Package Specification 1.0.1, www.imsglobal.org/profiles/lipinfo01.html#5.1/
4. Saccol, A.Z., Kich, M., Schlemmer, E., Reinhard, N., Barbosa, J.L.V., Hahn, R.: A Framework for the Design of Ubiquitous Learning Applications. In: 42nd Hawaii International Conference on System Sciences Proceedings (2009)
5. Hummel, K.A., Kopecny, R., Kotsis, G.: Peer Profile Driven Group Support for Mobile Learning Teams. In: Proceedings of Computers and Advanced Technology in Education, Rhodes, Greece (2003)

6. Doherty, B.C., et al.: Entre-pass: Personalising u-Learning with Intelligent Agents. In: Proceedings of Fourth IEEE International Workshop on Wireless, Mobile and Ubiquitous Technology in Education (WMUTE 2006), Athens, Greece (2006)

7. Meere, D., Ganchev, I., Stojanov, S., O'Dróma, M.: Adaptation for Assimilation: The Role of Adaptable M-Learning Services in the Modern Educational Paradigm. International Journal Information Technologies and Knowledge **3**, 101–110 (2009)

8. Bull, S., Quigley, S., Mabbott, A.: Computer-based Formative Assessment to Promote Reflection and Learner Autonomy. Engineering Education **1**(1), 8–18 (2006)

9. Bull, S., Vatrapu, R.: Supporting Collaborative Interaction with Open Learner Models: Existing Approaches and Open Questions. In: Proceedings of the Computer Supported Collaborative Learning (CSCL) (2011)

10. Santos, L.N., Castro, A.N., Menezes, C.S.: Flexible Virtual Environments for Teaching and Learning. In: 42nd ASEE/IEEE Frontiers in Education Conference Proceedings (FIE), Seattle, WA, USA, pp. 1388–1393 (2012)

11. Oliveira, E.A., Tedesco, P.: i-Collaboration in Practice: Results from our Investigation within the Cleverpal Environment. In: Proceedings of IEEE International Conference on Intelligent Computing and Intelligent Systems (ICIS), pp. 347–351 (2009)

12. Bastos Filho, O.C., Axt, M., Labidi, S., Machado, C.T.: Intelligent Open Challenges System: A possibility of adaptation of Piaget Clinical Method in Multi-agents Systems. In: Proceedings of IADIS Virtual Multi Conference on Computer Science and Information Systems, Lisboa, Portugal (2006)

13. Latham, A., Crockett, K., McLean, D.: An adaptation algorithm for an intelligent natural language tutoring system. Computers & Education **71**, 97–110 (2013)

14. Graf, S., Kinshuk: Adavanced Adaptivity in Learning Management Systems by Considering Learning Sytles. In: Proceedings of IEEE/WIC/ACM International Conference on Web Inteligence and Intelligent Agent Technology (2009)

15. Ahmad, N.: Self-Directed Learning: Student's Interest in Viewing the Learner Model. In: Proceeding of 3rd International Conference on Research and Innovation in Information Systems (ICRIIS), Malaysia, pp. 493–498 (2013)

16. Moodle: A Free, Open Source Course Management System for Online Learning, www.moodle.org/

17. Soloman, B.A., Felder, R.M.: Index of Learning Styles Questionnaire, www.engr.ncsu.edu/learningstyles/ilsweb.html

18. Honey and Mumford's Learning Styles Questionnaire, www.nwlink.com/~donclark/hrd/styles/honey_mumford.html

19. Scilab. Open source software for numerical computation, www.scilab.org/

20. JADE: Java Agent DEvelopment Framework, www.jade.tilab.com/

21. JADEX Active Components, www.activecomponents.org/bin/view/About/Features

22. Georgeff, M., Pell, B., Pollack, M.E., Tambe, M., Wooldridge, M.J.: The Belief-Desire-Intention Model of Agency. In: Papadimitriou, C., Singh, M.P., Müller, J.P. (eds.) ATAL 1998. LNCS (LNAI), vol. 1555, pp. 1–10. Springer, Heidelberg (1999)

23. Burden, R.L., Faires, J.D.: Numerical Analysis. Brooks/Cole, Cengage Learning, 9th edn., Boston, USA (2010)

24. CC/PP. Composite Capabilities/Preference Profiles, www.w3.org/Mobile/CCPP/

25. Protégé. The Ontology Editor, www.protege.stanford.edu/

26. Bremgartner, V., Netto, J.M.: Improving Collaborative Learning by Personalization in Virtual Learning Environments Using Agents and Competency-Based Ontology. In: Proceedings of IEEE Frontiers in Education Conference (FIE 2012), Seattle, USA (2012)

Recognizing the Brazilian Signs Language Alphabet with Neural Networks over Visual 3D Data Sensor

Gabriel de Souza Pereira Moreira[✉], Gustavo Ravanhani Matuck,
Osamu Saotome, and Adilson Marques da Cunha

ITA – Brazilian Aeronautics Institute of Technology, São José dos Campos, SP, Brazil
gspmoreira@gmail.com, {gmatuck,osaotome,cunha}@ita.br

Abstract. This paper describes an investigation of the Brazilian Signs Language (*LInguagem BRAsileira de Sinais* - LIBRAS) alphabet recognition using neural networks. The LIBRAS alphabet is represented by static postures and dynamic gestures. In this investigation, gestures were recorded with a 3D camera sensor and its associated library, providing coordinates from hands' fingertips. Deaf people, LIBRAS teachers and students were involved in the recording process. The pre-processing data involved frames sampling, normalization and 3D geometric transformations. Neural network models with different settings were trained, compared, and assessed to verify classification accuracy.

Keywords: Sign Language Recognition · Gesture Recognition · LIBRAS · Neural Networks · 3D Cameras

1 Introduction

The Brazilian 2010 Census depicted 1,799,885 citizens in the country having great difficulty to hear [1]. Signs languages are the natural languages of deaf communities. The Brazilian Signs Language (*Linguagem Brasileira de Sinais* - LIBRAS) is the sign language used by the majority of the deaf people in the Brazilian urban regions. It is similar to other signs languages from Europe and America. It was standardized and recognized as the second official language by the Brazilian courts, on laws 10.436 (2002)[1] [2] and 5.626 (2005)[2] [3].

For many deaf-and-dumb people in Brazil, LIBRAS is the only way they can communicate. But, unfortunately, very few hearing people are knowledgeable and skilled on LIBRAS. That leads difficulties for deaf people to be assisted on hospitals, schools and universities, government services, and many other sites.

This paper describes an investigation of the recognition of LIBRAS alphabet signs, what would allow the spelling of any word in Portuguese. For the recognition, it was

---

[1] The Brazilian Law 10,436, from April 24, 2002, addresses LIBRAS issues.
[2] The Brazilian Decree 5,626, from December 22, 2005, regulates the Brazilian Law 10,436, from April 24, 2002, and the Article 18 from the 10,098 Law, from December 19, 2000, also addresses some LIBRAS issues.

© Springer International Publishing Switzerland 2014
A.L.C. Bazzan and K. Pichara (Eds.): IBERAMIA 2014, LNAI 8864, pp. 637–648, 2014.
DOI: 10.1007/978-3-319-12027-0_51

used a 3D sensor to capture hand and fingers coordinates, some pre-processing strategies, and neural networks to classify gestures.

2   Literature Research

Many attempts have been made to recognize signs languages gestures, generally represented by hands postures and gestures, and translate them to spoken languages letters, words, and expressions. The two major classes of hand tracking systems are: (1) data-glove-based, which requires electromechanical gloves with sensors, and (2) vision-based, which works with continuous image frames [25], usually regular RGB cameras or 3D sensors (like Microsoft Kinect [5]).

For recognition models, some studies have been using machine-learning techniques, mostly Neural Networks and Hidden Markov Models.

Caputo et al. [4] present a 3D hand and gesture recognition system using Microsoft Kinect sensor, for dynamic gestures, and HD color sensor, for static gestures recognition.

In Kulshreshth et al. [5], a real-time finger tracking technique was developed, using Kinect sensor signals, based on feature vectors calculation, using Fourier descriptors of equidistant points. The result was compared using the K-curvature technique algorithm.

A French Sign Language recognition system using Hidden Markov Models (HMM) was proposed by Braffort [7]. Gao et al. proposed a Chinese Sign Language recognition system, based on dynamic programming [8]. Vogler and Metaxas described an American Sign Language (ASL) recognition system, applying HMM [9]. German Sign Language recognition system applying HMM was proposed by Bauer and Kriss [10]. Holden et al. proposed an Australian Sign Language recognition system, based on HMM [11]. A British Sign Language recognition system based on Markov chains was developed by Bowdwn et al. Yang et al. [12] have proposed an ASL recognition system based on a time-delay neural network.

Researches addressing the Brazilian Signs Language have been conducted in the last years. Anjo et al. [26] present a real-time system to recognize a set of Libras alphabet (only static gestures), using MS Kinect and neural networks. They extended their work in [6], by usage of HMM to tackle with temporality of gestures.

Souza et al. [27] use HMM to recognize 47 Libras gestures types, captured with regular RGB cameras.

In this work, we report the usage of Creative Senz3D GestureCam™ [13], a set of pre-processing approaches, and neural network models to recognize all letters of Brazilian Signs Language (LIBRAS) alphabet, represented by static and dynamic gestures.

3   The Investigation

This section introduces LIBRAS alphabet and describes the conducted investigation process.

3.1   Brazilian Signs Language Alphabet

The LIBRAS alphabet signs are composed by static postures, for some letters, and dynamic gestures with movement, for others. Figure 1 shows the 26 LIBRAS alphabet (A-Z) letters, 20 represented by static hand postures, and 6 by dynamic gestures (H, J, K, X, Y, Z), depicted with a red arrow indicating the expected movement.

All alphabet signs are made with just one hand. Therefore, this investigation considers only one-hand's data for recording and recognition.

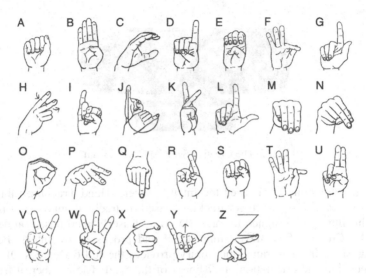

Fig. 1. The LIBRAS alphabet

3.2   Investigation Process

The objective of this investigation was to train a neural model on recorded gestures of LIBRAS alphabet and to recognize the same gestures from other samples. That would allow deaf people to spell letters using LIBRAS gestures, supporting the communication with hearing people.

The investigation stages were Data Acquisition, Pre-processing, Models Training, and Results Analysis, as shown in Figure 2, and described in the following sections.

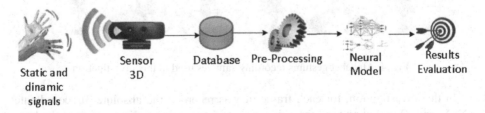

Fig. 2. The Investigation Process

3.3   Data Acquisition

In this stage, the gestures were recorded by using the low-cost 3D sensor Creative Senz3D GestureCam™ [13], presented in Figure 3. Intel made its beta-release available on the third quarter of 2013. This camera targets hand and finger tracking near of the computer, in the range from 15cm to 1m. As an infrared camera, it captures depth data with QVGA quality (320x240) on up to 30 frames per second. These features allowed this sensor to be chosen for this initial investigation.

Fig. 3. The Creative Senz3D Gesture Cam

In this investigation, it was used the Intel® Skeletal Hand Tracking Library (Experimental Release) [14] for finger tracking, based on tracking approaches presented in [24]. This library is designed to track 3D pose of user's hand based on depth data provided by Creative Senz3D GestureCam™ and processed by Intel® Perceptual Computing SDK. In each frame, the library provides the full 6 Degrees Of Freedom (6-DOF) position and orientation of 17 bones of the hand. The number of frames per second (fps) rate varied from 20-30 during recording.

As shown in Figure 4, 6 people volunteered to be recorded when making LIBRAS alphabet signs, divided in three groups: deaf people (2), LIBRAS teachers (2), and students (2). For all of them, it was recorded two samples of all alphabets, except for person 2, which had only one recorded sample. That resulted in 11 complete alphabet samples (268 letter gestures).

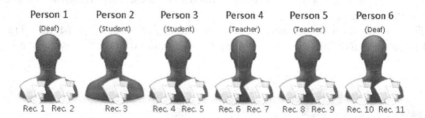

Fig. 4. Alphabet gestures recording samples used in this investigation

In this investigation, for each frame, it was recorded the absolute 3D coordinates (X, Y, and Z), based on the sensor distance, of 5 fingertips and the center of the hand. That resulted in 18 attributes with continuous positions of hands and fingers.

3.4   Pre-processing

In order to prepare data for models learning, a pre-processing stage was conducted. The performed steps are described in the following sections.

The Data Sets of Training, Validation, and Test. The alphabet gesture samples were divided into three data sets named training, validation, and test, of 7, 2, and 2, as shown in Table 1. This division was made in such a way that in training and test sets there were samples from specialists in LIBRAS (deaf people and teachers) and all sets had samples for every alphabet character.

Table 1. The division of data sets in training, validation, and test

Recording	Person	Profile	Sets		
			Training	Validation	Test
1	1	Deaf	X		
2	1	Deaf			X
3	2	Student		X	
4	3	Student	X		
5	3	Student		X	
6	4	Teacher	X		
7	4	Teacher	X		
8	5	Teacher	X		
9	5	Teacher			X
10	6	Deaf	X		
11	6	Deaf	X		
TOTAL			7	2	2

Normalization to Hand Relative Coordinates. The fingertips coordinates provided by the camera were relative to sensor's distance. It was necessary to convert them to coordinates relative to hand's center, because each hand position can vary in relation to the sensor for the same gesture. After this normalization, hand's center positions is discarded and models only considers relative fingertips coordinates.

Frames Sampling. For each gesture, it was recorded a different number of frames, because gesture time length varies, depending on alphabet letter and person style. The used sensors frames per second (fps) rate also varied, ranging from 20 to 30 fps.

So, as the input for neural network model is fixed, it was necessary to normalize the input size, sampling a fixed number of frames for each gesture. This process selected 18 equidistant frames for each gesture and fingertips 3D coordinates, which represented that gesture as input for neural models.

In Figure 5, it is presented the relative finger coordinates by recording frames for letters B and J, for example. It can be seen that, for a static posture (letter B), coordinates present a low variation during time while dynamic gestures present a high variation, as expected. Black dots over the lines point to the frames selected for sampling (as input for neural network).

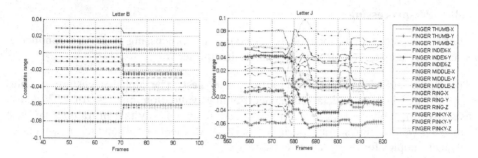

Fig. 5. Finger Relative Coordinates by Frame for letters B and J gestures

Training Samples Transformations. In this investigation, there were only 11 samples for each alphabet letter. Therefore, a strategy was created and implemented to generate new samples based on training samples, by rotation and scaling transformations.

Those transformations did not lead to any information loss or precision, but emulated new samples like different hand positions attitudes in relation to the sensor, in case of rotation transformations, or different hand sizes, in the case of scale transformations.

Rotations were simultaneously applied for X, Y and Z angles, for combinations of -20, -10, 0, 10, and 20 angles. These transformations have increased training samples by 5^5 (3125).

The scale transformation has increased by factors of 0.8, 0.9, 1.0, 1.1, and 1.2, multiplying training samples also by a factor of 5.

3.5   Neural Network Model

The neural network used in this investigation was the traditional Multi-Layer Perceptron (MLP). In Figure 6, it is presented the general MLP Neural Network architecture and the involved equations, comprised of one input layer, one or more hidden layers, and the output layer. The stimulus between the neurons and the input data is measured by equation (a). By the neuron output signal (Y) showed in equation (b), the sigmoidal function was applied on the hidden and output neurons. The network error and the weights adaptation were measured by equations (c) and (d), respectively.

The training data are presented to the input layer, propagating the information through one or more hidden layers. Mathematically, only one hidden layer of neurons is enough to perform nonlinear mapping [15]. Finally, the information is transmitted throughout the output layer, which produces the output response for the stimulus received from data in the input layer.

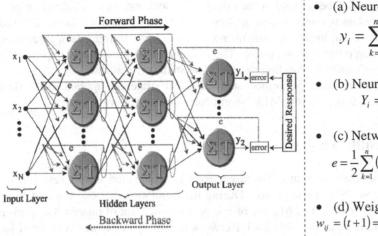

- (a) Neuron output:

$$y_i = \sum_{k=1}^{n} x_i w_j \geq \theta$$

- (b) Neuron output:

$$Y_i = F(y_i)$$

- (c) Network error:

$$e = \frac{1}{2} \sum_{k=1}^{n} (y_i(t) - d_i(t))^2$$

- (d) Weights adaptation:

$$w_{ij} = (t+1) = w_{ij}(t) + \eta \cdot e \cdot x(t)$$

Fig. 6. The general MLP Neural Network architecture [16]

For MLP network simulations, the well-known back-propagation learning algorithm [16] was used and the Sum Squared Error (SSE) parameter applied to measure the network performance, during the learning process [17][18]. The SSE parameter minimized the errors among the network output and desired values (supervised learning) from all patterns (gestures signals). More information about MLP Neural Network can be found in [20][21] and [22].

On this investigation, the MLP Network was composed by one input layer (pre-processed gestures signals), only one hidden layer (tested with 50 to 400 neurons, stepped by 50) and one output layer (with 26 output, each one representing an alphabet letter).

All data obtained from gestures signals were divided into training, validation, and test sets, as shown in Figure 7. The neural network learning process used the training data set for extracting important characteristics of each pattern and its specific data behaviors. Finally, the test data set was presented to the network, verifying the classification capability to detect new alphabet gestures samples, unseen by the neural model during the learning process.

Fig. 7. The data division in the three sets

In order to provide a better way to train the neural network, a cross-validation process and a *momentum* parameter were applied. The cross-validation process allowed the MLP network to minimize the over-fitting problem (over training set), finding an adequate time to stop the learning phase. The *momentum* parameter can improve the learning phase performance, avoiding local *minima* in the error surface.

Several simulations were performed, with different strategies applied to the data processing, as well as to different MLP Neural Networks configurations.

4   The Results Analysis

The main results obtained from different experiments conducted in this research investigation are described in this section. During the simulation process, the best MLP Network configuration reached 61.54% of correct classification of unseen data during the network training (test set). This MLP Network training process was conducted for 1,000 epochs, measuring the performance on SSE parameter. The learning rate parameter used by the model had started with the value of 0.2, adopted during the training process. It was observed that, after 1,000 epochs of training, simulations conducted by the MLP network have shown that the performance did not have any significant changes.

In Figure 8, it is presented the learning process from the best-found MLP network, with SEE evaluations applied into training and validation sets. The training phase has progressed until 375 epochs, when the cross-validation process stopped the network learning. After that training epoch, the use of new data patterns start decreasing the MLP network classification performance for unseen patterns (validation set).

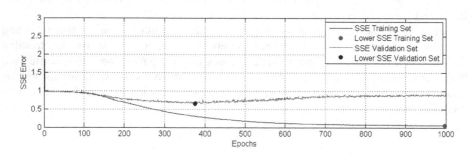

Fig. 8. MLP Neural Network training performance

Other simulations showed that, in this scenario, increasing the number of neurons in the hidden layer did not improve the MLP Network performance, thus, the increased computer power of the neural network could not help the network to correctly classify the test data set. This means that, in the training process, the MLP stopped learning important characteristics of each pattern and started to suffer from the influence of noise, decreasing the power of the MLP to detect new gestures signals patterns.

Figure 9 depicts the learning rate variation over training epochs, based on classification performance for validation set.

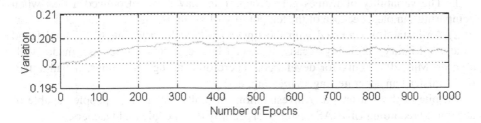

Fig. 9. The learning rate adaptation during the MLP Network training process

The best-found MLP network architecture was composed of 200 neurons on the hidden layer, and has correctly classified 61.53% patterns of the test set, that is, with 32/52 unseen patterns, as shown in Figure 10.

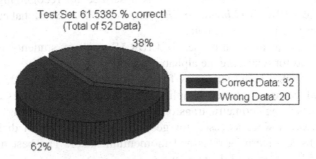

Fig. 10. The MLP test set performance classification

By analyzing the confusion model to diagnose gestures signals, in Table 2, it can be observed that the MLP Neural Network had difficulties to recognize some letters, like "f", "k", "t", "x" and "z". On the other hand, the neural model correctly classified 10 letters with 100% of success ("a", "c", "d", "j", "l", "m", "o", "u", "v" and "w").

Table 2. The Alphabet Test Set classification analysis

a	b	c	d	e	f	g	h	i	j	k	l	m	n	o	p	q	r	s	t	u	v	w	x	y	z
✓	✓	✓	✓	✓	✗	✓	✓	✓	✓	✗	✓	✓	✓	✓	✓	✓	✗	✓	✓	✗	✓	✓	✓	✓	✗
✓	✗	✓	✓	✗	✗	✗	✗	✓	✓	✗	✓	✓	✓	✗	✓	✗	✓	✗	✗	✓	✓	✓	✗	✗	✗

5   Limitations

This research investigation had some data acquisition quality limitations. The Creative Senz3D camera was chosen because its layout was considered: adequate for recording in front of computers; and suitable for capturing distance range, finger tracking library, and also its affordable price (COTS product).

Therefore, during this investigation, the camera presented the following limitations:

1) The variability of frames per seconds rate may have introduced a bias when comparing samples, because of the temporality of gestures; and

2) An instability occurred with the finger tracking library (Intel® Skeletal Hand Tracking Library), probably because it was an Intel experimental release, made available on May 2013, only for developers. Therefore, during recordings, it had sometimes mislead an accurate fingers tracking; and

Despite of the sensor, other investigation difficulty was to find people capable of accurately recording LIBRAS gestures, especially deaf people and teachers.

Those three factors may have limited in some way the proposed neural network models accuracy.

6   Conclusion and Future Works

In this investigation, an initial research was described for recognizing the Brazilian signs language LIBRAS (*LInguagem BRAsileira de Sinais*) alphabet using Neural Networks over visual 3D sensor data.

During the data acquisition phase, six LIBRAS teachers, students and deaf people have volunteered for recording the alphabet gestures.

It were developed some strategies for pre-processing gestures data to deal with temporality of gestures (frames sampling), normalizing coordinates and increasing training samples using geometric transformations (rotation and scaling)

Neural networks were assessed for gestures recognition, with different settings, training epochs and learning rates and momentum factor. The best model correctly classified 61.53% patterns of the test set.

Analyzing the results from this investigation, it can be observed that the MLP network was not as effective as expected when operating over noisy gestures data. Improvements in recognition models can be evaluated using more representative samples of gestures data.

As a natural continuation of this research, a statistical analysis should be conducted, using Student-t Distribution, a common procedure to validate neural networks. In that approach, the best MLP Neural Network architecture found would be trained many times, measuring the confidential interval (CI), as shown in [28]. Different confidence intervals can be applied, aiming to ensure that the whole network is within that range.

The authors of this research group have the intent to extend this investigation, still on its beginning phase. As the main limitations in this initial study were related to data acquisition, the next steps on this research are collecting more samples, assessing other 3D sensors, like Leap Motion and Kinect v2, as well as different pre-processing strategies, involving time series and geometric normalizations, and exploring other learning techniques, like Support Vector Machines and Hidden Markov Models. A near future points out the development of a real time prototype for LIBRAS alphabet recognition.

Acknowledgements. The authors would like to thank the Brazilian Aeronautics Institute of Technology (*Instituto Tecnológico de Aeronáutica – ITA*) for its academic support and to the Inilibras School [23] for providing domain knowledge and collaborating with sets of gestures recordings.

References

1. Brazilian Census 2010 – Preliminary Data, http://www.ibge.gov.br/home/estatistica/populacao/censo2010/resultados_preliminares_amostra/default_resultados_prelimi-nares_amostra.shtm
2. Law n° 10436 (March 24, 2002), http://www.planalto.gov.br/ccivil_03/Leis/2002/L10436.htm
3. Decree n° 5626 (December 22, 2005), http://www.planalto.gov.br/ccivil_03/_Ato2004-2006/2005/Decreto/D5626.htm
4. Caputo, M., Denker, K., Dums, B., Umlauf, G.: 3D Hand Gesture Recognition Based on Sensor Fusion of Commodity Hardware. Mensch & Computer (2012)
5. Kulshreshth, A., Zorn, C., LaViola Jr., J.J.: Real-time Markerless Kinect based Finger Tracking and Hand Gesture Recognition for HCI. In: IEEE Symposium on 3D User Interfaces, Orlando, FL, USA, March 16-17 (2013)
6. Anjo, M., Pizzolato, E., Feuerstack, S.: An evaluation of real-time requirements for automatic sign language recognition using ANNs and HMMs – The LIBRAS use case. SBC Journal on 3D Interactive Systems 4(1) (2013)
7. Braffort, A.: ARGo: An Architecture for Sign Language Recognition and Interpretation. In: Proc. Int'l Gesture Workshop Progress in Gestural Interaction, pp. 17–30 (April 1996)
8. Gao, W., Fang, G., Zhao, D., Chen, Y.: Transition Movement Models for Large vocabulary Continuous Sign Language Recognition. In: Sixth IEEE Int'l Conf. Automatic Face and Gesture Recognition, pp. 553–558 (May 2004)
9. Vogler, C., Metaxas, D.: A Framework for Recognizing the Simultaneous Aspects of American Sign Language. Computer Vision and Image Understanding 81(3), 358–384 (2001)
10. Bauer, B., Kraiss, K.F.: Video-Based Sign Recognition Using Self-Organizing Subunits, In: 16th Int'l Conf. Pattern Recognition, pp. 434–437 (August 2002)
11. Holden, E.-J., Lee, G., Owens, R.: Australian Sign Language Recognition. Machine Vision and Applications 16(5), 312–320 (2005)
12. Yang, M., Ahuja, N., Tabb, M.: Extraction of 2D Motion Trajectories and Its Application to Hand Gesture Recognition. IEEE Trans. Pattern Analysis and Machine Intelligence 24(8), 1061–1074 (2002)
13. Creative Senz3D Gesture Camera (2013), - http://software.intel.com/sites/default/files/article/325946/creativelabs-camera-productbrief-final.pdf
14. Intel® Skeletal Hand Tracking Library SDK (Experimental Release) (2013), http://software.intel.com/en-us/articles/the-intel-skeletal-hand-tracking-library-experimental-release
15. Russell, S., Norvig, P.: Artificial Intelligence - A Modern Approach. Prentice Hall (2003)
16. Montini, D.Á., Matuck, G.R., Dias, L.A.V., Cunha, A.M., Ribeiro, A.L.P.: A Sampling Diagnostics Model for Neural System Training Optimization. In: 10th International Conference on Information Technology: New Generations, ITNG 2013, Las Vegas, Nevada, USA, April 27–29 (2013)

17. Haykin, S.: Neural Networks: A Comprehensive Foundation. Macmillan College Publish Company, New York (1995)
18. Addison, J.F.D., Wermter, S., Macintyre, J.: Effectiveness of Feature Extraction in Neural Network Architectures for Novelty Detection. In: School of Computing, Engineering and Technology. University of Sunderland (1999)
19. Matuck, G.R., Barbosa, J.R., Bringhenti, C., Lima, I.: Multiple Faults Detection of Gas Turbine By MLP Neural Network. In: ASME Turbo Expo 2009, Power for Land, Sea, and Air, World Marriott Resort, Orlando, LF USA, GT2009-59964, June 08-12 (2009)
20. Yu, C.C., Liu, B.: A Back propagation Algorithm with Adaptive Learning Rate and Momentum Coefficient. IEEE (2002)
21. Freeman, J.A.; Skapura, D.M.: Neural Networks - Algorithms, Applications and Programming Techniques. Addison-Wesley Publishing Company (1991)
22. Matuck, G.R., Bringhenti. C., Barbosa, J.R., Lima, I.: 2007: Gas Turbine Fault Detection and Isolation Using MLP Artificial Neural Network. In: ASME Turbo Expo 2007, Power for Land, Sea, and Air, Palais des Congrès, Montreal, Canada, GT2007-27987, May 14-17 (2007); Bringhenti, C.: Variable Geometry Gas Turbine Performance Analysis. Ph.D. Thesis, ITA, Brazil (2003)
23. Inilibras – Libras School, http://www.inilibras.com.br
24. Melax, S., Keselman, L., Orsten, S.: Dynamics based 3D skeleton tracking. In: Proc. Graphics Interface Conference, Saskatchewan, Canada (May 2013)
25. Pistori, H., Neto, J.J.: An Experiment on Handshape Sign Recognition Using Adaptive Technology: Preliminary Results. In: Bazzan, A.L., Labidi, S. (eds.) SBIA 2004. LNCS (LNAI), vol. 3171, pp. 464–473. Springer, Heidelberg (2004)
26. Anjo, M., Pizzolato, E., Feuerstack, S.: A Real-Time System to Recognize Static Gestures of Brazilian Sign Language (Libras) alphabet using Kinect. In: Proc. of Simpósio Brasileiro sobre Fatores Humanos em Sistemas Computacionais, Cuiabá, Brazil (2012)
27. Souza, K., Dias, J., Pistori, H.: Reconhecimento Automático de Gestos da Língua Brasileira de Sinais utilizando Visão Computacional. In: III WVC - Workshop de Visão Computacional, São José do Rio Preto, Brazil (October 2007)
28. Matuck, G.R., Barbosa, J.R., Bringhenti. C., Lima, I.: 2010: Hybrid Neural System for Gas Turbine Diagnostics: An Optimization Strategy. In: ASME Turbo Expo 2010, Power for Land, Sea, and Air, Glasgow, UK, GT2010-22132, June 14-18 (2010)

Distributed Stock Exchange Scenario Using Artificial Emotional Knowledge

Daniel Cabrera-Paniagua[1(✉)], Tiago Thompsen Primo[2], and Claudio Cubillos[3]

[1] Escuela de Ingeniería Comercial, Universidad de Valparaíso,
Pasaje La Paz 1301, Viña del Mar, Chile
daniel.cabrera@uv.cl
[2] Samsung Research Institute Brasil,
Av. Cambacica 1200, Prédio 01, Campinas, SP, Brasil
tiago.t@samsung.com
[3] Escuela de Ingeniería Informática, Pontificia Universidad Católica de Valparaíso,
Av. Brasil 2241, Valparaíso, Chile
claudio.cubillos@ucv.cl

Abstract. The current globalization and distribution of markets has meant that companies and organizations frequently need to adapt their internal structure and operating processes, in order to demonstrate efficiency and effectiveness for every customers and users, specially when considering aspects that are beyond logical definitions, such as the emotions. To cope with that, this work proposes an alternative to model the distributed Stock Exchange Scenario with ontologies. The proposed model considers that each investor can invest using information obtained by communication with different traders or investors. Each investor has its own knowledge represented by ontologies, which is composed by technical knowledge together with internal emotional states. Our preliminary results, shows the possibility to use ontologies as knowledge representation mechanisms for domains that consider the human emotional dimension for decision-making processes.

Keywords: Investor · Emotions · Ontology

1   Introduction

People make decisions in different scenarios: individually or in interactive environments, either cooperating or negotiating. Despite of the contextual problem (coordination or negotiation), effective communication must be supported on three main aspects: knowledge of the domain (general vocabulary and specific technical concepts), knowledge of the language used (in terms of syntax, semantic, and timing), and assertiveness, that is, the ability to express own or personal ideas with clarity, without showing aggressiveness or passiveness. Any problem existing over these three main aspects will probably affect negatively the accomplishment of goals. Which leads us to the following question: Would be emotions a central component of assertiveness, and how could it be used by intelligent agents?

© Springer International Publishing Switzerland 2014
A.L.C. Bazzan and K. Pichara (Eds.): IBERAMIA 2014, LNAI 8864, pp. 649–659, 2014.
DOI: 10.1007/978-3-319-12027-0_52

The capital market domain represents a very interesting study area, mainly because the behavior of global stock markets has a highly impact in the world economy. The investment can be addressed thought different risk instruments (for example, stocks, venture capital funds, bonds, among others). In a real scenario, each investor, considering several aspects (knowledge available, own technical investment criteria, own emotional states, only to mention a few) can buy, maintain, or sell investment instruments in each period, a rich environment to explore the usage of intelligent agents.

The usage of agents was explored by Kendall and Su where they presented a multi-agent based model of a simulated stock market within which active stock traders are modeled as heterogeneous adaptive artificial agents, considering an approach of integrating individual learning and social learning to co-evolve these artificial agents with the aim of evolving successful trading strategies [1], a concept that was used in this work, but, based on the use of ontologies.

This idea was also explored by, Pu Qiu Mei *et al.* [5] where they presented an e-negotiation model based on multiagent and ontology. In particular, their work presented a novel agent construction model that enables agents to communicate in the Semantic Web [13].

Our proposal considers that each stock market has an independently context (knowledge, specific vocabulary, own process), so, it is important for each agent investor to have access to all available information (in our case represented by an ontology) in order to perform its own decision-making process and share such knowledge among other agents. Thus, considering an electronic stock market, each investor agent must consider, firstly, internal information and investment preferences, and secondly, the information associated with each specific stock market in order to make a decision.

This work proposes to simulate a distributed scenario of stock exchange market, where each investor can invest using internal information, general knowledge of stock market, and specific knowledge. This allows to incorporate the notion of globality of the market in an environment of electronic trading stock market. Each investor has its own knowledge represented by ontologies, and also can to interact with other investors or traders (for example, to increase own knowledge), allocated in any stock exchange market. Thus, each investor can move from a stock market to another one.

The remaining of the paper is organized as: Section 2 presents some selected works associated with study area; section 3 presents concepts of human decision-making processes, concepts of stock market domain and a subsection about ontologies and knowledge representation; section 4 explains the use of an ontology model for the stock exchange market scenario; and finally, section 5 presents conclusions of the developed work.

2   Related Work

In 2008, Boer-Sorbán provided a computational agent-based continuous-time simulation approach that supports a flexible representation of stock market organizations and traders' variable behavior [2]. Kodia *et al.* [3] describe the behavioral and cognitive attitudes of the investor at the micro level and explains their effects to his decision-making. The authors used an agent-based simulation identifing three types of investors: novice investors; expert investors and market intermediary. Outkin [4] presents an agent-based model of a dealer-mediated market, similar to Nasdaq. The author does not include an agent-based diagram, or another type of explanation to their model.

Smith et al. [6] defined an ontology for coordination, in which agents dynamically manage the interdependencies that arise during their interactions. A proof-of-concept implementation in the insurance domain is described and empirically evaluated. The proposed ontology has several concepts: agent, resources (viable, consumable, shareable, cloneable, owner), activity (coordinableActivity, nonCoordinableActivity), interdependency, and operationaRelationships. The evaluation of the ontology proposal was based on study case using a sample scenario, taken from the domain of car insurance fraud, to which a centralized coordination mechanism could be applied to successfully coordinate a number of activities.

Hai Dong *et al.* [7] presented a brief overview on the current negotiation ontology researches. Additionally, the authors presented a unique ontology notation system, unifying the notations used in some ontologies, to maximally promote knowledge sharing outcome in this field. This notation system is derived from UML [8]. Their results suggest that, in general, ontologies models are mainly defined for e-commerce applications. Furthermore, the proposed ontologies available in the literature do not have evaluation results. This raises the need to formally develop the scope of the use of ontologies in multiagent negotiation.

An example of integrated electronic stock exchange markets is MILA (Integrated Latin American Market) [15], composed of the stock exchanges markets of Chile, Colombia and Peru. MILA supports electronic transactions for buy/sale of stocks, by providing real-time information of the above three markets.

Our work proposes the use of integrated knowledge of different stock exchange markets in a distributed environment of different stock exchange markets with the support of a domain ontology. This allows us to conceive an unique electronic platform for trading stocks. In addition, each investor can incorporate an emotional dimension when deciding to invest in a determinate market, such aspect is not present in the previous related works.

3   Theoretical Background

With the aim to design a mechanism to facilitate stock market business, with distributed investors, it is necessary to consider some theoretical human aspects: decision-making process; knowledge about the stock markets, and a knowledge representation of stock information and investor information (knowledge and emotions).

3.1   Human Decision-Making Process

A decision encompasses several options to be done. Usually, it requires an evaluation of the specific characteristics and scope of each alternative to determine the fittest option. This explanation made sense if the entity that must take a decision has all necessary information. Usually, the decisions are made on uncertainty scenarios, with partial information and limited available time. Thus, humans developed internal mechanisms to take decisions quickly. Sometimes, the decision that is taken does not represent the best option, but, may be a "satisfactory solution". Two major aspects are crucial in a decision-making process: the probably result, and the value that each option represents for the person [12].

The expected utility model offers a rational perspective: the expected utility corresponds to utility of a specific result, considering the probability that this results may be obtained. However, risk aversion (for example, prefer an option with a minor but sure gain) or loss aversion (for example, prefer an option with minor utility, but less likely to lose investment) constitutes two cases of evidence that humans, usually, make decisions on uncertainty environments, and under a ratio-emotional schema.

3.2   Stock Market Domain

To invest is to put money into financial schemes, stocks, property, or a commercial venture with the expectation of achieving a profit [10]. An investment corresponds to the acquisition of an asset on which is possible to allocate funds, with the intention to protect or increase their value to generate positive returns [11]. A market corresponds to a physical or nonphysical space where suppliers and demanders interact over any good or service. When talking about financial markets, the instruments, which are traded, correspond, for example, to financial stocks. Stocks represent a property title over a company, that is, represent a "fragment" of company, allowed to stocks' owns to be company's owns. The investor is transformed in partner, and shares company earnings. Figure 1 presents a general process of stock market exchange. The Investor role corresponds to person or entity, which buys stocks in a Stock Exchange Market. In the same sense, the trader role is the entity that acts as intermediary between different investors.

3.3   Ontologies and Knowledge Representation

Ontologies are formal representations of a consensual knowledge [14]. It can be used as a mechanism to represent information and knowledge, forming a structured knowledge base, which allows to model concepts, relationships and properties. An ontology can be understood as a hierarchy of concepts. Each concept may have attributes and relationships. The hierarchy defines an agreed terminology associated with a specific domain or environment, allowing a common knowledge vocabulary to share information between agents.

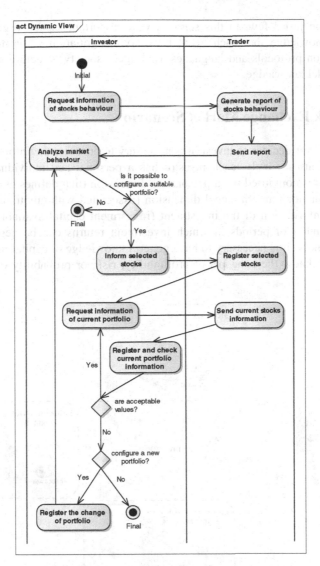

Fig. 1. General process of stock exchange

The use of domain ontology allows the agents of a negotiation to share the knowledge necessary to communicate its intentions, comprehend the intentions of other agents, and in general, perform all actions associated with a negotiation process.

In multiagent system scenarios, the automated negotiation is typically based on the assumption that agents can only participate to a negotiation if they commit to a shared protocol [9]. In most traditional negotiation scenarios, the protocol is fixed and implicitly assumed. A traditional negotiation schema has a set of constraints on the type of interactions that can take place among agents: number of participants, interaction protocols allowed in negotiation process, technology used in agents implementation, for to mention just a few. In this sense, a very important aspect to consider corresponds to knowledge that each agent has about negotiation environment, that is, communication protocols and languages used agent society, structure messages, and business model knowledge.

4   Stock Exchange Market Scenario

When an investor decides to invest, it is necessary to consider the information related to different senses. Firstly, each investor has a personal and individual investment profile, which is composed by: a personality dimension (that defines essential aspects of human behavior); an emotional dimension (associated with emotional states); and specifically information of the investment (investment capital available, time of investment, number of periods in which investment returns can be negative, among others). Secondly, it is necessary to have general knowledge of capital market domain (for example, know the concepts of profitability, risk, or probability of loss, just to name a few).

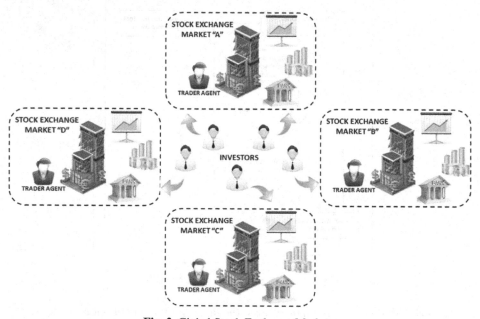

Fig. 2. Global Stock Exchange Markets

And finally, it is necessary to have knowledge of each specific stock exchange market in which an investor intends to invest, that is, knowledge of locally normative and legal aspects: normative over investment capital (tax for new foreign investment capital, and tax for withdrawal of investment); country risk index; and market volume (quantity of company traded, and number of transactions associated with each company).

Table 1. General terms of stock exchange market

Name	Description	Type	Ontology Type
Investor	Corresponds to person or entity which buys stocks in a Stock Exchange Market.	Concept	Class
Investment Capital	It is the risk capital used by an investor to buy stocks.	Concept	Class
Company	The Company is the entity which offers stocks of it, in the Stock Exchange Market. These stocks are purchased by different investors (this is called "Primary Market"). Then, an investor can sell its stocks to others investors (this is called "Secondary Market").	Concept	Class
Stock	It is the unit that is sold by a company (first time) or by an investor "X", and purchased by an investor "Y". Represents "a fragment" of the company.	Concept	Class
Stock Exchange Market	It is the place where stocks are buyed / selled.	Concept	Class
Country	It is the country where each Stock Exchange Market is available for investors	Concept	Class
Business Rule	Corresponds to specific rule or policy that is applied in each Stock Exchange Market.	Concept	Class, Data Property Or Axiom
Risk Index	Corresponds to valuation of several dimensions of a country. While most highest is it value, more risk represents this country for investment.	Instance attribute	Class Data Property
Tax	It is a legal tax, defined in each country, which can be applied to both incoming or outbound investment capital. Usually, the tax is defined as a percentage of investment capital value.	Concept	Class
Trader	The trader corresponds to entity who acts as intermediary between different investors.	Concept	Class
Transaction	Every time a stock is bought or sold, a transaction is generated	Concept	Class
Portfolio	An investment portfolio contains a set of stocks, usually, of different companies.	Concept	Class
Stock Price	It is the price defined by company (and then, by market) required to obtained one stock.	Instance attribute	Class Data Property
Profitability	It is a variation of stock value, represented in a percentage of stock price. Can be positive, zero, or negative.	Instance attribute	Class Data Property
Risk	Represents the standard deviation associated with a stock.	Instance attribute	Class Data Property
Probability of Loss	Represents the probability of profitability can be negative, that is, the probability that a stock can lose value.	Instance attribute	Class Data Property
Period (Date)	It is each instant of Stock Exchange Market calendar. Usually, the U.S. Stock Exchange Market has 250 to 252 periods per year.	Concept	Class

A stock exchange market with more companies, and in addition, with a highest number of transactions by market period, forms an interesting market with high liquidity. The proposed scenario assumes that an investor decides on which market is more attractive for investment, that is, defines an investment portfolio. For this, the investor uses information about your investment profile, general knowledge of capital markets, and specific knowledge of each market. At any time, the investor can check the performance of its investment, and then, he decides to modify the investment portfolio, or invest in another market (see figure 2).

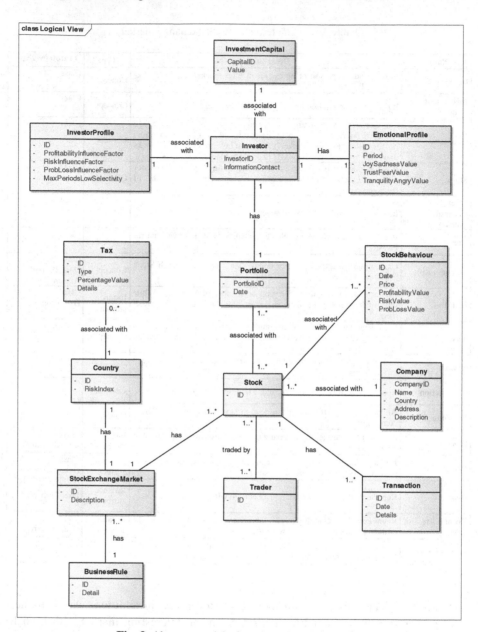

Fig. 3. Abstract model of stock exchange concepts

Concepts can be identified within this scenario. The table 1 presents a list of concepts, with a brief description and its corresponding type. In the same sense, the figure 3 shows an abstract model of terms associated with table 1.

In order to build an ontology to represent such domain, we have chose to use the OWL language. This decision is grounded in the fact that such language is able to build a decidable knowledge representation (based in description logics), and, it is quite popular when we consider the Semantic Web domain. To demonstrate our scenario we present the description of an Agent Investor. This agent, for the purpose of this article, has associated emotional characteristics like Tranquility, Influence Factors, Risk Influence, Trust, Timeframe for Low Selectivity and his Joy and Sadness. Figure 4, presents an overall view of the developed ontology. Each aspect is represented by a numerical representation. The number 1, is the class hierarch for the class auction domain; the number 2 is the Data Properties defined to describe the individuals that will compose this model; the number 3 is an example of the hasRiskValue characteristics, meaning that it belongs to the class Behaviour and the acceptable values are float; the number 4 is a the representation of four individuals, the number five are a set of object properties that were defined to describe relationships between the individuals and the number 6 represents the Data Properties of the AgentInvestor1 individual.

Fig. 4. Ontologies Classes, Properties and Individuals

The potential of this representation is mainly related to the potential to describe different contexts in which it is involved the stock market actors. Also, we can explore the usage of reasoning rules and derive knowledge to cope with the agent decision process. As usage example, we could make use of ontologies to cope with a transaction between two agent investors and two agent traders. In this situation, we could consider a few aspects such as the local context, un-emotional aspects and the same country. With this proposal we can envision more complex situations, were the emotional state of the investor is an important variable to consider. It is important to mention, that we are not proposing the usage of such emotional representation by any ontological reasoning method, but, to provide an alternative to engage and share such information among the agents' beliefs at a standardized matter. To describe the emotional characteristics of an investor, we could use properties from the EmotionalProfile class, and, with such information the trader agent can determine, in cases where two stocks have the same price, which one would be more appropriated to the investor profile. An example of communication between an investor and two

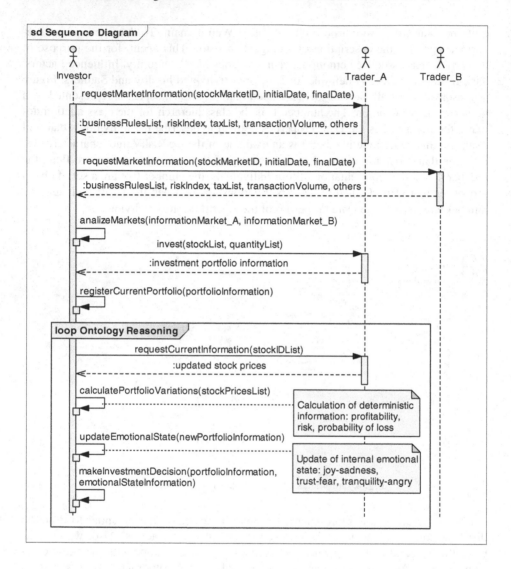

Fig. 5. Illustrative sequence of communication between investor and traders

different traders (associated with different stocks exchange markets), that could be benefit from the proposed ontology, is presented in the figure 5.

The presented scenario was build to illustrate the potential to use an ontology with emotional aspects to cope with a multiagent model for stock market. This proposal advances the state of the art by incorporating the possibility to decide, not only, by logical factors, but also, by the investor emotional state. Those aspects can be further extended within the proposed ontology, or, by adding new ontologies that are build using the same ontology engineering approach.

5   Conclusion

An approach of an ontology for knowledge representation of a distributed scenario of stock exchange market has been presented along with an multiagent model for stock exchange. The real human investors make their decisions considering both technical as internal emotional state information. Thus, the proposed ontology incorporates two dimensions (technical and emotional) with the idea to incorporate among agents the possibility to consider emotional aspects for human decisions. The future work will address, firstly, to increase the proposed scenario, in terms of concepts, relationships, and interactivity between actors, and secondly, to test the ontology representation on a functional prototype.

References

1. Kendall, G., Su, Y.: Co-evolution of Successful Trading Strategies in A Multi-agent Based Simulated Stock Market. In: Proceedings of The 2003 International Conference on Machine Learning and Applications (ICMLA 2003), Los Angeles, pp. 200–206 (2003)
2. Boer-Sorbán, K.: Agent-Based Simulation of Financial Markets: A Modular Continuous-Time Approach. Erasmus University Rotterdam (2008), ISBN: 90–5892–155–0
3. Kodia, Z., Ben Said, L., Ghedira, K.: SiSMar: Social Multi-agent Based Simulation of Stock Market. In: 8th International Conference on Autonomous Agents and Multiagent Systems AAMAS, Budapest, May 10-15 (2009)
4. Outkin, A.: An Agent-based Model of the Nasdaq Stock Market: Historic Validation and Future Directions. In: 2012 CSSSA Annual Conference, Santa Fe, New Mexico, USA, September 18-21 (2012)
5. Mei, P.Q., Hong, Z., Cun, C.Y., Qin, P.X.: An E-negotiation model based on Multi-agent and Ontology. In: International Conference on Computational Intelligence and Natural Computing CINC 2009, Wuhan, pp. 107–110 (2009)
6. Smith, B., Tamma, V., Wooldridge, M.: An Ontology for Coordination. Journal of Applied Artificial Intelligence 25(3), 235–265 (2011)
7. Dong, H., Hussain, F.K., Chang, E.: State of the Art in Negotiation Ontologies for Enhancing Business Intelligence. In: 4th International Conference on Next Generation Web Services Practices, NWESP 2008, Seoul, pp. 107–112 (2008)
8. Booch, G., Jacobson, I., Rumbaugh, J.: El Lenguaje Unificado de Modelado. Segunda Edición. Adisson Wesley (2006)
9. Tamma, V., Phelps, S., Dickinson, I., Wooldridge, M.: Ontologies for supporting negotiation in e-commerce. Engineering Applications of Artificial Intelligence 18, 223–236 (2005)
10. Invest. Oxford Dictionary, http://oxforddictionaries.com/definition/english/invest
11. Martín, M.: Inversiones. Instrumentos de Renta Fija, Valoración de Bonos y Análisis de Cartera, 1st edn. Pearson Prentice Hall (2007)
12. Smith, E., Kosslyn, S.: Procesos Cognitivos: Modelos y Bases Neurales. Pearson Prentice Hall (2008)
13. Shadbolt, N., Berners-Lee, T., Hall, W.: The Semantic Web Revisited. IEEE Intelligent Systems 21(3), 96–101 (2006)
14. Guarino, N., Giaretta, P.: Ontologies and knowledge bases: towards a terminological clarification. In: Mars, N.J.I. (ed.) Towards Very Large Knowledge Bases: Knowledge Building and Knowledge Sharing, pp. 25–32. IOS Press, Amsterdam (1995)
15. Mercado Integrado Latinoamericano, http://www.mercadomila.com

An Ontology-Based Framework for Relevant Guidance

Elaine H.T. Oliveira[1(✉)], Erika H. Nozawa[2], and Rosa Maria Vicari[3]

[1] Federal University of Amazonas, Manaus, Brazil
[2] IATECAM, Manaus, Brazil
[3] Federal University of Rio Grande do Sul, Porto Alegre, Brazil
elaine@icomp.ufam.edu.br, erika@iatecam.org.br, rosa@inf.ufrgs.br

Abstract. Nowadays there is a huge amount of information available in so many places. It is a hard task to decide where and what to look at, therefore a little guidance would be helpful. Towards this direction, this paper proposes a framework that uses ontologies to suggest relevant topics. This framework is based on a cognitive theory called Relevance Theory. In this particular case, we used a domain ontology to represent a proficiency test context and an application ontology to represent the relevance method. A proof of concept was conducted in order to demonstrate the validity of the framework. Some preliminary results point that the suggestion made from the system took to slightly more focused learning paths.

Keywords: Framework · Ontology · Relevance Theory · Learning path

1 Introduction

Students and teachers usually have a huge amount of information available on a specific theme in the web. Sometimes it is hard to decide what to take a look at. We are busy people. So it seems that relevance is a keyword nowadays. We seek for relevant information, we try to study relevant topics so we spend time and effort in what is really worth it. This is the case in the context of proficiency tests such as JLPT (Japanese Language Proficiency Test). Hours of practice and study are necessary to become proficient in a language. This could be a frustrating experience without appropriate guidance.

Considering similar situations, some works try to deliver appropriate information to users [1], guide them dynamically through information systems [2] or offer the best services based on user's intention [3]. Aligned to this motivation, we propose a framework that considers the complexity of a particular domain and tries to suggest relevant topics of study to the user. This framework is based on a cognitive theory called Relevance Theory.

To better place our research, in the next section, we present some related work on the use of ontologies as knowledge representation structures. The theory and its application to our problem are explained next. The proposed framework is presented along with its proof of concept. The framework was instantiated and some preliminary

© Springer International Publishing Switzerland 2014
A.L.C. Bazzan and K. Pichara (Eds.): IBERAMIA 2014, LNAI 8864, pp. 660–671, 2014.
DOI: 10.1007/978-3-319-12027-0_53

results are shown. Finally we bring up some guidance for future work and concluding remarks.

2 Related Work

Ontologies have been used as knowledge structures in several areas. They are useful for modeling domain knowledge, tasks to be performed and applications involving procedures and knowledge, thus providing semantic information that can be understood by machines.

There are many ways to model a context and to use ontologies to personalize information. In [4], they propose an architecture of an ontology-based adaptive e-learning decision support system which recommends adaptive learning paths personalized to particular learners. They use the Item Response Theory [5] in order to calculate learner's abilities. In our approach we propose a framework to represent and suggest relevant topics based on the Relevance Theory [11].

In pervasive computing area, context is usually represented mainly by location information. For example, in [6], ontologies are used to model personalized information about location. In our approach, context is seen from a cognitive perspective and what matters is how the information should be supposedly organized. In the work presented at [6], the population of the ontology is done by many different sources (location sensors, construction plans, direct data input by the user, etc.) and each source can have different reliability degrees and relevance in different contexts. It accomplishes it by using the accretion-resolution approach [7]. The domain ontology used in this paper has been populated by the researchers themselves, with the help of experts, based on books and other learning materials. Validation process was also carried out by experts. Evaluation of their ontology was performed using an application-based approach [8]. Our domain ontology was partially evaluated according to *oQual*, a model of ontology validation [9].

3 Application of the Relevance Theory

In the search for a cognitive theory that would support the semantic approach proposed by this work, we found the Relevance Theory proposed by [11]. It was very helpful guiding the development of the two ontologies presented in this paper.

According to this theory, a stimulus should be relevant enough to deserve audience's processing effort and the communicator should explicitly provide a set of assumptions that are adequately relevant to the audience. The focus is on how people share thoughts with one another, considering communication mainly as an inferential process.

The theory discusses many concepts from which five have been widely used in this project: context, relevance, contextual effect, processing effort and manifestability. For each concept presented next, we tried to make the relationship with the researched area and the proposed method.

3.1   Context

Context, in a cognitive perspective, is a psychological construct, a subset of the individual's assumptions about the world [11].

It is not the intention to represent the entire cognitive context of an individual, which would be probably impossible. For now, the context of JLPT level N4 was represented through a domain ontology. It consists of a class that represents the larger context and subclasses that represent subordinate contexts. In this case, the ontology plays the role of a general representation of the area, acting as a sort of a course agenda. It has all the necessary vocabulary for either a human or an artificial agent to communicate about the domain.

3.2   Relevance

Although relevance may be a multidimensional concept [10] and highly applied in Information Retrieval research, we look at relevance from a cognitive viewpoint. According to [11], relevance is a potential property of inputs to cognitive processes. The authors say that information is relevant if it changes or improves an individual's representation of the world.

Relevance to an individual can be defined in both classificatory and comparative terms [12]. For classifications, we may think that an assumption is relevant to an individual in a given time if and only if it has some positive cognitive effect in one or more contexts available to him at that time. In terms of comparisons, we may consider that an assumption is relevant to an individual as the positive cognitive effects achieved when optimally processed are large and the effort required to achieve these cognitive effects is small.

In the case of e-JLPT, relevance is a property of topics of study. As the theory goes through a qualitative comparative approach [12], assuming both a classificatory and a comparative definition, we decided to ask experts to attribute relevance values to each of the topics. The value itself has no quantitative meaning and do not have a unit of measurement, but is there for the purpose of classification and comparison. The expert was asked to carry out the process according to his/her experience, knowing that the result would be subjective.

3.3   Contextual Effect

For some assumption to be relevant there must be contextual effects. The greater the contextual effects generated by new information, the greater the relevance. Contextual effects are necessary and sufficient condition for relevance.

Contextual effects may occur primarily through three ways:

- Adding contextual implications – as a result of the interaction of new and old information, with contextual implications, i.e., there is an improvement in the individual's representation of the world;

- Reinforcement of prior assumptions – through evidence in favor of prior assumptions, modifying the strength of some assumptions in the context;
- Elimination of false assumptions – through evidence contrary to previous assumptions, in the case of contradictions, where there is the deletion of some assumptions in the context.

In the case of e-JLPT, contextual effects may occur in the following ways:

- Adding contextual implications – each new topic visited by the student, as long as it is related to a topic already visited, modifies the individual's representation of e-JLPT context;
- Reinforcement of prior assumptions – the strength of an assumption is related to the student performance in already visited topics. As the performance improves the strength of the topic in the context increases;
- Elimination of false assumptions – this case does not apply to e-JLPT context the way it has been modeled.

In the process of evaluation, experts were asked to compare the topics of the same level and assign values as contextual effects. Among a range of five topics, for example, they would have to identify the most relevant and assign a value from zero to ten according to their opinion about the benefits that would come from studying a particular topic. They also should give a degree of confidence on their own knowledge and experience.

The student's context is always improved as he improves his knowledge. As he is progressing and mastering other topics, his context is being expanded.

3.4   Processing Effort

Although contextual effects are necessary and sufficient condition for relevance, we should also consider another factor: the cost to produce some input to cognitive processes, the effort required to assimilate a new assumption.   There are cases where there are two assumptions with the same contextual effect; so the relevance difference is given by the processing effort of that assumption.

"Processing effort is a negative factor: other things being equal, the greater the processing effort, the lower the relevance" [13]. According to the authors, "human beings are efficient information-processing devices." The search for more benefits at lower costs is the search for efficiency. On the effort (cost) side, human beings tend to spend the least amount of resources possible. These features can be, for example: time, money, energy, etc. On the effect or benefit side, human beings tend to seek for the best possible gain.

In the case of e-JLPT, the processing effort was also a value assigned by experts based on their experience and knowledge about JLPT domain. They were asked to think on hours of study, i.e., how many hours of study would be required to master a particular topic. The only restriction was that the value should be greater than zero.

3.5 Manifestability

Manifestability is one concept related to the availability of information in individual's cognitive context. Information can simply be manifested to someone. This person perceives it, but the strength with which it is part of the cognitive environment may be quite weak, that is, it may be something that gets much less attention and soon after it is already forgotten. With a little more strength, assumptions are a bit beyond the notion of manifestation. The assumption may not necessarily be true. It is something that requires the attention of the individual, but needs to be proved to become knowledge. The knowledge of information, in a stronger sense, involves the mental representation of such information. In a weaker sense, may be the deduction of knowledge from something already known.

Claiming that the student knows the entire content of a topic of study is quite strong, it would be necessary to know all the individual's mental representations and all that could be deduced from that knowledge within the cognitive context represented. So this work adopted the notion of degree of manifestability. When the student performs the test, this points to some degree of manifestability, i.e., it is known that the topic was manifest to him in a certain degree. This avoids the commitment to assume that his performance is a complete and unrestricted reflection of his knowledge about the topic.

All topics visited by the student are in his learning path, with a higher or lower degree of manifestability, which varies according to the performance achieved in each topic. These topics with values varying according to performance, i.e., with different degrees of manifestability, are part of the student's context which is a subset of the general context.

Next we present the framework which is the basis for this proposal.

4 The Relevance Framework

The Relevance Framework is a conceptual and semantic framework designed to encapsulate and represent specific areas where knowledge and recommendation of relevant contexts are essential (or desirable) for some applications.

Some system design requirements were identified in this scenario:

- The deduction of new facts from existing facts and statements would be fundamental to represent a domain knowledge. It would use a declarative approach for the explanation of the concepts, rules and entities about any domain and then, allow their reuse and sharing with other possible domains;
- A particular application is required to recommend relevant contexts in a specific domain knowledge, a procedural approach to explicit the strategy and method of communication and inference engine, such as an application (function class) or an application ontology;

- In order to make use of the association that outcome from the knowledge inference, an application that can make exchanges of data (messages) within a well-defined, secure and unambiguous semantics is required. This application should enable browsing, selecting and using relevant information in a particular context. The application is the interface with the user which drives him into the recommended context.

Given the identified requirements, the framework has the components presented in Figure 1, with its development based on OWL by W3C recommendations:

- One or more domain ontologies for the declarative approach. These ontologies represent the set of concepts into specialized domain with explicit inference rules that add value to knowledge to solve a particular problem into this context (what need to be relevant). These domain ontologies should reflect the Relevance Theory. Concepts such as context, relevance, contextual effect, processing effort and manifestability should be used in modelling. All engineering process should be supported by domain experts;
- One or more application ontology for the procedural approach (strategy of knowledge inference). These ontologies guide in how to acquire relevant context based on user's goal parameters. The engine of ontology has a strategy to learn from this environment to guide to more and more relevant context. These ontologies may differ from each other according to the application and should be chosen by the educational tutor. Each tutor may decide the best approach for that domain. For example, one may think that it is better to study one topic in depth instead of study all the topics superficially;
- An interface application to interact with the user and capture the elements from the environment to guide the navigation into relevant context at a specific domain.

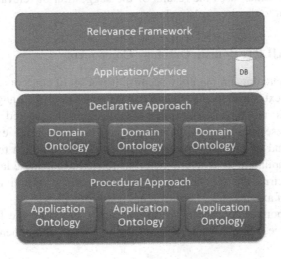

Fig. 1. Relevance Framework

5   Instantiation of the Framework

An instantiation of the framework, as a proof of concept, was done in an educational environment (e-JLPT Adapt). It was built based on a previous version of e-JLPT application that uses the domain ontology without the application ontology for relevant procedural approach. According to the Relevance Framework, suggestions of relevant topics are provided to the student assisting him in his goals and avoiding information overloads.

Summarizing and applying to JLPT case, we may say that as a static structure, the domain ontology acts as a course agenda with all the topics of study and their relationships among themselves. As a dynamic structure, it serves as the basis for navigation and suggestion of relevance.

The value for Relevance ($R_{i,j}$) of each topic of study i given by the specialist j is obtained by the ratio between Contextual Effect ($CE_{i,j}$) and Processing Effort ($PE_{i,j}$), as can be seen in the equation:

$$R_{i,j} = EC_{i,j}/PE_{i,j}$$

The final value for Relevance of topic i (R_i) is obtained by taking the average of the Relevance proposed by each of the t experts, considering the Confidence Degree ($CD_{i,j}$) of each expert j:

$$R_i = (\sum_{j=1}^{t} (R_{i,j} CD_{i,j}))/t$$

The instantiation of the framework is performed by considering the following components: *JLPT* ontology domain, *MethodOfSuggestingRT* ontology and the application or service which uses the results of the suggestion of relevant topics (e-JLPT Adapt). Both ontologies are explained next.

5.1   ontologiaJLPT: Domain Ontology Component

This is a taxonomic domain ontology because it is a set of concepts and hierarchies in a particular context, developed with OWL 1.0 (Web Ontology Language) using Protégé Editor. This ontology is an explicit specification of a shared conceptualization that holds Japanese language proficiency test context in N4 level, evaluated by JLPT course experts and by ontology experts. It is represented through the course agenda, result of the compilation of different materials related to Japanese language grammar. The ontology metrics are: 69 classes, 19 object properties, 76 individuals (instances), 111 subclasses of axioms and 24 equivalent classes of axioms.

The most important component in this ontology, based on the framework, is the hasRelevance object property: it explicits the relevance component at JLPT expert point of view.

5.2   Method of Suggesting RT: Application Ontology Component

For this case study, *MethodOfSuggestingRT* ontology was developed in OWL 2.0. This is a proposal of an application ontology, domain ontology dependent, that represents the hierarchy and semantic structure to apply the Relevance Theory Method by providing the suggestion of relevant topics from a given domain ontology.

The assumptions considered for this ontology are:

- It must meet student's goals and purposes to acquire relevant course agenda in JLPT context simulation;
- It shall allow its reuse and import in other contexts (domain independence);
- It shall allow reuse and import of existing domain ontology in the context of the case study, avoiding the need to formalize the domain knowledge and vocabulary.

MethodOfSuggestingRT ontology metric are: 2 classes (*GoalsTopics* and *RelevantTopics*), 4 object properties, 6 instances, 6 subclasses of axioms and 1 equivalent class axioms.

This ontology represents the relevant context suggestion method, based on student learning goals and recalculated by the manifestability degree of the context and the goals.

The most important component in this ontology is the *isRelevantTopic*. It represents the structure of a function that returns the Relevant Topics (defined by the student based on his goals) from the Goals Topics (based on hasRelevance component inherited from importation of *ontologiaJLPT* ontology). This function comes from the application of Dijkstras's algorithm in a method based on Relevance Theory, using and matching the student's manifestability degree property.

This ontology model was designed as a case study to maximize the revelant context considering the semantic approach through the inferred axiom. Figure 2 presents, in a sample query, the automatic extraction of all relevant topics from JLPT ontology to a student who is interested in '*Gobi*' and '*Subject*' topics. This result is obtained using the Pellet Reasoner and DL Query plugin by Protégé Editor.

Fig. 2. Relevant topic query result using Pellet Reasoner in MethodOfSuggestingRT ontology

5.3   E-JLPT Adapt: User Interface Application Component

For this case study, the e-JLPT Adapt interface was implemented adopting the declarative approach as in ontologiaJLPT and the implementation of the MethodOfSuggestingRT as a procedural approach. It was developed in Ruby, using Ruby on Rails framework, with MySQL database.

6   Preliminary Results

The proposal of this work was to adapt the navigation of students applying to JLPT test. It was done by using a method of suggestion of topics of study, according to the cognitive perspective of Relevance Theory. The expectation was that this would lead to a better performance in the process of exercise and practice to JLPT.

The initial version of the system was put on trial for 15 volunteers who could use it, in order to observe the relevance of the learning paths. The users interacted freely with two systems: one which had the suggestions, called e- JLPT Adapt, and other with no interference, called simply e-JLPT. Data were collected on the number of topics visited.

All volunteers used both systems freely and visited some topics of study. A topic of study was considered visited when it was part of the simulated test that the student had made. We noticed a considerable difference between the numbers of topics visited in the two systems. Some students used learning goals with many topics, which led to this difference. Figure 3 presents data collected by the system for all interactions conducted.

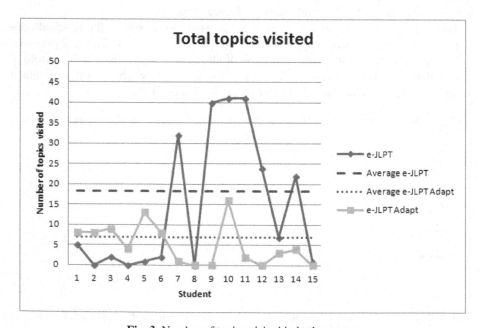

Fig. 3. Number of topics visited in both systems

In this case, it appears that the suggestion of relevance influence navigation, leading to a smaller number of topics chosen for the simulated tests. In adaptive version of the system, several users were more focused, selecting a few topics, instead of selecting all available topics.

This also can be seen on the following pictures. Figure 4a shows a volunteer's learning paths in traditional e-JLPT system, represented by the orange lines. The blue lines show what the suggested paths would be if it was in the adaptive system. It shows that student's learning paths are very different from the one generated by the suggestion method.

Figure 4b shows the interaction of the same volunteer in the adaptive system. In this case, the suggestion was explicitly made. As he responded to the suggestion of the system, his learning path was really close to it.

These are not conclusive data but illustrate some of the interaction of the users with the system, corroborating to the proof of concept of the framework. More observation shall be done in order to confirm the benefit of this proposal.

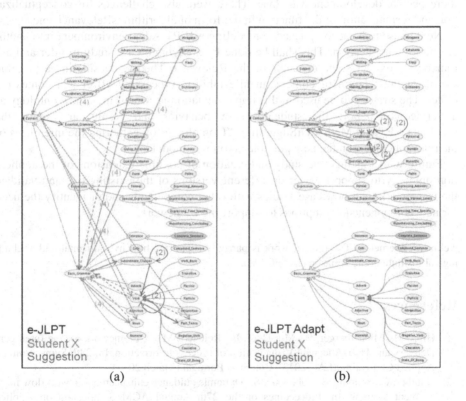

(a)   (b)

Fig. 4. User's interaction with e-JLPT system

7   Future Work and Conclusions

This project comes with several outcomes. In this section we list some of them and present some future work.

The proposed framework was validated: it is a conceptual and semantic one. It is part of a project that began with the development process of the domain ontology, where the method was validated and then identified the possibility of instantiation of the method for different scenarios, resulting in the specification of the framework.

The strategy adopted to formalize the concepts of the application ontology enabled knowledge explicitation in a safe and non-ambiguous vocabulary. It also get results from inferences directly from the ontology of general application, as well as the reuse, sharing and ease of maintenance of the ontology modeling, since it is application independent.

The decision to include a semantic component to the domain also benefits by allowing reuse, ease of maintenance and information sharing.

The validation of the ontology with the definition of application requirements and its respective development was done. There were also challenges for conceptualization and formalization of the function in the form of algorithm isRelevantTopic.

Next phase to be accomplished is modeling e-JLPT Adapt environment into another ontology application. This shall be done by applying a case study to infer and automatically extract some concepts of the Relevance Theory, considering a possible metric of the relation of context, manifestability, processing effort and contextual effect. The strategy to be used in this implementation is structuring a new ontology as a service to import the student's path behavior and results and reuse the ontologiaJLPT and MethodOfSuggestingRT ontologies by gathering the inferences of the relevant context in the new possible taxonomy model.

Future works include the study and creation of possible extensions of the application ontology to support newer or different versions of the existing one and validate the framework with new case studies with other components and/or identify the need for new components/assumptions to support the framework.

Acknowledgements. The present work is partially supported by Environmental and Technological Institute of the Amazon (IATECAM).

References

1. Hipp, M., Michelberger, B., Mutschler, B., Reichert, M.: A Framework for the Intelligent Delivery and User-Adequate Visualization of Process Information. In: 28th Symposium on Applied Computing (SAC 2013), Coimbra, Portugal (March 2013)
2. Günther, C., Schönig, S., Jablonski, S.: Dynamic guidance enhancement in workflow management systems. In: Proceedings of the 27th Annual ACM Symposium on Applied Computing (SAC 2012), pp. 1717–1719. ACM, New York (2012)
3. Guidara, I., Chaari, T., Fakhfakh, K.: Intention based semantic approach for service sourcing. In: Proceedings of the 27th Annual ACM Symposium on Applied Computing (SAC 2012), pp. 401–402. ACM, New York (2012)

4. Yarandi, M., Jahankhani, H., Tawil, A.-R.H.: Towards adaptive E-learning using decision support systems. International Journal of Emerging Technologies in Learning **8** (Spl. issue), 44–51 (2013)
5. Hambleton, R.K., Swaminathan, H., Rogers, H.J.: Fundamentals of Item Response Theory. Sage Publications, The International Professional Publishers, London (1991)
6. Niu, W.T., Kay, J.: PERSONAF: Framework for personalised ontological reasoning in pervasive computing. User Modeling and User-Adapted Interaction **20**(1), 1–40 (2010)
7. Carmichael, D.J., Kay, J., Kummerfeld, B.: Consistent modelling of users, devices and sensors in a ubiquitous computing environment. User Modeling and User-Adapted Interaction **15**, 197–234 (2005)
8. Brank, J., Grobelnik, M., Mladenić, D.: A survey of ontology evaluation techniques. In: Conference on Data Mining and Data Warehouses (2005)
9. Gangemi, A., Catenacci, C., Ciaramita, M., Lehmann, J.: Modelling Ontology Evaluation and Validation. In: Sure, Y., Domingue, J. (eds.) ESWC 2006. LNCS, vol. 4011, pp. 140–154. Springer, Heidelberg (2006)
10. Borlund, P.: The concept of relevance in IR. Journal of the American Society for Information Science and Technology **54**, 913–925 (2003)
11. Sperber, D., Wilson, D.: Relevance: communication and cognition. MIT Press, Cambridge (1986)
12. Sperber, D., Wilson, D.: Relevance: communication and cognition. Blackwell, Oxford (1995)
13. Yus, F.: Ciberpragmática 2.0: Nuevos usos del lenguaje en Internet. Ariel, Barcelona (2010)

Applications of AI

Recognition and Recommendation
of Parking Places

Andrew Koster[✉], Allysson Oliveira, Orlando Volpato, Viviane Delvequio,
and Fernando Koch

Samsung Research Institute, Campinas, Brazil
{andrew.k,allysson.o,orlando.f,v.franco,fernando.koch}@samsung.com

Abstract. Current solutions to recommend available parking spaces
rely on options like: intentional user feedback; installing data collectors
in volunteering fleet vehicles, or; installing static sensors to monitor available parking spaces. In this paper we propose a solution based application
that runs on commodity smartphones and makes use of the advanced sensor capabilities in these devices, along with methods of statistical analysis of the collected sensor data to provide useful recommendations. We
exploit a combination of k-medoid clustering and Conditional Random
Fields to reliably detect a user parking with a limited sensor capability. Next, we outline a method based on Markov Chains to calculate
the probability of finding a parking space near a given location. We also
enhance the solution with more sensor capability to discover desirable
properties in parking spaces.

1 Introduction

Finding parking spaces in big cities is aggravating. Reports indicate that from
30% to 40% of light vehicle traffic is made up of drivers actually searching for a
free parking space [3]. This represents a lot of wasted time and fuel, and increased
emissions of pollutant and green-house gases.

Current solutions to indicate available parking spaces rely on orthodox
approaches like: a) intentional user feedback, i.e. tapping a button to indicate
an available parking space; b) installing sensors, and its corresponding processing equipment in volunteering fleet vehicles, like taxi drivers, to detect available
parking spaces; or c) installing sensors and/or cameras on the parking lots with
an associated system to process those signals.

We introduce an alternative solution consisting of a mobile app to automatically detect that the user is parking, and a server-based system to recommend
available parking spaces. This solution is grounded on the concept of serendipitous recommendation: that is, providing useful and pleasant information based
on automatically collected environmental data and some form of understanding
of users' demands. Exemplary solutions are SAMSUNG S-Health[1] and Google
Now[2].

---

[1] http://content.samsung.com/us/contents/aboutn/sHealthIntro.do
[2] http;//www.google.com/landing/now/

© Springer International Publishing Switzerland 2014
A.L.C. Bazzan and K. Pichara (Eds.): IBERAMIA 2014, LNAI 8864, pp. 675–685, 2014.
DOI: 10.1007/978-3-319-12027-0_54

In our case, we developed new models of statistical analysis of smartphone's sensor data to detect salient movement signature such as "leaving a parking space" or "entering a park space". The mobile app performs statistical analysis upon sensor data and, once these signatures are detected, notifies the Parking Space Recommender server. The new information is stored in a repository, which in turn is used to calculate the probability of available spots, when this is requested. Simultaneously the recognized movement signature is evaluated in the app, to improve the recognition algorithm, and adapt it to better function in the user's context. By collecting historic parking information, contextualized by geographic region, calendar day, time of day, weather condition, ephemerides, real time traffic information and special events; a model can be built to predict free parking spaces generation and consumption rates.

Finally, we describe how our app presents the information about a parking space: along with the information about availability of spaces, we collect information about the desirability of these spaces. For instance, how far is it from the user's destination, does it have shade, or a street lamp, and any additional problems in the area. In Figure 1 we give an overview of how the system works. In the following, we describe the various computational methods used to achieve this.

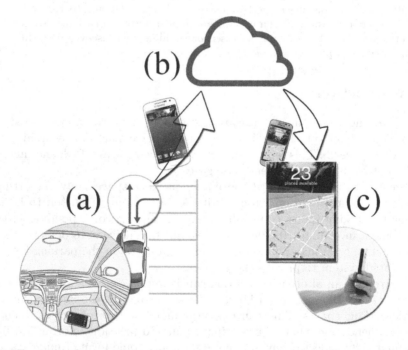

Fig. 1: Functional overview: (a) movements are automatically recognised and (b) notifications sent to a cloud-based service, which groups and classifies information from many devices; (c) the service is able to identify nearby available parking spaces to reply to users' geolocated requests.

2 Related Work

There are many systems envisioned to inform and manage available parking spaces in a context of smart city. Generally these require the installation of sensors as part of a city's infrastructure. Some of them are based on installing sensors on every parking space to detect directly whether there is a parked vehicle or not [10,13], which places a large demand on standardisation of sensors, data collection and processing equipment. Moreover, it demands a large monetary investment on procurement, installation and maintenance.

Other solutions use a fleet of voluntary vehicles to detect parking occupancy. Suhr et al. [16] proposes a free parking space detection system by using a fish-eye camera installed on the rear end of a vehicle to detect available spots when a user drives by them. Mathur et al. [9] describe a system for detection of available parking spaces by having a fleet of vehicles equipped with ultrasonic sensors in the vehicle's passenger door, which detects available spaces on the street. These solutions demand the use of dedicated equipment to be installed on vehicles that should be continuously passing on most of the streets. They are intended mostly for detecting street parking, as the vehicles are not meant to go to inside parking lots. However, these solution imply capital expenditure and continuous operation costs to fleets of vehicles such as taxi or buses, who are not the primary consumers of the product.

Rather than explicitly instrumenting the city, some solutions envision that the citizens report free parking spaces. Some require intentional action by the user, for instance, by tapping a button on their mobile phone's application indicating that they parked, or just left, a parking space [4,6]. Google's "Open Spot" application [4] continuously shows vacant parking spaces in a 1 mile radius of the user's location. The availability of parking spaces should be indicated as the user enters or leaves a space. This application did not become popular because it required the intentional action of the user, despite a system of points intended to incentivise the use of the system [12]. Instead, the recognition of a parking space should be automatic, as suggested in "PhonePark" [15], which uses, in addition to other things, GPS location and the connection/disconnection of the Smartphone with the Bluetooth based hands free system of the vehicle. The main disadvantage of this approach is that not all vehicles have a hands free system, especially in Brazil, where most of the fleet is composed of low technology content vehicles. For recognizing parking spaces we use a system similar to the Phonepark System, but make less assumptions on the available technology. In order to recognize a parking space, we require an accelerometer, a gyroscope and some method of sensing location (whether it be through triangulation in the cellphone grid, or GPS). However, our system builds upon these reports by using statistical machine learning techniques to better report the available parking spaces.

3   Detecting Parking Spaces

Whilst various methods are able to distinguish between different activities [7,14], they are not sufficiently precise to recognise parking movements. For instance, in commercially available software, the SAMSUNG Motion package in the Mobile SDK[3] recognises an elevator as a vehicle, which is clearly a problem: if we were to use the mode change from walking to vehicular transport and vice versa to recognise parking spaces, this would result in a large number of false positives. A second problem with the state-of-the-art is that they rely on labelled data. While this is fairly easy to obtain for rough categories like transportation mode, more detailed activities are harder to label manually, and of the data we have obtained, only a small part is unreliably labelled, whereas the rest is entirely unlabelled.

In order to deal with these shortcomings, we propose to combine the recognition of rough categories, such as changes in transportation mode, with what we call "parking signatures". In Figure 2 we have graphed a typical signature we captured for a park-out manoeuvre, reconstructed from accelerometer and gyroscope data. The motion is normalised to start at (0, 0) in the north direction. It is easy to see that the car reversed out, turned, and drove away. While not all moves are as easy to recognise visually, all park-out manoeuvres have, as a bare minimum, in common that they start from standstill, and accelerate in the XY-plane. Nevertheless, this description also includes other movements, such as starting from a traffic light, and if we do not take initial velocity into account (which must be computed, rather than sensed directly) these signatures may be confused with a host of other signatures, such as going around a corner.

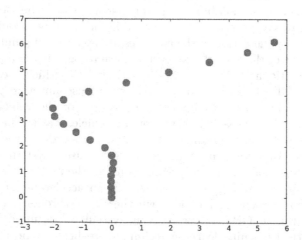

Fig. 2: Reconstruction of the car's position in the XY-plane over time

---
[3] http://developer.samsung.com/samsung-mobile-sdk

Rather than attempting to describe all potential movements manually in a rule-based system, we use machine learning. In specific, we use k-medoids [5], an unsupervised learning algorithm, to cluster a set of mostly unlabelled sensor readings, collected by volunteer motorists. As a distance measure we use Dynamic Time Warping (DTW) [11], a well-known distance measure for time series data that, despite its age, is still among the most accurate measures [1].

While there are other learning algorithms that work with unlabelled data, the most common are clustering algorithms. These algorithms aim to group together similar samples, while maintaining the groupings themselves as distinct as possible. Out of the possible clustering algorithms we choose to use k-medoids, because almost all other algorithms rely on a method for calculating a central point for each cluster. This is a notoriously hard problem for time series data, and an initial experiment using k-means and the arithmetic mean of the points in a cluster led to unsatisfactory results: often the algorithm would not even converge. k-medoids avoids entirely the calculation of a central point by choosing the most central of the data points as the representative of the cluster.

Based on preliminary research, we found that the best results are obtained with $k = 50$, with a Davies-Bouldin index of 0.066 (in comparison, with just 5 clusters, the best Davies-Bouldin index obtained was 0.209). The labelled samples we have serve to label each cluster as containing park-in manoeuvres, park-out manoeuvres or other manoeuvres. The result is a large collection of *labelled* movement signatures. These, in turn are used as input to train a Conditional Random Field (CRF) [8] model to recognise new series of sensor readings in real-time. By using cross-validation, we can test the CRF part, however this does not truly test whether the label assignment by the clustering algorithm was performed correctly. As such, sufficiently testing the classifier requires the composition of a set of labelled data, and will be performed when the parking app goes into beta testing: it will include a button to give feedback about whether a manoeuvre was recognised correctly by the algorithm, thus providing labelled samples.

4   Reporting Probable Spaces

Detected parking spaces are reported by the app to the server, which collects both current, and historic data about parking spaces. When an app requests information about available spaces, it reports the central location, around which a space should be found. This can be the user's current location, or anticipating the user travelling, his or her destination. The server performs two computations. Based on historic data, and using a Bayesian approach, it computes the distance around the point for which the probability of finding a parking spot at the given time is sufficiently high. Secondly, for the actual known spaces that are within the calculated distance, the probability of them in fact being free, given their last reported status, at the given time is calculated using a Hidden Markov Model.

4.1 Calculating Parking Distance

The historic data that is collected on the server can be interpreted as a time series for each individual parking space. In an ideal scenario, the sensor readings would be perfect, and would give a record of when any parking space was occupied or not, and we could use this to calculate the probability of the space being available, based on its availability at similar times in the past. However, in reality, the data will be very sparse, and we will be missing data for many parking spaces, and for those we do have data it may be updated infrequently: not everybody (or even most people) use the app, and even those that do may switch it off. It is thus important to assume (very) incomplete information regarding the availability of parking spaces in an area.

We solve this, by calculating a distance threshold, for which the expectation of finding a parking space is above a configurable probability threshold. Algorithm 1 computes this. For each distance, the algorithm collects all the historic sensor readings within range, and calculates for each location the probability that it is occupied using the beta probability distribution, and a hill-climbing method is used to find the optimum distance. For any location (or parking space), we generate the entire time series, by simply assuming that each reading is the status for the entire time period until the next reading. We discretise time and use the maximum likelihood estimation to calculate the parameters of a beta probability distribution for whether or not a position is occupied. Due to the law of large numbers, with sufficient readings, the errors from having sparse data will average out; hence the need to average over an area, rather than considering each parking space individually.

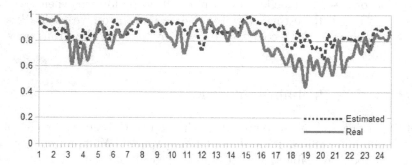

Fig. 3: Probabilities of a parking space being free

We tested the efficacy of the estimator of availability using the data set from the NYC Department of Traffic [4], averaged over 15 minute time windows during a day. The results are plotted in Fig. 3 and have a Pearson correlation coefficient of 0.57.

---

[4] http://www.nyc.gov/html/dot/html/motorist/realtimeparking.shtml

Algorithm 1. ParkingDistance

Input: Historic sensor readings of parking spaces, central location
Input: Probability threshold that is required
Result: Minimum distance from central location within which there is an
        available parking space with probability above the threshold

tested $\longleftarrow \emptyset$
distance $\longleftarrow$ initialdistance
repeat
    | tested $\longleftarrow$ tested $\cup$ {distance}
    | Readings $\longleftarrow$ getDataWithinRange(distance)
    | probability $\longleftarrow$ 1.0
    | **for** *location* $\in$ *getLocations(Readings)* **do**
    | | probOccupied $\longleftarrow$
    | | BetaDistrib(Readings.at(location))
    | | probability $\longleftarrow$ probability * probOccupied
    | **if** *probability* > *threshold* **then**
    | | distance $\longleftarrow$ getNearer(distance)
    | **else**
    | | distance $\longleftarrow$ getFarther(distance)
until $(1 - probability) > threshold \wedge distance \in tested$

4.2 Calculating Parking Space Probability

After finding a region for which the probability is sufficiently high, we can further help the user by computing the actual probability of the known parking spaces being available, given their last known status. For this, we use a Hidden Markov Model (HMM) [2] to model the conditional probability that a space is occupied, given its last known status, and the time of day. To learn the HMM, we consider all spaces, and thus all readings within the area as sufficiently similar, in order to give sufficient data for the parameter estimation. For the time-of-day we consider 15-minute intervals, and for the time since the last report, we consider anything longer than 30 minutes previous as "long ago". This gives us a space of 60×96 possible values for the observable signals, and 2 possible labels (occupied, or free) for the target. An example of a data point is:

(reported occupied 23 minutes ago, 13:00-13:15) $\rightarrow$ **occupied**.

The parking spaces with a sufficient probability of being free are sent to the app for reporting to the user.

5 Recommending Desirable Spaces

Finally, the mobile app provides parking recommendations using the data above. Available parking spaces are colour coded according to the estimated probability of them being free, and upon selecting any one of them, additional information is displayed: the estimated traffic density, and if a destination is provided, the

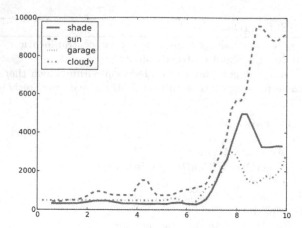

Fig. 4: Light, in lumens, upon exiting the car when parked in varying situations

time to walk there from the parking space is given. Note that this destination is not necessarily input by the user, but can be inferred from historical data about the user's behaviour, or extracted from his calendar.

Moreover, the system learns whether a parking space has shade during the day and light at night. As with the rest of the app, this data is also collected without needing any action from the user beyond normal use of his or her smartphone. When a parking signature is detected, as described in Section 2, the smartphone's photometer is activated. A rule-based system is used to detect whether the spot is shady or sunny during the day, and illuminated or dark during night-time. In Fig. 4 we graphed the luminosity readings for exiting the car in a sunny spot, and exiting the car in a shady spot. While the rules require more sophistication, depending on the time-of-day, weather, season, and location to estimate how big a jump in luminosity triggers a positive reading for either sunny or shady, the graph shows how to go about it. The rule-based system can additionally fuse data from other sensors; for instance, by using the proximity sensor to distinguish between dark of night and it being dark because the mobile phone is in the user's pocket.

This information is sent to the server, and maximum likelihood estimation is used to obtain the most likely situation. When searching for a spot, this situation is displayed. Screenshots of the mobile app are in Fig. 5.

We apply special interface marks to represent different park space categories, e.g. green dots for regular spaces and blue stars for recommended spaces. Currently we just choose the most likely to be free, but an extension of the app is to learn from user behaviour, and recommend spaces according to his or her preferences: for instance, if the user prefers to park slightly further away, but in a shady spot, this can be taken into account.

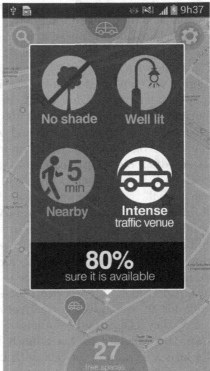

(a) Map display of the available parking spots, and the number of parking spots within range.

(b) Display with details for the selected parking spot.

Fig. 5: Screenshots of the parking recommender app

6   Conclusion and Future Work

In this paper we present a serendipitous solution to finding parking spaces: our vision is that this app works seamlessly with the user to collect and provide information when required without intruding or interrupting his or her day-to-day rhythm. The information is collected automatically when a park-in or park-out event is recognized using the activity recognition method we presented in Section 3, it is processed intelligently to calculate, as accurately as possible, the availability of parking spaces, and is reported to users who are detected to be searching, or will soon be needing, a parking spot.

The system is currently entering the last stages of development, and will soon enter alpha testing, when we will extensively test the algorithms developed in internal experiments. In particular this will serve to fine-tune our recognition algorithm and start populating our repository of historical parking data. While our current focus is on rolling out this service as fast as possible, in order to

684 A. Koster et al.

collect more data and better train our algorithms, we realise that the usability of the app should be at the forefront. Therefore there are already a number of improvements planned for its use in a car.

Because the app is meant to be used in a car, it is necessary to minimise the need to fiddle with the phone. The app will respond to voice commands, and in addition to the map interface of Fig. 5a, it will output suggestions and directions using spoken language. Additionally, we intend to use a similar system to the one outlined in Section 3 to predict that a user is looking for a parking space. Search patterns are fairly typical and we expect that a similar approach will allow us to recognise these. Furthermore, if the user's routines are known, or he has saved appointment locations in his agenda, we can use this information to predict when and where a user will search for a space. Any one of these approaches will trigger the app to ask the user if he is indeed in need of a free space (in spoken language), and upon confirmation, display the available spaces and guide the user to the best one. In this scenario, the user does not have to touch his phone, or even look at it, to get the desired functionality.

Moreover, the method we use to calculate the expected distance for finding a parking space in Section 4.1 can be used in anticipation to help users to plan for future decisions. The service can estimate how many free spaces will be available for an area, given a time period and date. When users are planning their day, they can obtain information about the availability of parking. For instance, they might have their lunch break slightly earlier to avoid parking hassles near a restaurant, or take such information into account when planning meetings. Additionally, city planners could use this information to easily see where parking problems are greatest and plan new projects accordingly.

As next steps, we are looking at reinforcement learning techniques [17] to adapt the general model described in Section 3 to detect a user's parking signature. Every person has different ways of doing things, and this is no different for driving. We thus expect that by adapting the parameters of the learned graphical model to the user's behaviour will lead to a more accurate classifier.

References

1. Ding, H., Trajcevski, G., Scheuermann, P., Wang, X., Keogh, E.: Querying and mining of time series data: experimental comparison of representations and distance measures. Proceedings of the VLDB Endowment 1(2), 1542–1552 (2008)
2. Elliott, R.J., Aggoun, L., Moore, J.B.: Hidden Markov Models. Springer, Heidelberg (1995)
3. Gallivan, S.D.: IBM global parking survey: Drivers share worldwide parking woes. Technical report, IBM (2011)
4. Hildenbrand, J.: Google releases open spot for android – find and share parking (July 10, 2010) http://www.androidcentral.com/googl-releases-open-spot-android-find-and-share-parking (retrieved June 24, 2013)
5. Kaufman, L., Rousseeuw, P.: Clustering by means of medoids. In: Statistical Data Analysis Based on the L1 Norm and Related Methods, pp. 405–416. Springer, Amsterdam (1987)

6. Koster, A., Koch, F., Bazzan, A.L.C.: Incentivising crowdsourced parking solutions. In: Nin, J., Villatoro, D. (eds.) CitiSens 2013. LNCS(LNAI), vol. 8313, pp. 36–43. Springer, Heidelberg (2014)

7. Kwapisz, J.R., Weiss, G.M., Moore, S.A.: Activity recognition using cell phone accelerometers. ACM SIGKDD Explorations Newsletter 12(2), 74–82 (2010)

8. Lafferty, J.D., McCallum, A., Pereira, F.C.N.: Conditional random fields: Probabilistic models for segmenting and labeling sequence data. In: ICML, pp. 282–289. Morgan Kaufmann, San Francisco (2001)

9. Mathur, S., Tong, J., Kasturirangan, N., Chandrasekaran, J., Xue, W., Gruteser, M., Trappe, W.: ParkNet: drive-by sensing of road-side parking statistics. In: Proc. of MobiSys 2010, pp. 123–136. ACM (2010)

10. Park, W.J., Kim, B.S., Kim, D.S., Lee, K.H.: Parking space detection using ultrasonic sensor in parking assistance system. In: Proc. of the IEEE Intelligent VEhicles Symposium, pp. 1039–1044. IEEE (2008)

11. Sakoe, H., Chiba, S.: Dynamic programming algorithm optimization for spoken word recognition. IEEE Transactions on Acoustics, Speech and Signal Processing 26(1), 43–49 (1978)

12. Sherwin, I.: Google Labs' Open Spot: A useful application that no one uses (July 10, 2011) http://www.androidauthority.com/google-labs-open-spot-a-useful-application-that-no-one-uses-15186/ (retrieved May 15, 2014)

13. Srikanth, S., Pramod, P.J., Dileep, K.P., Tapas, S., Patil, M.U., Sarat, C.B.N.: Design and implementation of a prototype smart PARKing (SPARK) system using wireless sensor networks. In: Proceedings of the Advanced Information Networking and Applications Workshops (WAINA 2009), pp. 401–406 (2009)

14. Stenneth, L., Wolfson, O., Xu, B., Yu, P.S.: Transportation mode detection using mobile phones and GIS information. In: Proc. of the 19th ACM SIGSPATIAL International Converence on Advances in Geographic Information Systems, pp. 54–63. ACM (2011)

15. Stenneth, L., Wolfson, O., Xu, B., Yu, P.S.: PhonePark: Street parking using mobile phones. In: Proceedings of the 13th IEEE International Conference on Mobile Data Management (MDM 2012), pp. 278–279. IEEE (2012)

16. Suhr, J.K., Jung, H.G., Bae, K., Kim, J.: Automatic free parking space detection by using motion stereo-based 3D reconstruction. Machine Vision and Applicatons 21(2), 163–176 (2010)

17. Sutton, R.S., Barto, A.: Reinforcement Learning: An Introduction. MIT Press (1998)

Using String Information
for Malware Family Identification

Prasha Shrestha[1]([⊠]), Suraj Maharjan[1], Gabriela Ramírez de la Rosa[2],
Alan Sprague[1], Thamar Solorio[1], and Gary Warner[1]

[1] University of Alabama at Birmingham, Birmingham, AL, USA
{prasha,suraj,gabyrr,sprague,solorio,gar}@cis.uab.edu
[2] Universidad Autónoma Metropolitana, Unidad Cuajimalpa, Mexico, Mexico
gramirez@correo.cua.uam.mx

Abstract. Classifying malware into correct families is an important task
for anti-virus vendors. Currently, only some of them will recognize a
particular malware. Even when they do, they either classify them into
different families or use a generic family name, which does not provide
much information. Our method for malware family identification is based
on the observation that closely related malware have heavy overlap of
strings. We first created two kinds of prototypes from printable strings in
the malware: one using term frequency–inverse document frequency (tf-
idf) and the other using the prominent strings extracted from the vocabulary. We then used these prototypes for classification. We achieved an
accuracy of 91.02 % by considering the entire vocabulary and an accuracy of 80.52 % by considering 20 prominent strings for each malware
family. Our accuracy is high enough for our system to be used to classify
even those malware that can confuse the anti-virus vendors.

Keywords: Malware · Prototype based classification · Prominent
strings · Tf-idf · Cosine similarity

1 Introduction

Malware is defined as malicious or malevolent software that threatens computers
and computer systems and often damages or disables them. Malware can also
gain access to private and sensitive information like social security number, bank
and credit card numbers. Malwares created by a hacker group and then modified
and improved successively by the same group or other different groups fall under
a malware family. Malware belonging to the same family exhibits similar behavior and performs similar system calls. For instance, Zeus family of malwares
can steal a victim's bank credentials and other valuable information like Social
Security Number. Users need to periodically scan and update their system by
using anti-virus software to protect it from the hazardous attacks of malware.
But these scans only make your machine as safe as the malware detecting and
correct family labeling capacity of the anti-virus vendors that you are using.

© Springer International Publishing Switzerland 2014
A.L.C. Bazzan and K. Pichara (Eds.): IBERAMIA 2014, LNAI 8864, pp. 686–697, 2014.
DOI: 10.1007/978-3-319-12027-0_55

Knowledge about malware has great importance for anti-virus vendors and there is a lot of research dedicated to this task. Being able to classify a malware into the correct family is crucial as one can predict the characteristics of the malware based upon its family. By using these characteristics, we can design better solutions to control malware. Manually classifying them is tedious, time consuming and does not scale well with their ever-growing quantity. Hence, automatic classification systems are needed to address this problem and ease the study of malware behaviours. Automatic classification systems have many applications, such as prediction of malware behaviour and of damage it may cause to the system, potential solutions to disable it, and even deeper analysis of its behaviour. Today, there is a lot of discrepancy between anti-virus vendors in assigning family labels to malware. Furthermore, sometimes these vendors are unable to recognize a particular malware.

Most of the earlier research on malware family identification is based on dynamic analysis of the malware by running it on a virtual sandbox environment. Park et al. (2010) have created system call dependency graph of the malware by running it on a virtual domain. They then measured edit distance based upon the maximal common subgraph between two dependency graphs and used a predefined threshold to classify them as being similar or different in behavior [1]. Bailey et al. (2007) used behaviour characteristics of malware rather than just sequences and patterns of system calls to classify malware [2]. They gathered the behavioural data from system logs after running malware in a virtual environment.

Some of the researches also focus on static analysis on disassembled malware. Recently, Tian et al. (2009) explored the classification of unpacked malware using features such as string frequency with AdaBoost and Random Forest classification algorithms [3]. In addition, Shabtai et al. concluded that a framework could be designed that could detect new malicious code with great accuracy [4]. They suggested using features like OpCode and byte n-grams with different classification algorithms and then ensemble results based on weights.

Our method is also a static method. A clear advantage that static methods have over dynamic ones is that dynamic analysis is harder than static since it requires running the malware on a virtual sandbox. Our method focuses on the information contained in the printable strings of an unpacked malware file. We assign a weight per family to each of these printable strings as a relative indication of its association with that family. By using these strings and their weights we construct the prototypes that will represent a family. All of the strings in the vocabulary of the training set along with their corresponding weights for a given family form a prototype for that family. The other prototype we use is based upon prominent strings and is a more concise representation of that family. The strings with the highest weights for a family are considered as the prominent strings for that family of malware. These prominent strings and their corresponding weights form the prototype for that family. In order to do the classification, we compute the cosine similarity between strings in the prototype and strings in the test malware file. The file gets classified into the family that results in the highest similarity. Furthermore, by using our prominent strings prototype, we experimented with soft-string matching using Levenshtein distance and Jaccard coefficient. Additionally, we hypothesized that the absence of prominent strings in a given malware test sample will give us some clue about incorrect labeling of the malware family by the anti-virus vendors. We leveraged this idea to detect the wrongly labeled malware samples. In short, we used the information encoded in the printable strings to classify malware into their respective families.

2 Prototypes

The core of our method is prototypes. In this section we describe the creation of our prototypes and also the prototype based classification method that we have used.

2.1 Prototype Based Classification

To classify an unseen malware file into a set of known families we use a prototype-based classification approach. The prototype based approach is one of the traditional methods for supervised text classification. There are two phases in this approach: training and testing. The training phase involves the construction of one single representative instance, called prototype, for each class or family. Then, in test phase, each given unlabeled file is compared against all prototypes and is assigned the family having the greatest similarity score. There are several ways to build a prototype in the training phase [5]. The assignation of a family or category to the vector representation of a given file f is based on the following criterion:

$$\text{family}(f) = \underset{i}{\text{argmax}}(\text{sim}(f, P_i)) \tag{1}$$

where, P_i is the prototype vector for family i and

$$\text{sim}(f, P_i) = \frac{f \cdot P_i}{||f|| \, ||P_i||} \tag{2}$$

2.2 Weighting Scheme

Our weighing scheme should assign weights to strings according to their relevance to a malware family such that the string could be useful in discriminating that family from other families. In natural language processing, three different metrics are commonly used to measure the importance of each term according to three observations: a) terms that appear many times in a single file should be more important; b) terms that appear in many files should be less important; and c) a file that contains many terms should be less important.

$$\text{tf}(t, d) = \frac{\text{freq}(t, d)}{\max\{\text{freq}(s, d) : s \in d\}} \tag{3}$$

$$idf(t, D) = \log \frac{|D|}{|\{d \in D : t \in d\}|} \qquad (4)$$

$$tf \times idf(t, d, D) = tf(t, d) \times idf(t, D) \qquad (5)$$

The tf factor as shown in Equation 3 takes into consideration the first observation, the idf from Equation 4 accounts for the second one and the third is considered in the normalization during the computation of tf. The tf-idf function as shown in Equation 5 (as [6] well noted) combines the tf and idf factors and thus incorporates all three criteria.

2.3   Prominent Strings Set (PSS)

We define a prominent string (PS) as a string that appears very frequently in a given malware family but appears rarely in any other family. The set of strings with top k weights for a family is defined as its prominent strings set. We hypothesized that a set of prominent strings PSS for a given family can distinguish one family from another such that its PSS can be seen as the signature of that family. In other words, a PSS should be enough to identify the family of a given unseen malware file.

2.4   Building Prototypes

In order to build prototypes, we first merged all the files labeled as belonging to that family into a single file. We call this new file, $TrainingFile_i$. Then, we computed the tf-idf factor for each unique string in $TrainingFile_i$. We repeated this process for each of the F families in the training dataset. We then used the strings and their tf-idf values to build two different types of prototypes.

To build the first type of prototype, we started out by creating a global vocabulary consisting of all the unique strings in the training dataset, i.e., all the unique strings of each $TrainingFile_i$. Then for each family, we formed a single vector consisting of the corresponding tf-idf values of all the strings in the global vocabulary. This vector is representative of a family and thus is our first kind of prototype.

In the second method, instead of considering the entire vocabulary, we reduced the number of strings that represents a family by only considering the prominent strings. For each $TrainingFile_i$, we ranked the strings in the file according to tf-idf values. Finally, we took the top k strings with highest tf-idf values as the set of prominent strings for that family i. We repeated this process for all F families. After this, we had F different sets of prominent strings along with their tf-idf values, one for each family. This forms our second kind of prototype.

Our prototype is a vector space model representation of a family, where each string in the prototype is a dimension of the vector $\{s_1, s_2, ..., s_d\}$ and the weight of each s_i is given by the tf-idf values computed in the previous phase. For our first prototype, the dimension d of this vector will be equal to the length of global vocabulary while for the second prototype it will be equal to k.

In the test phase, we will represent an unseen malware file as a vector as well, of equal dimension as the prototype vector. We will then use the Equations 1 and 2 to determine the family for each malware file in the test set. This process is described in the section below.

3   Malware Family Identification

In order to assign a family label to a test malware file, we used prototype based classification as described in Section 2.1. For each test malware file, we created a test vector consisting of the strings in the prototype. This is described in Section 3.1. For both kinds of prototypes, we performed malware family identification for each malware file by using this method. For the prototype based upon prominent strings, we further explored its use in two different ways, which we describe in Sections 3.2 and 3.3.

3.1   Exact Match

In this method, in order to classify a malware file, we first calculated a list of tf-idf values for the unique strings in that file. We then tested this file against the prototype of each family. For every string in the prototype, we took the tf-idf value from the above list in order to construct a test vector of that file. Those strings that are in the prototype but not in the file will have a value of 0. In the case where we use the whole vocabulary as a prototype, this vector will mostly be a sparse vector. For the prominent strings prototype, the vector will usually be sparse when we test against the prototype of a family that the file does not belong to. We then calculated the similarity between this vector and the vector of tf-idf values for the prototype by using cosine similarity between these two vectors (Equation 2). This process corresponds to the general schema of prototype-based approach.

3.2   Nearest Match

Nearest Matches captures not only exact same strings but also strings that are similar to the prominent strings. Two strings are considered similar if their Jaccard Coefficient is higher than certain threshold. Wei et al. (2009) generalised the definition of Jaccard Coefficient to strings [7]. Their definition of Jaccard Coefficient is as follows:

$$\text{Jaccard}(s,t) = \frac{\text{ILD}(s,t)}{|s| + |t| - \text{ILD}(s,t)} \tag{6}$$

where ILD is the Levenshtein distance that computes the minimum number of edits (insertions, deletions and substitutions) required to convert the string s to the string t. It is worth mentioning that ILD is taking into account the order of the letters in the strings, thus strings like 'silent' and 'listen' are not the exact same strings according to the distance measure.

The prominent strings set with their normalized term frequency values were used as prototype for classification. Each of the prominent strings was compared with strings in the test file in order to find similar strings. The sum of tf values of all these similar strings is taken as the value representing that prominent string in the test query vector. We weighted the strings by only using the tf and not the tf-idf because strings found to be similar to the prominent strings might not appear in the training dataset at all, which means that we do not have their idf.

3.3 Absence of PS

Since prominent strings are representatives of a malware family, lack of these strings in any sample labeled as a certain family raises dubiousness about its labeling. We used this idea to check the labeling of files done by anti-virus vendors. If the intersection between prominent strings sets and the set of all unique words in the test file is low, then the label is said to be incorrect. This is two class classification since we can only classify a file as either being correctly classified or misclassified. Although this method cannot predict the correct class of a given file, it is beneficial in terms of speed because it will need very low number of computations after we have built the prototype.

4 Dataset

We used a dataset consisting of 1504 malware files from our university's malware database. For each malware file, family labels were obtained by using Virustotal[1], which takes the MD5, SHA1 or SHA256 of a malware file and provides the family labels for a sample from different anti-virus vendors. When the data was collected, Virustotal provided results from 47 anti-virus products. For each malware file, n-way vendor agreement was found out, where n denotes the highest number of vendors that agreed upon the same family for the file. For example, given a malware file f, if out of a set of family labels $\{l_1, l_2, ..., l_m\}$, the label l_i was assigned by n malware vendors to f while all the other labels were assigned by less than n malware vendors, then f is said to have n-way vendor agreement. Our dataset contains only those files with at least *5-way vendor agreement*, i.e. at least five vendors assigned that same family label to the malware file. The Table 1 shows the distribution of files with n-way vendor agreement.

Our dataset has malware files belonging to 10 families. The distribution of files across these families is not uniform. The distribution of the files by family is given in Table 2. The data files we used were unpacked by our university's Malware and Forensic Research Lab and contain only printable strings. We extracted the strings from the file by splitting at null character and also performed a preprocessing step to remove all those strings whose length is less than five characters. The rationale behind removing small strings is that these are repeated across families, making them less likely to be prominent. They only increase the noise in the data, as well as the processing time.

---

[1] https://www.virustotal.com/

Table 1. File Distribution with n-way Vendor Agreement

Vendors (n)	Number of Files
5 - 10	424
11 - 15	235
16 - 20	269
21 - 25	314
26 - 30	206
31 - 35	56

Table 2. Number of files per family

Family	Files in the family
Bifros	333
Buzus	166
Gamevance	286
Kazy	99
Kbot	107
Medfos	100
Ramnit	115
Sality	92
Virut	93
Zeus	113
Total	**1504**

5   Experiments and Results

We conducted four types of experiments to classify malware files: 1) using the global vocabulary as a prototype to test using exact matches, which we referred to as *Exact Matches: Global vocabulary*; 2) using a prominent strings set as prototype for each family to test using exact matches, which we referred to as *Exact Matches: PS*; 3) relaxation of experiment 2 to allow the consideration of strings that are not a perfect match but are similar, which we referred to as *Nearest Matches*; and 4) using absence of exact matches of prominent strings to find files that are wrongly labeled, which we referred to as *Absence of PS*. There are several parameters being used in our experiments, such as number of prominent strings (N), absence threshold and string similarity threshold. We performed tuning of these parameters by running experiments on a smaller dataset containing 20 files per family. In addition, we used 10 fold cross validation to test the consistency of our classification model.

Figure 1(a) shows the results for our first experiment *Exact Match: Global Vocabulary*. This method uses prototypes based on global vocabulary and has been described in Section 3.1. As the graphs show, the global accuracy is 91.02% and the accuracy values are almost above 80% for every family except for *Kbot*.

In Table 3 we have listed some of the prominent strings (PS) captured by our model for each family. As the table suggests, the prominent strings are

Table 3. Prominent Strings (PS) per family

Family	Prominent Strings
Bifros	!This program cannot be run in DOS mode.\r\r\n, GetProcessHeap, HeapAlloc, kernel32.dll
Buzus	Boolean, TObject, 333333333333333333, comctl32.dll
Gamevance	Are you sure you want to cancel XOBNI Outlook Plugin Installation?, NativeQuad, Rd long, userenv.dll
Kazy	__vbaCyMulI2, MyComputer, __vbaUI1I2, ThreadSafeObjectProvider'1
Kbot	MSVCRT.dll, .rdata, MSVCRT.dll, uEKKxGLup
Medfos	CoGetCallContext, DeleteTimerQueueTimer, GetProcessPriorityBoost, StgCreatePropStg
Ramnit	.data, @h4a@, ;;;;;;;;;, strrchr
Sality	SAF.ocx, CustomizationManager.SAFDesigner, SAF.SAFFloat, SAF.SAFMaskedText
Virut	__p__commode, _exit, wwwwwwwwwww, _controlfp
Zeus	abcdefghijklmnopqrstuvwxyz, ^+*;W, GetLastInputInfo, /2ABj37

highly disjoint across the families. We created a prototype based upon prominent strings and used it to perform our other experiment *Exact Match: PSS* described in Section 3.1. Each of the prototypes consists of 20 such prominent strings per family. The goal of this experiment was to determine the performance of applying prominent strings in the identification of malware files. Figure 1(b) shows the accuracy obtained for each family as well as the accuracy for the entire test set by using this method. The global accuracy is 80.52%. The families with less accuracy and thus more errors are *Kbot*, *Kazy* and *Sality*. When we calculated the average number of prominent strings per malware sample, *Kbot* had the lowest value of 1.31. This might be the reason that the accuracy for *Kbot* is so low. Similarly, *Kazy* also has the second lowest value of 4.62. The *Exact Match: PSS* experiment was completed within 23 minutes while the *Exact Match: Global Vocabulary* took around 44 minutes to complete. The *Exact Match: PSS* experiment takes only half of the time than the *Exact Match: Global Vocabulary* experiment while still giving reasonable accuracy.

Our *Nearest Match* experiment was designed to analyze change in performance when a more relaxed comparison than exact matches is performed, as we explained in Section 3.2. We used a fixed number (0.8) as the similarity threshold between two strings. Figure 1(c) shows the accuracy obtained for this experiment. The graphs show a decrease in the global accuracy to 59.57%. *Ramnit* and *Kbot* families show an error of nearly 100%, which indicates that this method is not good enough to distinguish among families. Since the worst results were obtained by using *Nearest match* we also tried using just intersections instead of a prototype based approach on *Nearest Match* to check if we can get better results this way. To test a file against a PSS, we took an intersection between the set of all strings in the test file and the PSS. Since we are using the *Nearest Match* method, we also consider similar strings as belonging to the intersection (string similarity is the same as before). The results of this experiment are

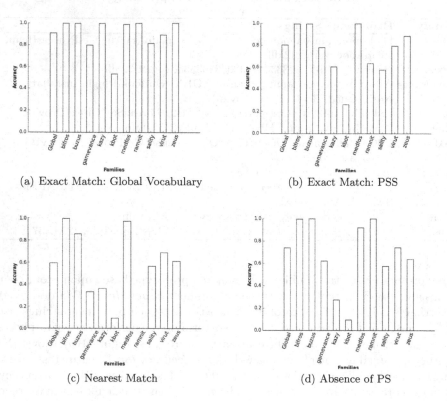

(a) Exact Match: Global Vocabulary

(b) Exact Match: PSS

(c) Nearest Match

(d) Absence of PS

Fig. 1. Accuracy for four different methods: Exact Match: PSS, Nearest Match, Absence of PS and Exact Match: Global Vocabulary. (*PS* = Prominent Strings, *PSS* = Prominent Strings Sets)

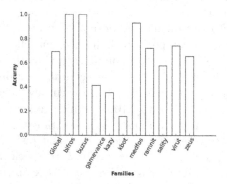

Fig. 2. Accuracy for Nearest Matches using intersections

presented in Figure 2. As we can see the performance was increased to 69.21%, but we still have families with less that 50% accuracy.

5.1 Absence of PS

We designed this experiment to investigate if the absence of PS in a given file indicates that a wrong family label was given to that particular file, as we described in Section 3.3. But since we do not have the ground truth to compare against and we only have the vendor agreement data, we cannot really report the accuracy for this case because any instance found as mislabeled will be counted as an error. We can only compare with the vendor agreement data. Figure 1(d) shows a graph of the percentage of files that were found by this method to be correctly labeled by the vendors across different malware families. The total agreement is around 74.1%. For families like *Bifros*, *Buzus* and *Ramnit*, the label given by vendors seems to be correct as this method also agrees with the vendors 100% for these families. However, for certain families like *kbot* and *kazy*, this method does not really agree with the vendor labels. These are the same families for which other methods too have lower accuracy. As shown by this method, the lower accuracy may have been the result of the files actually being mislabeled by the vendors.

5.2 Correlation with Vendor Agreement

We tried to find the correlation between n-way vendor agreement and the accuracy that our method achieves. Since we use vendor agreement as the gold standard to find the accuracy, this relation is important. We observed that for higher vendor agreement, our method also has higher accuracy.

Figure 3 shows the accuracy of our system per n-way vendor agreement for Experiments *Exact Match: Global Vocabulary* and *Exact Match: PSS*. Among the 47 vendors, if 30-35 of them agree upon the family of a malware file, the average accuracy for such a file is mostly between 80% to 100% in both experiments. On the other hand, if only 5-10 vendors agree upon the family, the average accuracy drops to 30% for Experiment *Exact Match: PSS* and to 56% for Experiment

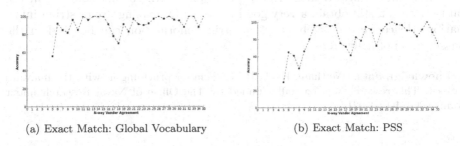

(a) Exact Match: Global Vocabulary   (b) Exact Match: PSS

Fig. 3. Accuracy per n-way vendor agreement

Exact Match: Global Vocabulary. In this case, since the vendor agreement is so low, the family label assigned by these vendors might not even be correct for that malware file. So, even when our results do not agree with the vendor label, our method could be correctly classifying these malware files. But we have no way of knowing this right now. In Figure 3(a), the relative change in accuracy is not that pronounced across vendor agreement since the accuracy of this method is very high in itself and thus, most of the accuracy values are in a small range.

6   Conclusion and Future Work

The accuracy for all our methods is above 80% except for the nearest match method. Our *Exact Match: Global Vocabulary* method that considered all the unique strings in the training files was the best with an accuracy of 91.02%. The low accuracy just for the nearest match method could be due to the fact that we allowed a high degree of freedom for detecting near similar strings. Also, as evidenced by our experiments, by using exact matches of prominent strings, we are getting good accuracy. So, there is no need to perform extra computations to find nearest matches and use the *Nearest Match* method. Even though *Exact Match: PSS* cannot achieve the accuracy as obtained by *Exact Match: Global Vocabulary*, PSS highly reduces the dimension of the prototype vector. So, *Exact Match: PSS* will help to decrease the computational time while still being highly accurate.

The malware dataset was collected by using the 5-way vendor agreement method. For the time being, we chose to believe that we are taking a good gold standard as each malware sample's labeling is agreed upon by at least five anti-virus vendors. But we do acknowledge that there might be some labeling errors in this dataset, especially when n is low. During prototype creation, this might have instilled some errors into our models. Also, we could be correctly classifying the malware even when our label does not agree with the vendor label. In the future, we need to explore a more rigorous approach to gather a good gold standard dataset. Although our family labels were sourced from the 5-way vendor agreement method, our system can very well be used when fewer than 5 vendors are in agreement. Also, it could be applied to newly arrived malwares, before most of the vendors have given their verdict.

Our results clearly demonstrate that despite of these shortcomings in the dataset, we can still obtain a very good accuracy by making use of string information. Hence we can safely say that string information can be used in the classification of malware.

Acknowledgments. We thank Kevin R Mitchem for providing us with the malware dataset. This research was partially funded by The Office of Naval Research under grant N00014-12-1-0217.

References

1. Park, Y., Reeves, D., Mulukutla, V., Sundaravel, B.: Fast malware classification by automated behavioral graph matching. In: Proceedings of the Sixth Annual Workshop on Cyber Security and Information Intelligence Research, CSIIRW 2010, pp. 45:1–45:4. ACM, New York (2010)
2. Bailey, M., Oberheide, J., Andersen, J., Mao, Z.M., Jahanian, F., Nazario, J.: Automated classification and analysis of internet malware. In: Kruegel, C., Lippmann, R., Clark, A. (eds.) RAID 2007. LNCS, vol. 4637, pp. 178–197. Springer, Heidelberg (2007)
3. Tian, R., Batten, L., Islam, M., Versteeg, S.: An automated classification system based on the strings of trojan and virus families. In: 2009 4th International Conference on Malicious and Unwanted Software (MALWARE), pp. 23–30 (2009)
4. Shabtai, A., Moskovitch, R., Elovici, Y., Glezer, C.: Detection of malicious code by applying machine learning classifiers on static features: A state-of-the-art survey. Information Security Technical Report 14, 16–29 (2009)
5. Han, E.-H.S., Karypis, G.: Centroid-based document classification: Analysis and experimental results. In: Zighed, D.A., Komorowski, J., Żytkow, J.M. (eds.) PKDD 2000. LNCS (LNAI), vol. 1910, pp. 424–431. Springer, Heidelberg (2000)
6. Debole, F., Sebastiani, F.: Supervised term weighting for automated text categorization. In: Proceedings of the 2003 ACM Symposium on Applied Computing, SAC 2003, pp. 784–788. ACM, New York (2003)
7. Wei, C., Sprague, A., Warner, G.: Clustering malware-generated spam emails with a novel fuzzy string matching algorithm. In: Proceedings of the 2009 ACM Symposium on Applied Computing, pp. 889–890. ACM (2009)

Applying Data Mining in Urban Environments Using the Roles Model Approach

Claudia Liliana Zúñiga-Cañón[1,2](✉) and Juan Carlos Burguillo[1]

[1] Information Technologies Group GTI, Department of Telematics Engineering,
University of Vigo, Vigo, Spain
[2] Research Group COMBA R & D, Department of Engineering,
University of Santiago de Cali, Cali, Colombia
clzuniga@ieee.org,{clzuniga,J.C.Burguillo}@uvigo.es

Abstract. One of the main challenges in urban computing is to interpret the behaviors of the individuals, and so to provide services for suppling their needs. Data mining offers very powerful tools that can be used to analyze data in urban environments. Our research uses the UrbanContext roles model to identify the states of the individuals within urban environments. Then, it applies supervised classification data mining techniques to the results obtained, and uses decision trees in order to facilitate the analysis of the individuals' behavior. Finally, we present the prediction results obtained from a study made about the roles that individuals adopt depending on their context. From these data we successfully predict the different types of services we can offer in an urban environment.

Keywords: Urban computing · Data mining · Decision tree · Weka

1 Introduction

Information and knowledge is growing very fast every day due to new devices, social networks, new trends like the Internet of Things, the search for ubiquitous spaces and intelligent environments. All this complexity lead to the identification of the real needs of individuals taking into account such a big database containing all types of information.

However, applying techniques to predict situations and behaviors is not enough. An understanding about how an individual interacts from the human point of view is needed to complement the different theories have been developed in the anthropological field along time to describe the Human behavior.

Thus, we have developed UrbanContext [1], a model based on the Theory of Roles by Erving Goffman [2], that allows the modeling of the information obtained from the individuals, and the interpretation of their states in order to understand their behavior within urban environments.

The main contribution of this paper is the use of the UrbanContext roles model, and data mining techniques, to analyze different individuals' states and

© Springer International Publishing Switzerland 2014
A.L.C. Bazzan and K. Pichara (Eds.): IBERAMIA 2014, LNAI 8864, pp. 698–709, 2014.
DOI: 10.1007/978-3-319-12027-0_56

to apply decision trees over these data to predict, with good outcomes, the type of services that should be provided within an urban environment.

This paper is organized as follows: The next section introduces the state of the art. Sections 3 and 4 describe our UrbanContext architecture and the roles model respectively. Section 5 describes the use of data mining techniques in urban environments, and section 6 presents an experimental scenario based on the states of the individuals obtained through the roles model. Then, we analyze in section 7 the data obtained by using knowledge algorithms as decision trees, and we analyze the results. Finally, we present our conclusions and future work.

2   State of Art

Pervasive computing has evolved in the last decades, through different stages for building a brand new ubiquitous world, and along such evolution it has experimented three main generations [3]:

- A first generation oriented for the connectivity.
- A second generation oriented for knowledge representation, as well as context-awareness.
- A third, more complex, generation extends the two previous ones, and it is mainly focused on discovering services and interactions; and it is oriented to social context, live data mining, and real-time social observatories.

Under this framework we address urban computing, an area defined by Paulos and Jenkins [4] as the intersection between mobile and social computing. In urban computing, to model the context, and to understand the individual states in the urban environment is very relevant, so it covers many aspects of sensing and data mining in urban atmospheres.

Several works are focusing on understanding the individuals needs, as well as discovering the individual interactions and relationships to develop fully adapted systems. One of the first works was developed by Paulos and Goodman [5] who used the concept "Familiar Strangers" defined by the psychologist Stanley Milgram [6]. Familiar Strangers are individuals that we repeatedly observe but yet do not interact with directly. This work uses such model to identify the properties, and the phenomenon, of the relations among familiar strangers in public environments.

Others proposals use sensor networks technologies to identify the behavior and the interactions of individuals in urban environments. Some examples are the Cityware Project [7] that maps social encounters using Bluetooth as the network technology, or the project made by [8] that uses the NFC (Near Field Communication) technology to find similar characteristics among the users located in the same place at the same time, in order to make recommendations.

Nowadays, different projects are applying data mining techniques in urban environments. Zhang [9] is developing a study about the relevance of temporal dimension to model the urban activity through the LBSN (Location-based Social

Network). Meanwhile Silva [10] is comparing data from participatory sensors networks to extract information, and to observe the patterns of user movements.

These works have obtained good results regarding different perspectives of the global picture. But if we combine these experiences, and also state human behavior theories as a basic foundation, we would be able to design systems more adapted to the overcoming ubiquitous World.

Taking all together, our research is grounded by these previous works and by human behavior theories to perform a structured data mapping. We have created UrbanContext [1], a model based on the Theory of Roles [2] that allows mapping the urban context in order to obtain a database of the different individuals' states.

3   UrbanContext: Architecture

UrbanContext architecture defines five components for modeling urban computing systems [1]: Roles, Semantics, Information Management (Cloud), Services and Interface. Among them, the Roles Component is in charge of interpreting the different states that an individual assume in his daily interaction, in order to provide adapted services suitable to his needs. This Roles Component has four subcomponents [11]: Urban Agent, Urban Atmosphere, Context, and Context Management (see Fig. 1). Each of those subcomponents has a specific function defined next.

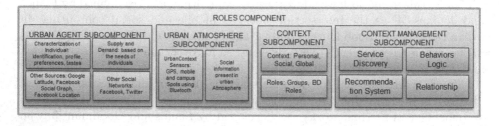

Fig. 1. Roles Component in UrbanContext

The Urban Agent Subcomponent is in charge of obtaining the complete characterization of the individual.

The Urban Atmosphere Subcomponent is the one that captures the information from the environment, regarding space, time and the type of available technology.

The Context Subcomponent identifies the context where the individual participates, whether a personal, a social or a global context. In this subcomponent the roles adopted by an individual are identified. Those might belong to a series of predetermined groups such as: personal roles, family roles, professional roles or others. For each group of roles there are different states as friend, boyfriend/girlfriend, brother/sister, son/daughter, among others.

The Context Management Subcomponent is in charge of processing all the information that has been obtained, and it returns the correspondent services suggested for each state of the individual.

4   UrbanContext: Roles Model

UrbanContext is based on the Theory of Roles [2] by Erving Goffman, which states that an individual is constantly playing different roles that condition his behavior, somehow similar to the work of an actor in a big play.

The UrbanContext roles model is making a characterization of the individual, and identifies the atmosphere where he is involved. This model is cataloguing physical and social environments through their context: public, private, social, and it uses the Theory of Roles to understand individual interactions.

Besides, the UrbanContext roles model uses a multi-tier approach to manage the context, dividing it in three main parts: global, social and personal:

- *Global Context* is fixed to an individual in an open space of the urban atmosphere. This context manages all what people publicly share through a set of services around a public place: a concert, the meeting in a square or a spontaneous congregation.
- *Social Context* corresponds to what is obtained from socializing with other individuals; for example, friends, acquaintances and people the individual get in contact with.
- *Personal Context* is based on the individual's own world, the one that is only available to him. In this space, the user is represented as a big bubble with some needs, fears, concerns, ideas and tastes.

The UrbanContext roles model defines a second ranking of abstraction that allows to offer customization, and most importantly user privacy. Therefore for every context in the urban atmosphere an individual can play different roles hierarchically structured as:

- *Role Groups:* Personal, Family, Professional or Academic, Social and Rest of the World Roles.
- *Role Categories:* Within each Role Group we have created several categories that identify the role the individual is playing, i.e., father, uncle, teacher, friend, or just himself.

Hence, we can illustrate a series of steps that describe the behavior of the Roles Component in Figure 2.

The UrbanContext roles model can characterize several individuals' states, defining if they want to be disconnected from the system or if the user wants to play a certain role in a particular spatial or temporal scenario in the urban environment.

Individuals can release public information and needs according to the role and the context they are at a certain moment. This information is fed into a knowledge base that identifies the role of the individual in an urban environment to be able to provide the right services adapted to his needs.

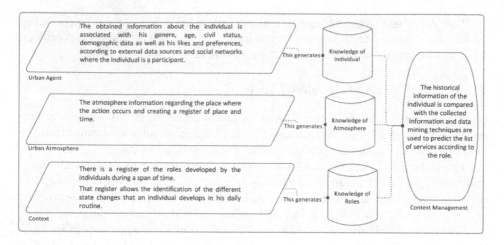

Fig. 2. Identification Process for the States of the Individual

5   Data Mining Techniques in Urban Environments

The use of data mining techniques in urban environments allows us to understand and to discover new relevant information in order to model urban systems. Data mining is a part of the knowledge discovery process and is in charge of extracting interesting information that has not been known before, but could be potentially useful regarding user services [12].

The data mining techniques are classified in: non-supervised techniques (descriptive) and supervised techniques (predictive). Non-supervised techniques are used to induce patterns from non-labeled data; these patterns are useful for the exploratory data analysis through clustering and association. The supervised techniques are used to induce models or theories from labeled class data; these induced models can be typically used to predict and to classify [13].

Hence, the selection of a particular data mining technique will depend on the research problem to be tackled. In a study realized by Pan [14], different scenarios to apply data mining in urban environments were presented. A classification technique was described as appropriate to work when recognizing the activities performed by the individual.

A classification technique must identify the class to which each sample belongs, from a model evolved from a set of labelled data training. Thus, within the classification techniques, we can find different alternatives such as: decision trees, neural networks, rule induction, bayesian network and genetic algorithms.

Decision trees share some similarities with the human behavior, so they can be useful when analyzing individuals. Decision trees are a subset of supervised learning methods, which are trained with historical data, and they use the results obtained from these data to generate predictions. The use of decision trees in data mining offers a vast variety of algorithms to predict such as: ID3 [15], C4.5 [16] (J48 Weka), Decision Stump [17] as well as other algorithms used to work with trees like: AD Tree, BF Tree, FT, J48 Graft, LAD Tree, LMT, M5P, NBTree, Random Tree, REP Tree, Simple Cart, y Random Forest.

Hence, our main objective was to apply supervised classification techniques (predictive) through decision trees over the behavior states of the individual identified by the UrbanContex roles model. The expected outcome is to obtain the appropriate classification rules to predict services.

6   Data Description Obtained with the UrbanContext Roles Model

We performed a previous study using the UrbanContext roles model, through a focus group composed by 20 people of different age and sex. We monitored their interaction during 24 hours. In the experiment, participants were asked to select an active day in urban environments in order to identify the different change of roles they experienced.

The tests were developed in different places and times. Each individual had an assigned week, and was free to select the day for the application of the test. The test begins at waking up and finishes at the end of the day. Each individual had to report the context, the place, the time, the assumed roles as well as the information (s)he wanted to publish, together with the needs (s)he had when playing the different roles along the test.

The purpose of this test is twofold. First to know the different states that individuals may face along the day. And then, from the results obtained, we can to set up an initial user model, with a set of generic services that will be adapted automatically on the run to every user by means of his personal device: mobile phone, tablet, etc.

As a result from this experiment, three sources of information were obtained. They were gathered in a database of the individual, a database of the atmosphere and a database of the roles played by the users (see Table 1).

These three knowledge bases were filtered, and then a classification of the information was performed identifying for each individual:

- *The number of daily interactions.*
- *Frequency of state changing.*
- *Needs for interaction.*
- *The services to be offered according to the played role.*

Thus we create a clean and post-processed data source named *"Experimen-tRoles.arff"*, and we have defined the class *"services"* for every register (we will refer to these two elements in the next section). In the experiment we have identified 25 types of roles played by individuals, and we have defined 13 services corresponding to these roles.

7   Data Analysis of the Roles Model Using Decision Trees

A decision tree is a structure of nodes and branches that has internal nodes associated with a decision and leaf nodes associated with a class label [18]. The trees are built following a top-down procedure, starting with the root node, until

Table 1. Knowledge DB

Roles Component –Subcomponent	Entity	Knowledge Base	Attributes
Urban Agent Subcomponent	Individual	BD Knowledge of the Individual	Name, Age, Marital status, Demographic data, Likes and preferences
Urban Atmosphere Subcomponent	Atmosphere	BD Knowledge of the Urban Atmosphere	Time and Place
Context Subcomponent	Roles	BD Knowledge of the Roles	Context (personal, social, global), Role Category, Role Type, Needs according to the role.

getting the specific structure. In decision trees the most important step is the identification of the selected attribute as a root node [13], then a classification can be built.

To start the analysis of the decision tree, we use the training dataset *"ExperimentRoles.arff"* obtained from the historical data collected in the previous experiment.

7.1 Applying the Classifier

To build the classifier we have to choose the decision algorithm which will be applied to the data. For this, we selected a group of five decision tree algorithms:

- **C4.5 (J48)** [16] is part of the induction methods TDIDT (Top Down Induction Trees). C4.5 generates decision trees and rules from pre-classified data. C4.5 is a divide-and-conquer method, and it is based on the dataset partition derived from the Gain Ratio criterium.
- **LAD Tree** [19] algorithm generates a multi-class alternating decision tree using the LogitBoost strategy.
- **NBTree** [20] algorithm generates a decision tree with naive Bayes classifiers at the leaves.
- **Random Tree** [21] algorithm builds a tree that considers K randomly chosen attributes at each node, and performs no pruning.
- **REP Tree** [21] is a fast-learning method that creates decision trees using the Information Gain criterium.

These algorithms were applied on the training dataset *"ExperimentRoles.arff"* using the data mining tool Weka (machine learning software workbench) [22][23].

Weka is an open source tool developed by Weikato University, and it allows to apply different data mining techniques on big data sources.

The training dataset *"ExperimentRoles.arff"* is composed by 90 selected registers from individual interactions collected in the experiment detailed in section 6. We apply the algorithms, according to the size of the data, calculating the accuracy percentage using cross-validation with $k = 10$. Cross-validation calculates the accuracy percentage making a cross validation of k folds. See the percentage of accuracy for every algorithm over the training data set in Table 2.

Table 2. Accuracy of Services Prediction

Algorithm	Accuracy %	Feature of the Decision Tree
C4.5(J48)	72.2%	Root Node RoleType
LAD Tree	72.2%	CAC
NBTree	77.7%	Root Node RoleCategory
Random Tree	77.8%	Root Node Location
REP Tree	**78.88%**	**Root Node RoleType**

The **REP Tree algorithm** offered the best results with an accuracy percentage of 78.8%. From this result, we can get the decision tree for services prediction according to individuals' states, where the root node is the **RoleType** attribute.

7.2 Identification of the Attribute Evaluator

The REP Tree algorithm discovers what is the best attribute to classify the data. To illustrate this result we present here an analysis of the available attributes in the training dataset. We present next four main attributes:

- *ContextType* identifies the context of individual: Personal, Social or Global.
- *RoleCategory* identifies the group of roles: Personal, Family, Professional or Academic, Social and Rest of the World.
- *RoleType* identifies the type of role inside every Category, such as: friend, father, teacher, partner, user, or pedestrian.
- *Location* identifies the place where the individual is located.

From this selection, the REP Tree algorithm evaluates each one of the four attributes to discover the best one, in order to classify the data, attending the Information Gain criterium. This criterium is based on entropy, i.e., the uncertainty in a training dataset for having more than one possible classification [24]. The Information Gain measures the reduction of entropy produced by the partition of the training set according to a selected attribute. To calculate the Information Gain for every selected attribute we use the equations (1,2,3).

– *Entropy of a Set*

$$H(X) = \sum_{i=1}^{n} [-P(x_i) \log_2 P(x_i)] \tag{1}$$

– *Entropy of the Result Sets*

$$H(X,Y) = \sum_{i=1}^{n} [(P(x_i) * H(x_i)]] \tag{2}$$

– *Gain*

$$Gain(X,Y) = H(X) - H(X,Y) \tag{3}$$

We present the results obtained after calculating the values of Information Gain for those four attributes in Table 3.

Table 3. Results of Attribute Analysis

Attribute	Information Gain
RoleCategory	1.515
RoleType	2.464
Location	2.192
ContextType	0.702

Therefore, REP Tree selects an attribute evaluator, which is an edge attribute that separates the data from the different services. For the Information Gain criterium the attribute with mayor gain becomes the best option, and in this case *RoleType* with a Gain = 2,464, is the attribute evaluator selected.

7.3 Analysis of the Results

The REP Tree algorithm works in two stages, first creating a set of rules which over-fits the training data, and second pruning the rules set using the part of the dataset that were not used in the training phase [21]. The data evaluation through REP Tree generated successful results in the services prediction for the individuals according to the *RoleType* attribute. As said before, we have obtaining a prediction percentage of 78.8%. Besides, the tree structure generated by REP Tree during the evaluation is simple and adequate.

We represent in Figure 3 the relation between *RoleType* attribute vs. *"Services Class"*. We can see the distribution of roles identified during the experiment, and the services assigned to every individual's state. For example we identified that when the individual plays *User* or *Client* roles the services assigned are the *Commercials* ones (see Fig. 3).

This after-test evaluation allowed us to identify a set of 25 roles, played by the individuals, for those we have assigned 13 different services according to their

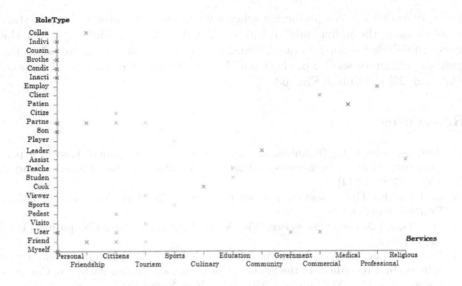

Fig. 3. Services by Type of Role (RoleType)

status (Personal, Friendship, Citizens, Tourism, Sports, Culinary, Education, Community, Government, Commercial, Medical, Professional and Religious).

Besides, during the experience we have identified situations where individuals play more than a role at the same time, making necessary to have additional mechanisms to determinate the role priority for service prediction. So, we consider the intersection or union set operators to provide the right set of services when an individual submits more than one role in the same time window.

8   Conclusions and Future Work

In this work we have obtained three individual knowledge bases using the Urban-Context roles model. From these results and applying data mining techniques, by means of decision trees, we were able to identify the attribute *RoleType* as the best classifier for the services prediction.

We have evaluated five classification algorithms on a total of 90 generated registers for the 20 participants of this experience, succeeding in identifying that the algorithm REP Tree is the more appropriate for the services prediction, obtaining an accuracy of 78.88%.

From the results obtained, after applying these data mining techniques, we have shown that the UrbanContext roles model allow us to identify, with good prediction indexes, the services according to the roles and the environment where the individual is involved. As a result, we were able to predict 13 different types of services for a set of 25 identified roles in the experiment.

As future work, we plan to make a modification of the basic prediction algorithm, involving a weighting function for the prediction of services under a adaptive scheme. This prediction scheme would allow to handle the cold start problem using the individuals' historical data. We also consider important the use of time-based services in our UrbanContext model. So we plan to adapt the basic algorithm for service prediction and to implement it in an Open Ubiquous Platform [25] at Oulu in Finland.

References

1. Zuniga-Canon, C.L., Burguillo, J.: Urbancontext: A management model for pervasive environments in user-oriented urban computing. Computer Science Journal **15**(1), 75–88 (2014)
2. Goffman, E.: The presentation of self in everyday life. Doubleday anchor books, Doubleday (1959)
3. Ferscha, A.: 20 years past weiser: What's next? IEEE Pervasive Computing **11**(1), 52–61 (2012)
4. Paulos, E., Jenkins, T.: Urban probes: Encountering our emerging urban atmospheres. In: Proceedings of the SIGCHI Conference on Human Factors in Computing Systems, CHI 2005, pp. 341–350. ACM, New York (2005)
5. Paulos, E., Goodman, E.: The familiar stranger: Anxiety, comfort, and play in public places. In: Proceedings of the SIGCHI Conference on Human Factors in Computing Systems, CHI 2004, pp. 223–230. ACM, New York (2004)
6. Milgram, S.: The individual in a social world: essays and experiments. Addison-Wesley series in social psychology. Addison-Wesley Pub. Co. (1977)
7. Kostakos, V., O'Neill, E.: Urban computing to bridge online and real-world social networks, ch. 13, pp. 196–205. IGI Global (2008)
8. Munoz-Organero, M., Ramíez-González, G.A., Munoz-Merino, P.J., Delgado Kloos, C.: A collaborative recommender system based on space-time similarities. IEEE Pervasive Computing **9**(3), 81–87 (2010)
9. Zhang, K., Jin, Q., Pelechrinis, K., Lappas, T.: On the importance of temporal dynamics in modeling urban activity. In: Proceedings of the 2nd ACM SIGKDD International Workshop on Urban Computing, UrbComp 2013, pp. 7:1–7:8. ACM, New York (2013)
10. Silva, T.H., Vaz de Melo, P.O.S., Almeida, J.M., Salles, J., Loureiro, A.A.F.: A comparison of foursquare and instagram to the study of city dynamics and urban social behavior. In: Proceedings of the 2nd ACM SIGKDD International Workshop on Urban Computing, UrbComp 2013, pp. 4:1–4:8. ACM, New York (2013)
11. Cañón, C.L.Z., Rial, J.C.B.: Modeling the urban context through the theory of roles. In: O'Grady, M.J., Vahdat-Nejad, H., Wolf, K.-H., Dragone, M., Ye, J., Röcker, C., O'Hare, G. (eds.) AmI Workshops 2013. CCIS, vol. 413, pp. 257–265. Springer, Heidelberg (2013)
12. Fayyad, U.M., Piatetsky-Shapiro, G., Smyth, P.: From Data Mining to Knowledge Discovery: An Overview. In: Advances in Knowledge Discovery and Data Mining, pp. 1–34. American Association for Artificial Intelligence, Menlo Park (1996)
13. Furnkranz, J., Gamberger, D., Lavrac, N.: Machine learning and data mining. In: Foundations of Rule Learning, Cognitive Technologies, pp. 1–17. Springer, Heidelberg (2012)
14. Pan, G., Qi, G., Zhang, W., Li, S., Wu, Z., Yang, L.: Trace analysis and mining for smart cities: issues, methods, and applications. IEEE Communications Magazine **51**(6), 120–126 (2013)

15. Quinlan, J.R.: Induction of decision trees. Mach. Learn. **1**, 81–106 (1986)
16. Quinlan, J.R.: C4.5: Programs for Machine Learning. Morgan Kaufmann Publishers Inc., San Francisco (1993)
17. Freund, Y., Schapire, R.E.: A decision-theoretic generalization of on-line learning and an application to boosting. J. Comput. Syst. Sci. **55**(1), 119–139 (1997)
18. Murty, M., Devi, V.: Decision trees. In: Pattern Recognition. Undergraduate Topics in Computer Science, pp. 123–146. Springer, London (2011)
19. Holmes, G., Pfahringer, B., Kirkby, R., Frank, E., Hall, M.: Multiclass alternating decision trees. In: Elomaa, T., Mannila, H., Toivonen, H. (eds.) ECML 2002. LNCS (LNAI), vol. 2430, pp. 161–172. Springer, Heidelberg (2002)
20. Kohavi, R.: Scaling up the accuracy of naive-bayes classifiers: a decision-tree hybrid. In: Proceedings of the Second International Conference on Knowledge Discovery and Data Mining, pp. 202–207. AAAI Press (1996)
21. Witten, I.H., Frank, E., Hall, M.A.: Data Mining: Practical Machine Learning Tools and Techniques, 3rd edn. Morgan Kaufmann Publishers Inc., San Francisco (2011)
22. WEKA, in: Waikato Environment for Knowledge Analysis, http://www.cs.waikato.ac.nz/ml/index.html (review in May 2014)
23. Hall, M., Frank, E., Holmes, G., Pfahringer, B., Reutemann, P., Witten, I.H.: The weka data mining software: An update. SIGKDD Explor. Newsl. **11**(1), 10–18 (2009)
24. Bramer, M.: Decision tree induction: Using entropy for attribute selection. In: Principles of Data Mining, Undergraduate Topics in Computer Science, pp. 49–62. Springer, London (2013)
25. UBI, in: Open Ubiquitous Oulu-Finland, http://www.ubioulu.fi/en/ (review in May 2014)

Prostate Cancer Biopsy Recommendation through Use of Machine Learning Classification Techniques

André A. Del Grossi[✉], Helen C. de Mattos Senefonte, and Vinícius G. Quaglio

Universidade Estadual de Londrina, Rodovia Celso Garcia Cid, Km 380 - Campus Universitário, Londrina, PR 86057-970, Brasil
{andredg91,viniciusquaglio}@gmail.com, helen@uel.br

Abstract. This study proposes the investigation and application of machine learning techniques in order to aid prostate cancer diagnosis through classification in order to either recommend or spare patients from biopsy, an essential procedure for confirmation of diagnosis. Pre-treatment variables collected from patients of the Academic Hospital of State University of Londrina, Brazil (HU-UEL) from 2005 to 2010 include age, PSA (prostate specific antigen) marker, DRE (digital rectum examination), free/total PSA and PSA density value. Models have been generated using logistic regression, two artificial neural networks (*MultiLayer-Perceptron*, *MLPClassifier*) and two decision tree algorithms (*ADTree*, *PART*). Obtained accuracy indicators for models were 69.4 %, 70.5 %, 71.14 %, 71.8 % and 71.48 % respectively.

1 Introduction

Diagnosing prostate cancer in patients is an intricate process and requires biopsy, a procedure that consists in obtaining samples of prostate cell for laboratory analysis, in the majority of cases. While biopsy can aid in the confirmation of cancerous tumors, it is considered an invasive and inconvenient process– 50% of men who undergo biopsy report nuisance and discomfort during the procedure [10]. In attempts to reduce the odds a patient has to be submitted to biopsy, techniques that use clinical data obtained throughout the investigation process are used to predict and determine the need for biopsy. However, even with use of exam results, prostate cancer diagnosis is not exempt of uncertainty– Djavan et al. [9] state that high levels of PSA serum do not affirm presence of prostate cancer since elevated markers can also occur in benign prostatic diseases. Therefore, evaluating PSA solely is ineffective for it recommends patients to biopsy without necessity [29].

Recent studies suggest the introduction of mathematical and computational methods in order to support the problem such as the construction of nomograms[1] [18] based on attributes such as clinical stage, PSA and Gleason score[2] to infer a diagnostic (nomogram proposed by Kattan et al.[19]) Another widely used technique is logistic regression (LR, for short), a variant from regression analysis that aims to predict a binary

---

[1] Diagram representing relationships among values of variables [1] in such way that a line intercepting the scales of these variables provides an associated value[2].

[2] Ranking scale for prostate cancer tumors obtained from biopsy; a higher value indicates a more aggressive tumor.

© Springer International Publishing Switzerland 2014
A.L.C. Bazzan and K. Pichara (Eds.): IBERAMIA 2014, LNAI 8864, pp. 710–721, 2014.
DOI: 10.1007/978-3-319-12027-0_57

or multinomial outcome from discrete and/or continuous independent variables. Lastly, generalizable and flexible classification methods based on machine learning techniques like for example artificial neural networks (ANN) and support vector machines (SVM) arised as alternatives with implied advantages due to the capability of recognizing patterns and non-linear interrelationships among variables [9].

This work aims to evaluate and apply machine learning techniques to predict the necessity of prostate cancer biopsy using data collected from patients of the Academic Hospital of the State University of Londrina, Brazil monitored by doctor and Urology professor Horácio Moreira. It is structured as follows: in section 2 a brief overview on prostate cancer is given highlighting important concepts and problem motivation; section 3 presents and constrasts related work; materials and methods for this study, including techniques, algorithms and data set are introduced in section 4; classification results follow in section 5. Lastly, final considerations are provided in section 6 along with difficulties and suggestions for future studies.

2   Prostate Cancer

Prostate cancer is the sixth leading cause of cancer-related mortality [3] with risk factors such as age, family history and ethnicity [9]. Due to the diseases's broad biological heterogeneity [15], it is inherently difficult to detect and diagnose especially because a great deal of prostate cancers bearers do not display aggravating symptoms and are therefore not submitted to any kind of therapy [8]. Added to that is a tumor's lack of palpability, often indistiguishable via ultrassound and magnetic resonance imaging [19]. Furthermore, only a small portion of patients among confirmed diagnostics are at risk: even though one in six men will develop prostate cancer at some point in his life, only one out of ten in these cases manifest aggressive tumors [28]. Patients that lack clinical data indicative of high risk do not benefit from prostate cancer biopsy, which can cause complications such as anxiety, ache, bleeding and chance of infection as well as additional medical charges and expenses.

Prostate specific antigen (PSA) is the most widely used parameter to prematurely diagnose prostate cancer [23]– this enzyme is normally found in small quantities in the prostate, however it is often elevated in the presence of prostate cancer or other prostate disorders [6].

Due to the high number of false positives obtained through the exclusive use of PSA for prostate cancer screening, it is considered ineffective in the diagnostic inference process [26]. Despite the existence of PSA reference values according to age, values higher than 4ng/ml suggest some prostatic anomaly mostly non-cancer related such as urinary retention, prostatitis, ejaculation problems and benign prostatic hyperplasia (BPH) [7], which cause prostate inflammation with a consequential rise in PSA production [25]. Conversely, it is estimated that 20% of patients diagnosed with clinically significate prostate cancer manifest PSA markers inferior to 4ng/ml [5]. Other variables indicative of biopsy include digital rectum examination (DRE) used to identify a variation in prostate volume and free/total PSA ratio, obtained through the proportion of respective hemograms.

Similarly, an increased prostate volume does not necessarily indicate a cancerous tumor. PSA density, obtained as the ratio between PSA and prostate volume was introduced to perform a discriminatory adjustment among patients and has a threshold value of approximately 0.15 to distinguish a benign hypertrophy from a probable tumor [4]. However, daily fluctuation of the PSA indicator as well as a 10% to 30% inaccuracy in prostate volume calculation limit the clinical use of this parameter [7]– PSA readings that remain elevated during a three months window are highly indicative of prostate cancer while persistent oscillations suggest a benign disorder [27]. For the free/total PSA indicator, values lower than 0.15 (15%) suggest prostate cancer with probability above 50%; the range from 0.15 to 0.25 is considered an uncertainty zone and values higher than 0.25 indicate prostate cancer probability inferior to 10% [17].

Available treatments for confined prostate cancer include watchful monitoring, radical prostatectomy[3], brachytherapy[4] and external radiation [19]. The choice of treatment relies heavily on the diagnostic results– factors such as clinical cancer stage, additional health complications (cardiovascular problems, diabetes and other diseases), age and treatment availability are taken into consideration when a practicioner must establish the most adequate treatment for his patients [16].

3   Related Work

The application of machine learning concepts and techniques to assist in cancer related tasks is a recurring theme– it is estimated that more than 500 academic publications in medical periodicals every year [11]. However, clinical trials are published less frequently as well as studies that evaluate classification performance of computational techniques in contrast to statistical methods and nomograms [21]. Related studies mentioned below are summarized in table 1, containing key characteristics such as methods and attributes used, purpose and overall AUC measurement (area under a receiver operating characteristic (ROC) curve, a technique used to display model accuracy over distinct threshold values for classification).

Cinar et al. [15] drew a comparison between artificial neural networks and support vector machines using data from 300 patients of the Hospital of Bornova Sifa in Turkey. Attributes of the data set included weight, height, BMI, free and total PSA serum markers, prostate volume, PSA density, blood pressure, heart rate and Gleason score. Authors attained an average accuracy of 79% through usage of three distinct training techniques in ANNs and 77.2%, 81.1% e 78.9% for support vector machines with linear, polynomial and gaussian kernels respectively.

Recent studies such as Regnier-Coudert et al. [24] analyzed statistical techniques, artificial neural networks and Bayesian networks. Clinical data was supplied by the British Association of Urological Surgeons (BAUS) with variables PSA, Gleason score and clinical cancer stage to predict the pathological state of 1701 patients. Likewise, the performance of Partin tables was evaluated on the British sample of patients concluding that demographical differences between British and American patients

---

[3] Partial or full surgical removal of the prostatic gland.

[4] A form of radiotherapy where the radiation source is positioned internally or next to the area requiring treatment.

(where Partin tables are generated originally) affects classification accuracy, which resulted in 61%. The introduction of bayesian networks and artificial neural networks increase accuracy to 67% and 65% respectively.

The study conducted by Lawrentschuk et al. [20] was performed with a sample of 3025 patients from the University Health Network (UHN) in Toronto, Canada with attributes age, DRE, TRUS (transrectal ultrasound) and prostate volume. It attempts to contrast logistic regression and artificial neural networks techniques to classify patients into four categorical biopsy results. Benign tumors were identified with an average accuracy of 87%, although clinically significant prostate cancer (CSPC) and non-significative prostate cancer (NSPC) were correctly classified with a rate of 22% and 2% respectively. The original data set contained 7758 instances, however more than half of the sample data was discarded due to lack of data integrity. Marin et al. [22] proposed tactics to reduce such problems using a data set with 950 entries for prostate cancer diagnosis where 95% was compromised. These strategies include filling in average attribute values for null fields, normalization through frequency histograms, outlier detection and relevant attributes selection.

Table 1. Summary of related case studies

Authors	Techniques	Goal	Data	AUC
Cinar et al (2009) [15]	ANN; SVM	Prediction of cancer prognostic	n=300; Weight, height, BMI, PSA (total, free, density), volume, Gleason score, blood pressure	79%; 81%
Regnier-Coudert et al (2012) [24]	LR, ANN, BN	Prediction of pathological state	n=1701; PSA, Gleason score, clinical stage	61%; 65%; 67%
Djavan et al (2002) [9]	ANN	Premature cancer detection	n=1246; PSA (total, free, density) and volume	91%
Lawrentschuk et al (2011) [20]	ANN, LR	Biopsy recommendation	n=3025; PSA, DRE, TRUS, prostate volume	55%; 57%
Garzotto et al (2005) [12]	CART, LR	Biopsy recommendation	n=1433; age, family history, DRE, TRUS, PSA density	74%; 72%

Garzotto et al. [12] drew results from tests with classification and regression trees (CART) and logistic regression algorithms, reaching similar accuracy– 74% and 72% respectively. The data set comprised 1433 patients with PSA indicators lower than 10ng/mL and other attributes such as age, demographic region, family history and laboratory data (DRE, PSA density and Gleason score). The decision tree model obtained classified instances with sensibility and specificity of 95% and 37.9% respectively. Gülkesen et al. [13] conducted similar experiments using QUEST (Quick, Unbiased and Efficient Statistical Tree), a CART variant where attribute selection criteria is more flexible and missing data is imputed. With a data set containing 1830 patients, the resulting decision tree held a 0.99 sensibility rate and 0.97 specificity rate, with an estimate of 13% of patients being spared from biopsy.

4   Materials and Methods

The classifiers used in our experiments were built using Weka [14], a collection of machine learning algorithms widely adopted by academics and professionals, licensed under *GNU Public License*. Three classes of algorithms have been selected for this trial:

1. Logistic regression
2. Artificial neural networks
   (a) *MultiLayerPerceptron*
   (b) *MLPClassifier*
3. Decision trees
   (a) *ADTree*
   (b) *PART*

Standard 10-fold cross validation was performed on all tests. In section 4.1, the selected data set for training and validation of classifiers is introduced with results presented in section 5.

4.1   Data Set

Clinical data obtained from Dr. Horácio A. Moreira, urologist at the Academic Hospital of Londrina included information on 500 patients monitored by the practitioner from 2005 to 2010 along with exam results for the investigation of cancerous tumors.

Attributes in the set originated from digital rectum examination (DRE) (1 - altered, 0 - normal), total PSA hemogram results, prostate volume ultrassound, free PSA hemogram and prostate biopsy. The *adjustment* attribute is a variable computed by the physician in hopes to fine tune PSA values to patient age, regardless of prostate volume– the value for this attribute is obtained through the rules presented in figure 1.

Continuous numerical variables are displayed in table 2a. Similarly, discrete binary characteristics are shown in table 2b.

Table 2. Data set attributes (n = 500)

(a) Continuous variables

Attribute	Min	Max	Mean	Std. Dev.	Missing
age	30	100	64.4	8.4	1
prostate volume	10	405	59.26	32.38	2
psa	1.8	809.1	19.12	61.4	-
free/total psa	0.01	0.94	0.18	0.17	183

(b) Categorical variables

Attribute	T	F	Missing
adjustment	458	42	-
dre	168	306	26
biopsy	193	307	-

Out of the initial 500 patients, it is estimated that approximately 40% were not submitted to all exams, particularly free/total PSA which brings out the largest amount of missing values. Once additional factors influenced most patients towards early biopsy, subsequent exams were not recorded.

The original dataset containing all 500 cases is used as default for training and testing of classifiers with a missing values filter applied to fill null attributes. The subset with full integrity holding 305 cases is also supplied to the classifiers aiming to assess the impact caused by the number of instances in the classification performance.

if $45 \leq$ age ≤ 55 **then**
    if PSA $\leq 2,5$ **then**
        adjustment = 1
    else
        adjustment = 0
else if $55 <$ age ≤ 65 **then**
    if PSA $\leq 3,5$ **then**
        adjustment = 1
    else
        adjustment = 0
else if $65 <$ age ≤ 75 **then**
    if PSA $\leq 4,5$ **then**
        adjustment = 1
    else
        adjustment = 0
else if idade > 75 **then**
    if PSA $\leq 6,5$ **then**
        adjustment = 1
    else
        adjustment = 0

Fig. 1. Rules for obtaining *adjustment* attribute value

5   Results

5.1   Logistic Regression

A logistic regression based classifier rendered moderate performance; 69.4% (fig. 3a), equivalent to 347 of all 500 cases. Regression coefficients and odds ratios[5] obtained with confidence intervals of 95% are shown in table 3.

The probability of positive classification for an instance in the sample is given by the sum of the products between regression coefficients and its associated attribute value. The threshold value (cutoff value that defines whether an instance is classified as

---

[5] Ratio between relative odds of the occurence of the expected output, given an individual variable.

Table 3. Regression coefficients for logistic regression classifier

Attribute	Value	Odds Ratio
age	0.0424	1.0433
volume	-0.0237	0.9766
psa	0.0054	1.0054
free/total psa	0.7547	2.127
adjustment	-0.7381	0.478
dre	-0.9931	0.3704
free coefficient (c_0)	-1.4102	N/A

positive or negative) that optimized classification for the obtained logistic regression model was 0.4642.

5.2 *MultiLayerPerceptron*

Highest accuracy of the classifier using the *MultiLayerPerceptron* algorithm was reached using three hidden layers, 0.5 learning rate and 0.2 momentum– epoch sizes larger than 500 caused a reduction in performance.

By using the smaller data set containing 305 instances, accuracy rose from 68.8% to 70.49%, indicating that *MultiLayerPerceptron* algorithm is sensible to filter manipulations for correction of data content.

When false positives rate approaches 0.15 it is possible to notice through the ROC (fig. 4) that the classifier borders on random decision, holding a high threshold value at roughly 0.68; the threshold for best accuracy rate was 0.49.

5.3 *MLPClassifier*

MLPClassifier showed a slight increase in accuracy when compared to *MultiLayerPerceptron* for both data sets, with model performance using the set which null instances were discarded at 71.14% and an associated threshold value of 0.51.

Table 4 displays the connection weight values between input and hidden neurons. Additionally, three bias neurons for each neuron in the hidden layer were created, with weight equal to 1.68314, 0.30868 and -1.58390.

5.4 *ADTree*

The *ADTree* algorithm yielded a classifier with an accuracy marker of 71.8%, a slight performance gain over logistic regression and neural networks techniques.

Whereas the true negative rate is shown to be reduced, there was a significant increase in the number of true positives. This is due to a lower threshold value of 0.4687, which in turn assigns a more conservative behavior to the model.

Table 4. Connection weight values for *MLPClassifier* based model

Attribute	Weight #1	Weight #2	Weight #3
age	0.99678	0.97959	-3.63784
volume	1.715815	1.38124	1.00791
psa	-0.23637	0.25022	-0.11938
free/total psa	0.39286	-0.78210	-0.64545
adjustment	-0.74715	1.37455	0.55101
dre	-0.36268	2.29051	-0.07021

The probability of positive classification is obtained by a full depth-first traversal of the tree; for every decision node reached, the resulting branch value is accumulated and the final value represents the probability.

5.5 *PART*

The *PART* algorithm attempts to extract rules from a constructed decision tree; its accuracy resembles what was obtained for artificial neural networks, but produced a compact set of six rules in total– these are shown in figure 2. While using all 500 cases, the classifier reached a 66.4% accuracy rate; when discarding instances with null values, accuracy rose to 71.48%.

if dre = F **and** volume > 53 **and** psa ≤ 14.2 **then**
    biopsy = F
else if age ≤ 59 **then**
    biopsy = F
else if dre = T **and** 0.21 < free/total psa ≤ 0.58 **then**
    biopsy = F
else if dre = T **then**
    biopsy = T
else if volume ≤ 46 **then**
    biopsy = F
else
    biopsy = T

Fig. 2. Decision rules generated by *PART* classifier

Rules in figure 2 are evaluated sequentially: if a condition is met, the value for the dependent variable is immediatly set. Otherwise, the following rules are tested for a match. If none of the conditions are satisfied, a default value is assigned.

Similarities among conventions adopted by physicians to infer the need for biopsy and the decision rules obtained by the classifier can be drawn; In the second test condition, a patient bearing a negative DRE exam and a free/total PSA value between 0.21

and 0.58 (uncertainty and low probability zone) can be spared from biopsy. On the contrary, a patient with a positive DRE exam is strongly recommended to biopsy, regardless of other markers.

5.6   Summary

Figure 3 illustrates the percent values of true positives, false positives, true negatives and false negatives for the highest ranking classifiers of each used technique. Receiver operating curves for the models are given in figure 4.

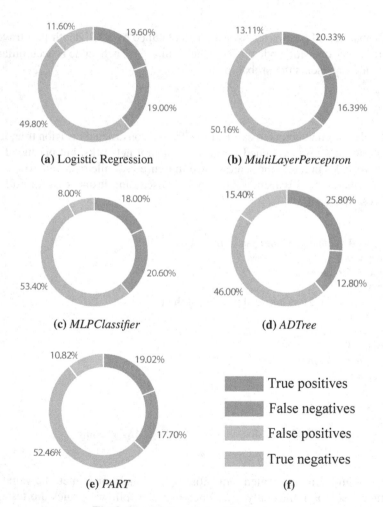

Fig. 3. Distribution of classified instances

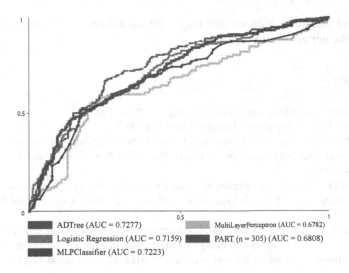

ADTree (AUC = 0.7277)

MultiLayerPerceptron (AUC = 0.6782)

Logistic Regression (AUC = 0.7159)

PART (n = 305) (AUC = 0.6808)

MLPClassifier (AUC = 0.7223)

Fig. 4. Receiver Operator Curves (ROC) for the obtained classifiers

6   Final Remarks

The field of study for the application of machine learning techniques in cancer related tasks although appealing and highly beneficial, remains complex and intricate due to numerous issues envolved in diagnosis inference as well as detection and identification of tumors and associated risks. Reviewed studies comprised several different techniques that led this current study's diverse experimentation with distinct classes of algorithms, allowing for a wide interpretation of results according to each particular technique.

The results obtained with the application of the given data set reached similar accuracy to a great number of clinical trials alike, i.e. none of the techniques or algorithms used in the study showed a significant difference when compared to existing clinical trials. Limiting factors for the classifiers' performance as well as for additional proposed tests originated from the narrow number of cases for a problem so diverse and filled with uncertainty that is the recommendation to prostate cancer biopsy. Additionally, the intrinsic characteristics of the data set such as the low dimensionality (few number of attributes) and features' specificity and granularity, no solid conclusions about the data sample as well as correlation among pre-treatment variables were able to be drawn– only the most commonly used markers obtained during monitoring and tracking of prostate cancer suspicion have been supplied by the physician. In an attempt to overcome these limitations, incorporating additional attributes and characteristics that also serve as risk factors for prostate cancer is a definite priority for enhancing accuracy and obtaining more insight about the data.

Given the slightly superior accuracy from the use of decision tree algorithms along with other machine learning resources such as *boosting* and rule extraction, it is expected that the design and construction of hybrid classifiers may come to benefit from advantages present in distinct algorithms. Moreover, advanced validation techniques such as temporal and external validation that may offer an enhanced estimate of classifiers' accuracy indicator are firmly suggested.

References

1. The Oxford English Dictionary. Oxford University Press (2007)
2. American Heritage Dictionary. Houghton Mifflin (2009)
3. Baade, P.D., Youlden, D.R., Krnjacki, L.J.: International epidemology of prostate cancer: geographical distribution and secular trends. Molecular Nutrition & Food Research **53**(2), 171–184 (2009)
4. Benson, M.C., Whang, I.S., Pantuc, P., et al.: Prostate specific antigen density: a means for distinguishing benign prostatic hypertrophy and prostate cancer. Journal of Urology **147**(3), 815–816 (1992)
5. Catalona, W.J., Ornstein, D.K.: Prostate cancer detection in men with serum PSA concentrations of 2.6 to 4.0 ng/ml and benign prostate examination: enhancement of specificity with free psa measurements. Journal of American Medical Association **277**(18), 1452–1455 (1977)
6. Catalona, W.J., Richie, J.P., Ahmann, F.R., Hudson, M.A., Scardino, P.T., Flanigan, R.C., Dekernion, J.B., Ratliff, T.L., et al.: Comparison of digital rectal examination and serum prostate specific antigen in the early detection of prostate cancer: Results of a multicenter clinical trial of 6630 men. Journal of Urology **151**(5), 1283–1290 (1994)
7. Cookson, M.M.: Prostate cancer: screening and early detection. Cancer Control **8**(2), 133–140 (2001)
8. van der Cruijsen-Koeter, I.W., Vis, A.N., Roobol, M.J., Wildhagen, M.F., de Koning, H.J., van der Kwast, T.H., Schroder, F.H.: Comparison of screen detected and clinically diagnosed prostate cancer in the european randomized study of screening for prostate cancer, section rotterdam. Journal of Urology **174**(1), 121–125 (2005)
9. Djavan, B., Remzi, M., Zlotta, A., et al.: Novel artificial neural network for early detection of prostate cancer. Journal of Clinical Oncology **20**(4), 921–929 (2002)
10. Essink-Bot, M.L., de Koning, J.H., et al.: Short-term effects of population-based screening for prostate cancer on health-related quality of life. Journal of National Cancer Institute **90**(12), 925–931 (1998)
11. Gant, V., Rodway, S., Wyatt, J.: Artificial neural networks: Practical considerations for clinical applications. Cambridge University Press (2001)
12. Garzotto, M., Beer, T.M., Hudson, R.G., Peters, L., Hsieh, Y., Barrera, E., Klein, T., Mori, M.: Improved detection of prostate cancer using classification and regression tree analysis. Journal of Clinical Oncology **23**(19), 4322–4329 (2005)
13. Gülkesen, K.H., Köksal, I.T., Özdem, S., Saka, O.: Prediction of prostate cancer using decision tree algorithm. Turkish Journal of Medicinal Science **40**(5), 681–686 (2010)
14. Hall, M., Frank, E., Holmes, G., Pfahringer, B., Reutemann, P., Witten, I.H.: The weka data mining software: An update. SIGKDD Explorations **11**(1) (2009)
15. Çinar, M., Engin, M., Engin, E.Z., Ateşçi, Y.Z.: Early prostate cancer diagnosis by using artificial neural networks and support vector machines. Expert Systems with Applications **36**(3), 6357–6361 (2009)
16. National Cancer Institute: Treatment choices for men with early-stage prostate cancer (January 2011)
17. Ito, K., Yamamoto, T., Ohi, M., Kurokawa, K., Suzuki, K., Yamanaka, H.: Free/total PSA ratio is a powerful predictor of future prostate cancer morbidity in men with initial PSA levels of 4.1 to 10.0 ng/ml. Journal of Urology **61**(4), 760–764 (2003)

18. Karakiewicz, P.I., Benayoun, S., Kattan, M.W., et al.: Development and validation of a nomogram predicting the outcome of prostate biopsy based on patient age, digital rectal examination and serum prostate specific antigen. The Journal of Urology 173(6), 1930–1934 (2005)
19. Kattan, M.W., Scardino, P.T.: Prediction of progression: nomograms of clinical utility. Clinical Prostate Cancer 1(2), 90–96 (2002)
20. Lawrentschuk, N., Lockwood, G., Davies, P., Evans, A., Sweet, J., Toi, A., Fleshner, N.E.: Predicting prostate biopsy outcome: artificial neural networks and polychotomous regression are equivalente models. International Urology and Nephrology 43(1), 23–30 (2010)
21. Lisboa, P.J.: A review of evidence of health benefit from artificial neural networks in medical intervention. Neural Networks 15(1), 11–39 (2002)
22. Marin, O.R., Ruiz, D., Soriano, A., Delgado, F.J.: Automatic decision using dirty databases: Application to prostate cancer diagnosis. In: 32nd Annual International Conference of the IEEE EMBS, Buenos Aires, Argentina (September 2010)
23. Partin, A.W., Oesterling, J.E.: The clinical usefulness of prostate specific antigen: Update 1994. Journal of Urology 152(5), 1358–1368 (1994)
24. Regnier-Coudert, O., McCall, J., Lothian, R., Lam, T., McClinton, S., N'Dow, J.: Machine learning for improved pathological staging of prostate cancer: A performance comparison on a range of classifiers. Artificial Intelligence in Medicine 55(1), 25–35 (2012)
25. Saritas, I., Ozkan, I.A., Sert, I.U.: Prognosis of prostate cancer by artificial neural networks. Expert Systems and Applications 37, 6646–6650 (2010)
26. Stephan, C., Meyer, H.A., Kwiatkowski, M., Recker, F., Cammann, H., Loening, S.A., et al.: A (-5, -7) propsa based artificial neural network to detect prostate cancer. European Urology 50(5), 1014–1020 (2006)
27. Strum, S.B., Pogliano, D.: What every doctor who treats male patients should know. PCRI Insights 8, 4–5 (2005)
28. Oregon Health and Science University: Presence of high-risk prostate cancer can be predicted without a biopsy, new study says (May 2005), http://www.sciencedaily.com/releases/2005/05/050522112707.htm
29. Vickers, A.J., Cronin, A.M., Aus, G., Pihl, C., Becker, C., Pettersson, K., Scardino, P.T., Hugosson, J., Lilja, H.: Impact of recent screening on predicting the outcome of prostate cancer biopsy in men with elevated PSA: data from the european randomized study of prostate cancer screening in gothenburg, Sweden. Cancer 116(11), 2612–2620 (2010)

Comparison of a New Qualifier Method for Multiple Object Tracking in RoboCup 2D Simulation League

Nelson I. González[✉] and Leonardo Garrido

Departamento de Ciencias Computacionales, Tecnológico de Monterrey,
Monterrey, México
ni.gonzalez.phd.mty@itesm.mx, leonardo.garrido@itesm.mx

Abstract. In this document two methods for a multiple object tracking problem are tested and compared in a 2D environment with quantisied vision considering the tracking problem as a constraint satisfaction problem as a general approach. The first method is a qualifier method which uses three probabilistic models (identity, distance, and movement direction) to compute the belief of the path of a given object considering the path a Markov process. The second method are particle filters with penalised predictions which expands the belief of a given objects in order to get the best match for it. Each method was tested in two situations. In the first situation the observer was static in a fixed position while the second situation involves a dynamic observer. The methods obtained an almost perfect result of 98 % of correct matches for the first situation and achieved a result of nearly 78 % of correct matches in the second situation.

1 Introduction

An autonomous mobile agent senses the world and performs actions in order to modify the surrounding ambient. An observer object is an object which senses the world (normally using a visual sensor) and make decisions using the information about the world. The kinematic model of an object in the world permits to infer movements and intentions for that object from an observer point of view. This can be extremely useful for prediction and planning in a multi-agent system. However, it is not always easy to generate the kinematic model or the observer just has no access to that model. Noise in the observer sensors and actuators, non-linear measure nature, and unpredictable object behaviour make this task difficult.

A Multiple Object Tracking (MOT) problem involves the path generation of the path followed for any dynamic object in the observer vision range. A MOT problem may also involve the object identification: each object in the word has an unique identity, and this identity can be given by the object physical appearance, the object name, the object type, etc, and may not always be known for the observer.

A.L.C. Bazzan and K. Pichara (Eds.): IBERAMIA 2014, LNAI 8864, pp. 722–733, 2014.
DOI: 10.1007/978-3-319-12027-0_58

In a 2D world such as the RoboCup 2D Simulation League a MOT problem is traduced to the path generation for each player in the field. There are two possible observers in the field: an omniscient observer (called the trainer) which has access to all the information in the field without noise in its measurements, and a normal observer (called a player) which is inside the field and has access only to the data its vision sensor permits.

The generation path for the trainer can be useful to test, compare and communicate global strategies to the teams, while is useful for a player to predict movements and intentions of the nearest players in order to choose the best action to perform in function of the current state of the world. The dynamic nature of the observer adds complexity to the MOT problem since the observer behaviour affects the relative measurements received in the visual sensor.

2   The RoboCup 2D Simulation League

RoboCup 2D Simulation League [11] is a 2D soccer simulator,where eleven players plus one coach play in one team versus another eleven players plus one coach in the other team. The simulation takes place in discrete simulation cycles of 100 ms of duration.

The league aims to simulate a complete soccer match with realistic physics and boundaries for a 2D soccer field. In this league each object is modelled by an absolute position $o^t_{xy\theta} :< x, y, \theta >$ composed of a simulation time t, coordinates x and y in the x-axis and y-axis, and a direction in sexagesimal degrees given by its facing angle θ measured from the x axis. Let $S : f(< d, \alpha >) \rightarrow < d', \alpha' >$ be the vision sensor model used to sense the world around the observer where d and α are respectively the real distance and real relative direction from an object inside the vision range, and d' and α' are respectively the measured distance and relative direction returned by the sensor for a given object inside the vision range. This vision sensor also has an aperture γ and an update frequency Δt. According to the RoboCup 2D manual [10], the raw data received in the vision sensor S is modelled by 1, where $QS = 0.1$ for dynamic objects (players and ball) and $QS = 0.01$ for static objects (flags, lines, and goals).

$$d' = \left\lceil \frac{e^{\left\lceil \frac{\ln d}{QS} \right\rceil \cdot QS}}{0.1} \right\rceil \cdot 0.1 \tag{1}$$

From 1 it can be deduced that the floor value in the quantisation for a real distance d is given by $e^{\ln d' - 0.1 - QS}$ while the ceil value is d'. In consequence, the average error ϵ for a measurement d' is considered as 2.

$$\epsilon = \frac{d' - e^{\ln d' - 0.1 - QS}}{2} \tag{2}$$

The vision range for an observer in the field can be of 60, 120 or 180 sexagesimal degrees of aperture and it affects the measurement frequency inversely: an aperture of 60 degrees receives measures every simulation cycle, an aperture of 120 degrees every two simulation cycles, and an aperture of 180 degrees every three simulation cycles. In a normal game, a solution to a MOT problem is necessary to infer movements and intentions from the opponent team and also from the partner players when the communication is limited.

3   Related Work

A MOT problem appears in applications such as radars, autonomous driving, person identification and tracking, and has been attacked by many approaches. However, most of them uses a static observer. Kalman Filters are used in [9] to update the belief in the position and velocity of an object. The authors in [12] generalise the Kalman Filter to implement data association and then use the data to update the object paths. One of the assumptions of Kalman Filters is linearity in the information and a Gaussian model in the system [16]. An Unscented Kalman Filter is used to overcome this assumptions and it was successfully implemented in [8] and compared against an Extended Kalman Filter and achieved a better performance.

Particle Filters [6,13] have also be used in order to get over the non-linear nature of the systems. One of the problems the authors in [6] deal with is the similar like hood of two objects for the same particle filter, they address this problem using a Markov random field prior motion. Most of the time the particle filters is used to identify the objects in a video frame and this identification is then used to track the object just as in [1].

In context of the RoboCup leagues, Particles Filters and Kalman Filters have been implemented in dynamic observers. In [7] the robots AIBO use a Kalman Filter along a Particles Filter to self-localise and to track the ball while the robots move. In [15] the robots Nao use the Unscented Kalman Filter in Self - Localisation and Mapping (SLAM) to self-localise and to construct the world model. This methods track a single object (the ball) or just generate the world model for a single frame.

Other authors propose the use of Markov Chain Monte Carlo (MCMC) data association [17] to create probability distribution for each tracked object. In [4] two problems related to MOT are solved using particle filters along with a MCMC: the problem of generate the path of all the objects, and the problem of assign the measurements to the exact object.

On other side, since the MOT problem can be addressed as linking objects from one frame to another some authors have proposed the use of network algorithms such as the k-shortest algorithm in [3] and even the use of linear programming [5] to optimise the solution of the problem. Even, in [2] the authors focused in energy estimation: they used continuos energy minimisation with a gradient descent for all the objects in order to construct the path followed by each target in the frame sequence. However this methods uses all the information received in several previous cycles.

4 The Kinematic Model

Each simulation cycle c_t the observer receives a list of players O^t of size s_t in its visual sensor. A MOT problem can be addressed as a problem of matching an object from c_{t-1} to an object in c_t. This matching must satisfy the constraint: *any object from c_t can only be matched to a single object in c_{t-1}, and any object from c_{t-1} can only be matched to a single object in c_t*, in order to avoid objects with more than one possible path.

The stated constraint is satisfied following the general approach shown in Algorithm 1. Each match from an object in c_{t-1} to an object in c_t is weighted and added to a constraints matrix $M_{s_{t-1} \times s_t}$. The cells of M are then ordered from the heaviest cell to the lightest cell, and in that order the matches are chosen. Once a match has been chosen the correspondent cells in the row and column of the chosen cell are dominated and cannot be chosen later. In this way it is ensured that an object in c_t has at most one correspondent object in c_{t-1} and viceversa. The algorithm ends after all the rows and columns are dominated or $\min(s_{t-1}, s_t)$ cells have been chosen.

Algorithm 1 The General Tracking Algorithm

```
 1: M[s_{t-1}][s_t]
 2: for all o_i in O^{t-1} do
 3:     for all o_j in O^t do
 4:         M[i][j] ← weight(o_i, o_j)
 5:     end for
 6: end for
 7: ordered[s_{t-1} × s_t] ← order(M)
 8: for all cell_k in ordered do
 9:     if cell_k is not dominated and is accepted then
10:         row ← row of cell_k
11:         column ← column of cell_k
12:         match(O^{t-1}[row], O^t[column])
13:         set row dominated
14:         set column dominated
15:     end if
16: end for
```

A match defined by $cell_k$ is only accepted if the distance between the two objects involved is less than the multiplication of the sum of its average errors and a threshold factor $THF > 1$. This last step is necessary in order to avoid the match of two objects which its displacement is higher than the maximum physical displacement detected by the vision sensor, in this case, the sum of the average errors.

Once two objects are matched the kinematic model is constructed using the difference vector $\Delta p = o^t_{xy\theta} - o^{t-1}_{xy\theta}$. If the facing angle is not known for the object o_j then it is inferred using the previously defined difference vector $\theta =$

arctan($\Delta y, \Delta x$). Finally, if the identity of o_i is known then this identity can be inherited to the matched object o_j. In this research two weighting methods are proposed and tested: a qualifier method, and particle filters.

5   The Qualifier Method

The main idea is to rate the matches among objects from c_{t-1} to objects in c_t using probabilistic models. The matches are modelled as Markov processes, which means that each match only needs information about the prior state and the new state to be fully described.

Consider the match between two objects in two consecutive frames each one, let o_i be an object from c_{t-1} (of size s_{t-1} objects) and o_j be and object from c_t (of size s_t objects). There are three probabilistic models for the kinematic model with its own probability distribution $P(\text{model})$ for the match m_{ij}, which attempts to match the object o_i and object o_j: the objects identities id_i and id_j, the euclidean distance d_{ij} between both of them, and the movement direction v_i of the object o_i.

The three models are considered independents among themselves, however, as will be seen below, if the identities of both objects are fully known and equal then the rating is immediately equals to 1. Therefore, the rating for a given match considering the three probabilistic models is given by 3.

$$P(m_{ij}) = \begin{cases} 1 & \text{if } \text{id}_i = \text{id}_j \\ P(v_i) \cdot P(d_{ij}) \cdot P(\text{id}_i \wedge \text{id}_j) & \text{otherwise} \end{cases} \quad (3)$$

5.1   Identities

The identity of each object is given by an unique id_i in any simulation cycle c_t. This model is the most critical since known identities may lead to a fully identification and the match is accepted immediately, as stated in 3. Since the object o_i and object o_j has an identity, the probability distribution is given by $P(\text{id}_i \wedge \text{id}_j)$.

The identity for any object is defined by a set of characteristics which identify the object: a number, a group, a function, a physical aspect, etc. In the context of RoboCup 2D, two characteristics are considered: team and number. Any object belongs to a single team and it is assigned a unique number inside that team. There could be two objects with the same number but of different team. The visual sensor, as stated in the manual, receives information about the identity of the objects in function of the object distance. The visual sensor receives the object team and number if it is close, the sensor receives only the team if the object is far, and the sensor receives no identity information about the object if it is very far.

In order to compute $P(\text{id}_i \wedge \text{id}_j)$ the pair $(\text{id}_i, \text{id}_j)$ is rated following the rules:

- If the teams and numbers are known and equal then the rate is 0, and all the other pairs receives a rate of 3.

- If the teams are known and equal then the rate is 1
- If at least one of the teams are not known then the rate is 2
- Otherwise the rate is 3

The rate 3 is achieved by the cases when the teams are equal but the numbers are not, and when the the teams are known but they are not equal. Then, the probabilistic model distributes the beliefs following 4 where $p = \frac{1}{2 \cdot n + m}$, n is the amount of pairs with rate 1 and m is the amount of pairs with rate 2, when there is no pair with rate 0.

$$P(\mathrm{id}_i \wedge \mathrm{id}_j) = \begin{cases} 1 & \text{if rate} = 0 \\ 2 \cdot p & \text{if rate} = 1 \\ p & \text{if rate} = 2 \\ 0 & \text{if rate} = 3 \end{cases} \qquad (4)$$

5.2 Euclidean Distance

The euclidean distance between two objects id_i and id_j is define as $d_{ij} = \sqrt{(o_{i_x} - o_{j_x})^2 + (o_{i_y} - o_{j_y})^2}$. The probability distribution for the euclidean distance is stated in 5. The distribution assigns a higher probability to objects nearest to o_i since the displacement from c_{t-1} to c_t is supposed to not be higher than a certain threshold.

$$P(d_{ij}) = \frac{\frac{1}{d_{ij}}}{\sum\limits_{j} \frac{1}{d_{ij}}} \qquad (5)$$

Equation 5 distributes the belief for object o_i from cycle c_{t-1} to be in the positions defined by all the objects received by the visual sensor in the cycle c_t.

5.3 Movement Direction

The visual sensor can receives information about an object direction if it is close. If the object is far then the visual sensor will receive no information about the object direction. This probabilistic model works along with the distance model since it distributes the belief for the object o_i to have moved in the direction defined by 6.

$$\text{direction} = \arctan\left(o_{i_y} - o_{j_y}, o_{i_x} - o_{j_x}\right) \qquad (6)$$

The variable α to be evaluated is the absolute difference between the direction of object o_i (θ_i) and the direction defined by 6: $\alpha = |\theta_i - \text{direction}|$. Since the direction θ_i can be or not be known the probabilist model used is a Gaussian model with mean 0 and standard deviation 90 when the direction is known, and a uniform model when the direction is not known. Therefore, the probabilistic model is given by

$$P(\text{direction}) = \begin{cases} \mathcal{N}(0, 90, \alpha) & \text{if } \theta_i \text{ is known} \\ 1/s_t & \text{otherwise} \end{cases} \tag{7}$$

Equation 7 distributes the belief for an object o_i to have moved to the position o_j, the equation states that an object o_j is more likely to have moved to position o_i if o_i is in the facing direction of o_j.

6   Particle Filters

Particle Filters represent the probability distribution of a variable by a set of random state samples drawn from this distribution [14,16]. Each particle in the filter has a weight representing the belief for the system given the current particle state. Supposing a initial set P_N^0 of N particles randomly distributed is space for a given object o, the basic particle filter algorithm is as stated in Algorithm 2.

Algorithm 2 Particle filter basic algorithm

1: **for all** p in P_N^t **do**
2:     $p_{weight} \leftarrow \frac{1}{N}$
3: **end for**
4: **for all** t **do**
5:     **for all** p in P_N^t **do**
6:         $p_{xy\theta} \leftarrow p_{xy\theta} + < o_x, o_y, o_\theta >$
7:         $p_{weight} \leftarrow \text{update}(o, p)$
8:     **end for**
9:     **for all** n in P_N **do**
10:         resample n_i with replacement from P_N^t
11:         add n to P_N^{t+1}
12:     **end for**
13: **end for**

In line 6 of Algorithm 2 the particle is moved with the same belief about the object movement, and in line 7 the belief of the particle is re-computed given the new object state. Lines 10 and 11 are called the resample step, which re-distribute the particles in order to obtain a better belief dispersion about the object.

To implement particle filters in a MOT problem, a particle filter is assigned to each tracked object and the particles distribution is used to match the objects in cycle c_t to the object in cycle c_{t-1}. Since the observer has no access to the object kinematic model or the players intention, it has to guess the prediction phase (line 6 of Algorithm 2). This prediction is guessed computing the fit value F_{ij} in 8 for the particle filter assuming the object moved to any of the new object positions, and this fit value is penalised by the euclidean distance between the object and the new assumed position (in order to avoid inconsistent jumps such as in the direction movement in the qualifier method).

$$F_{ij} = \sum_N \frac{d_{\max} - d_{ni}}{d_{\max}} \cdot \frac{1}{d_{ij}} \tag{8}$$

The prediction step for each object is performed with the distance and angle differences between it and an object from cycle c_{t-1}. In case the body angle is not known the angle difference is considered 0. This prediction permit to scatter in space the belief about the new object. The algorithm for the MOT using particle filters is stated in Algorithm 3.

Algorithm 3 Particle filter for tracking objects

1: **for all** o in O_0 **do**
2:      generate particle set for o
3: **end for**
4: **for all** t **do**
5:      **for all** o_i in O_t **do**
6:          **for all** o_j in O_{t-1} **do**
7:              predict set from o_j for o_i
8:              compute A_{ij} for o_i and o_j
9:          **end for**
10:     **end for**
11:     link objects from A values
12:     generate set for new objects in sight
13:     remove sets for objects no longer in sight
14: **end for**

---

7   Experiments and Results

The RoboCup2D server and the Phoenix2D framework[1] were used to run the experiments. Two kinds of experiments were performed. The first experiments used controlled settings to test the generation path using each of the proposed methods where the observer is always in a fixed position. Each experiment consisted in 200 simulation cycles and a threshold factor $THF = 1.5$ was used. It was found that any value $THF > 1.5$ performs equal, and performs better than a value of $THF < 1.5$. Two settings were first implemented to test the matching methods, and an omniscient agent (the trainer) was used to obtain free-noise and complete information:

Setting 1. The observer is static and there are five opponent players moving inside the observer vision range, the real paths are shown in Figure 1a.

Setting 2. The observer is static and there are three opponent players and two partner players moving in and out the observer vision range, the real paths are shown in Figure 1b.

---

[1] https://github.com/ivanGzz/Phoenix2D

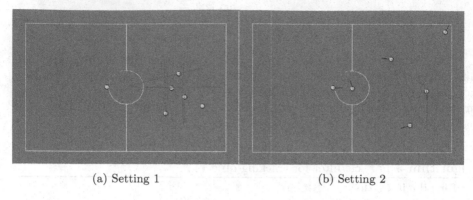

(a) Setting 1   (b) Setting 2

Fig. 1. Trainer

The particle filters were tested using 100 particles for each object. For each setting the correct matches were compared against the total matches. The results for each setting for the qualifier method and the particle filters are summarised in Table 1. The generated paths after the experiments for the qualifier method are shown in Figures 2a and 2b for Settings 1 and 2 respectively, and the generated paths for the particle filter are shown in Figures 3a and 3b for Settings 1 and 2 respectively. Table 1 shows that both of the methods matched correctly 98% of all the possible matches during the 200 cycles of duration.

Table 1. Correct matches

	Qualifier method	Particles Filter
Setting 1	98.79%	97.98%
Setting 2	98.87%	99.53%

Because the RoboCup 2D Simulation League is a highly stochastic and dynamic environment the second kind of experiments uses a randomised environment to test the matching methods. This experiments used five players for both teams and each player is given a list of random positions to follow during an experiment. Each experiment has a duration of 2000 simulation cycles, and 100 experiments were performed. Just like the previous experiments, a value of $THF = 1.5$ was used, and the information collected was the proportion of correct matches over all the matches chosen by the methods. The results obtained after the 100 iterations are shown in Table 2.

From the results shown in Table 2 it is deduced that there is no significative statistical difference between the two methods, and can be inferred that both methods performs equal in a dynamic environment. It must be noted that the particle filters are used to compute only the belief about the position of the objects while the qualifier method also uses information about the identities of the objects.

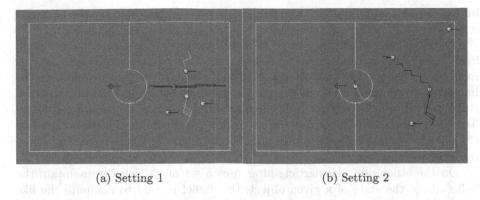

(a) Setting 1   (b) Setting 2

Fig. 2. Qualifier method

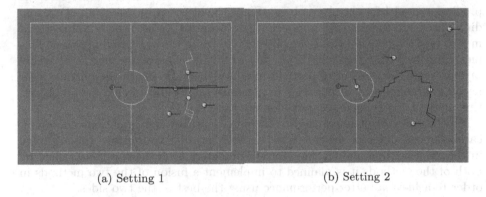

(a) Setting 1   (b) Setting 2

Fig. 3. Particle Filters

Table 2. Correct matches

	Qualifier method	Particles Filter
Average	77.82%	77.38%
Standard deviation	2.8%	2.49%

8 Conclusions

A general approach to a multiple objective tracking, shown in Algorithm 1 was
proposed and implemented to compute the path of each player in the RoboCup
2D Simulation League. The general approach implemented two methods to perform the matching among players in consecutive simulation cycles: a qualifier
method with probabilistic models, and particle filters. The methods were tested
and compared in static and dynamic environments and the two methods performed statistically equal. It was expected for the methods to performs better
when used in static observers since the errors received in the visual sensor are not

influenced by the observer movement, and it was corroborated by the obtained results.

The qualifier method uses three probabilistic models to rate a given match: identities, distance, and movement direction. One of the advantages of this method is that it only uses the information about the current cycle and the immediately previous cycle, in consequence it does not require an initialisation stage and can quickly recover from the loss of information. Considering 4, 5 and 6 to compute the cells of the constraints matrix M, the method has a complexity of $O(3 \cdot n^2)$ where n represents the maximum number of objects inside the vision range of the observer.

On the other side, the particle filter uses a set of particles to maintain the belief about the state of a given object, this belief is used to compute the like hood of another object to be in the next state for the given object. This method only requires the belief of a given object to be in its current state and the prediction model for the given object. Since the observer in RoboCup 2D has no direct access to the prediction model, it was proposed to uses the fit value stated in 8 to rate the belief of the given object to move to the evaluated position. This method runs with complexity $O(m \cdot n^2)$ to fill the constraints matrix M where m represents the number of particles used by the filter. Since the particle filter needs a large number of particles to generate an accurate belief for an object, this method can become computationally expensive.

As future work it is planned to include identities and intentions communication among different observers in the field in order to improve the accuracy in the identification and tracking for the objects. Given the results obtained by both of the methods it is planned to implement a fusion of the two methods in order to achieve a better performance using the best of the two sides.

References

1. Almeida, A., Almeida, J., Araujo, R.: Real-time tracking of moving objects using particle filters. In: Proceedings of the IEEE International Symposium on Industrial Electronics, ISIE 2005, vol. 4, pp. 1327–1332 (June 2005)
2. Andriyenko, A., Schindler, K.: Multi-target tracking by continuous energy minimization. In: CVPR (2011)
3. Berclaz, J., Fleuret, F., Turetken, E., Fua, P.: Multiple object tracking using k-shortest paths optimization. IEEE Transactions on Pattern Analysis and Machine Intelligence 33(9), 1806–1819 (2011)
4. Hue, C., Le Cadre, J.P., Perez, P.: Sequential monte carlo methods for multiple target tracking and data fusion. IEEE Transactions on Signal Processing (2002)
5. Jiang, H., Fels, S., Little, J.J.: A linear programming approach for multiple object tracking. In: IEEE Conference on Computer Vision and Pattern Recognition, CVPR 2007 (2007)
6. Khan, Z., Balch, T., Dellaert, F.: Mcmc-based particle filtering for tracking a variable number of interacting targets. IEEE Transactions on Pattern Analysis and Machine Intelligence 27 (2005)
7. Lastra, R.A., Vallejos, P.A., del Solar, J.R.: Integrated self-localization and ball tracking in the four-legged robot soccer league. In: Proceedings of the 1st IEEE Latin American Robotics Symposium, LARS 2004 (2004)

8. Leven, W., Lanterman, A.: Unscented kalman filters for multiple target tracking with symmetric measurement equations. IEEE Transactions on Automatic Control **54**(2), 370–375 (2009)
9. Li, X., Wang, K., Wang, W., Li, Y.: A multiple object tracking method using kalman filter. In: 2010 IEEE International Conference on Information and Automation (ICIA) (2010)
10. The RoboCup Federation: RoboCup Soccer Server: Users Manual
11. The Robocup Federation: Robocup (September 2012), www.robocup.org
12. Meng, L., Grimm, W., Donne, J.: Radar detection improvement by integration of multi-object tracking. In: Proceedings of the Fifth International Conference on Information Fusion (2002)
13. Okuma, K., Taleghani, A., de Freitas, N., Little, J.J., Lowe, D.G.: A boosted particle filter: multitarget detection and tracking. In: Pajdla, T., Matas, J.G. (eds.) ECCV 2004. LNCS, vol. 3021, pp. 28–39. Springer, Heidelberg (2004)
14. Ristic, B., Arulampalam, S., Gordon, N.: Beyond the Kalman Filter: Particle Filters for Tracking Applications. Artech House (2004)
15. Tasse, S., Hofmann, M., Urbann, O.: SLAM in the dynamic context of robot soccer games. In: Chen, X., Stone, P., Sucar, L.E., van der Zant, T. (eds.) RoboCup 2012. LNCS, vol. 7500, pp. 368–379. Springer, Heidelberg (2013)
16. Thrun, S., Burgard, W., Fox, D.: Probabilistic Robotics. The MIT Press (2005)
17. Yu, Q., Medioni, G.: Multiple-target tracking by spatiotemporal monte carlo markov chain data association. IEEE Trans. Pattern Anal. Mach. Intell. **31**(12), 2196–2210 (2009)

Artificial Neural Networks Ensemble Applied to the Electrical Impedance Tomography Problem to Determine the Cardiac Ejection Fraction

Rogério G.N. Santos Filho, Luciana C.D. Campos$^{(\boxtimes)}$,
Rodrigo Weber dos Santos, and Luis Paulo S. Barra

Federal University of Juiz de Fora, Juiz de Fora, Brazil
rogerio.gns@gmail.com, luciana.campos@ice.ufjf.br,
{rodrigo.weber,luis.barra}@ufjf.edu.br

Abstract. Cardiac Ejection Fraction (EF) is a parameter that indicates how much blood the heart is pumping to the body. It is a very important clinical parameter since it is highly correlated to the functional status of the heart. To measure the EF, diverse non-invasive techniques have been applied such as Magnetic Resonance. The method studied in this work is the Electrical Impedance Tomography (EIT) which consists in generate an image of the inner body using measures of electrical potentials - some electrodes are attached to the body boundary and small currents are applied in the body, the potentials are then measured in these electrodes. This technique presents lower costs and a high portability compared to others. It can be done in the patient bed and does not use ionizing radiation. The EIT problem consists in define the electrical distribution of the inner parts that results in the potentials measured. Therefore, it is considered as a non-linear inverse problem. To solve that, this work propose the application of an Artificial Neural network (ANN) Ensemble since it is simple to understand and implement. Our results show that the ANN Ensemble presents fast and good results, which are crucial for the continuous monitoring of the heart.

Keywords: Cardiac mechanics · Medical applications · Cardiac ejection fraction · Electrical impedance tomography · Artificial neural networks

1 Introduction

The cardiac ejection fraction (EF) is a clinical parameter that determines the amount of blood pumped from the heart in each heart cycle. During each heart cycle, the ventricle relaxes, refilling with blood, and contracts, ejecting part of the blood out of the heart. The Ejection Fraction is the percentage of blood ejected from the heart in its contraction [1]. The left ventricle is the heart's main pumping chamber and is often used to determine the cardiac ejection fraction, because he is the one who ejects blood to the whole body, while the right ventricle pumps deoxygenated blood to the lungs. EF is calculated as follows:

© Springer International Publishing Switzerland 2014
A.L.C. Bazzan and K. Pichara (Eds.): IBERAMIA 2014, LNAI 8864, pp. 734–741, 2014.
DOI: 10.1007/978-3-319-12027-0_59

$$EF = \frac{PV}{EDV} = \frac{EDV - ESV}{EDV}, \tag{1}$$

where PV denotes the volume of blood pumped, given by the difference between the end-diastolic volume (EDV) and the end-systolic volume (ESV).

An EF outside of the considered normal range indicates that the heart is contracting abnormally (abnormalities in the heart wall moviments), which may indicate a malfunction of the heart. It is a relevant parameter because of its high correlation with the functional status of the heart - a low EF number may indicate a heart failure, where the heart doesn't pump enough blood to the body. Diverse non-invasive methods can be applied to measure EF, like Computer Tomography, Magnetic Resonance, and others. Nevertheless, these techniques cannot be used to the continuous monitoring of EF, once they require the movement of the patient to a scanner into another room. On the other hand, Electrical Impedance Tomography (EIT) may be applied in the patient's bed, obtaining continuous EF estimations of the heart. In addition, it doesn't use ionizing radiation, it has low costs and high portability, justifying researches for solutions involving this technique for monitoring EF.

The EIT consists in fixing a number of electrodes on the boundary of the tomography body and small electric currents are injected. The electrical potentials are then measured in the electrodes. By the measurements of the potentials and current injection taken on the boundary of the domain, an image of the inner body can be generated based on the already known resistivity and conductivity distribution of the body parts - lungs, torso and heart. This technique has been applied to many fields (e.g. industrial monitoring [2], geophysics [3], and biomedical engineering [4–7]), although recent works [8] and [9] have shown results in obtaining the cardiac EF, where the viability of EIT to continuos monitoring was also discussed. These works have generated a 2D image of the ventricles and the their areas are used instead of the volume for calculation the EF.

In our work, the goal is not to generate an image, instead we use the electrical potentials measured to straightforward determine the EF. The [10] used a single ANN to solve this same problem obtained good results compared to [9]. Moreover, the single ANN is simpler to implement than the method presented in [9] and it requires less computational complexity, since it is only necessary the measures of the electrical potentials obtained in the EIT. In this work, we used an Artificial Neural Networks (ANN) Ensemble.

The ANN Ensemble, after trained, presents fast and good results, since its parts also present fast results. Therefore, it is ideal to use them in the EIT problem, since it requires the result to be accurate and quickly computed, in order to keep the continuous monitoring of the patient.

The ANN Ensemble has been used in many problems to improve the performance and generalization error (see e.g. [11–13]). Our results show that it also helps in the EIT problem improving the stability and confidence of the single ANN, which is important in a medical environment [14,15].

The potential protocols taken by the EIT are used as the ANN Ensemble's inputs and the areas of both ventricles are the ANN Ensemble's output. Due to a lack of real data of EIT, a synthetic data set was generated as described in [10]. The electrical potentials were computationally simulated using a representation of the body. In order to represent the body parts, a segmentation is made based on a magnetic resonance image. This segmentation represents the curves approaching the boundaries of the body cavities using parameters defined by a mathematical method of spline. By changing the parameters of the spline, it is possible to generate new curves that represent new body cavities. Our interest is to generate new heart configurations. The generation of new synthetical hearts is made by creating new parameters settings. Each new setting is then passed to a function that compute the correspondent electrical potentials used as input of the ANN Ensemble.

This paper is organized as follows. The second section describes the ANN ensemble. The third section, a detailed explanation of how our dataset was done and its properties. In the fourth section, we present all the results obtained using ANN ensemble to the EIT problem, also a comparison with previous methods. Finally, a conclusion is made and some ideas for future works are presented.

2   ANN Ensemble

The idea of an ensemble is to use a finite number of a predictor and combine their predictions in one single prediction. The combination of these predictions can be done in several ways - averaging is one of them. An ANN ensemble consists of training some ANNs, usually it is done by changing the training set of each ANN. But different methods can be used, such as change the number of hidden neurons or use different training function in the ensemble parts. After all ANN's of the ensemble have been trained, a test set is used in all trained network and the outputs of each tested network are combined to generate one single prediction. This single prediction is said to be the output of the ANN ensemble and its error is calculated, which define the ensemble's generalization error.

The ANN ensemble have became very popular since the work by Hansen and Salamon [11], which concludes that using a combination of several ANNs performs better than using only one single model. The reason of it is that in order to performs well, each part of an ensemble has to be well trained - diverging in their predictions with different inputs in such a way that the inaccurate output of ones are the accurate output of others ([16,17]). The combination of these predictions converges to the target. Since ANNs are unstable predictors, small changes in the training process can produce very different results. Therefore, it is possible to train a number of ANNs in different ways that produce good, and at the same time, different results. The combination of these networks results in a prediction smoother and more stable than the one from its parts.

There are a few popular methods that ensure a good ensemble performance [12]. The technique used in this work for training the ANNs ensemble is the Bootstrap aggregating (bagging) [18]. The bagging algorithm consists in training each ANNs of the ensemble using bootstrapped samples of the training data set. The bootstrap method consists in resampling with replacement the data set into

N new samples, where N is the number of ANNs in our ensemble. 20% of the dataset is reserved as test set and used to measure the performance of the ANN Ensemble after the training phase. The other part of the data set is used for the bootstrap method to complete a training set, and a validation set is filled with data that was not used in the training set. The validation set on each ANN is used to apply the early stopping.

Firstly, part of the database is reserved to calculate the generalization error of the ensemble - the test set. After that, bootstrapped samples are generated from the remaining database, one for each ANN in the Ensemble. The bootstrap samples are used as the training set and the data of the remaining database that was not used in that training set is chosen as the validation set. In this work, after all ANN are trained, an averaged combination of their predictions is made to compute the ANN Ensemble's prediction. Its generalization error is then calculated in the test set.

As said before, the goal of this work is to use an ANN ensemble to determine the areas of the ventricles of a heart represented in a 2D-model. This area is then used to calculate the cardiac ejection fraction, which is a very important parameter to analyze the functional status of the heart. The ANN ensemble used in this work receive as input the electrical potentials that are measured by the electrodes attached to the body and the areas of both ventricules are calculated as output.

The implementation of the ANN ensemble is done using Matlab [19]. To determine the best ANN ensemble configuration, several previous test are made changing the number of neurons in the hidden layer of the ANNs, once the optimal number changes for different training sets. Two different training functions are used to train the ANNs - the Backpropagation Algorithm with the Levenberg-Marquardt (LM) optimization [20]; and the second also uses the LM optmization to update the weights and bias of the ANN, the difference is that it uses the Bayesian regulation in the determination of the weights and reduces the number of parameters after the training phase. The use of Bayesian regulation is inspired in a previous work that have shown good results when applied to an ANN ensemble [21]. The Mean Absolute Percent Error (MAPE) is used to measure the performance of each configuration and the results are shown in the conclusion section.

3   Results

In this work, an ANN Ensemble is used with 10 ANNs and the bagging technique, this choice was based on good results of previous tests. Also, as said before, we compare two training functions. In order to do this comparison, the ANN Ensembles for each training function received the same datasets for the training and test phases. The tests were made by changing the number of hidden neurons on each neural network from 1 to 20. Many different test sets were used in order to calculate the mean error. As the figure 1 suggests, the ANN Ensemble trained with the trainbr algorithm achieves better results than the other. The best configuration for the ANN Ensemble trained with the trainbr algorithm uses 11 neurons in the hidden layer of the ANNs parts and it obtained a MAPE of 0.7226. The best configuration for the ANN Ensemble trained with the trainlm algorithm uses 10 neurons in its hidden layer and obtained a MAPE of 0.7759. The ANN Ensemble training phase took 0.2 hours for the trainlm algorithm and 4.4 hours for the trainbr algorithm. After trained, both configurations take less than 0.07 seconds to compute their outputs. These tests were taken in a computer with Intel Core I5 2.4Ghz and 4GB of RAM.

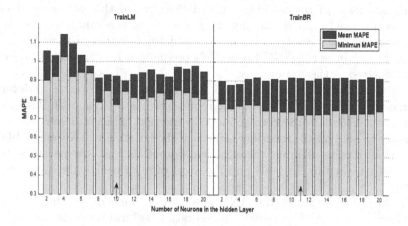

Fig. 1. Results for both training function

In [10] a single ANN was used to solve the EIT problem. Figure 2 makes a comparison between the best configuration achieved in that work and the ANN Ensemble trained with the trainbr algorithm. Both models use the test set that achieved a best result in [10]. The best MAPE achieved for the ANN Ensemble trained with the trainbr algorithm is 0.6551, while the best for the single ANN trained with the trainlm algorithm is 0.7253. Look at the figure 2 that the ensemble achieves a smaller error in majority configurations than the single ANN, following an error around 0.7%.

Until now, all results shown are in respect to the MAPE of the ANN Ensemble outputs that is related to the ventricules area of the heart. To show the errors in respect to the Cardiac ejection fraction, simulations are made and the results are compared with previous works.

In this work, we use a 2D representation of the body, therefore the following equation is used to calculate the EF:

$$EF = \frac{EDA - ESA}{EDA}, \qquad (2)$$

where EDA and ESA are the area of the heart at the end of diastole and at the end of systole, respectively. Note that the area is now used instead of the volumes.

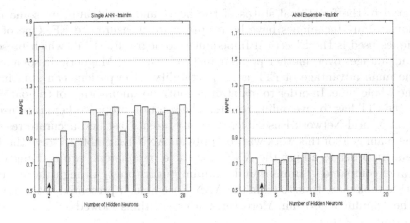

Fig. 2. Comparison between single ANN and ANN Ensemble

The table 1 shows the relative error obtained for three simulations compared in three methods - Levenberg-Marquardt Method [9], Single ANN [10], ANN Ensemble trainend with the trainbr algorithm, in both Right (RV) and Left Ventricle (LV). The simulations are done by the generation of an artificial cardiac malfunction where the first simulation expects the heart to have a normal diastole and only the systole is abnormal. The second one, expects the heart to have a normal systole and abnormal diastole. The last one does not represent a disease, instead it represents a heart that is pumping more efficiently and has a systolic area smaller than the one obtained in the resonance magnetic image (i.e. it is contracting more than expected).

Table 1. Comparison between LM Method [9], Single ANN [10] and ANN Ensemble

| | Relative Errors (%) | | | | | |
| | Bad Systole | | Bad Diastole | | Efficient | |
Method	RV	LV	RV	LV	RV	LV
LM [9]	2.410	0.090	-	-	-	-
Single ANN	4.490	1.060	4.837	0.555	3.222	5.262
ANN Ensemble	3.210	0.046	1.995	0.009	1.289	4.79

4   Conclusions

The Cardiac Ejection Fraction (EF) indicates how much blood the heart is pumping to the body. It is a very important clinical parameter since it is highly correlated to the functional status of the heart and might indicate some malfunctions. Many techniques have been applied to measure the EF. One of the techniques used is the Electrical Impedance Tomography (EIT) which presents some advantages over another popular methods such as Magnetic Resonance.

The main advantage of EIT is its portability - the patient can stay in his bed the whole time. In order to maintain a continuos monitoring of the patient's heart, the EIT has to give online results. The solution proposed here is to use an Artificial Neural Network Ensemble, since it presents fast and accurate results.

The main goal of this work was to apply an ANN Ensemble to solve the EIT problem. In order to adjust the ANN Ensemble parameters, two training functions were compared - 'trainbr' and 'trainlm' algorithms. Altough the 'trainbr' algorithm took more time to train the ANN Ensemble, it presented better results than the 'trainlm' algorithm. Moreover, both algorithms showed online execution time results.

Another comparison is made with another method used to solve the EIT problem applied in the EF, which uses the Levenberg-Marquardt optimization [9].

As future work we plan to use a three-dimension model that can better represent the body and the heart cavities. We also plan to use multiple resonance magnetic images and generate the potentials based on that, in this process the usage of a spline is not necessary and the amount of parameters is reduced. Another plan is to use real EIT data.

Acknowledgments. The first author would like to thank Departamento de Ciência da Computação of Universidade Federal de Juiz de Fora. All authors would like to thank the Programa de Pós-graduação em Modelagem Computacional of Universidade Federal de Juiz de Fora, FAPEMIG, CNPq, CAPES and FINEP.

References

1. American Heart Association: Ejection fraction heart failure measurement (2013), http://www.heart.org
2. Kim, M., Kim, K., Kim, S.: Phase boundary estimation in two-phase flows with electrical impedance tomography. Int. Comm. Heat Transfer **31**, 1105–1114 (2004)
3. Trigo, F., Lima, R., Amato, M.: Electrical impedance tomography using extended kalman filter. I3ETBE **51**, 72–81 (2004)
4. Polydorides, N., Lionheart, W.R.B., McCann, H.: Krylov subspace iterative thechniques: On the brain activity with electrical impedance tomography. I3ETMI **21**, 596–603 (2002)
5. Seo, J., Kwon, O., Ammari, H., Woo, E.: A mathematical model for breast cancer lesion estimation: Electrical impedance technique using ts2000 commercial system. I3ETBE **51**, 1898–1906 (2004)
6. Moura, F.S., Lima, R.G., Aya, J.C.C., Fleury, A.T., Amato, M.B.P.: Dynamic imaging in electrical impedance tomography of the human chest with online transition matrix identification. IEEE Trans. Biomed. Engineering **57**, 422–431 (2010)
7. Isaacson, D., Mueller, J.L., Newell, J.C., Siltanen, S.: Imaging cardiac activity by the d-bar method for electrical impedance tomography. Physiological Measurement **27**, S43 (2006)

8. Peters, F.C., Barra, L.P.S., dos Santos, R.W.: Determination of cardiac ejection fraction by electrical impedance tomography - numerical experiments and viability analysis. In: Allen, G., Nabrzyski, J., Seidel, E., van Albada, G.D., Dongarra, J., Sloot, P.M.A. (eds.) ICCS 2009, Part I. LNCS, vol. 5544, pp. 819–828. Springer, Heidelberg (2009)
9. Peters, F.C., Barra, L.P.S., Santos, R.W.: Determination of cardiac ejection fraction by electrical impedance tomography. In: Erondu, O.F. (ed.) Medical Imaging, pp. 253–270. InTech (2011)
10. Filho, R.G.N.S., Campos, L.C.D., dos Santos, R.W., Barra, L.P.S.: Determination of cardiac ejection fraction by electrical impedance tomography using an artificial neural network. In: Castro, F., Gelbukh, A., González, M. (eds.) MICAI 2013, Part II. LNCS, vol. 8266, pp. 130–138. Springer, Heidelberg (2013)
11. Hansen, L.K., Salamon, P.: Neural network ensembles. IEEE Transactions on Pattern Analysis and Machine Intelligence 12, 993–1001 (1990)
12. Opitz, D., Maclin, R.: Popular ensemble methods: An empirical study. Journal of Artificial Intelligence Research 11, 169–198 (1999)
13. Gheyas, I.A., Smith, L.S.: A novel neural network ensemble architecture for time series forecasting. Neurocomputing 74, 3855–3864 (2011)
14. Zhou, Z.H., Jiang, Y., Yang, Y.B., Chen, S.F.: Lung cancer cell identification based on artificial neural network ensembles. Artificial Intelligence in Medicine 24, 25–36 (2002)
15. Cunningham, P., Carney, J., Jacob, S.: Stability problems with artificial neural networks and the ensemble solution. Artificial Intelligence in Medicine 20, 217–225 (2000)
16. Hashem, S.: Optimal linear combinations of neural networks. Neural Networks 10, 599–614 (1997)
17. Maclin, R., Shavlik, J.W.: Combining the predictions of multiple classifiers: Using competitive learning to initialize neural networks. In Proceedings of the Fourteenth International Joint Conference on Artificial Intelligence, pp. 524–530. Morgan Kaufmann (1995)
18. Breiman, L.: Bagging predictors. Machine Learning 24, 123–140 (1996)
19. MATLAB: Neural Network Toolbox. The MathWorks, Inc. (R2009b)
20. Hagan, M.T., Menhaj, M.: Training feed-forward networks with the marquardt algorithm. IEEE Transactions on Neural Networks 5, 989–993 (1999)
21. Linares-Rodriguez, A., Ruiz-Arias, J.A., Pozo-Vazquez, D., Tovar-Pescador, J.: An artificial neural network ensemble model for estimating global solar radiation from meteosat satellite images. Energy 61, 636–645 (2013)

Towards Better Propagation of Geographic Location in Digital Photo Collections

Davi Oliveira Serrano de Andrade[1](✉), Savyo Igor da Nóbrega Santos[1],
Hugo Feitosa de Figueirêdo[2], Cláudio de Souza Baptista[1],
and Joseana Macêdo Fechine Régis de Araújo[1]

[1] Federal University of Campina Grande, Campina Grande, Paraíba, Brasil
{davi,savyo}@copin.ufcg.edu.br,
baptista@dsc.ufcg.edu.br, joseana@computacao.ufcg.edu.br
[2] Federal Institute of Education, Science and Technology of Paraíba – Monteiro, Paraíba, Brasil
hugo.figueiredo@ifpb.edu.br

Abstract. The integration of GPS in smartphones, tablets and digital cameras become increasingly popular, but GPS receivers does not work well indoors. This malfunction can generate erroneous location information from where the picture was really taken, or no information at all. In order to overcome this problem, this paper proposes an automatic selection of techniques that couples different solutions to the problem from multiple regression. The focus of the work is to minimize the error generated by existing techniques with an automatic selection of techniques that uses Artificial Intelligence methods to automatically select the best technique. Also, we execute an experiment to validate the results achieved. After validation, the tests indicated that the proposed automatic selection technique improved the results in five of the six scenarios. In the sixth scenario the results were the same.

Keywords: Geographic Location Propagation · Multimedia · Photographs Collection · Location Prediction · Multiple Linear Regression

1 Introduction

The technology in photograph market has grown considerably, making the process of image capture very simple and accessible to many people. This growth, together with decreasing cost of storage, has led to a large use of electronic devices, such as digital cameras, smartphones and tablets. As a consequence, people have generated a large number of multimedia files, making it difficult to organize and further retrieve them.

Some approaches have been proposed for automatic organization of photographs aiming to minimize user work [4, 5, 12]. At the same time, the creation of photo organizing systems using metadata has also improved the organization of photograph collections. Examples of such metadata include date, time, geographic location, and tags. Geographic location plays an important role on improving photo collection organization. The use of GPS devices facilitates the gathering of photograph locations, but the failures of the device itself cause extra work for the user. Correcting the

© Springer International Publishing Switzerland 2014
A.L.C. Bazzan and K. Pichara (Eds.): IBERAMIA 2014, LNAI 8864, pp. 742–753, 2014.
DOI: 10.1007/978-3-319-12027-0_60

failures caused by GPS receptor manually is very laborious. Therefore research on location propagation and location prediction has been encouraged to improve the results of multimedia retrieval [8, 11, 13].

However, many geographic location propagation techniques [4, 6, 7, 8, 10, 12, 18] were created to solve this problem. Because of this, another difficulty arises, i.e. the choice of the technique that best suits a given database.

Andrade et al. [18] present a comparative study of four geographic location propagation techniques. The results indicate that the choice of location propagation technique depends on the database and user profiles. Thus, the technique must be chosen based on these profiles.

Once most existing photograph databases are large and can dynamically change their profile, the manual identification of the best technique may take a long time. Therefore, there are studies that demonstrate the use of methods to assist this decision making [15, 16, 17].

This paper proposes an automatic selection of techniques for solving the problem described above. The main contribution of the proposed automatic selection of techniques is the error mitigation generated by other techniques by using Multiple-Criteria Decision-Making (MCDM) methods. MCDM methods are mathematical models that help the decision making to find the alternative that best satisfy the goals and pre-established conditions [3, 17].

2   Related Work

This section focuses on related work to geographic location problem, as well as the use of MCDM techniques in many contexts, e.g., Artificial Intelligence.

2.1   Geographic Location Annotation

Gong et al. [7] work on the idea of providing people's location for improving mobile services. Their proposed idea uses a model of social correlation to predict people's location, taking as basis their contact locations. The model is simple and can be easily adapted, but demands people annotation and assumes that the temporal difference between a photograph with location and another without location is small, which can generate unusual results.

Hays and Efros [8] propose an algorithm called "im2gps" estimating the geographic location of a photograph based on the geographic location of photographs with high visual similarity. The "im2gps" uses a database of photographs, so the location found is closely linked to the number of photographs in database. Also image processing takes long time.

Ivanov et al. [10] propose the propagation of geotags, i.e. geographic information about the location where the photo was taken, based on the combination of repeated object detection and modeling the user's confidence. These approaches are not indicated to be used for personal photograph collections, because at various times people present in the photograph cover the largest area of the image. This may decrease the quality of the results.

Hollenstein and Purves [9] suggest geographic location should be defined from the way users describe the place instead of using latitude and longitude coordinates. Hence, tags such as "Eiffel tower", for example, would represent the photograph location. However, it is hard to ensure consistency using user defined tags and to suggest tags not defined by users.

Lacerda et al. [12] address inconsistencies in photograph locations and location propagation. The proposed idea uses a temporal clustering to find the location from the nearest photograph in time and gives good results. However, a photograph collection with a large time interval between the photographs implies in a low precision temporal clustering, which results in locations far from reality.

Andrade et al. [18] propose two techniques: one based on the users trajectory and other based on shared events. The techniques present good results for different test scenarios. However, the work does not propose a way to unite the techniques to improve the results in all tested scenarios.

2.2   MCDM and Artificial Intelligence

Hwang, Kao e Yu [1] propose an integration mechanism based on MCDM and the Collaborative Filtering recommendation technique. The proposed system consists of two main parts. Firstly, the weight of each user for each feature is computed by using Multiple Linear Regression [14]. After this phase, the weight of feature is incorporated into the Collaborative Filtering process to provide the recommendation to users. The experimental results showed that the proposed hybrid approach was better than that used only the technical recommendation.

Adomavicius and Kwon [2] propose two approaches for recommendation, one based on similarity and other based an aggregation function to incorporate and enhance confidence in the prediction based on multi-criteria in recommender systems. Multiple linear regression techniques are used in the construction of the aggregation function. Through a set of real data, the authors showed that using multi-criteria classification recommendation improves item prediction compared to the single classification approach.

Pal, Gupta and Chakraborti [15] present an approach to stochastic simulation-based genetic algorithm (GA) that may be used to model and solve problems based on multi-criteria decision-making. The parameters used in this simulation were obtained randomly according to a lognormal probability distribution and, from them, the GA found the most suitable values according to two predefined regression models: minsum and minmax, which minimizes potential errors associated with the variables defining the objective function of the problem. The proposed technique was tested in decision-making problems encountered in the literature.

Bennett and Hauser [16] develop a framework based on Artificial Intelligence to help in decision-making in a clinical environment. This simulated environment explored health policies and methods of payment as well as being able to "think like a doctor". For this, the technique combined Markov decision processes and dynamic decision networks to learn the clinical data and develop such plans and policies. The results demonstrated the feasibility of the technique concerning performance and implementation cost.

3   Automatic Selection of Propagation Techniques

This section highlights the automatic selection of the location propagation techniques from multiple linear regression. Figure 1 presents the proposed automatic selection model. The techniques used are Social Correlation [7], Temporal Clustering [12], Shared Events [18] and Trajectory [18].

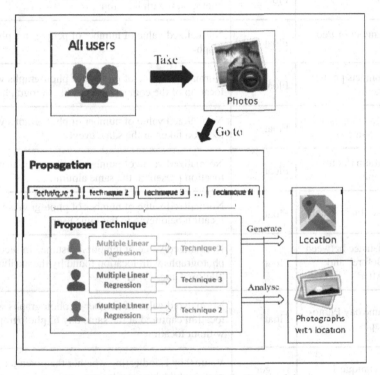

Fig. 1. Proposed automatic selection model

This work proposes an automatic selection of propagation techniques to select which of the four techniques should be used. The selection is made by multiple linear regression, in which each user will have its multiple linear regression models to predict which technique produces the smallest error, and then use it in the propagation of a particular photo. For that regression happens, it is necessary to have a training set. Thus, a metadata table associated with photographs (receiving location via propagation) is created to be used by the regression models. In addition to the metadata, each technique used in the selection process must contain a column in the table. Table 1 describes those columns.

Table 1. Data dictionary

#	Attribute	Type	Comment
1	Photo ID	Integer	Photo's id
2	User ID	Integer	User's id (photograph owner)
3	Before	Float	Normalized value of distance in seconds of the last photograph with location
4	After	Float	Normalized value of distance in seconds of the next photograph with location
5	Number of People	Float	Normalized value of number of people in a photograph
6	Contacts photographs	Float	Normalized value of number of photographs with location of the contacts present in photograph
7	Photographs at the same event	Float	Normalized value of number of photographs with location taken at the same event
8	Album Photographs	Float	Normalized value of number of photographs with location present at the same album
9	User Photographs	Float	Normalized value of number of photographs with location belonging to the same user
10	Distance between "Before" and "After"	Float	Normalized value of temporal distance in seconds of photographs with location found by the attributes "Before" and "After"
11	Same day Photographs	Float	Normalized value of number of photographs with location captured at the same day of photograph without location
12	Technique 1	Integer	Value 0 or 1, indicating whether the given technique produced the best result (1) or not (0)
13	Technique 2	Integer	Value 0 or 1, indicating whether the given technique produced the best result (1) or not (0)
14	Technique 3	Integer	Value 0 or 1, indicating whether the given technique produced the best result (1) or not (0)
15	Technique 4	Integer	Value 0 or 1, indicating whether the given technique produced the best result (1) or not (0)

Through the use of Table, four linear models will be built for each user. Each model is combined with a technique of the automatic selection. The linear models of each user will be used to predict which technique possibly generates the smallest error. Thus, the technique is automatically chosen from that prediction.

4   Methodology

This section discusses the database used and how the results of proposed automatic selection of propagation techniques were collected and tested. Additionally, we highlight the way the data were normalized; how the linear models were tested; and which test scenarios were considered in this study.

4.1   Database

We used a database of approximately 7,900 photographs divided into 41 users. Each photograph contains the following metadata: date and time, geographic location, people in the photographs and personal related event. The owners of the photographs indicated the geographic location for cameras that does not have GPS. Only 13% of the photographs came from cameras that have GPS integrated, 87% of locations were indicated by the observed users.

4.2   Result Gathering

This subsection focuses on how the results were obtained and validated. To collect the results, the database previously mentioned was used and only users with a minimal number ten pictures in their collection were considered.

Data gathering was divided into the followings stages:

1. Calculation of Propagation Error from the Techniques in the Automatic Selection;
2. Table Construction to be Used in the Multiple Linear Regression;
3. Linear Model's Test.

4.2.1   Stage 1 – Calculation of Propagation Error

At this stage, the propagation error generated by the techniques, used in automatic selection, will be calculated. The Pseudocode 1 represents the first stage of the collection of results. For all users in the system, half of the photographs will have their geographic locations temporarily removed and the remainder will serve as the training set for the techniques to perform the location suggestions. The selection of photographs that have temporarily removed the location is taken randomly.

Current techniques in the automatic selection perform the propagation of location and the error of each technique is calculated using the geodesic distance function between the suggested geographic coordinates and the original coordinates of the photograph. The first step is completed when the error of each technique is related to the respective photographs with locations temporarily removed.

```
for (User u in users) {
   toRemoveTemp = getPhotosToRemove(50%, u);
   for (Technique tec in existingTechniques) {
      removeTemporarily(toRemoveTemp);
      for (Photo p in toRemoveTemp) {
          suggestLocation = tec.suggestLocation(p);
          saveSuggestion(suggestedLocation);
      }
      restoreLocation(toRemoveTemp);
   }
}
```

[**Pseudocode 1.** Calculation of propagation error from the techniques in the automatic selection]

4.2.2 Stage 2 – Table Construction

The second stage of data collection consists in data preparation for applying the technique of multiple linear regression. In order to do the regression, it is necessary to mount the table with the associated metadata to photographs and columns indicating whether the technique generates the lowest error among the techniques of the selection.

The process to find the values of the columns is as follows:

- **"User ID"** and **"Photo ID"**: receive the gross amount , without any modification , no need for normalization;
- **"Before"**, **"After"** and **"Distance between 'Before' and 'After' "**: get the standard value from the N2 function shown in Equation 2, whose **"maxx"** parameter indicates the largest value found in the set of values from the concerned column before normalization;
- **"Contacts photographs"**, **"Number of People"**, **"Photographs at the same event"**, **"Album Photographs"**, **"User Photographs"** and **"Same day Photographs"**: receive the normalized value from the N1 function shown in Equation 1 whose **"maxx"** parameter indicates the largest value found in the set of values of the column in question before normalization;
- **"Technique 1"**, **"Technique 2"**, **"Technique 3"** and **"Technique 4"**: receive the normalized value by means of the function N3 shown in Equation 3 or function N4 function shown in Equation 4, where **"minn"** is the parameter that contains the lowest error found among the four techniques of automatic selection for the given photograph.

$$N1(x, maxx) = (^x/_{maxx}) \tag{1}$$

$$N2(x, maxx) = 1 - (^x/_{maxx}) \tag{2}$$

$$N3(x, minn) = \begin{cases} 1, & IF\ (x \leq 100)\ AND\ (x \leq minn) \\ 0, & Otherwise \end{cases} \tag{3}$$

$$N4(x, minn) = \begin{cases} 1, & IF\ (x \leq 100)\ OR\ (x \leq minn) \\ 0, & Otherwise \end{cases} \tag{4}$$

Thus, at the end of the second stage, we have a large table storing all the metadata associated with photographs and a column for each technique that indicates whether this technique should be chosen for the photo or not.

4.2.3 Stage 3 – Linear Model's Test

The third stage is concerned with the test of the linear models created in Stage 2. At the end of the second stage, there is a table with all the metadata associated with the photos that received propagation in step 1. To test the automatic selection of techniques from the regression, the table built in step 2 is divided into training set and testing set for the regression. The training set will be used for the construction of linear models and will consist of 70% of the rows in the metadata table, the choice of lines that will be part of the training set is randomly taken.

With the table divided into training and testing data, linear models of the users are created from the training data. With the linear models created, the metadata of the testing data are used to test the models.

If the technique chosen by linear models has the value 1 in table built in step 2, then it is considered a hit of the proposed automatic selection. In other words, let T1 be the table with the values of linear models constructed in multiple linear regression and T2 the table with the techniques values in the table built in step 2, then:

- $L1_n$ a list representing the row n ($L1_n \in T1$) formatted as $[v1, v2, v3, v4]$;
- $L2_n$ a list representing the row n ($L2_n \in T2$) formatted as $[t1, t2, t3, t4]$;
- indexHighestValue([x,y,z,w]) the function that returns the position of the highest value;
- rowIsCorrect($L1_i, L2_j$) the function shown by Equation 5.

$$\text{rowIsCorrect}(L1_i, L2_j) = L2_j[\text{indexHighestValue}(L1_i)] \tag{5}$$

The precision rate is shown by Equation 6:

$$precision = \frac{\sum_{k=0}^{n} \text{rowIsCorrect}(L1_i, L2_j)}{n} \tag{6}$$

4.3   Testing Scenarios

The steps outlined in the previous subsections were performed considering different testing scenarios. The temporary removal of the location of the photographs was made based on three strategies: random, by user and by event.

In the random removal, as the name suggests, photographs were chosen randomly from the entire set. Thus, the probability of containing either a user or an event with all the photos without location is low.

The removal by user is made by selecting random users and removing the location of all their photographs.

Finally, the removal by event chooses random events and removes the location of all the photographs associated with it.

The stage 1 was repeated 30 times for each removal scenario in which each of them had 10 replicas. Besides the replicas during the stage 1, stage 3 was repeated 30 times for each replica from stage 1. Replicas serve to ensure a set of training not biased.

5   Results and Discussion

The propagation techniques have different behavior according to the database and user profiles [18]. Thus, each testing scenario used the technique that presents the best results.

Therefore, to check the applicability of the proposed automatic selection, the following hypotheses were tested:

- H1: The proposed automatic selection presents a higher minimization percentage than the technique with the best results for the specific scenario;
- H2: The proposed automatic selection presents an equal minimization percentage to the technique with the best results for the specific scenario.

About the data normality, the Shapiro-Wilk [20] and Anderson Darling [21] tests were used to check if the sets came from a normal distribution. Furthermore, to test the hypothesis, the Student-t and Wilcox tests were used [19].

Tests results using N3 and N4 functions are shown in Table 2. It is seen that H1 is rejected only in test scenario 1 using the N3 function. In other cases, it is accepted.

Table 2. Hyphotesis Confirmatiom

	With Function N3	**With Function N4**
Scenario 1	H1 is rejected H2 is rejected	H1 is accepted H2 is rejected
Scenario 2	H1 is accepted H2 is rejected	H1 is accepted H2 is rejected
Scenario 3	H1 is accepted H2 is rejected	H1 is accepted H2 is rejected

The boxplots presented in Figure 2 are the precision percentages of the proposed automatic selection and the best technique for each scenario, considering the N3 function. It is seen in scenario 1, where H1 is rejected, that the values are close, indicating a low mean difference. In the other scenarios the proposed automatic selection presented improvements. The values of the mean differences between the proposed automatic selection and the technique with the best results for the specific scenario are shown in Table 3.

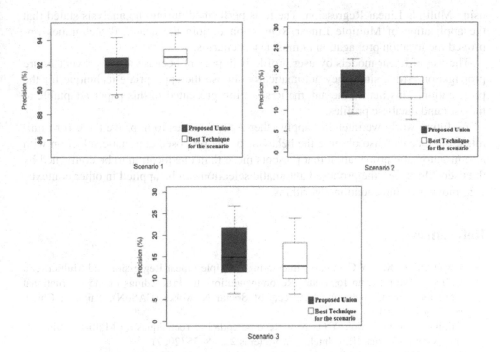

Fig. 2. Precision Boxplots with N3 function

Table 3. Mean Difference between the proposed automatic selection and the technique with the best results for the specific scenario

	With Function N3	With Function N4
Scenario 1	-0.56 %	0.23 %
Scenario 2	1.78 %	1.37 %
Scenario 3	1.66 %	3.13 %

Still in Figure 2, precision rates compared with the proposed automatic selection do not always correspond to the same technique. Thus, the proposed automatic selection presented good results in all tested scenarios, unlike other techniques, considering that for each scenario there is an approach that provides the best results. Therefore, although the proposed automatic selection was not the best choice for scenario 1, in the others tested scenarios some improvements were introduced over the best technique.

6   Conclusion and Future Work

In this work, we present a proposal to minimize the error generated by the automatic selection of four location propagation techniques for the collections of photographs using Multiple Linear Regression. The tests performed during the analysis stated that the application of Multiple Linear Regression to join the analyzed techniques improved the location propagation in most test scenarios.

The use of linear models by user profile is important because it can prevent future propagation errors, since they automatically choose the appropriate technique for the propagation. This makes the automatic selection presented in this paper adaptable to the user and database profiles.

As future work, we intend to apply other AI techniques to improve the error minimization. One can also observe the behavior of the proposed automatic selection with a semi-automatic propagation that presents more than one location to be confirmed by the user. Moreover, the proposed automatic selection can be applied in other contexts, e.g., movie recommendation algorithms.

References

1. Hwang, C.S., Kao, Y.C., Yu, P.: Integrating Multiple Linear Regression and Multicriteria Collaborative Filtering for Better Recommendation. In: Proceedings of the International Conference on Computational Aspects of Social Networks (CASoN), Taiyuan, China, pp. 229–232 (2010)
2. Adomavicius, G., Kwon, Y.O.: New Recommendation Techniques for Multi-Criteria Rating Systems. Journal IEEE Intelligent Systems 22, 48–55 (2007)
3. Vieira, F.M.P.: A Multicriteria Model for Managing Conflict in Aspects Composition. Master's thesis at New University of Lisbon (2006)
4. De Figueirêdo, H.F., Lacerda, Y.A., De Paiva, A.C., Casanova, M.A., De Souza Baptista, C.: PhotoGeo: a photo digital library with spatial-temporal support and self-annotation. Multimedia Tools and Applications 59(1), 279–305 (2012)
5. Shimizu, K., Nitta, N., Babaguchi, N.: Learning people co-occurrence relations by using relevance feedback for retrieving group photos. In: Proceedings of the 1st ACM International Conference on Multimedia Retrieval – ICMR 2011. ACM Press, New York (2011)
6. Gao, H., Tang, J., Liu, H.: Mobile location prediction in spatio-temporal context. In: Nokia Mobile Data Challenge 2012 Workshop. p. Dedicated task, vol. 2(1) (2012)
7. Gong, Y., Li, Y.; Jin, D., Su, L., Zeng, L.: A location prediction scheme based on social correlation. In: IEEE 73rd Vehicular Technology Conference (VTC Spring), pp. 1–5 (2011)
8. Hays, J., Efros, A.: A IM2GPS: estimating geographic information from a single image. In: 2008 IEEE Conference on Computer Vision and Pattern Recognition. IEEE (2008)
9. Hollenstein, L., Purves, R.: Exploring place through user-generated content: Using Flickr tags to describe city cores. Journal of Spatial Information Science, 21–48 (2013)
10. Ivanov, I., Vajda, P., Lee, J.S., Goldmann, L., Ebrahimi, T.: Geotag propagation in social networks based on user trust model. Multimedia Tools and Applications, 155–177 (2012)
11. Lacerda, Y.A., De Figueirêdo, H.F., de Souza Baptista, C., Sampaio, M.C.: PhotoGeo: A Self-Organizing System for Personal Photo Collections. In: 2008 Tenth IEEE International Symposium on Multimedia. IEEE (2008)
12. Lacerda, Y.A., de Figueirêdo, H.F., Da Silva, J.P.R., et al.: On Improving Geotag Quality in Photo Collections. In: The Fifth International Conference on Advanced Geographic Information Systems, Applications, and Services (GEOProcessing 2013), Nice, France: IARIA (2013)

13. Joshi, D., Gallagher, A., Yu, J., Luo, J.: Inferring photographic location using geotagged web images. Multimedia Tools and Applications **56**(1), 131–153 (2012)
14. Montgomery, D.C.: Design and Analysis of Experiments. John Wiley, Hoboken (2009)
15. Pal, B.B., Gupta, S., Chakraborti, D.A.: Genetic Algorithm Based Stochastic Simulation Approach to Chance Constrained Interval Valued Multiobjective Decision Making Problems. In: Proceedings of Second International Conference on Computing, Communication and Networking Technologies, Karur, India, 29 July-31 July (2010)
16. Bennett, C.C., Hauser, K.: Artificial Intelligence Framework for Simulating Clinical Decision-Making: A Markov Decision Process Approach. In: Artificial Intelligence in Medicine (2013)
17. Pohekar, S.D., Ramachandran, M.: Application of multi-criteria decision making to sustainable energy planning - A review. Renewable and Sustainable Energy Reviews **8**, 365–381 (2004)
18. Andrade, D.O.S., de Figueirêdo, H.F., de Souza Baptista, C., de Paiva, A.C.: New Approaches for Geographic Location Propagation in Digital Photograph Collections. In: 16th International Conference on Enterprise Information Systems, ICEIS 2014, Lisbon, Portugal, April 27-30 (in press, 2014)
19. Boslaugh, S.; Watters, P.: Statistics in a Nutshell. O'Reilly (2008)
20. Shapiro, S.S.; Wilk, M.B.: An Analysis of Variance Test for Normality. Biometrika, 591–611 (1965)
21. Anderson, T.W.; Darling, D.A.: Asymptotic Theory of Certain "Goodness-of-Fit" Criteria Based on Stochastic Processes. In: Annals of Mathematical Statistics, pp. 193–212 (1952)

Applying Multiple Regression Analysis to Adjust Operational Limits in Condition-Based Maintenance

Ana Cristina Garcia Bicharra[1], Inhaúma Neves Ferraz[1],
José Viterbo[1(✉)], and Daniel Costa de Paiva[2]

[1] Active Documentation and Design Laboratory (ADDLabs), Instituto de Computação,
Universidade Federal Fluminense (UFF), Niterói, RJ, Brazil
{cristina,ferraz,viterbo}@addlabs.uff.br
[2] Departamento de Informática (DAINF), Universidade Tecnológica Federal do Paraná,
Campus Ponta Grossa (UTFPR), Curitiba, Brazil
professordanielpaiva@gmail.com

Abstract. Condition-based maintenance (CBM) seeks to implement a policy wherein maintenance management decisions are based on the identification of the current condition of monitored machinery. It involves not only collecting data but also comparing them with reference values and, if necessary generating alerts based on preset operational limits. This approach is adopted by a system responsible for monitoring turbomachinery plants in oil platforms, to identify when a machine deserves special attention. With the purpose of extending the functionalities of such system for dynamically adjusting the detection limits and thus improving the precision in setting the appropriate time for maintenance, we proposed an approach based on the identification of clusters of correlated variables and multiple regression analysis. In this paper, we describe our approach and discuss our experience in implementing such functionalities.

Keywords: Condition-based maintenance · Multiple regression analysis · Variable selection

1 Introduction

Maintenance activities fall into two broad categories, which are corrective maintenance and preventive maintenance. Corrective maintenance, also known as breakdown maintenance, is performed as an action to restore the functional capabilities of failed or malfunctioned equipment or systems. It is a reactive approach triggered by the unscheduled abnormal event of an equipment failure. This kind of maintenance policy usually imposes elevated costs due to the high cost of restoring equipment to an operable condition under emergency. There may be extra costs due to secondary damage and safety/health hazards inflicted by the failure and to penalties associated with lost production. On the other hand, preventive maintenance is the approach developed to avoid this kind of waste (Tsang, 1995).

In oil platforms, the equipment used for oil extraction and exploration operates under severe conditions. High pressure, high temperatures, aggressive working

© Springer International Publishing Switzerland 2014
A.L.C. Bazzan and K. Pichara (Eds.): IBERAMIA 2014, LNAI 8864, pp. 754–764, 2014.
DOI: 10.1007/978-3-319-12027-0_61

conditions, high throughput and long shifts can have a critical effect on any component. In this scenario, the turbomachinery systems are the most sensitive equipment, since any interruption causes total shutdown of platform activity, resulting in extremely high financial cost (Ferraz and Garcia, 2014). As such, to avoid interruption in turbomachinery operation, it is very important to carry out preventive maintenance that is scheduled to occur during circumstances and at times when there is a high degree of control.

There are different approaches to preventive maintenance. Time-based maintenance (TBM), also known as periodic-based maintenance, is the most common approach. Following this approach, maintenance is performed to prevent or retard failures at hard time intervals regardless of other information that may be available when the preset time occurs. Such task also requires an intrusion into the equipment, thereby rendering it out of service until the task is completed (Tsang, 1995). An inadequate TBM strategy, however, may lead to unnecessarily high downtime – if it is carried out earlier than needed –, or accidental breakdown of a machine – if it is performed too late –, in both cases causing loss of money (Pham e Yang, 2009). Hence, maintenance optimization is a topic of great interest to researchers for its significant appeal to the safety and financial aspects involved (Marseguerra et al., 2002).

When the system condition can be continuously monitored, a Condition-Based Maintenance (CBM) strategy can be implemented, according to which the decision of maintaining the system is taken dynamically, based on the observed condition of the system (Marseguerra et al., 2002). CBM is assessed as the most effective technology that can identify incipient faults before they become critical. While other approaches such as corrective and time-based maintenance have shown to be costly in many applications, CBM enables more accurate planning of maintenance (Pham e Yang, 2009).

CBM seeks to implement a policy wherein maintenance management decisions are based on the identification of the current condition of monitored machinery (Emmanouilidis et al., 2006). Nowadays, advanced equipment and sensor technologies provide a great variety of timely data to reveal a machine's condition. Such data has to be analyzed in real-time to allow observing and evaluating the equipment condition in a more timely fashion (Chen and Wu, 2007). Condition monitoring data are very versatile. It can be vibration data, acoustic data, oil analysis data, temperature, pressure, moisture, humidity, weather or environment data, etc (Jardine et al., 2006).

Condition monitoring involves not only collecting such data but also comparing it with reference values and, if necessary generating alerts based on preset operational limits (Niu and Yang, 2010). In general, such operational limits are established based on manufacturers' recommendations, and utility and industry operating experience. However, as machines may operate in different environments, and thus, subject to different work conditions, in some situations such nominal values may not be the most adequate references. Therefore, artificial intelligence techniques may be useful to adjust such operational limits to the specific conditions of a machinery apparatus.

In this work we discuss our experience in a project for implementing new functionalities for a system responsible for monitoring turbomachinery plants in oil platforms. This system collects data from different sensors distributed all over a plant, each representing a variable. The collected signals are compared with a set of lower and upper reference values and when they cross pre-defined limits, the respective equipment may go under maintenance.

Our project aimed at developing new computational algorithms to be aggregated as new functionalities to the original system, introducing a degree of techniques based on artificial intelligence in the analysis of the turbomachine variables. We proposed several approaches with the purpose of dynamically adjusting the detection limits and thus improving the precision in setting the appropriate time for maintenance. In this work we focus on an approach based in the identification of clusters of correlated variables. The correlation coefficients are used to assess the influence of the variables in one another, thus allowing to calculate narrower limits based on this influence. In this paper, we discuss the fundaments for this novel approach and how it was implemented. In the next section, we present the scenario of our project. In Section 3, we present some fundamental concepts involved in our solution. In Section 4, we explain how the approach was implemented. In Section 5, we describe a case study. Finally, in Section 6 we draw our conclusions.

2   Scenario

In this work we discuss our experience in a project for implementing new functionalities for a system that consists in a center for monitoring the health of turbo machinery plants in oil platforms operated by a large energy corporation. The overall monitoring is performed via the remote monitoring of a set of variables collected from several sensors distributed along the plants, applying a Condition-Based Maintenance (CBM) strategy.

In the referred system, abnormal conditions of the machines are detected when any of the variables related with a given machine go above or below some predefined values. Such values define a set of alarms, in which there are 3 levels above (high, very high and critically high), and 3 levels below (low, very low and critically low). Only when the value of a monitored variable crosses one of the defined levels, the operator will check the variable. Because there is no continuous monitoring, many transients are not perceived at the time to issue a warning. The large number of variables that must be visually monitored by the operator causes the scan time to become too long.

As usual, at beginning of operation, such operational limits were set based on manufacturers' recommendations. As the machines operate subject to different work conditions in each plant of each platform, such limits were gradually and manually adjusted along time, based on the operators experience. This option reflects believes of the operators, the thresholds could be adjusted to alert a long time or a little time before the effective operator interference.

The purpose of our project was to develop new computational algorithms to be aggregated as new functionalities to the original system, introducing a degree of techniques based on Artificial Intelligence in the analysis of the turbomachine variables. Such functionalities should make the system capable of making more accurate and faster problem identification, contributing to increase the availability of the platforms main compression and generation systems, thus reducing losses in the oil and gas production. The main purpose was propose algorithms to automatically and dynamically adjust the reference limits for each variable.

In the specification of the new functionalities, a set of functional requirements were proposed by the client. Among them, the following are tackled in this paper:

- R1: The project should provide a functionality to calculate new monitoring limits of a variable, based on the historical values of such variable.
  - R1.1 The user should choose the variables for having new limits calculated;
  - R1.2 The user should decide for the adoption or not of the new limit calculated.
- R2: The project should provide a functionality to calculate new monitoring limits of a variable based on the influence other variables may have on this one.
  - R2.1: The user should define, based on their experience. a set of variables that he believes are strongly correlated. This option is related to time of reaction, some of the users prefer alerts with a comfortable time and others on a limit that they have to interfere;
  - R2.2: Along the process, the user should be capable of defining (or redefining default values) each parameter involved in such calculation.

In order to achieve such purposes, the project team had to surpass a number of challenges. As a first task, it was necessary to understand the behavior of the huge number of variables. In a set of approximately 150 machines, on average 100 variables were monitored by machine, totaling about 15,000 variables. Such large number of variables comprises different plants in different platforms and also different types (such, as external temperature, oil temperature, vibration, etc). Besides, the frequency of data acquisition and data acquisition time-window were two extra parameters to be studied in the pursue of the most adequate data sample conditions. After overcoming such challenges, the implementation of the first requirement was straightforward.

For meeting the second requirement, however, it was necessary to propose an innovative algorithm to identify groups of corrclated variables. In Section 4, we describe the technique we proposed to dynamically calculate a more precise set of alarms for each monitored variable, based on the natural interdependency among some of the variables in a plant. As this proposal involves multiple regression analysis and this topic is discussed in the next section.

3   Fundamental Concepts

In this section, we discuss some concepts on which this work was based and which are necessary for a clear understanding of the proposed approach, such as multiple regression analysis and variable selection.

3.1   Multiple Regression Analysis

According to Aiken *et al.* (2003), multiple regression analysis is a general system for examining the relationship of a collection of independent variables to a single dependent variable. Multiple regression analysis provides an assessment of how well a set of independent variables taken as a whole account for the dependent variable. Multiple regression (MR) analysis involves the estimation of a multiple regression equation that summarizes the relationship of a set of predictors to the observed criterion.

According to Møller *et al.* (2005), in multiple linear regression, the response variable Y_i is regressed on k explanatory variables $(X_{i1},...,X_{ik})$ in the model:

$$Y_i = b_0 + b_1 X_{i1} + ... + b_k X_{ik} + \varepsilon_i$$

where Y is a dependent variable, X_j are the independent variables, b_0 is the regression intercept, b_j are partial regression coefficients (or regression weights) and ε is the residual error. Considering $\hat{Y}$ the predicted value for the dependent variable, and Y the observed value. In multiple regression, the values of each regression weight b_0, b_1, ... , b_k are chosen so as to minimize the sum of the squared residuals across the participants. That is, the regression weights b_0, b_1, ... , b_k are chosen so that

$$\sum_{i=1}^{n} \varepsilon_i^2 = \sum_{i=1}^{n}(Y_i - \hat{Y}_i)^2 \text{ is minimum.}$$

This criterion is termed ordinary least squares. Multiple regression computed using ordinary least squares produces optimal estimates of the regression weights in that the correlation between the predicted score $\hat{Y}$ and the observed dependent variable Y is maximized.

Variable Selection

A crucial problem in building a multiple regression model is the selection of the independent variables that will form the best model (George and McCulloch, 1993). Stepwise regression is a standard procedure for variable selection, which is based on the procedure of sequentially introducing the predictors into the model one at a time. The stepwise regression is classified into three methods: forward selection, backward elimination and stepwise method. The forward selection adds predictors to the model one at a time. In contrast to the forward selection, the backward elimination begins with the full model and successively eliminates one predictor at a time. The stepwise method starts as the forward selection, but at each stage the possibility of deleting a predictor, as backward elimination, is considered (Chong and Jun, 2005).

In these methods, the number of variables retained in the final model is determined by some criteria assumed for inclusion (or exclusion) of variables in a model, such as the covariance index (Edwards, 1985) or the level of significance. Thus, in our approach we based our decision of including or not a variable in a group for regression on the covariance index, as will be further explained in the next section.

4   The Proposed Approach

Our purpose was to propose a technique to dynamically calculate a more precise set of alarms (variable monitoring limits) for each monitored variable, based on the natural interdependency among some of the variables in a plant. The rationale behind this approach goes as follows:

> *If the value of a given variable Y can be estimated by applying the values of a set of variables X_j in a multiple regression model, the set of limits of Y can be recalculated using the same model and taking as input the set of limits of each variables X_j, thus allowing the definition of tighter limits.*

This is true because, given a multiple regression model that represents this system, if we admit that each variable X_j assumes exactly the same value corresponding to a limit associated with a specific alarm level, the expected value of Y for this situation can be estimated as $\bar{Y}$. As this situation deserves the level of attention associated with that given alarm level, if Y reaches the value $\bar{Y}$, it may indicate a malfunctioning deserving the same level of attention. Thus, if this value is tighter then the previous limit of Y for that alarm level, the value calculated by regression $\bar{Y}$ may be considered as a tighter limit for alarming. We call this the "multivariate limit".

4.1   Multivariate Limit Algorithm

The algorithm for calculating the multivariate limit for a given dependent variable was implemented meeting some functional requirements defined by the users during the specification phase:

- R2.1: At the beginning of the process, the users should define, based on their experience. a set of variables that she or he believes are strongly correlated;
- R2.2: Along the process, the users should be capable of defining (or redefining default values) each parameter of the algorithm.

Therefore, in the process of calculating the multivariate limits, the user has to interacts with the system in several steps to set or change each parameter of the algorithm. Figure 1 illustrates this process, enumerating the eight steps executed and indicating if they are performed by the user or by the system. Each step is explained ahead.

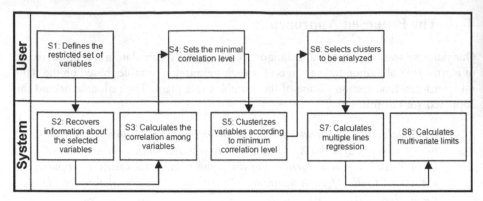

Fig. 1. Steps for calculating the multivariate limits

Step 1: Defining the restricted set of variables and time period

At first the user must define a restricted set of variables to be analyzed. This decision is based on the user's own experience, i.e., the user will select a set of variables that he thinks are strongly correlated, so that they will be the ones considered in the further steps for the calculation of the multivariate limits. The user must also define the time window for data samples that will be used in the calculation. This step was implemented to meet functional requirements elicited in the specification phase.

Step 2: Recovering information about the selected variables

Once the variables were selected and the time period to be considered in the calculation was defined by the user in the previous step, it is necessary to retrieve the respective data sample from the database. The calculation of the correlation between all the variables is carried out using such data set.

Step 3: Calculating the correlation among variables

As we discussed in Section 2.2, it is necessary to identify in the restricted set of variables which ones should be included in the final model. To assess the correlation among variables, we opted to calculate the covariance between each of the variables of the set. We generate the covariance matrix, a matrix whose element C_{ij} in the position i, j is the covariance between the ith and j^{th} variables. Thus, the covariance matrix gives a hint on how each pair of variables is correlated.

Step 4: Setting the minimal correlation level

Once again abiding to the elicited requirements, this steps allows the user to set the minimal correlation level that will be used to identify variables that belong to the same cluster, i.e., selecting variables to compose a model. As such, the covariance matrix is presented to the user, so that he can define which is the minimum correlation value for determining the clusters of variables.

Step 5: Clusterizing variables according to minimum correlation level
To generate the clusters we used an agglomerative algorithm, which takes the correlation value as the measure of similarity. The algorithm gathers the variables in a same cluster until the highest value of this correlation in the matrix is less than the minimum correlation value defined by the user. The generated clusters are exclusive and partial, whereas a variable can only belong to one group and not all variables are grouped together due to the defined minimum level of correlation. As our purpose is to identify a set of strongly correlated variables, the covariance is adopted as criteria to separate clusters of correlated variables that can be represented by a multivariate regression model, according with Algorithm 1:

Algorithm 1. Clustering strongly correlated variables

```
1   Calculate the covariance matriz
2   While there is a C_{ij} > C_{min} and matrix dimension > 1
3       Select the biggest C_{ij}
4       Group i^{th} and j^{th} variables
5       Recalculate the covariance matrix
```

In this algorithm, C_{min} is the minimal covariance for which we consider that two variables are strongly correlated, and as such, should be included in the same set for defining a multivariate regression model. In each step of the algorithm (line 4) the most correlated variable are linearly combined, forming a new derived variable. Given n variables, at the end of the algorithm, we may have 1 to n groups (clusters) of variables.

Step 6: Selecting clusters to be analyzed
The algorithm gathers the variables in a same cluster until the highest value of this correlation in the matrix is less than the minimum correlation value defined by the user. The generated clusters are exclusive and partial, whereas a variable can only belong to one group and not all variables are grouped together due to the defined minimum level of correlation.

Step 7: Calculating the multiple linear model
Once the clusters are defined, the multiple linear regression is calculated for each group in several iterations, each assuming one variable as the dependent (or target) variable (as discussed in Section 3).

Step 8: Calculating multivariate limits
Finally, the multivariable restrictive limits are calculated.

5   Case Study

For this case study, we selected a set of ten variables named Var_1 to Var_{10}, for each of which we have collected a hundred sample values. The graph presented in Figure 2 shows the behavior of such variables along the time.

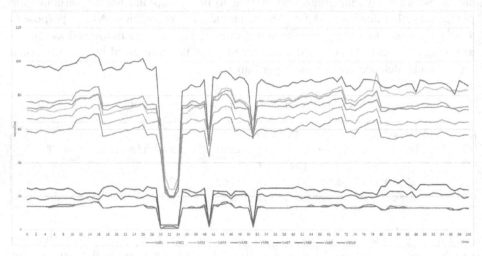

Fig. 2. Graph showing the behavior one of each the ten selected variables

In this same figure, it is possible to identify that in general there is some interdependency among these variables, as they vary similarly along the time. In fact, applying the clustering algorithm, according to minimum correlation level, previously discussed, the following clusters were formed:

- Cluster 1: Var_1, Var_2, Var_3, Var_6, Var_9, Var_{10}
- Cluster 2: Var_7, Var_8
- Cluster 3: Var_4
- Cluster 4: Var_5

Variables Var_4 and Var_5, formed individual clusters, what means in fact that these variables weren't groupped in any of the clusters, i.e., they don't influence or are influenced by any other in the group.

After the clusters are formed, it is possible to calculate the multivariate limits by applying the multiple linear regression. Figure 3 shows the visualization that is presented for the user indicating the limits for Var_3. The green stripe is limited by the high and low limits, the yellow stripe is limited below by the high limit and above by the very high limit, the orange stripe is limited bellow by the very high limited and above by the critically high limit. Then there is the red stripe above all the other stripes.

The multivariate limits can also be seen in the same figure as two black lines, one above and the other below the time series of the variable. Their respective values are 70.83 and 63.67, which are limits very much tighter than the previous limits indicated in the figure, which are 80 and 13, the borders of the green stripe.

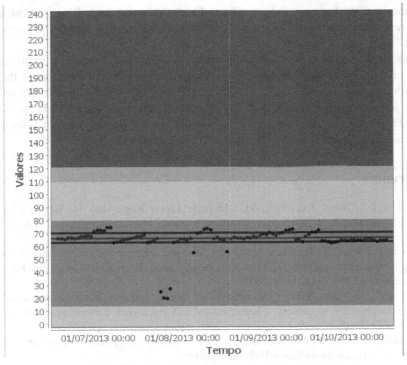

Fig. 3. Visualization of the limits and behavior of variable Var_3

6   Conclusions

In this work, we discussed our experience in a project for implementing new functionalities for a system responsible for monitoring turbomachinery plants in oil platforms. This system collects data from different sensors distributed all over a plant, each representing a variable. Abnormal conditions of the machines are detected when any of the variables related with a given machine go above or below some predefined values. At beginning of operation, such operational limits were set based on manufacturers' recommendations. As the machines operate subject to different work conditions in each plant of each platform, such limits were gradually and manually adjusted along time, based on the operators experience.

The purpose of our project was to develop new computational algorithms to be aggregated as new functionalities to the original system, introducing a degree of techniques based on artificial intelligence in the analysis of the turbomachine variables. The main purpose was propose algorithms to automatically and dynamically adjust the reference limits for each variable reducing the dependence of the operators experiences.

In this work we focused on an approach based in identification of clusters of correlated variables. The correlation coefficients are used to assess the influence of the variables in one another, thus allowing the calculation of narrower limits based on this influence. We explained the techniques applied and how such functionality was implemented. With a case study we showed how the multivariate limits are calculated and presented to the users, which may use this information to update the monitoring limits.

The implementation of such functionalities met the users requirements and received a satisfactory evaluation from the client, which in fact adopted the new algorithm in the original system. However, the evaluation if the new limits will improve the overall performance of the plant maintenance could not be performed immediately. In fact, it requires a long time of data collection and analysis on the turbomachines' maintenance cycles and will presented in the future.

References

1. Aiken, L.S., West, S.G., Pitts, S.C.: Multiple Linear Regression. In: Weiner I.B., et al. (eds.) Handbook of Psychology. Research methods in psychology, vol. 2, pp. 483–507. Wiley (2003)
2. Chen, A., Wu, G.S.: Real-time health prognosis and dynamic preventive maintenance policy for equipment under aging Markovian deterioration. International Journal of Production Research 45(15), 3351–3379 (2007)
3. Chong, I.G., Jun, C.H.: Performance of some variable selection methods when multicollinearity is present. Chemometrics and Intelligent Laboratory Systems 78(1), 103–112 (2005)
4. Edwards, A.L.: Multiple regression and the analysis of variance and covariance. WH Freeman/Times Books/Henry Holt & Co (1985)
5. Emmanouilidis, Christos, Jantunen, Erkki, MacIntyre, John: Flexible software for condition monitoring, incorporating novelty detection and diagnostics. Computers in Industry 57(6), 516–527 (2006)
6. Ferraz, I.N., Garcia, A.C.B.: Turbo machinery failure prognostics. In: Proceedings of the IEA-AIE The 27th International Conference on Industrial, Engineering & Other Applications of Applied Intelligent Systems (2014)
7. George, E.I., McCulloch, R.E.: Variable selection via Gibbs sampling. Journal of the American Statistical Association 88(423), 881–889 (1993)
8. Jardine, A.K.S., Lin, D., Banjevic, D.: A review on machinery diagnostics and prognostics implementing condition-based maintenance. Mechanical Systems and Signal Processing 20(7), 1483–1510 (2006)
9. Kuo, L., Mallick, B.: Variable selection for regression models. Sankhyā: The Indian Journal of Statistics, Series B, 65–81 (1998)
10. Marseguerra, Marzio, Zio, Enrico, Podofillini, Luca: Condition-based maintenance optimization by means of genetic algorithms and Monte Carlo simulation. Reliability Engineering & System Safety 77(2), 151–165 (2002)
11. Møller, S., von Frese Frosch, J., Rasmus, B.: Robust methods for multivariate data analysis. Journal of Chemometrics 19(10), 549–563 (2005)
12. Niu, Gang, Yang, Bo-Suk: Intelligent condition monitoring and prognostics system based on data-fusion strategy. Expert Systems with Applications 37(12), 8831–8840 (2010)
13. Pham, Hong Thom, and Bo-Suk Yang. Estimation and forecasting of machine health condition using ARMA/GARCH model. Mechanical Systems and Signal Processing 24.2: 546–558. (2010)
14. Tsang, A.H.C.: Condition-based maintenance: tools and decision making. Journal of Quality in Maintenance Engineering 1(3), 3–17 (1995)

Ambient Intelligence

EKG Intelligent Mobile System for Home Users

Gabriel Villarrubia[1(✉)], Juan F. De Paz[1], Juan M. Corchado[1], and Javier Bajo[2]

[1] Department of Computer Science and Automation, University of Salamanca,
Plaza de la Merced, s/n, 37008, Salamanca, Spain
{gvg,fcofds,corchado}@usal.es
[2] Department of Artificial Intelligence, Faculty of Computer Science,
Technical University of Madrid, Madrid, Spain
jbajo@fi.upm.es

Abstract. Medical diagnosis is a fundamental field to detect potential diseases and illness in patients. Nowadays, decision support systems used to detect health problems present several technical advances with respect to the existing systems 20 or 30 years ago. This work is associated to this evolution in diagnostic systems. In this work, a low cost electrocardiography system is developed. The system is able of acquiring patient medical information and send it to a medical center in execution time. This system can be used as an alternative to the current Holter monitors in daily life to record heart activity for 24 hours.

Keywords: EKG mobile · Information fusion · Physical activity monitor · Electrocardiogram · Health sensors

1 Introduction

Due to the advances occurred during last years in mobile technologies, the decreasing price of the terminals, and the ease of access of mobile devices, more and more people have a Smartphone on their daily activities. According to a report from Strategy Analytics [1] the sales of smartphones grew 40% to reach around 990.0 million units sold; this report give us an idea of the great impact of the smartphones in our society [2][3][4]. Smartphones can be explored as technological tools that can help humans in different ways and a critical field where smartphones can be applied is health care.

Nowadays, it is possible to find a variety of "silent" diseases. These diseases don't have symptoms but they are in continuous evolution. Some examples of these diseases are diabetes, hypertension or hypercholesterolemia [5][6], they can lead to important pathologies in the future such as myocardial infarction and stroke, associated with a high mortality among adults.

However, an early diagnosis and a correct treatment and control, can notably help the patients to avoid the consequences of these diseases and to prolong the quality of life [7][8].

© Springer International Publishing Switzerland 2014
A.L.C. Bazzan and K. Pichara (Eds.): IBERAMIA 2014, LNAI 8864, pp. 767–778, 2014.
DOI: 10.1007/978-3-319-12027-0_62

In this sense, the use of mobile devices provides a very useful and versatile tool to prevent and control diseases [10][11]. An example can be our previous work [24], where we pay special attention to the use of multi-agent systems for the detection and monitoring of the patients.

A clear example is the report of "Global Mobile Health Market Report 2010-2015" [9] carried out by expert of research2guidance establishes that in 2015 around 500 million of people in the world will use some application to interact with him/her doctor.

As to Global Mobile Health [9] there are over 4,200 mobile apps in the health sector available in the Apple and Android market places. These kinds of services allow the remote monitoring of the patient by doctors, helping people to control their health status remotely, in their homes.

In this work we present a system for mobile devices that can be used as an alternative to the Holter measurement systems available in medical centers. A Holter monitor is a portable device that measures and records the patient's heart activity EKG (*Elektrokardiogramm*) continuously for 24 to 48 hours [12][13]. The size of a Holter is similar to a compact camera and it has a series of cables connected to electrodes attached to the patient's skin.

A Holter monitor is a device used by the medical staff to observe the activity of the heart during the daily life of the patient. Abnormal heart rhythms and cardiac symptoms may appear and disappear intermittently, which is why physicians may need to evaluate the patient's heartbeat through your daily activities.

The data recorded by the device can be used to check the heartbeat and to establish if it is slow, fast or irregular. The information of an EKG can be used to check whether a certain medicine is working, or to check if a pacemaker is working correctly. This information can help the doctors to improve the patients' treatment.

A Holter monitor has no risks for the patient and it is painless [14]. The main drawback of these devices is their high price, which makes them unaffordable to the vast majority of patients who may need it. These devices are acquired by medical centers, but due to the high cost, medical centers usually don't have a sufficient number of available devices to meet the demand. Because of this, there are waiting lists, with the corresponding health risk for patients.

Another drawback with the Holter monitors is that the patient must register accurately all movements and activities carried out throughout the duration of the test. The patients have to register their daily activity, which also means a loss of precision, because some of the annotations cannot fully correspond to reality.

In this work a simple system, low cost and fully integrated with Smartphone is presented to emulate a Holter monitor. The system combines Arduino device with a smartphone to design an advanced and ubiquitous system. Arduino [15] has been used to record the heart rates continuously, using a set of electrodes. The system design scheme is shown in Figure 6. All the hardware used for the prototype is commercially available at a very low cost.

The data acquired by the EKG are displayed in real time in the user's Smartphone. One of the main advances of the system is its ability to fuse the EKG data with the values of the GPS and accelerometer of the device. This information will serve to monitor the daily activities performed by the user, wearing the device in similar way than a Holter monitor. If the user is at rest, the accelerometer or GPS values will indicate that there is not significant activity [16]. In other case, if the user is walking or performing physical activity, the accelerometers will register this activity.

Thanks to all this information, we will have a collection of values about the patient's heart rhythm and that activities performed. This information is received and processed in real time on the Smartphone, and it is sent to the doctor in charge of monitoring the patient.

Additionally, the proposed system will incorporate models to predict possible heart problems, through the comparison of the processed data with a collection of statistical data. The system not only records the sensor values, it will also process them in real time for detecting anomalies and send alerts to medical centers.

2   Literature Review

This section presents the state of the art of existing Holter systems, electrocardiograms readers systems and systems used to monitor daily physical activity of users.

First, we start reviewing the Holter monitor systems that can be found on the market. The vast majority of these devices are intended to provide services in medical centers and hospitals and not to the general public. The main reason is that the prices of these devices are very high. Besides, medical professionals are qualified to use them, because managing these devices requires technical knowledge and previous experience about their management.

The Dutch company Philips sells professional Holters devices, specifically the model DigiTrak XT Holter Recorder (Figure 1) which is priced at about $15,000.

Fig. 1. Philips DigiTrak XT Holter Recorder

The Phillips Holter monitor is one of the lightest devices on the market; it has an integrated display to provide information to the user. It has 12 referrals for heart rate measurement, pacemaker detector sensitivity settings, and can make a recording for up to 7 days on a single AAA battery. Another example of commercial systems like this is the BMS1200 of biomedical systems. The price is around € 20,000, and has very similar characteristics the Philips device.

There are many commercial examples of Holter monitors, they are very similar in price and features, and they are aimed at doctors and centers handled by qualified professionals.

Apart from this, it is possible to find more alternatives for a domestic use but equally effective and integrated with smartphones. The Israeli company SHL Tele-medicine offers a product called SmartHeart. This device is a household electrocardi-ogram that connects wirelessly to any SmartPhone and is able to record the user's ECKG and later sending the information to a doctor in order to make an analysis of the data.

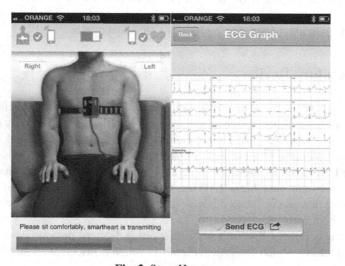

Fig. 2. SmartHeart app

This device simplifies the process of obtaining an EKG, especially compared to the Holter monitors used in medical centers. It's very simple to use since it only consists of an elastic band, it is placed on the chest and that the electrodes are integrated to the monitor that will record and send data to the Smartphone. The application interface is also very simple to use, since the user simple has to connect the device and link it via Bluetooth as illustrated in Figure 2.

This system has a cost of around $ 500, is less than the price Holter devices but still high for most users. Also note that this monitor only records heart activity over a peri-od of 30 seconds, while the Holter devices can monitor a person from 24h onwards.

The American company AliveCor has developed the AliveCor Heart Monitor, a sheath for Smartphones able to record the EKG through a single channel in the rear, Figure 3.

This device is integrated within the cover of a smartphone, and its price is $ 200 lower than other systems making it accessible to the public. It was created by Dr. David Albert, a cardiologist with over thirty years of experience. His main goal was to create an accessible EKG to everyone. The manufacturing cost in China per device is less than $ 15, which represents a very affordable price.

Fig. 3. EKG sheath for Smartphones

This monitor fits into the back side of a smartphone, and provides capacities to record, view, store and transfer wirelessly, the rhythms of the single EKG channel with the AliveECG application. It is not necessary a link between the Smartphone and the heart monitor. The heart rate data is recorded and can be of any length. It can be stored in the smartphone and in a cloud. The system provides a report in PDF format to be reviewed, analyzed and printed through the website AliveCor, which meets the HIPAA (Health Insurance Portability and Accountability) requirements.

Another open source alternative is found in the American College of South Carolina, Dr. Chris Rorden's research group has developed a prototype EKG open source system based on Arduino controller and a bluetooth system [17] shown in Figure 4.

An interesting feature of the ADS129n chip used in this project is that it provides 24 bits of precision. This allows that a single hardware design will be used for different applications. In contrast, a 16-bit design has to be adjusted for small and slow signals from the scalp to perform a rapid test or EEG signals generated by relatively large superficial muscles in EMG test. The chip also contains a number of more sophisticated data filtering to EKG acquisition. The recent ADS1299 chip provides better accuracy, but requires higher energy power.

Fig. 4. Prototype of South Carolina's college

The documentation, source code and hardware schemes of the project are available on the website of the university. Although the system still does not have a medical validation, the test results can provide a degree of accuracy similar to that of professional medical devices.

Regarding the activity meters that exist in the market, we can highlight the Fitbit Flex bracelets (Figure 5) from company Fitbit [21]. This is a watch to measure your daily activity: steps, calories burned, the walking distance and even the quality of your sleep.

Fig. 5. Fitbit Flex bracelets

This kind of bracelets takes a series of accelerometers and altimeter to monitor the activity values.

3   Proposed System

This paper proposes a system composed of an Open Source Arduino electrocardio-gram to merge the data of an EKG with the values of the sensors of Smartphone and monitor the physical activity of a patient shown in Figure 6. The obtained data will be analyzed by an intelligent algorithm that will be able to detect heart episodes and trigger a series of actions, such as contacting with a doctor.

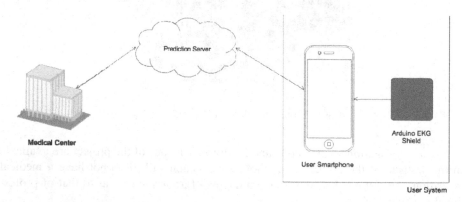

Fig. 6. Scheme of the proposed system

3.1   Low Cost EKG

As previously mentioned, the components of the prototype are based on Arduino technology because this technology is hardware and software free and it allow easily integrating a wide range of chip components and sensors. The prototype consists of 2 plates Ardunio (one Board and Shield) and electrodes compatible with the electronics.

Arduino Bluetooth: This is a kind of Arduino Board, it is responsible to interpret and process the information from the Shield plate and send the information via a bluetooth to the Smartphone user.

Olimex Arduino Shield SHIELD-EKG-EMG: The board receives the information from the electrodes and encode, Figure 7. The prototype and the example code, can be found in https://www.olimex.com/Products/Duino/Shields/SHIELD-EKG-EMG/open-source-hardware.

Fig. 7. Olimex Arduino SHIELD-EKG-EMG

Electrodes SHIELD-EKG-EMG-PA: they will be connected to the patient (Figure 8).

Fig. 8. Electrodes for EKG shield

The firmware of the Arduino executes the source code to read the data of the EKG. We used the Arduino programming language with Mstimer2 TimerOne and libraries provided by the manufacturer.

The functionality of the firmware is to obtain the values of the attached sensors in the shield and provides the information thought bluethooth connection.

In the Figure 9 is seen the graphics obtained by using the values obtained by the electrodes.

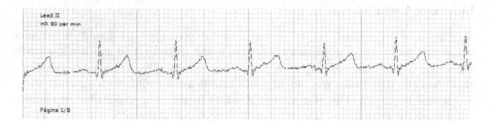

Fig. 9. EKG graphics

3.2 Algorithms for Detecting Cardiac Events

Currently many algorithms have been proposed for the detection of cardiac events. However, the recognition of the heart rate is still unsatisfactory due to unreliable extraction features in the analysis of the characteristic signal. It is possible to find advanced works in this area that allows learning patterns on electrocardiograms to predict pathologies.

In this work, the EKG introduces more noise than a professional EKG, and the calculation of P, QRS and T waves is more complicated. Thus, instead of calculating the length of each ware, the system calculates the maximum point or each wave P, QRS and T that can be easily observed in Figure 10.

First the R-wave is detected. The process to detect the R-wave peak is simple. The system looks for a sequence of values higher than a threshold tr according to the work [23], then the maximum value is selected. To find the minimum value of the P wave, the system follows the same procedure; the threshold is set tp and minimum value in the interval Ip prior to the wave time tr is calculated. Similarly the proceeds with the p-wave, s and t.

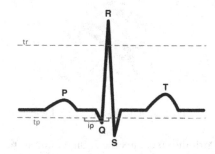

Fig. 10. EKG wave diagram

To detect anomalies, some basic rules were introduced based on the type of problem detected. Specifically, we have analyzed: sinus tachycardia up to 150 beats, sinus arrhythmia beats variation depending on the breathing apparatus is observed easily, SA nodal blocking a pause in a multiple of p-p interval, sinus pause is not a pause interval is multiple of p. This type of pathologies is analyzed using a set of rules according to a given definition. Apart from this pathology, it is possible to find many other pathologies so that it is necessary to introduce new rules.

One alert is sent automatically if a wave is not detected. Usually, it will be a symptom of a serious disease or malfunction of the system.

3.3   Sensors to Monitorize Daily Life

In this paper we use the sensors available in a Smartphone to merge this data with the information obtained from the EKG system weared by the user. Specifically, to obtain these values the system accesses to the values of the accelerometer and GPS.

The accelerometers can be used to detect the physical activity and detect if the person is walking, standing. Also, in outdoors environments, the GPS can determine the route of the patients and the walking speed. The detection step with the accelerometer is performed according to this work [18].

These values are useful to determine the activity performed by the user and to merge them with the values of the EKG. The system can determine if those values are normal or if there is a real problem instead. For this purpose, a case-based reasoning system is designed to determine if the situation is abnormal or not. A CBR system is chosen because the capacities for learning and adaptation as well as for the active participation of medical experts in the supervised evaluation and learning of the system. The proposed reasoning system makes use of past experiences to propose new solutions. CBR systems execute a CBR cycle composed of 4 stages: retrieve (to recover past experiences), reuse (to obtain a new solution based on the retrieved past experiences), revise (to evaluate the obtained solution) and retain (to learn from the new experience). The CBR system proposed in this paper recovers a set of variables for a group of patients. This dataset is used as an input for the reuse phase of the CBR system. The reuse phase incorporates new classification techniques during the reuse phase, not previously used for this kind of problems, in order to generate a classification for the new patient. The system defines a time series composed of 30 measures, each measure ei contains the elements showed in the table 1.

Table 1. EKG waves and times

Wave	Time
Pi	Milliseconds from the last value pi-1
Qi	Milliseconds from the last value qi-1
Ri	Milliseconds from the last value ri-1
Si	Milliseconds from the last value si-1
Ti	Milliseconds from the last value ti-1
Dpqi	Milliseconds between the maximum value of the p wave and minimum value of q wave.
Dqri	Milliseconds between the minimum value of the q wave and maximum value of r wave.
Drsi	Milliseconds between the maximum value of the r wave and minimum value of s wave.
Dsti	Milliseconds between the minimum value of the s wave and maximum value of t wave.

In addition, the case also introduced 5 measures associated with the accelerometers and GPS of the smartphone. Each measure s_i and v_i contains information about steps per second and speed. Measurements are taken homogeneously and distributed throughout the 30 measurements in the electrocardiogram.

State information has been added to indicate whether this case is a normal case or a pathology. Thus, the case is defined as follows.

$$c = \{e_1,...e_{30}, s_1,..., s_5, v_1,..., v_5, state\}$$

Once a new case is received, the CBR cycle of the system is applied. The CBR cycle is composed of four stages: retrieve, reuse, review and retain phases. During the retrieve phase the most similar case to the current case is retrieved by applying Manhattan distance. Cases with a distance less than the predefined threshold u1 are recovered, as a percentage of the difference between two heart beats. The retrieve phase only considers variables shown in Table 1. Then cases are filtered as the speed and steps, the system selects the cases with a distance lower than the threshold u2 as a percentage determined experimentally. When the system is not able to retrieve cases, then an alert is sent to the health center. Otherwise, the system uses the retrieved cases to build a J48 decision tree, and uses the decision tree to calculate the probability of belonging to a disease class or to a normal class. The interpretation of the tree is considered relevant if the kappa index is above 0.8 otherwise is ignored and always sends the alert. The alert will be sent if the probability of disease is greater than 0.2 to avoid false negatives.

The review and retain phases are performed online with the cases with a detected pathology while other cases are reviewed offline. The system send to the doctor the data associated with EKG and physical activity, due to some variations in the heart rate can be associated to some physical activity.

The initial cases of the CBR where created from the data available at the hospital and the state was defined by the medical staff that participated in the experiments.

4   Results

A mobile application for smartphones was developed to monitor the EKG in real time.

Some characteristics of the graphical user interface are as follows:

Previously to star using the system, the user has to configure the device to introduce IP address of the remote server to send the data, as shown in Figure 11.a. The second screenshot, shown in Figure 11.b, indicates the time from the EKG was started, and the last image show the EKG of the user.

The system has been tested with simulated data according to 100 sequences belonging to 4 pathologies and a normal state. The system has not been tested with real patients in daily life situations because it is in early stages and it is only a prototype. The successful rate of the first state of the algorithm was analyzed, and the system is able to discriminate between disease and normal behavior by 94% in a sequence, taking 10 consecutives sequences, all pathologies were detected.

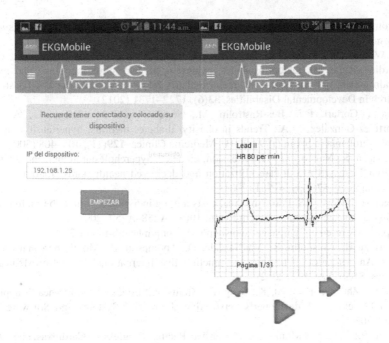

Fig. 11. a) Screenshot of previously version. b) Screenshot of EKG graphic

The functionality of the monitoring physical activity was also analyzed. The system helps the doctor to determine for example if the hearth rate is associated with a physical activity, improving the results and helping to detect a normal behavior with hearth rate 60-100 beats with a sinus tachycardia to 150 beats. However, this section is necessary to check more detail.

Although the work is in an early stage, it was proven that the hardware provides good enough data to analyze the EKG and this information can be used to make a clinical analysis. However, the hardware introduces a meaningful quantity of noise if we compare it with commercial existing devices. As further work it is needed to includes new pathologies and analyze alternatives such as [19] for the detection of pathologies. It will be necessary to introduce a public database as [20] to analyze the system performance.

References

1. http://blogs.strategyanalytics.com/WSS/post/2014/01/27/Global-Smartphone-Shipments-Reach-a-Record-990-Million-Units-in-2013.aspx
2. L., Sang Yup: Examining the factors that influence early adopters' smartphone adoption: The case of college students. Telematics and Informatics. **31**(2), 308–318 (2014)
3. Tseng, F., Liu, Y., Wu, H.: Market penetration among competitive innovation products: The case of the Smartphone Operating System. Journal of Engineering and Technology Management (2013)

4. Ström, R., Vendel, M., Bredican, J.: Mobile marketing: A literature review on its value for consumers and retailers. Journal of Retailing and Consumer Services (2014)
5. de Winter, C.F., Bastiaanse, L.P., Hilgenkamp, T.I.M., Evenhuis, H.M., Echteld, M.A.: Cardiovascular risk factors (diabetes, hypertension, hypercholesterolemia and metabolic syndrome) in older people with intellectual disability: Results of the HA-ID study. Research in Developmental Disabilities. 33(6), 1722–1731 (2012)
6. Basterra-Gortari, F.J., Bes-Rastrollo, M., Seguí-Gómez, M., Forga, L., Alfredo, J., Martínez-González, M.A.: Trends in obesity, diabetes mellitus, hypertension and hypercholesterolemia in Spain (1997-2003). Medicina Clinica. 129(11), 405–408 (2007)
7. Natarajan, S., Nietert, P.J.: Hypertension, diabetes, hypercholesterolemia, and their combinations increased health care utilization and decreased health status. Journal of Clinical Epidemiology. 57(9), 954–961 (2004)
8. Lage, M.J.: Boye, KS. Pdb17 medical costs among individuals with diabetes, hypertension or hypercholesterolemia. Value in Health 10(6), A258–A259 (2007)
9. http://www.research2guidance.com/shop/index.php/mhealth-report-2
10. Kharrazi, H., Chisholm, R., VanNasdale, D., Thompson, B.: Mobile personal health records: An evaluation of features and functionality. International Journal of Medical Informatics. 81(9), 579–593 (2012)
11. Liu, C., Zhu, Q., Holroyd, K., Seng, E.: Status and trends of mobile-health applications for iOS devices: A developer's perspective. Journal of Systems and Software. 84(11), 2022–2033 (2011)
12. Ritter, P.: Holter in Monitoring of Cardiac Pacing. Progress in Cardiovascular Diseases. 56(2), 211–223 (2013)
13. Enriquez, A., Bittner, A., Almehairi, M., Baranchuk, A.: Electrophysiology study without intracardiac catheters. The value of proper Holter interpretation: A case report. Journal of Electrocardiology (2013)
14. Mehairi, M., Ghamdi, S., Dagriri, K., Fagih, A.: The importance of utilizing 24-h Holter monitoring as a non-invasive method of predicting the mechanism of supraventricular tachycardia. Journal of the Saudi Heart Association 23(4), 241–243 (2011)
15. http://www.arduino.cc/
16. Taylor, K., Abdulla, U., Helmer, R., Lee, J., Blanchonette, I.: Activity classification with smart phones for sports activities. 13, 428–433 (2011)
17. http://www.mccauslandcenter.sc.edu/CRNL/tools/ads1298
18. Villarrubia, G., Bajo, J.; De Paz, J.F.; Corchado, J.M.: Real time positioning system using different sensors. In: 16th International Conference on Information Fusion (FUSION), pp. 604–609 (2013)
19. Shen, C., Kao, W., Yang, Y., Hsu, M., Wu, Y., Lai, F.: Detection of cardiac arrhythmia in electrocardiograms using adaptive feature extraction and modified support vector machines. Expert Systems with Applications 39(9), 7845–7852 (2012)
20. http://www.physonet.org/physiobank/database/mitdb (Last Visited: 28/07/2014)
21. http://www.fitbit.com (Last Visited: 28/07/2014)
22. Shiozaki, A., Senra, T., Arteaga, E.: Myocardial fibrosis detected by cardiac CT predicts ventricular fibrillation/ventricular tachycardia events in patients with hypertrophic cardiomyopathy. Journal of Cardiovascular Computed Tomography, 171–181 (2003)
23. Chen, S.W., Chen, H.C., Chan, H.L.: A real-time QRS detection method based on moving-averaging incorporating with wavelet denoising. Comput. Methods Programs Biomed. 82, 187–195 (2006)
24. Villarrubia G., De Paz J.F., Bajo, J., Corchado, J.M.: EKG Mobile. Advanced Science and Technology Letters, 49 (SoftTech 2014), pp. 95–100 (2014)

Improving Conflict Support Environments with Information Regarding Social Relationships

Marco Gomes[1]([✉]), Javier Alfonso-Cendón[2], Pilar Marqués-Sánchez[3],
Davide Carneiro[1], and Paulo Novais[1]

[1] Department of Informatics, University of Minho, Braga, Portugal
{marcogomes,dcarneiro,pjon}@di.uminho.pt
[2] Department of Mechanical, Computing and Aerospace Engineerings,
University of Leon, Leon, Spain
javier.alfonso@unileon.es
[3] Department of Nursing and Physiotherapy, University of Leon, Leon, Spain
pilar.marques@unileon.es

Abstract. Having knowledge about social interactions as a basis for informed decision support in situations of conflict can be determinant. However, lower attention is given to the social network interpretation process in conflict management approaches. The main objective of the work presented here is to identify how the parties' social networks correlate to their negotiation performance and how this can be formalized. Therefore, an experiment was set up in which was tried to streamline all the relevant aspects of the interaction between the individual and its environment that occur in a rich sensory environment (where the contextual modalities were monitored). This research explicitly focuses on the idea that an Ambient Intelligence system can create scenarios that augment the possibilities of reaching a positive outcome taking into account the role of contextualized social relationships in various conflict management strategies.

Keywords: Ambient intelligence · Social network analysis · Negotiation · Context-aware

1 Introduction

Conflicts arise from the complexity of society and the human mind. They may have positive or negative consequences depending on how conflicts are handled or managed. To learn to lead with them correctly is a complex, challenging but essential task. Especially when, these days, the conflict is brought to the digital environment where new business processes (buying and selling products on the internet) are already sufficiently widespread. Therefore, it is necessary that the conflict that arises in digital environments or the ones that are brought to must be properly managed. With conflicts now also emerging in virtual environments, a new field of research has been developed in which Artificial Intelligence and

© Springer International Publishing Switzerland 2014
A.L.C. Bazzan and K. Pichara (Eds.): IBERAMIA 2014, LNAI 8864, pp. 779–790, 2014.
DOI: 10.1007/978-3-319-12027-0_63

particularly Ambient Intelligence (AmI) are interesting. However, the development of tools for this purpose is insufficient. Therefore, it is important to develop conflict management platforms covering important aspects that are present in traditional processes of resolution and conflict management, including context-dependent aspects that have a significant role in human behavior.

Contextual information can influence the course of the process and, therefore, the result of the conflict setting. Moreover, it is accepted that the type of relationship that exists between conflicting parties will often determine the intensity of the conflict and its outcome. Having the knowledge to mapping and measuring the relationships between the parties will allow the conflict manager to measure the relationship, communication, and information flow between the parties through relations and focuses on uncovering the patterns of parties' interactions in the network. This kind of information can be obtained using the well-known Social Network Analysis (SNA) theory. This approach has been used to connote complex sets of relationships between members of social systems. Nevertheless, this kind of social network perspective of the conflict will benefice both researchers and practitioners of conflict management by encouraging the assessment of conflict in broader social systems instead of focusing on the primary parties involved in the conflict. To do so, we base our approach on the idea that our AmI system creates scenarios that augment the possibilities of reaching a positive outcome taking into account the role of contextualized social relationships in various conflict management strategies [6]. In that sense, this work tries to give a general overview of how one can apply social network approaches to shed light on the conflict and establishes a description of how valuable knowledge may be used to further the understanding of conflict [8].

With this purpose was developed a technological framework that will support the decision-making of the conflict manager by facilitating access to information such as the conflict handling style of the parties or their social context. In this work, it is introduced a new module that takes into account the social context by means of social network analysis. The development of such a framework results in a set of services or functionalities that will support the work of the conflict manager. The underlying aim is to release him so that he can have a more inform and practical approach to deal with complex issues such as the improvement of interpersonal communication and relationships.

2   Conflict and Conflict Handling Styles

Conflicts occur frequently in everyday life, as people show divergent opinions about problems and methods and vie for their preferred strategies. All parties involved in a conflict make decisions, whether they make it consciously or not, thinking this will avail them get what they want and need. These decisions may be spontaneous or calculated, constructive or destructive. One should be wary of making the mundane mistake of surmising that conflict is obligatorily a problem and is something to be evaded at all costs. That is far too simplistic approach to the complex subject of conflict management. It is difficult to define and reach a universally accepted definition of conflict. One view of conflict stands it as a disagreement. One should be wary of making the mundane mistake of postulating that conflict is obligatorily a problem and is something to be avoided at all costs. That is far too simplistic approach to the complex subject of conflict management. It is difficult to define and to reach a universally accepted definition of conflict. One define it as a disagreement through which the parties involved perceive a threat to their needs, interests or concerns [4]. Similarly, it can also be seen as the opposition of interests that disrupt or block the action or making-decision process [9]. Thus, a conflict may be seen as a process that begins when a party feels that the other has or is about to affect any interest negatively. The ideal conflict management process is one in which the parties are better in the end than they were in the beginning. Not all conflicts have such conclusion. In order to improve this, one believe that it is a meaningful context and behavioral information and its relevance for conflict management of utmost importance to: (1) provide the parties and manager with relevant knowledge about the conflict and (2) potentiate the role of the parties throughout all the process. Having this kind of information one can lead to a reduction in the severity of the conflict, in which parties continue the conflict but adopt less extreme or harmful tactic.

Conflicts can develop in stages and consequently may involve many different responses as the conflict proceeds. People involved develop various strategies, solutions or behaviors, to deal with the conflict. The style of dealing with a conflict that each one has must be seen as having a preponderant role in the outcome of a conflict resolution process, especially on those in which parties interact directly (e.g., negotiation, mediation). To classify the conflict style, must be analysed the proposals, namely in terms of their utility. In that sense, in each stage of the negotiation the parties' proposals are analysed according to their utility value and a range of possible outcomes defined by the values of the Worst Alternative to a Negotiated Agreement (WATNA) and Best Alternative to a Negotiated Agreement (BATNA) of each party. This approach uses a mathematical model [3], which classifies a party's conflict style considering the range of possible outcomes, the values of WATNA and BATNA as boundaries, and the utility of the proposal. Regarding that utility quantifies how good a given outcome is for a party, it is acceptable to argue that a competing party will propose solutions that maximize its own utility in expense of that of the other party (the utility of the proposal is higher than the WATNA of the other party). In the other hand, for example, a compromising party will most likely search for solutions in an intermediary region (the utility of the proposal falls within the range of the zone of possible agreement, the range of overlapped outcomes that would benefit both parties). Essentially, one were able to classify the personal conflict style of the party by continually analyzing the utility of the proposals created. Once the styles are identified, strategies can be implemented that aim to improve the success rate of procedures for resolution and conflict management.

This information and other insights about how an individual's conflict style is classified can be found in [3] work.

3   An Intelligent Conflict Support Environment

An AmI system consists of a series of interconnected computing and sensing devices which circumvent the user pervasively in his environment and are transparent to him. It is clear that when one designs a system with these characteristics there are some challenges that are raised by the heterogeneity and number of devices and technologies present in this kind of environment. Is not just a bunch of devices interconnected but instead a group of devices working together and sharing information towards a common goal. To cover it, the system must ensure that these devices interact and exchange information in a proper way and compatibility must be ensured between the different technologies and components.

One aim is to provide a service that is dynamically adapted to the interaction context, so that users (parties and the conflict manager) can take advantage of interacting with the system and thus enhance the conflict management process. It can be stated that underlying intent of this work is to extend the traditional technology-based conflict resolution or management methods, in which the user naturally interacts with the system, with a new component, an Intelligent Environment (IE). These environments should be made in a pervasive and transparent way, since when people are aware that they are under monitorization, they tend to behave differently. Therefore, towards an intelligent conflict support system the following ambient intelligence system was developed (Fig. 1).

The system general working is to sense conflict context, acquire it and then make reasoning on the acquired context and thus acting in on the parties' behalf. To achieve this, the system buildup a profile of each party and can link that profile subsequently with the correct individual performance within the conflict process that is been monitored by the system. In other words, while the user conscientiously interacts with the system and takes his or her decisions and actions, a parallel and transparent process takes place in which contextual and behavioural information is sent in a synchronized way to the conflict support platform. The platform allows to conflict manager for a contextualized analysis of the user's data, after converting the sensory information into useful data. The contextualized analysis of user's data is more critical than when the data is from heterogeneous sources of diverse nature like sensors, user profile, and social media and also at different timestamps. To tackle this, the features are extracted from various sensor observations and combined into a single concatenated feature vector which is introduced into different classification modules (conflict styles, stress recognition, and so forth). To integrate all the multimodal evidences is used a decision level integration strategy. Examples of decision level fusion methods used in this work include weighted decision methods and machine-learning techniques and are detailed in previous work [5].

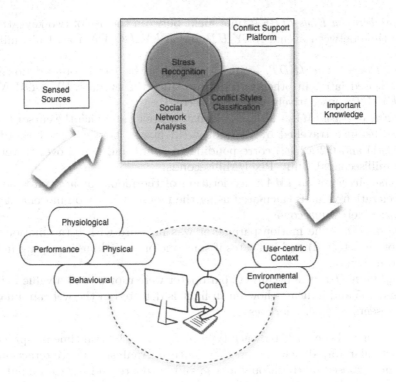

Fig. 1. Conceptual framework to support the decision-making of the conflict manager

3.1 Multimodal Approach to Gathering Behavorial and Context Data

Human behaviour can be understood as an all-encompassing spectrum of what people do including thinking and feeling, which are influenced, for example, by culture, attitudes or emotions. So one can stand that nothing characterizes an individual better than his or her behavior. Knowing how an individual reacts to stimuli allows one to foresee their future states. Therefore, this work addresses learning and recognition of human behavior from a multimodal approach in a conflict support environment in order to enrich the knowledge about user states in negotiation processes. It is a challenging task due to the presence of complex nonlinear correlations and interactions across modalities. Several multimodal recordings showing different situations have been conducted in order to evaluate the proposed approach. To do it a set of features were selected to this end. From between more than two dozen features that can be extracted in a non-invasive and transparent way, the following were selected from keyboard, mouse and webcam sensory data available when a user interacts with our platform:

- *Time between Keys (TBK):* time spent between the use of two keys, that is, the time between events KEY_UP and KEY_DOWN row. Unit: millisecond;
- *Key Down Time (KDT)* - time spent since the key is pressed down and is released later, in other words, time since the event KEY_DOWN and KEY_UP consecutively. Unit: milliseconds;
- *Mouse Velocity (MV)* - Mouse Velocity - velocity at which the cursor travels. The distance travelled by the mouse (in pixels) between a $C1$ coordinate $(x1, y1)$ and $C2(x2, y2)$ corresponding to $time1$ and $time2$ over travel time (in milliseconds). Unit: Pixel/Milliseconds;
- *Mouse Acceleration (MA):* acceleration of the mouse at a given time. The acceleration value is calculated using the mouse velocity on movement time. Unit: Pixel/Milliseconds;
- *Motion (M)* - the motion parameter was measure with 0 (no motion) or 1 (motion detected) and indicates if someone or something is moving in front of the camera;
- *Brightness (B)* - the brightness parameter were represented a value between 0 and 255 and indicates how much light is detected in the webcam image (0 represents complete darkness).

Once data have been gathered each type of data is to be real time pre-processed in a particular way depending on their nature. Analysing any interaction and experience exposed by traditional mouse and keyboard and webcam input these categories are organized around the user's current profile and the information is presented to the conflict manager.

3.2 Incorporation of Social Network Analysis in Conflict Characterization

The study detailed later in the article used a social network analysis method to map and measure the participants' relationships. The network analysis was based on the intuitive notion that these patterns are important features of the activities of the individuals who display them through their interaction, namely in the conflict situation. The Advice, Hindrance and Friendship measurements were considered to analyse the participant's network. Meanwhile, in this analysis we have emphasized friendship relations (Fig. 2) because they can be especially important in [7] [1]. The underlying intent was to study how friendship ties within a group of individuals is correlated with their conflict performance. The data to extract each of the aforementioned measurements were obtained through a questionnaire (carefully adapted) of social networks. According to studies Sparrowe [10], the Advice Network, in our experiment, was measured by asking respondents two questions:

- Do you go to this people to ask for help or advice on work-related matter? [10]
- Do you talk with this people about confidential work-related matters? [10]

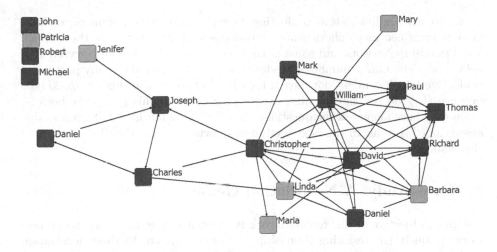

Fig. 2. Was used a questionnaire to collect data on friendship network. The network surveys listed the names of each individual in a respondent's friendships group.

To test the Hindrance Network, the question used was:

– Does he / she makes it difficult for you to carry out your job responsibilities? [10]

Friendship Network was measured by asking respondents:

– Do you consider this people like "personal friend'? [7]

Since the interest of the research was to analyze the strength of relationships, we use responses in a 5-point Likert Scale from "not at all" (1) to "very much" (5). With the data obtained, was measured the in-degree centrality scores for each individual. The in-degree is a measure of centrality, which measures the number of nominations received by a person. This variable was calculated for all individuals in the Advice, Hindrance and Friendship Network. At the individual level, one can also calculate the position of individuals who may be intermediaries (Betweenness Centrality), influential (Eigenvector Centrality) or conflicting (In-degree Centrality in Hindrance Network). The questionnaire was sent to a network of 20 individuals, and the data was collected in binary format and were stored in square matrices of 20 x 20. Calculate relational variables were performed with the software program UCINET VI. The meta-analytic techniques used to analyze the data collected were as follows: Descriptive statistics, both standard deviations, etc. Correlations between the independent variables (centrality and density) and dependent variables (hindrance); Regressions to test the model. Gender was used as a control variable.

In conclusion, was noted that those individuals who do not have a great reputation or central position in the first networks are hypothetically those most drawn to other individuals as conflicting. One can also see how some of the individuals identified as conflicting are individuals with prestige as in the Council and Friendship Network and some of them designated as a bridge between subnets. There are a large number of nodes that have not pointed to any partner as conflictive by what might not have a high level of conflict in this group. Maybe because they do not have a high degree of conflict in this group, or because when they have answered the questionnaires they were not have felt comfortable answering this item. In the next section is spawned a more detailed analysis of this results.

4   Case-Study: A Negotiation Game

The main objective of this research work is to identify how the users' social networks (namely the resulting friendship network) correlate to their negotiation performance and how it can be pointed out. The experiment was set up to demonstrate the relationship discussed in the previous sections, in which was tried to estimate all the relevant aspects of the interaction between the individual and their environment that occur in a rich sensory environment (where contextual modalities were monitored). This environment was empowered with sensors that acquire different kinds of information from the user in a non-intrusive way (using the multimodal approach described in Sec. 3.1). The participants of the proposed experiment were volunteers socially connected with lab members. Twenty individuals participated both female and male, aged between 22 and 36. The first step of the test was to ask the volunteers to fill in a small individual questionnaire (depicted in Sec. 3.2). The following step was the monitoring of the individuals' interaction (where the stress conflict support platform was installed) with the developed web-based negotiation game.

During the experiments, the information about the user's context was provided through monitoring framework, which is customized to perform movement detection from a web cam and collect and treat the interaction data. This data were combined and synchronized with those provided by the keyboard typing and mouse clicking behavior to fully describe several important aspects of the behavior of the user. The participants played the web-based game through computers that allowed the analysis of the described features.

4.1   Experimental Setup

As stated before, with the purpose of simulating a conflict situation in real-life environments a web-based game was developed. It was designed to enable test participants in having a conflicting experience induced by the presence of Ambient Intelligence systems. In that sense, the game simulates a business situation (conflict) where each party has to achieve the desired result in the negotiation or go bankrupt. The desired result was a win/win situation for both parties. A performance-based reward was settled to increased participants' intrinsic motivation. The game starts with the application randomly giving one of the predetermined roles to each party. The instructions to win the game were to negotiate a successful deal and make sure that the party in question did not go bankrupt. Each party's instructions were clearly presented, visible to them through the application interfaces. The objectives and the persona for each party are depicted as:

- Role A - party A was a piano seller who specialized in selling cheap pianos. He was not the only supplier of this kind of pianos. In order to stay in business, he needed to sell 1000 euros or more per piano, knowing that piano prices vary greatly depending on the locale and the particular situation. If he did not achieve this, he would go bankrupt. He was also given the information that Party B needed to make this deal.
- Role B - party B represented a musician that need a piano urgently. He had recently received a contract to make a concert and need a piano to play it. The contractors were prepared to pay 1200 euros per concert. If Party B did not manage to negotiate with Party A to buy a piano at 1200 or less, then he would go bankrupt. Party B was told that party A was in a little financial trouble and needed to make a deal to survive.

Regarding the conflict styles analysis, the ZOPA (Zone Of Possible Agreement) was bounded by the BATNA (1000 euros) and WATNA (1200 euros) values. The range of possible agreement is 200, but the parties were not aware of this detail.

4.2   Results

In the preliminary data analysis, the experimental data is organized into two groups based on the analysis of the social network. One group contains the collection of some experimental data about how a user behaves when he or she negotiates with someone without any relationship. This enables the establishment of a baseline for comparison with the second group, that comprises the data gathered from parties that negotiate with someone socially related. In order to statistically deal with data concerning to the utility values of the parties' proposals, it was necessary to convert to an arbitrary numeric scale (zero is the least favourable style for the resolution and four the most favourable style). This type of scale means that the exact numeric quantity of a particular value has no significance beyond its ability to establish a ranking over a set of data points. Therefore, it was built rank-ordering (which describes the order), but not relative size or degree of difference between the items measured, a mandatory step to make the data suitable for statistical and machine-learning techniques.

Regarding the evolution of the conflict handling styles evidenced by the parties (Fig. 3), we conclude that the conflict style is in average more favourable (mutually beneficial) when the parties are friends. It was also concluded that the style tends to improve (shifting towards of more cooperative solutions) as the rounds advance. In what concerns the final value of the negotiation process, was concluded that friends reach more mutually satisfactory solutions, i.e.,

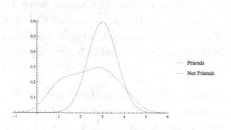

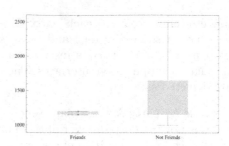

Fig. 3. Difference in the distribution (X axis) of the Conflict Handling Style (Y axis) used by the participants, when they where negotiating with a friend or not

Fig. 4. Distance of value of the final proposal to the optimum result when the participant are friends or not

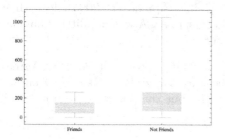

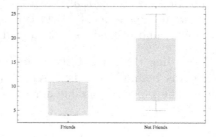

Fig. 5. Difference between the size of the messages exchanged when the participants are friends or not

Fig. 6. Difference in the necessary number of rounds to reach an agreement when the participants are friends or not

solutions that are closer to the optimum result (Fig. 4). Also interesting is the conclusion that participants who are friends need fewer rounds and exchange smaller messages to achieve a successful outcome (which is also more satisfactory, as described previously).

The data also collected shows that there is an apparent difference between the two groups regarding the conflict styles exhibited during the game. The main conclusion is that when participants are friends the frequency collaborative behaviours is far superior (42%) than when they are not friends (17%) (Fig. 7 (a)). This may mean that the relation of friendship between the parties will make them more sensitive to each other's concerns, despite being in a competitive game. In a similar analysis, but now concerning the roles played by participants, was concluded that the sellers are much more competitive than buyers (63% vs. 25%), while buyers are essentially collaborative (Fig. 7 (b)). To interpret the significance of these results it important to recall that participants were asked to negotiate a favorable deal in a competitive and win-lose scenario.

Nonetheless, it is shown that when participants are friends, they are more likely to transform it into a win/win situation. This is especially visible in the final results of the negotiations. On the one hand, 100% of the agreements made by friends accomplished were a favorable deal, i.e., between the range of solutions that would help both. On the other hand, only 50% of negotiations that occurred between non-friends opponents reached a mutual benefit agreement. It may be that they assumed they had to negotiate and get the best price (win/loose). However, that was not the objective. Their objective was to negotiate an agreement so they would not go bankrupt (win/win).

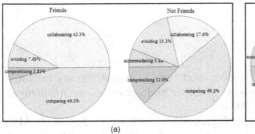 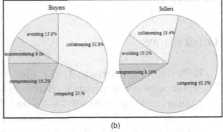

(a)   (b)

Fig. 7. Differences in the conflict styles concerning the social relationship (a) and the role in the game (b)

The preliminary evidence suggests a theoretical basis for expecting a connection between social networks and the use of conflict styles. Despite these results, one still do not know much about how internal configurations of social networks might facilitate (or inhibit) positive conflict outcomes. Therefore, we will perform more and deeper experiments in order to understand how to collect and analysis relational ties that can influence negotiation performance.

5   Conclusions

The main objective of this work was to investigate how to incorporate social conflict analysis in a conflict support environment. After the conceptualization and development of a conflict support framework within an intelligent environment, explained in the previous sections, a test environment was set up. During some weeks, several tests were performed. This included data gathering from a subjects' activities during the experiment, often using video analysis and software logging. The findings highlight the potential of social network analysis to further the understanding of conflict. They pointed out relationships between the features being monitored and the participants' social networks elicited through a small questionnaire. These relationships, especially those regarding the resulting friendship networks, have the potential to enable the characterization of individuals and enhance negotiation performance. The main contribution of this work is thus the identification of situations in which peoples' social networks influences the negotiation performance. It can be especially important when facing a conflict mediators, or conflict managers have the access to the knowledge which can facilitates processes and not let people lose efficiency when they get tangled by their own social and contextual circumstances.

Acknowledgments. This work is part-funded by ERDF - European Regional Development Fund through the COMPETE Programme (operational programme for competitiveness) and by National Funds through the FCT - Fundação para a Ciência e a Tecnologia (Portuguese Foundation for Science and Technology) within project FCOMP-01-0124-FEDER-028980 (PTDC/EEI-SII/1386/2012) and project PEst-OE/ EEI/UI0752/2014.

References

1. Balkundi, P., Harrison, D.A.: Ties, leaders, and time in teams: Strong inference about network structure's effects on team viability and performance. Academy of Management Journal **49**(1), 49–68 (2006)
2. Carneiro, D., Castillo, J.C., Novais, P., Fernández-Caballero, A., Neves, J.: Multimodal behavioral analysis for non-invasive stress detection. Expert Syst. Appl. **39**(18), 13376–13389 (2012). http://dx.doi.org/10.1016/j.eswa.2012.05.065
3. Carneiro, D., Gomes, M., Novais, P., Neves, J.: Developing dynamic conflict resolution models based on the interpretation of personal conflict styles. In: Antunes, L., Pinto, H.S. (eds.) EPIA 2011. LNCS, vol. 7026, pp. 44–58. Springer, Heidelberg (2011)
4. Deutsch, M.: The Resolution of Conflict: Constructive and Destructive Processes. Carl Hovland memorial lectures. Yale University Press (1977)
5. Gomes, M., Oliveira, T., Carneiro, D., Novais, P., Neves, J.: Studying the effects of stress on negotiation behavior. Cybernetics and Systems **45**(3), 279–291 (2014)
6. Judd, S., Kearns, M., Vorobeychik, Y.: Behavioral conflict and fairness in social networks. In: Chen, N., Elkind, E., Koutsoupias, E. (eds.) Internet and Network Economics. LNCS, vol. 7090, pp. 242–253. Springer, Heidelberg (2011)
7. Mehra, A., Dixon, A.L., Brass, D.J., Robertson, B.: The social network ties of group leaders: Implications for group performance and leader reputation. Organization Science **17**(1), 64–79 (2006)
8. Nelson, R.E.: The strength of strong ties: Social networks and intergroup conflict in organizations. The Academy of Management Journal **32**(2), 377–401 (1989)
9. Robbins, S.: Organizational behavior. Prentice Hall (2001)
10. Sparrowe, R.T., Liden, R.C., Wayne, S.J., Kraimer, M.L.: Social Networks and the Performance of Individuals and Groups. Academy of Management Journal **44**(2), 316–325 (2001)

A Formal Approach for Contextual Planning Management: Application to Smart Campus Environment

Ahmed-Chawki Chaouche[1,2]($\boxtimes$), Amal El Fallah Seghrouchni[1],
Jean-Michel Ilié[1], and Djamel Eddine Saïdouni[2]

[1] LIP6 Laboratory, University of Pierre and Marie Curie,
4 Place Jussieu, 75005 Paris, France
{ahmed.chaouche,amal.elfallah,jean-michel.ilie}@lip6.fr
[2] MISC Laboratory, University Constantine 2,
Ali Mendjeli Campus, 25000 Constantine, Algeria
saidouni@misc-umc.org

Abstract. In this paper, we address the building of ambient systems as autonomous and context-aware intelligent agents. The original contribution is an algebraic language, namely AgLOTOS, used to automatically build the plan of an agent from its intentions. As plans are formally conceived as a structured set of concurrent processes, we show how to define a guidance service, helping the agent to maximize the satisfaction of its intentions. The underlying structure, called Contextual Planning System (CPS), takes the contextual information into account to predict the ability to execute the processes in plans. The last part of the paper talks about our current experiment integrating the proposed technique to assist user in a smart campus university.

Keywords: Context-awareness · BDI agent · Planning language · Planning guidance · Smart campus

1 Introduction

Multi-agent System (MAS) approaches offer interesting frameworks for the development of ambient intelligence (AmI) systems, since their agents are considered as intelligent, proactive and autonomous [1]. This paper introduces an efficient planning management process into the architecture of the agent. In particular, we aim at offering to each AmI agent, a powerful predictive service. Like in other recent MAS approaches, e.g. [2,3], which are dedicated to the planning and the validation of agents in MAS, we focus on one agent rather than on the whole MAS. Regarding AmI systems, this eases us to consider whatever dynamic features in the environment for the agents and to propose solutions consistent with the openness of the system.

Belief-Desire-Intention (BDI) are well-known intentional structure emphasizing the reasoning tasks of the agent, up to obtain rationality properties. Such

© Springer International Publishing Switzerland 2014
A.L.C. Bazzan and K. Pichara (Eds.): IBERAMIA 2014, LNAI 8864, pp. 791–803, 2014.
DOI: 10.1007/978-3-319-12027-0_64

properties are really appreciate in AmI systems since this enforces the confidence on the system. The authors of [4] took profit from the fact that the plan of a BDI agent can be derived from its intentions, themselves resulting from the reasoning of the BDI interpreter [5]. In this context, the AgLOTOS language was defined to specify the plans accordingly to the following two criteria: *(1)* enhance the modular and concurrent aspects related to the execution of plans, up to see the plan as composed of concurrent processes, *(2)* handle the well-ordered composition of intentions, i.e. an agent can attribute weights to privilege execution with respect to some intentions.

In this paper, the AgLOTOS language is considered again but its semantics is enriched to automatically produce a state transition structure, namely *Contextual Planning System* (*CPS* for short). The aim is to capture the evolution of the plan in a predictive way, meaning that actions are supposed to be run successfully, but also that the context of the agent can evolve under the execution of actions. Automatic searches on this structure will allow us to propose guidance services, particularly helpful for the decision of agent in expected contexts.

Moreover, we aim at showing how our formal approach can be embedded in the development of the AmI agents. To our opinion, this contributes to making the operational bridge between AmI software engineering and formal approaches. Our project consisting in the design of a smart university campus is the very right place to embed our AmI agents architecture through a float of smart-devices dedicated to assisting users. In this project, the discovery of physical locations and the moves of users are taken into account. Unlike pure MAS approaches, this cannot be reduced to social problem and communication between software agents.

The outline of the paper is the following: Section 2 recalls the agent software architecture we consider, namely the HoA architecture, and its specific planning language used to associate plans with intentions. In Section 3, a contextual planning management is presented based on the building of the CPS structure. Section 4 details the concrete stages of the smart-campus project to conceive the AmI systems. A realistic scenario is given as an illustration of the concepts proposed in the paper. The last section concludes and brings out our next perspectives.

2   The HoA Architecture and Its Planning Language

Figure 1 highlights the agent architecture we consider for AmI systems. Called *Higher-order Agent architecture* (*HoA*), it enhances a clear separation in three processes:

– The *Context process* is in charge of the context information of the agent. It is triggered by new perceptions of the environment and also by internal events informing about the executions of actions. At a low level, it is in charge of observing the realization of the action executions, in order to state they are successfully achieved or not.

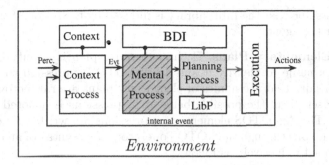

Fig. 1. Higher-order Agent architecture

- The *Mental process* corresponds to the reasoning part of the agent. It is notified by the context process so that it can be aware of the important context changes and can provoke possible revisions of the beliefs (B), desires (D), and intentions (I) data.
  As highlighted in Figure 1, the mental process represents the reasoning mechanism, which manages the BDI states of the agent. Triggered by the perceived events, it updates the B,D and I structures. In order to organize its selected intentions, the mental process is able to schedule them by associating with each one a given weight.
- The *Planning process* is called by the mental process. Helped by a library of plans (*LibP*), it mainly produces a plan of actions from the set of weighted intentions, but also offers some services related to the management of plans (see Section 3).

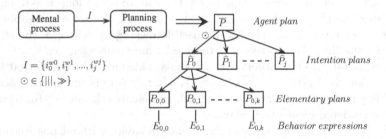

Fig. 2. Agent planning structure

In our approach for each BDI state, the plan of the agent is described by using the *AgLOTOS* language, as detailed in [4]. The language itself extends the LOTOS language [6] in order to specify concurrency between actions in plans. In addition as schemed by Figure 2, it refers to *two level planning structures*: *(1)* the *Agent plan* is made of sub-plans called *Intentions plans*, each one dedicated to achieve the associated selected intention; *(2)* each intention plan is an alternate of several sub-plans, called *Elementary plans*, extracted from the LibP library. This allows one to consider different ways to achieve the associated intention.

Further, we assume that the LibP library is indexed by the set of all the possible intentions for the agent.

Syntax of Elementary Plans. Each elementary plan is specified by a pair composed of a name to identify it and an AgLOTOS expression to feature its behavior. Consider that the names of elementary plans are ranged over $P, Q, \ldots$ and that the set of all the possible behavior expressions is denoted $\mathcal{E}$, ranged over $E, F, \ldots$. The AgLOTOS elementary expressions are written by composing (observable) actions through the LOTOS operators. The syntax of an elementary plan P is defined inductively as follows:

$$
\begin{aligned}
P &::= E & &\textit{Elementary plan} \\
E &::= \quad exit \mid stop & & \\
  &\quad \mid a; E \mid E \odot E & &(a \in \mathcal{O}) \\
  &\quad \mid hide\ L\ in\ E & & \\
\mathcal{H} &::= \mid move(\ell) & &(\mathcal{H} \subset \mathcal{O}, \ell \in \Theta) \\
  &\quad \mid x!(\nu) \mid x?(\nu) & &(x \in \Lambda, \nu \in \mathcal{M}) \\
\odot &= \{\ |||, |[L]|, ||, [\,], \gg, [> \ \}
\end{aligned}
$$

The expression of an elementary plan refers to a (finite) set $\mathcal{O}$ of observable actions which are practically described as instantiated predicates, below ranged over $a, b, \ldots$. This set includes the subset $\mathcal{H}$ of the so-called AmI primitives which represent the mobility and communication, based on the two following assumptions about the AmI system: *(1)* every agent can perceive the enter and leave of other agents in the AmI system, *(2)* it can suggest some move between the AmI system locations and *(3)* it can communicate with another agent in the system. In the syntax, the primitive $move(\ell)$ is used to represent the move of the assisted user to some location ℓ ($\ell \in \Theta$, a finite set of locations). The action $x!(\nu)$ specifies the emission to the agent x ($x \in \Lambda$, the set of neighbor agents) of the message ν ($\nu \in \mathcal{M}$, the set of possible messages), whereas, the expression $x?(\nu)$ means that the message ν is received from some agent x.

In addition, two non-observable actions are also introduced, so that the total set of actions is denoted $Act = \mathcal{O} \cup \{\tau, \delta\}$, where $\tau \notin \mathcal{O}$ is the internal action and $\delta \notin \mathcal{O}$ is a particular observable action which features the successful termination of the considered elementary plan.

The basic expression *stop* specifies a plan behavior without possible evolution and *exit* represents the successful termination of some plan. In the syntax, the set $\odot$ represents the standard LOTOS operators: $E\,[\,]\,E$ specifies a non-deterministic choice, $hide\ L\ in\ E$ a hiding of the actions of L that appear in E with L being any subset of $\mathcal{O}$, $E \gg E$ a sequential composition and $E\,[> E$ the interruption. The LOTOS parallel composition, denoted $E\,|[L]|\,E$ can model both synchronous composition, $E\,||\,E$ if $L = \mathcal{O}$, and asynchronous composition, $E\,|||\,E$ if $L = \emptyset$. In fact, the AgLOTOS language exhibits a rich expressivity such that the sequential executions of plans appears to be only a particular case.

Syntax of Agent Plans. The building of an agent plan requires adding the following AgLOTOS operators to compose some elementary plans:

- at the agent plan level, the parallel ||| and the sequential ≫ composition operators are used to build an agent plan from the intentions of the agent and the associated weights.
- the *alternate composition* operator, denoted ◊, allows to specify an alternate of elementary plans. In particular, an intention is satisfied iff at least one of the associated elementary plans is successfully terminated.

Let $\widehat{P}$ be the set of names used to identify the possible intention plans: $\widehat{P} \in \widehat{\mathcal{P}}$ and let $\overline{P}$ be the set of names qualifying the possible agent plans: $\overline{P} \in \overline{\mathcal{P}}$.

$$\widehat{P} ::= P \mid P \lozenge \widehat{P} \qquad\qquad \textit{Intention plan}$$
$$\overline{P} ::= \widehat{P} \mid \widehat{P} \mid\mid\mid \overline{P} \mid \widehat{P} \gg \overline{P} \quad \textit{Agent plan}$$

With respect to the set of intentions I of the agent, the agent plan is formed in two steps: *(1)* by an extraction mechanism of elementary plans from the LibP library, *(2)* by using the composition functions called *options* and *plan*:

- *options* : $\mathcal{I} \to \widehat{\mathcal{P}}$, yields for any $i \in \mathcal{I}$, an intention plan of the form $\widehat{P}_i = \lozenge_{P \in libP(i)} P$.
- *plan* : $2^I \to \overline{\mathcal{P}}$, creates the final agent plan $\overline{P}$ from the set of weighted intentions I. Depending on how I is ordered, the intention plans yielded by the different mappings $\widehat{P}_i = options(i)$ $(i \in I)$ are composed by using the AgLOTOS composition operators ||| and ≫.

The function *weight* : $I \longrightarrow \mathbb{N}$ that defines the weights of the intentions, in fact yields the way to compose the corresponding intention plans. The intention plans corresponding to the same weight are composed by using the concurrent parallel operator |||. In contrast, the intention plans corresponding to distinct weights are ordered by using the sequential operator ≫. For instance, let $I = \{i_0^1, i_1^2, i_2^1, i_3^0\}$ be the considered set of intentions, such that the superscript information denotes a weight value, and let $\widehat{P_0}, \widehat{P_1}, \widehat{P_2}, \widehat{P_3}$ be their corresponding intention plans, the constructed agent plan could be viewed (at a plan name level) as: $plan(I) = \widehat{P_1} \gg (\widehat{P_0}|||\widehat{P_2}) \gg \widehat{P_3}$.

A Simple AmI Example. Let us consider the following AmI scenario presented in [7], where Alice and Bob are two users of some University, each one assisted by a HoA software agent. The proposed problem of Alice is that she cannot make the two following tasks in the same time: *(1)* to meet with Bob in the location ℓ_1, and *(2)* to get her exam copies from the location ℓ_2. Clearly, the Alice's desires are conflicting since Alice cannot be in two distinct locations simultaneously. However, after having perceived that Bob is in ℓ_2, meaning in the same location as the exam copies, Alice asks for his help to bring her the copies.

The intentions of Alice and Bob are specified separately within their respective agents. These last ones can pervasively coordinate to help achieving the intentions of their assisted users. Here, the actions in plans are simply expressed by using instantiated predicates, like $get\_copies(\ell_2)$. Intention plans are composed from elementary plans which are viewed as concurrent processes, terminated by *exit*, *a la LOTOS*.

Alice's scenario
$I_A = \{meeting(Bob, \ell_1), asking(Bob, get\_copies(\ell_2))\}$
$\overline{P_A} = Bob!(get\_copies(\ell_2)); exit \gg meet(Bob); exit$

Bob's scenario
$I_B = \{meeting(Alice, \ell_1), getting\_copies(\ell_2)\}$
$\overline{P_B} = get\_copies(\ell_2); exit \;\|\|\; move(\ell_1); meet(Alice); exit$

The mental process of an HoA agent can order its set of intentions, according to some preferences of the assisted user. For instance, the intention set related to Alice $I_A = \{meeting(Bob, \ell_1), asking(Bob, get\_copies(\ell_2))\}$ can be ordered such that $weight(meeting(Bob, \ell_1)) < weight(asking(Bob, get\_copies(\ell_2))$. The corresponding agent plan expression of Alice is: $\overline{P_A} = Bob!(get\_copies(\ell_2)); exit \gg meet(Bob); exit$, which is built by using the *options* and *plan* mappings. Pay attention that some actions can be processed concurrently, so is the case in the agent plan $\overline{P_B}$, for the intention plans $get\_copies(\ell_2); exit$ and $move(\ell_1); meet(Alice); exit$.

3   Contextual Planning System

We show now how to build the *Contextual Planning System*, denoted *CPS* for short, from the specification of an agent plan. It is a transition system representing all the possible evolutions of the plan. The building of these last ones are formally driven by a semantics of AgLOTOS constrained by contextual information. As a service instance that can be defined at the planning process level, a guidance mechanism is defined, that works over the evolutions represented by the CPS.

Building of the Contextual Planning System. The AgLOTOS operational semantics is basically derived from the one of LOTOS. A pair (E, P) represents a process identified by P, such that its behavior expression is E. Basic LOTOS semantics is detailed in [7] which formalizes how a process can evolve under the execution of actions. In particular, the rule $\dfrac{P:=E \quad E \xrightarrow{a} E'}{P \xrightarrow{a} E'}$, specifies how (E, P) pair is changed to (E', P) under any action a. Actually, $P := E$ means to consider any (E, P) source pair and $P \xrightarrow{a} E'$ means changing E to E' for P under the execution of a. As far as AgLOTOS is concerned, these rules also represent the operational semantics of elementary plans, viewed as processes.

The next definition specifies how the expression of an *agent plan* is formed compositionally from the expressions of the *intentions plans* of the agent, themselves built from an alternate of *elementary plans* and their behavior expressions. With respect to some agent plan $\overline{P}$, we introduce a notion of configuration of plans in order to specify that a part of the plan can already be executed. Further, the notation $[\overline{P}]$ represents the configuration of the agent plan $\overline{P}$, it is an AgLOTOS expression, which is obtained by composition of the different intention plan configurations of the agent, like $(E, \widehat{P})$.

Definition 1. *Any agent plan configuration $[\overline{P}]$ has a generic representation defined by the following two rules:*

$$1. \quad \frac{\overline{P}::=\widehat{P} \qquad \widehat{P}::=\Diamond^{k=1..n}\,P_k \qquad P_k::=E_k}{[\overline{P}]::=(\Diamond^{k=1..n}\,E_k,\ \widehat{P})}$$

$$2. \quad \frac{\overline{P}::=\overline{P_1}\ \odot\ \overline{P_2} \qquad \odot\in\{|||,\gg\}}{[\overline{P}]::=[\overline{P_1}]\ \odot\ [\overline{P_2}]}$$

The planning state of the agent is now defined contextually, taking into account the agent location and the termination information about the different intention plans defined for the agent.

Definition 2. *A (contextual) planning state is a tuple (C,ℓ,T), where C is an agent plan configuration $[\overline{P}]$, ℓ corresponds to an expected location for the agent, and T is the subset of intention plans which will be terminated in this state.*

Table 1 shows the operational semantic rules defining the possible planning state changes for the agent. These rules are applied to produce the CPS, from an initial planning state, e.g. $([\overline{P}],\ell,\emptyset)$, meaning that the agent is initially at location ℓ, and its plan configuration is $[\overline{P}]$. There are two kinds of transition rules:

Table 1. Semantic rules of intention and agent plan configurations

Intention plan level		
(Action)	$\dfrac{E\xrightarrow{a}E' \quad a\in\mathcal{O}\cup\{\tau\}}{(E,\widehat{P})\xrightarrow{a}(E',\widehat{P})}$	$\dfrac{E\xrightarrow{\delta}E'}{(E,\widehat{P})\xrightarrow[\widehat{P}]{\tau}(E',\widehat{P})}$
Agent plan level		
(Action)	$\dfrac{C\xrightarrow{a}C' \quad a\in\mathcal{O}\cup\{\tau\}}{(C,\ell,T)\xrightarrow{a}(C',\ell,T)}$	$\dfrac{C\xrightarrow[\widehat{P}]{\tau}C'}{(C,\ell,T)\xrightarrow{\tau}(C',\ell,T\cup\{\widehat{P}\})}$
(Communication)	$\dfrac{C\xrightarrow{x!(\nu)}C' \quad x\in\Lambda}{(C,\ell,T)\xrightarrow{x!(\nu)}(C',\ell,T)}$	$\dfrac{C\xrightarrow{x?(\nu)}C' \quad x\in\Lambda}{(C,\ell,T)\xrightarrow{x?(\nu)}(C',\ell,T)}$
(Mobility)	$\dfrac{C\xrightarrow{move(\ell')}C' \quad \ell\neq\ell'}{(C,\ell,T)\xrightarrow{move(\ell')}(C',\ell',T)}$	$\dfrac{C\xrightarrow{move(\ell)}C'}{(C,\ell,T)\xrightarrow{\tau}(C',\ell,T)}$
(Sequence)	$\dfrac{C_1\xrightarrow{a}C_1' \quad a\in\mathcal{O}\cup\{\tau\}}{C_1\gg C_2\xrightarrow{a}C_1'\gg C_2}$	$\dfrac{C_1\xrightarrow[\widehat{P}]{\tau}C_1'}{C_1\gg C_2\xrightarrow[\widehat{P}]{\tau}C_1'\gg C_2}$
(Parallel)	$\dfrac{C_1\xrightarrow{a}C_1' \quad a\in\mathcal{O}\cup\{\tau\}}{C_1|||C_2\xrightarrow{a}C_1'|||C_2}$	$\dfrac{C_1\xrightarrow[\widehat{P}]{\tau}C_1'}{C_1|||C_2\xrightarrow[\widehat{P}]{\tau}C_1'|||C_2}$
	$\dfrac{C_1\xrightarrow{a}C_1' \quad a\in\mathcal{O}\cup\{\tau\}}{C_2|||C_1\xrightarrow{a}C_2|||C_1'}$	$\dfrac{C_1\xrightarrow[\widehat{P}]{\tau}C_1'}{C_2|||C_1\xrightarrow[\widehat{P}]{\tau}C_2|||C_1'}$

Intention plan level: When an intention plan is assumed to be treated, the left hand side transition $(\mathcal{C}_1, a, \widehat{P}, \mathcal{C}_2)$, denoted $\mathcal{C}_1 \xrightarrow[\widehat{P}]{a} \mathcal{C}_2$, expresses a change of intention plan configuration, from $\mathcal{C}_1$ to $\mathcal{C}_2$, and assumes the execution of the action a from $E \xrightarrow{a} E'$ and $P := E$. The right hand side transition highlights the termination case, keeping trace of the intention plan $\widehat{P}$ that is going to be terminated. By calling $\mathcal{CN}$ the set of all the possible intention plan configurations for the agent, the transition relation is a subset of $\mathcal{CN} \times \mathcal{O} \cup \{\tau\} \times \widehat{\mathcal{P}} \times \mathcal{CN}$. For sake of clarity, the transition $(\mathcal{C}_1, a, nil, \mathcal{C}_2)$ is simply denoted $\mathcal{C}_1 \xrightarrow{a} \mathcal{C}_2$. Observe that due to the fact we consider a predictive guidance in this paper, only expected successful executions are taken into account, thus abstracting that a plan may fail. Moreover, the semantics of the alternate operator is reduced to a simple non-deterministic choice of LOTOS: $\Diamond^{k=1..n} E_k \equiv [\ ]^{k=1..n} E_k$, in order to possibly take into account every elementary plan to achieve the corresponding intention.

Agent plan level: the possible changes of the planning states, like $(\mathcal{C}, \ell, T)$, are expressed at this level. In the Communication rules, the action send $x!(\nu)$ (resp. receive $x?(\nu)$) is constrained by the discovery of the agent x in its neighborhood. In the Mobility rule, the effect of the $move(\ell')$ action yields the agent to be placed in ℓ'. The Action rules refer to the ones of the intention plan level. The left hand side one exhibits the case of a regular action, whereas the right hand side one specifies the termination case of some intention plan, which is added to T.

The building of the CPS takes the three following contextual information into account: *(1)* the reached location in a planning state, *(2)* the set of intention plans that are terminated when reaching a planning state, and *(3)* more globally, the set Λ of neighbors currently known by the agent.

Definition 3. *Let I be a set of weighted intentions for the agent. The Contextual Planning System (CPS) is a labeled kripke structure $\langle S, s_0, Tr, \mathcal{L}, \mathcal{T} \rangle$ where:*

- *S is the set of (contextual) planning states,*
- *$s_0 = ([\overline{P}], \ell, \emptyset) \in S$ is the initial planning state of the agent, such that $[\overline{P}]$ is the agent plan configuration of the agent and ℓ represents its current location,*
- *$Tr \subseteq S \times \mathcal{O} \cup \{\tau\} \times S$ is the set of transitions which are denoted $s \xrightarrow{a} s'$,*
- *$\mathcal{L} : S \to \Theta$ is the location labeling function,*
- *$\mathcal{T} : S \to 2^{\widehat{P}}$ is the termination labeling function which captures the terminated intention plans.*

Application to the Scenario. We reconsider the scenario of Section 2. The pairs $(E_m, \widehat{P_m})$ and $(E_g, \widehat{P_g})$ are two intention plan configurations corresponding to Bob. The first one corresponds to the intention $meeting(Alice, \ell_1)$ and the second one to $getting\_copies(\ell_2)$, such that $E_m = move(\ell_1); meet(Alice); exit$ and $E_g = get\_copies(\ell_2); exit$.

The CPS corresponding to Bob, denoted CPS_B, is illustrated in Figure 3. It is built from the initial CPS state, $s_0 = ([\overline{P_B}], \ell_2, \emptyset)$, taking into account the current

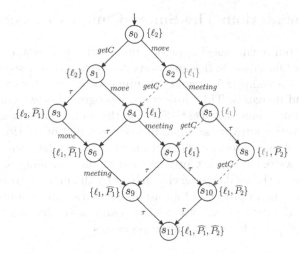

Fig. 3. The CPS_B corresponding to the agent plan $\overline{P_B}$

location ℓ_2 of Bob. In the figure, the dashed edges represent the unrealizable transitions from the states $s \in \{s_2, s_5, s_8\}$, because $pre(getC) = \ell_2 \notin \mathcal{L}(s)$.

In a CPS, the transitions from any state s only represent actions that are realizable. Like in STRIPS description language [3], actions to be executed are modeled by instantiated predicates submitted to preconditions and effects. In this paper, the preconditions only concern the contextual information known in that state. Let $pre(a)$ be the precondition of any action a, then $pre(x!(\nu)) = pre(x?(\nu)) = (x \in \Lambda)$ and for any other action a, $pre(a(\ell)) = \ell \in \mathcal{L}(s)$.

Planning Guidance. In order to guide the assisted user, the planning process can select an execution trace through the CPS such that the number of intention plan terminations is maximized, in respect to the mapping $\mathcal{T}$ of the planning states. This can be captured with the notion of Maximum trace, based on a trace mapping $end : \Sigma \longrightarrow 2^{\widehat{\mathcal{P}}}$ used to specify the set $end(\sigma)$ of the termination actions that occur in a trace $\sigma \in \Sigma$. From an algorithmical point of view, the configurations having the maximum number of terminated intention plans could be straightforwardly detected by parsing the CPS structure, with regards to the set of terminated intention plans of each built planning state. By labeling these states with a specific proposition MAX, the search of maximum traces is reduced to the traces which satisfies the (LTL) temporal logic property AF(MAX).

Considering again CPS_B corresponding to Bob, an example of maximum trace derived from s_0 is the following, expressing that Bob should get the copies before moving to the meeting with Alice:

$$((E_g, \widehat{P_g}) ||| (E_m, \widehat{P_m}), \ell_2, \emptyset) \xrightarrow{getC} ((E'_g, \widehat{P_g}) ||| (E_m, \widehat{P_m}), \ell_2, \emptyset) \xrightarrow[\widehat{P_g}]{\tau} ((E_m, \widehat{P_m}), \ell_2, \{\widehat{P_g}\})$$

$$\xrightarrow{move} ((E'_m, \widehat{P_m}), \ell_1, \{\widehat{P_g}\}) \xrightarrow{meet} ((E''_m, \widehat{P_m}), \ell_1, \{\widehat{P_g}\}) \xrightarrow{[\widehat{P_m}]} \tau ((stop, \widehat{P_m}), \ell_1, \{\widehat{P_g}, \widehat{P_m}\})$$

4   Experimentation: The Smart-Campus Project

We experiment our agent-based approach in a distributed system project called Smart-Campus. Our aim is to design a powerful system that assists users in their activities within a complex university campus to better interact and adapt to users' needs and demands. This project is in progress but we concretely equip a float of *Android Smart-Devices*[1] (SD) by the smart-campus application. In this application, the software architecture is composed of an HoA agent and a specific graphical user interface (GUI) to interact with the user to be assisted. Hence, this allows us an explicit presentation of the reasoning of an agent and the concrete use of the guidance service driven by the mental process, according to the change of context process information. From a smart-campus architecture, we now scheme the deployment of the smart-campus application in the SD, and the way to develop the HoA agent main processes.

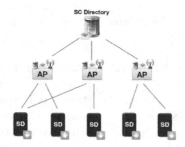

Fig. 4. Smart-campus architecture

Smart-Campus Architecture. The campus system is concretized by the smart-campus starting service which automatically runs the smart-campus application and connects the SD to the "CAMPUS" network, through one of the possible WiFi Access Points (AP). As illustrated in Figure 4, the SD can automatically access to the server *"SC Directory"* which is viewed as a middleware maintaining the persistence of contextual information like the discovery and the locations of other users (through their SD) and objects concerning the campus. The starting service is also dedicated to declare the public information of the user to the server, in particular its location. One of the specificity of this project is that the HoA agent embedded in the SD remains autonomous when the SC directory cannot be reached or when the user is exiting the campus. It can continue assisting the user, due to the context information and persistent data previously stored in the SD, can be pervasively updated with the help of other neighbor agents.

Context Process. The context process is based on services currently implemented over the smart-campus architecture, based on physical localization and

---

[1]   Devices: Google Nexus 5, 7 − Android 4.4 KitKat (API level 19).

(a)synchronous communication mechanisms. They are supported by the smart-device API facilities, in particular the WiFi API. As an example, the navigation service takes profit from the underlyied localization service to determine on the fly, the position and the move of the assisted user.

Observe that the localization service must work over the campus ground as well as the different stairs of the buildings. The best localization indoor technique is currently a research in progress e.g. [8]. Currently, we use different WiFi access points within the campus to compute the geographical locations, since this works in both indoor and outdoor locations. Anyway, the localization process requires a tune calibration phase to store specific information in the SC directory, concerning a set of physical reference points that must be selected over the campus, as mentioned in the fingerprinting approach.

In our case, information includes the physical location of the reference point (GPS), its symbolic name (place/room/corridor) and above all the perceived signal attenuation (RSSI[2]) from that location, in respect to the different WiFi access points. The localization service on the SD can then compare its proper perceptions of the WiFi attenuation in respect to the same references stored in the SC directory, so that to deduce an approximation of its position through statistical computations and trilateration concepts.

Mental and Planning Processes. To interact with the assisted user, the GUI is an important issue of our application. Figure 5 brings out an instance of three relevant screenshots of the developed GUI. Bob is here the assisted user, being notified on his SD in real time, of the evolution of its intentions, its current location and the (best) direction to meet Alice.

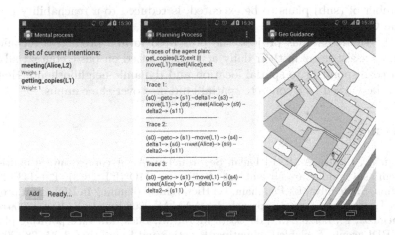

Fig. 5. Smart-campus scenario

---

[2] RSSI: Received Signal Strength Indication.

- The first one (left hand side) shows the current weighted intentions managed by the mental process, coming from the assisted user desires or the pervasive activity of the HoA agent.
- The second screen is a debug view showing the agent plan and all the possible CPS traces. The contextual guidance service allows the agent to assist the user in realizing his desires in proposing different alternatives of plans, optionally inducing the proposition of spatial paths.
- The last screen (right hand side) highlights the used navigation interface showing a global view of the campus during the execution of the Bob's scenario. As a specific GUI, graphical maps are modern and useful interfaces for the users. The application is able to manage the maps of the campus, over which additional layers are used to render maps interactive and to show different locations and paths.

5   Conclusion

The algebraic language AgLOTOS appears to be a powerful way to express an AmI agent plan as a set of concurrent processes, helped by an adapted plan library describing elementary plans. The proposed operational semantics of AgLOTOS allows one to build a Contextual Planning System (CPS), for any BDI state of the agent.

In respect to the current set of the agent intentions, the CPS structure allows to evaluate all the possible plans. Despite the concurrent execution of plans, the predictive mechanism we propose, allows to guide the agent contextually, over its next possible executions. The problem to search an optimal solution maximizing the number of (sub) plans to be executed, is reduced to a reachability problem over the CPS structure.

In the smart campus project, the presented formal predictive technique is applied to assist users in their daily activities, based on basic contextual information corresponding to spatial location and dynamic neighborhood. Hence, it can also be viewed as a concrete spatial guidance over the campus.

References

1. Olaru, A., Florea, A.M., El Fallah Seghrouchni, A.: A context-aware multi-agent system as a middleware for ambient intelligence. MONET **18**(3), 429–443 (2013)
2. Sardina, S., de Silva, L., Padgham, L.: Hierarchical planning in BDI agent programming languages: a formal approach. In: AAMAS 2006, pp. 1001–1008 (2006)
3. Meneguzzi, F., Zorzo, A.F., da Costa Móra, M., Luck, M.: Incorporating planning into BDI agents. Scalable Computing: Practice and Experience **8**, 15–28 (2007)
4. Chaouche, A.C., El Fallah Seghrouchni, A., Ilié, J.M., Saïdouni, D.E.: A dynamical plan revising for ambient systems. Procedia Computer Science **32**, 37–44 (2014)
5. Rao, A.S., Georgeff, M.P.: An abstract architecture for rational agents. In: Nebel, B., Rich, C., Swartout, W.R. (eds.) KR, pp. 439–449. Morgan Kaufmann (1992)
6. Brinksma, E. (ed.): ISO 8807, LOTOS - A Formal Description Technique Based on the Temporal Ordering of Observational Behaviour (1988)

7. Chaouche, A.C., El Fallah Seghrouchni, A., Ilié, J.M., Saïdouni, D.E.: A Higher-order Agent model for ambient systems. Procedia Computer Science **21**, 156–163 (2013)
8. Galván-Tejada, C.E., García-Vázquez, J.P., García-Ceja, E., Carrasco-Jiménez, J.C., Brena, R.F.: Evaluation of four classifiers as cost function for indoor location systems. Procedia Computer Science **32**, 453–460 (2014)

Author Index

Printed in the United States
By Bookmasters